THE
ROYAL &
ANCIENT
BOOK OF
GOLF
RECORDS

THE ROYAL & ANCIENT

BOOK OF

GOLF RECORDS

Edited by Laurence Viney

MACMILLAN

This edition published in 1991
by Macmillan Press
a division of Macmillan Publishers Ltd
4 Little Essex Street
London WC2R 3LF and Basingstoke.

Associated companies in Auckland, Delhi, Dublin, Gaborone, Hamburg,
Harare, Hong Kong, Johannesburg, Kuala Lumpur, Lagos, Manzini,
Melbourne, Mexico City, Nairobi, New York, Singapore and Tokyo

British Library Cataloguing in Publication Data
A CIP catalogue record for this book is available from the British Library

ISBN 0-333-54578-8

Correspondence
Letters on editorial matters should be addressed to:
The Editor, The Royal and Ancient Book of Golf Records,
Macmillan Press Ltd, 4 Little Essex Street, London WC2R 3LF.

Designed by Robert Updegraff
Typeset by Macmillan Production Ltd, 18–21 Cavaye Place,
London SW10 9PG
Printed and bound in Great Britain

Contents

Foreword

During the past two decades there has been a remarkable surge of interest in golf including an increase in the numbers who have taken up the game and others who wish to do so. The reasons for this are not hard to find. Among them are the TV coverage of championships so well presented by the BBC, the rapid development of the European Tour widely reported in the press, and the encouragement of youth by the Golf Foundation and many clubs.

As a result of heavy pressure on space in the *Royal & Ancient Golfer's Handbook*, so long the 'Bible' of golf and recorder of past records, in most events the lists of winners have had to be reduced to those of the last ten years. Both for the club tournaments which date back over a century and for the many more recent championships and tournaments, a complete roll of winners will be most welcome and a fitting record for all time.

Most golfers who love the game are fascinated with the results of the past and appreciate being able to refer to the achievements of the famous and those of lesser renown out of interest or to solve an argument with friends in the bar. I am sure the new *Book of Records*, which it is planned to be revised and published regularly, will be welcomed by all clubs, golf societies, golf historians and many others.

David Marsh

DAVID MARSH
Captain, Royal and
Ancient Golf Club
St. Andrews, October 1991

Acknowledgements

There are many friends and associates who have helped me in compiling this book and I am most grateful to them. To try to name them all is a task beyond me and I must ask them to be content with a general word of thanks, insufficient as it is. However there are a few who call for special mention.

Bobby Burnet, the Royal & Ancient Archivist and Librarian, has been of invaluable assistance, as has Mark Wilson, Editor of the *Golfer's Handbook*, and his communications staff at the European Tour at Wentworth. The Home Unions, the County Secretaries and the LGU and its constituent associations have each willingly contributed details required. Assistance beyond any call of duty has come from Alma Robertson, Administrator at the LGU, and Bill Hodge whose accumulated statistical knowledge is unrivalled. The help of Belle Robertson of Scotland and Marion Carr of ELGA must also be specially acknowledged.

Many of the area and county professional associations and the secretaries of clubs which hold open amateur tournaments drawing competitors from a wide area, have provided material and replied helpfully to queries.

Dorothy Robertson, as diligent a researcher as can be imagined, has been assiduous in her determination to be accurate and has raised countless points of doubt which the normal mortal would not pick up. Invariably she had a point and the book is the better for her many contributions.

LAURENCE VINEY

Introduction

For most new reference books the Editor must rely on many different sources for his text. Naturally for the *Book of Golf Records* I have leaned heavily on many earlier editions of the annual *Golfer's Handbook*. An essential aid for any golf historian, it has been affectionately known as the golfer's 'Bible'. Even so it has its snags. If accuracy and continuity are the hallmarks of such a work, the errors which have come to light in past issues and which have remained unchanged until recently, reveal the fallibility of former editorial efforts. I have tried to keep any remaining inaccuracies to a minimum.

The two most frequent variations are the names of players and courses. A player is usually listed under the name and initials which he used in his entry for an event. A few of the better known appear as winners of many tournaments, but use a selection of initials and first names. One of the best British amateurs between the wars, Cyril Tolley, appears as C.J.H. Tolley, C.J. Tolley, C. Tolley, Cyril J.H. Tolley and Cyril Tolley. A leading Portuguese amateur who played all over Europe for twenty years after the Second World War, J.L. de Sousa e Melo, betters Tolley and achieves thirteen variations on his name and initials in editions of the *Golfer's Handbook*. The principle I have adopted in most cases has been at least to keep to the same initials and name within a tournament won several times by the same individual. With ladies who have won events under two names, 'Smith (née Jones)' the first time she wins under her married or second surname will provide the clue to her being the same individual.

The problem of names is aggravated by the gradual change to the near universal use of first names today. Here again the aim has been consistency within a tournament, but sometimes switching from initials to first names some year after 1946. Before the 1939–45 war first names were seldom used.

Until about 1965 nearly every professional was attached to a club and entered from it. Today very few tournament players have a club attachment, but most have a sponsor. The earlier appellation 'unattached', under which for instance Max Faulkner won the Open at Portmarnock in 1951, is no longer in vogue. Usually today a player will have his country after his name, which is more appropriate, reflecting the world-wide entry in nearly all professional events.

As a general principle no tournaments in which handicaps are allowed have been included, except two. There would be no end to the number of pro–am and other competitions which would aspire to be included if the rule was rescinded. The two exceptions are the long established Sunningdale Foursomes played at the start of the season, when amateurs and professionals of both sexes play with fixed handicap allowances according to their status, and the Parliamentary Handicap. The latter is over one hundred years old and the winners include two Prime Ministers, Balfour and Bonar Law, Sir John (later Lord) Simon as Foreign Secretary and more recently Lord Whitelaw.

Inevitably there are tournaments included where it has not been possible to discover some of the early winners or venues. It is hoped that the next edition will remedy such omissions. The clubs of amateur winners have been left out for several reasons, but the venues of all tournaments each year have been included except occasionally when diligent research has failed to reveal the course. Some clubs have all their records; others are sadly lacking, quite often due to a club house fire.

Naming venues sounds easy. A venue is essentially the course on which a championship or tournament is played, but it may not be the same name as the club playing host. A Welsh championship, for instance, played at Harlech will have the Royal St David's Club as host. Again Hollinwell is the course where the Nottinghamshire Club plays. At Sandwich in Kent, both Royal St George's and Princes Clubs have held championships, the former many more than the latter. They are shown as St George's Sandwich and Princes Sandwich to designate which.

Research for this book has involved visits to many parts of the kingdom and to Eire, that land of great courses where the welcome is so warm and where golf, like rugby football, knows no divide. For one who can no longer play the game even with a buggy to assist arthritic limbs, it has been a joy to visit clubs and other golf organisations in search of material and meet so many with expert knowledge of the game.

With a new edition due in a year or two, comments and suggestions for improvements will be welcome. Apart from any errors of fact that there may be, there is no doubt room to widen the content with more overseas records.

LAURENCE VINEY
Berkhamsted,
October 1991

Part One
Men's Professionals

The Open Championship 1860–1990

The Open Championship was the first formal competitive golf tournament at stroke play. Except for about 15 years after the Second World War it has remained the most prestigious championship of all. Its history can be conveniently divided into seven periods, starting with the Prestwick Club's inspired initiative to hold a competitive tournament there in 1860. Seven players from Scotland and one from Blackheath, the only golf club in England at the time except for Old Manchester, completed the 36-hole contest in one day; the winner, Willie Park, took the Championship Belt and prize-money of £5. It has gradually grown to today's mammoth event, with its tented village, prize-money of £900,000, the winner taking £90,000, and up to 30,000 spectators a day for a week.

The first 11 championships were all held over three rounds of 12 holes at Prestwick, that fine course on Scotland's west coast in Ayrshire, and drew both amateur and professional players, mostly from the east coast where golf of a kind had been played for centuries. The winners of those first championships were limited to four: Willie Park with three, old Tom Morris four, Andrew Strath one and young Tom Morris three in succession. He thus won the Championship Belt outright.

With no contest in 1871, Scotland's three leading clubs, Prestwick, the Royal & Ancient of St Andrews and the Honourable Company of Edinburgh Golfers then at Musselburgh, together put up the famous Silver Claret Jug trophy for the Championship winner to hold for a year. It was never to be won outright and the Championship was to be played at each course in turn.

This second period until 1891 began with young Tom Morris's fourth and last win in 1872; he died tragically young three years later. In the next 20 years the entry grew steadily, but the winner was always a Scottish professional, mostly from St Andrews or Musselburgh. In 1888 for instance 38 players took part, including three amateurs. Twenty-one of the professionals came from St Andrews, where they earned a living at the game as club-makers, teachers and caddies. That year at St Andrews the first professional from an English club, Jack Burns of Warwick, an emigré Scot, won with a score of 171 for two rounds. In poor weather with a strong wind, this was a very good score considering the clothing, clubs and balls with which they played.

The Prestwick Open of 1890 was the first time the event was won by an Englishman and an amateur, John Ball of the Royal Liverpool Club at Hoylake. Only two other amateurs have been successful: Harold Hilton, also of Hoylake, who won twice in 1892 and 1897, and the great Bobby Jones three times in the 1920s.

The third phase began in 1892 when the Honourable Company of Edinburgh Golfers moved its club from Musselburgh to a new course at Muirfield near Gullane and the contest became one of four rounds of 18 holes. Hilton's winning total of 305, included a 72, a remarkable round with a gutty ball. Two years later the Open was played in England for the first time at Sandwich and was won by JH Taylor, the English professional who, with Harry Vardon and James Braid, became known as the Great Triumvirate. Between that year and 1914, they dominated the game, winning 16 Opens out of 21. No one else won it twice during that period, but Arnaud Massy from France was the first overseas winner in 1907 at Hoylake, where the Championship had been played twice before in 1897 and 1902. Deal in Kent was added in 1909 to be the seventh club to play host to the Open.

Very few Americans played over here before 1920, seldom more than a lone visitor, usually finishing well down the list, unlike the Amateur Championship which was won by Walter Travis from Garden City, Long Island, in 1904. But in the next period, 1920–39, led by Walter Hagen, many came across and from 1924 to 1933 they won every year, Hagen three times (he had also won in 1922), Bobby Jones also thrice, with Jim Barnes, Tommy Armour, Gene Sarazen and Densmore Shute once each. Henry Cotton broke the spell in 1934 and no American won again until 1946. Cotton had a second triumph at Carnoustie in 1937, when the entire US Ryder Cup team competed with little success, Byron Nelson heading the challenge in fifth place.

After the war in 1946 Sam Snead lifted the trophy, followed by Fred Daly, the only Irishman to win, and Henry Cotton's third title in 1948. Thereafter for a few years the Open became almost the exclusive property of the Commonwealth, except for Max Faulkner in 1951 and Ben Hogan on his only visit to the Open in 1953. Bobby Locke (South Africa) and Peter Thomson (Australia) each won four times, with their compatriots, respectively Gary Player and Kel Nagle, once each. True there was very little American participation in those years, but the Championship was still being run on pre-war lines and there was little incentive, either in terms of finance or even prestige, for US players to compete.

This all began to change in 1960, the year of the Centenary Open, when Arnold Palmer first made his challenge and finished second at St Andrews. Since then Palmer has missed only one Open, in 1964. With wins in 1961 and 1962, he and Jack Nicklaus, another devotee of the Championship and three times winner, have led the American invasion, made that much easier by transatlantic air travel. Encouraged by the then Secretary of the Royal & Ancient Club, Keith Mackenzie, whose promotional efforts were outstanding, together they have persuaded their fellow USPGA members to follow their lead. In doing so they have contributed much to make it what is now without doubt the world's greatest championship. Their support has coincided with the more forward-looking ideas of the Royal & Ancient Championship Committee, which promotes and runs the Open, and the growth of the worldwide TV coverage which contributes handsomely to the revenue.

The final phase from Nicklaus's last win in 1978, was at first largely Tom Watson's with four more successes (he had already won in 1975), but since that at Birkdale in 1983, no American won until Mark Calcavecchia at Troon in 1989. Seve Ballesteros twice, Sandy Lyle, Greg Norman and Nick Faldo, also twice, have successfully revived the challenge to US domination.

Where does the Open progress from here? The Championship Committee will ensure through sensible improvements and adjustments that it will never lose its appeal and will continue to be the most sought-after prize in golf. Developments there will be. The call for the Open to be played on a fine inland course will continue to be heard and, one hopes, ignored. Many feel, including the leading American proponents of the Open, that to leave the traditional links courses could destroy it as the greatest challenge of skill in the game. Fortunately there are but few who press for the change.

1860 *at Prestwick*

NAME	SCORE			
Willie Park (Musselburgh)	55	59	60	174
Tom Morris Sr (Prestwick)	58	59	59	176
Andrew Strath (St Andrews)				180
Robert Andrew (Perth)				191
George Brown (Blackheath)				192
Charles Hunter (Prestwick St Nicholas)				195
Alexander Smith (Bruntsfield)				
William Steel (Bruntsfield)				

1861 *at Prestwick*

NAME	SCORE			
Tom Morris Sr (Prestwick)	54	56	53	163
Willie Park (Musselburgh)	54	54	59	167
William Dow (Musselburgh)	59	58	54	171
David Park (Musselburgh)	58	57	57	172
Robert Andrew (Perth)	58	61	56	175
Peter McEwan (Bruntsfield)	56	60	62	178
William Dunn (Blackheath)	61	59	60	180
Col JO Fairlie (Prestwick)				184
George Brown (St Andrews)	60	65	60	185
Mr Robert Chambers Jr (Prestwick)				187
James Dunn (Blackheath)	63	62	63	188
Charles Hunter (Prestwick)	67	64	59	190

1862 *at Prestwick*

NAME	SCORE			
Tom Morris Sr (Prestwick)	52	55	56	163
Willie Park (Musselburgh)	59	59	58	176
Charles Hunter (Prestwick)	60	60	58	178
William Dow (Musselburgh)	60	58	63	181
Mr James Knight (Prestwick)	62	61	63	186
Mr JF Johnston (Prestwick)	64	69	75	208

1863 *at Prestwick*

NAME	SCORE			
Willie Park (Musselburgh)	56	54	58	168
Tom Morris Sr (Prestwick)	56	58	56	170
David Park (Musselburgh)	55	63	54	172
Andrew Strath (St Andrews)	61	55	58	174
George Brown (St Andrews)	58	61	57	176
Robert Andrew (Perth)	62	57	59	178
Charles Hunter (Prestwick St Nicholas)	61	61	62	184
Mr James Knight Jr (Prestwick St Nicholas)	66	65	59	190
Mr James Miller (Musselburgh)	63	63	66	192
James Paxton (Musselburgh)	65	65	66	196

NAME	SCORE			
Mr JF Johnston (Ayr Belleisle)	66	66	65	197
Mr Peter Chalmers (King James VI)	65	67	65	197
Mr William Mitchell (Prestwick)	70	70	66	206
Mr William Moffat (Musselburgh)	75	78	80	233

1864 *at Prestwick*

NAME	SCORE			
Tom Morris Sr (Prestwick)	54	58	55	167
Andrew Strath (St Andrews)	56	57	56	169
Robert Andrew (Perth)	57	58	60	175
Willie Park (Musselburgh)	55	67	55	177
William Dow (Musselburgh)	56	58	67	181
William Strath (St Andrews)	60	62	60	182

1865 *at Prestwick*

NAME	SCORE			
Andrew Strath (St Andrews)	55	54	53	162
Willie Park (Musselburgh)	56	52	56	164
William Dow (Musselburgh)				171
Bob Kirk (St Andrews)	64	54	55	173
Tom Morris Sr (St Andrews)	57	61	56	174
Mr William Doleman (Glasgow)	62	57	59	178
Robert Andrew (Perth)	61	59	59	179
William Strath (St Andrews)	60	60	62	182
William Miller	63	60	66	189
Tom Hood (Musselburgh)	66	66	66	198

1866 *at Prestwick*

NAME	SCORE			
Willie Park (Musselburgh)	54	56	59	169
David Park (Musselburgh)	58	57	56	171
Robert Andrew (Perth)	58	59	59	176
Tom Morris Sr (St Andrews)	61	58	59	178
Bob Kirk (St Andrews)	60	62	58	180
Andrew Strath (Prestwick)	61	61	60	182
Mr William Doleman (Glasgow)	60	60	62	182
John Allan (St Andrews)	60	63	60	183
Tom Morris Jr (Glasgow)	63	60	64	187
William Dunn (Leith)	64	63	62	189
Mr T Hood (Musselburgh)	61	69	61	191
James Hutchison (Musselburgh)	63	67	64	194

1867 *at Prestwick*

NAME	SCORE			
Tom Morris Sr (St Andrews)	58	54	58	170
Willie Park (Musselburgh)	58	56	58	172
Andrew Strath (St Andrews)	61	57	56	174
Tom Morris Jr (St Andrews)	58	59	58	175

NAME	SCORE			
Bob Kirk (St Andrews)	57	60	60	177
Mr William Doleman (Glasgow)	55	66	57	178
Robert Andrew (Perth)	56	58	65	179
William Dow (Musselburgh)	62	57	65	184
Mr T Hunter (Musselburgh)	62	60	62	184
Willie Dunn (Blackheath)	64	63	62	189

1868   *at Prestwick*

NAME	SCORE			
Tom Morris Jr (St Andrews)	50	55	52	157
Robert Andrew (Perth)	53	54	52	159
Willie Park (Musselburgh)	58	50	54	162
Bob Kirk (St Andrews)	56	59	56	171
John Allan (Westward Ho!)	54	55	63	172
Tom Morris Sr (St Andrews)	56	62	58	176
William Dow (Musselburgh)	61	58	60	179
Mr William Doleman (Glasgow)	57	63	61	181
Charles Hunter (Prestwick)	60	64	58	182
Willie Dunn (R Blackheath)	60	63	60	183

1869   *at Prestwick*

NAME	SCORE			
Tom Morris Jr (St Andrews)	51	54	49	154
Tom Morris Sr (St Andrews)	54	50	53	157
Mr S Mure Fergusson (Royal & Ancient)	57	54	54	165
Bob Kirk (St Andrews)	53	58	57	168
David Strath (St Andrews)	53	56	60	169
Jamie Anderson (St Andrews)	60	56	57	173
Mr William Doleman (Glasgow)	60	56	59	175
Mr G Mitchell-Innes (R North Devon)	64	58	58	180

1870   *at Prestwick*

NAME	SCORE			
Tom Morris Jr (St Andrews)	47	51	51	149
Bob Kirk (R Blackheath)	52	52	57	161
David Strath (St Andrews)	54	49	58	161
Tom Morris Sr (St Andrews)	56	52	54	162
Mr William Doleman (Musselburgh)	57	56	58	171
Willie Park (Musselburgh)	60	55	58	173
Jamie Anderson (St Andrews)	59	57	58	174
John Allan (Westward Ho!)	61	58	57	176
Mr A Doleman (Musselburgh)	61	59	58	178
Charles Hunter (Prestwick)	58	56	64	178
J Brown (Musselburgh)	66	55	59	180
J Millar (Musselburgh)	66	62	54	182
Mr T Hunter (Musselburgh)	62	63	60	185
F Doleman (Musselburgh)	65	64	60	189

NAME	SCORE			
J Hunter (Prestwick)	62	65	64	191
W Boyd (Prestwick)	65	59	67	191
William Dow (Musselburgh)	68	64	66	198

1871   *No Championship*

1872   *at Prestwick*

NAME	SCORE			
Tom Morris Jr (St Andrews)	57	56	53	166
David Strath (St Andrews)	56	52	61	169
Mr William Doleman (Musselburgh)	63	60	54	177
Tom Morris Sr (St Andrews)	62	60	57	179
David Park (Musselburgh)	61	57	61	179
Charles Hunter (Prestwick)	60	60	69	189
Hugh Brown (Prestwick)	65	73	61	199
Mr William Hunter (Prestwick)	65	63	74	202

1873   *at St Andrews*

NAME	SCORE		
Tom Kidd (St Andrews)	91	88	179
Jamie Anderson (St Andrews)	91	89	180
Tom Morris Jr (St Andrews)	94	89	183
Bob Kirk (R Blackheath)	91	92	183
David Strath (St Andrews)	97	90	187
Walter Gourlay (St Andrews)	92	96	188
Tom Morris Sr (St Andrews)	93	96	189
Mr Henry A Lamb (R Blackheath)	96	96	192
Robert Martin (St Andrews)	97	97	194
Willie Fernie (St Andrews)	101	93	194
Mr R Armitage (St Andrews)	96	99	195
J Fenton 'The Skipper' (St Andrews)	94	101	195
JOF Morris (St Andrews)	96	99	195
Mr S Mure Fergusson (St Andrews)	98	101	199
R Manzie (St Andrews)	96	104	200
Jack Morris (Hoylake)	106	100	206
David Ayton (St Andrews)	111	96	207
R Thomson (Edinburgh)	98	109	207
John Chisholm (St Andrews)	103	105	208
Robert Pringle (Musselburgh)	109	102	211
D Brand (St Andrews)	110	103	213

1874   *at Musselburgh*

NAME	SCORE		
Mungo Park (Musselburgh)	75	84	159
Tom Morris Jr (St Andrews)	83	78	161
George Paxton (Musselburgh)	80	82	162
Bob Martin (St Andrews)	85	79	164
Jamie Anderson (St Andrews)	82	83	165

NAME	SCORE		
David Park (Musselburgh)	83	83	166
W Thomson (Edinburgh)	84	82	166
Tom Kidd (St Andrews)	84	83	167
R Ferguson (Musselburgh)	83	84	167
G M'Cachnie (Musselburgh)	79	90	169
JOF Morris (St Andrews)	88	81	169
J Ferguson (Musselburgh)	87	82	169
Willie Park (Musselburgh)	83	87	170
T Hood (Musselburgh)	83	88	171
Robert Pringle (Musselburgh)	85	86	171
Mr T Hunter (Musselburgh)	88	86	174
T Brown (Musselburgh)	87	88	175
David Strath (St Andrews)	86	90	176
Tom Morris Sr (St Andrews)	90	86	176
Mr William Doleman (Musselburgh)	89	88	177
William Cosgrove (Musselburgh)	88	89	177

1875   *at Prestwick*

NAME	SCORE			
Willie Park (Musselburgh)	56	59	51	166
Bob Martin (St Andrews)	56	58	54	168
Mungo Park (Musselburgh)	59	57	55	171
Robert Ferguson (Musselburgh)	58	56	58	172
James Rennie (St Andrews)	61	59	57	177
David Strath (St Andrews)	59	61	58	178
Robert Pringle (Musselburgh)	62	58	61	181
Hugh Morrison (Prestwick)	62	59	62	183
Mr William Doleman (Musselburgh)	65	59	59	183
John Campbell (Musselburgh)	57	66	63	186
Neil Boon (Prestwick)	67	60	62	189
James Guthrie (Prestwick)	63	64	66	193
Matthew Allan (Prestwick)	67	65	62	194
James Boyd (Prestwick)	67	65	63	195

1876   *at St Andrews*

NAME	SCORE		
Bob Martin (St Andrews)	86	90	176
David Strath (North Berwick)	86	90	176
(Strath refused to play off)			
Willie Park (Musselburgh)	94	89	183
Tom Morris (St Andrews)	90	95	185
W Thompson (Elie)	90	95	185
Mungo Park (Musselburgh)	95	90	185
Mr Henry A Lamb (London)	94	92	186
George Paxton (Musselburgh)	95	92	187
W Gourlay (St Andrews)	98	89	187
Bob Kirk (St Andrews)	95	92	187
R Kinsman (St Andrews)	88	100	188
Mr David Lamb (London)	95	94	189
Jamie Anderson (St Andrews)	96	93	189
John Thompson (Bruntsfield)	89	101	190
D Anderson (St Andrews)	93	97	190

1877   *at Musselburgh*

NAME	SCORE				
Jamie Anderson (St Andrews)	40	42	37	41	160
Bob Pringle (Musselburgh)	44	38	40	40	162
Bob Ferguson (Musselburgh)	40	40	40	44	164
William Cosgrove (Musselburgh)	41	39	44	40	164
David Strath (North Berwick)	45	40	38	43	166
William Brown (Musselburgh)	39	41	45	41	166
Mungo Park (Musselburgh)					167

1878   *at Prestwick*

NAME	SCORE			
Jamie Anderson (St Andrews)	53	53	51	157
Bob Kirk (St Andrews)	53	55	51	159
JOF Morris (St Andrews)	50	56	55	161
Bob Martin (St Andrews)	57	53	55	165
Mr John Ball (Hoylake)	53	57	55	165
Willie Park (Musselburgh)	53	56	57	166
William Cosgrove (Musselburgh)	55	56	55	166
Jamie Allan (Westward Ho!)	62	53	52	167
Tom Dunn (Wimbledon)	54	60	54	168
John Allan (Westward Ho!)	55	55	58	168
Tom Morris (St Andrews)	55	53	63	171
Ben Sayers (Leith)	56	59	58	173
Edwin Paxton (Musselburgh)	58	59	58	175
George Strath (Glasgow)	63	62	51	176
A Patrick (Leven)	62	56	60	178
Jack Morris (Hoylake)	58	57	64	179
Mungo Park (Alnwick)	60	58	62	180
George Low (Hoylake)	57	61	63	181
Neil Boon (Prestwick)	63	54	66	183
Mr William Hunter (Prestwick St Nicholas)	67	65	55	187

1879   *at St Andrews*

NAME	SCORE		
Jamie Anderson (St Andrews)	84	85	169
James Allan (Westward Ho!)	88	84	172
Andrew Kirkaldy (St Andrews)	86	86	172
George Paxton (Musselburgh)			174
Tom Kidd (St Andrews)			175
Bob Ferguson (Musselburgh)			176
D Anderson (St Andrews)			178
JOF Morris (St Andrews)	92	87	179
Tom Dunn (Wimbledon)			179
W Gourlay (St Andrews)			179
Mr AW Smith (Glasgow)			180
J Rennie (St Andrews)			181
Willie Fernie (Musselburgh)			181
J Kirkaldy (St Andrews)			181
T Arundel (Musselburgh)			184

NAME	SCORE
David Ayton (St Andrews)	184
Mr Henry A Lamb (Wimbledon)	184
R Kinsman (St Andrews)	185
Tom Morris (St Andrews)	185
Mr William Doleman (Musselburgh)	185

1880   *at Musselburgh*

NAME	SCORE		
Bob Ferguson (Musselburgh)	81	81	162
Peter Paxton (Musselburgh)	81	86	167
Ned Cosgrove (Musselburgh)	82	86	168
George Paxton (Musselburgh)	85	84	169
Robert Pringle (Musselburgh)	90	79	169
David Brown (Musselburgh)	86	83	169
Andrew Kirkaldy (St Andrews)	85	85	170
W Brown (Musselburgh)	87	84	171
David Grant (Leith)	87	84	171
Willie Campbell (Musselburgh)	88	91	179
J Foreman (Musselburgh)	92	87	179
T Brown (Musselburgh)	90	89	179
T Arundel (Musselburgh)	86	93	179
Willie Park Sr (Musselburgh)	89	92	181
Willie Park Jr (Leith)	92	90	182
A Brown (Musselburgh)	91	92	183
D Corstorphine (St Andrews)	93	90	183
George Strath (Glasgow)	87	96	183
Ben Sayers (Leith)	91	93	184
Mungo Park (Alnmouth)	95	92	187

1881   *at Prestwick*

NAME	SCORE			
Bob Ferguson (Musselburgh)	53	60	57	170
Jamie Anderson (St Andrews)	57	60	56	173
Ned Cosgrove (Musselburgh)	61	59	57	177
Bob Martin (St Andrews)	57	62	59	178
Tom Morris (St Andrews)	58	65	58	181
Willie Campbell (Musselburgh)	60	56	65	181
Willie Park Jr (Musselburgh)	66	57	58	181
Willie Fernie (St Andrews)	65	62	56	183

1882   *at St Andrews*

NAME	SCORE		
Bob Ferguson (Musselburgh)	83	88	171
Willie Fernie (Dumfries)	88	86	174
Jamie Anderson (St Andrews)	87	88	175
John Kirkaldy (St Andrews)	86	89	175
Bob Martin (St Andrews)	89	86	175
Mr Fitz Boothby (St Andrews)	86	89	175
Willie Park Sr (Musselburgh)	89	89	178

NAME	SCORE		
David Ayton (St Andrews)	90	88	178
Mr James Mansfield (Edinburgh)	91	87	178
James Rennie (St Andrews)	90	88	178
Mr Henry A Lamb (Edinburgh)	88	92	180
Tom Kidd (St Andrews)	87	93	180
George Low (Hoylake)	95	86	181
Andrew Alexander (St Andrews)	93	88	181
Douglas Rolland (Earlsferry)	88	93	181
W Honeyman (St Andrews)	93	89	182
W Thomson (St Andrews)	95	87	182
Ben Sayers (Musselburgh)	92	91	183
Willie Park Jr (Musselburgh)	90	93	183
Tom Dunn (North Berwick)	93	90	183

1883   *at Musselburgh*

NAME	SCORE		
Willie Fernie (Dumfries)	75	84	159
Bob Ferguson (Musselburgh)	78	81	159
(Fernie won play-off 158 to 159)			
W Brown (Musselburgh)	83	77	160
Robert Pringle (Musselburgh)	79	82	161
Willie Campbell (Musselburgh)	80	83	163
G Paxton (Musselburgh)	80	83	163
Ben Sayers (Musselburgh)	81	83	164
Willie Park Jr (Ryton-on-Tyne)	77	88	165
Willie Dunn (North Berwick)	85	81	166
Tom Morris (St Andrews)	86	81	167
Peter Paxton (Malvern)	85	82	167
Mr D Rolland (Leith)	82	85	167
Ben Campbell (Musselburgh)	81	86	167
T Grossart (Musselburgh)	82	86	168
F Park (Musselburgh)	84	85	169
William Cosgrove (Musselburgh)	79	91	170
Mr J Simpson (Earlsferry)	90	81	171
Tom Dunn (North Berwick)	87	84	171
Mr G Miller (Leith)	80	92	172
Mr D Leitch (Leith)	88	86	174

1884   *at Prestwick*

NAME	SCORE		
Jack Simpson (Carnoustie)	78	82	160
D Rolland (Elie)	81	83	164
Willie Fernie (Felixstowe)	80	84	164
Willie Campbell (Musselburgh)	84	85	169
Willie Park Jr (Musselburgh)	86	83	169
Ben Sayers (North Berwick)	83	87	170
Tom Dunn (North Berwick)			171
G Fernie (Dumfries)			171
Peter Fernie (Oxford)			172
John Kirkaldy (St Andrews)			172
Willie Dunn (North Berwick)			173
Matthew Allan (Westward Ho!)			173

NAME	SCORE
Tom Morris (St Andrews)	174
JOF Morris (St Andrews)	174
Jamie Anderson (Ardeer)	175
William Cosgrove (Musselburgh)	178
Mr William Doleman (Glasgow)	178
Mr J Hunter (Royal & Ancient)	179
David Grant (St Andrews)	180
G Smith (Troon)	183

1885 *at St Andrews*

NAME	SCORE		
Bob Martin (St Andrews)	84	87	171
Archie Simpson (Carnoustie)	83	89	172
David Ayton (St Andrews)	89	84	173
Willie Fernie (Felixstowe)	89	85	174
Willie Park Jr (Musselburgh)	86	88	174
Bob Simpson (Carnoustie)	85	89	174
J Burns (St Andrews)	88	87	175
Peter Paxton (Malvern)	85	91	176
Willie Campbell (Musselburgh)	86	91	177
JOF Morris (St Andrews)	91	86	177
Mr Horace Hutchinson (Westward Ho!)	87	91	178
John Kirkaldy (St Andrews)	94	84	178
Jack Simpson (Carnoustie)	87	92	179
Mr JE Laidlay (Honourable Company)	87	92	179
Ben Sayers (North Berwick)	94	86	180
Mr Leslie Balfour (Royal & Ancient)	90	91	181
W Greig (St Andrews)	89	92	181
Mr HSC Everard (Royal & Ancient)	90	92	182
G Fernie (St Andrews)	87	95	182
J Rennie (Monifieth)	90	92	182

1886 *at Musselburgh*

NAME	SCORE		
David Brown (Musselburgh)	79	78	157
Willie Campbell (Musselburgh)	78	81	159
Ben Campbell (Musselburgh)	79	81	160
Archie Simpson (Carnoustie)	82	79	161
Willie Park Jr (Musselburgh)	84	77	161
Thomas Gossett (Musselburgh)	80	81	161
Bob Ferguson (Musselburgh)	82	79	161
Willie Fernie (St Andrews)	79	83	162
David Grant (Musselburgh)	86	76	162
Mr JE Laidlay (Honourable Company)	80	82	162
JOF Morris (St Andrews)	81	82	163
John Lambert (Musselburgh)	78	86	164
Thomas McWatt (Musselburgh)	81	83	164
Jack Simpson (Carnoustie)	83	81	164
Bob Simpson (Carnoustie)	84	81	165
Tom Dunn (North Berwick)	83	83	166
Mr Horace Hutchinson (Westward Ho!)	81	85	166
Bob Pringle (St Andrews)	80	86	166

NAME	SCORE		
Ben Sayers (Musselburgh)	84	82	166
Robert Tait (Musselburgh)	84	83	167
William Cosgrove (Musselburgh)	84	83	167

1887 *at Prestwick*

NAME	SCORE		
Willie Park Jr (Musselburgh)	82	79	161
Bob Martin (St Andrews)	81	81	162
Willie Campbell (Prestwick)	77	87	164
Mr JE Laidlay (Honourable Company)	86	80	166
Ben Sayers (North Berwick)	83	85	168
Archie Simpson (Carnoustie)	81	87	168
Willie Fernie (Troon)	86	87	173
David Grant (North Berwick)	89	84	173
David Brown (Musselburgh)	82	92	174
Mr Horace Hutchinson (Westward Ho!)	87	88	175
Ben Campbell (Musselburgh)	88	87	175
David Ayton (St Andrews)	89	87	176
J Simpson (Edinburgh)	85	91	176
J Kaye (Seaton Carew)	89	87	176
John Kirkaldy (St Andrews)	89	87	176
Bob Simpson (Carnoustie)	90	89	179
A Monoghan (Prestwick)	90	90	180
G Fernie (Troon)	92	88	180
Hugh Kirkaldy (St Andrews)	89	92	181
Mr P Wilson	90	92	182
J Boyd (Prestwick)	95	87	182

1888 *at St Andrews*

NAME	SCORE		
Jack Burns (Warwick)	86	85	171
D Anderson Jr (St Andrews)	86	86	172
Ben Sayers (North Berwick)	85	87	172
Willie Campbell (Prestwick)	84	90	174
Mr Leslie Balfour (Edinburgh)	86	89	175
Andrew Kirkaldy (St Andrews)	87	89	176
David Grant (North Berwick)	88	88	176
Alex Herd (St Andrews)	93	84	177
David Ayton (St Andrews)	87	91	178
Mr JE Laidlay (Honourable Company)	93	87	180
Willie Park Jr (Musselburgh)	90	92	182
Hugh Kirkaldy (St Andrews)	98	84	182
Mr HSC Everard (St Andrews)	93	89	182
Willie Fernie (Troon)	91	92	183
Laurie Auchterlonie (St Andrews)	91	93	184
Archie Simpson (Carnoustie)	91	93	184
Bob Martin (St Andrews)	86	98	184
Bob Tait (Musselburgh)	95	90	185
John Kirkaldy (St Andrews)	92	93	185
Mr AF Macfie (St Andrews)	94	91	185
Jamie Allen (Edinburgh)	95	90	185
Willie Auchterlonie (St Andrews)	92	93	185

1889   *at Musselburgh*

NAME	SCORE				
Willie Park Jr (Musselburgh)	39	39	39	38	155
Andrew Kirkaldy (St Andrews)	39	38	39	39	155
(Park won play-off 158 to 163)					
Ben Sayers (North Berwick)	39	40	41	39	159
Mr JE Laidlay (Honourable Company)	42	39	40	41	162
David Brown (Musselburgh)	43	39	41	39	162
Willie Fernie (Troon)	45	39	40	40	164
Willie Campbell (Bridge of Weir)	44	40	42	39	165
Willie Brown (Musselburgh)	44	43	41	37	165
David Grant (North Berwick)	41	41	41	42	165
Hugh Kirkaldy (Coventry)	44	39	43	40	166
William Thomson (Musselburgh)	43	42	40	41	166
Archie Simpson (Carnoustie)	44	45	37	41	167
Mr AM Ross (Edinburgh Burgess)	42	45	42	40	169
Jack Burns (Warwick)	47	39	42	42	170

1890   *at Prestwick*

NAME	SCORE		
Mr John Ball Jr (R Liverpool)	82	82	164
Willie Fernie (Troon)	85	82	167
Archie Simpson (Carnoustie)	85	82	167
Willie Park Jr (Musselburgh)	90	80	170
Andrew Kirkaldy (St Andrews)	81	89	170
Mr HG Hutchinson (R North Devon)	87	85	172
David Grant (North Berwick)	86	87	173
Hugh Kirkaldy (St Andrews)	82	91	173
W McEwan (Musselburgh)	87	87	174
David Brown (Musselburgh)	85	90	175
Mr JE Laidlay (Honourable Company)	89	88	177
J Kay (Seaton Carew)	86	91	177
Mr D Leitch (St Andrews)	86	93	179
D Anderson (Carnoustie)	90	90	180
Ben Campbell (Bridge of Weir)	93	88	181
John Allan (Prestwick)	93	88	181
Mr D Anderson (Carnoustie)	91	91	182
David Ayton (St Andrews)	97	85	182
Ben Sayers (North Berwick)	90	93	183
A Wright (Prestwick)	92	92	184

1891   *at St Andrews*

NAME	SCORE		
Hugh Kirkaldy (St Andrews)	83	83	166
Andrew Kirkaldy (St Andrews)	84	84	168
Willie Fernie (Troon)	84	84	168
Mr S Mure Fergusson (Royal & Ancient)	86	84	170
WD More (Chester)	84	87	171

NAME	SCORE		
Willie Park Jr (Musselburgh)	88	85	173
David Brown (Malvern)	88	86	174
Willie Auchterlonie (St Andrews)	85	90	175
Tom Vardon (St Anne's-on-Sea)	89	87	176
Ben Sayers (North Berwick)	91	85	176
Mr John Ball Jr (R Liverpool)	94	83	177
Archie Simpson (Carnoustie)	86	91	177
Alex Herd (St Andrews)	87	91	178
James Kay (Seaton Carew)	93	86	179
Bob Mearns (Aberdeen)	88	91	179
John Kirkaldy (St Andrews)	90	89	179
David Grant (North Berwick)	84	95	179
Laurie Auchterlonie (St Andrews)	87	93	180
Mr JE Laidlay (Honourable Company)	90	90	180
Mr Charles Hutchings (R Liverpool)	89	91	180
D Simpson (Earlsferry)	91	89	180

1892   *at Muirfield*

NAME	SCORE				
Mr HH Hilton (R Liverpool)	78	81	72	74	305
Mr John Ball Jr (R Liverpool)	75	80	74	79	308
Hugh Kirkaldy (St Andrews)	77	83	73	75	308
Alex Herd (Huddersfield)	77	78	77	76	308
J Kay (Seaton Carew)	82	78	74	78	312
Ben Sayers (North Berwick)	80	76	81	75	312
Willie Park Jr (Musselburgh)	78	77	80	80	315
Willie Fernie (Troon)	79	83	76	78	316
Archie Simpson (Prestwick)	81	81	76	79	317
Mr HG Hutchinson (St Andrews)	74	78	86	80	318
J White (North Berwick)	82	78	78	81	319
Tom Vardon (St Anne's-on-Sea)	83	75	80	82	320
Mr Edward BH Blackwell (St Andrews)	81	82	82	76	321
Andrew Kirkaldy (St Andrews)	84	82	80	75	321
Mr S Mure Fergusson (Royal & Ancient)	78	82	80	82	322
Ben Campbell (Bridge of Weir)	86	83	79	76	324
D Anderson Jr (St Andrews)	76	82	79	87	324
Mr RT Boothby (St Andrews)	81	81	80	82	324
Mr FA Fairlie (Prestwick)	83	87	79	76	325
W McEwan (Musselburgh)	79	83	84	79	325

1893   *at Prestwick*

NAME	SCORE				
Willie Auchterlonie (St Andrews)	78	81	81	82	322
Mr JE Laidlay (Honourable Company)	80	83	80	81	324
Alex Herd (Huddersfield)	82	81	78	84	325
Andrew Kirkaldy (St Andrews)	85	82	82	77	326
Hugh Kirkaldy (St Andrews)	83	79	82	82	326

NAME	SCORE				
J Kay (Seaton Carew)	81	81	80	85	327
Bob Simpson (Carnoustie)	81	81	80	85	327
Mr John Ball Jr (R Liverpool)	83	79	84	86	332
Mr HH Hilton (R Liverpool)	88	81	82	81	332
JH Taylor (Winchester)	75	89	86	83	333
Jack White (North Berwick)	81	86	80	86	333
Ben Sayers (North Berwick)	87	88	84	76	335
Mr Charles Hutchings (R Liverpool)	81	92	80	84	337
Archie Simpson (Carnoustie)	84	86	84	85	339
Mr S Mure Fergusson (Royal & Ancient)	83	85	85	87	340
J Hunter (Prestwick)	87	85	83	85	340
J Lloyd (Pau, France)	85	91	84	81	341
David Grant (North Berwick)	86	86	85	84	341
Willie Park Jr (Musselburgh)	82	89	86	85	342
Mr PC Anderson (St Andrews)	93	84	83	82	342
Mr LS Anderson (New North Berwick)	89	83	86	84	342

NAME	SCORE				
Archie Simpson (Aberdeen)	88	85	78	85	336
Willie Fernie (Troon)	86	79	86	86	337
David Brown (Malvern)	81	89	83	84	337
D Anderson Jr (St Andrews)	86	83	84	84	337
Ben Sayers (North Berwick)	84	87	85	82	338
A Toogood (Minchinhampton)	85	84	83	86	338
Harry Vardon (Bury)	80	85	85	88	338
Tom Vardon (Ilkley)	82	83	84	89	338
Laurie Auchterlonie (St Andrews)	84	84	85	87	340
J Robb (St Andrews)	89	88	81	82	340
Hugh Kirkaldy (St Andrews)	87	87	83	84	341
Mr FG Tait (Royal & Ancient)	87	86	82	86	341
Mr JE Laidlay (Honourable Company)	91	83	82	86	342
Mr John Ball Jr (R Liverpool)	85	85	88	86	344
L Waters (St Andrews)	86	83	85	90	344
David Herd (Bradford)	85	85	84	91	345

1894   *at St George's, Sandwich*

NAME	SCORE				
JH Taylor (Winchester)	84	80	81	81	326
R Rolland (Limpsfield)	86	79	84	82	331
Andrew Kirkaldy (St Andrews)	86	79	83	84	332
A Toogood (Eltham)	84	85	82	82	333
Willie Fernie (Troon)	84	84	86	80	334
Ben Sayers (North Berwick)	85	81	84	84	334
Harry Vardon (Bury)	86	86	82	80	334
Alex Herd (Huddersfield)	83	85	82	88	338
Mr FG Tait (Royal & Ancient)	90	83	83	84	340
James Braid (Elie)	91	84	82	84	341
Mr AD Blyth (R St George's)	91	84	84	82	341
Willie Park Jr (Musselburgh)	88	86	82	87	343
David Brown (Malvern)	93	83	81	87	344
Archie Simpson (Carnoustie)	90	86	86	82	344
Hugh Kirkaldy (Oxford)	90	85	80	89	344
Mr John Ball Jr (R Liverpool)	84	89	87	84	344
J Lloyd (Pau, France)	95	81	86	83	345
Mr S Mure Fergusson (R St George's)	87	88	84	87	346
Tom Vardon (Ilkley)	87	88	82	91	348
David Herd (Hoylake)	92	93	84	84	353
Mr CE Dick (R Liverpool)	85	89	89	90	353
David Grant (North Berwick)	91	84	87	91	353

1896   *at Muirfield*

NAME	SCORE				
Harry Vardon (Ganton)	83	78	78	77	316
JH Taylor (Winchester)	77	78	81	80	316
(Vardon won play-off 157 to 159)					
Mr FG Tait (Black Watch)	83	75	84	77	319
Willie Fernie (Troon)	78	79	82	80	319
Alex Herd (Huddersfield)	72	84	79	85	320
James Braid (Romford)	83	81	79	80	323
Ben Sayers (North Berwick)	83	76	79	86	324
David Brown (Malvern)	80	77	81	86	324
AH Scott (Earlsferry)	83	84	77	80	324
Tom Vardon (Ilkley)	83	82	77	83	325
P McEwan (Southport)	83	81	80	84	328
Willie Auchterlonie (St Andrews)	80	86	81	82	329
Archie Simpson (Aberdeen)	85	79	78	87	329
J Kay (Seaton Carew)	77	88	83	82	330
Willie Park Jr (Musselburgh)	79	80	83	88	330
Andrew Kirkaldy (St Andrews)	84	85	79	82	330
AH Toogood (Minchinhampton)	81	85	84	84	334
Mr JE Laidlay (Honourable Company)	85	82	82	86	335
David McEwan (Formby)	83	89	81	82	335
J Hunter (Prestwick)	85	79	83	88	335
J Ross (Seaford)	83	87	84	81	335

1895   *at St Andrews*

NAME	SCORE				
JH Taylor (Winchester)	86	78	80	78	322
Alex Herd (Huddersfield)	82	77	82	85	326
Andrew Kirkaldy (St Andrews)	81	83	84	84	332
G Pulford (Hoylake)	84	81	83	86	334

1897   *at Hoylake*

NAME	SCORE				
Mr HH Hilton (R Liverpool)	80	75	84	75	314
James Braid (Romford)	80	74	82	79	315
Mr FG Tait (Black Watch)	79	79	80	79	317
G Pulford (Hoylake)	80	79	79	79	317

NAME	SCORE				
Alex Herd (Huddersfield)	78	81	79	80	318
H Vardon (Ganton)	84	80	80	76	320
Tom Vardon (Ilkley)	81	81	79	83	324
Archie Simpson (Aberdeen)	83	81	81	79	324
David Brown (Malvern)	79	82	80	83	324
Andrew Kirkaldy (St Andrews)	83	83	82	82	330
JH Taylor (Wimbledon)	82	80	82	86	330
Ben Sayers (North Berwick)	84	78	85	84	331
Mr S Mure Fergusson (Royal & Ancient)	87	83	79	82	331
TG Renouf (Shipley)	86	79	83	84	332
P McEwan (Southport)	86	79	85	82	332
AH Scott (Earlsferry)	83	83	84	83	333
Mr John Ball Jr (R Liverpool)	78	81	88	87	334
Willie Auchterlonie (St Andrews)	84	85	85	81	335
Mr John Graham Jr (R Liverpool)	85	80	87	83	335
James Kinnell (Prestwick St Nicholas)	82	83	78	93	336
J Lloyd (Pau, France)	86	84	82	84	336

1898 *at Prestwick*

NAME	SCORE				
Harry Vardon (Ganton)	79	75	77	76	307
Willie Park Jr (Musselburgh)	76	75	78	79	308
Mr HH Hilton (R Liverpool)	76	81	77	75	309
JH Taylor (Winchester)	78	78	77	79	312
Mr FG Tait (Black Watch)	81	77	75	82	315
D Kinnell (Leven)	80	77	79	80	316
Willie Fernie (Troon)	79	85	77	77	318
John Hunter (Prestwick)	82	79	81	77	319
TG Renouf (Carlisle)	77	79	81	83	320
Philip Wynn (Mitcham)	83	79	81	78	321
James Braid (Romford)	80	82	84	75	321
James Kay (Seaton Carew)	81	81	77	83	322
G Pulford (Hoylake)	83	81	78	81	323
Jack White (Seaford)	82	81	77	83	323
Archie Simpson (Aberdeen)	83	80	82	79	324
James Kinnell (Prestwick)	77	81	78	88	324
Alex Herd (Huddersfield)	80	79	84	82	325
P McEwan (Southport)	83	83	77	82	325
Ben Sayers (North Berwick)	85	78	79	85	327
WG Toogood (Rochford)	82	84	83	78	327

1899 *at St George's, Sandwich*

NAME	SCORE				
Harry Vardon (Ganton)	76	76	81	77	310
Jack White (Seaford)	79	79	82	75	315
Andrew Kirkaldy (St Andrews)	81	79	82	77	319
JH Taylor (Richmond)	77	76	83	84	320
James Braid (Romford)	78	78	85	81	322
Willie Fernie (Troon)	79	83	82	78	322

NAME	SCORE				
Mr FG Tait (Black Watch)	81	82	79	82	324
James Kinnell (Prestwick)	76	84	80	84	324
A Tingey (West Herts)	81	81	79	85	326
T Williamson (Notts)	76	84	80	86	326
Ben Sayers (North Berwick)	81	79	82	86	328
Mr HH Hilton (R Liverpool)	86	80	80	83	329
TG Renouf (Carlisle)	79	82	84	84	329
Willie Park Jr (North Berwick)	77	79	85	89	330
W Aveston (Cromer)	77	86	82	86	331
Archie Simpson (Aberdeen)	84	84	81	83	332
Ted Ray (Jersey)	84	80	84	84	332
Alex Herd (Huddersfield)	82	81	80	89	332
P Rainford (Chevin)	79	83	83	87	332
WG Toogood (Rochford)	82	86	81	84	333

1900 *at St Andrews*

NAME	SCORE				
JH Taylor (Richmond)	79	77	78	75	309
Harry Vardon (Ganton)	79	81	80	77	317
James Braid (Romford)	82	81	80	79	322
Jack White (Seaford)	80	81	82	80	323
Willie Auchterlonie (St Andrews)	81	85	80	80	326
Willie Park Jr (R Musselburgh)	80	83	81	84	328
Mr Robert Maxwell (Tantallon)	81	81	86	81	329
Archie Simpson (Aberdeen)	82	85	83	79	329
Ben Sayers (North Berwick)	81	83	85	81	330
Andrew Kirkaldy (St Andrews)	87	83	82	79	331
Alex Herd (Huddersfield)	81	85	81	84	331
Tom Vardon (Ilkley)	81	85	84	81	331
Ted Ray (Churston)	88	80	85	81	334
T Simpson (Wakefield)	84	86	83	84	337
D Anderson Jr (St Andrews)	81	87	85	84	337
Mr HH Hilton (R Liverpool)	83	87	87	81	338
Mr W Greig (St Andrews)	93	84	80	81	338
JW Taylor (Redcar)	91	81	84	83	339
J Kirkaldy (St Andrews)	86	85	87	82	340
P Paxton (Tooting Bec)	87	87	79	87	340

1901 *at Muirfield*

NAME	SCORE				
James Braid (Romford)	79	76	74	80	309
Harry Vardon (Ganton)	77	78	79	78	312
JH Taylor (Richmond)	79	83	74	77	313
Mr HH Hilton (R Liverpool)	89	80	75	76	320
Alex Herd (Huddersfield)	87	81	81	76	325
Jack White (Seaford)	82	82	80	82	326
James Kinnell (R Norwich)	79	85	86	78	328
Mr JE Laidlay (Honourable Company)	84	82	82	80	328
PJ Gaudin (Manchester)	86	81	86	76	329

NAME	SCORE				
Mr J Graham Jr (R Liverpool)	82	83	81	83	329
Rowland Jones (Wimbledon Park)	85	82	81	83	331
T Yeoman (Frinton)	85	83	82	82	332
Ted Ray (Churston)	87	84	74	87	332
TG Renouf (Silloth)	83	86	81	82	332
F Collins (Llandudno)	89	80	81	84	334
Mr S Mure Fergusson (R St George's)	84	86	82	82	334
J Oke (Richmond)	91	83	80	80	334
A Lewis (Burton-on-Trent)	85	82	83	86	336
Andrew Kirkaldy (St Andrews)	82	87	86	81	336
Willie Park Jr (Huntercombe)	78	87	81	90	336
AH Scott (Earlsferry)	85	80	81	90	336

1902   *at Hoylake*

NAME	SCORE				
Alex Herd (Huddersfield)	77	76	73	81	307
Harry Vardon (Ganton)	72	77	80	79	308
James Braid (Romford)	78	76	80	74	308
Mr Robert Maxwell (Tantallon)	79	77	79	74	309
Tom Vardon (R St George's)	80	76	78	79	313
JH Taylor (Mid-Surrey)	81	76	77	80	314
James Kinnell (R Norwich)	78	80	79	77	314
Mr HH Hilton (R Liverpool)	79	76	81	78	314
Ted Ray (Churston)	79	74	85	80	318
Andrew Kirkaldy (St Andrews)	77	78	83	82	320
Arnaud Massy (France)	77	81	78	84	320
Rowland Jones (Wimbledon Park)	79	78	85	79	321
Willie Fernie (Troon)	76	82	84	79	321
Mr SH Fry (Mid-Surrey)	78	79	80	85	322
Mr John Ball Jr (Hoylake)	79	79	84	81	323
J Rowe (Forest Row)	79	78	85	81	323
J Sherlock (Oxford)	79	84	80	81	324
Jack White (Sunningdale)	82	75	82	86	325
Ben Sayers (North Berwick)	84	80	80	82	326
WG Toogood (Rochford Hundred)	83	83	80	81	327
TG Renouf (Silloth)	84	82	77	84	327

1903   *at Prestwick*

NAME	SCORE				
Harry Vardon (Totteridge)	73	77	72	78	300
Tom Vardon (R St George's)	76	81	75	74	306
Jack White (Sunningdale)	77	78	74	79	308
Alex Herd (Huddersfield)	73	83	76	77	309
James Braid (Romford)	77	79	79	75	310
AH Scott (Elie)	77	77	83	77	314
R Thomson (North Berwick)	83	78	77	76	314
WJ Leaver (Harlech)	79	79	77	80	315

NAME	SCORE				
GH Cawsey (Ashford Manor)	80	78	76	82	316
JH Taylor (Mid-Surrey)	80	82	78	76	316
Andrew Kirkaldy (St Andrews)	82	79	78	78	317
Tom Williamson (Notts)	76	80	79	82	317
W Hunter (Richmond)	81	74	79	84	318
Mr Robert Maxwell (Prestwick St Nicholas)	82	84	76	76	318
Willie Park Jr (Huntercombe)	78	86	80	75	319
J Kinnell (R Norwich)	78	86	76	79	319
E Gray (Littlehampton)	77	83	79	80	319
AH Toogood (Headingley)	86	77	80	77	320
G Pulford (Hoylake)	79	86	79	76	320
D Kinnell (Prestwick)	82	78	80	80	320

1904   *at St George's, Sandwich*

NAME	SCORE				
Jack White (Sunningdale)	80	75	72	69	296
JH Taylor (Mid-Surrey)	77	78	74	68	297
James Braid (Walton Heath)	77	80	69	71	297
Tom Vardon (R St George's)	77	77	75	72	301
Harry Vardon (South Herts)	76	73	79	74	302
J Sherlock (Oxford)	83	71	78	77	309
Andrew Kirkaldy (St Andrews)	78	79	74	79	310
Mr John Graham (R Liverpool)	76	76	78	80	310
Alex Herd (Huddersfield)	84	76	76	75	311
Mr Robert Maxwell (Tantallon)	80	80	76	77	313
Ben Sayers (North Berwick)	80	80	76	77	313
Ted Ray (Scarborough)	81	81	77	76	315
AH Toogood (Chingford)	88	76	74	77	315
Willie Park Jr (Huntercombe)	84	72	81	78	315
R Thomson (Romford)	75	76	80	84	315
J Rowe (Ashdown Forest)	86	82	75	73	316
G Coburn (Portmarnock)	79	82	75	80	316
Mr John Ball Jr (R Liverpool)	83	78	79	78	318
F Collins (Llandudno)	88	77	75	79	319
GH Cawsey (Malvern)	82	80	78	79	319
Ernest Gray (Littlehampton)	84	77	74	84	319

1905   *at St Andrews*

NAME	SCORE				
James Braid (Walton Heath)	81	78	78	81	318
Rowland Jones (Wimbledon Park)	81	77	87	78	323
JH Taylor (Mid-Surrey)	80	85	78	80	323
James Kinnell (Purley Downs)	82	79	82	81	324
Ernest Gray (Littlehampton)	82	81	84	78	325
Arnaud Massy (North Berwick)	81	80	82	82	325
R Thomson (Romford)	81	81	82	83	327
J Sherlock (Oxford)	81	84	80	83	328
T Simpson (St Anne's)	82	88	78	81	329
Harry Vardon (South Herts)	80	82	84	83	329

NAME	SCORE				
J Rowe (R Ashdown Forest)	87	81	80	82	330
Ted Ray (Ganton)	85	82	81	82	330
Willie Park (Huntercombe)	84	81	85	81	331
Tom Williamson (Notts)	84	81	79	87	331
Alex Herd (Huddersfield)	80	82	83	87	332
Alex Smith (USA)	81	88	86	78	333
TG Renouf (Silloth)	81	85	84	83	333
Jack White (Sunningdale)	86	83	83	83	335
T Watt (Southport)	86	85	79	85	335
J Johnstone (North Berwick)	85	86	84	80	335
Archie Simpson (Aberdeen)	87	84	81	83	335

1906   *at Muirfield*

NAME	SCORE				
James Braid (Walton Heath)	77	76	74	73	300
JH Taylor (Mid-Surrey)	77	72	75	80	304
Harry Vardon (South Herts)	77	73	77	78	305
Mr John Graham Jr (R Liverpool)	71	79	78	78	306
Rowland Jones (Wimbledon Park)	74	78	73	83	308
Arnaud Massy (France)	76	80	76	78	310
Mr Robert Maxwell (Tantallon)	73	78	77	83	311
Ted Ray (Ganton)	80	75	79	78	312
G Duncan (Timperley)	73	78	83	78	312
TG Renouf (Manchester)	76	77	76	83	312
D Kinnell (Prestwick St Nicholas)	78	76	80	79	313
Tom Vardon (R St George's)	76	81	81	77	315
W Hunter (Richmond)	79	76	80	80	315
WJ Leaver (Worsley)	80	76	78	81	315
WG Toogood (Ilkley)	83	79	83	71	316
GH Cawsey (Malvern)	79	80	79	78	316
Mr RW Whitecross (Dirleton Castle)	74	83	80	79	316
T Simpson (R Lytham & St Anne's)	78	78	81	79	316
H Hamill (Belfast)	83	78	79	77	317
D McEwan (Birkdale)	79	79	81	78	317
Alex Herd (Huddersfield)	81	79	77	80	317
PJ Gaudin (Fulwell)	77	77	80	83	317
Tom Williamson (Notts)	77	77	78	85	317

1907   *at Hoylake*

NAME	SCORE				
Arnaud Massy (La Boulie, France)	76	81	78	77	312
JH Taylor (Mid-Surrey)	79	79	76	80	314
Tom Vardon (R St George's)	81	81	80	75	317
G Pulford (Hoylake)	81	78	80	78	317
James Braid (Walton Heath)	82	85	75	76	318
Ted Ray (Ganton)	83	80	79	76	318

NAME	SCORE				
G Duncan (Timperley)	83	78	81	77	319
Tom Williamson (Notts)	82	77	82	78	319
Harry Vardon (South Herts)	84	81	74	80	319
T Ball (West Lancashire)	80	78	81	81	320
PJ Gaudin (Fulwell)	83	84	80	76	323
Alex Herd (Huddersfield)	83	81	83	77	324
Mr John Graham Jr (R Liverpool)	83	81	80	82	326
WG Toogood (Ilkley)	76	86	82	82	326
Mr John Ball Jr (R Liverpool)	88	83	79	77	327
F Collins (Llandudno)	83	83	79	82	327
CH Mayo (Burhill)	86	78	82	82	328
A Matthews (Rhyl)	82	80	84	82	328
TG Renouf (Manchester)	83	80	82	83	328
R Gray (R Guernsey)	83	85	81	80	329

1908   *at Prestwick*

NAME	SCORE				
James Braid (Walton Heath)	70	72	77	72	291
T Ball (West Lancashire)	76	73	76	74	299
Ted Ray (Ganton)	79	71	75	76	301
Alex Herd (Huddersfield)	74	74	79	75	302
Harry Vardon (South Herts)	79	78	74	75	306
D Kinnell (Prestwick)	75	73	80	78	306
JH Taylor (Mid-Surrey)	79	77	76	75	307
T Simpson (R Lytham & St Anne's)	75	77	76	79	307
PJ Gaudin (Fulwell)	77	76	75	80	308
Arnaud Massy (France)	76	75	76	81	308
T Watt (Timperley)	81	73	78	78	310
J Edmundson (Bangor, Co Down)	80	72	76	82	310
WJ Leaver (Worsley)	79	79	75	78	311
Tom Vardon (R St George's)	77	79	76	79	311
Fred Collins (Llandudno)	78	77	77	79	311
Mr John Ball Jr (R Liverpool)	74	78	78	81	311
Ernest Gray (Littlehampton)	68	79	83	81	311
G Duncan (Hanger Hill)	79	77	80	76	312
AH Toogood (Tramore)	82	76	77	77	312
Mr John Graham Jr (R Liverpool)	76	82	76	78	312
F Robson (Bromborough)	72	79	83	78	312
WG Toogood (Ilkley)	80	75	78	79	312
G Pulford (Hoylake)	81	77	74	80	312

1909   *at Deal*

NAME	SCORE				
JH Taylor (Mid-Surrey)	74	73	74	74	295
James Braid (Walton Heath)	79	75	73	74	301
T Ball (West Lancashire)	74	75	76	76	301
C Johns (Southdown)	72	76	79	75	302
TG Renouf (Manchester)	76	78	76	73	303
Ted Ray (Ganton)	77	76	76	75	304

NAME	SCORE				
WH Horne (Chertsey)	77	78	77	74	306
J Hepburn (Home Park)	78	77	76	76	307
Alex Herd (Huddersfield)	76	75	80	76	307
G Pulford (Hoylake)	81	76	76	75	308
B Nicolls (Walmer)	78	76	77	77	308
Mr EA Lassen (R Lytham & St Anne's)	82	74	74	78	308
Mr Robert Maxwell (Tantallon)	75	80	80	74	309
P Rainford (Llangammarch Wells)	78	76	76	80	310
EP Gaudin (Worplesdon)	76	77	77	80	310
GH Cawsey (Malvern)	79	76	78	78	311
R Thomson (North Berwick)	81	79	75	77	312
Ben Sayers Sr (North Berwick)	79	77	79	77	312
Tom Vardon (R St George's)	80	75	80	78	313
Capt CK Hutchison (Honourable Company)	75	81	78	79	313

1910   *at St Andrews*

NAME	SCORE				
James Braid (Walton Heath)	76	73	74	76	299
Alex Herd (Huddersfield)	78	74	75	76	303
G Duncan (Hanger Hill)	73	77	71	83	304
L Ayton (Bishop's Stortford)	78	76	75	77	306
J Robson (West Surrey)	75	80	77	76	308
W Smith (Mexico)	77	71	80	80	308
Ted Ray (Ganton)	76	77	74	81	308
F Kinnell (Purley Downs)	79	74	77	79	309
DJ Ross (USA)	78	79	75	77	309
TG Renouf (Manchester)	77	76	75	81	309
EP Gaudin (Worplesdon)	78	74	76	81	309
PJ Gaudin (Fulwell)	80	79	74	78	311
Tom Ball (Bramshot)	81	77	75	78	311
JH Taylor (Mid-Surrey)	76	80	78	78	312
Michael Moran (Dollymount)	77	75	79	81	312
WL Ritchie (Walton Heath)	78	74	82	79	313
F MacKenzie (St Andrews)	78	80	75	80	313
Harry Vardon (South Herts)	77	81	75	80	313
J Hepburn (Home Park)	78	82	76	78	314
Tom Williamson (Notts)	78	80	78	78	314
Mr John Ball Jr (R Liverpool)	79	75	78	82	314

1911   *at St George's, Sandwich*

NAME	SCORE				
Harry Vardon (South Herts)	74	74	75	80	303
Arnaud Massy (France)	75	78	74	76	303

(Vardon won play-off at the 35th hole)

NAME	SCORE				
Mr HH Hilton (R Liverpool)	76	74	78	76	304
Alex Herd (Coombe Hill)	77	73	76	78	304
James Braid (Walton Heath)	78	75	74	78	305
Ted Ray (Ganton)	76	72	79	78	305
JH Taylor (Mid-Surrey)	72	76	78	79	305
G Duncan (Hanger Hill)	73	71	83	79	306

NAME	SCORE				
L Ayton (Bishop's Stortford)	75	77	77	78	307
J Hepburn (Surbiton)	74	77	83	75	309
F Robson (West Sussex)	78	74	79	78	309
Fred Collins (Llandudno)	77	76	83	74	310
J Piper (Southerndown)	78	79	80	74	311
TG Renouf (Manchester)	75	76	79	81	311
T Ball (Raynes Park)	76	77	79	80	312
Rowland Jones (Wimbledon Park)	80	76	85	72	313
JG Sherlock (Stoke Poges)	73	80	76	84	313
Wilfred Reid (Banstead Downs)	78	79	80	76	313
CH Mayo (Burhill)	78	78	79	78	313
Mr HE Taylor (Richmond)	83	73	76	81	313

1912   *at Muirfield*

NAME	SCORE				
Ted Ray (Oxhey)	71	73	76	75	295
Harry Vardon (South Herts)	75	72	81	71	299
James Braid (Walton Heath)	77	71	77	78	303
G Duncan (Hanger Hill)	72	77	78	78	305
Alex Herd (Coombe Hill)	76	81	76	76	309
L Ayton (Bishop's Stortford)	74	80	75	80	309
Fred Collins (Llandudno)	76	79	81	74	310
J Gassiat (France)	76	80	78	76	310
RG Wilson (Berkhamsted)	82	75	75	78	310
Arnaud Massy (France)	74	77	82	78	311
CH Mayo (Burhill)	76	77	78	81	312
JH Taylor (Mid-Surrey)	75	76	77	84	312
G Fotheringham (Carnoustie)	75	78	79	81	313
R Thomson (North Berwick)	73	77	80	83	313
H McNeill (Portrush)	76	78	82	78	314
Michael Moran (R Dublin)	76	79	80	79	314
F Leach (Northwood)	75	82	81	77	315
Tom Williamson (Notts)	80	77	79	79	315
TG Renouf (Manchester)	77	80	80	79	316
WH Horne (Chertsey)	73	85	82	77	317
Wilfred Reid (Banstead Downs)	80	79	79	79	317
JD Edgar (Northumberland)	77	81	80	79	317

1913   *at Hoylake*

NAME	SCORE				
JH Taylor (Mid-Surrey)	73	75	77	79	304
Ted Ray (Ganton)	73	74	81	84	312
Michael Moran (R Dublin)	76	74	89	74	313
Harry Vardon (South Herts)	79	75	79	80	313
TG Renouf (Manchester)	75	78	84	78	315
JJ McDermott (USA)	75	80	77	83	315
J Sherlock (Stoke Poges)	77	86	79	75	317
J Bradbeer (Porters Park)	78	79	81	79	317
Arnaud Massy (France)	77	80	81	79	317
Tom Williamson (Notts)	77	80	80	80	317
Fred Collins (Llandudno)	77	85	79	77	318

NAME	SCORE				
Alex Herd (Coombe Hill)	73	81	84	80	318
Mr John Graham (R Liverpool)	77	79	81	81	318
C Roberts (Woolton)	78	79	84	78	319
Josh Taylor (Acton)	80	75	85	79	319
Mr EA Lassen (R Lytham & St Anne's)	79	78	80	82	319
PE Taylor (Littlehampton)	78	81	83	78	320
H McNeill (R Portrush)	80	81	81	79	321
E Jones (Chislehurst)	75	85	81	80	321
James Braid (Walton Heath)	80	79	82	80	321
C Gray (Beckenham)	80	81	79	81	321

1914   *at Prestwick*

NAME	SCORE				
Harry Vardon (South Herts)	73	77	78	78	306
JH Taylor (Mid-Surrey)	74	78	74	83	309
HB Simpson (St Anne's Old Links)	77	80	78	75	310
Abe Mitchell (Sonning)	76	78	79	79	312
Tom Williamson (Notts)	75	79	79	79	312
RG Wilson (Croham Hurst)	76	77	80	80	313
J Ockenden (West Drayton)	75	76	83	80	314
PJ Gaudin (Camberley Heath)	78	83	80	74	315
Mr JLC Jenkins (Troon)	79	80	73	83	315
George Duncan (Hanger Hill)	77	79	80	80	316
Ted Ray (Oxhey)	77	82	76	81	316
Arnaud Massy (France)	77	82	75	82	316
James Braid (Walton Heath)	74	82	78	82	316
JD Edgar (Northumberland)	79	75	84	79	317
J Bradbeer (Porters Park)	77	80	80	80	317
J Gassiat (France)	76	81	80	80	317
Mr EA Lassen (Bradford)	85	78	79	77	319
W Hunter (Richmond)	82	77	77	83	319
E Foord (Burnham)	82	81	82	76	321
C Hughes (Chester)	80	81	80	80	321

1915–19   *No Championship owing to the Great War*

1920   *at Deal*

NAME	SCORE				
G Duncan (Hanger Hill)	80	80	71	72	303
Alex Herd (Coombe Hill)	72	81	77	75	305
Ted Ray (Oxhey)	72	83	78	73	306
Abe Mitchell (North Foreland)	74	73	84	76	307
Len Holland (Northamptonshire)	80	78	71	79	308
Jim Barnes (USA)	79	74	77	79	309

NAME	SCORE				
S Wingate (Ravensworth)	81	74	76	82	313
AG Havers (West Lancashire)	80	78	81	74	313
WH Horne (unattached)	80	81	73	81	315
GR Buckle (Edgbaston)	80	80	77	78	315
A Compston (North Manchester)	79	83	75	78	315
JH Taylor (Mid-Surrey)	78	79	80	79	316
L Lafitte (France)	75	85	84	73	317
Harry Vardon (South Herts)	78	81	81	78	318
E Bannister (Sandy Lodge)	78	84	80	76	318
A Gaudin (Alwoodley)	81	82	77	79	319
Angel de la Torre (Spain)	84	78	78	79	319
PE Taylor (Fulwell)	78	84	77	80	319
C Johns (Purley Downs)	82	78	81	78	319
J Sherlock (Stoke Poges)	82	81	80	76	319

1921   *at St Andrews*

NAME	SCORE				
Jock Hutchison (USA)	72	75	79	70	296
Mr RH Wethered (Royal & Ancient)	78	75	72	71	296
(Hutchison won play-off 150 to 159)					
Tom Kerrigan (USA)	74	80	72	72	298
AG Havers (West Lancashire)	76	74	77	72	299
George Duncan (Hanger Hill)	74	75	78	74	301
F Leach (Northwood)	78	75	76	73	302
Walter Hagen (USA)	74	79	72	77	302
JH Kirkwood (Australia)	76	74	73	79	302
Arnaud Massy (France)	74	75	74	79	302
Alex Herd (Coombe Hill)	75	74	73	80	302
Jim Barnes (USA)	74	74	74	80	302
Tom Williamson (Notts)	79	71	74	78	302
Abe Mitchell (North Foreland)	78	79	76	71	304
W Pursey (East Devon)	74	82	74	74	304
JW Gaudin (Alwoodley)	78	76	75	76	305
Len Holland (Northampton)	78	78	76	74	306
W Mehlhorn (USA)	75	77	76	78	306
James Braid (Walton Heath)	77	75	78	76	306
WM Watt (Royal Automobile Club)	81	77	75	74	307
F Ball (Langley Park)	79	78	74	76	307
Dr P Hunter (USA)	75	78	76	78	307
Ted Ray (Oxhey)	76	72	81	78	307

1922   *at St George's, Sandwich*

NAME	SCORE				
Walter Hagen (USA)	76	73	79	72	300
George Duncan (Hanger Hill)	76	75	81	69	301
Jim Barnes (USA)	75	76	77	73	301
Jock Hutchison (USA)	79	74	73	76	302
CA Whitcombe (Dorchester)	77	79	72	75	303

NAME	SCORE				
JH Taylor (Mid-Surrey)	73	78	76	77	304
J Gassiat (France)	75	78	74	79	306
Harry Vardon (South Herts)	79	79	74	75	307
T Walton (Lytham & St Anne's)	75	78	77	77	307
Percy Alliss (Clyne)	75	78	78	77	308
C Johns (Purley)	78	76	80	75	309
AG Havers (West Lancashire)	78	80	78	74	310
Len Holland (Northampton)	79	81	74	76	310
George Gadd (Roehampton)	76	81	76	77	310
FC Jewell (North Middlesex)	75	80	78	77	310
ER Whitcombe (Marlborough)	77	78	77	78	310
AR Wheildon (Moseley)	80	80	76	75	311
Aubrey Boomer (France)	75	80	76	80	311
Abe Mitchell (North Foreland)	79	79	78	76	312
Hon M Scott (R North Devon)	77	83	79	74	313
HJ Osborne (Newquay)	80	81	76	76	313
JH Kirkwood (Australia)	79	76	80	78	313

1923   *at Troon*

NAME	SCORE				
AG Havers (Coombe Hill)	73	73	73	76	295
Walter Hagen (USA)	76	71	74	75	296
Macdonald Smith (USA)	80	73	69	75	297
JH Kirkwood (Australia)	72	79	69	78	298
TR Fernie (Turnberry)	73	78	74	75	300
George Duncan (Hanger Hill)	79	75	74	74	302
CA Whitcombe (Lansdown)	70	76	74	82	302
HC Jolly (Foxgrove)	79	75	75	74	303
J Mackenzie (Ilkley)	76	78	74	75	303
Abe Mitchell (North Foreland)	77	77	72	77	303
WM Watt (Royal Automobile Club)	76	77	72	78	303
Tom Williamson (Notts)	79	78	73	74	304
S Wingate (Wearside)	80	75	74	75	304
Ted Ray (Oxhey)	79	75	73	77	304
G Lockhart (Gleneagles)	78	71	76	79	304
T Barber (Alderley Edge)	78	80	76	71	305
Frank Ball (Langley Park)	76	77	77	75	305
F Collins (Llandudno)	76	78	72	79	305
Angel de la Torre (Spain)	78	80	74	74	306
T Walton (R Lytham & St Anne's)	77	74	78	77	306
JJ Farrell (USA)	79	73	75	79	306

1924   *at Hoylake*

NAME	SCORE				
Walter Hagen (USA)	77	73	74	77	301
ER Whitcombe (Came Down)	77	70	77	78	302
Frank Ball (Langley Park)	78	75	74	77	304
Macdonald Smith (USA)	76	74	77	77	304
JH Taylor (Mid-Surrey)	75	74	79	79	307
Len Holland (Northampton)	74	78	78	78	308

NAME	SCORE				
Aubrey Boomer (France)	75	78	76	79	308
George Duncan (Hanger Hill)	74	79	74	81	309
JM Barber (USA)	78	77	79	75	309
George Gadd (Roehampton)	79	75	78	77	309
PF Weston (Western Park)	76	77	77	79	309
JG Sherlock (Hunstanton)	76	75	78	80	309
Tom Williamson (Notts)	79	76	80	75	310
Gilbert Nicholls (USA)	75	78	79	78	310
Alex Herd (Moor Park)	76	79	76	79	310
JW Gaudin (Alwoodley)	79	78	80	76	313
C Johns (Purley Downs)	77	77	78	81	313
A Tingey Jr (Frinton)	82	81	76	75	314
James Braid (Walton Heath)	80	80	78	76	314
Mr Cyril Tolley (Walton Heath)	73	82	80	79	314

1925   *at Prestwick*

NAME	SCORE				
Jim Barnes (USA)	70	77	79	74	300
Ted Ray (Oxhey)	77	76	75	73	301
A Compston (North Manchester)	76	75	75	75	301
Macdonald Smith (USA)	76	69	76	82	303
Abe Mitchell (unattached)	77	76	75	77	305
JW Gaudin (Alwoodley)	78	81	77	74	310
Percy Alliss (Wanstead)	77	80	77	76	310
JH Taylor (Mid-Surrey)	74	79	80	77	310
WH Davies (Prenton)	76	76	80	78	310
S Wingate (Temple Newsam)	74	78	80	78	310
F Robson (Cooden Beach)	80	77	78	76	311
Mr Robert Harris (Royal & Ancient)	75	81	78	77	311
HA Gaudin (R Jersey)	76	79	77	80	312
J Kirkwood (Australia)	83	79	76	76	314
Alex Herd (Moor Park)	76	79	82	77	314
T Fernie (Turnberry)	78	74	77	85	314
Mr JI Cruickshank (Argentina)	80	78	82	75	315
Harry Vardon (South Herts)	79	80	77	79	315
J Smith (Wentworth)	75	78	82	80	315
RA Whitcombe (Came Down)	81	80	79	76	316
J Ockenden (Hanger Hill)	80	78	80	78	316
AG Havers (Coombe Hill)	77	80	80	79	316
D McCulloch (Troon)	76	77	84	79	316

1926   *at Lytham and St Anne's*

NAME	SCORE				
Mr RT Jones Jr (USA)	72	72	73	74	291
A Watrous (USA)	71	75	69	78	293
Mr G Von Elm (USA)	75	72	76	72	295
Walter Hagen (USA)	68	77	74	76	295
Abe Mitchell (unattached)	78	78	72	71	299
T Barber (Cavendish)	77	73	78	71	299

NAME	SCORE				
F McLeod (USA)	71	75	76	79	301
Jose Jurado (Argentina)	77	76	74	76	303
E French (USA)	76	75	74	78	303
W Mehlhorn (USA)	70	74	79	80	303
HA Gaudin (Wanstead)	78	78	71	77	304
JH Taylor (Mid-Surrey)	75	78	71	80	304
Tommy Armour (USA)	74	76	75	80	305
RA Whitcombe (Came Down)	73	82	76	75	306
Tom Williamson (Notts)	78	76	76	76	306
Mr WL Hartley (Cooden Beach)	74	77	79	76	306
J Walker (Sickleholme)	74	77	78	77	306
F Robson (Cooden Beach)	79	76	77	75	307
G Walker (USA)	79	71	80	77	307
Jim Barnes (USA)	77	80	72	78	307

1927 *at St Andrews*

NAME	SCORE				
Mr RT Jones (USA)	68	72	73	72	285
Aubrey Boomer (France)	76	70	73	72	291
Fred Robson (Cooden Beach)	76	72	69	74	291
ER Whitcombe (Bournemouth)	74	73	73	73	293
Joe Kirkwood (USA)	72	72	75	74	293
CA Whitcombe (Crews Hill)	74	76	71	75	296
AG Havers (Coombe Hill)	80	74	73	70	297
B Hodson (Newport Monmouthshire)	72	70	81	74	297
Henry Cotton (Langley Park)	73	72	77	76	298
Alex Herd (Moor Park)	76	75	78	71	300
Tom Williamson (Notts)	75	76	78	71	300
R Vickers (Heswall)	75	75	77	73	300
Mr WB Torrance (Edinburgh Burgess)	72	80	74	74	300
Mr TP Perkins (Castle Bromwich)	76	78	70	76	300
PH Rodgers (St Anne's Old Links)	76	73	74	77	300
Percy Alliss (Wannsee, Berlin)	73	74	73	80	300
O Johns (Purley Downs)	74	78	73	76	301
Jim Barnes (USA)	76	76	72	77	301
GR Buckle (Edgbaston)	77	69	77	78	301
DA Curtis (Bournemouth)	73	76	79	74	302
J Gassiat (France)	76	77	73	76	302
E Stevens (USA)	76	73	74	79	302

1928 *at St George's, Sandwich*

NAME	SCORE				
Walter Hagen (USA)	75	73	72	72	292
Gene Sarazen (USA)	72	76	73	73	294
A Compston (unattached)	75	74	73	73	295
Percy Alliss (Wannsee, Berlin)	75	76	75	72	298

NAME	SCORE				
Fred Robson (Cooden Beach)	79	73	73	73	298
Jim Barnes (USA)	81	73	76	71	301
Aubrey Boomer (France)	79	73	77	72	301
Jose Jurado (Argentina)	74	71	76	80	301
W Mehlhorn (USA)	71	78	76	77	302
WH Davies (Prenton)	78	74	79	73	304
A Whiting (R St George's)	78	76	76	75	305
F Taggart (Wilmslow)	76	74	77	78	305
Jack Smith (North Middlesex)	79	77	76	74	306
Mr TP Perkins (Castle Bromwich)	80	79	76	72	307
WT Twine (Bromley)	75	79	77	76	307
Stewart Burns (Cruden Bay)	76	74	75	83	308
Maj CO Hezlet (R Portrush)	79	76	78	76	309
Henry Cotton (Langley Park)	77	75	83	75	310
D McCulloch (Troon)	78	78	78	76	310
G Duncan (Wentworth)	75	77	78	80	310

1929 *at Muirfield*

NAME	SCORE				
Walter Hagen (USA)	75	67	75	75	292
J Farrell (USA)	72	75	76	75	298
L Diegel (USA)	71	69	82	77	299
Abe Mitchell (private)	72	72	78	78	300
Percy Alliss (Wannsee, Berlin)	69	76	76	79	300
R Cruickshank (USA)	73	74	78	76	301
Jim Barnes (USA)	71	80	78	74	303
Gene Sarazen (USA)	73	74	81	76	304
A Watrous (USA)	73	79	75	77	304
Tommy Armour (USA)	75	73	79	78	305
AG Havers (unattached)	80	74	76	76	306
A Compston (Coombe Hill)	76	73	77	81	307
J Golden (USA)	74	73	86	75	308
J Thomson (USA)	78	78	75	77	308
H Jolly (Foxgrove)	72	80	78	79	309
Macdonald Smith (USA)	73	78	78	80	309
Aubrey Boomer (France)	74	74	80	81	309
W Davies (Wallasey)	79	76	81	74	310
E Dudley (USA)	72	80	80	78	310
SF Brews (S Africa)	76	77	78	79	310
M Seymour (St Leonards)	75	74	78	83	310

1930 *at Hoylake*

NAME	SCORE				
Mr RT Jones (USA)	70	72	74	75	291
Macdonald Smith (USA)	70	77	75	71	293
L Diegel (Mexico)	74	73	71	75	293
Horton Smith (USA)	72	73	78	73	296
F Robson (Cooden Beach)	71	72	78	75	296
Jim Barnes (USA)	71	77	72	77	297
A Compston (Coombe Hill)	74	73	68	82	297
Henry Cotton (Langley Park)	70	79	77	73	299

NAME	SCORE				
T Barber (Derbyshire)	75	76	72	77	300
CA Whitcombe (Crews Hill)	74	75	72	79	300
A Boyer (France)	73	77	70	80	300
B Hodson (Chigwell)	74	77	76	74	301
Abe Mitchell (private)	75	78	77	72	302
RA Whitcombe (Parkstone)	78	72	73	79	302
Mr DK Moe (USA)	74	73	76	80	303
PH Rodgers (St Anne's Old Links)	74	73	76	80	303
AJ Young (Sonning)	75	78	78	74	305
W Large (Huyton)	78	74	77	76	305
ER Whitcombe (Meyrick Park)	80	72	76	77	305
Percy Alliss (Wannsee, Berlin)	75	74	77	79	305

1931   *at Carnoustie*

NAME	SCORE				
Tommy Armour (USA)	73	75	77	71	296
Jose Jurado (Argentina)	76	71	73	77	297
Percy Alliss (Wannsee, Berlin)	74	78	73	73	298
Gene Sarazen (USA)	74	76	75	73	298
J Farrell (USA)	72	77	75	75	299
Macdonald Smith (USA)	75	77	71	76	299
M Churio (Argentina)	76	75	78	71	300
WH Davies (Wallasey)	76	78	71	75	300
AJ Lacey (Selsdon Park)	74	80	74	73	301
Henry Cotton (Langley Park)	72	75	79	76	302
AG Havers (Sandy Lodge)	75	76	72	79	302
Horton Smith (USA)	77	79	75	72	303
G Faulkner (Bramley)	77	76	76	74	303
T Genta (Argentina)	75	78	75	75	303
Abe Mitchell (private)	77	74	77	75	303
Tom Williamson (Notts)	77	76	73	77	303
WG Oke (Fulwell)	74	80	75	75	304
M Dallemagne (France)	74	77	78	75	304
WI Hunter (USA)	76	75	74	79	304
RA Whitcombe (Parkstone)	75	78	71	80	304

1932   *at Prince's, Sandwich*

NAME	SCORE				
Gene Sarazen (USA)	70	69	70	74	283
Macdonald Smith (USA)	71	76	71	70	288
AG Havers (Sandy Lodge)	74	71	68	76	289
AH Padgham (R Ashdown Forest)	76	72	74	70	292
Percy Alliss (Beaconsfield)	71	71	78	72	292
CA Whitcombe (Crews Hill)	71	73	73	75	292
WH Davies (Wallasey)	71	73	74	75	293
AJ Lacey (Selsdon Park)	73	73	71	76	293
F Robson (Addington Palace)	74	71	78	71	294
Abe Mitchell (private)	77	71	75	72	295
Henry Cotton (Langley Park)	74	72	77	72	295
Archie Compston (Coombe Hill)	74	70	75	76	295
H Prowse (Lamberhurst)	75	75	75	73	298

NAME	SCORE				
S Easterbrook (Knowle)	74	75	72	77	298
Mr WL Hope (St George's Hill)	74	79	75	71	299
CS Denny (Thorpe Hall)	73	81	72	73	299
Bert Hodson (Chigwell)	77	73	77	73	300
CH Ward (Ladbrook Park)	73	77	77	73	300
A Perry (Leatherhead)	73	76	77	74	300
RA Whitcombe (Parkstone)	75	74	75	76	300
Tommy Armour (USA)	75	70	74	81	300

1933   *at St Andrews*

NAME	SCORE				
Densmore Shute (USA)	73	73	73	73	292
Craig Wood (USA)	77	72	68	75	292
(Shute won play-off, 149 to 154)					
Gene Sarazen (USA)	72	73	73	75	293
Leo Diegel (USA)	75	70	71	77	293
S Easterbrook (Knowle)	73	72	71	77	293
Olin Dutra (USA)	76	76	70	72	294
RA Whitcombe (Parkstone)	76	75	72	72	295
AH Padgham (R Ashdown Forest)	74	73	74	74	295
Ed Dudley (USA)	70	71	76	78	295
Henry Cotton (Waterloo, Belgium)	73	71	72	79	295
Abe Mitchell (private)	74	68	74	79	295
Archie Compston (Coombe Hill)	72	74	77	73	296
ER Whitcombe (Meyrick Park)	73	73	75	75	296
AG Havers (Sandy Lodge)	80	72	71	74	297
Horton Smith (USA)	73	73	75	76	297
A Boyer (France)	76	72	70	79	297
J Kirkwood (USA)	72	73	71	81	297
Mr Jack McLean (Hayston)	75	74	75	74	298
Aubrey Boomer (France)	74	70	76	78	298
Mr Cyril Tolley (R Eastbourne)	70	73	76	79	298

1934   *at St George's, Sandwich*

NAME	SCORE				
Henry Cotton (Waterloo, Belgium)	67	65	72	79	283
SF Brews (S Africa)	76	71	70	71	288
AH Padgham (Sundridge Park)	71	70	75	74	290
Macdonald Smith (USA)	77	71	72	72	292
M Dallemagne (France)	71	73	71	77	292
J Kirkwood (USA)	74	69	71	78	292
Bert Hodson (Chigwell)	71	74	74	76	295
CA Whitcombe (Crews Hill)	71	72	74	78	295
ER Whitcombe (Meyrick Park)	72	77	73	74	296
Percy Alliss (Beaconsfield)	73	75	71	77	296
WT Twine (Langley Park)	72	76	75	74	297

NAME	SCORE				
J Burton (Hillside)	80	72	72	74	298
EW Jarman (Prenton)	74	76	74	75	299
CH Ward (Moseley)	76	71	72	80	299
WH Davies (Wallasey)	76	68	73	82	299
RA Whitcombe (Parkstone)	75	76	74	75	300
Allan Dailey (Wanstead)	74	73	78	75	300
J McDowall (Turnberry)	73	74	77	76	300
Mr J McLean (Hayston)	77	76	69	78	300
Densmore Shute (USA)	71	72	80	78	301

1935   *at Muirfield*

NAME	SCORE				
Alfred Perry (Leatherhead)	69	75	67	72	283
AH Padgham (Sundridge Park)	70	72	74	71	287
CA Whitcombe (Crews Hill)	71	68	73	76	288
Mr W Lawson Little (USA)	75	71	74	69	289
B Gadd (Brand Hall)	72	75	71	71	289
H Picard (USA)	72	73	72	75	292
S Easterbrook (Knowle)	75	73	74	71	293
Henry Cotton (Waterloo, Belgium)	68	74	76	75	293
WJ Branch (Henbury)	71	73	76	74	294
L Ayton Sr (South Shields)	74	73	77	71	295
A Boyer (France)	74	75	76	71	296
WJ Cox (Addington)	76	69	77	75	297
JJ Busson (Pannal)	75	76	70	76	297
Aubrey Boomer (France)	76	69	75	77	297
EWH Kenyon (West Lancashire)	70	74	74	79	297
JA Jacobs (Lindrick)	78	74	75	71	298
Percy Alliss (Beaconsfield)	72	76	75	75	298
Mark Seymour (Crow Wood)	75	76	75	73	299
PH Rodgers (St Anne's Old Links)	74	76	74	75	299
ER Whitcombe (Meyrick Park)	75	72	74	78	299
Macdonald Smith (USA)	69	77	75	78	299
W Laidlaw (Malden)	74	71	75	79	299

1936   *at Hoylake*

NAME	SCORE				
AH Padgham (Sundridge Park)	73	72	71	71	287
J Adams (Romford)	71	73	71	73	288
M Dallemagne (France)	73	72	75	69	289
Henry Cotton (Waterloo, Belgium)	73	72	70	74	289
Percy Alliss (Temple Newsam)	74	72	74	71	291
Gene Sarazen (USA)	73	75	70	73	291
Tom Green (Burnham Beeches)	74	72	70	75	291
AJ Lacey (Berkshire)	76	74	72	72	294
RA Whitcombe (Parkstone)	72	77	71	74	294
Mr AD Locke (S Africa)	75	73	72	74	294

NAME	SCORE				
DJ Rees (Surbiton)	77	71	72	75	295
WJ Cox (Wimbledon Park)	70	74	79	73	296
R Burton (Hooton)	74	71	75	76	296
WH Davies (Wallasey)	72	76	73	77	298
Mr Hector Thomson (Williamwood)	76	76	73	74	299
T Turner (USA)	75	74	76	74	299
W Smithers (unattached)	75	73	77	74	299
Aubrey Boomer (France)	74	75	75	75	299
CA Whitcombe (Crews Hill)	73	76	79	72	300
G Good (Romiley)	75	73	79	73	300

1937   *at Carnoustie*

NAME	SCORE				
Henry Cotton (Ashridge)	74	73	72	71	290
RA Whitcombe (Parkstone)	72	70	74	76	292
C Lacey (USA)	76	75	70	72	293
CA Whitcombe (Crews Hill)	73	71	74	76	294
Byron Nelson (USA)	75	76	71	74	296
Ed Dudley (USA)	70	74	78	75	297
AJ Lacey (Berkshire)	75	73	75	75	298
W Laidlaw (Ashridge)	77	72	73	76	298
AH Padgham (Sundridge Park)	72	74	76	76	298
Horton Smith (USA)	77	71	79	72	299
Sam Snead (USA)	75	74	75	76	300
Ralph Guldahl (USA)	77	72	74	77	300
WJ Branch (Leicestershire)	72	75	73	81	301
Densmore Shute (USA)	73	73	76	80	302
Percy Alliss (Temple Newsam)	75	76	75	77	303
H Picard (USA)	76	77	70	80	303
AG Havers (Sandy Lodge)	77	75	76	76	304
F Robertson (Ashridge)	73	75	78	78	304
Mr AD Locke (S Africa)	74	74	77	79	304
J Adams (R Liverpool)	74	78	76	76	304

1938   *at St George's, Sandwich*

NAME	SCORE				
RA Whitcombe (Parkstone)	71	71	75	78	295
J Adams (R Liverpool)	70	71	78	78	297
Henry Cotton (Ashridge)	74	73	77	74	298
A Dailey (Wanstead)	73	72	80	78	303
JJ Busson (Pannal)	71	69	83	80	303
AH Padgham (Sundridge Park)	74	72	75	82	303
R Burton (Sale)	71	69	78	85	303
F Bullock (Sonning)	73	74	77	80	304
WJ Cox (Wimbledon Park)	70	70	84	80	304
AD Locke (S Africa)	73	72	81	79	305
CA Whitcombe (Crews Hill)	71	75	79	80	305
B Gadd (West Cheshire)	71	70	84	80	305
SF Brews (S Africa)	76	70	84	77	307
DJ Rees (Surbiton)	73	72	79	83	307

NAME	SCORE				
JH Ballingall (Balmore)	76	72	83	77	308
A Perry (Leatherhead)	71	74	77	86	308
AJ Lacey (Berkshire)	74	72	82	81	309
W Shankland (Haydock Park)	74	72	84	81	311
ER Whitcombe (Meyrick Park)	70	77	83	82	312
PJ Mahon (R Dublin)	73	74	83	83	313
JL Black (Rhos-on-Sea)	72	72	83	86	313

1939 *at St Andrews*

NAME	SCORE				
R Burton (Sale)	70	72	77	71	290
J Bulla (USA)	77	71	71	73	292
SL King (Knole Park)	74	72	75	73	294
RA Whitcombe (Parkstone)	71	75	74	74	294
A Perry (Leatherhead)	71	74	73	76	294
W Shankland (Temple Newsam)	72	73	72	77	294
J Fallon (Huddersfield)	71	73	71	79	294
M Pose (Argentina)	71	72	76	76	295
Percy Alliss (Ferndown)	75	73	74	74	296
EWH Kenyon (Beaconsfield)	73	75	74	74	296
AD Locke (S Africa)	70	75	76	75	296
DJ Rees (Hindhead)	71	74	75	77	297
E Bertolino (Argentina)	73	75	75	75	298
Mr J Bruen (Cork)	72	75	75	76	298
J Adams (R Liverpool)	73	74	75	76	298
Henry Cotton (Ashridge)	74	72	76	76	298
W Anderson (Murcar)	73	74	77	75	299
E Serra (Uruguay)	77	72	73	77	299
WH Green (Tynemouth)	75	75	72	78	300
Mr A Kyle (Sand Moor)	74	76	75	76	301
S Easterbrook (Knowle)	74	71	80	76	301
WH Davies (Wallasey)	71	79	74	77	301

1940–45 *No Championship owing to the Second World War*

1946 *at St Andrews*

NAME	SCORE				
Sam Snead (USA)	71	70	74	75	290
AD Locke (S Africa)	69	74	75	76	294
J Bulla (USA)	71	72	72	79	294
N von Nida (Australia)	70	76	74	75	295
CH Ward (Little Aston)	73	73	73	76	295
Henry Cotton (R Mid-Surrey)	70	70	76	79	295
DJ Rees (Hindhead)	75	67	73	80	295
F Daly (Balmoral, Belfast)	77	71	76	74	298
J Kirkwood (USA)	71	75	78	74	298
W Lawson Little (USA)	78	75	72	74	299
H Bradshaw (Kilcroney)	76	75	76	73	300

NAME	SCORE				
R Burton (Sale)	74	76	76	76	302
W Shankland (Temple Newsam)	76	76	77	75	304
W Anderson (Murcar)	76	76	78	75	305
RA Whitcombe (Parkstone)	71	76	82	76	305
LB Ayton Jr (Stoneham)	77	74	80	75	306
Percy Alliss (Ferndown)	74	72	82	79	307
F Jowle (Lees Hall)	78	74	76	80	308
A Compston (Wentworth)	77	74	77	80	308
A Lees (Dore & Totley)	77	71	78	82	308
G Knight (unattached)	77	75	82	76	310
EE Whitcombe (Porters Park)	75	79	77	79	310
RK Bell (Am) (Accrington)	81	73	81	77	312
JA Jacobs (Lindrick)	76	77	80	79	312
JC Wilson (Am) (Cawder)	78	76	81	78	313
A Perry (Reddish Vale)	78	77	78	80	313
F van Donck (Belgium)	76	78	83	78	315
AM Robertson (Whitley Bay)	79	75	80	81	315
A Dowie (Am) (St Andrews)	81	71	80	83	315
RJ White (Am) (Birkdale)	76	79	84	77	316
TB Haliburton (Knowle)	78	76	81	81	316
AH Padgham (Sundridge Park)	79	74	76	87	316
N Sutton (Leigh)	76	77	80	84	317
F Bullock (Holyhead)	80	75	87	76	318
WH Green (Tynemouth)	76	76	83	83	318
AJ Isherwood (Warrington)	77	78	83	81	319
JM Urry (Am) (Olton)	79	75	87	85	326

1947 *at Hoylake*

NAME	SCORE				
F Daly (Balmoral, Belfast)	73	70	78	72	293
RW Horne (Hendon)	77	74	72	71	294
FR Stranahan (Am) (USA)	71	79	72	72	294
W Shankland (Temple Newsam)	76	74	75	70	295
R Burton (Coombe Hill)	77	71	77	71	296
J Bulla (USA)	80	72	74	71	297
CH Ward (Little Aston)	76	73	76	72	297
SL King (Wildernesse)	75	72	77	73	297
A Lees (Dore & Totley)	75	74	72	76	297
N von Nida (Australia)	74	76	71	76	297
Henry Cotton (R Mid-Surrey)	69	78	74	76	297
J Adams (Beaconsfield)	73	80	71	75	299
AH Padgham (Sundridge Park)	75	75	76	76	300
RA Whitcombe (Parkstone)	75	77	71	77	300
F Bullock (Otley)	74	78	78	72	302
LB Ayton (Worthing)	69	80	74	79	302
N Sutton (Leigh)	77	76	73	77	303
EE Whitcombe (Porters Park)	77	76	74	77	304
V Ghezzi (USA)	75	78	72	79	304
A Perry (Reddish Vale)	76	77	70	81	304
F van Donck (Belgium)	73	76	81	75	305
DJ Rees (South Herts)	77	74	73	81	305
A Waters (Stand, Manchester)	75	78	76	77	306

NAME	SCORE				
J Burton (Hillside)	73	79	76	81	309
JA Jacobs (Lindrick)	75	80	76	79	310
JH Busson (Formby)	80	76	71	83	310
AG Havers (Moor Park)	80	76	79	76	311
B Shepard (Tehidy Park)	78	78	77	78	311
K Bousfield (Coombe Hill)	78	76	79	78	311
N Quigley (Windermere)	79	77	76	79	311
TE Odams (Grim's Dyke)	80	76	79	77	312
W Anderson (Rye)	74	81	80	79	314
F Howle (Lees Hall)	75	80	80	79	314
M Faulkner (Worlebury)	78	76	81	79	314
WB Thomson (Grange Park)	78	76	78	83	315
JD Henderson (Ilkley)	78	78	81	79	316
T Gardner (Sandiway)	77	76	77	89	319
B Hodson (Chigwell)	79	77	84	84	324
D McEwan (Northampton)	77	79	87	84	327

1948 *at Muirfield*

NAME	SCORE				
Henry Cotton (R Mid-Surrey)	71	66	75	72	284
F Daly (Balmoral, Belfast)	72	71	73	73	289
N von Nida (Australia)	71	72	76	71	290
J Hargreaves (Sutton Coldfield)	76	68	73	73	290
CH Ward (Little Aston)	69	72	75	74	290
R de Vicenzo (Argentina)	70	73	72	75	290
J Bulla (USA)	74	72	73	72	291
F van Donck (Belgium)	69	73	73	76	291
SL King (Knole Park)	69	72	74	76	291
AH Padgham (Sundridge Park)	73	70	71	77	291
Capt EC Kingsley (Am) (USA)	77	69	77	70	293
Mario Gonzales (Am) (Brazil)	76	72	70	75	293
A Waters (Stand, Manchester)	75	71	70	77	293
A Lees (Dore & Totley)	73	69	73	78	293
EE Whitcombe (Porters Park)	74	73	73	74	294
M Faulkner (Selsey)	75	71	74	74	294
DJ Rees (South Herts)	73	71	76	74	294
F Jowle (Lees Hall)	70	78	74	73	295
RA Whitcombe (Parkstone)	77	67	77	74	295
R Burton (Coombe Hill)	74	70	74	77	295
J Fallon (Huddersfield)	73	74	74	75	296
K Bousfield (Coombe Hill)	76	71	73	76	296
A Perry (Reddish Vale)	77	71	76	73	297
FR Stranahan (Am) (USA)	77	71	75	74	297
TB Haliburton (Knowle)	73	74	76	74	297
N Sutton (Leigh)	72	73	77	75	297
C Harmon (USA)	75	73	78	72	298
O Hayes (S Africa)	74	73	75	78	300
RW Horne (Hendon)	71	77	73	79	300
H Gould (R Porthcawl)	75	73	78	75	301
AE Clark (USA)	74	71	75	81	301
RA Cruickshank (USA)	74	74	77	77	302
W Lawson Little (USA)	72	76	76	78	302
WS Collins (North Wales)	77	69	77	79	302
CA Whitcombe (Crews Hill)	74	72	75	81	302
WB Lyle (Clober)	72	75	80	80	307

1949 *at St George's, Sandwich*

NAME	SCORE				
AD Locke (S Africa)	69	76	68	70	283
H Bradshaw (Kilcroney, Eire)	68	77	68	70	283
(Locke won play-off, 136 to 147)					
R de Vicenzo (Argentina)	68	75	73	69	285
CH Ward (Little Aston)	73	71	70	72	286
SL King (Knole Park)	71	69	74	72	286
A Lees (Dore & Totley)	74	70	72	71	287
M Faulkner (R Mid-Surrey)	71	71	71	74	287
WD Smithers (Long Ashton)	72	75	70	71	288
J Fallon (Huddersfield)	69	75	72	72	288
J Adams (Wentworth)	67	77	72	72	288
K Bousfield (Coombe Hill)	69	77	76	67	289
W Shankland (Temple Newsam)	69	73	74	73	289
FR Stranahan (Am) (USA)	71	73	74	72	290
WJ Branch (Berkhamsted)	71	75	74	71	291
J Knipe (R Mid-Surrey)	76	71	72	72	291
R Burton (Coombe Hill)	73	70	74	74	291
W Lees (Shipley)	74	72	69	78	293
A Waters (Stand, Manchester)	70	76	75	73	294
N Sutton (Leigh)	69	78	75	73	295
GW McIntosh (Ringway)	70	77	76	73	296
WA McMinn (Fairhaven)	70	75	78	73	296
RW Horne (Hendon)	73	74	75	74	296
EA Southerden (Lamberhurst)	69	76	74	77	296
AJ Lacey (Berkshire)	72	73	73	78	296
J Wade (Bradford)	71	74	77	75	297
HE Osborne (Newquay)	73	74	75	76	298
J Bulla (USA)	71	73	76	79	299
U Grappasonni (Italy)	70	76	77	77	300
EWH Kenyon (Worsley)	72	75	77	77	301
GM White (Coxmoor)	74	71	80	78	303
F Francis (Am) (Sunningdale)	72	74	82	79	307

1950 *at Troon*

NAME	SCORE				
AD Locke (S Africa)	69	72	70	68	279
R de Vicenzo (Argentina)	72	71	68	70	281
F Daly (Balmoral, Belfast)	75	72	69	66	282
DJ Rees (South Herts)	71	68	72	71	282
B Moore (S Africa)	74	68	73	68	283
M Faulkner (R Mid-Surrey)	72	70	70	71	283
F Bullock (R Lytham & St Anne's)	71	71	71	71	284
A Lees (Sunningdale)	68	76	68	72	284
FR Stranahan (Am) (USA)	77	70	73	66	286
F van Donck (Belgium)	73	71	72	70	286
SL King (Knole Park)	70	75	68	73	286
J Adams (Wentworth)	73	75	69	70	287
WD Smithers (Long Ashton)	74	70	73	70	287
H Thomson (unattached)	71	72	73	72	288
J Bulla (USA)	73	70	71	74	288
H Bradshaw (Portmarnock)	73	71	75	70	289
JB McHale (Am) (USA)	73	73	74	70	290

NAME	SCORE				
RW Horne (Hendon)	73	75	71	71	290
EE Whitcombe (Porters Park)	69	76	72	73	290
AH Padgham (Sundridge Park)	77	71	74	69	291
N von Nida (Australia)	74	72	76	69	291
J Panton (Glenbervie)	76	69	70	76	291
EC Brown (Haggs Castle)	73	73	73	73	292
GM White (Coxmoor)	74	74	73	72	293
N Sutton (Leigh)	71	75	74	73	293
WJ Branch (Berkhamsted)	71	69	78	75	293
SS Field (Dunstable Downs)	73	71	73	76	293
TW Allen (Richmond)	77	70	75	71	293
FG Allott (Enfield)	72	71	77	74	294
H Hassanein (Egypt)	73	72	77	73	295
Maj DA Blair (Am) (Nairn)	72	72	77	74	295
SS Scott (Carlisle City)	75	71	75	75	296
A Perry (Leatherhead)	73	74	76	75	298
J Carroll (Grange)	73	72	74	79	298
JC Wilson (Am) (Cawder)	72	76	79	72	299

1951   *at Portrush*

NAME	SCORE				
M Faulkner (unattached)	71	70	70	74	285
A Cerda (Argentina)	74	72	71	70	287
CH Ward (Little Aston)	75	73	74	68	290
J Adams (Wentworth)	68	77	75	72	292
F Daly (Balmoral, Belfast)	74	70	75	73	292
W Shankland (Temple Newsam)	73	76	72	72	293
AD Locke (S Africa)	71	74	74	74	293
H Weetman (Croham Hurst)	73	71	75	74	293
PW Thomson (Australia)	70	75	73	75	293
N Sutton (Leigh)	73	70	74	76	293
J Panton (Glenbervie)	73	72	74	75	294
DJ Rees (South Herts)	70	77	76	72	295
R Burton (Coombe Hill)	74	77	71	73	295
FR Stranahan (Am) (USA)	75	75	72	73	295
H Bradshaw (Portmarnock)	80	71	74	71	296
E Cremin (Australia)	73	75	75	74	297
A Waters (Worplesdon)	74	75	78	71	298
KE Enderby (Am) (Australia)	76	74	75	73	298
WJ Henderson (Nairn)	77	73	76	73	299
C O'Connor (Tuam)	79	74	72	74	299
KDG Nagle (Australia)	76	76	72	75	299
U Grappasonni (Italy)	73	73	77	76	299
J Hargreaves (Sutton Coldfield)	73	78	79	69	299
P Traviani (Italy)	74	79	73	74	300
EE Whitcombe (Chigwell)	74	74	76	76	300
F van Donck (Belgium)	72	76	76	76	300
JB Carr (Am) (Sutton)	75	76	73	76	300
A Poulton (Burhill)	77	77	73	75	302
J McKenna (Douglas, Cork)	74	76	76	76	302
WD Smithers (Long Ashton)	75	73	76	78	302

NAME	SCORE				
GN Roffe (Coventry)	78	76	78	71	303
C Rotan (USA)	76	76	76	75	303
Wing Cdr CH Beamish (Am) (R Portrush)	76	78	73	76	303
A Lees (Sunningdale)	75	74	76	78	303
SL King (Knole Park)	78	76	77	73	304
WCA Hancock (Stockport)	78	74	72	80	304
J Fallon (Huddersfield)	78	73	80	74	305
JA Jacobs (Lindrick)	76	77	77	75	305
FG Allott (Enfield)	74	79	77	75	305
EC Brown (Hartsbourne)	74	77	83	72	306
R Halsall (R Birkdale)	80	74	77	75	306
AJ Lacey (Berkshire)	75	76	79	76	306
GW McIntosh (Ringway)	76	71	80	79	306

1952   *at Lytham and St Anne's*

NAME	SCORE				
AD Locke (S Africa)	69	71	74	73	287
PW Thomson (Australia)	68	73	77	70	288
F Daly (Balmoral, Belfast)	67	69	77	76	289
Henry Cotton (R Mid-Surrey)	75	74	74	71	294
A Cerda (Argentina)	73	73	76	73	295
SL King (Knole Park)	71	74	74	76	295
F van Donck (Belgium)	74	75	71	76	296
F Bullock (Glasgow)	76	72	72	77	297
A Lees (Sunningdale)	76	72	76	74	298
N von Nida (Australia)	77	70	74	77	298
EC Brown (Sandy Lodge)	71	72	78	77	298
W Goggin (USA)	71	74	75	78	298
SS Scott (Carlisle City)	75	69	76	78	298
H Bradshaw (Portmarnock)	70	74	75	79	298
H Weetman (Croham Hurst)	74	77	71	77	299
J Panton (Glenbervie)	72	72	78	77	299
M Faulkner (St George's Hill)	72	76	79	73	300
Gene Sarazen (USA)	74	73	77	76	300
WD Smithers (Long Ashton)	73	74	76	77	300
N Sutton (Exeter)	72	74	79	76	301
E Noke (Dudley)	72	78	76	76	302
J Hine (USA)	73	78	74	77	302
FG Allott (Enfield)	77	71	76	78	302
K Bousfield (Coombe Hill)	72	73	79	78	302
JA Jacobs (Lindrick)	74	72	81	76	303
A Poulton (Burhill)	71	74	76	82	303
J Hargreaves (Sutton Coldfield)	75	75	79	75	304
DJ Rees (South Herts)	76	74	77	77	304
JRM Jacobs (unattached)	72	76	79	77	304
JW Jones (Am) (R Birkdale)	73	70	78	83	304
RW Horne (Hendon)	77	74	80	74	305
Peter Alliss (Ferndown)	72	72	80	81	305
D Rawlinson (Am) (Southport & Ainsdale)	74	73	79	80	306
AT Kyle (Am) (Sand Moor)	71	75	80	81	307
R Halsall (R Birkdale)	74	75	78	81	308

NAME	SCORE				
H de Lamaze (Am) (France)	73	72	80	83	308
TB Haliburton (Wentworth)	75	76	80	78	309
H Thomson (unattached)	73	77	80	79	309
JH Hawkins (Maidenhead)	76	72	82	79	309
FR Stranahan (Am) (USA)	75	76	78	80	309
G Johnson (South Staffs)	73	75	78	83	309
HAJ Young (Sonning)	70	77	77	85	309

1953   *at Carnoustie*

NAME	SCORE				
Ben Hogan (USA)	73	71	70	68	282
FR Stranhan (Am) (USA)	70	74	73	69	286
A Cerda (Argentina)	75	71	69	71	286
PW Thomson (Australia)	72	72	71	71	286
DJ Rees (South Herts)	72	70	73	71	286
R de Vicenzo (Argentina)	72	71	71	73	287
SL King (Knole Park)	74	73	72	71	290
AD Locke (S Africa)	72	73	74	72	291
Peter Alliss (Ferndown)	75	72	74	71	292
EC Brown (unattached)	71	71	75	75	292
F Daly (Balmoral, Belfast)	73	75	71	75	294
M Faulkner (St George's Hill)	74	71	73	77	295
A Lees (Sunningdale)	76	76	72	72	296
H Weetman (Croham Hurst)	80	73	72	72	297
JRM Jacobs (Sandy Lodge)	79	74	71	73	297
THT Fairbairn (Reddish Vale)	74	71	73	79	297
E Lester (Bristol & Clifton)	83	70	72	73	298
CH Ward (Little Aston)	78	71	76	73	298
H Hassanein (Egypt)	78	71	73	76	298
F van Donck (Belgium)	77	71	78	73	299
RW Horne (Hendon)	76	74	75	74	299
SS Scott (Carlisle City)	74	74	78	74	300
H Thomson (Scotland)	76	74	74	76	300
RA Knight (Wanstead)	74	79	74	74	301
C O'Connor (Bundoran)	77	77	72	75	301
L Mangrum (USA)	75	76	74	76	301
J Panton (Glenbervie)	79	74	76	73	302
U Grappasonni (Italy)	77	75	72	78	302
A Poulton (Burhill)	75	77	75	76	303
TB Haliburton (Wentworth)	75	76	76	76	303
R Ferguson (Donabate)	77	75	74	77	303
N Sutton (Exeter)	76	72	76	79	303
J Hargreaves (Sutton Coldfield)	81	73	76	74	304
K Bousfield (Coombe Hill)	78	76	79	72	305
JH Ballingall (Northumberland)	80	74	77	74	305
BJ Hunt (Atherstone)	79	74	77	75	305
EE Whitcombe (Chigwell)	76	78	73	78	305
RG French (West Surrey)	79	71	77	79	306
RP Mills (Wentworth)	80	73	72	81	306
JB Ado (France)	75	77	75	81	308

1954   *at Birkdale*

NAME	SCORE				
PW Thomson (Australia)	72	71	69	71	283
AD Locke (S Africa)	74	71	69	70	284
SS Scott (Carlisle City)	76	67	69	72	284
DJ Rees (South Herts)	72	71	69	72	284
J Adams (R Mid-Surrey)	73	75	69	69	286
J Turnesa (USA)	72	72	71	71	286
A Cerda (Argentina)	71	71	73	71	286
Peter Alliss (Ferndown)	72	74	71	70	287
SL King (Knole Park)	69	74	74	70	287
F van Donck (Belgium)	77	71	70	71	289
J Demaret (USA)	73	71	74	71	289
A Angelini (Italy)	76	70	73	71	290
H Bradshaw (Portmarnock)	72	72	73	73	290
JW Spence (Dartford)	69	72	74	75	290
R Halsall (R Birkdale)	72	73	73	73	291
P Toogood (Am) (Tasmania)	72	75	73	71	291
Gene Sarazen (USA)	75	74	73	70	292
U Grappasonni (Italy)	72	75	74	71	292
C Kane (R Dublin)	74	72	74	72	292
J Hargreaves (Sutton Coldfield)	77	72	77	67	293
JRM Jacobs (Sandy Lodge)	71	73	80	69	293
NV Drew (Am) (Rossmore)	76	71	74	72	293
L Topping (Old Links, Bolton)	75	76	69	73	293
M Faulkner (St George's Hill)	73	78	69	73	293
E Lester (Bristol & Clifton)	72	75	73	73	293
C O'Connor (Bundoran)	74	72	72	75	293
EB Williamson (Netherlands)	76	73	75	70	294
N Sutton (Exeter)	70	80	72	72	294
B Shelton (Ashridge)	74	77	71	73	295
J Hitchcock (Coombe Hill)	73	72	76	74	295
FR Stranahan (Am) (USA)	73	75	71	76	295
T Travena (S Africa)	75	74	75	72	296
J Garaialde (France)	76	73	72	75	296
RP Mills (Wentworth)	73	76	70	77	296
N von Nida (Australia)	76	74	74	73	297
WJ Branch (Ganton)	73	78	71	75	297
F Daly (Balmoral, Belfast)	74	72	74	77	297
JB Ado (France)	72	78	76	72	298
E Bertolino (Argentina)	74	76	74	74	298
A Casera (Italy)	75	73	72	78	298

1955   *at St Andrews*

NAME	SCORE				
PW Thomson (Australia)	71	68	70	72	281
J Fallon (Huddersfield)	73	67	73	70	283
F Jowle (Edgbaston)	70	71	69	74	284
AD Locke (S Africa)	74	69	70	72	285
K Bousfield (Coombe Hill)	71	75	70	70	286
A Cerda (Argentina)	73	71	71	71	286
BJ Hunt (Hartsbourne)	70	71	74	71	286

NAME	SCORE				
F van Donck (Belgium)	71	72	71	72	286
H Weetman (Croham Hurst)	71	71	70	74	286
C O'Connor (Bundoran)	71	75	70	71	287
R Barbieri (Argentina)	71	71	73	72	287
F Daly (Balmoral, Belfast)	75	72	70	71	288
JRM Jacobs (Sandy Lodge)	71	70	71	76	288
EC Brown (Buchanan Castle)	69	70	73	76	288
JS Anderson (Bruntsfield Links)	71	72	77	69	289
WJ Henderson (Troon)	74	71	72	72	289
A Sotto (Argentina)	72	73	72	73	290
DF Smalldon (Cardiff)	70	69	78	73	290
E Furgol (USA)	71	76	72	73	292
SS Scott (Carlisle City)	69	77	73	73	292
KDG Nagle (Australia)	72	72	74	74	292
Lt JW Conrad (Am) (USA)	72	76	74	71	293
RW Horne (Hendon)	72	75	75	71	293
R Halsall (R Birkdale)	71	74	76	72	293
WJ Branch (Ganton)	75	72	73	73	293
H Bradshaw (Portmarnock)	72	70	73	78	293
DJ Rees (South Herts)	69	79	73	73	294
H Hassanein (Egypt)	73	72	76	73	294
N Sutton (Exeter)	71	74	75	74	294
J Martin (Woodcote Park)	70	72	79	74	295
JB McHall (Am) (USA)	72	76	72	75	295
B Nelson (USA)	72	75	78	71	296
TB Haliburton (Wentworth)	75	72	73	76	296
Henry Cotton (Temple)	70	72	78	76	296
J Burton (Hillside)	75	73	75	74	297
M Faulkner (St George's Hill)	73	74	74	76	297
CC Potente (Spain)	73	75	76	74	298
W Shankland (Potters Bar)	73	74	77	74	298
B Wilkes (S Africa)	75	73	74	76	298
J Bulla (USA)	75	70	73	80	298

1956   *at Hoylake*

NAME	SCORE				
PW Thomson (Australia)	70	70	72	74	286
F van Donck (Belgium	71	74	70	74	289
R de Vicenzo (Argentina)	71	70	79	70	290
G Player (S Africa)	71	76	73	71	291
J Panton (Glenbervie)	74	76	72	70	292
Henry Cotton (Temple)	72	76	71	74	293
E Bertolino (Argentina)	69	72	76	76	293
M Souchak (USA)	74	74	74	72	294
A Cerda (Argentina)	72	81	68	73	294
C O'Connor (Bundoran)	73	78	74	70	295
H Weetman (Croham Hurst)	72	76	75	72	295
FR Stranahan (USA)	72	76	72	76	296
B Crampton (Australia)	76	77	72	72	297
DJ Rees (South Herts)	75	74	75	73	297
A Miguel (Spain)	71	74	75	77	297
JRM Jacobs (Sandy Lodge)	73	77	76	72	298
J Hargreaves (Sutton Coldfield)	72	80	75	73	300

NAME	SCORE				
A Balding (Canada)	70	81	76	73	300
CH Ward (Little Aston)	73	75	78	74	300
DC Thomas (Sudbury)	70	78	77	75	300
R Rossi (Argentina)	75	77	72	76	300
K Bousfield (Coombe Hill)	73	77	76	75	301
G de Wit (Netherlands)	76	73	74	78	301
EG Lester (Hazel Grove)	70	76	77	78	301
LB Ayton (Ipswich)	74	78	78	72	302
E Moore (S Africa)	75	75	78	74	302
J Adams (R Mid-Surrey)	75	76	76	75	302
KWC Adwick (Burhill)	77	76	74	76	303
SS Scott (Carlisle City)	78	74	74	77	303
DF Smalldon (Cardiff)	68	79	78	78	303
A Angelini (Italy)	73	80	76	75	304
BJ Hunt (Hartsbourne)	75	73	81	75	304
CP Chen (Formosa)	78	74	77	76	305
A Salas (Chile)	79	72	78	76	305
M Gonzales (Brazil)	72	81	75	77	305
JB Carr (Am) (Sutton)	73	77	79	77	306
C Greene (Milltown)	76	75	79	76	306
M Ishii (Japan)	74	77	77	78	306
J Martin (R Wimbledon)	74	79	78	75	306
S Miguel (Spain)	72	78	84	73	307
C Celles (Spain)	71	82	78	76	307
W Shankland (Potters Bar)	72	78	79	78	307

1957   *at St Andrews*

NAME	SCORE				
AD Locke (S Africa)	69	72	68	70	279
PW Thomson (Australia)	73	69	70	70	282
EC Brown (Buchanan Castle)	67	72	73	71	283
A Miguel (Spain)	72	72	69	72	285
DC Thomas (Sudbury)	72	74	70	70	286
WD Smith (Am) (Prestwick)	71	72	72	71	286
F van Donck (Belgium)	72	68	74	72	286
TB Haliburton (Wentworth)	72	73	68	73	286
Henry Cotton (Temple)	74	72	69	72	287
M Faulkner (St George's Hill)	74	70	71	72	287
A Cerda (Argentina)	71	71	72	73	287
Peter Alliss (Parkstone)	72	74	74	68	288
H Weetman (Croham Hurst)	75	71	71	71	288
C Middlecoff (USA)	72	71	74	72	289
S Miguel (Spain)	71	75	76	68	290
EG Lester (Hazel Grove)	71	76	70	73	290
J Panton (Glenbervie)	71	72	74	73	290
NV Drew (Knock)	70	75	71	74	290
FR Stranahan (USA)	74	71	74	72	291
C O'Connor (Bundoran)	77	69	72	73	291
H Bradshaw (Portmarnock)	73	74	69	75	291
J Fallon (Huddersfield)	75	67	73	76	291
J Hitchcock (Ashford Manor)	69	74	73	76	292
RW Horne (Hendon)	76	72	72	73	293
G Player (S Africa)	71	74	75	73	293
T Wilkes (S Africa)	75	73	71	74	293
SL King (Knole Park)	76	72	70	75	293

NAME	SCORE				
BJ Hunt (Hartsbourne)	72	72	74	75	293
H Henning (S Africa)	75	73	71	75	294
DJ Rees (South Herts)	73	72	79	71	295
PJ Butler (Harborne)	77	71	74	73	295
RA Knight (Wanstead)	71	73	75	76	295
N Sutton (Exeter)	69	76	73	77	295
LB Ayton (Ipswich)	67	76	75	77	295
K Bousfield (Coombe Hill)	74	73	75	74	296
R de Vicenzo (Argentina)	70	76	76	74	296
J Macdonald (Bedford & County)	73	71	76	76	296
RL Moffitt (Coventry Hearsall)	71	75	77	74	297
SS Scott (Carlisle City)	76	72	73	77	298
KA MacDonald (Hankley Common)	69	74	76	79	298
B Crampton (Australia)	68	73	78	79	298

1958 *at Lytham and St Anne's*

NAME	SCORE				
PW Thomson (Australia)	66	72	67	73	278
DC Thomas (Sudbury)	70	68	69	71	278
(Thomson won play-off, 139 to 143)					
EC Brown (Buchanan Castle)	73	70	65	71	279
C O'Connor (Killarney)	67	68	73	71	279
L Ruiz (Argentina)	71	65	72	73	281
F van Donck (Belgium)	70	70	67	74	281
G Player (S Africa)	68	74	70	71	283
H Weetman (Selsdon Park)	73	67	73	71	284
Henry Cotton (Temple)	68	75	69	72	284
EG Lester (Hazel Grove)	73	66	71	74	284
D Swaelens (Belgium)	74	67	74	70	285
Peter Alliss (Parkstone)	72	70	70	73	285
H Henning (S Africa)	70	71	72	73	286
DJ Rees (South Herts)	77	69	71	70	287
J Garaialde (France)	69	74	72	72	287
AD Locke (S Africa)	76	70	72	70	288
Gene Sarazen (USA)	73	73	70	72	288
E Moore (S Africa)	72	72	70	74	288
M Faulkner (Selsey)	68	71	71	78	288
C Greene (Milltown)	75	71	72	72	290
F Daly (Balmoral, Belfast)	71	74	72	73	290
NV Drew (Knock)	69	72	75	74	290
AB Coop (Dean Wood)	69	71	75	75	290
G de Wit (Netherlands)	71	75	72	73	291
H Bradshaw (Portmarnock)	70	73	72	76	291
S Miguel (Spain)	74	71	73	74	292
A Cerda (Argentina)	72	71	74	75	292
T Wilkes (S Africa)	76	70	69	77	292
A Miguel (Spain)	71	70	75	77	293
SL King (Knole Park)	71	73	76	75	295
D Snell (Worksop)	72	72	72	79	295
BJ Hunt (Hartsbourne)	70	70	76	79	295
JW Wilkshire (Crompton & Royton)	74	70	78	74	296

NAME	SCORE				
BBS Wilkes (S Africa)	73	73	75	76	297
SS Scott (Roehampton)	73	74	74	76	297
B Crampton (Australia)	73	73	75	76	297
JB Carr (Am) (Sutton)	70	74	77	77	298
DL Melville (Fulford)	76	71	76	79	302
CS Denny (North Middlesex)	74	73	77	79	303
W Large (Allerton)	70	72	81	80	303

1959 *at Muirfield*

NAME	SCORE				
G Player (S Africa)	75	71	70	68	284
F van Donck (Belgium)	70	70	73	73	286
F Bullock (Prestwick St Nicholas)	68	70	74	74	286
SS Scott (Roehampton)	73	70	73	71	287
C O'Connor (R Dublin)	73	74	72	69	288
J Panton (Glenbervie)	72	72	71	73	288
RR Jack (Am) (Dullatur)	71	75	68	74	288
SL King (Knole Park)	70	74	68	76	288
DJ Rees (South Herts)	73	73	69	74	289
L Ruiz (Argentina)	72	74	69	74	289
BJ Hunt (Hartsbourne)	73	75	71	71	290
AF Stickley (Ealing)	68	74	77	71	290
K Bousfield (Coombe Hill)	73	73	71	73	290
MF Bonallack (Am) (Thorpe Hall)	70	72	72	76	290
J Hitchcock (Ashford Manor)	75	68	70	77	290
Peter Alliss (Parkstone)	76	72	76	67	291
GB Wolstenholme (Am) (Kirby Muxloe)	78	70	73	70	291
H Weetman (Selsdon Park)	72	73	76	70	291
H Bradshaw (Portmarnock)	71	76	72	72	291
A Cerda (Argentina)	69	74	73	75	291
J Garaialde (France)	75	70	74	73	292
NC Coles (Burhill)	72	74	71	75	292
PW Thomson (Australia)	74	74	72	74	294
GM Hunt (Hartsbourne)	72	73	74	75	294
RP Mills (Pinner Hill)	75	71	72	76	294
H Henning (S Africa)	73	73	72	76	294
JR Moses (Sandwell Park)	72	73	73	76	294
RA Knight (Wanstead)	71	71	74	78	294
EE Whitcombe (Chigwell)	71	77	74	73	295
AD Locke (S Africa)	73	73	76	73	295
PJ Shanks (Wanstead)	76	70	75	74	295
J Adams (R Mid-Surrey)	71	74	75	75	295
TB Haliburton (Wentworth)	74	69	74	78	295
H Lewis (Altrincham)	73	73	78	72	296
NV Drew (Knock)	71	77	75	74	297
EG Lester (Hazel Grove)	73	71	78	75	297
CH Ward (Little Aston)	78	70	73	76	297
A Miguel (Spain)	73	75	73	77	298
JB Carr (Am) (Sutton)	72	73	74	79	298
C Kane (St Andrews)	77	69	77	76	299

1960 *at St Andrews*

NAME	SCORE				
KDG Nagle (Australia)	69	67	71	71	278
A Palmer (USA)	70	71	70	68	279
BJ Hunt (Hartsbourne)	72	73	71	66	282
H Henning (S Africa)	72	72	69	69	282
R de Vicenzo (Argentina)	67	67	75	73	282
GB Wolstenholme (Am) (Sunningdale)	74	70	71	68	283
G Player (S Africa)	72	71	72	69	284
JB Carr (Am) (Sutton)	72	73	67	73	285
DJ Rees (South Herts)	73	71	73	69	286
PW Thomson (Australia)	74	70	71	71	286
H Weetman (Selsdon Park)	74	70	71	71	286
EC Brown (Buchanan Castle)	75	68	72	71	286
Maj DA Blair (Am) (Royal & Ancient)	70	73	71	72	286
SS Scott (Roehampton)	73	71	67	75	286
R Sota (Spain)	74	72	71	70	287
A Miguel (Spain)	72	73	72	71	288
I Smith (Hesketh)	74	70	73	71	288
F de Luca (Argentina)	69	73	75	71	288
RR Jack (Am) (Dullatur)	74	71	70	73	288
RP Mills (Pinner Hill)	71	74	70	74	289
AM Deboys (Am) (Taymouth Castle)	76	70	73	71	290
R Moffitt (Coventry Hearsall)	72	71	76	71	290
GW Low (Enfield)	72	74	71	73	290
JA MacDonald (Bedford & County)	76	71	69	74	290
K Bousfield (Coombe Hill)	70	75	71	74	290
W Johnson (USA)	75	74	71	71	291
S Miguel (Spain)	73	68	74	76	291
FS Boobyer (Highgate)	74	74	73	71	292
GM Hunt (Hartsbourne)	76	69	72	75	292
LB Ayton (Ipswich)	73	69	75	75	292
J Martin (unattached)	72	72	72	76	292
L Ruiz (Argentina)	72	77	73	71	293
TB Haliburton (Wentworth)	77	70	74	72	293
JRM Jacobs (Sandy Lodge)	74	71	75	73	293
PJ Butler (Harborne)	76	72	75	71	294
C O'Connor (R Dublin)	80	67	76	72	295
D Miller (Stoneham)	75	73	74	73	295
P Shanks (unattached)	70	73	77	75	295
EB Williamson (Kingswood)	75	70	73	77	295
WD Smith (Am) (Selkirk)	74	71	78	74	297
JM Gonzales (Brazil)	72	74	75	76	297

1961 *at Birkdale*

NAME	SCORE				
A Palmer (USA)	70	73	69	72	284
DJ Rees (South Herts)	68	74	71	72	285
NC Coles (Coombe Hill)	70	77	69	72	288
C O'Connor (R Dublin)	71	77	67	73	288
EC Brown (unattached)	73	76	70	70	289

NAME	SCORE				
KDG Nagle (Australia)	68	75	75	71	289
PW Thomson (Australia)	75	72	70	73	290
K Bousfield (Coombe Hill)	71	77	75	68	291
Peter Alliss (Parkstone)	73	75	72	71	291
SS Scott (Roehampton)	76	75	71	71	293
H Henning (S Africa)	68	74	75	76	293
R Sota (Spain)	71	76	72	76	295
A Coop (Dean Wood)	71	79	73	74	297
A Miguel (Spain)	73	79	74	72	298
RA Knight (Wanstead)	71	80	73	74	298
S Miguel (Spain)	71	80	70	77	298
N Johnson (Haydock Park)	69	80	70	79	298
P Runyan (USA)	75	77	75	72	299
D Hutchinson (S Africa)	72	80	74	73	299
JRM Jacobs (Sandy Lodge)	71	79	76	74	300
H Bradshaw (Portmarnock)	73	75	78	74	300
P Butler (Harborne)	72	76	78	74	300
DC Thomas (Sunningdale)	71	77	77	75	300
L Platts (Thorndon Park)	70	80	71	79	300
RL Moffitt (Coventry Hearsall)	73	80	73	75	301
J Garaialde (France)	69	81	76	75	301
BGC Huggett (Romford)	72	77	75	77	301
EG Lester (Hazel Grove)	71	77	75	78	301
D Miller (Stoneham)	69	79	80	74	302
G Will (Walton Heath)	74	75	75	78	302
B Wilkes (S Africa)	72	76	77	78	303
GB Wolstenholme (St George's Hill)	72	80	77	75	304
Henry Cotton (Temple)	76	77	74	77	304
J Panton (Glenbervie)	73	78	75	78	304
W McHardy (Brough)	76	76	76	77	305
J Henderson (Clandeboye)	72	78	77	78	305
SL King (Knole Park)	70	77	79	79	305
E Green (Huyton & Prescot)	75	78	77	76	306
RJ White (Am) (R Birkdale)	71	79	80	76	306
GW Low (Enfield)	76	76	76	78	306

1962 *at Troon*

NAME	SCORE				
A Palmer (USA)	71	69	67	69	276
KDG Nagle (Australia)	71	71	70	70	282
BGC Huggett (Romford)	75	71	74	69	289
P Rodgers (USA)	75	70	72	72	289
RJ Charles (New Zealand)	75	70	70	75	290
PW Thomson (Australia)	70	77	75	70	292
Sam Snead (USA)	76	73	72	71	292
Peter Alliss (Parkstone)	77	69	74	73	293
DC Thomas (Sunningdale)	77	70	71	75	293
SS Scott (Roehampton)	77	74	75	68	294
RL Moffitt (Coventry Hearsall)	75	70	74	76	295
J Garaialde (France)	76	73	76	71	296
S Miguel (Spain)	72	79	73	72	296
H Weetman (Selsdon Park)	75	73	73	75	296
R Whitehead (Walton Heath)	74	75	72	75	296
J Panton (Glenbervie)	74	73	79	71	297

NAME	SCORE				
C O'Connor (R Dublin)	74	78	73	72	297
BJ Hunt (Hartsbourne)	74	75	75	73	297
R Foreman (Belfairs Park)	77	73	72	75	297
J Martin (Edmondstown)	73	72	76	76	297
D Hutchinson (S Africa)	78	73	76	70	297
AB Coop (Dean Wood)	76	75	75	72	298
D Swaelens (Belgium)	72	79	74	74	299
L Platts (Thorndon Park)	76	75	78	71	300
GB Wolstenholme (St George's Hill)	78	74	76	72	300
B Bamford (Wentworth)	77	73	74	76	300
HF Boyle (Coombe Hill)	73	78	74	76	301
KA MacDonald (Hankley Common)	69	77	76	79	301
GW Low (Enfield)	77	75	77	73	302
H Bradshaw (Portmarnock)	72	75	81	75	303
H Henning (S Africa)	74	73	79	77	303
J Hitchcock (Ashford Manor)	78	74	72	79	303
D Beattie (Addington Palace)	72	75	79	78	304
EC Brown (unattached)	74	78	79	74	305
J Nicklaus (USA)	80	72	74	79	305
JW Johnson (Arcot Hall)	76	74	81	76	307
CW Green (Am) (Dumbarton)	76	75	81	76	308
D Essig (USA)	76	72	79	81	308
D Miller (Stoneham)	76	74	81	78	309

1963   *at Lytham and St Anne's*

NAME	SCORE				
RJ Charles (New Zealand)	68	72	66	71	277
P Rodgers (USA)	67	68	73	69	277
(Charles won play-off, 140 to 148)					
J Nicklaus (USA)	71	67	70	70	278
KDG Nagle (Australia)	69	70	73	71	283
PW Thomson (Australia)	67	69	71	78	285
C O'Connor (R Dublin)	74	68	76	68	286
G Player (S Africa)	75	70	72	70	287
R Sota (Spain)	69	73	73	72	287
S Miguel (Spain)	73	69	73	73	288
J Garaialde (France)	72	69	72	75	288
AG King (Ganton)	71	73	73	72	289
BJ Hunt (Hartsbourne)	72	71	73	73	289
S Sewgolum (S Africa)	71	74	73	72	290
H Lewis (Altrincham)	71	77	69	74	291
BGC Huggett (Romford)	73	74	70	74	291
B Allen (Denton)	75	71	71	74	291
ID MacDonald (Farnham)	71	71	74	75	291
Peter Alliss (Parkstone)	74	71	77	70	292
F Phillips (Australia)	70	73	75	74	292
MT Leeder (Sheringham)	76	73	74	70	293
JA MacDonald (Bedford & County)	73	75	75	70	293
B Wilkes (S Africa)	70	77	74	72	293
NC Coles (Coombe Hill)	73	75	72	73	293
M Faulkner (Selsey)	77	71	71	74	293

NAME	SCORE				
H Henning (S Africa)	76	68	71	78	293
DC Thomas (Sunningdale)	74	74	75	71	294
J Hitchcock (Ashford Manor)	75	73	70	76	294
D Sewell (Wentworth)	75	72	73	74	294
A Palmer (USA)	76	71	71	76	294
A Jacklin (Potters Bar)	73	72	76	74	295
K Bousfield (Coombe Hill)	73	75	71	76	295
TB Haliburton (Wentworth)	68	73	77	77	295
E Large (Moortown)	78	71	76	71	296
B Devlin (Australia)	75	70	75	76	296
D Hutchinson (S Africa)	74	71	74	77	296
W Godfrey (New Zealand)	75	74	75	73	297
S Davies (S Africa)	76	69	79	73	297
FS Boobyer (Highgate)	76	70	74	77	297
L Platts (Thorndon Park)	74	75	78	71	298
AG Grubb (Coombe Hill)	77	72	74	75	298
GM Hunt (Hartsbourne)	71	76	75	76	298

1964   *at St Andrews*

NAME	SCORE				
A Lema (USA)	73	68	68	70	279
J Nicklaus (USA)	76	74	68	68	284
R de Vicenzo (Argentina)	76	72	70	67	285
BJ Hunt (Hartsbourne)	73	74	70	70	287
B Devlin (Australia)	72	72	73	73	290
C O'Connor (R Dublin)	71	73	74	73	291
H Weetman (Selsdon Park)	72	71	75	73	291
H Henning (S Africa)	78	73	71	70	292
G Player (S Africa)	78	71	73	70	292
A Miguel (Spain)	73	76	72	71	292
D Sanders (USA)	78	73	74	68	293
F Phillips (Australia)	77	75	72	70	294
DC Thomas (Sunningdale)	75	74	75	72	296
J Garaialde (France)	71	74	79	72	296
C Greene (Milltown)	74	76	73	73	296
RL Moffitt (Coventry Hearsall)	76	72	74	74	296
GA Caygill (Pannal)	77	74	71	75	297
RJ Charles (New Zealand)	79	71	69	78	297
P Rodgers (USA)	74	79	74	71	298
JA MacDonald (Bedford & County)	78	74	74	72	298
A Murray (S Africa)	77	73	76	72	298
SS Scott (Roehampton)	75	74	73	76	298
M Gregson (Moor Park)	78	70	74	76	298
D Ford (USA)	75	76	76	72	299
LH Lu (Hong Kong)	76	71	78	74	299
J Martin (Rush)	74	72	79	74	299
PW Thomson (Australia)	79	73	72	75	299
AB Coop (Dean Wood)	75	72	76	76	299
G Will (Sundridge Park)	74	79	71	76	300
PJ Butler (Harborne)	78	75	74	74	301
GM Hunt (Hartsbourne)	77	75	74	75	301
R Sota (Spain)	77	74	74	76	301
S Davies (S Africa)	74	77	71	80	302
J Panton (Glenbervie)	78	74	77	74	303

NAME	SCORE				
D Hutchinson (S Africa)	77	74	77	75	303
B Wilkes (S Africa)	77	76	74	76	303
M Murphy (R Dublin)	76	74	76	77	303
DJ Rees (South Herts)	76	77	77	74	304
M Faulkner (Selsey)	73	73	80	78	304
SWT Murray (Northants County)	80	73	78	74	305
NV Drew (Ralston)	76	76	79	74	305
B Allen (Manchester)	78	75	73	79	305
L Thomas (Australia)	76	75	82	72	305

1965 *at Birkdale*

NAME	SCORE				
PW Thomson (Australia)	74	68	72	71	285
BGC Huggett (Romford)	73	68	76	70	287
C O'Connor (R Dublin)	69	73	74	71	287
R de Vicenzo (Argentina)	74	69	73	72	288
BJ Hunt (Hartsbourne)	74	74	70	71	289
KDG Nagle (Australia)	74	70	73	72	289
A Lema (USA)	68	72	75	74	289
S Miguel (Spain)	72	73	72	73	290
B Devlin (Australia)	71	69	75	75	290
J Panton (Glenbervie)	74	74	75	70	293
M Faulkner (Selsey)	74	72	74	73	293
NC Coles (Coombe Hill)	73	74	77	70	294
J Nicklaus (USA)	73	71	77	73	294
HT Boyle (unattached)	73	69	76	76	294
L Platts (Wanstead)	72	72	73	77	294
A Palmer (USA)	70	71	75	79	295
C Legrange (S Africa)	76	73	75	72	296
T Horton (Ham Manor)	75	73	76	72	296
GB Wolstenholme (St George's Hill)	72	75	77	72	296
EC Brown (Cruden Bay)	72	70	77	77	296
C Greene (Milltown)	72	77	74	74	297
BJ Bamford (Tavistock)	72	76	74	75	297
D Hutchinson (S Africa)	74	72	76	75	297
G Will (Sundridge Park)	75	69	74	79	297
R Sota (Spain)	75	70	78	75	298
A Jacklin (Potters Bar)	75	73	73	77	298
D Sewell (Wentworth)	72	75	74	77	298
FS Boobyer (Whitefield)	74	73	73	78	298
MJ Burgess (Am) (West Sussex)	74	73	78	74	299
H Weetman (Selsdon Park)	76	69	80	74	299
AB Coop (Dean Wood)	78	71	78	74	301
W Large (Porters Park)	76	73	74	78	301
MF Bonallack (Am) (Thorpe Hall)	75	72	79	76	302
D Miller (Stoneham)	77	70	76	79	302
D Beattie (Addington Palace)	73	74	76	79	302
JB Carr (Am) (Sutton)	70	72	81	79	302
GW Low (Bush Hill)	74	75	77	77	303
W Hector (Seaton Carew)	76	70	79	78	303

NAME	SCORE				
DC Thomas (Dunham Forest)	73	73	78	80	304
J Gallardo (Spain)	77	71	80	77	305
TD Dill (USA)	75	72	79	79	305
RM Mandeville (West Herts)	72	76	77	80	305
D Talbot (Notts)	75	72	76	82	305

1966 *at Muirfield*

NAME	SCORE				
J Nicklaus (USA)	70	67	75	70	282
DC Thomas (Dunham Forest)	72	73	69	69	283
D Sanders (USA)	71	70	72	70	283
G Player (S Africa)	72	74	71	69	286
B Devlin (Australia)	73	69	74	70	286
KDG Nagle (Australia)	72	68	76	70	286
P Rodgers (USA)	74	66	70	76	286
D Marr (USA)	73	76	69	70	288
PW Thomson (Australia)	73	75	69	71	288
S Miguel (Spain)	74	72	70	72	288
A Palmer (USA)	73	72	69	74	288
RH Sikes (USA)	73	72	73	72	290
C O'Connor (R Dublin)	73	72	74	72	291
H Henning (S Africa)	71	69	75	76	291
J Boros (USA)	73	71	76	72	292
J Hitchcock (Croham Hurst)	70	77	74	72	293
PJ Butler (Harborne)	73	65	80	75	293
GA Gaygill (Cleckheaton)	72	71	73	77	293
RDBM Shade (Am) (Duddingston)	71	70	75	77	293
Peter Alliss (Parkstone)	74	72	75	73	294
D Sewell (Wentworth)	76	69	74	75	294
R de Vicenzo (Argentina)	74	72	71	77	294
EC Brown (Cruden Bay)	78	72	71	74	295
P Townsend (Am) (Potters Bar)	73	75	72	75	295
G Will (Sundridge Park)	74	75	73	73	295
KA MacDonald (Hankley Common)	75	74	70	77	296
MF Bonallack (Am) (Thorpe Hall)	73	76	75	73	297
D Hutchinson (S Africa)	74	73	73	77	297
RJ Stanton (Australia)	73	72	73	79	297
FS Boobyer (Whitefield)	72	76	77	73	298
C Greene (Milltown)	72	76	76	74	298
A Lema (USA)	71	76	76	75	298
A Jacklin (Potters Bar)	74	76	72	76	298
RE Cole (Am) (S Africa)	73	75	73	77	298
A Henning (S Africa)	73	73	74	78	298
DJ Rees (South Herts)	75	72	77	75	299
B Franklin (S Africa)	77	72	79	72	300
RJ Charles (New Zealand)	74	74	77	75	300
D Snell (Worksop)	73	75	76	76	300
R Bernardini (Italy)	76	73	73	78	300
GB Wolstenholme (St George's Hill)	73	76	73	78	300

1967 *at Hoylake*

NAME	SCORE				
R de Vicenzo (Argentina)	70	71	67	70	278
J Nicklaus (USA)	71	69	71	69	280
CA Clark (Sunningdale)	70	73	69	72	284
G Player (S Africa)	72	71	67	74	284
A Jacklin (Potters Bar)	73	69	73	70	285
H Henning (S Africa)	74	70	71	71	286
S Miguel (Spain)	72	74	68	72	286
HF Boyle (Jacobs Golf Centre)	74	74	71	68	287
T Horton (Ham Manor)	74	74	69	70	287
PW Thomson (Australia)	71	74	70	72	287
A Balding (Canada)	74	71	69	73	287
B Devlin (Australia)	70	70	72	75	287
S Peach (Australia)	71	75	73	70	289
GB Wolstenholme (St George's Hill)	74	71	73	71	289
M Hoyle (Castle Inn)	74	75	69	71	289
D Beman (USA)	72	76	68	73	289
L Platts (Pannal)	68	73	72	76	289
BJ Coxon (Australia)	73	76	71	70	290
D Sanders (USA)	71	73	73	73	290
HW Muscroft (Moor Allerton)	72	73	72	73	290
C O'Connor (R Dublin)	70	74	71	76	291
RP Mills (High Post)	72	75	73	72	292
D Hutchinson (S Africa)	73	72	71	76	292
KDG Nagle (Australia)	70	74	69	79	292
BGC Huggett (Warren)	73	75	72	73	293
BW Barnes (Burnham & Berrow)	71	75	74	73	293
RRW Davenport (North Hants)	76	69	75	73	293
B Franklin (S Africa)	70	74	73	76	293
FS Boobyer (Whitefield)	70	71	74	79	294
JM Hume (Formby)	69	72	73	80	294
B Allen (Denton)	71	77	76	71	295
H Weetman (Selsdon Park)	76	69	79	71	295
D Sewell (Ferndown)	71	77	74	73	295
G Cunningham (Stranraer)	74	74	73	74	295
D Snell (Worksop)	77	70	73	75	295
C Pennington (Trevose)	77	72	74	74	297
R Bernardini (Italy)	75	74	74	74	297
H Bannerman (R Aberdeen)	74	75	74	74	297
M Leeder (Sheringham)	72	76	75	74	297
D Melville (Ilkley)	74	74	74	75	297
NC Coles (Coombe Hill)	74	72	76	75	297
BJ Hunt (Hartsbourne)	74	73	73	77	297

1968 *at Carnoustie*

NAME	SCORE				
G Player (S Africa)	74	71	71	73	289
J Nicklaus (USA)	76	69	73	73	291
RJ Charles (New Zealand)	72	72	71	76	291
W Casper (USA)	72	68	74	78	292
M Bembridge (Little Aston)	71	75	73	74	293

NAME	SCORE				
BW Barnes (Burnham & Berrow)	70	74	80	71	295
NC Coles (Coombe Hill)	75	76	71	73	295
G Brewer (USA)	74	73	72	76	295
A Balding (Canada)	74	76	74	72	296
R de Vicenzo (Argentina)	77	72	74	74	297
B Devlin (Australia)	77	73	72	75	297
A Palmer (USA)	77	71	72	77	297
T Horton (Ham Manor)	77	74	73	74	298
KDG Nagle (Australia)	74	75	75	74	298
B Cole (S Africa)	75	76	72	75	298
Peter Alliss (Parkstone)	73	78	72	75	298
BGC Huggett (Betchworth Park)	76	71	75	76	298
EC Brown (Cruden Bay)	76	76	74	73	299
F Skerritt (St Anne's Dublin)	72	73	77	77	299
A Jacklin (Potters Bar)	72	72	75	80	299
DL Webster (Lundin)	77	71	78	74	300
S Miguel (Spain)	73	75	76	76	300
MF Bonallack (Am) (Thorpe Hall)	70	77	74	79	300
GA Caygill (Cleckheaton)	79	76	71	75	301
PW Thomson (Australia)	77	71	78	75	301
KA MacDonald (Hankley Common)	80	71	73	77	301
S Wilson (Selby)	73	81	74	74	302
M Gregson (Dyrham Park)	77	75	76	74	302
RJ Shaw (Australia)	75	76	73	78	302
DC Thomas (Dunham Forest)	75	71	78	78	302
J Gallardo (Spain)	78	71	78	76	303
D Huish (Berwick)	74	74	78	77	303
H Bannerman (R Aberdeen)	74	73	77	79	303
D Sanders (USA)	78	76	73	77	304
M Murphy (R Dublin)	77	74	77	77	305
J Martin (Rush)	81	72	74	78	305
G Cunningham (Troon Municipal)	80	70	75	80	305
H Habian (USA)	77	74	76	79	306
AG Grubb (Coombe Hill)	79	74	75	79	307
M Said Moussa (Egypt)	77	76	75	79	307
C Greene (Milltown)	75	77	76	79	307

1969 *at Lytham and St Anne's*

NAME	SCORE				
A Jacklin (Potters Bar)	68	70	70	72	280
RJ Charles (New Zealand)	69	69	75	72	282
R de Vicenzo (Argentina)	72	73	66	72	283
PW Thomson (Australia)	71	70	70	72	283
C O'Connor (R Dublin)	71	65	74	74	284
DM Love Jr (USA)	70	73	71	71	285
J Nicklaus (USA)	75	70	68	72	285
Peter Alliss (Parkstone)	73	74	73	66	286
KDG Nagle (Australia)	74	71	72	70	287
M Barber (USA)	69	75	75	69	288
NC Coles (Coombe Hill)	75	76	70	68	289
C Legrange (S Africa)	79	70	71	69	289

NAME	SCORE				
GB Wolstenholme (Australia)	70	71	76	72	289
T Horton (Ham Manor)	71	76	70	72	289
G Brewer (USA)	76	71	68	75	290
B Devlin (Australia)	71	73	75	72	291
P Townsend (Porters Park)	73	70	76	72	291
EC Brown (Braid Hills)	73	76	69	73	291
H Henning (S Africa)	72	71	75	73	291
O Moody (USA)	71	70	74	76	291
B Yancey (USA)	72	71	71	77	291
BGC Huggett (Betchworth Park)	72	72	69	78	291
BJ Hunt (Hartsbourne)	73	71	75	73	292
G Player (S Africa)	74	68	76	74	292
FS Boobyer (Whitefield)	74	70	76	73	293
GA Gaygill (Cleckheaton)	71	67	79	76	293
W Casper (USA)	70	70	75	78	293
LP Tupling (Am) (Tankersley Park)	73	71	78	72	294
HW Muscroft (Moor Allerton)	68	77	73	76	294
J Garaialde (France)	69	77	76	73	295
D Swaelens (Belgium)	72	73	76	74	295
M Faulkner (Ifield)	71	74	76	74	295
MB Ingham (Moor Allerton)	73	73	74	75	295
BJ Waites (Notts)	73	75	74	74	296
VB Hood (Bramley)	75	71	74	76	296
R Floyd (USA)	74	70	76	76	296
JR Garner (unattached)	72	71	76	77	296
L Trevino (USA)	75	72	71	78	296
G Cunningham (Troon Municipal)	74	72	71	79	296
BW Barnes (West Sussex)	73	73	76	75	297
J Hitchcock (Croydon Driving Range)	74	74	73	76	297

NAME	SCORE				
R Bernardini (Ita)	75	69	74	75	293
CA Clark (Eng)	69	70	77	77	293
C O'Connor (Ire)	72	68	74	79	293
W Godfrey (NZ)	71	75	74	74	294
GB Wolstenholme (Aus)	68	77	72	77	294
T Weiskopf (USA)	70	74	72	78	294
G Marsh (Aus)	75	72	74	74	295
B Devlin (Aus)	72	76	72	75	295
RDBM Shade (Sco)	72	75	69	79	295
BGC Huggett (Wal)	68	78	73	77	296
R Cole (SA)	71	76	71	78	296
SD Brown (Eng)	73	73	71	79	296
T Shaw (USA)	73	71	73	79	296
Peter Alliss (Eng)	69	74	78	76	297
F Molina (Arg)	67	75	78	77	297
D Douglass (USA)	75	71	73	78	297
EC Brown (Sco)	73	72	74	78	297
D Graham (Aus)	72	72	74	79	297
KDG Nagle (Aus)	71	74	73	79	297
BW Barnes (Sco)	69	74	75	79	297
DC Thomas (Eng)	70	72	76	79	297
G Brewer (USA)	69	74	74	80	297

1971   *at Birkdale*

NAME	SCORE				
L Trevino (USA)	69	70	69	70	278
Liang Huan Lu (Form)	70	70	69	70	279
A Jacklin (Eng)	69	70	70	71	280
C DeFoy (Wal)	72	72	68	69	281
C Coody (USA)	74	71	70	68	283
J Nicklaus (USA)	71	71	72	69	283
W Casper (USA)	70	72	75	67	284
G Player (SA)	71	70	71	72	284
D Sanders (USA)	73	71	74	67	285
PW Thomson (Aus)	70	73	73	69	285
KDG Nagle (Aus)	70	75	73	69	287
D Stockton (USA)	74	74	68	71	287
H Bannerman (Sco)	73	71	72	71	287
B Yancey (USA)	75	70	71	71	287
R Sota (Spain)	72	72	70	73	287
R de Vicenzo (Arg)	71	70	72	74	287
D Hayes (SA)	71	72	70	75	288
RJ Charles (NZ)	77	71	71	70	289
P Oosterhuis (Eng)	76	71	66	76	289
BJ Hunt (Eng)	74	73	73	70	290
H Johnson (USA)	69	76	72	73	290
NC Coles (Eng)	76	72	72	71	291
MF Bonallack (Am) (Eng)	71	72	75	73	291
H Jackson (N Ire)	71	73	72	75	291
V Fernandez (Arg)	69	79	73	71	292
W Large (Eng)	73	75	73	71	292
D Sewell (Eng)	73	74	74	71	292
BGC Huggett (Wal)	73	73	74	72	292
J Lister (NZ)	74	71	74	73	292
R Vines (Aus)	75	71	73	73	292

1970   *at St Andrews*

NAME	SCORE				
J Nicklaus (USA)	68	69	73	73	283
D Sanders (USA)	68	71	71	73	283
(Nicklaus won play-off, 72 to 73)					
H Henning (SA)	67	72	73	73	285
L Trevino (USA)	68	68	72	77	285
A Jacklin (Eng)	67	70	73	76	286
P Oosterhuis (Eng)	73	69	69	76	287
NC Coles (Eng)	65	74	72	76	287
H Jackson (N Ire)	69	72	73	74	288
J Panton (Sco)	72	73	73	71	289
PW Thomson (Aus)	68	74	73	74	289
T Horton (Eng)	66	73	75	75	289
A Palmer (USA)	68	72	76	74	290
RJ Charles (NZ)	72	73	73	74	292
M Bembridge (Eng)	67	74	75	76	292
B Yancey (USA)	71	71	73	77	292
JC Richardson (Eng)	67	72	76	77	292
R de Vicenzo (Arg)	71	76	71	75	293
W Casper (USA)	71	74	73	75	293

NAME	SCORE				
PJ Butler (Eng)	73	73	73	73	292
M Gregson (Eng)	71	71	73	77	292
Min Nan Hsieh (Form)	77	70	74	72	293
GB Wolstenholme (Aus)	75	72	73	73	293
C O'Connor (Ire)	74	72	76	72	294
J Garner (Eng)	76	74	71	73	294
B Gallacher (Sco)	72	76	75	72	295
T Horton (Eng)	70	72	79	74	295
B Devlin (Aus)	74	71	75	75	295
L Platts (Eng)	78	72	73	73	296
T Weiskopf (USA)	75	73	75	73	296
P Townsend (Eng)	73	75	75	73	296
W Godfrey (NZ)	72	79	71	74	296
J Kinsella (Ire)	64	68	80	74	296
J O'Leary (Ire)	70	75	75	76	296
EC Brown (Sco)	75	72	72	77	296
Peter Alliss (Eng)	74	76	72	75	297
J Miller (USA)	72	76	70	79	297
T Britz (SA)	73	78	73	74	298
S Melnyk (Am) (USA)	76	74	74	74	298
V Barrios (Spain)	72	74	77	75	298
AD Locke (SA)	75	73	74	76	298
J Wilkshire (Eng)	75	71	76	76	298
J Newton (Aus)	73	72	76	77	298
D Swaelens (Bel)	75	73	72	78	298
J Sharkey (Eng)	73	75	72	78	298
G Marsh (Aus)	75	73	72	79	299
D Snell (Eng)	75	75	74	76	300
B Waites (Eng)	70	79	72	79	300
M Bembridge (Eng)	75	73	76	77	301
M Barber (USA)	71	74	77	79	301
R Manning (SA)	73	72	76	80	301
D Talbot (Eng)	77	72	75	78	302
BW Barnes (Sco)	76	75	73	79	303

1972   *at Muirfield*

NAME	SCORE				
L Trevino (USA)	71	70	66	71	278
J Nicklaus (USA)	70	72	71	66	279
A Jacklin (Eng)	69	72	67	72	280
D Sanders (USA)	71	71	69	70	281
BW Barnes (Sco)	71	72	69	71	283
G Player (SA)	71	71	76	67	285
D Vaughan (Wal)	74	73	70	69	286
T Weiskopf (USA)	73	74	70	69	286
A Palmer (USA)	73	73	69	71	286
GL Hunt (Eng)	75	72	67	72	286
CA Clark (Eng)	72	71	73	71	287
D Marr (USA)	70	74	71	72	287
R Bernardini (Ita)	73	71	76	68	288
P Townsend (Eng)	70	72	76	70	288
PJ Butler (Eng)	72	75	73	69	289
RJ Charles (NZ)	75	70	74	70	289
J Dorrestein (Neth)	74	71	72	72	289
J Miller (USA)	76	66	72	75	289

NAME	SCORE				
H Bannerman (Sco)	77	73	73	67	290
F Beard (USA)	70	76	74	70	290
M Bembridge (Eng)	73	71	75	71	290
B Yancey (USA)	73	72	72	73	290
C O'Connor (Ire)	73	74	73	71	291
D McClelland (Eng)	73	74	72	72	291
C DeFoy (Wal)	70	75	71	75	291
BGC Huggett (Wal)	73	72	79	68	292
B Devlin (Aus)	75	70	77	70	292
P Oosterhuis (Eng)	75	75	73	70	293
J Heard (USA)	75	75	71	72	293
J Garner (Eng)	71	71	76	75	293
V Fernandez (Arg)	78	74	73	69	294
KDG Nagle (Aus)	79	72	74	69	294
Peter Alliss (Eng)	74	74	77	69	294
G Cunningham (Sco)	76	75	73	70	294
B Thomson (Eng)	74	77	72	71	294
Min Nan Hsieh (Tai)	75	75	73	71	294
RA Shearer (Aus)	77	75	68	74	294
D Stockton (USA)	72	72	76	74	294
PW Thomson (Aus)	71	72	74	77	294
VB Hood (Eng)	76	74	72	73	295
CH Kuo (Tai)	74	72	76	73	295
LH Lu (Tai)	77	73	71	74	295
W Casper (USA)	72	74	74	75	295
J Newton (Aus)	77	72	70	76	295
T Horton (Eng)	76	72	73	74	295
D Oakley (USA)	72	75	77	72	296
E Jones (Ire)	75	74	74	73	296
S Torrance (Sco)	72	74	76	74	296
LP Tupling (Eng)	68	74	73	81	296
G Marsh (Aus)	78	73	74	73	298
D Sewell (Eng)	75	74	75	74	298
D Talbot (Eng)	72	76	76	74	298
N Wood (Sco)	74	78	71	75	298
A Brooks (Sco)	74	74	75	75	298
B Hutchinson (Eng)	74	73	74	77	298
J O'Leary (Ire)	75	76	74	74	299
D Llewellyn (Wal)	72	73	79	75	299
RT Walker (Sco)	74	74	74	78	300
T Britz (SA)	75	77	73	76	301
A Garrido (Spa)	71	77	77	76	301
JM Hume (Eng)	77	70	77	77	301
G Baleson (SA)	76	73	73	80	302
J Fowler (Eng)	76	76	71	81	304
SD Brown (Eng)	81	70	74	80	305

1973   *at Troon*

NAME	SCORE				
T Weiskopf (USA)	68	67	71	70	276
NC Coles (Eng)	71	72	70	66	279
J Miller (USA)	70	68	69	72	279
J Nicklaus (USA)	69	70	76	65	280
B Yancey (USA)	69	69	73	70	281
PJ Butler (Eng)	71	72	74	69	286

NAME	SCORE				
RJ Charles (NZ)	73	71	73	71	288
C O'Connor (Ire)	73	68	74	73	288
L Wadkins (USA)	71	73	70	74	288
L Trevino (USA)	75	73	73	68	289
G Brewer (USA)	76	71	72	70	289
H Henning (SA)	73	73	73	70	289
BW Barnes (Sco)	76	67	70	76	289
G Player (SA)	76	69	76	69	290
A Jacklin (Eng)	75	73	72	70	290
A Palmer (USA)	72	76	70	72	290
D McClelland (Sco)	76	71	69	74	290
D Hill (USA)	75	74	74	69	292
DJ Good (Aus)	75	74	73	70	292
B Devlin (Aus)	72	78	71	71	292
P Oosterhuis (Eng)	80	71	69	72	292
E Polland (Ire)	74	73	73	72	292
B Crampton (Aus)	71	76	73	72	292
H Boyle (Ire)	75	75	69	73	292
PM Wilcock (Eng)	71	76	72	73	292
H Baiocchi (SA)	75	74	69	74	292
B Gallacher (Sco)	73	69	75	75	292
D Sanders (USA)	79	72	72	70	293
R de Vicenzo (Arg)	72	75	74	72	293
JA Rodriguez (Puerto Rico)	72	73	73	75	293
E Murray (Sco)	79	71	73	71	294
G Marsh (Aus)	74	71	78	71	294
PW Thomson (Aus)	76	75	70	73	294
R Wynn (Eng)	74	71	76	73	294
C DeFoy (Wal)	76	75	70	73	294
T Horton (Eng)	75	70	73	76	294
V Baker (SA)	72	74	75	74	295
D Vaughan (Wal)	78	70	72	75	295
GB Wolstenholme (Aus)	77	72	75	72	296
KDG Nagle (Aus)	74	76	73	73	296
D Hayes (SA)	76	72	73	75	296
P Elson (Port)	75	75	72	74	296
B Dassu (Ita)	75	75	73	73	296
D Gammon (Rho)	76	70	76	74	296
D Edwards (Am) (USA)	75	75	71	75	296
H Bannerman (Sco)	73	75	75	74	297
MJ Moir (Sco)	76	75	70	76	297
DK Webster (Sco)	73	76	72	76	297
BJ Hunt (Eng)	76	74	74	74	298
J Fourie (SA)	76	73	74	75	298
D Jagger (Eng)	76	74	74	75	299
RDBM Shade (Sco)	75	73	76	75	299
Peter Alliss (Eng)	76	71	76	76	299
J McTear (Sco)	76	74	71	78	299
P Townsend (Eng)	79	73	71	77	300
R Lambert (Eng)	78	74	72	77	301
WB Murray (Sco)	78	71	74	78	301
D Huish (Sco)	74	73	76	78	301
D Dunk (Eng)	73	74	74	82	303
G Mueller (Swe)	76	70	78	81	305

1974 *at Lytham and St Anne's*

NAME	SCORE				
G Player (SA)	69	68	75	70	282
P Oosterhuis (Eng)	71	71	73	71	286
J Nicklaus (USA)	74	72	70	71	287
H Green (USA)	71	74	72	71	288
D Edwards (USA)	70	73	76	73	292
LH Lu (Tai)	72	72	75	73	292
D Swaelens (Bel)	77	73	74	69	293
T Weiskopf (USA)	72	72	74	75	293
R Cole (SA)	70	72	76	75	293
J Miller (USA)	72	75	73	74	294
J Garner (Eng)	75	78	73	69	295
D Graham (Aus)	76	74	76	69	295
P Townsend (Eng)	79	76	72	69	296
A Tapie (USA)	73	77	73	73	296
NC Coles (Eng)	72	75	75	74	296
A Geiberger (USA)	76	70	76	74	296
J Morgan (Wal)	69	75	76	76	296
G Littler (USA)	77	76	70	74	297
D Weaver (USA)	73	80	70	74	297
A Jacklin (Eng)	74	77	71	75	297
P Dawson (Eng)	74	74	73	76	297
RDBM Shade (Sco)	78	75	73	72	298
L Wadkins (USA)	78	71	75	74	298
H Irwin (USA)	76	73	79	71	299
C O'Connor Jr (Ire)	78	76	72	73	299
A Gallardo (Spa)	74	77	75	73	299
B Gallacher (Sco)	76	72	76	75	299
B Crenshaw (USA)	74	80	76	70	300
D McClelland (Sco)	75	79	73	73	300
D Jagger (Eng)	80	71	76	73	300
AO Cerda (Mex)	80	74	77	70	301
T Horton (Eng)	78	76	76	71	301
PJ Butler (Eng)	75	77	77	72	301
H Jackson (N Ire)	78	76	73	74	301
D Chillas (Sco)	72	78	77	74	301
L Trevino (USA)	79	70	78	74	301
G Brewer (USA)	78	77	74	73	302
V Fernandez (Arg)	78	73	78	73	302
J Cook (Eng)	76	79	75	73	303
B Devlin (Aus)	81	74	73	75	303
GL Hunt (Eng)	78	73	72	80	303
BJ Hunt (Eng)	74	77	74	79	304
D Small (Barbados)	73	75	77	79	304
G Marsh (Aus)	79	75	77	74	305
BW Barnes (Sco)	74	79	78	74	305
JD Mahaffey (USA)	78	77	75	75	305
J O'Leary (Ire)	71	79	78	77	305
M Bembridge (Eng)	76	77	73	79	305
N Hunt (Eng)	73	73	79	80	305
SJ Levermore (Eng)	77	77	76	76	306
M Gregson (Eng)	79	76	76	76	307
R de Vicenzo (Arg)	80	74	77	76	307

NAME	SCORE				
BJ Waites (Eng)	78	74	74	81	307
MJ Slater (Eng)	77	74	80	77	308
N Wood (Sco)	74	78	78	78	308
IE Stanley (Aus)	77	79	75	78	309
C O'Connor Sr (Ire)	80	74	77	78	309
J Panton (Sco)	77	75	77	80	309
R Shearer (Aus)	77	79	73	81	310
J Fourie (SA)	79	73	77	81	310

1975 *at Carnoustie*

NAME	SCORE				
T Watson (USA)	71	67	69	72	279
J Newton (Aus)	69	71	65	74	279
(Watson won play-off, 71 to 72)					
J Nicklaus (USA)	69	71	68	72	280
J Miller (USA)	71	69	66	74	280
R Cole (SA)	72	66	66	76	280
G Marsh (Aus)	72	67	71	71	281
P Oosterhuis (Eng)	68	70	71	73	282
NC Coles (Eng)	72	69	67	74	282
H Irwin (USA)	69	70	69	75	283
G Burns (USA)	71	73	69	71	284
J Mahaffey (USA)	71	68	69	76	284
RJ Charles (NZ)	74	73	70	69	286
P Leonard (N Ire)	70	69	73	74	286
A Oosthuizen (SA)	69	69	70	78	286
T Weiskopf (USA)	73	72	70	72	287
M Bembridge (Eng)	75	73	67	73	288
A Palmer (USA)	74	72	69	73	288
A Tapie (USA)	70	72	67	79	288
L Hinkle (USA)	76	72	69	72	289
S Torrance (Sco)	72	74	71	72	289
T Horton (Eng)	72	71	71	75	289
B Gallacher (Sco)	72	67	72	78	289
MF Foster (Eng)	72	74	73	71	290
R Floyd (USA)	71	72	76	71	290
BW Barnes (Sco)	71	74	72	73	290
H Baiocchi (SA)	72	72	73	73	290
D Edwards (USA)	70	74	71	75	290
R de Vicenzo (Arg)	71	74	72	74	291
GL Hunt (Eng)	73	68	76	74	291
D Graham (Aus)	74	70	72	75	291
S Hobday (Rho)	70	70	76	75	291
P Dawson (Eng)	74	75	71	72	292
G Player (SA)	75	71	73	73	292
M Cahill (Aus)	71	73	74	74	292
T Britz (SA)	74	71	72	75	292
D Hayes (SA)	73	71	73	75	292
H Green (USA)	72	73	70	77	292
R Shearer (Aus)	69	72	74	77	292
D Huish (Sco)	69	67	76	80	292
R Gilder (USA)	75	71	75	72	293
N Wood (Sco)	74	74	71	74	293
L Trevino (USA)	76	69	73	75	293

NAME	SCORE				
KDG Nagle (Aus)	72	73	73	75	293
BGC Huggett (Wal)	72	71	75	75	293
BJ Waites (Eng)	74	72	69	78	293
I Stanley (Aus)	75	71	70	78	294
B Garrett (USA)	76	72	72	75	295
PM Wilcock (Eng)	77	68	75	75	295
L Graham (USA)	73	72	74	76	295
C O'Connor Jr (Ire)	72	73	73	77	295
B Brask (USA)	74	71	72	78	295
E Pearce (USA)	72	75	70	79	296
JA Jacobs (USA)	72	76	73	76	297
LH Lu (Tai)	76	72	72	77	297
V Fernandez (Arg)	76	70	74	77	297
DI Vaughan (Wal)	72	71	74	80	297
T Le Brocq (Eng)	72	76	72	78	298
P Townsend (Eng)	74	70	76	78	298
D Clark (NZ)	72	72	76	78	298
H Hansen (Den)	74	74	73	78	299
J Dorrestein (Neth)	75	73	73	79	300
SC Mason (Eng)	73	72	75	81	301
RJ Carr (Ire)	76	72	72	82	302

1976 *at Birkdale*

NAME	SCORE				
J Miller (USA)	72	68	73	66	279
J Nicklaus (USA)	74	70	72	69	285
S Ballesteros (Spa)	69	69	73	74	285
R Floyd (USA)	76	67	73	70	286
M James (Eng)	76	72	74	66	288
H Green (USA)	72	70	78	68	288
T Kite (USA)	70	74	73	71	288
C O'Connor Jr (Ire)	69	73	75	71	288
T Horton (Eng)	74	69	72	73	288
V Fernandez (Arg)	79	71	69	70	289
PJ Butler (Eng)	74	72	73	70	289
N Suzuki (Jpn)	69	75	75	70	289
G Burns III (USA)	75	69	75	70	289
BW Barnes (Sco)	70	73	75	72	290
E Darcy (Ire)	78	71	71	71	291
J Fourie (SA)	71	74	75	71	291
T Weiskopf (USA)	73	72	76	71	292
J Newton (Aus)	70	74	76	72	292
GB Wolstenholme (Aus)	76	72	71	73	292
G Marsh (Aus)	71	73	72	76	292
S Hobday (Rho)	79	71	75	68	293
R Shearer (Aus)	76	73	75	69	293
S Ginn (Aus)	78	72	72	71	293
D Graham (Aus)	77	70	75	71	293
Chi-San Hsu (Tai)	81	69	71	72	293
A Tapie (USA)	74	72	75	72	293
D Huish (Sco)	73	74	72	74	293
N Faldo (Eng)	78	71	76	69	294
D Sanders (USA)	77	73	73	71	294
NC Coles (Eng)	74	77	70	73	294
G Player (SA)	72	72	79	71	294

NAME	SCORE				
R de Vicenzo (Arg)	77	71	76	72	296
P McGuirk (Ire)	76	70	77	73	296
H Irwin (USA)	74	72	77	73	296
G Littler (USA)	75	74	73	74	296
GL Hunt (Eng)	76	68	76	76	296
R Cole (SA)	75	71	72	78	296
D Jagger (Tobago)	78	72	74	73	297
V Hood (Eng)	76	74	73	74	297
MF Foster (Eng)	74	71	77	75	297
I Mosey (Eng)	73	74	75	75	297
A Jacklin (Eng)	73	77	76	72	298
P Oosterhuis (Eng)	74	75	77	72	298
P Dawson (Eng)	80	72	73	73	298
BJ Burgess (Aus)	75	76	74	73	298
M Gregson (Eng)	73	75	76	74	298
W Humphreys (Eng)	73	77	73	75	298
B Garrett (USA)	74	74	78	73	299
R Murphy (USA)	75	77	73	74	299
CI Higgins (USA)	77	67	81	74	299
D McClelland (Sco)	74	73	77	75	299
P Berry (Eng)	80	72	71	76	299
SWR Adwick (Eng)	78	71	74	76	299
D Hayes (SA)	77	71	74	77	299
A O'Connor (Eng)	76	76	74	74	300
A Oosthuizen (SA)	75	73	78	74	300
JL Hammond (Eng)	74	76	73	77	300
A Palmer (USA)	75	72	76	77	300
D Talbot (Eng)	74	74	74	78	300
D Edwards (USA)	74	72	79	76	301
R Wynn (Eng)	79	70	75	77	301
B Gallacher (Sco)	74	72	76	79	301
WR Lockie (Sco)	78	74	74	76	302
GA Caygill (Fra)	80	71	75	76	302
L Higgins (Ire)	77	74	75	76	302
LP Tupling (Eng)	75	71	77	79	302

1977   *at Turnberry*

NAME	SCORE				
T Watson (USA)	68	70	65	65	268
J Nicklaus (USA)	68	70	65	66	269
H Green (USA)	72	66	74	67	279
L Trevino (USA)	68	70	72	70	280
G Burns (USA)	70	70	72	69	281
B Crenshaw (USA)	71	69	66	75	281
A Palmer (USA)	73	73	67	69	282
R Floyd (USA)	70	73	68	72	283
J Schroeder (USA)	66	74	73	71	284
M Hayes (USA)	76	63	72	73	284
T Horton (Eng)	70	74	65	75	284
J Miller (USA)	69	74	67	74	284
PW Thomson (Aus)	74	72	67	73	286
H Clark (Eng)	72	68	72	74	286
GL Hunt (Eng)	73	71	71	72	287
J Pate (USA)	74	70	70	73	287
R Cole (SA)	72	71	71	73	287
PJ Butler (Eng)	71	68	75	73	287
G Marsh (Aus)	73	69	71	74	287

NAME	SCORE				
R Shearer (Aus)	72	69	72	74	287
S Ballesteros (Spa)	69	71	73	74	287
G Player (SA)	71	74	74	69	288
T Weiskopf (USA)	74	71	71	72	288
P Dawson (Eng)	74	68	73	73	288
J Fourie (SA)	74	69	70	75	288
R Massengale (USA)	73	71	74	71	289
D Ingram (Sco)	73	74	70	72	289
MF Foster (Eng)	67	74	75	73	289
J O'Leary (Ire)	74	73	68	74	289
A Gallardo (Spa)	78	65	72	74	289
N Suzuki (Jpn)	74	71	69	75	289
G Burrows (USA)	69	72	68	80	289
R Maltbie (USA)	71	66	72	80	289
E Darcy (Ire)	74	71	74	71	290
K Brown (Sco)	74	73	71	72	290
M Pinero (Spa)	74	75	71	71	291
B Dassu (Ita)	72	74	72	73	291
Min Nan Hsieh (Tai)	72	73	73	73	291
BW Barnes (Sco)	79	69	69	74	291
J Morgan (Wal)	72	71	71	77	291
NC Coles (Eng)	74	74	71	73	292
DI Vaughan (Wal)	71	74	73	74	292
J Gonzales (USA)	78	72	71	72	293
A Jacklin (Eng)	72	70	74	77	293
RJ Charles (NZ)	73	72	70	78	293
S Ginn (Aus)	75	72	72	75	294
H Irwin (USA)	70	71	73	80	294
BGC Huggett (Wal)	72	77	72	74	295
V Fernandez (Arg)	75	73	73	74	295
MG King (Eng)	73	75	72	75	295
R de Vicenzo (Arg)	76	71	70	78	295
C O'Connor Jr (Ire)	75	73	71	77	296
JC Farmer (Sco)	72	74	72	78	296
BJ Waites (Eng)	78	70	69	79	296
R Davies (Aus)	77	70	70	79	296
M Bembridge (Eng)	76	69	75	77	297
V Tshabalala (SA)	71	73	72	81	297
I Mosey (Eng)	75	73	73	77	298
D Jones (N Ire)	73	74	73	78	298
Chi-San Hsu (Tai)	70	70	77	81	298
GD Jacobson (USA)	74	73	70	81	298
N Faldo (Eng)	71	76	74	78	299
S Locatelli (Ita)	72	72	76	79	299
V Baker (SA)	77	70	73	79	299

1978   *at St Andrews*

NAME	SCORE				
J Nicklaus (USA)	71	72	69	69	281
S Owen (NZ)	70	75	67	71	283
R Floyd (USA)	69	75	71	68	283
B Crenshaw (USA)	70	69	73	71	283
T Kite (USA)	72	69	72	70	283
P Oosterhuis (Eng)	72	70	69	73	284
I Aoki (Jpn)	68	71	73	73	285
R Shearer (Aus)	71	69	74	71	285

NAME	SCORE				
J Schroeder (USA)	74	69	70	72	285
N Faldo (Eng)	71	72	70	72	285
O Moody (USA)	73	69	74	70	286
M Cahill (Aus)	71	72	75	68	286
D Hayes (SA)	74	70	71	71	286
M Hayes (USA)	70	75	75	67	287
M Ozaki (Jpn)	72	69	75	71	287
T Watson (USA)	73	68	70	76	287
B Byman (USA)	72	69	74	73	288
T Nakajima (Jpn)	70	71	76	71	288
S Ballesteros (Spa)	69	70	76	73	288
GL Hunt (Eng)	71	73	71	73	288
T Weiskopf (USA)	69	72	72	75	288
B Gallacher (Sco)	72	71	76	70	289
N Job (Eng)	73	75	68	73	289
A Garrido (Spa)	73	71	76	70	290
H Irwin (USA)	75	71	76	68	290
J Newton (Aus)	69	76	71	74	290
SC Mason (Eng)	70	74	72	74	290
PW Thomson (Aus)	72	70	72	76	290
L Trevino (USA)	75	72	73	71	291
J Morgan (Wal)	74	68	77	72	291
T Britz (SA)	73	74	72	72	291
G Norman (Aus)	72	73	74	72	291
H Green (USA)	78	70	67	76	291
BW Barnes (Sco)	71	74	75	72	292
G Player (SA)	74	71	76	71	292
G Cullen (Eng)	73	67	79	73	292
K Brown (Sco)	73	72	71	76	292
A Palmer (USA)	71	71	75	75	292
N Price (SA)	74	73	74	72	293
M Krantz (USA)	75	72	75	71	293
P McEvoy (Am) (Eng)	71	74	76	72	293
GB Wolstenholme (Aus)	73	74	71	75	293
D Graham (Aus)	73	74	70	76	293
F Abreu (Spa)	73	73	76	72	294
H Clark (Eng)	70	75	73	76	294
M Miller (Am) (Sco)	70	74	74	76	294
M Ballesteros (Spa)	73	71	74	76	294
A Brodie (Am) (Sco)	73	72	75	75	295
A Bean (USA)	72	76	72	75	295
RJ Charles (NZ)	73	70	79	73	295
NC Coles (Eng)	71	73	73	78	295
V Somers (Aus)	72	72	76	76	296
R Thompson (USA)	73	73	76	74	296
J Bland (SA)	72	73	77	74	296
S Hobday (Rho)	73	71	77	75	296
W Longmuir (Sco)	75	71	75	75	296
D Good (Aus)	75	73	74	74	296
R Davis (Aus)	73	72	73	78	296
PJ Butler (Eng)	71	74	75	77	297
G Godwin (Am) (Eng)	74	73	75	76	298
R Wynn (Eng)	73	72	76	77	298
P Dawson (Eng)	75	72	75	77	299
E Murray (Sco)	76	70	76	78	300

1979 *at Lytham and St Anne's*

NAME	SCORE				
S Ballesteros (Spa)	73	65	75	70	283
B Crenshaw (USA)	72	71	72	71	286
J Nicklaus (USA)	72	69	73	72	286
M James (Eng)	76	69	69	73	287
R Davis (Aus)	75	70	70	73	288
H Irwin (USA)	68	68	75	78	289
G Marsh (Aus)	74	68	75	74	291
I Aoki (Jpn)	70	74	72	75	291
B Byman (USA)	73	70	72	76	291
RJ Charles (NZ)	78	72	70	72	292
M Ozaki (Jpn)	75	69	75	73	292
G Norman (Aus)	73	71	72	76	292
SM Owen (NZ)	75	76	74	68	293
W Armstrong (USA)	74	74	73	72	293
J O'Leary (Ire)	73	73	74	73	293
T Gale (Aus)	71	74	75	73	293
L Trevino (USA)	71	73	74	76	294
P McEvoy (Am) (Eng)	71	74	72	77	294
N Faldo (Eng)	74	74	78	69	295
AWB Lyle (Sco)	74	76	75	70	295
O Moody (USA)	71	74	76	74	295
G Player (SA)	77	74	69	75	295
K Brown (Sco)	72	71	75	77	295
A Jacklin (Eng)	73	74	76	73	296
T Nakamura (Jpn)	77	75	67	77	296
PW Thomson (Aus)	76	75	72	74	297
E Sneed (USA)	76	75	70	76	297
J Pate ((USA)	69	74	76	78	297
T Watson (USA)	72	68	76	81	297
M Hayes (USA)	75	75	77	71	298
FR Verwey (SA)	75	77	74	72	298
AE Saavedra (Arg)	76	76	73	73	298
T Kite (USA)	73	74	77	74	298
S Hobday (Zim)	75	77	71	75	298
W Longmuir (Sco)	65	74	77	82	298
C O'Connor Sr (Ire)	79	73	71	76	299
P Cowen (unattached)	79	72	72	76	299
L Elder (USA)	75	72	76	76	299
R Floyd (USA)	76	73	71	79	299
MG King (Eng)	75	70	73	81	299
MF Foster (Eng)	77	75	74	74	300
P Toussaint (Bel)	76	75	74	75	300
N Ratcliffe (Aus)	79	73	72	76	300
H Baiocchi (SA)	72	73	78	77	300
P Oosterhuis (Eng)	75	74	73	78	300
J Schroeder (USA)	74	75	72	79	300
H Green (USA)	77	71	73	79	300
DL Watson (SA)	75	70	76	79	300
DJ Clark (NZ)	72	69	76	83	300
BW Barnes (Sco)	78	71	77	75	301
SC Mason (Eng)	77	72	76	76	301
DW Weaver (USA)	73	71	80	77	301
G Cullen (Eng)	72	74	77	78	301

NAME	SCORE				
GL Parslow (Aus)	75	75	76	76	302
I Richardson (Eng)	75	73	77	77	302
K Shimada (Jpn)	75	74	75	78	302
J Miller (USA)	77	73	77	76	303
Y Yamamoto (Jpn)	76	74	77	76	303
J Newton (Aus)	76	73	78	76	303
GB Wolstenholme (Aus)	77	75	71	80	303
RP Fyfe (Sco)	74	73	79	81	307

1980 *at Muirfield*

NAME	SCORE				
T Watson (USA)	68	70	64	69	271
L Trevino (USA)	68	67	71	69	275
B Crenshaw (USA)	70	70	68	69	277
J Nicklaus (USA)	73	67	71	69	280
SC Mason (Eng)	72	69	70	69	280
C Stadler (USA)	72	70	69	71	282
A Bean (USA)	71	69	70	72	282
H Green (USA)	77	69	64	72	282
K Brown (Sco)	70	68	68	76	282
J Newton (Aus)	69	71	73	70	283
G Morgan (USA)	70	70	71	72	283
N Faldo (Eng)	69	74	71	70	284
L Nelson (USA)	72	70	71	71	284
AWB Lyle (Sco)	70	71	70	73	284
I Aoki (Jpn)	74	74	63	73	284
T Weiskopf (USA)	72	72	71	70	285
J Bland (SA)	73	70	70	72	285
J Pate (USA)	71	67	74	73	285
W Rogers (USA)	76	73	68	69	286
B Lietzke (USA)	74	69	73	70	286
N Suzuki (Jpn)	74	68	72	72	286
S Ballesteros (Spa)	72	68	72	74	286
P Oosterhuis (Eng)	72	71	75	69	287
M McNulty (SA)	71	73	72	71	287
W McColl (Sco)	75	73	68	71	287
G Cullen (Eng)	72	72	69	74	287
T Kite (USA)	72	72	74	70	288
N Price (Zim)	72	71	71	74	288
NC Coles (Eng)	75	69	69	76	289
H Baiocchi (SA)	76	67	69	77	289
D Graham (Aus)	73	71	68	77	289
M Hayes (USA)	70	73	76	71	290
T Horton (Eng)	76	71	71	72	290
A Jacklin (Eng)	72	74	71	73	290
J Mahaffey (USA)	77	71	69	73	290
BJ Waites (Eng)	75	72	69	74	290
H Clark (Eng)	72	70	70	78	290
J Sigel (Am) (USA)	72	72	74	73	291
S Torrance (Sco)	74	71	73	73	291
R Davis (Aus)	74	70	73	74	291
S Ginn (Aus)	77	70	70	74	291
B Brask Jr (USA)	74	71	71	75	291
T Nakamura (Jpn)	76	72	69	74	291

NAME	SCORE				
D Hayes (SA)	71	70	74	76	291
A North (USA)	75	72	72	73	292
W Armstrong (USA)	77	72	70	73	292
G Marsh (Aus)	73	72	72	75	292
M James (Eng)	69	72	75	76	292
E Darcy (Ire)	75	68	73	76	292
V Fernandez (Arg)	69	76	71	76	292
A Garrido (Spa)	74	71	73	75	293
R Gilder (USA)	75	71	72	75	293
B Langer (W Ger)	73	72	72	76	293
S Hobday (Zim)	76	71	71	75	293
H Henning (SA)	77	71	69	76	293
R Shearer (Aus)	76	71	70	76	293
D Cooper (Eng)	71	70	75	77	293
M Pinero (Spa)	72	72	75	75	294
BW Barnes (Sco)	73	72	71	78	294
RJ Charles (NZ)	75	71	73	76	295
D Jagger (Eng)	72	77	69	77	295
M Ozaki (Jpn)	73	68	73	81	295
LP Tupling (Eng)	76	70	73	77	296
SM Owen (NZ)	72	73	72	80	297
D Bies (USA)	73	74	72	79	298

1981 *at St George's, Sandwich*

NAME	SCORE				
W Rogers (USA)	72	66	67	71	276
B Langer (W Ger)	73	67	70	70	280
R Floyd (USA)	74	70	69	70	283
M James (Eng)	72	70	68	73	283
S Torrance (Sco)	72	69	73	70	284
B Lietzke (USA)	76	69	71	69	285
M Pinero (Spa)	73	74	68	70	285
H Clark (Eng)	72	76	70	68	286
B Crenshaw (USA)	72	67	76	71	286
B Jones (Aus)	73	76	66	71	286
L Trevino (USA)	77	67	70	73	287
I Aoki (Japan)	71	73	69	74	287
N Faldo (Eng)	77	68	69	73	287
BW Barnes (Sco)	76	70	70	72	288
D Graham (Aus)	71	71	74	72	288
E Darcy (Ire)	79	69	70	70	288
AWB Lyle (Sco)	73	73	71	71	288
N Job (Eng)	70	69	75	74	288
J Pate (USA)	73	73	69	74	289
P Townsend (Eng)	73	70	73	73	289
GJ Brand (Eng)	78	65	74	72	289
G Marsh (Aus)	75	71	72	71	289
A Jacklin (Eng)	71	71	73	75	290
SM Owen (NZ)	71	74	70	75	290
T Watson (USA)	73	69	75	73	290
A Palmer (USA)	72	74	73	71	290
J Nicklaus (USA)	83	66	71	70	290
H Green (USA)	75	72	74	69	290
M McNulty (SA)	74	74	74	68	290

NAME	SCORE				
N Price (SA)	77	68	76	69	290
T Powell (Wal)	75	68	73	75	291
D Smyth (Ire)	77	67	73	74	291
G Norman (Aus)	72	75	72	72	291
J Morgan (Wal)	77	72	73	69	291
RJ Charles (NZ)	77	71	71	73	292
M Ozaki (Jpn)	75	72	71	74	292
T Horton (Eng)	75	73	73	71	292
EW Dunk (Aus)	76	67	77	72	292
J Miller (USA)	71	73	73	76	293
R Davis (Aus)	74	71	74	74	293
F Molina (Arg)	78	68	74	73	293
S Ballesteros (Spa)	75	72	74	72	293
NC Coles (Eng)	74	73	73	73	293
T Gale (Aus)	73	73	71	77	294
R Streck (USA)	78	70	72	74	294
K Brown (Sco)	74	72	74	74	294
M O'Meara (USA)	74	73	73	75	295
H Sutton (Am) (USA)	71	77	73	74	295
J Gonzalez (Bra)	76	70	76	73	295
BJ Waites (Eng)	75	69	74	78	296
D Thorp (Eng)	76	69	74	77	296
D Jones (N Ire)	77	71	74	74	296
M Ferguson (Aus)	75	72	71	79	297
G Cullen (Eng)	78	70	73	76	297
E Polland (Ire)	75	75	72	75	297
W Humphreys (Eng)	76	71	74	77	298
N Hunt (Eng)	74	73	75	76	298
G Godwin (Am) (Eng)	75	71	72	81	299
P Stewart (USA)	73	75	74	77	299
J O'Leary (Ire)	73	74	75	77	299
R McClean (USA)	75	73	72	83	303

1982   *at Troon*

NAME	SCORE				
T Watson (USA)	69	71	74	70	284
P Oosterhuis (Eng)	74	67	74	70	285
N Price (SA)	69	69	74	73	285
TW Purtzer (USA)	76	66	75	69	286
N Faldo (Eng)	73	73	71	69	286
M Kuramoto (Jpn)	71	73	71	71	286
D Smyth (Ire)	70	69	74	73	286
F Zoeller (USA)	73	71	73	70	287
AWB Lyle (Sco)	74	66	73	74	287
J Nicklaus (USA)	77	70	72	69	288
R Clampett (USA)	67	66	78	77	288
S Torrance (Sco)	73	72	73	71	289
S Ballesteros (Spa)	71	75	73	71	290
B Langer (W Ger)	70	69	78	73	290
R Floyd (USA)	74	73	77	67	291
C Strange (USA)	72	73	76	70	291
B Crenshaw (USA)	74	75	72	70	291
D Watson (SA)	75	69	73	74	291
K Brown (Sco)	70	71	79	72	292
T Nakamura (Jpn)	77	68	77	71	293
I Aoki (Jpn)	75	69	75	74	293
JM Canizares (Spa)	71	72	79	72	294

NAME	SCORE				
J Miller (USA)	71	76	75	72	294
W Rogers (USA)	73	70	76	75	294
G Marsh (Aus)	76	76	72	71	295
B Gallacher (Sco)	75	71	74	75	295
J Haas (USA)	78	72	75	71	296
G Norman (Aus)	73	75	76	72	296
A Palmer (USA)	71	73	78	74	296
L Trevino (USA)	78	72	71	75	296
D Graham (Aus)	73	70	76	77	296
M Miller (Sco)	74	72	78	73	297
L Nelson (USA)	77	69	77	74	297
M Thomas (Wal)	72	74	75	76	297
E Darcy (Ire)	75	73	78	72	298
J Ferenz (USA)	76	69	80	73	298
P Way (Eng)	72	75	78	73	298
C Stadler (USA)	71	74	79	74	298
DJ Russell (Eng)	72	72	76	78	298
BW Barnes (Sco)	75	69	76	78	298
H Henning (SA)	74	74	76	75	299
R Shearer (Aus)	73	72	81	74	300
G Player (SA)	75	74	76	75	300
T Gale (Aus)	76	74	75	75	300
NC Coles (Eng)	73	73	72	82	300
ME Lewis (Am) (Eng)	74	74	77	75	300
W Longmuir (Sco)	77	72	77	75	301
T Britz (SA)	81	70	74	76	301
R Chapman (Eng)	75	76	74	76	301
BJ Waites (Eng)	75	77	73	76	301
M James (Eng)	74	73	79	76	302
Hsu Sheng-San (Tai)	75	75	75	77	302
M Pinero (Spa)	75	75	74	78	302
M McNulty (SA)	76	74	76	77	303
P Townsend (Eng)	76	73	76	78	303
M Poxon (Eng)	74	70	78	81	303
KR Waters (Eng)	73	78	71	81	303
P Harrison (Eng)	78	74	74	78	304
MG King (Eng)	73	78	74	80	305
MF Cahill (Aus)	73	76	77	80	306

1983   *at Birkdale*

NAME	SCORE				
T Watson (USA)	67	68	70	70	275
H Irwin (USA)	69	68	72	67	276
A Bean (USA)	70	69	70	67	276
G Marsh (Aus)	69	70	74	64	277
L Trevino (USA)	69	66	73	70	278
S Ballesteros (Spa)	71	71	69	68	279
H Henning (SA)	71	69	70	69	279
D Durnian (Eng)	73	66	74	67	280
C O'Connor Jr (Ire)	72	69	71	68	280
W Rogers (USA)	67	71	73	69	280
N Faldo (Eng)	68	68	71	73	280
P Jacobsen (USA)	73	69	70	70	281
C Stadler (USA)	64	70	72	75	281
M Sullivan (USA)	72	68	74	68	282
G Koch (USA)	75	71	66	70	282

NAME	SCORE				
F Zoeller (USA)	71	71	67	73	282
D Graham (Aus)	71	69	67	75	282
R Floyd (USA)	72	66	69	75	282
G Norman (Aus)	75	71	70	67	283
H Green (USA)	69	74	72	68	283
T Britz (SA)	71	74	69	69	283
BJ Waites (Eng)	70	70	73	70	283
B Gallacher (Sco)	72	71	70	70	283
S Hobday (SA)	70	73	70	70	283
J Haas (USA)	73	72	68	70	283
E Darcy (Ire)	69	72	74	69	284
H Clark (Eng)	71	72	69	72	284
R Davis (Aus)	70	71	70	73	284
C-S Lu (Tai)	71	72	74	68	285
L Wadkins (USA)	72	73	72	68	285
J Nicklaus (USA)	71	72	72	70	285
T Kite (USA)	71	72	72	70	285
M McCollough (USA)	74	69	72	70	285
H Sutton (USA)	68	71	75	71	285
M James (Eng)	70	70	74	71	285
T Nakamura (Jpn)	73	69	72	71	285
C Strange (USA)	74	68	70	73	285
T Gale (Aus)	72	66	72	75	285
A Jacklin (Eng)	71	75	71	69	286
K Arai (Jpn)	74	67	75	70	286
R Gilder (USA)	70	76	70	70	286
V Fernandez (Arg)	70	72	72	72	286
C Moody (Eng)	74	69	70	73	286
I Collins (Sco)	70	75	68	73	286
C Tucker (Eng)	73	71	73	70	287
M Kuramoto (Jpn)	70	74	73	70	287
M Pinero (Spa)	74	72	71	70	287
GR Burroughs (Eng)	71	74	71	71	287
T Weiskopf (USA)	73	73	69	72	287
T Simpson (USA)	73	69	72	73	287
VT Somers (Aus)	68	75	71	73	287
M McNulty (SA)	72	69	68	78	287
R Clampett (USA)	74	72	71	71	288
L Nelson (USA)	70	73	73	72	288
S Torrance (Sco)	68	73	74	73	288
B Langer (W Ger)	67	72	76	74	289
A Palmer (USA)	72	74	68	75	289
ME Johnson (Eng)	70	72	71	76	289
M Calero (Spa)	70	75	69	76	290
J O'Leary (Ire)	74	68	69	79	290
R Rafferty (N Ire)	75	67	73	76	291
M Ingham (Eng)	71	73	70	78	292
Y-S Hsieh (Tai)	71	72	74	78	295

1984   *at St Andrews*

NAME	SCORE				
S Ballesteros (Spa)	69	68	70	69	276
B Langer (W Ger)	71	68	68	71	278
T Watson (USA)	71	68	66	73	278
F Couples (USA)	70	69	74	68	281

NAME	SCORE				
L Wadkins (USA)	70	69	73	69	281
G Norman (Aus)	67	74	74	67	282
N Faldo (Eng)	69	68	76	69	282
M McCumber (USA)	74	67	72	70	283
G Marsh (Aus)	70	74	73	67	284
S Torrance (Sco)	74	74	66	70	284
R Rafferty (N Ire)	74	72	67	71	284
H Baiocchi (SA)	72	70	70	72	284
I Baker-Finch (Aus)	68	66	71	79	284
AWB Lyle (Sco)	75	71	72	67	285
K Brown (Sco)	74	71	72	68	285
A Bean (USA)	72	69	75	69	285
F Zoeller (USA)	71	72	71	71	285
P Senior (Aus)	74	70	70	71	285
W Bergin (USA)	75	73	66	71	285
H Irwin (USA)	75	68	70	72	285
L Trevino (USA)	70	67	75	73	285
C Pavin (USA)	71	74	72	69	286
B Crenshaw (USA)	72	75	70	69	286
T Kite (USA)	69	71	74	72	286
P Way (Eng)	73	72	69	72	286
P Jacobsen (USA)	67	73	73	73	286
G Morgan (USA)	71	71	71	73	286
T Gale (Aus)	71	74	72	70	287
J Gonzalez (Bra)	69	71	76	71	287
C Stadler (USA)	75	70	70	72	287
P Parkin (Wal)	73	73	73	69	288
R Drummond (Sco)	77	71	69	71	288
B Gallacher (Sco)	70	74	72	72	288
J Miller (USA)	75	71	70	72	288
J Nicklaus (USA)	76	72	68	72	288
M Pinero (Spa)	71	71	76	71	289
J Haas (USA)	73	71	73	72	289
G Levenson (SA)	74	70	73	72	289
J Heggarty (N Ire)	71	74	72	72	289
E Murray (Sco)	72	74	71	72	289
D Dunk (Eng)	71	72	73	73	289
T Nakajima (Jpn)	70	71	74	74	289
JM Canizares (Spa)	70	71	72	76	289
N Price (Zim)	74	73	72	71	290
M Poxon (Eng)	70	74	73	73	290
M James (Eng)	70	73	72	75	290
M Calero (Spa)	75	72	72	72	291
I Aoki (Japan)	71	74	73	73	291
D Frost (SA)	76	72	70	73	291
RJ Charles (NZ)	75	73	70	73	291
R Chapman (Eng)	72	74	70	75	291
H Clark (Eng)	74	74	71	73	292
J Chillas (Sco)	71	72	75	74	292
R Boxall (Eng)	71	74	73	74	292
M Mackenzie (Eng)	72	72	74	75	293
DJ Russell (Eng)	73	74	71	75	293
W Longmuir (Sco)	67	71	79	76	293
E Rodriguez (Spa)	74	74	69	76	293
S Fujiki (Jpn)	72	73	74	75	294
J Garner (Eng)	74	71	74	76	295
G Koch (USA)	75	73	70	77	295
R Hartmann (USA)	70	73	76	77	296
N Ozaki (Jpn)	72	76	70	78	296

1985 *at St George's, Sandwich*

NAME	SCORE				
AWB Lyle (Sco)	68	71	73	70	282
P Stewart (USA)	70	75	70	68	283
J Rivero (Spa)	74	72	70	68	284
C O'Connor Jr (Ire)	64	76	72	72	284
M O'Meara (USA)	70	72	70	72	284
D Graham (Aus)	68	71	70	75	284
B Langer (W Ger)	72	69	68	75	284
A Forsbrand (Swe)	70	76	69	70	285
DA Weibring (USA)	69	71	74	71	285
T Kite (USA)	73	73	67	72	285
E Darcy (Ire)	76	68	74	68	286
G Koch (USA)	75	72	70	69	286
JM Canizares (Spa)	72	75	70	69	286
F Zoeller (USA)	69	76	70	71	286
P Jacobsen (USA)	71	74	68	73	286
S Bishop (Eng)	71	75	72	69	287
S Torrance (Sco)	74	74	69	70	287
G Norman (Aus)	71	72	71	73	287
I Woosnam (Wal)	70	71	71	75	287
I Baker-Finch (Aus)	71	73	74	70	288
J Gonzalez (Bra)	72	72	73	71	288
L Trevino (USA)	73	76	68	71	288
G Marsh (Aus)	71	75	69	73	288
M James (Eng)	71	78	66	73	288
P Parkin (Wal)	68	76	77	68	289
K Moe (USA)	70	76	73	70	289
JM Olazabal (Am) (Spa)	72	76	71	70	289
M Cahill (Aus)	72	74	71	72	289
D Frost (SA)	70	74	73	72	289
GJ Brand (Eng)	73	72	72	72	289
M Pinero (Spa)	71	73	72	73	289
R Lee (Eng)	68	73	74	74	289
O Sellberg (Swe)	71	78	70	71	290
W Riley (Aus)	71	70	77	72	290
H Baiocchi (SA)	75	74	71	71	291
B Crenshaw (USA)	73	75	70	73	291
A Bean (USA)	72	72	73	74	291
R Shearer (Aus)	75	73	68	75	291
A Johnstone (Zim)	68	72	80	72	292
M Persson (Swe)	71	73	76	72	292
J Pinsent (Eng)	73	74	72	73	292
S Ballesteros (Spa)	75	74	70	73	292
C Pavin (USA)	70	74	72	76	292
P Senior (Aus)	70	71	80	72	293
R Rafferty (N Ire)	74	73	71	75	293
DA Russell (Eng)	74	72	71	76	293
D Watson (SA)	72	74	75	73	294
M Mouland (Wal)	72	75	74	73	294
G Brand Jr (Sco)	69	74	77	74	294
B Gallacher (Sco)	73	76	71	74	294
H Clark (Eng)	70	71	76	77	294
T Watson (USA)	72	73	72	77	294
N Faldo (Eng)	73	73	75	74	295
E Rodriguez (Spa)	71	70	77	77	295
L Nelson (USA)	70	75	75	77	297
P Fowler (Aus)	70	79	70	78	297

NAME	SCORE				
D Whelan (Eng)	69	74	75	80	298
D Williams (Eng)	74	71	74	81	300
V Somers (Aus)	76	72	73	80	301
RJ Charles (NZ)	70	76	69		Ret'd

1986 *at Turnberry*

NAME	SCORE				
G Norman (Aus)	74	63	74	69	280
GJ Brand (Eng)	71	68	75	71	285
B Langer (W Ger)	72	70	76	68	286
I Woosnam (Wal)	70	74	70	72	286
N Faldo (Eng)	71	70	76	70	287
S Ballesteros (Spa)	76	75	73	64	288
G Koch (USA)	73	72	72	71	288
F Zoeller (USA)	75	73	72	69	289
B Marchbank (Sco)	78	70	72	69	289
T Nakajima (Jpn)	74	67	71	77	289
C O'Connor Jr (Ire)	75	71	75	69	290
D Graham (Aus)	75	73	70	72	290
JM Canizares (Spa)	76	68	73	73	290
C Strange (USA)	79	69	74	69	291
A Bean (USA)	74	73	73	71	291
A Forsbrand (Swe)	71	73	77	71	292
JM Olazabal (Spa)	78	69	72	73	292
R Floyd (USA)	78	67	73	74	292
RJ Charles (NZ)	76	72	73	72	293
M Pinero (Spa)	78	71	70	74	293
R Rafferty (N Ire)	75	74	75	70	294
D Cooper (Eng)	72	79	72	71	294
V Somers (Aus)	73	77	72	72	294
B Crenshaw (USA)	77	69	75	73	294
R Lee (Eng)	71	75	75	73	294
P Parkin (Wal)	78	70	72	74	294
D Edwards (USA)	77	73	70	74	294
V Fernandez (Arg)	78	70	71	75	294
S Torrance (Sco)	78	69	71	76	294
I Stanley (Aus)	72	74	78	71	295
J Mahaffey (USA)	75	73	75	72	295
M Kuramoto (Jpn)	77	73	73	72	295
DA Weibring (USA)	75	70	76	74	295
AWB Lyle (Sco)	78	73	70	74	295
T Watson (USA)	77	71	77	71	296
R Chapman (Eng)	74	71	78	73	296
A Brooks (Sco)	72	73	77	74	296
R Commans (USA)	72	77	73	74	296
M James (Eng)	75	73	73	75	296
P Stewart (USA)	76	69	75	76	296
G Player (SA)	75	72	73	76	296
G Turner (NZ)	73	71	75	77	296
R Maltbie (USA)	78	71	76	72	297
M O'Meara (USA)	80	69	74	74	297
HM Chung (Tai)	77	74	69	77	297
M O'Grady (USA)	76	75	77	70	298
J Nicklaus (USA)	78	73	76	71	298
A Charnley (Eng)	77	73	76	72	298

NAME	SCORE				
F Couples (USA)	78	73	75	72	298
M Clayton (Aus)	76	74	75	73	298
L Mize (USA)	79	69	75	75	298
J Hawkes (SA)	78	73	72	75	298
Lu Hsi Chuen (Tai)	80	69	73	76	298
R Tway (USA)	74	71	76	77	298
T Armour III (USA)	76	70	75	77	298
S Randolph (USA)	72	76	77	75	300
G Marsh (Aus)	79	71	75	75	300
SC Mason (Eng)	76	73	73	78	300
M McNulty (SA)	80	71	79	71	301
M Mackenzie (Eng)	79	70	77	75	301
L Trevino (USA)	80	71	75	75	301
E Darcy (Ire)	76	75	75	75	301
T Lamore (USA)	76	71	77	77	301
F Nobilo (NZ)	76	75	71	79	301
A Chandler (Eng)	78	72	78	74	302
J Heggarty (N Ire)	75	72	80	75	302
M Gray (Sco)	75	76	76	75	302
D Hammond (USA)	74	71	79	78	302
S Simpson (USA)	78	71	75	78	302
O Moore (Aus)	76	74	79	74	303
P Fowler (Aus)	80	71	77	75	303
D Jones (N Ire)	75	76	79	75	305
R Drummond (Sco)	76	74	77	78	305
T Horton (Eng)	77	73	82	74	306
G Weir (Sco)	78	69	80	80	307
K Moe (USA)	76	74	82	82	314
H Green (USA)	77	73	81		Ret'd

1987 *at Muirfield*

NAME	SCORE				
N Faldo (Eng)	68	69	71	71	279
R Davis (Aus)	64	73	74	69	280
P Azinger (USA)	68	68	71	73	280
B Crenshaw (USA)	73	68	72	68	281
P Stewart (USA)	71	66	72	72	281
D Frost (SA)	70	68	70	74	282
T Watson (USA)	69	69	71	74	283
I Woosnam (Wal)	71	69	72	72	284
N Price (Zim)	68	71	72	73	284
C Stadler (USA)	69	69	71	75	284
M McNulty (Zim)	71	69	75	70	285
H Sutton (USA)	71	70	73	71	285
JM Olazabal (Spa)	70	73	70	72	285
M Ozaki (Jpn)	69	72	71	73	285
M Calcavecchia (USA)	69	70	72	74	285
G Marsh (Aus)	69	70	72	74	285
W Grady (Aus)	70	71	76	69	286
AWB Lyle (Sco)	76	69	71	70	286
E Darcy (Ire)	74	69	72	71	286
B Langer (W Ger)	69	69	76	72	286
L Trevino (USA)	67	74	73	72	286
M Roe (Eng)	74	68	72	72	286

NAME	SCORE				
K Brown (Sco)	69	73	70	74	286
R Floyd (USA)	72	68	70	76	286
G Taylor (Aus)	69	68	75	75	287
D Feherty (Ire)	74	70	77	67	288
G Brand Jr (Sco)	73	70	75	70	288
L Mize (USA)	68	71	76	73	288
L Wadkins (USA)	72	71	75	71	289
F Zoeller (USA)	71	70	76	72	289
K Green (USA)	67	76	74	72	289
D Edwards (USA)	71	73	72	73	289
A Forsbrand (Swe)	73	69	73	74	289
D Graham (Aus)	69	73	78	70	290
R Drummond (Sco)	79	66	77	69	291
M Calero (Spa)	71	74	75	71	291
J Haas (USA)	69	74	76	72	291
G Norman (Aus)	71	71	74	75	291
R Tway (USA)	67	72	75	77	291
D Cooper (Eng)	74	72	78	68	292
F Couples (USA)	70	74	78	70	292
A Bean (USA)	70	73	75	74	292
GJ Brand (Eng)	72	72	74	74	292
F Allem (SA)	74	69	77	73	293
B Marchbank (Sco)	72	72	76	73	293
O Moore (Aus)	71	72	76	74	293
SC Mason (Eng)	70	69	78	76	293
L Nelson (USA)	70	75	76	73	294
J Slaughter (USA)	72	71	76	75	294
M Lanner (Swe)	71	74	79	71	295
S Torrance (Sco)	76	69	77	73	295
S Ballesteros (Spa)	73	70	77	75	295
P Walton (Ire)	72	73	75	75	295
J O'Leary (Ire)	71	73	79	73	296
R Chapman (Eng)	70	73	79	74	296
W Andrade (USA)	74	69	78	75	296
O Sellberg (Swe)	71	72	78	76	297
P Mayo (Am) (Wal)	72	70	75	80	297
B Jones (Aus)	73	72	80	73	298
W McColl (Sco)	71	75	77	75	298
T Nakajima (Jpn)	73	72	77	76	298
S Simpson (USA)	75	71	82	71	299
N Hansen (Eng)	75	69	80	75	299
H Clark (Eng)	72	73	78	76	299
M Martin (Spa)	74	71	77	77	299
M O'Meara (USA)	73	72	82	73	300
G Player (SA)	72	74	79	75	300
T Ozaki (Jpn)	72	73	78	77	300
H Baiocchi (SA)	72	73	78	77	300
B Chamblee (USA)	73	72	77	78	300
W Westner (SA)	71	75	84	71	301
J Nicklaus (USA)	74	71	81	76	302
T Kite (USA)	73	72	81	76	302
J Hawkes (SA)	71	74	80	78	303
R Willison (Am) (Eng)	75	71	83	76	305
C Moody (Eng)	76	70	81	79	306
D Jones (Ire)	72	74	83	78	307
A Stevens (Eng)	71	75	82	84	312

1988   *at Lytham and St Anne's*

NAME	SCORE				
S Ballesteros (Spa)	67	71	70	65	273
N Price (Zim)	70	67	69	69	275
N Faldo (Eng)	71	69	68	71	279
F Couples (USA)	73	69	71	68	281
G Koch (USA)	71	72	70	68	281
P Senior (Aus)	70	73	70	69	282
D Frost (SA)	71	75	69	68	283
P Stewart (USA)	73	75	68	67	283
I Aoki (Jpn)	72	71	73	67	283
AWB Lyle (Sco)	73	69	67	74	283
DJ Russell (Eng)	71	74	69	70	284
B Faxon (USA)	69	74	70	71	284
E Romero (Arg)	72	71	69	73	285
L Nelson (USA)	73	71	68	73	285
C Strange (USA)	79	69	69	68	285
B Crenshaw (USA)	73	73	68	72	286
J Rivero (Spa)	75	69	70	72	286
D Pooley (USA)	70	73	69	74	286
A Bean (USA)	71	70	71	74	286
T Kite (USA)	75	71	73	68	287
R Tway (USA)	71	71	72	73	287
G Brand Jr (Sco)	72	76	68	71	287
RJ Charles (NZ)	71	74	69	73	287
R Davis (Aus)	76	71	72	68	287
J Nicklaus (USA)	75	70	75	68	288
I Woosnam (Wal)	76	71	72	69	288
M O'Meara (USA)	75	69	75	70	289
J Benepe (USA)	75	72	70	73	290
M McNulty (Zim)	73	73	72	72	290
T Watson (USA)	74	72	72	72	290
C Beck (USA)	72	71	74	73	290
T Armour III (USA)	73	72	72	73	290
H Clark (Eng)	71	72	75	72	290
W Riley (Aus)	72	71	72	76	291
L Wadkins (USA)	73	71	71	76	291
JM Olazabal (Spa)	73	71	73	75	292
GJ Brand (Eng)	73	74	72	73	292
B Marchbank (Sco)	73	74	73	73	293
J Haas (USA)	71	76	78	68	293
C Pavin (USA)	74	73	71	75	293
N Ratcliffe (Aus)	70	77	76	70	293
K Brown (Sco)	75	72	75	71	293
DA Russell (Eng)	72	73	72	76	293
R Rafferty (N Ire)	74	74	71	74	293
G Marsh (Aus)	75	73	71	74	293
W Grady (Aus)	69	76	72	76	293
S Torrance (Sco)	74	74	75	71	294
M McCumber (USA)	75	71	72	76	294
P Kent (Eng)	74	70	79	71	294
A North (USA)	77	68	74	75	294
P Azinger (USA)	72	75	73	74	294
P Walton (Ire)	72	74	75	74	295
P Fowler (Aus)	72	72	78	73	295
F Zoeller (USA)	72	74	76	73	295
H Green (USA)	74	73	73	75	295
J Miller (USA)	75	73	72	75	295
M Smith (USA)	75	71	76	74	296

NAME	SCORE				
SC Mason (Eng)	75	69	77	75	296
P Broadhurst (Am) (Eng)	73	73	74	76	296
G Player (SA)	72	76	73	76	297
C Stadler (USA)	72	68	81	76	297
S Bishop (Eng)	77	71	73	77	298
M James (Eng)	71	77	74	76	298
A Sherborne (Eng)	71	72	76	79	298
M Pinero (Spa)	75	73	77	74	299
P Carman (Eng)	77	71	80	73	301
G Bruckner (USA)	72	74	80	76	302
Hsieh Chin-Sheng (Tai)	74	73	73	82	302
B Langer (W Ger)	73	75	75	80	303
G Stafford (Eng)	76	72	78	79	305
P Mitchell (Eng)	73	75	79	81	308

1989   *at Troon*

NAME	SCORE				
M Calcavecchia (USA)	71	68	68	68	275
G Norman (Aus)	69	70	72	64	275
W Grady (Aus)	68	67	69	71	275
(Calcavecchia won play-off, over four holes)					
T Watson (USA)	69	68	68	72	277
J Mudd (USA)	73	67	68	70	278
D Feherty (N Ire)	71	67	69	72	279
F Couples (USA)	68	71	68	72	279
E Romero (Arg)	68	70	75	67	280
P Azinger (USA)	68	73	67	72	280
P Stewart (USA)	72	65	69	74	280
M McNulty (Zim)	75	70	70	66	281
N Faldo (Eng)	71	71	70	69	281
H Clark (Eng)	72	68	72	70	282
P Walton (Ire)	69	74	69	70	282
C Stadler (USA)	73	69	69	71	282
R Chapman (Eng)	76	68	67	71	282
M James (Eng)	69	70	71	72	282
S Pate (USA)	69	70	70	73	282
D Cooper (Eng)	69	70	76	68	283
D Pooley (USA)	73	70	69	71	283
T Kite (USA)	70	74	67	72	283
L Mize (USA)	71	74	66	72	283
D Love III (USA)	72	70	73	69	284
V Singh (Fiji)	71	73	69	71	284
JM Olazabal (Spa)	68	72	69	75	284
C Beck (USA)	75	69	68	73	285
S Bennett (Eng)	75	69	68	73	285
S Simpson (USA)	73	66	72	74	285
L Wadkins (USA)	72	70	69	74	285
G Koch (USA)	72	71	74	69	286
B Marchbank (Sco)	69	74	73	70	286
J Nicklaus (USA)	74	71	71	70	286
P Jacobsen (USA)	71	74	71	70	286
MA Martin (Spa)	68	73	73	72	286
M Ozaki (Jpn)	71	73	70	72	286
M Davis (Eng)	77	68	67	74	286
I Baker-Finch (Aus)	72	69	70	75	286
J Hawkes (SA)	75	67	69	75	286
J Woodland (Aus)	74	67	75	71	287

NAME	SCORE				
M Harwood (Aus)	71	72	72	72	287
T Armour III (USA)	70	71	72	74	287
J Rivero (Spa)	71	75	72	70	288
M O'Meara (USA)	72	74	69	73	288
L Trevino (USA)	68	73	73	74	288
R Floyd (USA)	73	68	73	74	288
AWB Lyle (Sco)	73	73	71	72	289
N Ozaki (Jpn)	71	71	69	78	289
M McCumber (USA)	71	68	70	80	289
I Woosnam (Wal)	74	72	73	71	290
J Miller (USA)	72	69	76	73	290
C O'Connor Jr (Ire)	71	73	72	74	290
B Ogle (Aus)	74	70	76	71	291
B Crenshaw (USA)	73	73	74	71	291
T Ozaki (Jpn)	75	71	73	72	291
M Roe (Eng)	74	71	73	73	291
M Allen (USA)	74	67	76	74	291
E Dussart (Fra)	76	68	73	74	291
A Johnstone (Zim)	71	71	74	75	291
R Boxall (Eng)	74	68	73	76	291
G Sauers (USA)	70	73	72	76	291
P Hoad (Eng)	72	71	77	72	292
M Reid (USA)	74	72	73	73	292
C Strange (USA)	70	74	74	74	292
R Tway (USA)	76	70	71	75	292
R Rafferty (N Ire)	70	72	74	76	292
D Graham (Aus)	74	72	69	77	292
W Stephens (Eng)	66	72	76	78	292
K Green (USA)	75	71	68	78	292
R Claydon (Am) (Eng)	70	74	74	75	293
L Carbonetti (Arg)	71	72	74	76	293
A Stephen (Sco)	71	74	71	77	293
C Gillies (Sco)	72	74	74	74	294
B Faxon (USA)	72	72	75	76	295
P Teravainen (USA)	72	73	72	78	295
E Aubrey (USA)	72	73	73	78	296
M Sludds (Ire)	72	74	73	78	297
R Karlsson (Am) (Swe)	75	70	76	78	299
S Ballesteros (Spa)	72	73	76	78	299
G Levenson (SA)	69	76	77	79	301
B Langer (W Ger)	71	73	83	82	309

1990 *at St Andrews*

NAME	SCORE				
N Faldo (Eng)	67	65	67	71	270
M McNulty (Zim)	74	68	68	65	275
P Stewart (USA)	68	68	68	71	275
I Woosnam (Wal)	68	69	70	69	276
J Mudd (USA)	72	66	72	66	276
I Baker-Finch (Aus)	68	72	64	73	277
G Norman (Aus)	66	66	76	69	277
S Pate (USA)	70	68	72	69	279
C Pavin (USA)	71	69	68	71	279
D Hammond (USA)	70	71	68	70	279
D Graham (Aus)	72	71	70	66	279
V Singh (Fiji)	70	69	72	69	280
T Simpson (USA)	70	69	69	72	280

NAME	SCORE				
R Gamez (USA)	70	72	67	71	280
P Broadhurst (Eng)	74	69	63	74	280
M Roe (Eng)	71	70	72	68	281
S Jones (USA)	72	67	72	70	281
AWB Lyle (Sco)	72	70	67	72	281
JM Olazabal (Spa)	71	67	71	72	281
P Jacobsen (USA)	68	70	70	73	281
F Nobilo (NZ)	72	67	68	74	281
E Darcy (Ire)	71	71	72	68	282
C Parry (Aus)	68	68	69	77	282
J Spence (Eng)	72	65	73	72	282
N Price (Zim)	70	67	71	75	283
F Couples (USA)	71	70	70	72	283
C O'Connor Jr (Ire)	68	72	71	72	283
L Trevino (USA)	69	70	73	71	283
J Rivero (Spa)	70	70	70	73	283
J Sluman (USA)	72	70	70	71	283
B Norton (USA)	71	72	68	73	284
L Mize (USA)	71	72	70	71	284
R Rafferty (N Ire)	70	71	73	70	284
B Crenshaw (USA)	74	69	68	73	284
M McCumber (USA)	69	74	69	72	284
M James (Eng)	73	69	70	72	284
V Fernandez (Arg)	72	67	69	76	284
G Powers (USA)	74	69	69	72	284
D Cooper (Eng)	72	71	69	73	285
N Ozaki (Jpn)	71	71	74	69	285
D Pooley (USA)	70	73	71	71	285
M Hulbert (USA)	70	70	70	75	285
M Reid (USA)	70	67	73	75	285
A North (USA)	71	71	72	71	285
S Simpson (USA)	73	70	69	73	285
R Floyd (USA)	72	71	71	71	285
S Torrance (Sco)	68	70	75	72	285
M O'Meara (USA)	70	69	73	74	286
C Montgomerie (Sco)	72	69	74	71	286
B Langer (W Ger)	74	69	75	68	286
P Fowler (Aus)	73	68	71	74	286
P Azinger (USA)	73	68	68	77	286
H Irwin (USA)	72	68	75	72	287
E Romero (Arg)	69	71	74	73	287
J Bland (SA)	71	72	72	72	287
M Allen (USA)	66	75	73	73	287
D Ray (Eng)	71	69	73	75	288
A Sorensen (Den)	70	68	71	79	288
B McCallister (USA)	71	68	75	74	288
J Rutledge (Can)	71	69	76	72	288
D Mijovic (USA)	69	74	71	74	288
M Clayton (Aus)	72	71	72	73	288
M Poxon (Eng)	68	72	74	75	289
P Baker (Eng)	73	68	75	73	289
J Nicklaus (USA)	71	70	77	71	289
R Chapman (Eng)	72	70	74	73	289
D Canipe (USA)	72	70	69	78	289
J Berendt (Arg)	75	66	72	77	290
D Feherty (N Ire)	74	69	71	76	290
A Saavedra (Arg)	72	69	75	75	291
M Mackenzie (Eng)	70	71	76	75	292
JM Canizares (Spa)	72	70	78	76	296

The US Open, US Masters and USPGA Championships

The 'Majors' is an unofficial but universally accepted appellation for the Open, the US Open, the US Masters and the USPGA Championships. It is not clear who originated the term but it is now invariably used by the press and most golfers. There is some pressure but little agreement for one or two other championships to be accepted as additional Majors but they have not been seriously considered.

US Open

As with the Open, the United States Open has a lengthy qualifying process. Thousands enter hoping for a place in the Championship itself and to play with those excused qualifying on their past records. The Masters is an invitation tournament; American professionals who have reached a given standard qualify to receive an invitation. Leading overseas professionals await one. Traditionally too the Amateur Champions of the United States and Great Britain are always invited. The USPGA is mainly confined to their own tour players, but a few European and overseas professionals are invited, especially if they have had some success on the USPGA tour. Fortunately in recent years the courses on which it has been played have, with one or two exceptions, been of a much higher standard than some of the earlier venues.

The US Open started soon after the first American clubs were founded in the late 1880s. Five clubs met to establish the Championship. The St Andrews Club in the Bronx near New York City was the instigator; the others were Southampton, Long Island, New York; the Chicago Club at Wheaton, Illinois; Newport, Rhode Island; and The Country Club, Brookline near Boston, Massachusetts. All of them staged the Championship in its early years. The first was in 1894 at St Andrews in the Bronx when Musselburgh-born Willie Dunn beat Willie Campbell his fellow-Scot in the 36-hole final over four rounds of the 9-hole course. For some reason the first US Open was decided by match play perhaps because the US Amateur, inaugurated the previous year, was a match play event. The Open in Britain had always been determined by stroke play and the next year its American counterpart followed suit at Newport.

For the first 17 years it was won by immigrant Scottish professionals — Willie Dunn, the brothers Alex and Willie Smith from Carnoustie, Willie Anderson thrice, and others. The only exception was Harry Vardon, who came across with JH Taylor in 1900 to play at Wheaton. Vardon duly won comfortably, with Taylor second.

In 1911 Jimmy McDermott became the first home-born professional to triumph. In the intervening 80 years Americans have won all but four: Ted Ray in 1920, Gary Player

(1965), Tony Jacklin (1970) and David Graham (1981), are the only successful overseas contestants.

The most sensational win was the 1913 success of the young amateur, Francis Ouimet, who had the temerity to tie with Vardon on his second visit, and Ted Ray at The Country Club, Brookline and beat them both on the play-off next day. Ouimet's triumph over two of the best players in the world heralded the coming United States superiority in all aspects of the game for the next 70 years. The Americans are still ahead overall, but not now at the highest level.

Ouimet was the first of five amateur winners, followed by Jerome Travers and Chick Evans in 1916 and 1917 respectively, Johnny Goodman (1933) and the incomparable Bobby Jones, four times between 1923 and 1930. Jones also lost a play-off in 1928. Walter Hagen won twice in 1914 and 1919 but surprisingly not again although he was often up with the leaders. Gene Sarazen also took the title twice in 1922 and again in 1932, when he held both the Open and the US Open at the same time, as Tony Jacklin did nearly 40 years later. Sam Snead, the winner of so many tournaments and each of the three other Majors, was never successful in the US Open. He often fell at the last fence, being second three times and third once over 20 years of competing.

The USGA always selects a tough course and sets stringent standards through the green. Fairways are narrow with little or no semi-rough; the rough itself is cut and maintained at 4–5 inches. Around heavily bunkered greens the grass is not cut short, making the pitch and run shot hardly ever an option. Accurate pitching on to the very fast greens is essential. While the star players may be trying to cut corners in their anxiety to win, lesser mortals play straight and steadily up the middle, are fortunate with their putts and can find themselves the winner.

This may explain why the leading trio of the 1960s and 1970s, Palmer, Nicklaus and Player, had only six wins between them, of which Nicklaus claimed four. In the Masters during the same period they amassed twelve.

Since 1952 only Julius Boros, Billy Casper, Lee Trevino and Curtis Strange have won twice, but Hale Irwin's 1990 win, when 44 years old, was his third. As long as the USGA continues the policy of holding its Open on the greatest courses and ensures that its demanding standards bring the best out of the players, so the US Open will be as hard to win as the Open in Britain.

The Masters

Not long after he retired at 29 in 1930, Bobby Jones had the vision of creating a classic course near his home in Georgia. Supported by Clifford Roberts and others, the unique Augusta course was designed and laid out under his meticulous direction. The consultant architect was Alistair Mackenzie, who had already been responsible for several famous courses, Cypress Point at Pebble Beach being the best known. The course which the combined genius of Jones and Mackenzie produced is now known as the Augusta National, and with only a few alterations, it has stood the test of time for nearly 60 years.

Soon after the course was opened in 1932, Jones conceived the idea of an invitation tournament for the best players in the country, which he named The Masters from the start. Horton Smith, a well-known Ryder Cup international, won the first time it was played in 1934 with a score of 284. That the course has never given in to the onslaught from the world-class competitors is underlined by the fact that there have since been more winning totals over Horton Smith's than below it. Occasionally a competitor has played a round in the middle 60s, but the best winning score over four rounds remains those of 271 by Jack Nicklaus in 1965 and Raymond Floyd in 1976.

The most sensational shot ever played in the Masters came in its second year. Craig Wood, was, to use today's expression, the leader in the clubhouse and appeared to have the title sewn up. Gene Sarazen, playing the 15th, hit his second shot to the par-5 hole with a wood and holed it for an albatross 2. This enabled him to tie with Wood and he beat him in the play-off next day.

It will be seen that only eleven players have won the Masters more than once. Nicklaus leads with six wins over a 23-year period, his last being a remarkable effort in 1986 when he was 46. Palmer with four in seven years when he was at his peak is next. Those with three wins each are Jimmy Demaret, Sam Snead and Gary Player.

Perhaps the luckiest win was that of Bob Goalby in 1968. He tied with the popular Argentinian Roberto de Vicenzo and was ready for the play-off next day. Vicenzo had signed and handed in his card but had not noticed his marker had recorded a 4 at a hole where he had in fact taken 3. According to the rules the higher score had to stand and Goalby was declared the winner. The manner and bearing of Vicenzo in his disappointment, when he blamed nobody but himself for the error, was admired by all. His only consolation was that he had won the Open at Hoylake the year before.

Since 1978 when Player, who in 1961 had been the first overseas winner, had his third victory, the Masters has been won six times by Europeans, the same number of wins as have been achieved by Americans. Ballesteros twice, Langer, Lyle and Faldo twice in successive years, have broken the US stranglehold on the tournament. Lyle's classic 5-iron shot from a bunker for a 3 at the 72nd to beat Norman, and Faldo's successive play-off wins have done much to consolidate European equality with the American players at the top level in recent years.

The USPGA

For its first 42 years the USPGA was played under match play rules. It began in 1916 when Cornish-born Jim Barnes, the Open Champion in 1925, beat Jock Hutchison, who himself was the Open Champion of 1921, by one hole. For seven years from 1921 Walter Hagen dominated the event, winning five times and losing in the final once. Gene Sarazen, Leo Diegel of the strange putting style, Densmore Shute, Paul Runyan, Byron Nelson, Sam Snead and Ben Hogan each won more than once.

The change to stroke play came in 1958. Since then only Nicklaus with four, Player, Dave Stockton, Floyd, Trevino and Larry Nelson with two each have been multiple winners. During those years there have been as many as six ties with a play-off the next day. Only Player and Australians David Graham and Wayne Grady have been overseas winners.

In 1986 Bob Tway, a largely unknown member of the US tour, was playing the 18th at Inverness, Toledo, Ohio, in the last round with Greg Norman, who had started four strokes in the lead. He caught Norman on the back nine and finished his round by holing his third shot from a greenside bunker to win by two strokes, so pushing Norman into second place in yet another Major.

United States Open Championship

INAUGURATED 1894

1894 *at St Andrews Club, The Bronx, New York*

Willie Dunn beat Willie Campbell 2 holes

1895 *at Newport, Rhode Island*

NAME	SCORE				
H Rawlins	45	46	41	41	173
W Dunn	43	46	44	42	175
J Foulis	46	43	44	43	176
AW Smith (Am)	47	43	44	42	176
WF Davis	45	49	42	42	178

1896 *at Shinnecock Hills, Southampton, New York*

NAME	SCORE		
J Foulis	78	74	152
H Rawlins	79	76	155
G Douglas	79	79	158
AW Smith (Am)	78	80	158
J Shippen	78	81	159
HJ Whigham (Am)	82	77	159

1897 *at Chicago Club, Wheaton, Illinois*

NAME	SCORE		
J Lloyd	83	79	162
W Anderson	79	84	163
J Foulis	80	88	168
W Dunn	87	81	168
WT Hoare	82	87	169

1898 *at Myopia Hunt Club, Hamilton, Massachusetts*

NAME	SCORE				
F Herd	84	85	75	84	328
A Smith	78	86	86	85	335
W Anderson	81	82	87	86	336
J Lloyd	87	80	86	86	339
W Smith	82	91	85	82	340

1899 *at Baltimore, Maryland*

NAME	SCORE				
W Smith	77	82	79	77	315
G Low	82	79	89	76	326
V Fitzjohn	85	80	79	82	326
WH Way	80	85	80	81	326
W Anderson	77	81	85	84	327

1900 *at Chicago Club, Wheaton, Illinois*

NAME	SCORE				
H Vardon (Eng)	79	78	76	80	313
JH Taylor (Eng)	76	82	79	78	315
D Bell	78	83	83	78	322
L Auchterlonie	84	82	80	81	327
W Smith	82	83	79	84	328

1901 *at Myopia Hunt Club, Hamilton, Massachusetts*

NAME	SCORE				
W Anderson	84	83	83	81	331
A Smith	82	82	87	80	331
(Anderson won play-off, 85 to 86)					
W Smith	84	86	82	81	333
S Gardner	86	82	81	85	334
L Auchterlonie	81	85	86	83	335
B Nicholls	84	85	83	83	335

1902 *at Garden City, New York*

NAME	SCORE				
L Auchterlonie	78	78	74	77	307
S Gardner	82	76	77	78	313
WJ Travis (Am)	82	82	75	74	313
W Smith	82	79	80	75	316
J Shippen	83	81	75	79	318
W Anderson	79	82	76	81	318

1903 *at Baltusrol, Springfield, New Jersey*

NAME	SCORE			
W Anderson	149	79	82	307
D Brown	156	75	76	307
(Anderson won play-off, 82 to 84)				
S Gardner	154	82	79	315
A Smith	154	81	81	316
DJ Ross	158	78	82	318

1904 *at Glen View, Illinois*

NAME	SCORE				
W Anderson	75	78	78	72	303
G Nicholls	80	76	79	73	308
F Mackenzie	76	79	74	80	309
L Auchterlonie	80	81	75	78	314
B Nicholls	80	77	79	78	314

1905 *at Myopia Hunt Club, Hamilton, Massachusetts*

NAME	SCORE				
W Anderson	81	80	76	77	314
A Smith(Bahamas)	81	80	76	79	316
P Robertson	79	80	81	77	317
PF Barrett (Can)	81	80	77	79	317
S Gardner	78	78	85	77	318

1906 *at Onwentsia Club, Lake Forest, Illinois*

NAME	SCORE				
A Smith (Bahamas)	73	74	73	75	295
W Smith (Mex)	73	81	74	74	302
L Auchterlonie	76	78	75	76	305
J Maiden	80	73	77	75	305
W Anderson	73	76	74	84	307

1907 *at Philadelphia Cricket Club, Pennsylvania*

NAME	SCORE				
A Ross	76	74	76	76	302
G Nicholls	80	73	72	79	304
A Campbell	78	74	78	75	305
J Hobens	76	75	73	85	309
P Robertson	81	77	78	74	310
G Low	78	76	79	77	310
F McLeod	79	77	79	75	310

1908 *at Myopia Hunt Club, Hamilton, Massachusetts*

NAME	SCORE				
F McLeod	82	82	81	77	322
W Smith (Mex)	77	82	85	78	322
(McLeod won play-off , 77 to 83)					
A Smith (Bahamas)	80	83	83	81	327
W Anderson	85	86	80	79	330
J Jones	81	81	87	82	331

1909 *at Englewood, New Jersey*

NAME	SCORE				
G Sargent	75	72	72	71	290
T McNamara	73	69	75	77	294
A Smith	76	73	74	72	295
I Mackie	77	75	74	73	299
W Anderson	79	74	76	70	299
J Hobens	75	78	72	74	299

1910 *at Philadelphia Cricket Club, Pennsylvania*

NAME	SCORE				
A Smith	73	73	79	73	298
JJ McDermott	74	74	75	75	298
Macdonald Smith	74	78	75	71	298
(Smith won play-off, 71 to 75 to 77)					
F McLeod	78	70	78	73	299
T McNamara	73	78	73	76	300
G Nicholls	73	75	77	75	300

1911 *at Chicago Club, Wheaton, Illinois*

NAME	SCORE				
JJ McDermott	81	72	75	79	307
MJ Brady	76	77	79	75	307
GO Simpson	76	77	79	75	307
(McDermott won play-off, 80 to 82 to 85)					
F McLeod	77	72	76	83	308
G Nicholls	76	78	74	81	309
J Hutchison	80	77	73	79	309

1912 *at Buffalo, New York*

NAME	SCORE				
JJ McDermott	74	75	74	71	294
T McNamara	74	80	73	69	296
A Smith	77	70	77	75	299
MJ Brady	72	75	73	79	299
A Campbell	74	77	80	71	302

1913 *at The Country Club, Brookline, Massachusetts*

NAME	SCORE				
F Ouimet (Am)	77	74	74	79	304
Harry Vardon (Eng)	75	72	78	79	304
Ted Ray (Eng)	79	70	76	79	304
(Ouimet won play-off, 72 to 77 to 78)					
Walter Hagen	73	78	76	80	307
Jim Barnes	74	76	78	79	307
Macdonald Smith	71	79	80	77	307
L Tellier (Fra)	76	76	79	76	307

1914 *at Midlothian, Blue Island, Illinois*

NAME	SCORE				
Walter Hagen	68	74	75	73	290
C Evans Jr (Am)	76	74	71	70	291
G Sargent	74	77	74	72	297
F McLeod	78	73	75	71	297
F Ouimet (Am)	69	76	75	78	298
MJ Brady	78	72	74	74	298
JA Donaldson	72	79	74	73	298

1915 *at Baltusrol, Springfield, New Jersey*

NAME	SCORE			
JD Travers (Am)	148	73	76	297
T McNamara	149	74	75	298
RG MacDonald	149	73	78	300
Jim Barnes	146	76	79	301
L Tellier	146	76	79	301

1916 *at Minikahda Club, Minneapolis, Minnesota*

NAME	SCORE				
C Evans Jr (Am)	70	69	74	73	286
J Hutchison	73	75	72	68	288
Jim Barnes	71	74	71	74	290
W Reid	70	72	79	72	293
G Nicholls	73	76	71	73	293
G Sargent	75	71	72	75	293

1917-18 *No Championship owing to the Great War*

1919 *at Brae Burn, West Newton, Massachusetts*

NAME	SCORE			
Walter Hagen	78	73	75	75	301
MJ Brady	74	74	73	80	301
(Hagen won play-off, 77 to 78)				
J Hutchison	78	76	76	76	306
T McNamara	80	73	79	74	306
G McLean	81	75	76	76	308
L Tellier	73	78	82	75	308

1920   *at Inverness, Toledo, Ohio*

NAME	SCORE				
Ted Ray (Eng)	74	73	73	75	295
Harry Vardon (Eng)	74	73	71	78	296
J Burke	75	77	72	72	296
L Diegel	72	74	73	77	296
J Hutchison	69	76	74	77	296

1921   *at Columbia, Chevy Chase, Maryland*

NAME	SCORE				
Jim Barnes	69	75	73	72	289
Walter Hagen	79	73	72	74	298
F McLeod	74	74	76	74	298
C Evans Jr (Am)	73	78	76	75	302
RT Jones Jr (Am)	78	71	77	77	303
E French	75	77	74	77	303
A Smith	75	75	79	74	303

1922   *at Skokie, Glencoe, Illinois*

NAME	SCORE				
Gene Sarazen	72	73	75	68	288
JL Black	71	71	75	72	289
RT Jones Jr (Am)	74	72	70	73	289
WE Mehlhorn	73	71	72	74	290
Walter Hagen	68	77	74	72	291

1923   *at Inwood, New York*

NAME	SCORE				
RT Jones Jr (Am)	71	73	76	76	296
RA Cruickshank	73	72	78	73	296
(Jones won play-off , 76 to 78)					
J Hutchison	70	72	82	78	302
J Forrester	75	73	77	78	303
JJ Farrell	76	77	75	76	304
F Gallett	76	72	77	79	304
WM Reekie (Am)	80	74	75	75	304

1924   *at Oakland Hills, Birmingham, Michigan*

NAME	SCORE				
C Walker	74	74	74	75	297
RT Jones Jr (Am)	74	73	75	78	300
WE Mehlhorn	72	75	76	78	301
RA Cruikshank	77	72	76	78	303
Walter Hagen	75	75	76	77	303
Macdonald Smith	78	72	77	76	303

1925   *at Worcester, Massachusetts*

NAME	SCORE				
W Macfarlane	74	67	72	78	291
RT Jones Jr (Am)	77	70	70	74	291
(Macfarlane won play-off, 147 to 148)					
JJ Farrell	71	74	69	78	292
F Ouimet (Am)	70	73	73	76	292
Gene Sarazen	72	72	75	74	293
Walter Hagen	72	76	71	74	293

1926   *at Scioto, Columbus, Ohio*

NAME	SCORE				
RT Jones Jr (Am)	70	79	71	73	293
J Turnesa	71	74	72	77	294
WE Mehlhorn	68	75	76	78	297
Gene Sarazen	78	77	72	70	297
L Diegel	72	76	75	74	297
JJ Farrell	76	79	69	73	297

1927   *at Oakmont, Pittsburgh, Pennsylvania*

NAME	SCORE				
T Armour	78	71	76	76	301
H Cooper	74	76	74	77	301
(Armour won play-off, 76 to 79)					
Gene Sarazen	74	74	80	74	302
E French	75	79	77	73	304
WE Mehlhorn	75	77	80	73	305

1928   *at Olympia Fields, Matteson, Illinois*

NAME	SCORE				
JJ Farrell	77	74	71	72	294
RT Jones Jr (Am)	73	71	73	77	294
(Farrell won play-off, 143 to 144)					
R Hancock	74	77	72	72	295
Walter Hagen	75	72	73	76	296
G von Elm (Am)	74	72	76	74	299
J Turnesa	74	77	74	74	299
Gene Sarazen	78	76	73	72	299
H Ciuci	70	77	72	80	299
WW Crowder	74	74	76	75	299
W Leach	72	74	73	80	299
Macdonald Smith	75	77	75	72	299
Densmore Shute	75	73	79	72	299
E Dudley	77	79	68	75	299

1929 *at Winged Foot, Mamaroneck, New York*

NAME	SCORE				
RT Jones Jr (Am)	69	75	71	79	294
A Espinosa	70	72	77	75	294
(Jones won play-off, 141 to 164)					
Gene Sarazen	71	71	76	78	296
Densmore Shute	73	71	76	76	296
T Armour	74	71	76	76	297
G von Elm (Am)	79	70	74	74	297

1930 *at Interlachen, Minneapolis, Minnesota*

NAME	SCORE				
RT Jones Jr (Am)	71	73	68	75	287
Macdonald Smith	70	75	74	70	289
Horton Smith	72	70	76	74	292
H Cooper	72	72	73	76	293
J Golden	74	73	71	76	294

1931 *at Inverness, Toledo, Ohio*

NAME	SCORE				
B Burke	73	72	74	73	292
G von Elm (Am)	75	69	73	75	292
(Burke won play-off, 148 to 149)					
L Diegel	75	73	74	72	294
W Cox	75	74	74	73	296
WE Mehlhorn	77	73	75	71	296
Gene Sarazen	74	78	74	70	296

1932 *at Fresh Meadow, Flushing, New York*

NAME	SCORE				
Gene Sarazen	74	76	70	66	286
TP Perkins	76	69	74	70	289
R Cruickshank	78	74	69	68	289
L Diegel	73	74	73	74	294
W Cox	80	73	70	72	295

1933 *at North Shore, Glen View, Illinois*

NAME	SCORE				
J Goodman (Am)	75	66	70	76	287
Ralph Guldahl	76	71	70	71	288
C Wood	73	74	71	72	290
Walter Hagen	73	76	77	66	292
T Armour	68	75	76	73	292

1934 *at Merion Cricket Club, Ardmore, Pennsylvania*

NAME	SCORE				
O Dutra	76	74	71	72	293
Gene Sarazen	73	72	73	76	294
R Cruickshank	71	71	77	76	295
W Cox	71	75	74	75	295
H Cooper	76	74	74	71	295

1935 *at Oakmont, Pittsburgh, Pennsylvania*

NAME	SCORE				
S Parks	77	73	73	76	299
J Thomson	73	73	77	78	301
Walter Hagen	77	76	73	76	302
R Mangrum	76	76	72	79	303
Densmore Shute	78	73	76	76	303

1936 *at Baltusrol, Springfield, New Jersey*

NAME	SCORE				
T Manero	73	69	73	67	282
H Cooper	71	70	70	73	284
C Clark	69	75	71	72	287
Macdonald Smith	73	73	72	70	288
HG Picard	70	71	74	74	289
W Cox	74	74	69	72	289
K Laffoon	71	74	70	74	289

1937   *at Oakland Hills, Birmingham, Michigan*

NAME	SCORE				
Ralph Guldahl	71	69	72	69	281
Sam Snead	69	73	70	71	283
R Cruickshank	73	73	67	72	285
H Cooper	72	70	73	71	286
Ed Dudley	70	70	71	76	287

1938   *at Cherry Hills, Denver, Colorado*

NAME	SCORE				
Ralph Guldahl	74	70	71	69	284
D Metz	73	68	70	79	290
H Cooper	76	69	76	71	292
T Penna	83	68	73	68	292
E Zimmerman	72	71	73	78	294
Byron Nelson	77	71	74	72	294

1939   *at Philadelphia, West Conshohocken, Pennsylvania*

NAME	SCORE				
Byron Nelson	72	73	71	68	284
C Wood	70	71	71	72	284
Densmore Shute	70	72	70	72	284
(Nelson won play-off, 138 to 141)					
M (Bud) Ward (Am)	69	73	71	72	285
Sam Snead	68	71	73	74	286

1940   *at Canterbury, Cleveland, Ohio*

NAME	SCORE				
W Lawson Little	72	69	73	73	287
Gene Sarazen	71	74	70	72	287
(Little won play-off, 70 to 73)					
Horton Smith	69	72	78	69	288
C Wood	72	73	72	72	289
Ben Hogan	70	73	74	73	290
Ralph Guldahl	73	71	76	70	290
L Mangrum	75	70	71	74	290
Byron Nelson	72	74	70	74	290

1941   *at Colonial Club, Fort Worth, Texas*

NAME	SCORE				
C Wood	73	71	70	70	284
Densmore Shute	69	75	72	71	287
J Bulla	75	71	72	71	289
Ben Hogan	74	77	68	70	289
H Barron	75	71	74	71	291
P Runyan	73	72	71	75	291

1942-45   *No Championship owing to the Second World War*

1946   *at Canterbury, Cleveland, Ohio*

NAME	SCORE				
L Mangrum	74	70	68	72	284
Byron Nelson	71	71	69	73	284
V Ghezzi	71	69	72	72	284
(Mangrum won play-off, 72 to 73 to 73)					
H Barron	72	72	72	69	285
Ben Hogan	72	68	73	72	285

1947   *at St Louis Club, Clayton, Missouri*

NAME	SCORE				
L Worsham	70	70	71	71	282
Sam Snead	72	70	70	70	282
(Worsham won play-off , 69 to 70)					
AD Locke (SA)	68	74	70	73	285
P Oliver Jr	73	70	71	71	285
M (Bud) Ward (Am)	69	72	73	73	287

1948   *at Riviera, Los Angeles, California*

NAME	SCORE				
Ben Hogan	67	72	68	69	276
J Demaret	71	70	68	69	278
J Turnesa	71	69	70	70	280
AD Locke (SA)	70	69	73	70	282
Sam Snead	69	69	73	72	283

1949 *at Medinah, Chicago, Illinois*

NAME	SCORE				
C Middlecoff	75	67	69	75	286
C Heafner	72	71	71	73	287
Sam Snead	73	73	71	70	287
J Turnesa	78	69	70	72	289
AD Locke (SA)	74	71	73	71	289

1950 *at Merion, Ardmore, Pennsylvania*

NAME	SCORE				
Ben Hogan	72	69	72	74	287
L Mangrum	72	70	69	76	287
G Fazio	73	72	72	70	287
(Hogan won play-off, 69 to 73 to 75)					
D Harrison	72	67	73	76	288
J Kirkwood Jr	71	74	74	70	289
J Ferrier	71	69	74	75	289
H Ransom	72	71	73	73	289

1951 *at Oakland Hills, Birmingham, Michigan*

NAME	SCORE				
Ben Hogan	76	73	71	67	287
C Heafner	72	75	73	69	289
AD Locke (SA)	73	71	74	73	291
L Mangrum	75	74	74	70	293
J Boros	74	74	71	74	293

1952 *at Northwood, Dallas, Texas*

NAME	SCORE				
J Boros	71	71	68	71	281
P Oliver Jr	71	72	70	72	285
Ben Hogan	69	69	74	74	286
J Bulla	73	68	73	73	287
G Fazio	71	69	75	75	290

1953 *at Oakmont, Pittsburgh, Pennsylvania*

NAME	SCORE				
Ben Hogan	67	72	73	71	283
Sam Snead	72	69	72	76	289
L Mangrum	73	70	74	75	292
P Cooper	78	75	71	70	294
G Fazio	70	71	77	76	294
J Demaret	71	76	71	76	294

1954 *at Baltusrol , Springfield, New Jersey*

NAME	SCORE				
E Furgol	71	70	71	72	284
G Littler	70	69	76	70	285
D Mayer	72	71	70	73	286
L Mangrum	72	71	72	71	286
AD Locke (SA)	74	70	74	70	288

1955 *at Olympic, San Francisco, California*

NAME	SCORE				
J Fleck	76	69	75	67	287
Ben Hogan	72	73	72	70	287
Sam Snead	79	69	70	74	292
T Bolt	67	77	75	73	292
J Boros	76	69	73	77	295
B Rosburg	78	74	67	76	295

1956 *at Oak Hill, Rochester, New York*

NAME	SCORE				
C Middlecoff	71	70	70	70	281
Ben Hogan	72	68	72	70	282
J Boros	71	71	71	69	282
T Kroll	72	70	70	73	285
E Furgol	71	70	73	71	285
PW Thomson (Aus)	70	69	75	71	285

1957   *at Inverness, Toledo, Ohio*

NAME	SCORE				
R Mayer	70	68	74	70	282
C Middlecoff	71	75	68	68	282
(Mayer won play-off , 72 to 79)					
J Demaret	68	73	70	72	283
J Boros	69	75	70	70	284
W Burkemo	74	73	72	65	284

1958   *at Southern Hills, Tulsa, Oklahoma*

NAME	SCORE				
T Bolt	71	71	69	72	283
G Player (SA)	75	68	73	71	287
J Boros	71	75	72	71	289
G Littler	74	73	67	76	290
B Rosburg	75	74	72	70	291
W Burkemo	75	74	70	72	291

1959   *at Winged Foot, Mamaroneck, New York*

NAME	SCORE				
W Casper	71	68	69	74	282
B Rosburg	75	70	67	71	283
C Harmon	72	71	70	71	284
M Souchak	71	70	72	71	284
D Ford	72	69	72	73	286
E Vossier	72	70	72	72	286
A Palmer	71	69	72	74	286

1960   *at Cherry Hills, Denver, Colorado*

NAME	SCORE				
A Palmer	72	71	72	65	280
J Nicklaus (Am)	71	71	69	71	282
D Harrison	74	70	70	69	283
J Boros	73	69	68	73	283
M Souchak	68	67	73	75	283
T Kroll	72	69	75	67	283
J Fleck	70	70	72	71	283
D Finsterwald	71	69	70	73	283

1961   *at Oakland Hills, Birmingham, Michigan*

G Littler	73	68	72	68	281
R Goalby	70	72	69	71	282
D Sanders	72	67	71	72	282
M Souchak	73	70	68	73	284
J Nicklaus (Am)	75	69	70	70	284

1962   *at Oakmont, Pittsburgh, Pennsylvania*

NAME	SCORE				
J Nicklaus	72	70	72	69	283
A Palmer	71	68	73	71	283
(Nicklaus won play-off, 71 to 74)					
P Rodgers	74	70	69	72	285
R Nichols	70	72	70	73	285
G Brewer	73	72	73	69	287

1963   *at The Country Club, Brookline, Massachusetts*

NAME	SCORE				
J Boros	71	74	76	72	293
JD Cupit	70	72	76	75	293
A Palmer	73	69	77	74	293
(Boros won play-off, 70 to 73 to 76)					
P Harney	78	70	73	73	294
W Maxwell	73	73	75	74	295
B Crampton (Aus)	74	72	75	74	295
A Lema	71	74	74	76	295

1964   *at Congressional , Bethesda, Maryland*

NAME	SCORE				
K Venturi	72	70	66	70	278
T Jacobs	72	64	70	76	282
RJ Charles (NZ)	72	72	71	68	283
W Casper	71	74	69	71	285
G Brewer	76	69	73	68	286
A Palmer	68	69	75	74	286

1965 *at Bellerive, St Louis, Missouri*

NAME					SCORE
G Player (SA)	70	70	71	71	282
KDG Nagle (Aus)	68	73	72	69	282
(Player won play-off, 71 to 74)					
F Beard	74	69	70	71	284
J Boros	72	75	70	70	287
A Geiberger	70	76	70	71	287

1966 *at Olympic, San Francisco, California*

NAME					SCORE
W Casper	69	68	73	68	278
A Palmer	71	66	70	71	278
(Casper won play-off , 69 to 73)					
J Nicklaus	71	71	69	74	285
A Lema	71	74	70	71	286
D Marr	71	74	68	73	286

1967 *at Baltusrol, Springfield, New Jersey*

NAME					SCORE
J Nicklaus	71	67	72	65	275
A Palmer	69	68	73	69	279
D January	69	72	70	70	281
W Casper	69	70	71	72	282
L Trevino	72	70	71	70	283

1968 *at Oak Hill, Rochester, New York*

NAME					SCORE
L Trevino	69	68	69	69	275
J Nicklaus	72	70	70	67	279
B Yancey	67	68	70	76	281
R Nichols	74	71	68	69	282
D Bies	70	70	75	69	284
S Spray	73	75	71	65	284

1969 *at Champions, Cypress Creek, Texas*

NAME					SCORE
O Moody	71	70	68	72	281
DR Beman	68	69	73	72	282
A Geiberger	68	72	72	70	282
B Rosburg	70	69	72	71	282
R Murphy	66	72	74	71	283

1970 *at Hazeltine, Minnesota*

NAME					SCORE
A Jacklin (Eng)	71	70	70	70	281
D Hill	75	69	71	73	288
R Lunn	77	72	70	70	289
RJ Charles (NZ)	76	71	75	67	289
K Still	78	71	71	71	291

1971 *at Merion, Ardmore, Pennsylvania*

NAME					SCORE
L Trevino	70	72	69	69	280
J Nicklaus	69	72	68	71	280
(Trevino won play-off, 68 to 71)					
B Rosburg	71	72	70	69	282
JJ Colbert	69	69	73	71	282
J Simons	71	71	65	76	283
J Miller	70	73	70	70	283
G Archer	71	70	70	72	283

1972 *at Pebble Beach, California*

NAME					SCORE
J Nicklaus	71	73	72	74	290
B Crampton (Aus)	74	70	73	76	293
A Palmer	77	68	73	76	294
L Trevino	74	72	71	78	295
H Blancas	74	70	76	75	295

1973 *at Oakmont, Pittsburgh, Pennsylvania*

NAME					SCORE
J Miller	71	69	76	63	279
J Schlee	73	70	67	70	280
T Weiskopf	73	69	69	70	281
A Palmer	71	71	68	72	282
L Trevino	70	72	70	70	282
J Nicklaus	71	69	74	68	282

1974 *at Winged Foot, Mamaroneck, New York*

NAME					SCORE
H Irwin	73	70	71	73	287
F Fezler	75	70	74	70	289
L Graham	71	75	74	70	290
B Yancey	76	69	73	72	290
A Palmer	73	70	73	76	292
J Colbert	72	77	69	74	292
T Watson	73	71	69	79	292

1975   *at Medinah, Chicago, Illinois*

NAME		SCORE			
L Graham	74	72	68	73	287
J Mahaffey	73	71	72	71	287
(Graham won play-off , 71 to 73)					
R Murphy	74	73	72	69	288
H Irwin	74	71	73	70	288
B Crenshaw	70	68	76	74	288
F Beard	74	69	67	78	288

1976   *at Atlanta Athletic Club, Duluth, Georgia*

NAME		SCORE			
J Pate	71	69	69	68	277
A Geiberger	70	69	71	69	279
T Weiskopf	73	70	68	68	279
B Baird	71	71	71	67	280
J Mahaffey	70	68	69	73	280

1977   *at Southern Hills, Tulsa, Oklahoma*

NAME		SCORE			
H Green	69	67	72	70	278
L Graham	72	71	68	68	279
T Weiskopf	71	71	68	71	281
T Purtzer	69	69	72	72	282
J Haas	72	68	71	72	283
G Jacobson	73	70	67	73	283

1978   *at Cherry Hills, Denver, Colorado*

NAME		SCORE			
A North	70	70	71	74	285
JC Snead	70	72	72	72	286
D Stockton	71	73	70	72	286
H Irwin	69	74	75	70	288
T Weiskopf	77	73	70	68	288

1979   *at Inverness, Toledo, Ohio*

NAME		SCORE			
H Irwin	74	68	67	75	284
J Pate	71	74	69	72	286
G Player (SA)	73	73	72	68	286
L Nelson	71	68	76	73	288
W Rogers	71	72	73	72	288
T Weiskopf	71	74	67	76	288

1980   *at Baltusrol, Springfield, New Jersey*

NAME		SCORE			
J Nicklaus	63	71	70	68	272
I Aoki (Jpn)	68	68	68	70	274
K Fergus	66	70	70	70	276
T Watson	71	68	67	70	276
L Hinkle	66	70	69	71	276

1981   *at Merion, Ardmore, Pennsylvania*

NAME		SCORE			
D Graham (Aus)	68	68	70	67	273
W Rogers	70	68	69	69	276
G Burns III	69	66	68	73	276
J Cook	68	70	71	70	279
J Schroeder	71	68	69	71	279

1982   *at Pebble Beach, California*

NAME		SCORE			
T Watson	72	72	68	70	282
J Nicklaus	74	70	71	69	284
B Clampett	71	73	72	70	286
D Pohl	72	74	70	70	286
W Rogers	70	73	69	74	286

1983 *at Oakmont, Pittsburgh, Pennsylvania*

NAME	SCORE				
L Nelson	75	73	65	67	280
T Watson	72	70	70	69	281
G Morgan	73	72	70	68	283
S Ballesteros (Spa)	69	74	69	74	286
C Peete	75	68	70	73	286

1984 *at Winged Foot, Mamaroneck, New York*

NAME	SCORE				
F Zoeller	71	66	69	70	276
G Norman (Aus)	70	68	69	69	276
(Zoeller won play-off , 67 to 75)					
C Strange	69	70	74	68	281
J Miller	74	68	70	70	282
J Thorpe	68	71	70	73	282

1985 *at Oakland Hills, Birmingham, Michigan*

NAME	SCORE				
A North	70	65	70	74	279
D Watson	72	65	73	70	280
D Barr	70	68	70	72	280
T-C Chen (Tai)	65	69	69	77	280
L Wadkins	70	72	69	70	281
P Stewart	70	70	71	70	281
S Ballesteros (Spa)	71	70	69	71	281

1986 *at Shinnecock Hills, Southampton, New York*

NAME	SCORE				
R Floyd	75	68	70	66	279
L Wadkins	74	70	72	65	281
C Beck	75	73	68	65	281
L Trevino	74	68	69	71	282
H Sutton	75	70	66	71	282

1987 *at Olympic, San Francisco, California*

NAME	SCORE				
S Simpson	71	68	70	68	277
T Watson	72	65	71	70	278
S Ballesteros (Spa)	68	75	68	71	282
R Wadkins	71	71	70	71	283
C Strange	71	72	69	71	283
B Langer (W Ger)	69	69	73	72	283
B Crenshaw	67	72	72	72	283
L Mize	71	68	72	72	283

1988 *at The Country Club, Brookline, Massachusetts*

NAME	SCORE				
C Strange	70	67	69	72	278
N Faldo (Eng)	72	67	68	71	278
(Strange won play-off , 71 to 75)					
DA Weibring	71	69	68	72	280
S Pate	72	69	72	67	280
M O'Meara	71	72	66	71	280

1989 *at Oak Hill, Rochester, New York*

NAME	SCORE				
C Strange	71	64	73	70	278
I Woosnam (Wal)	70	68	73	68	279
M McCumber	70	68	72	69	279
C Beck	71	69	71	68	279
B Claar	71	72	68	69	280

1990 *at Medinah, Chicago, Illinois*

NAME	SCORE				
H Irwin	69	70	74	67	280
M Donald	67	70	72	71	280
(Irwin won play-off, at 1st extra hole following a tied 18-hole play-off)					
N Faldo (Eng)	72	72	68	69	281
BR Brown	69	71	69	72	281
G Norman (Aus)	72	73	69	69	283
T Simpson	66	69	75	73	283
M Brooks	68	70	72	73	283

United States Masters Championship

INAUGURATED 1934

at Augusta National, Georgia

1934

NAME	SCORE				
Horton Smith	70	72	70	72	284
C Wood	71	74	69	71	285
W Burke	72	71	70	73	286
P Runyan	74	71	70	71	286
Ed Dudley	74	69	71	74	288

1935

NAME	SCORE				
Gene Sarazen	68	71	73	70	282
C Wood	69	72	68	73	282
(Sarazen won play-off, 144 to 149)					
O Dutra	70	70	70	74	284
H Picard	67	68	76	75	286
D Shute	73	71	70	73	287

1936

NAME	SCORE				
Horton Smith	74	71	68	72	285
H Cooper	70	69	71	76	286
Gene Sarazen	78	67	72	70	287
R Cruikshank	75	69	74	72	290
P Runyan	76	69	70	75	290

1937

NAME	SCORE				
Byron Nelson	66	72	75	70	283
Ralph Guldahl	69	72	68	76	285
Ed Dudley	70	71	71	74	286
H Cooper	73	69	71	74	287
K Laffoon	73	70	74	73	290

1938

NAME	SCORE				
H Picard	71	72	72	70	285
Ralph Guldahl	73	70	73	71	287
H Cooper	68	77	71	71	287
P Runyan	71	73	74	70	288
Byron Nelson	73	74	70	73	290

1939

NAME	SCORE				
Ralph Guldahl	72	68	70	69	279
Sam Snead	70	70	72	68	282
W Burke	69	72	71	70	282
W Lawson Little	72	72	68	70	282
Gene Sarazen	73	66	72	72	283

1940

NAME	SCORE				
J Demaret	67	72	70	71	280
L Mangrum	64	75	71	74	284
Byron Nelson	69	72	74	70	285
Ed Dudley	73	72	71	71	287
H Cooper	69	75	73	70	287
W Goggin	71	72	73	71	287

1941

NAME	SCORE				
C Wood	66	71	71	72	280
Byron Nelson	71	69	73	70	283
S Byrd	73	70	68	74	285
B Hogan	71	72	75	68	286
Ed Dudley	73	72	75	68	288

1942

NAME	SCORE				
Byron Nelson	68	67	72	73	280
B Hogan	73	70	67	70	280
(Nelson won play-off, 69 to 70)					
P Runyan	67	73	72	71	283
S Byrd	68	68	75	74	285
Horton Smith	67	73	74	73	287

1943-45 *No Championship owing to the Second World War*

1946

NAME	SCORE				
H Keiser	69	68	71	74	282
B Hogan	74	70	69	70	283
R Hamilton	75	69	71	72	287
K Laffoon	74	73	70	72	289
J Demaret	75	70	71	73	289
J Ferrier	74	72	68	75	289

1947

NAME	SCORE				
J Demaret	69	71	70	71	281
Byron Nelson	69	72	72	70	283
F Stranahan (Am)	73	72	70	68	283
B Hogan	75	68	71	70	284
H McSpaden	74	69	70	71	284

1948

NAME	SCORE				
C Harmon	70	70	69	70	279
C Middlecoff	74	71	69	70	284
C Harbert	71	70	70	76	287
J Ferrier	71	71	75	71	288
L Mangrum	69	73	75	71	288

1949

NAME	SCORE				
Sam Snead	73	75	67	67	282
J Bulla	74	73	69	69	285
L Mangrum	69	74	72	70	285
J Palmer	73	71	70	72	286
J Turnesa	73	72	71	70	286

1950

NAME	SCORE				
J Demaret	70	72	72	69	283
J Ferrier	70	67	73	75	285
Sam Snead	71	74	70	72	287
B Hogan	73	68	71	76	288
Byron Nelson	75	70	69	74	288

1951

NAME	SCORE				
B Hogan	70	72	70	68	280
S Riegel	73	68	70	71	282
L Mangrum	69	74	70	73	286
L Worsham, Jr	71	71	72	72	286
D Douglass	74	69	72	73	288

1952

NAME	SCORE				
Sam Snead	70	67	77	72	286
J Burke, Jr	76	67	78	69	290
A Besselink	70	76	71	74	291
T Bolt	71	71	75	74	291
J Ferrier	72	70	77	72	291

1953

NAME	SCORE				
B Hogan	70	69	66	69	274
P Oliver, Jr	69	73	67	70	279
L Mangrum	73	68	71	69	282
R Hamilton	71	69	70	73	283
T Bolt	71	75	68	71	285
C Harbert	68	73	70	74	285

1954

NAME	SCORE				
Sam Snead	74	73	70	72	289
B Hogan	72	73	69	75	289
(Snead won play-off , 70 to 71)					
BJ Patton (Am)	70	74	75	71	290
EJ Harrison	70	79	74	68	291
L Mangrum	71	75	76	69	291

1955

NAME	SCORE				
C Middlecoff	72	65	72	70	279
B Hogan	73	68	72	73	286
Sam Snead	72	71	74	70	287
B Rosburg	72	72	72	73	289
M Souchak	71	74	72	72	289
J Boros	71	75	72	71	289

1956

NAME	SCORE				
J Burke, Jr	72	71	75	71	289
K Venturi	66	69	75	80	290
C Middlecoff	67	72	75	77	291
L Mangrum	72	74	72	74	292
Sam Snead	73	76	72	71	292

1957

NAME	SCORE				
D Ford	72	73	72	66	283
Sam Snead	72	68	74	72	286
J Demaret	72	70	75	70	287
E Harvie Ward (Am)	73	71	71	73	288
P Thomson (Aus)	72	73	73	71	289

1958

NAME	SCORE				
A Palmer	70	73	68	73	284
D Ford	74	71	70	70	285
F Hawkins	71	75	68	71	285
S Leonard (Can)	72	70	73	71	286
K Venturi	68	72	74	72	286

1959

NAME	SCORE				
A Wall, Jr	73	74	71	66	284
C Middlecoff	74	71	68	72	285
A Palmer	71	70	71	74	286
D Mayer	73	75	71	68	287
S Leonard (Can)	69	74	69	75	287

1960

NAME	SCORE				
A Palmer	67	73	72	70	282
K Venturi	73	69	71	70	283
D Finsterwald	71	70	72	71	284
W Casper	71	71	71	74	287
J Boros	72	71	70	75	288

1961

NAME	SCORE				
G Player (SA)	69	68	69	74	280
A Palmer	68	69	73	71	281
C Coe (Am)	72	71	69	69	281
T Bolt	72	71	74	68	285
D January	74	68	72	61	285

1962

NAME	SCORE				
A Palmer	70	66	69	75	280
G Player (SA)	67	71	71	71	280
D Finsterwald	74	68	65	73	280
(Palmer won play-off, 68 to 71 to 77)					
G Littler	71	68	71	72	282
J Demaret	73	73	71	70	287
J Barder	72	72	69	74	287
M Souchak	70	72	74	78	287
W Maxwell	71	73	72	71	287

1963

NAME	SCORE				
J Nicklaus	74	66	74	72	286
A Lema	74	69	74	70	287
J Boros	76	69	71	72	288
Sam Snead	70	73	74	71	288
D Finsterwald	74	73	73	69	289
E Furgol	70	71	74	74	289
G Player (SA)	71	74	74	70	289

1964

NAME	SCORE				
A Palmer	69	68	69	70	276
D Marr	70	73	69	70	282
J Nicklaus	71	73	71	67	282
B Devlin (Aus)	72	72	67	73	284
W Casper	76	72	69	69	286
J Ferrier	71	73	69	73	286
P Harvey	73	72	71	70	286
G Player (SA)	69	72	72	73	286

1965

NAME	SCORE				
J Nicklaus	67	71	64	69	271
A Palmer	70	68	72	70	280
G Player (SA)	65	73	69	73	280
M Rudolf	70	75	66	72	283
D Sikes	67	72	71	75	285

1966

NAME	SCORE				
J Nicklaus	68	76	72	72	288
T Jacobs	75	71	70	72	288
G Brewer	74	72	72	70	288
(Nicklaus won play-off, 70 to 72 to 78)					
A Palmer	74	70	74	72	290
D Sanders	74	70	75	71	290

1967

NAME	SCORE				
G Brewer	73	68	72	67	280
R Nichols	72	69	70	70	281
B Yancey	67	73	71	73	284
A Palmer	73	73	70	69	285
J Boros	71	70	70	75	286

1968

NAME	SCORE				
R Goalby	70	70	71	66	277
R de Vicenzo (Arg)	69	73	70	66	278
B Yancey	71	71	72	65	279
B Devlin (Aus)	69	73	69	69	280
F Beard	75	65	71	70	281
J Nicklaus	69	71	74	67	281

1969

NAME	SCORE				
G Archer	67	73	69	72	281
T Weiskopf	71	71	69	71	282
G Knudson	70	73	69	70	282
W Casper	66	71	71	74	282
C Coody	74	68	69	72	283
D January	74	73	70	66	283

1970

NAME	SCORE				
W Casper	72	68	68	71	279
G Littler	69	70	70	70	279
(Casper won play-off, 69 to 74)					
G Player (SA)	74	68	68	70	280
B Yancey	69	70	72	70	281
T Aaron	68	74	69	72	283
D Hill	73	70	70	70	283
D Stockton	72	72	69	70	283

1971

NAME	SCORE				
C Coody	66	73	70	70	279
J Miller	72	73	68	68	281
J Nicklaus	70	71	68	72	281
D January	69	69	73	72	283
G Littler	72	69	73	69	283

1972

NAME	SCORE				
J Nicklaus	68	71	73	74	286
T Weiskopf	74	71	70	74	289
B Crampton	72	75	60	73	289
R Mitchell	73	72	71	73	289
H Blancas	76	71	69	74	290
B Devlin (Aus)	74	75	70	71	290
J Heard	73	71	72	74	290
J Jamieson	72	70	71	77	290
J McGee	73	74	71	72	290

1973

NAME	SCORE				
T Aaron	68	73	74	68	283
JC Snead	70	71	73	70	284
P Oosterhuis (Eng)	73	70	68	74	285
J Jamieson	73	71	70	71	285
J Nicklaus	69	77	73	66	285

1974

NAME	SCORE				
G Player (SA)	71	71	66	70	278
D Stockton	71	66	70	73	280
T Weiskopf	71	69	70	70	280
J Nicklaus	69	71	72	69	281
H Irwin	68	70	72	71	281
J Colbert	67	72	69	73	281

1975

NAME	SCORE				
J Nicklaus	68	67	73	68	276
J Miller	75	71	65	66	277
T Weiskopf	69	72	66	70	277
H Irwin	73	74	71	64	282
B Nichols	67	74	72	69	282

1976

NAME	SCORE				
R Floyd	65	66	70	70	271
B Crenshaw	70	70	72	67	279
J Nicklaus	67	69	73	73	282
L Ziegler	67	71	72	72	282
C Coody	72	69	70	74	285
H Irwin	71	77	67	70	285
T Kite	73	67	72	73	285

1977

NAME	SCORE				
T Watson	70	69	70	67	276
J Nicklaus	72	70	70	66	278
T Kite	70	73	70	67	280
R Massengale	70	73	67	70	280
H Irwin	70	74	70	68	282

1978

NAME	SCORE				
G Player (SA)	72	72	69	64	277
R Funseth	73	66	70	69	278
H Green	72	69	65	72	278
T Watson	73	68	68	69	278
W Armstrong	72	70	70	68	280
W Kratzert	70	74	67	69	280

1979

NAME	SCORE				
F Zoeller	70	71	69	70	280
T Watson	68	71	70	71	280
E Sneed	68	67	69	76	280
(Zoeller won play-off at 2nd extra hole)					
J Nicklaus	69	71	72	69	281
T Kite	71	72	68	72	283

1980

NAME	SCORE				
S Ballesteros (Spa)	66	69	68	72	275
G Gilbert	70	74	68	67	279
J Newton (Aus)	68	74	69	68	279
H Green	68	74	71	67	280
D Graham	68	73	72	70	281

1981

NAME	SCORE				
T Watson	71	68	70	71	280
J Nicklaus	70	65	75	72	282
J Miller	69	72	73	68	282
G Norman (Aus)	69	70	72	72	283
T Kite	74	72	70	68	284
J Pate	71	72	71	70	284

1982

NAME	SCORE				
C Stadler	75	69	67	73	284
D Pohl	75	75	67	67	284
(Stadler won play-off at 1st extra hole)					
S Ballesteros (Spa)	73	73	68	71	285
J Pate	74	73	67	71	285
T Kite	76	69	73	69	287
T Watson	77	79	70	71	287

1983

NAME	SCORE				
S Ballesteros (Spa)	68	70	73	69	280
B Crenshaw	76	70	70	68	284
T Kite	70	72	73	69	284
T Watson	70	71	71	73	285
R Floyd	67	72	71	75	285

1984

NAME	SCORE				
B Crenshaw	67	72	70	68	277
T Watson	74	67	69	69	279
D Edwards	71	70	72	67	280
G Morgan	73	71	69	67	280
L Nelson	76	69	66	70	281

1985

NAME	SCORE				
B Langer (W Ger)	72	74	68	68	282
C Strange	80	65	68	71	284
S Ballesteros (Spa)	72	71	71	70	284
R Floyd	70	73	69	72	284
J Haas	73	73	73	67	286

1986

NAME	SCORE				
J Nicklaus	74	71	69	65	279
T Kite	70	74	68	68	280
G Norman (Aus)	70	72	68	70	280
S Ballesteros (Spa)	71	68	72	70	281
N Price (Zim)	79	69	63	71	282

1987

NAME	SCORE				
L Mize	70	72	72	71	285
S Ballesteros (Spa)	73	71	70	71	285
G Norman (Aus)	73	74	66	72	285

(Mize won play-off at 2nd extra hole)

B Crenshaw	75	70	67	74	286
R Maltbie	76	66	70	74	286
J Mudd	74	72	71	69	286

1988

NAME	SCORE				
AWB Lyle (Sco)	71	67	72	71	281
M Calcavecchia	71	69	72	70	282
C Stadler	76	69	70	68	283
B Crenshaw	72	73	67	72	284
D Pooley	71	72	72	70	285
G Norman (Aus)	77	73	71	64	285

1989

NAME	SCORE				
N Faldo (Eng)	68	73	77	65	283
S Hoch	69	74	71	69	283

(Faldo won play-off at 2nd extra hole)

G Norman (Aus)	74	75	68	67	284
B Crenshaw	71	72	70	71	284
S Ballesteros (Spa)	71	72	73	69	285

1990

NAME	SCORE				
N Faldo (Eng)	71	72	66	69	278
R Floyd	70	68	68	72	278

(Faldo won play-off at 2nd extra hole)

J Huston	66	74	68	75	283
L Wadkins	72	73	70	68	283
F Couples	74	69	72	69	284

United States PGA Championship

INAUGURATED 1916

YEAR	WINNER	MARGIN	RUNNER-UP	VENUE
1916	Jim Barnes	1 hole	J Hutchison	Siwanoy, New York
1919	Jim Barnes	6 and 5	Fred McLeod	Engineers' Club, New York
1920	J Hutchison	1 hole	JD Edgar	Flossmoor, Illinois
1921	Walter Hagen	3 and 2	Jim Barnes	Inwood, New York
1922	Gene Sarazen	4 and 3	E French	Oakmont, Pennsylvania
1923	Gene Sarazen	38th hole	Walter Hagen	Pelham, New York
1924	Walter Hagen	2 holes	Jim Barnes	French Lick, Indiana
1925	Walter Hagen	6 and 4	WE Mehlhorn	Olympic Fields, Illinois
1926	Walter Hagen	4 and 3	L Diegel	Salisbury, New York
1927	Walter Hagen	1 hole	J Turnesa	Dallas, Texas
1928	L Diegel	6 and 5	A Espinosa	Five Farms, Maryland
1929	L Diegel	6 and 4	J Farrell	Hillcrest, California
1930	T Armour	1 hole	Gene Sarazen	Fresh Meadow, New York
1931	T Creavy	2 and 1	Densmore Shute	Wannamoisett, Rhode Island
1932	O Dutra	4 and 3	F Walsh	St Paul, Minnesota
1933	Gene Sarazen	5 and 4	W Goggin	Blue Mound, Wisconsin
1934	P Runyan	38th hole	C Wood	Buffalo, New York
1935	J Revolta	5 and 4	T Armour	Twin Hills, Oklahoma
1936	Densmore Shute	3 and 2	J Thomson	Pinehurst, North Carolina
1937	Densmore Shute	37th hole	H McSpaden	Oakmont, Pennsylvania
1938	P Runyan	8 and 7	Sam Snead	Shawnee, Pennsylvania
1939	H Picard	37th hole	Byron Nelson	Pomonok, New York
1940	Byron Nelson	1 hole	Sam Snead	Hershey, Pennsylvania
1941	V Ghezzie	38th hole	Byron Nelson	Denver, Colorado
1942	Sam Snead	2 and 1	J Turnesa	Atlantic City, New Jersey
1943	*No Championship*			
1944	R Hamilton	1 hole	Byron Nelson	Spokane, Washington
1945	Byron Nelson	4 and 3	S Byrd	Dayton, Ohio
1946	B Hogan	6 and 4	Ed Oliver	Portland, Oregon
1947	J Ferrier	2 and 1	C Harbert	Detroit, Michigan
1948	B Hogan	7 and 6	M Turnesa	Norwood Hills, Missouri
1949	Sam Snead	3 and 2	J Palmer	Richmond, Virginia
1950	C Harper	4 and 3	H Williams	Scioto, Ohio
1951	Sam Snead	7 and 6	W Burkemo	Oakmont, Pennsylvania
1952	J Turnesa	1 hole	C Harbert	Big Spring, Kentucky
1953	W Burkemo	2 and 1	F Lorza	Oakland Hills, Birmingham, Michigan
1954	C Harbert	4 and 3	W Burkemo	St Paul, Minnesota
1955	D Ford	4 and 3	C Middlecoff	Detroit, Michigan
1956	J Burk	3 and 2	T Kroll	Boston, Massachusetts
1957	L Hebert	3 and 1	D Finsterwald	Miami Valley, Ohio

Decided hereafter by stroke play.

1958   *at Llanerch, Haverton, Pennsylvania*

NAME	SCORE				
D Finsterwald	67	72	70	67	276
W Casper	73	67	68	70	278
Sam Snead	73	67	67	73	280
J Burke	70	72	69	70	281
J Hebert	68	71	73	73	285
T Bolt	72	70	73	70	285
J Boros	72	68	73	72	285

1959   *at St Louis Park, Minneapolis, Minnesota*

NAME	SCORE				
B Rosburg	71	72	68	66	277
J Barber	69	65	71	73	278
D Sanders	72	66	68	72	278
D Finsterswald	71	68	71	70	280
M Souchak	69	67	71	74	281
B Goalby	72	69	72	68	281
K Venturi	70	72	70	69	281

1960   *at Firestone, Akron, Ohio*

NAME	SCORE				
J Hebert	72	67	72	70	281
J Ferrier	71	74	66	71	282
Sam Snead	68	73	70	72	283
D Sanders	70	71	69	73	283
D January	70	70	72	72	284

1961   *at Olympia Fields, Illinois*

NAME	SCORE				
J Barber	69	67	71	70	277
D January	72	66	67	72	277
(Barber won play-off, 67 to 68)					
D Sanders	70	68	74	68	280
T Kroll	72	68	70	71	281
D Ford	69	73	74	66	282
G Littler	71	70	72	69	282
A Wall	67	72	73	70	282
W Ellis	71	71	68	72	282
J Pott	71	73	67	71	282
A Palmer	73	72	69	68	282

1962   *at Aronimink, Newtown Square, Pennsylvania*

NAME	SCORE				
G Player (SA)	72	67	69	70	278
B Goalby	69	72	71	67	279
J Nicklaus	71	74	69	67	281
G Bayer	69	70	71	71	281
D Ford	69	69	73	71	282

1963   *at Dallas Athletic, Dallas, Texas*

NAME	SCORE				
J Nicklaus	69	73	69	68	279
D Ragan	75	70	67	69	281
D Finsterwald	72	72	66	72	282
B Crampton (Aus)	70	73	65	74	282
B Maxwell	73	71	69	71	284
A Geiberger	72	73	69	70	284

1964   *at Columbus, Ohio*

NAME	SCORE				
B Nichols	64	71	69	67	271
A Palmer	68	68	69	69	274
J Nicklaus	67	73	70	64	274
M Rudolph	73	66	68	69	276
K Venturi	72	65	73	69	279
T Nieporte	68	71	68	72	279

1965   *at Laurel Valley, Ligonier, Pennsylvania*

NAME	SCORE				
D Marr	70	69	70	71	280
W Casper	70	70	71	71	282
J Nicklaus	69	70	72	71	282
B Wininger	73	72	72	66	283
G Dickinson	67	74	69	74	284

1966 *at Firestone, Akron, Ohio*

NAME			SCORE		
A Geiberger	68	72	68	72	280
D Wysong	74	72	66	72	284
W Casper	73	73	70	70	286
G Littler	75	71	71	70	286
G Player (SA)	73	70	70	73	286

1967 *at Columbine, Denver, Colorado*

NAME			SCORE		
D January	71	72	70	68	281
D Massengale	70	75	70	66	281
(January won play-off, 69 to 71)					
J Nicklaus	67	75	69	71	282
D Sikes	69	70	70	73	282
A Geiberger	73	71	69	70	283
J Boros	69	76	70	68	283

1968 *at Pecan Valley, San Antonio, Texas*

NAME			SCORE		
J Boros	71	71	70	69	281
RJ Charles (NZ)	72	70	70	70	282
A Palmer	71	69	72	70	282
G Archer	71	69	74	69	283
M Fleckman	66	72	72	73	283

1969 *at NCR, Dayton, Ohio*

NAME			SCORE		
R Floyd	69	66	67	74	276
G Player (SA)	71	65	71	70	277
B Greene	71	68	68	71	278
J Wright	71	68	69	71	279
L Ziegler	69	71	70	70	280
M Barber	73	75	64	68	280

1970 *at Southern Hills, Tulsa, Oklahoma*

NAME			SCORE		
D Stockton	70	70	66	73	279
R Murphy	71	73	71	66	281
A Palmer	70	72	69	70	281
G Littler	72	71	69	70	282
L Hinson	69	71	74	68	282

1971 *at PGA National, Palm Beach Gardens, Florida*

NAME			SCORE		
J Nicklaus	69	69	70	73	281
W Casper	71	73	71	68	283
T Bolt	72	74	69	69	284
M Barber	72	68	75	70	285
G Player (SA)	71	73	68	73	285

1972 *at Oakland Hills, Birmingham, Michigan*

NAME			SCORE		
G Player (SA)	71	71	67	72	281
T Aaron	71	71	70	71	283
J Jamieson	69	72	72	70	283
R Floyd	69	71	74	70	284
W Casper	73	70	67	74	284
Sam Snead	70	74	71	69	284

1973 *at Canterbury, Cleveland, Ohio*

NAME			SCORE		
J Nicklaus	72	68	68	69	277
B Crampton (Aus)	71	73	67	70	281
M Rudolph	69	70	70	73	282
L Wadkins	73	69	71	69	282
JC Snead	71	74	68	69	282

1974 *at Tanglewood, Clemens, North Carolina*

NAME			SCORE		
L Trevino	73	66	68	69	276
J Nicklaus	69	69	70	69	277
AD Cole	69	68	71	71	279
H Green	68	68	73	70	279
D Hill	74	69	67	69	279
Sam Snead	69	71	71	68	279

1975 *at Firestone, Akron, Ohio*

NAME			SCORE		
J Nicklaus	70	68	67	71	276
B Crampton (Aus)	71	63	75	69	278
T Weiskopf	70	71	70	68	279
A North	72	74	70	65	281
H Irwin	72	65	73	73	283
W Casper	69	72	72	70	283

1976 *at Congressional, Bethesda, Maryland*

NAME	SCORE				
D Stockton	70	72	69	70	281
R Floyd	72	68	71	71	282
D January	70	69	71	72	282
D Graham (Aus)	70	71	70	72	283
J Schlee	72	71	70	70	283
J Nicklaus	71	69	69	74	283
J Pate	69	73	72	69	283

1977 *at Pebble Beach, California*

NAME	SCORE				
L Wadkins	69	71	72	70	282
G Littler	67	69	70	76	282
(Wadkins won sudden-death play-off)					
J Nicklaus	69	71	70	73	283
C Coody	70	71	70	73	284
J Pate	73	70	69	73	285

1978 *at Oakmont, Pennsylvania*

NAME	SCORE				
J Mahaffey	75	67	68	66	276
J Pate	72	70	66	68	276
T Watson	67	69	67	73	276
(Mahaffey won sudden-death play-off)					
T Weiskopf	73	67	69	71	280
G Morgan	76	71	66	67	280

1979 *at Oakland Hills, Birmingham, Michigan*

NAME	SCORE				
D Graham (Aus)	69	68	70	65	272
B Crenshaw	69	67	69	67	272
(Graham won sudden-death play-off)					
R Caldwell	67	70	66	71	274
R Streck	68	71	69	68	276
G Gilbert	69	72	68	69	278
J Pate	69	69	69	71	278

1980 *at Oak Hill, Rochester, New York*

NAME	SCORE				
J Nicklaus	70	69	66	69	274
A Bean	72	71	68	70	281
L Hinkle	70	69	69	75	283
G Morgan	68	70	73	72	283
H Twitty	68	74	71	71	284
C Strange	68	72	72	72	284

1981 *at Atlanta Athletic Club, Duluth, Georgia*

NAME	SCORE				
L Nelson	70	66	66	71	273
F Zoeller	70	68	68	71	277
D Pohl	69	67	73	69	278
I Aoki (Jpn)	75	68	66	70	279
K Fergus	71	71	69	68	279
G Norman (Aus)	73	67	68	71	279
T Kite	71	67	69	72	279
B Lietzke	70	70	71	68	279
B Gilder	74	69	70	66	279
J Nicklaus	71	68	71	69	279

1982 *at Southern Hills, Tulsa Oklahoma*

NAME	SCORE				
R Floyd	63	69	68	72	272
L Wadkins	71	68	69	67	275
F Couples	67	71	72	66	276
C Peete	69	70	68	69	276
J Simons	68	67	73	69	277
J Haas	71	66	68	72	277
G Norman (Aus)	66	69	70	72	277

1983   *at Riviera, Pacific Palisades, California*

NAME	SCORE				
H Sutton	65	66	72	71	274
J Nicklaus	73	65	71	66	275
P Jacobsen	73	70	68	65	276
P McGowan	68	67	73	69	277
J Fought	67	69	71	71	278

1984   *at Shoal Creek, Birmingham, Alabama*

NAME	SCORE				
L Trevino	69	68	67	69	273
L Wadkins	68	69	68	72	277
G Player (SA)	74	63	69	71	277
C Peete	71	70	69	68	278
S Ballesteros (Spa)	70	69	70	70	279

1985   *at Cherry Hills, Denver, Colorado*

NAME	SCORE				
H Green	67	69	70	72	278
L Trevino	66	68	75	71	280
A Bean	71	70	72	68	281
T-M Chen (Tai)	69	76	71	65	281
N Price (SA)	73	73	65	71	282

1986   *at Inverness, Toledo, Ohio*

NAME	SCORE				
R Tway	72	70	64	70	276
G Norman (Aus)	65	68	69	76	278
P Jacobsen	68	70	70	71	279
DA Weibring	71	72	68	69	280
B Lietzke	69	71	70	71	281
P Stewart	70	67	72	72	281

1987   *at PGA National, Palm Beach, Florida*

NAME	SCORE				
L Nelson	70	72	73	72	287
L Wadkins	70	70	74	73	287
(Nelson won play-off)					
S Hoch	74	74	71	69	288
DA Weibring	73	72	67	76	288
M McCumber	74	69	69	77	289
D Pooley	73	71	73	72	289

1988   *at Oak Tree, Edmond, Oklahoma*

NAME	SCORE				
J Sluman	69	70	68	65	272
P Azinger	67	66	71	71	275
T Nakajima (Jpn)	69	68	74	67	278
T Kite	72	69	71	67	279
N Faldo (Eng)	67	71	70	71	279

1989   *at Kemper Lakes, Hawthorn Woods, Illinois*

NAME	SCORE				
P Stewart	74	66	69	67	276
A Bean	70	67	74	66	277
M Reid	66	67	70	74	277
C Strange	70	68	70	69	277
D Rummells	68	69	69	72	278

1990   *at Shoal Creek, Atlanta, Georgia*

NAME	SCORE				
W Grady (Aus)	72	67	72	71	282
F Couples	69	71	73	72	285
G Morgan	77	72	65	72	286
B Britton	72	74	72	71	289
C Beck	71	70	78	71	290
B Mayfair	70	71	75	74	290
L Roberts	73	71	70	76	290

The European Tour

Before 1971 professional competitive golf in the UK was limited to the Open Championship, which was and still is, promoted and managed by the R&A, a few other 72-hole tournaments, sponsored by newspapers and golf equipment manufacturers, and the *News of the World* Match Play Tournament. Little had changed in the professional world since 1939. The Open was the first to see the way ahead with the coming of Arnold Palmer, Jack Nicklaus and Gary Player to support it each year, and it was time for the PGA to broaden its base. In 1971, John Jacobs was appointed to bring direction to tournament activities.

Several factors had combined to create the situation Jacobs took over. Tony Jacklin's win at Lytham in 1969, followed by his remarkable triumph in the US Open at Chaska, Minnesota a year later, generated tremendous enthusiasm at home. Television was bringing golf to a far wider public and the Golf Foundation was starting its work in teaching golf to many more boys and girls in the schools, together spreading the message at the grassroots level.

Jacobs laid the foundations for the European Tour in his four years as tournament director. He was succeeded in 1975 by Ken Schofield, who inherited a programme of many more sponsored tournaments, but understandably with quite a few gaps; the annual prize fund had more than doubled to £500,000, and a rich vein of enthusiasm from tournament players showed great promise for the future. While many of the players were still attached to clubs, the day of the perpetually travelling tournament professional, with company or individual sponsorship, had arrived. A year later in 1976, qualifying at the Tour School became the hardest test a young professional was ever likely to face, and many were disappointed and are still each season. Nor is it a question of once qualified, always in. All those outside the top 120 in the Order of Merit in any year, must qualify again unless they are exempt under a number of other categories.

The Tour now had a board of directors and a Tournament Committee, comprised of playing professionals with management abilities. Neil Coles has followed his success as a tournament player with expert leadership of his fellow professionals and works effectively with John O'Leary of the Tournament Committee, other members of the Board and with the director Ken Schofield, Tony Grey, External Affairs Director, and George O'Grady, Managing Director of Tour Enterprises. Their efforts have been enhanced by the inclusion in the management since 1980 of representative professionals from Europe, such as Severiano Ballesteros, Bernhard Langer and other prominent players. Spain has produced between two and four representatives in each of the last four Ryder Cup teams, with Bernhard Langer from Germany playing in the last five matches.

The Tour now stretches from February to November and there is no week in the period without a tournament. Prize money available has reached a staggering total of £17 million and it says much for Ken Schofield and his staff that a steady rise looks likely to continue even in the face of a recession. Those tournaments which have no television coverage attract sponsors who must feel the outlay well worth it as there are so few changes from year to year.

The success of the Tour has been helped by the standard of play and behaviour of today's professionals. In no other sport, certainly none covered by television, except perhaps snooker, is there a better example of how to play to the rules of the game, show respect for one's opponent and hold the head high. All participants know that any display of dissent or intemperate frustration, if caught by the camera, will live with them for a long time.

AGF Open

1988 *at Biarritz*

NAME	SCORE				
D Llewellyn	64	69	60	65	258
C O'Connor Jr	66	66	65	68	265
B Lane	71	65	63	67	266
J Rivero	67	63	69	67	266
M James	67	69	65	66	267
G Brand Jr	64	69	68	66	267
M Allen	67	66	69	65	267
P Walton	65	66	67	69	267
S Bishop	64	70	68	66	268
N Hansen	68	66	66	68	268
J Rutledge	66	67	66	69	268
E Darcy	63	71	67	67	268

1989 *at La Grande Mott, Montpellier*

NAME	SCORE				
M James	69	67	69	72	277
M Mouland	72	73	70	65	280
B Norton	70	70	70	71	281
V Singh	73	68	73	68	282
R Stelten	65	68	72	77	282

NAME	SCORE				
S Torrance	68	67	73	74	282
G Turner	73	73	65	71	282
J Howell	70	75	70	68	283
A Sherborne	72	70	70	71	283
M Aparicio	74	72	73	65	284
S Bennett	70	71	71	72	284
M Besanceney	72	72	70	70	284
J Quiros	69	69	72	74	284
G Ralph	72	71	67	74	284
DJ Russell	74	73	66	71	284

1990 *at La Grande Mott, Montpellier*

NAME	SCORE				
B Ogle	72	66	70	70	278
P Curry	70	71	69	71	281
B Longmuir	71	72	69	69	281
D Durnian	71	71	71	69	282
M McNulty	72	71	68	71	282
M James	77	68	67	71	283
P McWhinney	73	69	70	72	284
MA Martin	68	74	72	71	285
R Claydon	73	71	70	71	285
M McLean	69	73	71	72	285

Vinho Verde Atlantic Open

1990 *at Campo Golfe, Estela, Oporto*

NAME	SCORE					NAME	SCORE				
S McAllister	71	71	72	74	288	S Bowman	71	73	73	72	289
R Rafferty	72	70	74	72	288	R Stelten	70	69	70	80	289
D Williams	70	71	73	74	288	S Richardson	72	70	71	76	289
S Hamill	71	67	74	76	288	R Drummond	70	73	70	76	289
R Boxall	71	73	73	71	288	MA Jimenez	73	68	72	76	289
A Sorensen	68	73	70	77	288						

(McAllister won play-off)

Austrian Open

1990 *at Gut Altentann, Salzburg*

NAME	SCORE					NAME	SCORE				
B Langer	65	66	72	68	271	C Moody	70	69	70	69	278
L Wadkins	67	68	68	68	271	DJ Russell	70	74	66	69	279
D Smyth	70	69	72	62	273	R Hartmann	70	70	66	73	279
M Moreno	74	67	67	67	275	R Drummond	72	70	71	67	280
MA Martin	68	69	70	68	275	S Stephen	70	77	66	67	280
G Manson	72	67	72	65	276						

Baleares Open

1988 *at Santa Ponsa, Majorca*

NAME	SCORE				
S Ballesteros	70	68	67	67	272
JM Olazabal	68	73	64	73	278
G Brand Jr	76	68	70	66	280
R Rafferty	73	70	70	70	283
B Lane	71	73	67	72	283
M Poxon	72	72	69	70	283
J Jacobs	71	73	68	72	284
D Smyth	73	71	72	69	285
M James	73	70	71	72	286
M Pinero	72	71	74	69	286
P Jones	72	72	71	71	286
P Baker	71	73	70	72	286
J Slaughter	68	72	73	73	286
C McClellan	71	73	73	69	286

1989 *at Santa Ponsa, Majorca*

NAME	SCORE				
O Sellberg	68	71	69	71	279
M McNulty	69	70	71	71	281
JM Olazabal	71	75	68	67	281
P Parkin	71	71	69	70	281
D Durnian	71	72	69	70	282
J Howell	68	74	70	70	282
B Malley	69	70	70	73	282
B Ogle	70	70	71	71	282
J Quiros	71	70	71	70	282
R Rafferty	72	69	69	72	282

1990 *at Son Vida, Majorca*

NAME	SCORE				
S Ballesteros	66	65	70	68	269
M Persson	65	65	66	73	269
(Ballesteros won play-off)					
J Quiros	68	64	71	68	271
M McNulty	67	70	69	66	272
J van de Velde	71	66	69	67	273
R Davis	70	64	70	69	273

NAME	SCORE				
A Saavedra	67	68	70	70	275
B Langer	66	70	70	70	276
C O'Connor Jr	68	68	70	71	277
P Mitchell	70	65	73	70	278
P O'Malley	70	68	69	71	278
R Rafferty	69	69	67	73	278
E Darcy	69	68	71	70	278
B Malley	63	72	73	70	278

Barcelona Open

1988 *El Prat, Barcelona*

NAME	SCORE				
D Whelan	68	65	74	69	276
M Mouland	71	68	69	68	276
N Faldo	66	68	71	71	276
B Lane	71	69	67	69	276
(Whelan won play-off)					
J Rystrom	70	69	68	71	278
S Torrance	75	68	68	68	279
D Gilford	68	73	68	71	280
M Mackenzie	72	68	68	72	280
P Harrison	71	68	73	68	280
C O'Connor Jr	72	69	71	68	280
P Teravainen	68	71	69	72	280
P Baker	75	69	70	66	280

NAME	SCORE				
C Montgomerie	73	68	72	67	280
JM Olazabal	70	71	68	71	280
D Durnian	73	68	71	69	281
H Clark	72	68	70	72	282
P O'Malley	72	69	69	72	282
G Turner	73	66	70	73	282
M Calero	68	76	69	71	284
D Ecob	68	72	75	70	285
M Persson	72	72	71	70	285

1990

Not played

1989 *at Pals, Gerona*

NAME	SCORE				
M Roe	69	70	69	71	279
G Brand Jr	73	67	70	70	280

Belgian Open

1978 *at Royal Golf Club of Belgium, Brussels*

NAME	SCORE				
N Ratcliffe	72	70	72	66	280
C Tickner	68	72	68	73	281
M Gregson	69	73	72	70	284
W Longmuir	73	71	68	72	284

NAME	SCORE				
A Jacklin	74	66	69	75	284
E Polland	68	73	77	67	285
N Faldo	71	71	71	72	285
SC Mason	71	71	70	73	285
S Torrance	69	73	72	72	286
S Ginn	74	69	69	74	286
K Brown	70	69	69	78	286

1979 *at Royal Waterloo, Brussels*

NAME	SCORE				
G Levenson	68	71	68	72	279
M King	70	73	71	68	282
RJ Cole	71	71	71	69	282
N Faldo	69	72	70	71	282
B Dassu	73	66	71	73	283
J Hall	69	74	73	67	283
S Owen	70	74	69	71	284
M James	71	68	73	72	284
K Brown	72	70	72	71	285
A Jacklin	68	72	71	74	285

1980-86

Not played

1987 *at Royal Waterloo, Brussels*

NAME	SCORE			
E Darcy	69	67	64	200
N Faldo	69	67	65	201
R Rafferty	72	65	64	201
I Woosnam	66	66	69	201
P Fowler	71	66	68	205
B Lane	73	64	68	205
G Levenson	71	68	67	206
W Westner	71	68	67	206
M Allen	73	68	66	207
A Oldcorn	69	69	69	207
DJ Russell	72	67	68	207
O Sellberg	69	73	65	207
M Tapia	72	69	66	207
G Turner	70	67	70	207
B Andrade	67	70	70	207

1988 *at Bercuit, Brussels*

NAME	SCORE				
JM Olazabal	67	69	64	69	269
M Smith	67	73	63	70	273

NAME	SCORE				
GJ Brand	69	70	67	71	277
O Sellberg	68	71	70	68	277
P Baker	68	73	67	70	278
E Romero	72	69	71	67	279
A Johnstone	69	68	71	71	279
R Rafferty	68	70	69	72	279
S Bennett	71	72	69	67	279
M Lanner	73	69	68	70	280
SC Mason	69	68	73	70	280

1989 *at Royal Waterloo, Brussels*

NAME	SCORE				
GJ Brand	67	69	68	69	273
K Dickens	70	67	67	73	277
M Davis	68	73	70	67	278
J Parnevik	74	70	67	68	279
R Boxall	69	70	66	75	280
M Farry	69	69	71	71	280
R Rafferty	70	73	67	70	280
M Mackenzie	70	72	71	67	280
D Cooper	71	71	71	67	280
E Darcy	68	72	72	69	281
A Murray	72	71	69	69	281
D Williams	71	70	72	68	281
G Turner	74	70	70	67	281
P Walton	75	69	70	67	281

1990 *at Royal Waterloo, Brussels*

NAME	SCORE				
O Sellberg	68	66	67	71	272
I Woosnam	66	70	70	70	276
E Romero	69	72	69	68	278
G Turner	68	74	68	70	280
JM Olazabal	69	71	71	69	280
R Rafferty	70	70	74	68	282
C Montgomerie	69	73	72	68	282
M Miller	68	72	74	68	282
J Spence	68	76	68	71	283
P Carman	69	70	71	74	284
G Ralph	71	73	73	67	284
B Malley	74	70	69	71	284

The Benson & Hedges International Open

at Fulford

1971

NAME	SCORE				
A Jacklin	73	67	72	67	279
PJ Butler	70	65	73	71	279
P Oosterhuis	70	68	72	70	280
BGC Huggett	70	73	70	70	283
R Floyd	67	74	73	70	284
A Grubb	73	70	71	70	284
J Garner	72	70	71	71	284
NC Coles	73	70	70	72	285
C O'Connor	69	69	74	73	285
J Panton	72	74	72	69	287
BW Barnes	72	71	72	72	287

1972

NAME	SCORE				
J Newton	73	70	67	71	281
H Bannerman	73	72	68	69	282
D Vaughan	73	72	68	70	283
P Oosterhuis	70	74	70	71	285
BGC Huggett	71	73	68	73	285
J O'Leary	72	73	72	69	286
V Hood	70	75	71	70	286
CA Clark	73	70	75	69	287
NC Coles	71	76	69	71	287
H Baiocchi	71	75	69	72	287

1973

NAME	SCORE				
V Baker	73	68	71	64	276
D Hayes	66	71	71	70	278
J O'Leary	74	70	68	68	280
J Newton	71	70	71	69	281
N Wood	72	67	72	71	282
RJ Charles	71	69	71	71	282
J Britz	69	71	70	72	282
GL Hunt	69	70	73	71	283
P Oosterhuis	71	67	72	73	283
E Polland	71	71	69	73	284
PJ Butler	70	73	68	73	284

1974

NAME	SCORE				
P Toussaint	71	70	71	64	276
R Shearer	65	66	75	70	276
(Toussaint won play-off)					
CA Clark	65	71	75	67	278
BGC Huggett	64	73	74	67	278
S Snead	69	71	68	71	279
E Polland	65	70	72	72	279
J Jacobs	70	68	69	73	280
M Gregson	68	68	71	73	280
D Chillas	66	73	71	71	281
NC Coles	67	73	68	73	281

1975

NAME	SCORE				
V Fernandez	65	64	65	72	266
M Bembridge	64	66	66	71	267
B Fleisher	69	64	67	69	269
R Shearer	66	67	68	70	271
L Platts	69	64	68	71	272
MS Moussa	69	64	67	73	273
D Sanders	68	69	62	74	273
J O'Leary	71	67	69	67	274
SC Mason	70	63	70	71	274
R Gilder	63	71	69	71	274

1976

NAME	SCORE				
G Marsh	67	66	71	68	272
M James	69	66	70	69	274
G Player	72	65	69	70	276
B Gallacher	70	68	64	77	279
M Gregson	70	70	70	70	280
I Mosey	69	70	72	70	281
S Hobday	69	69	69	74	281
S Ballesteros	76	67	72	67	282
E Darcy	71	71	71	69	282
D Sanders	68	70	72	72	282
BGC Huggett	68	70	71	73	282
T Horton	71	72	66	73	282

1977

NAME	SCORE				
A Garrido	72	68	72	68	280
RJ Charles	69	76	69	69	283
L Stubblefield	75	70	71	68	284
W Casper	73	69	71	72	285
E Darcy	74	74	72	65	285
M Gregson	75	69	72	70	286
B Waites	72	70	71	73	286
H Baiocchi	73	72	74	68	287
S Ballesteros	76	72	70	69	287
K Brown	74	70	75	68	287
V Fernandez	71	72	73	71	287
L Higgins	74	71	71	71	287
T Horton	72	71	75	69	287
A Jacklin	70	72	75	70	287

1978

NAME	SCORE				
L Trevino	69	67	72	66	274
NC Coles	69	71	67	67	274
N Ratcliffe	69	69	69	67	274
(Trevino won play-off)					
N Faldo	70	68	66	71	275
S Ballesteros	71	69	65	70	275
E Polland	71	69	67	69	276
T Horton	72	72	67	67	278
D Durnian	69	71	68	70	278
H Clark	72	67	69	70	278
B Langer	69	69	70	70	278
C O'Connor Jr	73	67	68	70	278

1979 *at St Mellion, Cornwall*

NAME	SCORE				
M Bembridge	67	67	69	69	272
K Brown	71	65	70	68	274
S Torrance	73	68	69	66	276
J Gonzalez	72	71	67	66	276
A Jacklin	76	67	67	67	277
JM Canizares	74	71	67	66	278
M King	72	73	65	68	278
H Henning	74	65	70	69	278
D Ingram	72	69	71	67	279
BGC Huggett	71	67	70	71	279
DJ Russell	76	69	64	70	279

1980

NAME	SCORE				
G Marsh	65	64	73	70	272
J Bland	73	69	65	67	274
AWB Lyle	68	70	65	72	275
M Calero	68	73	71	64	276
N Job	65	65	77	69	276
D Hayes	69	70	70	67	276
NC Coles	71	68	71	68	278
B Waites	68	68	71	71	278
BW Barnes	67	69	69	73	278
S Ginn	67	72	70	70	279
L Liang-Huan	70	71	69	69	279
S Torrance	70	64	71	74	279
D Smyth	64	73	70	72	279

1981

NAME	SCORE				
T Weiskopf	66	69	68	69	272
B Langer	66	71	67	69	273
E Darcy	63	73	66	71	273
(Weiskopf won play-off)					
G Marsh	66	69	73	70	278
B Waites	67	71	68	72	278
AWB Lyle	69	72	71	67	279
J Bland	74	72	64	69	279
RJ Charles	69	71	70	69	279
M King	71	70	69	69	279
M Bembridge	72	70	66	71	279

1982

NAME	SCORE				
G Norman	69	74	69	71	283
RJ Charles	71	69	74	70	284
G Marsh	72	69	72	71	284
I Woosnam	71	71	71	71	284
SC Mason	70	74	70	71	285
N Faldo	70	72	71	72	285
D Durnian	72	72	72	71	287
V Somers	74	71	72	71	288
J Bland	72	70	75	71	288
NC Coles	69	75	71	73	288
B Gallacher	71	71	72	74	288

1983

NAME	SCORE				
J Bland	68	70	67	68	273
B Langer	68	68	71	67	274
C Pavin	65	70	72	69	276
J Hall	70	70	64	72	276
J Anglada	70	68	71	68	277
N Job	69	72	70	68	279
J Rivero	70	71	69	69	279
M Pinero	68	70	71	70	279
GJ Brand	70	68	69	72	279

1984

NAME	SCORE				
S Torrance	63	68	70	69	270
W Grady	72	69	65	65	271
D Frost	72	67	66	67	272
AWB Lyle	70	70	67	66	273
R Chapman	69	72	70	64	275
J Anderson	67	70	73	66	276
R Davis	67	67	73	69	276
B Gallacher	69	69	72	67	277
V Fernandez	73	66	69	69	277
H Baiocchi	67	69	70	71	277
C O'Connor Jr	67	68	70	72	277
JM Canizares	71	70	64	72	277

1985

NAME	SCORE				
AWB Lyle	70	69	71	64	274
I Woosnam	70	73	70	62	275
D Smyth	69	68	71	68	276
S Torrance	70	67	71	68	276
R Davis	70	70	67	69	276
H Clark	71	71	69	66	277
H Baiocchi	70	72	68	68	278
M Mouland	74	68	68	69	279
I Baker-Finch	73	69	69	68	279
M James	68	73	68	70	279

1986

NAME	SCORE				
M James	65	70	69	70	274
H Baiocchi	66	70	70	68	274
L Trevino	66	67	73	68	274
G Brand Jr	65	67	72	71	275
M McNulty	68	69	72	67	276
J O'Leary	66	69	72	69	276

NAME	SCORE				
I Woosnam	71	68	70	67	276
C O'Connor Jr	72	65	72	68	277
JM Olazabal	67	71	67	72	277
R Lee	68	69	71	70	278
JM Canizares	68	72	68	70	278

1987

NAME	SCORE				
N Ratcliffe	69	70	70	66	275
O Sellberg	70	69	69	69	277
N Faldo	74	68	66	70	278
JM Olazabal	69	71	71	67	278
R McFarlane	69	72	68	70	279
I Baker-Finch	70	69	71	70	280
JM Canizares	68	73	70	69	280
A Garrido	69	68	72	71	280
M King	71	67	71	71	280
B Langer	69	67	71	73	280
M Mouland	70	68	71	71	280
D Pruitt	69	72	71	68	280
B Zabriski	76	66	70	68	280

1988

NAME	SCORE				
P Baker	68	68	66	69	271
N Faldo	68	68	66	69	271
(Baker won play-off)					
JM Olazabal	70	71	66	65	272
C Parry	68	68	69	67	272
M James	72	69	68	65	274
AWB Lyle	70	67	69	69	275
C O'Connor Jr	70	65	71	70	276
H Clark	72	70	68	67	277
E Dussart	68	71	69	69	277
D Smyth	70	70	65	72	277
M McNulty	68	68	68	73	277

1989

NAME	SCORE				
G Brand Jr	64	72	72	64	272
D Cooper	67	66	68	72	273
M Mackenzie	66	68	71	69	274
JM Canizares	65	72	70	69	276
C Parry	68	72	67	70	277
H Clark	69	67	69	72	277
I Mosey	69	67	69	72	277
J Bland	67	68	70	72	277
P Fowler	69	71	70	68	278
B Hughes	62	71	71	74	278

1990 *at St Mellion, Cornwall*

NAME	SCORE				
JM Olazabal	69	68	69	73	279
I Woosnam	69	69	69	73	280
B Langer	72	72	68	70	282
M McNulty	68	68	73	74	283
J Bland	68	71	75	72	286

NAME	SCORE				
M Harwood	71	68	75	72	286
P Walton	70	71	75	70	286
R Rafferty	62	72	74	74	287
C Montgomerie	69	72	70	76	287
G Brand Jr	72	71	71	73	287
A Oldcorn	75	65	72	75	287

Benson and Hedges Trophy

1988 *at Moralejo, Madrid*

NAME	SCORE
M McNulty and ML de Lorenzi Taya	276
JM Canizares and T Abitbol	277
W Longmuir and F Descampe	278
A Stubbs and S Strudwick	278
D Cooper and P Conley	280
A Sherborne and K Douglas	280
M Pinero and M Figueras-Dotti	282
J Rivero and X Wunsch-Ruiz	282
M Lanner and M Wennersten From	282
S Bishop and D Dowling	284

NAME	SCORE				
D Jones and C Panton	71	72	71	72	286
JM Canizares and T Abitbol	72	73	68	73	286
M Pinero and M Figueras-Dotti	72	70	70	74	286
D Cooper and P Conley	71	71	74	71	287
M Mouland and A Nicholas	71	71	73	72	287
D Llewellyn and M Walker	68	69	74	76	287

1990 *at El Bosque, Valencia*

NAME	SCORE				
JM Canizares and T Abitbol	66	67	66	68	267
M Mouland and A Nicholas	65	66	69	69	269
BW Barnes and L Davies	67	67	71	66	271
GJ Brand and J Hill	68	67	66	71	272
O Sellberg and F Descampe	69	64	65	74	272
A Forsbrand and C Soules	66	71	67	69	273
M Pinero and M Figueras-Dotti	65	72	67	70	274
J Quiros and K Lunn	71	71	64	71	277
A Charnley and D Reid	66	70	69	72	277
J Hawksworth and A Oxenstierna	68	72	66	72	278

1989 *at Aloha, Marbella*

NAME	SCORE				
MA Jimenez and X Wunsch-Ruiz	70	68	71	72	281
SC Mason and G Stewart	67	69	71	76	283
GJ Brand and F Descampe	69	71	72	72	284
A Sherborne and K Douglas	74	70	74	68	286
I Mosey and P Gonzalez	72	70	73	71	286

El Bosque Open

1990 *at El Bosque, Valencia*

NAME	SCORE				
V Singh	66	69	74	69	278
C Williams	68	71	70	71	280
R Boxall	70	69	70	71	280
J Rystrom	72	72	69	68	281
B Marchbank	69	69	75	68	281

NAME	SCORE				
P Parkin	68	72	71	71	282
A Charnley	72	72	67	71	282
MA Jimenez	74	70	66	72	282
J Hawksworth	73	72	68	69	282
J Rivero	73	70	68	72	283
M Clayton	71	69	70	73	283

BMW International Open

at Nord-Eichenried, Munich

1989

NAME	SCORE				
D Feherty	62	66	68	73	269
F Couples	68	69	67	70	274
P Walton	67	70	68	70	275
E Darcy	70	69	70	67	276
M Mouland	70	70	68	69	277
M Harwood	70	71	66	70	277
GJ Brand	68	68	70	72	278
T Purtzer	69	69	69	71	278
D Love III	65	73	70	71	279
O Sellberg	66	71	70	72	279

1990

NAME	SCORE				
P Azinger	63	73	73	68	277
D Feherty	62	72	71	72	277
P O'Malley	70	71	71	66	278
R Claydon	66	76	67	70	279
J Haas	73	70	68	69	280
DA Russell	66	79	69	67	281
JM Olazabal	70	73	69	69	281
V Singh	66	81	69	66	282
M Clayton	69	75	69	69	282
P Walton	71	73	71	67	282
J Parnevik	71	71	70	70	282

Car Care Plan International

1982   *at Moor Allerton, Leeds*

NAME	SCORE				
B Waites	68	69	66	73	276
P Hoad	70	69	69	69	277
BW Barnes	68	72	68	69	277
S Ballesteros	70	70	67	71	278
B Gallacher	70	68	69	72	279
J O'Leary	72	74	69	65	280
N Faldo	72	70	72	66	280
M Calero	68	66	76	70	280
AWB Lyle	72	73	69	68	282
G Norman	72	68	73	69	282
K Brown	69	67	71	75	282

NAME	SCORE				
R Chapman	69	69	65	72	275
B Gallacher	70	66	71	69	276
R Rafferty	70	69	71	67	277
C O'Connor Jr	67	70	72	68	277
S Torrance	70	68	70	69	277
D Frost	66	69	67	75	277

1983   *at Sand Moor, Leeds*

NAME	SCORE				
N Faldo	67	68	68	69	272
B Waites	67	68	71	67	273
H Clark	65	68	70	70	273
AWB Lyle	70	66	69	69	274
M Pinero	69	68	72	66	275

1984   *at Sand Moor, Leeds*

NAME	SCORE				
N Faldo	69	70	66	71	276
H Clark	68	68	69	72	277
J Rivero	72	67	70	69	278
B Waites	71	71	68	69	279
D Smyth	74	69	69	68	280
AWB Lyle	69	72	66	73	280
K Brown	70	71	73	67	281
E Darcy	69	73	70	72	282
M Pinero	72	68	74	69	283
D Frost	71	70	73	69	283
W Humphreys	71	72	71	69	283
C O'Connor Jr	69	74	70	70	283

1985 *at Moortown, Leeds*

NAME	SCORE				
DJ Russell	71	67	68	71	277
SC Mason	74	69	69	66	278
W Riley	70	72	64	73	279
J Anderson	75	67	69	68	279
AWB Lyle	69	67	71	72	279
I Woosnam	69	70	72	69	280
D Feherty	71	70	68	72	281
S Torrance	69	70	72	71	282
P Carrigill	71	72	70	69	282
T Johnstone	70	73	73	67	283
C O'Connor Jr	69	70	69	75	283
D Smyth	69	68	74	72	283

1986 *at Moortown, Leeds*

NAME	SCORE				
M Mouland	72	71	65	64	272
A Forsbrand	69	70	68	66	273
S Torrance	68	72	67	67	274
V Somers	70	67	69	69	275
JM Canizares	69	68	70	69	276
SC Mason	70	71	67	69	277
J Quiros	68	71	73	65	277
H Baiocchi	72	70	69	66	277
D Edwards	69	71	69	69	278
M James	69	72	67	70	278
M Clayton	70	71	67	70	278
L Stephen	65	67	76	70	278
V Fernandez	70	68	72	68	278

Cannes Open
at Cannes Mougins

1984

NAME	SCORE				
D Frost	72	72	68	68	280
J Morgan	65	75	73	69	282
G Brand Jr	70	70	72	70	282
P Teravainen	75	68	72	68	283
M King	73	74	69	68	284
S Bishop	70	70	73	71	284
E Polland	71	72	69	72	284

1985

NAME	SCORE				
R Lee	71	68	72	69	280
D Llewellyn	71	69	72	68	280
M Persson	70	74	70	67	281
M Pinero	71	70	70	70	281
R Rafferty	68	77	72	67	284
J Rivero	75	66	70	73	284
G Brand Jr	71	72	74	68	285
R Chapman	73	70	71	71	285
P Way	73	71	72	70	286
N Hansen	74	73	68	71	286

1986

NAME	SCORE				
J Bland	68	71	70	67	276
S Ballesteros	70	69	68	73	280
N Hansen	73	68	69	72	282
D Smyth	70	71	70	72	283
M Pinero	74	71	73	66	284
I Woosnam	70	72	69	73	284
M Mouland	75	73	67	70	285
G Brand Jr	74	70	70	71	285
H Clark	75	71	72	68	286
A Forsbrand	72	76	67	71	286
M Roe	70	74	70	72	286

1987

NAME	SCORE				
S Ballesteros	69	70	68	68	275
I Woosnam	73	64	68	70	275
(Ballesteros won play-off)					
M McNulty	68	74	70	71	283
P Walton	72	69	69	75	285
G Brand Jr	69	74	72	71	286

NAME	SCORE				
M Adcock	73	68	73	73	287
M Martin	70	73	73	71	287
GJ Brand	74	72	70	72	288
D Jones	71	70	76	71	288
C Moody	73	68	76	71	288
M Persson	71	72	72	73	288
G Ralph	73	70	77	68	288
S Torrance	72	70	72	74	288

1988

NAME	SCORE				
M McNulty	72	71	70	66	279
R Commans	70	68	72	72	282
J Sindelar	69	74	69	70	282
D Durnian	72	69	74	70	285
A Charnley	71	75	74	66	286
J Rutledge	72	75	71	68	286
H Clark	70	72	73	72	287
P Walton	71	73	68	76	288
JM Olazabal	74	69	72	73	288
O Sellberg	71	77	70	70	288
J Anglada	72	74	71	71	288

1989

NAME	SCORE			
P Broadhurst	65	70	72	207
J Heggarty	69	72	67	208

NAME	SCORE			
B Ogle	71	68	69	208
P Senior	70	66	72	208
R Rafferty	72	67	70	209
J van de Velde	71	69	70	210
A Charnley	71	68	71	210
M McNulty	71	70	69	210
D Cooper	73	64	73	210
D Smyth	70	72	69	211
J Rivero	72	68	71	211
M Calero	70	66	75	211
P Walton	74	71	66	211
M Persson	68	68	75	211

1990

NAME	SCORE				
M McNulty	69	71	69	71	280
R Rafferty	73	67	72	69	281
M Roe	72	71	66	73	282
V Singh	69	72	74	69	284
M O'Meara	70	70	75	69	284
J Parnevik	69	68	73	74	284
A Sorensen	68	68	75	73	284
M Persson	70	74	68	73	285
I Woosnam	69	72	67	77	285
H Clark	72	68	73	72	285

Desert Classic
at Dubai

1989

NAME	SCORE				
M James	69	68	72	68	277
P O'Malley	71	68	68	70	277
(James won play-off)					
P Broadhurst	72	66	70	72	280
B Ogle	77	69	67	69	282
M Persson	67	72	72	72	283
E Dussart	71	71	72	70	284
B Lane	71	73	73	67	284
M Miller	72	74	67	71	284
J Rutledge	73	70	70	71	284
S Torrance	70	71	71	72	284

1990

NAME	SCORE				
E Darcy	64	68	75	69	276
D Feherty	73	69	70	68	280
S Ballesteros	72	69	71	70	282
D Smyth	68	71	74	69	282
D Gilford	70	73	69	72	284
P Fowler	72	70	73	70	285
S Richardson	72	70	72	71	285
D Durnian	72	67	73	73	285
B Ogle	71	73	75	67	286
N Faldo	72	73	72	69	286
M McNulty	69	74	71	72	286
P O'Malley	68	70	77	71	286
W Longmuir	70	69	74	73	286

Dunhill British Masters
at Woburn, Bedfordshire

1985

NAME	SCORE				
L Trevino	74	68	69	67	278
R Davis	73	67	68	73	281
S Ballesteros	71	68	74	70	283
N Faldo	72	73	69	69	283
P Way	69	71	71	71	283
I Baker-Finch	70	70	72	73	285
R Chapman	70	68	75	72	285
V Fernandez	69	72	72	73	286
H Baiocchi	74	70	73	69	286
B Langer	72	74	71	70	287
E Darcy	76	71	69	71	287
GJ Brand	77	69	66	75	287

1986

NAME	SCORE				
S Ballesteros	67	68	70	70	275
G Brand Jr	70	71	69	67	277
B Langer	68	68	72	70	278
R Lee	69	65	73	71	278
B Marchbank	73	70	68	70	281
C O'Connor Jr	68	73	69	71	281
R Hartmann	66	72	70	73	281
A Chandler	72	70	69	71	282
S Torrance	70	73	68	72	283
N Faldo	73	71	72	68	283
M McNulty	71	70	73	69	283
J Rivero	70	73	74	66	283

1987

NAME	SCORE				
M McNulty	71	65	71	67	274
I Woosnam	67	68	72	68	275
H Baiocchi	67	70	72	69	278
C O'Connor Jr	71	66	71	70	278
J Rivero	74	67	71	68	280
M Clayton	72	69	71	69	281
R Davis	72	72	68	69	281
K Brown	71	69	71	71	282
E Darcy	70	66	77	69	282
B Marchbank	70	73	71	68	282

1988

NAME	SCORE				
AWB Lyle	66	68	68	71	273
N Faldo	72	67	67	69	275
M McNulty	69	69	72	65	275
JM Olazabal	69	68	71	68	276
R Rafferty	72	67	71	69	279
M James	68	75	71	67	281
P Walton	73	68	71	69	281
JM Canizares	74	71	69	68	282
K Brown	74	67	74	68	283
R Davis	70	71	70	72	283
R Shearer	70	71	71	71	283
L Trevino	69	75	70	69	283

1989

NAME	SCORE				
N Faldo	71	65	65	66	267
R Rafferty	70	65	67	69	271
C O'Connor Jr	69	66	73	68	276
O Sellberg	71	66	70	69	276
M Harwood	69	70	66	71	276
I Woosnam	71	70	70	66	277
R Hartmann	70	69	71	67	277
M Smith	71	69	66	71	277
M James	69	68	70	71	278
P Senior	74	66	66	72	278
P Mitchell	67	73	64	74	278

1990

NAME	SCORE				
M James	70	67	66	67	270
D Feherty	65	70	68	69	272
SC Mason	69	70	68	67	274
B Ogle	70	65	68	73	276
M McNulty	68	70	72	66	276
J Hawkes	69	69	72	66	276
V Singh	72	67	71	68	278
V Fernandez	69	71	69	70	279
C Parry	71	69	69	70	279
B Lane	70	69	75	65	279
W Longmuir	67	67	73	72	279
T Johnstone	71	68	72	68	279
P Senior	68	69	75	67	279
R Chapman	67	70	75	67	279

Dutch Open

1972   *at Haagsche, Wassenaar*

NAME	SCORE				
J Newton	64	75	69	69	277
P Oosterhuis	64	70	73	71	278
M Gregson	65	73	70	70	278
GB Wolstenholme	69	72	70	70	281
T Westbrook	71	72	69	70	282
BGC Huggett	66	72	74	70	282
PJ Butler	72	74	67	72	285
P Townsend	73	73	72	68	286
D Vaughan	70	73	73	70	286
NC Coles	77	70	68	71	286
S Rolley	70	72	70	74	286

1973   *at Haagsche, Wassenaar*

NAME	SCORE				
D McClelland	72	67	72	68	279
P Oosterhuis	72	74	70	64	280
D Swaelens	75	67	69	70	281
E Polland	74	71	67	70	282
H Jackson	72	72	69	71	284
D Hayes	72	73	69	70	284
A Gallardo	74	67	69	75	285
C O'Connor	73	73	70	69	285
B Dassu	73	71	72	70	286
J Newton	74	68	71	74	287
D Ingram	72	73	70	72	287
BW Barnes	69	71	75	72	287
PJ Butler	75	77	70	65	287

1974   *at Hilversum*

NAME	SCORE			
BW Barnes	71	69	71	211
P Oosterhuis	73	71	72	216
S Owen	73	70	73	216
E Polland	71	72	73	216
D Hayes	75	69	74	218
S Hobday	72	69	77	218
R Carrasco	76	70	73	219
D Small	73	73	73	219
D Swaelens	71	74	74	219
D Jones	73	72	74	219
P Wilcock	75	69	75	219

1975   *at Hilversum*

NAME	SCORE				
H Baiocchi	71	72	69	67	279
D Hayes	70	70	67	74	281
S Hobday	72	68	73	68	281
G Kelley	73	71	72	67	283
P Townsend	69	75	72	67	283
G Marsh	72	69	71	71	283
C DeFoy	71	69	73	71	284
J Gallardo	70	76	68	70	284
G Koch	67	75	73	70	285
MF Foster	72	73	72	70	287
R Gilder	74	70	72	71	287
J O'Leary	71	69	76	71	287
M Pinero	70	71	75	71	287
V Fernandez	71	70	72	74	287

1976   *at Kennemer*

NAME	SCORE				
S Ballesteros	65	73	68	69	275
H Clark	66	71	70	76	283
M Krantz	72	71	72	69	284
PJ Butler	69	67	78	71	285
E Polland	71	72	71	71	285
V Fernandez	69	72	72	72	285
S Hobday	77	69	67	72	285
D Vaughan	70	72	69	74	285
B Gallacher	71	74	71	70	286
T Horton	72	68	71	75	286

1977   *at Kennemer*

NAME	SCORE				
B Byman	69	70	68	71	278
H Baiocchi	70	67	70	72	279
B Risch	67	72	70	71	280
P Toussaint	72	70	70	69	281
K-H Gogele	70	68	71	73	282
P Townsend	69	70	73	70	282
E Darcy	74	67	69	73	283
M James	72	72	70	70	284
P Mateer	75	67	71	71	284
M Bembridge	71	72	69	73	285
M Gregson	74	71	71	69	285
J Bland	68	75	70	72	285

1978   *at Noordwijk*

NAME	SCORE			
B Byman	74	72	68	214
N Price	71	74	70	215
N Ratcliffe	72	77	67	216
A Garrido	73	74	72	219
J Bland	71	74	74	219
NC Coles	73	78	69	220
P Elson	76	72	72	220
SC Mason	71	73	77	221
C O'Connor Jr	70	78	74	222
M Pinero	74	74	74	222

1979   *at Noordwijk*

NAME	SCORE				
G Marsh	71	70	74	70	285
M Gregson	72	71	69	74	286
A Garrido	73	71	70	72	286
M Pinero	70	73	73	71	287
J Bland	72	66	72	77	287
D Watson	74	74	68	72	288
R Davis	72	72	72	72	288
M King	70	72	74	72	288
N Job	71	71	72	74	288
R Verwey	73	70	74	72	289
G Parslow	74	73	66	76	289

1980   *at Hilversum*

NAME	SCORE				
S Ballesteros	69	75	65	71	280
AWB Lyle	70	70	72	71	283
S Ginn	72	73	71	69	285
S Torrance	72	67	73	74	286
M Krantz	71	74	72	69	286
I Mosey	71	74	70	72	287
BW Barnes	75	71	72	70	288
RJ Charles	76	72	71	70	289
A Charnley	70	76	71	72	289
E Darcy	82	69	67	71	289
B Langer	75	73	72	69	289

1981   *at Haagsche, Wassenaar*

NAME	SCORE				
H Henning	71	68	70	71	280
R Floyd	69	73	69	70	281
N Price	67	68	70	76	281
K Brown	71	70	74	68	283

NAME	SCORE				
S Torrance	71	70	69	73	283
T Sieckmann	68	71	71	73	283
J Hall	69	68	75	73	285
T Gale	71	74	73	68	286
J Bland	72	70	74	70	286
C Moody	71	73	72	70	286
F Molina	69	70	74	73	286

1982   *at De Pan, Utrecht*

NAME	SCORE				
P Way	71	73	67	65	276
D Feherty	74	69	68	67	278
V Fernandez	72	69	69	68	278
E Polland	70	74	69	66	279
I Woosnam	70	70	73	66	279
J Hawkes	72	70	67	71	280
V Somers	71	71	69	70	281
G Brand Jr	70	75	69	68	282
J Dorrestein	72	71	70	69	282
H Clark	71	71	69	72	283
M Garcia	74	68	69	72	283
M Miller	70	65	73	75	283

1983   *at Kennemer*

NAME	SCORE				
K Brown	66	73	66	69	274
JM Canizares	69	73	68	65	275
V Somers	67	70	68	70	275
W Grady	65	70	72	72	279
G Ralph	66	65	74	74	279
M McLean	70	72	68	70	280
P Way	68	69	71	72	280
B Gallacher	71	71	70	69	281
P Harrison	72	71	68	70	281
T Horton	68	76	71	66	281

1984   *at Rosendaelsche, Arnhem*

NAME	SCORE				
B Langer	64	68	69	74	275
G Marsh	72	66	69	72	279
L Trevino	74	69	67	70	280
P Way	67	74	73	66	280
J Bland	73	71	67	70	281
A Magee	72	70	70	69	281
J Miller	69	70	72	74	285
B Waites	72	68	70	75	285
D Frost	75	73	71	67	286
K Han	70	72	70	74	286

1985   *at Noordwijk*

NAME	SCORE				
G Marsh	68	68	73	73	282
B Langer	68	72	75	68	283
E Romero	69	71	78	67	285
C O'Connor Jr	70	71	76	68	285
D Feherty	69	69	74	73	285
H Baiocchi	75	69	74	68	286
S Torrance	69	71	73	73	286
G Turner	71	71	73	72	287
R Rafferty	71	74	70	73	288
C Strange	71	71	75	72	289

1986   *at Noordwijk*

NAME	SCORE				
S Ballesteros	69	63	71	68	271
J Rivero	72	66	69	72	279
V Fernandez	68	69	71	72	280
P Parkin	71	74	73	72	280
I Baker-Finch	72	66	71	72	281
G Brand Jr	71	67	69	74	281
B Marchbank	73	66	72	70	281
M Pinero	70	66	71	74	281
D Smyth	75	63	73	70	281
G Marsh	72	66	75	69	282

1987   *at Hilversum*

NAME	SCORE				
G Brand Jr	69	67	67	69	272
DA Russell	66	68	73	66	273
M Persson	70	68	68	68	274
A Garrido	70	69	67	69	275
JM Olazabal	69	69	68	69	275
E Darcy	69	67	71	69	276
M Pinero	68	70	74	64	276
M Roe	68	66	72	70	276
S Ballesteros	67	72	68	70	277
D Feherty	65	72	70	70	277
B Malley	66	73	72	66	277

1988   *at Hilversum*

NAME	SCORE				
M Mouland	72	68	69	65	274
D Smyth	71	67	67	70	275
SC Mason	69	69	72	66	276
T Johnstone	68	66	68	74	276
MA Martin	71	72	68	66	277
JM Olazabal	69	67	71	71	278
C Parry	70	70	67	71	278
A Murray	65	76	67	71	279
D Williams	68	71	68	72	279
M McNulty	70	69	67	73	279

1989   *at Kennemer*

NAME	SCORE				
JM Olazabal	67	66	68	76	277
R Chapman	70	67	71	69	277
R Rafferty	72	66	66	73	277
(Olazabal won play-off)					
J Parnevik	69	67	72	70	278
G Brand Jr	65	68	74	72	279
S Torrance	69	70	72	69	280
C Parry	69	65	70	76	280
D Smyth	71	68	70	72	281
MA Martin	68	71	71	71	281
D Feherty	72	69	68	72	281

1990   *at Kennemer*

NAME	SCORE				
S McAllister	69	67	68	70	274
R Chapman	73	68	66	71	278
JM Olazabal	73	70	65	71	279
C Montgomerie	71	68	73	68	280
D Mijovic	71	70	71	68	280
P Baker	69	73	71	68	281
V Fernandez	72	69	69	71	281
P McWhinney	76	69	67	69	281
M Poxon	71	69	68	73	281
J Spence	71	72	69	69	281

English Open Championship

1988 *at Birkdale*

NAME	SCORE				
H Clark	72	71	67	69	279
P Baker	73	70	69	70	282
D Smyth	74	65	70	74	283
P McWhinney	75	67	74	67	283
S McAllister	73	69	73	69	284
MA Martin	74	71	72	67	284
DJ Russell	74	70	70	71	285
A Charnley	74	73	69	70	286
W Longmuir	74	70	72	70	286
R Boxall	74	71	76	66	287
M Mouland	75	73	70	69	287
M James	74	68	75	70	287

1989 *at The Belfry*

NAME	SCORE				
M James	72	70	69	68	279
E Darcy	70	71	67	72	280
C Parry	66	74	73	67	280
S Torrance	66	73	70	71	280
B Norton	74	70	67	71	282
J Bland	69	70	70	73	282

NAME	SCORE				
M Poxon	69	72	69	73	283
P Teravainen	71	75	69	68	283
C O'Connor Jr	71	73	68	71	283
J Davila	68	75	73	68	284
R Rafferty	72	67	73	72	284
M Lanner	72	71	69	72	284
J Hawkes	67	71	73	73	284
R Chapman	73	72	73	66	284
S Tinning	66	78	71	69	284
R Claydon (Am)	72	71	71	70	284

1990 *at The Belfry*

NAME	SCORE				
M James	76	68	65	75	284
S Torrance	75	67	69	73	284
(James won play-off)					
D Feherty	73	75	69	68	285
S Ballesteros	72	72	68	75	287
D Cooper	77	73	71	67	288
S McAllister	74	74	72	68	288
H Clark	76	73	69	70	288
M Harwood	74	73	69	72	288
G Brand Jr	71	75	72	71	289
S Richardson	71	76	67	75	289

The Equity & Law Challenge

at Royal Mid-Surrey

1987

NAME	BIRDIES	EAGLES	POINTS	PAR
B Lane	13	1	15	16
W Malley	12	1	14	15
NC Coles	12		12	19
W Longmuir	12		12	18
R Hartmann	11		11	21
A Charnley	11		11	20
M Roe	9	1	11	20
M Allen	9	1	11	19
DJ Russell	10		10	20
P Walton	8	1	10	19

1988

NAME	BIRDIES	EAGLES	POINTS	PAR
R Rafferty	19	1	21	31
B Lane	18	1	20	31
D Cooper	20		20	25
M Roe	19		19	34
E Romero	19		19	31
D Durnian	17	1	19	29
SC Mason	18		18	32
R Drummond	16	1	18	30
JM Olazabal	16		16	33
S Bennett	14	1	16	33

1989

NAME	BIRDIES	EAGLES	POINTS	PAR
B Ogle	23	1	25	24
C Montgomerie	21		21	31
D Feherty	20		20	29
R Boxall	20		20	24
P Senior	15	2	19	31
SC Mason	19		19	27
M Harwood	16	1	18	37
A Charnley	18		18	27

1990

NAME	BIRDIES	EAGLES	POINTS	PAR
B Marchbank	22		22	23
D Cooper	21		21	29
P Teravainen	19	1	21	29
B Ogle	17	1	19	27
P Broadhurst	18		18	32
P Parkin	14	2	18	29
V Singh	13	2	17	34
M Lanner	15	1	17	31
M McLean	17		17	30
GJ Brand	17		17	17

Europcar Cup

1988   *at Biarritz*

POSITION		SCORE
1	Sweden (M Lanner, J Rystrom, J Parnevik, M Persson)	810
2	Spain (A Garrido, I Gervas, J Anglada, MA Martin)	817
3	England (D Cooper, G Ralph, A Charnley, D Williams)	820
	Ireland (D Jones, J Heggarty, M Sludds, P Walton)	820
5	France	828
6	Wales (P Thomas, M Litton, G Davies, H Davies-Thomas)	830
7	Italy	832
8	West Germany	838
9	Scotland (W Longmuir, R Drummond, W McColl, M Miller)	840

(4 rounds of stroke play, the best 3 scores to count towards team total)

European Open

1978   *at Walton Heath*

NAME	SCORE				
R Wadkins	71	72	72	68	283
B Gallacher	71	71	71	70	283
G Morgan	70	73	71	69	283
(Wadkins won play-off)					
M McLendon	71	71	71	71	284
N Faldo	68	70	75	71	284
M Gregson	72	70	70	72	284
G Norman	69	72	69	74	284
J McGee	72	75	69	69	285
BW Barnes	72	73	73	68	286
E Sneed	71	75	72	68	286
NC Coles	70	73	72	71	286

1979   *at Ailsa Course, Turnberry*

NAME	SCORE				
AWB Lyle	71	67	72	65	275
D Hayes	72	72	70	68	282
P Townsend	72	68	70	72	282
T Horton	74	72	71	66	283
NC Coles	73	70	66	74	283
S Torrance	71	72	71	70	284
S Ballesteros	69	69	75	71	284
M James	73	72	64	75	284
H Clark	74	71	67	73	285
JM Canizares	70	70	72	73	285

1980 *at Walton Heath*

NAME	SCORE				
T Kite	71	67	71	75	284
L Thompson	72	70	72	71	285
L Hinkle	69	65	74	77	285
D Hayes	73	73	69	71	286
D Smyth	72	72	73	70	287
M James	69	71	77	70	287
S Torrance	71	71	73	72	287
B Langer	71	73	70	73	287
B Gallacher	69	73	71	74	287
G Norman	72	73	74	69	288

1981 *at Hoylake*

NAME	SCORE				
G Marsh	67	72	68	68	275
S Ballesteros	68	68	67	74	277
N Job	71	70	69	69	279
AWB Lyle	72	69	68	70	279
G Norman	66	71	71	71	279
B Waites	73	71	64	71	279
D Smyth	71	67	69	73	280
I Mosey	76	67	68	71	282
M King	71	71	72	69	283
B Langer	73	71	69	70	283
BW Barnes	68	75	69	71	283
B Gallacher	68	69	73	73	283

1982 *at Sunningdale*

NAME	SCORE				
M Pinero	68	68	67	63	266
S Torrance	67	70	64	67	268
G Norman	64	70	69	67	270
AWB Lyle	68	66	67	69	270
NC Coles	69	68	70	64	271
J Bland	68	72	66	67	273
V Fernandez	70	71	69	66	276
J O'Leary	69	69	69	69	276
R Davis	69	67	74	67	277
N Faldo	70	72	67	68	277

1983 *at Sunningdale*

NAME	SCORE				
I Aoki	65	70	70	69	274
S Ballesteros	68	75	69	64	276
SC Mason	69	73	66	68	276
N Faldo	68	69	68	71	276

NAME	SCORE				
G Norman	71	72	68	68	277
S Torrance	68	73	68	68	277
M Pinero	70	73	70	65	278
JM Canizares	70	70	70	68	278
J Bland	69	67	71	71	278
D Frost	67	73	72	68	280
M King	68	68	73	71	280

1984 *at Sunningdale*

NAME	SCORE				
G Brand Jr	67	66	73	74	270
N Ratcliffe	67	74	67	66	273
S Ballesteros	68	68	69	70	273
R Boxall	71	69	67	67	274
H Clark	66	65	72	71	274
L Wadkins	69	67	70	70	276
K Waters	72	69	68	68	277
B Gallacher	68	69	68	72	277
RJ Charles	73	67	70	68	278
M Pinero	69	69	71	69	278

1985 *at Sunningdale*

NAME	SCORE				
B Langer	66	72	64	67	269
J O'Leary	68	69	67	68	272
H Clark	66	72	68	67	273
D Smyth	69	67	69	68	273
G Brand Jr	69	67	66	71	273
I Woosnam	71	71	67	65	274
JM Canizares	66	71	66	72	275
S Ballesteros	70	68	69	68	275
T Nakajima	66	71	69	69	275
B Gallacher	68	68	68	71	275

1986 *at Sunningdale*

NAME	SCORE				
G Norman	67	67	69	66	269
K Brown	67	67	68	67	269
(Norman won play-off)					
B Langer	69	68	66	68	271
S Ballesteros	64	72	72	65	273
N Faldo	62	72	71	68	273
JM Olazabal	68	67	72	66	273
R Davis	71	67	69	67	274
P Fowler	65	68	73	68	274
J Bland	68	72	67	68	275
B Gallacher	65	68	73	69	275
MA Martin	67	73	67	68	275

1987   *at Walton Heath*

NAME	SCORE				
P Way	70	71	71	67	279
J Bland	69	72	70	70	281
G Brand Jr	70	69	72	70	281
C O'Connor Jr	70	70	72	70	282
I Woosnam	73	71	74	65	283
NC Coles	71	70	75	68	284
M Mouland	71	72	72	69	284
G Norman	71	72	69	72	284
R Rafferty	74	70	69	71	284
JM Canizares	67	74	78	66	285
R Davis	69	71	72	73	285
N Faldo	73	73	70	69	285
B Langer	70	67	73	75	285
R Lee	68	72	76	69	285
W Westner	72	73	73	67	285

1988   *at Walton Heath*

NAME	SCORE				
I Woosnam	65	66	64	65	260
N Faldo	66	65	66	66	263
JM Olazabal	65	70	64	67	266
AWB Lyle	69	65	67	65	266
M James	66	70	63	67	266
G Brand Jr	65	70	67	65	267
C Parry	68	70	67	63	268
J Rivero	68	65	66	70	269
B Ogle	71	68	66	65	270
P Baker	67	68	66	69	270

1989   *at Walton Heath*

NAME	SCORE				
A Murray	66	68	71	72	277
F Nobilo	70	69	69	70	278
S Torrance	70	71	69	70	280
C Parry	73	72	70	66	281
I Woosnam	71	68	70	72	281
R Claydon	70	68	71	74	283
R Drummond	70	69	71	73	283
AWB Lyle	69	74	71	70	284
R Davis	69	73	72	70	284
D Feherty	72	71	71	70	284

1990   *at Sunningdale*

NAME	SCORE				
P Senior	67	68	66	66	267
I Woosnam	65	68	68	67	268
JM Canizares	69	69	63	68	269
T Simpson	67	72	64	67	270
JM Olazabal	65	69	70	66	270
N Faldo	68	70	64	68	270
GJ Brand	70	65	65	70	270
E Romero	70	65	69	67	271
D Feherty	73	65	66	68	272
J Heggarty	72	70	66	64	272

French Open

1972   *at La Nivelle and Biarritz*

NAME	SCORE				
B Jaeckel	68	67	63	67	265
CA Clark	67	67	66	65	265
(Jaeckel won play-off)					
J Garaialde	72	64	65	67	268
R Fidler	71	68	66	64	269
P Oosterhuis	65	67	68	69	269
Hsieh Min-Nan	67	70	63	69	269
BW Barnes	67	68	64	70	269
R Bernardini	67	71	69	63	270
GL Hunt	71	68	66	65	270
V Barrios	72	65	66	67	270

1973   *at La Foret and La Vallée, Paris*

NAME	SCORE				
P Oosterhuis	75	69	68	68	280
A Jacklin	72	68	70	71	281
BW Barnes	75	75	67	68	285
M Bembridge	72	73	71	69	285
H Baiocchi	73	69	71	72	285
JM Canizares	75	70	70	72	287
D Swaelens	72	73	72	71	288
B Hunt	70	70	74	74	288
J Garaialde	72	74	73	70	289
P Wilcock	74	73	72	70	289
R Cerrudo	73	72	69	75	289

1974   *at Chantilly, Paris*

NAME	SCORE				
P Oosterhuis	71	72	68	73	284
P Townsend	72	73	69	72	286
V Fernandez	71	68	74	75	288
D Swaelens	73	72	73	70	288
T Horton	70	72	70	78	290
A Jacklin	78	69	69	74	290
D Chillas	71	73	72	74	290
A Brooks	74	73	70	73	290
R Bernardini	73	71	73	73	290
W Tape	75	74	69	72	290
P Dawson	75	73	72	70	290

1975   *at La Boulie, Paris*

NAME	SCORE				
BW Barnes	68	69	71	73	281
J O'Leary	68	69	75	71	283
NC Coles	64	71	75	73	283
D Hayes	71	71	68	73	283
E Darcy	72	69	71	71	283
N Wood	70	68	69	77	284
J Fourie	70	70	69	75	284
A Henning	69	71	72	72	284
A Jacklin	75	68	71	71	285
V Fernandez	70	70	71	74	285
D Chillas	66	72	72	75	285

1976   *at Le Touquet*

NAME	SCORE				
V Tshabalala	69	70	66	67	272
S Balbuena	67	66	69	72	274
S Torrance	69	74	63	70	276
NC Coles	69	69	68	70	276
S Hobday	69	67	69	71	276
F Abreu	68	68	69	72	277
A Oosthuizen	70	67	68	72	277
M Pinero	69	68	75	67	279
S Ballesteros	71	66	73	69	279
A Garrido	67	71	71	70	279
H Baiocchi	70	71	68	70	279
J Gallardo	70	71	67	71	279
M King	70	71	66	72	279
B Burgess	69	70	67	73	279
S Owen	70	66	69	74	279

1977   *at Le Touquet*

NAME	SCORE				
S Ballesteros	69	70	71	72	282
A Garrido	71	68	73	73	285
I Stanley	70	71	72	72	285
J Bland	71	74	69	71	285
M Pinero	69	72	70	74	285
H Baiocchi	70	74	73	71	288
M King	70	71	72	75	288
D Ingram	76	73	72	68	289
E Polland	71	71	74	73	289
SC Mason	71	70	72	76	289

1978   *at La Baule*

NAME	SCORE				
D Hayes	66	69	67	67	269
S Ballesteros	70	68	69	73	280
S Hobday	73	75	70	65	283
M James	73	69	68	73	283
K Brown	71	70	68	74	283
G Cullen	74	68	69	72	283
E Darcy	68	72	73	71	284
I Stanley	74	73	66	69	284
P Elson	69	73	71	72	285
R Davis	74	69	68	75	286

1979   *at Lyon*

NAME	SCORE				
B Gallacher	71	69	74	70	284
W Milne	76	70	67	72	285
S Ballesteros	73	74	71	68	286
H Baiocchi	73	69	69	75	286
W Longmuir	71	69	78	70	288
N Faldo	72	72	73	71	288
D Chillas	76	72	68	72	288
E Darcy	74	69	71	75	289
D Hayes	73	74	73	70	290
G Cullen	74	70	75	71	290
N Ratcliffe	75	72	71	72	290
A Jacklin	70	70	77	73	290
G Player	75	68	73	74	290

1980   *at St Cloud, Paris*

NAME	SCORE				
G Norman	67	66	68	67	268
I Mosey	66	72	71	69	278
AWB Lyle	69	69	73	68	279
G Cullen	72	71	71	66	280
BW Barnes	69	75	70	67	281
D Watson	68	71	71	71	281
S Ginn	70	71	69	71	281
P Townsend	71	72	70	69	282
M Ballesteros	69	69	73	71	282
M Bembridge	67	66	72	77	282

1981   *at St Germain, Paris*

NAME	SCORE				
AWB Lyle	70	66	67	67	270
B Langer	69	69	66	70	274
H Clark	71	69	70	66	276
S Ballesteros	72	67	68	69	276
S Torrance	68	71	68	70	277
J Anglada	70	70	71	67	278
M King	69	70	71	68	278
B Waites	69	70	70	69	278
JM Canizares	68	70	71	69	278
N Job	69	66	71	72	278

1982   *at St Nom-la-Bretêche*

NAME	SCORE				
S Ballesteros	71	70	72	65	278
AWB Lyle	72	64	79	67	282
J Anglada	73	75	71	68	287
M James	68	73	75	71	287
T Horton	73	69	73	72	287
M Pinero	69	76	73	71	289
J Anderson	75	71	71	72	289
A Garrido	71	71	74	73	289
P Hoad	75	71	70	73	289
M Calero	73	70	74	73	290

1983   *at La Boulie, Paris*

NAME	SCORE				
N Faldo	69	67	72	69	277
JM Canizares	72	68	70	67	277
DJ Russell	71	72	65	69	277
(Faldo won play-off)					
S Ballesteros	68	68	71	71	278
D Frost	70	70	73	67	280
D Sheppard	71	72	70	67	280

NAME	SCORE				
SC Mason	68	66	70	76	280
M James	72	70	73	67	282
P Harrison	72	69	73	68	282
J Cabo	72	72	69	69	282
A Garrido	70	70	69	73	282

1984   *at St Cloud, Paris*

NAME	SCORE				
B Langer	68	71	67	64	270
J Rivero	67	69	68	67	271
N Faldo	71	68	66	68	273
AWB Lyle	67	70	71	68	276
SC Mason	72	67	68	69	276
M King	72	66	70	69	277
A Charnley	71	69	68	69	277
J Crow	68	70	66	73	277
M Montes	70	70	70	68	278
B Gallacher	69	74	65	70	278
J Bland	71	69	66	72	278
GJ Brand	68	69	68	73	278

1985   *at St Germain, Paris*

NAME	SCORE				
S Ballesteros	62	68	64	69	263
AWB Lyle	69	64	68	64	265
B Langer	68	69	68	67	272
E Romero	67	69	66	70	272
D Llewellyn	70	68	69	66	273
S Torrance	65	68	68	72	273
I Woosnam	68	69	72	65	274
R Rafferty	69	68	68	69	274
M Tapia	68	69	70	69	276
R Lee	66	66	74	70	276
SC Mason	67	64	75	70	276

1986   *at La Boulie, Paris*

NAME	SCORE				
S Ballesteros	65	66	69	69	269
V Fernandez	69	65	69	68	271
B Langer	71	65	68	68	272
N Faldo	66	70	68	70	274
R Hartmann	71	69	67	68	275
A Saavedra	71	68	66	70	275
R Stewart	68	66	77	65	276
M Roe	70	68	70	68	276
R Lee	68	70	66	72	276
W Westner	69	69	72	72	277

1987   *at St Cloud, Paris*

NAME	SCORE				
J Rivero	68	67	71	63	269
H Clark	64	68	69	69	270
H Baiocchi	68	66	66	71	271
S Torrance	66	67	65	73	271
N Faldo	70	66	64	72	272
D Feherty	68	70	68	66	272
JM Olazabal	73	68	66	65	272
O Sellberg	68	68	69	67	272
P Senior	69	69	67	67	272
J Sindelar	70	64	66	72	272

1989   *at Chantilly, Paris*

NAME	SCORE				
N Faldo	70	70	64	69	273
H Baiocchi	69	67	68	70	274
M Roe	69	68	67	70	274
B Langer	70	67	71	66	274
M James	70	70	66	69	275
I Woosnam	67	70	69	69	275
M Harwood	68	68	69	70	275
P Parkin	71	68	72	64	275
R Rafferty	69	67	66	74	276
M McNulty	70	70	70	66	276
G Brand Jr	69	67	69	71	276

1988   *at Chantilly, Paris*

NAME	SCORE				
N Faldo	71	67	68	68	274
D Durnian	65	68	69	74	276
W Riley	72	67	67	70	276
C Moore	71	69	69	69	278
D Feherty	72	70	66	70	278
P Senior	70	69	68	72	279
R Rafferty	73	69	74	64	280
D Williams	73	67	69	71	280
M MacKenzie	72	70	68	72	282
S Torrance	69	73	70	70	282
MA Martin	75	68	65	74	282
A Forsbrand	72	72	67	71	282

1990   *at Chantilly, Paris*

NAME	SCORE				
P Walton	73	66	67	69	275
B Langer	71	65	72	67	275
(Walton won play-off)					
E Romero	68	69	69	70	276
N Faldo	68	69	68	72	277
R Hartmann	68	65	73	71	277
R Rafferty	70	70	66	72	278
M McNulty	71	65	69	73	278
R Boxall	70	69	66	73	278
B Gallacher	70	65	72	71	278
M Mackenzie	70	70	70	68	278

German Masters

at Monsheim, Stuttgart

1987

NAME	SCORE				
AWB Lyle	73	69	70	66	278
B Langer	68	69	71	70	278
(Lyle won play-off)					
S Ballesteros	72	70	67	70	279
G Brand Jr	74	71	67	69	281
JM Olazabal	70	74	67	71	282
I Woosnam	79	68	69	66	282
G Norman	77	68	69	68	282
M Allen	75	68	71	69	283
A Charnley	70	71	71	71	283
P Fowler	73	71	70	69	283

1988

NAME	SCORE				
JM Olazabal	69	72	70	68	279
A Forsbrand	75	68	70	68	281
D Smyth	71	68	71	71	281
T Purtzer	68	72	72	70	282
M McNulty	69	72	71	70	282
R Rafferty	75	69	72	68	284
S Ballesteros	72	70	68	74	284
J Hawkes	78	70	69	68	285
J Rivero	71	71	72	71	285
P Walton	70	71	75	70	286
M Lanner	69	70	71	76	286

1989

NAME	SCORE				
B Langer	67	71	70	68	276
P Stewart	69	67	70	71	277
JM Olazabal	73	66	69	69	277
B Ogle	73	68	71	68	280
F Couples	69	72	73	66	280
D Cooper	70	72	71	68	281
S Bennett	72	70	70	70	282
B Gallacher	73	71	70	68	282
N Faldo	69	66	74	73	282
R Davis	68	69	72	74	283

1990

NAME	SCORE				
S Torrance	70	65	64	73	272
B Langer	66	67	74	68	275
I Woosnam	75	69	69	62	275
JM Olazabal	69	70	69	69	277
M Harwood	71	67	70	69	277
D Feherty	69	68	74	67	278
S Simpson	72	67	71	70	280
M McNulty	71	68	72	70	281
AWB Lyle	69	72	71	69	281
P Broadhurst	67	73	69	72	281

German Open

1972 *at Frankfurt*

NAME	SCORE				
G Marsh	70	70	67	64	271
BGC Huggett	69	67	71	68	275
J Gallardo	68	70	71	70	279
N Job	74	66	69	70	279
NC Coles	69	69	75	67	280
P Oosterhuis	68	71	70	72	281
A Gallardo	67	71	72	71	281
M Ballesteros	73	65	77	67	282
P Townsend	70	71	72	69	282
D McClelland	73	75	69	68	285
V Fernandez	72	71	71	71	285

1974 *at Krefeld*

NAME	SCORE				
S Owen	69	68	79	69	276
P Oosterhuis	70	71	69	66	276
(Owen won play-off)					
B Gallacher	75	70	67	67	279
D Hayes	69	70	69	71	279
E Polland	68	71	72	69	280
D Swaelens	70	68	70	72	280
BW Barnes	70	72	72	68	282
M Bembridge	70	71	70	71	282
L Owens	72	70	69	71	282
J Monroy	70	73	71	69	283
GL Hunt	74	75	64	70	283
D Edwards	70	71	70	72	283

1973 *at Düsseldorf*

NAME	SCORE				
F Abreu	67	70	69	70	276
D Hayes	71	67	71	69	278
G Marsh	73	70	70	67	280
P Oosterhuis	72	67	71	71	281
T Britz	71	74	68	70	283
P Berry	69	68	74	73	284
D Swaelens	69	69	71	75	284
H Baiocchi	71	74	69	71	285
M Ballesteros	68	73	72	72	285
CA Clark	71	72	70	72	285
A Gallardo	70	70	74	71	285
O Gartenmaier	70	70	71	74	285

1975 *at Bremen*

NAME	SCORE				
M Bembridge	75	72	69	69	285
R Shearer	75	72	74	71	292
L Hinkle	72	75	69	76	292
BW Barnes	75	76	71	71	293
J Britz	71	71	76	75	293
NC Coles	74	76	74	69	293
J Darr	75	73	76	71	295
J Fourie	74	75	74	72	295
H Bannerman	74	78	72	71	295
P Townsend	71	73	74	77	295
R Gilder	74	72	69	80	295
A Gallardo	73	70	76	76	295

1976 *at Frankfurt*

NAME	SCORE				
S Hobday	67	68	65	66	266
A Garrido	66	66	63	72	267
S Ballesteros	70	67	68	68	273
S Torrance	68	65	73	69	275
E Darcy	71	71	71	63	276
M Krantz	72	65	68	72	277
V Fernandez	68	71	71	68	278
M Pinero	68	72	69	69	278
B Dassu	67	67	72	72	278
T Crandall	76	69	69	65	279
N Faldo	71	69	71	68	279
P Butler	69	70	71	69	279
H Baiocchi	70	67	72	70	279

1977 *at Düsseldorf*

NAME	SCORE				
T Britz	66	67	71	71	275
H Baiocchi	69	73	67	68	277
N Faldo	70	72	68	68	278
R Byman	70	66	72	70	278
A Garrido	68	71	69	70	278
F Abreu	69	74	66	71	280
G Parslow	72	72	71	66	281
S Balbuena	69	72	70	70	281
J Bland	72	74	71	66	283
M James	71	74	70	68	283
T Jones	73	68	71	71	283
P Townsend	70	70	71	72	283
J Hammond	69	69	71	74	283

1978 *at Refrath-Cologne*

NAME	SCORE				
S Ballesteros	64	67	70	67	268
NC Coles	71	68	66	65	270
J Bland	69	68	67	67	271
G Player	67	72	68	68	275
BW Barnes	71	70	66	68	275
G Norman	72	66	70	68	276
J Morgan	66	69	69	72	276
J Fourie	66	70	67	73	276
M Bembridge	67	69	71	70	277
E Acosta	71	69	67	70	277

1979 *at Frankfurt*

NAME	SCORE				
A Jacklin	68	68	70	71	277
A Garrido	70	71	71	67	279
L Wadkins	71	71	71	66	279
S Hobday	71	74	69	68	282

NAME	SCORE				
H Clark	69	71	70	73	283
J Edman	68	76	72	68	284
H Baiocchi	69	74	73	68	284
D Ingram	75	73	68	68	284
J Bland	73	69	72	70	284
M Bembridge	70	72	71	71	284
JM Canizares	69	73	69	73	284

1980 *at Wannsee, Berlin*

NAME	SCORE				
M McNulty	71	70	70	69	280
NC Coles	70	70	73	68	281
A Charnley	71	69	72	69	281
V Fernandez	76	65	72	70	283
J Bland	72	74	70	69	285
S Torrance	67	75	73	70	285
D Smyth	74	69	72	70	285
R Verwey	73	74	70	69	286
B Gallacher	71	71	72	72	286
S Ballesteros	72	69	70	75	286

1981 *at Hamburg Club, Falkenstein*

NAME	SCORE				
B Langer	67	69	64	72	272
A Jacklin	68	70	68	67	273
V Fernandez	68	72	65	70	275
M McNulty	71	70	68	67	276
E Darcy	69	73	70	65	277
K Brown	69	70	68	70	277
NC Coles	70	71	70	67	278
M Calero	71	70	70	68	279
M Steadman	74	71	67	68	280
GJ Brand	73	72	66	69	280
E Polland	69	68	72	71	280

1982 *at Solitude, Stuttgart*

NAME	SCORE				
B Langer	73	71	69	66	279
W Longmuir	69	72	70	68	279
(Langer won play-off)					
C O'Connor Jr	69	68	74	69	280
A Jacklin	72	71	70	70	283
B Gallacher	71	74	70	70	285
W Humphreys	72	68	71	74	285
M Thomas	66	72	73	74	285
G Brand Jr	72	71	73	70	286
E Darcy	71	70	71	74	286
D Frost	72	70	75	70	287
RJ Charles	73	69	72	73	287

1983 *at Cologne*

NAME	SCORE				
C Pavin	67	71	68	69	275
T Johnstone	75	69	68	66	278
S Ballesteros	68	73	69	68	278
S Bishop	75	68	68	69	280
M Clayton	68	74	68	70	280
R Davis	70	72	71	68	281
J Hall	72	68	70	71	281
GJ Brand	74	67	68	72	281

1984 *at Frankfurt*

NAME	SCORE				
W Grady	70	65	69	64	268
J Anderson	70	67	69	63	269
A Forsbrand	69	70	68	65	272
S Torrance	70	71	64	67	272
RJ Charles	68	68	65	71	272
P Carrigill	71	67	72	65	275
D Frost	67	68	69	71	275
M Bembridge	68	71	67	70	276
A Charnley	69	69	67	71	276
R Chapman	71	70	70	66	277
J Heggarty	75	70	66	66	277
G Brand Jr	69	69	71	68	277
S Bishop	68	70	71	68	277
I Mosey	67	71	70	69	277
J Bland	71	67	70	69	277

1985 *at Garstedt, Bremen*

NAME	SCORE			
B Langer	61	60	62	183
M McLean	65	63	62	190
M McNulty	59	65	66	190
M Mackenzie	64	63	64	191
J Bland	66	63	63	192
P Walton	63	66	63	192
V Somers	66	63	65	194
V Fernandez	62	67	65	194
J Gonzalez	67	66	62	195
H Baiocchi	66	67	62	195
M Lanner	62	69	64	195
A Russell	61	69	65	195
R Rafferty	65	65	65	195

1986 *at Hubbelrath, Düsseldorf*

NAME	SCORE				
B Langer	75	65	66	67	273
D Davis	68	72	68	64	273
(Langer won play-off)					
M McNulty	67	72	69	72	275
AWB Lyle	70	71	68	66	275
M Mouland	68	73	66	69	276
I Woosnam	74	68	68	66	276
I Baker-Finch	68	68	70	72	278
G Brand Jr	71	71	66	70	278
D Smyth	73	67	70	68	278
P Baker	67	70	70	72	279
I Mosey	72	67	70	70	279
S Ballesteros	69	69	73	66	279

1987 *at Frankfurt*

NAME	SCORE				
M McNulty	65	66	65	63	259
A Garrido	64	66	63	69	262
D Durnian	64	65	69	65	263
P Fowler	67	65	67	64	263
B Lane	67	64	66	66	263
O Eckstein	69	65	67	65	266
D Pruitt	69	64	68	65	266
D Smyth	70	64	67	65	266
G Brand Jr	68	69	68	62	267
JM Canizares	68	68	66	65	267
B Langer	68	67	67	65	267

1988 *at Frankfurt*

NAME	SCORE				
S Ballesteros	68	68	65	62	263
G Brand Jr	67	69	62	70	268
M Clayton	68	68	68	65	269
W Longmuir	71	67	67	64	269
M James	71	69	65	65	270
R Boxall	68	69	62	72	271
D Smyth	66	69	69	67	271
SC Mason	67	71	66	67	271
BE Smith	67	67	69	68	271
P Senior	67	69	66	70	272
F Nobilo	67	68	69	68	272
M Smith	71	66	67	68	272

1989 *at Frankfurt*

NAME	SCORE				
C Parry	66	70	66	64	266
M James	65	66	65	70	266
(Parry won play-off)					
M Allen	68	66	64	69	267
M Harwood	65	65	68	70	268
JM Canizares	66	72	62	69	269
J Haas	66	69	64	70	269
G Brand Jr	71	66	67	65	269
B Langer	68	69	67	65	269
R Hartmann	67	70	64	69	270
B Ogle	66	67	68	69	270
J Rivero	69	68	66	67	270
S Struever (Am)	73	62	66	69	270

1990 *at Hubbelrath, Düsseldorf*

NAME	SCORE				
M McNulty	67	68	70	65	270
C Parry	66	65	72	70	273
E Darcy	66	70	68	70	274
A Forsbrand	64	66	73	71	274
J Rivero	70	71	70	64	275
P Walton	69	67	69	70	275
D Smyth	68	66	73	68	275
M James	67	73	66	71	277
T Johnstone	70	70	66	71	277
S Torrance	70	70	70	67	277
P O'Malley	68	73	71	65	277
SC Mason	69	68	71	69	277

Gsi-L'Equipe Open

1985 *at Le Touquet*

NAME	SCORE				
M James	66	67	71	66	272
SC Mason	72	68	67	68	275
H Clark	69	64	72	72	277
J O'Leary	74	72	67	65	278
J Bland	70	66	72	70	278
M Lanner	74	72	66	67	279

NAME	SCORE				
G Brand Jr	72	71	69	67	279
P Parkin	68	72	69	70	279
M Mackenzie	67	72	69	71	279
W Riley	67	73	67	72	279
M King	67	72	68	72	279
G Taylor	74	65	68	72	279
R Rafferty	67	69	70	73	279
GJ Brand	65	64	75	75	279

Carrolls Irish Open

1972 *at Woodbrook*

NAME	SCORE				
C O'Connor Sr	73	69	75	67	284
D Talbot	74	71	71	72	288
B Dassu	74	74	68	73	289
P Townsend	74	71	77	68	290
E Polland	76	72	73	69	290
P Wilcock	78	71	71	70	290
T Horton	74	74	70	72	290
T Britz	75	71	75	70	291
J Newton	77	73	70	71	291
H Bannerman	74	77	68	72	291

1973 *at Woodbrook*

NAME	SCORE				
P McGuirk	67	72	72	66	277
H Baiocchi	71	70	70	68	279
M Bembridge	71	72	68	69	280
I Stanley	70	74	73	66	283
D Webster	70	71	76	66	283
C O'Connor Sr	69	72	72	70	283
RDBM Shade	73	74	71	66	284
J McTear	73	69	78	66	286
A Skerritt	72	73	70	71	286
BW Barnes	69	72	74	71	286
H Jackson	72	70	72	72	286

1974   *at Woodbrook*

NAME	SCORE				
B Gallacher	72	71	68	68	279
J Newton	73	68	71	70	282
P Townsend	76	68	69	70	283
C O'Connor Sr	75	69	69	70	283
SC Mason	70	68	73	73	284
D Hayes	75	67	70	72	284
D Llewellyn	75	66	73	71	285
C O'Connor Jr	73	71	70	72	286
B Hunt	73	69	71	73	286
S Ginn	74	72	68	72	286
T Halpin	75	74	68	69	286

1975   *at Woodbrook*

NAME	SCORE				
C O'Connor Jr	66	70	69	70	275
H Bannerman	69	69	70	68	276
E Darcy	69	71	72	67	279
PJ Butler	72	66	70	71	279
A Jacklin	74	66	69	71	280
D Hayes	74	68	71	68	281
GL Hunt	72	72	68	69	281
J Newton	72	71	70	69	282
I Stanley	69	66	74	73	282
R Shearer	74	69	73	67	283

1976   *at Portmarnock*

NAME	SCORE				
B Crenshaw	73	69	69	73	284
M Foster	69	69	75	73	286
W Casper	70	71	74	71	286
BW Barnes	71	69	74	72	286
S Ballesteros	70	75	70	73	288
T Horton	73	75	70	73	291
C O'Connor Jr	75	71	70	75	291
H Bannerman	73	73	73	73	292
G Player	71	75	72	74	292
L Platts	72	73	78	70	293
D McClelland	71	75	74	73	293

1977   *at Portmarnock*

NAME	SCORE				
H Green	70	69	74	70	283
B Crenshaw	72	69	72	71	284
J Kinsella	69	71	74	71	285
P Dawson	71	71	73	70	285
G Norman	72	68	75	70	285
S Ballesteros	70	72	72	72	286

NAME	SCORE				
K Brown	69	76	74	69	288
H Clark	70	73	74	71	288
SC Mason	71	73	76	69	289
D Durnian	72	72	76	69	289
N Faldo	73	72	71	73	289

1978   *at Portmarnock*

NAME	SCORE				
K Brown	70	71	70	70	281
S Ballesteros	71	72	74	65	282
J O'Leary	69	70	71	72	282
T Weiskopf	70	76	67	70	283
P Townsend	71	71	73	69	284
M James	70	73	71	70	284
H Green	67	76	69	72	284
H Clark	70	73	70	72	285
B Gallacher	70	70	72	73	285
B Langer	72	71	68	74	285

1979   *at Portmarnock*

NAME	SCORE				
M James	73	75	69	65	282
E Sneed	75	72	71	65	283
M McCumber	75	71	70	69	285
JM Canizares	73	73	73	68	287
BW Barnes	81	69	67	70	287
S Hobday	73	74	67	73	287
H Clark	71	69	73	75	288
A Jacklin	73	69	72	74	288
M King	73	71	75	70	289
GL Hunt	73	72	73	71	289
P Elson	76	70	71	72	289

1980   *at Portmarnock*

NAME	SCORE				
M James	71	66	74	73	284
BW Barnes	69	71	70	75	285
H Green	72	69	75	71	287
S Ballesteros	72	74	67	75	288
G Marsh	71	69	78	71	289
S Torrance	72	72	71	74	289
GJ Brand	71	68	79	72	290
H Irwin	72	73	71	74	290
G Norman	72	68	74	76	290
AWB Lyle	67	74	80	70	291
J Bland	74	73	74	70	291
M Pinero	68	76	76	71	291
A Charnley	69	78	73	71	291
D Jagger	71	70	76	74	291
M Bembridge	68	75	74	74	291

1981 *at Portmarnock*

NAME	SCORE				
S Torrance	68	67	69	72	276
N Faldo	68	70	71	72	281
D Jones	73	67	71	71	282
J Heggarty	69	71	70	72	282
D Smyth	70	69	70	73	282
E Polland	70	69	74	70	283
G Norman	70	70	73	70	283
B Langer	69	74	70	70	283
R Davis	66	73	70	74	283
V Fernandez	70	66	71	76	283

1982 *at Portmarnock*

NAME	SCORE				
J O'Leary	74	68	72	73	287
M Bembridge	71	71	72	74	288
G Norman	79	73	71	67	290
N Faldo	78	70	73	69	290
C O'Connor	74	74	70	72	290
M Pinero	75	70	74	72	291
M Poxon	75	72	75	70	292
E Darcy	76	70	72	74	292
T Kite	76	70	71	75	292
G Brand Jr	78	75	69	71	293
SC Mason	78	72	71	72	293
W Humphreys	75	71	74	73	293

1983 *at Royal Dublin*

NAME	SCORE				
S Ballesteros	67	67	70	67	271
BW Barnes	66	71	67	69	273
B Marchbank	71	65	70	70	276
N Faldo	69	68	68	71	276
M Pinero	68	76	69	65	278
M Cahill	72	69	70	67	278
A Jacklin	69	69	71	70	279
G Cullen	74	70	72	64	280
H Clark	70	69	72	69	280
JM Canizares	68	75	65	72	280
G Marsh	72	66	69	73	280
H Baiocchi	66	71	70	73	280
J Rivero	69	71	66	74	280

1984 *at Royal Dublin*

NAME	SCORE				
B Langer	68	66	67	66	267
M James	67	67	70	67	271
S Ballesteros	69	69	68	67	273
G Norman	69	65	71	68	273

NAME	SCORE				
G Marsh	70	67	67	69	273
DJ Russell	68	65	69	72	274
M Persson	66	65	76	68	275
A Magee	71	67	68	69	275
JM Canizares	71	67	70	68	276
J O'Leary	71	69	68	68	276
J Anderson	66	70	69	71	276
J Rivero	68	67	68	73	276

1985 *at Royal Dublin*

NAME	SCORE				
S Ballesteros	70	69	73	66	278
B Langer	74	71	70	63	278
I Woosnam	66	75	70	69	280
P Way	72	74	68	66	280
GJ Brand	71	75	69	67	282
R Chapman	72	75	67	68	282
P Parkin	72	68	71	71	282
C O'Connor Jr	74	69	73	67	283
R Rafferty	72	74	69	68	283
J Morgan	74	71	69	69	283

1986 *at Portmarnock*

NAME	SCORE				
S Ballesteros	68	75	68	74	285
M McNulty	74	72	71	70	287
R Davis	74	73	71	69	287
W Riley	67	78	71	74	290
JM Olazabal	68	78	73	71	290
H Clark	74	75	70	71	290
R Lee	66	79	73	73	291
G Turner	71	76	72	72	291
GJ Brand	71	78	72	70	291
R Chapman	72	79	70	70	291
D Jones	74	73	73	71	291

1987 *at Portmarnock*

NAME	SCORE				
B Langer	67	68	66	68	269
AWB Lyle	70	70	71	68	279
R Davis	69	72	69	72	282
I Woosnam	72	74	69	67	282
H Clark	71	71	73	68	283
J Bland	70	75	70	69	284
D Jones	73	72	75	65	285
G Brand Jr	73	70	73	71	287
R Chapman	72	73	71	73	289
M O'Meara	74	71	74	70	289
DA Russell	72	75	74	68	289
BE Smith	72	71	75	71	289

1988   *at Portmarnock*

NAME	SCORE				
I Woosnam	68	70	70	70	278
JM Olazabal	66	70	74	75	285
D Smyth	68	73	71	73	285
M Pinero	69	68	75	73	285
N Faldo	71	68	73	73	285
E Darcy	69	68	75	74	286
P Walton	69	68	75	74	286
R Shearer	69	70	77	70	286
M Sludds	70	72	71	73	286
R Chapman	73	71	69	73	286

1989   *at Portmarnock*

NAME	SCORE				
I Woosnam	70	67	71	70	278
P Walton	68	69	69	72	278
(Woosnam won play-off)					
B Ogle	69	69	74	70	282

NAME	SCORE				
R Rafferty	67	71	72	72	282
M McNulty	71	67	71	73	282
S Torrance	71	70	72	70	283
JM Olazabal	69	70	73	71	283
M Davis	73	71	66	73	283
P McWhinney	70	68	73	72	283
E Darcy	71	70	69	74	284

1990   *at Portmarnock*

NAME	SCORE				
JM Olazabal	67	72	71	72	282
M Calcavecchia	66	75	72	72	285
F Nobilo	73	70	69	73	285
R Hartmann	72	74	71	69	286
J Bland	71	69	73	74	287
R Claydon	71	71	72	73	287
E Darcy	70	70	74	74	288
B Marchbank	71	73	71	73	288
D Ray	71	73	72	73	289
M Sludds	72	72	76	69	289

Italian Open

1972   *at Villa d'Este*

NAME	SCORE				
N Wood	65	69	68	69	271
BGC Huggett	67	65	70	71	273
A Croce	69	70	67	68	274
RJ Charles	71	67	70	69	277
R Bernardini	72	67	67	71	277
GL Hunt	68	68	68	73	277
NC Coles	67	68	73	70	278
R de Vicenzo	69	69	70	70	278
D Vaughan	70	71	67	71	279
RDBM Shade	72	68	69	70	279
H Jackson	69	66	73	71	279
JM Canizares	70	69	70	70	279

1973   *at Olgiata and Roma, Rome*

NAME	SCORE				
A Jacklin	71	72	70	71	284
V Barrios	73	70	72	70	285
W Berry	72	70	74	70	286
J Garaialde	71	72	69	74	286

NAME	SCORE				
H Baiocchi	71	70	74	73	288
P Oosterhuis	71	70	72	75	288
M Bembridge	73	70	68	77	288
H Muscroft	76	66	75	72	289
D Wren	72	71	77	70	290
D Vaughan	72	72	75	71	290
C O'Connor Sr	75	70	72	73	290
D Swaelens	73	71	70	76	290

1974   *at Lido de Venice*

NAME	SCORE				
P Oosterhuis	*37	72	70	70	249
D Hayes	34	75	74	68	251
J Miller	34	70	74	73	251
S Owen	34	76	70	72	252
S Ballesteros	33	75	73	73	254
C DeFoy	36	76	71	73	256
A Croce	38	70	71	77	256
BW Barnes	37	71	74	74	256
LP Tupling	36	71	72	77	256
A Brooks	37	77	69	74	257
B Pascassio	37	74	70	76	257

First round restricted to 9 holes due to fog.

1975 *at Monticello, Como*

NAME	SCORE				
W Casper	74	69	70	73	286
BW Barnes	71	71	73	72	287
T Horton	76	70	71	71	288
M Pinero	74	71	72	71	288
E Polland	77	74	67	71	289
C DeFoy	71	74	71	76	292
J O'Leary	71	73	75	73	292
R Bernardini	68	75	75	74	292
H Clark	73	72	73	76	294
P Molteni	75	73	74	72	294
M Foster	72	70	72	80	294

1976 *at Is Molas, Sardinia*

NAME	SCORE				
B Dassu	71	71	69	69	280
M Pinero	76	70	72	70	288
SC Mason	70	74	72	72	288
S Torrance	72	70	74	73	289
T Horton	78	67	70	74	289
E Polland	74	71	76	70	291
W Casper	71	74	76	71	292
BW Barnes	75	75	73	70	293
B Murphy	76	75	72	70	293
A Garrido	77	74	71	71	293
M King	76	74	70	73	293

1977 *at Monticello, Como*

NAME	SCORE				
A Gallardo	71	69	72	74	286
BW Barnes	72	71	74	69	286
(Gallardo won play-off)					
P Dawson	72	72	70	73	287
S Balbuena	72	71	73	72	288
P Toussaint	71	70	75	73	289
S Ballesteros	70	75	72	72	289
F Abreu	70	74	73	73	290
E Polland	70	74	74	73	291
JM Canizares	72	76	70	73	291
M Cahill	76	69	76	71	292
C Strange	71	72	73	76	292

1978 *at Pevero, Costa Smeralda, Sardinia*

NAME	SCORE				
D Hayes	74	72	68	79	293
T Horton	73	71	75	77	296

NAME	SCORE				
V Baker	78	69	73	76	296
M King	71	76	74	76	297
J Bland	76	76	74	71	297
GJ Brand	70	80	73	75	298
E Polland	76	71	73	80	300
M Pinero	77	72	77	74	300
M McNulty	72	76	81	71	300
A Jacklin	72	78	77	73	300

1979 *at Monticello, Como*

NAME	SCORE				
BW Barnes	73	70	71	67	281
D Hayes	73	69	71	68	281
(Barnes won play-off)					
S Torrance	72	73	69	70	284
V Fernandez	72	74	67	71	284
S Ballesteros	73	72	72	68	285
A Garrido	73	73	68	71	285
A Jacklin	79	67	68	71	285
B Crenshaw	74	70	68	73	285
B Waites	72	71	71	72	286
M King	70	71	71	74	286

1980 *at Acquasanta, Rome*

NAME	SCORE				
M Mannelli	68	66	70	72	276
J Bland	69	68	69	75	281
K Brown	70	68	72	71	281
N Faldo	73	67	69	73	282
J O'Leary	70	68	73	71	282
M Foster	70	68	72	73	283
A Garrido	69	70	72	72	283
G Norman	70	74	69	70	283
R Campagnoli	70	69	72	73	284
I Woosnam	70	69	71	74	284

1981 *at Milano, Monza*

NAME	SCORE				
JM Canizares	68	71	70	71	280
R Clampett	71	72	66	71	280
(Canizares won play-off)					
B Langer	71	73	68	70	282
A Jacklin	71	76	68	69	284
P Hoad	70	76	71	69	286
AWB Lyle	71	74	68	73	286
H Clark	74	72	69	72	287
M Pinero	73	71	75	69	288
M James	68	74	73	73	288
J Bland	73	70	72	73	288

1982   *at Is Molas, Sardinia*

NAME	SCORE				
M James	70	67	71	72	280
I Woosnam	69	74	68	72	283
R Clampett	68	73	72	70	283
F Molina	72	76	68	69	285
B Langer	70	74	70	71	285
M Pinero	73	74	66	74	287
J Anglada	73	70	70	74	287
R Rafferty	71	75	71	70	287
JM Canizares	73	75	71	69	288
M Montes	71	77	67	73	288
J Bland	71	74	72	71	288
A Garrido	70	71	71	76	288

1983   *at Ugolino, Florence*

NAME	SCORE				
B Langer	67	69	67	68	271
K Brown	69	67	67	68	271
S Ballesteros	64	74	67	66	271
(Langer won play-off)					
B Waites	72	67	68	67	274
M Pinero	69	67	71	70	277
E Darcy	73	67	67	70	277
S Torrance	69	71	69	69	278
W Humphreys	69	66	71	72	278
J Anderson	70	73	69	67	279
B Gallacher	71	65	68	75	279

1984   *at Milano, Milan*

NAME	SCORE				
AWB Lyle	71	70	68	68	277
R Clampett	75	69	71	66	281
D Feherty	70	74	68	70	282
V Heafner	70	74	70	69	283
DJ Russell	72	74	67	71	284
J Rivero	74	72	68	70	284
JM Canizares	76	65	74	69	284
S Torrance	72	75	71	67	285
B Langer	71	75	66	73	285
H Clark	74	71	69	71	285
M King	77	71	68	69	285
D Lovato	71	71	74	69	285

1985   *at Molinetto, Milan*

NAME	SCORE				
M Pinero	69	66	66	66	267
S Torrance	65	67	69	67	268
AWB Lyle	69	67	68	66	270

NAME	SCORE				
R Chapman	68	68	71	64	271
S Ballesteros	70	68	64	70	272
JM Canizares	68	69	67	68	272
J Quiros	68	68	68	70	274
M McLean	70	74	67	65	276
J Bland	69	69	65	74	277
B McColl	69	69	68	71	277

1986   *at Isola di Albarella*

NAME	SCORE				
D Feherty	69	67	66	68	270
R Rafferty	69	69	68	64	270
(Feherty won play-off)					
A Chandler	72	69	65	66	272
E Darcy	73	67	69	64	273
S Ballesteros	70	67	65	71	273
J Slaughter	67	72	71	64	274
M Harwood	68	70	68	68	274
R Lee	72	66	71	65	274
M James	65	71	67	71	274
A Sowa	67	69	68	70	274

1987   *at Monticello, Milan*

NAME	SCORE				
S Torrance	64	68	71	68	271
J Rivero	68	69	68	66	271
(Torrance won play-off)					
N Faldo	70	67	69	66	272
P Senior	70	67	68	70	275
D Feherty	71	68	69	68	276
R Rafferty	70	71	68	67	276
MA Martin	69	71	67	71	278
DJ Russell	71	69	68	70	278
B Lane	70	69	73	67	279
R Lee	70	70	70	69	279
M Mackenzie	70	67	73	69	279

1988   *at Monticello, Milan*

NAME	SCORE				
G Norman	69	68	63	70	270
C Parry	65	68	67	71	271
R Rafferty	66	70	67	69	272
D Durnian	67	70	68	68	273
R Chapman	66	68	69	70	273
G Brand Jr	67	68	70	69	274
I Woosnam	68	68	69	69	274
P Parkin	65	72	68	70	275
P Senior	70	69	67	69	275
D Whelan	63	71	70	72	276
R Shearer	67	70	71	68	276

1989   *at Monticello, Milan*

NAME	SCORE				
R Rafferty	71	69	68	65	273
S Torrance	69	70	65	70	274
M Persson	66	72	69	68	275
R Lee	66	73	69	69	277
P Carman	70	69	67	72	278
A Sherborne	72	70	65	71	278
D Feherty	65	72	69	73	279
S Ballesteros	71	69	68	71	279
L Carbonetti	76	68	67	68	279
F Nobilo	71	70	71	67	279
N Hansen	71	72	71	65	279

1990   *at Milano, Monza*

NAME	SCORE				
R Boxall	65	64	70	68	267
JM Olazabal	67	69	68	68	272
E Romero	72	69	66	68	275
J Bland	67	74	68	68	277
S Ballesteros	75	68	66	69	278
G Cali	71	71	67	70	279
K Waters	70	70	71	68	279
A Sorensen	66	72	71	70	279
C Stadler	68	68	71	72	279
JM Canizares	73	72	66	69	280
J Rutledge	68	71	71	70	280
S Richardson	71	68	72	69	280

Jersey Open
at La Moye

1978

NAME	SCORE				
BGC Huggett	65	66	71	69	271
E Darcy	71	68	69	66	274
J Hawkes	70	68	71	66	275
V Baker	74	64	69	68	275
P Elson	69	67	72	68	276
N Price	67	69	69	71	276
D Hayes	69	67	73	69	278
J O'Leary	69	71	69	69	278
M Gregson	70	70	71	68	279
R Verwey	66	70	72	71	279
C Tickner	71	66	71	71	279

1980

NAME	SCORE				
JM Canizares	71	67	71	72	281
S Martin	71	69	73	70	283
H Baiocchi	68	70	77	70	285
N Faldo	74	67	75	70	286
C Moody	72	65	77	72	286
D Smyth	75	72	67	72	286
C O'Connor Jr	72	71	71	74	288
N Price	72	71	77	69	289
P Elson	72	70	77	70	289
T Britz	72	67	79	71	289
A Jacklin	70	70	79	70	289
RJ Charles	74	70	74	71	289
M Pinero	70	69	77	73	289

1979

NAME	SCORE				
AWB Lyle	66	71	66	68	271
H Clark	70	68	67	69	274
S Torrance	69	69	72	65	275
A Jacklin	64	75	68	68	275
B Gallacher	64	69	69	73	275
M King	69	70	67	69	275
H Baiocchi	68	71	71	66	276
N Ratcliffe	70	70	70	66	276
RJ Charles	72	68	69	67	276
P Cowen	70	72	71	64	277

1981

NAME	SCORE				
A Jacklin	71	68	72	68	279
B Langer	69	68	74	69	280
M Calero	70	69	72	70	281
D Smyth	69	72	72	69	282
S Rolley	70	71	72	70	283
J O'Leary	71	70	70	72	283
H Clark	67	74	73	70	284
A Charnley	73	66	70	75	284
S Ginn	70	69	73	73	285
JM Canizares	71	74	70	71	286
T Horton	70	70	75	71	286

1982

NAME	SCORE				
B Gallacher	69	66	68	70	273
E Darcy	65	71	69	68	273
D Smyth	65	68	67	73	273
(Gallacher won play-off)					
AWB Lyle	72	70	68	65	275
I Mosey	69	68	68	71	276
I Woosnam	73	70	68	66	277
E Polland	73	65	70	70	278
A Jacklin	71	69	71	68	279
S Bishop	69	69	70	71	279
N Ratcliffe	68	69	70	72	279

1983

NAME	SCORE				
J Hall	71	68	67	72	278
M King	66	72	70	71	279
B Gallacher	69	68	68	74	279
AWB Lyle	72	66	71	71	280
V Fernandez	69	62	74	76	281
J Morgan	72	69	73	68	282
D Smyth	71	71	70	70	282
JM Canizares	70	70	68	74	282
A Jacklin	75	72	68	68	283
I Woosnam	72	73	72	67	284
C Maltman	75	71	69	69	284

1984

NAME	SCORE				
B Gallacher	66	71	68	69	274
AWB Lyle	68	71	70	67	276
M King	69	67	71	70	277
JM Canizares	67	68	71	73	279
BW Barnes	71	67	73	69	280
E Murray	66	73	71	70	280
I Woosnam	72	69	69	70	280
H Clark	70	70	66	74	280
SC Mason	68	72	73	68	281
G Brand Jr	69	72	69	71	281
J Rivero	70	69	70	72	281

1985

NAME	SCORE				
H Clark	71	69	71	68	279
P Parkin	73	70	69	68	280
W Humphreys	69	68	71	72	280
I Woosnam	67	69	71	73	280
SC Mason	70	71	74	66	281

NAME	SCORE				
R Chapman	73	68	71	69	281
E Darcy	70	72	66	74	282
K Waters	73	71	70	69	283
P Senior	71	69	73	70	283

1986

NAME	SCORE				
J Morgan	65	68	71	71	275
P Fowler	65	71	70	69	275
(Morgan won play-off)					
H Clark	68	68	75	66	277
G Brand Jr	62	70	75	70	277
I Mosey	72	70	69	67	278
R Davis	64	73	69	72	278
H Baiocchi	72	64	69	73	278
B Marchbank	73	68	69	69	279
N Hansen	67	70	74	69	280
C Moody	69	70	72	69	280

1987

NAME	SCORE				
I Woosnam	68	67	72	72	279
B Malley	69	72	69	70	280
JM Canizares	68	74	67	72	281
DA Russell	69	67	71	74	281
B Gallacher	71	67	73	71	282
S Torrance	70	72	71	69	282
A Forsbrand	72	70	73	68	283
A Murray	70	69	73	71	283
DJ Russell	68	71	72	72	283
D Durnian	71	68	70	75	284
C O'Connor Jr	70	68	76	70	284

1988

NAME	SCORE				
D Smyth	69	68	69	67	273
R Chapman	68	68	68	69	273
(Smyth won play-off)					
SC Mason	66	68	69	71	274
P Way	71	69	65	69	274
R McFarlane	67	70	65	72	274
N Hansen	68	69	69	68	274
D Whelan	71	68	68	68	275
C O'Connor Jr	66	71	69	70	276
C Moody	64	71	69	72	276
S Bottomley	68	70	70	69	277
S Tinning	68	69	71	69	277
D Gilford	71	70	68	68	277

1989

NAME	SCORE				
C O'Connor Jr	73	70	66	72	281
D Durnian	70	71	67	73	281
(O'Connor won play-off)					
M Lanner	71	69	70	72	282
P Broadhurst	73	69	71	69	282
D Smyth	74	69	71	69	283
C Montgomerie	69	75	68	71	283
B Gallacher	71	70	70	72	283

NAME	SCORE				
S Torrance	72	70	69	72	283
R Rafferty	74	69	68	72	283
B Lane	76	70	65	73	284
P Fowler	74	71	69	70	284

1990

Not played

Lancôme Trophy
at St Nom-La-Bretêche

1970

NAME	SCORE			
A Jacklin	67	71	68	206
A Palmer	68	71	68	207
R Sota	71	70	66	207
R Floyd	70	73	67	210
G Player	70	72	68	210
RJ Charles	70	69	73	212
R Bernardini	75	70	71	216
J Garaialde	77	77	69	223

1971

NAME	SCORE			
A Palmer	66	65	71	202
G Player	68	66	70	204
CC Rodriguez	71	71	69	211
A Jacklin	68	72	72	212
LL Huan	68	73	74	215
J Garaialde	72	73	73	218
R de Vicenzo	71	71	76	218
R Sota	76	72	72	220

1972

NAME	SCORE				
T Aaron	71	71	67	70	279
T Weiskopf	74	74	67	67	282
G Player	71	71	71	70	283

NAME	SCORE				
A Palmer	74	68	73	70	285
D Sanders	74	69	72	71	286
A Gallardo	72	70	73	72	287
J Garaialde	72	72	74	74	292
D Swaelens	78	72	74	72	292

1973

NAME	SCORE				
J Miller	68	69	71	69	277
V Barrios	69	71	70	70	280
G Player	73	70	71	67	281
C Coody	70	70	70	71	281
D Hayes	71	71	67	73	282
T Aaron	73	72	69	71	285
J Garaialde	71	71	75	69	286
A Palmer	74	71	73	70	288

1974

NAME	SCORE				
W Casper	66	74	70	73	283
H Irwin	72	70	74	70	286
R Cole	73	74	69	71	287
A Palmer	73	71	71	77	298
J Garaialde	73	78	78	74	299
B Crenshaw	68	73	73	83	302
S Snead	73	78	76	75	302
M Pinero	77	73	79	75	304

1975

NAME	SCORE				
G Player	73	65	69	71	278
L Wadkins	73	70	72	70	284
S Ballesteros	71	74	71	70	286
A Jacklin	70	67	76	74	287
A Palmer	69	74	75	70	288
W Casper	75	73	71	71	290
R Shearer	73	73	73	72	291
J Garaialde	76	75	73	71	295

1976

NAME	SCORE				
S Ballesteros	73	73	68	69	283
A Palmer	75	70	69	70	284
G Player	73	72	71	72	288
D Graham	75	70	70	73	288
L Elder	76	71	72	74	293
A Jacklin	80	72	67	75	294
R Floyd	78	73	73	70	294
J Garaialde	75	70	74	76	295

1977

NAME	SCORE				
G Marsh	70	69	68	66	273
S Ballesteros	74	64	67	68	273
(Marsh won play-off)					
G Littler	71	70	70	70	281
N Faldo	67	69	73	74	283
G Player	74	70	70	70	284
J Garaialde	71	71	73	69	284
G Burns	73	72	75	68	288
A Palmer	75	73	75	69	292

1978

NAME	SCORE				
T Watson	68	71	68	70	277
G Player	72	69	66	70	277
G Marsh	68	77	67	70	282
R Byman	75	71	68	70	284
A North	73	71	67	73	284
I Aoki	74	70	71	71	286
P Cotton	72	75	72	71	290

1979

NAME	SCORE				
J Miller	70	71	69	71	281
AWB Lyle	71	71	72	70	284
L Trevino	74	72	68	70	284
R Floyd	72	65	74	74	285
M James	69	75	75	70	287
W Rogers	72	71	73	71	287
A Jacklin	72	67	74	75	288
A Palmer	72	75	73	72	292
BW Barnes	75	76	72	71	294
D Hayes	77	71	70	76	294

1980

NAME	SCORE				
L Trevino	68	72	71	69	280
G Hallberg	74	69	70	71	284
B Langer	72	67	74	72	285
J Miller	71	69	73	74	287
AWB Lyle	73	75	71	69	288
S Ballesteros	76	71	69	72	288
N Price	71	69	73	77	290
J Renner	71	73	71	75	290
B Gallacher	74	71	73	74	292
N Faldo	75	72	71	74	292

1981

NAME	SCORE				
D Graham	71	72	67	70	280
AWB Lyle	73	72	72	68	285
I Aoki	70	74	69	72	285
N Faldo	77	70	68	71	286
R Clampett	75	69	72	71	287
C Strange	72	72	70	73	287
R Alarcon	75	71	71	74	291
P Cotton	73	73	73	74	293
G Watine	75	73	71	74	293
JM Canizares	78	68	71	76	293

1982

NAME	SCORE				
D Graham	66	70	70	70	276
S Ballesteros	68	71	70	69	278

NAME	SCORE				
C Stadler	69	74	70	67	280
AWB Lyle	69	70	68	74	281
A Palmer	73	72	68	68	281
D Smyth	75	68	74	66	283
G Watine	72	72	71	68	283
G Brand Jr	71	73	70	69	283
M McNulty	73	71	72	67	283
P Jacobsen	74	69	70	71	284

1983

NAME	SCORE				
S Ballesteros	71	65	64	69	269
C Pavin	69	69	67	68	273
V Fernandez	70	66	70	70	276
P Way	66	68	70	72	276
G Norman	70	67	67	72	276
M King	70	70	69	68	277
S Torrance	67	71	68	71	277
M James	72	71	69	67	279
JM Canizares	68	72	71	68	279

1984

NAME	SCORE				
AWB Lyle	74	70	67	67	278
S Ballesteros	71	66	69	72	278
(Lyle won play-off)					
I Woosnam	75	70	69	65	279
E Darcy	67	73	68	72	280
J Miller	73	70	68	70	281
B Langer	70	70	68	73	281
B Gallacher	70	73	70	72	285
JM Canizares	75	70	71	70	286
H Clark	73	68	75	70	286
D Smyth	73	70	70	73	286
C Pavin	71	72	70	73	286

1985

NAME	SCORE				
N Price	66	71	67	71	275
M James	70	67	66	72	275
H Clark	73	72	64	70	279
S Torrance	75	68	64	73	280
M Pinero	72	69	73	67	281
S Ballesteros	74	69	72	67	282
R Rafferty	72	68	73	70	283
E Darcy	74	69	68	72	283

NAME	SCORE				
TC Chen	73	69	72	70	284
A North	71	70	69	74	284

1986

NAME	SCORE				
S Ballesteros	67	69	68	70	274
B Langer	73	66	66	69	274
(Ballesteros and Langer shared trophy)					
D Smyth	72	69	68	66	275
S Torrance	71	64	74	67	276
AWB Lyle	70	66	70	70	276
J Bland	72	71	68	66	277
GJ Brand	69	69	68	71	277
JM Olazabal	71	69	66	71	277
C Strange	69	67	70	72	278
H Baiocchi	69	70	73	67	279

1987

NAME	SCORE				
I Woosnam	65	64	69	66	264
M McNulty	68	67	67	64	266
A Johnstone	64	69	66	69	268
AWB Lyle	67	69	66	66	268
B Langer	64	70	72	63	269
R Rafferty	69	67	67	68	271
D Feherty	67	69	68	68	272
M James	66	71	70	65	272
R Floyd	69	69	65	69	272
A Charnley	71	67	70	66	274
B Lane	67	63	73	71	274

1988

NAME	SCORE				
S Ballesteros	64	66	68	71	269
JM Olazabal	69	66	69	69	273
G Norman	71	72	68	67	278
AWB Lyle	75	63	68	72	278
R Rafferty	71	70	75	63	279
R Davis	71	73	71	65	280
J Rivero	71	68	69	70	281
P Baker	70	67	74	70	281
C Moody	71	68	72	70	281
J Bland	71	69	69	72	281
C O'Connor Jr	72	72	70	67	281
A Johnstone	74	71	67	69	281
R Boxall	70	77	69	65	281
J Hawkes	75	68	67	71	281

1989

NAME	SCORE				
E Romero	69	65	66	66	266
B Langer	68	68	66	65	267
JM Olazabal	67	70	65	65	267
P Fowler	66	64	68	70	268
D Feherty	68	69	67	65	269
V Singh	70	71	66	67	274
H Clark	69	74	67	64	274
C Parry	68	69	68	69	274
S Torrance	72	68	69	66	275
A Murray	64	78	68	65	275
M Lanner	72	74	62	67	275

1990

NAME	SCORE				
JM Olazabal	68	66	70	65	269
C Montgomerie	69	63	71	67	270
A Johnstone	68	69	70	64	271
R Davis	69	66	71	69	275
C Parry	69	70	66	70	275
M James	72	64	68	71	275
E Darcy	70	70	67	69	276
S Ballesteros	70	69	70	67	276
E Romero	71	67	71	67	276
M Clayton	71	67	73	66	277
J Rivero	68	70	70	69	277

The Lawrence Batley International

1981 *at Bingley St Ives*

NAME	SCORE				
AWB Lyle	70	70	69	71	280
N Faldo	71	73	72	66	282
S Martin	67	73	72	72	284
M Pinero	73	69	73	70	285
M Miller	74	71	74	67	286
NC Coles	68	71	77	70	286
P Elson	71	72	74	70	287
I Mosey	71	77	73	67	288
F Zoeller	73	69	76	70	288
E Murray	72	77	74	71	288

1983 *at Bingley St Ives*

NAME	SCORE				
N Faldo	71	69	64	62	266
P Way	64	70	70	66	270
B Waites	68	70	65	67	270
W Humphreys	71	67	65	67	270
M King	68	70	68	65	271
M McLean	64	64	73	70	271
M Pinero	72	66	64	69	271
P Carrigill	66	69	73	64	272
M Clayton	68	69	70	65	272
P Hoad	66	70	70	66	272
T Gale	68	68	68	68	272
E Darcy	66	69	68	69	272
D Durnian	67	70	65	70	272

1982 *at Bingley St Ives*

NAME	SCORE				
AWB Lyle	70	66	67	66	269
M Pinero	71	66	69	65	271
R Caldwell	68	70	66	69	273
E Darcy	66	69	69	70	274
N Faldo	68	71	64	71	274
P Curry	69	67	67	71	274
B Gallacher	68	66	68	72	274
J Rassett	68	72	67	68	275
K Brown	67	70	64	74	275
B Waites	66	68	70	72	276

1984 *at The Belfry*

NAME	SCORE				
J Rivero	73	69	71	67	280
JM Canizares	75	69	70	67	281
S Torrance	68	72	71	72	283
N Ozaki	70	72	68	73	283
A Garrido	71	77	68	68	284
P Senior	70	74	68	72	284
K Brown	69	71	74	71	285
J Gonzalez	74	74	70	68	286
I Woosnam	72	71	72	71	286
AWB Lyle	70	74	70	72	286

1985   *at The Belfry*

NAME	SCORE				
G Marsh	69	71	70	73	283
R Hartmann	69	74	69	73	285
M King	72	68	73	73	286
JM Canizares	68	76	71	73	288
DA Weibring	70	72	74	73	289
R Davis	74	70	74	71	289
R Chapman	72	72	71	75	290
B Gallacher	72	75	73	70	290
G Brand Jr	75	71	73	71	290
O Sellberg	75	74	70	72	291
K Brown	76	72	72	71	291

1986   *at The Belfry*

NAME	SCORE				
I Woosnam	71	71	66	69	277
K Brown	73	70	72	69	284
JM Canizares	70	72	71	71	284
M Allen	70	72	72	72	286
R Drummond	76	67	70	73	286
N Hansen	73	71	71	71	286
J Hawkes	69	71	73	73	286
J Rivero	70	71	70	75	286
A Forsbrand	75	68	70	74	287

NAME	SCORE				
S Bennett	71	71	73	73	288
C O'Connor Jr	75	72	73	68	288
M Pinero	73	72	71	72	288
G Powers	72	72	72	72	288
R Stelten	71	69	74	74	288

1987   *at Birkdale*

NAME	SCORE				
M O'Meara	71	64	70	66	271
SC Mason	74	67	65	68	274
A Oldcorn	68	68	71	68	275
N Faldo	72	65	70	69	276
S Torrance	67	72	70	67	276
H Clark	72	65	72	68	277
A Johnstone	75	66	68	69	278
D Llewellyn	69	69	69	71	278
I Baker-Finch	73	66	69	71	279
S Bishop	70	69	73	67	279
J Bland	73	71	67	68	279
N Hansen	68	72	73	66	279
M King	74	66	67	72	279
B Lane	70	71	69	69	279
C O'Connor Jr	74	68	70	67	279
M Roe	73	70	68	68	279
D Smyth	70	71	70	68	279

Madrid Open

1973   *at Real Automovil Club de Espana and Real Club de la Puerta de Hierro*

NAME	SCORE				
G Garrido	67	74	73	73	287
E Perera	72	75	71	70	288
CA Clark	70	73	79	67	289
J Kinsella	74	79	70	67	290
D Hayes	69	79	71	71	290
H Baiocchi	71	72	73	74	290
R Bernardini	71	77	74	69	291
NC Coles	76	73	73	69	291
V Barrios	73	78	71	70	292
M Pinero	72	74	73	73	292
W Humphreys	75	72	72	73	292

1974   *at Real de la Puerta de Hierro and Club de Campo, Villa de Madrid*

NAME	SCORE				
M Pinero	73	71	69	70	283
V Barrios	75	67	69	72	283
(Pinero won play-off)					
R Bernardini	73	73	69	70	285
P Townsend	71	69	76	70	286
V Fernandez	69	70	76	71	286
J Fourie	72	73	73	70	288
D Hayes	75	67	68	78	288
N Job	76	69	69	74	288
I Stanley	70	76	74	70	290
M Sanchez	72	74	72	72	290
JM Canizares	78	72	68	72	290

1975   *at Lomas- Bosque*

NAME		SCORE	
R Shearer	68	67	135
D Hayes	68	70	138
N Wood	68	70	138
V Barrios	70	70	140
BW Barnes	69	72	141
M Montes	73	68	141
L Higgins	72	69	141
J Garner	70	72	142
A Rivadeneira	71	71	142
S Ballesteros	70	72	142

1976   *at Real Club de la Puerta de Hierro*

NAME		SCORE			
F Abreu	75	65	66	69	275
A Garrido	75	69	69	71	284
H Baiocchi	69	72	70	74	285
JM Canizares	72	72	68	73	285
P Townsend	72	70	73	71	286
J Cabo	74	70	72	70	286
B Langer	69	76	71	70	286
M Calero	71	72	73	70	286
D Jagger	71	74	72	69	286
M Sanchez	72	71	74	70	287

1977   *at Hipica Espana Club de Campo, Madrid*

NAME		SCORE			
A Garrido	71	68	68	71	278
F Abreu	66	73	73	69	281
JM Canizares	73	71	72	68	284
N Faldo	70	72	73	69	284
J Bland	71	70	72	71	284
S Hobday	71	72	68	73	284
M James	69	72	79	65	285
E Polland	68	71	73	73	285
J Fourie	75	70	70	72	287
M Pinero	74	75	66	73	288
A Gallardo	71	75	69	73	288

1978   *at Real Club de la Puerta de Hierro*

NAME		SCORE			
H Clark	70	70	72	70	282
JM Canizares	75	69	68	72	284
S Ballesteros	66	72	74	73	285

NAME		SCORE			
H Baiocchi	73	71	67	75	286
V Barrios	73	70	71	73	287
P Townsend	71	71	70	75	287
J Fourie	77	73	69	71	290
D Hayes	75	73	69	73	290
S Balbuena	75	72	74	70	291
T Britz	73	74	72	72	291

1979   *at Real Club de la Puerta de Hierro*

NAME		SCORE			
S Hobday	67	73	71	74	285
GJ Brand	69	73	76	69	287
T Britz	73	76	69	69	287
F Abreu	70	70	74	73	287
B Gallacher	67	76	73	72	288
S Balbuena	75	77	70	67	289
H Baiocchi	67	74	75	73	289
M King	70	72	71	76	289
JM Canizares	74	74	71	71	290
A Garrido	73	74	68	75	290
S Ballesteros	73	74	68	75	290

1980   *at Real Club de la Puerta de Hierro*

NAME		SCORE			
S Ballesteros	68	63	70	69	270
M Pinero	67	69	69	68	273
N Price	70	68	71	70	279
P Elson	75	70	73	65	283
J Bland	71	68	68	76	283
D Watson	76	72	67	69	284
J Rivero	71	70	71	72	284
W Humphreys	72	75	69	69	285
A Jacklin	72	68	72	73	285
V Barrios	75	70	67	74	286
AWB Lyle	71	72	73	70	286

1981   *at Real Club de la Puerta de Hierro*

NAME		SCORE			
M Pinero	70	68	69	72	279
D Smyth	73	65	77	69	284
B Dassu	70	72	74	70	288
B Langer	72	71	72	73	288
A Garrido	74	70	70	74	288
JM Canizares	71	70	72	75	288
M King	77	69	73	70	289

NAME	SCORE				
W McColl	78	71	72	70	291
BW Barnes	73	69	75	74	291
E Polland	71	73	73	74	291

1982   *at Real Club de la Puerta de Hierro*

NAME	SCORE				
S Ballesteros	70	69	66	68	273
JM Canizares	70	64	69	71	274
A Garrido	67	70	69	69	275
V Fernandez	69	71	71	67	278
S Torrance	71	67	68	74	280
AWB Lyle	71	67	68	76	282
J Rivero	72	72	68	71	283
I Mosey	72	75	69	68	284
J Rassett	72	69	72	71	284
D Smyth	71	71	68	74	284
J Anderson	70	69	70	75	284

1983   *at Real Club de la Puerta de Hierro*

NAME	SCORE				
AWB Lyle	70	69	76	70	285
GJ Brand	70	72	71	74	287
R Rafferty	75	70	75	69	289
A Garrido	69	77	72	71	289
S Ballesteros	71	72	73	73	289
T Sieckmann	69	71	77	74	291
P Way	73	71	71	76	291
M Calero	73	78	72	69	292
B Gallacher	72	77	74	70	293
B Langer	71	72	76	75	294

1984   *at Real Club de la Puerta de Hierro*

NAME	SCORE				
H Clark	66	68	69	71	274
JM Canizares	68	71	70	68	277
D Frost	69	69	71	69	278
E Darcy	71	68	71	69	279
M Johnson	68	70	73	70	281
M Poxon	70	72	68	71	281
M Ballesteros	73	70	67	72	282
A Garrido	69	74	71	68	282
DJ Russell	72	69	69	72	282
D Smyth	71	69	70	72	282
S Ballesteros	71	72	70	69	282

1985   *at Real Club de la Puerta de Hierro*

NAME	SCORE				
M Pinero	67	71	67	73	278
JM Canizares	69	70	70	69	278
V Fernandez	69	74	72	64	279
S Torrance	73	67	70	69	279
D Smyth	72	71	70	68	281
C Moody	71	71	69	70	281
J Rivero	71	71	67	72	281
O Sellberg	71	72	68	71	282
D Feherty	70	68	72	72	282
B Marchbank	71	65	71	75	282

1986   *at Real Club de la Puerta de Hierro*

NAME	SCORE				
H Clark	70	68	67	69	274
S Ballesteros	69	67	69	70	275
I Woosnam	69	69	70	71	279
JM Olazabal	72	68	71	69	280
O Sellberg	67	70	72	72	281
B Waites	71	69	69	73	282
R Rafferty	70	70	71	71	282
R Drummond	71	73	71	67	282
G Ralph	73	71	68	70	282
G Brand Jr	69	70	71	73	283
S Torrance	70	71	73	69	283
M King	70	67	73	73	283
A Chandler	73	70	70	70	283

1987   *at Real Club de la Puerta de Hierro*

NAME	SCORE				
I Woosnam	67	67	69	66	269
W Grady	67	73	68	64	272
S Ballesteros	69	67	71	66	273
N Faldo	70	71	69	64	274
J Rivero	69	70	72	66	277
H Clark	72	68	71	68	279
O Sellberg	71	72	69	69	281
J Bland	68	74	69	71	282
M Mouland	73	70	70	69	282
R Rafferty	70	74	69	69	282

1988 *at Real Club de la Puerta de Hierro*

NAME	SCORE				
D Cooper	70	68	69	68	275
M Pinero	69	69	67	71	276
MA Martin	69	69	68	70	276
S Ballesteros	69	68	69	72	278
H Clark	69	76	71	64	280
M McNulty	71	67	71	71	280
J Morgan	68	72	68	72	280
M James	71	70	69	70	280
B Gallacher	69	71	70	70	280
I Gervas	65	69	73	74	281
D Ray	72	73	69	67	281

1989 *at Real Club de la Puerta de Hierro*

NAME	SCORE				
S Ballesteros	67	67	69	69	272
H Clark	65	68	70	70	273
P Walton	70	67	70	68	275
M Lanner	70	70	68	68	276

NAME	SCORE				
D Cooper	67	72	67	71	277
A Charnley	70	69	70	69	278
R Davis	69	72	70	68	279
M Persson	64	70	75	70	279
E Dussart	69	71	68	72	280
SC Mason	70	68	71	71	280
M James	70	68	68	74	280
M Smith	69	72	69	70	280

1990 *at Real Club de la Puerta de Hierro*

NAME	SCORE				
B Langer	70	67	66	67	270
R Davis	67	70	68	66	271
B Ogle	72	66	73	61	272
M Sunesson	72	65	66	70	273
R Stelten	73	68	67	68	276
P Walton	70	69	71	67	277
J Rivero	67	71	70	69	277
J Hawksworth	69	68	72	69	278
G Brand Jr	68	70	72	68	278
G Turner	70	70	70	69	279
J Rutledge	71	69	69	70	279

American Express Mediterranean Open

1990 *at Las Brisas, Marbella*

NAME	SCORE			
I Woosnam	68	68	74	210
E Romero	70	71	71	212
MA Martin	69	69	74	212
C O'Connor Jr	71	71	71	213
M James	67	71	76	214

NAME	SCORE			
P Smith	72	72	72	216
A Murray	74	70	72	216
J Morgan	74	75	68	217
P Fowler	71	72	74	217
M McNulty	72	69	76	217
M Lanner	70	71	76	217

Monte Carlo Open
at La Turbie, Mont Agel

1984

NAME	SCORE		
I Mosey	68	63	131
M Calero	68	67	135
P Fowler	67	68	135
J Gonzalez	69	67	136
G Brand Jr	69	67	136
I Baker-Finch	69	67	136
I Aoki	67	69	136
M McLean	66	70	136
C Moody	70	67	137
T Horton	69	68	137
L Trevino	68	69	137

1985

NAME	SCORE				
S Torrance	69	63	62	70	264
I Aoki	63	68	64	70	265
AWB Lyle	67	69	65	68	269
R Lee	61	68	73	69	271
B Langer	69	69	67	67	272
G Player	68	67	70	67	272
JM Canizares	71	69	66	68	274
A Garrido	73	67	69	65	274
C Moody	69	69	70	66	274
M McLean	68	68	70	68	274
RJ Charles	65	70	71	68	274
P Carrigill	69	67	71	67	274

1986

NAME	SCORE				
S Ballesteros	66	71	64	64	265
M McNulty	69	69	63	67	267
J Bland	66	68	65	69	268
A Garrido	67	66	65	70	268
M McLean	67	64	67	70	268
P Senior	66	67	66	69	268
G Cali	70	67	63	69	269
J Rivero	68	68	66	67	269
MA Martin	72	63	66	68	269
S Elkington	67	66	66	70	269

1987

NAME	SCORE				
P Senior	66	63	65	66	260
R Davis	71	63	65	62	261
P Walton	66	65	73	62	266
S Ballesteros	68	66	68	65	267
P Curry	67	69	63	68	267
I Baker-Finch	69	62	69	69	269
GJ Brand	70	66	68	65	269
G Levenson	69	65	65	70	269
B Marchbank	63	70	65	71	269
F Allem	68	70	68	64	270
S Grappasonni	67	68	69	66	270

1988

NAME	SCORE				
J Rivero	65	64	67	65	261
M McNulty	66	62	68	67	263
S Ballesteros	65	66	67	68	266
L Stephen	72	68	62	66	268
H Baiocchi	67	68	67	68	270
N Faldo	71	65	69	67	272
J Hawkes	66	70	71	66	273
BE Smith	71	67	68	67	273
G Levenson	67	66	70	71	274
P Senior	70	68	67	69	274

1989

NAME	SCORE				
M McNulty	68	64	64	65	261
J Hawkes	64	72	67	64	267
JM Canizares	68	66	65	68	267
P Senior	66	66	67	69	268
R Lee	68	70	69	64	271
P Mitchell	65	68	67	71	271
P Fowler	66	72	70	64	272
L Carbonetti	68	66	71	67	272
G Levenson	70	70	67	66	273
M Allen	71	67	70	65	273
B Langer	66	68	71	68	273
J Rivero	67	71	67	68	273
MA Jimenez	72	64	68	69	273

1990

NAME	SCORE				
I Woosnam	66	67	65	60	258
C Rocca	67	66	67	63	263
M McNulty	67	66	66	65	264
M Mouland	63	67	65	69	264
M Lanner	68	66	72	63	269

NAME	SCORE				
J Hawkes	70	66	67	66	269
C Williams	70	70	66	64	270
J Anglada	70	64	69	67	270
S Ballesteros	72	66	63	69	270
D Williams	69	71	66	65	271
H Baiocchi	64	69	70	68	271

Moroccan Open

1987   *at Rabat*

NAME	SCORE				
H Clark	73	73	66	72	284
M James	71	70	72	74	287
P Baker	71	72	77	68	288
S Torrance	75	73	71	70	289
R Commans	74	72	71	73	290

NAME	SCORE				
M Pinero	75	73	70	72	290
I Woosnam	72	71	73	74	290
JM Olazabal	71	75	72	73	291
I Young	75	71	69	76	291
J Heggarty	70	78	69	75	292
W Riley	75	76	70	71	292

Motorola Classic

1989   *at Burnham & Berrow*

NAME	SCORE				
D Llewellyn	64	69	72	67	272
D Williams	70	68	67	71	276
R Weir	70	67	71	69	277
P Carrigill	71	71	71	65	278

NAME	SCORE				
D Prosser	71	69	69	70	279
R Stelten	70	69	72	69	280
BW Barnes	73	66	68	73	280
S Richardson	71	70	69	71	281
P Teravainen	71	68	72	71	282
D Jagger	69	70	73	71	283

Murphy's Cup

1989 *at St Pierre*
(Stableford Points Format)

NAME	POINTS				
H Baiocchi	35	40	39	42	156
J Hawkes	36	39	37	42	154
J Bland	38	37	39	40	154
M McNulty	38	38	37	39	152
AR Stephen	37	38	37	39	151
C Peete	35	42	35	37	149
SC Mason	38	38	36	37	149
W Longmuir	31	36	39	42	148
S Hoch	35	34	40	39	148
BW Barnes	32	38	41	37	148

1990 *at Fulford, York*
(Modified Stableford Points Format)

NAME	POINTS				
A Johnstone	6	23	6	15	50
M Mackenzie	8	13	16	11	48
R Claydon	10	15	7	12	44
AWB Lyle	9	10	8	13	40
M Poxon	7	7	9	16	39
B Lane	5	13	10	9	37
G Krause	7	17	9	3	36
C O'Connor Jr	8	8	11	9	36
P Way	4	9	10	13	36
P Baker	2	11	9	12	34

PLM Open

1986 *at Falsterbo*

NAME	SCORE				
P Senior	69	72	64	68	273
M Lanner	73	70	65	67	275
O Sellberg	76	66	68	66	276
T Armour III	70	68	70	69	277
M Persson	71	70	71	66	278
GJ Brand	69	70	70	69	278
DA Russell	71	65	70	72	278
G Turner	68	66	72	72	278
E Darcy	76	70	65	68	279
R Stewart	74	68	69	68	279
R Rafferty	72	68	73	66	279

1987 *at Ljunghusen, Malmo*

NAME	SCORE				
H Clark	68	73	67	63	271
O Moore	73	63	69	68	273
P Senior	67	69	67	71	274
GJ Brand	70	68	70	68	276
V Fernandez	72	68	70	66	276

NAME	SCORE				
R Rafferty	68	71	69	69	277
C Moody	71	68	67	72	278
A Forsbrand	70	72	69	68	279
B Lane	70	70	71	68	279
M Persson	70	70	67	72	279
D Smyth	68	72	70	69	279

1988 *at Flommen, Falsterbo*

NAME	SCORE				
F Nobilo	63	68	71	68	270
H Clark	68	69	68	66	271
P Fowler	65	69	72	70	276
A Forsbrand	67	66	72	71	276
C Montgomerie	66	67	74	69	276
O Sellberg	69	68	72	69	278
A Sorensen	69	68	71	71	279
C Parry	67	67	76	70	280
A Charnley	66	66	76	72	280
M Persson	68	71	72	69	280
S Bennett	72	69	67	72	280
M Mouland	68	74	69	69	280

1989   *at Bokskogen, Malmo*

NAME	SCORE				
M Harwood	66	70	67	68	271
P Senior	68	67	65	72	272
S Torrance	71	67	65	70	273
M Lanner	70	68	69	67	274
B Langer	68	66	69	71	274
R Rafferty	69	69	66	72	276
P Walton	67	72	66	71	276
O Sellberg	69	73	65	70	277
L Hederstrom	71	66	70	70	277
M Moreno	68	68	73	69	278

1990   *at Bokskogen, Malmo*

NAME	SCORE				
R Rafferty	64	67	70	69	270
V Singh	69	71	69	65	274
B Langer	72	68	67	68	275
O Sellberg	68	66	72	70	276
F Couples	70	72	69	65	276
C Cookson	68	71	72	67	278
R Davis	70	70	73	65	278
J Pinsent	71	69	71	67	278
F Nobilo	67	70	72	71	280
M Clayton	73	70	65	72	280
J Van de Velde	68	70	68	74	280

Portuguese Open

1973   *at Penina*

NAME	SCORE				
J Benito	73	74	72	75	294
B Gallacher	77	69	75	73	294
(Benito won play-off)					
M Bembridge	69	75	75	77	296
T Britz	72	75	74	76	297
J Garner	74	74	73	76	297
H Baiocchi	77	70	75	76	298
BGC Huggett	78	72	73	75	298
A Brooks	72	74	78	74	298
C O'Connor Sr	71	78	76	73	298
PJ Butler	76	71	79	73	299
S Torrance	79	73	75	72	299

1975   *at Penina*

NAME	SCORE				
H Underwood	73	72	71	76	292
V Fernandez	77	73	70	75	295
S Hobday	76	70	76	75	297
J Benito	70	77	77	74	298
NC Coles	72	72	74	80	298
N Wood	81	74	72	72	299
M Ballesteros	79	73	73	74	299
S Ballesteros	74	74	76	75	299
PJ Butler	76	71	75	78	300
E Darcy	74	73	79	74	300

1974   *at Estoril*

NAME	SCORE				
BGC Huggett	71	66	68	67	272
J Fourie	73	65	68	68	274
J O'Leary	68	71	72	67	278
E Darcy	67	69	70	72	278
C O'Connor Jr	68	75	68	67	278
A Gallardo	73	68	69	68	278
M Pinero	69	67	73	69	278
P Townsend	74	69	68	68	279
F Abreu	70	67	74	68	279
GL Hunt	73	67	71	68	279
J Kinsella	72	71	66	70	279

1976   *at Quinta do Lago*

NAME	SCORE				
S Balbuena	69	68	74	72	283
S Torrance	75	73	69	70	287
C DeFoy	73	76	68	71	288
PJ Butler	70	72	73	73	288
S Ballesteros	74	72	70	73	289
T Horton	73	73	72	72	290
A Garrido	72	73	73	72	290
M Pinero	74	72	71	73	290
BW Barnes	74	74	71	72	291
JM Canizares	71	73	74	73	291

1977 *at Penina*

NAME	SCORE				
M Ramos	70	74	75	68	287
H Baiocchi	74	73	69	73	289
V Baker	73	74	74	70	291
A Garrido	74	70	76	71	291
P Townsend	70	79	70	72	291
B Gallacher	71	78	72	71	292
BW Barnes	74	74	75	70	293
K Brown	73	75	71	74	293
J O'Leary	69	76	73	75	293
C Witcher	74	70	75	74	293

1978 *at Penina*

NAME	SCORE				
H Clark	71	75	71	74	291
BW Barnes	73	79	74	66	292
S Hobday	72	76	73	71	292
A Garrido	73	77	68	75	293
M James	72	72	78	72	294
K Brown	74	72	74	74	294
D McClelland	78	73	74	72	296
J Gallardo	77	67	77	75	296
A Gallardo	79	72	72	73	296
JM Canizares	74	76	76	71	297
SC Mason	77	73	76	71	297
J Hammond	75	75	71	76	297

1979 *at Vilamoura*

NAME	SCORE				
BW Barnes	69	75	71	72	287
F Abreu	71	70	73	75	289
D Hayes	73	77	69	72	291
M James	74	73	75	70	292
E Darcy	71	75	75	71	292
A Garrido	73	72	76	72	293
T Horton	76	75	71	73	295
AWB Lyle	77	71	71	76	295
A Jacklin	74	73	72	76	295
K Brown	76	70	76	74	296
S Hobday	73	75	74	74	296

1980–81 *Not played*

1982 *at Penina*

NAME	SCORE			
S Torrance	71	67	69	207
N Faldo	70	69	72	211
J Hall	69	72	72	213
J Anglada	69	71	74	214
H Clark	75	69	71	215
T Horton	74	71	71	216
A Garrido	72	73	71	216
C O'Connor Jr	70	74	73	217
K Brown	72	70	75	217
SC Mason	70	77	71	218
AWB Lyle	73	71	74	218
G Ralph	73	70	75	218

1983 *at Tróia, Setúbal*

NAME	SCORE				
S Torrance	72	73	71	70	286
C Moody	70	73	78	68	289
P Cargill	75	70	76	71	292
H Baiocchi	70	73	74	76	293
J O'Leary	74	72	73	75	294
M King	76	74	74	71	295
M Miller	75	73	74	74	296
P Way	77	73	71	75	296
A Johnstone	74	75	70	77	296
P Teravainen	74	75	74	75	298

1984 *at Quinta do Lago*

NAME	SCORE				
A Johnstone	70	69	67	68	274
M King	67	70	69	69	277
S Torrance	68	71	73	67	279
M Montes	67	71	71	70	279
D Frost	77	65	64	73	279
R Rafferty	76	66	70	68	280
A Garrido	72	68	70	70	280
JM Canizares	73	61	69	71	280
M James	69	71	68	72	280
R Chapman	70	69	73	69	281

1985   *at Quinta do Lago*

NAME	SCORE				
W Humphreys	69	68	71	71	279
H Baiocchi	73	66	73	68	280
M Poxon	69	70	72	70	281
GJ Brand	70	70	71	70	281
N Crosby	70	72	69	70	281
R Cromwell	70	77	67	68	282
J O'Leary	73	67	72	70	282
L Jones	71	70	71	70	282
S Ballesteros	69	72	68	73	282
DJ Russell	70	69	71	72	282
G Ralph	69	72	67	74	282
R Boxall	68	69	71	74	282

1986   *at Quinta do Lago*

NAME	SCORE				
M McNulty	66	69	69	66	270
I Mosey	69	69	69	67	274
J Bland	67	66	71	72	276
JM Canizares	68	70	72	66	276
A Forsbrand	72	66	71	68	277
A Johnstone	69	71	66	71	277
AWB Lyle	66	67	71	73	277
GJ Brand	68	70	72	69	279
R Chapman	73	71	69	66	279
J Higgins	72	67	68	72	279

1987   *at Estoril*

NAME	SCORE			
R Lee	61	67	67	195
S Torrance	67	64	65	196
O Sellberg	69	65	63	197
A Sherborne	65	67	65	197
I Young	69	66	63	198
P Walton	71	63	64	198
C O'Connor Jr	69	65	64	198
J Rivero	70	66	63	199
P Baker	64	69	66	199
J O'Leary	66	66	68	200

3 rounds only played due to weather

1988   *at Quinta do Lago*

NAME	SCORE				
M Harwood	73	70	68	69	280
E Darcy	69	70	72	70	281

NAME	SCORE				
P Baker	74	68	67	73	282
D Smyth	70	74	68	70	282
P Fowler	71	68	73	71	283
I Gervas	74	70	69	71	284
P Harrison	69	73	73	70	285
J Rivero	73	72	71	69	285
R Boxall	74	71	69	72	286
GJ Brand	73	73	73	67	286
A Johnstone	72	71	71	72	286
M Mackenzie	74	70	70	72	286
R Rafferty	71	71	70	74	286
W Westner	74	70	73	69	286

1989   *at Quinta do Lago*

NAME	SCORE				
C Montgomerie	67	65	69	63	264
M Smith	70	69	66	70	275
M Moreno	71	69	69	66	275
R Davis	66	72	69	68	275
M Pinero	68	70	72	66	276
C O'Connor Jr	69	68	71	68	276
S Stephen	71	69	68	69	277
D Feherty	70	71	67	69	277
GJ Brand	70	71	67	69	277
P Senior	73	65	71	68	277
A Garrido	69	71	67	70	277
P Fowler	69	68	73	67	277

1990   *at Quinta do Lago*

NAME	SCORE				
M McLean	69	69	65	71	274
G Brand Jr	68	70	68	69	275
M Harwood	70	68	71	66	275
M James	68	69	70	69	276
P Broadhurst	70	69	68	69	276
P Hartmann	68	68	73	69	277
O Sellberg	67	68	70	72	277
M Poxon	73	68	69	68	278
D Williams	72	69	69	68	278
J Quiros	72	68	68	71	279
S Bennett	73	69	70	67	279

Sanyo Open

1982 *at Sant Cugat, Barcelona*

NAME	SCORE				
NC Coles	71	67	64	64	266
G Cullen	71	68	64	64	267
M Montes	65	70	64	70	269
M Pinero	69	66	68	67	270
K Waters	70	67	69	65	271
J Anglada	66	69	68	68	271
D Jones	68	69	70	65	272
W Humphreys	67	65	72	69	273
T Horton	68	70	64	71	273
M Calero	66	70	72	66	274
DJ Russell	71	64	71	68	274

1983 *at El Prat, Barcelona*

NAME	SCORE				
D Smyth	72	66	70	71	279
M James	70	75	69	66	280
H Baiocchi	68	73	75	64	280
G Cullen	67	77	68	69	281
E Darcy	72	71	67	73	283
J Fowler	74	73	70	67	284
M Miller	73	67	72	72	284
M King	69	77	70	69	285
JM Canizares	69	74	73	69	285
G Brand Jr	70	72	72	71	285

1984 *at El Prat, Barcelona*

NAME	SCORE				
S Torrance	71	69	70	71	281
D Smyth	71	71	67	72	281
(Torrance won play-off)					
D Frost	69	70	75	69	283

NAME	SCORE				
M Clayton	72	72	72	68	284
R Rafferty	70	67	77	70	284
P Way	70	72	69	73	284
JM Canizares	73	72	70	70	285
C O'Connor Jr	72	67	75	71	285
V Fernandez	74	70	70	71	285
M Montes	74	69	73	70	286

1985 *at El Prat, Barcelona*

NAME	SCORE				
S Ballesteros	66	70	65	71	272
J Hawkes	72	68	64	71	275
C O'Connor Jr	69	67	69	71	276
JM Canizares	74	69	72	63	278
J Rivero	70	68	71	69	278
M Pinero	70	68	70	71	279
I Woosnam	72	71	71	66	280
P Fowler	71	68	73	68	280
D Smyth	70	69	71	70	280
M James	72	68	71	70	281

1986 *at El Prat, Barcelona*

NAME	SCORE				
JM Olazabal	69	68	69	67	273
H Clark	72	68	69	67	276
I Mosey	73	67	68	69	277
S Ballesteros	67	67	73	71	278
O Sellberg	70	71	65	72	278
I Woosnam	71	68	69	70	278
J Anglada	67	74	67	71	279
G Brand Jr	69	70	68	72	279
E Darcy	71	70	70	68	279
A Oldcorn	73	67	71	68	279
R Rafferty	69	71	70	69	279

Scandinavian Enterprise Open

1973 *at Drottningholm, Stockholm*

NAME	SCORE				
RJ Charles	69	69	70	70	278
V Baker	70	72	70	68	280
H Muscroft	71	70	69	70	280
A Jacklin	69	74	67	70	280
G Marsh	73	70	70	69	282
V Barrios	68	72	71	71	282
P Townsend	68	76	68	72	284
M Ballesteros	71	73	68	72	284
S Hobday	71	71	69	73	284
A Gallardo	71	68	69	77	285
N Hunt	73	74	68	70	285
BGC Huggett	73	71	70	71	285

1974 *at Bokskogen, Malmo*

NAME	SCORE				
A Jacklin	70	65	69	75	279
JM Canizares	73	72	74	71	290
S Torrance	72	68	74	77	291
N Job	73	73	74	72	292
D Hayes	76	73	74	69	292
RJ Charles	71	70	78	74	293
J Garaialde	72	74	71	76	293
J O'Leary	72	75	71	75	293
M Pinero	76	71	73	73	293
R Shearer	73	70	79	72	294

1975 *at Bokskogen, Malmo*

NAME	SCORE				
G Burns	70	70	70	69	279
G Marsh	69	70	68	72	279
(Burns won play-off)					
BGC Huggett	71	69	71	69	280
R Gilder	73	69	70	69	281
W Brask	68	73	72	71	284
C O'Connor Jr	74	68	73	70	285
A Garrido	74	70	70	71	285
J Pate	71	68	74	72	285
A Gallardo	70	73	74	70	287
R Shearer	73	73	66	75	287

1976 *at Drottningholm, Stockholm*

NAME	SCORE				
H Baiocchi	68	65	70	68	271
E Darcy	68	70	69	66	273
S Ballesteros	72	68	69	66	275
L Higgins	67	72	69	68	276
B Garrett	72	72	64	68	276
V Fernandez	69	73	71	67	280
P Townsend	67	71	74	68	280
D Hayes	71	72	69	68	280
M Pinero	70	73	68	69	280
M Lye	70	67	71	72	280

1977 *at Drottningholm, Stockholm*

NAME	SCORE				
R Byman	70	69	68	68	275
H Baiocchi	73	68	68	67	276
S Ballesteros	71	69	70	67	277
A Gallardo	72	70	69	67	278
L Hinkle	71	73	67	67	278
H Clark	71	67	69	71	278
G Hallberg (Am)	70	69	72	67	278
B Gardner	72	69	72	67	280
D Vaughan	69	71	69	71	280
G Norman	67	71	69	73	280

1978 *at Vasatorp, Helsingborg*

NAME	SCORE				
S Ballesteros	73	69	68	69	279
D Hayes	67	71	72	70	280
B Gallacher	71	70	70	70	281
M James	72	69	71	70	282
S Torrance	72	70	74	68	284
A Gallardo	70	68	76	70	284
K Brown	75	69	69	72	285
N Ratcliffe	70	74	71	70	285
H Clark	74	69	73	69	285
G Cullen	73	70	71	71	285
M Foster	74	68	73	70	285
S Hobday	70	70	70	75	285

1979   *at Vasatorp, Helsingborg*

NAME	SCORE				
AWB Lyle	73	69	65	69	276
S Ballesteros	70	72	68	69	279
M Krantz	71	72	65	73	281
K Brown	71	70	72	71	284
D Hayes	70	72	71	71	284
E Darcy	70	73	74	68	285
M King	73	71	69	72	285
T Gale	72	72	74	70	288
E Polland	71	73	71	73	288
A Saavedra	71	72	70	75	288
P Townsend	70	73	70	75	288

1980   *at Vasatorp, Helsingborg*

NAME	SCORE				
G Norman	76	66	70	64	276
M James	69	71	68	71	279
S Ballesteros	71	71	71	67	280
RJ Charles	74	70	68	68	280
AWB Lyle	71	70	67	72	280
S Torrance	72	70	67	72	281
K Brown	71	73	66	72	282
M McNulty	71	71	70	71	283
GJ Brand	71	71	69	72	283
M Krantz	69	68	69	77	283

1981   *at Linkoping*

NAME	SCORE				
S Ballesteros	69	70	68	66	273
A Garrido	73	69	71	65	278
N Faldo	72	71	68	70	281
M Pinero	71	70	69	72	282
B Langer	69	70	72	72	283
S Martin	70	71	71	72	284
E Darcy	74	72	67	72	285
A Jacklin	74	68	74	70	286
M James	76	68	72	71	287
RJ Charles	75	70	70	73	288

1982   *at Linkoping*

NAME	SCORE				
R Byman	69	69	66	71	275
S Torrance	71	69	69	69	278
S Ballesteros	68	69	70	72	279
G Cullen	73	73	66	69	281
T Sieckmann	73	70	65	73	281
M James	71	74	69	69	283

NAME	SCORE				
J Gonzalez	69	69	74	71	283
D Smyth	71	73	71	69	284
I Mosey	73	70	72	69	284
J Morgan	75	66	70	73	284
K Kinell (Am)	68	72	70	74	284

1983   *at Lindö, Stockholm*

NAME	SCORE				
S Torrance	73	69	68	70	280
C Stadler	70	69	70	72	281
C Pavin	72	73	70	68	283
W Grady	69	72	74	69	284
M King	70	70	74	70	284
I Woosnam	75	69	70	71	285
SC Mason	70	74	73	69	286
C O'Connor Jr	71	70	74	71	286
M Ferguson	73	71	69	73	286
J Morgan	74	76	63	73	286
P Hoad	74	67	71	74	286

1984   *at Sven Tomba*

NAME	SCORE				
I Woosnam	71	70	69	70	280
P Teravainen	67	74	76	66	283
M Clayton	70	71	72	73	286
AWB Lyle	65	72	81	69	287
C Stadler	73	74	71	69	287
W Longmuir	70	71	74	72	287
I Aoki	77	68	75	68	288
SC Mason	70	70	73	75	288
H Clark	74	68	71	75	288
A Johnstone	71	72	74	72	289
G Marsh	69	73	74	73	289
O Moore	72	71	73	73	289
M Pinero	74	71	69	75	289

1985   *at Ullna, Stockholm*

NAME	SCORE				
I Baker-Finch	68	72	68	66	274
G Marsh	67	70	68	71	276
G Brand Jr	71	69	70	67	277
T Gale	69	73	66	69	277
R Hartmann	69	70	68	70	277
J Miller	66	69	69	73	277
C O'Connor Jr	72	67	72	67	278
B Waites	68	70	68	72	278
M Mouland	67	71	72	69	279
AWB Lyle	68	67	69	75	279

1986   *at Ullna, Stockholm*

NAME	SCORE				
G Turner	69	62	69	70	270
C Stadler	66	66	66	72	270
I Baker-Finch	65	67	71	71	274
J Rivero	70	67	67	72	276
R Rafferty	67	66	68	75	276
H Clark	72	70	66	70	278
M James	66	71	71	72	280
O Sellberg	71	72	72	66	281
R Stewart	71	70	71	69	281
M Lanner	69	73	70	69	281
M Clayton	71	71	69	70	281
T Gale	70	67	72	72	281
R Davis	73	65	71	72	281

1987   *at Ullna, Stockholm*

NAME	SCORE				
G Brand Jr	64	71	71	71	277
M Persson	72	68	69	68	277
(Brand won play-off)					
D Llewellyn	68	67	72	71	278
SC Mason	72	68	67	72	279
R Rafferty	68	65	69	77	279
R Shearer	70	71	69	70	280
D Williams	74	69	68	70	281
I Woosnam	66	74	70	71	281
J Hall	71	69	72	70	282
R Hartmann	68	66	72	76	282
M Hoegberg	74	67	66	75	282
D Smyth	65	66	72	79	282
M Sunesson	70	68	70	74	282

1988   *at Ullna, Stockholm*

NAME	SCORE				
S Ballesteros	67	70	66	67	270
G Taylor	67	68	71	69	275
G Marsh	66	66	77	67	276
P Senior	66	68	72	70	276
KH Han	68	69	69	71	277
G Brand Jr	65	71	68	73	277

NAME	SCORE				
C Stadler	68	69	69	72	278
C Parry	64	69	73	72	278
R Boxall	72	66	66	72	278
B Ogle	73	67	69	70	279
P McWhinney	66	68	78	67	279
R Rafferty	70	68	72	69	279
DJ Russell	68	68	66	77	279

1989   *at Drottningholm, Stockholm*

NAME	SCORE				
R Rafferty	70	69	64	65	268
M Allen	67	71	67	65	270
P Senior	64	70	73	67	274
G Brand Jr	70	70	66	69	275
V Singh	69	70	67	69	275
B Ogle	68	70	70	68	276
D Cooper	70	70	69	67	276
D Whelan	68	73	72	64	277
M Mouland	70	71	67	69	277
J Haas	71	68	68	70	277

1990   *at Drottningholm, Stockholm*

NAME	SCORE				
C Stadler	68	72	67	61	268
C Parry	66	70	69	67	272
R Rafferty	70	71	65	67	273
M Lanner	69	71	70	64	274
MA Jimenez	67	69	72	67	275
M Harwood	68	69	69	69	275
P McWhinney	67	68	71	70	276
G Brand Jr	69	66	68	73	276
R Chapman	72	68	65	71	276
J Morgan	67	70	71	69	277
P Curry	66	72	71	68	277
P Senior	67	67	72	71	277
I Woosnam	70	69	71	67	277
G Turner	70	68	68	71	277
M Mackenzie	73	68	66	70	277

Bell's Scottish Open

(formerly Glasgow Golf Classic;
1983–85)

1983 *at Haggs Castle, Glasgow*

NAME	SCORE				
B Langer	70	66	66	72	274
V Fernandez	70	68	67	70	275
K Brown	69	67	70	73	279
N Faldo	72	69	67	71	279
D Frost	73	65	71	72	281
E Polland	71	70	68	72	281
R Rafferty	68	73	73	68	282
A Garrido	74	70	68	70	282
C O'Connor Jr	70	66	74	72	282
H Baiocchi	71	70	69	72	282
W Grady	71	68	66	67	282

1984 *at Haggs Castle, Glasgow*

NAME	SCORE				
K Brown	63	65	67	71	266
S Torrance	76	70	62	69	277
AWB Lyle	72	71	70	65	278
SC Mason	68	73	74	64	279
D Cooper	70	71	69	69	279
R Drummond	70	70	68	71	279
B Marchbank	69	66	72	72	279
E Darcy	68	72	68	71	279
DJ Russell	71	67	69	72	279
I Baker-Finch	73	70	64	72	279
B Langer	69	69	68	73	279

1985 *at Haggs Castle, Glasgow*

NAME	SCORE				
H Clark	71	65	70	68	274
AWB Lyle	70	66	71	67	274
P Parkin	69	69	72	67	277
I Woosnam	68	69	70	73	280
M James	69	72	71	69	281
R Rafferty	73	67	69	72	281
G Turner	69	70	70	72	281
G Brand Jr	67	74	72	69	282
S Reese	71	71	71	69	282
E Polland	69	71	71	71	282

1986 *at Haggs Castle, Glasgow*

NAME	SCORE				
D Feherty	69	68	66	67	270
C O'Connor Jr	67	66	69	68	270
I Baker-Finch	66	66	66	72	270
R Drummond	71	71	65	65	272
H Baiocchi	68	68	67	70	273
P Thomas	72	66	68	68	274
AWB Lyle	70	69	66	71	276
B Waites	67	69	72	68	276
M Roe	73	68	71	65	277
G Brand Jr	69	70	71	67	277

1987 *at King's Course, Gleneagles*

NAME	SCORE				
I Woosnam	65	65	66	68	264
P Senior	68	66	65	72	271
R Davis	68	67	69	68	272
A Forsbrand	68	68	67	69	272
JM Olazabal	74	62	71	66	273
S Ballesteros	68	65	72	70	275
R Chapman	68	64	71	72	275
F Couples	70	70	65	71	276
E Darcy	73	69	69	66	277
R Drummond	69	70	68	70	277
M James	70	72	68	67	277

1988 *at King's Course, Gleneagles*

NAME	SCORE				
B Lane	70	67	66	68	271
J Rivero	64	70	72	68	274
AWB Lyle	68	69	69	68	274
R Chapman	68	68	67	72	275
P Fowler	71	63	69	73	276
JM Olazabal	71	70	67	69	277
M Lanner	71	71	72	63	277
D Gilford	69	70	70	69	278
R Davis	74	66	68	70	278
R Weir	66	72	67	73	278
D Graham	71	69	70	68	278

1989 *at King's Course, Gleneagles*

NAME	SCORE				
M Allen	73	66	70	63	272
JM Olazabal	67	70	68	69	274
I Woosnam	65	70	71	68	274
R Rafferty	69	67	70	70	276
D Feherty	71	67	69	69	276
M McNulty	69	71	67	70	277
E Romero	72	66	70	69	277
R Chapman	69	70	70	69	278
L Rinker	73	66	68	71	278
AWB Lyle	70	66	72	71	279
M Poxon	68	70	71	70	279
D Smyth	67	72	74	66	279
P Fowler	72	69	68	70	279
R Boxall	72	69	69	69	279
P Senior	71	66	68	74	279

1990 *at King's Course, Gleneagles*

NAME	SCORE				
I Woosnam	72	62	67	68	269
M McNulty	73	67	64	69	273
G Brand Jr	65	67	72	71	275
M Mackenzie	71	72	65	67	275
N Faldo	72	73	67	65	277
D Feherty	69	72	68	68	277
D Cooper	68	69	68	72	277
P Fowler	74	70	65	69	278
C Parry	67	74	71	67	279
R Drummond	71	69	68	71	279
M Roe	74	68	66	71	279

Spanish Open

1972 *at Pals, Gerona*

NAME	SCORE				
A Garrido	77	71	71	74	293
V Barrios	72	70	78	73	293
(Garrido won play-off)					
GL Hunt	76	70	73	75	294
A Gallardo	71	76	73	74	294
D Oakley	70	78	71	75	294
C O'Connor Sr	76	70	74	75	295
L Platts	74	76	70	76	296
H Baiocchi	76	75	73	72	296
J Benito	74	79	71	73	297
A Sadler	76	74	72	75	297
D Hayes	73	75	72	77	297
BGC Huggett	77	75	69	76	297

1974 *at La Manga, Cartagena*

NAME	SCORE				
J Heard	72	67	70	70	279
G Player	72	72	70	71	285
P Townsend	74	67	75	72	288
D Chillas	79	68	74	68	289
D Hayes	77	71	72	69	289
R Panasiuk	73	67	79	71	290
BGC Huggett	78	72	69	71	290
JM Canizares	69	75	73	73	290
C DeFoy	71	77	72	72	292
T Lopez	73	73	73	73	292

1973 *at La Manga, Cartagena*

NAME	SCORE				
NC Coles	67	71	72	72	282
T Britz	69	70	71	75	285
C DeFoy	71	74	71	69	285
PJ Butler	70	72	72	72	286
BW Barnes	71	78	67	71	287
A Jacklin	67	74	72	75	288
J Benito	70	78	70	71	289
M Bembridge	71	72	72	74	289
J Fourie	72	74	74	70	290
BJ Hunt	72	76	72	70	290

1975 *at La Manga, Cartagena*

NAME	SCORE				
A Palmer	72	69	69	73	283
J Fourie	71	72	67	74	284
A Garrido	72	75	67	72	286
V Barrios	70	71	72	73	286
GL Hunt	70	69	73	74	286
NC Coles	71	73	71	72	287
J Heard	74	73	68	72	287
S Ballesteros	73	72	70	72	287
A Gallardo	72	72	69	74	287
BW Barnes	73	70	71	74	288
J O'Leary	73	65	73	77	288

1976 *at La Manga, Cartagena*

NAME	SCORE				
E Polland	72	68	72	70	282
R Shearer	70	68	72	74	284
P Townsend	71	73	71	70	285
G Garrido	71	68	72	74	285
M Ballesteros	71	72	69	73	285
D Jagger	74	67	76	69	286
A Gallardo	76	69	72	69	286
S Ballesteros	70	71	75	70	286
A Garrido	71	72	72	71	286
S Hobday	72	74	72	69	287
M Pinero	67	72	73	75	287
B Gallacher	69	75	70	73	287
A Rivadeneira	68	76	70	73	287

1977 *at La Manga, Cartagena*

NAME	SCORE				
B Gallacher	70	68	70	69	277
F Abreu	71	70	67	71	279
S Ballesteros	72	66	74	69	281
B Dassu	69	71	70	71	281
J Fourie	72	70	69	71	282
M Sanchez	70	70	71	72	283
P Elson	70	71	68	74	283
S Balbuena	74	71	71	68	284
J Benito	71	69	75	69	284
S Torrance	71	74	70	69	284
M Montes	71	70	68	75	284

1978 *at El Prat, Barcelona*

NAME	SCORE				
BW Barnes	67	75	70	64	276
H Clark	67	67	74	70	278
S Balbuena	73	69	69	69	280
A Garrido	66	70	74	70	280
M King	72	68	72	69	281
S Ballesteros	72	68	70	71	281
M James	71	71	65	74	281
M Ballesteros	70	72	72	69	283
D Hayes	69	71	74	69	283
JM Canizares	69	71	69	74	283

1979 *at Torrequebrada, Malaga*

NAME	SCORE				
D Hayes	70	75	67	66	278
BW Barnes	69	73	66	72	280
B Gallacher	74	70	69	68	281
JM Canizares	67	70	73	71	281
B Dassu	71	71	68	72	282
J Morgan	74	71	70	68	283

NAME	SCORE				
M Poxon	67	70	76	70	283
AWB Lyle	70	70	71	72	283
A Garrido	74	71	70	69	284
N Price	74	68	70	72	284

1980 *at Escorpion, Valencia*

NAME	SCORE				
E Polland	70	69	68	69	276
M James	69	70	70	72	281
S Ballesteros	68	72	69	72	281
K Brown	72	71	68	71	282
S Ginn	71	70	73	70	284
H Baiocchi	72	71	71	70	284
V Fernandez	72	70	68	74	284
D Smyth	70	72	72	71	285
AWB Lyle	73	66	74	72	285
J Purcell	72	70	70	73	285
N Faldo	69	72	71	73	285
B Dassu	71	71	69	74	285
JM Canizares	73	70	69	73	285
G Norman	70	72	69	74	285
A Johnstone	71	67	68	74	285
M Pinero	68	69	74	74	285

1981 *at El Prat, Barcelona*

NAME	SCORE				
S Ballesteros	71	67	70	65	273
S Martin	67	72	67	68	274
V Fernandez	67	67	69	72	275
A Garrido	69	69	71	68	277
W Longmuir	69	70	68	70	277
S Torrance	65	72	75	66	278
A Johnstone	68	67	71	72	278
JM Canizares	67	69	67	75	278
E Polland	72	68	69	70	279
M Pinero	70	71	70	68	279

1982 *at Club de Campo, Villa de Madrid*

NAME	SCORE				
S Torrance	71	65	67	70	273
I Woosnam	71	69	69	72	281
AWB Lyle	71	68	70	72	281
R Chapman	69	71	67	74	281
H Clark	70	69	69	74	282
M Pinero	69	70	69	74	282
G Cullen	74	68	71	70	283
P Hoad	71	70	68	74	283
J Anglada	73	68	68	74	283
JM Canizares	71	76	67	70	284
M King	71	70	72	71	284

1983 *at Las Brisas, Marbella*

NAME	SCORE				
E Darcy	67	71	67	72	277
M Pinero	76	70	65	67	278
JM Canizares	70	71	65	74	280
M Montes	70	66	72	72	280
R Chapman	70	73	71	68	282
A Johnstone	68	75	68	74	282
S Ballesteros	68	75	68	72	283
R Rafferty	71	74	70	68	283
E Murray	73	72	71	68	284
D Jones	70	72	73	69	284
A Forsbrand	71	73	71	69	284
NC Coles	71	72	70	71	284

1984 *at El Saler, Valencia*

NAME	SCORE				
B Langer	73	68	72	62	275
H Clark	66	73	67	71	277
M McLean	71	71	70	68	280
S Ballesteros	71	71	69	70	281
I Woosnam	68	71	71	71	281
M Pinero	77	68	73	65	283
J Anderson	73	70	73	68	284
GJ Brand	71	73	68	72	284
D Frost	71	72	73	69	285

1985 *at Vallromanes, Barcelona*

NAME	SCORE				
S Ballesteros	67	68	65	66	266
G Brand Jr	67	68	66	69	270
M Pinero	66	69	67	69	271
D Cooper	70	66	66	70	272
E Darcy	69	64	72	68	273
R Chapman	66	67	69	71	273
R Drummond	68	68	68	69	273
H Baiocchi	65	70	68	71	274
J Rivero	69	70	65	71	275
B McColl	69	70	65	71	275
M Poxon	69	67	72	67	275

1986 *at La Moraleja, Madrid*

NAME	SCORE				
H Clark	68	71	66	67	272
I Baker-Finch	69	68	68	68	273
S Ballesteros	74	66	68	68	276
R Lee	72	70	65	71	278
R Drummond	68	72	72	68	280
M Pinero	73	69	70	68	280

NAME	SCORE				
J Rivero	72	68	67	74	281
I Mosey	74	70	68	70	282
R Davis	75	71	72	64	282
P Parkin	72	70	71	70	283
M McNulty	73	71	68	71	283

1987 *at Las Brisas, Marbella*

NAME	SCORE				
N Faldo	72	71	71	72	286
H Baiocchi	73	69	72	74	288
S Ballesteros	70	72	74	72	288
J Anderson	75	72	72	72	291
M James	77	72	72	71	292
M McNulty	77	70	74	72	293
R Rafferty	72	72	76	73	293
R Davis	71	78	73	72	294
AWB Lyle	74	70	75	75	294
L Stephen	73	71	77	73	294

1988 *at Real Pedrena, Santander*

NAME	SCORE				
M James	63	68	63	68	262
N Faldo	68	67	62	68	265
R Boxall	63	64	70	69	266
GJ Brand	70	66	64	68	268
C O'Connor Jr	67	66	69	66	268
E Darcy	71	68	67	64	270
JM Olazabal	71	66	65	68	270
MA Martin	70	67	65	68	270
G Brand Jr	69	68	68	66	271
D Cooper	69	71	63	68	271
D Williams	67	66	69	69	271
C Montgomerie	69	64	70	68	271

1989 *at El Saler, Valencia*

NAME	SCORE				
B Langer	70	72	67	72	281
JM Canizares	72	72	70	70	284
P Carrigill	70	69	72	73	284
JM Olazabal	70	72	70	73	285
M Lanner	71	72	71	72	286
G Brand Jr	71	73	69	74	287
B Lane	72	69	75	71	287
D Feherty	70	70	74	74	288
S Ballesteros	75	68	74	72	289
J Rystrom	72	73	72	72	289

1990 *at Club de Campo, Villa de Madrid*

NAME	SCORE				
R Davis	74	69	68	66	277
N Faldo	70	71	72	65	278
B Langer	70	71	69	68	278
P Fowler	72	68	69	69	278
S McAllister	74	71	65	70	280

NAME	SCORE				
Y Beamonte	71	75	67	68	281
S Ballesteros	74	70	68	69	281
JM Olazabal	71	67	71	72	281
S Bowman	71	70	68	72	281
J Parnevik	70	72	72	68	282
M McNulty	69	70	72	71	282
MA Martin	68	70	72	72	282

Swiss Open
at Crans-sur-Sierre

1972

NAME	SCORE				
G Marsh	67	67	66	70	270
A Jacklin	74	65	64	68	271
S Hobday	68	66	70	69	273
A Gallardo	67	66	71	70	274
J Gallardo	69	66	67	72	274
M Ballesteros	70	70	68	67	275
N Job	70	71	67	68	276
G Baleson	69	68	67	72	276
R Bernardini	65	71	66	74	276
M Bembridge	71	69	70	67	277
P Oosterhuis	68	70	71	68	277
J Garner	70	67	71	69	277
S Cook	65	69	71	72	277

1974

NAME	SCORE				
RJ Charles	70	70	67	68	275
A Jacklin	72	72	64	68	276
D Hayes	71	64	72	72	279
J Newton	69	69	72	70	280
H Baiocchi	70	71	67	72	280
V Fernandez	72	71	71	68	282
GL Hunt	69	74	70	69	282
D Swaelens	68	69	70	75	282
J Garaialde	73	72	67	71	283
F Abreu	72	72	71	69	284
A Brooks	70	75	68	71	284
D Edwards	69	71	71	73	284

1973

NAME	SCORE				
H Baiocchi	70	68	71	69	278
E Polland	71	70	70	68	279
J Newton	73	71	67	68	279
D Jagger	72	70	70	68	280
D Hayes	67	71	69	73	280
A Jacklin	70	67	70	73	280
V Barrios	68	69	72	72	281
S Torrance	69	72	74	67	282
P Molteni	72	72	71	67	282
N Job	74	70	69	69	282
M Pinero	70	70	72	70	282

1975

NAME	SCORE				
D Hayes	68	69	66	70	273
T Britz	68	69	69	68	274
B Gallacher	69	66	70	69	274
G Player	69	67	69	69	274
E Ball	68	68	74	67	277
G Koch	67	71	71	68	277
D Jagger	69	70	68	70	277
D Pooley	72	68	70	68	278
S Ballesteros	71	68	70	69	278
G Groh	68	70	70	70	278
R Shearer	70	71	67	70	278

1976

NAME	SCORE				
M Pinero	69	67	70	68	274
D Hill	70	68	69	70	277
S Ballesteros	72	70	66	70	278
M Foster	70	70	70	71	281
V Fernandez	73	67	70	71	281
T Crandall	68	71	72	71	282
E Darcy	67	73	70	73	283
J Fourie	73	69	69	72	283
S Torrance	71	67	73	73	284
A Rivadeneira	70	69	73	72	284

1977

NAME	SCORE				
S Ballesteros	68	66	70	69	273
J Schroeder	69	70	71	66	276
F Abreu	71	69	66	71	277
J Garaialde	69	69	72	68	278
R Thompson	65	71	74	69	279
M Bembridge	69	69	70	71	279
A Garrido	71	70	66	72	279
G Burrows	71	72	69	68	280
A Gallardo	68	67	75	70	280
L Hinkle	71	70	67	72	280

1978

NAME	SCORE				
S Ballesteros	68	68	68	68	272
M Pinero	71	67	67	70	275
RJ Charles	71	66	70	69	276
JM Canizares	71	67	64	74	276
H Irwin	69	70	68	69	276
S Torrance	70	69	73	65	277
D Hayes	71	69	70	68	278
B Gallacher	73	67	68	70	278
H Clark	70	69	67	72	278
H Baiocchi	71	72	70	66	279

1979

NAME	SCORE				
H Baiocchi	68	67	73	67	275
A Garrido	69	71	72	68	280
D Hayes	68	71	68	73	280
D Lovato	67	70	68	75	280
K Brown	72	70	71	68	281
B Langer	72	69	70	70	281
M Adcock	66	72	72	71	281
E Murray	73	67	68	74	282

NAME	SCORE				
T Britz	72	70	73	68	283
M Pinero	73	68	71	71	283
R Botts	68	67	75	73	283
A Geiberger	69	68	72	74	283

1980

NAME	SCORE				
N Price	65	69	67	66	267
M Calero	74	66	68	65	273
G Norman	69	69	68	68	274
D Hayes	68	70	67	70	275
J Hall	73	68	68	68	277
J Miller	71	67	69	70	277
H Clark	67	70	73	68	278
P Townsend	71	67	69	71	278
P Hoad	67	66	73	73	279
H Henning	69	70	70	71	280
E Polland	67	72	67	74	280
GJ Brand	72	67	67	74	280

1981

NAME	SCORE				
M Pinero	69	73	69	66	277
A Johnstone	69	69	71	68	277
A Garrido	70	69	67	71	277
(Pinero won play-off)					
H Baiocchi	69	70	69	70	278
F Molina	66	72	70	71	279
E Polland	76	67	69	68	280
J Bland	72	69	71	68	280
LP Tupling	71	71	68	70	280
R Botts	67	67	73	73	280
G Burns	73	70	69	69	281
J Cabo	70	68	72	71	281
RJ Charles	67	69	73	72	281
JM Canizares	67	68	69	77	281
G Cullen	68	72	67	74	281

1982

NAME	SCORE				
I Woosnam	68	68	66	70	272
W Longmuir	69	70	67	66	272
(Woosnam won play-off)					
JM Canizares	67	72	70	67	276
H Green	69	71	70	67	277
J Anglada	71	72	66	68	277
M Runge	69	68	67	74	278
B Waites	72	74	66	67	279
J Anderson	73	67	70	69	279

NAME	SCORE				
J Higgins	71	70	67	72	280
S Locatelli	70	71	72	67	280

1983

NAME	SCORE				
N Faldo	70	64	68	66	268
AWB Lyle	64	63	70	71	268
(Faldo won play-off)					
V Fernandez	66	69	72	68	275
S Torrance	63	73	70	70	276
S Ballesteros	72	66	68	70	276
I Woosnam	68	70	66	73	277
RJ Charles	67	68	69	75	279
B Langer	70	67	73	69	279
B Dassu	69	68	73	71	281
B Waites	75	68	70	69	282
M Miller	68	68	73	73	282
B Gallacher	70	74	70	68	282
D Feherty	72	70	70	70	282

1984

NAME	SCORE				
J Anderson	63	66	66	66	261
H Clark	63	71	68	64	266
B Langer	68	65	66	68	267
A Forsbrand	67	70	67	64	268
AWB Lyle	65	68	69	66	268
JM Canizares	68	67	66	68	269
H Green	67	65	71	68	271
I Woosnam	70	71	64	67	272
R Rafferty	71	66	67	68	272
L Wadkins	67	75	64	67	273
P Teravainen	72	65	68	68	273
S Bishop	70	67	68	68	273

1985

NAME	SCORE				
C Stadler	68	65	67	67	267
D Feherty	70	66	67	66	269
O Sellberg	71	66	67	66	269
R Rafferty	70	66	68	66	270
DJ Russell	68	71	65	66	270
JM Canizares	68	68	65	70	271
R Chapman	61	69	67	74	271
R Drummond	68	69	69	66	272
D Smyth	68	67	70	67	272
I Woosnam	66	68	67	71	272
G Levenson	66	66	67	73	272

1986

NAME	SCORE				
JM Olazabal	64	66	66	66	262
A Forsbrand	69	68	63	65	265
GJ Brand	68	65	63	71	267
I Baker-Finch	70	63	65	69	267
R Rafferty	64	66	68	70	268
H Baiocchi	65	68	68	67	268
M McNulty	69	66	68	66	269
JM Canizares	71	68	69	61	269
S Torrance	66	70	69	64	269
T Armour III	71	69	64	65	269
C Stadler	67	67	65	70	269

1987

NAME	SCORE				
A Forsbrand	71	64	66	62	263
M Mouland	66	66	69	65	266
G Ralph	68	66	67	66	267
J Rivero	70	65	68	65	268
I Mosey	66	66	67	70	269
AWB Lyle	71	65	66	68	270
P Walton	68	66	69	67	270
JM Canizares	68	67	65	71	271
N Faldo	71	67	67	66	271
M Harwood	70	69	66	66	271
W Longmuir	65	68	67	71	271
M McNulty	69	67	69	66	271
D Smyth	66	71	65	69	271

1988

NAME	SCORE				
C Moody	68	68	67	65	268
I Woosnam	68	66	66	69	269
S Ballesteros	65	68	68	68	269
A Forsbrand	67	71	67	64	269
P Senior	70	68	64	68	270
R Rafferty	70	66	69	67	272
G Brand Jr	70	68	67	68	273
D Frost	70	68	72	63	273
JM Olazabal	73	69	65	66	273
B Ogle	73	68	65	67	273
N Faldo	67	67	71	68	273

1989

NAME	SCORE				
S Ballesteros	65	68	66	67	266
C Parry	66	69	66	67	268
S Bennett	65	67	66	71	269
J Rivero	66	64	67	73	270
P Quirici	72	67	66	65	270
B Lane	67	65	67	72	271
C Montgomerie	68	66	67	71	272
G Levenson	68	66	71	68	273
M Lanner	65	72	65	71	273
JM Olazabal	69	70	69	65	273

1990

NAME	SCORE				
R Rafferty	70	65	66	66	267
J Bland	70	66	66	67	269
J Spence	66	67	68	69	270
C Parry	72	65	66	68	271
H Clark	64	66	72	69	271
M McNulty	65	72	68	67	272
JM Canizares	69	67	65	71	272
M Mouland	68	72	66	68	274
M Lanner	73	67	66	68	274
D Gilford	70	71	64	69	274
K Waters	68	68	69	69	274
A Forsbrand	68	67	71	68	274
D Williams	69	66	71	68	274
AWB Lyle	67	66	71	70	274

Tenerife Open

1989   *at Golf del Sur, Tenerife*

NAME	SCORE				
JM Olazabal	69	68	68	70	275
D Gilford	72	70	69	67	278
JM Canizares	70	66	70	72	278
M King	74	70	69	67	280
P Walton	70	70	68	72	280
J Quiros	70	73	69	68	280
J Rystrom	72	72	68	68	280
J Rivero	70	72	68	71	281
M Roe	68	69	69	75	281
D Smyth	66	75	68	72	281
R Chapman	74	70	67	70	281

1990   *at Amarilla*

NAME	SCORE				
V Fernandez	67	74	72	69	282
M Mouland	70	73	71	68	282
(Fernandez won play-off)					
C O'Connor Jr	74	71	66	73	284
E Dussart	71	74	69	70	284
A Charnley	71	74	66	73	284
MA Jimenez	68	72	75	70	285
G Turner	70	76	69	71	286
M Pinero	68	73	73	72	286
B Hughes	71	71	74	70	286
D Jones	72	71	71	74	288
J Parnevik	70	71	71	76	288
S Bottomley	73	71	67	77	288
P Carrigill	71	74	70	73	288
J Rivero	71	73	72	72	288
P O'Malley	71	74	72	71	288
J Rutledge	70	72	72	74	288

Timex Open

at Le Phare, Biarritz

1983

NAME	SCORE				
S Ballesteros	67	65	66	64	262
N Faldo	65	65	67	67	264
JM Canizares	67	70	64	64	265
V Fernandez	67	65	67	70	269
R Chapman	70	69	67	66	272
GJ Brand	69	64	71	68	272
G Cullen	65	69	66	72	272
R Craig	68	69	69	67	273
M Tapia	67	67	71	68	273
P Leglise	67	68	69	69	273

1984

NAME	SCORE				
M Clayton	67	65	61	67	260
S Torrance	69	68	61	65	263
P Teravainen	63	66	64	70	263
M Johnson	64	66	68	67	265
R Davis	64	67	66	68	265
E Darcy	68	67	64	67	266
R Hartmann	66	68	64	68	266
J Gonzalez	70	65	67	65	267
P Fowler	69	66	64	68	267
B Langer	67	68	64	68	267

Tunisian Open

at Sousse

1982

NAME	SCORE				
A Garrido	71	73	70	72	286
M Calero	75	69	70	72	286
(Garrido won play-off)					
M Pinero	73	70	75	69	287
D Smyth	71	74	71	71	287
G Brand Jr	76	72	68	71	287
AWB Lyle	74	69	73	72	288
K Brown	74	67	71	76	288
I Mosey	74	72	73	70	289
S Torrance	76	71	69	74	290
SC Mason	72	73	71	74	290
K Williams	70	74	73	73	290

1983

NAME	SCORE				
M James	74	69	69	72	284
GJ Brand	76	70	69	71	286
G Brand Jr	75	68	72	71	286
T Sieckmann	68	70	74	74	286
M Calero	73	71	72	72	288
D Smyth	72	68	74	74	288
I Mosey	68	71	76	74	289
A Garrido	69	72	79	70	290

NAME	SCORE				
B Waites	72	71	74	73	290
M Pinero	72	71	73	74	290

1984

NAME	SCORE				
S Torrance	66	71	75	70	282
B Waites	71	69	68	75	283
E Darcy	68	72	70	74	284
M James	65	70	72	78	285
R Rafferty	72	69	70	78	289
D Feherty	72	72	73	73	290
JM Canizares	75	71	71	74	291
GJ Brand	74	71	68	78	291
DJ Russell	73	70	71	78	292
P Way	72	71	71	79	293

1985

NAME	SCORE				
S Bennett	72	70	68	75	285
P Way	71	71	73	70	285
J Rivero	71	70	69	76	286

NAME	SCORE					NAME	SCORE				
M Pinero	69	70	75	73	287	M Tapia	73	73	70	73	289
E Darcy	70	69	75	74	288	D Smyth	77	72	69	72	290
I Mosey	71	73	69	75	288	D Llewellyn	77	72	71	71	291
D Feherty	74	71	72	72	289	M McLean	71	68	74	78	291

Volvo Masters

at Valderrama, Cadiz

1988

NAME	SCORE				
N Faldo	74	71	71	68	284
S Ballesteros	68	72	74	72	286
AWB Lyle	68	71	75	74	288
I Woosnam	75	74	70	70	289
R Chapman	71	77	70	75	293
E Darcy	74	71	74	74	293
M Lanner	77	70	74	73	294
A Sorensen	76	67	76	75	294
P Fowler	77	71	71	75	294
C O'Connor Jr	78	73	70	73	294

NAME	SCORE				
M James	77	70	71	72	290
H Clark	73	70	74	73	290
C Parry	73	68	75	75	291
V Fernandez	75	73	73	71	292
E Romero	73	73	74	72	292
O Sellberg	75	74	73	70	292

1989

NAME	SCORE				
R Rafferty	72	69	70	71	282
N Faldo	74	68	72	69	283
JM Olazabal	69	70	74	74	287
AWB Lyle	70	76	69	74	289
P Fowler	75	72	69	74	290

1990

NAME	SCORE				
M Harwood	70	72	73	71	286
S Torrance	69	73	72	73	287
S Richardson	71	73	70	73	287
B Langer	72	71	72	73	288
A Forsbrand	75	69	71	73	288
JM Olazabal	72	69	74	73	288
M McNulty	73	73	71	71	288
C Montgomerie	71	72	71	75	289
D Feherty	70	77	67	75	289
R Davis	74	71	74	72	291

Volvo Open

1989   *at Is Molas, Sardinia*

NAME	SCORE				
V Singh	72	68	68	68	276
P Fowler	71	69	71	68	279
GJ Brand	69	72	70	72	283
W Longmuir	71	69	72	71	283
C Bolling Jr	68	72	71	73	284
C O'Connor Jr	70	72	69	73	284
M Mannelli	73	72	71	69	285
P O'Malley	72	70	68	75	285
R Rafferty	72	68	71	74	285
D Williams	73	72	72	68	285

1990   *at Ugolino, Florence*

NAME	SCORE				
E Romero	68	66	64	67	265
C Montgomerie	65	64	67	70	266
R Claydon	63	68	66	69	266
R Davis	69	63	71	66	269
M Hallberg	71	63	67	68	269
P O'Malley	67	64	68	71	270
R Chapman	65	66	70	71	272
P Senior	69	67	68	68	272
J Rutledge	72	65	64	71	272
S Hamill	66	69	67	71	273
M Mouland	68	71	67	67	273

Volvo Senior's British Open

at Ailsa Course, Turnberry

1988

NAME	SCORE				
G Player	65	66	72	69	272
W Casper	68	65	72	68	273
H Henning	70	68	68	68	274
RJ Charles	70	69	68	70	277
J O'Hern	70	70	68	73	281
A Palmer	69	70	73	71	283
NC Coles	70	65	69	79	283
B Devlin	69	70	76	69	284
G Will	70	73	73	70	286
C O'Connor Sr	70	73	71	72	286

NAME	SCORE				
C O'Connor Sr	76	70	70	68	284
A Palmer	74	72	70	70	286
A Grubb	73	72	70	73	288
B Yancey	75	68	71	75	289
L Mancour	72	68	73	76	289
D Dalziel	72	76	71	70	289

1989

NAME	SCORE				
RJ Charles	70	68	65	66	269
W Casper	67	69	65	75	276
B Hiskey	71	71	65	72	279
G Player	74	68	69	71	282
PJ Butler	72	74	67	69	282
NC Coles	70	74	70	69	283

1990

NAME	SCORE				
G Player	69	65	71	75	280
D Beman	67	66	67	81	281
B Waites	66	70	69	76	281
A Palmer	66	68	69	79	282
S Hobday	67	70	67	79	283
W Casper	70	70	70	74	284
RJ Charles	68	67	73	76	284
D Simon	71	68	66	80	285
H Henning	72	75	62	76	285
L Mowry	70	66	71	79	286
J Fourie	68	72	69	77	286

Wang Four Stars National Pro-Celebrity

(formerly Bob Hope British Classic 1980 – 83)
at Moor Park, Rickmansworth from 1981

1980   *at RAC, Epsom*

NAME	SCORE				
JM Canizares	68	67	70	64	269
S Ballesteros	66	68	70	66	270
L Trevino	66	67	68	69	270
B Waites	68	65	65	72	270
B Langer	66	67	67	71	271
AWB Lyle	70	69	67	66	272
M James	68	73	64	68	273
E Darcy	64	70	69	70	273
G Norman	70	64	69	70	273
BGC Huggett	69	68	70	67	274
H Clark	66	71	69	68	274

1981

NAME	SCORE			
B Langer	67	65	68	200
P Oosterhuis	69	66	70	205
E Murray	69	69	68	206
BW Barnes	70	68	69	207
NC Coles	71	70	66	207
J Bland	70	67	70	207
AWB Lyle	68	67	72	207
D Smyth	73	67	68	208
W Longmuir	68	70	70	208
B Marchbank	71	69	69	208
W Humphreys	70	65	73	208

1982

NAME	SCORE				
G Brand Jr	65	73	65	69	272
M James	70	66	66	73	275
RJ Charles	68	69	71	68	276
H Clark	72	72	67	66	277
B Gallacher	65	72	69	71	277
BW Barnes	68	70	65	75	278
D Feherty	66	73	68	72	279
AWB Lyle	73	69	65	73	280
M King	72	72	69	69	282
S Ballesteros	70	70	72	70	282
T Horton	72	73	66	71	282
E Murray	73	71	66	72	282
JM Canizares	69	71	70	72	282
V Fernandez	65	75	69	73	282

1983

NAME	SCORE				
JM Canizares	70	65	68	66	269
D Feherty	66	67	68	67	270
B Langer	70	66	65	70	271
RJ Charles	68	71	70	64	273
G Cullen	71	68	68	66	273
SC Mason	69	68	67	69	273
J Anderson	68	70	70	66	274
M King	71	69	63	71	274
P Teravainen	63	72	73	67	275
AWB Lyle	69	70	69	68	276
I Woosnam	70	70	66	70	276
M Clayton	68	71	67	70	276
S Torrance	69	71	66	70	276

1984 *Not played*

1985

NAME	SCORE				
K Brown	71	68	69	69	277
G Brand Jr	76	67	65	70	278
H Clark	69	71	71	68	279
A Garrido	72	69	68	71	280
R Davis	74	67	68	71	280
O Moore	70	70	70	70	280
M McLean	71	68	73	68	280
GJ Brand	75	67	68	70	280
G Levenson	72	70	68	71	281

NAME	SCORE				
S Bishop	69	72	72	68	281
A Johnstone	74	67	73	67	281
MA Martin	73	68	70	70	281

1986

NAME	SCORE				
A Garrido	69	67	71	68	275
R Rafferty	71	67	68	70	276
JM Olazabal	68	68	72	68	276
M Clayton	69	72	67	69	277
H Baiocchi	71	65	74	69	279
M McNulty	70	70	71	69	280
P Parkin	73	68	69	70	280
B Marchbank	70	72	69	70	281
H Clark	71	69	74	67	281
A Johnstone	72	72	69	68	281
I Woosnam	68	71	74	68	281

1987

NAME	SCORE				
M McNulty	70	67	69	67	273
S Torrance	67	69	72	65	273
(McNulty won play-off)					
A Charnley	68	69	72	67	276
P Senior	69	68	70	70	277
D Smyth	69	70	70	68	277
R Chapman	70	69	71	68	278
J Rutledge	70	70	70	68	278
D Cooper	69	66	69	75	279
B Marchbank	69	68	75	67	279
L Stephen	70	70	68	71	279

1988

NAME	SCORE				
R Davis	60	63	71	72	276
JM Canizares	69	67	69	71	276
E Darcy	67	68	69	72	276
D Ray	67	69	69	74	279
M Harwood	69	70	70	72	281
B Lane	71	69	69	72	281
G Brand Jr	69	70	71	72	282
E Dussart	70	74	67	71	282
M Roe	72	71	66	73	282
J Slaughter	68	73	71	70	282
D Smyth	71	71	71	69	282

1989

NAME	SCORE				
C Parry	67	71	66	69	273
I Woosnam	67	72	68	66	273
D Gilford	71	69	65	69	274
M Harwood	66	72	67	69	274
B Lane	72	68	68	68	276
G Brand Jr	72	67	72	65	276
J Anderson	70	69	69	69	277
B Marchbank	73	69	67	69	278
P Senior	72	67	68	71	278
R Shearer	69	72	65	72	278
J Hawkes	71	70	66	71	278
R McFarlane	68	74	67	69	278

1990

NAME	SCORE				
R Davis	67	72	65	67	271
M McNulty	68	69	69	65	271
M Clayton	68	70	66	67	271
B Malley	68	66	67	70	271
(Davis won play-off)					
P Mitchell	66	66	69	71	272
P Hoad	69	69	67	69	274
R Hartmann	66	66	73	70	275
P Way	69	67	67	72	275
DJ Russell	71	66	71	68	276
K Brown	69	68	72	67	276
J Bennett	71	66	67	72	276

World Match Play
at Wentworth

YEAR	WINNER	RUNNER-UP	MARGIN
1964	A Palmer	NC Coles	2 and 1
1965	G Player	PW Thomson	3 and 2
1966	G Player	J Nicklaus	6 and 4
1967	A Palmer	PW Thomson	1 hole
1968	G Player	RJ Charles	1 hole
1969	RJ Charles	G Littler	37th hole
1970	J Nicklaus	L Trevino	2 and 1
1971	G Player	J Nicklaus	5 and 4
1972	T Weiskopf	L Trevino	4 and 3
1973	G Player	G Marsh	40th hole
1974	H Irwin	G Player	3 and 1
1975	H Irwin	A Geiberger	4 and 2
1976	D Graham	H Irwin	38th hole
1977	G Marsh	R Floyd	5 and 3
1978	I Aoki	S Owen	3 and 2
1979	W Rogers	I Aoki	1 hole
1980	G Norman	AWB Lyle	1 hole
1981	S Ballesteros	B Crenshaw	1 hole
1982	S Ballesteros	AWB Lyle	37th hole
1983	G Norman	N Faldo	3 and 2
1984	S Ballesteros	B Langer	2 and 1
1985	S Ballesteros	B langer	6 and 5
1986	G Norman	AWB Lyle	2 and 1
1987	I Woosnam	AWB Lyle	1 hole
1988	AWB Lyle	N Faldo	2 and 1
1989	N Faldo	I Woosnam	1 hole
1990	I Woosnam	M McNulty	4 and 2

Sony Ranking

In the spring of 1986 the Sony Corporation announced the launch of a world ranking system for professional golf. The Sony Ranking, which is sanctioned by the Championship Committee of the Royal & Ancient Golf Club of St Andrews, is a specially developed computerised ranking which provides an authoritative reference source to the relative performance of the world's leading players.

The official events from all the geographical circuits are taken into account and points awarded according to the quality and strength of the players participating in each event. The number of points distributed to each player is dependent upon his finishing position and the scale of bonus points allocated on the basis of the number and ranking of the players in the field. The four Major Championships and the Players Championship have been weighted separately to reflect the higher quality of the events and the strong fields participating.

The Sony Ranking is based on a three year 'rolling' period weighted in favour of the more recent results, and a divisor is used to take account of the number of tournaments played by each ranked player.

As at 28 December 1986

POS	PLAYER	TOUR		TOTAL POINTS
1	G Norman	ANZ	1	1507
2	B Langer	Eur	1	1181
3	S Ballesteros	Eur	2	1175
4	T Nakajima	Jpn	1	899
5	A Bean	USA	1	694
6	R Tway	USA	2	687
7	H Sutton	USA	3	674
8	C Strange	USA	4	653
9	P Stewart	USA	5	652
10	M O'Meara	USA	6	639

As at 27 December 1987

POS	PLAYER	TOUR		TOTAL POINTS
1	G Norman	ANZ	1	1231
2	S Ballesteros	Eur	1	1169
3	B Langer	Eur	2	1112
4	AWB Lyle	Eur	3	879
5	C Strange	USA	1	873
6	I Woosnam	Eur	4	830
7	P Stewart	USA	2	717
8	L Wadkins	USA	3	697
9	M McNulty	SA	1	673
10	B Crenshaw	USA	4	668

As at 31 December 1988

POS	PLAYER	TOUR		TOTAL POINTS
1	S Ballesteros	Eur	1	1458
2	G Norman	ANZ	1	1365
3	AWB Lyle	Eur	2	1297
4	N Faldo	Eur	3	1103
5	C Strange	USA	1	1092
6	B Crenshaw	USA	2	898
7	I Woosnam	Eur	4	854
8	D Frost	Afr	1	843
9	P Azinger	USA	3	825
10	M Calcavecchia	USA	4	819

As at 31 December 1989

POS	PLAYER	TOUR		POINTS AVG.
1	G Norman	ANZ	1	17.76
2	N Faldo	Eur	1	16.25
3	S Ballesteros	Eur	2	15.03
4	C Strange	USA	1	13.79
5	P Stewart	USA	2	12.82
6	T Kite	USA	3	12.41
7	JM Olazabal	Eur	3	12.00
8	M Calcavecchia	USA	4	11.81
9	I Woosnam	Eur	4	11.56
10	P Azinger	USA	5	10.95

As at 31 December 1990

POS	PLAYER	TOUR		POINTS AVG.
1	G Norman	ANZ	1	18.95
2	N Faldo	Eur	1	18.54
3	JM Olazabal	Eur	2	17.22
4	I Woosnam	Eur	3	15.47
5	P Stewart	USA	1	12.75
6	P Azinger	USA	2	11.63
7	S Ballesteros	Eur	4	10.15
8	T Kite	USA	3	10.10
9	M McNulty	Afr	1	10.06
10	M Calcavecchia	USA	4	9.96

Other Men's Professional Tournaments

Asahi Glass Four Tours World Championship

(formerly Nissan Cup and Kirin Cup)

1986 *at Yomiuri, Tokyo*

POS	TEAM
1	PGA Japan Tour
2	PGA European Tour
3	Australia/New Zealand Tour
4	USPGA Tour

1987 *at Yomiuri, Tokyo*

POS	TEAM
1	USPGA Tour
2	PGA European Tour
3	Australia/New Zealand Tour
4	PGA Japan Tour

1988 *at Kapalua, Maui, Hawaii*

POS	TEAM
1	USPGA Tour
2	PGA European Tour
3	Australia/New Zealand Tour
4	PGA Japan Tour

1989 *at Yomiuri, Tokyo*

POS	TEAM
1	USPGA Tour
2	PGA European Tour
3	PGA Japan Tour
4	Australia/New Zealand Tour

1990 *at Yomiuri, Tokyo*

POS	TEAM
1	Australia/New Zealand Tour
2	USPGA Tour
3	PGA European Tour
4	PGA Japan Tour

Dunhill Nations Cup

INAUGURATED 1985

The Dunhill Cup has been played at St Andrews each year since it began in 1985. No other international professional tournament is played under similar conditions. Many countries enter teams of three. After regional qualifying matches 16 countries arrive for the finals at St Andrews in October. Four teams are seeded and do not play until the first round, when they are kept apart in the draw. In the Dunhill, the four home countries enter separate teams: so far England and Ireland have won, England beating Scotland in 1987, and Ireland defeating Australia in 1988, and England in 1990.

Matches are over 18 holes of stroke play, with the winner of each three scoring one point for his team. It is a hybrid form of golf, but is match play suited to television, each match being played out to the full 18. In the event of the third match being even when 18 holes have been completed, it is decided in a sudden-death finish. On occasions two games of a match have had to go to extra holes. In 1989 and 1990 the finals were played over 36 holes.

There have been several exciting semi-finals and finals, providing excellent television viewing. Each year usually produces unexpected upsets in the form-book. In 1990 France, a side not renowned for its prowess, which had to qualify to reach St Andrews, surprisingly beat the strong USA team of Calcavecchia, Strange and Kite, the favourites. In the same round unsung New Zealand beat the might of Norman, O'Grady and Baker-Finch playing for Australia. England eventually beat Japan in the semi-final in sudden-death extra holes. Japan had looked certain to win having led in two matches on the 18th tee. In the final the match was again tied, Ireland's David Feherty at last subduing Howard Clark on the third extra hole.

1985

First Round

NEW ZEALAND		Matches
RJ Charles	70	1
F Nobilo	70	1
S Reese	77	0
		2

CANADA		Matches
D Barr	71	0
J Anderson	74	0
D Halldorson	72	1
		1

USA		
R Floyd	70	1
M O'Meara	66	1
C Strange	70	1
		3

FRANCE		
M Tapia	73	0
P Pascassio	72	0
G Watine	73	0
		0

JAPAN		
J Aoki	71	1
M Kuramoto	73	1
K Arai	73	1
		3

PHILIPPINES		
J Rates	77	0
E Bagtas	82	0
M Siodina	74	0
		0

AUSTRALIA		
G Norman	71	1
G Marsh	73	1
D Graham	73	0
		2

HONG KONG		
A Tang	84	0
L Parker	83	0
Y Sui Ming	72	1
		1

SCOTLAND		
AWB Lyle	75	0
G Brand Jr	71	1
S Torrance	71	1
		2

BRAZIL		
R Navarro	73	1
J Gonzalez	73	0
F German	76	0
		1

ENGLAND		
H Clark	67	1
N Faldo	68	1
P Way	76	0
		2

IRELAND		
C O'Connor Jr	72	0
D Feherty	72	0
D Smyth	70	1
		1

WALES		
I Woosnam	69	1
D Llewellyn	77	0
P Parkin	70	1
		2

TAIWAN		
TC Chen	72	0
L Huan Lu	74	1
TM Chen	75	0
		1

SPAIN		
S Ballesteros	67	1
M Pinero	70	1
JM Canizares	73	1
		3

NIGERIA		
P Akakasiaka	72	0
C Okwu	78	0
T Uduimoh	79	0
		0

Second Round

USA	Matches		NEW ZEALAND	Matches	
M O'Meara	69	1	RJ Charles	70	0
C Strange	67	1	F Nobilo	75	0
R Floyd	69	1	S Reese	72	0
		3			0

SCOTLAND			JAPAN		
AWB Lyle	67	1	M Kuramoto	70	0
S Torrance	68	1	I Aoki	71	0
G Brand Jr	72	1	K Arai	73	0
		3			0

WALES			SPAIN		
I Woosnam	69	1	M Pinero	70	0
D Llewellyn	71	½	S Ballesteros	71	½
P Parkin	67	1	JM Canizares	69	0
		2½			½

AUSTRALIA			ENGLAND		
G Norman	69	1	H Clark	70	0
D Graham	69	1	P Way	72	0
G Marsh	73	0	N Faldo	69	1
		2			1

Semi-Finals

AUSTRALIA	Matches		WALES	Matches	
G Norman	70	1	P Parkin	73	0
G Marsh	74	0	D Llewellyn	69	1
D Graham	69	1	I Woosnam	74	0
		2			1

USA			SCOTLAND		
M O'Meara	69	1	AWB Lyle	72	0
C Strange	72	1	S Torrance	73	0
R Floyd	72	0	G Brand Jr	71	1
		2			1

Play-off for 3rd and 4th places

SCOTLAND	Matches		WALES	Matches	
AWB Lyle	70	1	I Woosnam	71	0
G Brand Jr	70	1	D Llewellyn	76	0
S Torrance	74	0	P Parkin	71	1
		2			1

Final

AUSTRALIA	Matches		USA	Matches	
G Norman	65	1	M O'Meara	71	0
G Marsh	71	1	R Floyd	74	0
D Graham	69	1	C Strange	72	0
		3			0

1986

First Round

WALES	Matches		NEW ZEALAND	Matches	
M Mouland	69	1	G Turner	77	0
I Woosnam	66	1	F Nobilo	71	0
P Parkin	69	1	RJ Charles	73	0
		3			0

JAPAN			SOUTH KOREA		
T Nakajima	68	1	Y-S Choi	78	0
T Ozaki	71	1	S-H Choi	79	0
N Ozaki	67	1	H-S Cho	74	0
		3			0

CANADA			SWEDEN		
D Barr	69	1	M Lanner	74	0
R Zokol	75	0	O Sellberg	72	1
D Halldorson	69	1	A Forsbrand	71	0
		2			1

USA			ZAMBIA		
R Floyd	72	1	P Sinyana	81	0
M O'Meara	70	1	S Mwanza	83	0
L Wadkins	70	1	P Tembo	79	0
		3			0

SCOTLAND			INDONESIA		
S Torrance	69	1	S Sumarno	76	0
G Brand Jr	71	1	M Naasim	83	0
AWB Lyle	69	1	E Tachyana	83	0
		3			0

ARGENTINA			ENGLAND		
V Fernandez	67	1	H Clark	70	0
A Sowa	69	1	GJ Brand	70	0
A Saavedra	72	0	N Faldo	69	1
		2			1

AUSTRALIA			ITALY		
R Davis	65	1	C Rocca	70	0
G Norman	67	1	G Cali	77	0
D Graham	68	1	B Dassu	79	0
		3			0

IRELAND			SPAIN		
R Rafferty	67	1	S Ballesteros	74	0
D Feherty	73	0	J Rivero	71	1
D Smyth	71	1	JM Olazabal	73	0
		2			1

Second Round

USA		Matches	CANADA		Matches
M O'Meara	74	1	R Zokol	76	0
L Wadkins	68	0	D Barr	66	1
R Floyd	68	1	D Halldorson	70	0
		2			1

JAPAN			ARGENTINA		
T Nakajima	67	1	V Fernandez	68	0
N Ozaki	69	1	A Sowa	71	0
T Ozaki	72	0	A Saavedra	69	1
		2			1

AUSTRALIA			WALES		
R Davis	71	1	M Mouland	73	0
G Norman	67	1	I Woosnam	71	0
D Graham	68	1	P Parkin	69	0
		3			0

SCOTLAND			IRELAND		
G Brand Jr	68	1	R Rafferty	70	0
S Torrance	70	1	D Smyth	72	0
AWB Lyle	70	1	D Feherty	72	0
		3			0

Semi-Finals

JAPAN		Matches	USA		Matches
T Ozaki	77	0	M O'Meara	70	1
N Ozaki	69	1	L Wadkins	74	0
T Nakajima	69	1	R Floyd	76	0
		2			1

AUSTRALIA			SCOTLAND		
R Davis	72	1	G Brand Jr	74	0
D Graham	70	0	AWB Lyle	68	1
G Norman	70	1	S Torrance	72	0
		2			1

Play-off for 3rd and 4th places

SCOTLAND	Matches		USA	Matches	
G Brand Jr	75	1	M O'Meara	78	0
S Torrance	78	0	R Floyd	73	1
AWB Lyle	73	1	L Wadkins	78	0
		2			1

Final

AUSTRALIA	Matches		JAPAN	Matches	
R Davis	76	1	T Ozaki	81	0
D Graham	81	1	N Ozaki	82	0
G Norman	73	1	T Nakajima	76	0
		3			0

1987

First Round

CANADA	Matches		NEW ZEALAND	Matches	
D Carr	71	1	B Soulsby	75	0
D Halldorson	74	$\frac{1}{2}$	G Turner	74	$\frac{1}{2}$
R Zokol	72	1	F Nobilo	74	0
		$2\frac{1}{2}$			$\frac{1}{2}$

JAPAN			MALAYSIA		
K Suzuki	75	0	M Ramayah	74	1
N Serizawa	70	1	S Yusof	76	0
N Yuhara	75	1	ZA Yusof	80	0
		2			1

USA			ITALY		
C Strange	71	1	C Rocca	72	0
DA Weibring	69	1	S Grappasonni	77	0
M O'Meara	70	1	G Cali	75	0
		3			0

SPAIN			PHILIPPINES		
J Rivero	68	1	F Minoza	75	0
JM Olazabal	71	1	R Lavares	80	0
JM Canizares	72	1	E Bagtas	77	0
		3			0

IRELAND			FRANCE		
R Rafferty	71	1	M Tapia	76	0
E Darcy	72	1	G Watine	76	0
D Smyth	74	1	E Dussart	76	0
		3			0

SCOTLAND			ZIMBABWE		
AWB Lyle	71	1	T Price	73	0
G Brand Jr	70	1	A Edwards	72	0
S Torrance	72	1	W Koen	73	0
		3			0

ENGLAND			MEXICO		
H Clark	71	$1/2$	EP Acosta	71	$1/2$
N Faldo	70	1	C Espinosa	75	0
GJ Brand	74	1	F Esparza	81	0
		$2^1/2$			$1/2$

AUSTRALIA			SWEDEN		
R Davis	75	0	O Sellberg	69	1
G Norman	70	1	M Lanner	71	0
P Senior	67	1	A Forsbrand	70	0
		2			1

Second Round

USA		Matches	JAPAN		Matches
C Strange	68	1	K Suzuki	70	0
DA Weibring	75	0	N Yuhara	69	1
M O'Meara	70	1	N Serizawa	70	0
(at 3rd extra hole)					
		2			1

AUSTRALIA			CANADA		
P Senior	73	0	D Barr *(at 1st extra hole)*	73	1
G Norman *(at 5th extra hole)*	71	1	R Zokol	71	0
R Davis	63	1	D Halldorson	73	0
		2			1

SCOTLAND			IRELAND		
S Torrance	69	1	R Rafferty	74	0
AWB Lyle	67	1	E Darcy	72	0
G Brand Jr	73	0	D Smyth	67	1
		2			1

ENGLAND			SPAIN		
H Clark	77	0	J Rivero	72	1
N Faldo	71	1	JM Olazabal	77	0
GJ Brand	71	1	JM Canizares	74	0
		2			1

Semi-Finals

SCOTLAND		Matches	USA		Matches
S Torrance	69	1	C Strange	74	0
AWB Lyle	70	1	M O'Meara	71	0
G Brand Jr	73	1	DA Weibring	74	0
		3			0

ENGLAND			AUSTRALIA		
H Clark	73	1	P Senior	74	0
GJ Brand	69	0	G Norman	68	1
N Faldo	71	1	R Davis	72	0
		—			—
		2			1

Play-off for 3rd and 4th places

USA	Matches		AUSTRALIA	Matches	
M O'Meara	71	1	P Senior	72	0
DA Weibring	71	0	R Davis	70	1
C Strange	62	1	G Norman	76	0
		—			—
		2			1

Final

ENGLAND	Matches		SCOTLAND	Matches	
N Faldo	66	1	AWB Lyle	69	0
GJ Brand	64	1	S Torrance	69	0
H Clark	73	0	G Brand Jr	68	1
		—			—
		2			1

1988

First Round

USA	Matches		PHILIPPINES	Matches	
C Strange	70	1	E Bagtas	75	0
C Beck	68	1	R Lambares	81	0
M McCumber	72	1	F Minoza	75	0
		—			—
		3			0

IRELAND			CANADA		
R Rafferty	69	0	D Barr	67	1
E Darcy	69	1	D Halldorson	72	0
D Smyth	69	1	R Zokol	76	0
		—			—
		2			1

SPAIN			ZIMBABWE		
S Ballesteros	72	1	T Price	74	0
J Rivero	68	1	A Edwards	72	0
JM Olazabal	74	1	M Shumba	78	0
		—			—
		3			0

AUSTRALIA			BRAZIL		
R Davis	69	1	R Navarro	73	0
D Graham	68	1	C Dluosh	79	0
G Norman	71	1	P Diniz	73	0
		—			—
		3			0

ENGLAND			FRANCE		
M James	66	1	F Regard	75	0
B Lane	70	1	M Tapia	75	0
N Faldo	65	1	E Dussart	70	0
		3			0

SCOTLAND			THAILAND		
G Brand Jr	74	1	B Ruangkit	76	0
C Montgomerie	72	1	S Meesawad	80	0
AWB Lyle	70	1	S Springsangar	73	0
		3			0

JAPAN			DENMARK		
N Ozaki	69	1	J Rasmussen	77	0
T Ozaki	68	1	S Tinning	69	0
H Meshiai	72	1	A Sorensen	75	0
		3			0

WALES			SWEDEN		
D Llewellyn	72	1	M Persson	75	0
M Mouland	70	1	O Sellberg	71	0
I Woosnam	69	1	A Forsbrand	75	0
		3			0

Second Round

AUSTRALIA		Matches	WALES		Matches
D Graham	67	1	M Mouland	76	0
R Davis	69	1	D Llewellyn	70	0
G Norman	73	0	I Woosnam	71	1
		2			1

IRELAND			USA		
R Rafferty	71	1	M McCumber	72	0
D Smyth	71	$\frac{1}{2}$	C Beck	71	$\frac{1}{2}$
E Darcy	66	1	C Strange	68	0
		$2\frac{1}{2}$			$\frac{1}{2}$

SPAIN			JAPAN		
S Ballesteros	72	1	N Ozaki	74	0
J Rivero	65	1	H Meshiai	68	0
JM Olazabal	68	1	T Ozaki	69	0
		3			0

ENGLAND			SCOTLAND		
B Lane	73	0	G Brand Jr	71	1
M James	69	1	C Montgomerie	71	0
N Faldo	67	1	AWB Lyle	68	0
		2			1

Semi-Finals

AUSTRALIA		Matches		SPAIN		Matches	
G Norman	67	1		S Ballesteros	69	0	
R Davis	71	1		J Rivero	72	0	
D Graham	73	0		JM Olazabal	69	1	
		—				—	
		2				1	

IRELAND		Matches		ENGLAND		Matches	
R Rafferty	68	0		B Lane	65	1	
D Smyth	69	1		N Faldo	70	0	
E Darcy	68	1		M James	72	0	
		—				—	
		2				1	

Play-off for 3rd and 4th places

SPAIN		Matches		ENGLAND		Matches	
JM Olazabal	67	0		N Faldo	66	1	
S Ballesteros	71	1		B Lane	72	0	
J Rivero	69	1		M James	70	0	
		—				—	
		2				1	

Final

IRELAND		Matches		AUSTRALIA		Matches	
D Smyth	71	1		R Davis	73	0	
R Rafferty	69	1		D Graham	74	0	
E Darcy	70	0		G Norman	63	1	
		—				—	
		2				1	

1989

First Round

ARGENTINA		Matches		WALES		Matches	
E Romero	68	1		P Parkin	75	0	
V Fernandez	70	½		M Mouland	70	½	
M Fernandez	69	1		I Woosnam	72	0	
		—				—	
		2½				½	

USA		Matches		KOREA		Matches	
M Calcavecchia	71	0		PN Shin	70	1	
T Kite	72	1		CY Soo	75	0	
C Strange	67	1		CS Ho	79	0	
		—				—	
		2				1	

SWEDEN			SPAIN		
M Lanner	70	0	JM Olazabal	67	1
O Sellberg	71	1	JM Canizares	72	0
M Persson	71	1	J Rivero	72	0
		2			1

IRELAND			TAIPEI		
P Walton	69	1	LC Soon	76	0
R Rafferty	73	0	YC Han	71	1
C O'Connor Jr *(at 4th extra hole)*	73	1	HC Sheng	73	0
		2			1

SCOTLAND			NEW ZEALAND		
G Brand Jr	76	0	S Owen	72	1
S Torrance	67	1	G Waite	70	0
AWB Lyle	65	1	F Nobilo	70	0
		2			1

JAPAN			ITALY		
K Suzuki	74	1	H Mannelli	76	0
N Ozaki	68	1	C Rocca	73	0
H Meshiai	73	0	A Binaghi	72	1
		2			1

FRANCE			AUSTRALIA		
E Dussart	72	1	I Baker-Finch	73	0
M Pendaries	71	1	G Norman	73	0
G Watine	70	0	W Grady	67	1
		2			1

ENGLAND			CANADA		
D Durnian *(at 2nd extra hole)*	72	1	R Zokol	72	0
M James	73	0	D Barr	71	1
H Clark	71	1	D Halldorson	72	0
		2			1

Second Round

JAPAN		Matches	FRANCE		Matches
N Ozaki	71	1	E Dussart	73	0
K Suzuki	73	1	M Pendaries	75	0
H Meshiai	72	1	G Watine	74	0
		3			0

USA			ARGENTINA		
T Kite	70	1	V Fernandez	72	0
M Calcavecchia	72	1	M Fernandez	77	0
C Strange	68	1	E Romero	70	0
		3			0

IRELAND			SWEDEN		
P Walton	72	1	M Lanner	74	0
R Rafferty	68	1	O Sellberg	78	0
C O'Connor Jr	73	1	M Persson	76	0
		3			0

ENGLAND			SCOTLAND		
H Clark	67	1	S Torrance	69	0
D Durnian	78	0	G Brand Jr	71	1
M James *(at 1st extra hole)*	70	1	AWB Lyle	70	0
		2			1

Semi-Finals

USA		Matches	IRELAND		Matches
M Calcavecchia	69	1	P Walton	71	0
T Kite *(at 1st extra hole)*	71	1	C O'Connor Jr	71	0
C Strange	72	0	R Rafferty	71	1
		2			1

JAPAN			ENGLAND		
N Ozaki	70	1	D Durnian	72	0
K Suzuki	66	1	H Clark	70	0
H Meshiai	73	0	M James	71	0
		2			1

Play-off for 3rd and 4th places

ENGLAND		Matches	IRELAND		Matches
D Durnian	72	0	P Walton	71	1
H Clark	72	1	R Rafferty	75	0
M James	69	1	C O'Connor Jr	76	0
		2			1

Final

USA		Matches	JAPAN		Matches
M Calcavecchia	67	1	H Meshiai	68	0
T Kite	68	½	N Ozaki	68	½
C Strange	72	1	K Suzuki	75	0
M Calcavecchia	66	1	H Meshiai	68	0
T Kite	74	0	K Suzuki	71	1
C Strange	71	0	N Ozaki	69	1
		3½			2½

1990

First Round

JAPAN	Matches		ARGENTINA	Matches	
S Higashi	68	1	M Guzman	70	0
Y Kaneko	72	1	V Fernandez	73	0
H Meshiai	76	0	E Romero	73	1
		2			1

FRANCE			USA		
M Farry	70	1	M Calcavecchia	73	0
J Van de Velde	69	1/2	C Strange	69	1/2
E Dussart	73	1	T Kite	74	0
		2 1/2			1/2

SPAIN			SWEDEN		
MA Jimenez	67	1	O Sellberg	72	0
J Rivero	69	1	M Persson	77	0
JM Canizares	71	0	M Lanner	68	1
		2			1

ENGLAND			THAILAND		
R Boxall	74	1	S Oncham	77	0
H Clark	68	1	S Meesawat	78	0
M James	70	1	B Ruengkit	79	0
		3			0

SCOTLAND			MEXICO		
AWB Lyle	68	1	R Alarcon	73	0
S McAllister	73	1	E Serna	77	0
S Torrance	69	1/2	C Espinosa	69	1/2
		2 1/2			1/2

IRELAND			KOREA		
R Rafferty	70	1	CS Ho	73	0
P Walton	71	1	PN Shin	74	0
D Feherty	69	1	CY Soo	81	0
		3			0

WALES			TAIWAN		
I Woosnam	71	1	HY Shu	78	0
M Mouland	73	0	CL Hsi	72	1
P Parkin	77	1	KC Hsiung	78	0
		2			1

NEW ZEALAND			AUSTRALIA		
F Nobilo	67	1	G Norman	76	0
S Owen	74	1	W Grady	78	0
G Turner	75	0	R Davis	66	1
		2			1

Second Round

JAPAN	Matches		FRANCE	Matches	
S Higashi	71	1	M Farry	80	0
Y Kaneko	71	1	E Dussart	75	0
H Meshiai	70	1	J Van de Velde	72	0
		3			0

IRELAND			SPAIN		
D Feherty	76	1	MA Jimenez	77	0
R Rafferty	71	0	JM Canizares	70	1
P Walton	70	1	J Rivero	82	0
		2			1

NEW ZEALAND			WALES		
F Nobilo	70	0	I Woosnam	67	1
S Owen	72	1	M Mouland	83	0
G Turner	72	1	P Parkin	76	0
		2			1

ENGLAND			SCOTLAND		
R Boxall	73	1	S McAllister	75	0
H Clark	77	0	AWB Lyle	75	1
M James	72	1	S Torrance	73	0
		2			1

Semi-Finals

IRELAND	Matches		NEW ZEALAND	Matches	
P Walton	70	1	S Owen	71	0
R Rafferty	68	1/2	F Nobilo	68	1/2
D Feherty	68	1	G Turner	69	0
		2 1/2			1/2

ENGLAND			JAPAN		
H Clark *(at 1st extra hole)*	70	1	S Higashi	70	0
R Boxall	70	0	Y Kaneko	69	1
M James *(at 4th extra hole)*	70	1	H Meshiai	70	0
		2			1

Play-off for 3rd and 4th places

NEW ZEALAND	Matches		JAPAN	Matches	
G Turner	72	1	S Higashi	75	0
S Owen	77	0	Y Kaneko	74	1
F Nobilo	73	1	H Meshiai	77	0
		2			1

Final

IRELAND			ENGLAND		
	Matches			Matches	
P Walton	72	½	M James	72	½
R Rafferty	71	1	R Boxall	73	0
D Feherty	74	0	H Clark	73	1
P Walton	77	0	M James	76	1
R Rafferty	71	1	R Boxall	77	0
D Feherty *(at 3rd extra hole)*	75	1	H Clark	75	0
	3½			2½	

World Cup of Golf
Until 1966, called Canada Cup

YEAR	WINNER	SCORE	RUNNERS-UP	VENUE
1953	Argentina (A Cerda and R De Vicenzo)	287	Canada (S Leonard and B Kerr)	Montreal
	(Individual: A Cerda, Argentina, 104)			
1954	Australia (PW Thomson and KDG Nagle)	556	Argentina (A Cerda and R De Vicenzo)	Laval-Sur-Lac
1955	United States (C Harbert and E Furgol)	560	Australia (PW Thomson and KDG Nagle)	Washington
	(Individual: E Furgol, USA, after a play-off with PW Thomson and F van Donck, 279)			
1956	United States (B Hogan and S Snead)	567	South Africa (AD Locke and G Player)	Wentworth
	(Individual: B Hogan, USA, 277)			
1957	Japan (T Nakamura and K Ono)	557	United States (S Snead and J Demaret)	Tokyo
	(Individual: T Nakamura, Japan, 274)			
1958	Ireland (H Bradshaw and C O'Connor Sr)	579	Spain (A Miguel and S Miguel)	Mexico City
	(Individual: A Miguel, Spain, after a tie with H Bradshaw, 286)			
1959	Australia (PW Thomson and KDG Nagle)	563	United States (S Snead and C Middlecoff)	Melbourne
	(Individual: S Leonard, Canada, 275, after a play-off with PW Thomson, Australia)			
1960	United States (S Snead and A Palmer)	565	England (H Weetman and BJ Hunt)	Portmarnock
	(Individual: F van Donck, Belgium, 279)			
1961	United States (S Snead and J Demaret	560	Australia (PW Thomson and KDG Nagle)	Puerto Rico
	(Individual: S Snead, USA, 272)			
1962	United States (S Snead and A Palmer)	557	Argentina (F de Luca and R De Vicenzo)	Buenos Aires
	(Individual: R De Vicenzo, Argentina, 276)			
1963	United States (A Palmer and J Nicklaus) (63 holes)	482	Spain (S Miguel and R Sota)	St Nom-La-Bretêche
	(Individual: J Nicklaus, USA, 237)			
1964	United States (A Palmer and J Nicklaus)	554	Argentina (R De Vicenzo and L Ruiz)	Maui, Hawaii
	(Individual: J Nicklaus, USA, 276)			

YEAR	WINNER	SCORE	RUNNERS-UP	VENUE
1965	South Africa (G Player and H Henning)	571	Spain (A Miguel and R Sota)	Madrid
	(Individual: G Player, South Africa, 281)			
1966	United States (J Nicklaus and A Palmer)	548	South Africa (G Player and H Henning)	Tokyo
	(Individual: G Knudson, Canada, and H Sugimoto, Japan, each 272; Knudson won play-off)			
1967	United States (J Nicklaus and A Palmer)	557	New Zealand (RJ Charles and W Godfrey)	Mexico City
	(Individual: A Palmer, USA, 276)			
1968	Canada (A Balding and G Knudson)	569	United States (J Boros and L Trevino)	Olgiata, Rome
	(Individual: A Balding, Canada, 274)			
1969	United States (O Moody and L Trevino)	552	Japan (T Kono and H Yasuda)	Singapore
	(Individual: L Trevino, USA, 275)			
1970	Australia (B Devlin and D Graham)	545	Argentina (R De Vicenzo and V Fernandez)	Buenos Aires
	(Individual: R De Vicenzo, Argentina, 269)			
1971	United States (J Nicklaus and L Trevino)	555	South Africa (H Henning and G Player)	Palm Beach, Florida
	(Individual: J Nicklaus, USA, 271)			
1972	Taiwan (H Min-Nan and LL Huan) [3 rounds only]	438	Japan (T Kono and T Murakami)	Melbourne
	(Individual: H Min-Nan, Taiwan, 217)			
1973	United States (J Nicklaus and J Miller)	558	South Africa (G Player and H Baiocchi)	Marbella, Spain
	(Individual: J Miller, USA, 277)			
1974	South Africa (R Cole and D Hayes)	554	Japan (I Aoki and M Ozaki)	Caracas
	(Individual: R Cole, South Africa, 271)			
1975	United States (J Miller and L Graham)	554	Taiwan (H Min-Nan and KC Hsiung)	Bangkok
	(Individual: J Miller, USA, 275)			
1976	Spain (S Ballesteros and M Pinero)	574	United States (J Pate and D Stockton)	Palm Springs, USA
	(Individual: E Acosta, Mexico, 282)			
1977	Spain (S Ballesteros and A Garrido)	591	Philippines (R Lavares and B Arda)	Manila, Philippines
	(Individual: G Player, South Africa, 289)			
1978	United States (J Mahaffey and A North)	564	Australia (G Norman and W Grady)	Hawaii
	(Individual: J Mahaffey, USA, 281)			
1979	United States (J Mahaffey and H Irwin)	575	Scotland (AWB Lyle and K Brown)	Glyfada, Greece
	(Individual: H Irwin, USA, 285)			
1980	Canada (D Halldorson and J Nelford	572	Scotland (AWB Lyle and S Martin)	Bogota
	(Individual: AWB Lyle, Scotland, 282)			
1981	Not played			
1982	Spain (M Pinero and JM Canizares)	563	United States (B Gilder and R Clampett)	Acapulco
	(Individual: M Pinero, Spain, 281)			
1983	United States (R Caldwell and J Cook)	565	Canada (D Barr and J Anderson)	Pondok Inah, Jakarta
	(Individual: D Barr, Canada, 276)			
1984	Spain (JM Canizares and J Rivero) (54 holes due to storm)	414	Scotland (S Torrance and G Brand Jr)	Olgiata, Rome
	(Individual: JM Canizares, Spain, 205)			

YEAR	WINNER	SCORE	RUNNERS-UP	VENUE
1985	Canada (D Halldorson and D Barr)	559	England (H Clark and P Way)	La Quinta, California
(Individual: H Clark, England, 272)				
1986	*Not played*			
1987	Wales (I Woosnam and D Llewellyn)	574	Scotland (S Torrance and AWB Lyle)	Kapalua, Hawaii
(Wales won play-off)				
(Individual: I Woosnam, Wales, 274)				
1988	United States (B Crenshaw and M McCumber)	560	Japan (T Ozaki and M Ozaki)	Royal Melbourne, Australia
(Individual: B Crenshaw, USA, 275)				
1989	Australia (P Fowler and W Grady) (36 holes due to storms)	278	Spain (JM Olazabal and JM Canizares)	Las Brisas, Spain
(Individual: P Fowler, Australia, 135)				
1990	Germany (B Langer and T Giedeon)	556	England (M James and R Boxall)	
			Ireland (R Rafferty and D Feherty)	Grand Cypress Resort, Orlando, Florida

(Individual: P Stewart, USA, 271)

British Isles International Players, Professional Men

Since 1979 the 'Great Britain and Ireland' team format for the Ryder Cup match against the United States has been widened to include professionals from the Continent of Europe.

Adams, J
(Scotland): v England 1932-33-34-35-36-37-38; v Wales 1937-38; v Ireland 1937-38. (GBI): v America 1947-49-51-53

Ainslie, T
(Scotland): v Ireland 1936

Alliss, Percy
(England): v Scotland 1932-33-34-35-36-37; v Ireland 1932-38; v Wales 1938. (GBI): v France 1929; v America 1929-31-33-35-37

Alliss, Peter
(England): in Canada Cup 1954-55-57-58-59-61-62-64-66; in World Cup 1967. (GBI): v America 1953-57-59-61-63-65-67-69

Anderson, Joe
(Scotland): v Ireland 1932

Anderson, W
(Scotland): v Ireland 1936; v England 1937; v Wales 1937

Ayton, LB
(Scotland): v England 1910-12-13-33-34

Ayton, JB, jr
(Scotland): v England 1937. (GBI): v America 1949

Ballantine, J
(Scotland): v England 1932-36

Ballingall, J
(Scotland): v England 1938; Ireland 1938; v Wales 1938

Bamford, BJ
(England): in Canada Cup 1961

Bannerman, H
(Scotland): in World Cup 1967-72. (GBI): v America 1971

Barber, T
(England): v Ireland 1932-33

Barnes, BW
(Scotland): in World Cup 1974-75-76-77. (GBI): v America 1969-71-73-75-77-79; v Europe 1974-76-78-80; v South Africa 1976

Batley, JB
(England): v Scotland 1912

Beck, AG
(England): v Wales 1938; v Ireland 1938

Bembridge, M
(England): in World Cup 1974-75.
(GBI): v America 1969-71-73-75; v South Africa 1976

Boomer, A
(England): (GBI): v America 1926-27-29

Bousfield, K
(England): in Canada Cup 1956-57.
(GBI): v America 1949-51-55-57-59-61

Boxall, R
(England): in Dunhill Cup 1990; in World Cup 1990

Boyle, HF
(Ireland): in World Cup 1967. (GBI): v America 1967

Bradshaw, H
(Ireland): in Canada Cup 1954-55-56-57-58-59; v Scotland 1937-38; v Wales 1937; v England 1938. (GBI): v America 1953-55-57

Braid, J
(Scotland): v England 1903-04-05-06-07-09-10-12. (GBI): v America 1921

Branch, WJ
(England): v Scotland 1936

Brand, G, jr
(Scotland): in World Cup 1984-85-88-89-90; in Dunhill Cup 1985-86-87-88-89; (Eur): in Nissan Cup 1985; Kirin Cup 1988; Four Tours World Chp 1989; (GBI): v America 1987-89; v Australia 1988

Brand,GJ
(England): in World Cup 1983; in Dunhill Cup 1986-87 (winners). (GBI): v America 1983; (Eur) Nissan Cup 1986

Brown, EC
(Scotland): in Canada Cup 1954-55-56-57-58-59-60-61-62-65-66; in World Cup 1987-68. (GBI): v America 1953-55-57-59

Brown, K
(Scotland): in World Cup 1977-78-79-83. (GBI): v America 1977-79-83-85-87; v Europe 1978; (Eur) Kirin Cup 1987

Burns, S
(Scotland): v England 1932. (GBI): v America 1929

Burton, J
(England): v Ireland 1933

Burton, R
(England): v Scotland 1935-36-37-38; v Ireland 1938; v Wales 1938. (GBI): v America 1935-37-49

Busson, JH
(England): v Scotland 1938

Busson, JJ
(England): v Scotland 1934-35-36-37. (GBI): v America 1935

Butler, PJ
(England): in World Cup 1969-70-73. (GBI): v America 1965-69-71-73; v Europe 1976

Callum, WS
(Scotland): v Ireland 1935

Campbell, J
(Scotland): v Ireland 1936

Carrol, LJ
(Ireland): v Scotland 1937-38; v Wales 1937; v England 1938

Cassidy, J
(Ireland): v England 1933; v Scotland 1934-35

Cassidy, D
(Ireland): v Scotland 1936-37; v Wales 1937

Cawsey, GH
(England): v Scotland 1906-07

Caygill, GA
(England): (GBI): v America 1969

Clark, C
(England): (GBI): v America 1973

Clark, HK
(England): in World Cup 1978-84-85-87; in Dunhill Cup 1985-86-87 (winners)-89-90 (r/u). (GBI): v America 1977-81-85-87-89; v Australia 1988; v Europe 1978-84. (Eur): in Nissan Cup 1985

Coles, NC
(England): in Canada Cup 1963; in World Cup 1968. (GBI): v America 1961-63-65-67-69-71-73-77; v Europe 1974-76-78-80

Collinge, T
(England): v Scotland 1937

Collins, JF
(England): v Scotland 1903-04

Coltart, F
(Scotland): v England 1909

Compston, A
(England): v Scotland 1932-35; v Ireland 1932. (GBI): v America 1926-27-29-31; v France 1929

Cotton, TH
(England): (GBI): v America 1929-37-47; v France 1929

Cox, S
(Wales): in World Cup 1975

Cox, WJ
(England): v Scotland 1935-36-37. (GBI): v America 1935-37

Curtis, D
(England): v Scotland 1934-38; v Ireland 1938; v Wales 1938

Dabson, K
(Wales): in World Cup 1972

Dailey, A
(Scotland): v England 1932-33-34-35-36-38; v Ireland 1938; v Wales 1938. (GBI): v America 1933

Daly, F
(Ireland): v Scotland 1936-37-38; v England 1938; v Wales 1937; in Canada Cup 1954-55. (GBI): v America 1947-49-51-53

Darcy, E
(Ireland): in World Cup 1976-77-83-84-85-87; Dunhill Cup 1987-88 (winners). (GBI): v America 1975-77-81-87; v Europe 1976-84; v South Africa 1976

Davies, R
(Wales): in World Cup 1968

Davies, WH
(England): v Scotland 1932-33; v Ireland 1932-33. (GBI): v America 1931-33

Davis, W
(Scotland): v Ireland 1933-34-35-36-37-38; v England 1937-38; v Wales 1937-38

Dawson, P
(England): in World Cup 1977. (GBI): v America 1977

De Foy, CB
(Wales): in World Cup 1971-73-74-75-76-77-78

Denny, CS
(England): v Scotland 1936

Dobson, T
(Scotland): v England 1932-33-34-35-36-37; v Ireland 1932-33-34-35-36-37-38; v Wales 1937-38

Don, W
(Scotland): v Ireland 1935-36

Donaldson, J
(Scotland): v England 1932-35-38; v Ireland 1937; v Wales 1937

Dornan, R
(Scotland): v Ireland 1932

Drew, NV
(Ireland): in Canada Cup 1960-61. (GBI): v America 1959

Duncan, G
(Scotland): v England 1906-07-09-10-12-13-32-34-35-36-37. (GBI): v America 1921-26-27-29-31

Durnian, D
(England): in World Cup 1989; in Dunhill Cup 1989

Durward, JG
(Scotland): v Ireland 1934; v England 1937

Easterbrook, S
(England): v Scotland 1932-33-34-35-38; v Ireland 1933. (GBI): v America 1931-33

Edgar, J
(Ireland): v Scotland 1938

Fairweather, S
(Ireland): v England 1932; v Scotland 1933. (Scotland): v England 1933-35-36; v Ireland 1938; v Wales 1938

Faldo, NA
(England): in World Cup 1977; in Dunhill Cup 1985-86-87 (winners) -88. (GBI): v America 1977-79-81-83-85-87-89; v Europe 1978-80-82-84; v Rest of World 1982. (Eur) Nissan Cup 1986. Kirin Cup 1987; Four Tours World Chp 1990

Fallon, J
(Scotland): v England 1936-37-38; v Ireland 1937-38; v Wales 1937-38. (GBI): v America 1955

Faulkner, M
(England): (GBI): v America 1947-49-51-53-57

Feherty, D
(Ireland): in World Cup 1990; in Dunhill Cup 1985-86-90 (winners); (Eur): in Four Tours World Chp 1990

Fenton, WB
(Scotland): v England 1932; v Ireland 1932-33

Fernie, TR
(Scotland): v England 1910-12-13-33

Foster, M
(England): in World Cup 1976. (GBI): v Europe 1976

Gadd, B
(England): v Scotland 1933-35-38; v Ireland 1933-38; v Wales 1938

Gadd, G
(England): (GBI): v America 1926-27

Gallacher, BJ
(Scotland): in World Cup 1969-71-74-82-83. (GBI): v America 1969-71-73-75-77-79-81-83-91 (Captain); v Europe 1974-78-82-84; v South Africa 1976; v Rest of World 1982

Garner, JR
(England): (GBI): v America 1971-73

Gaudin, PJ
(England): v Scotland 1905-06-07-09-12-13

Good, G
(Scotland): v England 1934-36

Gould, H
(Wales): in Canada Cup 1954-55

Gow, A
(Scotland): v England 1912

Grabham, C
(Wales): v England 1938; v Scotland 1938

Grant, T
(Scotland): v England 1913

Gray, E
(England): v Scotland 1904-05-07

Green, E
(England): (GBI): v America 1947

Green, T
(England): v Scotland 1935. (Wales): v Scotland 1937-38; v Ireland 1937; v England 1938

Greene, C
(Ireland): in Canada Cup 1965

Gregson, M
(England): in World Cup 1967. (GBI): v America 1967

Haliburton, TB
(Scotland): v Ireland 1935-36-38; v England 1938; v Wales 1938; in Canada Cup 1954. (GBI): v America 1961-63

Hamill, J
(Ireland): v Scotland 1933-34-35; v England 1932-33

Hargreaves, J
(England): (GBI): v America 1951

Hastings, W
(Scotland): England 1937-38; v Wales 1937-38; v Ireland 1937-38

Havers, AG
(England): v Scotland 1932-33-34; v Ireland 1932-33. (GBI): v America 1921-26-27-31-33; v France 1929

Healing, SF
(Wales): v Scotland 1938

Hepburn, J
(Scotland): v England 1903-05-06-07-09-10-12-13

Herd, A
(Scotland): v England 1903-04-05-06-09-10-12-13-32

Hill, EF
(Wales): v Scotland 1937-38; v Ireland 1937; v England 1938

Hitchcock, J
(England): (GBI): v America 1965

Hodson, B
(England): v Ireland 1933. (Wales): v Scotland 1937-38; v Ireland 1937; v England 1938. (GBI): v America 1931

Holley, W
(Ireland): v Scotland 1933-34-35-36-38; v England 1932-33-38

Horne, R
(England): (GBI): v America 1947

Horton, T
(England): in World Cup 1976. (GBI): v Europe 1974-76; v America 1975-77

Houston, D
(Scotland): v Ireland 1934

Huggett, BGC
(Wales): in Canada Cup 1963-64-65; in World Cup 1968-69-70-71-76-79. (GBI): v America 1963-67-69-71-73-75; v Europe 1974-78

Huish, D
(Scotland): in World Cup 1973

Hunt, BJ
(England): in Canada Cup 1958-59-60-62-63-64; in World Cup 1968. (GBI): v America 1953-57-59-61-63-65-67-69

Hunt, GL
(England): in World Cup 1972-75. (GBI): v Europe 1974; v America 1975

Hunt, Geoffrey M
(England): (GBI): v America 1963

Hunter, W
(Scotland): v England 1906-07-09-10

Hutton, GC
(Scotland): v Ireland 1936-37; v England 1937-38; v Wales 1937

Ingram, D
(Scotland): in World Cup 1973

Jacklin, A
(England): in Canada Cup 1966; in World Cup 1970-71-72. (GBI): v America 1967-69-71-73-75-77-79-83 (captain) -85(captain) -87(captain) -89(captain); v Europe 1976-82; v Rest of World 1982

Jackson, H
(Ireland): in World Cup 1970-71

Jacobs, JRM
(England): (GBI): v America 1955

Jagger, D
(England): (GBI): v Europe 1976

James, G
(Wales): v Scotland 1937; v Ireland 1937

James, MH
(England): in World Cup 1978-79-82-84-87-88; in Dunhill Cup 1988-89-90 (r/u). (GBI): v America 1977-79-81-89; v Europe 1978-80-82; v Rest of World 1982; v Australia 1988; (Eur): Kirin Cup 1988; Four Tours World Chp 1989-90

Jarman, EW
(England): v Scotland 1935. (GBI): v America 1935

Job, N
(England): (GBI): v Europe 1980

Jolly, HC
(England): (GBI): v America 1926-27; v France 1929

Jones, DC
(Wales): v Scotland 1937-38; v Ireland 1937; v England 1938

Jones, E
(Ireland): in Canada Cup 1965

Jones, R
(England): v Scotland 1903-04-05-06-07-09-10-12-13

Jones, T
(Wales): v Scotland 1936; v Ireland 1937; v England 1938

Kenyon, EWH
(England): v Scotland 1932; v Ireland 1932

King, M
(England): in World Cup 1979. (GBI): v America 1979

King, SL
(England): v Scotland 1934-36-37-38; v Wales 1938;
v Ireland 1938. (GBI): v America 1937-47-49

Kinsella, J
(Ireland): in World Cup 1968-69-72-73

Kinsella, W
(Ireland): v Scotland 1937-38; v England 1938

Knight, G
(Scotland): v England 1937

Lacey, AJ
(England): v Scotland 1932-33-34-36-37-38; v Ireland
1932-33-38; v Wales 1938. (GBI): v America 1933-37

Laidlaw, W
(Scotland): v England 1935-36-38; v Ireland 1937;
v Wales 1937

Lane, B
(England): in World Cup 1988; in Dunhill Cup 1988

Lees, A
(England): v Scotland 1938; v Wales 1938; v Ireland 1938.
(GBI): v America 1947-49-51-55

Llewellyn, D
(Wales): in World Cup 1974-85-87 (winners)-88; in Dunhill
Cup 1985-88. (GBI): v Europe 1984

Lloyd, F
(Wales): v Scotland 1937-38; v Ireland 1937;
v England 1938

Lockhart, G
(Scotland): v Ireland 1934-35

Lyle, AWB
(Scotland): in World Cup 1979-80-87; in Dunhill Cup 1985-
86-87-88-89-90. (GBI): v America 1979-81-83-85-87; v Europe
1980-82-84; v Rest of World 1982; v Australia 1988. (Eur): in
Nissan Cup 1985-86; Kirin Cup 1987.

McCartney, J
(Ireland): v Scotland 1932-33-34-35-36-37-38;
v England 1932-33-38; v Wales 1937

McCulloch, D
(Scotland): v England 1932-33-34-35-36-37;
v Ireland 1932-33-34-35

McDermott, M
(Ireland): v England 1932; v Scotland 1932

McDowall, J
(Scotland): v England 1932-33-34-35-36;
v Ireland 1933-34-35-36

McEwan, P
(Scotland): v England 1907

McIntosh, G
(Scotland): v England 1938; v Ireland 1938;
v Wales 1938

McKenna, J
(Ireland): v Scotland 1936-37-38; v Wales 1937-38;
v England 1938

McKenna, R
(Ireland): v Scotland 1933-35; v England 1933

McMillan, J
(Scotland): v England 1933-34-35; v Ireland 1933-34

McMinn, W
(Scotland): v England 1932-33-34

McNeill, H
(Ireland): v England 1932

Mahon, PJ
(Ireland): v Scotland 1932-33-34-35-36-37-38;
v Wales 1937-38; v England 1932-33-38

Martin, J
(Ireland): in Canada Cup 1962-63-64-66;
in World Cup 1970. (GBI): v America 1965

Martin, S
(Scotland): in World Cup 1980

Mason, SC
(England): in World Cup 1980. (GBI): v Europe 1980

Mayo, CH
(England): v Scotland 1907-09-10-12-13

Mills, RP
(England): (GBI): v America 1957

Mitchell, A
(England): v Scotland 1932-33-34. (GBI): v America
1921-26-29-31-33

Moffitt, R
(England): (GBI): v America 1961

Montgomerie, C
(Scotland): in World Cup 1988; in Dunhill Cup 1988

Mouland, M
(Wales): in World Cup 1988-89-90; in Dunhill Cup 1986-87-
88-89. (Eur): Kirin Cup 1988.

Mouland, S
(Wales): in Canada Cup 1965-66; in World Cup 1967

O'Brien, W
(Ireland): v Scotland 1934-36-37; v Wales 1937

Ockenden, J
(England): (GBI): v America 1921

O'Connor, C
(Ireland): in Canada Cup 1956-57-58-59-60-61-62-63-64-66;
in World Cup 1967-68-69-71-73. (GBI): v America 1955-57-
59-61-63-65-67-69-71-73

O'Connor, C, jr
(Ireland): in World Cup 1974-75-78-85-89; in Dunhill Cup
1985-89. (GBI): v Europe 1974-84; v America
1975-89; v South Africa 1976

O'Connor, P
(Ireland): v Scotland 1932-33-34-35-36; v England 1932-33

Oke, WG
(England): v Scotland 1932

O'Leary, JE
(Ireland): in World Cup 1972-80-82. (GBI): v America 1975;
v Europe 1976-78-82; v Rest of World 1982

O'Neill, J
(Ireland): v England 1933

O'Neill, M
(Ireland): v Scotland 1933-34; v England 1933

Oosterhuis, PA
(England): in World Cup 1971. (GBI): v America 1971-73-75-
77-79-81; v Europe 1974

Padgham, AH
(England): v Scotland 1932-33-34-35-36-37-38; v Ireland
1932-33-38; v Wales 1938. (GBI): v America 1933-35-37

Panton, J
(Scotland): in Canada Cup 1955-56-57-58-59-60-61-62-63-64-
65-66; in World Cup 1968. (GBI): v America 1951-53-61

Park, J
(Scotland): v England 1909

Parkin, P
(Wales): in World Cup 1984-89; in Dunhill Cup 1985-86-87-
89-90. (GBI): v Europe 1984

Patterson, E
(Ireland): v Scotland 1933-34-35-36; v England 1933;
v Wales 1937

Perry, A
(England); v Ireland 1932; v Scotland 1933-36-38.
(GBI): v America 1933-35-37

Pickett, C
(Wales): v Scotland 1937-38; v Ireland 1937; v England 1938

Platts, L
(Wales): (GBI): v America 1965

Polland, E
(Ireland): in World Cup 1973-74-76-77-78-79.
(GBI): v America 1973; v Europe 1974-76-78-80;
v South America 1976

Pope, CW
(Ireland): v England 1932; v Scotland 1932

Rafferty, R
(Ireland): in World Cup 1983-84-87-88-90; in Dunhill Cup
1986-87-88 (winners)-89-90 (winners); (GBI): v Europe 1984;
v Australia 1988. (Eur): v America 1989; Kirin Cup 1988; Four
Tours World Chp 1989-90

Rainford, P
(England): v Scotland 1903-07

Ray, E
(England): v Scotland 1903-04-05-06-07-09-10-12-13.
(GBI): v America 1921-26-27

Rees, DJ
(Wales): v Scotland 1937-38; v Ireland 1937; England 1938; in
Canada Cup 1954-56-57-58-59-60-61-62-64.
(GBI): v America 1937-47-49-51-53-55-57-59-61

Reid, W
(England): v Scotland 1906-07

Renouf, TG
(England): v Scotland 1903-04-05-10-13

Ritchie, WL
(Scotland): v England 1913

Robertson, F
(Scotland): v Ireland 1933; v England 1938

Robertson, P
(Scotland): v England 1932; v Ireland 1932-34

Robson, F
(England): v Scotland 1909-10. (GBI): v America
1926-27-29-31

Roe, M
(England): in World Cup 1989

Rowe, AJ
(England): v Scotland 1903-06-07

Sayers, B, jr
(Scotland): v England 1906-07-09

Scott, SS
(England): (GBI): v America 1955

Seymour, M
(England): v Scotland 1932-33; v Ireland 1932-33.
(Scotland): v Ireland 1932

Shade, RDBM
(Scotland): in World Cup 1970-71-72

Sherlock, JG
(England): v Scotland 1903-04-05-06-07-09-10-12-13.
(GBI): v America 1921

Simpson, A
(Scotland): v England 1904

Smalldon, D
(Wales): in Canada Cup 1955-56

Smith, CR
(Scotland): v England 1903-04-07-09-13

Smith, GE
(Scotland): v Ireland 1932

Smyth, D
(Ireland): in World Cup 1979-80-82-83-88-89; in Dunhill Cup
1985-86-87-88 (winners). (GBI): v America 1979-81; v Europe
1980-82-84; v Rest of World 1982

Snell, D
(England): in Canada Cup 1965

Spark, W
(Scotland): v Ireland 1933-35-37; v England 1935;
v Wales 1937

Stevenson, P
(Ireland): v Scotland 1933-34-35-36-38;
v England 1933-38

Sutton, M
(England): in Canada Cup 1955

Taylor, JH
(England): v Scotland 1903-04-05-06-07-09-10-12-13
(GBI): v America 1921

Taylor, JJ
(England): v Scotland 1937

Taylor, Josh
(England): v Scotland 1913. (GBI): v America 1921

Thomas, DC
(Wales): in Canada Cup 1957-58-59-60-61-62-63-66; in
World Cup 1967-69-70. (GBI): v America 1959-63-65-67

Thompson, R
(Scotland): v England 1903-04-05-06-07-09-10-12

Tingey, A
(England): v Scotland 1903-05

Torrance, S
(Scotland): in World Cup 1976-78-82-84-85-87-89-90; in
Dunhill Cup 1985-86-87-89-90. (GBI): v Europe 1976-78-80-
82-84; v America 1981-83-85-87-89; v Rest of World 1982.
(Eur): in Nissan Cup 1985

Townsend, P
(England): in World Cup 1969-74. (GBI): v America
1969-71; v Europe 1974

Twine, WT
(England): v Ireland 1932

Vardon, H
(England): (GBI): v America 1921

Vaughan, DI
(Wales): in World Cup 1972-73-77-78-79-80

Waites, BJ
(England): in World Cup 1980-82-83. (GBI): v Europe
1980-82-84; v Rest of World 1982; v America 1983

Walker, RT
(Scotland): in Canada Cup 1964

Wallace, L
(Ireland): v England 1932; v Scotland 1932

Walton P
(Ireland): in Dunhill Cup 1989-90 (winners)

Ward, CH
(England): v Ireland 1932. (GBI): v America 1947-49-51

Watt, T
(Scotland): v England 1907

Watt, W
(Scotland): v England 1912-13

Way, P
(England): in Dunhill Cup 1985; in World Cup 1985.
(GBI): v America 1983-85

Weetman, H
(England): in Canada Cup 1954-56-60. (GBI): v America
1951-53-55-57-59-61-63

Whitcombe, CA
(England): v Scotland 1932-33-34-35-36-37-38;
v Ireland 1933. (GBI): v America 1927-29-31-33-35-37;
v France 1929

Whitcombe, EE
(England): v Scotland 1938; v Wales 1938; v Ireland 1938

Whitcombe, ER
(England): v Scotland 1932; v Ireland 1933.
(GBI): v America 1926-29-31-35; v France 1929

Whitcombe, RA
(England): v Scotland 1933-34-35-36-37-38.
(GBI): v America 1935

White, J
(Scotland): v England 1903-04-05-06-07-09-12-13

Wilcock, P
(England): in World Cup 1973

Will, G
(Scotland): in Canada Cup 1963; in World Cup 1969-70.
(GBI): v America 1963-65-67

Williams, K
(Wales): v Scotland 1937-38; v Ireland 1937;
v England 1938

Williamson, T
(England): v Scotland 1904-05-06-07-09-10-12-13

Wilson, RG
(England): v Scotland 1913

Wilson, T
(Scotland): v England 1933-34; v Ireland 1932-33-34

Wolstenholme, GB
(England): in Canada Cup 1965

Wood, N
(Scotland): in World Cup 1975. (GBI): v America 1975

Woosnam, I
(Wales): in World Cup 1980-82-83-84-85-87 (winners)-90;
Dunhill Cup 1985-86-87-88-89-90. (GBI): v Europe 1982-84; v
Rest of World 1982; v America 1983-85-87-89; v Australia
1988. (Eur): in Nissan Cup 1985-86. Kirin Cup 1987; Four
Tours World Chp 1989-90

The Ryder Cup

INAUGURATED 1927

Samuel Ryder, the seed merchant from St Albans and keen golfer, presented the Ryder Cup for competition between American and British Professionals in 1927. It was to be played every two years alternately in the United States and Britain.

The first match was at Worcester, Massachusetts. The two sides were fairly well matched, with the USA just having the edge. Before 1939 the USA won four and the British two matches. Both participants selected sides for the 1939 match, due to be played that September in the USA, but at the outbreak of war the contest was cancelled. During those early years Walter Hagen had usually captained the USA, with Ted Ray, George Duncan, JH Taylor or Charles Whitcombe the British. The most exciting match was in 1933 at Southport and Ainsdale when Sid Easterbrook from Devon, playing Densmore Shute, who won the Open that year at St Andrews, was left with a three-foot putt to win the whole match, which he sank after Shute had taken three putts.

The British record in the pre-1939 series was no more than adequate. However, for 30 years after the war the British were ineffective, especially when the match was played in the USA. There was only one win during that period, in 1957 at Lindrick, Yorkshire, when Dai Rees captained the side. Rees was one of the best professionals never to win the Open, although he was often in contention. This was a notable win against a strong US side. Britain had nearly won at Wentworth four years before, but two young contestants, Bernard Hunt and Peter Alliss, both later to make their names in the golf world, failed with three-foot putts to clinch their matches on the last green.

In 1959 the format of the match was changed. Previously it had always been 36 holes foursomes on the first day and 36 holes singles on the second. Four-ball matches were introduced, either two matches of foursomes one day and two four-balls the next, or one of each on both days. Then in 1963 it was extended to three days and ten years later a new arrangement was adopted: 18 holes of foursomes and four-balls on each of the first two days and all eight players on each side playing two singles on the third day. This format lasted until 1975. At Lytham in the next match, a poor format was played to accommodate television. So in 1979 it was revised yet again to 18 holes of foursomes and four-ball matches on each day of the first two days and twelve 18-hole singles on the third day. So it has remained and has provided a side down by, say, three matches at the end of the second day, the opportunity still to have a chance of winning by capturing the singles 9–3.

In 1979 a major change occurred when the USPGA agreed that European players on the European Tour would be eligible for selection. Since then the match has been more closely contested and players of the quality of Ballesteros, Langer and Olazabal have been available. Indeed, the Spanish element, supplemented by Rivero and Canizares has been a major factor in Europe's recent victories.

In matches in the USA, the British never looked like winning until the 1980s. In 1979 it was very even for the first two days, but Europe lost the singles by a wide margin. After the outstanding win at the Belfry in 1985, Europe's first victory in the USA occurred two years later at Muirfield Village, Jack Nicklaus's course in Ohio. In a thrilling climax in the 12 singles, Europe began with a handsome lead, but the Americans fought back and at one time were leading in eight matches; but Europe counter-attacked with effect and ran out the winners 16½–11½.

The 1989 contest was halved at the Belfry amid great excitement, Europe retaining the cup which has now been held for six years, a record never before achieved by the team from this side of the Atlantic.

The change in fortune in recent years has been largely, if not entirely, due to the US's opponents now being Europe and not Great Britain and Ireland only. While the match is still run by the PGA, as the largest and most influential professional body in Europe, the seven top men in the European Order of Merit are automatically nominated, with the captain able to pick three others, who may not have featured high in the order. Tony Jacklin, non-playing captain of the last four European sides, has proved himself an outstanding leader and has done much to inspire his team to success.

The Europeans have added a potent force to the side, with Ballesteros an outstanding competitor, resulting in a much more even contest. The honour of playing for either team is still much sought after in the professional ranks, even though, or perhaps because, it is the only event in which they take part where there is no remuneration for playing.

1927   *at Worcester, Massachusetts*

Foursomes

USA	Matches	GREAT BRITAIN	Matches
W Hagen and J Golden (2 and 1)	1	E Ray and F Robson	0
J Farrell and J Turnesa (8 and 6)	1	G Duncan and A Compston	0
G Sarazen and A Watrous (3 and 2)	1	AG Havers and H Jolly	0
L Diegel and W Mehlhorn	0	A Boomer and CA Whitcombe (7 and 5)	1
	3		1

Singles

USA	Matches	GREAT BRITAIN	Matches
W Mehlhorn (1 hole)	1	A Compston	0
J Farrell (5 and 4)	1	A Boomer	0
J Golden (8 and 7)	1	H Jolly	0
L Diegel (7 and 5)	1	E Ray	0
G Sarazen	½	CA Whitcombe	½
W Hagen (2 and 1)	1	AG Havers	0
A Watrous (3 and 2)	1	F Robson	0
J Turnesa	0	G Duncan (1 hole)	1
	6½		1½

Match Aggregate: USA 9½; Great Britain 2½.
Captains: E Ray, Great Britain, and W Hagen, USA.

1929 *at Moortown, Leeds*

Foursomes

GREAT BRITAIN	Matches	USA	Matches
CA Whitcombe and A Compston	½	J Farrell and J Turnesa	½
A Boomer and G Duncan	0	L Diegel and A Espinosa (7 and 5)	1
A Mitchell and F Robson (2 and 1)	1	G Sarazen and E Dudley	0
ER Whitcombe and TH Cotton	0	J Golden and W Hagen (2 holes)	1
	1½		2½

Singles

GREAT BRITAIN		USA	
CA Whitcombe (8 and 6)	1	J Farrell	0
G Duncan (10 and 8)	1	W Hagen	0
A Mitchell	0	L Diegel (9 and 8)	1
A Compston (6 and 4)	1	G Sarazen	0
A Boomer (4 and 3)	1	J Turnesa	0
F Robson	0	H Smith (4 and 2)	1
TH Cotton (4 and 3)	1	A Watrous	0
ER Whitcombe	½	A Espinosa	½
	5½		2½

Match Aggregate: Great Britain 7; USA 5.
Captains: G Duncan, Great Britain, and W Hagen, USA.

1931 *at Scioto, Columbus, Ohio*

Foursomes

USA	Matches	GREAT BRITAIN	Matches
G Sarazen and J Farrell (8 and 7)	1	A Compston and WH Davies	0
W Hagen and D Shute (10 and 9)	1	G Duncan and AG Havers	0
L Diegel and A Espinosa	0	A Mitchell and F Robson (3 and 1)	1
W Burke and W Cox (3 and 2)	1	S Easterbrook and ER Whitcombe	0
	3		1

Singles

USA		GREAT BRITAIN	
W Burke (7 and 6)	1	A Compston	0
G Sarazen (7 and 6)	1	F Robson	0
J Farrell	0	WH Davies (4 and 3)	1
W Cox (3 and 1)	1	A Mitchell	0
W Hagen (4 and 3)	1	CA Whitcombe	0
D Shute (8 and 6)	1	B Hodson	0
A Espinosa (2 and 1)	1	ER Whitcombe	0
C Wood	0	AG Havers (4 and 3)	1
	6		2

Match Aggregate: USA 9 ; Great Britain 3.
Captains: CA Whitcombe, Great Britain, and W Hagen, USA.

1933   *at Southport and Ainsdale, Southport*

Foursomes

GREAT BRITAIN	Matches	USA	Matches
Percy Alliss and CA Whitcombe	¹/₂	G Sarazen and W Hagen	¹/₂
A Mitchell and AG Havers (3 and 2)	1	O Dutra and D Shute	0
WH Davies and S Easterbrook (1 hole)	1	C Wood and P Runyan	0
AH Padgham and A Perry	0	E Dudley and W Burke (1 hole)	1
	—		—
	2¹/₂		1¹/₂

Singles

GREAT BRITAIN		USA	
AH Padgham	0	G Sarazen (6 and 4)	1
A Mitchell (9 and 8)	1	O Dutra	0
AJ Lacey	0	W Hagen (2 and 1)	1
WH Davies	0	C Wood (4 and 3)	1
Percy Alliss (2 and 1)	1	P Runyan	0
AG Havers (4 and 3)	1	L Diegel	0
S Easterbrook (1 hole)	1	D Shute	0
CA Whitcombe	0	H Smith (2 and 1)	1
	—		—
	4		4

Match Aggregate: Great Britain 6¹/₂; USA 5¹/₂.
Captains: JH Taylor, Great Britain (non-playing), and W Hagen, USA.

1935   *at Ridgewood, New Jersey*

Foursomes

USA	Matches	GREAT BRITAIN	Matches
G Sarazen and W Hagen (7 and 6)	1	A Perry and JJ Busson	0
H Picard and J Revolta (6 and 5)	1	AH Padgham and Percy Alliss	0
P Runyan and H Smith (9 and 8)	1	W Cox and EW Jarman	0
O Dutra and K Laffoon	0	CA Whitcombe and ER Whitcombe (1 hole)	1
	—		—
	3		1

Singles

USA		GREAT BRITAIN	
G Sarazen (3 and 2)	1	JJ Busson	0
P Runyan (5 and 3)	1	R Burton	0
J Revolta (2 and 1)	1	CA Whitcombe	0
O Dutra (4 and 2)	1	AH Padgham	0
C Wood	0	Percy Alliss (1 hole)	1
H Smith	¹/₂	W Cox	¹/₂
H Picard (3 and 2)	1	ER Whitcombe	0
S Parks	¹/₂	A Perry	¹/₂
	—		—
	6		2

Match Aggregate: USA 9; Great Britain 3.
Captains: CA Whitcombe, Great Britain, and W Hagen, USA.

1937 *at Southport and Ainsdale, Southport*

Foursomes

GREAT BRITAIN	Matches	**USA**	Matches
AH Padgham and TH Cotton	0	E Dudley and B Nelson (4 and 2)	1
AJ Lacey and W Cox	0	R Guldahl and A Manero (2 and 1)	1
CA Whitcombe and DJ Rees	½	G Sarazen and D Shute	½
Percy Alliss and R Burton (2 and 1)	1	H Picard and J Revolta	0
	1½		2½

Singles

GREAT BRITAIN		**USA**	
AH Padgham	0	R Guldahl (8 and 7)	1
SJ King	½	D Shute	½
DJ Rees (3 and 1)	1	B Nelson	0
TH Cotton (5 and 3)	1	A Manero	0
Percy Alliss	0	G Sarazen (1 hole)	1
R Burton	0	S Snead (5 and 4)	1
A Perry	0	E Dudley (2 and 1)	1
AJ Lacey	0	H Picard (2 and 1)	1
	2½		5½

Match Aggregate: USA 8; Great Britain 4.
Captains: CA Whitcombe, Great Britain, and W Hagen, USA (non-playing).

1939

Due to be played at Ponte Vedra, Jacksonville, 18–19 November, 1939.
No contest owing to European War.
British players chosen for 1939 were: TH Cotton (captain), R Burton, RA Whitcombe, SL King, AH Padgham, CA Whitcombe, DJ Rees, J Adams. Selection of two more players had been deferred.
The US team chosen for 1939 was: V Ghezzi, R Guldahl, J Hines, H McSpaden, R Metz, B Nelson, H Picard, P Runyan, H Smith, and S Snead, with W Hagen as non-playing captain.
In 1941 the US again chose a team comprising: J Demaret, V Ghezzi, B Hogan, H McSpaden, L Mangrum, B Nelson, G Sarazen, H Smith, S Snead and C Wood, with W Hagen as non-playing captain.
No further teams were chosen until 1947, when the Second World War was over.

1947 *at Portland, Oregon*

Foursomes

USA	Matches	**GREAT BRITAIN**	Matches
E Oliver and L Worsham (10 and 9)	1	TH Cotton and A Lees	0
S Snead and L Mangrum (6 and 5)	1	F Daly and CH Ward	0
B Hogan and J Demaret (2 holes)	1	J Adams and M Faulkner	0
B Nelson and H Barron (2 and 1)	1	DJ Rees and SL King	0
	4		0

Singles

USA		GREAT BRITAIN	
EJ Harrison (5 and 4)	1	F Daly	0
L Worsham (3 and 2)	1	J Adams	0
L Mangrum (6 and 5)	1	M Faulkner	0
E Oliver (4 and 3)	1	CH Ward	0
B Nelson (2 and 1)	1	A Lees	0
S Snead (5 and 4)	1	TH Cotton	0
J Demaret (3 and 2)	1	DJ Rees	0
H Keiser	0	SL King (4 and 3)	1
	7		1

Match Aggregate: USA 11; Great Britain 1.
Captains: TH Cotton, Great Britain, and B Hogan, USA.

1949 *at Ganton, Scarborough*

Foursomes

GREAT BRITAIN	Matches	USA	Matches
M Faulkner and J Adams (2 and 1)	1	EJ Harrison and J Palmer	0
F Daly and K Bousfield (4 and 2)	1	R Hamilton and S Alexander	0
CH Ward and SL King	0	J Demaret and C Heafner (4 and 3)	1
R Burton and A Lees (1 hole)	1	S Snead and L Mangrum	0
	3		1

Singles

GREAT BRITAIN		USA	
M Faulkner	0	EJ Harrison (8 and 7)	1
J Adams (2 and 1)	1	J Palmer	0
CH Ward	0	S Snead (6 and 5)	1
DJ Rees (6 and 4)	1	R Hamilton	0
R Burton	0	C Heafner (3 and 2)	1
SL King	0	C Harbert (4 and 3)	1
A Lees	0	J Demaret (7 and 6)	1
F Daly	0	L Mangrum (1 hole)	1
	2		6

Match Aggregate: USA 7; Great Britain 5.
Captains (non-playing): CA Whitcombe, Great Britain, and B Hogan, USA.

1951 *at Pinehurst, North Carolina*

Foursomes

USA	Matches	GREAT BRITAIN	Matches
C Heafner and J Burke (5 and 3)	1	M Faulkner and DJ Rees	0
E Oliver and H Ransom	0	CH Ward and A Lees (2 and 1)	1
L Mangrum and S Snead (5 and 4)	1	J Adams and J Panton	0
B Hogan and J Demaret (5 and 4)	1	F Daly and K Bousfield	0
	3		1

Singles

USA		GREAT BRITAIN	
J Burke (4 and 3)	1	J Adams	0
J Demaret (2 holes)	1	DJ Rees	0
C Heafner	½	F Daly	½
L Mangrum (6 and 5)	1	H Weetman	0
E Oliver	0	A Lees (2 and 1)	1
B Hogan (3 and 2)	1	CH Ward	0
S Alexander (8 and 7)	1	J Panton	0
S Snead (4 and 3)	1	M Faulkner	0
	6½		1½

Match Aggregate: USA 9½; Great Britain 2½.
Captains: AJ Lacey, Great Britain (non-playing), and S Snead, USA.

1953 *at Wentworth, Surrey*

Foursomes

GREAT BRITAIN	Matches	USA	Matches
H Weetman and Peter Alliss	0	D Douglas and E Oliver (2 and 1)	1
EC Brown and J Panton	0	L Mangrum and S Snead (8 and 7)	1
J Adams and BJ Hunt	0	T Kroll and J Burke (7 and 5)	1
F Daly and H Bradshaw (1 hole)	1	W Burkemo and C Middlecoff	0
	1		3

Singles

GREAT BRITAIN		USA	
DJ Rees	0	J Burke (2 and 1)	1
F Daly (9 and 7)	1	T Kroll	0
EC Brown (2 holes)	1	L Mangrum	0
H Weetman (1 hole)	1	S Snead	0
M Faulkner	0	C Middlecoff (3 and 1)	1
Peter Alliss	0	J Turnesa (1 hole)	1
BJ Hunt	½	D Douglas	½
H Bradshaw (3 and 2)	1	F Haas	0
	4½		3½

Match Aggregate: USA 6½; Great Britain 5½.
Captains: TH Cotton, Great Britain (non-playing), and L Mangrum, USA.

1955 *at Palm Springs, California*

Foursomes

USA	Matches	GREAT BRITAIN	Matches
C Harper and J Barber	0	J Fallon and JR Jacobs (1 hole)	1
D Ford and T Kroll (5 and 4)	1	EC Brown and SS Scott	0
J Burke and T Bolt (1 hole)	1	A Lees and H Weetman	0
S Snead and C Middlecoff (3 and 2)	1	DJ Rees and H Bradshaw	0
	3		1

Singles

USA		**GREAT BRITAIN**	
T Bolt (4 and 2)	1	C O'Connor	0
C Harbert (3 and 2)	1	SS Scott	0
C Middlecoff	0	JR Jacobs (1 hole)	1
S Snead (3 and 1)	1	DJ Rees	0
M Furgol	0	A Lees (3 and 1)	1
J Barber	0	EC Brown (3 and 2)	1
J Burke (3 and 2)	1	H Bradshaw	0
D Ford (3 and 2)	1	H Weetman	0
	—		—
	5		3

Match Aggregate: USA 8; Great Britain 4.
Captains: DJ Rees, Great Britain, and C Harbert, USA.

1957   *at Lindrick, Sheffield*

Foursomes

GREAT BRITAIN	Matches	**USA**	Matches
Peter Alliss and BJ Hunt	0	D Ford and D Finsterwald (2 and 1)	1
K Bousfield and DJ Rees (3 and 2)	1	A Wall and F Hawkins	0
M Faulkner and H Weetman	0	T Kroll and J Burke (4 and 3)	1
C O'Connor and EC Brown	0	R Mayer and T Bolt (7 and 5)	1
	—		—
	1		3

Singles

GREAT BRITAIN		**USA**	
EC Brown (4 and 3)	1	T Bolt	0
RP Mills (5 and 3)	1	J Burke	0
Peter Alliss	0	F Hawkins (2 and 1)	1
K Bousfield (4 and 3)	1	L Hebert	0
DJ Rees (7 and 6)	1	E Furgol	0
BJ Hunt (6 and 5)	1	D Ford	0
C O'Connor (7 and 6)	1	D Finsterwald	0
H Bradshaw	¹/₂	R Mayer	¹/₂
	—		—
	6¹/₂		1¹/₂

Match Aggregate: Great Britain 7¹/₂; USA 4¹/₂.
Captains: DJ Rees, Great Britain, and J Burke, USA.

1959   *at Palm Desert, California*

Foursomes

USA	Matches	**GREAT BRITAIN**	Matches
R Rosburg and M Souchak (5 and 4)	1	BJ Hunt and EC Brown	0
D Ford and A Wall	0	C O'Connor and Peter Alliss (3 and 2)	1
J Boros and D Finsterwald (2 holes)	1	DJ Rees and K Bousfield	0
S Snead and C Middlecoff	¹/₂	H Weetman and DC Thomas	¹/₂
	—		—
	2¹/₂		1¹/₂

Singles

USA | | **GREAT BRITAIN** |
| --- | --- | --- | --- |
| D Ford | ½ | NV Drew | ½ |
| M Souchak (3 and 2) | 1 | K Bousfield | 0 |
| R Rosburg (6 and 5) | 1 | H Weetman | 0 |
| S Snead (6 and 5) | 1 | DC Thomas | 0 |
| D Finsterwald (1 hole) | 1 | DJ Rees | 0 |
| J Hebert | ½ | Peter Alliss | ½ |
| A Wall (7 and 6) | 1 | C O'Connor | 0 |
| C Middlecoff | 0 | EC Brown (4 and 3) | 1 |
| | 6 | | 2 |

Match Aggregate: USA 8½; Great Britain 3½.
Captains: DJ Rees, Great Britain, and S Snead, USA.

1961 *at Royal Lytham and St Anne's*

Foursomes

GREAT BRITAIN	Matches	**USA**	Matches
C O'Connor and Peter Alliss (4 and 3)	1	G Littler and D Ford	0
J Panton and BJ Hunt	0	A Wall and J Hebert (4 and 3)	1
DJ Rees and K Bousfield	0	W Casper and A Palmer (2 and 1)	1
TB Haliburton and NC Coles	0	M Souchak and W Collins (1 hole)	1
	1		3

AFTERNOON

C O'Connor and Peter Alliss	0	A Wall and J Hebert (1 hole)	1
J Panton and BJ Hunt	0	W Casper and A Palmer (5 and 4)	1
DJ Rees and K Bousfield (4 and 2)	1	M Souchak and W Collins	0
TB Haliburton and NC Coles	0	J Barber and D Finsterwald (1 hole)	1
	1		3

First Day Aggregate: Great Britain 2; USA 6.

Singles

MORNING

GREAT BRITAIN		**USA**	
H Weetman	0	D Ford (1 hole)	1
RL Moffitt	0	M Souchak (5 and 4)	1
Peter Alliss	½	A Palmer	½
K Bousfield	0	W Casper (5 and 3)	1
DJ Rees (2 and 1)	1	J Hebert	0
NC Coles	½	G Littler	½
BJ Hunt (5 and 4)	1	J Barber	0
C O'Connor	0	D Finsterwald (2 and 1)	1
	3		5

AFTERNOON

H Weetman	0	A Wall (1 hole)	1
Peter Alliss (3 and 2)	1	W Collins	0
BJ Hunt	0	M Souchak (2 and 1)	1
TB Haliburton	0	A Palmer (2 and 1)	1
DJ Rees (4 and 3)	1	D Ford	0
K Bousfield (1 hole)	1	J Barber	0
NC Coles (1 hole)	1	D Finsterwald	0
C O'Connor	$^1/_2$	G Littler	$^1/_2$
	—		—
	$4^1/_2$		$3^1/_2$

Second Day Total: Great Britain $7^1/_2$; USA $8^1/_2$.
Match Aggregate: Great Britain $9^1/_2$; USA $14^1/_2$.
Captains: DJ Rees, Great Britain, and J Barber, USA.

1963   *at Atlanta, Georgia*

Foursomes

USA		**GREAT BRITAIN**	
	Matches		Matches
A Palmer and J Pott	0	BGC Huggett and G Will (3 and 2)	1
W Casper and D Ragan (1 hole)	1	Peter Alliss and C O'Connor	0
J Boros and A Lema	$^1/_2$	NC Coles and BJ Hunt	$^1/_2$
G Littler and D Finsterwald	$^1/_2$	DC Thomas and H Weetman	$^1/_2$
	—		—
	2		2

AFTERNOON

W Maxwell and R Goalby (4 and 3)	1	DC Thomas and H Weetman	0
A Palmer and W Casper (5 and 4)	1	BGC Huggett and G Will	0
G Littler and D Finsterwald (2 and 1)	1	NC Coles and GM Hunt	0
J Boros and A Lema (1 hole)	1	TB Haliburton and BJ Hunt	0
	—		—
	4		0

First Day Aggregate: USA 6; Great Britain 2.

Four-Balls

MORNING

USA		**GREAT BRITAIN**	
A Palmer and D Finsterwald (5 and 4)	1	BGC Huggett and DC Thomas	0
G Littler and J Boros	$^1/_2$	Peter Alliss and BJ Hunt	$^1/_2$
W Casper and W Maxwell (3 and 2)	1	H Weetman and G Will	0
R Goalby and D Ragan	0	NC Coles and C O'Connor (1 hole)	1
	—		—
	$2^1/_2$		$1^1/_2$

AFTERNOON

A Palmer and D Finsterwald (3 and 2)	1	NC Coles and C O'Connor	0
A Lema and J Pott (1 hole)	1	Peter Alliss and BJ Hunt	0
W Casper and W Maxwell (2 and 1)	1	TB Haliburton and GM Hunt	0
R Goalby and D Ragan	$^1/_2$	BGC Huggett and DC Thomas	$^1/_2$
	—		—
	$3^1/_2$		$^1/_2$

Second Day Total: USA 6; Great Britain 2.
Match Aggregate: USA 12; Great Britain 4.

Singles

MORNING

USA		GREAT BRITAIN	
A Lema (5 and 3)	1	GM Hunt	0
J Pott	0	BGC Huggett (3 and 1)	1
A Palmer	0	Peter Alliss (1 hole)	1
W Casper	1/2	NC Coles	1/2
R Goalby (3 and 2)	1	DC Thomas	0
G Littler (1 hole)	1	C O'Connor	0
J Boros	0	H Weetman (1 hole)	1
D Finsterwald	0	BJ Hunt (2 holes)	1
	3¹/₂		4¹/₂

AFTERNOON

A Palmer (3 and 2)	1	G Will	0
D Ragan (2 and 1)	1	NC Coles	0
A Lema	1/2	Peter Alliss	1/2
G Littler (6 and 5)	1	TB Haliburton	0
J Boros (2 and1)	1	H Weetman	0
W Maxwell (2 and 1)	1	C O'Connor	0
D Finsterwald (4 and 3)	1	DC Thomas	0
R Goalby (2 and 1)	1	BJ Hunt	0
	7¹/₂		¹/₂

Third Day Total: USA 11; Great Britain 5.
Match Aggregate: USA 23; Great Britain 9.
Captains: J Fallon (non-playing), Great Britain, and A Palmer, USA; .

1965   *at Royal Birkdale*

Foursomes

MORNING

GREAT BRITAIN	Matches	USA	Matches
DC Thomas and G Will (6 and 5)	1	D Marr and A Palmer	0
C O'Connor and Peter Alliss (5 and 4)	1	K Venturi and D January	0
L Platts and PJ Butler	0	J Boros and A Lema (1 hole)	1
BJ Hunt and NC Coles	0	W Casper and G Littler (2 and 1)	1
	2		2

AFTERNOON

DC Thomas and G Will	0	D Marr and A Palmer (6 and 5)	1
J Martin and J Hitchcock	0	J Boros and A Lema (5 and 4)	1
C O'Connor and Peter Alliss (2 and 1)	1	W Casper and G Littler	0
BJ Hunt and NC Coles (3 and 2)	1	K Venturi and D January	0
	2		2

First Day Aggregate: Great Britain 4; USA 4.

Four-Balls

MORNING

DC Thomas and G Will	0	D January and T Jacobs (1 hole)	1
L Platts and PJ Butler	½	W Casper and G Littler	½
Peter Alliss and C O'Connor	0	D Marr and A Palmer (5 and 4)	1
NC Coles and BJ Hunt (1 hole)	1	J Boros and A Lema	0
	1½		**2½**

AFTERNOON

P Alliss and C O'Connor (1 hole)	1	D Marr and A Palmer	0
DC Thomas and G Will	0	D January and T Jacobs (1 hole)	1
L Platts and PJ Butler	½	W Casper and G Littler	½
NC Coles and BJ Hunt	0	A Lema and K Venturi (1 hole)	1
	1½		**2½**

Second Day Total: Great Britain 3; USA 5.
Match Aggregate: Great Britain 7; USA 9.

Singles

MORNING

GREAT BRITAIN		USA	
J Hitchcock	0	A Palmer (3 and 2)	1
L Platts	0	J Boros (4 and 2)	1
PJ Butler	0	A Lema (1 hole)	1
NC Coles	0	D Marr (2 holes)	1
BJ Hunt (2 holes)	1	G Littler	0
Peter Alliss (1 hole)	1	W Casper	0
DC Thomas	0	T Jacobs (2 and 1)	1
G Will	½	D January	½
	2½		**5½**

AFTERNOON

PJ Butler	0	A Palmer (2 holes)	1
J Hitchcock	0	J Boros (2 and 1)	1
C O'Connor	0	A Lema (6 and 4)	1
Peter Alliss (3 and 1)	1	K Venturi	0
BJ Hunt	0	D Marr (1 hole)	1
NC Coles (3 and 2)	1	W Casper	0
G Will	0	G Littler (2 and 1)	1
L Platts (1 hole)	1	T Jacobs	0
	3		**5**

Third Day Total: Great Britain 5½; USA 10½.
Match Aggregate: Great Britain 12½; USA 19½.
Captains (non-playing): H Weetman, Great Britain, and B Nelson, USA.

1967   *at Houston, Texas*

Foursomes
MORNING

USA	Matches	GREAT BRITAIN	Matches
W Casper and J Boros	½	BGC Huggett and G Will	½
A Palmer and G Dickinson (2 and 1)	1	Peter Alliss and C O'Connor	0
D Sanders and G Brewer	0	A Jacklin and DC Thomas (4 and 3)	1
B Nichols and J Pott (6 and 5)	1	BJ Hunt and NC Coles	0
	2½		1½

AFTERNOON

J Boros and W Casper (1 hole)	1	BGC Huggett and G Will	0
G Dickinson and A Palmer (5 and 4)	1	M Gregson and HF Boyle	0
G Littler and A Geiberger	0	A Jacklin and DC Thomas (3 and 2)	1
B Nichols and J Pott (2 and 1)	1	Peter Alliss and C O'Connor	0
	3		1

First Day Aggregate: USA 5½; Great Britain 2½

Four-Balls
MORNING

USA		GREAT BRITAIN	
W Casper and G Brewer (3 and 2)	1	Peter Alliss and C O'Connor	0
B Nichols and J Pott (1 hole)	1	BJ Hunt and NC Coles	0
G Littler and A Geiberger (1 hole)	1	A Jacklin and DC Thomas	0
G Dickinson and D Sanders (3 and 2)	1	BGC Huggett and G Will	0
	4		0

AFTERNOON

W Casper and G Brewer (5 and 3)	1	BJ Hunt and NC Coles	0
G Dickinson and D Sanders (3 and 2)	1	Peter Alliss and M Gregson	0
A Palmer and J Boros (1 hole)	1	G Will and HF Boyle	0
G Littler and A Geiberger	½	A Jacklin and DC Thomas	½
	3½		½

Second Day Total: USA 7½; Great Britain ½.
Match Aggregate: USA 13; Great Britain 3.

Singles
MORNING

USA		GREAT BRITAIN	
G Brewer (4 and 3)	1	HF Boyle	0
W Casper (2 and 1)	1	Peter Alliss	0
A Palmer (3 and 2)	1	A Jacklin	0
J Boros	0	BGC Huggett (1 hole)	1
D Sanders	0	NC Coles (2 and 1)	1
A Geiberger (4 and 2)	1	M Gregson	0
G Littler	½	DC Thomas	½
B Nichols	½	BJ Hunt	½
	5		3

AFTERNOON

A Palmer (5 and 3)	1	BGC Huggett	0
G Brewer	0	Peter Alliss (2 and 1)	1
G Dickinson (3 and 2)	1	A Jacklin	0
B Nichols (3 and 2)	1	C O'Connor	0
J Pott (3 and 1)	1	G Will	0
A Geiberger (2 and 1)	1	M Gregson	0
J Boros	$1/2$	BJ Hunt	$1/2$
D Sanders	0	NC Coles (2 and 1)	1
	5$1/2$		2$1/2$

Third Day Total: USA 10$1/2$; Great Britain 5$1/2$.
Match Aggregate: USA 23$1/2$; Great Britain 8$1/2$.
Captains (non-playing): B Hogan, USA, and DJ Rees, Great Britain.

1969   *at Royal Birkdale*

Foursomes

MORNING

GREAT BRITAIN	Matches	USA	Matches
NC Coles and BGC Huggett (3 and 2)	1	M Barber and R Floyd	0
B Gallacher and M Bembridge (2 and 1)	1	L Trevino and K Still	0
A Jacklin and P Townsend (3 and 1)	1	D Hill and T Aaron	0
C O'Connor and Peter Alliss	$1/2$	W Casper and F Beard	$1/2$
	3$1/2$		$1/2$

AFTERNOON

NC Coles and BGC Huggett	0	D Hill and T Aaron (1 hole)	1
B Gallacher and M Bembridge	0	L Trevino and G Littler (2 holes)	1
A Jacklin and P Townsend (1 hole)	1	W Casper and F Beard	0
BJ Hunt and PJ Butler	0	J Nicklaus and D Sikes (1 hole)	1
	1		3

First Day Aggregate: Great Britain 4$1/2$; USA 3$1/2$.

Four-Balls

MORNING

C O'Connor and P Townsend (1 hole)	1	D Hill and D Douglass	0
BGC Huggett and GA Caygill	$1/2$	R Floyd and M Barber	$1/2$
BW Barnes and Peter Alliss	0	L Trevino and G Littler (1 hole)	1
A Jacklin and NC Coles (1 hole)	1	J Nicklaus and D Sikes	0
	2$1/2$		1$1/2$

AFTERNOON

P Townsend and PJ Butler	0	W Casper and F Beard (2 holes)	1
BGC Huggett and B Gallacher	0	D Hill and K Still (2 and 1)	1
M Bembridge and BJ Hunt	$1/2$	T Aaron and R Floyd	$1/2$
A Jacklin and NC Coles	$1/2$	L Trevino and M Barber	$1/2$
	1		3

Second Day Total: Great Britain 3$1/2$; USA 4$1/2$.
Match Aggregate: Great Britain 8; USA 8.

Singles
MORNING

Peter Alliss	0	L Trevino (2 and 1)	1
P Townsend	0	D Hill (5 and 4)	1
NC Coles (1 hole)	1	T Aaron	0
BW Barnes	0	W Casper (1 hole)	1
C O'Connor (5 and 4)	1	F Beard	0
M Bembridge (1 hole)	1	K Still	0
PJ Butler (1 hole)	1	R Floyd	0
A Jacklin (4 and 3)	1	J Nicklaus	0
	5		**3**

AFTERNOON

BW Barnes	0	D Hill (4 and 2)	1
B Gallacher (4 and 3)	1	L Trevino	0
M Bembridge	0	M Barber (7 and 6)	1
PJ Butler (3 and 2)	1	D Douglass	0
C O'Connor	0	G Littler (2 and 1)	1
BGC Huggett	1/2	W Casper	1/2
NC Coles	0	D Sikes (4 and 3)	1
A Jacklin	1/2	J Nicklaus	1/2
	3		**5**

Third Day Total: Great Britain 8; USA 8.
Match Aggregate: Great Britain 16; USA 16.
Captains (non-playing): EC Brown, Great Britain, and S Snead, USA.

1971 *at St Louis, Missouri*

Foursomes
MORNING

USA	Matches	GREAT BRITAIN AND IRELAND	Matches
W Casper and M Barber	0	NC Coles and C O'Connor (2 and 1)	1
A Palmer and G Dickinson (2 holes)	1	P Townsend and P Oosterhuis	0
J Nicklaus and D Stockton	0	BGC Huggett and A Jacklin (3 and 2)	1
C Coody and F Beard	0	M Bembridge and PJ Butler (1 hole)	1
	1		**3**

AFTERNOON

W Casper and M Barber	0	H Bannerman and B Gallacher (2 and 1)	1
A Palmer and G Dickinson (1 hole)	1	P Townsend and P Oosterhuis	0
L Trevino and M Rudolph	1/2	BGC Huggett and A Jacklin	1/2
J Nicklaus and JC Snead (5 and 3)	1	M Bembridge and PJ Butler	0
	2 1/2		**1 1/2**

First Day Aggregate: USA 3 1/2; Great Britain and Ireland 4 1/2.

Four-Balls
MORNING

L Trevino and M Rudolph (2 and 1)	1	C O'Connor and BW Barnes	0
F Beard and JC Snead (2 and 1)	1	NC Coles and J Garner	0
A Palmer and G Dickinson (5 and 4)	1	P Oosterhuis and B Gallacher	0
J Nicklaus and G Littler (2 and 1)	1	P Townsend and H Bannerman	0
	4		**0**

AFTERNOON

L Trevino and W Casper	0	B Gallacher and P Oosterhuis (1 hole)	1
G Littler and JC Snead (2 and 1)	1	A Jacklin and BGC Huggett	0
A Palmer and J Nicklaus (1 hole)	1	P Townsend and H Bannerman	0
C Coody and F Beard	½	NC Coles and C O'Connor	½
	2½		1½

Second Day Total: USA 6½; Great Britain and Ireland 1½.
Match Aggregate: USA 10; Great Britain and Ireland 6.

Singles

MORNING

L Trevino (1 hole)	1	A Jacklin	0
D Stockton	½	B Gallacher	½
M Rudolph	0	BW Barnes (1 hole)	1
G Littler	0	P Oosterhuis (4 and 3)	1
J Nicklaus (3 and 2)	1	P Townsend	0
G Dickinson (5 and 4)	1	C O'Connor	0
A Palmer	½	H Bannerman	½
F Beard	½	NC Coles	½
	4½		3½

AFTERNOON

L Trevino (7 and 6)	1	BGC Huggett	0
JC Snead (1 hole)	1	A Jacklin	0
M Barber	0	BW Barnes (2 and 1)	1
D Stockton (1 hole)	1	P Townsend	0
C Coody	0	B Gallacher (2 and 1)	1
J Nicklaus (5 and 3)	1	NC Coles	0
A Palmer	0	P Oosterhuis (3 and 2)	1
G Dickinson	0	H Bannerman (2 and 1)	1
	4		4

Third Day Total: USA 8½; Great Britain and Ireland 7½.
Match Aggregate: USA 18½; Great Britain and Ireland 13½.
Captains (non-playing): EC Brown, Great Britain and Ireland, and J Hebert, USA .

1973   *at Muirfield*

First Day–Foursomes

GREAT BRITAIN AND IRELAND	Matches	USA	Matches
BW Barnes and B Gallacher (1 hole)	1	L Trevino and W Casper	0
C O'Connor and NC Coles (3 and 2)	1	T Weiskopf and JC Snead	0
A Jacklin and P Oosterhuis	½	J Rodriguez and L Graham	½
M Bembridge and E Polland	0	J Nicklaus and A Palmer (6 and 5)	1
	2½		1½

Four-Balls

BW Barnes and B Gallacher (5 and 4)	1	T Aaron and G Brewer	0
M Bembridge and BGC Huggett (3 and 1)	1	A Palmer and J Nicklaus	0
A Jacklin and P Oosterhuis (3 and 1)	1	T Weiskopf and W Casper	0
C O'Connor and NC Coles	0	L Trevino and H Blancas (2 and 1)	1
	3		1

First Day Aggregate: Great Britain and Ireland 5½; USA 2½.

Second Day–Foursomes

BW Barnes and PJ Butler	0	J Nicklaus and T Weiskopf (1 hole)	1
P Oosterhuis and A Jacklin (2 holes)	1	A Palmer and D Hill	0
M Bembridge and BGC Huggett (5 and 4)	1	J Rodriguez and L Graham	0
NC Coles and C O'Connor	0	L Trevino and W Casper (2 and 1)	1
	2		2

Four-Balls

BW Barnes and PJ Butler	0	JC Snead and A Palmer (2 holes)	1
A Jacklin and P Oosterhuis	0	G Brewer and W Casper (3 and 2)	1
CA Clark and E Polland	0	J Nicklaus and T Weiskopf (3 and 2)	1
M Bembridge and BGC Huggett	½	L Trevino and H Blancas	½
	½		3½

Second Day Totals: Great Britain and Ireland 2½; USA 5½.
Match Aggregate: Great Britain and Ireland 8; USA 8.

Third Day–Singles

MORNING

BW Barnes	0	W Casper (2 and 1)	1
B Gallacher	0	T Weiskopf (3 and 1)	1
PJ Butler	0	H Blancas (5 and 4)	1
A Jacklin (3 and 1)	1	T Aaron	0
NC Coles	½	G Brewer	½
C O'Connor	0	JC Snead (1 hole)	1
M Bembridge	½	J Nicklaus	½
P Oosterhuis	½	L Trevino	½
	2½		5½

AFTERNOON

BGC Huggett (4 and 2)	1	H Blancas	0
BW Barnes	0	JC Snead (3 and 1)	1
B Gallacher	0	G Brewer (6 and 5)	1
A Jacklin	0	W Casper (2 and 1)	1
NC Coles	0	L Trevino (6 and 5)	1
C O'Connor	½	T Weiskopf	½
M Bembridge	0	J Nicklaus (2 holes)	1
P Oosterhuis (4 and 2)	1	A Palmer	0
	2½		5½

Third Day Aggregate: Great Britain and Ireland 5; USA 11.
Match Aggregate: Great Britain and Ireland 13; USA 19.
Captains (non-playing): BJ Hunt, Great Britain and Ireland, and J Burke, USA.

1975 *at Laurel Valley, Pennsylvania*

First Day–Foursomes

USA	Matches	GREAT BRITAIN AND IRELAND	Matches
J Nicklaus and T Weiskopf (5 and 4)	1	BW Barnes and B Gallacher	0
G Littler and H Irwin (4 and 3)	1	N Wood and M Bembridge	0
A Geiberger and J Miller (3 and 1)	1	A Jacklin and P Oosterhuis	0
L Trevino and JC Snead (2 and 1)	1	T Horton and J O'Leary	0
	4		0

Four-Balls

W Casper and R Floyd	0	P Oosterhuis and A Jacklin (2 and 1)	1
T Weiskopf and L Graham (3 and 2)	1	E Darcy and C O'Connor	0
J Nicklaus and R Murphy	½	BW Barnes and B Gallacher	½
L Trevino and H Irwin (2 and 1)	1	T Horton and J O'Leary	0
	2½		1½

First Day Aggregate: USA 6½; Great Britian and Ireland 1½.

Second Day–Four-Balls

W Casper and J Miller	½	P Oosterhuis and A Jacklin	½
J Nicklaus and JC Snead (4 and 2)	1	T Horton and N Wood	0
G Littler and L Graham (5 and 3)	1	BW Barnes and B Gallacher	0
A Geiberger and R Floyd	½	E Darcy and GL Hunt	½
	3		1

Foursomes

L Trevino and R Murphy	0	A Jacklin and BW Barnes (3 and 2)	1
T Weiskopf and J Miller (5 and 3)	1	C O'Connor and J O'Leary	0
H Irwin and W Casper (3 and 2)	1	P Oosterhuis and M Bembridge	0
A Geiberger and L Graham (3 and 2)	1	E Darcy and GL Hunt	0
	3		1

Second Day Totals: USA 6; Great Britain and Ireland 2.
Match Aggregate: USA 12½; Great Britain and Ireland 3½.

Third Day– Singles

MORNING

R Murphy (2 and 1)	1	A Jacklin	0
J Miller	0	P Oosterhuis (2 holes)	1
L Trevino	½	B Gallacher	½
H Irwin	½	T Horton	½
G Littler (4 and 2)	1	BGC Huggett	0
W Casper (3 and 2)	1	E Darcy	0
T Weiskopf (5 and 3)	1	GL Hunt	0
J Nicklaus	0	BW Barnes (4 and 2)	1
	5		3

AFTERNOON

R Floyd (1 hole)	1	A Jacklin	0
JC Snead	0	P Oosterhuis (3 and 2)	1
A Geiberger	½	B Gallacher	½
L Graham	0	T Horton (2 and 1)	1
H Irwin (2 and 1)	1	J O'Leary	0
R Murphy (2 and 1)	1	M Bembridge	0
L Trevino	0	N Wood (2 and 1)	1
J Nicklaus	0	BW Barnes (2 and 1)	1
	3½		4½

Third Day Totals: USA 8½; Great Britain and Ireland 7½.
Match Aggregate: USA 21; Great Britain and Ireland 11.
Captains (non-playing): A Palmer, USA, and BJ Hunt, Great Britain and Ireland.

1977   *at Royal Lytham and St Anne's*

First Day–Foursomes

GREAT BRITAIN AND IRELAND	Matches	USA	Matches
B Gallacher and BW Barnes	0	L Wadkins and H Irwin (3 and 1)	1
NC Coles and P Dawson	0	D Stockton and J McGee (1 hole)	1
N Faldo and P Oosterhuis (2 and 1)	1	R Floyd and L Graham	0
E Darcy and A Jacklin	1/2	E Sneed and D January	1/2
T Horton and M James	0	J Nicklaus and T Watson (5 and 4)	1
	1½		3½

Second Day–Four-Balls

	Matches		Matches
BW Barnes and T Horton	0	T Watson and H Green (5 and 4)	1
NC Coles and P Dawson	0	E Sneed and L Wadkins (5 and 3)	1
N Faldo and P Oosterhuis (3 and 1)	1	J Nicklaus and R Floyd	0
A Jacklin and E Darcy	0	D Hill and D Stockton (5 and 3)	1
M James and K Brown	0	H Irwin and L Graham (1 hole)	1
	1		4

Third Day–Singles

	Matches		Matches
H Clark	0	L Wadkins (4 and 3)	1
NC Coles	0	L Graham (5 and 3)	1
P Dawson (5 and 4)	1	D January	0
BW Barnes (1 hole)	1	H Irwin	0
T Horton	0	D Hill (5 and 4)	1
B Gallacher (1 hole)	1	J Nicklaus	0
E Darcy	0	H Green (1 hole)	1
M James	0	R Floyd (2 and 1)	1
N Faldo (1 hole)	1	T Watson	0
P Oosterhuis (2 holes)	1	J McGee	0
	5		5

Match Aggregate: Great Britain and Ireland 7½; USA 12½.
Captains (non-playing): BGC Huggett, Great Britain and Ireland, and D Finsterwald,USA.

1979   *at Greenbrier, West Virginia*

From 1979 players from Europe became available for selection in addition to those from Great Britain and Ireland.

First Day–Four-Balls

USA	Matches	EUROPE	Matches
L Wadkins and L Nelson (2 and 1)	1	A Garrido and S Ballesteros	0
L Trevino and F Zoeller (3 and 2)	1	K Brown and M James	0
A Bean and L Elder (2 and 1)	1	P Oosterhuis and N Faldo	0
H Irwin and J Mahaffey	0	B Gallacher and BW Barnes (2 and 1)	1
	3		1

Foursomes

H Irwin and T Kite (7 and 6)	1	K Brown and D Smyth	0
F Zoeller and H Green	0	S Ballesteros and A Garrido (3 and 2)	1
L Trevino and G Morgan	½	AWB Lyle and A Jacklin	½
L Wadkins and L Nelson (4 and 3)	1	B Gallacher and BW Barnes	0
	2½		1½

First Day Aggregate: USA 5½; Europe 2½.

Second Day–Foursomes

L Elder and J Mahaffey	0	A Jacklin and AWB Lyle (5 and 4)	1
A Bean and T Kite	0	N Faldo and P Oosterhuis (6 and 5)	1
F Zoeller and M Hayes	0	B Gallacher and BW Barnes (2 and 1)	1
L Wadkins and L Nelson (3 and 2)	1	S Ballesteros and A Garrido	0
	1		3

Four-Balls

L Wadkins and L Nelson (5 and 4)	1	S Ballesteros and A Garrido	0
H Irwin and T Kite (1 hole)	1	A Jacklin and AWB Lyle	0
L Trevino and F Zoeller	0	B Gallacher and BW Barnes (3 and 2)	1
L Elder and M Hayes	0	N Faldo and P Oosterhuis (1 hole)	1
	2		2

Second Day Total: USA 3; Europe 5.
Match Aggregate: USA 8½; Europe 7½.

Third Day–Singles

L Wadkins	0	B Gallacher (3 and 2)	1
L Nelson (3 and 2)	1	S Ballesteros	0
T Kite (1 hole)	1	A Jacklin	0
M Hayes (1 hole)	1	A Garrido	0
A Bean (4 and 3)	1	M King	0
J Mahaffey (1 hole)	1	BW Barnes	0
L Elder	0	N Faldo (3 and 2)	1
H Irwin (5 and 3)	1	D Smyth	0
H Green (2 holes)	1	P Oosterhuis	0
F Zoeller	0	K Brown (1 hole)	1
L Trevino (2 and 1)	1	AWB Lyle	0
G Morgan (match not played)	½	M James (match not played, injured)	½
	8½		3½

Match Aggregate: USA 17; Europe 11.
Captains (non-playing): J Jacobs, Europe, and W Casper, USA .

1981 *at Walton Heath*

First Day–Foursomes

EUROPE	Matches	USA	Matches
B Langer and M Pinero	0	L Trevino and L Nelson (1 hole)	1
AWB Lyle and M James (2 and 1)	1	W Rogers and B Lietzke	0
B Gallacher and D Smyth (3 and 2)	1	H Irwin and R Floyd	0
P Oosterhuis and N Faldo	0	T Watson and J Nicklaus (4 and 3)	1
	2		2

Four-Balls

S Torrance and H Clark	½	T Kite and J Miller	½
AWB Lyle and M James (3 and 2)	1	B Crenshaw and J Pate	0
D Smyth and JM Canizares (6 and 5)	1	W Rogers and B Lietzke	0
B Gallacher and E Darcy	0	H Irwin and R Floyd (2 and 1)	1
	2½		**1½**

First Day Aggregate: USA 4½; Europe 3½.

Second Day–Four-Balls

N Faldo and S Torrance	0	L Trevino and J Pate (7 and 5)	1
AWB Lyle and M James	0	L Nelson and T Kite (1 hole)	1
B Langer and M Pinero (2 and 1)	1	R Floyd and H Irwin	0
JM Canizares and D Smyth	0	J Nicklaus and T Watson (3 and 2)	1
	1		**3**

Foursomes

P Oosterhuis and S Torrance	0	L Trevino and J Pate (2 and 1)	1
B Langer and M Pinero	0	J Nicklaus and T Watson (3 and 2)	1
AWB Lyle and M James	0	W Rogers and R Floyd (3 and 2)	1
D Smyth and B Gallacher	0	T Kite and L Nelson (3 and 2)	1
	0		**4**

Second Day Total: Europe 1; USA 7.
Match Aggregate: Europe 5½; USA 10½ .

Third Day–Singles

S Torrance	0	L Trevino (5 and 3)	1
AWB Lyle	0	T Kite (3 and 2)	1
B Gallacher	½	W Rogers	½
M James	0	L Nelson (2 holes)	1
D Smyth	0	B Crenshaw (6 and 4)	1
B Langer	½	B Lietzke	½
M Pinero (4 and 2)	1	J Pate	0
JM Canizares	0	H Irwin (1 hole)	1
N Faldo (2 and 1)	1	J Miller	0
H Clark (4 and 3)	1	T Watson	0
P Oosterhuis	0	R Floyd (2 holes)	1
E Darcy	0	J Nicklaus (5 and 3)	1
	4		**8**

Match Aggregate: Europe 9½; USA 18½.
Captains (non-playing): J Jacobs, Europe, and D Marr, USA.

1983 *at PGA National, Florida*

First Day–Foursomes

USA	Matches	EUROPE	Matches
T Watson and B Crenshaw (5 and 4)	1	B Gallacher and AWB Lyle	0
L Wadkins and C Stadler	0	N Faldo and B Langer (4 and 2)	1
R Floyd and R Gilder	0	JM Canizares and S Torrance (4 and 3)	1
T Kite and C Peete (2 and 1)	1	S Ballesteros and P Way	0
	2		**2**

Four-Balls

G Morgan and F Zoeller	0	B Waites and K Brown (2 and 1)	1
T Watson and J Haas (2 and 1)	1	N Faldo and B Langer	0
R Floyd and C Strange	0	S Ballesteros and P Way (1 hole)	1
B Crenshaw and C Peete	½	S Torrance and I Woosnam	½
	1½		2½

First Day Aggregate: USA 3½; Europe 4½.

Second Day–Foursomes

R Floyd and T Kite	0	N Faldo and B Langer (3 and 2)	1
L Wadkins and G Morgan (7 and 5)	1	S Torrance and JM Canizares	0
R Gilder and T Watson	0	S Ballesteros and P Way (2 and 1)	1
J Haas and C Strange (3 and 2)	1	K Brown and B Waites	0
	2		2

Four-Balls

C Stadler and L Wadkins (1 hole)	1	K Brown and B Waites	0
C Peete and B Crenshaw	0	N Faldo and B Langer (2 and 1)	1
G Morgan and J Haas	½	S Ballesteros and P Way	½
T Watson and R Gilder (5 and 4)	1	S Torrance and I Woosnam	0
	2½		1½

Second Day Total: USA 4½; Europe 3½.
Match Aggregate: USA 8; Europe 8.

Third Day–Singles

F Zoeller	½	S Ballesteros	½
J Haas	0	N Faldo (2 and 1)	1
G Morgan	0	B Langer (2 holes)	1
R Gilder (2 holes)	1	GJ Brand	0
B Crenshaw (3 and 1)	1	AWB Lyle	0
C Peete (1 hole)	1	B Waites	0
C Strange	0	P Way (2 and 1)	1
T Kite	½	S Torrance	½
C Stadler (3 and 2)	1	I Woosnam	0
L Wadkins	½	JM Canizares	½
R Floyd	0	K Brown (4 and 3)	1
T Watson (2 and 1)	1	B Gallacher	0
	6½		5½

Match Aggregate: USA 14½; Europe 13½.
Captains (non-playing): A Jacklin, Europe, and J Nicklaus, USA .

1985   *at The Belfry, Sutton Coldfield*

First Day–Foursomes

EUROPE	Matches	USA	Matches
S Ballesteros and M Pinero (2 and 1)	1	C Strange and M O'Meara	0
B Langer and N Faldo	0	C Peete and T Kite (3 and 2)	1
AWB Lyle and K Brown	0	L Wadkins and R Floyd (4 and 3)	1
H Clark and S Torrance	0	C Stadler and H Sutton (3 and 2)	1
	1		3

Four-Balls

P Way and I Woosnam (1 hole)	1	F Zoeller and H Green	0
S Ballesteros and M Pinero (2 and 1)	1	A North and P Jacobsen	0
B Langer and JM Canizares	½	C Stadler and H Sutton	½
S Torrance and H Clark	0	R Floyd and L Wadkins (1 hole)	1
	—		—
	2½		1½

First Day Aggregate: Europe 3½; USA 4½.

Second Day–Four-Balls

S Torrance and H Clark (2 and 1)	1	T Kite and A North	0
P Way and I Woosnam (4 and 3)	1	H Green and F Zoeller	0
S Ballesteros and M Pinero	0	M O'Meara and L Wadkins (3 and 2)	1
B Langer and AWB Lyle	½	C Stadler and C Strange	½
	—		—
	2½		1½

Foursomes

JM Canizares and J Rivero (7 and 5)	1	T Kite and C Peete	0
S Ballesteros and M Pinero (5 and 4)	1	C Stadler and H Sutton	0
P Way and I Woosnam	0	C Strange and P Jacobsen (4 and 2)	1
B Langer and K Brown (3 and 2)	1	R Floyd and L Wadkins	0
	—		—
	3		1

Second Day Total: Europe 5½; USA 2½.
Match Aggregate: Europe 9; USA 7.

Third Day–Singles

M Pinero (3 and 1)	1	L Wadkins	0
I Woosnam	0	C Stadler (2 and 1)	1
P Way (2 holes)	1	R Floyd	0
S Ballesteros	½	T Kite	½
AWB Lyle (3 and 2)	1	P Jacobsen	0
B Langer (5 and 4)	1	H Sutton	0
S Torrance (1 hole)	1	A North	0
H Clark (1 hole)	1	M O'Meara	0
N Faldo	0	H Green (3 and 1)	1
J Rivero	0	C Peete (1 hole)	1
JM Canizares (2 holes)	1	F Zoeller	0
K Brown	0	C Strange (4 and 2)	1
	—		—
	7½		4½

Match Aggregate: Europe 16½; USA 11½.
Captains (non-playing): A Jacklin, Europe, and L Trevino, USA.

1987   *at Muirfield Village, Ohio*

Foursomes

USA	Matches	EUROPE	Matches
C Strange and T Kite (4 and 2)	1	S Torrance and H Clark	0
H Sutton and D Pohl (2 and 1)	1	K Brown and B Langer	0
L Wadkins and L Mize	0	N Faldo and I Woosnam (2 holes)	1
L Nelson and P Stewart	0	S Ballesteros and JM Olazabal (1 hole)	1
	—		—
	2		2

Four-Balls

B Crenshaw and S Simpson	0	G Brand Jr and J Rivero (3 and 2)	1
A Bean and M Calcavecchia	0	AWB Lyle and B Langer (1 hole)	1
H Sutton and D Pohl	0	N Faldo and I Woosnam (2 and 1)	1
C Strange and T Kite	0	S Ballesteros and JM Olazabal (2 and 1)	1
	0		**4**

First Day Aggregate: USA 2; Europe 6.

Second Day–Foursomes

C Strange and T Kite (3 and 1)	1	J Rivero and G Brand Jr	0
H Sutton and L Mize	½	N Faldo and I Woosnam	½
L Wadkins and L Nelson	0	AWB Lyle and B Langer (2 and 1)	1
B Crenshaw and P Stewart	0	S Ballesteros and JM Olazabal (1 hole)	1
	1½		**2½**

Four-Balls

T Kite and C Strange	0	I Woosnam and N Faldo (5 and 4)	1
A Bean and P Stewart (3 and 2)	1	E Darcy and G Brand Jr	0
H Sutton and L Mize (2 and 1)	1	S Ballesteros and JM Olazabal	0
L Wadkins and L Nelson	0	AWB Lyle and B Langer (1 hole)	1
	2		**2**

Second Day Total: USA 3½; Europe 4½.
Match Aggregate: USA 5½; Europe 10½.

Third Day–Singles

A Bean (1 hole)	1	I Woosnam	0
D Pohl	0	H Clark (1 hole)	1
L Mize	½	S Torrance	½
M Calcavecchia (1 hole)	1	N Faldo	0
P Stewart (2 holes)	1	JM Olazabal	0
S Simpson (2 and 1)	1	J Rivero	0
T Kite (3 and 2)	1	AWB Lyle	0
B Crenshaw	0	E Darcy (1 hole)	1
L Nelson	½	B Langer	½
C Strange	0	S Ballesteros (2 and 1)	1
L Wadkins (3 and 2)	1	K Brown	0
H Sutton	½	G Brand Jr	½
	7½		**4½**

Match Aggregate: USA 13; Europe 15.
Captains (non-playing): A Jacklin, Europe, and J Nicklaus, USA.

1989   *at The Belfry, Sutton Coldfield*

First Day–Foursomes

EUROPE		USA	
	Matches		Matches
N Faldo and I Woosnam	½	T Kite and C Strange	½
H Clark and M James	0	L Wadkins and P Stewart (1 hole)	1
S Ballesteros and JM Olazabal	½	T Watson and C Beck	½
B Langer and R Rafferty	0	M Calcavecchia and K Green (2 and 1)	1
	1		**3**

Four-Balls

S Torrance and G Brand Jr (1 hole)	1	C Strange and P Azinger	0
H Clark and M James (3 and 2)	1	F Couples and L Wadkins	0
N Faldo and I Woosnam (1 hole)	1	M Calcavecchia and M McCumber	0
S Ballesteros and JM Olazabal (6 and 5)	1	T Watson and M O'Meara	0
	—		—
	4		0

First Day Aggregate: Europe 5; USA 3.

Second Day–Foursomes

I Woosnam and N Faldo (3 and 2)	1	L Wadkins and P Stewart	0
G Brand Jr and S Torrance	0	C Beck and P Azinger (4 and 3)	1
C O'Connor Jr and R Rafferty	0	M Calcavecchia and K Green (3 and 2)	1
S Ballesteros and JM Olazabal (1 hole)	1	T Kite and C Strange	0
	—		—
	2		2

Four-Balls

N Faldo and I Woosnam	0	C Beck and P Azinger (2 and 1)	1
B Langer and JM Canizares	0	T Kite and M McCumber (2 and 1)	1
H Clark and M James (1 hole)	1	P Stewart and C Strange	0
S Ballesteros and JM Olazabal (4 and 2)	1	M Calcavecchia and K Green	0
	—		—
	2		2

Second Day Total: Europe 4; USA 4.
Match Aggregate: Europe 9; USA 7.

Third Day–Singles

S Ballesteros	0	P Azinger (1 hole)	1
B Langer	0	C Beck (3 and 1)	1
JM Olazabal (1 hole)	1	P Stewart	0
R Rafferty (1 hole)	1	M Calcavecchia	0
H Clark	0	T Kite (8 and 7)	1
M James (3 and 2)	1	M O'Meara	0
C O'Connor Jr (1 hole)	1	F Couples	0
JM Canizares (1 hole)	1	K Green	0
G Brand Jr	0	M McCumber (1 hole)	1
S Torrance	0	T Watson (3 and 1)	1
N Faldo	0	L Wadkins (1 hole)	1
I Woosnam	0	C Strange (1 hole)	1
	—		—
	5		7

Match Aggregate: Europe 14; USA 14.
Captains (non-playing): A Jacklin, Europe and R Floyd, USA.

Individual Records

(Matches were contested as Great Britain v USA from 1927-71; as Great Britain and Ireland from 1973-7; and as Europe v USA from 1979.)

Bold type indicates captain; in brackets did not play

Europe

Name	Year	Played	Won	Lost	Halved
Jimmy Adams	*1939-47-49-51-53	7	2	5	0
Percy Alliss	1929-33-35-37	6	3	2	1
Peter Alliss	1953-57-59-61-63-65-67-69	30	10	15	5
Laurie Ayton	1949	0	0	0	0
Severiano Ballesteros	1979-83-85-87-89	25	13	8	4
Harry Bannerman	1971	5	2	2	1
Brian Barnes	1969-71-73-75-77-79	25	10	14	1
Maurice Bembridge	1969-71-73-75	16	5	8	3
Aubrey Boomer	1927-29	4	2	2	0
Ken Bousfield	1949-51-55-57-59-61	10	5	5	0
Hugh Boyle	1967	3	0	3	0
Harry Bradshaw	1953-55-57	5	2	2	1
Gordon J Brand	1983	1	0	1	0
Gordon Brand Jr	1987-89	7	2	4	1
Eric Brown	1953-55-57-59-(69)-(71)	8	4	4	0
Ken Brown	1977-79-83-85-87	13	4	9	0
Stewart Burns	1929	0	0	0	0
Dick Burton	1935-37-*39-49	5	2	3	0
Jack Busson	1935	2	0	2	0
Peter Butler	1965-69-71-73	14	3	9	2
Jose Maria Canizares	1981-83-85-89	11	5	4	2
Alex Caygill	1969	1	0	0	1
Clive Clark	1973	1	0	1	0
Howard Clark	1977-81-85-87-89	13	6	6	1
Neil Coles	1961-63-65-67-69-71-73-77	40	12	21	7
Archie Compston	1927-29-31	6	1	4	1
Henry Cotton	1929-37-*39-47-(53)	6	2	4	0
Bill Cox	1935-37	3	0	2	1
Allan Dailey	1933	0	0	0	0
Fred Daly	1947-49-51-53	8	3	4	1
Eamonn Darcy	1975-77-81-87	11	1	8	2
William Davies	1931-33	4	2	2	0
Peter Dawson	1977	3	1	2	0
Norman Drew	1959	1	0	0	1
George Duncan	1927-29-31	5	2	3	0
Syd Easterbrook	1931-33	3	2	1	0
Nick Faldo	1977-79-81-83-85-87-89	27	16	9	2
John Fallon	1955-(63)	1	1	0	0
Max Faulkner	1947-49-51-53-57	8	1	7	0
George Gadd	1927	0	0	0	0
Bernard Gallacher	1969-71-73-75-77-79-81-83-(91)	31	13	13	5
John Garner	1971-73	1	0	1	0
Antonio Garrido	1979	5	1	4	0
Eric Green	1947	0	0	0	0
Malcolm Gregson	1967	4	0	4	0
Tom Haliburton	1961-63	6	0	6	0
Jack Hargreaves	1951	0	0	0	0

Name	Year	Played	Won	Lost	Halved
Arthur Havers	1927-31-33	6	3	3	0
Jimmy Hitchcock	1965	3	0	3	0
Bert Hodson	1931	1	0	1	0
Reg Horne	1947	0	0	0	0
Tommy Horton	1975-77	8	1	6	1
Brian Huggett	1963-67-69-71-73-75-(77)	25	9	10	6
Bernard Hunt	1953-57-59-61-63-65-67-69-(73)-(75)	28	6	16	6
Geoffrey Hunt	1963	3	0	3	0
Guy Hunt	1975	3	0	2	1
Tony Jacklin	1967-69-71-73-75-77-79-(83)-(85)-(87)-(89)	35	13	14	8
John Jacobs	1955-(79)-(81)	2	2	0	0
Mark James	1977-79-81-89	14	5	8	1
Edward Jarman	1935	1	0	1	0
Herbert Jolly	1927	2	0	2	0
Michael King	1979	1	0	1	0
Sam King	1937-*39-47-49	5	1	3	1
Arthur Lacey	1933-37-(51)	3	0	3	0
Bernhard Langer	1981-83-85-87-89	22	10	8	4
Arthur Lees	1947-49-51-55	8	4	4	0
Sandy Lyle	1979-81-83-85-87	18	7	9	2
Jimmy Martin	1965	1	0	1	0
Peter Mills	1957-59	1	1	0	0
Abe Mitchell	1929-31-33	6	4	2	0
Ralph Moffitt	1961	1	0	1	0
Christy O'Connor, Jr	1975-89	4	1	3	0
Christy O'Connor, Sr	1955-57-59-61-63-65-67-69-71-73	36	11	21	4
Jose Maria Olazabal	1987-89	10	7	2	1
John O'Leary	1975	4	0	4	0
Peter Oosterhuis	1971-73-75-77-79-81	28	14	11	3
Alf Padgham	1933-35-37-*39	6	0	6	0
John Panton	1951-53-61	5	0	5	0
Alf Perry	1933-35-37	4	0	3	1
Manuel Pinero	1981-85	9	6	3	0
Lionel Platts	1965	5	1	2	2
Eddie Polland	1973	2	0	2	0
Ronan Rafferty	1989	3	1	2	0
Ted Ray	1927	2	0	2	0
Dai Rees	1937-*39-47-49-51-53-55-57-59-61-(67)	18	7	10	1
Jose Rivero	1985-87	5	2	3	0
Fred Robson	1927-29-31	6	2	4	0
Syd Scott	1955	2	0	2	0
Des Smyth	1979-81	7	2	5	0
Dave Thomas	1959-63-65-67	18	3	10	5
Sam Torrance	1981-83-85-87-89	18	4	10	4
Peter Townsend	1969-71	11	3	8	0
Brian Waites	1983	4	1	3	0
Charlie Ward	1947-49-51	6	1	5	0
Paul Way	1983-85	9	6	2	1
Harry Weetman	1951-53-55-57-59-61-63-(65)	15	2	11	2
Charles Whitcombe	1927-29-31-33-35-37-*39-(49)	9	3	2	4
Ernest Whitcombe	1929-31-35	6	1	4	1
Reg Whitcombe	1935-*39	1	0	1	0
George Will	1963-65-67	15	2	11	2
Norman Wood	1975	3	1	2	0
Ian Woosnam	1983-85-87-89	17	7	7	3

(Great Britain named eight members of their 1939 side, but the match was not played because of the Second World War.)

United States of America

Name	Year	Played	Won	Lost	Halved
Tommy Aaron	1969-73	6	1	4	1
Skip Alexander	1949-51	2	1	1	0
Paul Azinger	1989	4	3	1	0
Jerry Barber	1955-61	5	1	4	0
Miller Barber	1969-71	7	1	4	2
Herman Barron	1947	1	1	0	0
Andy Bean	1979-87	6	4	2	0
Frank Beard	1969-71	8	2	3	3
Chip Beck	1989	4	3	0	1
Homero Blancas	1973	4	2	1	1
Tommy Bolt	1955-57	4	3	1	0
Julius Boros	1959-63-65-67	16	9	3	4
Gay Brewer	1967-73	9	5	3	1
Billy Burke	1931-33	3	3	0	0
Jack Burke	1951-53-55-57-59-(73)	8	7	1	0
Walter Burkemo	1953	1	0	1	0
Mark Calcavecchia	1987-89	7	3	4	0
Billy Casper	1961-63-65-67-69-71-73-75-(79)	37	20	10	7
Bill Collins	1961	3	1	2	0
Charles Coody	1971	3	0	2	1
Fred Couples	1989	2	0	2	0
Wilfred Cox	1931	2	2	0	0
Ben Crenshaw	1981-83-87	9	3	5	1
Jimmy Demaret	**1941-47-49-51	6	6	0	0
Gardner Dickinson	1967-71	10	9	1	0
Leo Diegel	1927-29-31-33	6	3	3	0
Dale Douglass	1969	2	0	2	0
Dave Douglas	1953	2	1	0	1
Ed Dudley	1929-33-37	4	3	1	0
Olin Dutra	1933-35	4	1	3	0
Lee Elder	1979	4	1	3	0
Al Espinosa	1927-29-31	4	2	1	1
Johnny Farrell	1927-29-31	6	3	2	1
Dow Finsterwald	1957-59-61-63-(77)	13	9	3	1
Ray Floyd	1969-75-77-81-83-85-(89)	23	7	13	3
Doug Ford	1955-57-59-61	9	4	4	1
Ed Furgol	1957	1	0	1	0
Marty Furgol	1955	1	0	1	0
Al Geiberger	1967-75	9	5	1	3
Vic Ghezzi	*1939-**41	0	0	0	0
Bob Gilder	1983	4	2	2	0
Bob Goalby	1963	5	3	1	1
Johnny Golden	1927-29	3	3	0	0
Lou Graham	1973-75-77	9	5	3	1
Hubert Green	1977-79-85	7	4	3	0
Ken Green	1989	4	2	2	0
Ralph Guldahl	1937-*39	2	2	0	0
Fred Haas, Jr	1953	1	0	1	0
Jay Haas	1983	4	2	1	1
Walter Hagen	1927-29-31-33-35-(37)	9	7	1	1
Bob Hamilton	1949	2	0	2	0
Chick Harbert	1949-55	2	2	0	0
Chandler Harper	1955	1	0	1	0
Dutch (EJ) Harrison	1947-49-51	3	2	1	0
Fred Hawkins	1957	2	1	1	0
Mark Hayes	1979	3	1	2	0

Name	Year	Played	Won	Lost	Halved
Clayton Heafner	1949-51	4	3	0	1
Jay Hebert	1959-61-(71)	4	2	1	1
Lionel Hebert	1957	1	0	1	0
Dave Hill	1969-73-77	9	6	3	0
Jimmy Hines	*1939	0	0	0	0
Ben Hogan	**1941-47-(49)-51-(67)	3	3	0	0
Hale Irwin	1975-77-79-81	16	11	4	1
Tommy Jacobs	1965	4	3	1	0
Peter Jacobsen	1985	3	1	2	0
Don January	1965-77	7	2	3	2
Herman Keiser	1947	1	0	1	0
Tom Kite	1979-81-83-85-87-89	24	13	7	4
Ted Kroll	1953-55-57	4	3	1	0
Ky Laffoon	1935	1	0	1	0
Tony Lema	1963-65	11	8	1	2
Bruce Lietzke	1981	3	0	2	1
Gene Littler	1961-63-65-67-69-71-75	27	14	5	8
John Mahaffey	1979	3	1	2	0
Mark McCumber	1989	3	2	1	0
Jerry McGee	1977	2	1	1	0
Harold McSpaden	*1939-**41	0	0	0	0
Tony Manero	1937	2	1	1	0
Lloyd Mangrum	**1941-47-49-51-53	8	6	2	0
Dave Marr	1965-(81)	6	4	2	0
Billy Maxwell	1963	4	4	0	0
Dick Mayer	1957	2	1	0	1
Bill Mehlhorn	1927	2	1	1	0
Dick Metz	*1939	0	0	0	0
Cary Middlecoff	1953-55-59	6	2	3	1
Johnny Miller	1975-81	6	2	2	2
Larry Mize	1987	4	1	1	2
Gil Morgan	1979-83	6	1	2	3
Bob Murphy	1975	4	2	1	1
Byron Nelson	1937-*39-**41-47-(65)	4	3	1	0
Larry Nelson	1979-81-87	13	9	3	1
Bobby Nichols	1967	5	4	0	1
Jack Nicklaus	1969-71-73-75-77-81-(83)-(87)	28	17	8	3
Andy North	1985	3	0	3	0
Ed Oliver	1947-51-53	5	3	2	0
Mark O'Meara	1985-89	5	1	4	0
Arnold Palmer	1961-63-65-67-71-73-(75)	32	22	8	2
Johnny Palmer	1949	2	0	2	0
Sam Parks	1935	1	0	0	1
Jerry Pate	1981	4	2	2	0
Calvin Peete	1983-85	7	4	2	1
Henry Picard	1935-37-*39	4	3	1	0
Dan Pohl	1987	3	1	2	0
Johnny Pott	1963-65-67	7	5	2	0
Dave Ragan	1963	4	2	1	1
Henry Ransom	1951	1	0	1	0
Johnny Revolta	1935-37	3	2	1	0
Chi Chi Rodriguez	1973	2	0	1	1
Bill Rogers	1981	4	1	2	1
Bob Rosburg	1959	2	2	0	0
Mason Rudolph	1971	3	1	1	1
Paul Runyan	1933-35-*39	4	2	2	0
Doug Sanders	1967	5	2	3	0
Gene Sarazen	1927-29-31-33-35-37-**41	12	7	2	3

Name	Year	Played	Won	Lost	Halved
Densmore Shute	1931-33-37	6	2	2	2
Dan Sikes	1969	3	2	1	0
Scott Simpson	1987	2	1	1	0
Horton Smith	1929-31-33-35-37-*39-**41	4	3	0	1
JC Snead	1971-73-75	11	9	2	0
Sam Snead	1937-*39-**41-47-49-51-53-55-59-(69)	13	10	2	1
Ed Sneed	1977	2	1	0	1
Mike Souchak	1959-61	6	5	1	0
Craig Stadler	1983-85	8	4	2	2
Payne Stewart	1987-89	8	3	5	0
Ken Still	1969	3	1	2	0
Dave Stockton	1971-77-(91)	5	3	1	1
Curtis Strange	1983-85-87-89	17	6	9	2
Hal Sutton	1985-87	9	3	3	3
Lee Trevino	1969-71-73-75-79-81-(85)	30	17	7	6
Jim Turnesa	1953	1	1	0	0
Joe Turnesa	1927-29	4	1	2	1
Ken Venturi	1965	4	1	3	0
Lanny Wadkins	1977-79-83-85-87-89	25	15	9	1
Art Wall, Jnr	1957-59-61	6	4	2	0
Al Watrous	1927-29	3	2	1	0
Tom Watson	1977-81-83-89	15	10	4	1
Tom Weiskopf	1973-75	10	7	2	1
Craig Wood	1931-33-35-**41	4	1	3	0
Lew Worsham	1947	2	2	0	0
Fuzzy Zoeller	1979-83-85	10	1	8	1

(US teams were selected in 1939 (*) and 1941 (**), but the matches were not played because of the Second World War.)

European Opens
Prior to becoming part of European Tour

Golf courses in Europe before the Great War were sparse and still very few until the 1970s. It is true that the course at Pau in the foothills of the Pyrenees, founded in 1856 by British ex-patriates, pre-dates all English courses apart from Blackheath and Old Manchester, but it is the only exception.

The large number of new courses constructed in the last twenty years has provided opportunities for far more European nationals to play the game and has produced a high standard of performance; this is particularly evident in Spain where playing conditions are good throughout the year.

Several countries staged open and amateur championships before 1914, encouraged by British ex-patriates, who provided the winners of many of the amateur events, with leading British professionals successful in most of the opens.

Both wars meant gaps of up to eight years in some of the continental championships and it was not until 1971 that the national opens began to be absorbed into the European Tour circuit. Since then most have found sponsorship and are established in the Tour programme; at present they are the Opens of Austria, Belgium, France, Germany, Netherlands, Italy, Portugal, Spain and Switzerland.

Belgian Open

INAUGURATED 1910

NAME	WINNER	VENUE	NAME	WINNER	VENUE
1910	A Massy	Brussels	1931	AJ Lacey	Spa
1911	CH Mayo	Brussels	1932	AJ Lacey	Brussels
1912	G Duncan	Brussels	1933	A Boyer	Spa
1913	T Ball	Lombartzyde	1934	TH Cotton	Waterloo
1914	T Ball	Antwerp	1935	WJ Branch	Brussels
1915–20	*Not played due to Great War*		1936	A Boyer	Spa
1920	R Jones	Le Zoute	1937	M Dallemagne	Le Zoute
1921	E Lafitte	Brussels	1938	TH Cotton	Waterloo
1922	A Boomer	Brussels	1939	F van Donck	Spa
1923	P Boomer	Brussels	1940–45	*Not played due to Second World*	
1924	W Hagen	Le Zoute		*War*	
1925	E Lafitte	Antwerp	1946	F van Donck	Waterloo
1926	A Boomer	Le Zoute	1947	F van Donck	Spa
1927	M Dallemagne	Le Zoute	1948	WS Forrester	Brussels
1928	A Tingey Jr	Brussels	1949	J Adams	Spa
1929	SF Brews	Antwerp	1950	R de Vicenzo	Le Zoute
1930	TH Cotton	Brussels	1951	A Pelissier	Ghent

NAME	WINNER	VENUE	NAME	WINNER	VENUE
1952	A Cerda	Spa	1956	F van Donck	Ghent
1953	F van Donck	Waterloo	1957	BJ Hunt	Ghent
1954	DJ Rees	Antwerp	1958	K Bousfield	Ravenstein
1955	DC Thomas	Spa	1959 – 77	*No Competition*	

Dutch Open

INAUGURATED 1919

YEAR	WINNER	SCORE	VENUE	YEAR	WINNER	SCORE	VENUE
1919	D Oosterveer	158*	The Hague	1950	R de Vicenzo	269	Breda
1920	H Burrows	155*	Haarlem	1951	F van Donck	281	Kennemer
1921	H Burrows	151*	Domburg	1952	C Denny	284	Hilversum
1922	G Pannell	169*	Noordwijk	1953	F van Donck	286	Eindhoven
1923	H Burrows	153*	Hilversum	1954	U Grappasonni	295	The Hague
1924	A Boomer	138*	The Hague	1955	A Angelini	280	Zandvoort
1925	A Boomer	144*	The Hague	1956	A Cerda	277	Eindhoven
1926	A Boomer	151*	The Hague	1957	J Jacobs	284	Hilversum
1927	P Boomer	147*	The Hague	1958	DC Thomas	277	Zandvoort
1928	ER Whitcombe	141*	The Hague	1959	S Sewgolum	283	The Hague
1929	JJ Taylor	153*	Hilversum	1960	S Sewgolum	280	Eindhoven
1930	J Oosterveer	152*	The Hague	1961	BBS Wilkes	279	Zandvoort
1931	F Dyer	145*	Haarlem	1962	BGC Huggett	274	Hilversum
1932	A Boyer	137*	The Hague	1963	R Waltman	279	Wassenaar
1933	M Dallemagne	143*	Zandvoort	1964	S Sewgolum	275	Eindhoven
1934	SF Brews	286	Utrecht	1965	A Miguel	278	Breda
1935	SF Brews	275	Zandvoort	1966	R Sota	276	Zandvoort
1936	F van Donck	285	Hilversum	1967	P Townsend	282	The Hague
1937	F van Donck	286	Utrecht	1968	J Cockin	292	Hilversum
1938	AH Padgham	281	The Hague	1969	GB Wolstenholme	277	Utrecht
1939	AD Locke	281	Zandvoort	1970	V Fernandez	279	Eindhoven
1940–47	*Not played due to Second World War*			1971	R Sota	277	Zandvoort
1948	C Denny	290	Hilversum	* *Played over 36 holes*			
1949	J Adams	294	The Hague				

French Open

INAUGURATED 1906

YEAR	WINNER	SCORE	VENUE	YEAR	WINNER	SCORE	VENUE
1906	A Massy	292	La Boulie	1912	J Gassiat	289	La Boulie
1907	A Massy	298	La Boulie	1913	George Duncan	304	Chantilly
1908	JH Taylor	300	La Boulie	1914	J Douglas Edgar	288	Le Touquet
1909	JH Taylor	293	La Boulie	1915–19	*Not played due to Great War*		
1910	J Braid	298	La Boulie	1920	W Hagen	298	La Boulie
1911	A Massy	284	La Boulie	1921	A Boomer	284	Le Touquet

YEAR	WINNER	SCORE	VENUE	YEAR	WINNER	SCORE	VENUE
1922	A Boomer	286	La Boulie	1951	H Hassanein	278	St Cloud
1923	J Ockenden	288	Dieppe	1952	AD Locke	268	St Germain
1924	CJH Tolley (Am)	290	La Boulie	1953	AD Locke	276	La Boulie
1925	A Massy	291	Chantilly	1954	F van Donck	275	St Cloud
1926	A Boomer	280	St Cloud	1955	Byron Nelson	271	La Boulie
1927	George Duncan	299	St Germain	1956	A Miguel	277	Deauville
1928	CJH Tolley (Am)	283	La Boulie	1957	F van Donck	266	St Cloud
1929	A Boomer	283	Fourqueux	1958	F van Donck	276	St Germain
1930	ER Whitcombe	282	Dieppe	1959	DC Thomas	276	La Boulie
1931	A Boomer	291	Deauville	1960	R de Vicenzo	275	St Cloud
1932	AJ Lacey	295	St Cloud	1961	KDG Nagle	271	La Boulie
1933	B Gadd	283	Chantilly	1962	A Murray	274	St Germain
1934	SF Brews	284	Dieppe	1963	B Devlin	273	St Cloud
1935	SF Brews	293	Le Touquet	1964	R de Vicenzo	272	Chantilly
1936	M Dallemagne	277	St Germain	1965	R Sota	268	St Nom-la-Bretêche
1937	M Dallemagne	278	St Cloud				
1938	M Dallemagne	282	Fourqueux	1966	DJ Hutchinson	274	La Boulie
1939	M Pose	285	Le Touquet	1967	BJ Hunt	271	St Germain
1940–45	*Not played due to Second World War*			1968	PJ Butler	272	St Cloud
1946	TH Cotton	269	St Cloud	1969	J Garaialde	277	St Nom-la-Bretêche
1947	TH Cotton	285	Chantilly				
1948	F Cavalo	287	St Cloud	1970	D Graham	268	St Jean de Luz
1949	U Grappasonni	275	St Germain				
1950	R de Vicenzo	279	Chantilly	1971	Liang Huan Lu	262	Biarritz

German Open

INAUGURATED 1911

YEAR	WINNER	SCORE	VENUE	YEAR	WINNER	SCORE	VENUE
1911	H Vardon	279	Baden-Baden	1953	F van Donck	271	Frankfurt
1912	JH Taylor	279	Baden-Baden	1954	AD Locke	277	Krefeld
1913–25	*No championship*			1955	K Bousfield	279	Hamburg
1926	Percy Alliss	284	Berlin	1956	F van Donck	271	Frankfurt
1927	Percy Alliss	288	Berlin	1957	H Weetman	279	Cologne
1928	Percy Alliss	280	Berlin	1958	F de Luca	275	Krefeld
1929	Percy Alliss	285	Berlin	1959	K Bousfield	271	Hamburg
1930	A Boyer	266	Baden-Baden	1960	PW Thomson	281	Cologne
1931	R Golias	298	Berlin	1961	BJ Hunt	272	Krefeld
1932	A Boyer	282	Bad Ems	1962	R Verwey	276	Hamburg
1933	Percy Alliss	284	Bad Ems	1963	BGC Huggett	278	Cologne
1934	AH Padgham	285	Bad Ems	1964	R de Vicenzo	275	Krefeld
1935	A Boyer	280	Bad Ems	1965	HR Henning	274	Hamburg
1936	A Boyer	291	Berlin	1966	R Stanton	274	Frankfurt
1937	TH Cotton	274	Bad Ems	1967	D Swaelens	273	Krefeld
1938	TH Cotton	285	Frankfurt	1968	B Franklin	265	Cologne
1939	TH Cotton	280	Bad Ems	1969	J Garaialde	272	Frankfurt
1940–50	*No championship*			1970	J Garaialde	276	Krefeld
1951	A Cerda	286	Hamburg	1971	NC Coles	279	Bremen
1952	A Cerda	283	Hamburg				

Italian Open

INAUGURATED 1925

YEAR	WINNER	SCORE	VENUE	YEAR	WINNER	SCORE	VENUE
1925	F Pasquali	154*	Stresa	1949	H Hassanein	263	Villa d'Este
1926	A Boyer	147*	Stresa	1950	U Grappasonni	281	Rome
1927	Percy Alliss	145*	Stresa	1951	J Adams	289	Milan
1928	A Boyer	145*	Villa d'Este	1952	EC Brown	273	Milan
1929	R Golias	143*	Villa d'Este	1953	F van Donck	267	Villa d'Este
1930	A Boyer	140*	Villa d'Este	1954	U Grappasonni	272	Villa d'Este
1931	A Boyer	141*	Villa d'Este	1955	F van Donck	287	Venice
1932	A Boomer	143*	Villa d'Este	1956	A Cerda	284	Milan
1933	*No championship*			1957	H Henning	273	Villa d'Este
1934	N Nutley	132*	San Remo	1958	Peter Alliss	282	Varese
1935	Percy Alliss	262	San Remo	1959	PW Thomson	269	Villa d'Este
1936	TH Cotton	268	Sestriere	1960	B Wilkes	285	Venice
1937	M Dallemagne	276	San Remo	1961–70	*No championship*		
1938	F van Donck	276	Villa d'Este	1971	R Sota	282	Garlenda,
1939–46	*Not played due to Second World War*						Alassio
1947	F van Donck	263	San Remo		*Played over 36 holes*		
1948	A Casera	267	San Remo				

Portuguese Open

INAUGURATED 1953

at Estoril

YEAR	WINNER	SCORE	YEAR	WINNER	SCORE
1953	EC Brown	260	1962	A Angelini	269
1954	A Miguel	263	1963	R Sota	204
1955	F van Donck	267	1964	A Miguel	279
1956	A Miguel	268	1966	A Angelini	273
1957	*No championship*		1967	A Gallardo	214
1958	Peter Alliss	264	1968	M Faulkner	273
1959	S Miguel	265	1969	R Sota	270
1960	K Bousfield	268	1970	R Sota	274
1961	K Bousfield	263	1971	L Platts	277

Spanish Open

INAUGURATED 1912

YEAR	WINNER	VENUE	YEAR	WINNER	VENUE
1912	A Massy	Polo, Madrid	1946	M Morcillo	Pedrena
1913–15	*No championship*		1947	M Gonzalez	Puerta de Hierro
1916	A de la Torre	Puerta de Hierro		M Morcillo } tie	
1917	A de la Torre	Puerta de Hierro	1948	M Morcillo	Negun
1918	*No championship*		1949	M Morcillo	Puerta de Hierro
1919	A de la Torre	Puerta de Hierro	1950	A Cerda	Cedana
1920	*No championship*		1951	M Provencio	Puerta de Hierro
1921	E Lafitte	Puerta de Hierro	1952	M Faulkner	Puerta de Hierro
1922	*No championship*		1953	M Faulkner	Puerta de Hierro
1923	A de la Torre	Puerta de Hierro	1954	S Miguel	Puerta de Hierro
1924	*No championship*		1955	H de Lamaze (Am)	Puerta de Hierro
1925	A de la Torre	Puerta de Hierro	1956	Peter Alliss	El Prat
1926	J Bernardino	Puerta de Hierro	1957	M Faulkner	Club de Campo,
1927	A Massy	Puerta de Hierro			Madrid
1928	A Massy	Puerta de Hierro	1958	Peter Alliss	Puerta de Hierro
1929	E Lafitte	Puerto de Hierro	1959	PW Thomson	El Prat
1930	J Bernardino	Puerto de Hierro	1960	S Miguel	Club de Campo,
1931	*No championship*				Madrid
1932	G Gonzalez	Puerto de Hierro	1961	A Miguel	Puerta de Hierro
1933	G Gonzalez	Puerto de Hierro	1963	R Sota	El Prat
1934	J Bernardino	Puerto de Hierro	1964	A Miguel	Tenerife
1935	A de la Torre	Puerto de Hierro	1966	R de Vicenzo	Sotogrande
1936–40	*No championship*		1967	S Miguel	Sant Cugat,
1941	M Provencio	Puerto de Hierro			Barcelona
1942	G Gonzalez	Sant Cugat,	1968	R Shaw	La Galea
		Barcelona	1969	J Garaialde	RACE, Madrid
1943	M Provencio	Puerta de Hierro	1970	A Gallardo	Nueva Andalucia
1944	N Sagardia	Pedrena	1971	D Hayes	El Prat
1945	C Celles	Puerta de Hierro			

Swiss Open

INAUGURATED 1923

YEAR	WINNER	SCORE	VENUE	YEAR	WINNER	SCORE	VENUE
1923	A Ross	149	Engen	1938	J Saubaber	139	Zumikon
1924	P Boomer	150	Engen	1939	F Cavalo	273	Crans-sur-
1925	A Ross	148	Engen				Sierre
1926	A Ross	145	Lucerne	1940–47	*No championship*		
1927–28	*No championship*			1948	U Grappasonni	285	Crans-sur-
1929	A Wilson	142	Lucerne				Sierre
1930	A Boyer	150	Samedan	1949	M Dallemagne	270	Crans-sur-
1931	M Dallemagne	150	Lucerne				Sierre
1932–33	*No championship*			1950	A Casera	276	Crans-sur-
1934	A Boyer	133	Lausanne				Sierre
1935	A Boyer	137	Lausanne	1951	EC Brown	267	Crans-sur-
1936	F Francis (Am)	134	Lausanne				Sierre
1937	M Dallemagne	138	Samedan				

YEAR	WINNER	SCORE	VENUE	YEAR	WINNER	SCORE	VENUE
1952	U Grappasonni	267	Crans-sur-Sierre	1962	RJ Charles	272	Crans-sur-Sierre
1953	F van Donck	267	Crans-sur-Sierre	1963	DJ Rees	278	Crans-sur-Sierre
1954	AD Locke	276	Crans-sur-Sierre	1964	H Henning	276	Crans-sur-Sierre
1955	F van Donck	277	Crans-sur-Sierre	1965	H Henning	208 (54 holes)	Crans-sur-Sierre
1956	DJ Rees	278	Crans-sur-Sierre	1966	A Angelini	271	Crans-sur-Sierre
1957	A Angelini	270	Crans-sur-Sierre	1967	R Vines	272	Crans-sur-Sierre
1958	K Bousfield	272	Crans-sur-Sierre	1968	R Bernardini	272	Crans-sur-Sierre
1959	DJ Rees	274	Crans-sur-Sierre	1969	R Bernardini	277	Crans-sur-Sierre
1960	H Henning	270	Crans-sur-Sierre	1970	G Marsh	274	Crans-sur-Sierre
1961	KDG Nagle	268	Crans-sur-Sierre	1971	P Townsend	270	Crans-sur-Sierre

Discontinued Professional Tournaments

Bowmaker Amateur Professional Tournament

YEAR	WINNER		SCORE	VENUE	YEAR	WINNER	SCORE	VENUE
1957	AD Locke / F Jowle	}tie	135	The Berkshire	1965	KDG Nagle	133	Sunningdale
					1966	F Boobyer	135	Sunningdale
1958	R Mills / BJ Hunt	}tie	129	Sunningdale	1967	PJ Butler	131	Sunningdale
					1968	CA Clark	136	Sunningdale
1959	AD Locke		132	Sunningdale	1969	BGC Huggett / A Grubb }tie	135	Sunningdale
1960	PW Thomson		132	Sunningdale				
1961	RJ Charles		132	Sunningdale	1970	NC Coles	132	Royal Mid-Surrey
1962	KDG Nagle		133	Sunningdale				
1963	PJ Butler		132	Sunningdale	1971	P Oosterhuis	132	Royal Mid-Surrey
1964	NC Coles		136	Sunningdale				

Coca-Cola Young Professionals

YEAR	WINNER	SCORE	VENUE	YEAR	WINNER	SCORE	VENUE
1968	PM Townsend	270	Coventry	1972	P Oosterhuis	278	Long Ashton
1969	BW Barnes	280	Bristol and Clifton	1973	B Gallacher	277	Bristol and Clifton
1970	P Oosterhuis	274	Morecambe and Heysham	1974	D Hayes	274	Long Ashton
1971	J Garner	273	Stoneham		*Taken over by Tournament Players Section of PGA.*		

Daily Mail Tournament

YEAR	WINNER	SCORE	VENUE
1919	A Mitchell	312	St Andrews
1920	G Duncan	291	Westward Ho!
1921	A Hallam	291	Formby
1922	G Duncan	300	St Andrews
1923	E Ray	288	Lytham St Annes
1924	CA Whitcombe	289	Deal
1925	C Johns	293	Hollinwell
1926	A Boomer	297	St Andrews
1927	A Mitchell	294	Wentworth
1928–35	*No competition*		
1936	AH Padgham	284	Bramshot

YEAR	WINNER	SCORE	VENUE
1937	S King	283	Little Aston
1938	A Perry	284	Gosforth Park
1939	TH Cotton	292	Bournemouth
1940	R Burton	280	Sundridge Park
1941–45	*Not played due to Second World War*		
1946	AH Padgham	301	Lytham St Annes
1947	DJ Rees	279	Barassie
1948	N Von Nida	270	Sunningdale
1949	T Haliburton	271	Killermont
1950	CH Ward	290	Walton Heath

Daks Tournament

YEAR	WINNER	SCORE	VENUE
1950	N Sutton	272	Royal Mid-Surrey
1951	J Panton	282	Sunningdale
1952	F Daly	280	Wentworth
1953	DJ Rees	280	Wentworth
1954	Peter Alliss	279	Little Aston
1955	J Pritchett	275	Sunningdale
1956	T Wilkes	276	Wentworth
1957	AD Locke	281	Wentworth
1958	PW Thomson } H Henning } tie	275	Wentworth
1959	C O'Connor	274	Wentworth
1960	PW Thomson	279	Wentworth
1961	BJ Hunt	279	Wentworth

YEAR	WINNER	SCORE	VENUE
1962	DJ Rees } RJ Charles } tie	278	Wentworth
1963	Peter Alliss } NC Coles } tie	280	Wentworth
1964	NC Coles	282	Wentworth
1965	PW Thomson	275	Wentworth
1966	H Boyle	286	Wentworth
1967	M Gregson	279	Wentworth
1968	M Gregson	284	Wentworth
1969	BGC Huggett	289	Wentworth
1970	NC Coles	281	Wentworth
1971	BGC Huggett } NC Coles } tie	284	South Herts

Dunlop Masters

YEAR	WINNER	SCORE	VENUE	YEAR	WINNER	SCORE	VENUE
1946	AD Locke ⎱ tie J Adams ⎰	286	Stoneham	1965	BJ Hunt	283	Portmarnock
				1966	NC Coles	278	Lindrick
1947	A Lees	288	Little Aston	1967	A Jacklin	274	St George's,
1948	N Von Nida	272	Sunningdale				Sandwich
1949	CH Ward	290	St Andrews	1968	PW Thomson	274	Sunningdale
1950	DJ Rees	281	Hoylake	1969	C Legrange	281	Little Aston
1951	M Faulkner	281	Wentworth	1970	BGC Huggett	293	Lytham St
1952	H Weetman	281	Mere				Anne's
1953	H Bradshaw	272	Sunningdale	1971	M Bembridge	273	St Pierre
1954	AD Locke	291	Prince's,	1972	RJ Charles	277	Northumber-
			Sandwich				land
1955	H Bradshaw	277	Little Aston	1973	A Jacklin	272	St Pierre
1956	C O'Connor	277	Prestwick	1974	B Gallacher	282	St Pierre
1957	EC Brown	275	Hollinwell	1975	B Gallacher	289	Ganton
1958	H Weetman	276	Little Aston	1976	B Dassu	271	St Pierre
1959	C O'Connor	276	Portmarnock	1977	GL Hunt	291	Lindrick
1960	J Hitchcock	275	Sunningdale	1978	T Horton	279	St Pierre
1961	PW Thomson	284	Porthcawl	1979	G Marsh	283	Woburn
1962	DJ Rees	278	Wentworth	1980	B Langer	270	St Pierre
Sponsored by Silk Cut 1963–83				1981	G Norman	273	Woburn
1963	BJ Hunt	282	Little Aston	1982	G Norman	267	St Pierre
1964	C Legrange	288	Birkdale	1983	I Woosnam	269	St Pierre

English Golf Classic
at The Belfry

YEAR	WINNER	SCORE	YEAR	WINNER	SCORE
1979	S Ballesteros	286	1982	G Norman	279
1980	M Pinero	286	1983	H Baiocchi	279
1981	R Davis	284			

Great Britain & Ireland v Continent of Europe (Hennessy Cup)

INAUGURATED 1974

Cup presented 1976
Format changed 1982 and 1984

YEAR	WINNER	SCORE	VENUE
1974	Great Britain & Ireland	31 – 25	Sotogrande
1976	Great Britain & Ireland	20 – 10	Bondues, Lille
1978	Great Britain & Ireland	17½ – 14½	The Belfry
1980	Great Britain & Ireland	16½ – 13½	Sunningdale
1982	Great Britain & Ireland	106	Ferndown
	Rest of World	86	
	Europe	67	
1984	Scotland	394	Ferndown

Irish Open Championship

YEAR	WINNER	SCORE	VENUE	YEAR	WINNER	SCORE	VENUE
1927	G Duncan	312	Portmarnock	1938	AD Locke	292	Portmarnock
1928	ER Whitcombe	288	Newcastle	1939	A Lees	287	Newcastle
1929	A Mitchell	309	Portmarnock	1940–45	*Not played due to Second World War*		
1930	CA Whitcombe	289	Portrush	1946	F Daly	288	Portmarnock
1931	EW Kenyon	291	Dollymount	1947	H Bradshaw	290	Portrush
1932	AH Padgham	283	Cork	1948	DJ Rees	295	Portmarnock
1933	EW Kenyon	286	Malone	1949	H Bradshaw	286	Belvoir Park
1934	S Easterbrook	284	Portmarnock	1950	H Pickworth	287	Dollymount
1935	ER Whitcombe	292	Newcastle	1951–52	*No championship*		
1936	RA Whitcombe	281	Dollymount	1953	EC Brown	272	Belvoir Park
1937	B Gadd	284	Portrush	*Suspended. From 1975 see European Tour*			

Martini International Tournament

YEAR	WINNER	SCORE	VENUE	YEAR	WINNER	SCORE	VENUE
1961	BJ Hunt	270	Sundridge Park	1967	M Gregson / BGC Huggett } tie	279	Fulford
1962	PW Thomson	275	St Andrews	1968	BGC Huggett	278	Southerndown
1963	NC Coles / C O'Connor } tie	298	Hoylake	1969	G Henning / G Caygill } tie	282	Bournemouth
1964	C O'Connor	286	Wentworth	1970	PW Thomson / D Sewell } tie	268	Conwy
1965	P Butler	275	Little Aston	1971	B Gallacher	282	Norwich
1966	Peter Alliss / W Large } tie	275	Long Ashton	1972	BW Barnes	277	Abridge

YEAR	WINNER	SCORE	VENUE	YEAR	WINNER	SCORE	VENUE
1973	M Bembridge	279	Barnton	1978	S Ballesteros	270	RAC, Epsom
1974	S Ginn	286	Pannal	1979	G Norman	288	Wentworth
1975	I Stanley, C O'Connor Jr } tie	279	Westward Ho!	1980	S Ballesteros	286	Wentworth
				1981	G Norman	287	Wentworth
1976	S Torrance	280	Ashburnham	1982	B Gallacher	277	Lindrick
1977	G Norman	277	Blairgowrie	1983	N Faldo	268	Wilmslow

News Chronicle Tournament

YEAR	WINNER	SCORE	VENUE	YEAR	WINNER	SCORE	VENUE
1936	D Curtis	283	East Brighton	1948	A Dailey, RW Horne } tie		Hollingbury Park
1937	ER Whitcombe	268	East Brighton				
1938	RA Whitcombe	300	East Brighton	1949	R Burton	266	Hollingbury Park
1939	AH Padgham	279	East Brighton				
1940–45	*Not played due to Second World War*			1950	DJ Rees	277	Hollingbury Park
1945	TH Cotton	301	Hollingbury Park				
1946	N Von Nida	285	Hollingbury Park	1951	K Bousfield	279	Hollingbury Park
1947	DJ Rees	275	Hollingbury Park				

Penfold Tournament

(Match play format 1949–50)

YEAR	WINNER	SCORE	VENUE	YEAR	WINNER	SCORE	VENUE
1932	Percy Alliss	278	Porthcawl	1956	EG Lester	275	Barnton
1933	J Burton	292	Porthcawl	1957	H Weetman	270	Killermont
1934	RA Whitcombe	284	Fairhaven	1958	H Weetman	289	Prestwick
1935	Percy Alliss	273	Gleneagles	1959	PJ Butler	280	Barnton
1936	J Adams	287	Ayr Belleisle	1960	H Weetman	271	Copt Heath
1937–45	*Not played*			1961	K Bousfield	266	Stoneham
1946	N Sutton	283	Sutton Coldfield	1962	H Weetman	280	Maesdu
	DJ Rees, RA Whitcombe, N Von Nida } tie			1963	BJ Hunt	272	Ayr Belleisle
1947		270	Stoke Poges	1964	Peter Alliss	293	Maesdu
				1965	A Miguel	287	Pannal
1948	F Daly	273	Gleneagles	1966	D Thomas	281	Little Aston
1949	M Faulkner and J Burton	1 hole	South Herts	1967	J Cockin	275	Blackpool, North Shore
1950	Mrs A Gee and N Sutton	1 hole	Sutton Coldfield	1968	PJ Butler	281	Maesdu
				1969	G Caygill	278	Worthing Hill Barn
1951	A Lees	278	Bournemouth	1970	BJ Hunt	271	Worthing Hill Barn
1952	EC Brown	6 and 5	Maesdu				
1953	A Lees	2 holes	Maesdu	1971	NC Coles	284	Bournemouth
1954	TH Cotton	5 and 4	Maesdu	1972	P Oosterhuis	285	Bournemouth
1955	C O'Connor	292	Southport and Ainsdale	1973	E Polland	281	Bournemouth
				1974	T Horton	272	Worthing Hill Barn

PGA (News of the World) Match Play Tournament

Sponsored by The News of the World 1903–69

In the last century challenge matches between two or more professionals, usually sponsored by individuals backing their fancied man for the large sum in those days of £100 or more a side, were, apart from the Open, the only public tests of their skill. The first regular tournament solely for professionals was the *News of the World* Match Play, which began in 1903 and lasted until 1969. For many years it was considered second in importance only to the Open and provided a formidable test of match play, a form of golf which has now largely lost its appeal to sponsors and professionals. Interest in challenge matches was already fading in the 1920s and 1930s, although two in 1937 and 1938 at Walton Heath featuring Henry Cotton at his peak, were exciting enough and drew large crowds.

The list of early winners in the *News of the World* contains many famous names and continued so while it lasted under that newspaper's aegis. It was a test of endurance as well as skill. The two players, who met in the 36-hole final, had played five 18-hole matches in three days. Play was much faster then; before the Second World War, seldom did 18 holes last for more than two and a half hours, unless extra holes were needed. Twenty years after his first *News of the World* win in 1906, Sandy Herd, aged 58, beat James Bloxham of Coventry at Mid-Surrey in the 36-hole final. He may even have travelled to Richmond and back from Moor Park, Rickmansworth, each day by train. Such stamina would have been matched by others of his generation and was not considered exceptional.

As match play sometimes brings to the fore the lesser-known professional, so there are finalists' and semi-finalists' names few can remember. In 1906 Herd had beaten a C Mayo in the final and in 1923 RG Wilson and T Renouf were the finalists at Walton Heath; that they had beaten Abe Mitchell and Tom Williamson respectively in the semi-finals must have come as a surprise.

In the early days of the competition, James Braid won four times between 1903 and 1909. The only other man to equal Braid's figure was Dai Rees, whose four wins were two sides of the Second World War. At Oxhey and Walton Heath in the first two he was still an assistant professional at Surbiton before being appointed to Hindhead and later to Harry Vardon's old post at South Herts.

The *News of the World* was usually played on a course close to London, with Walton Heath the venue more than any other course as, for many years, the club had strong ties with the sponsors. It was not until 1946 that the match ventured north to Hoylake and later to Lytham and Birkdale and further afield to Scotland at St Andrews, Carnoustie and Turnberry. During its last eight years with new sponsors, when it was sometimes staged on not so well known courses, the match play format proved difficult to televise and the tournament inevitably lost its appeal.

YEAR	WINNER	RUNNER-UP	SEMI-FINALISTS		VENUE
1903	J Braid	E Ray	JH Taylor	G Coburn	Sunningdale
1904	JH Taylor	A Toogood	J Hepburn	A Herd	Mid-Surrey
1905	J Braid	T Vardon	R Jones	A Mitchell	Walton Heath
1906	A Herd	C Mayo	G Duncan	R Jones	Hollinwell
1907	J Braid	JH Taylor	E Ray	H Vardon	Sunningdale
1908	JH Taylor	F Robson	C Mayo	JG Sherlock	Mid-Surrey
1909	T Ball	A Herd	H Vardon	J Hepburn	Walton Heath
1910	JG Sherlock	G Duncan	E Bannister	C Hughes	Sunningdale
1911	J Braid	E Ray	T Williamson	H Vardon	Walton Heath
1912	H Vardon	E Ray	RG Wilson	H Cawsey	Sunningdale
1913	G Duncan	J Braid	RG Wilson	W Watt	Walton Heath
1914 – 18	*Not played due to Great War*				
1919	A Mitchell	G Duncan	P Rainford	F Robson	Walton Heath
1920	A Mitchell	Josh Taylor	B Seymour	L Holland	Mid-Surrey
1921	B Seymour	J Gaudin	E Ray	C Wingate	Oxhey
1922	G Gadd	F Leach	ER Whitcombe	C Johns	Sunningdale
1923	RG Wilson	T Renouf	A Mitchell	T Williamson	Walton Heath
1924	ER Whitcombe	G Gadd	A Herd	T Barber	St George's Hill
1925	A Compston	G Gadd	G Duncan	L Holland	Moor Park
1926	A Herd	J Bloxham	RG Wilson	WH Ball	Mid-Surrey
1927	A Compston	J Braid	T Williamson	ER Whitcombe	Walton Heath
1928	CA Whitcombe	TH Cotton	JJ Taylor	HC Jolly	Stoke Poges
1929	A Mitchell	P Rogers	A Compston	A Beck	Wentworth
1930	CA Whitcombe	TH Cotton	A Mitchell	S Easterbrook	Oxhey
1931	AH Padgham	M Seymour	CH Ward	CW Thomson	Mid-Surrey
1932	TH Cotton	A Perry	AJ Lacey	JH Jolly	Moor Park
1933	Percy Alliss	M Seymour	ER Whitcombe	A Compston	Purley Downs
1934	JJ Busson	CA Whitcombe	A Chevalier	RA Whitcombe	Walton Heath
1935	AH Padgham	Percy Alliss	R Burton	RA Whitcombe	Mid-Surrey
1936	DJ Rees	ER Whitcombe	Percy Alliss	JJ Taylor	Oxhey
1937	Percy Alliss	J Adams	D Curtis	CA Whitcombe	Stoke Poges
1938	DJ Rees	EE Whitcombe	AG Havers	L Ayton Jr	Walton Heath
1939	*No competition*				
1940	TH Cotton	AH Padgham	RG French	AJ Lacey	Mid-Surrey
1941–44	*Not played due to Second World War*				
1945	RW Horne	Percy Alliss	RA Knight	TE Odams	Walton Heath
1946	TH Cotton	J Adams	AD Locke	R Burton	Hoylake
1947	F Daly	F Van Donck	CH Ward	TH Cotton	Lytham St Annes
1948	F Daly	L Ayton	SL King	CH Ward	Birkdale
1949	DJ Rees	TH Cotton	SL King	L Mangrum	Walton Heath
1950	DJ Rees	F Jowle	K Bousfield	TH Cotton	Carnoustie
1951	H Weetman	J Adams	AS Waters	SL King	Hoylake
1952	F Daly	F Van Donck	J Panton	G Johnson	Walton Heath
1953	M Faulkner	DJ Rees	JRM Jacobs	F Daly	Ganton
1954	PW Thomson	J Fallon	F Jowle	N Sutton	St Andrews
1955	K Bousfield	EC Brown	A Lees	F Jowle	Walton Heath
1956	J Panton	H Weetman	K Bousfield	RP Mills	Hoylake
1957	C O'Connor	TB Haliburton	H Bradshaw	EC Brown	Turnberry
1958	H Weetman	BJ Hunt	C O'Connor	AM Fox	Walton Heath
1959	D Snell	H Weetman	N Sutton	DC Thomas	Birkdale
1960	EC Brown	H Weetman	TB Haliburton	DC Thomas	Turnberry
1961	PW Thomson	RL Moffitt	NC Coles	BJ Hunt	Walton Heath
1962	EC Brown	E Whitehead	DC Thomas	TA Fisher	Walton Heath
1963	DC Thomas	J MacDonald	G Will	I Wright	Turnberry
1964	NC Coles	PJ Butler	M Faulkner	HW Muscroft	Walton Heath
1965	NC Coles	L Platts	C Greene	A Jacklin	Walton Heath
1966	PW Thomson	NC Coles	A King	Peter Alliss	Walton Heath

YEAR	WINNER	RUNNER-UP	SEMI-FINALISTS		VENUE
1967	PW Thomson	DJ Rees	M Faulkner	NC Coles	Walton Heath
1968	BGC Huggett	J Panton	NC Coles	J Martin	Walton Heath
1969	M Bembridge	DJ Rees	BGC Huggett	D Talbot	Walton Heath
Sponsored by Long John Scotch Whisky					
1970	T Horton	RDBM Shade	RT Walker	R Bernardini	Moor Park
1971	*No competition*				
Sponsored by Benson & Hedges					
1972	JR Garner	NC Coles	RDBM Shade	D Stockton	Moor Park
1973	NC Coles	D McClelland	P Wilcock	H Muscroft	Hillside
1974	J Newton	C Sunado	NC Coles	D Jagger	Downfield
Sponsored by Sun Alliance					
1975	E Polland	PJ Butler	D Hayes	RDBM Shade	Lindrick
1976	BW Barnes	CB DeFoy	J O'Leary	S Hobday	King's Norton
1977	H Baiocchi	BGC Huggett	NC Coles	C O'Connor Jr	Stoke Poges
1978	M James	NC Coles	S Torrance	M Pinero	Dalmahoy
1979	D Smyth	N Price	A Garrido	C Mason	Fulford

Piccadilly Tournament

From 1962 – 67 a 72-hole stroke event. In 1968 a four-ball match play event decided on strokes then in 1976 returned to 72-hole stroke play.

YEAR	WINNER	SCORE	RUNNER-UP	VENUE
1962	PW Thomson	283	C O'Connor	Southport and Ainsdale
1963	*No competition*			
1964	J Martin	268	BJ Hunt	Wentworth
1965	PJ Butler	267	DJ Rees	Wentworth
1966	BJ Hunt	262	PO Green	Wentworth
1967	PJ Butler	263	BGC Huggett	Wentworth
1968	H Jackson and RH Emery	2 and 1	NC Coles and B Hutchison	Wentworth
1969	Peter Alliss (149)	37th hole	G Will (149)	Prince's, Sandwich
1970	J Lister (134)	–	T Horton (137)	Southerndown
1971	P Oosterhuis (75, 56)	–	EC Brown (73, 63, ret)	Southerndown
1972	T Horton (80, 77)	–	GL Hunt (80, 78)	Hillside
1973	P Oosterhuis (67)	–	T Westbrook (73)	Finham Park, Coventry
1974	M Bembridge (65)	–	P Oosterhuis (70)	Finham Park, Coventry
1975	RA Shearer (70)	19th hole	A Oosthuizen (70)	Finham Park, Coventry
1976	S Torrance	277		Finham Park, Coventry

Silver King Tournament
at Moor Park

YEAR	WINNER	SCORE		YEAR	WINNER		SCORE
1936	AH Padgham	230		1948	J Adams }tie		283
1937	TH Cotton	279			CH Ward		
1938	CA Whitcombe	276		1949	R Burton		281
1939	AH Padgham	285		1950	J Panton		276
1940–45	*Not played due to Second World War*			1951	F van Donck		285
1946	DJ Rees	288		1952	R Horne		276
1947	AH Padgham	285		1953	F van Donck		274

Spalding Tournament

YEAR	WINNER	SCORE	VENUE		YEAR	WINNER	SCORE	VENUE
1947	TH Cotton	288	St Andrews		1955	C Denny	278	Moor Park
1948	N Von Nida	289	St Andrews		1956	C O'Connor }tie	276	Moor Park
1949	CH Ward	273	Worthing			H Weetman		
1950	AD Locke	267	Worthing		1957	BJ Hunt	278	Moor Park
1951	J Hargreaves	281	Worthing		1958	F Jowle	277	Moor Park
1952	H Weetman	271	Worthing		1959	EG Lester }tie	278	Moor Park
1953	BJ Hunt	273	Worthing			HR Henning		
1954	DJ Rees	272	Moor Park		1960	H Weetman	273	Moor Park

Sumrie Better-Ball Tournament

YEAR	WINNER	SCORE	VENUE		YEAR	WINNER	SCORE	VENUE
1969	M Bembridge and A Gallardo	263	Pannal, Harrogate		1974	CA Clark and PJ Butler	267	Queen's Park, Bournemouth
1970	NC Coles and BJ Hunt	257	Pannal, Harrogate		1975	J Newton and J O'Leary	256	Queen's Park Bournemouth
1971	*No competition*				1976	E Darcy and C O'Connor Jr	260	Queen's Park Bournemouth
1972	BGC Huggett and M Gregson	264	Blairgowrie		1977	*No competition*		
1973	NC Coles and BJ Hunt	265	Blairgowrie		1978	E Darcy and C O'Connor Jr	255	Queen's Park Bournemouth

Yorkshire Evening News Tournament

Match play 1923–39
Stroke play 1944–58

YEAR	WINNER	MARGIN	VENUE	YEAR	WINNER	MARGIN	VENUE
1923	N Jolly	2 holes	Headingley	1940–43	*Not played due to Second World War*		
1924	F Robson	37th hole	Headingley	1944	SL King	133	Roundhay
1925	L Holland	3 and 2	Moortown	1945	A Compston	148	Moortown
1926	CA Whitcombe	9 and 8	Moortown	1946	AD Locke	283	Moortown
1927	ER Whitcombe	9 and 8	Headingley	1947	N Von Nida } TH Cotton } tie	277	Moortown
1928	CA Whitcombe	3 and 2	Moortown				
1929	J Turnesa	37th hole	Moortown	1948	CH Ward	275	Moortown
1930	H Jolly	3 and 1	Headingley	1949	SL King	6 and 5	Moortown
1931	ER Whitcombe	39th hole	Sand Moor	1950	DJ Rees	276	Sand Moor
1932	B Hodson	39th hole	Moortown	1951	DJ Rees } N Von Nida } tie	281	Moortown
1933	AJ Lacey	2 and 1	Temple Newsam				
				1952	DJ Rees	283	Moortown
1934	AH Padgham	37th hole	Moortown	1953	F van Donck	278	Sand Moor
1935	TH Cotton	3 and 2	Sand Moor	1954	J Panton	284	Moortown
1936	R Burton	3 and 2	Temple Newsam	1955	A Cerda	276	Sand Moor
				1956	DJ Rees } K Bousfield } tie	281	Moortown
1937	AJ Lacey	2 and 1	Moortown	1957	PW Thomson	264	Sand Moor
1938	A Perry	8 and 6	Cobble Hall				
1939	DJ Rees	37th hole	Temple Newsam	1958	EC Brown } H Henning } tie	280	Moortown

British Regional and County Professional Tournaments

The County Professional Associations tend to change their officials in rapid order; this is not surprising as professional golfers sometimes move from club to club to widen their experience, or they quickly find increased responsibility leaves them no time for voluntary work. Hence records of past winners and venues tend to be lost.

Every effort has been made to discover missing names and venues. There may also be some events which warrant inclusion of which there has been no mention in the golfing press. There will doubtless be wider coverage in the next edition of the *Book of Golf Records*.

Derbyshire Professional Championship

INAUGURATED 1921

YEAR	WINNER	VENUE	YEAR	WINNER	VENUE
1921	HW Woolscroft	Matlock	1937	A Norton	Derbyshire
1922	DC Tunbridge	Derbyshire	1938	A Norton	Chesterfield
1923	F Hocking	Chesterfield	1939	A Norton	Mellor
1924	EF Woolscroft	Buxton and High Peak	1940–46	*Not played due to Second World War*	
			1947	W Walker	Buxton and High Peak
1925	S Harrison	Markeaton			
1926	T Barber	Burton-on-Trent	1948	E Lester	Derby Municipal
1927	T Barber	Matlock	1949	W Walker	Burton-on-Trent
1928	T Barber	Chevin	1950	W Walker	Erewash Valley
1929	T Barber	Chapel-en-le-Frith	1951	EB Williamson	Buxton and High Peak
1930	T Barber	Erewash Valley			
1931	T Barber	Derby Municipal	1952	JE Wiggett	Chevin
1932	A Norton	Chesterfield	1953	W Walker	Cavendish, Buxton
1933	A Norton	Mickleover	1954	H Lester	Kedleston Park
1934	T Jarman	Markeaton	1955	H Lester	Derby Municipal
1935	TB Robertson	Burton-on-Trent	1956	H Lester	Chesterfield
1936	A Norton	Buxton and High Peak	1957	W Walker	Burton-on-Trent
			1959	H Lester	Erewash Valley

YEAR	WINNER	VENUE	YEAR	WINNER	VENUE
1960	W Walker	Chevin	1978	P Seal	Chevin
1961	H Lester	Cavendish, Buxton	1979	D Russell	Burton-on-Trent
1962	H Lester	Kedleston Park	1980	P Taylor	Kedleston Park
1963	H Lester	Burton-on-Trent	1981	J Lower	Cavendish, Buxton
1964	H Lester	Matlock	1982	A Wardle	Erewash Valley
1967	H Lester	Derby Municipal	1983	PK Seal	Matlock
1968	LJ Feeney	Cavendish, Buxton	1984	W Bird	Chevin
1969	KD Pickup	Erewash Valley	1985	J Turnbull	Chesterfield
1970	DT Parsonage	Chevin	1986	J Lower	Erewash Valley
1971	K Oliver	Kedleston Park	1987	AR Skingle	Kedleston Park
1972	C Jepson	Burton-on-Trent	1988	M McLean	Cavendish, Buxton
1973	E Darcy	Matlock	1989	N Hallam	Buxton and High
1974	E Darcy	Chesterfield			Peak
1975	RH Lambert	Cavendish	1990	M Deesey	Mickleover
1976	C Jepson	Erewash Valley			
1977	E Darcy	Buxton and High Peak			

East Region PGA Championship

YEAR	WINNER	YEAR	WINNER
1987	J Pinsent ⎫ tie P Kent ⎭	1989	*Not played*
1988	L Farmer	1990	R Mann

Hampshire Professional Match Play Championship

INAUGURATED 1921

YEAR	WINNER	VENUE	YEAR	WINNER	VENUE
1971	F Gilbride	Hockley	1980	J Hay	Corhampton
1972	J Sharkey	Crookhorn, Portsmouth	1981	D Miller	Corhampton
			1982	A Gillard	Fleming Park, Eastleigh
1973	I Macdonald	Crookhorn, Portsmouth	1983	H Stott	Lee-on-the-Solent
1974	D Miller	Crookhorn, Portsmouth	1984	J Hay	Lee-on-the-Solent
			1985	P Dawson	Lee-on-the-Solent
1975	J Morgan	Hockley	1986	K Bowden	Southwick Park
1976	C Bonner	Bramshott Hill	1987	M Desmond	Waterlooville
1977	D Miller	Bramshott Hill	1988	K Bowden	Waterlooville
1978	T Healy	Bramshott Hill	1989	I Young	Basingstoke
1979	T Healy	Bramshott Hill	1990	K Bowden	Royal Winchester

Hampshire Professional Stroke Play Championship

INAUGURATED 1950

YEAR	WINNER	VENUE	YEAR	WINNER	VENUE
1950	JE Watt	Stoneham	1971	I Macdonald	Lee-on-the-Solent
1951	G West	Hayling Island	1972	J Sharkey	Highcliffe Castle
1952	BW Spanner	Blackmoor	1973	D Miller	Corhampton
1953	WH Wiltshire	Brokenhurst	1974	J Sharkey	Bramshaw
		Manor	1975	D Miller	Brokenhurst
1954	G West	Liphook			Manor
1955	A Freemantle	Hayling Island	1976	C Bonner	Brokenhurst
1956	DA Nash	Stoneham			Manor
1957	CL Cargill	Brokenhurst	1977	A Bridge	Tidworth Garrison
		Manor	1978	J Hay	Crookhorn,
1958	CL Cargill	Liphook			Portsmouth
1959	D Miller	North Hants, Fleet	1979	C Bonner	Meon Valley
1960	JA McGee	Hayling Island	1980	T Pinner	Meon Valley
1961	D Miller	Brokenhurst	1981	J Grant	Meon Valley
		Manor	1982	J Garner	Stoneham
1962	D Miller	Stoneham	1983	I Pinner	Meon Valley
1963	D Miller	Royal Winchester	1984	G Stubbington	Royal Winchester
1964	J Stirling	Hockley	1985	T Healy	Hockley
1965	D Miller	Lee-on-the-Solent	1986	M Desmond	Blackmoor
1966	D Miller	Lee-on-the-Solent	1987	T Healy	Brokenhurst
1967	R Davenport	Hockley			Manor
1968	A White	Royal Winchester	1988	G Stubbington	Stoneham
1969	JC Richardson	Hayling Island	1989	J Coles	Bramshaw
1970	J Sharkey	Lee-on-the-Solent	1990	S Watson	Hayling Island

Kent Professional Championship

INAUGURATED 1912

YEAR	WINNER	VENUE	YEAR	WINNER	VENUE
1912	JB Ross		1929	TH Cotton	
1913	C Gray		1930	TH Cotton	
1914	JB Ross		1931	WT Twine	
1915–18	*Not played due to Great War*		1932	SL King	
1919	S Guard		1933	SL King	
1920	Abe Mitchell		1934	SL King	
1921	HC Jolly		1935	SL King	
1922	HC Jolly		1936	SL King	
1923	F Ball		1937	SL King	
1924	HC Jolly		1938	AH Padgham	
1925	WT Twine		1939–45	*Not played due to Second World War*	
1926	TH Cotton		1946	SL King	
1927	TH Cotton		1947	SL King	
1928	TH Cotton		1948	SL King	

YEAR	WINNER	VENUE	YEAR	WINNER	VENUE
1949	SL King		1972	G Will	
1950	SL King		1973	R Fidler	
1951	SL King		1974	G Will	
1952	F Taylor		1975	G Will	
1953	L Roberts		1976	G Will	
1954	AH Padgham		1977	K Ashdown	
1955	SL King		1978	G Will	
1956	W West		1979	R Fidler	
1957	N Quigley		1980	R Fidler	
1958	FL Roberts		1981	D Russell	
1959	C Whiting		1982	R Watkins	
1960	SL King		1983	G Potter	
1961	N Quigley		1984	R Cameron	
1962	W Dawson		1985	J Bennett	Broome Park
1966	RS Fidler		1986	P Mitchell	Sundridge Park
1967	D Bonthron		1987	S Barr	Cranbrook
1968	R Game		1988	R Cameron	Chislehurst
1969	N Job		1989	P Lyons	Prince's, Sandwich
1970	RS Fidler		1990	R Cameron	Gillingham
1971	G Norton				

Kent Match Play Championship

YEAR	WINNER	VENUE	YEAR	WINNER	VENUE
1986	B Impett	Mid Kent	1989	P Lyons	Dartford
1987	P Mitchell	Mid Kent	1990	L Batchelor	Dartford
1988	R Cameron	Mid Kent			

Midland Professional Stroke Play Championship

INAUGURATED 1897

YEAR	WINNER	VENUE	YEAR	WINNER	VENUE
1897	T Williamson		1912	G Buckle	Skegness
1898	T Williamson		1913	GV Tuck	Little Aston
1899	T Toogood		1914–18	*Not played due to Great War*	
1900	T Williamson		1919	BS Weastell	Sandwell Park
1901	JG Sherlock		1920	T Williamson	Moseley
1903	JG Sherlock		1921	W Robertson	Robin Hood,
1904	A Lewis				Solihull
1906	J Fulford		1922	T Williamson	Copt Heath
1907	T Williamson		1923	GR Buckle	Edgbaston
1909	G Coburn	Sutton Coldfield	1924	J Bloxham	Olton
1910	E Veness	Stourbridge	1925	GR Buckle	Walmley, Wilde
1911	T Williamson	Ladbrook Park			Green

YEAR	WINNER	VENUE	YEAR	WINNER	VENUE
1926	ES Douglas	Coventry	1961	PJ Butler	Hawkstone Park
1927	T Barber	Harborne	1962	A Rees	Luffenham Heath
1928	PF Weston	Handsworth	1963	CH Ward	Edgbaston
1929	GR Buckle	North	1964	SWT Murray	Rushcliffe
		Worcestershire	1965	SA Hunt	Hawkstone Park
1930	T Green	Copt Heath	1966	J Anderson	Coxmoor
1931	T Green	Castle Bromwich	1967	SWT Murray	Whittington
1932	T Barber	Henbury			Barracks
1933	CH Ward	Little Aston	1968	SWT Murray	Olton
1934	CH Ward	Olton	1969	TR Squires	Shifnal
1935	WR Firkins	Little Aston	1970	D Llewellyn	Moor Hall
1936	WJ Branch	Sandwell Park	1971	RA Beattie	South
1937	AG Beck	Harborne			Staffordshire
1938	HR Manton	Beau Desert	1972	BJ Waites	Kedleston Park
1939	WJ Martin	Woodhall Spa	1973	RDS Livingston	Handsworth
1939–45	*Not played due to Second World War*		1974	M Gallacher	Stratford-upon-
1946	W Lees	Sandwell Park			Avon
1947	KWC Adwick	North Shore,	1975	HFJ Boyle	Peterborough
		Skegness			Milton
1948	A Lees	Dore and Totley	1976	PR Herbert	Longcliffe
1949	A Lees	Blackwell	1977	BJ Waites	Coxmoor
1950	CH Ward	Sutton Coldfield	1978	BJ Waites	Ladbrook Park
1951	JR Moses	Sandwell Park	1979	BJ Waites	Lincoln Torksey
1952	J Hargreaves	Copt Heath	1980	DI Vaughan	Barnham Broom
1953	CH Ward	Harborne	1981	D Stewart	Burton-on-Trent
1954	A Cunningham	Olton	1982	P Elson	
1955	CH Ward	South	1983	AR Minshall	
		Staffordshire	1984	M Mouland	
1956	RL Hastelow	Robin Hood,	1985	K Hayward	
		Solihull	1986	A Skingle	
1957	D Snell	Seacroft	1987	M Mouland	
1958	JH Cawsey	Hawkstone Park	1988	G Farr	
1959	GA Maisey	Luffenham Heath	1989	J Higgins	
1960	J Hargreaves	Ladbrooke Park	1990	G Stafford	Forest of Arden

Midland Challenge Cup

INAUGURATED 1899

YEAR	WINNER	YEAR	WINNER
1899		1912	WE Reid
1900	JG Sherlock	1913	WE Reid
1901	JG Sherlock	1914	T Williamson
1902	JG Sherlock	1915–18	*Not played due to Great War*
1903	T Williamson	1919	T Williamson
1904	A Herd	1920	H Roberts
1905	T Williamson	1921	L Holland
1906	J Sherlock	1922	J Adwick
1907	P Wynne	1923	MJ Bingham
1908	G Coburn	1924	L Holland
1909	CH Mayo	1925	T Williamson
1910	CV Tuck	1926	T Williamson
1911	WE Reid	1927	T Williamson

YEAR	WINNER	YEAR	WINNER
1928	T Barber	1940–45	*Not played due to Second World War*
1929	T Barber	1946	TB Haliburton
1930	PF Weston	1948	CH Ward
1931	WR Firkins	1949	KWC Adwick
1932	GR Buckle	1950	CH Ward
1933	T Green	1951	EB Williamson
1934	WJ Martin	1954	R Moffitt
1935	WJ Martin	1955	F Jowle
1936	J McMillan	1958	CH Ward
1937	K Hooker	1959	F Jowle
1938	G Johnson	1960	R Moffitt
1939	J McMillan		

Midland Professional Match Play

INAUGURATED 1972

YEAR	WINNER	VENUE	YEAR	WINNER
1972	BJ Waites	Moor Hall	1982	P Elson
1973	BJ Waites	Gay Hill	1983	PG Ackerley
1974	BJ Waites	Walmley	1984	P Elson
1975	PJ Weaver	Shirley	1985	D Ridley
1976	M Gallagher	King's Norton	1986	J Higgins
1977	J Rhodes	Rothley Park	1987	K Hayward
1978	DT Steele	The Belfry	1988	J Higgins
1979	RDS Livingston	Burton-on-Trent	1989	K Hayward
1980	RDS Livingston	Staverton Park	1990	G Farr
1981	P Elson	Staverton Park		

Midland Masters

INAUGURATED 1988

YEAR	WINNER	VENUE
1988	BJ Waites	Abbey Park
1989	C Haycock	Abbey Park
1990	J King	Patshull Park

Norfolk Professional Championship

INAUGURATED 1921

YEAR	WINNER	VENUE	YEAR	WINNER	VENUE
1921	R Donald	Royal West Norfolk	1959	M Leeder	Eaton
1922	JG Sherlock	Sheringham	1960	M Leeder	Great Yarmouth and Caister
1923	JG Sherlock	Royal Norwich	1961	Alan Poulton	Sheringham
1924	JG Sherlock	Hunstanton	1962	MT Leeder	Kings Lynn
1925	T King Jr	Royal West Norfolk	1963	MT Leeder	Thetford
1926	T King Jr	Royal Cromer	1964	MT Leeder	Royal Norwich
1927	T King Jr	Great Yarmouth and Caister	1965	J Carter	Hunstanton
1928	JG Sherlock	Sheringham	1966	J Carter	Sheringham
1929	JG Sherlock	Royal Norwich	1967	J Carter	Eaton
1930	JG Sherlock	Hunstanton	1968	J Carter	Royal Cromer
1931	G Johnson	Cromer	1969	MT Leeder	Royal West Norfolk
1932	E Risebro	Royal West Norfolk	1970	TG Symmons	Great Yarmouth and Caister
1933	RJ Knight	Kings Lynn	1971	MT Leeder	Kings Lynn
1934	CJ Holland	Eaton	1972	MT Leeder	Thetford
1935	R Donald	Royal Norwich	1973	MT Leeder	Royal Norwich
1936	J Mackie	Thetford	1974	MT Leeder	Hunstanton
1937	J Mackie	Sheringham	1975	N Catchpole	Sheringham
1938	BR Kelly	Great Yarmouth and Caister	1976	MT Leeder	Royal Cromer
1939–47	*Not played due to Second World War*		1977	MT Leeder	Eaton
1948	BR Kelly	Royal Norwich	1978	MT Leeder	Royal West Norfolk
1949	L Ball	Hunstanton	1979	MT Leeder	Great Yarmouth and Caister
1950	BR Kelly	Eaton			
1951	J Mackie	Great Yarmouth and Caister	1980	MT Leeder	Kings Lynn
1952	M Leeder	Sheringham	1981	SLH Beckham	Thetford
1953	M Leeder	Kings Lynn	1982	RJ Page	
1954	BR Kelly	Thetford	1983	RG Foster	
1955	BR Kelly	Royal Norwich	1984	MJ Elsworthy	
1956	Alan Poulton	Earlham	1985	M Spooner	
1957	L Ball	Royal West Norfolk	1986	M Spooner	
1958	L Ball	Royal Cromer	1987	MJ Elsworthy	
			1988	M Few	
			1989	M Few	
			1990	M Few	

Norfolk Professional Match Play Championship

INAUGURATED 1986

YEAR	WINNER	VENUE	YEAR	WINNER	VENUE
1986	MT Leeder	Great Yarmouth and Caister	1989	NJ Catchpole	Great Yarmouth and Caister
1987	RG Foster	Great Yarmouth and Caister	1990	A Collison	Thetford
1988	M Few	Great Yarmouth and Caister			

Northern (England) Professional Championship

INAUGURATED 1920

YEAR	WINNER	VENUE	YEAR	WINNER	VENUE
1920	TG Renouf	Hopwood Park	1955	DA Lewis	Blackpool, North Shore
1921	AG Havers	Alwoodley			
1922	AG Havers	Blackpool	1956	J Fallon	Stanley Park, Blackpool
1923	G Sarazen	Lytham St Anne's			
1924	G Gadd	Wilmslow	1957	F Bullock	Blackpool, North Shore
1925	A Mitchell	Lytham St Anne's			
1926	G Gadd	Formby	1958	A Coop	Scarcroft, Leeds
1927	CA Whitcombe	Blackpool	1959	E Green	Moor Allerton, Leeds
1928	W Large	Birkdale			
1929	TG Renouf	Pleasington	1960	E Large	Garforth, Leeds
1930	CH Gadd	Brancepeth Castle	1961	JW Wilkshire	Hopwood Park
1931	WH Davies	Lytham St Anne's	1962	IG Smith	Pannal, Harrogate
1932	PH Rodgers	Barrow	1963	GA Caygill	Swinton Park, Manchester
1933	C Fryer	Fleetwood			
1934	R Burton	Fleetwood	1964	HW Muscroft	Hillside, Southport
1935	WH Davies	Moortown			
1936	Percy Alliss	Heysham	1965	JW Wilkshire	Huddersfield
1937	Percy Alliss	Mere	1966	M Hoyle	St Annes Old
1938–45	*Not played due to Second World War*		1967	G Parton	Blackpool North Shore
1946	N Sutton	Sand Moor			
1947	E Green	Morecombe	1968	AC Gillies	Blackpool North Shore
1948	A Perry	North Manchester			
1949	N Quigley	Fulford	1969	BH Allen	Hillside, Southport
1950	J Fallon	Stand, Manchester			
1951	N Sutton	Heysham	1970	L Platts	Swinton Park, Manchester
1952	HW Myers	Crompton and Royton			
			1971	L Platts	Moortown
1953	J Fallon	Northenden, Manchester	1972	W Ferguson	Woodsome Hall, Huddersfield
1954	J Burton	Seaton Carew			

YEAR	WINNER	VENUE	YEAR	WINNER	VENUE
1973	D Jagger	West Lancs, Blundellsands	1982	H Muscroft	Oakdale, Harrogate
1974	GA Caygill	Oakdale, Harrogate	1983	D Muscroft	Moortown
1975	D Dunk	Heysham	1984	A Chandler	Furness
1976	W Ferguson	Rotherham	1985	A Murray	Bolton Old Links
1977	B Hutchinson	Whitefield and Stand	1986	D Stirling	Windermere
1978	J Morgan	Manchester/N Manchester	1987	D Jagger	Haigh Hall Municipal
1979	*Not played*		1988	K Waters	Haigh Hall Municipal
1980	G Townhill	Moor Allerton, Leeds	1989	S Bottomley	Walton Hall Municipal
1981	B Evans	Pannal, Harrogate	1990	J Morgan	Warrington

Scottish Professional Championship

INAUGURATED 1907

YEAR	WINNER	VENUE	YEAR	WINNER	VENUE
1907	J Hunter	Barry	1938	J Ballingall	Lundin Links
1908	R Thomson	Cardross	1939	W Davis	Inverness
1909	TR Fernie	Montrose	1940–45	*Not played due to Second World War*	
1910	TR Fernie	Lossiemouth	1946	W Anderson	Nairn
1911	E Sinclair	Turnberry	1947	J McCondichie	Luffness
1912	WM Watt	Dunbar	1948	J Panton	Prestwick
1913	A Marling	Cruden Bay	1949	J Panton	Nairn
1914	DP Watt	North Berwick Burgh	1950	J Panton	Longniddry
			1951	J Panton	Ayr, Belleisle
1915–18	*Not played due to Great War*		1952	J Campbell	Lossiemouth
1919	TR Fernie	Monifieth	1953	H Thomson	Gullane
1920	TR Fernie	Gleneagles	1954	J Panton	Turnberry
1921	P Robertson	Gleneagles	1955	J Panton	Elie
1922	GE Smith	Gleneagles	1956	EC Brown	Nairn
1923	AW Butchart	Western Gailes	1957	EC Brown	Barassie
1924	P Robertson	North Berwick Burgh	1958	EC Brown	Dornoch
			1959	J Panton	Turnberry
1925	S Burns	Lossiemouth	1960	EC Brown	West Kilbride
1926	T Wilson	Bruntsfield	1961	RT Walker	Forres
1927	S Burns	Gleneagles	1962	EC Brown	Dunbar
1928	S Burns	Balgownie	1963	WM Miller	Crieff
1929	D McCulloch	Bogside	1964	RT Walker	Machrihanish
1930	D McCulloch	Nairn	1965	EC Brown	Forfar
1931	M Seymour	Dalmahoy	1966	EC Brown } tie J Panton	Cruden Bay
1932	R Dornan	Forfar			
1933	M Seymour	Lossiemouth	1967	H Bannerman	Montrose
1934	M Seymour	Nairn	1968	EC Brown	Monktonhall
1935	J McDowall	Longniddry	1969	G Cunningham	Machrihanish
1936	J Forrester	Lossiemouth	1970	RDBM Shade	Montrose
1937	WM Hastings	Barassie	1971	BJ Gallacher	Lundin Links

YEAR	WINNER	VENUE	YEAR	WINNER	VENUE
1972	H Bannerman	Strathaven	1981	B Barnes	Dalmahoy
1973	BJ Gallacher	Kings Links, Aberdeen	1982	B Barnes	Dalmahoy
			1983	BJ Gallacher	Dalmahoy
1974	BJ Gallacher	Drumpellier	1984	I Young	Dalmahoy
1975	D Huish	Duddingston	1985	S Torrance	Dalmahoy
1976	J Chillas	Haggs Castle	1986	R Drummond	Glenbervie
1977	BJ Gallacher	Barnton	1987	R Drummond	Glenbervie
1978	S Torrance	Strathaven	1988	S`Stephen	Haggs Castle
1979	AWB Lyle	Glasgow Gailes	1989	R Drummond	Monktonhall
1980	S Torrance	East Kilbride	1990	R Drummond	Deer Park

South Region PGA Championship

(formerly Southern (England) Professional Championship)

INAUGURATED 1952

YEAR	WINNER	VENUE	YEAR	WINNER	VENUE
1952	F van Donck	Dunstable Downs	1972	JH Cook	Fulwell
1953	TE Odhams	Mill Hill	1973	N Job	Fulwell
1954	DJ Rees	Fulwell	1974	K Bousfield	Bramley
1955	J Adams	Calcot	1975	DJ Rees	Crews Hill, Enfield
1956	A Lees	Stoneham	1976	R Jewell	Selsdon Park
1957	K Bousfield	Sundridge Park	1977	GR Burroughs	Brookmans Park
1958	H Weetman	Prince's, Sandwich	1978	VB Hood	West Malling
1959	BJ Hunt	Hill Barn	1979	*Not played*	
1960	BJ Hunt	Southampton	1980	PR Mitchell	Windmill Hill and Abbey Hill
1961	GB Wolstenholme	Maidenhead			
1962	BJ Hunt	Selsdon Park	1981	P Milton	Addington Court
1963	H Weetman	Seaford	1982	D McClelland	Eastbourne Downs
1964	Max Faulkner	Hollingbury Park, Brighton	1983	M McLean	Worthing
			1984	M McLean	Mannings Heath
1965	I Macdonald	Hollingbury Park, Brighton	1985	C Mason	West Malling
			1986	P Mitchell	West Malling
1966	DJ Rees	Southampton	1987	*Not played*	
1967	BJ Hunt	Bognor Regis	1988	J Spence	Hollingbury Park, Brighton
1968	GL Hunt	Sonning			
1969	T Grubb	Crews Hill, Enfield	1989	W Grant	Hollingbury Park, Brighton
1970	NC Coles	Bramley			
1971	P Oosterhuis	Fulwell	1990	*Not played*	

Staffordshire and Shropshire Professional Championship

INAUGURATED 1947

YEAR	WINNER	VENUE	YEAR	WINNER	VENUE
1947	CH Ward	Walsall	1950	CH Ward	Calthorpe Park
1948	CH Ward	Penn, Wolverhampton	1951	CH Ward	Leek
			1952	CH Ward	Brocton Hall, Stafford
1949	CA Winks	Trentham			

YEAR	WINNER	VENUE	YEAR	WINNER	VENUE
1953	CH Ward	Oxley Park, Wolverhampton	1970	AR Sadler	Shifnal
1954	CH Ward	Drayton Park, Tamworth	1971	AR Sadler	Shifnal
			1972	RDS Livingston	Shifnal
1955	CH Ward	Tamworth	1973	A Stadler	Shifnal
1956	CH Ward	Hawkstone Park, Shrewsbury	1974	J Rhodes	Shifnal
1957	CH Ward	Whittington Barracks, Lichfield	1975	J Rhodes ⎱ tie A Sadler ⎰	Shifnal
1958	JR Moses	Wolstanton	1976	P McGarry	Leek
1959	CH Ward	Enville	1977	H Boyle	Great Barr, Birmingham
1960	CH Ward	Walsall			
1961	CH Ward	Hawkstone Park, Shrewsbury	1978	A Sadler	Great Barr, Birmingham
1962	CH Ward	Sandwell Park, West Bromwich	1979	J Rhodes	Bloxwich
			1980	A Sadler	Shifnal
1963	CH Ward	Brocton Hall, Stafford	1981	A Griffiths	Drayton Park
			1982	A Griffiths	Drayton Park
			1983	CM Holmes	Drayton Park
1964	CH Ward ⎱ tie E Large ⎰	Little Aston	1984	A Minshall	Drayton Park
			1985	A Stubbs	Brocton Hall
1965	D Fitton	Bloxwich	1986	A Minshall	Drayton Park
			1987	J Higgins	Drayton Park
1966	E Large	South Staffs	1988	J Annable	Bloxwich
1967	M Bembridge	Shifnal	1989	J Higgins	Drayton Park
1968	CH Ward	Leek	1990	G Farr	Penn
1969	J Rhodes	South Staffs			

Staffordshire and Shropshire Professional Match Play Championship

INAUGURATED 1980

YEAR	WINNER	VENUE	YEAR	WINNER
1980	A Sadler	Shifnal	1986	J Annable
1981	A Griffiths	Drayton Park	1987	J Annable
1982	A Griffiths	Beau Desert, Cannock	1988	J Annable
			1989	J Higgins
1983	C Holmes	Drayton Park	1990	G Farr
1984	A Minshall	Drayton Park		
1985	A Stubbs	Brocton Hall, Stafford		

Suffolk Professional Championship

INAUGURATED 1927

YEAR	WINNER	VENUE	YEAR	WINNER	VENUE
1927			1966	J Frew	Thorpeness
1928			1967	AA Butcher	Gorleston
1929			1968	SJ Whymark	Woodbridge
1930	SG Rush	Woodbridge	1969	JW Johnson	Rushmere, Ipswich
1931	SG Rush	Thorpeness			
1932	CH Kennett	Felixstowe	1970	J Frew	Aldeburgh
1933	AH Monk	Bury St Edmunds	1971	JW Johnson	Bury St Edmunds
1934	CH Kennett	Aldeburgh	1972	J Frew	Purdis Heath, Ipswich
1935	SG Rush	Ipswich			
1936	RA Knight	Woodbridge	1973	JW Johnson	Bungay
1937	RA Knight	Thorpeness	1974	RW Mann	Thorpeness
1938	E Gray	Gog Magog	1975	J Frew	Bury St Edmunds
1939–47	*Not played due to Second World War*		1976	J Frew	Woodbridge
1948	EE Beverley	Bury St Edmunds	1977	RW Mann	Stowmarket
1949	FJ Davis	Ipswich	1978	RW Mann	Felixstowe Ferry
1950	RA Knight	Woodbridge	1979	R Webb	Stoke-By-Nayland
1951	FJ Davis	Aldeburgh	1980	T Pennock	Stoke-By-Nayland
1952	J Proudfoot	Thorpeness	1981	M Elsworthy	Purdis Heath, Ipswich
1953	FT Davies	Ipswich			
1954	DA Levermore	Woodbridge	1982	M Elsworthy	Woodbridge
1955	LB Ayton	Aldeburgh	1983	RW Mann	Rookery Park
1956	LB Ayton	Thorpeness	1984	RW Mann	Rookery Park
1957	LB Ayton	Ipswich	1985	S Beckham	Rookery Park
1958	LB Ayton	Woodbridge	1986	RW Mann	Rookery Park
1959	JW Johnson	Aldeburgh	1987	S Beckham	Thorpeness
1960	LA Jones	Thorpeness	1988	S Whymark	Purdis Heath, Ipswich
1961	BJ Proudfoot	Aldeburgh			
1963	LB Ayton	Bury St Edmunds	1989	S Whymark	Woodbridge
1964	LA Jones	Aldeburgh	1990	RW Mann	Felixstowe Ferry
1965	C Aldred	Felixstowe			

Warwickshire Professional Championship

INAUGURATED 1937

YEAR	WINNER	VENUE	YEAR	WINNER	VENUE
1937	WJ Martin	Handsworth	1952	J Hargreaves	Coventry Hearsall
1938	HR Manton	Robin Hood	1953	BJ Hunt	Stratford-on-Avon
1939	GA Maisey	Ladbrook Park	1954	GA Maisey	Robin Hood
1940–46	*Not played due to Second World War*		1955	F Jowle	Copt Heath
1947	J Cawsey	Ladbrook Park	1956	F Jowle	Sutton Coldfield
1948	T Hassall	Harborne	1957	F Jowle	Coventry, Finham
1949	J Hargreaves	Pype Hayes, Walmley	1958	PJ Butler	Sutton Coldfield
			1959	F Jowle	Copt Heath
1950	J Hargreaves	Sutton Coldfield	1960	T Collinge	Moor Hall
1951	J Hargreaves	Copt Heath	1961	GA Maisey	Stratford-on-Avon

YEAR	WINNER	VENUE	YEAR	WINNER	VENUE
1962	NR McDonald	Coventry Hearsall	1977	J Higgins	Leamington and
1963	GA Maisey	Ladbrook Park			County
1964	RL Moffitt	Handsworth	1978	AFC Miller	Stratford-on-Avon
1965	PJ Butler	Coventry, Finham	1979	RDS Livingston	Rugby
1966	PJ Butler	Olton	1980	D Steele	Shirley
1967	PJ Butler	Coventry Hearsall	1981	PJ Weaver	Coventry, Finham
1968	M Reece	Moor Hall	1982	N Selwyn-Smith	Maxstoke Park
1969	RL Moffitt	Coventry, Finham	1983	PJ Weaver	Walmley
1970	J Byard	Nuneaton	1984	A Bownes	Robin Hood
1971	J Byard	Robin Hood	1985	P Elson	Sutton Coldfield
1972	PJ Butler	Edgbaston	1986	P Elson	Shirley
1973	PJ Weaver	Shirley	1987	P Elson	Kenilworth
1974	RDS Livingston	Walmley	1988	C Wicketts	Nuneaton
1975	PR Herbert	Ladbrook Park	1989	T Rouse	Nuneaton
1976	BJ Barton	Copt Heath	1990	N McEwan	Nuneaton

Welsh Professional Championship

INAUGURATED 1904

YEAR	WINNER	VENUE	YEAR	WINNER	VENUE
1904	A Day	Radyr	1948	H Gould	Aberdovey
1905	Fred Collins	Conwy	1949	H Gould	Radyr
1906	Jack Ross	Radyr	1950	G James	Newport
1907	S Whiting	Porthcawl	1951	H Gould	Llandudno
1908	TJ Brace	Bridgend	1952	WS Collins	Southerndown
1909	A Matthews	Rhyl	1953		
1910	A Matthews	Swansea	1954		
1911	P Rainford	Conwy	1955		
1912	Cyril Hughes	Porthcawl	1956	D Smalldon	Porthcawl
1913	G Gadd	Chester	1957	J Black	Llandudno
1914–19	*Not played due to Great War*		1958	RH Kemp Jr	Radyr
1920	Percy Alliss	Aberdovey	1959	D Smalldon	Newport
1921	Percy Alliss	Southerndown	1960	RH Kemp	Llandudno
1922	G Falkner	Rhos-on-Sea	1961	S Mouland	Southerndown
1923	JW Milner	Porthcawl	1962	S Mouland	Porthcawl
1924	BS Weastell	Llandudno	1963	H Gould	Wrexham
1925	J Horn	Pennard	1964	B Bielby	Tenby
1926	BS Weastell	Harlech	1965	S Mouland	Penarth
1927	B Hodson	Tenby	1966	S Mouland	Conway
1928	R Walker	Llandudno	1967	S Mouland	Pyle and Kenfig
1929	B Hodson	Porthcawl	1968	RJ Davies	Southerndown
1930	H Palferman	Wrexham	1969	S Mouland	Llandudno
1931	R Watts	Newport	1970	W Evans	Tredegar Park
1932	WG Smalldon	Porthcawl	1971	J Buckley	St Pierre,
1933	F Collins	Rhyl			Chepstow
1934	CA Pickett	Swansea Bay	1972	J Buckley	Porthcawl
1935	F Hill	Penarth	1973	A Griffiths	Newport, Gwent
1936	F Lloyd	Prestatyn	1974	M Hughes	Cardiff
1937	F Hill	Clyne	1975	C DeFoy	Whitchurch
1938	WS Collins	St Mellons	1976	S Cox	Radyr
1939	C Grabham	Harlech	1977	C DeFoy	Glamorganshire
1940–45	*Not played due to Second World War*		1978	BGC Huggett	Whitchurch
1946	H Gould	Porthcawl	1979	*No Championship*	
1947	K Williams	Llandrindod	1980	A Griffiths	Cardiff

YEAR	WINNER	VENUE	YEAR	WINNER	VENUE
1981	C Defoy	Cardiff	1987	A Dodman	Cardiff
1982	C Defoy	Cardiff	1988	I Woosnam	Cardiff
1983	S Cox	Cardiff	1989	K Jones	Porthcawl
1984	K Jones	Cardiff	1990	P Mayo	Fairwood Park,
1985	D Llewellyn	Whitchurch			Swansea
1986	P Parkin	Whitchurch			

West Region PGA Championship

(formerly West of England Professional Championship)

INAUGURATED 1922

YEAR	WINNER	VENUE	YEAR	WINNER	VENUE
1922	RA Whitcombe	Dorchester	1961	BJ Hunt	Knowle
1923	CH Reith	Broadstone	1962	Peter Alliss	High Post
1924	CA Whitcombe	Burnham and	1963	EG Lester	Lelant
		Berrow	1964	FS Boobyer	Westward Ho!
1925	HL Osborne	Newquay	1965	J McAllister	Swindon
1926	GR Buckle	Long Ashton	1966	Peter Alliss	Trevose
1927	E Hore	Ferndown	1967	T Lebrocq	High Post
1928	J Horn	Lelant	1968	D Sewell	Broadstone
1929	CA Whitcombe	Yelverton	1969	S Peach	Trevose
1930	L Holland	Newquay	1970	D Sewell	Broadstone
1931	RA Whitcombe	Came Down	1971	RM Anderson	Torquay
1932	WJ Branch	Torquay	1972	P Green	Lansdown, Bath
1933	RA Whitcombe	Parkstone	1973	T Pinner	Tehidy Park
1934	RA Whitcombe	Burnham and	1974	FS Boobyer	Filton
		Berrow	1975	A MacDonald	Moretonhampstead
1935	A Easterbrook	St Enodoc	1976	J Yeo	Clevedon
1936	A Perry	Yelverton	1977	G Smith	St Mellion
1937	CH Ward	Exeter	1978	G Smith	Trevose
1938	RA Whitcombe	Lelant	1979	S Brown	Queen's Park,
1939	S Easterbrook	Westward Ho!			Bournemouth
1940–45	*Not played due to Second World War*		1980	P Ward	Broadstone
1946	TB Haliburton	Budleigh Salterton	1981	G Brand Jr	Launceston
1947	M Faulkner	Whitsand Bay	1982	G Smith	Gloucester
1948	RA Whitcombe	Torquay	1983	G Marks	Manor House,
1949	WD Smithers	Knowle, Bristol			Mortonhampstead
1950	RA Whitcombe	Newquay	1984	M Thomas	Lansdown, Bath
1951	WD Smithers	High Post	1985	D Sheppard	Manor House,
1952	WD Smithers	Cotswold Hills			Mortonhampstead
1953	E Lester	Teignmouth	1986	S Little	Launceston
1954	WD Smithers	Bristol & Clifton	1987	A Sherborne	Pyle and Kenfig
1955	H Weetman	Exeter	1988	M Thomas	Pyle and Kenfig
1956	Peter Alliss	Saltford	1989	G Laing	Pyle and Kenfig
1957	H Weetman	Budleigh Salterton	1990	P Price	Mountain Lakes,
1958	Peter Alliss	Tehidy Park			Mid Glamorgan
1959	WD Smithers	Moretonhampstead			
1960	BJ Hunt	Parkstone			

Wiltshire Professional Championship

Now known as the 'Hills' Wiltshire Pro-Champ

INAUGURATED 1925

YEAR	WINNER	VENUE	YEAR	WINNER	VENUE
1925	F Webb	Warminster	1959	AJ Harman	Salisbury and South Wilts
1926	HV Orford	Salisbury and South Wilts	1960	D Haslam	High Post
1927	J Webb	Marlborough	1961	D Haslam	Swindon
1928	FW Goldsmith	Chippenham	1962	AJ Harman	Warminster
1929	J Webb	Warminster	1963	D Haslam	Tidworth
1930	J Webb	Devizes	1964	AJ Harman	Salisbury and South Wilts
1931	J Webb	Tidworth			
1932	J Webb	Swindon	1965	AJ Harman	High Post
1933	C Easterbrook	Kingsdown, Corsham	1966	AJ Harman	Swindon
			1967	P Coombs	Warminster
1934	J Webb	Salisbury and South Wilts	1968	P Coombs	Tidworth
			1969	D Haslam	Salisbury and South Wilts
1935	J Webb	High Post			
1936	RV Redmond	High Post	1970	P Coombs	High Post
1937	C Easterbrook	Swindon	1971	P Coombs	Swindon
1938	AW Edmonds	Salisbury and South Wilts	1972	P Coombs	Warminster
			1973	G Pickup	Kingsdown
1939	J Webb	Warminster	1974	AJ Harman	Tidworth Garrison
1940–45	*Not played due to Second World War*		1975	B Sandry	Salisbury and South Wilts
1946	A Illingworth ⎱ tie RA Brown ⎰	High Post	1976	B Sandry	Swindon
1947	RV Redmond	Swindon	1977	L Bowen	High Post
1948	J Webb	Warminster	1978	G Smith	North Wilts
1949	AS Illingworth	Salisbury and South Wilts	1979	B Sandry	Chippenham
			1980	B Sandry	Marlborough
1950	RA Brown	High Post	1981	Gary Smith	Marlborough
1951	RA Brown	Swindon	1982	R Emery	Swindon
1952	SEG Slocombe	Warminster	1983	I Bolt	Marlborough
1953	J Powell	Tidworth	1984	G Laing	Chippenham
1954	SEG Slocombe	Salisbury and South Wilts	1985	G Laing	Tidworth
			1986	B Sandry	Broome Manor
1955	SEG Slocombe	High Post	1987	G Laing	North Wilts
1956	SEG Slocombe	Swindon	1988	R Emery	Marlborough
1957	D Haslam	Warminster	1989	G Emerson	Marlborough
1958	D Haslam	Tidworth	1990	G Clough	Marlborough

Worcestershire Professional Championship

INAUGURATED 1937

YEAR	WINNER	VENUE	YEAR	WINNER	VENUE
1937	K Hooker	Worcester	1968	JR Moses	Blackwell
1938	E Cawsey	Worcester	1969	S Fogarty	Fulford Heath
1939–46	*Not played due to Second World War*		1970	JR Moses	Gay Hill
1947	L Cliffe	Worcester	1971	WH Firkins	Moseley
1948	WR Firkins	Stourbridge	1972	S Fogarty	Kidderminster
1949	HE Lewis	Cock Moor	1973	N Underwood	Dudley
		Woods	1974	I Richardson	Fulford Heath
1950	WR Firkins	Kidderminster	1975	DJ Russell	Droitwich
1951	WE Booy	Worcester	1976	I Richardson	Moseley
1952	WR Firkins	King's Norton	1977	I Richardson	Churchill and
1953	FT Sumner				Blakedown
1954	WR Firkins		1978	I Richardson	Worcester
1955	FE Miller	Fulford Heath	1979	I Richardson	Worcestershire,
1956	FE Miller	King's Norton			Malvern
1957	WR Firkins	Stourbridge	1980	WH Firkins	Worcester
1958	FE Miller	North	1981	WH Firkins	North Worcester
		Worcestershire	1982	WH Firkins	Kings Norton
1959	JE Wiggett	Moseley	1983	KA Hayward	Blackwell
1960	JE Wiggett	Kidderminster	1984	KA Hayward	Kings Norton
1961	WE Booy	Gay Hill	1985	D Dunk	Kidderminster
1962	JE Wiggett	Fulford Heath	1986	KA Hayward	Moseley
1963	JE Wiggett	Redditch	1987	G Mercer	Gay Hill
1964	RDS Livingston	King's Norton	1988	C Haycock	Blackwell
1965	JR Moses	Blackwell	1989	KA Hayward	Moseley
1966	FE Miller	Dudley	1990	KA Hayward	Worcestershire,
1967	S Fogarty	Droitwich			Malvern

Worcestershire Professional Match Play Championship

YEAR	WINNER	VENUE	YEAR	WINNER	VENUE
1982	KA Hayward	Moseley	1986	KA Hayward	Gay Hill
1983	N Underwood	North	1987	R Cameron	King's Norton
		Worcestershire	1988	C Thompson	Redditch
1984	C Thompson	Droitwich	1989	G Broadbent	North
1985	K Williams	North			Worcestershire
		Worcestershire	1990	WH Firkins	Stourbridge

Yorkshire Professional Championship

INAUGURATED 1921

YEAR	WINNER	VENUE	YEAR	WINNER	VENUE
1921	JW Gaudin	Oakdale, Harrogate	1959	WJ Branch	West Bowling
			1960	WJ Branch	Redcar
1922	JW Gaudin	Halifax	1961	GA Caygill	Hawksworth
1923	J Mackenzie	Hull	1962	B Hutchinson	Oakdale, Harrogate
1924	JW Gaudin	Horsforth			
1925	W Button	Halifax	1963	B Hutchinson	Halifax West End
1926	H Walker	Dore and Totley	1964	GA Gaygill	Crosland Heath
1927	H Crapper	Wakefield	1965	B Hutchinson	Scarcroft
1928	O Sanderson	Woodsome Hall	1966	GA Caygill	Hornsea
1929	L Hetherington	Huddersfield	1967	H Muscroft	Moor Allerton
1930	JW Gaudin	Strensall	1968	L Platts	Horsforth
1931	JW Gaudin	Alwoodley	1969	H Muscroft	Fulford
1932	A Dailey	Fulford	1970	B Hutchinson	Moortown
1933	BS Weastell	Brough	1971	H Muscroft	Abbeydale
1934	RE Ballantine	West Bowling	1972	W Ferguson	Ilkley
1935	A Lees	Oakdale, Harrogate	1973	S Rolley	Pannal, Harrogate
1936	JJ Busson	Pannal, Harrogate	1974	P Cowen	Abbeydale
			1975	M Ingham	Scarcroft
1937	Percy Alliss	Brough	1976	RH Emery	Huddersfield
1938	JJ Busson	Headingley	1977	P Cowen	Moor Allerton
1939 – 45	*Not played due to Second World War*		1978	A Swaine	Fulford
1946	F Jowle	Garforth	1979	G Manson	Garforth
1947	WH Green	Moor Allerton	1980	M Ingham	Otley
1948	J Fallon	Oakdale, Harrogate	1981	G Townhill	York
			1982	M Mackenzie	Abbeydale
1949	A Lees	Fulford	1983	P Cowen	Fulford
1950	F Jowle	Alwoodley	1984	B Hutchinson	Oakdale, Harrogate
1951	JA Jacobs	Pontefract			
1952	WJ Branch	Hillsborough	1985	D Jagger	Woodsome Hall
1953	J Fallon	Cobble Hall	1986	M Ingham	Huddersfield
1954	S Stenhouse	Horsforth	1987	D Stirling	Huddersfield
1955	WJ Branch	Scarcroft	1988	M Higginbottom	Hallamshire
1956	J Fallon	Sickleholme	1989	D Stirling	Leeds
1957	WJ Branch	Kirk Ella, Hull	1990	D Stirling	Ilkley
1958	M Law	Moor Allerton			

PGA Club Professional Championship

YEAR	WINNER	SCORE	VENUE	YEAR	WINNER	SCORE	VENUE
1973	D Sewell	276	Calcot Park	1983	J Farmer	270	Heaton Park
1974	B Murray	275	Calcot Park	1984	D Durnian	278	Old Links,
1975	D Sewell	276	Calcot Park				Bolton
1976	B Ferguson	283	Moortown	1985	Robin Mann	291	The Belfry
1977	D Huish	284	Hollinwell	1986	D Huish	278	Birkdale
1978	D Jones	281	Pannal	1987	R Weir	273	Sandiway
1979	D Jones	278	Pannal	1988	R Weir	269	Harlech
1980	D Jagger	286	Turnberry	1989	BW Barnes	280	Prince's,
1981	M Steadman	289	Woburn				Sandwich
1982	D Durnian	285	Hill Valley	1990	A Webster	280	Carnoustie

PGA Seniors' Championship

YEAR	WINNER	SCORE	VENUE	YEAR	WINNER	SCORE	VENUE
1957	J Burton	213	Fulwell	1976	C O'Connor Sr	276	North Berwick
1958	N Sutton	214	Copt Heath	1977	C O'Connor Sr	284	Cambridge Moat
1959	A Lees	204	Royal Mid-				House Hotel
			Surrey	1978	P Skerritt	288	Cambridge Moat
1960	R Horne	213	Mere				House Hotel
1961	SL King	208	Hill Barn	1979	C O'Connor Sr	280	Cambridge Moat
1962	SL King	214	Harrogate				House Hotel
1963	G Evans	222	Weston-super-	1980	P Skerritt	286	Gleneagles
			Mare	1981	C O'Connor Sr	287	North Berwick
1964	S Scott	213	Gosforth Park	1982	C O'Connor Sr	285	Longniddry
1965	CH Ward	210	Ashford Manor	1983	C O'Connor Sr	277	Burnham and
1966	DJ Rees	215	Coventry				Berrow
1967	J Panton	282	Ayr Belleisle	1984	E Jones	280	Stratford-on-Avon
1968	M Faulkner	283	Aldeburgh	1985	NC Coles	284	Pannal, Harrogate
1969	J Panton	281	West Kilbride	1986	NC Coles	276	Mere
1970	M Faulkner	288	Longniddry	1987	NC Coles	206	Coventry
1971	KDG Nagle	269	Elie	1988	PW Thomson	287	North Berwick
1972	K Bousfield	291	Longniddry	1989	NC Coles	277	West Hill
1973	KDG Nagle	270	Elie	1990	B Waites	278	Brough
1974	E Lester	282	Lundin Links				
1975	KDG Nagle	268	Longniddry				

PGA Records and Awards

Presidents

DATE	NAME	DATE	NAME
1901 – 30	Rt Hon The Earl of Balfour	1950 – 54	Rt Hon Lord Lyle of Westbourne
1930 – 36	HRH The Prince of Wales	1954 – 64	Rt Hon Lord Brabazon of Tara MC
1936 – 42	HRH The Duke of Kent	1964 –	Rt Hon The Earl of Derby MC
1946 – 49	Rt Hon Lord Wardington		

Chairmen

DATE	NAME	DATE	NAME
1923 – 24	JH Taylor	1946 – 49	R McKenzie
1924 – 25	WR Reith	1949 – 51	Arthur Lacey
1926 – 26	R McKenzie	1951 – 53	Alf Padgham
1926 – 27	B Gadd	1953 – 55	Fred Taylor
1927 – 28	Josh Taylor	1955 – 57	Ernest Bradbeer
1928 – 29	James Batley	1957 – 58	Henry Crapper
1929 – 30	Herbert Jolly	1958 – 59	Ernest Cawsey
1931 – 31	WG Oke	1959 – 62	Arthur Harrison
1931 – 32	James Braid	1962 – 67	Thomas Jones
1932 – 33	HC Kinch	1967 – 69	Geoff Cotton
1933 – 34	C Johns	1970 – 72	Eddie Whitcombe
1934 – 35	WB Smith	1973 – 75	Doug Smith
1935 – 36	Charles Whitcombe	1976 – 81	Michael Bonallack
1936 – 37	JH Taylor	1982 – 84	Ronnie Alexander
1937 – 38	Josh Taylor	1985 – 88	Derek Nash
1938 – 39	Fred Taylor	1989 –	Philip Weaver
1939 – 40	R McKenzie		
1940 – 45	*Chairmen elected on ad hoc basis due to Second World War*		

Captains

DATE	NAME	DATE	NAME
1901 – 2	James Braid	1950 – 51	Percy Alliss
1902 – 3	Alex Herd	1951 – 52	Max Faulkner
1903 – 4	Harry Vardon	1952 – 53	Henry Crapper
1904 – 5	Jack White	1953 – 54	Fred Taylor
1905 – 6	James Braid	1955	Ernest Cawsey
1906 – 7	James Braid	1956	Allan Dailey
1907 – 8	Arnaud Massy	1957	Thomas Jones
1908 – 9	James Braid	1958	William Davies
1909 – 10	JH Taylor	1959	George Robins
1910 – 11	James Braid	1960	Ernest Bradbeer
1911 – 12	Harry Vardon	1961	Alfred Beck
1912 – 13	Ted Ray	1962	Peter Alliss
1913 – 14	JH Taylor	1963	Arthur Harrison
1914 – 15	Harry Vardon	1964	Joseph Baker
1915 – 18	*No Captains elected due to Great War*	1965	Joseph Baker
1920 – 21	George Duncan	1966	Bernard Hunt
1921 – 22	WR Reith	1967	Dai Rees
1922 – 23	J Rowe	1968	Hugh Lewis
1923 – 24	Arthur Havers	1969	Tom Haliburton
1924 – 25	W Philpot	1970	Eric Brown
1925 – 26	Archie Compston	1971	Geoff Cotton
1926 – 27	Adrian Wheildon	1972	Peter Butler
1927 – 28	Josh Taylor	1973	Reg Cox
1928 – 29	Ted Williamson	1974	Byron Hutchinson
1929 – 30	Rowland Jones	1975	Harry Riseborough
1930 – 31	CH Corlett	1976	Dai Rees
1931 – 32	TG Renouf	1977	Jack Hargreaves
1932 – 33	P Robertson	1978	Tommy Horton
1933 – 34	Abe Mitchell	1979	Bill Watson
1934 – 35	Henry Cotton	1980	David Talbot
1935 – 36	Alf Padgham	1981	Doug Smith
1936 – 37	Alf Padgham	1982	Angel Gallardo
1937 – 38	R McKenzie	1983	Keith Hockey
1938 – 39	Reg Whitcombe	1984	Peter Townsend
1939 – 40	Dick Burton	1985	Norman McDonald
1940 – 46	*No Captains elected due to Second World War*	1986	Charles Hughes
		1987	Peter Alliss
1946 – 47	James Braid	1988	David Huish
1947 – 48	Fred Daly	1989	John Stirling
1948 – 49	Henry Cotton	1990	Richard Bradbeer
1949 – 50	Bobby Locke		

Ryle Memorial Medal

Awarded to the winner of the Open Championship if the winner is a member of the Association

DATE	NAME	SCORE	VENUE	DATE	NAME	SCORE	VENUE
1901	J Braid	309	Muirfield	1951	M Faulkner	285	Portrush
1902	A Herd	307	Hoylake	1952	AD Locke	287	Lytham St
1903	H Vardon	300	Prestwick				Annes
1904	J White	296	St George's,	1954	PW Thomson	283	Birkdale
			Sandwich	1955	PW Thomson	281	St Andrews
1905	J Braid	318	St Andrews	1956	PW Thomson	286	Hoylake
1906	J Braid	300	Muirfield	1957	AD Locke	279	St Andrews
1907	A Massy	312	Hoylake	1958	PW Thomson	278	Lytham St
1908	J Braid	291	Prestwick				Annes
1909	JH Taylor	295	Deal	1959	G Player	284	Muirfield
1910	J Braid	299	St Andrews	1960	KDG Nagle	278	St Andrews
1911	H Vardon	303	St George's,	1963	RJ Charles	277	Lytham St
			Sandwich				Annes
1912	T Ray	295	Muirfield	1965	PW Thomson	285	Birkdale
1913	JH Taylor	304	Hoylake	1967	R de Vicenzo	278	Hoylake
1914	H Vardon	306	Prestwick	1968	G Player	289	Carnoustie
1920	G Duncan	303	Deal	1969	A Jacklin	280	Lytham St
1923	A Havers	295	Troon				Annes
1934	TH Cotton	283	St George's,	1974	G Player	282	Lytham St
			Sandwich				Annes
1935	A Perry	283	Muirfield	1979	S Ballesteros	276	Lytham St
1936	A Padgham	287	Hoylake				Annes
1937	TH Cotton	290	Carnoustie	1984	S Ballesteros	276	St Andrews
1938	R Whitcombe	295	St George's,	1985	AWB Lyle	282	St George's,
			Sandwich				Sandwich
1939	R Burton	290	St Andrews	1987	N Faldo	279	Muirfield
1947	F Daly	293	Hoylake	1988	S Ballesteros	273	Lytham St
1948	TH Cotton	284	Muirfield				Annes
1949	AD Locke	283	St George's,	1990	N Faldo	270	St Andrews
			Sandwich				
1950	AD Locke	279	Troon				

Braid Taylor Memorial Medal

Awarded to the member of the Association born in the United Kingdom or Republic of Ireland or has one or both parents born in the United Kingdom or Republic of Ireland, who finishes highest in the Open Championship

DATE	NAME	SCORE	VENUE	DATE	NAME	SCORE	VENUE
1966	D Thomas	283	Muirfield	1975	NC Coles / P Oosterhuis	282 } tie	Carnoustie
1967	CJ Clark	284	Hoylake				
1968	M Bembridge	293	Carnoustie		T Horton		
1969	A Jacklin	280	Lytham St	1976	C O'Connor Jr / M James	288 } tie	Birkdale
			Annes				
1970	A Jacklin	286	St Andrews	1977	T Horton	284	Turnberry
1971	A Jacklin	280	Birkdale	1978	P Oosterhuis	284	St Andrews
1972	A Jacklin	280	Muirfield	1979	M James	287	Lytham St
1973	NC Coles	279	Troon				Annes
1974	P Oosterhuis	286	Lytham St	1980	SC Mason	280	Muirfield
			Annes				

DATE	NAME	SCORE	VENUE		DATE	NAME	SCORE	VENUE
1981	M James	283	St George's, Sandwich		1986	GJ Brand	285	Turnberry
1982	P Oosterhuis C O'Connor Jr	285	Troon		1987	N Faldo	279	Muirfield
1983	N Faldo D Durnian	280 } tie	Birkdale		1988	N Faldo	279	Lytham St Annes
1984	N Faldo	282	St Andrews		1989	D Feherty	279	Troon
1985	AWB Lyle	282	St George's, Sandwich		1990	N Faldo	270	St Andrews

Tooting Bec Cup

Awarded to the member of the PGA born in the United Kingdom or Republic of Ireland or who has one or both parents born in the United Kingdom or Republic of Ireland, who returns the lowest single round score in the Open Championship. From 1901-22 the Tooting Bec Trophy was contested over 36 holes prior to its association with the Open Championship.

DATE	NAME	SCORE	VENUE
1901	JH Taylor	149	Tooting
1902	J Braid	148	Romford
1903	J Braid	148	Hanger Hill
1904	J Braid	148	West Middlesex
1905	AH Toogood	150	Northwood
1906	WR Lonie	152	Ashford Manor
1907	J Braid	151	South Herts
1908	R Jones	153	Neasden
1909	J Sherlock	149	Maidenhead
1910	J Sherlock	148	Stoke Poges
1911	H Vardon	154	Banstead Downs
1912	PJ Gaudin	147	West Herts
1913–19	*Discontinued due to the Great War*		
1920	E Ray	149	Worplesdon
1921	A Massy	147	Cooden Beach
1922	G Duncan	142	Purley Downs
1923	*Held in abeyance*		
1924	ER Whitcombe	70	Hoylake
1925	E Ray	73	Prestwick
1926	*Held in abeyance*		
1927	F Robson	69	St Andrews
1928	*Held in abeyance*		
1929	Percy Alliss	69	Muirfield
1930	A Compston	68	Hoylake
1931	*Held in abeyance*		
1932	A Havers	68	Prince's, Sandwich
1933	A Mitchell	68	St Andrews
1934	W Davies	68	St George's, Sandwich
1935	A Perry	67	Muirfield
1936	WJ Branch	68	Hoylake
1937	RA Whitcombe	70	Carnoustie
1938	J Busson R Burton } tie	69	St George's, Sandwich

DATE	NAME	SCORE	VENUE
1939	R Burton M Faulkner J Busson } tie	70	St Andrews
1940–45	*Discontinued due to Second World War*		
1946	D Rees	67	St Andrews
1947	L Ayton TH Cotton } tie	69	Hoylake
1948	TH Cotton	66	Muirfield
1949	K Bousfield J Adams } tie	67	St Georges, Sandwich
1950	F Daly	66	Troon
1951	C Ward J Adams } tie	68 68	Portrush
1952	F Daly	67	Lytham St Annes
1953	E Lester D Rees } tie	70	Carnoustie
1954	J Hargreaves S Scott } tie	67	Birkdale
1955	J Fallon	67	St Andrews
1956	D Smalldon	68	Hoylake
1957	E Brown L Ayton J Fallon } tie	67	St Andrews
1958	E Brown	65	Lytham St Annes
1959	Peter Alliss	67	Muirfield
1960	B Hunt	66	St Andrews
1961	C O'Connor Sr	67	Birkdale
1962	S Scott	68	Troon
1963	C O'Connor Sr T Haliburton } tie	68	Lytham St Annes
1964	M Gregson B Hunt } tie	67	St Andrews
1965	B Huggett	68	Birkdale
1966	PJ Butler	65	Muirfield

DATE	NAME		SCORE	VENUE
1967	L Platts / H Boyle	tie	68	Hoylake
1968	G Cunningham / B Barnes	tie	70	Carnoustie
1969	C O'Connor Sr		65	Lytham St Annes
1970	N Coles		65	St Andrews
1971	P Oosterhuis		66	Birkdale
1972	G Hunt / A Jacklin / H Bannerman	tie	67	Muirfield
1973	N Coles		66	Troon
1974	P Townsend / J Morgan	tie	69	Lytham St Annes
1975	B Gallacher / N Coles / M Bembridge	tie	67	Carnoustie
1976	M James		66	Birkdale
1977	T Horton		65	Turnberry

DATE	NAME		SCORE	VENUE
1978	G Cullen		67	St Andrews
1979	W Longmuir		65	Lytham St Annes
1980	W McColl / K Brown / E Darcy	tie	68	Muirfield
1981	G Brand Jr		65	St George's, Sandwich
1982	AWB Lyle		66	Troon
1983	D Durnian		66	Birkdale
1984	S Torrance		66	St Andrews
1985	C O'Connor Jr		64	St George's, Sandwich
1986	GJ Brand		68	Turnberry
1987	R Drummond		66	Muirfield
1988	AWB Lyle		67	Lytham St Annes
1989	W Stephens		66	Troon
1990	P Broadhurst		63	St Andrews

Harry Vardon Trophy

Awarded to the leader of the Order of Merit

DATE	NAME	DATE	NAME
1937	CA Whitcombe	1967	MC Gregson
1938	TH Cotton	1968	BGC Huggett
1939	RA Whitcombe	1969	BJ Gallacher
1940 – 45 *No award owing to the Second World War*		1970	NC Coles
1946	AD Locke	1971	P Oosterhuis
1947	N von Nida	1972	P Oosterhuis
1948	CH Ward	1973	P Oosterhuis
1949	CH Ward	1974	P Oosterhuis
1950	AD Locke	1975	D Hayes
1951	J Panton	1976	S Ballesteros
1952	H Weetman	1977	S Ballesteros
1953	F Van Donck	1978	S Ballesteros
1954	AD Locke	1979	AWB Lyle
1955	DJ Rees	1980	AWB Lyle
1956	H Weetman	1981	B Langer
1957	EC Brown	1982	G Norman
1958	BJ Hunt	1983	N Faldo
1959	DJ Rees	1984	B Langer
1960	BJ Hunt	1985	AWB Lyle
1961	C O'Connor Sr	1986	S Ballesteros
1962	C O'Connor Sr	1987	I Woosnam
1963	NC Coles	1988	S Ballesteros
1964	Peter Alliss	1989	R Rafferty
1965	BJ Hunt	1990	I Woosnam
1966	Peter Alliss		

Part Two

Men's Amateur Tournaments

British Open Amateur Championship

INAUGURATED 1885

The proposal for an Amateur Championship in Britain — *The* Amateur because it was the first national tournament for non-professionals — came from the Royal Liverpool Club. In 1885 they invited most of the clubs then in existence to send their best players to take part in a championship at Hoylake. There were 44 entries and the winner, A.F. MacFie, beat Horace Hutchinson in the final. The haphazard nature of the first effort is clear from the draw for partners; it was probably made in the morning of the first day when it was known how many wished to play, but was so inexpertly conducted that there were eventually only three semi-finalists, MacFie receiving a bye into the final.

The next year the Royal Liverpool Club suggested that the Royal & Ancient Club should run the championship and that it should be open to all amateurs, not just to invited players. Horace Hutchinson won and for 30 years was recognised as the first Amateur Champion, but when the Royal & Ancient took full control of the championship in 1920, it was agreed that the 1885 event should be considered the first.

Until 1911 the Amateur Championship was played at only five courses, Hoylake, St Andrews, Prestwick, Sandwich and Muirfield. For many of those years Hoylake, that nursery which produced so many champions, provided the winners in A.F. MacFie, John Ball and Harold Hilton. Others such as Horace Hutchinson and John Laidlay were Hoylake members but it was not their home club.

The first break from these five courses came in 1912 when John Ball won the last of his eight amateur titles, beating Abe Mitchell of the Ashdown Forest Canteloupe (Artisan) Club before he turned professional, at the 38th hole at Westward Ho! Ball's record is never likely to be equalled. Nearest to it is Michael Bonallack's remarkable five wins in ten years starting in 1961, when the fields were so much larger and stronger.

Between the wars Deal, Lytham and Troon were added to the roster. Since then three Irish courses, Portmarnock, Portrush and Newcastle, Co. Down, Turnberry and Dornoch in Scotland, Porthcawl in Wales, three Lancastrian at Birkdale, Formby and Hillside, and Ganton in North Yorkshire have all been visited, some on several occasions.

The format of the Amateur Championship has changed little in the 106 years since it began. The final became a 36-hole match early on and, but for three years in the 1950s when the quarter- and semi-finals (1956–57) and the semi-finals (1958) were also extended to 36 holes, it has been so since.

Entries did not reach 100 until 1899, were 200 by 1907 and 283 in 1936. After 1945 enthusiasm to take part rose further, reaching a peak in 1958 with an entry of 488 at St Andrews. It was the year of the second of Joe Carr's three championships. Thereafter, due to stricter handicap limits, the entry stayed at 256, with perhaps a few preliminary matches to contract the field to that number, which is the most that can play in six rounds, semi-finals and final. In spite of handicap restrictions, entries again increased and in 1983 36-hole stroke play qualifying was introduced, played over two courses, the leading 64 reverting to match play over four days.

The overseas entry in the Amateur Championship has been considerable for 70 years, especially from the United States. The first American to win was W.J. Travis as early as 1904 at Sandwich. He used a centre-staffed Schenectady putter, which was banned soon after in the U.K. In the 1920s and 1930s there were six American victories: Jesse Sweetser in 1926, Bobby Jones in 1930, Lawson Little (1934–35), Bob Sweeney (1937) and Charlie Yates in 1938. It is noticeable that in four of those years the Walker Cup preceded the Amateur Championship bringing over all the best US players to compete. Since the war, Americans have won 14 Amateurs, with Stranahan (1948 and 1950) and Siderowf (1973 and 1976) both successful twice. Yet no American has won since Joe Sigel, a frequent and popular visitor, in 1979; this was the last of seven occasions when two Americans contested the final.

Until 1981 only two other countries, Australia (D.W. Bachli, 1954) and South Africa (Bobby Cole, 1966) had provided the winner. More recently, after Pierre Ploujoux became the first Frenchman to win in 1981, there have followed the Spaniard Jose Maria Olazabal (1984), C. Hardin of Sweden (1988) and R. Muntz of the Netherlands (1990). Olazabal is the sole winner to have become a highly successful professional. As an amateur he is also the only man to have won the British Boys', Youths' and the Amateur titles.

Not that the British challenge has ever been lacking in the Amateur Championship. In the early years with much smaller fields, apart from John Ball, Harold Hilton won four times up to 1913, Horace Hutchinson, Freddie Tait and Jimmy Laidlay twice each. Robert Maxwell's two wins spanned the First World War, but only Ernest Holderness, Cyril Tolley and Lawson Little won twice between 1920 and 1939. Michael Scott won in 1933 at the age of 56 and two years later Lawson Little beat James Wallace, a local Scot, at Prestwick by the vast margin of 14 and 13. Next year, he scraped home at Lytham against Dr William Tweddell, the 1927 winner, by 1 hole.

Michael Bonallack's and Joe Carr's many wins have already been mentioned, but in the past 20 years only Trevor Homer and Peter McEvoy of the British have won more than once. Several Irishmen and recently Welshmen have won in the past ten years. Since 1945, the Scottish effort has been most disappointing. The last Scot to win was David Jack in 1957; apart from him only Robert Harris, Alex Kyle and Hector Thomson were successful after 1920. In the early days of the championship Tait, Laidlay, Balfour-Melville and others won, but since then the number of Scottish winners has not been worthy of the nation where the game as we know it began.

YEAR	WINNER	RUNNER-UP	MARGIN	VENUE
1885	AF MacFie	HG Hutchinson	7 and 6	Hoylake
1886	HG Hutchinson	H Lamb	7 and 6	St Andrews
1887	HG Hutchinson	J Ball	1 hole	Hoylake
1888	J Ball	JE Laidlay	5 and 4	Prestwick
1889	JE Laidlay	LMB Melville	2 and 1	St Andrews
1890	J Ball	JE Laidlay	4 and 3	Hoylake
1891	JE Laidlay	HH Hilton	20th hole	St Andrews
1892	J Ball	HH Hilton	3 and 1	Sandwich
1893	P Anderson	JE Laidlay	1 hole	Prestwick
1894	J Ball	SM Fergusson	1 hole	Hoylake
1895	LMB Melville	J Ball	19th hole	St Andrews
1896	FG Tait	HH Hilton	8 and 7	Sandwich
36 holes played on and after this date				
1897	AJT Allan	J Robb	4 and 2	Muirfield
1898	FG Tait	SM Fergusson	7 and 5	Hoylake
1899	J Ball	FG Tait	37th hole	Prestwick
1900	HH Hilton	J Robb	8 and 7	Sandwich

YEAR	WINNER	RUNNER-UP	MARGIN	VENUE
1901	HH Hilton	JL Low	1 hole	St Andrews
1902	C Hutchings	SH Fry	1 hole	Hoylake
1903	R Maxwell	HG Hutchinson	7 and 5	Muirfield
1904	WJ Travis (USA)	E Blackwell	4 and 3	Sandwich
1905	AG Barry	Hon O Scott	3 and 2	Prestwick
1906	J Robb	CC Lingen	4 and 3	Hoylake
1907	J Ball	CA Palmer	6 and 4	St Andrews
1908	EA Lassen	HE Taylor	7 and 6	Sandwich
1909	R Maxwell	Capt CK Hutchison	1 hole	Muirfield
1910	J Ball	CC Aylmer	10 and 9	Hoylake
1911	HH Hilton	EA Lassen	4 and 3	Prestwick
1912	J Ball	A Mitchell	38th hole	Westward Ho!
1913	HH Hilton	R Harris	6 and 5	St Andrews
1914	JLC Jenkins	CO Hezlet	3 and 2	Sandwich
1915–19	*Not played due to Great War*			
1920	CJH Tolley	RA Gardner (USA)	37th hole	Muirfield
1921	WI Hunter	AJ Graham	12 and 11	Hoylake
1922	EWE Holderness	J Caven	1 hole	Prestwick
1923	RH Wethered	R Harris	7 and 6	Deal
1924	EWE Holderness	EF Storey	3 and 2	St Andrews
1925	R Harris	KF Fradgley	13 and 12	Westward Ho!
1926	J Sweetser (USA)	AF Simpson	6 and 5	Muirfield
1927	Dr W Tweddell	DE Landale	7 and 6	Hoylake
1928	TP Perkins	RH Wethered	6 and 4	Prestwick
1929	CJH Tolley	JN Smith	4 and 3	Sandwich
1930	RT Jones (USA)	RH Wethered	7 and 6	St Andrews
1931	E Martin Smith	J De Forest	1 hole	Westward Ho!
1932	J De Forest	EW Fiddian	3 and 1	Muirfield
1933	Hon M Scott	TA Bourn	4 and 3	Hoylake
1934	W Lawson Little (USA)	J Wallace	14 and 13	Prestwick
1935	W Lawson Little (USA)	Dr W Tweddell	1 hole	Lytham St Annes
1936	H Thomson	J Ferrier (Aus)	2 holes	St Andrews
1937	R Sweeney Jr (USA)	LO Munn	3 and 2	Sandwich
1938	CR Yates (USA)	RC Ewing	3 and 2	Troon
1939	AT Kyle	AA Duncan	2 and 1	Hoylake
1940–45	*Not played due to Second World War*			
1946	J Bruen	R Sweeney (USA)	4 and 3	Birkdale
1947	WP Turnesa (USA)	RD Chapman (USA)	3 and 2	Carnoustie
1948	FR Stranahan (USA)	C Stowe	5 and 4	Sandwich
1949	SM McCready	WP Turnesa (USA)	2 and 1	Portmarnock
1950	FR Stranahan (USA)	RD Chapman (USA)	8 and 6	St Andrews
1951	RD Chapman (USA)	CR Coe (USA)	5 and 4	Porthcawl
1952	E Harvie Ward (USA)	FR Stranahan (USA)	6 and 5	Prestwick
1953	JB Carr	E Harvie Ward (USA)	2 holes	Hoylake
1954	DW Bachli (Aus)	WC Campbell (USA)	2 and 1	Muirfield
1955	JW Conrad (USA)	A Slater	3 and 2	Lytham St Annes
1956	JC Beharrell	LG Taylor	5 and 4	Troon
1957	R Reid Jack	HB Ridgeley (USA)	2 and 1	Formby
1958	JB Carr	A Thirlwell	3 and 2	St Andrews
1959	DR Beman (USA)	W Hyndman (USA)	3 and 2	Sandwich
1960	JB Carr	R Cochran (USA)	8 and 7	Portrush
1961	MF Bonallack	J Walker	6 and 4	Turnberry
1962	RD Davies (USA)	J Povall	1 hole	Hoylake
1963	MSR Lunt	JG Blackwell	2 and 1	St Andrews
1964	GJ Clark	MSR Lunt	39th hole	Ganton
1965	MF Bonallack	CA Clark	2 and 1	Porthcawl

YEAR	WINNER	RUNNER-UP	MARGIN	VENUE
1966	RE Cole (SA)	RDBM Shade	3 and 2	Carnoustie
1967	RB Dickson (USA)	RJ Cerrudo (USA)	2 and 1	Formby
1968	MF Bonallack	JB Carr	7 and 6	Troon
1969	MF Bonallack	W Hyndman (USA)	3 and 2	Hoylake
1970	MF Bonallack	W Hyndman (USA)	8 and 7	Newcastle Co Down
1971	S Melnyk (USA)	J Simons (USA)	3 and 2	Carnoustie
1972	T Homer	A Thirlwell	4 and 3	Sandwich
1973	R Siderowf (USA)	PH Moody	5 and 3	Porthcawl
1974	T Homer	J Gabrielsen (USA)	2 holes	Muirfield
1975	MM Giles (USA)	M James	8 and 7	Hoylake
1976	R Siderowf (USA)	JC Davies	37th hole	St Andrews
1977	P McEvoy	HM Campbell	5 and 4	Ganton
1978	P McEvoy	PJ McKellar	4 and 3	Troon
1979	J Sigel (USA)	S Hoch (USA)	3 and 2	Hillside
1980	D Evans	D Suddards (USA)	4 and 3	Porthcawl
1981	P Ploujoux (Fr)	J Hirsch (USA)	4 and 2	St Andrews
1982	M Thompson	A Stubbs	4 and 3	Deal
1983	AP Parkin	J Holtgrieve (USA)	5 and 4	Turnberry
1984	JM Olazabal (Spa)	CS Montgomerie	5 and 4	Formby
1985	G McGimpsey	G Homewood	8 and 7	Dornoch
1986	D Curry	G Birtwell	11 and 19	Lytham St Annes
1987	PM Mayo	P McEvoy	3 and 1	Prestwick
1988	C Hardin (Swe)	B Fouchee (SA)	1 hole	Porthcawl
1989	S Dodd	C Cassells	5 and 3	Birkdale
1990	R Muntz (Neth)	A Macara	7 and 6	Muirfield

Senior Open Amateur Championship

INAUGURATED 1969

The British Seniors Trophy was inaugurated in 1969 under the Royal & Ancient Championship Committee's aegis. It is contested over 54 holes of stroke play; until 1976 it was 36 holes only and such is now the size of the entry, two courses are used for the first 36 holes, the leading 50 players qualifying for the third and last round over the main course. The entry is limited to 252, divided proportionally into four age-groups from 55 to over 70.

The winners of 1978–79 and 1988–90, Ronnie White and Charlie Green respectively, are the two best known British winners, both having long Walker Cup experience in separate decades. The entry from US Seniors has increased recently and Americans took the title four times between 1983 and 1987.

Venues have been spread over the kingdom from Blairgowrie to Deal and Western Gailes to The Berkshire and many other top rank courses, about evenly divided between England and Scotland, with a switch to Harlech in Wales in 1979.

YEAR	WINNER	SCORE	VENUE
1969	R Pattinson	154	Formby
1970	K Bamber	150	Prestwick
1971	GH Pickard	150	Deal
1972	TC Hartley	147	St Andrews
1973	JT Jones	149	Hoylake
1974	MA Ivor-Jones	149	Moortown
1975	HJ Roberts	138	Turnberry
1976	WM Crichton	149	The Berkshire
1977	Dr TE Donaldson	228	Panmure
1978	RJ White	225	Formby
1979	RJ White	226	Harlech
1980	JM Cannon	218	Prestwick St Nicholas
1981	T Branton	227	Hoylake
1982	RL Glading	218	Blairgowrie
1983	AJ Swann (USA)	222	Walton Heath
1984	JC Owens (USA)	222	Western Gailes
1985	D Morey (USA)	223	Hesketh
1986	AN Sturrock	229	Panmure
1987	B Soyers (USA)	226	Deal
1988	CW Green	221	Barnton, Edinburgh
1989	CW Green	226	Moortown
1990	CW Green	207	The Berkshire

The Walker Cup

INAUGURATED 1922

Donated by George H. Walker, President of the USGA in 1920 and grandfather of President George Bush, the Walker Cup was the first trophy given for regular competition between teams of British and US players. At the time the standard of amateur play was little short of that of the professionals. As many as a dozen would qualify for the Open. In 1921 Roger Wethered, one of the best English amateurs, tied with Jock Hutchison, but lost the 36-hole play-off, and the incomparable Bobby Jones was to win the Open in 1926, 1927 and 1930 and the US Open four times between 1923 and 1930.

George Walker's gift was probably the result of an unofficial match before the 1920 Amateur Championship at Hoylake when the Americans won decisively by 9 matches to 3, playing four foursomes and eight singles, each over 36 holes on consecutive days; this was the format which remained in force until 1963.

The first match for the trophy was played the next year at the National Links, Long Island, New York, with the USA again winning comfortably 8 matches to 4. It was notable for the effort of Bernard Darwin, who, accompanying the side as golf correspondent of *The Times*, took the place of the captain, Robert Harris, who was ill, and was one of the three Britons to win in the singles. After two more American wins by 6–5 at St Andrews the next year and 9–3 at Garden City, New York the year after, it was decided to stage the match every two years.

There was a succession of dreary defeats for the British, 11–1, 10–2, 8–1 with 3 halved and 9–2 with 1 halved in the years leading up to 1938 at St Andrews. Here the British, led by the first non-playing captain, John Beck, turned the tables with a win by 7–4 and one halved. The victory was to a large extent inspired by the play in the pre-match trials and practice rounds of the young Irishman Jimmy Bruen, who galvanised the side with the feeling that they could win. In the event he halved his foursomes match playing with Harry Bentley and lost a close single to Charles Yates, but his brilliant example in practice was a vital element in the victory.

For a decade after 1945 when the war ended, British teams felt at a disadvantage to the US players who had not suffered similar wartime privations of a lack of playing opportunity and twelve years of rationing. Again the matches were usually one-sided, especially when played in the USA.

For ten years and more Ronnie White and Joe Carr were outstanding British players. In the ten matches he played White lost only three, an unsurpassed British record. Their mantle was taken over by Michael Bonallack, who in 1971 captained the side which took the Cup at St Andrews by 13–11, a splendid and unexpected achievement amid a depressing succession of defeats. Yet six years before, Joe Carr's side had achieved a remarkable halved match, the USA therefore retaining the Cup, at Baltimore, Maryland. Having lead 8–3 on the first day and 10–5 before the last singles, it was only a long putt by Clive Clark to win the 18th hole and halve his match that saved the day. Similarly at St Andrews the vital shot was played by Dr David Marsh to the 17th green to take the lead over William Hyndman.

After the 1971 British win, the Americans continued their comfortable victories, but the margins were less than before. All matches were played on championship courses in both countries, the closest result being at Hoylake in 1983 when the margin was 13½–10½ to the USA. Usually during this period the first day's play was fairly even, but the Americans invariably improved the next day to win. This ability to play better under pressure was often their strongest point.

Come 1987 the match was played inland for the first time in Britain at Sunningdale and there were high hopes of a home win. Alas! The British lost the first morning's foursomes 0–4 and the day's play 3–9. The second day was no more successful and Great Britain and Ireland lost by 7½ to 16½. So much for high hopes!

They were, however, to be amply fulfilled in the next match at Peachtree, Atlanta, Georgia in 1989. Great Britain and Ireland came out well in a very close match with a victory by 12½ to 11½. Leading by 11–5 going in to the second day singles, the whole side were confident of winning. Once again the USA staged a wonderful recovery and it was only the three halves obtained under intense pressure by Hare, O'Connell and Milligan that enabled Great Britain and Ireland to scrape home by 12½–11½. Nevertheless it was a splendid win, the first in the Walker Cup on American soil. As a result that year Great Britain and Ireland held each of the three trophies, the Ryder, Curtis and Walker Cups, for the first time.

1922 *at National Golf Links, New York*

Foursomes

UNITED STATES	Matches	GREAT BRITAIN AND IRELAND	Matches
JP Guilford and FD Ouimet (8 and 7)	1	CJH Tolley and B Darwin	0
C Evans Jr and RA Gardner	0	RH Wethered and CC Aylmer (5 and 4)	1
RT Jones Jr and JW Sweetser (3 and 2)	1	WB Torrance and CVL Hooman	0
MR Marston and WC Fownes Jr (2 and 1)	1	J Caven and WW Mackenzie	0
	3		1

Singles

JP Guilford (2 and 1)	1	CJH Tolley	0
RT Jones Jr (3 and 2)	1	RH Wethered	0
C Evans Jr (5 and 4)	1	J Caven	0
FD Ouimet (8 and 7)	1	CC Aylmer	0
RA Gardner (7 and 5)	1	WB Torrance	0
MR Marston	0	WW Mackenzie (6 and 5)	1
WC Fownes Jr	0	B Darwin (3 and 1)	1
JW Sweetser	0	CVL Hooman (37th)	1
	5		3

Aggregate: USA 8 matches; Great Britain and Ireland 4 matches.
Captains: WC Fownes Jr, USA, and R Harris, Great Britain and Ireland (Harris was unable to play through illness).

1923 *at St Andrews*

Foursomes

GREAT BRITAIN AND IRELAND	Matches	UNITED STATES	Matches
CJH Tolley and RH Wethered (6 and 5)	1	FD Ouimet and JW Sweetser	0
R Harris and CVL Hooman	0	RA Gardner and MR Marston (7 and 6)	1
EWE Holderness and WL Hope (1 hole)	1	GV Rotan and SD Herron	0
J Wilson and WA Murray (4 and 3)	1	HR Johnston and JF Neville	0
	3		1

Singles

GREAT BRITAIN AND IRELAND	Matches	UNITED STATES	Matches
RH Wethered	½	FD Ouimet	½
CJH Tolley (4 and 3)	1	JW Sweetser	0
R Harris	0	RA Gardner (1 hole)	1
WW Mackenzie	0	GV Rotan (5 and 4)	1
WL Hope	0	MR Marston (6 and 5)	1
EWE Holderness	0	FJ Wright Jr (1 hole)	1
J Wilson (1 hole)	1	SD Herron	0
WA Murray	0	OF Willing (2 and 1)	1
	2½		5½

Aggregate: USA 6½ matches; Great Britain and Ireland 5½ matches.
Captains: R Harris, Great Britain and Ireland, and RA Gardner, USA.

1924 *at Garden City, New York*

Foursomes

UNITED STATES	Matches	GREAT BRITAIN AND IRELAND	Matches
MR Marston and RA Gardner (3 and 1)	1	EF Storey and WA Murray	0
JP Guilford and FD Ouimet (2 and 1)	1	CJH Tolley and CO Hezlet	0
RT Jones Jr and WC Fownes Jr	0	Hon M Scott and R Scott Jr (1 hole)	1
JW Sweetser and HR Johnston (4 and 3)	1	TA Torrance and OC Bristowe	0
	3		1

Singles

MR Marston	0	CJH Tolley (1 hole)	1
RT Jones Jr (4 and 3)	1	CO Hezlet	0
C Evans Jr (2 and 1)	1	WA Murray	0
FD Ouimet (1 hole)	1	EF Storey	0
JW Sweetser	0	Hon M Scott (7 and 6)	1
RA Gardner (3 and 2)	1	WL Hope	0
JP Guilford (2 and 1)	1	TA Torrance	0
OF Willing (3 and 2)	1	DH Kyle	0
	6		**2**

Aggregate: USA 9 matches; Great Britain and Ireland 3 matches.
Captains: RA Gardner, USA, and CJH Tolley, Great Britain and Ireland.

1926 *at St Andrews*

Foursomes

GREAT BRITAIN AND IRELAND	Matches	UNITED STATES	Matches
RH Wethered and EWE Holderness (5 and 4)	1	FD Ouimet and JP Guilford	0
CJH Tolley and A Jamieson Jr	0	RT Jones Jr and W Gunn (4 and 3)	1
R Harris and CO Hezlet	0	G Von Elm and JW Sweetser (8 and 7)	1
EF Storey and Hon WGE Brownlow	0	RA Gardner and RR MacKenzie (1 hole)	1
	1		**3**

Singles

CJH Tolley	0	RT Jones Jr (12 and 11)	1
EWE Holderness	0	JW Sweetser (4 and 3)	1
RH Wethered (5 and 4)	1	FD Ouimet	0
CO Hezlet	1/2	G Von Elm	1/2
R Harris (2 and 1)	1	JP Guilford	0
Hon WGE Brownlow	0	W Gunn (9 and 8)	1
EF Storey (2 and 1)	1	RR MacKenzie	0
A Jamieson Jr (5 and 4)	1	RA Gardner	0
	4½		**3½**

Aggregate: USA 6½ matches; Great Britain and Ireland 5½ matches.
Captains: R Harris, Great Britain and Ireland, and RA Gardner, USA.

1928 *at Wheaton, Chicago, Illinois*

Foursomes

UNITED STATES		GREAT BRITAIN AND IRELAND	
	Matches		Matches
JW Sweetser and G Von Elm (7 and 6)	1	TP Perkins and W Tweddell	0
RT Jones Jr and C Evans Jr (5 and 3)	1	CO Hezlet and WL Hope	0
FD Ouimet and HR Johnston (4 and 2)	1	TA Torrance and EF Storey	0
W Gunn and RR MacKenzie (7 and 5)	1	JB Beck and GNC Martin	0
	4		0

Singles

	Matches		Matches
RT Jones Jr (13 and 12)	1	TP Perkins	0
G Von Elm (3 and 2)	1	W Tweddell	0
FD Ouimet (8 and 7)	1	CO Hezlet	0
JW Sweetser (5 and 4)	1	WL Hope	0
HR Johnston (4 and 2)	1	EF Storey	0
C Evans Jr	0	TA Torrance (1 hole)	1
W Gunn (11 and 10)	1	RH Hardman	0
RR MacKenzie (2 and 1)	1	GNC Martin	0
	7		1

Aggregate: USA 11 matches; Great Britain and Ireland 1 match.
Captains: RT Jones Jr, USA, and W Tweddell, Great Britain and Ireland.

1930 *at St George's, Sandwich*

Foursomes

GREAT BRITAIN AND IRELAND		UNITED STATES	
	Matches		Matches
CJH Tolley and RH Wethered (2 holes)	1	G Von Elm and GJ Voigt	0
RW Hartley and TA Torrance	0	RT Jones Jr and OF Willing (8 and 7)	1
EWE Holderness and JA Stout	0	RR MacKenzie and DK Moe (2 and 1)	1
W Campbell and JN Smith	0	HR Johnston and FD Ouimet (2 and 1)	1
	1		3

Singles

CJH Tolley	0	HR Johnston (5 and 4)	1
RH Wethered	0	RT Jones Jr (9 and 8)	1
RW Hartley	0	G Von Elm (3 and 2)	1
EWE Holderness	0	GJ Voigt (10 and 8)	1
JN Smith	0	OF Willing (2 and 1)	1
TA Torrance (7 and 6)	1	FD Ouimet	0
JA Stout	0	DK Moe (1 hole)	1
W Campbell	0	RR MacKenzie (6 and 5)	1
	—		—
	1		7

Aggregate: USA 10 matches; Great Britain and Ireland 2 matches.
Captains: RH Wethered, Great Britain and Ireland, and RT Jones Jr, USA.

1932   *at The Country Club, Brookline, Massachusetts*

Foursomes

UNITED STATES	Matches	GREAT BRITAIN AND IRELAND	Matches
JW Sweetser and GJ Voigt (7 and 6)	1	RW Hartley and WL Hartley	0
CH Seaver and GT Moreland (6 and 5)	1	TA Torrance and JG de Forest	0
FD Ouimet and GT Dunlap Jr (7 and 6)	1	JA Stout and J Burke	0
DK Moe and W Howell (5 and 4)	1	EW Fiddian and EA McRuvie	0
	—		—
	4		0

Singles

FD Ouimet	½	TA Torrance	½
JW Sweetser	½	JA Stout	½
GT Moreland (2 and 1)	1	RW Hartley	0
J Westland	½	J Burke	½
GJ Voigt	0	LG Crawley (1 hole)	1
MJ McCarthy Jr (3 and 2)	1	WL Hartley	0
CH Seaver (7 and 6)	1	EW Fiddian	0
GT Dunlap Jr (10 and 9)	1	EA McRuvie	0
	—		—
	5½		2½

Aggregate: USA 9½ matches; Great Britain and Ireland 2½ matches.
Captains: FD Ouimet, USA, and TA Torrance, Great Britain and Ireland.

1934   *at St Andrews*

Foursomes

GREAT BRITAIN AND IRELAND	Matches	**UNITED STATES**	Matches
RH Wethered and CJH Tolley	0	JG Goodman and WL Little Jr (8 and 6)	1
HG Bentley and EW Fiddian	0	GT Moreland and J Westland (6 and 5)	1
Hon M Scott and SL McKinlay	0	HC Egan and MR Marston (3 and 2)	1
EA McRuvie and J McLean (4 and 2)	1	FD Ouimet and GT Dunlap Jr	0
	1		3

Singles

	Matches		Matches
Hon M Scott	0	JG Goodman (7 and 6)	1
CJH Tolley	0	WL Little Jr (6 and 5)	1
LG Crawley	0	FD Ouimet (5 and 4)	1
J McLean	0	GT Dunlap Jr (4 and 3)	1
EW Fiddian	0	JW Fischer (5 and 4)	1
SL McKinlay	0	GT Moreland (3 and 1)	1
EA McRuvie	¹/₂	J Westland	¹/₂
TA Torrance (4 and 3)	1	MR Marston	0
	1¹/₂		6¹/₂

Aggregate: USA 9¹/₂ matches; Great Britain and Ireland 2¹/₂ matches.
Captains: Hon M Scott, Great Britain and Ireland, and FD Ouimet, USA.

1936   *at Pine Valley, New Jersey*

Foursomes

UNITED STATES	Matches	**GREAT BRITAIN AND IRELAND**	Matches
JG Goodman and AE Campbell (7 and 5)	1	H Thomson and HG Bentley	0
R Smith and E White (8 and 7)	1	J McLean and JDA Langley	0
CR Yates and W Emery	¹/₂	GB Peters and JM Dykes	¹/₂
HL Givan and GJ Voigt	¹/₂	GA Hill and RC Ewing	¹/₂
	3		1

Singles

JG Goodman (3 and 2)	1	H Thomson	0
AE Campbell (5 and 4)	1	J McLean	0
JW Fischer (8 and 7)	1	RC Ewing	0
R Smith (11 and 9)	1	GA Hill	0
W Emery (1 hole)	1	GB Peters	0
CR Yates (8 and 7)	1	JM Dykes	0
GT Dunlap Jr	½	HG Bentley	½
E White (6 and 5)	1	JDA Langley	0
	—		—
	7½		½

Aggregate: USA 10½ matches; Great Britain and Ireland 1½ matches.
Captains: FD Ouimet, USA, and W Tweddell, Great Britain and Ireland.

1938 *at St Andrews*

Foursomes

GREAT BRITAIN AND IRELAND		UNITED STATES	
	Matches		Matches
HG Bentley and J Bruen Jr	½	JW Fischer and CR Kocsis	½
GB Peters and H Thomson (4 and 2)	1	JG Goodman and MH Ward	0
AT Kyle and C Stowe	0	CR Yates and RE Billows (3 and 2)	1
JJF Pennink and LG Crawley (3 and 1)	1	R Smith and F Haas Jr	0
	—		—
	2½		1½

Singles

J Bruen Jr	0	CR Yates (2 and 1)	1
H Thomson (6 and 4)	1	JG Goodman	0
LG Crawley	0	JW Fischer (3 and 2)	1
C Stowe (2 and 1)	1	CR Kocsis	0
JJF Pennink	0	MH Ward (12 and 11)	1
RC Ewing (1 hole)	1	RE Billows	0
GB Peters (9 and 8)	1	R Smith	0
AT Kyle (5 and 4)	1	F Haas Jr	0
	—		—
	5		3

Aggregate: Great Britain and Ireland 7½ matches; USA 4½ matches.
Captains: JB Beck, Great Britain and Ireland, and FD Ouimet, USA.

1947   *at St Andrews*

Foursomes

GREAT BRITAIN AND IRELAND	Matches	UNITED STATES	Matches
JB Carr and RC Ewing	0	SE Bishop and RH Riegel (3 and 2)	1
LG Crawley and PB Lucas (5 and 4)	1	MH Ward and SL Quick	0
AT Kyle and JC Wilson	0	WP Turnesa and AF Kammer Jr (5 and 4)	1
RJ White and C Stowe (4 and 3)	1	FR Stranahan and RD Chapman	0
	2		2

Singles

	Matches		Matches
LG Crawley	0	MH Ward (5 and 3)	1
JB Carr (5 and 3)	1	SE Bishop	0
GH Micklem	0	RH Riegel (6 and 5)	1
RC Ewing	0	WP Turnesa (6 and 5)	1
C Stowe	0	FR Stranahan (2 and 1)	1
RJ White (4 and 3)	1	AF Kammer Jr	0
JC Wilson	0	SL Quick (8 and 6)	1
PB Lucas	0	RD Chapman (4 and 3)	1
	2		6

Aggregate: USA 8 matches; Great Britain and Ireland 4 matches.
Captains: JB Beck, Great Britain and Ireland, and FD Ouimet, USA.

1949   *at Winged Foot, New York*

Foursomes

UNITED STATES	Matches	GREAT BRITAIN AND IRELAND	Matches
RE Billows and WP Turnesa	0	JB Carr and RJ White (3 and 2)	1
CR Kocsis and FR Stranahan (2 and 1)	1	J Bruen Jr and SM McCready	0
SE Bishop and RH Riegel (9 and 7)	1	RC Ewing and GH Micklem	0
JW Dawson and BN McCormick (8 and 7)	1	KG Thom and AH Perowne	0
	3		1

Singles

WP Turnesa	0	RJ White (4 and 3)	1
FR Stranahan (6 and 5)	1	SM McCready	0
RH Riegel (5 and 4)	1	J Bruen Jr	0
JW Dawson (5 and 3)	1	JB Carr	0
CR Coe (1 hole)	1	RC Ewing	0
RE Billows (2 and 1)	1	KG Thom	0
CR Kocsis (4 and 2)	1	AH Perowne	0
JB McHale Jr (5 and 4)	1	GH Micklem	0
	—		—
	7		1

Aggregate: USA 10 matches; Great Britain and Ireland 2 matches.
Captains: FD Ouimet, USA, and PB Lucas, Great Britain and Ireland.

1951 *at Birkdale*

Foursomes

GREAT BRITAIN AND IRELAND	Matches	UNITED STATES	Matches
RJ White and JB Carr	¹/₂	FR Stranahan and WC Campbell	¹/₂
RC Ewing and JDA Langley	¹/₂	CR Coe and JB McHale Jr	¹/₂
AT Kyle and I Caldwell	0	RD Chapman and RW Knowles Jr (1 hole)	1
J Bruen Jr and JL Morgan	0	WP Turnesa and S Urzetta (5 and 4)	1
	—		—
	1		3

Singles

SM McCready	0	S Urzetta (4 and 3)	1
JB Carr (2 and 1)	1	FR Stranahan	0
RJ White (2 and 1)	1	CR Coe	0
JDA Langley	0	JB McHale Jr (2 holes)	1
RC Ewing	0	WC Campbell (5 and 4)	1
AT Kyle (2 holes)	1	WP Turnesa	0
I Caldwell	¹/₂	HD Paddock Jr	¹/₂
JL Morgan	0	RD Chapman (7 and 6)	1
	—		—
	3¹/₂		4¹/₂

Aggregate: USA 7¹/₂ matches; Great Britain and Ireland 4¹/₂ matches.
Captains: RH Oppenheimer, Great Britain and Ireland, and WP Turnesa, USA.

1953 *at Kittansett, Massachusetts*

Foursomes

UNITED STATES	Matches	GREAT BRITAIN AND IRELAND	Matches
S Urzetta and K Venturi (6 and 4)	1	JB Carr and RJ White	0
EH Ward Jr and J Westland (9 and 8)	1	JDA Langley and AH Perowne	0
JG Jackson and GA Littler (3 and 2)	1	JC Wilson and RC MacGregor	0
WC Campbell and CR Coe	0	GH Micklem and JL Morgan (4 and 3)	1
	3		1

Singles

	Matches		Matches
EH Ward Jr (4 and 3)	1	JB Carr	0
RD Chapman	0	RH White (1 hole)	1
GA Littler (5 and 3)	1	GH Micklem	0
J Westland (7 and 5)	1	RC MacGregor	0
DR Cherry (9 and 7)	1	NV Drew	0
K Venturi (9 and 8)	1	JC Wilson	0
CR Coe	0	JL Morgan (3 and 2)	1
S Urzetta (3 and 2)	1	JDA Langley	0
	6		2

Aggregate: USA 9 matches; Great Britain and Ireland 3 matches.
Captains: CR Yates, USA, and AA Duncan, Great Britain and Ireland.

1955

at St Andrews

Foursomes

GREAT BRITAIN AND IRELAND	Matches	UNITED STATES	Matches
JB Carr and RJ White	0	EH Ward Jr and DR Cherry (1 hole)	1
GH Micklem and L Morgan	0	WJ Patton and RL Yost (2 and 1)	1
I Caldwell and EB Millward	0	JW Conrad and D Morey (3 and 2)	1
DA Blair and JR Cater	0	BH Cudd and JG Jackson (5 and 4)	1
	0		4

Singles

RJ White	0	EH Ward Jr (6 and 5)	1
PF Scrutton	0	WJ Patton (2 and 1)	1
I Caldwell (1 hole)	1	D Morey	0
JB Carr	0	DR Cherry (5 and 4)	1
DA Blair (1 hole)	1	JW Conrad	0
EB Millward	0	BH Cudd (2 holes)	1
RC Ewing	0	JG Jackson (6 and 4)	1
JL Morgan	0	RL Yost (8 and 7)	1
	—		—
	2		6

Aggregrate: USA 10 matches; Great Britain and Ireland 2 matches.
Captains: GA Hill, Great Britain and Ireland, and WC Campbell, USA.

1957 *at Minikahda, Minnesota*

Foursomes

UNITED STATES	Matches	GREAT BRITAIN AND IRELAND	Matches
R Baxter Jr and WJ Patton (2 and 1)	1	JB Carr and FWG Deighton	0
WC Campbell and FM Taylor Jr (4 and 3)	1	AF Bussell and PF Scrutton	0
AS Blum and CR Kocsis	0	RR Jack and D Sewell (1 hole)	1
H Robbins Jr and EM Rudolph	½	AE Shepperson and GB Wolstenholme	½
	—		—
	2½		1½

Singles

WJ Patton (1 hole)	1	RR Jack	0
WC Campbell (3 and 2)	1	JB Carr	0
R Baxter Jr (4 and 3)	1	A Thirlwell	0
W Hyndman III (7 and 6)	1	FWG Deighton	0
JE Campbell	0	AF Bussell (2 and 1)	1
FM Taylor Jr (1 hole)	1	D Sewell	0
EM Rudolph (3 and 2)	1	PF Scrutton	0
H Robbins Jr	0	GB Wolstenholme (2 and 1)	1
	—		—
	6		2

Aggregate: USA 8½ matches; Great Britain and Ireland 3½ matches.
Captains: CR Coe, USA, and GH Micklem, Great Britain and Ireland.

1959 *at Muirfield*

Foursomes

GREAT BRITAIN AND IRELAND	Matches	UNITED STATES	Matches
RR Jack and DN Sewell	0	EH Ward Jr and FM Taylor Jr (1 hole)	1
JB Carr and GB Wolstenholme	0	W Hyndman III and TD Aaron (1 hole)	1
MF Bonallack and AH Perowne	0	WJ Patton and CR Coe (9 and 8)	1
MSR Lunt and AE Shepperson	0	HW Wettlaufer and JW Nicklaus (2 and 1)	1
	—		—
	0		4

Singles

	Matches		Matches
JB Carr (3 and 1)	1	CR Coe	0
GB Wolstenholme	0	EH Ward Jr (9 and 8)	1
RR Jack (5 and 3)	1	WJ Patton	0
DN Sewell	0	W Hyndman III (4 and 3)	1
AE Shepperson (2 and 1)	1	TD Aaron	0
MF Bonallack	0	DR Beman (2 holes)	1
MSR Lunt	0	HW Wettlaufer (6 and 5)	1
WD Smith	0	JW Nicklaus (5 and 4)	1
	—		—
	3		5

Aggregate: USA 9 matches; Great Britain and Ireland 3 matches.
Captains: GH Micklem, Great Britain and Ireland, and CR Coe, USA.

1961 *at Seattle, Washington*

Foursomes

UNITED STATES	Matches	GREAT BRITAIN AND IRELAND	Matches
DR Beman and JW Nicklaus (6 and 5)	1	J Walker and BHG Chapman	0
CR Coe and DR Cherry (1 hole)	1	DA Blair and MJ Christmas	0
W Hyndman III and RW Gardner (4 and 3)	1	JB Carr and G Huddy	0
RE Cochran and ES Andrews (4 and 3)	1	MF Bonallack and RDBM Shade	0
	—		—
	4		0

Singles

DR Beman (3 and 2)	1	MF Bonallack	0
CR Coe (5 and 4)	1	MSR Lunt	0
FM Taylor Jr (3 and 2)	1	J Walker	0
W Hyndman III (7 and 6)	1	DW Frame	0
JW Nicklaus (6 and 4)	1	JB Carr	0
CB Smith	0	MJ Christmas (3 and 2)	1
RW Gardner (1 hole)	1	RDBM Shade	0
DR Cherry (5 and 4)	1	DA Blair	0
	—		—
	7		1

Aggregate: USA 11 matches; Great Britain and Ireland 1 match.
Captains: J Westland, USA, and CD Lawrie, Great Britain and Ireland.

1963 *at Turnberry*

First Series

Foursomes

GREAT BRITAIN AND IRELAND		UNITED STATES	
	Matches		Matches
MF Bonallack and SWT Murray (4 and 3)	1	WJ Patton and RH Sikes	0
JB Carr and CW Green	0	AD Gray Jr and LE Harris Jr (2 holes)	1
MSR Lunt and DB Sheahan	0	DR Beman and CR Coe (5 and 3)	1
JFD Madeley and RDBM Shade	½	RW Gardner and ER Updegraff	½
	—		—
	1½		2½

Singles

SWT Murray (3 and 1)	1	DR Beman	0
MJ Christmas	0	WJ Patton (3 and 2)	1
JB Carr (7 and 5)	1	RH Sikes	0
DB Sheahan (1 hole)	1	LE Harris Jr	0
MF Bonallack (1 hole)	1	RD Davies	0
AC Saddler	½	CR Coe	½
RDBM Shade (4 and 3)	1	AD Gray Jr	0
MSR Lunt	½	CB Smith	½
	—		—
	6		2

First Series Total: Great Britain and Ireland 7½; United States 4½.

Second Series

Foursomes

MF Bonallack and SWT Murray	0	WJ Patton and RH Sikes (1 hole)	1
MSR Lunt and DB Sheahan	0	AD Gray Jr and LE Harris Jr (3 and 2)	1
CW Green and AC Saddler	0	RW Gardner and ER Updegraff (3 and 1)	1
JFD Madeley and RDBM Shade	0	DR Beman and CR Coe (3 and 2)	1
	—		—
	0		4

Singles

SWT Murray	0	WJ Patton (3 and 2)	1
DB Sheahan (1 hole)	1	RD Davies	0
JB Carr	0	ER Updegraff (4 and 3)	1
MF Bonallack	0	LE Harris Jr (3 and 2)	1
MSR Lunt	0	RW Gardner (3 and 2)	1
AC Saddler	½	DR Beman	½
RDBM Shade (2 and 1)	1	AD Gray Jr	0
CW Green	0	CR Coe (4 and 3)	1
	2½		5½

Second Series Total: Great Britain and Ireland 2½; United States 9½.

Grand Aggregate: USA 14 matches; Great Britain and Ireland 10 matches.
Captains: CD Lawrie, Great Britain and Ireland, and RS Tufts, USA.

1965   *Five Farms, Maryland*

First Series

Foursomes

UNITED STATES		**GREAT BRITAIN AND IRELAND**	
	Matches		Matches
WC Campbell and AD Gray Jr	0	MSR Lunt and GB Cosh (1 hole)	1
DR Beman and DC Allen	½	MF Bonallack and CA Clark	½
WJ Patton and EM Tutwiler (5 and 4)	1	R Foster and G Clark	0
JM Hopkins and D Eichelberger	0	P Townsend and RDBM Shade (2 and 1)	1
	1½		2½

Singles

WC Campbell (6 and 5)	1	MF Bonallack	0
DR Beman (2 holes)	1	R Foster	0
AD Gray Jr	0	RDBM Shade (3 and 1)	1
JM Hopkins	0	CA Clark (5 and 3)	1
WJ Patton	0	P Townsend (3 and 2)	1
D Morey	0	AC Saddler (2 and 1)	1
DC Allen	0	GB Cosh (2 holes)	1
ER Updegraff	0	MSR Lunt (2 and 1)	1
	2		6

First Series Total: United States 3½; Great Britain and Ireland 8½.

Second Series

Foursomes

WC Campbell and AD Gray Jr (4 and 3)	1	AC Saddler and R Foster	0
DR Beman and D Eichelberger	0	RDBM Shade and P Townsend (2 and 1)	1
EM Tutwiler and WJ Patton (2 and 1)	1	GB Cosh and MSR Lunt	0
DC Allen and D Morey	0	CA Clark and MF Bonallack (2 and 1)	1
	2		2

Singles

WC Campbell (3 and 2)	1	R Foster	0
DR Beman (1 hole)	1	AC Saddler	0
EM Tutwiler (5 and 3)	1	RDBM Shade	0
DC Allen	0	GB Cosh (4 and 3)	1
AD Gray Jr (1 hole)	1	P Townsend	0
JM Hopkins	1/2	CA Clark	1/2
D Eichelberger (5 and 3)	1	MF Bonallack	0
WJ Patton (4 and 2)	1	MSR Lunt	0
	6 1/2		1 1/2

Second Series Total: United States 8 1/2; Great Britain and Ireland 3 1/2.

Grand Aggregate: USA 12 matches; Great Britain and Ireland 12 matches.
Captains: JW Fischer, USA, and JB Carr, Great Britain and Ireland.

1967 *at St George's, Sandwich*

First Series

Foursomes

GREAT BRITAIN AND IRELAND	Matches	UNITED STATES	Matches
RDBM Shade and P Oosterhuis	1/2	RJ Murphy Jr and RJ Cerrudo	1/2
R Foster and AC Saddler	0	WC Campbell and W Lewis Jr (1 hole)	1
MF Bonallack and MF Attenborough	0	AD Gray Jr and EM Tutwiler (4 and 2)	1
JB Carr and T Craddock	0	RB Dickson and JA Grant (3 and 1)	1
	1/2		3 1/2

Singles

RDBM Shade	0	WC Campbell (2 and 1)	1
R Foster	0	RJ Murphy Jr (2 and 1)	1
MF Bonallack	¹/₂	AD Gray Jr	¹/₂
MF Attenborough	0	RJ Cerrudo (4 and 3)	1
P Oosterhuis	0	RB Dickson (6 and 4)	1
T Craddock	0	JW Lewis Jr (2 and 1)	1
AK Pirie	¹/₂	DC Allen	¹/₂
AC Saddler (3 and 2)	1	MA Fleckman	0
	—		—
	2		6

First Series Total: Great Britain and Ireland 2¹/₂; United States 9¹/₂.

Second Series

Foursomes

MF Bonallack and T Craddock (2 holes)	1	RJ Murphy Jr and RJ Cerrudo	0
AC Saddler and AK Pirie	0	WC Campbell and W Lewis Jr (1 hole)	1
RDBM Shade and P Oosterhuis (3 and 1)	1	AD Gray Jr and EM Tutwiler	0
R Foster and DJ Millensted (2 and 1)	1	DC Allen and MA Fleckman	0
	—		—
	3		1

Singles

RDBM Shade	0	WC Campbell (3 and 2)	1
MF Bonallack (4 and 2)	1	RJ Murphy Jr	0
AC Saddler (3 and 2)	1	AD Gray Jr	0
R Foster	¹/₂	RJ Cerrudo	¹/₂
AK Pirie	0	RB Dickson (4 and 3)	1
T Craddock (5 and 4)	1	JW Lewis Jr	0
P Oosterhuis	0	JA Grant (1 hole)	1
DJ Millensted	0	EM Tutwiler (3 and 1)	1
	—		—
	3¹/₂		4¹/₂

Second Series Total: Great Britain and Ireland 6¹/₂; United States 5¹/₂.

Grand Aggregate: USA 15 matches; Great Britain and Ireland 9 matches.
Captains: JB Carr, Great Britain and Ireland, JW Sweetser, USA.

1969 *at Milwaukee, Wisconsin*

First Series

Foursomes

UNITED STATES	Matches	GREAT BRITAIN AND IRELAND	Matches
M Giles III and S Melnyk (3 and 2)	1	MF Bonallack and T Craddock	0
B Fleisher and A Miller III	1/2	PJ Benka and B Critchley	1/2
L Wadkins and RL Siderowf	0	CW Green and A Brooks (3 and 2)	1
W Hyndman III and J Inman Jr (2 and 1)	1	R Foster and GC Marks	0
	2 1/2		1 1/2

Singles

	Matches		Matches
B Fleisher	1/2	MF Bonallack	1/2
M Giles III (1 hole)	1	CW Green	0
A Miller III (1 hole)	1	B Critchley	0
RL Siderowf (6 and 5)	1	LP Tupling	0
S Melnyk	0	PJ Benka (3 and 1)	1
L Wadkins	0	GC Marks (1 hole)	1
J Bohmann (2 and 1)	1	MG King	0
ER Updegraff (6 and 5)	1	R Foster	0
	5 1/2		2 1/2

First Series Total: United States 8; Great Britain and Ireland 4.

Second Series

Foursomes

M Giles III and S Melnyk	1/2	CW Green and A Brooks	1/2
B Fleisher and A Miller III	0	PJ Benka and B Critchley (2 and 1)	1
RL Siderowf and L Wadkins (6 and 5)	1	R Foster and MG King	0
ER Updegraff and J Bohmann	0	MF Bonallack and LP Tupling (4 and 3)	1
	1 1/2		2 1/2

Singles

B Fleisher	0	MF Bonallack (5 and 4)	1
RL Siderowf	1/2	B Critchley	1/2
A Miller III (1 hole)	1	MG King	0
M Giles III	1/2	T Craddock	1/2
J Inman Jr (2 and 1)	1	PJ Benka	0
J Bohmann	0	A Brooks (4 and 3)	1
W Hyndman III	1/2	CW Green	1/2
ER Updegraff	0	GC Marks (3 and 2)	1
	3 1/2		4 1/2

Second Series Total: United States 5; Great Britain and Ireland 7.

Grand Aggregate: USA 13 matches; Great Britain and Ireland 11 matches.
Captains: WJ Patton, USA, and MF Bonallack, Great Britain and Ireland.

1971 *at St Andrews*

First Series

Foursomes

GREAT BRITAIN AND IRELAND	Matches	UNITED STATES	Matches
MF Bonallack and W Humphreys (1 hole)	1	L Wadkins and JB Simons	0
CW Green and RJ Carr (1 hole)	1	S Melnyk and M Giles III	0
DM Marsh and G Macgregor (2 and 1)	1	AL Miller III and J Farquhar	0
JS Macdonald and R Foster (2 and 1)	1	WC Campbell and T Kite	0
	4		0

Singles

CW Green	0	L Wadkins (1 hole)	1
MF Bonallack	0	M Giles III (1 hole)	1
GC Marks	0	AL Miller III (1 hole)	1
JS Macdonald	0	S Melnyk (3 and 2)	1
RJ Carr	1/2	W Hyndman III	1/2
W Humphreys	0	JR Gabrielsen (1 hole)	1
HB Stuart (3 and 2)	1	J Farquhar	0
R Foster	0	T Kite (3 and 2)	1
	1 1/2		6 1/2

First Series Total: Great Britain and Ireland 5 1/2; United States 6 1/2.

Second Series

Foursomes

GC Marks and CW Green	0	S Melnyk and M Giles III (1 hole)	1
HB Stuart and RJ Carr (1 hole)	1	L Wadkins and R Gabrielsen	0
DM Marsh and MF Bonallack	0	AL Miller III and J Farquhar (5 and 4)	1
JS Macdonald and R Foster	1/2	WC Campbell and T Kite	1/2
	1 1/2		2 1/2

Singles

MF Bonallack	0	L Wadkins (3 and 1)	1
HB Stuart (2 and 1)	1	M Giles III	0
W Humphreys (2 and 1)	1	S Melnyk	0
CW Green (1 hole)	1	AL Miller III	0
RJ Carr (2 holes)	1	JB Simons	0
G Macgregor (1 hole)	1	JR Gabrielsen	0
DM Marsh (1 hole)	1	W Hyndman III	0
GC Marks	0	T Kite (3 and 2)	1
	6		2

Second Series Total: Great Britain and Ireland 7 1/2; United States 4 1/2.

Grand Aggregate: Great Britain and Ireland 13 matches; USA 11 matches.
Captains: MF Bonallack, Great Britain and Ireland, and JM Winters Jr, USA.

1973 *at The Country Club, Brookline, Massachusetts*

First Series

Foursomes

UNITED STATES		GREAT BRITAIN AND IRELAND	
	Matches		Matches
M Giles III and G Koch	½	MG King and P Hedges	½
RL Siderowf and M Pfeil (5 and 4)	1	HB Stuart and J Davies	0
D Edwards and J Ellis (2 and 1)	1	CW Green and WT Milne	0
M West and D Ballenger (2 and 1)	1	R Foster and TWB Homer	0
	3½		½

Singles

M Giles III (5 and 4)	1	HB Stuart	0
RL Siderowf (4 and 2)	1	MF Bonallack	0
G Koch	0	J Davies (1 hole)	1
M West	0	HK Clark (2 and 1)	1
D Edwards (2 holes)	1	R Foster	0
M Killian	0	MG King (1 hole)	1
W Rodgers	0	CW Green (1 hole)	1
M Pfeil	0	WT Milne (4 and 3)	1
	3		5

First Series Total: United States 6½; Great Britain and Ireland 5½.

Second Series

Foursomes

M Giles III and G Koch (7 and 5)	1	TWB Homer and R Foster	0
RL Siderowf and M Pfeil	½	HK Clark and JC Davies	½
D Edwards and J Ellis (2 and 1)	1	P Hedges and MG King	0
W Rodgers and M Killian (1 hole)	1	HB Stuart and WT Milne	0
	3½		½

Singles

J Ellis	0	HB Stuart (5 and 4)	1
RL Siderowf	0	JC Davies (3 and 2)	1
D Edwards (2 and 1)	1	TWB Homer	0
M Giles III	½	CW Green	½
M West (1 hole)	1	MG King	0
M Killian	0	WT Milne (2 and 1)	1
G Koch	½	P Hedges	½
M Pfeil (1 hole)	1	HK Clark	0
	4		4

Second Series Total: United States 7½; Great Britain and Ireland 4½.

Grand Aggregate: USA 14 matches; Great Britain and Ireland 10 matches.
Captains: JW Sweetser, USA, and DM Marsh, Great Britain and Ireland.

1975 *at St Andrews*

First Series

Foursomes

GREAT BRITAIN AND IRELAND	Matches	UNITED STATES	Matches
M James and GRD Eyles (1 hole)	1	J Pate and RL Siderowf	0
JC Davies and MA Poxon	0	GF Burns and C Stadler (5 and 4)	1
CW Green and HB Stuart	0	J Haas and C Strange (2 and 1)	1
G Macgregor and IC Hutcheon	0	M Giles III and G Koch (5 and 4)	1
	1		3

Singles

M James (2 and 1)	1	J Pate	0
JC Davies	1/2	C Strange	1/2
P Mulcare (1 hole)	1	RL Siderowf	0
HB Stuart	0	G Koch (3 and 2)	1
MA Poxon	0	J Grace (3 and 1)	1
IC Hutcheon	1/2	WC Campbell	1/2
GRD Eyles	0	J Haas (2 and 1)	1
G Macgregor	0	M Giles III (5 and 4)	1
	3		5

First Series Total: Great Britain and Ireland 4; United States 8.

Second Series

Foursomes

P Mulcare and IC Hutcheon (1 hole)	1	J Pate and RL Siderowf	0
CW Green and HB Stuart	0	GF Burns and C Stadler (1 hole)	1
M James and GRD Eyles (5 and 3)	1	WC Campbell and J Grace	0
P Hedges and JC Davies	0	J Haas and C Strange (3 and 2)	1
	2		2

Singles

IC Hutcheon (3 and 2)	1	J Pate	0
P Mulcare	0	C Strange (4 and 3)	1
M James	0	G Koch (5 and 4)	1
JC Davies (2 and 1)	1	GF Burns	0
CW Green	0	J Grace (2 and 1)	1
G Macgregor	0	C Stadler (3 and 2)	1
GRD Eyles	0	WC Campbell (2 and 1)	1
P Hedges	1/2	M Giles III	1/2
	2 1/2		5 1/2

Second Series Total: Great Britain and Ireland 4 1/2; United States 7 1/2.

Grand Aggregate: USA 15 1/2 matches; Great Britain and Ireland 8 1/2 matches .
Captains: DM Marsh, Great Britain and Ireland, and ER Updegraff, USA.

1977 *at Shinnecock Hills, New York*

First Series

Foursomes

UNITED STATES	Matches	GREAT BRITAIN AND IRELAND	Matches
J Fought and V Heafner (4 and 3)	1	AWB Lyle and P McEvoy	0
S Simpson and L Miller (5 and 4)	1	JC Davies and MJ Kelley	0
RL Siderowf and G Hallberg	0	IC Hutcheon and PD Deeble (1 hole)	1
J Sigel and M Brannan (1 hole)	1	A Brodie and S Martin	0
	3		1

Singles

L Miller (2 holes)	1	P McEvoy	0
J Fought (4 and 3)	1	IC Hutcheon	0
S Simpson (7 and 6)	1	GH Murray	0
V Heafner (4 and 3)	1	JC Davies	0
B Sander	0	A Brodie (4 and 3)	1
G Hallberg	0	S Martin (3 and 2)	1
F Ridley (2 holes)	1	AWB Lyle	0
J Sigel (5 and 3)	1	P McKellar	0
	6		2

First Series Total: United States 9; Great Britain and Ireland 3.

Second Series

Foursomes

J Fought and V Heafner (4 and 3)	1	IC Hutcheon and PD Deeble	0
L Miller and S Simpson (2 holes)	1	P McEvoy and JC Davies	0
RL Siderowf and B Sander	0	A Brodie and S Martin (6 and 4)	1
F Ridley and M Brannan	0	GH Murray and MJ Kelley (4 and 3)	1
	2		2

Singles

L Miller (1 hole)	1	S Martin	0
J Fought (2 and 1)	1	JC Davies	0
B Sander	0	A Brodie (2 and 1)	1
G Hallberg (4 and 3)	1	P McEvoy	0
RL Siderowf	0	MJ Kelley (2 and 1)	1
M Brannan	0	IC Hutcheon (2 holes)	1
F Ridley (5 and 3)	1	AWB Lyle	0
J Sigel (1 hole)	1	PD Deeble	0
	5		3

Second Series Total: United States 7; Great Britain and Ireland 5.

Grand Aggregate: USA 16 matches; Great Britain and Ireland 8 matches.
Captains: LW Oehmig, USA, and AC Saddler, Great Britain and Ireland.

1979 *at Muirfield*

First Series

Foursomes

GREAT BRITAIN AND IRELAND	Matches	UNITED STATES	Matches
P McEvoy and B Marchbank	0	S Hoch and J Sigel (1 hole)	1
G Godwin and IC Hutcheon (2 holes)	1	M West and H Sutton	0
G Brand Jr and MJ Kelley	0	D Fischesser and J Holtgrieve (1 hole)	1
A Brodie and I Carslaw (2 and 1)	1	G Moody and M Gove	0
	2		2

Singles

	Matches		Matches
P McEvoy	½	J Sigel	½
JC Davies	0	D Clarke (8 and 7)	1
J Buckley	0	S Hoch (9 and 7)	1
IC Hutcheon	0	J Holtgrieve (6 and 4)	1
B Marchbank (1 hole)	1	M Peck	0
G Godwin (3 and 2)	1	G Moody	0
MJ Kelley (3 and 2)	1	D Fischesser	0
A Brodie	0	M Gove (3 and 2)	1
	3½		4½

First Series Total: Great Britain and Ireland 5½; United States 6½.

Second Series

Foursomes

	Matches		Matches
G Godwin and G Brand Jr	0	S Hoch and J Sigel (4 and 3)	1
P McEvoy and B Marchbank (2 and 1)	1	D Fischesser and J Holtgrieve	0
MJ Kelley and IC Hutcheon	½	M West and H Sutton	½
I Carslaw and A Brodie	½	D Clarke and M Peck	½
	2		2

Singles

	Matches		Matches
P McEvoy	0	S Hoch (3 and 1)	1
G Brand Jr	0	D Clarke (2 and 1)	1
G Godwin	0	M Gove (3 and 2)	1
IC Hutcheon	0	M Peck (2 and 1)	1
A Brodie (3 and 2)	1	M West	0
MJ Kelley	0	G Moody (3 and 2)	1
B Marchbank	0	H Sutton (3 and 1)	1
I Carslaw	0	J Sigel (2 and 1)	1
	1		7

Second Series Total: Great Britain and Ireland 3; United States 9.

Grand Aggregate: USA 15½ matches; Great Britain and Ireland 8½ matches .
Captains: R Foster, Great Britain and Ireland, and RL Siderowf, USA.

1981 *at Cypress Point, California*

First Series

Foursomes

UNITED STATES		GREAT BRITAIN AND IRELAND	
	Matches		Matches
H Sutton and J Sigel	0	P Walton and R Rafferty (4 and 2)	1
J Holtgrieve and F Fuhrer (1 hole)	1	R Chapman and P McEvoy	0
B Lewis and D von Tacky (2 and 1)	1	PD Deeble and IC Hutcheon	0
R Commans and C Pavin (5 and 4)	1	D Evans and P Way	0
	3		1

Singles

H Sutton (3 and 1)	1	R Rafferty	0
J Rassett (1 hole)	1	CR Dalgleish	0
R Commans	0	P Walton (1 hole)	1
B Lewis	0	R Chapman (2 and 1)	1
J Mudd (1 hole)	1	G Godwin	0
C Pavin (4 and 3)	1	IC Hutcheon	0
D von Tacky	0	P Way (3 and 1)	1
J Sigel (4 and 2)	1	P McEvoy	0
	5		3

First Series Total: United States 8; Great Britain and Ireland 4.

Second Series

Foursomes

H Sutton and J Sigel	0	R Chapman and P Way (1 hole)	1
J Holtgrieve and F Fuhrer	0	P Walton and R Rafferty (6 and 4)	1
B Lewis and D von Tacky	0	D Evans and CR Dalgleish (3 and 2)	1
J Rassett and J Mudd (5 and 4)	1	IC Hutcheon and G Godwin	0
	1		3

Singles

H Sutton	0	R Chapman (1 hole)	1
J Holtgrieve (2 and 1)	1	R Rafferty	0
F Fuhrer (4 and 3)	1	P Walton	0
J Sigel (6 and 5)	1	P Way	0
J Mudd (7 and 5)	1	CR Dalgleish	0
R Commans	½	G Godwin	½
J Rassett (4 and 3)	1	PD Deeble	0
C Pavin	½	D Evans	½
	6		2

Second Series Total: United States 7; Great Britain and Ireland 5.

Grand Aggregate: USA 15 matches; Great Britain and Ireland 9 matches.
Captains: J Gabrielsen, USA, and R Foster, Great Britain and Ireland.

1983   *at Hoylake*

First Series

Foursomes

GREAT BRITAIN AND IRELAND	Matches	UNITED STATES	Matches
G Macgregor and P Walton (3 and 2)	1	J Sigel and R Fehr	0
SD Keppler and A Pierse	0	W Wood and B Faxon (3 and 1)	1
ME Lewis and M Thompson	0	B Lewis Jr and J Holtgrieve (7 and 6)	1
LS Mann and A Oldcorn (5 and 4)	1	W Hoffer and D Tentis	0
	—		—
	2		2

Singles

	Matches		Matches
P Walton (1 hole)	1	J Sigel	0
SD Keppler	0	R Fehr (1 hole)	1
G Macgregor	1/2	W Wood	1/2
DG Carrick	0	B Faxon (3 and 1)	1
A Oldcorn (4 and 3)	1	B Tuten	0
P Parkin (5 and 4)	1	N Crosby	0
AD Pierse	0	B Lewis Jr (3 and 1)	1
LS Mann	0	J Holtgrieve (6 and 5)	1
	—		—
	3 1/2		4 1/2

First Series Total: Great Britain and Ireland 5 1/2; United States 6 1/2.

Second Series

Foursomes

	Matches		Matches
G Macgregor and P Walton	0	N Crosby and W Hoffer (2 holes)	1
P Parkin and ME Thompson (1 hole)	1	B Faxon and W Wood	0
LS Mann and A Oldcorn (1 hole)	1	B Lewis Jr and J Holtgrieve	0
SD Keppler and AD Pierse	1/2	J Sigel and R Fehr	1/2
	—		—
	2 1/2		1 1/2

Singles

	Matches		Matches
P Walton (2 and 1)	1	W Wood	0
P Parkin	0	B Faxon (3 and 2)	1
G Macgregor	0	R Fehr (2 and 1)	1
ME Thompson	0	B Tuten (3 and 2)	1
LS Mann	1/2	D Tentis	1/2
SD Keppler	0	B Lewis Jr (6 and 5)	1
A Oldcorn (3 and 2)	1	J Holtgrieve	0
DG Carrick	0	J Sigel (3 and 2)	1
	—		—
	2 1/2		5 1/2

Second Series Total: Great Britain and Ireland 5; United States 7.

Grand Aggregate: USA 13 1/2 matches; Great Britain and Ireland 10 1/2 matches.
Captains: CW Green, Great Britain and Ireland, and J Sigel, USA.

1985 *at Pine Valley, New Jersey*

First Series

Foursomes

UNITED STATES	Matches	GREAT BRITAIN AND IRELAND	Matches
S Verplank and J Sigel (1 hole)	1	CS Montgomerie and G Macgregor	0
D Waldorf and S Randolph	0	J Hawksworth and G McGimpsey (4 and 3)	1
R Sonnier and J Haas	0	P Baker and P McEvoy (6 and 5)	1
M Podolak and D Love	1/2	C Bloice and AR Stephen	1/2
	1½		2½

Singles

S Verplank (2 and 1)	1	G McGimpsey	0
S Randolph (5 and 4)	1	P Mayo	0
R Sonnier	1/2	J Hawksworth	1/2
J Sigel (5 and 4)	1	CS Montgomerie	0
B Lewis	0	P McEvoy (2 and 1)	1
C Burroughs	0	G Macgregor (2 holes)	1
D Waldorf (4 and 2)	1	D Gilford	0
J Haas	0	AR Stephen (2 and 1)	1
	4½		3½

First Series Total: United States 6; Great Britain and Ireland 6.

Second Series

Foursomes

S Verplank and J Sigel	1/2	P Mayo and CS Montgomerie	1/2
S Randolph and J Haas (3 and 2)	1	J Hawksworth and G McGimpsey	0
B Lewis and C Burroughs (2 and 1)	1	P Baker and P McEvoy	0
M Podolak and D Love (3 and 2)	1	C Bloice and AR Stephen	0
	3½		½

Singles

S Randolph	1/2	G McGimpsey	1/2
S Verplank (1 hole)	1	CS Montgomerie	0
J Sigel	0	J Hawksworth (4 and 3)	1
D Love (5 and 3)	1	P McEvoy	0
R Sonnier	0	P Baker (5 and 4)	1
C Burroughs	0	G Macgregor (3 and 2)	1
B Lewis (4 and 3)	1	C Bloice	0
D Waldorf	0	AR Stephen (2 and 1)	1
	3½		4½

Second Series Total: United States 7; Great Britain and Ireland 5.

Grand Aggregate: USA 13 matches; Great Britain and Ireland, 11 matches.
Captains: J Sigel, USA, and CW Green, Great Britain and Ireland.

1987 *at Sunningdale*

First Series

Foursomes

GREAT BRITAIN AND IRELAND		UNITED STATES	
	Matches		Matches
CS Montgomerie and G Shaw	0	B Alexander and B Mayfair (5 and 4)	1
D Currey and P Mayo	0	C Kite and L Mattice (2 and 1)	1
G Macgregor and J Robinson	0	B Lewis and B Loeffler (2 and 1)	1
J McHenry and P Girvan	0	J Sigel and B Andrade (3 and 2)	1
	0		4

Singles

D Currey (2 holes)	1	B Alexander	0
J Robinson	0	B Andrade (7 and 5)	1
CS Montgomerie (3 and 2)	1	J Sorenson	0
R Eggo	0	J Sigel (3 and 2)	1
J McHenry	0	B Montgomery (1 hole)	1
P Girvan	0	B Lewis (3 and 2)	1
DG Carrick	0	B Mayfair (2 holes)	1
G Shaw (1 hole)	1	C Kite	0
	3		5

First Series Total: Great Britain and Ireland 3; United States 9.

Second Series

Foursomes

D Currey and DG Carrick	0	B Lewis and B Loeffler (4 and 3)	1
CS Montgomerie and G Shaw	0	C Kite and L Mattice (5 and 3)	1
P Mayo and G Macgregor	0	J Sorenson and B Montgomery (4 and 3)	1
J McHenry and J Robinson (4 and 2)	1	J Sigel and B Andrade	0
	1		3

Singles

D Currey	0	B Alexander (5 and 4)	1
CS Montgomerie (4 and 2)	1	B Andrade	0
J McHenry (3 and 2)	1	B Loeffler	0
G Shaw	1/2	J Sorenson	1/2
J Robinson (1 hole)	1	L Mattice	0
DG Carrick	0	B Lewis (3 and 2)	1
R Eggo	0	B Mayfair (1 hole)	1
P Girvan	0	J Sigel (6 and 5)	1
	3 1/2		4 1/2

Second Series Total: Great Britain and Ireland 4 1/2; United States 7 1/2.

Grand Aggregate: Great Britain and Ireland 7 1/2 matches; USA 16 1/2 matches.
Captains: GC Marks, Great Britain and Ireland, and F Ridley, USA.

1989 *at Peachtree, Atlanta, Georgia*

First Series

Foursomes

UNITED STATES	Matches	GREAT BRITAIN AND IRELAND	Matches
R Gamez and D Martin (3 and 2)	1	R Claydon and D Prosser	0
D Yates and P Mickelson	1/2	SC Dodd and G McGimpsey	1/2
G Lesher and J Sigel	0	P McEvoy and E O'Connell (6 and 5)	1
D Eger and K Johnson	0	JW Milligan and AD Hare (2 and 1)	1
	1½		2½

Singles

	Matches		Matches
R Gamez (7 and 6)	1	JW Milligan	0
D Martin	0	R Claydon (5 and 4)	1
E Meeks	1/2	SC Dodd	1/2
R Howe	0	E O'Connell (5 and 4)	1
D Yates	0	P McEvoy (2 and 1)	1
P Mickelson (4 and 2)	1	G McGimpsey	0
G Lesher	0	C Cassells (1 hole)	1
J Sigel	1/2	RN Roderick	1/2
	3		5

First Series Total: United States 4½; Great Britain and Ireland 7½.

Second Series

Foursomes

	Matches		Matches
R Gamez and D Martin	1/2	P McEvoy and E O'Connell	1/2
J Sigel and G Lesher	0	R Claydon and C Cassells (3 and 2)	1
D Eger and K Johnson	0	JW Milligan and AD Hare (2 and 1)	1
P Mickelson and D Yates	0	G McGimpsey and SC Dodd (2 and 1)	1
	1/2		3½

Singles

	Matches		Matches
R Gamez (1 hole)	1	SC Dodd	0
D Martin	1/2	AD Hare	1/2
G Lesher (3 and 2)	1	R Claydon	0
D Yates (4 and 3)	1	P McEvoy	0
P Mickelson	1/2	E O'Connell	1/2
D Eger (4 and 2)	1	RN Roderick	0
GK Johnson (4 and 2)	1	C Cassells	0
J Sigel	1/2	JW Milligan	1/2
	6½		1½

Second Series Total: United States 7; Great Britain and Ireland 5.

Grand Aggregate: USA 11½ matches; Great Britain and Ireland 12½ matches.
Captains: F Ridley, USA, and GC Marks, Great Britain and Ireland.

Individual Records

Great Britain and Ireland

Name		Year	Played	Won	Lost	Halved
MF Attenborough	Eng	1967	2	0	2	0
CC Aylmer	Eng	1922	2	1	1	0
P Baker	Eng	1985	3	2	1	0
JB Beck	Eng	1928-(38)-(47)	1	0	1	0
PJ Benka	Eng	1969	4	2	1	1
HG Bentley	Eng	1934-36-38	4	0	2	2
DA Blair	Scot	1955-61	4	1	3	0
C Bloice	Scot	1985	3	0	2	1
MF Bonallack	Eng	1957-59-61-63-65-67-69-71-73	25	8	14	3
G Brand	Scot	1979	3	0	3	0
OC Bristowe	Eng	(1923)-24	1	0	1	0
A Brodie	Scot	1977-79	8	5	2	1
A Brooks	Scot	1969	3	2	0	1
Hon WGE Brownlow	Eng	1926	2	0	2	0
J Bruen	Ire	1938-49-51	5	0	4	1
JA Buckley	Wales	1979	1	0	1	0
J Burke	Ire	1932	2	0	1	1
AF Bussell	Scot	1957	2	1	1	0
I Caldwell	Eng	1951-55	4	1	2	1
W Campbell	Scot	1930	2	0	2	0
JB Carr	Ire	1947-49-51-53-55-57-59-61-63-(65)-67	20	5	14	1
RJ Carr	Ire	1971	4	3	0	1
DG Carrick	Scot	1983-87	5	0	5	0
IA Carslaw	Scot	1979	3	1	1	1
C Cassells	Eng	1989	3	2	1	0
JR Cater	Scot	1955	1	0	1	0
J Caven	Scot	1922	2	0	2	0
BHG Chapman	Eng	1961	1	0	1	0
R Chapman	Eng	1981	4	3	1	0
MJ Christmas	Eng	1961-63	3	1	2	0
*CA Clark	Eng	1965	4	2	0	2
GJ Clark	Eng	1965	1	0	1	0
*HK Clark	Eng	1973	3	1	1	1
R Claydon	Eng	1989	4	2	2	0
GB Cosh	Scot	1965	4	3	1	0
T Craddock	Ire	1967-69	6	2	3	1
LG Crawley	Eng	1932-34-38-47	6	3	3	0
B Critchley	Eng	1969	4	1	1	2
D Curry	Eng	1987	4	1	3	0
CR Dalgleish	Scot	1981	3	1	2	0
B Darwin	Eng	1922	2	1	1	0
JC Davies	Eng	1973-75-77-79	13	3	8	2
P Deeble	Eng	1977-81	5	1	4	0
FWG Deighton	Scot	(1951)-57	2	0	2	0
SC Dodd	Wales	1989	4	1	1	2
*NV Drew	Ire	1953	1	0	1	0
AA Duncan	Wales	(1953)	0	0	0	0
JM Dykes	Scot	1936	2	0	1	1

Name		Year	Played	Won	Lost	Halved
R Eggo	Eng	1987	2	0	2	0
D Evans	Wales	1981	3	1	1	1
RC Ewing	Ire	1936-38-47-49-51-55	10	1	7	2
GRD Eyles	Eng	1975	4	2	2	0
EW Fiddian	Eng	1932-34	4	0	4	0
J de Forest	Eng	1932	1	0	1	0
R Foster	Eng	1965-67-69-71-73-(79)-(81)	17	2	13	2
DW Frame	Eng	1961	1	0	1	0
D Gilford	Eng	1985	1	0	1	0
P Girvan	Scot	1987	3	0	3	0
G Godwin	Eng	1979-81	7	2	4	1
CW Green	Scot	1963-69-71-73-75-(83)-(85)	17	4	10	3
RH Hardman	Eng	1928	1	0	1	0
A Hare	Eng	1989	3	2	0	1
R Harris	Scot	(1922)-23-26	4	1	3	0
RW Hartley	Eng	1930-32	4	0	4	0
WL Hartley	Eng	1932	2	0	2	0
J Hawksworth	Eng	1985	4	2	1	1
P Hedges	Eng	1973-75	5	0	2	3
CO Hezlet	Ire	1924-26-28	6	0	5	1
GA Hill	Eng	1936-(55)	2	0	1	1
Sir EWE Holderness	Eng	1923-26-30	6	2	4	0
TWB Homer	Eng	1973	3	0	3	0
CVL Hooman	Eng	1922-23	3	1**	2	0**
WL Hope	Scot	1923-24-28	5	1	4	0
G Huddy	Eng	1961	1	0	1	0
W Humphreys	Eng	1971	3	2	1	0
IC Hutcheon	Scot	1975-77-79-81	15	5	8	2
RR Jack	Scot	1957-59	4	2	2	0
*M James	Eng	1975	4	3	1	0
A Jamieson, Jr	Scot	1926	2	1	1	0
MJ Kelley	Eng	1977-79	7	3	3	1
SD Keppler	Eng	1983	4	0	3	1
*MG King	Eng	1969-73	7	1	5	1
AT Kyle	Scot	1938-47-51	5	2	3	0
DH Kyle	Scot	1924	1	0	1	0
JA Lang	Scot	(1930)	0	0	0	0
JDA Langley	Eng	1936-51-53	6	0	5	1
CD Lawrie	Scot	(1961)-(63)	0	0	0	0
ME Lewis	Eng	1983	1	0	1	0
PB Lucas	Eng	(1936)-47-(49)	2	1	1	0
MSR Lunt	Eng	1959-61-63-65	11	2	8	1
*AWB Lyle	Scot	1977	3	0	3	0
AR McCallum	Scot	1928	1	0	1	0
SM McCready	Ire	1949-51	3	0	3	0
JS Macdonald	Scot	1971	3	1	1	1
P McEvoy	Eng	1977-79-81-85-89	18	5	11	2
G McGimpsey	Ire	1985-89	7	2	3	2
G Macgregor	Scot	1971-75-83-85-87-(91)	14	5	8	1
RC MacGregor	Scot	1953	2	0	2	0
J McHenry	Ire	1987	4	2	2	0
P McKellar	Scot	1977	1	0	1	0
WW Mackenzie	Scot	1922-23	3	1	2	0
SL McKinlay	Scot	1934	2	0	2	0
J McLean	Scot	1934-36	4	1	3	0
EA McRuvie	Scot	1932-34	4	1	2	1
JFD Madeley	Ire	1963	2	0	1	1
LS Mann	Scot	1983	4	2	1	1

Name		Year	Played	Won	Lost	Halved
B Marchbank	Scot	1979	4	2	2	0
GC Marks	Eng	1969-71-(87)-(89)	6	2	4	0
DM Marsh	Eng	(1959)-71-(73)-(75)	3	2	1	0
GNC Martin	Ire	1928	1	0	1	0
S Martin	Scot	1977	4	2	2	0
P Mayo	Wales	1985-87	4	0	3	1
GH Micklem	Eng	1947-49-53-55-(57)-(59)	6	1	5	0
DJ Millensted	Eng	1967	2	1	1	0
JW Milligan	Scot	1989	4	2	1	1
EB Millward	Eng	(1949)-55	2	0	2	0
WTG Milne	Scot	1973	4	2	2	0
CS Montgomerie	Scot	1985-87	8	2	5	1
JL Morgan	Wales	1951-53-55	6	2	4	0
P Mulcare	Ire	1975	3	2	1	0
GH Murray	Scot	1977	2	1	1	0
SWT Murray	Scot	1963	4	2	2	0
WA Murray	Scot	1923-24-(26)	4	1	3	0
E O'Connell	Ire	1989	4	2	0	2
A Oldcorn	Eng	1983	4	4	0	0
*PA Oosterhuis	Eng	1967	4	1	2	1
R Oppenheimer	Eng	(1951)	0	0	0	0
P Parkin	Wales	1983	3	2	1	0
JJF Pennink	Eng	1938	2	1	1	0
TP Perkins	Eng	1928	2	0	2	0
AH Perowne	Eng	1949-53-59	4	0	4	0
GB Peters	Scot	1936-38	4	2	1	1
AD Pierse	Ire	1983	3	0	2	1
AK Pirie	Scot	1967	3	0	2	1
MA Poxon	Eng	1975	2	0	2	0
D Prosser	Eng	1989	1	0	1	2
*R Rafferty	Ire	1981	4	2	2	0
J Robinson	Eng	1987	4	2	2	0
RN Roderick	Wales	1989	2	0	1	1
AC Saddler	Scot	1963-65-67-(77)	10	3	5	2
Hon M Scott	Eng	1924-34	4	2	2	0
R Scott, Jr	Scot	1924	1	1	0	0
PF Scrutton	Eng	1955-57	3	0	3	0
DN Sewell	Eng	1957-59	4	1	3	0
RDBM Shade	Scot	1961-63-65-67	14	6	6	2
G Shaw	Scot	1987	4	1	2	1
DB Sheahan	Ire	1963	4	2	2	0
AE Shepperson	Eng	1957-59	3	1	1	1
AF Simpson	Scot	(1926)	0	0	0	0
JN Smith	Scot	1930	2	0	2	0
WD Smith	Scot	1959	1	0	1	0
AR Stephen	Scot	1985	4	2	1	1
EF Storey	Eng	1924-26-28	6	1	5	0
JA Stout	Eng	1930-32	4	0	3	1
C Stowe	Eng	1938-47	4	2	2	0
HB Stuart	Scot	1971-73-75	10	4	6	0
A Thirlwell	Eng	1957	1	0	1	0
KG Thom	Eng	1949	2	0	2	0
MS Thompson	Eng	1983	3	1	2	0
H Thomson	Scot	1936-38	4	2	2	0
CJH Tolley	Eng	1922-23-24-26-30-34	12	4	8	0
TA Torrance	Scot	1924-28-30-32-34	9	3	5	1
WB Torrance	Scot	1922	2	0	2	0
*PM Townsend	Eng	1965	4	3	1	0

Name		Year	Played	Won	Lost	Halved
LP Tupling	Eng	1969	2	1	1	0
W Tweddell	Eng	1928-(36)	2	0	2	0
J Walker	Scot	1961	2	0	2	0
P Walton	Ire	1981-83	8	6	2	0
*P Way	Eng	1981	4	2	2	0
RH Wethered	Eng	1922-23-26-30-34	9	5	3	1
RJ White	Eng	1947-49-51-53-55	10	6	3	1
J Wilson	Scot	1923	2	2	0	0
JC Wilson	Scot	1947-53	4	0	4	0
GB Wolstenholme	Eng	1957-59	4	1	2	1

Notes: Bold Type indicates captain; in brackets, did not play.
  *Players who have also played in the Ryder Cup.
  **CVL Hooman and J Sweetser in 1922 were all square after 36 holes; instructions to the contrary not being readily available, they played on and Hooman won at the 37th. On all other occasions halved matches have counted as such.

United States of America

Name	Year	Played	Won	Lost	Halved
*TD Aaron	1959	2	1	1	0
B Alexander	1987	3	2	1	0
DC Allen	1965-67	6	0	4	2
B Andrade	1987	4	2	2	0
ES Andrews	1961	1	1	0	0
D Ballenger	1973	1	1	0	0
R Baxter, jr	1957	2	2	0	0
DR Beman	1959-61-63-65	11	7	2	2
RE Billows	1938-49	4	2	2	0
SE Bishop	1947-49	3	2	1	0
AS Blum	1957	1	0	1	0
J Bohmann	1969	3	1	2	0
M Brannan	1977	3	1	2	0
GF Burns	1975	3	2	1	0
C Burroughs	1985	3	1	2	0
AE Campbell	1936	2	2	0	0
JE Campbell	1957	1	0	1	0
WC Campbell	1951-53-(55)-57-65-67-71-75	18	11	4	3
RJ Cerrudo	1967	4	1	1	2
RD Chapman	1947-51-53	5	3	2	0
D Cherry	1953-55-61	5	5	0	0
D Clarke	1979	3	2	0	1
RE Cochran	1961	1	1	0	0
CR Coe	1949-51-53-(57)-59-61-63	13	7	4	2
R Commans	1981	3	1	1	1
JW Conrad	1955	2	1	1	0
N Crosby	1983	2	1	1	0
BH Cudd	1955	2	2	0	0
RD Davies	1963	2	0	2	0
JW Dawson	1949	2	2	0	0
RB Dickson	1967	3	3	0	0
GT Dunlap Jr	1932-34-36	5	3	1	1
D Edwards	1973	4	4	0	0
HC Egan	1934	1	1	0	0
HC Eger	1989	3	1	2	0
D Eichelberger	1965	3	1	2	0
J Ellis	1973	3	2	1	0

Name	Year	Played	Won	Lost	Halved
W Emery	1936	2	1	0	1
C Evans Jr	1922-24-28	5	3	2	0
J Farquhar	1971	3	1	2	0
B Faxon	1983	4	3	1	0
R Fehr	1983	4	2	1	1
JW Fischer	1934-36-38-(65)	4	3	0	1
D Fischesser	1979	3	1	2	0
MA Fleckman	1967	2	0	2	0
B Fleisher	1969	4	0	2	2
J Fought	1977	4	4	0	0
WC Fownes Jr	1922-24	3	1	2	0
F Fuhrer	1981	3	2	1	0
JR Gabrielsen	1977-(81)	3	1	2	0
R Gamez	1989	4	3	0	1
RA Gardner	1922-23-24-26	8	6	2	0
RW Gardner	1961-63	5	4	0	1
M Giles	1969-71-73-75	15	8	2	5
HL Givan	1936	1	0	0	1
JG Goodman	1934-36-38	6	4	2	0
M Gove	1979	3	2	1	0
J Grace	1975	3	2	1	0
JA Grant	1967	2	2	0	0
AD Gray Jr	1963-65-67	12	5	6	1
JP Guilford	1922-24-26	6	4	2	0
W Gunn	1926-28	4	4	0	0
*F Haas Jr	1938	2	0	2	0
*J Haas	1975	3	3	0	0
J Haas	1985	3	1	2	0
G Hallberg	1977	3	1	2	0
GS Hamer Jr	(1947)	0	0	0	0
LE Harris Jr	1963	4	3	1	0
V Heafner	1977	3	3	0	0
SD Herron	1923	2	0	2	0
S Hoch	1979	4	4	0	0
W Hoffer	1983	2	1	1	0
J Holtgrieve	1979-81-83	10	6	4	0
JM Hopkins	1965	3	0	2	1
R Howe	1989	1	0	1	0
W Howell	1932	1	1	0	0
W Hyndman	1957-59-61-69-71	9	6	1	2
J Inman	1969	2	2	0	0
JG Jackson	1953-55	3	3	0	0
K Johnson	1989	3	1	2	0
HR Johnston	1923-24-28-30	6	5	1	0
RT Jones Jr	1922-24-26-28-30	10	9	1	0
AF Kammer	1947	2	1	1	0
M Killian	1973	3	1	2	0
C Kite	1987	3	2	1	0
*TO Kite	1971	4	2	1	1
RE Knepper	(1922)	0	0	0	0
RW Knowles	1951	1	1	0	0
G Koch	1973-75	7	4	1	2
CR Kocsis	1938-49-57	5	2	2	1
G Lesher	1989	4	1	3	0
B Lewis Jr	1981-83-85-87	14	10	4	0
JW Lewis	1967	4	3	1	0
WL Little Jr	1934	2	2	0	0
*GA Littler	1953	2	2	0	0

Name	Year	Played	Won	Lost	Halved
B Loeffler	1987	3	2	1	0
D Love	1985	3	2	0	1
MJ McCarthy Jr	(1928)-32	1	1	0	0
BN McCormick	1949	1	1	0	0
JB McHale	1949-51	3	2	0	1
RR Mackenzie	1926-28-30	6	5	1	0
MR Marston	1922-23-24-34	8	5	3	0
D Martin	1989	4	1	1	2
L Mattiace	1987	3	2	1	0
B Mayfair	1987	3	3	0	0
E Meeks	1989	1	0	0	1
SN Melnyk	1969-71	7	3	3	1
P Mickelson	1989	4	1	1	2
AL Miller	1969-71	8	4	3	1
L Miller	1977	4	4	0	0
DK Moe	1930-32	3	3	0	0
B Montgomery	1987	2	2	0	0
G Moody	1979	3	1	2	0
GT Moreland	1932-34	4	4	0	0
D Morey	1955-65	4	1	3	0
J Mudd	1981	3	3	0	0
*RJ Murphy	1967	4	1	2	1
JF Neville	1923	1	0	1	0
*JW Nicklaus	1959-61	4	4	0	0
LW Oehmig	(1977)	0	0	0	0
FD Ouimet	1922-23-24-26-30-32-34-(36)-(38)-(47)-(49)	16	9	5	2
HD Paddock Jr	1951	1	0	0	1
*J Pate	1975	4	0	4	0
WJ Patton	1955-57-59-63-65-(69)	14	11	3	0
C Pavin	1981	3	2	0	1
M Peck	1979	3	1	1	1
M Pfeil	1973	4	2	1	1
M Podolak	1985	2	1	0	1
SL Quick	1947	2	1	1	0
S Randolph	1985	4	2	1	1
J Rassett	1981	3	3	0	0
F Ridley	1977-(87)-(89)	3	2	1	0
RH Riegel	1947-49	4	4	0	0
H Robbins Jr	1957	2	0	1	1
*W Rogers	1973	2	1	1	0
GV Rotan	1923	2	1	1	0
*EM Rudolph	1957	2	1	0	1
B Sander	1977	3	0	3	0
CH Seaver	1932	2	2	0	0
RL Siderowf	1969-73-75-77-(79)	14	4	8	2
J Sigel	1977-79-81-83-85-87-89	27	14	8	5
RH Sikes	1963	3	1	2	0
JB Simons	1971	2	0	2	0
*S Simpson	1977	3	3	0	0
CB Smith	1961-63	2	0	1	1
R Smith	1936-38	4	2	2	0
R Sonnier	1985	3	0	2	1
J Sorensen	1987	3	1	1	1
*C Stadler	1975	3	3	0	0
FR Stranahan	1947-49-51	6	3	2	1
*C Strange	1975	4	3	0	1
*H Sutton	1979-81	7	2	4	1

Name	Year	Played	Won	Lost	Halved
JW Sweetser	1922-23-24-26-28-32-(67)-(73)	12	7	4**	1**
FM Taylor	1957-59-61	4	4	0	0
D Tentis	1983	2	0	1	1
RS Tufts	(1963)	0	0	0	0
WP Turnesa	1947-49-51	6	3	3	0
B Tuten	1983	2	1	1	0
EM Tutweiler	1965-67	6	5	1	0
ER Updegraff	1963-65-69-(75)	7	3	3	1
S Urzetta	1951-53	4	4	0	0
K Venturi	1953	2	2	0	0
S Verplank	1985	4	3	0	1
GJ Voigt	1930-32-36	5	2	2	1
G Von Elm	1926-28-30	6	4	1	1
D von Tacky	1981	3	1	2	0
*JL Wadkins	1969-71	7	3	4	0
D Waldorf	1985	3	1	2	0
EH Ward	1953-55-59	6	6	0	0
MH Ward	1938-47	4	2	2	0
M West	1973-79	6	2	3	1
J Westland	1932-34-53-(61)	5	3	0	2
HW Wettlaufer	1959	2	2	0	0
E White	1936	2	2	0	0
OF Willing	1923-24-30	4	4	0	0
JM Winters Jr	(1971)	0	0	0	0
W Wood	1983	4	1	2	1
FJ Wright	1923	1	1	0	0
CR Yates	1936-38-(53)	4	3	0	1
D Yates	1989	4	1	2	1
RL Yost	1955	2	2	0	0

Notes: Bold type indicates captain: in brackets, did not play.

*Players who have also played in the Ryder Cup.

**CVL Hooman and J Sweetser in 1922 were all square after 36 holes; instructions to the contrary not being readily available, they played on and Hooman won at the 37th.

On all other occasions halved matches have counted as such.

International Amateur Events

Since the 1950s international amateur events have burgeoned beyond the pre-war Walker and Curtis Cups and the occasional matches between Britain and France. Air travel has made it much easier to stage these new events which take place annually, or with a gap of a year or two. While the British countries still dominate the European scene, it may not be long before the other countries gain the necessary strength in depth to provide winning teams regularly rather than occasionally.

St Andrews Trophy

Great Britain & Ireland v Continent of Europe

INAUGURATED 1956

Trophy presented 1962

In 1956 the first of the biennial matches between Great Britain and Ireland and the Continent of Europe was played. Contested alternately in Britain and a continental country, it was not until 1974 in the tenth meeting that Europe won at Punta Ala in Tuscany, Italy. Eight years later at Rosendaelsche near Arnhem in Holland, they won again by 14 matches to 10.

The match takes place over two days and from 1962 four foursomes and eight singles have been played. Previously it had been 36-hole matches on both days, but with the demise of the largely traditional 36-hole contests in other internationals, the St Andrews Trophy organisers decided to move into line.

The growing strength of golf on the continent is shown by the much closer winning margins since that 1974 win. The European Golf Union, now based in Geneva, selects the team for the continent, which is no easy task with so many countries spread over so wide an area to consider. The Championship Committee is responsible for selecting the side representing Great Britain and Ireland.

The St Andrews Trophy, a beautiful loving cup, was given by the Royal & Ancient Club in 1964. Competition to be selected for either side is keen and the match a popular one wherever it is played.

YEAR	WINNER	RESULT	VENUE
1956	Great Britain & Ireland	$12\frac{1}{2}$–$2\frac{1}{2}$	Wentworth
1958	Great Britain & Ireland	10–5	St Cloud, France
1960	Great Britain & Ireland	13–5	Walton Heath
1962	Great Britain & Ireland	18–12	Halmstad, Sweden
1964	Great Britain & Ireland	23–7	Muirfield
1966	Great Britain & Ireland	$19\frac{1}{2}$–$10\frac{1}{2}$	Bilbao, Spain
1968	Great Britain & Ireland	20–10	Portmarnock
1970	Great Britain & Ireland	$17\frac{1}{2}$–$12\frac{1}{2}$	La Zoute, Belgium
1972	Great Britain & Ireland	$19\frac{1}{2}$–$10\frac{1}{2}$	The Berkshire
1974	Continent of Europe	16–14	Punta Ala, Italy
1976	Great Britain & Ireland	$18\frac{1}{2}$–$11\frac{1}{2}$	St Andrews
1978	Great Britain & Ireland	$20\frac{1}{2}$–$9\frac{1}{2}$	Bremen, Germany
1980	Great Britain & Ireland	$19\frac{1}{2}$–$10\frac{1}{2}$	St George's, Sandwich
1982	Continent of Europe	14–10	Rosendaelsche, Netherlands
1984	Great Britain & Ireland	13–11	Saunton, Devon
1986	Great Britain & Ireland	$14\frac{1}{2}$–$9\frac{1}{2}$	Halmstad, Sweden
1988	Great Britain & Ireland	$15\frac{1}{2}$–$8\frac{1}{2}$	St Andrews
1990	Great Britain & Ireland	13–11	El Saler, Spain

European Amateur Team Championship

INAUGURATED 1959

YEAR	WINNER	SECOND	VENUE
1959	Sweden	France	Barcelona, Spain
1961	Sweden	England	Brussels, Belgium
1963	England	Sweden	Falsterbo, Sweden
1965	Ireland	Scotland	St George's, Sandwich, England
1967	Ireland	France	Turin, Italy
1969	England	W Germany	Hamburg, Germany
1971	England	Scotland	Lausanne, Switzerland
1973	England	Scotland	Penina, Portugal
1975	Scotland	Italy	Killarney, Ireland
1977	Scotland	Sweden	The Haagsche, Holland
1979	England	Wales	Esbjerg, Denmark
1981	England	Scotland	St Andrews, Scotland
1983	Ireland	Spain	Chantilly, France
1985	Scotland	Sweden	Halmstad, Sweden
1987	Ireland	England	Murhof, Austria
1989	England	Scotland	Porthcawl, Wales

Eisenhower Trophy (World Cup)

INAUGURATED 1956

Designated the World Cup for Amateurs, the first Eisenhower Trophy for teams of four from any country, playing 72 holes stroke play, with the three best scores to count, took place at St Andrews in 1958. Bobby Jones on his last visit to the UK, confined to a wheelchair, was captain of the American team and was given the Freedom of St Andrews in a memorable ceremony. His team tied with Australia on 918 but lost the play-off over 18 holes next day.

The Trophy is played every other year, and in 17 contests to 1990 has been held in 16 countries all over the world. The strength of the amateur game in the USA is shown in that country's nine wins. Great Britain and Ireland have three to their credit, Australia two, Japan and Canada one each.

Each country selects its best amateurs and the standard of play is high. There is an individual winner with the best four round score from any competitor. Quite often the individual winner is from a country with little chance of taking the Trophy, such as Taiwan and Mexico.

YEAR	WINNERS	SCORE	RUNNERS-UP	VENUE
1958	Australia (B Devlin,		United States (C Coe,	
	P Toogood,		WJ Patton,	
	RF Stevens,		Dr F Taylor,	
	D Bachli)	918	W Hyndman)	St Andrews
After a tie, Australia won the play-off by two strokes. Australia 222, United States 224.				
(Best individual score (unofficial), B Devlin, W Hyndman, RR Jack, 301.)				
1960	United States		Australia	
	(DR Beman,		(E Ball, J Coogan,	
	RW Gardner,		B Devlin,	
	W Hyndman,		EG Routley)	
	J Nicklaus)	834		Ardmore, USA
(Best individual score, J Nicklaus 269)				
1962	United States		Canada (G Cowan,	
	(DR Beman,		B Wakeham,	
	WJ Patton,		N Weslock,	
	R Silkes, L Harris)	854	R Wylie)	Kawana, Japan
(Best individual score, G Cowan, 280)				
1964	Great Britain and			
	Ireland		Canada (N Weslock,	
	(RDBM Shade,		D Silverberg,	
	R Foster,		RK Alexander)	
	MSR Lunt,			
	MF Bonallack)	895		Olgiata, Rome
(Best individual score, Min Nan Hsieh, Formosa, 294)				
1966	Australia		United States	
	(KW Hartley,		(DR Beman,	
	PK Billings,		RJ Murphy,	
	W Berwick,		RJ Cerrudo,	
	KK Donohoe)	877	D Gray)	Mexico City
(Best individual score, RDBM Shade, Great Britain, 281)				

YEAR	WINNERS	SCORE	RUNNERS-UP	VENUE
1968	United States (M Giles, B Fleisher, J Lewis Jr, R Siderowf)	868	Great Britain and Ireland (MF Bonallack, P Oosterhuis, RDBM Shade, GB Cosh)	Melbourne

(Best individual score, MF Bonallack and M Giles, 286)

1970	United States (M Giles, T Kite, A Miller, L Wadkins)	857	New Zealand (G Clarke, S Jones, T McDougall, R Murray)	Madrid

(Best individual score, V Regalado, Mexico, 280)

1972	United States (B Crenshaw, M Giles, M Hayes, M West)	865	Australia (M Cahill, T Gale, A Gresham, N Ratcliffe)	Buenos Aires

(Best individual score, A Gresham, Australia, 285)

1974	United States (G Burns, G Coch, J Pate, C Strange)	888	Japan (G Nakabe, T Irie, T Sakata, S Yamazaki)	Dominican Republic

(Best individual score, J Pate, USA, and J Gonzalez, Brazil, 294)

1976	Great Britain and Ireland (J Davies, I Hutcheon, M Kelley, S Martin)	892	Japan (M Kuramoto, M Mori, G Nakabe, T Sakata)	Penina, Portugal

(Best individual score, I Hutcheon, Great Britain, TM Chen, Taiwan, 293)

1978	United States (R Clampett, J Cook, S Hoch, J Sigel)	873	Canada (G Cowan, D Mick, D Roxburgh, Y Tremblay)	Fiji

(Best individual score, R Clampett, USA, 287)

1980	United States (H Sutton, J Holtgrieve, R Tway, J Sigel)	848	South Africa (D Suddards, E Groenwald, W Player, D Lindsay-Smith)	Pinehurst, USA

(Best individual score, H Sutton, USA, 276)

1982	United States (N Crosby, B Lewis, J Holtgrieve, J Sigel)	859	Sweden (K Kinell, O Sellberg, M Persson, P Andersson)	Lausanne

(Best individual score, L Carbonetti, Argentina, 284)

1984	Japan (K Kato, N Kimura, K Oie, T Sokata)	870	United States (J Inman, J Sigel, R Sonnier, S Verplank)	Hong Kong

(Best individual score, L Carbonetti, Argentina, 286)

1986	Canada (M Brewer, F Brent, K Kack Jr, S Warren)	860	United States (B Alexander, W Andrade, R Lewis, J Sigel)	Caracas, Venezuela

(Best individual score, M Brewer, Canada, 277)

1988	Great Britain & Ireland (P McEvoy, G McGimpsey, J Milligan, E O'Connell)	882	United States (K Johnson, E Meeks, J Sigel, D Yates)	Ullna, Sweden

(Best individual score, P McEvoy, Great Britain & Ireland, 284)

1990	Sweden (M Gronberg, G Hjertsedt, K Eriksson, P Nyman)	879	New Zealand (M Long, B Paterson, S Alker, G Moorhead)	Christchurch, New Zealand

(Best individual score, M Gronberg, Sweden, 286)

The Home Internationals

The first official meeting of the four countries was in 1932, but it was by no means the first occasion any of the countries had played each other. England and Scotland had their first match in 1902, the day before the Amateur Championship. Thus both countries were able to field strong sides. The next year a cup was presented for the match, giving it official status. It was named the Walker Cup, which must not be confused with the later trophy of that name given for the USA–GB competition. From 1903 to 1912 the format was a match of nine-a-side 36-hole singles. After the war, in 1922, it was changed to five 18-hole foursomes and ten 18-hole singles.

Ireland and Wales played a match in 1913, Ireland winning comfortably. Before 1932 Ireland played both Scotland and England intermittently at different venues to the England *v* Scotland match, and Wales occasionally. The 1932 meeting when the four countries, with teams selected by their Unions, met for the first time to play each other on the same course, was held at Troon. Newcastle (Co. Down), Porthcawl and Lytham followed and each country has since selected the venue in the same progression. In the early years, Wales, the weakest of the four, usually finished at the bottom of the pack, with either England or Scotland the winner. Each has 17 wins: Scotland has shared the result six times, England and Ireland five each. Ireland has three outright wins.

The Walker Cup between England and Scotland was dropped after the four Unions all competed together and later the English international, Raymond Oppenheimer, gave a Challenge Cup in 1953.

ENGLAND	APPEARANCES	YEARS	ENGLAND	APPEARANCES	YEARS
John Ball	11	1902–12	Arthur Perowne	9	1947–57
Harry Bentley	8	1932–47	Alan Thirlwell	9	1951–64
Michael Bonallack	19	1957–74	Cyril Tolley	12	1922–38
Ian Caldwell	11	1950–61	Tony Torrance	8	1922–33
Leonard Crawley	11	1932–55	Roger Wethered	9	1922–30
Bernard Darwin	8	1902–24			
Peter Deeble	8	1975–84			
Rodney Foster	9	1963–72			
Peter Hedges	9	1970–84			
Harold Hilton	10	1902–12	SCOTLAND	APPEARANCES	YEARS
Cecil Hutchison	9	1904–12	Ernley Blackwell	11	1902–25
Michael Kelley	9	1974–88	David Blair	8	1948–57
Michael Lunt	9	1956–66	Allan Brodie	9	1970–80
Peter McEvoy	12	1976–89	David Carrick	9	1981–89
Geoffrey Marks	9	1963–82	Dr Frank Deighton	8	1950–60
Dr David Marsh	12	1956–72	John Graham	10	1902–11
Gerald Micklem	9	1947–55	Charlie Green	17	1961–78

SCOTLAND	APPEARANCES	YEARS
Robert Harris	12	1905–28
Iain Hutcheon	9	1971–80
Sandy Stephen	9	1971–85
Reid Jack	9	1950–61
John Laidlay	10	1902–11
Gregor Macgregor	16	1969–87
William McLeod	8	1935–51
Robert Maxwell	8	1902–10
Alex Pirie	10	1966–75
Ronnie Shade	10	1957–68
Gordon Simpson	9	1906–26
Hugh Stuart	8	1967–76
John Thomson	9	1981–89
James Walker	8	1954–63

WALES	APPEARANCES	YEARS
Clive Brown	10	1970–88
Ted Davies	16	1959–74
Tony Duncan	17	1933–59
Peter Dunn	9	1957–66
Albert Evans	15	1932–61
Hugh Evans	9	1976–88
Henry Howell	13	1923–47
John Jones	11	1970–85
Mervyn Jones	8	1947–57
Stephen Jones	8	1981–89
Robert de Lloyd	10	1931–48

WALES	APPEARANCES	YEARS
David McLean	18	1968–88
John Moody	9	1947–61
John Morgan	17	1948–68
John Povall	17	1960–77
Sam Roberts	14	1932–54
Hew Squirrell	20	1955–75
David Stevens	10	1963–82
Jeff Toye	13	1963–78
Iestyn Tucker	26	1969–75
Jim Breen Turner	8	1947–56

IRELAND	APPEARANCES	YEARS
Joe Brown	9	1933–53
John Burke	10	1932–49
Joe Carr	23	1947–69
Tom Cleary	8	1976–86
Tom Craddock	10	1934–58
Brenie Edwards	9	1961–73
Cecil Ewing	16	1934–58
Mark Gannon	11	1973–89
L Macnamara	8	1973–89
Pat Mulcare	8	1968–80
Garth McGimpsey	11	1978–89
Michael O'Brian	8	1968–77
William O'Sullivan	12	1934–54
Arthur Pierce	11	1976–88
David Sheahan	8	1961–70

Home Internationals

1932 *at Troon*

Winners: Scotland

Scotland beat England	8 matches to 7
Scotland beat Ireland	11½ matches to 3½
Scotland beat Wales	9 matches to 6
England beat Ireland	12 matches to 3
England beat Wales	11½ matches to 3½
Ireland beat Wales	9½ matches to 5½

1933 *at Newcastle, Co Down*

Winners: Scotland

Scotland beat England	9½ matches to 5½
Scotland beat Ireland	9 matches to 6
Scotland beat Wales	11 matches to 4
England beat Ireland	9½ matches to 5½
England beat Wales	9 matches to 6
Ireland beat Wales	11 matches to 4

1934 *at Porthcawl*

Winners: Scotland

Scotland beat England	10 matches to 5
Scotland beat Ireland	10½ matches to 4½
Scotland beat Wales	9½ matches to 5½
Ireland beat Wales	10 matches to 5
Ireland beat England	12 matches to 3
England beat Wales	10 matches to 5

1938 *at Porthcawl*

Winners: England

England beat Ireland	10 matches to 5
England beat Wales	10½ matches to 4½
England beat Scotland	8½ matches to 6½
Scotland beat Wales	8½ matches to 6½
Scotland beat Ireland	9½ matches 5½
Ireland beat Wales	9 matches to 6

1939–46 *Not played due to Second World War*

1935 *at Lytham St Annes*

Winners: England, Scotland, Ireland (tie)

Scotland beat Wales	10½ matches to 4½
Scotland beat England	12½ matches to 2½
England beat Ireland	8½ matches to 6½
England beat Wales	10½ matches to 4½
Ireland beat Scotland	9 matches to 6
Ireland beat Wales	10½ matches to 4½

1947 *at Hoylake*

Winners: England

England beat Wales	14 matches to 1
England beat Ireland	9 matches to 6
England beat Scotland	8 matches to 7
Scotland beat Ireland	10 matches to 5
Scotland beat Wales	11 matches to 4
Ireland beat Wales	12 matches to 3

1936 *at Prestwick*

Winners: Scotland

Scotland beat Wales	9½ matches to 5½
Scotland beat Ireland	8 matches to 7
Scotland beat England	8 matches to 7
England beat Ireland	13 matches to 2
England beat Wales	12 matches to 3
Ireland beat Wales	11 matches to 4

1948 *at Muirfield*

Winners: England

England beat Scotland	10½ matches to 4½
England beat Wales	8½ matches to 6½
England beat Ireland	8 matches to 7
Ireland beat Scotland	10½ matches to 4½
Ireland beat Wales	12½ matches to 2½
Scotland beat Wales	11 matches to 4

1937 *at Portmarnock*

Winners: Scotland

Scotland beat Ireland	9½ matches to 5½
Scotland beat England	9 matches to 6
Scotland halved with Wales	7½ matches each
England beat Ireland	8 matches to 7
England beat Wales	8½ matches to 6½
Ireland beat Wales	9 matches to 6

1949 *at Portmarnock*

Winners: England

England beat Ireland	8 matches to 7
England beat Wales	10 matches to 5
England beat Scotland	10 matches to 5
Ireland beat Wales	10½ matches to 4½
Ireland beat Scotland	10½ matches to 4½
Wales beat Scotland	8½ matches to 6½

1950 *at Harlech*

Winners: Ireland

Ireland beat Wales	10 matches to 5
Ireland halved with Scotland	7½ matches each
Ireland beat England	8½ matches to 6½
Scotland beat England	9 matches to 6
Scotland halved with Wales	7½ matches each
England beat Wales	10 matches to 5

1951 *at Lytham St Annes*

Winners: Ireland, Scotland (tie)

Ireland beat Scotland	8½ matches to 6½
Ireland beat England	8 matches to 7
Scotland beat Wales	8 matches to 7
Scotland beat England	8 matches to 7
Wales beat England	9½ matches to 5½
England beat Wales	10 matches to 5

1952 *at Troon (for Raymond Trophy presented 1952)*

Winners: Scotland

Scotland beat Wales	10 matches to 5
Scotland beat England	9 matches to 6
Scotland beat Ireland	9½ matches to 5½
England beat Wales	9 matches to 6
Ireland halved with England	7½ matches each
Ireland halved with Wales	7½ matches each

1953 *at Killarney*

Winners: Scotland

Scotland beat Wales	10 matches to 5
Scotland beat England	8½ matches to 6½
Scotland halved with Ireland	7½ matches each
Ireland beat England	9 matches to 6
England beat Wales	9 matches to 6
Wales beat Ireland	8½ matches to 6½

1954 *at Porthcawl*

Winners: England

England beat Wales	12 matches to 3
England beat Scotland	9 matches to 6
England beat Ireland	8½ matches to 6½
Ireland beat Scotland	9 matches to 6
Scotland beat Wales	9 matches to 6
Wales beat Ireland	8 matches to 7

1955 *at Southport & Ainsdale*

Winners: Ireland

Ireland beat Scotland	9 matches to 6
Ireland beat Wales	9 matches to 6
Ireland halved with England	7½ matches each
Scotland beat Wales	8 matches to 7
Scotland beat England	8 matches to 7
England beat Wales	9½ matches to 5½

1956 *at Muirfield*

Winners: Scotland

Scotland beat Wales	10½ matches to 4½
Scotland beat Ireland	8 matches to 7
Scotland beat England	9½ matches to 5½
England beat Ireland	11 matches to 4
England beat Wales	10½ matches to 4½
Wales beat Ireland	9 matches to 6

1957 *at Newcastle, Co Down*

Winners: England

England beat Scotland	12 matches to 3
England beat Wales	9 matches to 6
England beat Ireland	10½ matches to 4½
Scotland beat Ireland	13 matches to 2
Scotland beat Wales	10 matches to 5
Wales beat Ireland	8½ matches to 6½

1958 *at Porthcawl*

Winners: England

England beat Ireland	9 matches to 6
England beat Wales	11½ matches to 3½
England beat Scotland	8 matches to 7
Scotland beat Ireland	8½ matches to 6½
Scotland beat Wales	10½ matches to 4½
Wales beat Ireland	8 matches to 7

1959 *Lytham St Annes*

Winners: England, Ireland, Scotland (tie)

England beat Scotland	10 matches to 5
Ireland beat Wales	8 matches to 7
Scotland beat Wales	10 matches to 5
Ireland beat England	8½ matches to 6½
Scotland beat Ireland	8½ matches to 6½
England beat Wales	11½ matches to 3½

1960 *at Turnberry*

Winners: England

Scotland halved with England	7½ matches each
Scotland beat Wales	9 matches to 6
England beat Ireland	8 matches to 7
England beat Wales	11½ matches to 3½
Ireland beat Wales	12 matches to 3
Ireland beat Scotland	8 matches to 7

1961 *at Portmarnock*

Winners: Scotland

Scotland beat England	12½ matches to 2½
Scotland beat Ireland	11½ matches to 3½
Scotland beat Wales	8 matches to 7
Ireland beat Wales	11 matches to 4
Ireland beat England	8 matches to 7
Wales beat England	12 matches to 3

1962 *at Porthcawl*

Winners: Tie: England, Ireland, Scotland

Scotland beat England	9 matches to 6
Scotland beat Wales	9 matches to 6
England beat Ireland	8½ matches to 6½
England beat Wales	11½ matches to 3½
Ireland beat Scotland	8 matches to 7
Ireland beat Wales	10½ matches to 4½

1963 *at Lytham St Annes*

Winners: England, Ireland, Scotland (tie)

Scotland beat England	10½ matches to 4½
Scotland beat Wales	10½ matches to 4½
England beat Ireland	8½ matches to 6½
England beat Wales	9 matches to 6
Ireland beat Scotland	10 matches to 5
Ireland beat Wales	11 matches to 4

1964 *at Carnoustie*

Winners: England

England beat Wales	12½ matches to 2½
England beat Ireland	8½ matches to 6½
England beat Scotland	8 matches to 7
Ireland beat Scotland	8 matches to 7
Ireland beat Wales	10 matches to 5
Scotland beat Wales	12½ matches to 2½

1965 *at Portrush*

Winners: England

England beat Wales	8 matches to 7
England beat Scotland	11½ matches to 3½
England beat Ireland	8½ matches to 6½
Ireland beat Wales	10½ matches to 4½
Ireland beat Scotland	9½ matches to 5½
Scotland beat Wales	9 matches to 6

1966 *at Porthcawl*

Winners: England

England beat Scotland	8 matches to 7
England beat Ireland	12½ matches to 2½
England beat Wales	8 matches to 7
Ireland beat Scotland	10½ matches to 4½
Ireland beat Wales	9 matches to 6
Scotland beat Wales	8 matches to 7

1967 *at Ganton*

Winners: Scotland

Scotland beat England	8 matches to 7
Scotland beat Ireland	8½ matches to 6½
Scotland beat Wales	8 matches to 7
England beat Ireland	10½ matches to 4½
England beat Wales	10½ matches to 4½
Ireland beat Wales	8½ matches to 6½

1968 *at Gullane*

Winners: England

England beat Scotland	9½ matches to 5½
England beat Ireland	12 matches to 3
England beat Wales	11 matches to 4
Scotland beat Ireland	8 matches to 7
Scotland beat Wales	9 matches to 6
Ireland beat Wales	9 matches to 6

1969 *at Killarney*

Winners: England

England beat Scotland	10½ matches to 4½
England halved with Ireland	7½ matches each
England beat Wales	11 matches to 4
Scotland beat Ireland	9½ matches to 5½
Wales beat Scotland	8 matches to 7
Ireland beat Wales	8 matches to 7

1970 *at Porthcawl*

Winners: Scotland

Scotland beat Ireland	10 matches to 5
Scotland beat Wales	10 matches to 5
Scotland beat England	9½ matches to 4½
Ireland beat Wales	8 matches to 7
Ireland halved with England	7½ matches each
Wales beat England	8½ matches to 6½

1971 *at Formby*

Winners: Scotland

Scotland beat England	8 matches to 7
Scotland beat Ireland	8½ matches to 6½
Scotland beat Wales	12 matches to 3
England beat Ireland	12 matches to 3
England beat Wales	8½ matches to 6½
Ireland beat Wales	9½ matches to 5½

1972 *at Troon*

Winners: Scotland, England (tie)

Scotland halved with England	7½ matches each
Scotland beat Ireland	8½ matches to 6½
Scotland beat Wales	10½ matches to 4½
England beat Ireland	8 matches to 7
England beat Wales	10½ matches to 4½
Ireland beat Wales	12 matches to 3

1973 *at Lytham St Annes*

Winners: England

England beat Scotland	9 matches to 6
England beat Ireland	10½ matches to 4½
England beat Wales	9½ matches to 5½
Scotland beat Ireland	9½ matches to 5½
Scotland halved with Wales	7½ matches each
Ireland beat Wales	10½ matches to 4½

1977 *at Hillside*

Winners: England

England beat Scotland	8 matches to 7
England beat Wales	9 matches to 6
England beat Ireland	8½ matches to 6½
Scotland beat Wales	10 matches to 5
Scotland beat Ireland	11½ matches to 3½
Wales beat Ireland	9 matches to 6

1974 *at Harlech*

Winners: England

England beat Scotland	10½ matches to 4½
England beat Ireland	11 matches to 4
England halved with Wales	7½ matches each
Scotland beat Ireland	9 matches to 6
Scotland beat Wales	9 matches to 6
Ireland beat Wales	8 matches to 7

1978 *at Ashburnham*

Winners: England

England beat Wales	8½ matches to 6½
England beat Scotland	9 matches to 6
England beat Ireland	8½ matches to 6½
Wales beat Scotland	8 matches to 7
Scotland beat Ireland	9 matches to 6
Ireland beat Wales	8 matches to 7

1975 *at Portmarnock*

Winners: Scotland

Scotland beat England	9½ matches to 5½
Scotland beat Ireland	10½ matches to 4½
Scotland beat Wales	13 matches to 2
England beat Ireland	10½ matches to 4½
England beat Wales	11 matches to 4
Ireland beat Wales	9 matches to 6

1979 *Cancelled*

In place of the Home International Matches
Scotland beat England 17–13 at Troon and Wales
beat Ireland 17–15 at Porthcawl

1976 *at Muirfield*

Winners: Scotland

Scotland beat England	10 matches to 5
Scotland beat Ireland	10 matches to 5
Scotland beat Wales	9 matches to 6
England beat Ireland	10½ matches to 4½
England beat Wales	10 matches to 5
Ireland beat Wales	8 matches to 7

1980 *at Dornoch*

Winners: England

England halved with Ireland	7½ matches each
England beat Wales	10 matches to 5
England beat Scotland	11 matches to 4
Ireland halved with Wales	7½ matches each
Ireland beat Scotland	9 matches to 6
Wales halved with Scotland	7½ matches each

1981   *at Woodhall Spa*

Winners: Scotland

Scotland beat Ireland	9 matches to 6
Scotland beat England	11½ matches to 3½
Scotland beat Wales	9½ matches to 5½
Ireland beat England	8 matches to 7
Ireland beat Wales	10½ matches to 4½
Wales halved with England	7½ matches each

1982   *at Porthcawl*

Winners: Scotland

Scotland beat England	8 matches to 7
Scotland beat Wales	9½ matches to 5½
England beat Ireland	8½ matches to 6½
England beat Wales	8 matches to 7
Ireland beat Scotland	8 matches to 7
Ireland halved with Wales	7½ matches each

1983   *at Portmarnock*

Winners: Ireland

Ireland beat Scotland	9½ matches to 5½
Ireland halved with England	7½ matches each
Ireland beat Wales	10 matches to 5
Scotland beat England	8½ matches to 6½
Scotland beat Wales	8 matches to 7
England beat Wales	9 matches to 6

1984   *at Troon*

Winners: England

Ireland halved with Wales	7½ matches each
England beat Scotland	8 matches to 7
Scotland beat Ireland	10 matches to 5
England beat Wales	12½ matches to 2½
Scotland beat Wales	7 matches to 3
Ireland beat England	6 matches to 4

(Foursomes of third series of matches cancelled due to torrential rain.)

1985   *at Formby*

Winners: England

England beat Wales	11 matches to 4
England beat Scotland	8 matches to 7
England beat Ireland	8½ matches to 6½
Wales beat Scotland	8 matches to 7
Wales beat Ireland	9½ matches to 5½
Ireland beat Scotland	11½ matches to 3½

1986   *at Harlech*

Winners: Scotland

Scotland beat England	9½ matches to 5½
Scotland beat Ireland	10½ matches to 4½
Scotland beat Wales	10 matches to 5
England beat Wales	9 matches to 6
Ireland beat England	8 matches to 7
Wales halved with Ireland	7½ matches each

1987   *at Lahinch*

Winners: Ireland

Ireland beat England	6 matches to 4
Ireland beat Scotland	10½ matches to 4½
Ireland beat Wales	8 matches to 7
England beat Scotland	9 matches to 6
England halved with Wales	7 matches each
Scotland beat Wales	6½ matches to 3½

(On the first day the foursomes were abandoned due to bad weather, singles only being played.)

1988   *at Muirfield*

Winners: England

England beat Wales	11 matches to 4
England beat Scotland	9 matches to 6
England beat Ireland	8 matches to 7
Ireland halved with Wales	7½ matches each
Ireland beat Scotland	10 matches to 5
Wales beat Scotland	8 matches to 7

1989 *at Ganton*

Winners: England

England beat Ireland	8 matches to 7
England beat Scotland	9 matches to 6
England beat Wales	12 matches to 3
Ireland beat Wales	11 matches to 4
Scotland beat Wales	8 matches to 7
Scotland beat Ireland	8½ matches to 6½

1990 *at Conwy*

Winners: Ireland

England beat Wales	10 matches to 5
Ireland beat Scotland	9 matches to 6
Scotland beat England	9½ matches to 5½
Ireland beat Wales	11 matches to 4
Wales beat Scotland	8 matches to 7
Ireland beat England	8 matches to 7

British Isles International Players, Amateur Men

Abbreviations:

Com Tnmt   Commonwealth Tournament
Eur T Ch   played in European Team Championship for home country;
Home Int   played in Home International matches

Adams, MPD
(Wales): Home Int 1969-70-71-72-75-76-77; Eur T Ch 1971

Aitken, AR
(Scotland): v England 1906-07-08

Alexander, DW
(Scotland): Home Int 1958; v Scandinavia 1958

Allison, A
(Ireland): v England 1928; v Scotland 1929

Anderson, N
(Ireland): Home Int 1985-86-87-88-89-90. Eur T Ch 1989.
(GBI): v Europe 1988

Anderson, RB
(Scotland): v Scandinavia 1960-62; Home Int 1962-63

Andrew, R
(Scotland): v England 1905-06-07-08-09-10

Armour, A
(Scotland): v England 1922

Armour, TD
(GBI): v America 1921

Ashby, H
(England): Home Int 1972-73-74. (GBI): in Dominican Int
1973. (GBI): v Europe 1974

Atkinson, HN
(Wales): v Ireland 1913

Attenborough, M
(England): Home Int 1964-66-67-68; Eur T Ch 1967.
(GBI): v Europe 1966-68; v America 1967

Aylmer, CC
(England): v Scotland 1911-22-23-24. (GBI): v America
1921-22

Babington, A
(Ireland): v Wales 1913

Baker, P
(England): Home Int 1985. (GBI): v America 1985;
v Europe 1986

Baker, RN
(Ireland): Home Int 1975

Ball, J
(England): v Scotland 1902-03-04-05-06-07-08-09-10-11-12

Bamford, JL
(Ireland): Home Int 1954-56

Banks, C
(England): Home Int 1983

Banks, SE
(England): Home Int 1934-38

Bannerman, S
(Scotland): Home Int 1988; v Sweden 1990

Bardsley, R
(England): Home Int 1987; v France 1988

Barker, HH
(England): v Scotland 1907

Barnett, A
(Wales): Home Int 1989-90

Barrie, GC
(Scotland): Home Int 1981-83

Barry, AG
(England): v Scotland 1906-07

Bathgate, D
(England): Home Int 1990

Bayliss, RP
(England): v Ireland 1929; Home Int 1933-34

Bayne, PWGA
(Wales): Home Int 1949

Beamish, CH
(Ireland): Home Int 1950-51-53-56

Beck, JB
(England): v Scotland 1926-30; Home Int 1933.
(GBI): v America 1928-38 (Captain) -47 (Captain)

Beddard, JB
(England): v Wales/Ireland 1925; v Ireland 1929;
v Scotland 1927-28-29

Beharrell, JC
(England): Home Int 1956

Bell, HE
(Ireland): v Wales 1930; Home Int 1932

Bell, RK
(England): Home Int 1947

Benka, PJ
(England): Home Int 1967-68-69-70: Eur T Ch 1969.
(GBI): v America 1969; v Europe 1970

Bennett, H
(England): Home Int 1948-49-51

Bennett, S
(England): v Scotland 1979

Bentley, AL
(England): Home Int 1936-37; v France 1937-39

Bentley, HG
(England): v Ireland 1931; v Scotland 1931. Home Int 1932-
33-34-35-36-37-38-47; v France 1934-35-36-37-39-54.
(GBI): v America 1934-36-38

Berry, P
(England): Home Int 1972. (GBI): v Europe 1972

Bevan, RJ
(Wales): Home Int 1964-65-66-67-73-74

Beveridge, HW
(Scotland): v England 1908

Birtwell, SG
(England): Home Int 1968-70-73

Black, D
(Scotland): Home Int 1966-67

Black, FC
(Scotland): Home Int 1962-64-65-66-68; v Scandinavia 1962; Eur T Ch 1965-67. (GBI): v Europe 1966

Black, GT
(Scotland): Home Int 1952-53; v South Africa 1954

Black, JL
(Wales): Home Int 1932-33-34-35-36

Black, WC
(Scotland): Home Int 1964-65

Blackwell, EBH
(Scotland): v England 1902-04-05-06-07-09-10-12-23-24-25

Blair, DA
(Scotland): Home Int 1948-49-51-52-53-55-56-57; v Scandinavia 1956-58-62. (GBI): v America 1955-61; in Com Tnmt 1954

Blakeman, D
(England): Home Int 1981; v France 1982

Bloice, C
(Scotland): Home Int 1985-86. (GBI): v America 1985

Bloxham, JA
(England): Home Int 1966

Blyth, AD
(Scotland): v England 1904

Bonallack,MF
(England): Home Int 1957-58-59-60-61-62-63-64-65-66-67-68-69-70-71-72-73-74; Eur T Ch 1969-71. (GBI): v America 1957-59-61-63-65-67-69 (Captain) -71 (Captain) -73; v Europe 1958-62-64-66-68-70-72; in Com Tnmt 1959-63-67-71; in World Team Ch 1960-62-64-66-68-70-72

Bonnell, DJ
(Wales): Home Int 1949-50-51

Bookless, JT
(Scotland): v England 1930-31; v Ireland 1930; v Wales 1931

Bottomley, S
(England): Home Int 1986

Bourn, TA
(England): v Ireland 1928; v Scotland 1930; Home Int 1933-34; v France 1934. (GBI): v Australia 1934

Bowen, J
(Ireland): Home Int 1961

Bowman, TH
(England): Home Int 1932

Boxall, R
(England): Home Int 1980-81-82; v France 1982

Boyd, HA
(Ireland): v Wales 1913-23

Bradshaw, AS
(England): Home Int 1932

Bradshaw, EI
(England): v Scotland 1979; Eur T Ch 1979

Braid, H
(Scotland): v England 1922-23

Bramston, JAT
(England): v Scotland 1902

Brand, GJ
(England): Home Int 1976. (GBI) v Europe 1976

Brand, G
(Scotland): Home Int 1978-80; v England 1979; Eur T Ch 1979; v Italy 1979; v Belgium 1980; v France 1980. (GBI); v Europe 1978-80; in World Team Ch 1978-80; v America 1979; v France 1981

Branigan, D
(Ireland): Home Int 1975-76-77-80-81-82-86; Eur T Ch 1977-81; v West Germany, France, Sweden 1976

Bretherton, CF
(England): v Scotland 1922-23-24-25; v Wales/Ireland 1925

Briscoe, A
(Ireland): v England 1928-29-30-31; v Scotland 1929-30-31; v Wales 1929-30-31; Home Int 1932-33-38

Bristowe, OC
(GBI): v America 1923-24

Broad, RD
(Wales): v Ireland 1979; Home Int 1980-81-82-84; Eur T Ch 1981

Broadhurst, P
(England): Home Int 1986-87; v France 1988. (GBI) v Europe 1988

Brock, J
(Scotland) v Ireland 1929; Home Int 1932

Brodie, Allan
(Scotland): Home Int 1970-72-73-74-75-76-77-78-80; Eur T Ch 1973-77-79; v England 1979; v Italy 1979; v Belgium 1977; v Spain 1977; v France 1978. (GBI): v America 1977-79; v Europe 1974-76-78-80;in World Team Ch 1978

Brodie, Andrew
(Scotland): Home Int 1968-69; v Spain 1974

Bromley-Davenport, E
(England): Home Int 1938-51

Brooks, A
(Scotland): Home Int 1968-69; Eur T Ch 1969. (GBI): v America 1969

Brooks, CJ
(Scotland): Home Int 1984-85. (GBI): v Europe 1986

Brotherton, IR
(Scotland): Home Int 1984-85

Brough, S
(England): Home Int 1952-55-59-60; v France 1952-60. (GBI): v Europe 1960

Brown, CT
(Wales): Home Int 1970-71-72-73-74-75-77-78-80-88 (captain); Eur T Ch 1973; v Denmark 1977-80; v Ireland 1979; v Switzerland, Spain 1980

Brown, D
(Wales): v Ireland 1923-30-31; v England 1925; v Scotland 1931

Brown, JC
(Ireland): Home Int 1933-34-35-36-37-38-48-52-53

Brownlow, Hon WGE
(GBI): v America 1926

Bruen, J
(Ireland): Home Int 1937-38-49-50. (GBI): v America 1938-49-51

Bucher, AM
(Scotland): Home Int 1954-55-56; v Scandinavia 1956

Buckley, JA
(Wales): Home Int 1967-68-69-76-77-78; Eur T Ch 1967-69; v
Denmark 1976-77. (GBI): v America 1979

Burch, N
(England): Home Int 1974

Burgess, MJ
(England): Home Int 1963-64-67; Eur T Ch 1967

Burke, J
(Ireland): v England 1929-30-31; v Wales 1929-30-31;
v Scotland 1930-31; Home Int 1932-33-34-35-36-37-38-47-
48-49. (GBI): v America 1932

Burns, M
(Ireland): Home Int 1973-75-83

Burnside, J
(Scotland): Home Int 1956-57

Burrell, TM
(Scotland): v England 1924

Bussell, AF
(Scotland): Home Int 1956-57-58-61; v Scandinavia
1956-60. (GBI): v America 1957; v Europe 1956-62

Butterworth, JR
(England): v France 1954

Cairnes, HM
(Ireland): v Wales 1913-25; v England 1904; v Scotland
1904-27

Caldwell, I
(England): Home Int 1950-51-52-53-54-55-56-57-58-59-61;
v France 1950. (GBI): v America 1951-55

Calvert, M
(Wales): Home Int 1983-84-86-87-89

Cameron, D
(Scotland): Home Int 1938-51

Campbell, Bart, Sir Guy C
(Scotland): v England 1909-10-11

Campbell, HM
(Scotland): Home Int 1962-64-68; v Scandinavia 1962;
v Australia 1964; Eur T Ch 1965.(GBI): v Europe 1964

Campbell, JGS
(Scotland): Home Int 1947-48

Campbell, W
(Scotland): v Ireland 1927-28-29-30-31; v England 1928
-29-30-31; v Wales 1931; Home Int 1933-34-35-36.
(GBI): v America 1930

Cannon, JHS
(England): v Ireland/Wales 1925

Cannon, JM
(Scotland): Home Int 1969; v Spain 1974

Carman, A
(England): v Scotland 1979; Home Int 1980

Carr, FC
(England): v Scotland 1911

Carr, JB
(Ireland): Home Int 1947-48-49-50-51-52-53-54-55-56-57-58-
59-60-61-62-63-64-65-66-67-68-69; Eur T Ch 1965-67-69.
(GBI): v America 1947-49-51-53-55-57-59-61-63-65
(Captain) -67 (Captain); v Europe 1954-56-64-66-68;
in World Team Ch 1958-60

Carr, JJ
(Ireland): Home Int 1981-82-83

Carr, JP
(Wales): v Ireland 1913

Carr JR
(Ireland): v Wales 1930-31; v England 1931; Home Int 1933

Carr, R
(Ireland): Home Int 1970-71; Eur T Ch 1971.
(GBI): v America 1971

Carrgill, PM
(England): Home Int 1978

Carrick, DG
(Scotland): Home Int 1981-82-83-84-85-86-87-88-89; v West
Germany 1987; v Italy 1988; v France 1989; Eur T Ch 1989.
(GBI): v America 1983-87; v Europe 1986

Carroll, CA
(Ireland): v Wales 1924

Carroll, JP
(Ireland): Home Int 1948-49-50-51-62

Carroll, W
(Ireland): v Wales 1913-23-24-25; v England 1925;
v Scotland 1929; Home Int 1932

Carslaw, LA
(Scotland): Home Int 1976-77-78-80-81; Eur T Ch 1977-79;
v England 1979; v Italy 1979; v Spain 1977;
v Belgium 1978; v France 1978. (GBI): v Europe 1978;
v America 1979

Carvill, J
(Ireland): Home Int 1989; Eur T Ch 1989. (GBI): v Europe
1990

Cashell, BG
(Ireland): Home Int 1978; v France, West Germany, Sweden
1978

Cassells, C
(England): Home Int 1989

Castle, H
(England): v Scotland 1903-04

Cater, JR
(Scotland): Home Int 1952-53-54-55-56. (GBI): v America
1955

Caul, P
(Ireland): Home Int 1968-69-71-72-73-74-75

Caven, J
(Scotland): v England 1926. (GBI): v America 1922

Chapman, BHG
(England): Home Int 1961-62. (GBI): v America 1961;
v Europe 1962

Chapman, JA
(Wales): v Ireland 1923-29-30-31; v Scotland 1931;
v England 1925

Chapman, R
(Wales): v Ireland 1929; Home Int 1932-34-35-36

Chapman, R
(England): v Scotland 1979; Home Int 1980-81; Eur T Ch
1981. (GBI): v Europe 1980; v America 1981

Charles, WB
(Wales): v Ireland 1924

Chillas, D
(Scotland): Home Int 1971

Christmas, MJ
(England): Home Int 1960-61-62-63-64. (GBI): v America
1961-63; v Europe 1962-64; in World Team Ch 1962

Clark, CA
(England): Home Int 1964. (GBI): v Europe 1964;
v America 1965

Clark, D
(Ireland): Home Int 1987-89. (GBI): v Europe 1990

Clark, GJ
(England): Home Int 1961-64-66-67-68-71.
(GBI): v Europe 1964-66; v America 1965.

Clark, HK
(England): Home Int 1973. (GBI): v America 1973

Clark, MD
(Wales): v Ireland 1947

Clay, G
(Wales): Home Int 1962

Claydon, R
(England): Home Int 1988; Eur T Ch 1989: (GBI): v America 1989

Cleary, T
(Ireland): Home Int 1976-77-78-82-83-84-85-86; v Wales 1979; v France, West Germany, Sweden 1976

Clement, G
(Wales): v Ireland 1979

Cochran, JS
(Scotland): Home Int 1966

Colt, HS
(England): v Scotland 1908

Coltart, A
(Scotland): Home Int 1988-89-90; Eur T Ch 1989; v Sweden 1990; v Italy 1990; Nixdorf Nations Cup 1990; (GBI): v Europe 1990; World Cup 1990

Cook, J
(England): Home Int 1989-90

Cook, JH
(England): Home Int 1969

Corridan, T
(Ireland): Home Int 1983-84

Corcoran, DK
(Ireland): Home Int 1972-73; Eur T Ch 1973

Cosh, GB
(Scotland): Home Int 1964-65-66-67-68-69; Eur T Ch 1965-69. (GBI): v America 1965; v Europe 1966-68; in Com Tnmt 1967; in World Team Ch 1966-68

Coulter, JG
(Wales): Home Int 1951-52

Coutts, FJ
(Scotland): Home Int 1980-81-82; Eur T Ch 1981; v France 1981-82

Cox, S
(Wales): Home Int 1970-71-72-73-74; Eur T Ch 1971-73

Crabbe, JL
(Ireland): v Wales 1925; v Scotland 1927-28

Craddock, T
(Ireland): Home Int 1955-56-57-58-59-60-67-68-69-70; Eur T Ch 1971. (GBI): v America 1967-69

Craigan, RM
(Ireland): Home Int 1963-64

Crawford, D
(Scotland): Home Int 1990

Crawley, LG
(England): v Ireland 1931; v Scotland 1931; Home Int 1932-33-34-36-37-38-47-48-49-54-55; v France 1936-37-38-49. (GBI): v America 1932-34-38-47

Critchley, B
(England): Home Int 1962-69-70; Eur T Ch 1969. (GBI): v America 1969; v Europe 1970

Crosbie, GF
(Ireland): Home Int 1953-55-56-57-88 (captain)

Crowley, M
(Ireland): v England 1928-29-30-31; v Wales 1929-31; v Scotland 1929-30-31; Home Int 1932

Cuddihy, J
(Scotland): Home Int 1977

Curry, DH
(England): Home Int 1984-86-87; v France 1988. (GBI): v Europe 1986-88 v America 1987

Dalgleish, CR
(Scotland): Home Int 1981-82-83-89; v France 1982; Eur T Ch 1981; Nixdorf Nations Cup 1989. (GBI): v America 1981

Darwin, B
(England): v Scotland 1902-04-05-08-09-10-23-24. (GBI): v America 1922

Davies, EN
(Wales): Home Int 1959-60-61-62-63-64-65-66-67-68-69-70-71-72-73-74; Eur T Ch 1969-71-73

Davies, JC
(England) Home Int 1969-71-72-73-74-78; Eur T Ch 1973-75-77. (GBI): v Europe 1972-74-76-78; v America 1973-75-77-79; in World Team Ch 1974-76

Davies, FE
(Ireland): v Wales 1923

Davies, G
(Wales): v Denmark 1977; Home Int 1981-82-83

Davies, HE
(Wales): Home Int 1933-34-36

Davies, M
(England): Home Int 1984-85

Davies, TJ
(Wales): Home Int 1954-55-56-57-58-58-60

Davison, C
(England): Home Int 1989

Dawson, JE
(Scotland): v Ireland 1927-29-30-31; v England 1930-31; v Wales 1931; Home Int 1932-33-34-37

Dawson, M
(Scotland): Home Int 1963-65-66

Dawson, P
(England): Home Int 1969

Deboys, A
(Scotland): Home Int 1956-59-60; v Scandinavia 1960

Deeble, P
(England): Home Int 1975-76-77-78-80-81-83-84; v Scotland 1979; Eur T Ch 1979-81. (GBI): v America 1977-81; v Europe 1978; v France 1982; in Colombian Int 1978

Deighton, FWG
(Scotland): Home Int 1950-52-53-56-57-58-59-60. (GBI): v America 1951-57; v South Africa 1952; in Com Tnmt 1954-59

Denholm, RB
(Scotland): v Ireland 1929-31; v Wales 1931; v England 1931; Home Int 1932-33-34-35

Dewar, FG
(Scotland): Home Int 1952-53-55

Dick, CE
(Scotland): v England 1902-03-04-05-09-12

Dickson, HM
(Scotland): v Ireland 1929-31

Dickson, JR
(Ireland): Eur T Ch 1977; Home Int 1980

Disley, A
(Wales): Home Int 1976-77-78; v Denmark 1977;
v Ireland 1979

Dodd, SC
(Wales):Home Int 1985-87-88-89. (GBI): v America 1989

Donellan, B
(Ireland): Home Int 1952

Dowie, A
(Scotland): Home Int 1949

Downes, P
(England): Home Int 1976-77-78-80-81-82;
Eur T Ch 1977-79-81. (GBI): v Europe 1980

Downie, JJ
(England): Home Int 1974

Draper, JW
(Scotland): Home Int 1954

Drew, NV
(Ireland): Home Int 1952-53. (GBI): v America 1953

Duffy, I
(Wales): Home Int 1975

Duncan, AA
(Wales): Home Int 1933-34-36-38-47-48-49-50-51-52-53-
54-55-56-57-58-59. (GBI): v America (Captain) 1953

Duncan, GT
(Wales): Home Int 1952-53-54-55-56-57-58

Duncan, J, jr
(Wales): v Ireland 1913

Duncan, J
(Ireland): Home Int 1959-60-61

Dunn, NW
(England): v Ireland 1928

Dunn, P
(Wales): Home Int 1957-58-59-60-61-62-63-65-66

Dunne, E
(Ireland): Home Int 1973-74-76-77; v Wales 1979;
Eur T Ch 1975

Durrant, RA
(England): Home Int 1967; Eur T Ch 1967

Dykes, JM
(Scotland): Home Int 1934-35-36-48-49-51.
(GBI): v America 1936

Easingwood, SR
(Scotland): Home Int 1986-87-88-90; v Italy 1988-90; v France
1989; Eur T Ch 1989

Eaves, CH
(Wales): Home Int 1935-36-38-47-48-49

Edwards, B
(Ireland): Home Int 1961-62-64-65-66-67-68-69-73

Edwards, M
(Ireland): Home Int 1956-57-58-60-61-62

Edwards, TH
(Wales): Home Int 1947

Egan, TW
(Ireland): Home Int 1952-53-59-60-62-67-68;
Eur T Ch 1967-69

Eggo, R
(England): Home Int 1986-87-88-89-90; v France 1988.
(GBI): v America 1987; v Europe 1988

Elliot, A
(Scotland): Home Int 1989; v France 1989; Eur T Ch 1989

Elliot, C
(Scotland): Home Int 1982

Elliot, IA
(Ireland): Home Int 1975-77-78; Eur T Ch 1975,
v France, West Germany, Sweden 1978

Ellis, HC
(England): v Scotland 1902-12

Ellison, TF
(England): v Scotland 1922-25-26-27

Emerson, T
(Wales): Home Int 1932

Emery, G
(Wales): v Ireland 1925; Home Int 1933-36-38

Errity, D
(Ireland): Home Int 1990

Evans, AD
(Wales): v Scotland 1931-35; v Ireland 1931; Home Int 1932-
33-34-35-38-47-49-50-51-52-53-54-55-56-61

Evans, C
(Wales): Home Int 1990

Evans, Duncan
(Wales): Home Int 1978-80-81; v Ireland 1979;
Eur T Ch 1981. (GBI) v Europe 1980; v America 1981

Evans, G
(England): Home Int 1961

Evans, G
(England): Home Int 1990. (GBI) World Cup 1990

Evans, HJ
(Wales): Home Int 1976-77-78-80-81-84-85-87-88;
v France 1976; v Denmark 1977-80; v Ireland 1979;
Eur T Ch 1979-81; v Switzerland, Spain 1980

Evans, M Gear
(Wales): v Ireland 1930-31; v Scotland 1931

Everett, C
(Scotland): Home Int 1988-89-90; v Italy 1988-90;
v France 1989; Eur T Ch 1989; Nixdorf Nations Cup 1989-90;
v Sweden 1990;

Ewing, RC
(Ireland): Home Int 1934-35-36-37-38-47-48-49-50-51-53-
54-55-56-57-58. (GBI): v America 1936-38-47-49-51-55

Eyles, GR
(England): Home Int 1974-75; Eur T Ch 1975. (GBI): v
America 1975; v Europe 1974; in World Team Ch 1974

Fairbairn, KA
(England): Home Int 1988

Fairchild, CEL
(Wales): v Ireland 1923; v England 1925

Fairchild, LJ
(Wales): v Ireland 1924

Fairlie, WE
(Scotland): v England 1912

Faldo, N
(England): Home Int 1975. (GBI): in Com Tnmt 1975

Fanagan, J
(Ireland): Home Int 1989-90

Farmer, JC
(Scotland): Home Int 1970

Ferguson, M
(Ireland): Home Int 1952

Ferguson, WJ
(Ireland): Home Int 1952-54-55-58-59-61

Fergusson, S Mure
(Scotland): v England 1902-03-04

Ffrench, WF
(Ireland): v Scotland 1929; Home Int 1932

Fiddian, EW
(England): v Scotland 1929-30-31; v Ireland 1929-30-31;
Home Int 1932-33-34-35; v France 1934. (GBI): v America
1932-34

Fitzgibbon, JF
(Ireland): Home Int 1955-56-57

Fitzsimmons, J
(Ireland): Home Int 1938-47-48

Flaherty, JA
(Ireland): Home Int 1934-35-36-37

Flaherty, PD
(Ireland): Home Int 1967; Eur T Ch 1967-69

Fleming, J
(Scotland): Home Int 1987

Fleury, RA
(Ireland): Home Int 1974

Flockhart, AS
(Scotland): Home Int 1948-49

Fogarty, GN
(Ireland): Home Int 1956-58-63-64-67

Fogg, HN
(England): Home Int 1933

Forest, J de (now Count J de Bendern)
(England): v Ireland 1931; v Scotland 1931.
(GBI): v America 1932

Foster, MF
(England): Home Int 1973

Foster, R
(England): Home Int 1963-64-66-67-68-69-70-71-72;
Eur T Ch 1967-69-71-73. (GBI): v Europe 1964-66-68-70;
v America 1965-67-69-71-73-79 (Captain) -81 (Captain);
in Com Tnmt 1967-71; in World Team Ch 1964-70

Fowler, WH
(England): v Scotland 1903-04-05

Fox, SJ
(England): Home Int 1956-57-58

Frame, DW
(England): Home Int 1958-59-60-61-62-63.
(GBI): v America 1961

Francis, F
(England): Home Int 1936; v France 1935-36

Frazier, K
(England): Home Int 1938

Froggatt, P
(Ireland): Home Int 1957

Fry, SH
(England): v Scotland 1902-03-04-05-06-07-09

Gairdner, JR
(Scotland): v England 1902

Gallacher, BJ
(Scotland): Home Int 1967

Galloway, RF
(Scotland): Home Int 1957-58-59;
v Scandinavia 1958

Gannon, MA
(Ireland): Home Int 1973-74-77-78-80-81-83-84-87-88-89-90;
v France, West Germany, Sweden 1978-80;
Eur T Ch 1979-81-89. (GBI): v Europe 1974-78

Garbutt, I
(England): Home Int 1990

Garner, PF
(England): Home Int 1977-78-80; v Scotland 1979

Garnet, LG
(England): v France 1934. (GBI): v Australia 1934

Garson, R
(Scotland): v Ireland 1928-29

Gent, J
(England): v Ireland 1930; Home Int 1938

Gibb, C
(Scotland): v England 1927; v Ireland 1928

Gibson, WC
(Scotland): Home Int 1950-51

Gilford, CF
(Wales): Home Int 1963-64-65-66-67

Gilford, D
(England): Home Int 1983-84-85. (GBI): v America 1985;
v Europe 1986

Gill, WJ
(Ireland): v Wales 1931; Home Int 1932-33-34-35-36-37

Gillies, HD
(England): v Scotland 1908-25-26-27

Girvan, P
(Scotland): Home Int 1986; West Germany 1987.
(GBI): v America 1987

Glossop, R
(Wales): Home Int 1935-37-38-47

Glover, J
(Ireland): Home Int 1951-52-53-55-59-60-70

Godwin, G
(England): Home Int 1976-77-78-80-81; v Scotland 1979;
v France 1982; Eur T Ch 1979-81. (GBI): v America 1979-81

Goulding, N
(Ireland): Home Int 1988-89-90

Graham, AJ
(Scotland): v England 1925

Graham, J
(Scotland): v England 1902-03-04-05-06-07-08-09-10-11

Graham, JSS
(Ireland): Home Int 1938-50-51

Gray, CD
(England): Home Int 1932

Green, CW
(Scotland): Home Int 1961-62-63-64-65-67-68-69-70-71-72-
73-74-75-76-77-78; Eur T Ch 1965-67-69-71-73-75-77-79;
v Scandinavia 1962; v Belgium 1973-75-77-78; v Spain 1977; v
Italy 1979; v England 1979. (GBI): v Europe 1962-66-68-70-
72-74-76; v America 1963-69-71-73-75-83 (Captain) -85
(Captain) in Com Tnmt 1971; in World Team Ch 1970-72

Green, HB
(England): v Scotland 1979

Green, PO
(England): Home Int 1961-62-63. (GBI): in Com Tnmt 1963

Greene, R
(Ireland): Home Int 1933

Greig, DG
(Scotland): Home Int 1972-73-75. (GBI): in Com Tnmt 1975

Greig, K
(Scotland): Home Int 1933

Griffiths, HGB
(Wales): v Ireland 1923-24-25

Griffiths, HS
(Wales): v England 1958

Griffiths, JA
(Wales): Home Int 1933

Guild, WJ
(Scotland): v England 1925-27-28; v Ireland 1927-28

Hales, JP
(Wales): v Scotland 1963

Hall, AH
(Scotland): Home Int 1962-66-69

Hall, D
(Wales): Home Int 1932-37

Hall, K
(Wales): Home Int 1955-59

Hambro, AV
(England): v Scotland 1905-08-09-10-22

Hamilton, CJ
(Wales): v Ireland 1913

Hamilton, ED
(Scotland): Home Int 1936-37-38

Hamer, S
(England): Home Int 1983-84

Hanway, M
(Ireland): Home Int 1971-74

Hardman, RH
(England): v Scotland 1927-28. (GBI): v America 1928

Hare, A
(England): Home Int 1988; Eur T Ch 1989. (GBI) v America 1989

Hare, WCD
(Scotland): Home Int 1953

Harrhy, A
(Wales): Home Int 1988-89

Harrington, J
(Ireland): Home Int 1960-61-74-75-76; Eur T Ch 1975; v Wales 1979

Harrington, P
(Ireland): Home Int 1990

Harris, IR
(Scotland): Home Int 1955-56-58-59

Harris, R
(Scotland): v England 1905-08-10-11-12-22-23-24-25-26-27-28 (GBI): v America 1922 (Captain) -23 (Captain) -26 (Captain)

Harrison, JW
(Wales): Home Int 1937-50

Hartley, RW
(England): v Scotland 1926-27-28-29-30-31; v Ireland 1928-29-30-31; Home Int 1933-34-35. (GBI): v America 1930-32

Hartley, WL
(England): v Ireland/Wales 1925; v Scotland 1927-31; v Ireland 1928-31; Home Int 1932-33; v France 1935. (GBI): v America 1932

Hassall, JE
(England): v Scotland 1923; v Ireland/Wales 1925

Hastings, JL
(Scotland): Home Int 1957-58; v Scandinavia 1958

Hawksworth, J
(England): Home Int 1984-85. (GBI): v America 1985

Hay, G
(Scotland): v England 1979; Home Int 1980-88-90; v Belgium 1980; v France 1980-82-89; v Italy 1988. (GBI): v Europe 1986

Hay, J
(Scotland): Home Int 1972

Hayes, JA
(Ireland): Home Int 1977

Hayward, CH
(England): v Scotland 1925; v Ireland 1928

Healy, TM
(Ireland): v Scotland 1931; v England 1931

Heather, D
(Ireland): Home Int 1976; v France, West Germany, Sweden 1976

Hedges, PJ
(England): Home Int 1970-73-74-75-76-77-78-82-83; Eur T Ch 1973-75-77. (GBI): v America 1973-75; v Europe 1974-76; in World Team Ch 1974

Hegarty, J
(Ireland): Home Int 1975

Hegarty, TD
(Ireland): Home Int 1957

Helm, AGB
(England): Home Int 1948

Henderson, J
(Ireland): v Wales 1923

Henderson, N
(Scotland): Home Int 1963-64

Henriques, GLQ
(England): v Ireland 1930

Henry, W
(England): Home Int 1987; v France 1988

Herlihy, B
(Ireland): Home Int 1950

Herne, KTC
(Wales): v Ireland 1913

Heverin, AJ
(Ireland): Home Int 1978; v France, West Germany, Sweden 1978

Hezlet, CO
(Ireland): v Wales 1923-25-27-29-31; v Scotland 1927-28-29-30-31; v England 1929-30-31. (GBI): v America 1924-26-28; v South Africa 1927

Higgins, L
(Ireland): Home Int 1968-70-71

Hill, GA
(England): Home Int 1936-37. (GBI): v America 1936-55 (Captain)

Hilton, HH
(England): v Scotland 1902-03-04-05-06-07-09-10-11-12

Hird, K
(Scotland): Home Int 1987-88-89; Nixdorf Nations Cup 1989;
v Italy 1990

Hoad, PGJ
(England): Home Int 1978; v Scotland 1979

Hodgson, C
(England): v Scotland 1924

Hoey, TBC
(Ireland): Home Int 1970-71-72-73-77-84; Eur T Ch 1971-77

Hogan, P
(Ireland): Home Int 1985-86-87-88

Holderess, Sir EWE
(England): v Scotland 1922-23-24-25-26-28.
(GBI): v America 1921-23-26-30

Holmes, AW
(England): Home Int 1962

Homer, TWB
(England): Home Int 1972-73; Eur T Ch 1973. (GBI): v
America 1973; v Europe 1972; in World Team Ch 1972

Homewood, G
(England): Home Int 1985

Hooman, CVL
(England): v Scotland 1910-22. (GBI): v America 1922-23

Hope, WL
(Scotland): v England 1923-25-26-27-28-29.
(GBI): v America 1923-24-28

Horne, A
(Scotland): Home Int 1971

Hosie, JR
(Scotland): Home Int 1936

Houston, G
(Wales): Home Int 1990

Howard, DB
(Scotland): v England 1979; Home Int 1980-81-82-83;
v Belgium 1980; v France 1980-81; Eur T Ch 1981.
(GBI): v Europe 1980.

Howell, HR
(Wales): v Ireland 1923-24-25-29-30-31; v England 1925;
v Scotland 1931; Home Int 1932-34-35-36-37-38-47

Howell, H Logan
(Wales): v Ireland 1925

Huddy, G
(England): Home Int 1960-61-62. (GBI): v America 1961

Huggan, J
(Scotland): Home Int 1981-82-83-84; v France 1982;
Eur T Ch 1981

Hughes, I
(Wales): Home Int 1954-55-56

Hulme, WJ
(Ireland): Home Int 1955-56-57

Humphrey, JG
(Wales): v Ireland 1925

Humphreys, AR
(Ireland): v England 1957

Humphreys, DI
(Wales): Home Int 1972

Humphreys, W
(England): Home Int 1970-71; Eur T Ch 1971.
(GBI): v Europe 1970; v America 1971

Hunter, NM
(Scotland): v England 1903-12

Hunter, WI
(Scotland): v England 1922

Hutcheon, I
(Scotland): Home Int 1971-72-73-74-75-76-77-78-80;
v Belgium 1973-75-77-78-80; v Spain 1977; v France 1978
-80-81; v Italy 1979; Eur T Ch 1973-75-77-79-81.
(GBI): v Europe 1974-76; v America 1975-77-79-81;
in World Team Ch 1974-76-80; in Com Tnmt 1975;
in Dominican Int 1973; in Colombian Int 1975

Hutchings, C
(England): v Scotland 1902

Hutchinson, HG
(England): v Scotland 1902-03-04-06-07-09

Hutchison, CK
(Scotland): v England 1904-05-06-07-08-09-10-11-12

Hyde, GE
(England): Home Int 1967-68

Illingworth, G
(England): v Scotland 1929; v France 1937

Inglis, MJ
(England): Home Int 1977

Isitt, GH
(Wales): v Ireland 1923

Jack, RR
(Scotland): Home Int 1950-51-54-55-56-57-58-59-61;
v Scandinavia 1958. (GBI): v America 1957-59; v
Europe 1956; in World Team Ch 1958; in Com Tnmt
1959

Jack, WS
(Scotland): Home Int 1955

Jacob, NE
(Wales): Home Int 1932-33-34-35-36

James, D
(Scotland): Home Int 1985

James, M
(England): Home Int 1974-75; Eur T Ch 1975
(GBI): v America 1975

James, RD
(England): Home Int 1974-75

Jameson, JF
(Ireland): v Wales 1913-24

Jamieson, A, jr
(Scotland): v England 1927-28-31; v Ireland 1928-31;
v Wales 1931; Home Int 1932-33-36-37.
(GBI): v America 1926

Jamieson, D
(Scotland): Home Int 1980

Jenkins, JLC
(Scotland): v England 1908-12-22-24-26-28;
v Ireland 1928. (GBI): v America 1921

Jermine, JG
(Wales): Home Int 1972-73-74-75-76-82; Eur T Ch
1975-77; v France 1975

Jobson, RH
(England): v Ireland 1928

Johnson, R
(Wales): Home Int 1990

Johnson, TWG
(Ireland): v England 1929

Johnston, JW
(Scotland): Home Int 1970-71

Jones, A
(Wales): Home Int 1989-90

Jones, DK
(Wales): Home Int 1973

Jones, EO
(Wales): Home Int 1983-85-86

Jones, JG Parry
(Wales): Home Int 1959-60

Jones, JL
(Wales): Home Int 1933-34-36

Jones, JR
(Wales): Home Int 1970-72-73-77-78-80-81-82-83-84-85;
Eur T Ch 1973-79-81; v Denmark 1976-80; v Ireland
1979; v Switzerland, Spain 1980; v Ireland 1979

Jones, JW
(England): Home Int 1948-49-50-51-52-54-55

Jones, KG
(Wales): Home Int 1988

Jones, MA
(Wales): Home Int 1947-48-49-50-51-53-54-57

Jones, Malcolm F
(Wales): Home Int 1933

Jones, SP
(Wales): Home Int 1981-82-83-84-85-86-88-89

Kane, RM
(Ireland): Home Int 1967-68-71-72-74-78; Eur T Ch
1971-79; v Wales 1979. (GBI): v Europe 1974

Kearney, K
(Ireland): Home Int 1988-89-90

Keenan, S
(Ireland): Home Int 1989

Kelleher, WA
(Ireland): Home Int 1962

Kelley, MJ
(England): Home Int 1974-75-76-77-78-80-81-82-88
(Captain); v France 1982; Eur T Ch 1977-79. (GBI): v America
1977-79; v Europe 1976-78; in World Team Ch 1976; in
Colombian Int 1978

Kelley, PD
(England): Home Int 1965-66-68

Kelly, NS
(Ireland): Home Int 1966

Keppler, SD
(England): Home Int 1982-83; v France 1982.
(GBI): v America 1983

Kilduff, AJ
(Ireland): v Scotland 1928

Killey, GC
(Scotland): v Ireland 1928

King, M
(England): Home Int 1969-70-71-72-73; Eur T Ch 1971-73
(GBI): v America 1969-73; v Europe 1970-72; in Com Tnmt
1971

Kissock, B
(Ireland): Home Int 1961-62-74-76; v France, West
Germany, Sweden 1978

Kitchin, JE
(England): v France 1949

Knight, B
(Wales): Home Int 1986

Knipe, RG
(Wales): Home Int 1953-54-55-56

Knowles, S
(Scotland): Home Int 1990

Knowles, WR
(Wales): v England 1948

Kyle, AT
(Scotland): Home Int 1938-47-49-50-51-52-53.
(GBI): v America 1938-47-51; v South Africa 1952

Kyle, D
(Scotland): v England 1924-30. (GBI): v America 1924

Kyle, EP
(Scotland): v England 1925

Laidlay, JE
(Scotland): v England 1902-03-04-05-06-07-08-09-10-11

Lake, AD
(Wales): Home Int 1958

Lang, JA
(Scotland): v England 1929-31; v Ireland 1929-30-31;
v Wales 1931. (GBI): v America 1930

Langley, JDA
(England): Home Int 1950-51-52-53; v France 1950.
(GBI): v America 1936-51-53

Langmead, J
(England): Home Int 1986

Lassen, EA
(England): v Scotland 1909-10-11-12

Last, CN
(Wales): Home Int 1975

Laurence, C
(England): Home Int 1983-84-85

Lawrie, CD
(Scotland): Home Int 1949-50-55-56-57-58; v Scandinavia
1958. (GBI): v South Africa 1952; v America 1961
(Captain) -63 (Captain)

Lawrie, G
(Scotland): Home Int 1990

Layton, EN
(England): v Scotland 1922-23-26; v Ireland/Wales 1925

Lee, IGF
(Scotland): Home Int 1958-59-60-61-62; v Scandinavia 1960

Lee, JN
(Wales): Home Int 1988-89

Lee, M
(England): Home Int 1950

Lee, MG
(England): Home Int 1965

Lehane, N
(Ireland): Home Int 1976; v France, West Germany,
Sweden 1976

Lewis, DH
(Wales): Home Int 1935-36-37-38

Lewis, DR
(Wales): v Ireland 1925-29-30-31; v Scotland 1931;
Home Int 1932-34

Lewis, ME
(England): Home Int 1980-81-82; v France 1982.
(GBI): v America 1983

Lewis, R Cofe
(Wales): v Ireland 1925

Leyden, PJ
(Ireland): Home Int 1953-55-56-57-59

Lincoln, AC
(England): v Scotland 1907

Lindsay, J
(Scotland): Home Int 1933-34-35-36

Lloyd, HM
(Wales): v Ireland 1913

Lloyd, RM de
(Wales): v Scotland 1931; v Ireland 1931; Home Int 1932-33-34-35-36-37-38-47-48

Llyr, A
(Wales): Home Int 1984-85

Lockhart, G
(Scotland): v England 1911-12

Lockley, AE
(Wales): Home Int 1956-57-58-62

Logan, GW
(England): Home Int 1973

Long, D
(Ireland): Home Int 1973-74-80-81-82-83-84; v Wales 1979; Eur T Ch 1979

Low, AJ
(Scotland): Home Int 1964-65; Eur T Ch 1965

Low, JL
(Scotland): v England 1904

Lowe, A
(Ireland): v Wales 1924; v England 1925-28; v Scotland 1927-28

Lowson, G
(Scotland): Home Int 1989-90; v Sweden 1990

Lucas, PB
(England): Home Int 1936-48-49; v France 1936. (GBI): v America 1936-47-49 (Captain)

Lunt, MSR
(England): Home Int 1956-57-58-59-60-62-63-64-66. (GBI): v America 1959-61-63-65; v Europe 1964; in Com Tnmt 1963; in World Team Ch 1964

Lunt, S
(England): Home Int 1932-33-34-35; v France 1934-35-39

Lygate, M
(Scotland): Home Int 1970-75-88 (Captain); Eur T Ch 1971

Lyle, AWB
(England): Home Int 1975-76-77; Eur T Ch 1977. (GBI): v America 1977; in Com Tnmt 1975; v Europe 1976

Lyon, JS
(England): Home Int 1937-38

Lyons, P
(Ireland): Home Int 1986

McAllister, SD
(Scotland): Home Int 1983

Macara, MA
(Wales): Home Int 1983-84-85-87-89-90

McArthur, W
(Scotland): Home Int 1952-54

McBeath, J
(Scotland): Home Int 1964

McBride, D
(Scotland): Home Int 1932

McCallum, AR
(Scotland): v England 1929. (GBI): v America 1928

McCarrol, F
(Ireland): Home Int 1968-69

McCart, DM
(Scotland): Home Int 1977; v Belgium 1978

McCarthy, L
(Ireland): Home Int 1953-54-55-56

McConnell, FP
(Ireland): v Wales 1929-30-31; v England 1929-30-31; v Scotland 1930-31; Home Int 1934

McConnell, RM
(Ireland): v Wales 1924-25-29-30-31; v England 1925-28-29-30-31; v Scotland 1927-28-29-31; Home Int 1934-35-36-37

McConnell, WG
(Ireland): v England 1925

McCormack, JD
(Ireland): v Wales 1913-24; v England 1928, Home Int 1932-33-34-35-36-37

McCrea, WE
(Ireland): Home Int 1965-66-67; Eur T Ch 1965

McCready, SM
(Ireland): Home Int 1947-49-50-52-54. (GBI): v America 1949-51

McDaid, B
(Ireland): v Wales 1979

MacDonald, GK
(Scotland): Home Int 1978-81-82; v England 1979; v France 1981-82

McDonald, H
(Scotland): Home Int 1970

Macdonald, JS
(Scotland): Home Int 1969-70-71-72; v Belgium 1973; Eur T Ch 1971. (GBI): v Europe 1970; v America 1971

McEvoy, P
(England): Home Int 1976-77-78-80-81-83-84-85-86-87-88-89; v Scotland 1979; v France 1982-88; Eur T Ch 1977-79-81-89; (GBI): v America 1977-79-81-85-89; v Europe 1978-80-86-88; in World Cup 1978-80-88 (winners)

Macfarlane, CB
(Scotland): v England 1912

McGimpsey, G
(Ireland): Home Int 1978-80-81-82-83-84-85-86-87-88-89-90; v Wales 1979; Eur T Ch 1981-89. (GBI): v America 1985-89; v Europe 1986-88-90; World Cup 1988 (winners)

McGinley, P
(Ireland): Home Int 1989-90

Macgregor, A
(Scotland): v Scandinavia 1956

Macgregor, G
(Scotland): Home Int 1969-70-71-72-73-74-75-76-80-81-82-83-84-85-86-87; v Belgium 1973-75-80; v England 1979; Eur T Ch 1971-73-75-81. (GBI): v Europe 1970-74; v America 1971-75-83-85-87-91 (Captain); in Com Tnmt 1971-75; v France 1981-82

MacGregor, RC
(Scotland): Home Int 1951-52-53-54. (GBI): v America 1953

McHenry, J
(Ireland): Home Int 1985-86. (GBI): v America 1987

McInally, H
(Scotland): Home Int 1937-47-48

McInally, RH
(Ireland): Home Int 1949-51

McIntosh, E
(Scotland): Home Int 1989

Macintosh, KW
(Scotland): v England 1979; Home Int 1980; v France 1980; v Belgium 1980. (GBI): v Europe 1980

McKay, G
(Scotland): Home Int 1969

McKay, JR
(Scotland): Home Int 1950-51-52-54

McKellar, PJ
(Scotland): Home Int 1976-77-78; v Belgium 1978; v France 1978; v England 1979. (GBI): v America 1977; v Europe 1978

Mackenzie, F
(Scotland): v England 1902-03

MacKenzie, S
(Scotland): Home Int 1990

Mackenzie, WW
(Scotland): v England 1923-26-27-29; v Ireland 1930. (GBI): v America 1922-23

Mackeown, HN
(Ireland): Home Int 1973; Eur T Ch 1973

Mackie, GW
(Scotland): Home Int 1948-50

McKinna, RA
(Scotland): Home Int 1938

McKinlay, SL
(Scotland): v England 1929-30-31; v Ireland 1930; v Wales 1931; Home Int 1932-33-35-37-47. (GBI): v America 1934

McKinnon, A
(Scotland): Home Int 1947-52

McLean, D
(Wales): Home Int 1968-69-70-71-72-73-74-75-76-77-78-80-81-82-83-85-86-88-90; Eur T Ch 1975-77-79-81; v France 1975-76; v Denmark 1976-80; v Ireland 1979; v Switzerland, Spain 1980

McLean, J
(Scotland): Home Int 1932-33-34-35-36. (GBI): v America 1934-36; v Australia 1934

McLeod, AE
(Scotland): Home Int 1937-38

McLeod, WS
(Scotland): Home Int 1935-37-38-47-48-49-50-51

McMenamin, E
(Ireland): Home Int 1981

McMullan, C
(Ireland): Home Int 1933-34-35

McNair, AA
(Scotland): v Ireland 1929

MacNamara, L
(Ireland): Home Int 1977-83-84-85-86-87-88-89-90; Eur T Ch 1977

McRuvie, EA
(Scotland): v England 1929-30-31; v Ireland 1930-31; v Wales 1931; Home Int 1932-33-34-35-36. (GBI): v America 1932-34

McTear, J
(Scotland): Home Int 1971

Madeley, JFD
(Ireland): Home Int 1959-60-61-62-63-64. (GBI): v Europe 1962; v America 1963

Mahon, RJ
(Ireland): Home Int 1938-52-54-55

Maliphant, FR
(Wales): Home Int 1932

Malone, B
(Ireland): Home Int 1959-64-69-71-75; Eur T Ch 1971-75

Manford, GC
(Scotland): v England 1922-23

Manley, N
(Ireland): v Wales 1924; v England 1928; v Scotland 1927-28

Mann, LS
(Scotland): Home Int 1982-83. (GBI): v America 1983

Marchbank, B
(Scotland): Home Int 1978; v Italy 1979; Eur T Ch 1979. (GBI): v Europe 1976-78; in World Team Ch 1978; v America 1979

Marks, GC
(England): Home Int 1963-67-68-69-70-71-74-75-82; Eur T Ch 1967-69-71-75. (GBI): v Europe 1968-70; v America 1969-71-87 (Captain)-89 (Captain); in World Team Ch 1970; in Com Tnmt 1975; in Colombian Int 1975. Non playing captain v France 1982

Marren, JM
(Ireland): v Wales 1925

Marsh, DM
(England): Home Int 1956-57-58-59-60-64-66-68-69-70-71-72; Eur T Ch 1971. (GBI): v Europe 1958; v America 1959-71-73 (Captain) -75 (Captain)

Marshman, A
(Wales): Home Int 1952

Marston, CC
(Wales): v Ireland 1929-30-31; v Scotland 1931

Martin, DHR
(England): Home Int 1938; v France 1934-49

Martin, GNC
(Ireland): v Wales 1923-29; v Scotland 1928-29-30; v England 1929-30. (GBI): v America 1928

Martin, S
(Scotland): Home Int 1975-76-77; Eur T Ch 1977; v Belgium 1977; v Spain 1977. (GBI): v America 1977; v Europe 1976; in World Team Ch 1976

Mason, SC
(England): Home Int 1973

Mathias-Thomas, FEL
(Wales): v Ireland 1924-25

Matthews, RL
(Wales): Home Int 1935-37

Maxwell, R
(Scotland): v England 1902-03-04-05-06-07-09-10

Mayo, PM
(Wales): Home Int 1982-87. (GBI): v America 1985-87

Meharg, W
(Ireland): Home Int 1957

Melia, TJ
(Wales): Home Int 1976-77-78-80-81-82; v Ireland 1979; Eur T Ch 1977-79; v Denmark 1976-80; v Switzerland, Spain 1980

Mellin, GL
(England): v Scotland 1922

Melville, LM Balfour
(Scotland): v England 1902-03
Melville, TE
(Scotland): Home Int 1974
Menzies, A
(Scotland): v England 1925
Metcalfe, J
(England): Home Int 1989. (GBI) v Europe 1990
Micklem, GH
(England): Home Int 1947-48-49-50-51-52-53-54-55.
(GBI): v America 1947-49-53-55-57 (Captain) -59 (Captain); in
World Team 1958
Mill, JW
(Scotland): Home Int 1953-54
Millensted, DJ
(England): Home Int 1966; Eur T Ch 1967. (GBI): v America
1967; in Com Tnmt 1967
Miller, AC
(Scotland): Home Int 1954-55
Miller, MJ
(Scotland): Home Int 1974-75-77-78; v Belgium 1978;
v France 1978
Milligan, JW
(Scotland): Home Int 1986-87-88-89-90; v West Germany
1987; v Italy 1988-90; v France 1989; Eur T Ch 1989; Nixdorf
Nations Cup 1989; v Sweden 1990. (GBI): v Europe 1988;
World Cup 1988 (winners)-90. (GBI): v America 1989
Mills, ES
(Wales): Home Int 1957
Millward, EB
(England): Home Int 1950-52-53-54-55. (GBI): v America
1949-55
Milne, WTG
(Scotland): Home Int 1972-73; Eur T Ch 1973;
v Belgium 1973. (GBI): v America 1973
Mitchell, A
(England): v Scotland 1910-11-12
Mitchell, CS
(England): Home Int 1975-76-78
Mitchell, FH
(England): v Scotland 1906-07-08
Mitchell, JWH
(Wales): Home Int 1964-65-66
Moffat, DM
(England): Home Int 1961-63-67; v France 1959-60
Moir, A
(Scotland): Home Int 1983-84
Montgomerie, CS
(Scotland): Home Int 1984-85-86; v West Germany 1987.
(GBI): v America 1985-87; v Europe 1986
Montgomerie, JS
(Scotland): Home Int 1957; v Scandinavia 1958
Montgomerie, RH de
(England): v Scotland 1908; v Wales/Ireland 1925;
v South Africa 1927. (GBI): v America 1921
Moody, JV
(West): Home Int 1947-48-49-51-56-58-59-60-61
Moody, PH
(England): Home Int 1971-72. (GBI): v Europe 1972
Moore, GJ
(Ireland): v England 1928; v Wales 1929

Morgan, JL
(Wales): 1948-49-50-51-52-53-54-55-56-57-58-59-60-61-62-
64-68. (GBI): v America 1951-53-55
Morris, FS
(Scotland): Home Int 1963
Morris, MF
(Ireland): Home Int 1978-80-82-83-84; v Wales 1979;
Eur T Ch 1979; v France, West Germany, Sweden 1980
Morris, R
(Wales): Home Int 1983-86-87
Morris, TS
(Wales): v Ireland 1924-29-30
Morrison, JH
(Scotland): v Scandinavia 1960
Morrison, JSF
(England): v Ireland 1930
Morrow, AJC
(Ireland): Home Int 1975-83
Morrow, JM
(Wales): v Ireland 1979; Home Int 1980-81; Eur T Ch
1979-81; v Denmark, Switzerland, Spain 1980
Mosey, IJ
(England): Home Int 1971
Moss, AV
(Wales): Home Int 1965-66-68
Mouland, MG
(Wales): Home Int 1978-81; v Ireland 1979; Eur T Ch 1979
Moxon, GA
(Wales): v Ireland 1929-30
Mulcare, P
(Ireland): Home Int 1968-69-70-71-72-74-78-80; v France,
West Germany, Sweden 1978-80; Eur T Ch 1975-79.
(GBI): v Europe 1972; v America 1975
Mulholland, D
(Ireland): Home Int 1988
Munn, E
(Ireland): v Wales 1913-23-24; v Scotland 1927
Munn, L
(Ireland): v Wales 1913-23-24; Home Int 1936-37
Munro, RAG
(Scotland): Home Int 1960
Murdoch, D
(Scotland): Home Int 1964
Murphy, AR
(Scotland): Home Int 1961-65-67
Murphy, P
(Ireland): Home Int 1985-86
Murray, GH
(Scotland): Home Int 1973-74-75-76-77-78-83; v Spain
1974-77; v Belgium 1975-77; Eur T Ch 1975-77.
(GBI): v America 1977; v Europe 1978
Murray, SWT
(Scotland): Home Int 1959-60-61-62-63; v Scandinavia
1960. (GBI): v Europe 1958-62; v America 1963
Murray, WA
(Scotland): v England 1923-24-25-26-27. (GBI): v America
1923-24
Murray, WB
(Scotland): Home Int 1967-68-69; Eur T Ch 1969
Muscroft, R
(England): Home Int 1986

Nash A
(England): Home Int 1988-89

Neech, DG
(England): Home Int 1961

Neill, JH
(Ireland): Home Int 1938-47-48-49

Neill, R
(Scotland): Home Int 1936

Nestor, JM
(Ireland): Home Int 1962-63-64

Nevin, V
(Ireland): Home Int 1960-63-65-67-69-72;
Eur T Ch 1967-69-73

Newey, AS
(England): Home Int 1932

Newman, JE
(Wales): Home Int 1932

Newton, H
(Wales): v Ireland 1929

Nicholson, J
(Ireland): Home Int 1932

Noon, GS
(Wales): Home Int 1935-36-37

Noon, J
(Scotland): Home Int 1987

O'Boyle, P
(Ireland): Eur T Ch 1977

O'Brien, MD
(Ireland): Home Int 1968-69-70-71-72-75-76-77; Eur T
Ch 1971; v France, West Germany, Sweden 1976

O'Carroll, C
(Wales): Home Int 1989-90

O'Connell, A
(Ireland): Home Int 1967-70-71-71

O'Connell, E
(Ireland): Home Int 1985; Eur T Ch 1989. (GBI): v Europe
1988; World Cup 1988 (winners). (GBI): v America 1989

O'Leary, JE
(Ireland): Home Int 1969-70; Eur T Ch 1969

O'Neill, JJ
(Ireland): Home Int 1968

Oldcorn, A
(England): Home Int 1982-83. (GBI): v America 1983

Oosterhuis, PA
(England): Home Int 1966-67-68. (GBI): v America 1967;
v Europe 1968; in World Team Ch 1968

Oppenheimer, RH
(England): v Ireland 1928-29-30; v Scotland 1930.
(GBI): v America 1957 (Captain)

O'Rourke, P
(Ireland): Home Int 1980-81-82-84-85

O'Sullivan, D
(Ireland): Home Int 1985-86-87

O'Sullivan, DF
(Ireland): Home Int 1976; Eur T Ch 1977

O'Sullivan, WM
(Ireland): Home Int 1934-35-36-37-38-47-48-49-50-51-53-54

Osgood, TH
(Scotland): v England 1925

Owen, JB
(Wales): Home Int 1971

Owens, GF
(Wales): Home Int 1960-61

Ownes, GH
(Ireland): Home Int 1935-37-38-47

Palferman, H
(Wales): Home Int 1950-53

Palmer, DJ
(England): Home Int 1962-63

Parfitt, RWM
(Wales): v Ireland 1924

Parkin, AP
(Wales): Home Int 1980-81-82. (GBI): v America 1983

Parry, JR
(Wales): Home Int 1966-75-76-77; v France 1976

Patey, IR
(England): Home Int 1952; v France 1948-49-50

Patrick, KG
(Scotland): Home Int 1937

Patterson, AH
(Ireland): v Wales 1913

Pattinson, R
(England): Home Int 1949

Payne, J
(England): Home Int 1950-51

Payne, J
(England): Home Int 1989-90. (GBI) v Europe 1990

Pearson, AG
(GBI): v South Africa 1927

Pearson, MJ
(England): Home Int 1951-52

Pease, JWB (*later* Lord Wardington)
(England): v Scotland 1903-04-05-06

Pennink, JJF
(England): Home Int 1937-38-47; v France 1937-38-39.
(GBI): v America 1938

Perkins, TP
(England): v Scotland 1927-28-29. (GBI): v America 1928

Perowne, AH
(England): Home Int 1947-48-49-50-51-53-54-55-57.
(GBI): v America 1949-53-59; in World Team Ch 1958

Peters, GB
(Scotland): Home Int 1934-35-36-37-38. (GBI): v America
1936-38

Peters, JL
(Wales): Home Int 1987-88-89

Phillips, LA
(Wales): v Ireland 1913

Pierse, AD
(Ireland): Home Int 1976-77-78-80-81-82-83-84-85-87-88;
v Wales 1979; v France, West Germany, Sweden 1980;
Eur T Ch 1981. (GBI): v Europe 1980; v America 1983

Pinch, AG
(Wales): Home Int 1969

Pirie, AK
(Scotland): Home Int 1966-67-68-69-70-71-72-73-74-75;
Eur T Ch 1967-69; v Belgium 1973-75; v Spain 1974.
(GBI): v America 1967; v Europe 1970

Plaxton, J
(England): Home Int 1983-84

Pollin, RKM
(Ireland): Home Int 1971; Eur T Ch 1973

Pollock, VA
(England): v Scotland 1908

Povall, J
(Wales): Home Int 1960-61-62-63-65-66-67-68-69-70-71-72-73-74-75-76-77; Eur T Ch 1967-69-71-73-75-77; v France 1975-76; v Denmark 1976, (GBI): v Europe 1962

Powell, WA
(England): v Scotland 1923-24; v Wales/Ireland 1925

Power, E
(Ireland): Home Int 1987-88

Power, M
(Ireland): Home Int 1947-48-49-50-51-52-54

Poxon, MA
(England): Home Int 1975-76; Eur T Ch 1975. (GBI): v America 1975

Pressdee, RNG
(Wales): Home Int 1958-59-60-61-62

Pressley, J
(Scotland): Home Int 1947-48-49

Price, JP
(Wales): Home Int 1986-87-88

Prosser, D
(England): Eur T Ch 1989

Pugh, RS
(Wales): v Ireland 1923-24-29

Purcell, J
(Ireland): Home Int 1973

Raeside, A
(Scotland): v Ireland 1929

Rafferty, R
(Ireland): v Wales 1979; Home Int 1980-81; v France, West Germany, Sweden 1980; Eur T Ch 1981. (GBI): v Europe 1980; in World Team Ch 1980; v America 1981

Rainey, WHE
(Ireland): Home Int 1962

Rawlinson, D
(England): Home Int 1949-50-52-53

Ray, D
(England): Home Int 1982; v France 1982

Rayfus, P
(Ireland): Home Int 1986-87-88

Reade, HE
(Ireland): v Wales 1913

Reddan, B
(Ireland): Home Int 1987

Rees, CN
(Wales): Home Int 1986-88-89

Rees, DA
(Wales): Home Int 1961-62-63-64

Renfrew, RL
(Scotland): Home Int 1964

Renwick, G, jr
(Wales): v Ireland 1923

Revell, RP
(England): Home Int 1972-73; Eur T Ch 1973

Ricardo, W
(Wales); v Ireland 1930-31; v Scotland 1931

Rice, JH
(Ireland): Home Int 1947-52

Rice-Jones, L
(Wales): v Ireland 1924

Richards, PM
(Wales): Home Int 1960-61-62-63-71

Richardson, S
(England): Home Int 1986-87-88

Risdon, PWL
(England): Home Int 1935-36

Robb, J, jr
(Scotland): v England 1902-03-05-06-07

Robb, WM
(Scotland): Home Int 1935

Roberts, AT
(Scotland): v Ireland 1931

Roberts, G
(Scotland): Home Int 1937-38

Roberts, GP
(England): Home Int 1951-53; v France 1949

Roberts, HJ
(England): Home Int 1947-48-53

Roberts, J
(Wales): Home Int 1937

Roberts, SB
(Wales): Home Int 1932-33-34-35-37-38-47-48-49-50-51-52-53-54

Roberts, WJ
(Wales): Home Int 1948-49-50-51-52-53-54

Robertson, A
(England): Home Int 1986-87; v France 1988

Robertson, CW
(Ireland): v Wales 1930; v Scotland 1930

Robertson, DM
(Scotland): Home Int 1973-74; v Spain 1974

Robertson-Durham, JA
(Scotland): v England 1911

Robinson, J
(England): v Ireland 1928

Robinson, J
(England): Home Int 1986. (GBI): v America 1987

Robinson, S
(England): v Scotland 1925; v Ireland 1928-29-30

Roderick, RN
(Wales): Home Int 1983-84-85-86-87-88. (GBI) v Europe 1988. (GBI): v America 1989

Rolfe, B
(Wales): Home Int 1963-65

Roobottom, EL
(Wales): Home Int 1967

Roper, HS
(England): v Ireland 1931; v Scotland 1931

Roper, MS
(Wales): v Ireland 1979

Roper, R
(England): Home Int 1984-85-86-87

Rothwell, J
(England): Home Int 1947-48

Rutherford, DS
(Scotland): v Ireland 1929

Rutherford, R
(Scotland): Home Int 1938-47

Saddler, AC
(Scotland): Home Int 1959-60-61-62-63-64-66; Eur T Ch 1965-67. (GBI): v Europe 1960-62-64—66; v America 1963-65-67-77 (Captain); in Com Tnmt 1959-63-67; in World Team Ch 1962

Sandywell, A
(England): Home Int 1990

Scannel, BJ
(Ireland): Home Int 1947-48-49-50-51-53-54

Scott, KB
(England): Home Int 1937-38; v France 1938

Scott, Hon M
(England): v Scotland 1911-12-23-24-25-26. (GBI): v America 1924-34 (Captain); v Australia 1934

Scott, Hon O
(England): v Scotland 1902-05-06

Scott, R, jr
(Scotland): v England 1924-28. (GBI): v America 1924

Scratton, EWHB
(England): v Scotland 1912

Scroggie: FH
(Scotland): v England 1910

Scrutton, PF
(England): Home Int 1950-55. (GBI): v America 1955-57

Sewell, D
(England): Home Int 1956-57-58-59-60. (GBI): v America 1957-59; in Com Tnmt 1959; in World Team Ch 1960

Shade, RDBM
(Scotland): Home Int 1957-60-61-62-63-64-65-66-67-68; v Scandinavia 1960-62; Eur T Ch 1965-67. (GBI): v America 1961-63-65-67; v Europe 1962-64-66-68; in World Team Ch 1962-64-66-68; in Com Tnmt 1963-67

Shaw, G
(Scotland): Home Int 1984-86-87-88-90; v West Germany 1987. (GBI): v America 1987

Sheals, HS
(Ireland): v Wales 1929; v England 1929-30-31; v Scotland 1930; Home Int 1932-33

Sheahan, D
(Ireland): Home Int 1961-62-63-64-65-66-67-70. (GBI): v Europe 1962-64-67; v America 1963

Sheilds, B
(Scotland):Home Int 1986

Sheppard, M
(Wales): Home Int 1990

Shepperson, AE
(England): Home Int 1956-57-58-59-60-62. (GBI): v America 1957-59

Sherborne, A
(England): Home Int 1982-83-84

Shingler, TR
(England): Home Int 1977

Shorrock, TJ
(England): v France 1952

Simcox, R
(Ireland): v Wales 1930-31; v Scotland 1930-31; v England 1931; Home Int 1932-33-34-35-36-38

Simpson, AF
(Scotland): v Ireland 1928; v England 1927

Simpson, JG
(Scotland): v England 1906-07-08-09-11-12-22-24-26. (GBI): v America 1921

Sinclair, A
(Scotland): Home Int 1950

Slark, WA
(England): Home Int 1957

Slater, A
(England): Home Int 1955-62

Slattery, B
(Ireland): Home Int 1947-48

Sludds, MF
(Ireland): Home Int 1982

Smith, Eric M
(England): v Ireland 1931; v Scotland 1931

Smith, Everard
(England): v Scotland 1908-09-10-12

Smith, GF
(England): v Scotland 1902-03

Smith, JN
(Scotland): v Ireland 1928-30-31; v England 1929-30-31; v Wales 1931; Home Int 1932-33-34. (GBI): v America 1930

Smith, JR
(England): Home Int 1932

Smith, LOM
(England): Home Int 1963

Smith, VH
(Wales): v Ireland 1924-25

Smith, W
(England): Home Int 1972. (GBI): v Europe 1972

Smith, WD
(Scotland): Home Int 1957-58-59-60-63; v Scandinavia 1958-60. (GBI): v Europe 1958; v America 1959

Smyth, D
(Ireland): Home Int 1972-73; Eur T Ch 1973

Smyth, DW
(Ireland): v Wales 1923-30; v England 1930; v Scotland 1931; Home Int 1933

Smyth, HB
(Ireland): Home Int 1974-75-76-78; Eur T Ch 1975-79; v France, West Germany, Sweden 1976. (GBI): v Europe 1976

Smyth, V
(Ireland): Home Int 1981-82

Snowdon, J
(England): Home Int 1934

Soulby, DEB
(Ireland): v Wales 1929-30; v England 1929-30; v Scotland 1929-30

Spiller, EF
(Ireland): v Wales 1924; v England 1928; v Scotland 1928-29

Squirrell, HC
(Wales): Home Int 1955-56-57-58-59-60-61-62-63-64-65-66-67-68-69-70-71-73-74-75; Eur T Ch 1967-69-71-75; v France 1975

Staunton, R
(Ireland): Home Int 1964-65-72; Eur T Ch 1973

Steel, DMA
(England): Home Int 1970

Stephen, AR
(Scotland): Home Int 1971-72-73-74-75-76-77-84-85;
Eur T Ch 1975; v Spain 1974; v Belgium 1975-77-78.
(GBI): v Europe 1972; v America 1985

Stevens, DI
(Wales): Home Int 1968-69-70-74-75-76-77-78-80-82;
Eur T Ch 1969-77; v France 1976; v Denmark 1977

Stevens, LB
(England): v Scotland 1912

Stevenson, A
(Scotland): Home Int 1949

Stevenson, JB
(Scotland): v Ireland 1931; Home Int 1932-38-47-49-50-51

Stevenson, JF
(Ireland): v Wales 1923-24; v England 1925

Stevenson, K
(Ireland): Home Int 1972

Stockdale, B
(England): Home Int 1964-65

Stoker, K
(Wales): v Ireland 1923-24

Stokoe, GC
(Wales): v England 1925; v Ireland 1929-30

Storey, EF
(England): v Scotland 1924-25-26-27-28-30; Home Int
1936; v France 1936. (GBI): v America 1924-26-28

Stott, HAN
(England): Home Int 1976-77

Stout, JA
(England): v Scotland 1928-29-30-31; v Ireland 1929-31.
(GBI): v America 1930-32

Stowe, C
(England): Home Int 1935-36-37-38-47-49-54; v
France 1938-39-49. (GBI): v America 1938-47

Strachan, CJL
(Scotland): Home Int 1965-66-67; Eur T Ch 1967

Straker, R
(England): Home Int 1932

Stuart, HB
(Scotland): Home Int 1967-68-70-71-72-73-74-76; Eur T
Ch 1969-71-73-75; v Belgium 1973-75. (GBI): v Europe
1968-72-74; v America 1971-73-75; in Com Tnmt 1971; in
World Team Ch 1972

Stuart, JE
(Scotland): Home Int 1959

Stubbs, AK
(England): Home Int 1982

Suneson, C
(England): Home Int 1988; Eur T Ch 1989

Sutherland, DMG
(England): Home Int 1947

Sutton, W
(England): v Scotland 1929-31; v Ireland 1929-30-31

Symonds, A
(Wales): v Ireland 1925

Taggart, J
(Ireland): Home Int 1953

Tait, AG
(Scotland): Home Int 1987-88-89; Nixdorf Nations Cup 1989

Tate, JK
(England): Home Int 1954-55-56

Taylor, GN
(Scotland): Home Int 1948

Taylor, HE
(England): v Scotland 1911

Taylor, JS
(Scotland): v England 1979; Home Int 1980; v Belgium 1980;
v France 1980

Taylor, LG
(Scotland): Home Int 1955-56

Taylor, TPD
(Wales): Home Int 1963

Thirlwell, A
(England): Home Int 1951-52-54-55-56-57-58-63-64.
(GBI): v Europe 1956-58-64; v America 1957; in Com Tnmt
1953-64

Thirsk, TJ
(England): v Ireland 1929; Home Int 1933-34-35-36-37-38;
v France 1935-36-37-38-39

Thom, KG
(England): Home Int 1947-48-49-53. (GBI): v America 1949

Thomas, I
(England): Home Int 1933

Thomas, KR
(Wales): Home Int 1951-52

Thompson, ASG
(England): Home Int 1935-37

Thompson, MS
(England): Home Int 1982. (GBI): v America 1983

Thomson, AP
(Scotland): Home Int 1970; Eur T Ch 1971

Thomson, H
(Scotland): Home Int 1934-35-36-37-38. (GBI): v America
1936-38

Thomson, JA
(Scotland): Home Int 1981-82-83-84-85-86-87-88-89;
v West Germany 1987; v Italy 1988-90; v Sweden 1990

Thorburn, K
(Scotland): v England 1928; v Ireland 1927

Timbey, JC
(Ireland): v Scotland 1928-31; v Wales 1931

Timmis, CW
(England): v Ireland 1930; Home Int. 1936-37

Tipping, EB
(England): v Ireland 1930

Tipple, ER
(England): v Ireland 1928-29; Home Int 1932

Tolley, CJH
(England): v Scotland 1922-23-24-25-26-27-28-29-30;
Home Int 1936-37-38; v Ireland/Wales 1925; v France 1938.
(GBI): v America 1921-22-23-24 (Captain) -26-30-34;
v South Africa 1927

Tooth, EA
(Wales): v Ireland 1913

Torrance, TA
(Scotland): v England 1922-23-25-26-28-29—30; Home Int
1933. (GBI): v America 1924-28-30-32 (Captain) -34

Torrance, WB
(Scotland): v England 1922-23-24-26-27-28-30; v Ireland
1928-29-30. (GBI): v America 1922

Townsend, PM
(England): Home Int 1965-66. (GBI): v America 1965;
v Europe 1966; in World Team Ch 1966

Toye, JL
(Wales): Home Int 1963-64-65-66-67-69-70-71-72-73-74-
76-78; Eur T Ch 1971-73-75-77; v France 1975

Tredinnick, SV
(England): Home Int 1950

Tucker, WI
(Wales): Home Int 1949-50-51-52-53-54-55-56-57-58-59-
60-61-62-63-64-65-66-67-68-69-70-71-72-74-75; Eur
T Ch 1967-69-75; v France 1975

Tulloch, W
(Scotland): v England 1929-30-31; v Ireland 1930-31;
v Wales 1931; Home Int 1932

Tupling, LP
(England): Home Int 1969; Eur T Ch 1969.
(GBI): v America 1969

Turnbull, CH
(Wales): v Ireland 1913-25

Turner, A
(England): Home Int 1952

Turner, GB
(Wales): Home Int 1947-48-49-50-51-52-55-56

Tweddell, W
(England): v Scotland 1928-29-30; Home Int 1935.
(GBI): v America 1928 (Captain) -36 (Captain)

Twynholm, S
(Scotland): Home Int 1990. Nixdorf Nations Cup 1990

Vannet, L
(Scotland): Home Int 1984

Waddell, G
(Ireland): v Wales 1925

Walker, J
(Scotland): Home Int 1954-55-57-58-60-61-62-63; v
Scandinavia 1958-62. (GBI): v Europe 1958-60; v America
1961

Walker, KH
(Scotland): Home Int 1985-86

Walker, MS
(England): v Ireland/Wales 1925

Walker, RS
(Scotland): Home Int 1935-36

Wallis, G
(Wales): Home Int 1934-36-37-38

Walls, MPD
(England): Home Int 1980-81-85

Walters, EM
(Wales): Home Int 1967-68-69; Eur T Ch 1969

Walton, AR
(England): Home Int 1934-35

Walton, P
(Ireland): v Wales 1979: Home Int 1980-81; v France,
Germany, Sweden 1980; Eur T Ch 1981. (GBI): v America
1981-83

Warren, KT
(England): Home Int 1962

Watt, A
(Scotland): Home Int 1987

Way, P
(England): Home Int 1981; Eur T Ch 1981,
(GBI): v America 1981.

Webster, A
(Scotland): Home Int 1978

Webster, F
(Ireland): Home Int 1949

Weeks, K
(England): Home Int 1987-88; v France 1988

Welch, L
(Ireland): Home Int 1936

Wemyss, DS
(Scotland): Home Int 1937

Werner, LE
(Ireland): v Wales 1925

West, CH
(Ireland): v England 1928; Home Int 1932

Wethered, RH
(England): v Scotland 1922-23-24-25-26-27-28-29-30.
(GBI): v America 1921-22-23-26-30 (Captain) -34

White, L
(England): Home Int 1990

White, RJ
(England): Home Int 1947-48-49-53-54.
(GBI): v America 1947-49-51-53-55

Whyte, AW
(Scotland): Home Int 1934

Wiggett, M
(England): Home Int 1990

Wilkie, D
(Scotland): Home Int 1962-63-65-67-68

Wilkie, G
(Scotland): v England 1911

Wilkie, GT
(Wales): Home Int 1938

Wilkinson, S
(Wales): Home Int 1990

Willcox, FS
(Wales): v Scotland 1931; v Ireland 1931

Williams, DF
(England): v Scotland 1979

Williams KH
(Wales): Home Int 1983-84-85-86-87

Williams, PG
(Wales): v Ireland 1925

Williamson, SB
(Scotland): Home Int 1947-48-49-51-52

Willison, R
(England): Home Int 1988-89-90; Eur T Ch 1989. (GBI) v
Europe 1990. World Cup 1990

Wills, M
(Wales): Home Int 1990

Wilson, F
(Scotland): Home Int 1985

Wilson, J
(Scotland): v England 1922-23-24-26. (GBI): v America 1923

Wilson, JC
(Scotland): Home Int 1947-48-49-51-52-53. (GBI): v America
1947-53; v South Africa 1952; in Com Tnmt 1954

Wilson, P
(Scotland): Home Int 1976; Belgium 1977

Winchester, R
(England): Home Int 1985-87-89

Winfield, HB
(Wales): v Ireland 1913

Wise, WS
(England): Home Int 1947

Wolstenholme, G
(England): Home Int 1953-55-56-57-58-59-60 (GBI): v
America 1957-59; in World Team Ch 1958-60; in Com Tnmt
1959

Wolstenholme, G
(England): Home Int 1988-89-90; v France 1988

Wood, DK
(Wales): Home Int 1982-83-84-85-86-87

Woollam, J
(England): Home Int 1933-34-35; v France 1935

Woolley, FA
(England): v Scotland 1910-11-12

Woosnam, I
(Wales): v France 1976

Worthington, JS
(England): v Scotland 1905

Wright, I
(Scotland): Home Int 1958-59-60-61; v Scandinavia 1960

Yeo, J
(England): Home 1971

Young, D
(Ireland): Home Int 1969-70-77

Young, ID
(Scotland): Home Int 1981-82; v France 1982

Young, JR
(Scotland): Home Int 1960-61-65; v Scandinavia 1960.
(GB): v Europe 1960

Zacharias, JP
(England): Home Int 1935

Zoete, HW de
(England): v Scotland 1903-04-06-07

The Home Unions

English, Irish, Scottish and Welsh Championships

The four Home Unions were founded in the reverse order to that one might expect. Ireland was founded in 1891, followed by Wales in 1895, Scotland in 1920 and finally England in 1924.

That there should be 33 years between the first and the last is surprising. Each has worked assiduously to promote and control golf through their county associations which cover all affiliated clubs. With many courses under construction and new clubs founded to play on them, the assistance of Unions will be in greater demand.

Apart from the many more championships which the Unions now control, such as Intermediate, Boys and Seniors, each is making positive moves to assist clubs by holding seminars for secretaries, club management and greenkeeping, to name but a few.

Finally, the Unions all contribute to the work of CONGU (Council of National Golf Unions), the body based at Formby which controls the system of handicapping for all male golfers in Great Britain and Ireland.

England

First played in 1925, only Michael Bonallack has won the English Amateur Championship more than twice; after being the runner-up in 1959 he took the title five times between 1962 and 1968. His supremacy in the amateur field between 1961 and 1970 was such that only in the two years 1964 and 1966 did he not hold either the British or English Amateur and in 1965 and 1968 he won both. He also won the Stroke Play Championship, formerly the Brabazon Trophy, four times in the same period. His outstanding record is unlikely now to be equalled. Of those who have won twice, four — Froes Ellison, Frank Pennink, Alan Thirlwell and Howard Ashby — made it in successive years.

The list of winners contains many Walker Cup players. Harry Bentley, who beat the 18-year-old schoolboy John Langley in the 1936 final at Deal, was runner-up 18 years later. His brother Arnold won in 1939 and, it can be said, held the title for seven years, because with the war intervening, it was not contested again until 1946. Stanley Lunt (1934) and Michael Lunt (1966) are the only father and son to have both been English champions.

After his second title in 1959 Guy Wolstenholme became the first winner to turn professional. He was followed down that road by Douglas Sewell, Mark James and Nick Faldo. Some others who made the change, have found the going tough in the paid ranks.

For its championship the English Golf Union (EGU) has spread its favours over many of England's best courses; it has returned to Ganton and Burnham and Berrow five times each and to Lytham, Formby and Birkdale on four occasions.

In 1947 Lord Brabazon of Tara, who had been EGU President in 1938, gave the Brabazon Trophy for a 72-hole Stroke Play Tournament. In 1957 it became the English Open Amateur Stroke Play for the Brabazon Trophy. As it is an open tournament, winners have included the Scots Ronnie Shade, Gordon Brand Jr, Sandy Lyle, and the Irishman Ronan Rafferty, each before turning professional, and Neil Roderick of Wales. Although he has only won it once, Peter McEvoy has been a leading contender for some time and has left his mark on English golf in many ways. His disappointment at never having captured the knockout championship is understandable.

The EGU now has several more championships under its wing: the Seniors in 1981, first played over 36 holes but now over 54, the English Mid-Amateur for those over 35, the Champion of Champions contested by those who have won each county title and the club championship for teams of four. All this activity must help to raise the standard of the country's golf.

English Amateur Championship

INAUGURATED 1925

YEAR	WINNER	RUNNER-UP	MARGIN	VENUE
1925	TF Ellison	S Robinson	1 hole	Hoylake
1926	TF Ellison	Sq Ldr CH Hayward	6 and 4	Walton Heath
1927	TP Perkins	JB Beddard	2 and 1	Little Aston
1928	JA Stout	TP Perkins	3 and 2	Lytham St Annes
1929	W Sutton	EB Tipping	3 and 2	Gosforth Park
1930	TA Bourn	CE Hardman	3 and 2	Burnham and Berrow
1931	LG Crawley	W Sutton	1 hole	Hunstanton
1932	EW Fiddian	AS Bradshaw	1 hole	St George's, Sandwich
1933	J Woollam	TA Bourn	4 and 3	Ganton
1934	S Lunt	LG Crawley	37th hole	Formby
1935	J Woollam	EW Fiddian	2 and 1	Hollinwell
1936	HG Bentley	JDA Langley	5 and 4	Deal
1937	JJ Pennink	LG Crawley	6 and 5	Saunton
1938	JJ Pennink	SE Banks	2 and 1	Moortown
1939	AL Bentley	W Sutton	5 and 4	Birkdale
1940–45	*Not played due to Second World War*			
1946	IR Patey	KG Thom	5 and 4	Mid-Surrey
1947	GH Micklem	C Stowe	1 hole	Ganton
1948	AGB Helm	HJR Roberts	2 and 1	Little Aston
1949	RJ White	C Stowe	5 and 4	Formby
1950	JDA Langley	IR Patey	1 hole	Deal
1951	GP Roberts	H Bennett	39th hole	Hunstanton
1952	EB Millward	TJ Shorrock	2 holes	Burnham and Berrow
1953	GH Micklem	RJ White	2 and 1	Birkdale
1954	A Thirlwell	HG Bentley	2 and 1	St George's, Sandwich
1955	A Thirwell	M Burgess	7 and 6	Ganton
1956	GB Wolstenholme	E Bennett	1 hole	Lytham St Annes
1957	A Walker	G Whitehead	4 and 3	Hoylake
1958	DN Sewell	DA Procter	8 and 7	Walton Heath

YEAR	WINNER	RUNNER-UP	MARGIN	VENUE
1959	GB Wolstenholme	MF Bonallack	1 hole	Formby
1960	DN Sewell	MJ Christmas	41st hole	Hunstanton
1961	I Caldwell	GJ Clark	37th hole	Wentworth
1962	MF Bonallack	MSR Lunt	2 and 1	Moortown
1963	MF Bonallack	A Thirlwell	4 and 3	Burnham and Berrow
1964	Dr D Marsh	R Foster	1 hole	Hollinwell
1965	MF Bonallack	CA Clark	3 and 2	The Berkshire
1966	MSR Lunt	DJ Millensted	3 and 2	Lytham St Annes
1967	MF Bonallack	GE Hyde	4 and 2	Woodhall Spa
1968	MF Bonallack	PD Kelley	12 and 11	Ganton
1969	JH Cook	P Dawson	6 and 4	St George's, Sandwich
1970	Dr D Marsh	SG Birtwell	6 and 4	Birkdale
1971	W Humphreys	JC Davies	9 and 8	Burnham and Berrow
1972	H Ashby	R Revell	5 and 4	Gosforth Park
1973	H Ashby	SC Mason	5 and 4	Formby
1974	M James	JA Watts	6 and 5	Woodhall Spa
1975	N Faldo	D Eccleston	6 and 4	Lytham St Annes
1976	P Deeble	JC Davies	3 and 1	Ganton
1977	TR Shingler	J Mayell	4 and 3	Walton Heath
1978	P Downes	P Hoad	1 hole	Birkdale
1979	R Chapman	A Carman	6 and 5	St George's, Sandwich
1980	P Deeble	P McEvoy	4 and 3	Moortown
1981	D Blakeman	A Stubbs	3 and 1	Burnham and Berrow
1982	A Oldcorn	I Bradshaw	4 and 3	Hoylake
1983	C Laurence	A Brewer	7 and 6	Wentworth
1984	D Gilford	M Gerrard	4 and 3	Woodhall Spa
1985	R Winchester	P Robinson	1 hole	Little Aston
1986	J Langmead	B White	2 and 1	Hillside
1987	K Weeks	R Eggo	37th hole	Frilford Heath
1988	R Claydon	D Currey	38th hole	Birkdale
1989	S Richardson	R Eggo	2 and 1	St George's, Sandwich
1990	I Garbutt	G Evans	8 and 7	Woodhall Spa

English Open Amateur Stroke Play Championship
(formerly Brabazon Trophy)

INAUGURATED 1947

YEAR	WINNER	SCORE	VENUE	YEAR	WINNER	SCORE	VENUE
1947	DMG Sutherland	306	Birkdale	1957	D Sewell	287	Moortown
1948	C Stowe	299	Lytham St Annes	1958	AH Perowne	289	Birkdale
1949	PB Hine	287	Stoneham	1959	D Sewell	300	Hollinwell
1950	RJ White	294	Birkdale	1960	GB Wolstenholme	286	Ganton
1951	RJ White	293	Formby	1961	RDBM Shade	284	Hoylake
1952	PF Scrutton	290	Ganton	1962	A Slater	209	Woodhall Spa
1953	C Stowe	283	Sunningdale	1963	RDBM Shade	306	Birkdale
1954	PF Scrutton	302	Woodhall Spa	1964	MF Bonallack	290	Deal
1955	PF Scrutton	283	Gosforth Park		CA Clark		
1956	SJ Fox	292	Burnham and Berrow	1965	DJ Millensted } tie 289 MJ Burgess		Formby

YEAR	WINNER	SCORE	VENUE		YEAR	WINNER	SCORE	VENUE
1966	PM Townsend	282	Hunstanton		1980	R Rafferty ⎱ tie	293	Hunstanton
1967	RDBM Shade	299	Saunton			P McEvoy ⎰		
1968	MF Bonallack	210	Walton Heath		1981	P Way	292	Hillside
1969	R Foster ⎱ tie	290	Moortown		1982	P Downes	299	Woburn
	MF Bonallack ⎰				1983	C Banks	294	Hollinwell
1970	R Foster	287	Little Aston		1984	M Davis	286	Deal
1971	MF Bonallack	294	Hillside		1985	R Roper ⎱ tie	296	Seaton Carew
1972	PH Moody	296	Hoylake			P Baker ⎰		
1973	R Revell	294	Hunstanton		1986	R Kaplan	286	Sunningdale
1974	N Sundelson	291	Moortown		1987	JG Robinson	287	Ganton
1975	AWB Lyle	298	Hollinwell		1988	R Eggo	289	Saunton
1976	PJ Hedges	294	Saunton		1989	C Rivet ⎱ tie	293	Hoylake
1977	AWB Lyle	293	Hoylake			RN Roderick ⎰		
1978	G Brand Jr	289	Woodhall Spa		1990	O Edmond ⎱ tie	287	Burnham and
1979	D Long	291	Little Aston			G Evans ⎰		Berrow

English Open Over 35s Championship

(formerly English Mid-Amateur)

INAUGURATED 1988

YEAR	WINNER	SCORE	VENUE
1988	P McEvoy	284	Little Aston
1989	A Mew	290	Moortown
1990	A Mew	214	Wentworth

English Seniors Championship

INAUGURATED 1981

Up to 1987 the championship was 36 holes over one course. Since 1988 it has been extended to 54 holes, competitors having one round on each of two courses. The leading 60 then play a third round on one of the courses.

YEAR	WINNER	SCORE	VENUE		YEAR	WINNER	SCORE	VENUE
1981	CR Spalding	152	Copt Heath		1987	I Caldwell	72	North Hants,
1982	JL Whitworth	152	Lindrick					Fleet
1983	B Cawthray	154	Ross-on-Wye			*(curtailed due to storm)*		
1984	RL Glading	150	Thetford		1988	G Edwards	222	Sandiway and
1985	JR Marriott	153	Bristol and					Delamere
			Clifton					Forest
1986	R Hiatt	153	Church		1989	G Clark	212	Ham Manor
			Brampton		1990	NA Paul	217	Enville

English Club Champions

YEAR	WINNER	SCORE	VENUE
1989	Ealing	289	Southport and Ainsdale
1990	Ealing	277	Goring and Streatley

English County Championship

The English County Championship was first played in 1926, two years after the English Golf Union was formed. The first winner was Cheshire's team of four which beat Surrey at Formby with a score of 663. In 1938 teams were reduced to three players, each playing two rounds. It continued in this way, apart from the war years of 1940–46, until 1955 when regional qualifying was held in the four EGU areas, comprising these counties:

North: Cheshire; Cumbria; Durham; Isle of Man; Lancashire; Northumberland; Yorkshire.

Midlands: Cambridgeshire; Derbyshire; Leicestershire and Rutland; Lincolnshire; Northamptonshire; Nottinghamshire; Shropshire and Herefordshire; Staffordshire; Warwickshire; Worcestershire.

South-East Bedfordshire; Berks, Bucks and Oxfordshire; Essex; Hampshire, Isle of Wight and the Channel Islands; Hertfordshire; Kent; Middlesex; Norfolk; Suffolk; Surrey; Sussex.

South-West: Cornwall; Devon; Dorset; Gloucestershire; Somerset; Wiltshire.

It will be noted that the EGU still retains the old county areas in their organisation; clubs in the new counties, such as Avon and Merseyside, remain within their previous counties.

The winners of each regional qualifying event sent teams of six players to play a semi-final and final of three foursomes and six singles each match, at a club selected by the EGU. This format continued for 26 years. In 1982 it was changed to enable each of the regional winners to play the other three in a round robin tournament over three days. This has proved popular and successful.

Yorkshire has had 11 wins, Surrey 9, Lancashire 7, Staffordshire 6 and Warwickshire and Northumberland 4 each. The courses most used over the years have been Formby, Burnham and Berrow, Ganton, Saunton, Little Aston and the Northumberland Club at Gosforth.

YEAR	WINNER	SCORE	RUNNER-UP	VENUE
1926	Cheshire	463	Surrey	Formby
1927	Surrey	650	Worcestershire	Little Aston
1928	Warwickshire	646	Yorkshire	Lytham St Annes
1929	Lancashire	631	Yorkshire	Gosforth Park

YEAR	WINNER	SCORE	RUNNER-UP	VENUE
1930	Lancashire	640	Surrey	Burnham and Berrow
1931	Yorkshire	654	Worcestershire	Hunstanton
1932	Surrey	620	Lancashire	St George's, Sandwich
1933	Yorkshire	619	Worcestershire	Ganton
1934	Worcestershire	610	Cheshire	Formby
1935	Worcestershire	607	Lancashire	Hollinwell
1936	Surrey	624	Kent	Deal
1937	Lancashire	622	Devon Surrey Yorkshire } tie	Saunton
1938	Staffordshire	452	Yorkshire	Moortown, Leeds
1939	Worcestershire	503	Yorkshire	Birkdale
1940–46	*Not played due to Second World War*			
1947	Staffordshire	476	Lancashire	Ganton
1948	Staffordshire	452	Worcestershire	Little Aston
1949	Lancashire	455	Norfolk Lincolnshire } tie	Formby
1950	*No competition*			
1951	Lancashire	455	Cheshire	Formby
1952	Yorkshire	452	Surrey	Ganton
1953	Yorkshire	422	Staffordshire	Sunningdale
1954	Cheshire	455	Northumberland	Woodhall Spa
1955	Yorkshire	7–2	Worcestershire	Formby
1956	Staffordshire	5–4	Surrey	Little Aston
1957	Surrey	5–4	Northumberland	Burnham and Berrow
1958	Surrey	6–3	Warwickshire	The Berkshire
1959	Yorkshire	6–3	Worcestershire	Ganton
1960	Northumberland	5–4	Surrey	Seacroft
1961	Lancashire	7–2	Middlesex	Saunton
1962	Northumberland	7–2	Staffordshire	Sunningdale
1963	Yorkshire	7½–1½	Hampshire, C.I. and Isle of Wight	Gosforth Park
1964	Northumberland	5½–3½	Worcestershire	Little Aston
1965	Northumberland	8–1	Gloucestershire	Burnham and Berrow
1966	Surrey	5½–3½	Worcestershire	Deal
1967	Lancashire	5½–3½	Hampshire, C.I. and Isle of Wight	Prestbury
1968	Surrey	5–4	Lancashire	Copt Heath
1969	Berks, Bucks and Oxon	5–4	Yorkshire	Saunton
1970	Gloucestershire	5–4	Staffordshire	Moor Park
1971	Staffordshire	6–3	Essex	Seascale
1972	Berks, Bucks and Oxon	5–4	Yorkshire	Woodhall Spa
1973	Yorkshire	6–3	Surrey	Burnham and Berrow
1974	Lincolnshire	7–2	Northumberland	Walton Heath
1975	Staffordshire	7–2	Essex	Brancepeth Castle
1976	Warwickshire	7–2	Yorkshire	Coventry
1977	Warwickshire	5½–3½	Gloucestershire	Saunton
1978	Kent	5–4	Northumberland	Frilford Heath
1979	Gloucestershire	6½–2½	Berks, Bucks and Oxon	Formby
1980	Surrey	5–4	Gloucestershire	Church Brampton
1981	Surrey	7½–1½	Nottinghamshire	Ferndown

1982: Orsett, Essex

1 Yorkshire
2 Staffordshire
3 Gloucestershire
4 Hampshire, Isle of Wight & C.I.

1983: Ganton

1 Berks, Bucks & Oxon
2 Warwickshire
3 Lancashire
4 Devon

1984: Hollinwell

1 Yorkshire
2 Gloucestershire
3 Warwickshire
4 Lancashire

1985: Burnham and Berrow

1 Devon
2 Hertfordshire
3 Yorkshire
4 Warwickshire

1986: John O'Gaunt

1 Hertfordshire
2 Lancashire
3 Devon
4 Staffordshire

1987: Gosforth Park

1 Yorkshire
2 Warwickshire
3 Hertfordshire
4 Devon

1988: Seacroft

1 Warwickshire
2 Cheshire
3 Kent
4 Dorset

1989: St Enodoc

1 Middlesex
2 Durham
3 Warwickshire
4 Gloucestershire

1990: Hayling Island

1 Warwickshire
2 Yorkshire
3 Hampshire, Isle of Wight & C.I.
4 Somerset

Ireland

The Golf Union of Ireland (GUI) which controls men's golf throughout the island, was the first Union to inaugurate a national championship in 1893, two years after the Union's foundation. It had started the Irish Open Amateur Match Play the year before, which lasted until 1959 when lack of support from the mainland amateurs caused it to be discontinued. It had always been played on four courses, Portmarnock, Portrush, Newcastle, Co. Down, and Dollymount, with Killarney and Rosses Point, Co. Sligo, being added in its last years. An attempt to revive interest in it by switching to 72 holes stroke play in 1958 unfortunately failed. The native amateur tournament, while also confining itself to the same four courses until 1912, has since been played far and wide in all areas of the island.

Both championships have provided notable winners, the most prominent being Lionel Munn, Major CO Hezlet, James Burke, Jimmy Bruen, Cecil Ewing and Joe Carr, all except Munn being Walker Cup internationals. Apart from Major Hezlet, the other five each held both championships in the same year once: Munn in 1911, Bruen in 1938, Burke in 1947, Ewing in 1948 and Carr in 1954.

The only recent winners of the Amateur Championship to turn professional are Philip Walton and Ronan Rafferty. Since Joe Carr's last win in 1967 only Michael O'Brien, David Sheahan and Declan Branigan have won the title more than once and there has been a new winner every year since 1982, including Garth McGimpsey, who has played for Ireland for 12 years, and won in 1988 at Portrush after many attempts.

The GUI also control the Boys', Youths' and Seniors' Championships.

Irish Amateur Championship

INAUGURATED 1893

YEAR	WINNER	RUNNER-UP	MARGIN	VENUE
1893	T Dickson	G Combe	2 holes	Portrush
1894	R Magill Jr	T Dickson	3 and 1	Newcastle
1895	WH Webb	J Stevenson	10 and 9	Dollymount
1896	J Stewart-Moore Jr	HAS Upton	8 and 7	Portrush
1897	HE Reade	WH Webb	2 and 1	Newcastle
1898	WH Webb	J Stewart-Moore Jr	9 and 8	Dollymount
1899	HE Reade	JP Todd	3 and 2	Portrush
1900	RGN Henry	J McAvoy	4 and 3	Portmarnock
1901	WH Boyd	HE Reade	7 and 5	Newcastle
1902	FB Newett	R Shaw	1 hole	Dollymount
1903	HE Reade	DRA Campbell	5 and 4	Portrush
1904	HA Boyd	JP Todd	4 and 2	Portmarnock
1905	FB Newett	B O'Brien	6 and 5	Newcastle

YEAR	WINNER	RUNNER-UP	MARGIN	VENUE
1906	HA Boyd	HM Cairnes	38th hole	Dollymount
1907	HM Cairnes	HA Boyd	7 and 6	Portrush
1908	LOM Munn	A Babbington	10 and 9	Portmarnock
1909	AH Patterson	EF Spiller	37th hole	Newcastle
1910	JF Jameson	LOM Munn	2 and 1	Dollymount
1911	LOM Munn	Capt HA Boyd	7 and 6	Portrush
1912	AH Craig	P Halligan	13 and 11	Castlerock
1913	LOM Munn	Capt HA Boyd	6 and 5	Portmarnock
1914	LOM Munn	Earl Annesley	10 and 8	Hermitage
1915–18	*Not played due to Great War*			
1919	E Carter	WG McConnell	9 and 7	Portmarnock
1920	CO Hezlet	CL Crawford	12 and 11	Castlerock
1921	E Carter	G Moore	9 and 8	Portmarnock
1922	E Munn	WK Tillie	3 and 1	Portrush
1923	Dr JD McCormack	LE Werner	2 and 1	Milltown
1924	Dr JD McCormack	DEB Soulby	4 and 2	Newcastle
1925	C Robertson	HM Cairnes	4 and 3	Portmarnock
1926	AC Allison	OW Madden	7 and 6	Portrush
1927	Dr JD McCormack	HM Cairnes	37th hole	Cork
1928	DEB Soulby	JO Wisdon	7 and 5	Castlerock
1929	DEB Soulby	FP McConnell	4 and 3	Dollymount
1930	J Burke	FP McConnell	6 and 5	Lahinch
1931	J Burke	FP McConnell	6 and 4	Rosses Point
1932	J Burke	M Crowley	6 and 5	Portrush
1933	J Burke	GT McMullan	3 and 2	Cork
1934	JC Brown	R McConnell	6 and 5	Rosslare
1935	R McConnell	J Burke	2 and 1	Galway
1936	J Burke	R McConnell	7 and 6	Castlerock
1937	J Bruen Jr	J Burke	3 and 2	Ballybunion
1938	J Bruen Jr	R Simcox	3 and 2	Rathfarnham Castle
1939	GH Owens	R McConnell	6 and 5	Rosses Point
1940	J Burke	WM O'Sullivan	4 and 3	Dollymount
1941–45	*Not played due to Second World War*			
1946	J Burke	RC Ewing	2 and 1	Dollymount
1947	J Burke	J Fitzsimmons	2 holes	Lahinch
1948	RC Ewing	BJ Scannell	3 and 2	Portrush
1949	J Carroll	Pat Murphy	4 and 3	Galway
1950	B Herlihy	BC McManus	4 and 3	Baltray
1951	M Power	JB Carr	3 and 2	Cork
1952	TW Egan	JC Brown	41st hole	Royal Belfast
1953	J Malone	M Power	2 and 1	Rosses Point
1954	JB Carr	I Forsythe	4 and 3	Carlow
1955	Dr J Mahon	G Crosbie	3 and 2	Lahinch
1956	G Love	G Crosbie	37th hole	Malone
1957	JB Carr	G Crosbie	2 holes	Galway
1958	RC Ewing	GA Young	5 and 3	Ballybunion
1959	T Craddock	JB Carr	38th hole	Portmarnock
1960	M Edwards	N Fogarty	6 and 5	Portstewart
1961	D Sheahan	J Brown	5 and 4	Rosses Point
1962	M Edwards	J Harrington	42nd hole	Baltray
1963	JB Carr	EC O'Brien	2 and 1	Killarney
1964	JB Carr	A McDade	6 and 5	Newcastle
1965	JB Carr	T Craddock	3 and 2	Rosses Point
1966	D Sheahan	J Faith	3 and 2	Dollymount
1967	JB Carr	PD Flaherty	1 hole	Lahinch
1968	M O'Brien	F McCarroll	2 and 1	Portrush
1969	V Nevin	J O'Leary	1 hole	Rosses Point

YEAR	WINNER	RUNNER-UP	MARGIN	VENUE
1970	D Sheahan	M Bloom	2 holes	Grange
1971	R Kane	M O'Brien	3 and 2	Ballybunion
1972	K Stevenson	B Hoey	2 and 1	Newcastle
1973	RKM Pollin	RM Staunton	1 hole	Rosses Point
1974	R Kane	M Gannon	5 and 4	Portmarnock
1975	M O'Brien	JA Bryan	5 and 4	Cork
1976	D Branigan	D O'Sullivan	2 holes	Portrush
1977	M Gannon	A Hayes	19th hole	Westport
1978	M Morris	T Cleary	1 hole	Carlow
1979	J Harrington	M Gannon	2 and 1	Ballybunion
1980	R Rafferty	MJ Bannon	8 and 7	Newcastle
1981	D Branigan	E McMenamin	19th hole	Rosses Point
1982	P Walton	B Smyth	7 and 6	Woodbrook
1983	T Corridan	E Power	2 holes	Killarney
1984	CB Hoey	L McNamara	20th hole	Malone
1985	D O'Sullivan	D Branigan	1 hole	Westport
1986	J McHenry	P Rayfus	4 and 3	Royal Dublin
1987	E Power	JP Fitzgerald	2 holes	Tramore
1988	G McGimpsey	D Mulholland	2 and 1	Portrush
1989	P McGinley	N Goulding	3 and 2	Rosses Point
1990	D Clarke	P Harrington	3 and 2	Baltray

East of Ireland Amateur Open Championship
at Baltray, Co Louth

YEAR	WINNER	SCORE	YEAR	WINNER	SCORE
1941	JB Carr	301	1960	JB Carr	290
1942	K Garvey	302	1961	JB Carr	291
1943	JB Carr	305	1962	TW Egan	290
1944	JW Hulme	306	1963	GN Fogarty	294
1945	JB Carr } tie	302	1964	JB Carr	292
	J Burke		1965	T Craddock	291
1946	JB Carr	316	1966	T Craddock	288
1947	BJ Scannell } tie	321	1967	GN Fogarty	293
	JW Hulme		1968	P Caul	289
1948	JB Carr	296	1969	JB Carr	292
1949	M Ferguson } tie	305	1970	RJ Carr	291
	JW Hulme		1971	P Mulcare	281
1950	JP Carroll	311	1972	P Mulcare	292
1951	M Power	297	1973	P Mulcare	291
1952	NV Drew	306	1974	HB Smyth	295
1953	JP Carroll	303	1975	ACJ Morrow	300
1954	BJ Scannell	298	1976	D White	295
1955	BJ Scannell	298	1977	T Cleary	299
1956	JB Carr	300	1978	M Gannon	295
1957	JB Carr	287	1979	AD Pierse	288
1958	JB Carr	288	1980	P Caul	292
1959	T Craddock	294	1981	D Branigan	292

YEAR	WINNER	SCORE	YEAR	WINNER	SCORE
1982	MF Sludds	285	1987	P Rayfus	297
1983	ACJ Morrow	291	1988	G McGimpsey	283
1984	BVM Reddan	293	1989	D Clarke	285
1985	F Ronan	286	1990	D O'Sullivan	291
1986	PF Hogan	291			

North of Ireland Amateur Open Championship

INAUGURATED 1947

at Portrush, Co Antrim

YEAR	WINNER	RUNNER-UP	MARGIN	YEAR	WINNER	RUNNER-UP	MARGIN
1947	J Fitzsimmons	JC Kissock	8 and 7	1969	MJC Hoey	J Faith	3 and 2
1948	J Fitzsimmons	WA McNeill	10 and 9	1970	J Faith	RJ Carr	20th hole
1949	F Webster ⎱tie J Taggart ⎰		311	1971	RKM Pollin	TBC Hoey	2 and 1
				1972	JL Bamford	J McAleese	5 and 4
1950	NV Drew	J Taggart	19th hole	1973	B Edwards	WJJ Ferguson	6 and 5
1951	Dr W Meharg	J Glover	2 and 1	1974	BJS Kissock	JC Moss	1 hole
1952	NV Drew	Dr W Meharg	2 and 1	1975	J Heggarty	WJJ Ferguson	2 and 1
1953	C Knox	JL Bamford	2 and 1	1976	BJS Kissock	M Patterson	4 and 3
1954	JL Bamford	JP Coulter	6 and 5	1977	DJF Young	JD Coey	5 and 4
1955	R McK Fleury	WI Forsythe	3 and 2	1978	G McGimpsey	G McGuckian	2 and 1
1956	M Edwards	M Macauley	7 and 6	1979	TBC Hoey	JA McDade	2 and 1
1957	M Edwards	C Knox	7 and 6	1980	M Malone	M Martin	6 and 4
1958	TE Dijon	SAG Cooley	5 and 3	1981	DC Long	BJS Kissock	1 hole
1959	J Duncan	D Sheahan	5 and 3	1982	DC Long	DJF Young	5 and 4
1960	WHE Rainey	M Edwards	3 and 2	1983	TBC Hoey	IA Elliott	2 and 1
1961	J Duncan	P Donnelly	3 and 1	1984	G McGimpsey	DC Long	6 and 5
1962	JFD Madeley	WHE Rainey	5 and 4	1985	IA Elliott	B Patton	1 hole
1963	JFD Madeley	JSG Muir	7 and 5	1986	D Ballentine	P O'Donnell	5 and 3
1964	FA McCorry	WE McCrea	3 and 2	1987	AD Pierse	RA Hanna	8 and 6
1965	WHE Rainey	NS Kelly	1 hole	1988	NH Anderson	B Norgard	4 and 3
1966	B Edwards	J Faith	3 and 2	1989	NH Anderson	D Baker	3 and 2
1967	WRA Tennant	J Faith	3 and 2	1990	D Clarke	P McGinley	1 hole
1968	MJC Hoey	JE O'Leary	1 hole				

South of Ireland Amateur Open Championship

INAUGURATED 1895

at Lahinch, Co Clare

YEAR	WINNER	RUNNER-UP	MARGIN	YEAR	WINNER	RUNNER-UP	MARGIN
1895	Dr GS Browning	WF McDonald	2 and 1	1946	J Burke	JB Carr	39th hole
1896	B O'Brien	DM Wilson	9 and 7	1947	B Slattery	J Burke	6 and 5
1897	F Ballingall	JR Gairdner	2 and 1	1948	JB Carr	JP Carroll	3 and 2
1898	F Ballingall	HM Ballingall	3 and 1	1949	JP Carroll	B Slattery	1 hole
1899	JR Gairdner	J Livingstone	6 and 5	1950	M Power	PJ Leydon	12 and 10
1900	F Ballingall	T Fullerton	5 and 4	1951	G Gilligan	TW Egan	5 and 3
1901	W Dodd	SH Fry	2 and 1	1952	M Power	NV Drew	1 hole
1902	W Ballingall	Dr GS Browning	2 and 1	1953	PJ Leydon	M Power	9 and 8
1903	JB Ballingall	JS Worthington	2 and 1	1954	P Bugler	JR Mahon	3 and 2
1904	D Foster	H Castle	1 hole	1955	PJ Leydon	B Slattery	4 and 3
1905	H Castle	AC Lincoln	5 and 3	1956	PJ Leydon	M Power	6 and 5
1906	Lord Glenrawly	AE Browning	10 and 8	1957	PJ Leydon	M Power	8 and 7
1907	JJ Hurley	HD Gillies	4 and 2	1958	JC Brown	G McLennon	5 and 4
1908	AR Aitken	Rev P Gannon	10 and 8	1959	G Roberts	P Donnelly	6 and 5
1909	JD Little	C Taylor	12 and 11	1960	P Sullivan	P Morrison	1 hole
1910	Dr GR Girdlestone	SH Fry	4 and 2	1961	M Guerin	JL Bamford	7 and 6
1911	LOM Munn	JS Kennedy	7 and 5	1962	M Guerin	M Skerritt	4 and 3
1912	GVM Boyd	JS Jennings	1 hole	1963	M Guerin	D Sheahan	2 and 1
1913	AW Murray	TS Jennings	2 and 1	1964	WA Kelleher	JM Nestor	2 and 1
1914–19	*Not played due to Great War*			1965	R de L Staunton	GA Young	5 and 3
1920	EC Carter	DJ O'Brien	10 and 9	1966	JB Carr	GA Young	1 hole
1921	J Murphy	DDB Soulby	1 hole	1967	GN Fogarty	S MacDonald	3 and 2
1922	*No Championship*			1968	JD Smyth	GA Young	3 and 2
1923	F Murphy	Dr TM Healy	2 and 1	1969	JB Carr	GN Fogarty	2 and 1
1924	J Crabbe	WG McConnell	2 holes	1970	JE O'Leary	GA Young	1 hole
1925	M Crowley	J Crabbe	5 and 4	1971	P Mulcare	E Higgins	1 hole
1926	R Simcox	M Crowley	7 and 4	1972	R de L Staunton	GA Young	20th hole
1927	R Simcox	WG McConnell	2 and 1	1973	M Gannon	DC Long	1 hole
1928	J Burke	DF Sweeney	6 and 5	1974	DC Long	RA Fleury	19th hole
1929	J Burke	DF Sweeney	8 and 5	1975	BP Malone	M Skerritt	2 holes
1930	J Burke	O Brown	6 and 4	1976	V Nevin	P Mulcare	6 and 5
1931	J Burke	E Dwyer	10 and 8	1977	L MacNamara	MF Morris	4 and 3
1932	JC Brown	SW Martyn	4 and 3	1978	V Nevin	M Guerin	2 and 1
1933	JC Brown	SW Martyn	3 and 1	1979	P O'Rourke	T Cleary	4 and 3
1934	RM Saunders	PF Murray	3 and 1	1980	M Burns	MF Morris	4 and 3
1935	RM Saunders	J Garrahey	4 and 2	1981	P O'Rourke	RJ Carr	2 and 1
1936	TF Ryan	R Simcox	4 and 3	1982	MF Morris	C McCarroll	1 hole
1937	M O'Loughlin	D Torrens	2 and 1	1983	ACJ Morrow	M Burns	3 and 2
1938	M O'Loughlin	RM Saunders	2 and 1	1984	N Anderson	MF Morris	19th hole
1939	J Burke	T Lenihan	6 and 4	1985	P O'Rourke	P Lyons	3 and 2
1940	PF Murray	JA English	8 and 7	1986	J McHenry	L MacNamara	3 and 2
1941	J Burke	F Hannon	9 and 8	1987	BVM Reddan	M Gannon	20th hole
1942	J Burke	P Garihy	8 and 7	1988	M Gannon	PF Hogan	3 and 2
1943	J Burke	B Slattery	1 hole	1989	S Keenan	J Flanagan	22nd hole
1944	J Burke	JC Brown	5 and 4	1990	D Clarke	J Carvill	4 and 3
1945	J Burke	C Ewing	4 and 3				

West of Ireland Amateur Open Championship

INAUGURATED 1923

at Rosses Point, Co Sligo

YEAR	WINNER	RUNNER-UP	MARGIN	YEAR	WINNER	RUNNER-UP	MARGIN
1923	LP Vernon	BN Cook	3 and 2	1957	JR Mahon	J Fitzgibbon	3 and 1
1924	JL Crabbe	WG McConnell	3 and 2	1958	JB Carr	C Ewing	4 and 3
1925	WG McConnell	JD MacCormack	6 and 4	1959	WJJ Ferguson	PJ Leydon	38th hole
1926	JL Crabbe	WG McConnell	3 and 2	1960	JB Carr	T Craddock	39th hole
1927	HG McCallum	AW Briscoe	4 and 3	1961	JB Carr	M Edwards	1 hole
1928	AW Briscoe	C Ewing	1 hole	1962	JB Carr	B O'Beirne	7 and 5
1929	WG McConnell	EPJ O'Flynn	4 and 2	1963	RM Craigan	TM Duggan	1 hole
1930	C Ewing	C McMullen	4 and 3	1964	BP Malone	WA Kelleher	5 and 4
1931	AW Briscoe	J O'Mara	6 and 4	1965	RM Craigan	V Nevin	1 hole
1932	C Ewing	G O'Connor	10 and 8	1966	JB Carr	R de L Staunton	2 and 1
1933	J Burke	G O'Connor	13 and 12	1967	RKM Pollin	A O'Connor	1 hole
1934	J Burke	C Ewing	3 and 2	1968	DA Nelson	J Boston	20th hole
1935	C Ewing	J Burke	3 and 2	1969	RKM Pollin	MJC Hoey	1 hole
1936	J Burke	JF McLoughlin	11 and 10	1970	J McTear	JE O'Leary	4 and 3
1937	JF McLoughlin	C Ewing	3 and 2	1971	RJ Carr	BP Malone	1 hole
1938	J Burke	M Aherne	8 and 7	1972	V Nevin	BP Malone	4 and 3
1939	C Ewing	J Burke	3 and 1	1973	HB Smyth	V Nevin	2 and 1
1940	J Burke	WJ Gill	4 and 3	1974	M Gannon	E Dunne	1 hole
1941	C Ewing	JF McLoughlin	5 and 4	1975	IA Elliott	D Branigan	1 hole
1942	C Ewing	GH Owens	4 and 3	1976	D Branigan	T Cleary	5 and 4
1943	C Ewing	L Howley	10 and 8	1977	TBC Hoey	L MacNamara	1 hole
1944	J Burke	C Ewing	3 and 2	1978	BVM Reddan	K Stevenson	3 and 2
1945	C Ewing	J Burke	4 and 3	1979	DC Long	AD Pierse	26th hole
1946	JB Carr	BJ Scannell	11 and 9	1980	AD Pierse	P Walton	3 and 2
1947	JB Carr	C Ewing	3 and 2	1981	D Branigan	D Conway	7 and 5
1948	JB Carr	C Ewing	5 and 3	1982	AD Pierse	MJ Malone	3 and 1
1949	C Ewing	F Webster	5 and 4	1983	C Glasgow	G McGimpsey	2 and 1
1950	C Ewing	B Slattery	1 hole	1984	G McGimpsey	F Gannon	5 and 4
1951	JB Carr	M Ferguson	3 and 2	1985	J Feeney	G Moore	1 hole
1952	JC Brown	NV Drew	2 and 1	1986	P Rayfus	E McMenamin	1 hole
1953	JB Carr	RH McInnally	1 hole	1987	N McGrane	E McMenamin	1 hole
1954	JB Carr	BJ Scannell	9 and 8	1988	G McGimpsey	C Carew	3 and 2
1955	Dr WI Forsythe	TD Hegarty	2 and 1	1989	P McInerney	K Kearney	2 and 1
1956	JB Carr	C Ewing	4 and 3	1990	N Goulding	AD Pierse	3 and 2

Irish Seniors' Open Amateur Championship

INAUGURATED 1970

YEAR	WINNER	SCORE	VENUE	YEAR	WINNER	SCORE	VENUE
1970	C Ewing	153	Lahinch	1981	GN Fogarty	149	Bundoran
1971	J O'Sullivan	159	Rosslare	1982	J Murray	141	Douglas
1972	BJ Scannell	152	Rosses Point	1983	F Sharpe	153	Courtown
1973	JW Hulme	147	Warrenpoint	1984	J Boston	155	Connemara
1974	Rev P Walsh	155	Cork	1985	J Boston	155	Newcastle
1975	SA O'Connor	152	Woodbrook	1986	J Coey	153	Waterford
1976	BJ Scannell	150	Athlone	1987	J Murray	150	Castletroy
1977	DB Somers	150	Warrenpoint	1988	WB Buckley	154	Westport
1978	DP Herlihy	150	Limerick	1989	B McCrea	149	Royal Belfast
1979	P Kelly	156	Royal Tara	1990	C Hartland	149	Cork
1980	GN Fogarty	144	Galway				

Connacht Championships

INAUGURATED 1953

YEAR	WINNER	VENUE	YEAR	WINNER	VENUE
1953	E O'Beirn		1972	V Hassett	
1954	N O'Donovan		1973	T Winslow	
1955	PG McCann		1974	M O'Donnell	
1956	E O'Grady		1975	I Hadden	
1957	E O'Grady		1976	M O'Donnell	
1958	HE Colhoun		1977	Margaret Keon	
1959	HE Colhoun		1978	J McHugh	
1960	HE Colhoun		1979	M Gorry	
1961	B Sexton		1980	B Gearty	Ennis
1962	E O'Beirn		1981	J Gillespie	Rosses Point
1963	E O'Beirn		1982	P Wickham	Galway
1964	E O'Beirn		1983	L Sweeney	Bundoran
1965	I Burke		1984	L Sweeney	Athlone
1966	T Winslow		1985	P Wickham	Donegal
1967	V Hendron		1986	Y McQuillan	Westport
1968	T Winslow		1987	P Wickham	Connemara
1969	M O'Donnell		1988	D McCarthy	Co Longford
1970	J Mark		1989	D Mahon	Enniscrone
1971	M O'Donnell		1990	P Wickham	Rosses Point

Connacht Seniors' Amateur Open

INAUGURATED 1990

YEAR	WINNER	SCORE	VENUE
1990	JJ Bryne	149	Athlone

Leinster Seniors' Amateur Open

INAUGURATED 1987

YEAR	WINNER	SCORE	VENUE
1987	A Foran	148	Clontarf
1988	H McQuillan	148	Laytown and Bettystown
1989	H Hood	154	Clontarf
1990	T O'Donoghue	156	Kilkenny

Munster Seniors' Amateur Open

INAUGURATED 1990

YEAR	WINNER	SCORE	VENUE
1990	M Kearse	150	Ennis

Ulster Seniors' Amateur Open

INAUGURATED 1988

YEAR	WINNER	SCORE	VENUE
1988	HB Smith	158	Royal Belfast
1989	B McCrea	151	Bangor
1990	JP Daly	153	Shandon Park

Scotland

Scotland had several open amateur tournaments run by clubs at the end of the last century, which may be a reason why the Scottish Golf Union (SGU), founded in 1920, did not hold its first Amateur Championship until 1922. It has always had a strong field, the game in Scotland being so universally played by all sections of the community. In these days there is little comment if a leading amateur joins the professionals, but when Jack McLean, Hector Thomson, Eric Brown and Ronnie Shade changed status, it was much more unusual.

Ronnie Shade won five years in succession 1963–67 and Jack McLean thrice on the trot 1932–34. Generally Scottish amateurs seem not to continue to win over a period of years, Charlie Green and Ian Hutcheon being notable exceptions in the Match Play and Stroke Play Championships respectively. Other Walker Cup players have won only once, including Hector Thomson, Morton Dykes, David Blair, David Carrick, Allan Brodie, Hugh Stuart, Iain Carslaw, James Milligan and Colin Montgomerie.

The 72-hole Stoke Play Championship is an open event but usually the natives have seen off the invaders. The first in 1967 was won by Bernard Gallacher, then an amateur, before his distinguished professional career and captaincy of the Ryder Cup team. So far no man has held both Match Play and Stroke Play titles concurrently. In 1989 the age-old Franco-Scottish accord was under some strain when François Illouz won the stroke play title for France.

The Seniors' 36-hole Stroke Play, started in 1978, is also open. The Boys have both a Match Play (1960) and a Stroke Play (1970) which is open, although here again there has been only one winner from outside Scotland. It is also of interest that few winners of either of the Boys' events have progressed on to take the titles in the Senior championships.

Most Scottish championships are played on the wide variety of first-class courses to be found in nearly every area. Only the Boys' Match Play has stuck to North Berwick (1960–75) and Dunbar (1976–90), except for a solitary foray to West Kilbride in 1979.

Scottish Amateur Championship

INAUGURATED 1922

YEAR	WINNER	RUNNER-UP	MARGIN	VENUE
1922	J Wilson	E Blackwell	19th hole	St Andrews
1923	TM Burrell	Dr AR McCallum	1 hole	Troon
1924	WW Mackenzie	W Tulloch	3 and 2	Balgownie
1925	JT Dobson	WW Mackenzie	3 and 2	Muirfield
1926	WJ Guild	SO Shepherd	2 and 1	Leven
1927	A Jamieson Jr	Rev DS Rutherford	22nd hole	Western Gailes
1928	WW Mackenzie	WE Dodds	5 and 3	Muirfield

YEAR	WINNER	RUNNER-UP	MARGIN	VENUE
1929	JT Bookless	JE Dawson	5 and 4	Balgownie
1930	K Greig	T Wallace	9 and 8	Carnoustie
1931	J Wilson	A Jamieson Jr	2 and 1	Prestwick
1932	J McLean	K Greig	5 and 4	Dunbar
1933	J McLean	KC Forbes	6 and 4	Balgownie
1934	J McLean	W Campbell	3 and 1	Western Gailes
1935	H Thomson	J McLean	2 and 1	St Andrews
1936	ED Hamilton	R Neill	1 hole	Carnoustie
1937	H McInally	KG Patrick	6 and 5	Barassie
1938	ED Hamilton	R Rutherford	4 and 2	Muirfield
1939	H McInally	H Thomson	6 and 5	Prestwick
1940–45	*Not played due to Second World War*			
1946	EC Brown	R Rutherford	3 and 2	Carnoustie
1947	H McInally	J Pressley	10 and 8	Glasgow Gailes
1948	AS Flockhart	GN Taylor	7 and 6	Balgownie
1949	R Wright	H McInally	1 hole	Muirfield
1950	WC Gibson	DA Blair	2 and 1	Prestwick
1951	JM Dykes	JC Wilson	4 and 2	St Andrews
1952	FG Dewar	JC Wilson	4 and 3	Carnoustie
1953	DA Blair	JW McKay	3 and 1	Western Gailes
1954	JW Draper	WGH Gray	4 and 3	Nairn
1955	RR Jack	AC Miller	2 and 1	Muirfield
1956	Dr FWG Deighton	A MacGregor	8 and 7	Troon
1957	JS Montgomerie	J Burnside	2 and 1	Balgownie
1958	WD Smith	IR Harris	6 and 5	Prestwick
1959	Dr FWG Deighton	RMK Murray	6 and 5	St Andrews
1960	JR Young	S Saddler	5 and 3	Carnoustie
1961	J Walker	SWT Murray	4 and 3	Western Gailes
1962	SWT Murray	RDBM Shade	2 and 1	Muirfield
1963	RDBM Shade	N Henderson	4 and 3	Troon
1964	RDBM Shade	J McBeath	8 and 7	Nairn
1965	RDBM Shade	GB Cosh	4 and 2	St Andrews
1966	RDBM Shade	CJL Strachan	9 and 8	Western Gailes
1967	RDBM Shade	A Murphy	5 and 4	Carnoustie
1968	GB Cosh	RL Renfrew	4 and 3	Muirfield
1969	JM Cannon	AH Hall	6 and 4	Troon
1970	CW Green	HB Stuart	1 hole	Balgownie
1971	S Stephen	CW Green	3 and 2	St Andrews
1972	HB Stuart	AK Pirie	3 and 1	Prestwick
1973	IC Hutcheon	Allan Brodie	3 and 2	Carnoustie
1974	GH Murray	AK Pirie	2 and 1	Western Gailes
1975	D Greig	GH Murray	7 and 6	Montrose
1976	GH Murray	HB Stuart	6 and 5	St Andrews
1977	Allan Brodie	PJ McKellar	1 hole	Troon
1978	IA Carslaw	J Cuddihy	7 and 6	Downfield
1979	K Macintosh	PJ McKeller	5 and 4	Prestwick
1980	D Jamieson	CW Green	2 and 1	Balgownie
1981	C Dalgleish	A Thomson	7 and 6	Western Gailes
1982	CW Green	G McGregor	1 hole	Carnoustie
1983	CW Green	J Huggan	1 hole	Gullane
1984	A Moir	K Buchan	3 and 2	Renfrew
1985	DG Carrick	D James	4 and 2	Southerness
1986	C Brooks	A Thomson	3 and 2	Monifieth
1987	C Montgomerie	AW Watt	9 and 8	Nairn
1988	J Milligan	A Colthart	1 hole	Barassie
1989	A Thomson	A Tait	1 hole	Lossiemouth
1990	C Everett	M Thomson	7 and 5	Gullane

Scottish Open Amateur Stroke Play Championship

INAUGURATED 1967

YEAR	WINNER	SCORE	VENUE
1967	BJ Gallacher	291	Muirfield
1968	RDBM Shade	282	Prestwick
1969	JS Macdonald	288	Carnoustie
1970	D Hayes	275	Glasgow Gailes and Barassie
1971	IC Hutcheon	277	Leven and Lundin Links
1972	BN Nicholson	290	Dalmahoy and Ratho Park
1973	DM Robertson } tie GJ Clark	284	Dunbar
1974	IC Hutcheon	283	Blairgowrie
1975	CW Green	295	Nairn and Nairn Dunbar
1976	S Martin	283	Monifieth and Carnoustie
1977	PJ McKellar	299	Muirfield and Gullane
1978	AR Taylor	281	Keir and Cawder
1979	IC Hutcheon	286	Blairgowrie
1980	G Brand Jr	207 (54 holes)	Musselburgh and Royal Musselburgh
1981	F Walton	287	Erskine and Renfrew
1982	G Macgregor	287	Downfield and Camperdown
1983	C Murray	291	Irvine
1984	CW Green	287	Blairgowrie
1985	CS Montgomerie	274	Dunbar
1986	KH Walker	289	Carnoustie
1987	DG Carrick	282	Lundin Links
1988	S Easingwood	277	Cathkin Braes
1989	F Illouz (Fra)	281	Blairgowrie
1990	G Hay	133 (36 holes)	Balgownie

Scottish Open Amateur Seniors' Championship

INAUGURATED 1978

YEAR	WINNER	SCORE	VENUE
1978	JM Cannon ⎱ tie GR Carmichael ⎰	149	Glasgow Killermont
1979	A Sinclair	143	Glasgow Killermont
1980	JM Cannon	149	Barnton
1981	IR Harris ⎱ Dr J Hastings ⎰ tie AN Sturrock ⎰	146	Glasgow Killermont
1982	JM Cannon ⎱ tie J Niven ⎰	143	Barnton
1983	WD Smith	145	Glasgow Killermont
1984	A Sinclair	148	Barnton
1985	AN Sturrock	143	Glasgow Killermont
1986	RL Glading	153	Barnton
1987	I Hornsby	145	Glasgow Killermont
1988	J Hayes	143	Barnton
1989	AS Mayer		Glasgow Killermont
1990	G Hartland	146	Barnton

Wales

The Welsh followed quickly after the Irish with their first national championship in 1895 at Aberdovey, one of the venues most visited since, the others being Porthcawl, Harlech, Southerndown and Ashburnham. Before the first war James Hunter won five championships and between the wars, Henry Howell eight, a fine record which still did not gain him a place in the Walker Cup team in spite also of countless wins in the Home Internationals. He is one of the few to have won all six matches in a series.

Colonel Tony Duncan, whose father and mother were both Welsh champions, who won the Welsh Championship four times and captained the Walker Cup team in 1953, was a strong influence in Welsh golf. John Morgan, the first Welshman to play in the Walker Cup match, and Hew Squirrell, winner five times between 1958 and 1965, helped him to bring Welsh golf to the fore and laid the groundwork for future Welsh success. They were ably assisted by Albert Evans and Iestyn Tucker, both double-winners and stalwart internationals over many years.

More recently the young British champions Duncan Evans, Philip Parkin, Paul Mayo, Neil Roderick and Stephen Dodd have led a new Welsh challenge to the established order and have fully justified the Welsh Golf Union's encouragement of junior golf in the Principality.

The Welsh Boys' Championship was first played in 1954, the Men's Stroke Play in 1967 and the Seniors in 1975.

Welsh Amateur Championship

INAUGURATED 1895

YEAR	WINNER	RUNNER-UP	MARGIN	VENUE
1895	J Hunter	TM Barlow	2 holes	Aberdovey
1896	J Hunter	P Plunkett	1 hole	Rhyl
1897*	FE Woodhead	J Hunter	4 and 3	Penarth
From 1897 the final played over 36 holes.				
1898	FE Woodhead	Dr E Reid	5 and 4	Aberdovey
1899	FE Woodhead	TD Cummins	6 and 5	Conwy
1900	TM Barlow	H Ludlow	2 and 1	Porthcawl
1901	Major Green	P Plunkett	8 and 7	Aberdovey
1902	J Hunter	H Ludlow	5 and 4	Penarth
1903	J Hunter	TM Barlow	2 holes	Rhos-on-Sea
1904	H Ludlow	RM Brown	13 and 11	Ashburnham
1905	J Duncan	AP Cary Thomas	6 and 5	Conwy
1906	G Renwick	WT Davies	9 and 7	Radyr

YEAR	WINNER	RUNNER-UP	MARGIN	VENUE
1907	LA Phillips	LH Gottwaltz	3 and 1	Porthcawl
1908	G Renwick	LA Phillips	7 and 5	Southerndown
1909	J Duncan	EJ Bryne	9 and 8	Rhyl
1910	G Renwick	RM Brown	2 holes	Swansea
1911	HM Lloyd	TC Mellor	4 and 2	Conwy
1912	LA Phillips	CH Turnbull	4 and 3	Porthcawl
1913	HN Atkinson	CJ Hamilton	38th hole	Chester
1914–19	*Not played due to Great War*			
1920	HR Howell	J Duncan	2 holes	Southerndown
1921	CEL Fairchild	E Rowe	1 hole	Aberdovey
1922	HR Howell	EDSN Carne	12 and 11	Tenby
1923	HR Howell	CEL Fairchild	3 and 1	Rhyl
1924	HR Howell	C Turnbull	2 and 1	Radyr
1925	CEL Fairchild	GS Emery	10 and 8	Rhyl
1926	DR Lewis	K Stoker	1 hole	Porthcawl
1927	DR Lewis	JL Jones	4 and 3	Tenby
1928	CC Maston	DR Lewis	37th hole	Harlech
1929	HR Howell	R Chapman	4 and 3	Southerndown
1930	HR Howell	DR Lewis	2 and 1	Tenby
1931	HR Howell	WG Morgan	7 and 6	Aberdovey
1932	HR Howell	HE Davies	7 and 6	Ashburnham
1933	JL Black	AA Duncan	2 and 1	Porthcawl
1934	SB Roberts	GS Noon	4 and 3	Prestatyn
1935	R Chapman	GS Noon	1 hole	Tenby
1936	RM de Lloyd	G Wallis	1 hole	Aberdovey
1937	DH Lewis	R Glossop	2 holes	Porthcawl
1938	AA Duncan	SB Roberts	2 and 1	Rhyl
1939–45	*Not played due to Second World War*			
1946	JV Moody	A Marshman	9 and 8	Porthcawl
1947	SB Roberts	G Breen Turner	8 and 7	Harlech
1948	AA Duncan	SB Roberts	2 and 1	Porthcawl
1949	AD Evans	MA Jones	2 and 1	Aberdovey
1950	JL Morgan	DJ Bonnell	9 and 7	Southerndown
1951	JL Morgan	WI Tucker	3 and 2	Harlech
1952	AA Duncan	JL Morgan	4 and 3	Ashburnham
1953	SB Roberts	D Pearson	5 and 3	Prestatyn
1954	AA Duncan	K Thomas	6 and 5	Tenby
1955	TJ Davies	P Dunn	38th hole	Harlech
1956	A Lockley	WI Tucker	2 and 1	Southerndown
1957	ES Mills	H Griffiths	2 and 1	Harlech
1958	HC Squirrell	AD Lake	4 and 3	Conwy
1959	HC Squirrell	N Rees	8 and 7	Porthcawl
1960	HC Squirrell	P Richards	2 and 1	Aberdovey
1961	AD Evans	JL Toye	3 and 2	Ashburnham
1962	JKD Povall	HC Squirrell	3 and 2	Harlech
1963	WI Tucker	JKD Povall	4 and 3	Southerndown
1964	HC Squirrell	WI Tucker	1 hole	Harlech
1965	HC Squirrell	G Clay	6 and 4	Porthcawl
1966	WI Tucker	EN Davies	6 and 5	Aberdovey
1967	JKD Povall	WI Tucker	3 and 2	Ashburnham
1968	J Buckley	JKD Povall	8 and 7	Conwy
1969	JL Toye	EN Davies	1 hole	Porthcawl
1970	EN Davies	JKD Povall	1 hole	Harlech
1971	CT Brown	HC Squirrell	6 and 5	Southerndown
1972	EN Davies	JL Toye	40th hole	Prestatyn
1973	D McLean	T Holder	6 and 4	Ashburnham
1974	S Cox	EN Davies	3 and 2	Caernarvonshire
1975	JL Toye	WI Tucker	5 and 4	Porthcawl
1976	MPD Adams	WI Tucker	6 and 5	Harlech

YEAR	WINNER	RUNNER-UP	MARGIN	VENUE
1977	DL Stevens	JKD Povall	3 and 2	Southerndown
1978	D McLean	A Ingram	11 and 10	Conwy
1979	TJ Melia	MS Roper	5 and 4	Ashburnham
1980	DL Stevens	G Clement	10 and 9	Prestatyn
1981	S Jones	C Davies	5 and 3	Porthcawl
1982	DK Wood	C Davies	8 and 7	Harlech
1983	JR Jones	AP Parkin	2 holes	Southerndown
1984	JR Jones	A Llyr	1 hole	Prestatyn
1985	ED Jones	MA Macara	2 and 1	Ashburnham
1986	C Rees	B Knight	1 hole	Conwy
1987	PM Mayo	DK Wood	2 holes	Porthcawl
1988	K Jones	RN Roderick	40th hole	Harlech
1989	S Dodd	K Jones	2 and 1	Tenby
1990	A Barnett	A Jones	1 hole	Prestatyn

Welsh Amateur Stroke Play Championship

INAUGURATED 1967

YEAR	WINNER	SCORE	VENUE	YEAR	WINNER	SCORE	VENUE
1967	EN Davies	295	Harlech	1979	D McLean	289	Holyhead
1968	JA Buckley	294	Harlech	1980	TJ Melia	291	Tenby
1969	DL Stevens	288	Tenby	1981	D Evans	270	Wrexham
1970	JKD Povall	292	Newport	1982	JR Jones	287	Cradoc
1971	EN Davies } tie	296	Harlech	1983	G Davies	287	Aberdovey
	JL Toye			1984	RN Roderick	292	Newport
1972	JR Jones	299	Pyle and Kenfig	1985	MA Macara	291	Harlech
1973	JR Jones	300	Llandudno	1986	M Calvert	299	Pyle and Kenfig
1974	JL Toye	307	Tenby	1987	MA Macara	290	Llandudno
1975	D McLean	288	Wrexham	1988	RN Roderick	283	Tenby
1976	WI Tucker	282	Newport	1989	SC Dodd	304	Conwy
1977	JA Buckley	302	Prestatyn	1990	G Houston	288	Pyle and Kenfig
1978	HJ Evans	300	Pyle and Kenfig				

Welsh Team Championship

INAUGURATED 1895

YEAR	WINNER	VENUE	YEAR	WINNER	VENUE
1895	Rhyl	Aberdovey	1949	Llandudno (Maesdu)	Aberdovey
1896	Rhyl	Rhyl	1950	Southerndown	Southerndown
1897	Rhyl	Penarth	1951	Royal St David's	Harlech
1898	Rhyl	Aberdovey	1952	Prestatyn	Ashburnham
1899	Aberdovey	Conwy	1953	Llandudno (Maesdu)	Prestatyn
1900	Aberdovey	Porthcawl	1954	Aberystwyth	Tenby
1901	Aberdovey	Aberdovey	1955	Rhyl	Harlech
1902	Glamorganshire	Penarth	1956	Southerndown	Southerndown
1903	Rhyl	Rhos-on-Sea	1957	Ashburnham	Harlech
1904	Glamorganshire	Ashburnham	1958		
1905	Glamorganshire	Conwy	1959	Royal St David's	Porthcawl
1906	Radyr	Radyr	1960	Newport	Aberdovey
1907	Glamorganshire	Porthcawl	1961	Ashburnham	Ashburnham
1908	Glamorganshire	Southerndown	1962	Royal St David's	Harlech
1909	Glamorganshire	Rhyl	1963	Cardiff	Southerndown
1910	Royal Porthcawl	Swansea	1964	Royal St David's	Harlech
1911	Rhyl	Conwy	1965	Royal St David's	Porthcawl
1912	Glamorganshire	Porthcawl	1966	Whitchurch	Aberdovey
1913	Chester	Chester	1967	Whitchurch	Ashburnham
1914–19	*Not played due to Great War*		1968	Holyhead	Conwy
1920	Glamorganshire	Southerndown	1969	Whitchurch	Porthcawl
1921	Southerndown	Aberdovey	1970	Royal Porthcawl	Harlech
1922	Glamorganshire	Tenby	1971	St Pierre	Southerndown
1923	Newport	Rhyl	1972	Whitchurch	Prestatyn
1924	Radyr	Radyr	1973	Caernarfonshire	Ashburnham
1925	Ashburnham	Rhyl	1974	Whitchurch	Conwy
1926	Glamorganshire	Porthcawl	1975	Caernarfonshire	Porthcawl
1927	Ashburnham	Tenby	1976	Caernarfonshire	Harlech
1928	Royal St David's	Harlech	1977	Wenvoe	Southerndown
1929	Glamorganshire	Southerndown	1978	Pontypool	Conwy
1930	Newport	Tenby	1979	Pontypool	Ashburnham
1931	Glamorganshire	Aberdovey	1980	Radyr	Prestatyn
1932	Glamorganshire	Ashburnham	1981	Radyr	Porthcawl
1933	Southerndown	Porthcawl	1982	Newport	Harlech
1934	Glamorganshire	Prestatyn	1983	Pontypridd	Southerndown
1935	Glamorganshire	Tenby	1984	Whitchurch	Prestatyn
1936	Ashburnham	Aberdovey	1985	Whitchurch	Ashburnham
1937	Brecon	Porthcawl	1986	Pontnewydd	Conwy
1938	Prestatyn	Rhyl	1987	Llandudno (Maesdu)	Porthcawl
1939–46	*Not played due to Second World War*		1988	Ashburnham	Harlech
1947	Brecon	Clyne	1989	Cardiff	Tenby
1948	Rhyl	Llandudno	1990	Whitchurch	Prestatyn

Welsh Seniors' Amateur Championship

INAUGURATED 1975

at Aberdovey

YEAR	WINNER	SCORE	YEAR	WINNER	SCORE
1975	A Marshaman	77 (18 holes)	1983	WS Gronow	153
1976	AD Evans	156	1984	WI Tucker	150
1977	AE Lockley	154	1985	NA Lycett	149
1978	AE Lockley	75 (18 holes)	1986	ES Mills	154
1979	CR Morgan	158	1987	WS Gronow	146
1980	ES Mills	152	1988	NA Lycett	150
1981	T Branton	153	1989	WI Tucker	160
1982	WI Tucker	147	1990	I Hughes	159

COUNTY AND DISTRICT CHAMPIONSHIPS

The inauguration years of the English County and District Championships vary widely from Hampshire and Yorkshire in 1894, Cornwall 1896, Sussex 1899, to Cambridge in 1950. Match play was the usual method of deciding who was county champion. Some which started later, however, chose stroke play, and since 1950 many counties have had a stroke play championship in addition, from which the leading 16 or 32 players proceed to match play for the county title. Each county champion, whether decided by match play or stroke play, represents his county in the County Champions Tournament later in the year.

About half the County Unions now also hold an open championship, most of which have started since 1950. These opens are sometimes organised by the County PGAs, but more often by the Unions. Occasionally an amateur will win a county open, but usually professionals prevail.

England

Bedfordshire Amateur Championship

INAUGURATED 1923

YEAR	WINNER	VENUE	YEAR	WINNER	VENUE
1923	WL Goddard	Dunstable Downs	1939	WG Groves	South Beds
1924	WL Goddard	Bedfordshire	1940–45	*Not played due to Second World War*	
1925	CN Loake	South Beds	1946	LG Randall	Dunstable Downs
1926	WL Goddard	Dunstable Downs	1947	AL Day	Bedfordshire
1927	Captain Hime	Bedford and County	1948	LG Randall	South Beds
			1949	LG Randall	Dunstable Downs
1928	WL Goddard	Bedfordshire	1950	LG Randall	Bedfordshire
1929	Rev AJW Pym	South Beds	1951	I Anderson	Dunstable Downs
1930	HC Longhurst	Bedford and County	1952	LG Randall	John O' Gaunt
			1953	I Anderson	Bedfordshire
1931	WL Goddard	South Beds	1954	LG Randall	South Beds
1932	HC Longhurst	Bedfordshire	1955	AL Day	Bedford and County
1933	DS Redman	Dunstable Downs			
1934	HC Longhurst	Bedford and County	1956	LG Randall	Dunstable Downs
			1957	AL Day	John O'Gaunt
1935	HC Longhurst	South Beds	1958	AL Day	Bedfordshire
1936	LG Randall	Bedfordshire	1959	AL Day	South Beds
1937	RG Field	Dunstable Downs	1960	AL Day	Bedford and County
1938	WG Groves	Bedford and County	1961	AL Day	Dunstable Downs

YEAR	WINNER	VENUE	YEAR	WINNER	VENUE
1962	E Woodward	John O'Gaunt	1976	S Evans	Dunstable Downs
1963	AJ Southam	Bedfordshire	1977	R Drew	John O'Gaunt
1964	AL Day	South Beds	1978	A Rose	Apsley Guise
1965	CW Day	Bedford and	1979	P Wharton	Bedfordshire
		County	1980	D Ellis	South Beds
1966	R Sharp	Dunstable Downs	1981	C Beard	Bedford and
1967	RA Durrant	John O'Gaunt			County
1968	RA Durrant	Bedfordshire	1982	A Rose	Dunstable Downs
1969	F Rowden	South Beds	1983	A Rose	John O'Gaunt
1970	RA Durrant	Bedford and	1984	MA Stokes	Apsley Guise
		County	1985	R Harris	Bedfordshire
1971	R Coogan	Dunstable Downs	1986	M Wharton	Beadlow Manor
1972	N Wharton	John O'Gaunt	1987	P Wharton	Bedford and
1973	R Coogan	Bedfordshire			County
1974	R Coogan	South Beds	1988	P Wharton	South Beds
1975	S Evans	Bedford and	1989	C Staroscik	John O'Gaunt
		County	1990	D Charlton	Dunstable Downs

Berks, Bucks and Oxfordshire Amateur Championship

INAUGURATED 1924

(Until 1936 and 1952–54 decided by match play)

YEAR	WINNER	VENUE	YEAR	WINNER	VENUE
1924	Geoffrey McCallum	Stoke Poges	1957	NJ Niven	East Berks
1925	Geoffrey McCallum	Beaconsfield	1958	FB Reed	Frilford Heath
1926	RWA Speed	Sonning	1959	JK Tullis	Beaconsfield
1927	Geoffrey McCallum	Frilford Heath	1960	WOT Cocker	Maidenhead
1928	Geoffrey McCallum	Burnham Beeches	1961	J Lawrence	Burnham Beeches
1929	CH Brickhill	Maidenhead	1962	J Lawrence	Stoke Poges
1930	CB Booth	Huntercombe	1963	J Coomber	Sonning
1931	D Provan	Flackwell Heath	1964	J Lawrence	The Berkshire
1932	R Fortescue	Sonning	1965	J Coomber	Frilford Heath
1933	GR Girdlestone	Frilford Heath	1966	J Lawrence	Denham
1934	JOH Greenly	Stoke Poges	1967	RWT Addey	East Berks
1935	CW Mole	Burnham Beeches	1968	MG King	Calcot
1936	EH Chambers	Beaconsfield	1969	MG King	Beaconsfield
1937	A Keith	Frilford Heath	1970	MG King	Maidenhead
1938	CB Booth	Sonning	1971	K Borrett	Sonning
1939	HC Stone	Denham	1972	JA Putt	Denham
1940–45	*Not played due to Second World War*		1973	MG King	The Berkshire
1946	R Sweeney Jr	Stoke Poges	1974	MG King	Burnham Beeches
1947	R Sweeney Jr	The Berkshire	1975	A Parsons	Gerrards Cross
1948	AR Strong	Burnham Beeches	1976	WS Gronow	East Berks
1949	JE Kitchin	Maidenhead	1977	MD Owers	Temple
1950	BW Parmenter	Huntercombe	1978	A Parsons	Stoke Poges
1951	NRM Philcox	Beaconsfield	1979	A Miller	Frilford Heath
1952	Dr GMF Bisset	The Berkshire	1980	DG Lane	Beaconsfield
1953	IR Harris	Frilford Heath	1981	M Rapley	Calcot Park
1954	RK Pitamber	Sonning	1982	DG Lane	Maidenhead
1955	RSG Scott	Denham	1983	M Orris	The Berkshire
1956	JJ MacBeth	Calcot	1984	NG Webber	Ellesborough

YEAR	WINNER	VENUE	YEAR	WINNER	VENUE
1985	M Rapley	Denham	1988	F George	East Berks
1986	DG Lane	Burnham Beeches	1989	H Bareham	Temple
1987	F George	Gerrards Cross	1990	S Barwick	Frilford Heath

Cambridge Area GU Amateur Championship
(HA Newport Cup)

INAUGURATED 1950

YEAR	WINNER	VENUE	YEAR	WINNER	VENUE
1950	IN Reynolds	Gog Magog	1971	Dr AW Garner	Gog Magog
1951	Sq Ldr GH Duncan	Newmarket	1972	GP Powell	Royston
1952	LW Wheeler	Gog Magog	1973	RW Guy	Newmarket
1953	WB Dunn	Newmarket	1974	MT Seaton	Gog Magog
1954	GG Kerr	Gog Magog	1975	S Derbyshire	Royston
1955	A Peck	Newmarket	1976	BJ McCulloch	Newmarket
1956	WB Dunn	Gog Magog	1977	RW Guy	Gog Magog
1957	FG Rand	Royston	1978	MT Seaton	Newmarket
1958	JF Goddard	Newmarket	1979	RW Guy	Gog Magog
1959	Flt Lt AJA Heyns	Gog Magog	1980	MT Seaton	Ely City
1960	JF Goddard	Newmarket	1981	MT Seaton	Saffron Walden
1961	JF Goddard	Gog Magog	1982	RW Guy	Gog Magog
1962	FG Rand	Royston	1983	JR Gray	St Neots
1963	KA Cameron	Newmarket	1984	NK Hughes	Ely City
1964	RJ Brown	Gog Magog	1985	DWG Wood	Royston
1965	FG Rand	Newmarket	1986	JGR Miller	Newmarket
1966	CP Harrison	Royston	1987	R Claydon	Saffron Walden
1967	B McCulloch	Newmarket	1988	R Claydon	Gog Magog
1968	RAC Blows	Gog Magog	1989	B Jackson	Ely City
1969	WS Harrison	Royston	1990	GN Stevenson	St Neots
1970	RW Guy	Newmarket			

Cambridgeshire Match Play Championship
(Wheeler Salver)
1970–71 at Royston; 1972–1990 at Gog Magog

YEAR	WINNER	YEAR	WINNER
1970	RW Guy	1977	RW Guy
1971	RAC Blows	1978	RW Guy
1972	RW Guy	1979	MT Seaton
1973	S Derbyshire	1980	MT Seaton
1974	RW Guy	1981	RW Guy
1975	GPL Collins	1982	DF Tiplady
1976	RC Maltman	1983	MT Seaton

YEAR	WINNER	YEAR	WINNER
1984	RW Guy	1988	R Claydon
1985	KM Diss	1989	RW Guy
1986	B Jackson	1990	KM Diss
1987	R Claydon		

Cheshire Amateur Championship

INAUGURATED 1921

YEAR	WINNER	VENUE	YEAR	WINNER	VENUE
1921	G Tweedale	Delamere Forest	1959	JT Jones	Hoylake
1922	G Tweedale	Prenton	1960	JT Jones	Wilmslow
1923	I Sidebottom	Stockport	1961	JT Jones	Mere
1924	MS Walker	Wallasey	1962	GM Edwards	Wallasey
1925	D Eadie	Wilmslow	1963	MJ Pearson	Stockport
1926	W Sutton	Hoylake	1964	A O'Connor	Delamere Forest
1927	W Sutton	Prestbury	1965	MJ Pearson	Hoylake
1928	N Sutton	Sandiway	1966	GM Edwards	Prestbury
1929	J Braid Jr	Timperley	1967	A O'Connor	Wilmslow
1930	HW Heslop	Prenton	1968	NB Moir	Sandiway
1931	E Coventry	Sale	1969	DP Jones	Hoylake
1932	HD Porter	Wallasey	1970	B Stockdale	Mere
1933	HN Fogg	Stockport	1971	TD Frost	Wallasey
1934	CW Timmis	Leasowe	1972	DK Jones	Sandiway
1935	J Abraham	Ringway	1973	GM Edwards	Prestbury
1936	W Sutton	Delamere Forest	1974	PH Dennett	Wilmslow
1937	HE Walker	Hoylake	1975	EI Bradshaw	Bromborough
1938	E Bromley-Davenport	Warrington	1976	RA Biggs	Hoylake
1939	MW Budd	Prestbury	1977	EI Bradshaw	Delamere Forest
1940–45	*Not played due to Second World War*		1978	CR Smethurst	Stockport
1946	CW Timmis	Hoylake	1979	PT Bailey	Sandiway
1947	P Clark	Mere	1980	EI Bradshaw	Caldy
1948	CW Timmis	Hoylake	1981	CR Harrison	Romiley
1949	S Mettam	Wilmslow	1982	CR Smethurst	Delamere Forest
1950	HC Humphreys	Sandiway	1983	CR Smethurst	Heswall
1951	HC Humphreys	Prestbury	1984	I Spencer	Prestbury
1952	DHL Shone	Hoylake	1985	NW Briggs	Hoylake
1953	S Mettam	Mere	1986	PT Bailey	Wilmslow
1954	MJ Pearson	Stockport	1987	PT Jones	Bromborough
1955	E Crimes	Wallasey	1988	PT Bailey	Sandiway
1956	AE Billington	Delamere Forest	1989	PT Bailey	Caldy
1957	P Clark	Prestbury	1990	JR Berry	Wilmslow
1958	S Ball	Sandiway			

Cheshire Amateur Match Play Championship

INAUGURATED 1964

YEAR	WINNER	VENUE	YEAR	WINNER	VENUE
1964	GM Edwrds	Mere	1978	PT Bailey	Wallasey
1965	GM Edwards	Mere	1979	SR Williams	Warrington
1966	CJ Farey	Mere	1980	EI Bradshaw	Dunham Forest
1967	GF Lloyd	Delamere Forest	1981	SH Roberts	Bromborough
1968	AP O'Connor	Delamere Forest	1982	CC Harrison	Wilmslow
1969	PH Dennett	Delamere Forest	1983	P Lovall	Stockport
1970	JR Bennett	Sandiway	1984	EI Bradshaw	Caldy
1971	IH Ainsworth	Stockport	1985	CC Harrison	Romiley
1972	AW Brindle	Mere	1986	GM Edwards	Wallasey
1973	RA Briggs	Delamere Forest	1987	AE Hill	Bramhall Park
1974	GM Edwards	Hoylake	1988	AE Hill	Heswall
1975	PH Dennett	Mere	1989	A Sandywell	Delamere Forest
1976	KP Geddes	Prestbury	1990	JR Berry	Heswall
1977	JE Cann	Ringway			

Cornwall Amateur Championship

INAUGURATED 1896

YEAR	WINNER	VENUE	YEAR	WINNER	VENUE
1896	EM Bannerman	Royal Cornwall	1926	Dr FH Cleveland	Newquay
1897	L Stuart Anderson	Lelant	1927	HP Bazeley	Mullion
1898	L Stuart Anderson	St Enodoc	1928	PC Thornton	Bude
1899	L Stuart Anderson	St Enodoc	1929	HP Bazeley	Lelant
1900	L Stuart Anderson	Newquay	1930	WH Ricardo	St Enodoc
1901	L Stuart Anderson	Mullion	1931	FH Wills	Newquay
1902	J Knowlden Willis	Bude	1932	JF Jackson	Mullion
1903	A Basil Reece	Newquay	1933	P Buchanan	Bude
1904	EF Wood	Lelant	1934	EL Thomas	Lelant
1905	A Basil Reece	St Enodoc	1935	Cdr Bannerman	St Enodoc
1906	G Kellner	Mullion	1936	RM Jewson	Newquay
1907	J Knowlden Willis	Newquay	1937	AD Stocks	Mullion
1908	J Knowlden Willis	Mullion	1938	AI Roberts	Lelant
1909	EJS Jenner	Bude	1939	Col GL Tyringham	St Enodoc
1910	TM Rogers	St Enodoc	1940–45	*Not played due to Second World War*	
1911	TM Rogers	Lelant	1946	H Hutchinson	Trevose
1912	JK Willis	St Enodoc	1947	AJ Billing	Newquay
1913	EJS Jenner	Falmouth	1948	PC Vardon	Lelant
1914	H Hargreaves	Newquay	1949	H Hutchinson	St Enodoc
1915–19	*Not played due to Great War*		1950	E Bennett	Trevose
1920	H Hargreaves	Newquay	1951	E Bennett	Newquay
1921	E Coppin	Bude	1952	E Bennett	Tehidy Park
1922	BG Ware	Newquay	1953	H Hutchinson	Lelant
1923	ER Campbell	St Enodoc	1954	H Hutchinson	St Enodoc
1924	JM Thomson	Lelant	1955	H Hutchinson	Trevose
1925	Cdr Bannerman	St Enodoc	1956	H Hutchinson	Newquay

YEAR	WINNER	VENUE	YEAR	WINNER	VENUE
1957	G Medlyn	Tehidy Park	1974	CS Carveth	Carlyon Bay
1958	DM Payne	Lelant	1975	P Hasson	St Enodoc
1959	GN Bicknell	St Enodoc	1976	JW Bradley	St Enodoc
1960	GN Bicknell	Trevose	1977	JW Bradley	Newquay
1961	DM Payne	Newquay	1978	AJK Rowe	Tehidy Park
1962	E Holland	Tehidy Park	1979	PA Gilbert	Lelant
1963	RGW Sanders	Lelant	1980	M Boggia	Carlyon Bay
1964	GN Bicknell	St Enodoc	1981	JR Hirst	Launceston
1965	PJ Yeo	Trevose	1982	MC Edmunds	Trevose
1966	PJ Yeo	Newquay	1983	MC Edmunds	Tehidy Park
1967	PJ Yeo	Tehidy Park	1984	RJ Simmons	Newquay
1968	JV Brown	Lelant	1985	CD Phillips	St Enodoc
1969	HG Champion	St Enodoc	1986	RJ Simmons	Lelant
1970	PJ Yeo	Trevose	1987	P Clayton	Launceston
1971	PJC Ward	Newquay	1988	P Clayton	Trevose
1972	G Medlyn	Tehidy Park	1989	CD Phillips	Tehidy Park
1973	RE Libby	Lelant	1990	MC Edmunds	Newquay

County Champions' Tournament (England)

For President's Bowl

INAUGURATED 1962

YEAR	WINNER	VENUE
1962	GM Edwards, Cheshire A Thirlwell, Northumberland }tie	Sherwood Forest
1963	MJ Burgess, Sussex R Foster, Yorks }tie	Little Aston
1964	MF Attenborough, Kent	Sandiway
1965	MG Lee, Lincs	Royal Worlington and Newmarket
1966	RP Stephenson, Middx	Church Brampton
1967	PJ Benka, Surrey	Lindrick
1968	GE Hyde, Sussex	Liphook
1969	AW Holmes, Herts	Luffenham Heath
1970	MG King, Berks, Bucks and Oxon	Frilford Heath
1971	M Lee, Yorkshire	Lincoln
1972	P Berry, Glos	Moseley
1973	AH Chandler, Lancs	Whittington Barracks
1974	GE Hyde, Sussex AWB Lyle, Shrops & Hereford }tie	Ross-on-Wye
1975	N Faldo, Herts	Kedleston Park
1976	RPF Brown, Devon	Shifnal
1977	M Walls, Cumbria	Gog Magog
1978	IT Simpson, Notts	Pleasington
1979	N Burch, Essex	Olton
1980	DG Lane, Berks, Bucks & Oxon	Ashridge
1981	MJ Kelly, Yorks	Hallamshire
1982	PG Deeble, Northumberland	Prestbury
1983	N Chesses, Warwickshire	Aldeburgh

YEAR	WINNER	VENUE
1984	N Briggs, Herts P McEvoy, Warwickshire } tie	South Staffs
1985	R Robinson, Herts	Stoke Poges
1986	A Gelsthorpe, Yorks	Trentham
1987	F George, Berks, Bucks & Oxon D Fay, Sussex } tie	Sherwood Forest
1988	R Claydon, Cambridge	Alwoodley
1989	R Willison, Middx	Woodbridge
1990	P Streeter, Lincs R Sloman, Kent } tie	Olton

Cumbria Amateur Championship
Cumberland and Westmorland Amateur Championship until 1973

INAUGURATED 1910

YEAR	WINNER	VENUE	YEAR	WINNER	VENUE
1910	CF Pennington	Silloth	1956	WD Longcake	Silloth
1911	WM Reed	Kendal	1957	WA Anderson	Furness
1912	SW Fleming	Cockermouth	1958	WR Sharp	Workington
1913	SW Fleming	Appleby	1959	WD Longcake	Carlisle
1914	HJ Watt	Carlisle	1960	WR Sharp	Penrith
1915–9	*Not played due to Great War*		1961	W Anderson	Ulverston
1920	MS Walker	Seascale	1962	A Grieve	Cockermouth
1921	T Cape	Silloth	1963	WD Longcake	Barrow
1922	E Swan	Kendal	1964	WR Sharp	Appleby
1923	WJH Horrocks	Cockermouth	1965	JB Carr	Seascale
1924	F Williamson	Penrith	1966	JB Carr	Kendal
1925	Capt WM Reed	Appleby	1967	WD Longcake	Silloth
1926	WJH Horrocks	Carlisle	1968	J Terris	Carlisle
1927	CF Pennington	Seascale	1969	JH French	Ulverston
1928	WJH Horrocks	Ulverston	1970	ID Stavert	Appleby
1929	R Lomas	Silloth	1971	ID Stavert	Seascale
1930	Dr G Irving	Kendal	1972	M Wallis	Penrith
1931	AH Foster	Workington	1973	JDM Dodds	Carlisle
1932	LH Wilson	Cockermouth	1974	M Walls	Ulverston
1933	Dr JL Cowan	Penrith	1975	M Walls	Appleby
1934	JW Brough	Ulverston	1976	E Gulliksen	Seascale
1935	A Grieve	Carlisle	1977	M Walls	Silloth
1936	A Grieve	Appleby	1978	M Barrand	Furness
1937	A Grieve	Kendal	1979	AJ Payne	Carlisle
1938	TS Hartley	Seascale	1980	AR Morrison	Ulverston
1939	L Steele	Workington	1981	J Kirkpatrick	Penrith
1940–46	*Not played due to Second World War*		1982	E Gulliksen	Appleby
1947	F Todd	Silloth	1983	A Drabble	Workington
1948	F Todd	Carlisle	1984	M Lowe	Seascale
1949	F Todd	Penrith	1985	J Longcake	Silloth
1950	F Todd	Ulverston	1986	M Ruddick	Brampton
1951	F Todd	Cockermouth	1987	J Longcake	Furness
1952	RS Furness	Barrow	1988	G Waters	Carlisle
1953	LE Kilshaw	Kendal	1989	G Winter	Barrow
1954	A Grieve	Appleby	1990	G Winter	Penrith
1955	WD Longcake	Seascale			

Cumbria Match Play Championship

YEAR	WINNER	VENUE	YEAR	WINNER	VENUE
1974	E Gulliksen	Penrith	1983	AR Morrison	Seascale
1975	M Walls	Barrow	1984	M Ruddick	Carlisle
1976	M Barrand	Brampton	1985	J Longcake	Furness
1977	M Walls	Kendal	1986	M Ruddick	Kendal
1978	E Gulliksen	Penrith	1987	G Winter	Appleby
1979	E Gulliksen	Seascale	1988	P Chapman	Kendal
1980	P Jack	Carlisle	1989	G Winter	Appleby
1981	J Brennand	Appleby	1990	A Atkinson	Ulverston
1982	AR Morrison	Brampton			

Derbyshire Amateur Championship

INAUGURATED 1913

YEAR	WINNER	VENUE	YEAR	WINNER	VENUE
1913	Dr H Barber	Burton-on-Trent	1947	R Pattinson	Erewash Valley
1914–20	*Not played due to Great War*		1948	R Pattinson	Burton-on-Trent
1921	G Nutt	Derbyshire	1949	R Pattinson	Chesterfield
1922	EPW Davis	Chesterfield	1950	J Armitt	Cavendish
1923	BW Maltby	Erewash Valley	1951	R Pattinson	Chevin
1924	TGM Ward	Markeaton	1952	H Bennett	Buxton and High
1925	JC Harrison	Burton-on-Trent			Peak
1926	C Thorpe	Buxton and High	1953	H Bennett	Erewash Valley
		Peak	1954	H Bennett	Burton-on-Trent
1927	C Thorpe	Matlock	1955	H Bennett	Kedleston Park
1928	TB Farrington	Duffield	1956	H Bennett	Chesterfield
1929	C Thorpe	Cavendish	1957	H Bennett	Cavendish
1930	C Thorpe	Chesterfield	1958	R Pattinson	Chevin
1931	C Thorpe	Erewash Valley	1959	D Mason	Buxton and High
1932	C Thorpe	Derbyshire			Peak
1933	J Long	Marketon	1960	H Bennett	Erewash Valley
1934	C Thorpe	Burton-on-Trent	1961	H Bennett	Burton-on-Trent
1935	A Robinson	Buxton and High	1962	R Pattinson	Kedleston Park
		Peak	1963	JM Booth	Chesterfield
1936	E Ashmore	Matlock	1964	R Pattinson	Cavendish
1937	A Robinson	Chevin	1965	DP Cross	Chevin
1938	J Armitt	Cavendish	1966	WT Easson	Buxton and High
1939	H Bennett	Derby Municipal			Peak
1940–45	*Not played due to Second World War*		1967	JC Thomas	Derby
1946	J Armitt	Buxton and High	1968	JE Beddington	Burton-on-Trent
		Peak	1969	PM Baxter	Erewash Valley

YEAR	WINNER	VENUE	YEAR	WINNER	VENUE
1970	TJ Hanson	Kedleston Park	1981	RJ Hall	Chevin
1971	JC Thomas	Chesterfield	1982	RRW Davenport	Cavendish
1972	N Rogers	Cavendish	1983	RRW Davenport	Breadsall Priory
1973	PM Baxter	Chevin	1984	G Shaw	Matlock
1974	D Mason	Buxton and High	1985	RRW Davenport	Erewash Valley
		Peak	1986	J Feeney	Burton-on-Trent
1975	JK Lawton	Matlock	1987	RP Green	Buxton and High
1976	RRW Davenport	Erewash Valley			Peak
1977	JE Roberts	Burton-on-Trent	1988	NC Wylde	Kedleston Park
1978	PM Baxter	Kedleston Park	1989	PM Eastwood	Mickleover
1979	RRW Davenport	Mickleover	1990	RP Fletcher	Chesterfield
1980	JC Thomas	Chesterfield			

Derbyshire Match Play Championship

INAUGURATED 1971

YEAR	WINNER	VENUE	YEAR	WINNER	VENUE
1971	JC Thomas	Chevin	1981	N Rowland	Kedleston Park
1972	PM Baxter	Kedleston Park	1982	MP Higgins	Chevin
1973	PM Baxter	Chesterfield	1983	G Shaw	Chesterfield
1974	PM Baxter	Erewash Valley	1984	G Shaw	Erewash Valley
1975	AT Bird	Burton-on-Trent	1985	CRJ Ibbotson	Burton-on-Trent
1976	PM Baxter	Matlock	1986	J Feeney	Buxton and High
1977	PM Baxter	Cavendish			Peak
1978	CRJ Ibbotson	Breadsall Priory	1987	G Shaw	Matlock
1979	N Rowland	Buxton and High	1988	MP Higgins	Cavendish
		Peak	1989	G Shaw	Kedleston Park
1980	CRJ Ibbotson	Mickleover	1990	RP Fletcher	Chevin

Derbyshire Open Championship

INAUGURATED 1924

YEAR	WINNER	VENUE	YEAR	WINNER	VENUE
1924	WH Wolliscroft	Burton-on-Trent	1961	LJ Feeney	Chevin
1925	H Walker	Derbyshire	1962	LJ Feeney	Burton-on-Trent
1926	T Barber	Chesterfield	1963	LJ Feeney	Cavendish
1927	S Harrison	Chevin	1964	RI Tickle	Derby
1928	T Barber	Markeaton	1965	AF Simms	Buxton and High
1929	T Barber	Matlock			Peak
1930	T Barber	Erewash Valley	1966	D Mason (Am)	Kedleston Park
1931	J Fallin	Buxton and High	1967	JC Thomas (Am)	Matlock
		Peak	1968	H Lester	Chesterfield
1932	J Armitt (Am)	Mickleover	1969	CRJ Ibbotson (Am)	Chevin
1933	J Armitt (Am)	Allestree	1970	JB Flanders	Burton-on-Trent
1934	C Thorpe (Am)	Derby	1971	R Lambert	Cavendish
1935	A Norton	Markeaton	1972	E Darcy	Erewash Valley
1936	J Armitt (Am)	Burton-on-Trent	1973	E Darcy	Buxton and High
1937	F Jowle	Chesterfield			Peak
1938	A Norton	Erewash Valley	1974	MJ Ronan	Kedleston Park
1939	A Norton	Chevin	1975	A Ellis	Cavendish
1940–45	*Not played due to Second World War*		1976	MC Orme	Chesterfield
1946	C Thorpe (Am)	Cavendish	1977	RRW Davenport (Am)	Matlock
1947	J Armitt (Am)	Matlock	1978	RH Lambert	Chevin
1948	E Lester	Derby Municipal	1979	RRW Davenport (Am)	Burton-on-Trent
1949	*No championship*		1980	I Gretton (Am)	Erewash Valley
1950	W Walker	Chesterfield	1981	RRW Davenport (Am)	Buxton and High
1951	H Lester	Buxton and High			Peak
		Peak	1982	RRW Davenport (Am)	Mickleover
1952	H Bennett (Am)	Burton-on-Trent	1983	C Radford (Am)	Kedleston
1953	SM McCready (Am)	Kedleston Park	1984	J Feeney (Am)	Cavendish
1954	WW Walker	Chevin	1985	M McLean	Chesterfield
1955	WW Walker	Cavendish	1986	N Furniss (Am)	Matlock
1956	H Bennett (Am)	Derby Municipal	1987	SA Smith	Erewash Valley
1957	WW Walker	Matlock	1988	G Shaw	Chevin
1958	H Lester	Kedleston Park	1989	DL Clarke (Am)	Burton-on-Trent
1959	D Ferguson	Chesterfield	1990	M Deeley	Buxton and High
1960	LJ Feeney	Buxton and High			Peak
		Peak			

Devon Amateur Championship

INAUGURATED 1912

After 1924 decided by match play

YEAR	WINNER	VENUE
1912	CC Aylmer	Tavistock
1913	CC Aylmer	Budleigh Salterton
1914	LCH Palairet	Warren
1915–19	*Not played due to Great War*	
1920	KF Fradgley	Churston
1921	OL Trenchman	Saunton
1922	C Chard	Yelverton
1923	C Chard	Westward Ho!
1924	LF Fradgley	Torquay
1925	C Chard	Tavistock
1926	C Chard	Saunton
1927	C Chard	Yelverton
1928	C Chard	Budleigh Salterton
1929	JH Greathead	Westward Ho!
1930	FH Carroll	Tavistock
1931	AG Skinner	Saunton
1932	AG Skinner	Torquay
1933	AGT Rees	Tavistock
1934	HP Reed	Yelverton
1935	AG Skinner	Budleigh Salterton
1936	AG Skinner	Westward Ho!
1937	LC Lake	Churston
1938	LC Lake	Exeter
1939	AGT Rees	Yelverton
1940–46	*Not played due to Second World War*	
1947	Dr RM Munro	Torquay
1948	JP Phillips	Budleigh Salterton
1949	Dr RM Munro	Yelverton
1950	ED Trapnell	Westward Ho!
1951	R Thairlwall	Warren
1952	Dr DI Stirk	Exeter
1953	ED Trapnell	Thurlestone
1954	LC Lake	Saunton
1955	AD Inglis	Churston
1956	ED Trapnell	Budleigh Salterton

YEAR	WINNER	VENUE
1957	LC Lake	Warren
1958	CH Scott	Tavistock
1959	ED Trapnell	Westward Ho!
1960	RPF Brown	Exeter
1961	TDW Slater	Saunton
1962	RPF Brown	Yelverton
1963	RB Redfern	Teignmouth
1964	RB Redfern	Westward Ho!
1965	BG Steer	Budleigh Salterton
1966	RB Redfern	Thurlestone
1967	TB Jones Jr	Churston
1968	BG Steer	Exeter
1969	RM Leach	Saunton
1970	D Lang	Tavistock
1971	RW Holmes	Thurlestone
1972	RB Williams	Yelverton
1973	MW Hampton	Westward Ho!
1974	RPF Brown	Budleigh Salterton
1975	AP Vivary	Saunton
1976	RPF Brown	Westward Ho!
1977	R Knott	Churston
1978	MJ Jewell	Teignmouth
1979	MW Hampton	Tavistock
1980	MG Symons	Budleigh Salterton
1981	MJ Jewell	Yelverton
1982	MG Symons	Westward Ho!
1983	A Richards	Exeter
1984	JN May	Saunton
1985	J Langmead	Teignmouth
1986	P Newcombe	Thurlestone
1987	J Langmead	Churston
1988	J Langmead	Westward Ho!
1989	R Barrow	Tiverton
1990	G Milne	Tavistock

Devon Open Championship

INAUGURATED 1923

YEAR	WINNER	VENUE	YEAR	WINNER	VENUE
1923	E Hore	Tavistock	1959	JJ Spencer	Thurlestone
1924	W Pursey	Budleigh Salterton	1960	N Sutton	Saunton
1925	CH Reith	Yelverton	1961	N Sutton	Budleigh Salterton
1926	E Hooker	Yelverton	1963	B Bamford	Tavistock .
1927	A Easterbrook	Torquay and South Devon	1964	Dr DI Stirk (Am)	Westward Ho!
			1965	B Bamford	Exeter
1928	S Easterbrook	Churston	1966	AM MacDonald	Churston
1929	E Hooker	Tavistock	1967	B Jolly	Yelverton
1930	E Hooker	Torquay and South Devon	1968	TB Jones Jr	Saunton
			1969	N Sutton	Budleigh Salterton
1931	A Robins	Saunton	1970	N Sutton	Teignmouth
1932	A Hooker	Yelverton	1971	R Radway (Am)	Thurlestone
1933	E Hooker	Exeter	1972	Dr DI Stirk (Am)	Westward Ho!
1934	A Robins	Westward Ho!	1973	K Whitfield (Am)	Tiverton
1935	E Hooker	Churston	1974	RB Williams	Torquay
1936	W Ivory	Budleigh Salterton	1975	J Green	Tavistock
1937	E Hooker	Yelverton	1976	J Green	Yelverton
1938	CH Ward	Tavistock	1977	A Valentine	Saunton
1939–46	*Not played due to Second World War*		1978	BG Steer (Am)	Exeter
1947	KJ Hooker	Thurlestone	1979	MJ Jewell (Am)	Teignmouth
1948	KJ Hooker	Exeter	1980	M Kemp	Bigbury
1949	KJ Hooker	Stover	1981	D Sheppard	Westward Ho!
1950	KJ Hooker	Westward Ho!	1982	MJ Jewell (Am)	Tiverton
1951	KJ Hooker	Tavistock	1983	T Valentine	Churston
1952	N Sutton	Saunton	1984	M Symons (Am)	Exeter
1953	C Easterbrook	Budleigh Salterton	1985	AM MacDonald	Yelverton
1954	N Sutton	Teignmouth	1986	P Newcombe	Budleigh Salterton
1955	N Sutton	Yelverton	1987	G Milne	Westward Ho!
1956	N Sutton	Westward Ho!	1988	D Sheppard	Teignmouth
1957	N Sutton	Exeter	1989	D Sheppard	Teignmouth
1958	S Taggart	Churston	1990	G Tomkinson	Churston

Dorset Amateur Championship

INAUGURATED 1924

YEAR	WINNER	VENUE	YEAR	WINNER	VENUE
1924	FA Stephens	Came Down	1935	A Dore	Broadstone
1925	V Weldon	Ferndown	1936	HE Botting	Ferndown
1926	FA Stephens	Parkstone	1937	RM Chadwick	Came Down
1927	E Hunter	Broadstone	1938	EJ Nicholl	Broadstone
1928	WR Wills-Sanford	Ferndown	1939	C Glass Hooper	Ferndown
1929	Sq Ldr JP Shorten	Came Down	1940–45	*Not played due to Second World War*	
1930	CL Gordon Steward	Parkstone	1946	KJ Longmore	Parkstone
1931	MR Gardner	Parkstone	1947	O Austreng	Ferndown
1932	CL Gordon Steward	Ferndown	1948	EB Millward	Parkstone
1933	C Glass Hooper	Came Down	1949	J Santall	Ferndown
1934	MR Gardner	Parkstone	1950	EB Millward	Broadstone

YEAR	WINNER	VENUE	YEAR	WINNER	VENUE
1951	RE Garrett	Parkstone	1972	GJ Butler	Parkstone
1952	EB Millward	Came Down	1973	AK Jones	Broadstone
1953	K Clarke	Northbourne	1974	J Lawrence	Lyme Regis
1954	RE Garrett	Ferndown	1975	GJ Butler	Came Down
1955	R Lawford	Broadstone	1976	GJ Butler	Isle of Purbeck
1956	K Longmore	Yeovil	1977	D Scholes	Ferndown
1957	K Longmore	Parkstone	1978	GJ Butler	Yeovil
1958	P Saunders	Came Down	1979	M Farley	Parkstone
1959	GJ Butler	Ferndown	1980	J Nash	Broadstone
1960	K Longmore	Broadstone	1981	R Hearn	Lyme Regis
1961	GJ Butler	Yeovil	1982	R Miles	Came Down
1962	AJ Richmond	Parkstone	1983	R Miles	Isle of Purbeck
1963	GJ Butler	Lyme Regis	1984	JD Gordon	Ferndown
1964	AJ Richmond	Came Down	1985	J Bloxham	Knighton Heath
1965	GJ Butler	Ferndown	1986	AW Lawrence	Yeovil
1967	GJ Butler	Parkstone	1987	AW Lawence	Parkstone
1968	RG Peach	Broadstone	1988	AW Lawrence	Broadstone
1969	JG Butler	Came Down	1989	AW Lawrence	Sherborne
1970	R Lawford	Ferndown	1990	P McMullen	Lyme Regis
1971	EJS Garrett	Yeovil			

Dorset Stroke Play Championship

YEAR	WINNER	VENUE	YEAR	WINNER	VENUE
1980	RA Francis	Lyme Regis	1986	M Welch	Came Down
1981	J Tynor	Weymouth	1987	AW Lawrence	Sherborne
1982	AW Lawrence	Yeovil	1988	S Edgley	Knighton Heath
1983	R Hearn	Broadstone	1989	R Mabb	Yeovil
1984	R Hearn	Parkstone	1990	AW Lawrence	Ferndown
1985	AW Lawrence	Isle of Purbeck			

Durham Amateur Championship

INAUGURATED 1908

YEAR	WINNER	VENUE	YEAR	WINNER	VENUE
1908	AC Patterson	Seaton Carew	1926	J Clark	Brancepeth Castle
1909	AC Patterson	Coxgreen	1927	TS Wraith	Cleadon
1910	JS Roddam	South Shields	1928	FG Harland	Ravensworth
1911	AJ Graham	Seaton Carew	1929	J Clark	Seaton Carew
1912	AC Patterson	Coxgreen	1930	A Harrison	Seaham Harbour
1913	HW Cummins	Ryton	1931	A Harrison	Brancepeth Castle
1914	JS Roddam	Seaton Carew	1932	A Harrison	Dinsdale Spa
1915–18	*Not played due to Great War*		1933	JV Todd	Ryton
1919	AC Patterson	Coxgreen	1934	JV Todd	Coxgreen
1920	DA Haggie	Seaton Carew	1935	JV Todd	Darlington
1921	S Armitage	Ravensworth	1936	JV Todd	South Shields
1922	FG Harland	Seaham Harbour	1937	Dr RR Dodd	Ravensworth
1923	Dr GJ Moore	Dinsdale Spa	1938	Dr RR Dodd	Hartlepool
1924	J Bate	Tyneside	1939	C Crosthwaite	Seaton Carew
1925	FG Harland	Coxgreen	1940–45	*Not played due to Second World War*	

YEAR	WINNER	VENUE	YEAR	WINNER	VENUE
1946	W Irvine	Brancepeth Castle	1969	DW McClelland	Seaton Carew
1947	C Moffitt	Ravensworth	1970	R Clark	Brancepeth Castle
1948	JV Todd	Seaton Carew	1971	RW Green	Darlington
1949	Col WHH Aitken	Brancepeth Castle	1972	RW Renaut	Seaton Carew
1950	Brig WHH Aitken	Darlington	1973	H Ashby	Brancepeth Castle
1951	TH Tooley	Seaton Carew	1974	JW Ord	Seaton Carew
1952	W Moffitt	Brancepeth Castle	1975	A Doxford	South Shields
1953	W Moffitt	Ryton	1976	D Oughton	Brancepeth Castle
1954	G Pickering	Seaton Carew	1977	JL Naisby	Wearside
1955	WR Thomas	Brancepeth Castle	1978	AJ McLure	Seaton Carew
1956	TE Jones	South Shields	1979	JL Naisby	Tyneside
1957	D Hunter	Seaton Carew	1980	AJ McLure	Brancepeth Castle
1958	IR Hornsby	Brancepeth Castle	1981	D Hawkins	Seaton Carew
1959	KT Thompson	Dinsdale Spa	1982	J Ellwood	Bishop Auckland
1960	R Clark	Seaton Carew	1983	M Ure	Darlington
1961	R Clark	Brancepeth Castle	1984	M Ure	Eaglescliffe
1962	JA Sanderson	Wearside	1985	A Robertson	Brancepeth Castle
1963	H Ashby	Seaton Carew	1986	H Ashby	Whickham
1964	IR Hornsby	Brancepeth Castle	1987	P Highmoor	Seaton Carew
1965	J Wrigley	Hartlepool	1988	JR Ellwood	South Shields
1966	G Hedley	Seaton Carew	1989	GR Bell	Seaton Carew
1967	RW Green	Brancepeth Castle	1990	R Walker	Brancepeth Castle
1968	JW Ord	South Moor			

Durham Match Play Championship

INAUGURATED 1950

YEAR	WINNER	VENUE	YEAR	WINNER	VENUE
1950	Dr JWA Rodgers	Ravensworth	1971	R Hindhaugh	South Moor
1951	WW Nichol	Tyneside	1972	R Clark	Consett
1952	WC Welsh	Seaton Carew	1973	D Oughton	Seaton Carew
1953	PJ Thubron	Brancepeth Castle	1974	JL Naisby	Wearside
1954	SG Ward	South Moor	1975	BH Skipper	Eaglescliffe
1955	JA Owen	Darlington	1976	G Wraith	Bishop Auckland
1956	D Hunter	Ravensworth	1977	D Oughton	Boldon
1957	D Hunter	Durham City	1978	M Latham	South Moor
1958	NR Rutherford	Wearside	1979	HK Walton	Darlington
1959	WC Welsh	Hartlepool	1980	JL Still	Castle Eden
1960	D Hunter	Brancepeth Castle	1981	D Patrickson	Hartlepool
1961	R Clark	Seaton Carew	1982	B Collingwood	Whitburn
1962	R Hindhaugh	Tyneside	1983	G Bell	Tyneside
1963	J Hall	South Shields	1984	AK Green	South Shields
1964	R Clark	Seaton Carew	1985	D Moralee	Dinsdale Spa
1965	BL Bolam	Ravensworth	1986	D Wood	Seaham
1966	IR Hornsby	Darlington	1987	NAR Hall	Durham City
1967	IR Hornsby	Tyneside	1988	GR Bell	Billingham
1968	A Doxford	Dinsdale Spa	1989	AJ McLure	Seaton Carew
1969	RW Green	Durham City	1990	HK Walton	Consett
1970	JW Ord	Hartlepool			

East Anglian Open Championship

YEAR	WINNER	VENUE	YEAR	WINNER	VENUE
1951	RA Knight	Aldeburgh	1971	G Burroughs	Ipswich
1952	AH Perowne	Gt Yarmouth and	1972	J Frew	Bury St Edmonds
		Caister	1973	MF Bonallack (Am)	Colchester
1953	EE Whitcombe	Frinton-on-Crouch	1974	H Flatman	Aldeburgh
1954	LB Ayton	Burnham	1975	F Flatman	Stowmarket
1955	K Budd	Eaton, Norwich	1976	G Schader	Felixstowe
1956	EE Whitcombe	Chigwell	1977	W Longmuir	Bury St Edmonds
1957	A Poulton	Woodbridge	1978	G Schader	Ipswich
1958	R Foreman	Thetford	1979	N Burch	Gog Magog
1959	RA Knight	Gog Magog	1980	S Levermore	Felixstowe
1960	PJ Shanks	Thorpe Hall	1981	F Hill	Stoke-by-Nayland
1961	MT Leeder	Aldeburgh	1982	RW Mann	Gt Yarmouth &
1962	BGC Huggett	Sheringham			Caister
1963	L Platts	Chelmsford	1983	RW Mann	Stoke-by-Nayland
1964	EE Whitcombe	Ipswich	1984	M Stokes } tie	Stoke-by-Nayland
1965	R Foreman	Royal Norwich		K Ashdown }	
1966	H Flatman	Colchester	1985	C Platts	Stoke-by-Nayland
1967	BGC Huggett	Woodbridge	1986	M Stokes	Frinton
1968	M Leeder	Gog Magog	1987	*No competition*	
1969	A Ibberson	Gt Yarmouth and	1988	P Kent	Stoke-by-Nayland
		Caister	1989	RY Mitchell	Thorpe Hall
1970	H Flatman	Woodbridge	1990	N Wichelow	Stoke-by-Nayland

Essex Amateur Championship

INAUGURATED 1924

YEAR	WINNER	VENUE	YEAR	WINNER	VENUE
1924	C Law	Wanstead	1952	HM Clarke	Thorndon Park
1925	JJ Murray	Romford	1953	KG Budd	Romford
1926	WA Murray	Rochford Hundred	1954	MF Bonallack	Chigwell
1927	J Esplin	Thorndon Park	1955	KG Budd	Maylands
1928	E Baldwin	Thorndon Park	1956	KG Budd	Chelmsford
1929	BC Crouch	Romford	1957	MF Bonallack	Thorndon Park
1930	E Baldwin	Wanstead	1958	P O'Connor	Thorndon Park
1931	E Baldwin	Thorndon Park	1959	MF Bonallack	Romford
1932	AW McClure	Rochford Hundred	1960	MF Bonallack	Orsett
1933	AE Hutton	Romford	1961	MF Bonallack	Wanstead
1934	WP Nairn	Thorndon Park	1962	E Bullman	Thorndon Park
1935	KS Duncan	Orsett	1963	MF Bonallack	Thorpe Hall
1936	JH Rogers	Thorndon Park	1964	MF Bonallack	Thorndon Park
1937	KS Duncan	Thorndon Park	1965	CK Jones	Chigwell
1938	WH Ferns	Chigwell	1966	J Thorogood	Colchester
1939–45	*Not played due to Second World War*		1967	J Thorogood	Orsett
1946	AW McClure	Thorndon Park	1968	MF Bonallack	Warren
1947	KS Duncan	Romford	1969	MF Bonallack	Rochford Hundred
1948	CD Cocks	Romford	1970	MF Bonallack	West Essex
1949	Major NA Gray	Thorndon Park	1971	A Budd	Romford
1950	W Kennedy	Thorndon Park	1972	MF Bonallack	Maylands
1951	KG Budd	Thorndon Park	1973	N Burch	Thorpe Hall

YEAR	WINNER	VENUE	YEAR	WINNER	VENUE
1974	H Weber	Wanstead	1983	M Davis	Channels
1975	G Turner	Canons Brook	1984	M Stokes	Rochford Hundred
1976	J Darling	Orsett	1985	D Wood	West Essex
1977	G Turner	Chigwell	1986	M Davis	Braintree
1978	G Godwin	Chelmsford	1987	V Cox	Romford
1979	N Burch	Warren	1988	R Scott	Orsett
1980	G Godwin	Frinton	1989	V Cox	Upminster
1981	C Davies	Thorndon Park	1990	*No competition*	
1982	C Laurence	Braintree			

Gloucestershire Amateur Championship

INAUGURATED 1906

YEAR	WINNER	VENUE	YEAR	WINNER	VENUE
1906	TK Ashton	Cheltenham	1950	WS Wise	Stinchcombe Hill
1907	CD Stephens	Minchinhampton	1951	LF Brown	Knowle
1908	J Bryan	Rodway Hill	1952	RE Strange	Cotswold Hills
1909	TK Ashton	Stinchcombe Hill	1953	Dr WG Hunt	Bristol & Clifton
1910	TK Ashton	Cheltenham	1954	CGE Randel	Stinchcombe Hill
1911	G Grieve	Henbury	1955	Dr DS Maunsell	Long Ashton
1912	DW Smith	Stinchcombe Hill	1956	CG Griffith	Cotswold Hills
1913	Dr A Brown	Minchinhampton	1957	G Jackson	Knowle
1914	Dr JH Beavis	Filton	1958	WS Wise	Stinchcombe Hill
1915–19	*Not played due to Great War*		1959	RJ Gardiner	Bristol & Clifton
1920	JH Baker	Stinchcombe Hill	1960	JM Clarke	Cotswold Hills
1921	HSB Tubbs	Long Ashton	1961	JM Clarke	Long Ashton
1922	JH Baker	Stinchcombe Hill	1962	RJ Gardiner	Stinchcombe Hill
1923	HSB Tubbs	Bristol & Clifton	1963	JN Littler	Knowle
1924	W Baglin	Minchinhampton	1964	RW Clarke	Cotswold Hills
1925	GC Brooks	Long Ashton	1965	GM Brand	Bristol & Clifton
1926	GC Brooks	Cheltenham	1966	RF Brown	Stinchcombe Hill
1927	GC Brooks	Knowle	1967	RJ Gardiner	Long Ashton
1928	FW Jacob	Gloucester	1968	JKR Graveney	Cotswold Hills
1929	Cdr RD Howard	Bristol & Clifton	1969	GM Brand	Knowle
1930	HP Bazeley	Cheltenham	1970	AG Clay	Stinchcombe Hill
1931	GC Brooks	Long Ashton	1971	P Berry	Bristol & Clifton
1932	GC Brooks	Stinchcombe Hill	1972	P Berry	Cirencester
1933	HG Pruett	Knowle	1973	JA Bloxham	Long Ashton
1934	GC Killey	Gloucester	1974	DJ Carroll	Cotswold Hills
1935	WSJ Watson	Bristol & Clifton	1975	CS Mitchell	Knowle
1936	GC Brooks	Stinchcombe Hill	1976	S Dunlop	Ross-on-Wye
1937	GC Brooks	Long Ashton	1977	G Brand Jr	Bristol & Clifton
1938	GC Brooks	Cotswold Hills	1978	CS Mitchell	Broadway
1939	DM Anderson	Knowle	1979	RD Broad	Henbury
1940–45	*Not played due to Second World War*		1980	ME Lewis	Lilley Brook
1946	WSJ Watson	Stinchcombe Hill	1981	J Durbin	Chipping Sodbury
1947	WSJ Watson	Knowle	1982	D Ray	Cotswold Hills
1948	WSJ Watson	Cotswold Hills	1983	D Rollo	Bristol & Clifton
1949	WSJ Watson	Long Ashton	1984	C Robinson	Cirencester

YEAR	WINNER	VENUE	YEAR	WINNER	VENUE
1985	DJ Carroll	Shirehampton Park	1988	J Webber	Ross-on-Wye
1986	RD Broad	Stinchcombe Hill	1989	RD Broad	Minchinhampton
1987	M Bessell	Long Ashton	1990	D Hares	Knowle

Hampshire, Isle of Wight and Channel Islands Amateur Championship

INAUGURATED 1894

YEAR	WINNER	VENUE	YEAR	WINNER	VENUE
1894	FG Tait	Winchester	1935	IR Patey	Bramshot
1895	JW Duncan	Bembridge	1936	IR Patey	Liphook
1896	JW Duncan	Hayling	1937	IR Patey	Stoneham
1897	EH Buckland	Lyndhurst	1938	EW Spencer	Shanklin & Sandown
1898	EH Buckland	Bembridge	1939	JE Mellor	Hayling
1899	EH Buckland	Haslar	1940–45	*Not played due to Second World War*	
1900	WR Reid	Hayling	1946	AP Sharpe	Brokenhurst
1901	WR Reid	Guernsey			Manor
1902	JAT Bramston	Winchester	1947	D Lewcock	North Hants, Fleet
1903	JAT Bramston	Bembridge	1948	IR Patey	Liphook
1904	Capt P Balfour	Haslar	1949	PB Hine	Stoneham
1905	Major CB Collins	Hayling	1950	J Earl	Blackmoor
1906	Rev FN Harvey	Jersey	1951	S Cole	Hayling
1907	P Millar	Bramshot	1952	S Cole	Meyrick Park,
1908	EL Horsburgh	Shanklin & Sandown			Bournemouth
1909	HG Biden	Meyrick Park,	1953	JF Cripps	Shanklin & Sandown
		Bournemouth	1954	HP Lock	North Hants, Fleet
1910	HLF Nicholls	North Hants, Fleet	1955	SJ Fox	Brokenhurst
1911	JC Cragie	Needles			Manor
1912	Dr HW Lamplough	Winchester	1956	SJ Fox	Liphook
1913	J Burnet Cragie	Hayling	1957	AA Sutcliffe	Stoneham
1914	Dr JL Jackson	Stoneham	1958	C Burke	Hayling
1915–20	*Not played due to Great War*		1959	EH James	Blackmoor
1921	Cdr PH Waterer	Shanklin & Sandown	1960	JE Rush	Shanklin & Sandown
1922	Fl Lt CH Hayward	Brokenhurst	1961	CW Cole	North Hants, Fleet
		Manor	1962	RJ Mahy	Royal Jersey
1923	Ft Lt CH Hayward	Hayling	1963	SWT Murray	Brokenhurst
1924	Sir CBW Magnay	Stoneham			Manor
1925	Sq Ldr CH Hayward	Lee-on-Solent	1964	CW Cole	Liphook
1926	Sir CBW Magnay	Bramshot	1965	DJ Harrison	Stoneham
1927	Cdr AHD Field	Brokenhurst	1966	JB Airth	Hayling
		Manor	1967	JB Airth	Royal Guernsey
1928	Lt Cdr H McMaster	Shanklin & Sandown	1968	T Koch de	
1929	Sq Ldr CH Hayward	Liphook		Gooreynd	North Hants, Fleet
1930	AE Phillips	Stoneham	1969	DJ Harrison	Shanklin & Sandown
1931	Com HE Raymond	Hayling	1970	DJ Harrison	Blackmoor
1932	AP Sharpe	Blackmoor	1971	G Foden	Liphook
1933	WL Barnett	Meyrick Park	1972	G Binding	La Moye, Jersey
1934	IR Patey	Lee-on-Solent	1973	DJ Harrison	Brokenhurst Manor

YEAR	WINNER	VENUE	YEAR	WINNER	VENUE
1974	DJ Harrison	Stoneham	1983	KJ Weeks	Brokenhurst Manor
1975	BJ Winteridge	Hayling	1984	R Eggo	Stoneham
1976	DJ Harrison	Royal Guernsey	1985	RA Alker	Hayling
1977	BJ Winteridge	North Hants	1986	R Eggo	North Hants, Fleet
1978	KJ Weeks	Blackmoor	1987	A Mew	Royal Guernsey
1979	T Whittaker	Shanklin & Sandown	1988	S Richardson	Blackmoor
1980	RW Johnson	Liphook	1989	M Smith	Shanklin & Sandown
1981	BJ Winteridge	Army, Aldershot	1990	M Wiggett	Liphook
1982	BJ Winteridge	Royal Jersey			

Hampshire Open Championship

INAUGURATED 1967

YEAR	WINNER	VENUE	YEAR	WINNER	VENUE
1967	W McHardy	Hayling	1978	R Pinner	Liphook
1968	W Woodman	Queens Park, Bournemouth	1979	I Young	Army, Aldershot
			1980	R Doig	Blackmoor
1969	D Miller	Stoneham	1981	B Winteridge (Am)	Stoneham
1970	I Macdonald	Hayling	1982	J Hay	Hayling
1971	J Stirling	Queens Park, Bournemouth	1983	J Hay	North Hants, Fleet
			1984	M Desmond	Lee-on-Solent
1972	D Miller	Stoneham	1985	I Young	Brokenhurst Manor
1973	A Bridge	Blackmoor			
1974	J Morgan	Hayling	1986	M Desmond	Blackmoor
1975	D Miller	Stoneham	1987	T Healy	Blackmoor
1976	B Winteridge (Am)	Blackmoor	1988	K Bowden	Meon Valley
1977	T Pinner	Brokenhurst, Manor	1989	J Coles	Hockley
			1990	R Watkins	Hayling

Isle of Wight Amateur Championship

INAUGURATED 1924

YEAR	WINNER	VENUE	YEAR	WINNER	VENUE
1924	ST Ricketts	Needles	1937	FH Hayward	Shanklin & Sandown
1925	JE Mellor	Shanklin & Sandown	1938	Capt AC Newnham	Needles
1926	H McMaster	Bembridge	1939	JE Mellor	Bembridge
1927	JE Mellor	Needles	1940–45	*Not played due to Second World War*	
1928	H McMaster	Shanklin & Sandown	1946	IR Patey	Shanklin & Sandown
1929	ST Ricketts	St Helen's	1947	FH Hayward	Shanklin & Sandown
1930	Lt Cdr M McMaster	Needles	1948	C Haworth	Shanklin & Sandown
1931	AD Dickson	Shanklin & Sandown	1949	C Haworth	Bembridge
1932	PH White	St Helen's	1950	C Haworth	Shanklin & Sandown
1933	Dr AS Drummond	Needles	1951	GT White	Shanklin & Sandown
1934	JE Mellor	Shanklin & Sandown	1952	K Chiverton	Needles
1935	JE Mellor	Needles	1953	GT White	Shanklin & Sandown
1936	JE Mellor	Bembridge	1954	C Haworth	Shanklin & Sandown

YEAR	WINNER	VENUE	YEAR	WINNER	VENUE
1955	C Haworth	Shanklin & Sandown	1969	K Johnston	Osborne
1956	GT White	Shanklin & Sandown	1970	C Haworth	Shanklin & Sandown
1957	HD Robinson	Shanklin & Sandown	1971	S Trueman	Shanklin & Sandown
1958	S Trueman	Shanklin & Sandown	1972	P Nuttall	Shanklin & Sandown
1959	EA Young	Shanklin & Sandown	1973	P Cridland	Shanklin & Sandown
1960	JT Shiel	Shanklin & Sandown	1974	P Nuttall	Shanklin & Sandown
1961	C Haworth	Shanklin & Sandown	1975	RA Lock	Shanklin & Sandown
1962	L Scovell	Shanklin & Sandown	1976	BA Claridge	Shanklin & Sandown
1963	H Minchin	Shanklin & Sandown	1977	T Underwood	Shanklin & Sandown
1964	A Pemberton	Shanklin & Sandown	1978	D Green	Shanklin & Sandown
1965	C Haworth	Shanklin & Sandown	1979	H Brownsdon	Shanklin & Sandown
1966	MV Lyon	Shanklin & Sandown	1980	RJ Beach	Shanklin & Sandown
1967	C Haworth	Shanklin & Sandown	1981	DJ Maidment	Shanklin & Sandown
1968	WA Close	Shanklin & Sandown	*Discontinued*		

Hertfordshire Amateur Championship

INAUGURATED 1922

YEAR	WINNER	VENUE	YEAR	WINNER	VENUE
1922	HW Beveridge	Oxhey	1959	GH Dudley	Ashridge
1923	AR Nall Caine	Old Fold Manor	1960	WJ Glennie	Porters Park
1924	CN Flint	Porters Park	1961	SN Perry	Brookmans Park
1925	CN Flint	Oxhey	1962	BHG Chapman	West Herts
1926	RC Young	Bushey Hall	1963	HC Squirrell	Old Fold Manor
1927	LG Lambourne	Old Fold Manor	1964	P Townsend	South Herts
1928	JB Anderson	Verulam	1965	BHG Chapman	West Herts
1929	GG Bennett	West Herts	1966	DC Allen	Sandy Lodge
1930	PL Smith	Moor Park	1967	A Holmes	Berkhamsted
1931	REA Bott	Sandy Lodge	1968	PN Wingfield	Ashridge
1932	HE Rance	Porters Park	1969	AW Holmes	Porters Park
1933	JH Neal	Berkhamsted	1970	M Hastings	Brookmans Park
1934	J McKay	Oxhey	1971	AW Holmes	Old Fold Manor
1935	J McKay	South Herts	1972	D Woolmer	Moor Park
1936	J McKay	Old Fold Manor	1973	HC Squirrell	Berkhamsted
1937	MGS Fox	West Herts	1974	RA Durrant	Sandy Lodge
1938	WS Gronow	Oxhey	1975	N Faldo	Ashridge
1939	CW Measor	Porters Park	1976	RA Durrant	South Herts
1940–45	*Not played due to Second World War*		1977	C Allen	Porters Park
1946	PB Lucas	Moor Park	1978	RA Durrant	West Herts
1947	PB Lucas	Sandy Lodge	1979	DF Williams	Brookmans Park
1948	K Leslie Smith	Moor Park	1980	JE Ambridge	Knebworth
1949	GA Hill	Berkhamsted	1981	RY Mitchell	Old Ford Manor
1950	EH Holt	Ashridge	1982	JE Ambridge	Moor Park
1951	BM Atkinson	Porters Park	1983	C McKay	Berkhamsted
1952	ER Anscombe	Brookmans Park	1984	NJ Briggs	Sandy Lodge
1953	EH Holt	South Herts	1985	PR Robinson	Ashridge
1954	CG Ostler	Old Fold Manor	1986	PJ Cherry	South Herts
1955	EH Holt	Moor Park	1987	A Clark	Porters Park
1956	BHG Chapman	West Herts	1988	JE Ambridge	West Herts
1957	TS Waddell	Sandy Lodge	1989	S Hankin	Hadley Wood
1958	GAD Dailey	Berkhamsted	1990	NA Leconte	Knebworth

Kent Amateur Championship

INAUGURATED 1925

YEAR	WINNER	VENUE	YEAR	WINNER	VENUE
1925	L Schon	Deal	1960	JR Langridge	Prince's, Sandwich
1926	T Chilton	Sidcup	1961	A LePage	Deal
1927	WC Wright	Littlestone	1962	RA Hogg	Littlestone
1928	AJ Evans	Rochester and	1963	MF Attenborough	Knole Park
		Cobham	1964	MF Attenborough	Prince's, Sandwich
1929	F Parry	West Kent	1965	MF Attenborough	Deal
1930	ER Tipple	Knole Park	1966	PBC Gracey	Littlestone
1931	JCV Moberley	Royal Blackheath	1967	M Bills	Wildernesse
1932	F McGloin	Sundridge Park	1968	PJ Hedges	Prince's, Sandwich
1933	HS Mitchell	Wildernesse	1969	RJ Redsull	Deal
1934	O Austreng	Langley Park	1970	RH Mummery	Littlestone
1935	F McGloin	Deal	1971	PJ Hedges	St Georges,
1936	O Austreng	Littlestone			Sandwich
1937	O Austreng	Rochester and	1972	J Ryan	Knole Park
		Cobham	1973	G Brown	Prince's, Sandwich
1938	AT Wilson	Faversham	1974	RH Mummery	Littlestone
1939	Dr JA Flaherty	Sidcup	1975	J Powell	Ashford
1940–45	*Not played due to Second World War*		1976	P Hoad	Prince's, Sandwich
1946	TD Page	Knole Park	1977	P Hoad	Deal
1947	Dr MG Heugh	Canterbury	1978	P Hoad	Langley Park
1948	AGS Penman	Sundridge Park	1979	PJ Hedges	Littlestone
1949	AGS Penman	Deal	1980	M McLean	Prince's, Sandwich
1950	AGS Penman	Wildernesse	1981	M McLean	Sundridge Park
1951	AGS Penman	Littlestone	1982	S Baldwin	Rochester and
1952	MD Asprey	Rochester and			Cobham
		Cobham	1983	M Lawrence	Prince's, Sandwich
1953	TA Torrance	Prince's, Sandwich	1984	M Lawrence	Wildernesse
1954	JD Lyons	Langley Park	1985	J Simmance	Littlestone
1955	SM McCready	Deal	1986	M Lawrence	Canterbury
1956	SM McCready	Wildernesse	1987	L Batchelor	Mid Kent
1957	G Darlington	Knole Park	1988	W Hodkin	Littlestone
1958	JD Lyons	Littlestone	1989	S Green	Royal Blackheath
1959	MF Wisher	Sundridge Park	1990	R Sloman	Faversham

Kent Open Championship

INAUGURATED 1962

YEAR	WINNER	VENUE	YEAR	WINNER	VENUE
1962	R Fidler	Deal	1972	G Will	Deal
1963	R Fidler	Deal	1973	N Job	Deal
1964	R Fidler	Deal	1974	PJ Hedges (Am)	Deal
1965	C Whiting	Deal	1975	G Will	Deal
1966	SL King / M Henderson } tie	Deal	1976	P Gill	Deal
			1977	R Chapman (Am)	Deal
1967	R Fidler	Deal	1978	R Cameron (Am)	Deal
1968	G Will	Deal	1979	PGJ Hoad	Deal
1969	G Will	Deal	1980	I Grant	Wildernesse
1970	PJ Hedges (Am)	Deal	1981	G Potter	Deal
1971	B Sandry	Deal	1982	P Mitchell	Deal

YEAR	WINNER	VENUE	YEAR	WINNER	VENUE
1983	G Potter	Deal	1987	M Goodin	Prince's, Sandwich
1984	R Cameron	Sundridge Park	1988	J Bennett	Prince's, Sandwich
1985	G Will	Deal	1989	R Cameron	Broome Park
1986	J Bennett	West Malling	1990	S Barr	Broome Park

Lancashire Amateur Championship

INAUGURATED 1910

YEAR	WINNER	VENUE	YEAR	WINNER	VENUE
1910	GF Smith	Hesketh	1955	D Anderson	Fairhaven
1911	RW Crummack	Lancaster	1956	D Rawlinson	Southport and
1912	RW Crummack	St Anne's Old Links			Ainsdale
1913	R Jennison	Hopwood Park	1957	D Anderson	St Anne's Old Links
1914	S Robinson	Southport and	1958	EJ Riley	Hesketh
		Ainsdale	1959	EJ Riley	Birkdale
1915–19	*Not played due to Great War*		1960	D Rawlinson	Lytham St Anne's
1920	RW Crummack	Worsley	1961	MJ Reece	Formby
1921	AT Dixon	Hesketh	1962	AB Kidd	Fairhaven
1922	TLC Heald	Formby	1963	GP Roberts	Hillside
1923	RH Hardman	Lytham St Anne's	1964	EJ Threlfall	Fleetwood
1924	DEB Soulby	Birkdale	1965	RH Tupling	West Lancs
1925	S Robinson	St Anne's Old Links	1966	AV Moss	Ormskirk
1926	S Robinson	West Lancs	1967	SG Birtwell	St Anne's Old Links
1927	RH Hardman	Fairhaven	1968	SG Birtwell	Southport and
1928	S Robinson	Southport and			Ainsdale
		Ainsdale	1969	PH Evans	Hesketh
1929	S Robinson	Blackpool South	1970	J Glover	Pleasington
		Shore	1971	MJ Reece	Lytham St Anne's
1930	RH Hardman	Lytham St Anne's	1972	SG Birtwell	Birkdale
1931	HG Bentley	Hesketh	1973	AH Chandler	West Lancs
1932	HG Bentley	Birkdale	1974	JB Dickinson	Bolton Old Links
1933	J Kennedy Jr	St Anne's Old Links	1975	A Squires	Fairhaven
1934	AR Walton	West Lancs	1976	MJ Reece	Formby
1935	E Halliwell	Fleetwood	1977	JB Dickinson	Clitheroe
1936	DS Coates	Formby	1978	HAN Scott	St Anne's Old Links
1937	IW Calder	Fairhaven	1979	MPD Walls	Southport and
1938	IW Calder	Southport and			Ainsdale
		Ainsdale	1980	A Squires	Bolton
1939	HG Bentley	Lytham St Anne's	1981	MJ Wild	Ormskirk
1940–45	*Not played due to Second World War*		1982	A Squires	West Lancs
1946	RK Bell	Hesketh	1983	MPD Walls	Hillside
1947	WK Hargreaves	Fairhaven	1984	SG Birtwell	Pleasington
1948	RJ White	Birkdale	1985	RA Bardsley	Hesketh
1949	JW Jones	Fleetwood	1986	MJ Wild	Fairhaven
1950	JW Calder	West Lancs	1987	T Foster	Lancaster
1951	JR Wroe	St Anne's Old Links	1988	M Kingsley	Birkdale
1952	DT Stevenson	Formby	1989	RA Bardsley	Formby
1953	GP Roberts	Lytham St Anne's	1990	T Foster	Manchester
1954	JW Jones	Hillside			

Lancashire Open Championship

INAUGURATED 1973

YEAR	WINNER	VENUE	YEAR	WINNER	VENUE
1973	GA Caygill	St Anne's Old Links	1983	S Hamer (Am)	Crompton and Royton
1974	IJ Mosey	St Anne's Old Links			
1975	K Hornby (Am)	Bolton	1984	R Longworth	Crompton and Royton
1976	AH Chandler	Shaw Hill			
1977	F Till (Am)	Crompton and Royton	1985	R Green	Crompton and Royton
1978	IJ Mosey	Crompton and Royton	1986	T Foster (Am)	Crompton and Royton
1979	IJ Mosey	Crompton and Royton	1987	S Hamer (Am)	Crompton and Royton
1980	D Clarke	Crompton and Royton	1988	P Wesselingh	Crompton and Royton
1981	D Durnian	Crompton and Royton	1989	M Jones	Crompton and Royton
1982	S Hadfield	Crompton and Royton	1990	P Allan	Crompton and Royton

Leicestershire and Rutland Amateur Championship

INAUGURATED 1910

YEAR	WINNER	VENUE	YEAR	WINNER	VENUE
1910	ME Whitehead	Leicestershire	1937	ST Matthews	Kirby Muxloe
1911	REB Overton	Longcliffe	1938	ST Matthews	Longcliffe
1912	TP Harrison	Birstall	1939	ST Matthews	Rothley Park
1913	REB Overton	Leicestershire	1940–45	*Not played due to Second World War*	
1914	WI Nelson	Charnwood Forest	1946	ST Matthews	Longcliffe
1915–19	*Not played due to Great War*		1947	ST Matthews	Leicestershire
1920	PR Wykes	Leicestershire	1948	CM Warren	Birstall
1921	AF Percival	Rothley Park	1949	ST Matthews	Willesley Park
1922	WMW Sutton	Leicestershire	1950	ST Matthews	Luffenham Heath
1923	DS Bruce	Luffenham Heath	1951	ST Matthews	Rothley Park
1924	JT Loach	Birstall	1952	EF Bayden	Longcliffe
1925	WMW Sutton	Longcliffe	1953	GB Wolstenholme	Kirby Muxloe
1926	JT Loach	Rothley Park	1954	P Wood	Leicestershire
1927	JT Loach	Willesley Park	1955	GB Wolstenholme	Birstall
1928	RB Weston-Webb	Leicestershire	1956	GB Wolstenholme	Willesley Park
1929	DE Cameron	Luffenham Heath	1957	GB Wolstenholme	Luffenham Heath
1930	H King	Birstall	1958	EF Bayden	Rothley Park
1931	T Haslam	Longcliffe	1959	EF Bayden	Longcliffe
1932	CR Smith	Rothley Park	1960	ES Blackadder	Kirby Muxloe
1933	KHR Gibbs	Willesley Park	1961	RD Christian	Leicestershire
1934	GH Richardson	Leicestershire	1962	TR Shingler	Birstall
1935	RB Weston-Webb	Luffenham Heath	1963	TR Shingler	Willesley Park
1936	DB May	Birstall	1964	TR Shingler	Luffenham Heath

YEAR	WINNER	VENUE	YEAR	WINNER	VENUE
1965	W Ridgway	Luffenham Heath	1978	IR Middleton	Leicestershire
1966	RD Christian	Glen Gorse	1979	IR Middleton	Birstall
1967	W Ridgway	Longcliffe	1980	A Harrison	Rothley Park
1968	JR Riley	Scraptoft	1981	EW Hammond	Longcliffe
1969	RR Campbell	Kirby Muxloe	1982	CJ Gotla	Willesley Park
1970	RJ Taylor	Leicestershire	1983	T Stephens	Glen Gorse
1971	RR Campbell	Luffenham Heath	1984	A Martinez	Kirby Muxloe
1972	P Wood	Willesley Park	1985	EW Hammond	Leicestershire
1973	JM Hayles	Rothley Park	1986	IR Middleton	Luffenham Heath
1974	P Haddon	Birstall	1987	GN Marshall	Birstall
1975	RJ Taylor	Longcliffe	1988	A Martinez	Rothley Park
1976	EW Hammond	Glen Gorse	1989	JD Cayless	Longcliffe
1977	MC Dayus	Kirby Muxloe	1990	D Gibson	Scraptoft

Leicestershire and Rutland Match Play Championship

INAUGURATED 1932

(The Philip R Wykes Bowl)

YEAR	WINNER	VENUE	YEAR	WINNER	VENUE
1932	KHR Gibbs		1964	W Ridgway	Luffenham Heath
1933	KHR Gibbs		1965	RD Christian	Luffenham Heath
1934	KHR Gibbs		1966	JJ Jeffery	Glen Gorse
1935	RB Weston-Webb		1967	RD Christian	Longcliffe
1936	SR Ellis		1968	W Ridgway	Scraptoft
1937	HD Greenlees		1969	RS Bulloch	Kirby Muxloe
1938	CD Elliott		1970	RD Christian	Leicestershire
1939	RB Weston-Webb		1971	RR Campbell	Luffenham Heath
1940–45	*Not played due to Second World War*		1972	KTR Clarke	Willesley Park
1946	ST Matthews		1973	P Haddon	Rothley Park
1947	ST Matthews		1974	R Hayes	Birstall
1948	GB Wolstenholme		1975	DP Hughes	Willesley Park
1949	EF Bayden		1976	EW Hammond	Luffenham Heath
1950	WR Hope		1977	IP Dickinson	Rothley Park
1951	GB Wolstenholme		1978	EE Feasey	Birstall
1952	GB Wolstenholme		1979	R Spence	Rothley Park
1953	GB Wolstenholme		1980	MP Nutt	Longcliffe
1954	EF Bayden		1981	R Hayes	Willesley Park
1955	GB Wolstenholme		1982	A Martinez	Glen Gorse
1956	ES Blackadder		1983	A Martinez	Kirby Muxloe
1957	EF Bayden		1984	G Wolstenholme	Leicestershire
1958	ES Blackadder		1985	G Wolstenholme	Luffenham Heath
1959	WE Scott		1986	G Wolstenholme	Birstall
1960	WE Scott		1987	D Gibson	Scraptoft
1961	RD Christian		1988	G Wolstenholme	Kirby Muxloe
1962	RD Christian		1989	D Gibson	Rothley Park
1963	ES Blackadder	Leicestershire	1990	D Gibson	Longcliffe

Leicestershire and Rutland Open Championship

INAUGURATED 1963

YEAR	WINNER	VENUE	YEAR	WINNER	VENUE
1963	BN Davies	Luffenham Heath	1977	K Barnes	Birstall
1964	P Wood (Am)	Rothley Park	1978	B Edmundson	Glen Gorse
1965	TR Shingler (Am)	Birstall	1979	R Swain	Willesley Park
1966	TR Shingler (Am)	Longcliffe	1980	EW Hammond (Am)	Longcliffe
1967	RD Christian (Am)	Kirby Muxloe	1981	SH Adams (Am)	Rothley Park
1968	E Martin	Glen Gorse	1982	IR Middleton (Am)	Scraptoft
1969	BJ Bates	Birstall	1983	EE Feasey (Am)	Kibworth
1970	P Wood (Am)	Willesley Park	1984	S Sherratt	Leicestershire
1971	JD Morgan	Rothley Park	1985	RT Adams	Birstall
1972	KD Pickup	Leicestershire	1986	R Stephenson	Kirby Muxloe
1973	D Kirkland	Longcliffe	1987	*Not played*	
1974	RD Christian (Am)	Luffenham Heath	1988	D Gibson (Am)	Glen Gorse
1975	*Not played*		1989	RT Adams	Willesley Park
1976	*Not played*		1990	RS Larratt	Kibworth

Lincolnshire Amateur Championship

INAUGURATED 1925

YEAR	WINNER	VENUE	YEAR	WINNER	VENUE
1925	TH Bowman	Woodhall Spa	1954	Dr L Jones	Lincoln
1926	TH Bowman	Skegness	1955	PJ Butler	Holme Hall
1927	TH Bowman	Belton Park	1956	Dr L Jones	Seacroft
1928	TH Bowman	Grimsby	1957	PJ Butler	Woodhall Spa
1929	NJ Bacon	Lincoln	1958	DJ Baxter	Lincoln
1930	TH Bowman	Skegness	1959	S Kennedy	Holme Hall
1931	RL Bacon	Sutton	1960	JW Ellmore	Seacroft
1932	RL Bacon	Woodhall Spa	1961	MG Lee	Woodhall Spa
1933	TH Bowman	Woodhall Spa	1962	Flt Lt RD Shrivell	Holme Hall
1934	NW Dunn	Scunthorpe	1963	JC Baggott	Seacroft
1935	Dr L Jones	Woodhall Spa	1964	KP Allan	Lincoln
1936	Dr L Jones	North Shore, Skegness	1965	MG Lee	Woodhall Spa
			1966	F Wood	Seacroft
1937	JF Sharp	Belton Park	1967	F Wood	Holme Hall
1938	Dr L Jones	Grimsby	1968	RJ Barrell	Lincoln
1939	R Pumfrey	Lincoln	1969	RJ Nix	Woodhall Spa
1940–45	*Not played due to Second World War*		1970	RJ Barrell	Seacroft
1946	JW Ellmore	Holme Hall	1971	A Thain	Holme Hall
1947	CH Caswell	Seacroft	1972	RJ Barrell	Lincoln
1948	Dr L Jones	North Shore, Skegness	1973	F Woods	Woodhall Spa
			1974	PG Shillington	Seacroft
1949	DJ Baxter	Woodhall Spa	1975	M James	Holme Hall
1950	AM Tew	Lincoln	1976	K Waters	Lincoln
1951	CH Beamish	Holme Hall	1977	S Bennett	Woodhall Spa
1952	TA Saul	Seacroft	1978	S Bennett	Seacroft
1953	JW Ellmore	Woodhall Spa	1979	PK Allen	Holme Hall

YEAR	WINNER	VENUE	YEAR	WINNER	VENUE
1980	A Thain	Lincoln	1986	JA Purdy	Seacroft
1981	L Brumpton	Woodhall Spa	1987	P Stenton	Holme Hall
1982	CS Graves	Seacroft	1988	P Streeter	Lincoln
1983	P Stenton	Holme Hall	1989	JA Payne	Woodhall Spa
1984	JA Purdy	Lincoln	1990	P Streeter	Elsham
1985	JGS Robinson	Woodhall Spa			

Lincolnshire Amateur Match Play Championship

INAUGURATED 1986

YEAR	WINNER	VENUE
1986	AD Hare	Seacroft
1987	JR Payne	Holme Hall
1988	AD Hare	Lincoln
1989	GH Lee	Woodhall Spa
1990	GH Lee	Elsham

Lincolnshire Open Championship

YEAR	WINNER	VENUE	YEAR	WINNER	VENUE
1947	A Fixter	Lincoln	1968	B Thompson	North Shore, Skegness
1948	DJ Baxter (Am)	North Shore, Skegness	1969	P Leslie	Seacroft
1949	A Fixter	Seacroft	1970	TR Squires	Woodhall Spa
1950	A Fixter	Holme Hall	1971	B Simpson	Lincoln
1951	A Fixter	Woodhall Spa	1972	B Thompson	Seacroft
1952	A Fixter	Lincoln	1973	TR Squires	Holme Hall
1953	JH Ellis	North Shore, Skegness	1974	B Thompson	Lincoln
1954	PJ Butler (Am)	Seacroft	1975	H Jackson	Woodhall Spa
1955	Dr L Jones (Am)	Woodhall Spa	1976	J Wraith	Seacroft
1956	J Wiggett	Holme Hall	1977	K Waters (Am)	Holme Hall
1957	J Wiggett	Lincoln	1978	M James	Lincoln
1958	J Wiggett	North Shore, Skegness	1979	S Bennett (Am)	Woodhall Spa
1959	CJ Norton	Seacroft	1980	K Daubney (Am)	Seacroft
1960	JW Elmore (Am)	Woodhall Spa	1981	P Davies	Holme Hall
1961	A Jacklin	Holme Hall	1982	TR Squires	Belton Park
1962	RD Shrivell (Am)	Lincoln	1983	SR Dickinson (Am)	Woodhall Spa
1963	TR Squires	North Shore, Skegness	1984	J Taylor	Seacroft
1964	IH Stackhouse (Am)	Woodhall Spa	1985	A Carter	Holme Hall
1965	R Issitt	Seacroft	1986	GE Stafford	Lincoln
1966	TR Squires	Holme Hall	1987	SR Dickinson (Am)	Woodhall Spa
1967	TR Squires	Lincoln	1988	J Heib	Seacroft
			1989	AD Hare	Holme Hall
			1990	A Butler (Am)	Lincoln

Manx Amateur Championship

INAUGURATED 1926

YEAR	WINNER	VENUE	YEAR	WINNER	VENUE
1926	GR Trustrum	Castletown	1961	B Jones	Ramsey
1927	JE McArd	Peel	1962	M Anderson	Rowany
1928	JS Corrin	Castletown	1963	WE Ashworth	Douglas
1929	H MacHarrie	Castletown	1964	WE Ashworth	Peel
1930	JS Corrin	Peel	1965	WCA Stead	Ramsey
1931	JS Corrin	Castletown	1966	A Copley	Rowany
1932	JS Corrin	Ramsey	1967	D Jones	Castletown
1933	JS Corrin	Peel	1968	R Moore	Douglas
1934	RE Cowell	Douglas	1969	A Copley	Peel
1935	JS Corrin	Ramsey	1970	WCA Stead	Ramsey
1936	JS Corrin	Ramsey	1971	J Sutton	Douglas
1937	F Dalgleish	Castletown	1972	J Sutton	Peel
1938	WS Kennedy	Peel	1973	J Sutton	Ramsey
1939	WA Kirkpatrick	Douglas	1974	MJ Kewley	Douglas
1940–45	*Not played due to Second World War*		1975	SJ Boyd	Peel
1946	WA Kirkpatrick	Douglas	1976	SJ Boyd	Ramsey
1947	WA Kirkpatrick	Douglas	1977	WR Ennett	Douglas
1948	CH Cain	Howstrake	1978	G Wilson	Peel
1949	CW Jackson	Ramsey	1979	G Wilson	Ramsey
1950	WA Kirkpatrick	Castletown	1980	SJ Boyd	Douglas
1951	WA Kirkpatrick	Peel	1981	G Kelley	Douglas
1952	WCA Stead	Douglas	1982	J Sutton	Ramsey
1953	WA Kirkpatrick	Ramsey	1983	J Sutton	Douglas
1954	D Jones	Castletown	1984	J Sutton	Peel
1955	WA Kirkpatrick	Peel	1985	J Sutton	Ramsey
1956	D Ball	Douglas	1986	AM Cain	Douglas
1957	SA Ashworth	Douglas	1987	J Sutton	Peel
1958	NC Corlett	Ramsey	1988	G Kelley	Ramsey
1959	KJ Skillicorn	Castletown	1989	G Ashe	Douglas
1960	R Ennett	Douglas	1990	M Pugh	Peel

Middlesex Amateur Championship

INAUGURATED 1925

YEAR	WINNER	VENUE	YEAR	WINNER	VENUE
1925	DJ Tymms	Northwood	1938	Dr LF Clarke	Sudbury
1926	LA Wilson	Home Park	1939	LA Wilson	Hadley Wood
1927	LA Wilson	Crews Hill	1940–45	*Not played due to Second World War*	
1928	C Buchan	Hendon	1946	WH Macdonald	Fulwell
1929	LA Wilson	Hadley Wood	1947	KG Thom	Crews Hill
1930	FH Rouse	Sudbury	1948	KG Thom	Hendon
1931	WC Hewitt	Fulwell	1949	E Gibbs	Grim's Dyke
1932	CJ Anderson	Hendon	1950	CE Hetherington	Northwood
1933	LA Wilson	West Middlesex	1951	DJ Scott	Pinner Hill
1934	E Gibbs	Pinner Hill	1952	JRB Johnstone	Hadley Wood
1935	LA Wilson	Northwood	1953	DJ Scott	Sudbury
1936	CJ Anderson	Fulwell	1954	JA Rancome	Hendon
1937	CJ Anderson	Mote Mount	1955	DJ Scott	Fulwell

YEAR	WINNER	VENUE	YEAR	WINNER	VENUE
1956	J Kirkham	Northwood	1974	R Kane	Northwood
1957	AB Simmonds	Mill Hill	1975	R Kane	Finchley
1958	GT Mills	Finchley	1976	IM Stungo	Sudbury
1959	N Frazer	Ashford Manor	1977	SR Warrin	Crews Hill
1960	K Warren	Finchley	1978	IM Stungo	Pinner Hill
1961	AB Simmonds	Northwood	1979	IM Stungo	Ashford Manor
1962	N Brown	Hadley Wood	1980	NM Curtis	Muswell Hill
1963	JA Ransome	Hendon	1981	GA Homewood	Fulwell
1964	JA Ransome	Sudbury	1982	ML Wear	Mill Hill
1965	JA Ransome	Crews Hill	1983	GA Homewood	Hadley Wood
1966	RP Stephenson	Pinner Hill	1984	R Willison	Ealing
1967	SR Warrin	Ashford Manor	1985	R Willison	Hendon
1968	T Lane	Muswell Hill	1986	A Rogers	Northwood
1969	SR Warrin	Fulwell	1987	R Willison	Finchley
1970	M Whelan	Mill Hill	1988	A Rogers	Sudbury
1971	SR Warrin	Hadley Wood	1989	R Willison	Crews Hill
1972	I Buchan	Ealing	1990	A Rogers	Pinner Hill
1973	M Devetta	Hendon			

Middlesex Open Championship

YEAR	WINNER	VENUE	YEAR	WINNER	VENUE
1966	R Emery	Sudbury	1979	J Reynolds	Mill Hill
1967	JK Ramsden	Mill Hill	1980	P Buchan	West Middlesex
1968	K Warren	Finchley	1981	P Glozier	Stanmore
1969	J Hudson	Mill Hill	1982	L Farmer	
1970	GW Low	Pinner Hill	1983	N Wichelow	
1971	T Lane	Hendon	1984	L Fickling	
1972	S Murray	Muswell Hill	1985	P Golding	
1973	S Murray	Bush Hill Park	1986	*Not played*	
1974	A Toner (Am)	Crews Hill	1987	L Fickling	Highgate
1975	JN Paramor (Am)	Ealing	1988	L Fickling	Enfield
1976	J Hamilton	Wyke Green	1989	L Fickling	Bush Hill Park
1977	SJ Levermore	North Middlesex	1990	R Willison (Am)	Sudbury
1978	J Reynolds	Sudbury			

Norfolk Amateur Championship

INAUGURATED 1894

YEAR	WINNER	VENUE	YEAR	WINNER	VENUE
1921	DH Fish	Sheringham	1929	Rev ES Ulyat	Hunstanton
1922	JA Bott	Royal Norwich	1930	WD Robinson	Cromer
1923	O Bunn	Hunstanton	1931	JH Thompson	Brancaster
1924	O Bunn	Brancaster	1932	JA Bott	Great Yarmouth
1925	JA Bott	Cromer			and Caister
1926	WD Robinson	Great Yarmouth	1933	Lt Col AW Tate	Sheringham
		and Caister	1934	FA Brett	Hunstanton
1927	HR Craske	Sheringham	1935	WD Robinson	Cromer
1928	JA Bott	Royal Norwich	1936	WD Robinson	Brancaster

YEAR	WINNER	VENUE	YEAR	WINNER	VENUE
1937	GP Burroughs	Great Yarmouth and Caister	1967	G Williams	Sheringham
			1968	RJ Trower	Thetford
1938	WD Robinson	Sheringham	1969	J Nudds	Hunstanton
1939	JH Thompson	Hunstanton	1970	PR Johnston	Great Yarmouth
1940–46	*Not played due to Second World War*				and Caister
1947	JPA Clymer	Sheringham	1971	S Cranmer	Brancaster
1948	AH Perowne	Hunstanton	1972	S Cranmer	Sheringham
1949	JA Floyd	Brancaster	1973	MM Orr	Hunstanton
1950	FA Brett	Sheringham	1974	BJ Ashton	Great Yarmouth
1951	AH Perowne	Royal Norwich			and Caister
1952	AH Perowne	Hunstanton	1975	JD Crawford	Brancaster
1953	AH Perowne	Great Yarmouth and Caister	1976	DC Hatton	Sheringham
			1977	MJF Bell	Hunstanton
1954	AH Perowne	Brancaster	1978	DJ Hood	Great Yarmouth
1955	AH Perowne	Sheringham			and Caister
1956	AH Perowne	Hunstanton			
1957	AH Perowne	Great Yarmouth and Caister	1979	JG Parkhill	Royal Norwich
			1980	JG Parkhill	Brancaster
			1981	MR Few	Sheringham
1958	AH Perowne	Brancaster	1982	DW Rains	Thetford
1959	JPA Clymer	Sheringham	1983	MN Sperrin	Hunstanton
1960	AH Perowne	Hunstanton	1984	T Hurrell	Great Yarmouth
1961	AH Perowne	Great Yarmouth and Caister			and Caister
			1985	CJ Lamb	Royal Norwich
1962	DW Rains	Brancaster	1986	ID Sperrin	Brancaster
1963	A Cook	Sheringham	1987	NJ Williamson	Sheringham
1964	J Nudds	Hunstanton	1988	NJ Williamson	Cromer
1965	RJ Trower	Great Yarmouth and Caister	1989	NJ Williamson	Royal Norwich
			1990	PR Little	Hunstanton
1966	RJ Trower	Brancaster			

Norfolk Open Championship

YEAR	WINNER	VENUE	YEAR	WINNER	VENUE
1963	MT Leeder	Thetford	1977	MT Leeder	Eaton
1964	AH Perowne (Am)	Royal Norwich	1978	RE Clarke	Brancaster
1965	J Carter	Hunstanton	1979	MT Leeder	Great Yarmouth and Caister
1966	J Carter	Sheringham			
1967	J Carter	Eaton	1980	MT Leeder	Kings Lynn
1968	J Carter	Cromer	1981	JG Parkhill (Am)	Thetford
1969	MT Leeder	Brancaster	1982	RJ Page	Hunstanton
1970	J Nudds	Great Yarmouth and Caister	1983	RG Foster	Royal Norwich
			1984	MJ Elsworthy	Sheringham
1971	MT Leeder	Kings Lynn	1985	T Hurrell (Am)	Cromer
1972	MT Leeder	Thetford	1986	M Spooner	Eaton
1973	MT Leeder	Royal Norwich	1987	MJ Elsworthy	Brancaster
1974	MT Leeder	Hunstanton	1988	MR Few	Barnham Broom
1975	NJ Catchpole	Sheringham	1989	MR Few	Great Yarmouth
1976	DC Hatton	Cromer	1990	AD Brydon	Kings Lynn

Northamptonshire Amateur Championship

INAUGURATED 1927

YEAR	WINNER	VENUE	YEAR	WINNER	VENUE
1927	WJ Thompson	Kettering	1964	RG Aitken	Church Brampton
1928	LF Brown	Church Brampton	1965	JE Saxby	Peterborough
1929	GN Somers	Northampton	1966	RG Aitken	Church Brampton
1930	L Bostock	Church Brampton	1967	JM Pettigrew	Northampton
1931	FC Roe	Kettering	1968	RG Aitken	Kettering
1932	RW Kilsby	Church Brampton	1969	RG Aitken	Kingsthorpe
1933	RW Kilsby	Kingsthorpe	1970	RG Aitken	Peterborough
1934	CS Catlow	Church Brampton			Milton
1935	RW Kilsby	Kettering	1971	RS Larratt	Church Brampton
1936	RW Kilsby	Church Brampton	1972	RJ Gray	Northampton
1937	CS Catlow	Northampton	1973	CR Cieslewicz	Peterborough
1938	CS Catlow	Church Brampton			Milton
1939	CS Catlow	Kingsthorpe	1974	JC Hodgson	Kingsthorpe
1940–45	*Not played due to Second World War*		1975	CR Cieslewicz	Kettering
1946	M Gear Evans	Kettering	1976	TJ Giles	Church Brampton
1947	CS Catlow	Church Brampton	1977	RG Aitken	Northampton
1948	CS Catlow	Peterborough	1978	CR Cieslewicz	Wellingborough
1949	FG Roe	Church Brampton	1979	CR Cieslewicz	Northampton
1950	CS Catlow	Kingsthorpe	1980	CR Cieslewicz	Peterborough
1951	AJ Harrison	Northampton			Milton
1952	FG Roe	Church Brampton	1981	MJ Haddon	Staverton Park
1953	MJ Worley	Peterborough	1982	S McDonald	Kingsthorpe
1954	RL Mobbs	Kettering	1983	DJJ Warren	Church Brampton
1955	CS Catlow	Church Brampton	1984	M Scott	Kettering
1956	CS Catlow	Northampton	1985	M McNally	Peterborough
1957	GF Clarke	Kingsthorpe			Milton
1958	CS Catlow	Northampton	1986	M Scott	Wellingborough
1959	RG Halliday	Kettering	1987	D Jones	Northampton
1960	CS Catlow	Peterborough	1988	DK Ellson	Church Brampton
1961	EJ Kingdon	Church Brampton	1989	N Goodman	Kingsthorpe
1962	RG Aitken	Northampton	1990	A Print	Peterborough
1963	RG Aitken	Kingsthorpe			Milton

Northamptonshire Match Play Championship

YEAR	WINNER	VENUE
1987	DK Ellson	Church Brampton
1988	MS Herson	Wellingborough
1989	M Scott	Northampton
1990	I Marshall	Kettering

Northumberland Amateur Championship

INAUGURATED 1907

YEAR	WINNER	VENUE	YEAR	WINNER	VENUE
1907	JB Pease	Gosforth Park	1953	JK Tate	Ponteland
1908	H Miller	Alnmouth	1954	JK Tate	City of Newcastle
1909	NRE Wilkinson	Newbiggin	1955	A Thirlwell	Gosforth
1910	J Miller	Goswick	1956	GJ Clark	Gosforth Park
1911	NRE Wilkinson	Three Mile Bridge	1957	JE Hayes	Ponteland
1912	H Miller	Hexham	1958	DMcM Moffat	City of Newcastle
1913	MR Philipson	Alnmouth	1959	DMcM Moffat	Gosforth Park
1914	H Miller	Gosforth Park	1960	N Dunn	Ponteland
1915–18	*Not played due to Great War*		1961	DMcM Moffat	Gosforth Park
1919	T Heads Jr	Gosforth Park	1962	A Thirlwell	City of Newcastle
1920	RG Macnaughton	Alnmouth	1963	JE Hayes	Tynemouth
1921	JJ Harrison	Three Mile Bridge	1964	A Thirlwell	Morpeth
1922	H Bates	Hexham	1965	JE Hayes	Arcot Hall
1923	JJ Harrison	Gosforth Park	1966	JE Hayes	Gosforth
1924	CW Howie	Alnmouth	1967	DMcM Moffat	Ponteland
1925	G Renwick	Three Mile Bridge	1968	DP Davidson	Tynemouth
1926	GS Sowerby	Gosforth Park	1969	DMcM Moffat	City of Newcastle
1927	RE Grey	Gosforth Park	1970	JE Hayes	Morpeth
1928	R Thompson	Three Mile Bridge	1971	GJ Clark	Whitley Bay
1929	J Snowdon	Gosforth	1972	DP Davidson	Alnmouth
1930	R Thompson	Gosforth Park	1973	DP Davidson	Tynemouth
1931	JK Fraser	Three Mile Bridge	1974	JK Tate	Gosforth Park
1932	JE Common	Gosforth	1975	P Deeble	Arcot Hall
1933	J Snowdon	Gosforth Park	1976	JE Hayes	Ponteland
1934	RE Grey	Three Mile Bridge	1977	JE Hayes	Gosforth
1935	R Thompson	Gosforth	1978	D Faulder	Hexham
1936	R Thompson	Gosforth Park	1979	S Elliott	City of Newcastle
1937	J Snowdon	City of Newcastle	1980	S Smith	Morpeth
1938	ACR Stephenson	Gosforth	1981	D George	Westerhope
1939	RE Grey	Gosforth	1982	P Deeble	Whitley Bay
1940–45	*Not played due to Second World War*		1983	P Deeble	Gosforth Park
1946	RE Grey	Gosforth	1984	J Straker	Newbiggen
1947	RJ Rutherford	City of Newcastle	1985	D Faulder	Arcot Hall
1948	DL Couves	Gosforth Park	1986	D Martin	Tynemouth
1949	GRB Fairbairn	Bridle Path, Gosforth	1987	K Fairbairn	Alnmouth
			1988	J Metcalfe	Ponteland
1950	WB Blake	City of Newcastle	1989	J Metcalfe	Gosforth
1951	W Embleton	Gosforth Park	1990	K Fairbairn	Berwick
1952	A Thirlwell	Gosforth Park			

Northumberland Amateur Stroke Play Championship

INAUGURATED 1963

YEAR	WINNER	VENUE	YEAR	WINNER	VENUE
1963	DMcM Moffat	Ponteland	1977	P Deeble	Morpeth
1964	DMcM Moffat	Gosforth	1978	P Deeble	Ponteland
1965	JPB Nichol	Hexham	1979	P Deeble	Berwick
1966	JK Tate	Alnmouth	1980	D George	Tynemouth
1967	GJ Clark	Tynemouth	1981	GA Knighting	Arcot Hall
1968	GRB Fairbairn	Morpeth	1982	N Macdonald	Alnmouth
1969	JE Hayes	Alnmouth	1983	R Farrelly	Westerhope
1970	JE Hayes	Ponteland	1984	DH Curry	Berwick
1971	GJ Clark	Hexham	1985	DH Curry	City of Newcastle
1972	T Leigh	Arcot Hall	1986	DH Curry	Whitley Bay
1973	P Deeble	City of Newcastle	1987	KP Robson	Morpeth
1974	DP Davidson	Whitley Bay	1988	I Donaldson	Hexham
1975	P Deeble	Hexham	1989	G Pickup	Gosforth Park
1976	DMcM Moffat	Northumberland	1990	MD Hall	Whitley Bay

Nottinghamshire Amateur Championship

INAUGURATED 1924

YEAR	WINNER	VENUE	YEAR	WINNER	VENUE
1924	Dr HK Sparrow	Rushcliffe	1953	DC Gardner	Sherwood Forest
1925	S Roper	Hollinwell	1954	DC Gardner	Chilwell Manor
1926	AV Campbell	Radcliffe-on-Trent	1955	AE Shepperson	Hollinwell
1927	S Roper	Hollinwell	1956	DC Gardner	Wollaton Park
1928	FL Snook	Beeston Fields	1957	V Kregel	Rushcliffe
1929	S Roper	Sherwood Forest	1958	AE Shepperson	Coxmoor
1930	TM Kirkland	Chilwell Manor	1959	AF Bussell	Stanton-on-the-Wolds
1931	HW Street	Bulwell Hall			
1932	DS Robinson	Hollinwell	1960	AF Bussell	Radcliffe-on-Trent
1933	C Sellick	Wollaton Park	1961	AE Shepperson	Beeston Fields
1934	FA Naylor	Rushclifffe	1962	AF Bussell	Sherwood Forest
1935	HW Street	Radcliffe-on-Trent	1963	AF Bussell	Coxmoor
1936	J Unwin	Beeston Fields	1964	AF Bussell	Chilwell Manor
1937	TH Copeland	Sherwood Forest	1965	AE Shepperson	Hollinwell
1938	SCH Elliott	Chilwell Manor	1966	AD McLuckie	Wollaton Park
1939	FA Naylor	Bulwell Hall	1967	FK Shaw	Rushcliffe
1940–45	*Not played due to Second World War*		1968	AF Bussell	Stanton-on-the-Wolds
1946	AP Burgass	Hollinwell			
1947	WAC Glennie	Wollaton Park	1969	AF Bussell	Radcliffe-on-Trent
1948	Dr J Angus	Rushcliffe	1970	GAL Coleman	Newark
1949	CHV Elliott	Sutton-in-Ashfield	1971	JD Hall	Worksop
1950	CHV Elliott	Stanton-on-the-Wolds	1972	P Shaw	Sherwood Forest
			1973	P Shaw	Beeston Fields
1951	HS Johnson	Radcliffe-on-Trent	1974	AWP White	Coxmoor
1952	Dr J Angus	Beeston Fields	1975	I Simpson	Chilwell Manor

YEAR	WINNER	VENUE	YEAR	WINNER	VENUE
1976	RP Naylor	Hollinwell	1983	TM Estrop	Sherwood Forest
1977	P Shaw	Wollaton Park	1984	G Krause	Beeston Fields
1978	I Simpson	Rushcliffe	1985	M Scothern	Coxmoor
1979	PM Baxter	Stanton-on-the-	1986	G Krause	Chilwell Manor
		Wolds	1987	RJ Sallis	Wollaton Park
1980	T Leigh	Newark	1988	CA Banks	Hollinwell
1981	CA Banks	Radcliffe-on-Trent	1989	P Shaw	Rushcliffe
1982	CA Banks	Worksop	1990	L White	Radcliffe-on-Trent

Nottinghamshire Match Play Championship

YEAR	WINNER	VENUE	YEAR	WINNER	VENUE
1982	CA Banks	Worksop	1987	RJ Sallis	Wollaton Park
1983	J Vaughan	Sherwood Forest	1988	G Krause	Hollinwell
1984	S Riley	Beeston Fields	1989	P Shaw	Rushcliffe
1985	RJ Sallis	Coxmoor	1990	P Edwards	Radcliffe-on-Trent
1986	B Moir	Chilwell Manor			

Nottinghamshire Open Championship

INAUGURATED 1933

YEAR	WINNER	VENUE	YEAR	WINNER	VENUE
1933	T Williamson	Hollinwell	1964	S Hunt	Chilwell Manor
1934	AG Beck	Sherwood Forest	1965	D Talbot	Hollinwell
1935	AG Beck	Radcliffe-on-Trent	1966	AD McLuckie	Wollaton Park
1936	AG Beck	Beeston Fields	1967	D Talbot	Rushcliffe
1937	AG Beck	Sherwood Forest	1968	D Snell	Stanton-on-the-
1938	G Johnson	Chilwell Manor			Wolds
1939	G Johnson	Bulwell Hall	1969	BJ Waites	Radcliffe-on-Trent
1940–46	*Not played due to Second World War*		1970	P Bottell	Newark
1947	G Johnson	Sherwood Forest	1971	BJ Waites	Worksop
1948	G Thomson	Rushcliffe	1972	GM White	Sherwood Forest
1949	G Johnson	Coxmoor	1973	BJ Waites	Beeston Fields
1950	EB Williamson	Stanton-on-the-	1974	BJ Waites	Coxmoor
		Wolds	1975	G Tickell	Chilwell Manor
1951	W Hill	Radcliffe-on-Trent	1976	RP Naylor (Am)	Hollinwell
1952	CA Winks	Sherwood Forest	1977	P Shaw (Am)	Wollaton Park
1953	DC Gardner (Am)	Sherwood Forest	1978	BJ Waites	Rushcliffe
1954	DC Gardner (Am)	Chilwell Manor	1979	DJ Ridley	Stanton-on-the-
1955	AE Shepperson				Wolds
	(Am)	Hollinwell	1980	CA Banks (Am)	Newark
1956	GM White	Wollaton Park	1981	CA Banks (Am)	Radcliffe-on-Trent
1957	MW Youngs	Rushcliffe	1982	BJ Waites	Worksop
1958	AE Shepperson		1983	CA Banks (Am)	Sherwood Forest
	(Am)	Coxmoor	1984	CD Hall	Beeston Fields
1959	D Snell	Stanton-on-the-	1985	C Jepson	Coxmoor
		Wolds	1986	BJ Waites	Chilwell Manor
1960	AF Bussell (Am)	Radcliffe-on-Trent	1987	CD Hall	Wollaton Park
1961	GM White	Beeston Fields	1988	CA Banks (Am)	Hollinwell
1962	AF Bussell (Am)	Sherwood Forest	1989	P Hinton	Rushcliffe
1963	D Smart	Coxmoor	1990	CD Hall	Radcliffe-on-Trent

Shropshire and Herefordshire Amateur Championship

INAUGURATED 1913

YEAR	WINNER	VENUE	YEAR	WINNER	VENUE
1913	HH Clarke	Church Stretton	1959	CG Griffith	Oswestry
1914–19	*Not played due to Great War*		1960	CG Griffith	Hereford
1920	FG Corser	Wrekin	1961	D Mercer	Wrekin
1921–22	*No championship*		1962	RP Yates	Ludlow
1923	FG Corser	Wrekin	1963	RP Yates	Shrewsbury
1924	R Roberts	Wrekin	1964	A Parsonage	Oswestry
1925	FG Corser	Shrewsbury	1965	CG Griffith	Hereford
1926	FG Corser	Wrekin	1966	RP Yates	Wrekin
1927	J Custance	Shrewsbury	1967	DJ Humphreys	Lilleshall Hall
1928	GH Darlington	Shrewsbury	1968	R Issitt	Shifnal
1929	DG Heasman	Shrewsbury	1969	DJ Humphreys	Ludlow
1930	CEL Fairchild	Wrekin	1970	J Black	Shrewsbury
1931	GH Darlington	Shrewsbury	1971	GH Roberts	Hereford
1932	SW Jacobs	Wrekin	1972	DJ Humphreys	Oswestry
1933	CEL Fairchild	Shrewsbury	1973	MA Smith	Lilleshall Hall
1934	AG Sheppard	Wrekin	1974	AWB Lyle	Kington
1935	AG Sheppard	Oswestry	1975	I Woosnam	Bridgnorth
1936	CW Plant	Ludlow	1976	AWB Lyle	Shifnal
1937	GH Darlington	Shrewsbury	1977	MA Smith	Wrekin
1938	JH Jones	Wrekin	1978	JR Burn	Shrewsbury
1939	GH Darlington	Ludlow	1979	MA Smith	Llanymynech
1940–47	*Not played due to Second World War*		1980	MA Smith	Hereford
1948	GH Darlington	Shrewsbury	1981	JA Wilson	Oswestry
1949	FR Wingate Hughes	Oswestry	1982	NS Kelly	Ludlow
1950	W Turner	Wrekin	1983	PA Baker	Lilleshall Hall
1951	GG Williams	Hawkstone Park	1984	PA Baker	Bridgnorth
1952	FR Wingate Hughes	Ludlow	1985	PA Baker	Oswestry
1953	CEL Fairchild	Shrewsbury	1986	C Bufton	Wrekin
1954	FR Wingate Hughes	Oswestry	1987	R Dixon	Kington
1955	DW Kent	Wrekin	1988	S Thomas	Church Stretton
1956	RP Yates	Hawkstone Park	1989	M Welch	Shrewsbury
1957	CG Griffith	Ludlow	1990	M Welch	Hereford
1958	CG Griffith	Shrewsbury			

Somerset Amateur Championship

INAUGURATED 1911

YEAR	WINNER	VENUE	YEAR	WINNER	VENUE
1911	RA Ridell		1924	AB James	
1912	RA Ridell		1925	SL Dickinson	Burnham and Berrow
1913	RW May				
1914	Capt Cunningham		1926	RG Cleveland	Weston-super-Mare
1915–20	*Not played due to Great War*		1927	SL Dickinson	Burnham and Berrow
1921	SL Dickinson				
1922	K Whetstone		1928	SL Dickinson	Weston-super-Mare
1923	K Whetstone		1929	SL Dickinson	Burnham and Berrow

YEAR	WINNER	VENUE	YEAR	WINNER	VENUE
1930	H Grey	Weston-super-Mare	1961	GT Irlam	Burnham and Berrow
1931	SHR Hornby	Burnham and Berrow	1962	PO Green	Bath
1932	HD Grey	Weston-super-Mare	1963	RN Jutsum	Weston-super-Mare
1933	P MacAllister	Burnham and Berrow	1964	BW Barnes	Weston-super-Mare
			1965	RN Jutsum	Burnham and Berrow
1934	Dr G Cook	Weston-super-Mare			
1935	EJ Poole Jr	Burnham and Berrow	1966	DE Jones	Weston-super-Mare
			1967	GK Baker	Weston-super-Mare
1936	BR Feaver	Weston-super-Mare	1968	DJ Jacobs	Weston-super-Mare
1937	EJ Poole	Burnham and Berrow	1969	RN Jutsum	Weston-super-Mare
			1970	WR Hartree	Weston-super-Mare
1938	RN Jutsum	Weston-super-Mare	1971	LF Millar	Burnham and Berrow
1939	EP Tomkinson	Burnham and Berrow	1972	WP Hucker	Bath
1940–46	*Not played due to Second World War*		1973	NJ Roseff	Weston-super-Mare
1947	RN Jutsum	Burnham and Berrow	1974	TW Jones	Burnham and Berrow
1948	RN Jutsum	Burnham and Berrow	1975	TE Knott	Weston-super-Mare
			1976	AJ Hill	Burnham and Berrow
1949	RN Jutsum	Sham Castle			
1950	J Payne	Burnham and Berrow	1977	PC Emery	Burnham and Berrow
1951	JWR Swayne	Weston-super-Mare	1978	NJ Roseff	Bath
1952	J Payne	Burnham and Berrow	1979	D Meredith	Weston-super-Mare
			1980	LF Millar	Burnham and Berrow
1953	GT Irlam	Weston-super-Mare			
1954	RC Champion	Burnham and Berrow	1981	J Clifford	Weston-super-Mare
			1982	BJ Reeves	
1955	A Cook	Sham Castle	1983	DJ Huxtable	
1956	RN Jutsum	Weston-super-Mare	1984	CS Edwards	
1957	RN Jutsum	Burnham and Berrow	1985	PR Hare	
			1986	CS Edwards	
1958	RN Jutsum	Weston-super-Mare	1987	G Hickman	
1959	RC Champion	Burnham and Berrow	1988	CS Edwards	
			1989	CS Edwards	
1960	GT Irlam	Weston-super-Mare	1990	CS Edwards	

South-Western Counties Amateur Championship

INAUGURATED 1924

YEAR	WINNER	VENUE	YEAR	WINNER	VENUE
1924	AV Hambro	Westward Ho!	1932	GC Brooks	Broadstone
1925	RA Riddell	Long Ashton	1933	SHR Hornby	St Enodoc
1926	CH Young	Broadstone	1934	PBM Wallace	Westward Ho!
1927	JA Pierson	Burnham and Berrow	1935	SHR Hornby	Burnham and Berrow
1928	E Hunter	Broadstone	1936	GE Newton	Broadstone
1929	C Chard	St Enodoc	1937	EJ Poole	St Enodoc
1930	Cdr RD Howard	Saunton	1938	LC Lake	Saunton
1931	F Smith	Burnham and Berrow	1939	EJ Poole	Burnham and Berrow

YEAR	WINNER	VENUE	YEAR	WINNER	VENUE
1940–46	*Not played due to Second World War*		1969	DJ Carroll	Trevose
1947	LF Brown	Ferndown	1970	PJ Yeo	Westward Ho!
1948	EB Millward	Trevose	1971	JA Bloxham	St Enodoc
1949	J Payne	Westward Ho!	1972	JH Davis	Saunton
1950	J Payne	Burnham and	1973	RW Tugwell	Ferndown
		Berrow	1974	CS Mitchell	Burnham and
1951	EB Millward	Ferndown			Berrow
1952	EB Millward	Trevose	1975	R Abbott	Trevose
1953	ED Trapnell	Westward Ho!	1976	GT Irlam	Westward Ho!
1954	EB Millward	Burnham and	1977	GJ Brand	St Enodoc
		Berrow	1978	GJ Brand	Saunton
1955	R Lawford	Broadstone	1979	S Davidson	Ferndown
1956	RG Peach	St Enodoc	1980	CS Mitchell	Burnham and
1957	ED Trapnell	Saunton			Berrow
1958	RC Champion	Burnham and	1981	P Newcombe	St Mellion
		Berrow	1982	D Ray	Westward Ho!
1959	G Butler	St Enodoc	1983	CS Edwards	St Enodoc
1960	ED Trapnell	Westward Ho!	1984	M Blaber	Saunton
1961	RN Jutsum	Saunton	1985	C Phillips	Ferndown
1962	GN Bicknell	Trevose	1986	C Phillips	Trevose
1963	RN Jutsum	Westward Ho!	1987	P Newcombe	Burnham and
1964	BW Barnes	Burnham and			Berrow
		Berrow	1988	J Langmead	Westward Ho!
1965	JA Bloxham	St Enodoc	1989	K Jones	St Enodoc
1966	R Lawford	Ferndown	1990	S Amor	Saunton
1967	PJ Yeo	Saunton			
1968	BG Steer	Burnham and			
		Berrow			

Staffordshire Amateur Championship

INAUGURATED 1924

YEAR	WINNER	VENUE	YEAR	WINNER	VENUE
1924	JB Beddard	Sandwell Park	1946	C Stowe	Little Aston
1925	JB Beddard	Little Aston	1947	E Perry	Sandwell Park
1926	JB Beddard	Brocton Hall	1948	C Stowe	South Staffs
1927	*Twice abandoned owing to weather*		1949	P Squire	Brocton Hall
1928	JB Beddard	South Staffs	1950	MB Morgan	Whittington
1929	JB Beddard	Trentham			Barracks
1930	Dr GJ Moore	Beau Desert	1951	SM Sangster	Trentham
1931	RMW Pritchard	Leek	1952	J Beales	Beau Desert
1932	GS Beharrell	Sandwell Park	1953	C Stowe	Bloxwich
1933	RB Bayliss	Bloxwich	1954	C Stowe	Leek
1934	C Stove	Little Aston	1955	RB Bayliss	Little Aston
1935	TR Deighton	Trentham	1956	RB Bayliss	South Staffs
1936	TR Deighton	Beau Desert	1957	C Stowe	Brocton Hall
1937	KW Chaundy	Whittington	1958	Gp Capt CH Beamish	Sandwell Park
		Barracks	1959	GC Marks	Enville
1938	G Mills	Oxley Park,	1960	GC Marks	Trentham
		Wolverhampton	1961	JPG Windsor	Whittington
1939	C Stowe	Leek			Barracks
1940–45	*Not played due to Second World War*		1962	Gp Capt CH Beamish	Little Aston

YEAR	WINNER	VENUE	YEAR	WINNER	VENUE
1963	GC Marks	Trentham	1977	D Blakeman	South Staffs
1964	C Stowe	Bloxwich	1978	D Blakeman	Enville
1965	RD James	Trentham	1979	D Evans	Leek
1966	GC Marks	South Staffs	1980	AR Eden	Little Aston
1967	GC Marks	Enville	1981	M Hassall	Walsall
1968	GC Marks	Beau Desert	1982	AK Stubbs	Trentham Park
1969	GC Marks	Little Aston	1983	M Hassall	Sandwell Park
1970	K Hodgkinson	Brocton Hall	1984	M Hassall	Whittington
1971	AN Dathan	Leek			Barracks
1972	PH Minton	Sandwell Park	1985	M Hassall	Trentham
1973	GC Marks	Whittington	1986	M Scarrett	Bloxwich
		Barracks	1987	M Hassall	Beau Desert
1974	K Hodgkinson	Bloxwich	1988	P Sweetsur	South Staffs
1975	AN Dathan	Trentham	1989	CG Poxon	Newcastle
1976	MA Payne	Beau Desert	1990	P Sweetsur	Drayton Park

Staffordshire Match Play Championship

INAUGURATED 1974

at Little Aston (1990 at South Staffs)

YEAR	WINNER	YEAR	WINNER
1974	MA Poxon	1983	CS White
1975	AN Dathan	1984	CG Poxon
1976	MW Baker	1985	M Hassall
1977	MA Payne	1986	P Griffiths
1978	MA Payne	1987	PCR Smith
1979	CP Hodgkinson	1988	P Sweetsur
1980	G Broadbent	1989	SB Perry
1981	G Broadbent	1990	M McGuire
1982	AK Stubbs		

Staffordshire Open Championship

YEAR	WINNER	VENUE	YEAR	WINNER	VENUE
1948	C Stowe (Am)	Sandwell Park	1970	R Janes	Enville
1949	CH Ward	Little Aston	1971	H Jones (Am)	Walsall
1950	CH Ward	South Staffs	1972	P Hinton (Am)	Bloxwich
1951	CH Ward	Enville	1973	J Rhodes	Beau Desert
1952	CH Ward	Walsall	1974	A Sadler	South Staffs
1953	G Johnson	Little Aston	1975	J Rhodes	Sandwell Park
1954	CH Ward	Brocton Hall	1976	MA Poxon (Am)	Little Aston
1955	CH Ward	Oxley Park	1977	J Anderson	Oxley Park
1956	JR Moses	Sandwell Park	1978	J Anderson	Whittington
1957	CH Ward	Trentham			Barracks
1958	RL Hastelow	Whittington	1979	J Anderson	Walsall
		Barracks	1980	P Robinson (Am)	Penn
1959	J Sharkey	Bloxwich	1981	J Rhodes	Bloxwich
1960	G Johnson	South Staffs	1982	A Stubbs (Am)	Enville
1961	G Johnson	Enville	1983	C Poxon (Am)	Beau Desert
1962	JR Moses	Brocton Hall	1984	D Gilford (Am)	South Staffs
1963	RD James (Am)	Walsall	1985	J Annable	Whittington
1964	E Large	Sandwell Park			Barracks
1965	A Smith (Am)	Little Aston	1986	J Higgins	Brocton Hall
1966	R Janes	Bloxwich	1987	J Annable	Sandwell Park
1967	E Large	Oxley Park	1988	J Rhodes	Sandwell Park
1968	M Bembridge	South Staffs	1989	M Passmore	Sandwell Park
1969	A Smith (Am)	Whittington	1990	J Rhodes	Sandwell Park
		Barracks			

Suffolk Amateur Championship

INAUGURATED 1924

YEAR	WINNER	VENUE	YEAR	WINNER	VENUE
1924	FEB Moritz	Aldeburgh	1950	Dr SJS Pitts	Thorpeness
1925	FEB Moritz	Woodbridge	1951	WJ Brooks	Ipswich
1926	WSJ Watson	Bury St Edmunds	1952	J Newson	Woodbridge
1927	FWT Layton	Felixstowe	1953	P Rush	Aldeburgh
1928	VC Longstaffe	Aldeburgh	1954	C Branch	Thorpeness
1929	Abdy-Collins	Ipswich	1955	H Ridgeley	Ipswich
1930	FWT Layton	Woodbridge	1956	RJ Taylor	Woodbridge
1931	WE Winstanley	Thorpeness	1957	HW Howlett	Thorpeness
1932	Dr KW Mackenzie	Rushmere	1958	HW Howlett	Ipswich
1933	ASG Thompson	Aldeburgh	1959	Flt Lt AD Mencer	Woodbridge
1934	O Bunn	Ipswich	1960	RF Long	Thorpeness
1935	T Wright	Woodbridge	1961	RF Long	Ipswich
1936	RB Beare	Thorpeness	1962	RJ Taylor	Thorpeness
1937	ASG Thompson	Felixstowe	1963	HW Howlett	Woodbridge
1938	ED Keeble	Rushmere	1964	RR Sparrow	Aldeburgh
1939	Dr KW Mackenzie	Aldeburgh	1965	DC Whinney	Ipswich
1940–46	*Not played due to Second World War*		1966	PJ Parsons	Thorpeness
1947	RM Fell	Ipswich	1967	DC Whinney	Woodbridge
1948	HW Howlett	Woodbridge	1968	DC Whinney	Ipswich
1949	HW Howlett	Aldeburgh	1969	DC Whinney	Aldeburgh

YEAR	WINNER	VENUE	YEAR	WINNER	VENUE
1970	RF Long	Thorpeness	1981	P Buckle	Bury St Edmunds
1971	IL Pearce	Woodbridge	1982	CJC Lloyd	Aldeburgh
1972	RW Mann	Ipswich	1983	M Turner	Stowmarket
1973	JC Broad	Aldeburgh	1984	S Goodman	Woodbridge
1974	J Marks	Thorpeness	1985	R Barrell	Ipswich
1975	P Saggers	Woodbridge	1986	M Clark	Aldeburgh
1976	J Doe	Ipswich	1987	CN Coulton	Bury St Edmunds
1977	S Block	Aldeburgh	1988	J Whitby	Ipswich
1978	R Taylor	Thorpeness	1989	M Turner	Woodbridge
1979	J Cook	Woodbridge	1990	JR Booth	Aldeburgh
1980	I Whinney	Ipswich			

Suffolk Amateur Match Play Championship

(President's Mashie)

INAUGURATED 1982

YEAR	WINNER	VENUE	YEAR	WINNER	VENUE
1982	R Taylor	Aldeburgh	1987	C Woods	Bury St Edmunds
1983	R Taylor	Stowmarket	1988	M Clark	Ipswich
1984	K Woods	Woodbridge	1989	J Maddocks	Woodbridge
1985	B Bell	Ipswich	1990	P Buckle	Aldeburgh
1986	M Harvey	Aldeburgh			

Suffolk Open Championship

INAUGURATED 1936

YEAR	WINNER	VENUE	YEAR	WINNER	VENUE
1936	SG Rush	Aldeburgh	1962	LB Ayton	Ipswich
1937	JD Freeman	Ipswich	1963	LB Ayton	Aldeburgh
1938	Dr KW Mackenzie (Am)	Woodbridge	1964	DA Levermore	Thorpeness
1939–46	*Not played due to Second World War*		1965	DC Whinney (Am)	Woodbridge
1947	AD Stewart (Am) ⎫ tie EE Beverley ⎭	Aldeburgh	1966	J Frew	Aldeburgh
			1967	JW Johnson	Thorpeness
1948	EE Beverley	Thorpeness	1968	TE Sutton	Aldeburgh
1949	FJ Davis	Ipswich	1969	DC Whinney (Am)	Ipswich
1950	RA Knight	Woodbridge	1970	C Aldred	Woodbridge
1951	FJ Davis	Aldeburgh	1971	J Frew	Thorpeness
1952	HB Ridgeley (Am)	Thorpeness	1972	SJ Whymark	Aldeburgh
1953	HB Ridgeley (Am)	Ipswich	1973	SJ Whymark	Ipswich
1954	DA Levermore	Woodbridge	1974	RG Webb	Woodbridge
1955	LB Ayton	Aldeburgh	1975	J Cook (Am)	Thorpeness
1956	LB Ayton	Aldeburgh	1976	T Bird (Am)	Bury St Edmunds
1957	LB Ayton	Ipswich			
1958	LB Ayton	Woodbridge	1977	JW Johnson	Ipswich
1959	JW Johnson	Aldeburgh	1978	RA Knight	Aldeburgh
1960	LA Jones	Thorpeness	1979	C Jervis	Stoke-by-Nayland
1961	BJ Proudfoot	Aldeburgh			

YEAR	WINNER	VENUE	YEAR	WINNER	VENUE
1980	SJ Whymark	Felixstowe Ferry	1985	K Preston	Aldeburgh
1981	P Buckle (Am)	Ipswich	1986	SL Beckham	Thorpeness
1982	RW Mann	Thorpeness	1987	MR Turner	Ipswich
1983	SJ Whymark	Woodbridge	1988	J Maddock	Woodbridge
1984	JVT Marks	Stoke-by-Nayland	1989	N Elsworthy	Aldeburgh
			1990	S Crosby (Am)	Gorleston

Surrey Amateur Championship

INAUGURATED 1924

YEAR	WINNER	VENUE	YEAR	WINNER	VENUE
1924	D Grant	Addington	1958	D Sewell	Walton Heath
1925	Sir E Holderness	Walton Heath	1959	DW Frame	Wentworth
1926	D Grant	Sunningdale	1960	JL McClue	St Georges Hill
1927	Major SK Thorburn	Wentworth	1961	I Caldwell	Sunningdale
1928	Major CO Hezlet	St Georges Hill	1962	R Hunter	Walton Heath
1929	DB Anderson	St Georges Hill	1963	RH Miller	Wentworth
1930	R Straker	West Hill	1964	PD Flaherty	Worplesdon
1931	J de Forest	Sunningdale	1965	D Millensted	Sunningdale
1932	Brig Gen AC Critchley	Addington	1966	KG Thom	Addington
1933	D Grant	Royal Mid-Surrey	1967	PJ Benka	Wentworth
1934	WL Hartley	Royal Wimbledon	1968	PJ Benka	Sunningdale
1935	Major SK Thorburn	Sunningdale	1969	B Critchley	Walton Heath
1936	F Francis	Walton Heath	1970	RL Glading	West Hill
1937	WA Stevenson	Worplesdon	1971	JC Davies	Wentworth
1938	Brig Gen AC Critchley	Woking	1972	JC Davies	Sunningdale
1939	C Gray	West Hill	1973	RP Revell	Walton Heath
1940–45	Not played due to Second World War		1974	PD Flaherty	Royal Mid-Surrey
1946	F Francis	Walton Heath	1975	PD Flaherty	Worplesdon
1947	A McNair	Sunningdale	1976	Dr HUS McMichen	Sunningdale
1948	WA Slark	Royal Mid-Surrey	1977	JC Davies	Royal Mid-Surrey
1949	Count John de Bendern (formerly de Forest)	Worplesdon	1978	PF Garner	Walton Heath
			1979	M Devetta	Woking
1950	EM Pollitt	West Hill	1980	JG Bennet	Wentworth
1951	PF Scrutton	Addington	1981	SD Keppler	Sunningdale
1952	RH Miller	Camberley	1982	R Boxall	Royal Mid-Surrey
1953	WA Slark	Coombe Hill	1983	G Lashford	Walton Heath
1954	D Sewell	Woking	1984	PM Talbot	West Hill
1955	JR Thornhill	West Hill	1985	G Walmsley	Sunningdale
1956	D Sewell	Addington	1986	B White	Wentworth
1957	D Sewell	Burhill	1987	JN Paramor	Royal Mid-Surrey
			1988	A Carter	Worplesdon
			1989	T Lloyd	Walton Heath
			1990	J Good	West Hill

Sussex Amateur Championship

INAUGURATED 1899

YEAR	WINNER	VENUE	YEAR	WINNER	VENUE
1899	GH Peacock	Royal Eastbourne	1950	A Warnett	Crowborough
1900	AWH Murray	Seaford			Beacon
1901	OC Bevan	Royal Ashdown	1951	J McKay	Cooden Beach
		Forest	1952	JJF Pennink	Seaford
1902	SH Fry	Littlehampton	1953	WG Pierce	Rye
1903	Dr Bruce E Gott	Brighton and Hove	1954	DD Grant-White	Littlehampton
1904	AWH Murray	Lewes	1955	WG Pierce	Royal Ashdown
1905	P Winterscale	Rye			Forest
1906	GH Peacock	East Brighton	1956	WG Pierce	West Sussex
1907	DF Ranson	Southdown	1957	WG Pierce	Cooden Beach
1908	WS Lurcott	Royal Ashdown	1958	WG Pierce	Seaford
		Forest	1959	WG Pierce	Littlehampton
1909	WS Lurcott	Crowborough	1960	MJ Burgess	Rye
		Beacon	1961	RB Carroll	Royal Ashdown
1910	Hon B Butler	Littlehampton			Forest
1911	Capt JS Armstrong	Seaford	1962	G Hyde	Pulborough
1912	OC Bevan	Royal Ashdown	1963	MJ Burgess	Nevill
		Forest	1964	MJ Burgess	Seaford
1913	GH Peacock	Royal Eastbourne	1965	I Shepherd	Pulborough
1914	TBC Piggott	Cooden Beach	1966	AG Clay	Crowborough
1915–19	*Not played due to Great War*				Beacon
1920	D Sundias-Smith	Littlehampton	1967	T Frost	Cooden Beach
1921	CJH Tolley	Crowborough	1968	HG Hyde	Littlehampton
		Beacon	1969	P Royle	Royal Ashdown
1922	CJH Tolley	Seaford			Forest
1923	RA Reid	Royal Ashdown	1970	G Hyde	Worthing
		Forest	1971	G Hyde	Seaford
1924	CJH Tolley	Royal Eastbourne	1972	C King	Highwoods
1925	FG Mirfield	Brighton and Hove	1973	G Hyde	Crowborough
1926	RW Hartley	Rye			Beacon
1927	CJH Tolley	Worthing	1974	G Hyde	Pulborough
1928	WL Hartley	Cooden Beach	1975	MV Jones	Cooden Beach
1929	R Howell	Littlehampton	1976	MIR Ross	Royal Ashdown
1930	RVJ Findlay	Goodwood			Forest
1931	EB Tipping	Crowborough	1977	SC Illingworth	Worthing
		Beacon	1978	AW Schofield	Seaford
1932	D Watson	Royal Ashdown	1979	AP Higgins	Crowborough
		Forest			Beacon
1933	CJH Tolley	Seaford	1980	N Mitchell	Mannings Heath
1934	D Watson	Pulborough	1981	N Mitchell	Ham Manor
1935	FG Mirfield	Cooden Beach	1982	DJ Sewell	Rye
1936	DD Grant-White	Littlehampton	1983	P Scarles	Pulborough
1937	RA Howell	Royal Eastbourne	1984	JS Spence	Royal Ashdown
1938	L Green	Worthing			Forest
1939	RK Furneaux	Royal Ashdown	1985	MS Jarvis	Seaford
		Forest	1986	AW Schofield	Nevill
1940–46	*Not played due to Second World War*		1987	D Fay	Worthing
1947	A Heasman	Royal Ashdown	1988	DW Alderson	Cooden Beach
		Forest	1989	P Hurring	Crowborough
1948	HG Francis	Worthing			Beacon
1949	JH Langmead	Pulborough	1990	D Arnold	Pulborough

Sussex Open Championship

INAUGURATED 1946

YEAR	WINNER	VENUE	YEAR	WINNER	VENUE
1946	J McLean	Goodwood	1969	P Huggett	Crowborough
1947	LB Ayton	Pulborough	1970	SR Bassil	Bognor Regis
1948	W Anderson	Seaford	1971	B Firkins	Cooden Beach
1949	AG Harrison	Littlehampton	1972	BA Morrison	Worthing
1950	AG Harrison	Royal Ashdown Forest	1973	AJ Lowles	Royal Ashdown Forest
1951	AG Harrison	East Brighton	1974	AJ Lowles	Rye
1952	K Beckett	Dyke	1975	G Hyde (Am)	Ham Manor
1953	LB Ayton	Pulborough	1976	JRM Jewell	Highwoods
1954	W Anderson	East Brighton	1977	CR Jones (Am)	Nevill
1955	AG Harrison	Hill Barn	1978	JC Burrell	Littlehampton
1956	WG Pierce (Am)	Royal Ashdown Forest	1979	JC Burrell	Royal Ashdown Forest
1957	W Anderson	Worthing	1980	JC Burrell	Pulborough
1958	JT Baker	Piltdown	1981	J Pinsent (Am)	Seaford
1959	HA Padgham	Pulborough	1982	CR Jones	Dyke
1960	MJ Burgess (Am)	Seaford	1983	ACB Giddins	Cooden Beach
1961	*Not played*		1984	J Dodds (Am)	Worthing
1962	MJ Christmas (Am)	Bognor Regis	1985	JS Spence (Am)	Crowborough Beacon
1963	RJ McLean	Littlehampton			
1964	HT Riseborough	Hill Barn	1986	ACB Giddins	Mannings Heath
1965	HA Padgham	Royal Ashdown Forest	1987	BW Barnes	Ham Manor
			1988	S Rolley	Rye
1966	B Bamford	Dyke	1989	M Groombridge (Am)	Bognor Regis
1967	B Bamford	Pulborough			
1968	JR Hollands (Am)	Highwoods	1990	*Not played*	

Warwickshire Amateur Championship

INAUGURATED 1906

YEAR	WINNER	VENUE	YEAR	WINNER	VENUE
1906	B Norbury	Olton	1925	TP Perkins	Whitnash
1907	TS Fishwick	Harborne	1926	TP Perkins	Harborne
1908	FW Clive	Sutton Coldfield	1927	TP Perkins	Sutton Coldfield
1909	FW Clive	Coventry, Whitley Common	1928	TP Perkins	Ladbrook Park
			1929	TP Perkins	Walmley
1910	WF Hutchings	Castle Bromwich	1930	WA Stockwin	Handsworth
1911	HB Barker	Whitnash	1931	H Hall	Castle Bromwich
1912	HB Barker	Olton	1932	SA Dark	Copt Heath
1913	HB Barker	Harborne	1933	SA Dark	Coventry, Finham
1914–19	*Not played due to Great War*		1934	V Gerstenberg	Robin Hood
1920	W Archdale	Castle Bromwich	1935	KR Frazier	Olton
1921	TP Perkins	Copt Heath	1936	KR Frazier	Moor Hall
1922	TP Perkins	Coventry, Finham	1937	KR Frazier	Harborne
1923	TP Perkins	Robin Hood	1938	DM Sutherland	Whitnash
1924	TP Perkins	Olton	1939	RJ Nauen	Sutton Coldfield

YEAR	WINNER	VENUE	YEAR	WINNER	VENUE
1940–45	*Not played due to Second World War*		1969	JA Fisher	Coventry, Finham
1946	JM Urry	Sutton Coldfield	1970	JMH Mayell	Walmley
1947	BJ Newey	Pype Hayes	1971	JA Fisher	Edgbaston
1948	AW Pullar	Ladbrook Park	1972	JA Fisher	Moor Hall
1949	AW Pullar	Robin Hood	1973	JMH Mayell	Harborne
1950	WL Smart	Sutton Coldfield	1974	P McEvoy	Kenilworth
1951	JL Morgan	Olton	1975	P Pritchard	Leamington and
1952	T Mannion	Copt Heath			County
1953	E Walton	Walmley	1976	P McEvoy	Stratford-on-Avon
1954	JM Urry	Handsworth	1977	P McEvoy	Robin Hood
1955	T Mannion	Coventry, Finham	1978	TM Allen	Sutton Coldfield
1956	P Skerritt	Edgbaston	1979	M Biddle	Olton
1957	RJ Nauen	Coventry Hearsall	1980	P McEvoy	Handsworth
1958	P Skerritt	Moor Hall	1981	B Wilkes	Maxstoke Park
1959	JL Whitworth	Harborne	1982	A Roach	Walmley
1960	PG Jones	Pype Hayes	1983	NM Chesses	Copt Heath
1961	AW Pullar	Stratford-on-Avon	1984	P McEvoy	Harborne
1962	AW Holmes	Leamington and	1985	C Suneson	Leamington and
		County			County
1963	P Skerritt	Ladbrook Park	1986	P Downes	Coventry, Finham
1964	GW Barton	Robin Hood	1987	W Bladon	Kenilworth
1965	P Skerritt	Sutton Coldfield	1988	TM Allen	Sutton Coldfield
1966	RG Hiatt	Olton	1989	J Cook	Moor Hall
1967	CC Back	Handsworth	1990	J Cook	Edgbaston
1968	JM Lower	Copt Heath			

Warwickshire Open Championship

YEAR	WINNER	VENUE	YEAR	WINNER	VENUE
1946	GA Maisey	Olton	1965	PJ Butler	Ladbrook Park
1947	GA Maisey	Robin Hood	1966	PJ Butler	Copt Heath
1948	J Hargreaves	Sutton Coldfield	1967	RL Moffitt	Coventry, Finham
1949	JH Cawsey	Ladbrook Park	1968	TM Collinge	Kenilworth
1950	GA Maisey	Pype Hayes	1969	RL Moffitt	Stratford-on-
1951	J Hargreaves	Coventry, Finham			Avon
1952	GA Maisey	Moor Hall	1970	RL Moffitt	Leamington and
1953	GA Maisey	Copt Heath			County
1954	J Hargreaves	Coventry	1971	JM Lower	Coventry
		Hearsall			Hearsall
1955	PJ Butler	Harborne	1972	PJ Weaver	Coventry Finham
1956	J Hargreaves	Stratford-on-	1973	P McEvoy (Am)	Nuneaton
		Avon	1974	P McEvoy (Am)	Leamington and
1957	GR Maisey	Handsworth			County
1958	F Jowle	Leamington	1975	PJ Weaver	Harborne
1959	PJ Butler	Sutton Coldfield	1976	PJ Weaver	Robin Hood
1960	F Jowle	Kenilworth	1977	N Selwyn-Smith	Walmley
1961	PJ Butler	Edgbaston	1978	J Higgins	Nuneaton
1962	PJ Butler	Coventry, Finham	1979	R Livingston	Leamington and
1963	PJ Butler	Olton			County
1964	PJ Butler	Coventry	1980	D Steele	Edgbaston
		Hearsall	1981	TM Allen (Am)	Coventry, Finham

YEAR	WINNER	VENUE	YEAR	WINNER	VENUE
1982	TM Allen (Am) PM Downes (Am) } tie	Harborne	1986	PJ Weaver	The Belfry
			1987	PJ Weaver	Edgbaston
1983	PJ Weaver	Nuneaton	1988	TM Allen (Am)	Moor Hall
1984	P Broadhurst	Olton	1989	TM Allen (Am)	Kenilworth
1985	J Gould	Forest of Arden	1990	M Biddle (Am)	Harborne

Wiltshire Amateur Championship

INAUGURATED 1924

YEAR	WINNER	VENUE	YEAR	WINNER	VENUE
1924	LJ Fairchild	Warminster	1959	DL Pugsley	Salisbury and South Wilts
1925	LJ Fairchild	Warminster			
1926	LJ Fairchild	Salisbury and South Wilts	1960	Major RG Kelley	Swindon
			1961	DL Pugsley	Swindon
1927	AS Hoare	Warminster	1962	PE Edgington	Warminster
1928	NG Holt	Salisbury and South Wilts	1963	PE Edgington	Tidworth
			1964	RB Robertson	Salisbury and South Wilts
1929	NG Holt	Warminster			
1930	Rev KG Hoare	Tidworth	1965	PE Edgington	High Post
1931	AT Warren	Salisbury	1966	SML Morgan	Swindon
1932	EWC Lonnen	Warminster	1967	PE Edgington	Warminster
1933	AJ Combes	High Post	1968	RE Searle	Tidworth
1934	LW Toomber	Swindon	1969	RE Searle	Salisbury and South Wilts
1935	JG Anderson	High Post			
1936	EI Hobden	High Post	1970	RB Robertson	High Post
1937	LF Webb	Swindon	1971	RE Searle	Swindon
1938	EI Hobden	Salisbury and South Wilts	1972	MR Lovett	Warminster
			1973	BF McCallum	Kingsdown
1939	RP Bowie Jr	Warminster	1974	BM Townsend	Tidworth
1940–45	*Not played due to Second World War*				
1946	RP Bowie	High Post	1975	RE Searle	Salisbury and South Wilts
1947	RP Bowie CF Macpherson } tie	Ogbourne			
			1976	BM Townsend	Swindon
1948	DL Pugsley	Warminster	1977	BM Townsend	High Post
1949	EI Hobden	Salisbury and South Wilts	1978	RE Searle	North Wilts
			1979	KA Clark	Chippenham
1950	Major R Davenport	High Post	1980	RE Searle	Marlborough
1951	MC Swift	Swindon	1981	JN Fleming	Swindon
1952	AS Mayer	Warminster	1982	BF McCallum	North Wilts
1953	AS Mayer	Tidworth	1983	D Kingsman	Chippenham
1954	DL Pugsley	Salisbury and South Wilts	1984	DC Garfoot	Tidworth
			1985	S Amor	Warminster
			1986	G Clough	Swindon
1955	DL Pugsley MC Swift } tie	High Post	1987	RE Searle	High Post
			1988	G Clough	Salisbury and South Wilts
1956	H Watson	Swindon			
1957	AS Mayer	Warminster	1989	A Burch	Broome Manor
1958	EN Davis	Tidworth	1990	NM Williams	Marlborough

Wiltshire Match Play Championship

INAUGURATED 1972

YEAR	WINNER	VENUE	YEAR	WINNER	VENUE
1972	WG Ellis	Swindon	1982	A Cook	High Post
1973	BM Townsend	Salisbury and	1983	RE Searle	Kingsdown
		South Wilts	1984	BF McCallum	Swindon
1974	BM Townsend	Warminster	1985	DC Garfoot	North Wilts
1975	MR Lovett	Tidworth	1986	RE Searle	Broome Manor
1976	RE Searle	Kingsdown	1987	G Clough	Tidworth
1977	G Stewart	North Wilts	1988	NM Williams	Warminster
1978	J Rowell	Chippenham	1989	JWG Tomlinson	Salisbury and
1979	BM Townsend	Marlborough			South Wilts
1980	JN Fleming	Kingsdown	1990	NJ Tait	Chippenham
1981	RE Searle	Swindon			

Worcestershire Amateur Championship

INAUGURATED 1906

YEAR	WINNER	VENUE	YEAR	WINNER	VENUE
1906	JM Challinor	The Worcestershire	1932	JT Mitchley	Brand Hall
1907	FA Woolley	King's Norton	1933	JR Fraser	The Worcestershire
1908	FA Woolley	The Worcestershire	1934	Dr GH Marshall	Blackwell
1909	GM Archdale	Worcester	1935	JT Mitchley	North
1910	F Gordon Smith	Stourbridge			Worcestershire
1911	FA Woolley	Moseley	1936	S Lunt	Moseley
1912	FA Woolley	King's Norton	1937	Dr WM Robb	King's Norton
1913	JP Humphries	The Worcestershire	1938	Dr W Tweddell	Stourbridge
1914	FA Woolley	North	1939	Dr W Anderson	Kidderminster
		Worcestershire	1940–45	*Not played due to Second World War*	
1915–19	*Not played due to Great War*		1946	Dr WM Robb	Stourbridge
1920	RP Humphries	Moseley	1947	HJ Roberts	Halesowen
1921	SC Craven	Stourbridge	1948	SL Elliott	Blackwell
1922	RP Humphries	King's Norton	1949	Dr WM Robb	Stourbridge
1923	CJ Reece	Brand Hall	1950	EW Fiddian	Worcester
1924	E Somers Smith	The Worcestershire	1951	JS Mitchley	Kidderminster
1925	S Lunt	Blackwell	1952	NA Seers	King's Norton
1926	GNP Humphries	North	1953	JR Butterworth	Stourbridge
		Worcestershire	1954	JR Butterworth	Moseley
1927	ST Matthews	Moseley	1955	JR Butterworth	Blackwell
1928	EW Fiddian	King's Norton	1956	FL Wilkinson	Fulford Heath
1929	Dr W Tweddell	Kidderminster	1957	HJ Roberts	North
1930	EW Fiddian	Stourbridge			Worcestershire
1931	Dr W Tweddell	Boughton Park	1958	HJ Roberts	Stourbridge

YEAR	WINNER	VENUE	YEAR	WINNER	VENUE
1959	HJ Roberts	Worcester	1975	D Turner	North
1960	RW Sandilands	King's Norton			Worcestershire
1961	RA Jowle	Blackwell	1976	R Hobbis	Stourbridge
1962	JR Butterworth	Moseley	1977	SJ Pimley	Blackwell
1963	HJ Roberts	Stourbridge	1978	M Curry	King's Norton
1964	R Hobbis	Kidderminster	1979	PD Kelley	The Worcestershire
1965	PD Kelley	Worcester	1980	PR Swinburne	Fulford Heath
1966	A Forrester	King's Norton	1981	MC Reynard	Moseley
1967	MWL Hampton	North	1982	DJ Eddiford	Droitwich
		Worcestershire	1983	TR Shingler	Redditch
1968	A Thomson	Blackwell	1984	T Martin	Gay Hill
1969	A Forester	Moseley	1985	SJ Pimley	North
1970	J Toddington	King's Norton			Worcestershire
1971	J Toddington	Stourbridge	1986	DJ Eddiford	Kidderminster
1972	TR Shingler	Gay Hill	1987	D Prosser	Worcester
1973	TR Shingler	Kidderminster	1988	D Prosser	Stourbridge
1974	R Langridge	Worcester	1989	S Braithwaite	The Worcestershire
			1990	DJ Eddiford	Moseley

Worcestershire Match Play Championship
(Derek Grey Cup)

YEAR	WINNER	VENUE	YEAR	WINNER	VENUE
1975	TR Shingler	Blackwell	1984	MC Reynard	Stourbridge
1976	TR Shingler	Kidderminster	1985	NR Hunter	North
1977	SJ Pimley	Redditch			Worcestershire
1978	WR Painter	Gay Hill	1986	PA Adams	Kings Norton
1979	TR Shingler	Worcestershire	1987	CK Norman	Gay Hill
1980	MC Reynard	Fulford Heath	1988	J Bickerton	Blackwell
1981	RA Jowle	Moseley	1989	M Daw	Halesowen
1982	DJ Eddiford	Droitwich	1990	J Bickerton	Droitwich
1983	CK Norman	Redditch			

Worcestershire Open Championship

YEAR	WINNER	VENUE	YEAR	WINNER	VENUE
1949	JS Mitchley (Am)	Blackwell	1971	PD Kelley (Am)	Blackwell
1950	WR Firkins	Stourbridge	1972	K Bayliss	Stourbridge
1951	Dr WM Robb (Am)	Worcester	1973	H Macdonald	North
1952	FE Miller	Moseley			Worcestershire
1953	FE Miller	Blackwell	1974	TR Shingler (Am)	King's Norton
1954	FE Miller	Stourbridge	1975	I Richardson	Kidderminster
1955	HJ Roberts (Am)	Worcester	1976	R Hobbis (Am)	Stourbridge
1956	HJ Roberts (Am)	Kidderminster	1977	SJ Carpenter (Am)	North
1957	GF Reynolds	King's Norton			Worcestershire
1958	FE Miller	Moseley	1978	RA Jowle (Am)	Moseley
1959	SS Seymour (Am)	Blackwell	1979	I Richardson	The Worcestershire
1960	WH Firkins	Stourbridge	1980	RA Jowle (Am)	Redditch
1961	RA Jowle (Am)	Kidderminster	1981	W Firkins	North
1962	HJ Roberts Am)	Worcester			Worcestershire
1963	FE Miller	North	1982	MC Reynard (Am)	Worcester
		Worcestershire	1983	AJ Hill	Fulford Heath
1964	FE Miller	King's Norton	1984	KA Hayward	King's Norton
1965	JE Wiggett	Moseley	1985	DJ Eddiford (Am)	Droitwich
1966	JE Wiggett	Blackwell	1986	WR Painter (Am)	Blackwell
1967	FE Miller	Stourbridge	1987	KA Hayward	Stourbridge
1968	PD Kelley (Am)	Kidderminster	1988	DJ Eddiford (Am)	Moseley
1969	H Macdonald	Worcester	1989	KA Hayward	Kidderminster
1970	TR Shingler (Am)	Moseley	1990	J Bickerton	The Worcestershire

Yorkshire Amateur Championship

INAUGURATED 1894

YEAR	WINNER	VENUE	YEAR	WINNER	VENUE
1894	FE Woodhead	Huddersfield	1915–18	*Not played due to Great War*	
1895	FE Woodhead	Ganton	1919	DM Smith	Starbeck,
1896	GH Peacock	Redcar			Harrogate
1897	HB McCarthy	Lindrick	1920	C Hodgson	Lindrick
1898	FE Woodhead	Huddersfield	1921	B Wragg	Huddersfield
1899	FE Woodhead	Ganton	1922	C Hodgson	Ganton
1900	EA Lassen	Redcar	1923	WC Macfarlane	Starbeck,
1901	HB McCarthy	Lindrick			Harrogate
1902	WP Wightman	Huddersfield	1924	B Wragg	Lindrick
1903	HD Gaunt	Ganton	1925	J Robinson	Ganton
1904	HH Barker	Lindrick	1926	NW Dunn	Moortown
1905	JS Roddam	Redcar	1927	J Robinson	Huddersfield
1906	HH Barker	Huddersfield	1928	J Robinson	Lindrick
1907	C Hodgson	Bradford	1929	JE Gent	Ganton
1908	EA Lassen	Sandygate	1930	J Robinson	Moortown
1909	EA Lassen	Ganton	1931	A Fell	Kirk Ella, Hull
1910	L Butler Smith	Lindrick	1932	TJ Thirsk	Lindrick
1911	HD Gaunt	Redcar	1933	G Marwood	Redcar
1912	JL Crowther	Huddersfield	1934	J Robinson	Ganton
1913	EA Lassen	Ganton	1935	AT Kyle	Huddersfield
1914	EA Lassen	Redcar	1936	AT Kyle	Redcar

YEAR	WINNER	VENUE	YEAR	WINNER	VENUE
1937	JE Gent	Lindrick	1967	R Foster	Moortown
1938	JE Gent	Ganton	1968	LP Tupling	Lindrick
1939	SE Banks	Moortown	1969	M Kelley	Pannal
1940–45	*Not played due to Second World War*		1970	R Foster	Ganton
1946	WV Hembry	Ganton	1971	M Lee	Huddersfield
1947	JE Gent	Huddersfield	1972	M Holliday	Alwoodley
1948	Dr JR Acfield	Sand Moor	1973	H Clark	Ganton
1949	M Lee	Lindrick	1974	M Kelley	Moortown
1950	M Lee	Ganton	1975	R Mitchell	Lindrick
1951	R Arend	Moortown	1976	GJ Brand	Ganton
1952	M Lee	Huddersfield	1977	MJ Mackenzie	Huddersfield
1953	A Turner	Ganton	1978	P Carrigill	Alwoodley
1954	DF Livingston	Lindrick	1979	KJ Miller	Ganton
1955	SJ Brough	Moortown	1980	MJ Mackenzie	Lindrick
1956	M Lee	Ganton	1981	M Kelley	Moortown
1957	SJ Brough	Fulford	1982	S East	Fulford
1958	SJ Brough	Ganton	1983	JL Paxton	Huddersfield
1959	SJ Brough	Moortown	1984	J Whiteley	Ganton
1960	G Ash	Ganton	1985	G Field	Alwoodley
1961	B Meldrum	Lindrick	1986	AR Gelsthorpe	Hull
1962	J Greenwood	Huddersfield	1987	RM Roper	Cleveland
1963	R Foster	Ganton	1988	S Field	Pannal
1964	R Foster	Ilkley	1989	G Harland	Ganton
1965	R Foster	Alwoodley	1990	PI Wood	Moortown
1966	C Bland	Ganton			

Yorkshire Amateur Stroke Play Championship

INAUGURATED 1986

YEAR	WINNER	VENUE
1986	P Hall	Bradford
1987	P Hall }tie RM Roper	Fulford
1988	CG Rawson	Moor Allerton
1989	S East	Alwoodley
1990	L Walker	Cleveland

Yorkshire Open Championship

INAUGURATED 1927

YEAR	WINNER	VENUE	YEAR	WINNER	VENUE
1927	JW Gaudin	Ganton	1955	SJ Brough (Am)	Sand Moor and
1928	S Wingate	Wakefield			Moortown
1929	H Crapper	Kirk Ella, Hull	1956	W Lees	Sand Moor and
1930	*No competition due to bad weather*				Moortown
1931	O Sanderson	Huddersfield	1957	E Large	Sand Moor and
1932	A Dailey	Sand Moor			Moortown
1933	A Dailey	Halifax	1958	J Fallon	Sand Moor and
1934	JJ Busson	Sand Moor and			Moortown
		Moortown	1959	G Weston	Sand Moor and
1935	A Lees	Abbeydale			Moortown
1936	Percy Alliss	Halifax	1960	B Hutchinson	Sand Moor and
1937	Percy Alliss	Sand Moor and			Moortown
		Moortown	1961	CE Hughes	Huddersfield
1938	H Crapper	Abbeydale	1962	B Hutchinson	Ganton
1939	A Lees	Moortown	1963	B Hutchinson	Abbeydale
1940–45	*Not played due to Second World War*		1964	B Hutchinson	Fulford
1946	A Lees	Sand Moor and	1965	HW Muscroft	Sand Moor
		Moortown	1966	BJ Waites	Kirk Ella, Hull
1947	J Fallon	Sand Moor and	1967	HW Muscroft	Hallamshire
		Moortown	1968	L Platts	Pannal
1948	JD Henderson	Sand Moor and	1969	M Kelley (Am)	Moor Allerton
		Moortown	1970	S Evans	Bradford
1949	F Jowle	Sand Moor and	1971	GA Caygill	Abbeydale
		Moortown	1972	B Hutchinson	Fulford
1950	J Shanks	Sand Moor and	1973	R Emery	Ilkley
		Moortown	1974	N Melvin	Sand Moor
1951	J Fallon	Sand Moor and	1975	M Kelley (Am)	Hull
		Moortown	1976	R Hardcastle	Cleveland
1952	J Wade	Sand Moor and	1977	RS Mitchell (Am)	Scarcroft
		Moortown	1978	M Ingham	Rotherham
1953	B Shelton	Sand Moor and	1979	A Bickerdike	Halifax
		Moortown	1980	D Jagger	Ilkley
1954	J Fallon	Sand Moor and	1981	D Jagger	Abbeydale
		Moortown	*Discontinued*		

Scotland

Angus Amateur Championship

YEAR	WINNER
1988	D Downie
1989	T Peebles
1990	D Leith

Argyll and Bute Amateur Championship

YEAR	WINNER	VENUE	YEAR	WINNER	VENUE
1979	AF Gallacher	Rothesay	1985	G Reynolds	Rothesay
1980	GJ Tyre	Cowal	1986	GJ Tyre	Cowal
1981	M Cannon	Machrihanish	1987	S Campbell	Machrihanish
1982	J Ewing	Rothesay	1988	G Bolton	Rothesay
1983	GJ Tyre	Cowal	1989	GJ Tyre	Cowal
1984	D McIntyre	Machrihanish	1990	G Reynolds	Cowal

Ayrshire Amateur Championship

YEAR	WINNER	VENUE	YEAR	WINNER	VENUE
1950	A Stevenson	Ayr Belleisle	1965	CJL Strachan	Bogside
1951	HC Maclaine	Barassie	1966	JH Morrison	Ayr Belleisle
1952	J Armour	Troon	1967	M Lygate	Troon
1953	JM Cannon	Bogside	1968	WR Lockie	Troon Darley
1954	JR McKay	Turnberry	1969	A Cruickshanks	Caprington
1955	M Alexander	Prestwick St Nicholas	1970	JM Cannon	Ayr Belleisle
			1971	JT Moffat	West Kilbride
1956	JR McKay } tie J Walker	Ayr Belleisle	1972	AMB Sym	Prestwick
			1973	JM Cannon	Barassie
1957	JH Morrison	Troon Lochgreen	1974	M Rae	Prestwick St Nicholas
1958	JM Cannon	Irvine			
1959	JH Morrison	Largs	1975	L Crawford	Bogside
1960	A MacGregor	Ayr Belleisle	1976	JT Moffat	Barassie
1961	JH Morrison	West Kilbride	1977	B Stevely	Prestwick
1962	RR Davidson	Ayr Belleisle	1978	A Thomson	Loudoun
1963	S Anderson	Troon Lochgreen	1979	JT Moffat	Prestwick St Nicholas
1964	D Murdoch	Bogside			

YEAR	WINNER	VENUE	YEAR	WINNER	VENUE
1980	J Bunting	Ballochmyle	1986	G Armstrong	
1981	D Murdoch	Barassie	1987	B Gemmell	
1982	C Evans		1988	G Blair	
1983	L Crawford		1989	D Hawthorn	
1984	J Milligan		1990	RL Crawford	
1985	P Girvan				

Border Golfers' Association Amateur Championship

INAUGURATED 1893

YEAR	WINNER	VENUE	YEAR	WINNER	VENUE
1893	TDC Smith	Kelso and Selkirk	1920	HM Duncan	Kelso and Ladhope
1894	C Todd	Innerleithen and Hawick	1921	WR Welsh	Melrose and Innerleithen
1895	A Robertson	Melrose and Peebles	1922	CS Rennie	Jedburgh and Peebles
1896	J Hardie	Jedburgh and Selkirk	1923	W Burnet	Torwoodlee and Hawick
1897	W Rutherford	Kelso and Hawick	1924	CJ Anderson	Kelso and Selkirk
1898	HL Purdom	Innerleithen and Torwoodlee	1925	W Burnet	Melrose and Galashiels
1899	W Rutherford	Melrose and Peebles	1926	W Burnet	Innerleithen and Jedburgh
1900	W Rutherford	Jedburgh and Selkirk	1927	R Thomson	Torwoodlee and Peebles
1901	J Barrie	Hawick and Goswick	1928	WR Welsh	St Boswells and Hawick
1902	GP Ross	Innerleithen and Torwoodlee	1929	AT Kyle	Kelso and Selkirk
1903	J Barrie	Kelso and West Linton	1930	AT Kyle	Melrose and Galashiels
1904	HM Duncan	Jedburgh and Hawick	1931	TT Sanderson	Jedburgh and Peebles
1905	T Ballantyne	Torwoodlee and Innerleithen	1932	TT Sanderson	Torwoodlee and Hawick
1906	HM Duncan	St Boswells and Melrose	1933	TT Sanderson	Selkirk and Galashiels
1907	HM Duncan	Kelso and West Linton	1934	AT Cleghorn	Melrose and Kelso
1908	T Ballantyne	Selkirk and Peebles	1935	JC Conn	Torwoodlee
1909	HM Duncan	Jedburgh and Torwoodlee	1936	TT Sanderson	Selkirk
1910	HM Duncan	Innerleithen and Hawick	1937	JA Brown	Peebles
			1938	JA Brown	Hawick
1911	A Elder	Kelso and Melrose	1939	JW Gladstone	Ladhope
1912	RJ Inglis	Selkirk and Peebles	1940–46	*Not played due to Second World War*	
1913	HM Duncan	Jedburgh and Torwoodlee	1947	TT Sanderson	Peebles
1914 – 19	*Not played due to Great War*		1948	TA Fairbairn	Hawick
			1949	WD Smith	Torwoodlee
			1950	TW Fraser	Peebles
			1951	WD Smith	Hawick
			1952	WW Cowe	Galashiels

YEAR	WINNER	VENUE	YEAR	WINNER	VENUE
1953	R Livingstone	Torwoodlee	1973	K Allan	Peebles
1954	WW Cowe	Peebles	1974	JK Wells	Galashiels
1955	CW Telfer	Hawick	1975	MD Cleghorn	Torwoodlee
1956	CW Telfer	Torwoodlee	1976	DF Campbell	Melrose and
1957	WD Smith	Selkirk			Selkirk
1958	TT Sanderson	Peebles	1977	J Hume	Hawick
1959	JA Brown	Hawick	1978	PWJ Gallagher	Kelso
1960	TT Sanderson	Ladhope	1979	PWJ Gallagher	Peebles
1961	I Turnbull	Kelso	1980	PWJ Gallagher	Melrose
1962	TT Sanderson	Torwoodlee	1981	PWJ Gallagher	Galashiels
1963	WD Smith	Selkirk	1982	DF Campbell	
1964	TT Sanderson	Ladhope	1983	B Reid	
1965	JF Thomas	Torwoodlee	1984	A Turnbull	
1966	JK Wells	Peebles	1985	L Wallace	
1967	R McAllan	Hawick	1986	L Wallace	
1968	JF Thomas	Kelso	1987	D Ballantyne	
1969	JK Wells	Selkirk	1988	W Renwick	
1970	JK Wells	Ladhope	1989	A Turnbull	
1971	WD Simpson	Peebles	1990	MG Thomson	
1972	AR Potts	Hawick			

Clackmannanshire Amateur Championship

YEAR	WINNER
1988	R Stewart
1989	J Gullen
1990	P Macleod

Dumbartonshire Amateur Championship

YEAR	WINNER	VENUE	YEAR	WINNER	VENUE
1949	Dr FWG Deighton		1957	RI Ross	Lenzie
1950	Dr FWG Deighton	Hilton Park	1958	MN Ferguson	Douglas Park
1951	JG Campbell	Cardross	1959	MN Ferguson	Balmore
1952	D Cameron	Milngavie	1960	CW Green	Hilton Park
1953	Dr FWG Deighton	Hayston	1961	J Wallace	Cardross
1954	Dr FWG Deighton	Clydebank	1962	GD Gray	Milngavie
1955	J Wallace	Kirkintilloch	1963	AH Hill	Hayston
1956	J Munro	Helensburgh	1964	AM Grant	Clydebank

YEAR	WINNER	VENUE	YEAR	WINNER	VENUE
1965	RM Douglas	Helensburgh	1978	L Hulme	Douglas Park
1966	DC Penman	Lenzie	1979	DG Carrick	Dougalston
1967	CW Green	Douglas Park	1980	DG Carrick	Windyhill
1968	CW Green	Cardross	1981	J Graham	Hilton Park
1969	JS Cochrane	Milngavie	1982	DG Carrick	Milngavie
1970	D Black	Hilton Park	1983	DG Carrick	Cardross
1971	CJ Smith	Windyhill	1984	T Eckford	Douglas Park
1972	JMJ McMahon	Cardross	1985	SR Miller	Windyhill
1973	CW Green	Douglas Park	1986	DG Carrick	Cardross
1974	D Weir	Helensburgh	1987	D Shaw	Dullatur
1975	Allan Brodie	Hilton Park	1988	J Laird	Dumbarton
1976	Allan Brodie	Milngavie	1989	D Shaw	Milngavie
1977	CW Green	Cardross	1990	JL Kinloch	Helensburgh

Dumbartonshire Amateur Match Play Championship
at Hayston

YEAR	WINNER	YEAR	WINNER
1980	KW Macintosh	1986	WG Thom
1981	GF Jack	1987	Allan Brodie
1982	C White	1988	R Blair
1983	G Millar	1989	CD Stewart
1984	RG Fraser	1990	D Shaw
1985	DG Carrick		

East of Scotland Open Amateur Stroke Play Championship
at Lundin Links

YEAR	WINNER	YEAR	WINNER
1974	S Stephen	1983	S Stephen
1975	AK Pirie	1984	S Stephen
1976	S Martin	1985	A McQueen
1977	S Stephen	1986	S Knowles
1978	GK MacDonald	1987	T Cochrane
1979	G Macgregor	1988	C Everett
1980	D Greig	1989	K Hird
1981	K Gray	1990	G Lawrie
1982	G Macgregor		

Fife Amateur Championship

INAUGURATED 1925

YEAR	WINNER	VENUE	YEAR	WINNER	VENUE
1925	JN Smith	Kinghorn	1961	A Cunningham	Leven
1926	W Murray	Leven	1962	W Moyes	Scotscraig
1927	W Ogg	North Queensferry	1963	W Moyes	Leven
1928	D Scott	St Andrews	1964	I Clark	Ladybank
1929	JN Smith	Lundin Links	1965	A Drysdale	Dunfermline
1930	GE Hutton	Kinghorn	1966	WMO Petrie	Scotscraig
1931	EA McRuvie	Leven	1967	AN Wilson	Pitreavie
1932	CL Muir	Burntisland	1968	GT Russell	Lundin Links
1933	EA McRuvie	St Andrews	1969	J Farmer	Dunnikier Park
1934	JEG Ballingall	Dunfermline	1970	G Milne	Scotscraig
1935	DM Stewart	Elie	1971	GT Russell	Dunfermline
1936	JN Smith	Lundin Links	1972	WA Thomson	Burntisland
1937	W Murray	Leven	1973	S Stephen	Leven
1938	JH Mathieson	Burntisland	1974	TE Melville	Pitreavie
1939	A Dowie	St Andrews New	1975	JA McIntyre	Ladybank
1940–46	Not played due to Second World War		1976	TM Cochrane	Dunnikier Park
1947	R Easson	St Andrews Eden	1977	ST Reith	Scotscraig
1948	HG Rodger	Leven	1978	TM Cochrane	Dunfermline
1949	D Foulis	Burntisland	1979	DJ Gray	Elie
1950	A Dowie	St Andrews	1980	JW Noble	Kirkcaldy
1951	WRM Foulis	Dunfermline	1981	D Ross	Lundin Links
1952	GW Low	Scotscraig	1982	DR Weir	Burntisland
1953	A Dowie	Leven	1983	DM Lawrie	St Andrews
1954	JT Pearson	Burntisland	1984	C Birrell	Dunnikier Park
1955	I Reid	Crail	1985	DR Weir	Thornton
1956	AS Melville	Lundin Links	1986	D Spriddle	Crail
1957	G Will	Pitreavie	1987	SR Meiklejohn	Aberdour
1958	JF Ferguson	Scotscraig	1988	A Mathers	Kinghorn
1959	J Clark	Lundin Links	1989	D Spriddle	Canmore
1960	A Reid	Burntisland	1990	D Spriddle	Dunnikier Park

Glasgow Open Amateur Championship

INAUGURATED 1897

at Pollok

YEAR	WINNER	YEAR	WINNER
1897	JG Macfarlane	1907	R Scott Jr
1898	CB Macfarlane	1908	A Buchanan
1899	A Reid	1909	D Bone
1900	D Bone	1910	R Scott Jr
1901	G Fox	1911	HE Higgins
1902	CB Macfarlane	1912	JH Irons
1903	CB Macfarlane	1913	R Scott Jr
1904	WH Thomson	1914–18 Not played due to Great War	
1905	R Bone	1919	R Scott Jr
1906	R Bone	1920	WP Nairn

YEAR	WINNER	YEAR	WINNER
1921	J Crerar	1959	WS Jack
1922	J Smith	1960	SWT Murray
1923	RM White	1961	A Sinclair
1924	J Brodie	1962	AD Gray
1925	A Jamieson Jr	1963	WS Jack
1926	W Campbell	1964	CJL Strachan
1927	JA Lang	1965	JE Stuart
1928	W Campbell	1966	AH Hall
1929	W Tulloch	1967	EW Hammond
1930	JA Lang	1968	JS Cochran
1931	J McLean	1969	GB Cosh
1932	W Campbell	1970	EW Hammond
1933	J McLean	1971	J McTear
1934	GB Peters	1972	Andrew Brodie
1935	H Thomson	1973	K MacIntosh
1936	SL McKinlay	1974	I Gillan
1937	JC More	1975	EW Hammond
1938	SL McKinlay	1976	I Gillan
1939	D Cameron	1977	JT Moffat
1940–46	*Not played due to Second World War*	1978	IA Carslaw
1947	ED Hamilton	1979	CW Green
1948	WS McLeod	1980	DG Carrick
1949	D Cameron	1981	DG Carrick
1950	SL McKinlay	1982	B Pearson
1951	Dr FWG Deighton	1983	B Pearson
1952	D Cameron	1984	IA Carslaw
1953	RR Jack	1985	S Savage
1954	RR Jack	1986	G Shaw
1955	Dr FWG Deighton	1987	S Dixon
1956	MN Ferguson	1988	J Finnigan
1957	JE Stuart	1989	J McLaughlin
1958	RR Jack	1990	C Barrowman

Glasgow Stroke Play Championship

YEAR	WINNER	VENUE	YEAR	WINNER	VENUE
1955	WS Jack	Sandyhills	1973	S Barclay	Cathcart Castle
1956	ED Hamilton	Cathkin Braes	1974	GB Cosh	Cowglen
1957	JR Cater	Haggs Castle	1975	D McCart	Haggs Castle
1958	WS Jack	Williamwood	1976	D McCart	Cathkin Braes
1959	JR Young	Cathcart Castle	1977	M Miller	Bishopbriggs
1960	W Norris	Cowglen	1978	M Miller	Cathcart Castle
1961	WS Jack	Bishopbriggs	1979	J Cubbage	
1962	A Cribbes	Cawder	1980	WC Black	
1963	RL Renfrew	Ralston	1981	BA Pearson	
1964	WC Black	Sandyhills	1982	R Gregan	
1965	JW Campbell	Cathkin Braes	1983	IA Carslaw	
1966	JW Campbell	Haggs Castle	1984	IA Carslaw	
1967	JR Young	Williamwood	1985	IA Carslaw	
1968	EW Hammond		1986	A Maclaine	
1969	G Hewitt	Bishopbriggs	1987	S Machin	
1970	EW Hammond	Cawder	1988	D Martin	
1971	WC Black	Sandyhills	1989	G Shaw	
1972	GB Cosh	Haggs Castle	1990	H Kemp	

Lanarkshire Amateur Championship

YEAR	WINNER	VENUE	YEAR	WINNER	VENUE
1950	G Parker	Hamilton	1971	J McTear	East Kilbride
1951	JS Montgomerie	Lanark	1972	W Smeaton	Hamilton
1952	A Sinclair Jr	Easter Moffat	1973	DC Longmuir	Easter Moffat
1953	GR Morgan	Drumpellier	1974	DC Longmuir	Strathaven
1954	JS Montgomerie	Hamilton	1975	EAE Quinn	Crow Wood
1955	JW Gardner	Easter Moffat	1976	J Johnston	Colville Park
1956	I Young	Lanark	1977	W Paterson	Airdrie
1957	RJ Jameson	Colville Park	1978	H Milligan	Lanark
1958	DA Walkinshaw	Bothwell Castle	1979	R Smith	Drumpellier
1959	A Sinclair	Airdrie	1980	H Miller	Bellshill
1960	JF Milligan	Crow Wood	1981	G Banks	Carluke
1961	A Sinclair	Drumpellier	1982	G Jones	Hamilton
1962	J Abernethy	Hamilton	1983	R Lynch	Strathaven
1963	AV Baxter	Lanark	1984	WS Bryson	Carnwath
1964	A Neil	Airdrie	1985	J Reid	Lanark
1965	DB Mackie	Easter Moffat	1986	WS Bryson	Torrance House
1966	I Frame	Bothwell Castle	1987	S Henderson	Strathaven
1967	W Redpath	Colville Park	1988	G Jones	Bellshill
1968	J McTear	Crow Wood	1989	JS Taylor	Colville Park
1969	TB Main	Drumpellier	1990	G Shanks	Shotts
1970	J Howieson	Lanark			

Lanarkshire Match Play Championship

YEAR	WINNER	VENUE	YEAR	WINNER	VENUE
1964	JF Milligan	Drumpellier	1978	HS Milligan	Crow Wood
1965	AA McLarty	Bothwell Castle	1979	G Sinclair	Kirkhill
1966	J Nielan	Hamilton	1980	J Simpson	Airdrie
1967	DB Mackie	Crow Wood	1981	R Lynch	Hamilton
1968	J McTear	Cambuslang	1982	K Ross	Bellshill
1969	R McTavish	Bothwell Castle	1983	JS Taylor	Kirkhill
1970	J Thomson	East Kilbride	1984	WS Bryson	Drumpellier
1971	G O'Keane	Airdrie	1985	J Simpson	Airdrie
1972	DC Longmuir	Colville Park	1986	JS Taylor	Hamilton
1973	A Grant	Cambuslang	1987	WS Bryson	Drumpellier
1974	A Orr	Cambuslang	1988	WS Bryson	Airdrie
1975	D Martin	Drumpellier	1989	R Jenkins	Bothwell Castle
1976	G Russo	Bellshill	1990	W Denholm	Colville Park
1977	N Good	Hamilton			

Lothians Amateur Championship

INAUGURATED 1921

YEAR	WINNER	VENUE	YEAR	WINNER	VENUE
1921	WB Torrance	Duddingston	1960	DW Alexander	Murrayfield
1922	WW Mackenzie	Gullane	1961	HC Brownlee	New Luffness
1923	WW Mackenzie	Murrayfield	1962	HM Campbell	Prestonfield
1924	C Mann	Gullane	1963	A Lourie	Barnton
1925	GC Killey	Baberton	1964	RDBM Shade	Dalmahoy
1926	WB Torrance	Gullane	1965	AJ Low	Duddingston
1927	WB Torrance	Barnton	1966	GE Robertson	Bruntsfield
1928	RB Denholm	Royal Musselburgh	1967	B Gallacher	Monktonhall
1929	GC Killey	Duddingston	1968	G McGregor Jr	Dalmahoy
1930	H Watt	Gullane	1969	DF Campbell	Longniddry
1931	JA Lang	Dalmahoy	1970	C McCulloch	Prestonfield
1932	RB Denholm	Luffness	1971	AGG Miller	Duddingston
1933	DC Murray	Longniddry	1972	P Bucher	Longniddry
1934	WGF Scott	Baberton	1973	W Davidson	Dalmahoy
1935	RB Denholm	North Berwick	1974	L Morton	Barnton
1936	GN Tweedale	Barnton	1975	RE Muir	Monktonhall
1937	DS Wemyss	Luffness	1976	N Fisher	Prestonfield
1938	HS Mackersy	Prestonfield	1977	ID Stavert	Bruntsfield
1939–46	*Not played due to Second World War*		1978	S Stephen	Duddingston
1947	AS Flockhart	Murrayfield	1979	CP Christy	Longniddry
1948	RM Lees	Bruntsfield	1980	ST Knowles	Barnton
1949	CM Meek	Baberton	1981	B Dunlop	Musselburgh
1950	I Macniven	Dalmahoy	1982	R Bradley	
1951	AB Taylor	Murrayfield	1983	A Roy	
1952	WCD Hare	Turnhouse	1984	PJ Smith	
1953	WCD Hare	New Luffness	1985	S Easingwood	
1954	S Smith	Barnton	1986	S Smith	
1955	AMM Bucher	Longniddry	1987	D Kirkpatrick	
1956	PR Bryce	Gullane	1988	B Shields	
1957	DW Alexander	Prestonfield	1989	K Hastings	
1958	JR Kyle	Duddingston	1990	S Middleton	
1959	AHH Campbell	Bruntsfield			

Northern Scottish Open Championship

YEAR	WINNER	VENUE	YEAR	WINNER	VENUE
1931	J McDowall	Balgownie	1940–45	*Not played due to Second World War*	
1932	JT Henderson	Nairn	1946	WS Forrester	Murcar
1933	J McLean (Am)	Murcar	1947	JH Ballingall	Peterhead
1934	J Forrester	Inverness	1948	J Panton	Inverness
1935	RS Walker (Am)	Dornoch	1949	JH Ballingall	Balgownie
1936	RS Walker (Am)	Deeside	1950	EC Brown	Lossiemouth
1937	J McLean	Lossiemouth	1951	J Panton	Nairn
1938	TB Haliburton	Peterhead	1952	J Panton	Balgownie
1939	J McLean	Nairn	1953	EC Brown	Cruden Bay

YEAR	WINNER	VENUE	YEAR	WINNER	VENUE
1954	EC Brown	Dornoch	1973	D Huish	Dornoch
1955	EC Brown	Murcar	*From 1974 sponsored by Clydesdale Bank*		
1956	J Panton	Lossiemouth	1974	W Milne	Murcar
1957	EC Brown	Nairn	1975	W Milne	Nairn
1958	G Will	Cruden Bay	1976	D Chillas	Balgownie
1959	J Panton	Peterhead	1977	JE Murray	Dornoch
1960	J Panton	Dornoch	1978	BW Barnes	Elgin
1961	H Weetman	Murcar	1979	JC Farmer	Nairn
1962	J Panton	Lossiemouth	1980	D Huish	Balgownie
1963	G Will	Cruden Bay	1981	A Thomson	Lossiemouth
1964	LR Taylor	Nairn	1982	T Minshall	
1965	JT Brown	Balgownie	1983	D Cooper	
1966	R Liddle	Elgin	1984	D Huish	
1967	H Bannerman	Dornoch	1985	BW Barnes	
1968	DK Webster	Murcar	1986	R Weir	
1969	H Bannerman	Lossiemouth	1987	A Hunter	
1970	AK Price (Am)	Cruden Bay	1988	D Huish	
1971	F Rennie	Nairn	1989	C Brooks	
1972	H Bannerman	Balgownie	1990	C Brooks	

North of Scotland Open Amateur Stroke Play Championship

INAUGURATED 1970

YEAR	WINNER	VENUE	YEAR	WINNER	VENUE
1970	WTG Milne	Nairn	1981	NS Grant	Lossiemouth
1971	RM Grant	Lossiemouth	1982	IC Hutcheon	
1972	S Stephen	Elgin	1983	D Kryzanowski	
1973	BM Nicholson	Nairn	1984	JS Macdonald	
1974	HB Stuart	Elgin	1985	JS Macdonald	
1975	IC Hutcheon	Nairn	1986	S Cruickshank	
1976	IC Hutcheon	Nairn	1987	S McIntosh	
1977	S Stephen	Elgin	1988	KS Hird	
1978	NS Grant	Nairn	1989	GB Hickman	
1979	ID Grant	Nairn	1990	S McIntosh	
1980	BC Milne	Elgin			

Perth and Kinross Amateur Stroke Play Championship

INAUGURATED 1930

YEAR	WINNER	YEAR	WINNER
1946	KT Thomson	1969	DJ Donaldson
1947	J Wilson	1970	DA Steven
1948	RL Haggart	1971	G Simpson
1949	J Wilson	1972	JBT Douglas
1950	JT Smith	1973	W Milne
1951	E Tanser	1974	G Simpson
1952	RL Haggart	1975	CP Christy
1953	TL Jackson	1976	JBT Douglas
1954	E Tanser	1977	BRN Grieve
1955	K Doig	1978	A Munro
1956	AG Robertson	1979	CP Christy
1957	JG Moir	1980	GT Russell
1958	JPG Windsor	1981	AG Campbell
1959	WR Brown	1982	M Niven
1960	KS Thomson	1983	ER Lindsay
1961	WI MacDonald	1984	G Lowson
1962	GR Sinclair	1985	G Lowson
1963	J Freeman	1986	C Bloice
1964	GR Sinclair	1987	BRM Grieve
1965	HC Miller	1988	EJ Lindsay
1966	J Freeman	1989	AG Campbell
1967	DA Steven	1990	G Smith
1968	JL Leith		

Renfrewshire Amateur Championship

INAUGURATED 1950

YEAR	WINNER	VENUE	YEAR	WINNER	VENUE
1950	WS McLeod	Kilmacolm	1965	FC Black	Caldwell
1951	JC Russell	Old Ranfurly	1966	IL Rae	Greenock
1952	J Winning	East Renfrew	1967	FC Black	Old Ranfurly
1953	WA Stewart	Erskine	1968	FC Black	Bonnyton
1954	JC Russell	Ranfurly Castle	1969	FC Black	Ranfurly Castle
1955	AF Russell	Kilmacolm	1970	J Armstrong	Kilmacolm
1956	J Fulton	Paisley	1971	AD Sutherland	Greenock
1957	WB McIntyre	East Renfrewshire	1972	TC Houston	Erskine
1960	LG Taylor	Ranfurly Castle	1973	N Douglas	East Renfrewshire
1961	DD Cameron	Kilmacolm	1974	SG Cairns	Old Ranfurly
1962	J Gardner	Elderslie	1975	JA Jones	Cochrane Castle
1963	DD Cameron	Paisley	1976	I Bell	Fereneze
1964	FC Black	East Renfrewshire	1977	R Blackwood	Elderslie

YEAR	WINNER	VENUE	YEAR	WINNER	VENUE
1978	DB Howard	Caldwell	1985	J McDonald	Ranfurly Castle
1979	R Blackwood	Whitecraigs	1986	IG Riddell	Kilmacolm
1980	N Skinner	Gourock	1987	DB Howard	Paisley
1981	DB Howard	Eastwood	1988	ES Gray	East Renfrewshire
1982	A Hunter	Renfrew	1989	RA Clark	Ranfurly Castle
1983	G Thomson	Cochrane Castle	1990	RA Clark	Greenock
1984	DB Howard	Erskine			

Scottish Area Team Championship

INAUGURATED 1977

YEAR	WINNER	VENUE	YEAR	WINNER	VENUE
1977	North	Lanark	1984	Glasgow	Bruntsfield
1978	Lothians	Duddingston	1985	Lothians	Stranraer
1979	North East	Ladybank	1986	Ayrshire	Murcar
1980	Dunbartonshire	Haggs Castle	1987	Lothians	Glenbervie
1981	Stirlingshire	Alloa	1988	Lothians	Downfield
1982	Renfrewshire	Cardross	1989	Lanarkshire	West Kilbride
1983	Lothians	Lossiemouth	1990	North East	Glasgow Gailes

Scottish Champion of Champions

INAUGURATED 1970

at Leven

YEAR	WINNER	YEAR	WINNER
1970	A Horne	1981	IC Hutcheon
1971	D Black	1982	G Macgregor
1972	RS Strachan	1983	DG Carrick
1973	*Not played*	1984	S Stephen
1974	MM Niven	1985	IR Brotherston
1975	Allan Brodie	1986	IC Hutcheon
1976	Allan Brodie	1987	G Shaw
1977	V Reid	1988	IC Hutcheon
1978	DG Greig	1989	JW Milligan
1979	B Marchbank	1990	JW Milligan
1980	IC Hutcheon		

Scottish Foursomes Tournament – Glasgow Evening Times Trophy

INAUGURATED 1891

YEAR	WINNER	VENUE	YEAR	WINNER	VENUE
1891	Carlton	Prestwick	1933	Lothianburn	Barnton
1892	St Andrews	St Andrews	1934	Ayr Academy	Killermont
1893	Edinburgh Thistle	Troon	1935	Ayr Academy	Lundin Links
1894	St Andrews	Leven	1936	Ayr Academy	Pollok
1895	St Andrews Thistle	Glasgow Gailes	1937	Ayr Academy	Dunbar
1896	Leven Thistle	North Berwick	1938	Western Gailes	Glasgow Gailes
1897	Leven Thistle	Bridge of Weir	1939–45	*Not played due to Second World War*	
1898	Scottish Liberal	Barnton	1946	New Club	
1899	Western	Troon		(St Andrews)	North Berwick
1900	Troon	Elie	1947	Western Gailes	Prestwick
1901	Leven Thistle	Bogside	1948	Melville College	Bruntsfield
1902	Leven Thistle	Musselburgh	1949	Troon Portland	Barassie
1903	Cathcart Castle	Glasgow Gailes	1950	'36 Club	Ayr Belleisle
1904	Edinburgh St		1951	Troon Portland	Barnton
	Matthew's	Gullane	1952	Western Gailes	Killermont
1905	Edinburgh		1953	Irvine	Gullane
	Watsonians	Barassie	1954	Glasgow University	Troon
1906	Prestwick St		1955	Haggs Castle	Longniddry
	Nicholas	Bruntsfield	1956	Prestonfield	Glenbervie
1907	Pollok	Killermont	1957	Falkirk Tryst	Douglas Park
1908	Edinburgh New		1958	Troon St Meddans	Prestwick St
	Alban	Burntisland			Nicholas
1909	Prestwick St	Prestwick St	1959	Cambuslang	Bruntsfield
	Nicholas	Nicholas	1960	Irvine	Gailes
1910	Prestwick St		1961	Falkirk Tryst	Barnton
	Nicholas	Elie	1962	Irvine	Bogside
1911	Prestwick St		1963	Clydebank and	
	Nicholas	Troon Municipal		District	Gullane
1912	Troon Portland	Carnoustie	1964	Scottish Building	
1913	Prestwick St			Contractors	Lanark
	Nicholas	Pollok	1965	Falkirk Tryst	Dunblane
1914–18	*Not played due to Great War*		1966	Bathgate	Erskine
1919	Mortonhall	Lundin Links	1967	Prestonfield	Dalmahoy
1920	Prestwick St		1968	Troon St Meddans	Barassie
	Nicholas	Prestwick	1969	Irvine	Dunbar
1921	Carnoustie	Eden (St Andrews)	1970	Cardross	Cardross
1922	New Club		1971	Airdrie	Longniddry
	(St Andrews)	Glasgow Gailes	1972	Scottish Building	
1923	Gullane Comrades	Gullane		Contractors	West Kilbride
1924	New Club		1973	Glasgow Insurance	Dunblane New
	(St Andrews)	Gleneagles	1974	Baberton	Irvine Bogside
1925	New Club		1975	Prestwick St	
	(St Andrews)	Troon		Cuthbert	Barnton
1926	Pollok	Leven	1976	Wishaw	Hamilton
1927	Erskine	Erskine	1977	Stirlingshire JYS	Baberton
1928	Earlsferry Thistle	Carnoustie	1978	Helensburgh	Prestwick
1929	Pollok	Barassie	1979	Helensburgh	Hamilton
1930	Mortonhall	Lanark	1980	Helensburgh	Dunblane
1931	Royal Burgess	Longniddry	1981	Duddingston	Baberton
1932	Hayston	Ayr Belleisle	1982	Haggs Castle	West Kilbride

YEAR	WINNER	VENUE	YEAR	WINNER	VENUE
1983	Haggs Castle	Hamilton	1987	Drumpellier	Drumpellier
1984	Royal Musselburgh	Baberton	1988	Irvine Ravenspark	Baberton
1985	East Renfrewshire	Drumpellier	1989	Cochrane Leith	Dunblane New
1986	Hamilton	Hamilton	1990	Dunblane, New	Prestwick

South-East District Open Championship

YEAR	WINNER	VENUE
1987	SR Easingwood	Mortonhall
1988	SR Easingwood	Dunbar
1989	C Cassells	Mortonhall
1990	S Knowles	Mortonhall

South of Scotland Championship

INAUGURATED 1905

YEAR	WINNER	VENUE	YEAR	WINNER	VENUE
1932	JG Carver	Portpatrick	1961	RB Anderson	Stranraer
1933	TB Manson	Moffat	1963	RB Anderson	Powfoot
1934	TB Manson	Dumfries and County	1965	R Murray	Southerness
			1966	R Smith	Powfoot
1935	R Murray	Stranraer	1967	E Shamash	Creachmore
1936	TB Manson	Powfoot	1968	E Shamash	Powfoot
1937	JH Hill	Dumfries and Galloway	1969	E Shamash	Southerness
			1970	J Miller	Creachmore
1938	RH Stevenson	Portpatrick	1971	W Jackson	Powfoot
1939	S Hastings	Moffat	1972	R Nairn	Southerness
1940–46	*Not played due to Second World War*		1973	D MacRae	Powfoot
1947	JG Carver	Portpatrick	1974	W Jackson	Southerness
1948	R Murray	Southerness	1975	B Wilson	Stranraer
1949	RB Anderson	Southerness	1976	I Brotherston	Powfoot
1950	R Murray	Dumfries and County	1977	D Ireland	Southerness
			1978	I Brotherston	Stranraer
1951	S Hastings	Portpatrick	1979	I Brotherston	Powfoot
1952	A Hall	Dumfries and Galloway	1980	A Clark	Southerness
			1981	D James	Stranraer
1953	MH Forrest	Stranraer	1982	I Brotherston	Powfoot
1954	D Maxwell	Powfoot	1983	I Brotherston	Southerness
1955	D Maxwell	Southerness	1984	D Ireland	Stranraer
1956	Dr JB Cochran	Moffat	1985	I Brotherston	Powfoot
1957	RB Anderson	Dumfries and County	1986	I Semple	Southerness
			1987	I Brotherston	Stranraer
1958	MC Douglas	Stranraer	1988	A Coltart	Southerness
1959	MC Douglas	Dumfries and Galloway	1989	V Reid	Powfoot
			1990	B Kerr	Stranraer
1960	MC Douglas	Powfoot			

Stirlingshire Amateur Championship

YEAR	WINNER	VENUE	YEAR	WINNER	VENUE
1936	KG Patrick	Stirling	1967	EC Gibson	Falkirk
1937	JNK Clarkson	Grangemouth	1968	AJ Macnaught	Dunblane
1938	J Lindsay	Falkirk	1969	R Thomas	Falkirk Tryst
1939	J Lindsay	Stirling	1970	HM Campbell	Buchanan Castle
1940–46	*Not played due to Second World War*		1971	HM Campbell	Glenbervie
1947	KG Patrick	Glenbervie	1972	WJ Dalling	Stirling
1948	J Lindsay	Falkirk Tryst	1973	WJ Dalling	Falkirk
1949	GN Taylor	Stirling	1974	JAS Zuill	Dunblane
1950	TD Wilson	Falkirk	1975	DJ Smith	Falkirk Tryst
1951	KG Patrick	Buchanan Castle	1976	AY Wilson	Buchanan Castle
1952	KT Thomson	Falkirk Tryst	1977	GK MacDonald	Glenbervie
1953	DW Anderson	Glenbervie	1978	AC MacLaren	Stirling
1954	J Lindsay	Falkirk	1979	AJ Liddle	Falkirk Carmuirs
1955	DW Anderson	Stirling	1980	DF Wilkie	Callander
1956	T Harrower	Dunblane	1981	A Liddle	Falkirk Tryst
1957	HM Campbell	Falkirk Tryst	1982	A Liddle	
1958	J Nimmo	Buchanan Castle	1983	C Gillies	
1959	AM Grant	Glenbervie	1984	G Barrie	
1960	D Macintosh	Stirling	1985	W Fleming	
1961	IA MacMillan	Falkirk	1986	RA Godfrey	
1962	DF Wilkie	Dunblane	1987	SA Lee	
1963	HM Campbell	Falkirk Tryst	1988	H Anderson	
1964	WJ Dalling	Buchanan Castle	1989	S Russell	
1965	M Murray	Glenbervie	1990	KW Goodwin	
1966	C McLachlan	Stirling			

West of Scotland Close Amateur Championship

INAUGURATED 1977

YEAR	WINNER	VENUE	YEAR	WINNER	VENUE
1977	R Blackwood	Dumfries and County	1984	W Erskine	Grangemouth
			1985	S Savage	Hagg's Castle
1978	AP McDonald	Caldwell	1986	S Savage	Wishaw
1979	N Skinner	Cochrane Castle	1987	R Jenkins	Hayston
1980	PJ McKellar	East Kilbride	1988	G King	Stirling
1981	DB Howard	East Renfrewshire	1989	G Lawrie	Bellshill
1982	G Shaw	Helensburgh	1990	B Smith	Cawder
1983	D Murdoch	Ardeer			

West of Scotland Open Amateur Championship

INAUGURATED 1950

YEAR	WINNER		YEAR	WINNER	VENUE
1950	A Sinclair		*From 1972 became open event*		
1951	JR Cater		1972	AK Pine	Troon
1952	J Campbell		1973	GH Murray	Cawder
1953	J Mill		1974	Allan Brodie	Cawder
1954	J Walker		1975	S Stephen	Cawder
1955	JR Cater		1976	GH Murray	Cawder
1956	HVS Thomson		1977	MJ Miller	Cawder
1957	Dr JL Hastings		1978	GH Murray	Paisley
1958	SWT Murray		1979	CW Green	Renfrew
1959	Dr FWG Deighton		1980	DB Howard	Cardross
1960	IGF Lee		1981	H McMorran	Prestwick
1961	GB Cosh		1982	G MacDonald	East Kilbride
1962	CW Green		1983	G Barrie	Stirling
1963	FS Morris		1984	G Shaw	Cathkin Braes
1964	GB Cosh		1985	JA Thomson	Paisley
1965	GB Cosh		1986	C Brooks	Dullatur
1966	GB Cosh		1987	R Jenkins	Barassie
1967	CJL Strachan		1988	S Savage	Lanark
1968	AM Grant		1989	AJ Elliott	Bellshill
1969	W Smeaton		1990	ST Knowles	Cawder
1970	CW Green				
1971	GH Murray				

Wigtownshire Golf Championship

INAUGURATED 1903

YEAR	WINNER	VENUE	YEAR	WINNER	VENUE
1903	WT Scott-Douglas	Glenluce	1927	WHS Mactier	Dunskey
1904	WT Hawthorn	Newton Stewart	1928	EG Paton	Stranraer
1905	JH Thomson	Glenluce	1929	JGC Carver	Dunskey
1906	R Gordon	Newton Stewart	1930	JGC Carver	Stranraer
1907	R Gordon	Glenluce	1931	W McMillan	Dunskey
1908	R Gordon	Newton Stewart	1932	J Stewart	Stranraer
1909	WT Hawthorn	Glenluce	1933	JS Buchanan	Dunskey
1910	JH Thomson	Newton Stewart	1934	JGC Carver	Stranraer
1911	R Goodall	Glenluce	1935	AW Mackay	Dunskey
1912	C Hunter	Stranraer	1936	R Murray	Stranraer
1913	WT Hawthorn	Newton Stewart	1937	JGC Carver	Dunskey
1914–19	*Not played due to Great War*		1938	RHU Stevenson	Stranraer
1920	NH Wilson	Stranraer	1939	J Stewart	Dunskey
1921	WHS Mactier	Newton Stewart	1940–45	*Not played due to Second World War*	
1922	WHS Mactier	St Medan	1946	RHU Stevenson	Dunskey
1923	RR Kay	Stranraer	1947	MH Forrest	Dunskey
1924	WHS Mactier	Newton Stewart	1948	MH Forrest	Dunskey
1925	WHS Mactier	Dunskey	1949	R Murray	Kirroughtree
1926	FC Smith	Stranraer	1950	R Murray	Kirroughtree

YEAR	WINNER	VENUE	YEAR	WINNER	VENUE
1951	R Murray	Dunskey	1971	MC Gibson	Stranraer
1952	R Murray	Dunskey	1972	K Wallace	Dunskey
1953	T Stangoe	Creachmore	1973	MC Gibson	Stranraer
1954	R Murray	Dunskey	1974	R McGinn	Dunskey
1955	JS Boyd	Creachmore	1975	MC Gibson	Stranraer
1956	GM Cook	Dunskey	1976	K Russell	Dunskey
1957	R Murray	Creachmore	1977	MC Gibson	Stranraer
1958	R Murray	Dunskey	1978	AV Plant	Dunskey
1959	A Simpson	Creachmore	1979	MC Gibson	Stranraer
1960	CG Findlay	Dunskey	1980	RNC Douglas	Dunskey
1961	A Simpson	Creachmore	1981	JK Young	Stranraer
1962	J Gibson	Dunskey	1982	RNC Douglas	Dunskey
1963	R Murray	Creachmore	1983	K Hardie	Stranraer
1964	R Murray	Dunskey	1984	RA Burns	Dunskey
1965	R McGinn	Creachmore	1985	MC Gibson	Stranraer
1966	A Johnstone	Dunskey	1986	A Cunningham	Dunskey
1967	CG Findlay	Creachmore	1987	J Burns	Stranraer
1968	CG Findlay	Dunskey	1988	K Hardie	Dunskey
1969	MC Gibson	Stranraer	1989	D Taylor	Stranraer
1970	R McGinn	Dunskey	1990	RA Burns	Wigtownshire

Wales

Anglesey Amateur Championship

YEAR	WINNER	VENUE	YEAR	WINNER	VENUE
1977	D Walsh	Anglesey	1984	A Llyr	Holyhead
1978	D McLean	Holyhead	1985	I Furlong	Bull Bay
1979	D McLean	Bull Bay	1986	M Perdue	Anglesey
1980	D McLean	Anglesey	1987	S Owen	Holyhead
1981	D McLean	Holyhead	1988	EO Jones	Bull Bay
1982	D McLean	Bull Bay	1989	M Robinson	Anglesey
1983	I Cooper	Anglesey	1990	D McLean	Holyhead

Brecon and Radnor Amateur Championship

YEAR	WINNER	VENUE
1986	AS Beetham	Cradoc
1987	C Davies	Brecon
1988	C Davies	Llandrindod Wells
1989	C Davies	Builth Wells
1990	R Dixon	Cradoc

Caernarfonshire and District Amateur Championship

INAUGURATED 1922

YEAR	WINNER	VENUE	YEAR	WINNER	VENUE
1922	LE Richards	Maesdu, Llandudno	1930	J Morris	Criccieth
1923	N Roberts	Criccieth	1931	JL Black	Bangor
1924	L Riley	Bull Bay	1932	JL Black	Nevin
1925	W Roberts	Pwllheli	1933	JL Black	Conway
1926	HN Thomas	Rhos-on-Sea	1934	JL Black	Bull Bay
1927	HN Thomas	Criccieth	1935	JL Black	Pwllheli
1928	LE Richards	Holyhead	1936	SB Roberts	North Wales, Llandudno
1929	J Morris	North Wales, Llandudno	1937	SB Roberts	Rhosneigr

YEAR	WINNER	VENUE	YEAR	WINNER	VENUE
1938	AH Wright	Maesdu, Llandudno	1967	E Mills	Maesdu, Llandudno
1939	GE Roberts	Rhos-on-Sea	1968	D McLean	Nefyn
1940	James Roberts	Holyhead	1969	D McLean	Bangor
1941–45	*Not played due to Second World War*		1970	D McLean } tie	Rhos-on-Sea
1946	Mervyn Jones	North Wales,		J Roger Jones	
		Llandudno	1971	WG Jones	Conwy
1947	AM Goodwin	Nevin	1972	J Roger Jones	Maesdu, Llandudno
1948	AM Goodwin	Bangor	1973	C Brown	Harlech
1949	JB Wilson	Rhosneigr	1974	J Roger Jones	Conwy
1950	CG Guy	Pwllheli	1975	J Roger Jones	Maesdu, Llandudno
1951	WW Prytherch	Conwy	1976	GW Jones	Harlech
1952	H Palferman	Harlech	1977	D McLean	Conwy
1953	W Vale	North Wales,	1978	C Brown	Nefyn
		Llandudno	1979	D McLean	Holyhead
1954	H Palferman	Bull Bay	1980	A Llyr	Maesdu, Llandudno
1955	H Palferman	Holyhead	1981	WG Jones	Pwllheli
1956	W Vale	North Wales,	1982	D McLean	Bull Bay
		Llandudno	1983	JR Parry } tie	Porthmadog
1957	P Mills	Nevin		WG Jones	
1958	ES Mills	Bangor	1984	S Owen	Harlech
1959	EC Roberts	Rhosneigr	1985	MA Macara	North Wales,
1960	WJ Hobson	Pwllheli			Llandudno
1961	A Moss	Conwy	1986	JT Roberts	Caernarfon
1962	C Hobley Eaves	Harlech	1987	D McLean	Rhosneigr
1963	W Vale	Maesdu, Llandudno	1988	D McLean	Conwy
1964	WJ Hobson	North Wales,	1989	WE Jones	Nefyn
		Llandudno	1990	D McLean	Pwllheli
1965	WJ Roberts	Maesdu, Llandudno			
1966	D McLean	North Wales,			
		Llandudno			

Caernarfonshire Amateur Championship Cup

INAUGURATED 1989

YEAR	WINNER	VENUE
1989	M Sheppard	Harlech
1990	I Jones	Caernarfon

Carmarthenshire Open Championship

INAUGURATED 1966

YEAR	WINNER	YEAR	WINNER
1966	HC Squirrell	1978	MS Roper
	CI Morgan	1979	JR Jones
1967	JKD Povall } tie	1980	JR Jones
	G Gilford	1981	B Rolfe
1968	B Rolfe	1982	RN Roderick
1969	JKD Povall	1983	RN Roderick
1970	RE Phillips	1984	JR Jones
1971	T Rickard	1985	CW Jones
1972	AB Morgan	1986	RN Roderick
1973	I Duffy	1987	RN Roderick
1974	S Cox	1988	RN Roderick
1975	B Rolfe	1989	M Macara
1976	RE Phillips	1990	
1977	G Davies		

Denbigh Amateur Championship

INAUGURATED 1967

YEAR	WINNER	VENUE	YEAR	WINNER	VENUE
1967	J Buckley	Wrexham	1979	G Pattison	Llangollen
1968	J Buckley	Wrexham	1980	C Wright	Wrexham
1969	JR Jones	Wrexham	1981	I Hughes	Abergele
1970	P Riley	Wrexham	1982	A Jones	Llangollen
1971	JR Jones	Wrexham	1983	D Chidley	Wrexham
1972	P Riley	Wrexham	1984	A Jones	Abergele
1973	C Wright	Wrexham	1985	JD Jones-Roberts	Llangollen
1974	C Wright	Wrexham	1986	N Chidley	Wrexham
1975	C Wright	Wrexham	1987	D Davies	Abergele
1976	J Buckley	Wrexham	1988	S Edwards	Llangollen
1977	C Wright	Wrexham	1989	H Parry	Denbigh
1978	J Buckley	Abergele	1990	S Edwards	Wrexham

Dyfed (Three Counties) Championship

INAUGURATED 1952

YEAR	WINNER	VENUE	YEAR	WINNER	VENUE
1952	T Henry Edwards	Ashburnham	1972	B Rolfe	Ashburnham
1953	D Carew	Tenby	1973	K Beynon	Tenby
1954			1974	J Priestland	Cardigan
1955			1975	L Goodchild	Carmarthen
1956		Ashburnham	1976	A Jones	Ashburnham
1957	TW Treharne	Carmarthen	1977	I Duffy	Tenby
1958	DJ Bonnel	Tenby	1978	C Jones	Carmarthen
1959	BEJ Wheeler	Carmarthen	1979	C Jones	Ashburnham
1960	DJ Howells	Ashburnham	1980	B Cramb	Tenby
1961	G Childs	Tenby	1981	W Pugh	Cardigan
1962	D Rees	Ashburnham	1982	R Collins	Ashburnham
1963	RL Yorath	Carmarthen	1983	G Evans	Carmarthen
1964	B Rolfe	Tenby	1984	B Rolfe	Tenby
1965	AW Kelly	Ashburnham	1985	W Farrell	Ashburnham
1966	DB Rees	Tenby	1986	C Jones	Carmarthen
1967	RL Yorath	Ashburnham	1987	P Neysmith	Tenby
1968	JV Dinsdale	Tenby	1988	M Stimson	Ashburnham
1969	JV Dinsdale	Ashburnham	1989	C Hill	Carmarthen
1970	B Rolfe	Tenby	1990	M Stimson	Tenby
1971	B Rolfe	Carmarthen			

Glamorgan Amateur Championship

INAUGURATED 1928

YEAR	WINNER	VENUE	YEAR	WINNER	VENUE
1928	GS Emery	Porthcawl	1953	RM de Lloyd	Southerndown
1929	J Duncan	Southerndown	1954	G Knipe	Porthcawl
1930	FS Wilcox	Swansea Bay	1955	G Knipe	Southerndown
1931	G Llewellin	Radyr	1956	AE Lockley	Porthcawl
1932	JW Jones	Pyle and Kenfig	1957	G Knipe	Southerndown
1933	J Lyndon Jones	Porthcawl	1958	RJ Pressdee	Porthcawl
1934	DH Lewis	Southerndown	1959	HC Squirrell	Southerndown
1935	N Jacob	Pyle and Kenfig	1960	JKD Povall	Porthcawl
1936	GS Emery	Porthcawl	1961	G Clay	Southerndown
1937	HR Howell	Southerndown	1962	AE Lockley	Porthcawl
1938	J Lyndon Jones	Pyle and Kenfig	1963	JKD Povall	Southerndown
1939	GS Emery	Clyne	1964	G Clay	Porthcawl
1940–46	*Not played due to Second World War*		1965	HC Squirrell	Southerndown
1947	HR Howell	Porthcawl	1966	JL Toye	Porthcawl
1948	RM de Lloyd	Porthcawl	1967	JKD Povall	Pyle and Kenfig
1949	AD Lake	Southerndown	1968	JHM Jones	Southerndown
1950	AE Lockley	Porthcawl	1969	JKD Povall	Porthcawl
1951	RM de Lloyd	Southerndown	1970	JG Jermine	Pyle and Kenfig
1952	AE Lockley	Porthcawl	1971	CT Brown	Southerndown

YEAR	WINNER	VENUE	YEAR	WINNER	VENUE
1972	PE Light	Porthcawl	1982	T Melia	Pyle and Kenfig
1973	JG Jermine	Pyle and Kenfig	1983	P Bloomfield	Southerndown
1974	DL Stevens	Southerndown	1984	RN Roderick	Porthcawl
1975	CN Last	Pyle and Kenfig	1985	R Brown	Pyle and Kenfig
1976	DL Stevens	Southerndown	1986	LP Price	Southerndown
1977	JR Jones	Pyle and Kenfig	1987	RN Roderick	Pyle and Kenfig
1978	HJ Evans	Porthcawl	1988	I Booth	Porthcawl
1979	JR Jones	Southerndown	1989	BR Knight	Southerndown
1980	DL Stevens	Pyle and Kenfig	1990	P Bloomfield	Pyle and Kenfig
1981	T Melia	Southerndown			

Gwent Amateur Championship

INAUGURATED 1920

Formerly Monmouthshire Amateur Championship

YEAR	WINNER	VENUE	YEAR	WINNER	VENUE
1920	WC Baddeley	Newport	1959	WI Tucker	St Mellons
1921	G Williams	Blackwood	1960	WI Tucker	Llanwern
1922	VH Smith	West Monmouth	1961	WI Tucker	West Monmouth
1923	VH Smith	Abergavenny	1962	WI Tucker	Monmouthshire
1924	VH Smith	Tredegar Park	1963	WI Tucker	Pontypool
1925	WC Baddeley	Newport	1964	C Gilford	St Pierre
1926	VH Smith	Pontypool	1965	C Gilford	Newport
1927	AJ Bunce	Tredegar Park	1966	W Windsor	St Mellons
1928	VH Smith	Newport	1967	WI Tucker	Llanwern
1929	RB Bennet	Pontypool	1968	K Dabson	Tredegar Park
1930	AW Morris	Tredegar Park	1969	WI Tucker	West Monmouth
1931	R Chapman	West Monmouth	1970	W Dwyer	Monmouthshire
1932	JA Chapman	Newport	1971	A Morgan	Pontypool
1933	JH Burland	Llanwern	1972	G Pinch	St Pierre
1934	R Chapman	Pontypool	1973	A Disley	Tredegar Park
1935	JA Chapman	Tredegar Park	1974	WI Tucker	Newport
1936	RB Bennett	West Monmouth	1975	T Branton	St Mellons
1937	LJ Rowlands	Newport	1976	WI Tucker	Monmouthshire
1938	K Llewellyn	Tredegar Park	1977	AB Morgan	Pontypool
1939	RB Bennett	Pontypool	1978	M Wilce	St Pierre
1940–46	*Not played due to Second World War*		1979	A Jones	St Mellons
1947	H Lloyd	Newport	1980	A Disley	Newport
1948	HW Wright	Tredegar Park	1981	A Disley	Tredegar Park
1949	WI Tucker	Pontypool	1982	PM Mayo	Monmouthshire
1950	H Phillips	Newport	1983	NR Davies	Pontypool
1951	P Dunn	Newport	1984	PM Mayo	St Mellons
1952	WI Tucker	Newport	1985	M Brimble	St Pierre
1953	WI Tucker	Monmouthshire	1986	G Hughes	Llanwern
1954	WI Tucker	Llanwern	1987	M Bearcroft	Newport
1955	WI Tucker	West Monmouth	1988	A Williams	Tredegar Park
1956	WI Tucker	Tredegar Park	1989	P Glyn	Monmouthshire
1957	WI Tucker	Pontypool	1990	M Hayward	Tredegar Park
1958	WI Tucker	Monmouthshire			

Gwent Match Play Championship

YEAR	WINNER	VENUE	YEAR	WINNER	VENUE
1982	PM Mayo	Newport	1987	NR Davies	Newport
1983	G Davies	Newport	1988	M Roper	Tredegar Park
1984	M Roper	Newport	1989	C Dinsdale	Monmouthshire
1985	S Hewitt	Newport	1990	J Griffiths	Newport
1986	M Bearcroft	Pontypool			

Open Amateur Tournaments

Many clubs have well-known and old-established open amateur tournaments which draw competitors from a wide area, if not nationwide. Among them are the Leven Gold Medal, Tennant Cup and Edward Trophy in Scotland, and the St George's Challenge Cup and *Golf Illustrated* Gold Vase in the south. Others were inaugurated in the 1920–39 period, including the Royal Cinque Ports Prince of Wales Cup at Deal and the Royal St David's Gold Cross at Harlech. Many more have been started since 1950: the best known of these are the Berkshire and Lytham Trophies and Southerndown's Duncan Putter in Wales.

The other club open tournaments are those known to have players coming to take part from neighbouring counties as well as from nearby clubs. County Unions have suggested a few which were previously unknown nationally and it is anticipated that more may appear in the next edition when others worthy of inclusion are discovered.

Aberconwy Trophy

INAUGURATED 1976

at Conwy and Llandudno Maesdu

YEAR	WINNER	YEAR	WINNER
1976	JR Jones	1984	D McLean
1977	EN Davies	1985	MA Macara
1978	MG Mouland	1986	JR Berry
1979	JM Morrow	1987	M Sheppard
1980	JM Morrow	1988	MG Hughes
1981	D Evans	1989	JN Lee
1982	G Tuttle	1990	SM Wilkinson
1983	GH Brown		

The Antlers of Royal Mid-Surrey

INAUGURATED 1933

YEAR	WINNERS	SCORE
1933	TFB Law and PWL Risdon	147
1934	GA Hill and HS Malik	153
1935	EF Storey and Sir WS Worthington Evans	152
1936	HG Bentley and F Francis	144
1937	LG Crawley and C Stowe	145
1938	RW Hartley and PWL Risdon	149
1939	LG Crawley and H Thomson	148
1940–47	*Not played due to Second World War*	
1948	RC Quilter and E Bromley Davenport	151
1949	LG Crawley and JC Wilson	143
1950	L Gracey and I Caldwell	151
1951	LG Crawley and JC Wilson	147
1952	Major DA Blair and GH Micklem } tie / LG Crawley and JC Wilson }	145
1953	D Wilson and G Simmons	148
1954	JR Thornhill and PF Scrutton	147
1955	G Evans and D Sewell	147
1956	GH Micklem and AF Bussell	141
1957	Major DA Blair and CD Lawrie	138
1958	D Sewell and G Evans	143
1959	HC Squirrell and P Dunn	146
1960	MSR Lunt and JC Beharrell	139
1961	HC Squirrell and P Dunn	145
1962	AW Holmes and JM Leach	142
1963	RC Pickering and MJ Cooper	146
1964	MF Bonallack and Dr DM Marsh	145
1965	MSR Lunt and DE Rodway	146

YEAR	WINNERS	SCORE
1966	PD Kelley and Dr DM Marsh	144
1967	*Play abandoned*	
1968	H Broadbent and G Birtwell	144
1969	SR Warrin and JH Cook / J Povall and K Dabson / JC Davies and W Humphreys } tie / RD Watson-Jones and LOM Smith	146
1970	JB Carr and R Carr	142
1971	I Mosey and I Gradwell	144
1972	MJ Kelley and W Smith	144
1973	DOJ Albutt and P Flaherty	148
1974	BF Critchley and MC Hughesdon	140
1975	JC Davies and PJ Davies	140
1976	JK Tate and P Deeble	144
1977	JC Davies and PJ Davies	141
1978	R Chapman and R Fish	148
1979	N Roche and D Williams	143
1980	G Coles and M Johnson	148
1981	R Boxall and R Chapman	143
1982	IA Carslaw and J Huggan	139
1983	N Fox and G Lashford	147
1984	M Palmer and M Belsham	147
1985	S Blight and R Wilkins	143
1986	M Gerrard and B White	146
1987	IA Carslaw and J Huggan	141
1988	A Raitt and P Thornley	143
1989	A Howard and R Hunter	146
1990	AC Livesey and RG Payne	143

Ashton Vase

INAUGURATED 1924

at Long Ashton, Bristol

YEAR	WINNER	YEAR	WINNER
1924	CH Young	1964	M Clarke
1925	GC Brooks	1965	JW Harrison
1926	*No competition*	1966	P Clarke
1927	LtCdr RD Howard	1967	GJ Brand
1928	GC Brooks	1968	DR Hemming
1929	GC Brooks	1969	R Abbott
1930	GC Brooks	1970	JN Littler
1931	HG Pruett	1971	JKR Graveney
1932	GC Killey	1972	J Bloxham
1933	GC Brooks	1973	R Abbott
1934	W Gow Cook	1974	PJ Smith
1935–46	*No competition*	1975	ME Lewis
1947	J Payne	1976	M Little
1948	WS Wise	1977	M Bessell
1949	RJ Naven	1978	CS Ray
1950	WS Wise	1979	A Sherborne
1951	JW Harrison	1980	ME Lewis
1952	KP Lyon	1981	RD Broad
1953	WS Wise	1982	A Sherborne
1954	G Morgan	1983	M Few
1955	RST Cole	1984	AJ Hynam
1956	DS Maunsell	1985	SD Hurley ⎫ tie
1957	IR Patey		CS Edwards ⎭
1958	VC Harrison	1986	M Stokes
1959	LH Holley	1987	CS Edwards
1960	RJ Gardiner	1988	J Webber
1961	M Clarke	1989	ST Lee
1962	RJ Gardiner	1990	G Wolstenholme
1963	M Clarke		

Auchterlonie Spoon

INAUGURATED 1976

at Selby, North Yorkshire

YEAR	WINNER	YEAR	WINNER
1976	R Kelly	1984	R Mitchell
1977	S East	1985	AR Gelsthorpe
1978	PM Carrigill	1986	AR Whitworth
1979	H Green	1987	J Whiteley
1980	H Taylor	1988	L Walker
1981	PN Huddlestone	1989	N Ludwell
1982	MJ Kelley	1990	AF Thorpe
1983	L Walker		

Beau Desert Stag

INAUGURATED 1980

at Beau Desert, Cannock, Staffordshire

YEAR	WINNER	YEAR	WINNER
1980	DJ Fearns	1986	P Broadhurst
1981	J Loader	1987	M Hassall
1982	AK Stubbs	1988	TPC Owen
1983	GR Krause	1989	GR Krause
1984	AJ Hurst	1990	J Smethurst
1985	P Broadhurst		

Berkhamsted Trophy

INAUGURATED 1960

at Berkhamsted, Hertfordshire

YEAR	WINNER	YEAR	WINNER
1960	HC Squirrell	1976	JC Davies
1961	DW Frame	1977	AWB Lyle
1962	DG Neech	1978	JC Davies
1963	HC Squirrell	1979	JC Davies
1964	PD Flaherty	1980	R Knott
1965	LF Millar	1981	P Dennett
1966	P Townsend	1982	DG Lane
1967	DJ Millensted	1983	J Hawksworth
1968	PD Flaherty	1984	R Willison
1969	MM Niven	1985	F George
1970	R Hunter	1986	P McEvoy
1971	A Millar	1987	F George
1972	C Cieslewicz	1988	J Cowgill
1973	SC Mason	1989	J Payne
1974	P Fisher	1990	J Barnes
1975	PG Deeble		

Berkshire Trophy

INAUGURATED 1946

at The Berkshire

Started in 1946, this was the first open 72-hole stroke play tournament for amateurs to be established by an English club. It has had many distinguished winners, especially in its earlier years: a few have changed their status and two, Lyle and Faldo, have become Open Champions.

YEAR	WINNER	SCORE	YEAR	WINNER	SCORE
1946	R Sweeney } tie JB Beck	148	1968	MF Bonallack	273
			1969	JC Davies	278
1947	PB Lucas	298	1970	MF Bonallack	274
1948	LG Crawley	301	1971	MF Bonallack } tie JC Davies	277
1949	PB Lucas	300			
1950	PF Scrutton	296	1972	DP Davidson	280
1951	PF Scrutton	301	1973	PJ Hedges	278
1952	PF Scrutton	286	1974	J Downie	280
1953	JL Morgan	289	1975	N Faldo	281
1954	E Bromley-Davenport } tie Ft Lt K Hall	303	1976	PJ Hedges	284
			1977	AWB Lyle	279
1955	GH Micklem	282	1978	PJ Hedges	281
1956	GB Wolstenholme	285	1979	D Williams	274
1957	MF Bonallack	291	1980	P Downes	280
1958	GB Wolstenholme } tie AH Perowne	284	1981	D Blakeman	280
			1982	SD Keppler	278
1959	JB Carr	279	1983	S Hamer	288
1960	GB Wolstenholme	276	1984	JL Plaxton	276
1961	MF Bonallack	275	1985	P McEvoy	279
1962	SC Saddler	279	1986	R Muscroft	280
1963	DW Frame	289	1987	J Robinson	275
1964	R Foster	281	1988	R Claydon	276
1965	MF Bonallack	278	1989	J Metcalfe	272
1966	P Oosterhuis	287	1990	J O'Shea	271
1967	DJ Millensted	283			

Birkdale Silver Goblet

INAUGURATED 1968

at Royal Birkdale, Southport

YEAR	WINNER	YEAR	WINNER
1968	GJ Clark	1980	SG Birtwell
1969	JB Dickinson	1981	S Hamer
1970	N Sumner	1982	MP Thorpe
1971	S Rolley	1983	SM Bottomley
1972	JM Tyrer	1984	DJ Eccleston
1973	MG King	1985	RI Godley
1974	SG Birtwell	1986	RA Bardsley
1975	DJ Eccleston	1987	P McNally
1976	MPD Walls	1988	JS Cheetham
1977	DJ Eccleston	1989	T Foster
1978	RJ White	1990	M Sheppard
1979	J Glover		

Boyd Quaich Tournament

INAUGURATED 1946

at St Andrews

YEAR	WINNER	YEAR	WINNER
1946	AS Mayer	1969	PH Moody
1947	Harry Brews / Dr FWG Deighton } tie	1970	JT Moffatt
		1971	JW Johnston
1948	JL Lindsay	1972	D Greig
1949	FD Tatum	1973	J Rube
1950	GP Roberts	1974	G Cairns
1951	H Dooley	1975	S Dunlop
1952	G Parker	1976	R Watson
1953	JL Bamford	1977	R Watson
1954	I Caldwell	1978	R Watson
1955	HC Squirrell	1979	D McLeary
1956	JL Bamford	1980	ME Lewis
1957	DM Marsh	1981	P Gallagher
1958	R Mummery	1982	ME Lewis
1959–61	*No competition*	1983	R Risan
1962	DB Sheahan	1984	J Huggan
1963	S MacDonald	1985	S Elgie
1964	AJ Low	1986	A Roberts
1965	S MacDonald	1987	M Pask
1966	FE McCarroll	1988	A Mathers
1967	B Nicholson	1989	A Mathers
1968	JW Johnston	1990	A Mathers

Brokenhurst Bowl

INAUGURATED 1966

at Brokenhurst Manor, Hampshire

YEAR	WINNER	YEAR	WINNER
1966	JFR Brander	1979	K Weeks
1967	J Airth	1980	BJ Winteridge
1968	DM Lang	1981	AJ Wells
1969	PR Newton	1982	I Gray
1970	JFR Brander	1983	SD Keppler
1971	MA Butcher	1984	R Park
1972	P Edington	1985	MP Wiggett
1973	D Powell	1986	M Smith
1974	MA Butcher	1987	J Tomlinson
1975	JFR Brander	1988	D Wheeler
1976	JFR Brander	1989	M Smith
1977	M Edmunds	1990	NJ Graves
1978	K Weeks		

Burnham and Berrow Challenge Salver

INAUGURATED 1951

at Burnham and Berrow, Somerset

YEAR	WINNER	YEAR	WINNER
1951	JWR Swayne	1971	RE Searle
1952	IS Keelan	1972	P Dunn
1953	GC Griffiths	1973	AJ Hill
1954	SL Elliott	1974	WP Hucker
1955	F Griffin	1975	BJ Winteridge
1956	GC Griffiths	1976	BJ Winteridge
1957	F Griffin	1977	AR Dunlop
1958	F Smith	1978	JP Clifford
1959	F Smith	1979	PJ Smith
1960	WAJ Kinnersley	1980	N Rowland
1961	JM Clarke	1981	A Lyddon
1962	DM Brown	1982	PJ Smith
1963	GT Irlam	1983	N Holman
1964	GD Roberts	1984	DJ Huxtable
1965	T Schofield	1985	TS Crandon
1966	TJ Griffin	1986	NE Holman
1967	WP Hucker	1987	DM Powell
1968	HC Jessop	1988	NE Holman
1969	WP Hucker	1989	PA Vickers
1970	GT Irlam	1990	W Richardson

Caldy Quart

INAUGURATED 1975

at Mere, Cheshire

YEAR	WINNER	YEAR	WINNER
1975	RF Evans	1983	PT Bailey
1976	CM Edwards	1984	ME Jordan
1977	PT Bailey	1985	PT Bailey
1978	AD Jordan	1986	PT Bailey
1979	PT Bailey	1987	PT Bailey
1980	CR Smethurst	1988	PT Bailey
1981	PW Thomas	1989	PT Bailey
1982	CR Smethurst	1990	J Greenough

Cameron Corbett Vase

INAUGURATED 1897

at Haggs Castle, Glasgow

YEAR	WINNER	YEAR	WINNER
1897	AF Duncan	1927	RS Rodger
1898	AF Duncan	1928	SL McKinlay
1899	W Laidlaw	1929	D McBride
1900	GH Hutcheson	1930	HM Dickson
1901	G Fox Jr	1931	HM Dickson
1902	AF Duncan	1932	W Stringer
1903	G Fox Jr	1933	W Tulloch
1904	R Bone	1934	JM Dykes
1905	R Bone	1935	H Thomson
1906	W Gemmill	1936	J Gray
1907	G Wilkie	1937	TI Craig Jr
1908	AF Duncan	1938	JS Logan
1909	EB Tipping	1939	A Steel
1910	JH Irons	1940–41	*No competition*
1911	G Morris	1942	AC Taylor
1912	R Scott Jr	1943–45	*No competition*
1913	R Scott Jr	1946	JS Montgomerie
1914	D Martin	1947	W Maclaren
1915–18	*Not played due to Great War*	1948	J Pressley
1919	HR Orr	1949	GB Peters
1920	DJ Murray Campbell	1950	J Gray
1921	HM Dickson	1951	GB Peters
1922	WS Macfarlane	1952	J Stewart Thomson
1923	JO Stevenson	1953	J Orr
1924	JO Stevenson	1954	JR Cater
1925	A Jamieson Jr	1955	RC Macgregor
1926	G Chapple	1956	RC Macgregor

YEAR	WINNER	YEAR	WINNER
1957	I Rennie	1974	M Rae
1958	DH Reid	1975	D Barclay Howard
1959	AS Kerr	1976	GH Murray
1960	J Mackenzie	1977	MJ Miller
1961	GB Cosh	1978	GH Murray
1962	JH Richmond	1979	KW Macintosh
1963	JA Davidson	1980	IA Carslaw
1964	IA MacCaskill	1981	GH Murray
1965	H Frazer	1982	GH Murray
1966	D Black	1983	AS Oldcorn
1967	JRW Walkinshaw	1984	D Barclay Howard
1968	CW Green	1985	J McDonald
1969	A Brooks	1986	JW Milligan
1970	D Hayes ⎱ tie J McTear ⎰	1987	J Semple
		1988	C Everett
1971	G Macgregor	1989	AG Tait
1972	HB Stuart	1990	D Robertson
1973	MJ Miller		

Championship of Bath

INAUGURATED 1964

at Bath, Avon

YEAR	WINNER	YEAR	WINNER
1964	A Wells	1978	SR Butler
1965	WAJ Kinnersley	1979	RA Searle
1966	RO Aitken	1980	RD Broad
1967	P Pascall	1981	DJ Huxtable
1968	AL Scott	1982	DJ Huxtable
1969	GJ Brand	1983	CS Edwards
1970	B McCullum	1984	CS Edwards
1971	P Edgington	1985	CS Edwards
1972	R Abbott	1986	M Bloxham
1973	RA Searle	1987	T White
1974	LF Millar	1988	CS Edwards
1975	SR Davidson	1989	CS Edwards
1976	R Abbott	1990	CS Edwards
1977	D Streeter		

The Chanctonbury Ring

INAUGURATED 1936

at Pulborough, West Sussex

YEAR	WINNER	YEAR	WINNER
1936	JJF Pennink	1967	DJ Harrison
1937	JJF Pennink	1968	GI Stradling
1938	AA McNair	1969	MJ Burgess
1939–46	*Not played due to Second World War*	1970	JRG Cobbett
		1971	J Yeo
1947	KG Thom	1972	GE Hyde
1948	Sq Ldr CH Beamish	1973	GI Stradling
1949	N Stiller	1974	J Watts
1950	W/Cdr CH Beamish	1975	DJ Harrison
1951	Col JVC Moberly	1976	DJ Harrison
1952	Sir J Craddock-Hartopp	1977	MC Hughesdon
1953	SL Elliott	1978	P Garner
1954	WG Pierce	1979	PB Phillips
1955	GH Micklem	1980	P Garner
1956	G Evans	1981	R Lee
1957	GR Bristowe	1982	M Simpson
1958	G Evans	1983	NM Godin
1959	MW Steel	1984	JS Spence
1960	DJ Harrison	1985	S Graham
1961	DJ Harrison	1986	D Fay
1962	DJ Harrison	1987	S Robertson
1963	DJ Harrison	1988	P Hurring
1964	PD Kelley	1989	G Evans
1965	PD Kelley	1990	G Graham
1966	PMP Townsend		

Chigwell Bowl

INAUGURATED 1959

at Chigwell, Essex

YEAR	WINNER	YEAR	WINNER
1959	RA Bulgin	1970	JAR Darling
1960	MMD Laidlaw	1971	AT Bird
1961	PD Good	1972	G Godwin
1962	JM Howard	1973	G Godwin
1963	JM Howard	1974	N Burch
1964	J Thorogood	1975	G Turner
1965	HC Weber	1976	I Grant
1966	JAR Darling	1977	T Patmore
1967	NF Rochefort	1978	B Hilsdon
1968	D Miller	1979	B Hilsdon
1969	AT Bird	1980	NPO Coles

YEAR	WINNER	YEAR	WINNER
1981	C Platts	1986	M Davis
1982	C Laurence	1987	D Jones
1983	M Davis	1988	A Duffin
1984	D Jones	1989	J Robson
1985	J Robson	1990	A Duffin

Devil's Punch Bowl

INAUGURATED 1928

at Hindhead, Surrey

YEAR	WINNER	YEAR	WINNER
1928	Major AJ Jimeney	1962	AS Guthrie
1929	Captain DJ Steward	1963	A Leeson
1930	EC Hillard	1964	RL Glading
1931	PJ Urlwin-Smith	1965	J Hardy
1932	KAS Morrice	1966	G Pratt
1933	PB Lucas	1967	JL Raitt
1934	PWL Risdon	1968	RM Johnson
1935	K Martin Jones	1969	JW Kirkpatrick
1936	MR Gardner	1970	Dr K Bright
1937	AS Anderson	1971	AJ Holloway
1938	FH Tate	1972	W Rowland
1939–45	*Not played due to to Second World War*	1973	RH Mitchell
		1974	MI Farmer
1946	BAF Pelmore	1975	DM Swanston
1947	ADG Russell	1976	AD Swanston
1948	TW Drew	1977	WS Gronow
1949	SE Rudge	1978	W Rowland
1950	EH Pogson	1979	SW Pilgrim
1951	SK Proctor	1980	SW Pilgrim
1952	SK Proctor	1981	R Lee
1953	SE Emberton	1982	G Walmsley
1954	DAS Robertson	1983	APS Brewer
1955	CDD Gilmour	1984	M Jarvis
1956	BAF Pelmore	1985	M Stokes
1957	BAF Pelmore	1986	M Jarvis
1958	BAF Pelmore	1987	D Rosier
1959	IA Leeson	1988	G Orr
1960	J Whelan	1989	SP Horkan
1961	HGL Collins	1990	D Lee

The Duncan Putter

INAUGURATED 1959

at Southerndown

Before the 1939–45 war there were few 72-hole events for amateurs. With the advent of the Berkshire Trophy in 1946 and the Brabazon, now the English Open Stroke Play, a year later, they became important tournaments in the amateur season. In the later 1950s Welsh golfers were lamenting that while Scotland and Ireland both had a few 72-hole competitions, Wales had no such trophy. Colonel Tony Duncan, four times Welsh Amateur Champion, a Welsh international for 26 years from 1933 and Walker Cup Captain 1953, took up the challenge and with the enthusiastic support of his home club, Southerndown, inaugurated the Duncan Putter in 1959.

From the start it was an invitation tournament held over the Easter weekend. Leading Welsh golfers, especially the younger element, were invited, in addition to several guests from outside the Principality. In its 31 years it has been won 19 times by Welshmen and 15 by guest players. Iestyn Tucker, now president of the Welsh Golf Union, won it five times in the early years and guest player Peter McEvoy on four occasions between 1978 and 1987.

Colonel Duncan insisted that it should be a traditional amateur tournament from the start, with medal prizes for the leading three players and another for the most successful Welsh player under 25. There is no entrance fee and these conditions remain to this day. Five years ago Colonel Duncan, who still maintains a keen interest in the event, handed over the management of the Duncan Putter to Wing Commander Ken Cooper, a former secretary of the Southerndown Club.

YEAR	WINNER	SCORE	YEAR	WINNER	SCORE
1959	G Huddy	301	1976	WI Tucker ⎫ tie	286
1960	WI Tucker	289		H Stott ⎭	
1961	WI Tucker ⎫ tie	295	1977	H Stott	295
	G Huddy ⎭		1978	P McEvoy	295
1962	EN Davies	297	1979	HJ Evans	292
1963	WI Tucker	296	1980	P McEvoy	296
1964	JL Toye	293	1981	R Chapman ⎫ tie	294
1965	P Townsend	305		PG Way ⎭	
1966	MF Attenborough	291	1982	D McLean	283
1967	D Millensted	297	1983	JG Jermine	297
1968	JL Morgan	299	1984	JP Price	284
1969	WI Tucker	304	1985	P McEvoy	299
1970	JL Toye	305	1986	D Wood	300
1971	W Humphreys	295	1987	P McEvoy	278
1972	P Berry (3 rds. fog)	230	1988	S Dodd	290
1973	JKD Povall	299	1989	RN Roderick	280
1974	S Cox	302	1990	R Willison	311
1975	JG Jermine	295			

East Berkshire Stag

INAUGURATED 1976

at East Berks, Crowthorne

YEAR	WINNER	YEAR	WINNER
1976	AWB Lyle	1984	P Young
1977	PM Carrigill	1985	SM Bottomley
1978	JC Davies	1986	SM Bottomley
1979	SD Keppler	1987	J Robinson
1980	JC Davies	1988	A O'Neill
1981	P Garner	1989	J Cowgill
1982	M Few	1990	J Cowgill
1983	D Lane		

Edward Trophy

INAUGURATED 1892

at Glasgow Gailes from 1928

Presented by the Edward family in 1892 for amateur competition among West of Scotland club golfers, it was played in the west over numerous courses until 1928. Since that year it has been a 36-hole contest at Glasgow Gailes, the course of the Glasgow Club on the coast.

In 1968 Charlie Green, one of the most consistent Scottish amateurs of the post-war years, five times in the Walker Cup team and twice more as non-playing captain, in the first of his four Edward Trophy victories, holed the course in the second round in 62. The record stood for 20 years until the 14th hole was extended and Drew Elliott's 66 became the new record in 1989. William Tulloch has the greatest number of wins, with five between 1924 and 1931.

The Edward Trophy has always had a distinguished field; in recent years the catchment area of players has been extended, several winners coming from east-coast clubs. In 1987, the Glasgow Club's bi-centenary year, the winner, S. Easingwood, received a gold medal. Subsequent winners have been awarded a silver.

YEAR	WINNER	VENUE	YEAR	WINNER	VENUE
1892	DD Robertson	Troon	1901	CB Macfarlane	Western Gailes
1893	GHN Rennie	Prestwick St	1902	G Wilkie	Irvine
		Nicholas	1903	AH Colville	Milngavie
1894	Wm Doleman	Ardeer	1904	JW Cooper	Kilmacolm
1895	R Adam	Glasgow Gailes	1905	HC Dow	Cathcart Castle
1896	D Bone	Bridge of Weir	1906	G Wilkie	Prestwick St
1897	AF Duncan	Greenock			Nicholas
1898	IG Macfarlane	Skelmorlie	1907	F Peebles	Ranfurly Castle
1899	WB Hunter	Bogside	1908	I Ure	Cardross
1900	D Bone	Dumbarton	1909	R Scott	Erskine

YEAR	WINNER	VENUE	YEAR	WINNER	VENUE
1910	R Andrew	Barassie	1954	Dr FWG Deighton	Glasgow Gailes
1911	G Lockhart	Drumchapel	1955	LG Taylor	Glasgow Gailes
1912	PE Soutter	Hamilton	1956	JC Wilson	Glasgow Gailes
1913	W Fotheringham	Balmore	1957	WS Jack	Glasgow Gailes
1914	PE Soutter	Lanark	1958	Dr JL Hastings	Glasgow Gailes
1915–19	*Not played due to Great War*		1959	RR Jack	Glasgow Gailes
1920	G Lockhart	Prestwick St	1960	SWT Murray	Glasgow Gailes
		Nicholas	1961	SWT Murray	Glasgow Gailes
1921	DS Rutherford	Western Gailes	1962	JE Stuart	Glasgow Gailes
1922	HM Dickson	Glasgow,	1963	F Morris	Glasgow Gailes
		Killermont	1964	HM Campbell	Glasgow Gailes
1923	W Brock	Whitecraigs	1965	WT Thornton	Glasgow Gailes
1924	W Tulloch	Prestwick St	1966	JM Cannon	Glasgow Gailes
		Nicholas	1967	M Alexander	Glasgow Gailes
1925	W Tulloch	Glasgow N.	1968	CW Green	Glasgow Gailes
		Western	1969	WR Lockie	Glasgow Gailes
1926	W Tulloch	Glasgow Gailes	1970	JW Johnston	Glasgow Gailes
1927	D Russell	Hamilton	1971	IH Ritchie	Glasgow Gailes
1928	A Menzie	Glasgow Gailes	1972	B Nicholson	Glasgow Gailes
1929	W Tulloch	Glasgow Gailes	1973	CW Green	Glasgow Gailes
1930	JE Dawson	Glasgow Gailes	1974	CW Green	Glasgow Gailes
1931	W Tulloch	Glasgow Gailes	1975	CW Green	Glasgow Gailes
1932	T MacLean	Glasgow Gailes	1976	DM McCart	Glasgow Gailes
1933	SL McKinlay	Glasgow Gailes	1977	R Blackwood	Glasgow Gailes
1934	H Thomson	Glasgow Gailes	1978	R Blackwood	Glasgow Gailes
1935	D Cameron	Glasgow Gailes	1979	J Cuddity	Glasgow Gailes
1936	JM Dykes	Glasgow Gailes	1980	D Murdoch	Glasgow Gailes
1937	SL McKinlay	Glasgow Gailes	1981	DJ Liddle	Glasgow Gailes
1938	JB Stevenson	Glasgow Gailes	1982	AF Dunsmore	Glasgow Gailes
1939	WS McLeod	Glasgow Gailes	1983	S Morrison	Glasgow Gailes
1940–46	*Not played due to Second World War*		1984	RH Walker	Glasgow Gailes
1947	JB Stevenson	Glasgow Gailes	1985	GK MacDonald	Glasgow Gailes
1948	A Stevenson	Glasgow Gailes	1986	JM Noon	Glasgow Gailes
1949	JC Wilson	Glasgow Gailes	1987	S Easingwood	Glasgow Gailes
1950	J McKay	Glasgow Gailes	1988	R Blair	Glasgow Gailes
1951	JC Wilson	Glasgow Gailes	1989	AJ Elliot	Glasgow Gailes
1952	D Cameron	Glasgow Gailes	1990	A Gourlay	Glasgow Gailes
1953	RDR Walker	Glasgow Gailes			

The Failand Cup

INAUGURATED 1965

at Bristol and Clifton, Avon

YEAR	WINNER	YEAR	WINNER
1965	JG Parker	1973	RA Searle
1966	JG Parker	1974	R Abbott
1967	ET Jackson	1975	S Dunlop
1968	GM Brand	1976	R Abbott
1969	GM Brand	1977	CS Mitchell
1970	P French	1978	*No competition*
1971	IM Stungo	1979	ME Lewis
1972	M Lane	1980	A Sherborne

YEAR	WINNER	YEAR	WINNER
1981	S Davidson	1986	G Thomas
1982	CS Mitchell	1987	JG Stordy
1983	D Hares	1988	MW Plummer
1984	A Lyddon	1989	G Wolstenholme
1985	D Wood	1990	G Wolstenholme

Formby Hare

INAUGURATED 1949

at Formby

YEAR	WINNER	YEAR	WINNER
1949	AT Kyle	1970	DJ Eccleston
1950	CH Beamish	1971	H Ashby
1951	RJ White	1972	RJ White
1952	D Anderson	1973	SG Birtwell
1953	IW Calder	1974	TR Shingler
1954	DL Woon	1975	AF Warde
1955	F Fawcett	1976	JB Dickinson
1956	GH Foster	1977	JB Dickinson
1957	MJ Pearson	1978	PM Carrigill
1958	RJ White	1979	BA Williams
1959	G Huddy	1980	MS Thompson
1960	B Stockdale	1981	PT Bailey
1961	MJ Reece	1982	DJ Eccleston
1962	JB Carr	1983	P Snowden
1963	J Glover	1984	N Brazell
1964	B Stockdale	1985	G Boardman
1965	IR Harris	1986	RA Bardsley
1966	DI Rigby	1987	CJ Heneghan
1967	SG Birtwell	1988	A Mitchell
1968	DM Marsh	1989	S Hamer
1969	SG Birtwell	1990	TA Foster

Frame Trophy

INAUGURATED 1986

at Worplesdon, Surrey

YEAR	WINNER	YEAR	WINNER
1986	DW Frame	1989	JRW Walkinshaw
1987	JRW Walkinshaw	1990	WJ Williams
1988	DW Frame		

Frank Stableford Open Memorial Trophy

INAUGURATED 1969

at Wallasey, Merseyside

YEAR	WINNER	YEAR	WINNER
1969	NB Moir	1980	P Morgan
1970	C Foster	1981	A Sutcliffe
1971	TD Frost	1982	A Gibson
1972	PH Dennett	1983	CR Smethurst
1973	PH Dennett	1984	SH Roberts
1974	LJ Mooney	1985	A Hill
1975	B Williams	1986	S Fitzpatrick
1976	RWR Walker	1987	AP Jordon
1977	P Morgan	1988	B Hickey
1978	S Hadfield	1989	PT Bailey
1979	PH Dennett	1990	I McGurn

Frilford Gold Medal

INAUGURATED 1961

at Frilford Heath, Oxfordshire

YEAR	WINNER	YEAR	WINNER
1961	DW Frame	1976	CA Banks
1962	DW Frame	1977	MD Owers
1963	J Lawrence	1978	C Bezer
1964	AG Clay	1979	D Rosier
1965	J Lawrence	1980	S Scott
1966	DW Frame	1981	JB Berney
1967	JH Cook	1982	DH Niven
1968	DW Frame	1983	M Pinner
1969	A Millar	1984	A Cotton
1970	W Humphreys	1985	P Hall
1971	SC Mason	1986	S Walker
1972	MG King	1987	A Rogers
1973	SC Mason	1988	A Rogers
1974	MG King	1989	N Williamson
1975	WJ Reid	1990	P Sullivan

George Hillyard Memorial Cup

INAUGURATED 1949

at Pulborough, West Sussex

YEAR	WINNER	YEAR	WINNER
1949	R Quilter	1964	CS Wells / C Copus } tie
1950	GA Hill		
1951	JH Langmead	1965	CS Wells / B Fibbins } tie
1952	JS Whedbee		
1953	JF Cripps	1966	DJ Harrison
1954	WA Slark	1967	RL Glading
1955	GE Hampshire	1968	TD Frost
1956	LS Foster	1969	R Hunter
1957	PF Scrutton	1970	G Hyde
1958	GR Bristowe	1971	JC Davies
1959	MJ Burgess / G Evans } tie	1972	DJ Harrison
		1973	PJ Benka
1960	MJ Burgess / G Evans } tie	1974	PJ Benka
		1975	B Winteridge
1961	MJ Burgess / G Evans } tie	1976	PJ Benka
		1977	JC Davies
1962	M Dawson / R Hunter } tie	1978	AG Sykes
		1979	P Garner
1963	MJ Fisher / MW Steel } tie	1980	K Weeks
		1981	M Torrens

YEAR	WINNER	YEAR	WINNER
1982	R Lee	1987	DW Alderson
1983	P Talbot	1988	R Edwards
1984	JS Spence	1989	D Lee
1985	K Weeks	1990	M Galway
1986	D Fay		

Gogs Trophy

INAUGURATED 1974

at Gog Magog, Cambridge

YEAR	WINNER	YEAR	WINNER
1974	JG Parkhill	1983	RW Guy
1975	R Dew	1984	C McKay
1976	JG Parkhill	1985	BJ Harris
1977	WR Calderwood	1986	R Claydon
1978	C Cox	1987	E Wisbey
1979	C Cox	1988	RD Squire
1980	JM Skoulding	1989	GR Krause
1981	K Diss	1990	T Ryan
1982	BJ Hilsdon		

Golf Illustrated Gold Vase

INAUGURATED 1909

One of the oldest open amateur stroke play events, the *Golf Illustrated* Gold Vase has always drawn a distinguished field. There have been many Amateur Champions among the winners; they include Bobby Jones in 1930, his grand slam year, and Michael Bonallack with six wins between 1961 and 1975.

YEAR	WINNER	VENUE	SCORE	YEAR	WINNER	VENUE	SCORE
1909	CK Hutchinson	Mid-Surrey	146	1920	DS Crowther	St George's Hill	159
1910	A Mitchell	Sunningdale	150	1921	M Seymour	Sunningdale	144
1911	R Harris	Stoke Poges	145	1922	WA Murray	Stoke Poges	151
1912	R Harris	Mid-Surrey	147	1923	CJH Tolley	Oxhey	153
1913	A Mitchell	Walton Heath	152	1924	CC Aylmer	Moor Park	149
1914	HH Hilton	Sunningdale	151	1925	JB Beck	Addington	150
1915–18	*Not played due to Great War*			1926	CJH Tolley } tie TA Torrance	Addington	147
1919	B Darwin	Mid-Surrey	153				

YEAR	WINNER	VENUE	SCORE	YEAR	WINNER	VENUE	SCORE
1927	RH Wethered	Beaconsfield	151	1965	CA Clark	Sunningdale	139
1928	CJH Tolley	Northwood	150	1966	P Townsend	Sunningdale	142
1929	D Grant	Walton Heath	151	1967	RA Durrant ⎫ tie Sunningdale		141
1930	RT Jones (USA)	Sunningdale	143		MF Bonallack ⎭		
1931	WA Murray	West Hill	147	1968	MF Bonallack	Sunningdale	143
1932	RW Hartley	Woking	147	1969	MF Bonallack ⎫ tie Sunningdale		142
1933	RW Hartley	Stoke Poges	143		J Hayes ⎭		
1934	WL Hartley	Walton Heath	147	1970	DJ Harrison	Sunningdale	140
1935	J Thomas	The Berkshire	147	1971	MF Bonallack	Sunningdale	137
1936	J Ferrier (Aus)	Ashridge	139		H Ashby ⎫		
1937	R Sweeney Jr	West Herts	137	1972	DP Davidson ⎬ tie Sunningdale		143
1938	CJ Anderson	Bramshot	150		R Hunter ⎭		
1939	SB Roberts	Pulborough	143	1973	JC Davies	Walton Heath	142
1940–47	*Not played due to Second World War*			1974	PJ Hedges	Walton Heath	146
1948	RD Chapman (USA)	Sunningdale	143	1975	MF Bonallack	Walton Heath	142
1949	RJ White	Dollymount	142	1976	Allan Brodie	Walton Heath	141
1950	AW Whyte	Western Gailes	148	1977	JC Davies	Walton Heath	141
1951	JB Carr	Southerndown	143	1978	P Thomas	Walton Heath	141
1952	JDA Langley	Sunningdale	140	1979	KJ Miller	Walton Heath	140
1953	JDA Langley	Sunningdale	143	1980	G Brand Jr	Walton Heath	142
1954	H Ridgeley (USA)	Sunningdale	143	1981	P Garner	Walton Heath	143
1955	Maj DA Blair	Sunningdale	140	1982	I Carslaw	Walton Heath	140
1956	Maj DA Blair	Sunningdale	141	1983	SD Keppler	Walton Heath	143
1957	GB Wolstenholme	Sunningdale	138	1984	JV Marks	Walton Heath	146
1958	MSR Lunt	Sunningdale	141	1985	M Davis	Walton Heath	145
1959	AF Bussell	Sunningdale	141	1986	R Eggo	Walton Heath	106
1960	D Sewell	Sunningdale	142				(27 holes)
1961	DJ Harrison ⎫ tie Sunningdale		141	1987	D Lane	Walton Heath	144
	MF Bonallack ⎭			1988	M Turner	Walton Heath	141
1962	BHG Chapman	Sunningdale	145	1989	G Wolstenholme	Sunningdale	142
1963	RH Mummery	Sunningdale	143	1990	A Rogers	Walton Heath	137
1964	D Moffat	Sunningdale	148				

Grafton Morrish Trophy

INAUGURATED 1963

at Hunstanton and Brancaster

The Grafton Morrish Trophy draws entries from a wider range of schools than the Halford-Hewitt which is limited to 64. After five regional qualifying competitions, 32 schools, each consisting of three foursomes partnerships, compete over a weekend at Hunstanton and Brancaster.

YEAR	WINNER	YEAR	WINNER
1963	Tonbridge	1977	Haileybury
1964	Tonbridge	1978	Charterhouse
1965	Charterhouse	1979	Harrow
1966	Charterhouse	1980	Charterhouse
1967	Charterhouse	1981	Charterhouse
1968	Wellington	1982	Marlborough
1969	Sedbergh	1983	Wellington
1970	Sedbergh	1984	Sedbergh
1971	Dulwich	1985	Warwick
1972	Sedbergh	1986	Tonbridge
1973	Pangbourne	1987	Harrow
1974	Millfield	1988	Robert Gordon's
1975	Oundle	1989	Tonbridge
1976	Charterhouse	1990	Clifton

Graham Butler Trophy
(formerly Ferndown Fox)

INAUGURATED 1967

at Ferndown, Dorset

YEAR	WINNER	YEAR	WINNER
1967	Ferndown	1978	The Army
1968	Parkstone	1979	Royal Air Force
1969	Stoneham	1980	High Post
1970	Stoneham	1981	High Post
1971	Royal Air Force	1982	Brokenhurst
1972	High Post	1983	Parkstone
1973	High Post	1984–86	*Not played*
1974	Walton Heath	1987	Parkstone
1975	Worplesdon	1988	Ferndown
1976	Worplesdon	1989	Brokenhurst
1977	Newbury and Crookham	1990	Stoneham

Halford-Hewitt Cup

INAUGURATED 1924

at Deal

First played over several courses by the old boys of eleven public schools in 1924, the Halford-Hewitt soon found a permanent home at Deal where the Royal Cinque Ports Club has thrown open its doors to a vast horde of keen amateur players ever since 1926. The competition has always been for five pairs from each school playing foursomes with the fifth match often having to play extra holes to obtain a 3–2 result. As the entry grew to more than 50 schools, Deal was unable to complete the tournament in the necessary four days and the Royal St George's Club at nearby Sandwich has accommodated half the matches in the first two rounds. It is a remarkable feat of organisation when 640 players take part in the first round and 20 remain to contest the final in the afternoon of the fourth day.

Always played in late March or early April, often in cold and windy weather, it is nevertheless one of the most social of all tournaments and is played in the best spirit of amateur golf. Schools which seldom progress beyond the first or second round put a high value on keeping their place in the draw. With no seeding there are invariably upsets when a fancied school comes to grief in an early round at the hands of one with little hope, playing above its game on the day.

In the first 26 years the winner was always one of six schools: Eton, Harrow, Charterhouse, Rugby, Marlborough and Winchester. During the following 34 years only another ten schools have been added to the list of winners – although the semi-finals have included a far wider range than previously.

YEAR	WINNER	MATCHES	RUNNER-UP	MATCHES
1924	Eton	4	Winchester	1
1925	Eton	3	Harrow	2
1926	Eton	3	Winchester	2
1927	Harrow	3½	Rugby	1½
1928	Eton	3	Charterhouse	2
1929	Harrow	4	Charterhouse	1
1930	Charterhouse	4	Uppingham	1
1931	Harrow	3	Winchester	2
1932	Charterhouse	3½	Rugby	1½
1933	Rugby	3	Harrow	2
1934	Charterhouse	4	Watson's	1
1935	Charterhouse	4	Shrewsbury	1
1936	Charterhouse	3½	Rugby	1½
1937	Charterhouse	4	Liverpool	1
1938	Marlborough	3½	Harrow	1½
1939	Charterhouse	3	Harrow	2
1940 – 46 *Not played due to the Second World War*				
1947	Harrow	3½	Charterhouse	1½
1948	Winchester	3	Watson's	2
1949	Charterhouse	3	Rugby	2
1950	Rugby	3	Stowe	2
1951	Rugby	3	Harrow	2

YEAR	WINNER	MATCHES	RUNNER-UP	MATCHES
1952	Harrow	4	Rossall	1
1953	Harrow	4	Watson's	1
1954	Rugby	3	Wellington	2
1955	Eton	3½	Harrow	1½
1956	Eton	3½	Rugby	1½
1957	Watson's	3	Harrow	2
1958	Harrow	3	Charterhouse	2
1959	Wellington	3	Charterhouse	2
1960	Rossall	4	Fettes	1
1961	Rossall	4	Rugby	1
1962	Oundle	3	Stowe	2
1963	Repton	3	Fettes	2
1964	Fettes	3½	Shrewsbury	1½
1965	Rugby	3½	Merchiston	1½
1966	Charterhouse	4	Malvern	1
1967	Eton	4	Wellington	1
1968	Eton	3	Cranleigh	2
1969	Eton	4	Uppingham	1
1970	Merchiston	3½	Harrow	1½
1971	Charterhouse	3	Marlborough	2
1972	Marlborough	4½	Harrow	½
1973	Rossall	3	Loretto	2
1974	Charterhouse	4	Rugby	1
1975	Harrow	3½	Merchant Taylor's	1½
1976	Merchiston	3	Whitgift	2
1977	Watson's	4½	Marlborough	½
1978	Harrow	3½	Stowe	1½
1979	Stowe	3½	Marlborough	1½
1980	Shrewsbury	4½	Epsom	½
1981	Watson's	3	Charterhouse	2
1982	Charterhouse	4	Dulwich	1
1983	Charterhouse	3	Shrewsbury	1
1984	Charterhouse	3	Malvern	2
1985	Harrow	4	Shrewsbury	1
1986	Repton	3	Malvern	2
1987	Merchiston	3½	Tonbridge	1½
1988	Stowe	4½	Bradfield	½
1989	Eton	3	Shrewsbury	2
1990	Tonbridge	3	Malvern	2

The Hampshire Hog

INAUGURATED 1957

at North Hants, Fleet

YEAR	WINNER	YEAR	WINNER
1957	MF Bonallack	1974	TJ Giles
1958	PF Scrutton	1975	HAN Stott
1959	Col AA Duncan	1976	MC Hughesdon
1960	MF Attenborough	1977	AWB Lyle
1961	HC Squirrell	1978	GF Godwin
1962	FD Physick	1979	MF Bonallack
1963	Sqn Ldr WE McCrea	1980	RA Durrant
1964	DF Wilkie	1981	G Brand Jr
1965	T Koch de Gooreynd	1982	A Sherborne
1966	Maj DA Blair	1983	I Gray
1967	Maj DA Blair	1984	J Hawksworth
1968	MJ Burgess	1985	A Clapp
1969	B Critchley	1986	R Eggo
1970	Maj DA Blair	1987	A Rogers
1971	DW Frame	1988	S Richardson
1972	R Revell	1989	P McEvoy
1973	SC Mason	1990	J Metcalfe

Hawksworth Trophy

INAUGURATED 1971

at Bradford Golf Club, West Yorkshire

YEAR	WINNER	YEAR	WINNER
1971	B Cawthray	1981	S Hamer
1972	MJ Kelley	1982	S Hamer
1973	MJ Kelley	1983	IJA Stephenson
1974	MJ Kelley	1984	I Mackenzie
1975	D McCarthy	1985	JL Paxton
1976	PM Carrigill	1986	I Mackenzie
1977	R Foster	1987	J Whiteley
1978	S Williams	1988	SA Lax
1979	R Foster	1989	S East
1980	L Walker	1990	D Boughey

High Post Open

INAUGURATED 1973

at High Post, Salisbury, Wiltshire

YEAR	WINNER	YEAR	WINNER
1973	BM Townsend	1982	N Garfoot
1974	RE Searle	1983	A Sherborne
1975	BM Townsend	1984	R Willison
1976	BM Townsend	1985	RE Searle
1977	RE Searle	1986	N Graves
1978	RE Searle	1987	N Graves
1979	J Lawrence	1988	A Haworth
1980	K Weeks	1989	N Garfoot
1981	K Weeks	1990	N Graves

Howley Hall Scratch Trophy

INAUGURATED 1978

at Howley Hall, Leeds

YEAR	WINNER	YEAR	WINNER
1978	S Bennett	1985	G Boardman
1979	MJ Kelley	1986	A Squires
1980	MJ Kelley	1987	S Field
1981	MJ Wild	1988	G Boardman
1982	IJA Stephenson	1989	G Boardman
1983	R Roper	1990	I Mackenzie
1984	S Hamer		

John Cross Bowl

INAUGURATED 1957

at Worplesdon, Surrey

YEAR	WINNER	YEAR	WINNER
1957	DW Frame	1974	RPF Brown
1958	G Evans	1975	BJ Winteridge
1959	G Evans	1976	DW Frame
1960	DW Frame	1977	DW Frame
1961	DW Frame	1978	RPF Brown
1962	DW Frame	1979	JG Bennett
1963	PO Green	1980	JG Bennett
1964	RL Glading	1981	ME Johnson
1965	P Townsend	1982	R Boxall
1966	P Townsend	1983	DG Lane
1967	MJ Burgess	1984	I Gray
1968	PJ Benka	1985	M Devetta
1969	DW Frame	1986	C Rotheroe
1970	P Dawson	1987	B White
1971	PBQ Drayson	1988	B White
1972	AR Kerr	1989	KG Jones
1973	DW Frame	1990	D Lee

Lagonda Trophy

INAUGURATED 1975

at Camberley Heath (from 1990 at Gog Magog)

YEAR	WINNER	YEAR	WINNER
1975	WJ Reid	1983	I Sparkes
1976	JC Davies	1984	M Davis
1977	WS Gronow	1985	J Robinson
1978	JC Davies	1986	D Gilford
1979	JG Bennett	1987	DG Lane
1980	P McEvoy	1988	R Claydon
1981	N Mitchell	1989	T Spence
1982	A Sherborne	1990	L Parsons

Leven Gold Medal

INAUGURATED 1870

(now Standard Life Champion Medal)

First played in 1870, the Leven Club claims it is the oldest amateur tournament open to all. Other clubs record earlier medal competitions but for members only. Most of the winners before it was extended to 36 and then 72 holes after nearly 100 years, came from Fife Clubs with Edinburgh intervening occasionally. The Leven Thistle Club, which uses the Leven Links as its home course, has provided many winners, including Eric McRuvie who had seven successes between 1927 and 1950. The Innerleven Club, which also claimed many winners, joined the Leven Club to form the Leven Golfing Society some years ago.

Since 1969 winners have come from further away, several of them Scots Walker Cup players, Ian Hutcheon in 1976 having the lowest score of 266. The only winner from outside Scotland has been the Swede Per-Ulrik Johansson in 1986.

Standard Life presented the gold medal to the Innerleven Club in 1870.

YEAR	WINNER	SCORE	CLUB	YEAR	WINNER	SCORE	CLUB
1870	J Elder	85	Leven	1901	R Simpson	76	Leven Thistle
1871	R Wallace	91	Leven	1902	J Bell	76	Leven Thistle
1872	P Anderson	91	Leven	1903	W Henderson	76	Innerleven
1873	R Armit	95	St Andrews	1904	W Henderson	77	Innerleven
			Thistle	1905	G Wilkie	76	Leven Thistle
1874	D Campbell	93	Leven	1906	G Wilkie	78	Leven Thistle
1875	AM Ross	90	Warrender	1907	M Goodwillie	73	Leven Thistle
1876	AM Ross	88	Warrender	1908	W Henderson	77	Innerleven
1877	J Wilkie	88	Leven	1909	W Henderson	77	Innerleven
1878	R Wallace	90	Innerleven	1910	W Whyte	76	Leven Thistle
1879	C Anderson	89	Innerleven	1911	G Wilkie	73	Leven Thistle
1880	C Anderson	89	Innerleven	1912	G Wilkie	73	Leven Thistle
1881	J Foggo	91	Innerleven	1913	W Whyte	73	Leven Thistle
1882	J Wilkie	89	Leven Thistle	1914	GB Rattray	76	Leven Thistle
1883	J Foggo	86	Innerleven	1915–18 *Not played due to Great War*			
1884	C Anderson	89	Innerleven	1919	G Wilkie	77	Leven Thistle
1885	R Adam	84	Leven Thistle	1920	JJ Smith	76	Leven Thistle
1886	R Adam	87	Leven Thistle	1921	GV Donaldson	77	Innerleven
1887	J Foggo	81	Innerleven	1922	SO Shepperd	72	Innerleven
1888	DA Leitch	86	Edinburgh St	1923	GV Donaldson	73	Innerleven
			Andrew	1924	JN Smith	76	Earlsferry
1889	R Adam	81	Leven Thistle	1925	A Robertson	73	Leven Thistle
1890	W Marshall	80	Leven Thistle	1926	T Ainslie	75	Leven Thistle
1891	DM Jackson	80	Leven Thistle	1927	EA McRuvie	72	Leven Thistle
1892	Col DW		Royal &	1928	EA McRuvie	70	Leven Thistle
	Mackinnon	85	Ancient	1929	EA McRuvie	72	Leven Thistle
1893	HS Colt	79	Royal &	1930	EA McRuvie	68	Leven Thistle
			Ancient	1931	A Dunsire	71	Leven Thistle
1894	J Bell Nr	82	Leven Thistle	1932	J Ballingall	72	Lundin
1895	G Wilkie Jr	80	Leven Thistle	1933	CA Danks	73	Leven Thistle
1896	J Bell Jr	78	Leven Thistle	1934	EA McRuvie	67	Leven Thistle
1897	J Bell Jr	79	Leven Thistle	1935	EG Stoddart	71	Innerleven
1898	G Wilkie	82	Leven Thistle	1936	GA Buist	73	Leven Thistle
1899	G Wilkie Jr	78	Leven Thistle	1937	JY Strachan	75	Leven Thistle
1900	W Henderson	78	Innerleven	1938	S Macdonald	71	St Andrews

YEAR	WINNER	SCORE	CLUB	YEAR	WINNER	SCORE	CLUB
1939	D Jamieson	72	Leven Thistle	1955	JW Draper	72	Innerleven
1940–45	*Not played due to Second World War*			1956	R Dishart	72	Leven Thistle
1946	EA McRuvie	77	Leven Thistle	1957	I Pearson	72	Leven Thistle
1947	JE Young	74		1958	W McIntyre	71	Leven Thistle
1948	J Imrie	77	Leven Thistle	1959	W Moyes	71	Leven Thistle
1949	WM Ogg	76	Aberdour	1960	T Taylor	69	Leven Thistle
1950	E McRuvie	77	Leven Thistle	1961	A Cunningham	69	Leven Thistle
1951	J Imrie	72	Leven Thistle	1962	W Moyes	71	Leven Thistle
1952	HVS Thomson	69	Prestwick	1963	W Moyes	68	Leven Thistle
1953	O Rolland	70	Innerleven	1964	A Cunningham	68	Leven Thistle
1954	JW Draper	73	Innerleven	1965	PG Buchanan	71	Williamwood

YEAR	WINNER					SCORE	CLUB
1966	GM Rutherford	72	72			144	Williamwood
1967	AO Maxwell	66	74			140	Grange
1968	A Cunningham	66	74			140	Leven Thistle
1969	P Smith	71	70	72	71	284	Dalmahoy
1970	JC Farmer	70	67	69	71	277	St Andrews
1971	J Scott Macdonald	67	70	70		207	Dalmahoy
1972	J Rankine	69	71	71	71	282	Falkirk Tryst
1973	S Stephen	70	71	73	74	288	Leven
1974	P Smith	72	71	70	69	282	Dalmahoy
1975	HB Stuart	70	73	69	74	286	Forres
1976	IC Hutcheon	65	66	67	68	266	Monifieth
1977	IC Hutcheon	71	71	75	72	289	Monifieth
1978	R Wallace	75	71	69	72	287	Canmore
1979	B Marchbank	70	67	67	70	274	Auchterarder
1980	J Huggan	75	68	68	68	279	Dunbar
1981	IC Hutcheon	68	73	70	71	282	Monifieth
1982	IC Hutcheon	69	65	68	70	272	Monifieth
1983	J Huggan	70	67	70	67	274	Dunbar
1984	S Stephen	70	71	68	69	278	Broomieknowe
1985	AD Turnbull	78	68	69	66	281	Peebles
1986	P-U Johansson	68	72	65	70	275	Kalmar, Sweden
1987	G Macgregor	69	67	67	68	271	Glencorse
1988	CE Everett	68	70	68	74	280	Cambuslang
1989	AJ Coltart	69	72	73	66	280	Thornhill
1990	CE Everett	70	75	65	70	280	Cambuslang

Lytham Trophy

INAUGURATED 1965

at Royal Lytham and St Annes

The Lytham Trophy was founded by the Royal Lytham and St Annes Club to fill a gap in the amateur programme 25 years ago. The club felt there was a need for a prestigious open 72-hole stroke play tournament in the North, which would draw the best amateurs in Britain. A glance at the list of winners will show how successful the club's imaginative idea has been. Most of them have been Walker Cup internationals. Lytham is acknowledged as a tough course which will try the skills of the best players. It will be seen that only on six occasions has the winner's score been under 290 for 72 holes. The best have been Peter McEvoy's 279 in 1979 and 281 by Michael Bonallack in 1972. Several winners have come from Ireland, putting up a strong challenge to the English players.

YEAR	WINNER	SCORE	YEAR	WINNER	SCORE
1965	MF Bonallack ⎱ tie CA Clark ⎰	295	1976	MJ Kelley	292
			1977	P Deeble	296
1966	P Townsend	290	1978	B Marchbank	288
1967	R Foster	296	1979	P McEvoy	279
1968	R Foster	286	1980	IC Hutcheon	293
1969	T Craddock	290	1981	R Chapman (3 rounds)	221
	SG Birtwell ⎫		1982	MF Sludds	306
1970	JC Farmer ⎬ tie	296	1983	S McAllister	299
	CW Green ⎪		1984	J Hawksworth	289
	GC Marks ⎭		1985	L Macnamara	
1971	W Humphreys	282		(2 rounds)	144
1972	MF Bonallack	281	1986	S McKenna	297
1973	MG King ⎱ tie SG Birtwell ⎰	292	1987	D Wood	293
			1988	P Broadhurst	290
1974	CW Green	291	1989	N Williamson	286
1975	G Macgregor	299	1990	G Evans	291

Mere Trophy

INAUGURATED 1946

at Mere, Cheshire

YEAR	WINNER	YEAR	WINNER
1946	CW Timmis	1969	EJ Threlfall
1947	G Winterbottom	1970	AS Thornley
1948	JT Jones	1971	W Smith
1949	KE Woodward	1972	E Walsh
1950	Lt Col F Schuermann USAF	1973	B Stockdale
1951	GC Tuck	1974	B Stockdale
1952	JCW Daniels	1975	RA Briggs
1953	PB Scott	1976	A Squires
1954	HC Humphries	1977	GM Edwards
1955	ME Wesley	1978	CR Smethurst
1956	PB Allen	1979	PHH Dennett
1957	ND Howard	1980	M Hassall
1958	CV Keith	1981	PHH Dennett
1959	BJ Isaac	1982	A Hamer
1960	ME Wesley	1983	J Cartmell
1961	B Stockdale	1984	CR Smethurst
1962	KP Geddes	1985	S Hamer
1963	TB Taylor	1986	A Hill
1964	R Foster	1987	I Spencer
1965	MJ Pearson	1988	A Hill
1966	MSR Lunt	1989	E Els
1967	ND Howard	1990	PI Wood
1968	PHH Dennett		

Northamptonshire County Cup

INAUGURATED 1966

at Northants County, Church Brampton

YEAR	WINNER	YEAR	WINNER
1966	A Forrester	1979	P Downes
1967	A Forrester	1980	I Mackenzie
1968	JM Pettigrew	1981	JE Ambridge
1969	RA Durrant	1982	NL Roche
1970	D Butler	1983	GR Krause
1971	P Elson	1984	*No competition*
1972	GAL Colman	1985	J Vaughan
1973	RG Hiatt	1986	*No competition*
1974	P McEvoy	1987	PN Wharton
1975	M James	1988	AS King
1976	KR Waters	1989	N Williamson
1977	PM Harris	1990	PN Wharton
1978	T Leigh		

Oak Tree Cup

INAUGURATED 1988

at King's Norton, Hereford & Worcestershire

YEAR	WINNER
1988	J Bickerton
1989	C Bufton
1990	A Allen

Oxford v Cambridge University Match

INAUGURATED 1878

The Oxford *v* Cambridge University match, first played as early as 1878, is not the oldest team golf match still in existence. In Canada the Royal Montreal Club has played the Quebec Club since 1876. Although it is possible that there are matches in Scotland which are still played and which began earlier than that in Canada, undoubtedly the University Match is the oldest known in Britain.

Until 1907 the Universities played each other on the 'holes up' basis, each game of 18 holes being played out between 1876 and 1897 and 36 holes from 1898. The system, which is still occasionally used in team matches, has something to be said for it in that the weaker player cannot be 'hidden'. The method was discarded after 1907, Cambridge having won that year by 23 holes to 22. Ever since the games have been decided by the customary method of matches won, lost and halved. Not until 1921 was the match extended to two days, with 36 holes foursomes being added on the opening day.

The first venue was Wimbledon Common, one of the very few courses in 1878 which enabled both sides to reach the course, play 18 holes and still return to college before midnight. After 1896 it was decided to move the match to links courses including Royal St George's and the old Prince's at Sandwich, Hoylake and Rye, which soon became the unofficial home of the Oxford and Cambridge Golfing Society. Before 1914 Woking and Sunningdale, both inland courses, were used for the match. Between the wars four more links courses were chosen, Hunstanton, Burnham and Berrow, Formby and Westward Ho! Subsequently Lytham St Annes, Birkdale, Porthcawl, Saunton, Ganton and Woodhall Spa have been added. Each captain selects the course for the match in alternate years.

Until the Second World War many of the best amateurs were from the two universities. Most weekends both teams played matches against well-known clubs in the London area and further afield. The results were reported by the press and they were considered worthy events in the winter calendar. The University golf season was from October to March when the Oxford and Cambridge match was played; the date is still the same. The standard of play was formidable and most Walker Cup teams until 1951 contained two or three Blues. Between the wars seven Amateur Championships were won by former Blues: Cyril Tolley and Ernest Holderness each won twice, Roger Wethered, Eric Martin-Smith and Robert Sweeney once each.

While the two universities were fine nurseries for some of the best amateur golfers to develop their game, golf was played by many fewer people until the 1950s when the preponderance of Blues in the higher echelons of amateur competition was gradually eroded. The standard of play in the match now may have declined a little, but there is still keen rivalry between the two sides and the award of a Blue is much prized.

Cambridge has drawn steadily ahead in the last thirty years and lead by 58 matches to 38, with 5 halved.

YEAR	WINNER	VENUE	HOLES UP
1878	Oxford	Wimbledon	24
1879	Cambridge	Wimbledon	10
1880	Oxford	Wimbledon	8
1881	No match		
1882	Cambridge	Wimbledon	1
1883	Oxford	Wimbledon	2
1884	Oxford	Wimbledon	2
1885	Oxford	Wimbledon	38
1886	Oxford	Wimbledon	37
1887	Cambridge	Wimbledon	12
1888	Cambridge	Wimbledon	8
1889	Oxford	Wimbledon	9
1890	Cambridge	Wimbledon	1
1891	Cambridge	Wimbledon	11
1892	Cambridge	Wimbledon	12
1893	Cambridge	Wimbledon	32
1894	Oxford	Sandwich	13
1895	Cambridge	Sandwich	3
1896	Halved	Wimbledon	0
1897	Cambridge	Sandwich	5
1898	Cambridge	Sandwich	11
1899	Oxford	Sandwich	18
1900	Oxford	Sandwich	69
1901	Oxford	Sandwich	19
1902	Oxford	Sandwich	47
1903	Oxford	Sandwich	27
1904	Oxford	Woking	2
1905	Cambridge	Sunningdale	49
1906	Cambridge	Hoylake	23
1907	Cambridge	Hoylake	1

(After 1907 the result was arrived at by matches won)

YEAR	WINNER	VENUE	MARGIN
1908	Cambridge	Sunningdale	1 match
1909	Oxford	St George's, Sandwich	4 matches
1910	Cambridge	Hoylake	2 matches
1911	Oxford	Rye	2 matches
1912	Halved	Prince's, Sandwich	4 matches each

YEAR	WINNER	VENUE	MARGIN
1913	Halved	Hoylake	4 matches each
1914	Oxford	Rye	1 match
1915–19	No match due to the Great War		
1920	Cambridge	Sunningdale	3 matches
1921	Oxford	Hoylake	9 matches
1922	Cambridge	Prince's, Sandwich	1 match
1923	Oxford	Rye	3 matches
1924	Cambridge	Hoylake	3 matches
1925	Oxford	Hunstanton	3 matches
1926	Cambridge	Burnham and Berrow	3 matches
1927	Cambridge	Hoylake	3 matches
1928	Cambridge	Prince's, Sandwich	2 matches
1929	Cambridge	Rye	4 matches
1930	Oxford	Hoylake	9 matches
1931	Oxford	Prince's, Sandwich	3 matches
1932	Oxford	Lytham St Annes	3 matches
1933	Cambridge	Prince's, Sandwich	7 matches
1934	Oxford	Formby	2 matches
1935	Cambridge	Burnham and Berrow	1 match
1936	Cambridge	Hoylake	9 matches
1937	Cambridge	Prince's, Sandwich	3 matches
1938	Cambridge	Westward Ho!	6 matches
1939	Cambridge	St George's, Sandwich	6 matches
1940–45	No match due to Second World War		
1946	Cambridge	Lytham St Annes	5 matches
1947	Oxford	Rye	3 matches
1948	Oxford	St George's, Sandwich	7 matches
1949	Cambridge	Hoylake	1 match
1950	Oxford	Lytham St Annes	4 matches

YEAR	WINNER	VENUE	MARGIN	YEAR	WINNER	VENUE	MARGIN
1951	Cambridge	Rye	6 matches	1969	Cambridge	Formby	7 matches
1952	Cambridge	Rye	5 matches	1970	Halved	St George's,	7½ matches
1953	Cambridge	Rye	3 matches			Sandwich	each
1954	Cambridge	Rye	1 match	1971	Oxford	Rye	7 matches
1955	Cambridge	Rye	1 match	1972	Cambridge	Formby	1 match
1956	Oxford	Formby	5 matches	1973	Oxford	Saunton	1 match
1957	Oxford	St George's,		1974	Cambridge	Ganton	5 matches
		Sandwich	5 matches	1975	Cambridge	Hoylake	4 matches
1958	Cambridge	Rye	1 match	1976	Cambridge	Woodhall Spa	5 matches
1959	Cambridge	Burnham and		1977	Cambridge	Porthcawl	11 matches
		Berrow	2 matches	1978	Oxford	Rye	3 matches
1960	Cambridge	Lytham St		1979	Oxford	Harlech	2 matches
		Annes	3 matches	1980	Oxford	Hoylake	2 matches
1961	Oxford	St George's,		1981	Cambridge	Formby	6 matches
		Sandwich	7 matches	1982	Cambridge	Hunstanton	1 match
1962	Halved	Hunstanton	7½ matches	1983	Cambridge	St George's,	
			each			Sandwich	4 matches
1963	Cambridge	Birkdale	10 matches	1984	Cambridge	Sunningdale	8 matches
1964	Oxford	Rye	10 matches	1985	Oxford	Rye	3 matches
1965	Cambridge	St George's,		1986	Oxford	Ganton	7 matches
		Sandwich	12 matches	1987	Cambridge	Formby	6 matches
1966	Cambridge	Hunstanton	15 matches	1988	Cambridge	Porthcawl	4 matches
1967	Cambridge	Rye	15 matches	1989	Cambridge	Rye	8 matches
1968	Cambridge	Porthcawl	2 matches	1990	Cambridge	Muirfield	7 matches

Parliamentary Handicap

INAUGURATED 1891

The Parliamentary Golfing Society was founded in 1891, when its first competition under handicap was played over the course at Tooting Bec, long since a housing estate. It was won by H.P. St John, a Clerk in the House of Lords. The Society has always drawn its members from the Lords and Commons, parliamentary staff and the Press Gallery. From 1893 to 1899 Furzedown, just south of Tooting Bec Common, was the venue. Here, AJ Balfour, a keen golfer and a leading figure in the game, won in 1894 when Leader of the House.

In 1900 it was decided to move the tournament to a seaside course, alternating between Rye, Deal, Littlestone and the two Sandwich courses, Royal St George's and the old Prince's, later demolished in the Second World War. By 1912 at Rye, entries had grown to 150. Among the winners before 1914 were several well-known parliamentarians including Balfour, who also won a third time in 1910, another (future) prime minister, Arthur Bonar Law in 1907, Sir Frank Newnes MP and Lords Dalhousie and Northesk.

In 1920 the Hon. FS Jackson MP, the famous English cricket captain, later Sir Stanley Jackson, had the first of his three victories in four years. Lord Balfour of Burleigh twice,

Colonel JT Moore Brabazon MP in 1932 and Sir John Simon MP, the Foreign Secretary, in 1934, were each victorious; all three were to be Captain of the Royal & Ancient Club, as have been several other PGS members.

The handicap was resumed in 1946 and the winners since have included Lord Balfour of Burleigh again twice, Lord Aldington four times, Walker Cup captain P.B. (Laddie) Lucas MP, Earl Wavell, Selwyn Lloyd MP (later to be Speaker), Sir Robert Speed (Counsel to the Speaker), Lord Whitelaw, and Stanley Clinton Davis MP with three successive wins 1982–84.

Intermittently in the 1920s and continuously from 1931–73 Walton Heath was the home of the tournament. Afterwards, it was played at New Zealand, near Byfleet, for six years, followed by Royal Mid-Surrey until 1990 when it moved to Royal Wimbledon. In earlier years when it was a knock-out competition the later rounds were played at a course mutually agreed by remaining participants; for instance, in 1933 George Lambert MP beat the Prince of Wales in the final at Coombe Hill. The Prince had played Lady Astor in the semi-final at Walton Heath, a match which attracted a large crowd.

YEAR	WINNER	VENUE
1891	Mr HP St John	Tooting Bec Common
1892	Mr HJ Tollemache MP	Tooting Bec Common
1893	The Hon TW Legh MP	Furzedown
1894	Mr AJ Balfour MP	Furzedown
1895	Mr J Moore	Furzedown
1896	The Hon TW Legh MP	Furzedown
1897	Mr AJ Balfour MP	Furzedown
1898	Mr FW Fison MP	Furzedown
1899	Mr AJ Robertson	Furzedown
1900	Mr AJ Robertson	Rye
1901	Mr HJF Badeley	Littlestone
1902	Mr William Younger MP	Deal
1903	Mr HW Forster MP	Rye
1904	Mr AW Soames MP	Littlestone
1905	Sir Edgar Vincent MP	Deal
1906	Mr F Newnes MP	Littlestone
1907	Mr A Bonar Law MP	Rye
1908	Mr Oswald Partington MP	Deal
1909	Lord Dalhousie	Prince's, Sandwich
1910	Mr AJ Balfour MP	St George's, Sandwich
1911	Mr Guy L'Estrange	Littlestone
1912	Mr A Hambro MP	Rye
1913	Lord Northesk	Prince's, Sandwich
1914 – 19	No contest owing to the Great War	
1920	Hon FS Jackson MP	St George's, Sandwich
1921	Sir P Greame MP	Beaconsfield
1922	Hon FS Jackson MP	Felixstowe
1923	Hon FS Jackson MP	Prince's, Sandwich
1924	Major Entwistle MP	Walton Heath
1925	Lord Balfour of Burleigh	Prince's, Sandwich
1926	Sir A Steel Maitland MP	Walton Heath
1927	Lord Balfour of Burleigh	Walton Heath
1928	GM Garro Jones MP	Prince's, Sandwich

YEAR	WINNER	VENUE
1929	C Coote	Walton Heath
1930	Major McKenzie Wood MP	Deal
1931	Sir R Hutchison MP	Walton Heath
1932	Lt-Col JTC Moore Brabazon MP	Walton Heath
1933	George Lambert MP	Walton Heath
1934	Sir J Simon MP	Walton Heath
1935	Lord Fairfax	Walton Heath
1936	Sir C MacAndrew MP	Walton Heath
1937	Lord Sandhurst	Walton Heath
1938	HR Farmer	Walton Heath
1939	Lord Brocket	Walton Heath
1940–45	No contest owing to Second World War	
1946	Lord Balfour of Burleigh	Walton Heath
1947	HT Newport	Walton Heath
1948	Sir G Campion	Walton Heath
1949	Brig ARW Low MP	Walton Heath
1950	Selwyn Lloyd MP	Walton Heath
1951	Sir John A Stainton	Walton Heath
1952	Lord Balfour of Burleigh } Lord Wavell } tie	Walton Heath
1953	Cyril Osborne MP	Walton Heath
1954	The Master of Sinclair	Walton Heath
1955	R Gresham Cooke MP } KA Bradshaw } tie	Walton Heath
1956	Cyril Osborne MP	Walton Heath
1957	ARW Low MP	Walton Heath
1958	Cyril Osborne MP	Walton Heath
1959	PB Lucas MP	Walton Heath
1960	Sir Toby Low MP	Walton Heath
1961	HRM Farmer	Walton Heath
1962	KA Bradshaw	Walton Heath
1963	JR Rose	Walton Heath
1964	John Osborn MP	Walton Heath
1965	Lord Allerton	Walton Heath

YEAR	WINNER	VENUE	YEAR	WINNER	VENUE
1966	Lord Allerton ⎱ tie DS Gordon ⎰	Walton Heath	1978	Lord Allerton	New Zealand
			1979	Lord Windlesham	New Zealand
1967	HRM Farmer	Walton Heath	1980	GR Russell	New Zealand
1968	Sir Robert Speed	Walton Heath	1981	Rodney Foster	Royal Mid-Surrey
1969	HRM Farmer	Walton Heath	1982	Stanley Clinton Davis MP	Royal Mid-Surrey
1970	Lord Campbell of Eskan	Walton Heath	1983	Stanley Clinton Davis MP	Royal Mid-Surrey
1971	DS Gordon	Walton Heath	1984	Stanley Clinton Davis	Royal Mid-Surrey
1972	Graham Cawthorne	Walton Heath	1985	Michael Morris MP	Royal Mid-Surrey
1973	Lord Aldington	Walton Heath	1986	Sir Anthony Grant MP	Royal Mid-Surrey
1974	PA Rawstorne	New Zealand	1987	Sir Anthony Grant MP	Royal Mid-Surrey
1975	John Osborn MP	New Zealand	1988	Sir Peter Hordern	Royal Mid-Surrey
1976	WSI Whitelaw MP	New Zealand	1989	Lord Vaux	Royal Mid-Surrey
1977	Lord Allerton	New Zealand	1990	Timothy Raison MP	Royal Wimbledon

The President's Putter

INAUGURATED 1920

at Rye

The Oxford and Cambridge Golfing Society, whose members nearly all played in the Varsity match, has always held its annual tournament in early January at Rye in East Sussex. Remarkably, since its inception in 1920, only once has it been cancelled due to snow and ice. On one occasion it had to be hurriedly transferred to Littlestone down the road and twice the later rounds and finals have had to be postponed until March.

'*The* Society', as it is known to many golfers, has had as distinguished a list of members as any. The competition is played off scratch. Rye is a course which usually plays better in winter than in summer and the greens are normally as true and fast in January as in any season. It is a true links course where the low pitch and run is more effective than the high approach.

The average time taken to play an 18-hole match in the Putter (as it is always known) is a little over 2½ hours. This means than an entry of up to 128 players can have the first match off early on Thursday morning, with the final being contested on Sunday afternoon.

The standard of play in the Putter has always been high. In the 40 times it was played until the mid-1960s, only six winners had not been Walker Cup or international players. Since then the general standard of amateur golf has risen due to the far greater numbers having the opportunity to play the game. While The Society may not now be producing as many top amateurs as before, it still represents all that is best in the amateur game.

YEAR	WINNER	YEAR	WINNER
1920	EWE Holderness	1925	HD Gillies
1921	EWE Holderness	1926	EF Storey ⎱ tie RH Wethered ⎰
1922	EWE Holderness		
1923	EWE Holderness	1927	RH Wethered
1924	B Darwin	1928	RH Wethered

YEAR	WINNER	YEAR	WINNER
1929	Sir EWE Holderness	1963	JG Blackwell
1930	TA Bourn	1964	DMA Steel
1931	AG Pearson	1965	WJ Uzielli
1932	LG Crawley	1966	MF Attenborough
1933	AJ Peech	1967	JR Midgley
1934	DHR Martin	1968	AWJ Holmes
1935	RH Wethered	1969	P Moody
1936	RH Wethered	1970	DMA Steel
1937	JB Beck	1971	GT Duncan
1938	CJH Tolley	1972	P Moody
1939	JOH Greenly	1973	AD Swanston
1940–46	Not played due to Second World War	1974	R Biggs
1947	LG Crawley	1975	CJ Weight
1948	Major AA Duncan	1976	MJ Reece
1949	PB Lucas	1977	AWJ Holmes
1950	DHR Martin	1978	MJ Reece
1951	LG Crawley	1979	Cancelled due to snow
1952	LG Crawley	1980	S Melville
1953	GH Micklem	1981	AWJ Holmes
1954	G Huddy	1982	DMA Steel
1955	G Huddy	1983	ER Dexter
1956	GT Duncan	1984	A Edmond
1957	AE Shepperson	1985	ER Dexter
1958	Lt-Col AA Duncan	1986	J Caplan
1959	ID Wheater	1987	CD Meacher
1960	JME Anderson	1988	G Woollett
1961	ID Wheater	1989	M Froggatt
1962	MF Attenborough	1990	G Woollett

HRH Prince of Wales Challenge Cup

INAUGURATED 1927

at Deal

First played in 1928 at Prince's, Sandwich, it was transferred to Royal Cinque Ports at Deal after the Second World War, when the original Princes course had been commandeered for a tank training area. It has remained at Deal since. As with the St George's Cup it has had a distinguished list of winners and remains a formidable test for any amateur.

Before the War it was for five years from 1934 played as a 72-hole stroke play tournament. However, on its rebirth in 1948 it reverted to 36 holes and has remained so ever since.

YEAR	WINNER	SCORE	YEAR	WINNER	SCORE
1928	D Grant	142	1935	HG Bentley	301
1929	NR Reeves	153	1936	LOM Munn	301
1930	R Harris	156	1937	DHR Martin	291
1931	RW Hartley	149	1938	EA Head	291
1932	EN Layton	151	1939–46	Not played due to Second World War	
1933	JB Nash	148			
1934	R Sweeney	304	1947	PB Lucas	154

YEAR	WINNER	SCORE	YEAR	WINNER	SCORE
1948	Capt DA Blair	151	1970	J Butterworth	153
1949	C Stowe	142	1971	VE Barton	147
1950	I Caldwell	151	1972	PJ Hedges	162
1951	I Caldwell	151	1973	PJ Hedges	138
1952	I Caldwell	150	1974	PJ Hedges	146
1953	JG Blackwell	159	1975	JC Davies	150
1954	DLW Woon	143	1976	MJ Inglis	162
1955	C Taylor ⎱ tie GT Duncan ⎰	153	1977 1978	PJ Hedges ER Dexter	154 145
1956	PF Scrutton	151	1979	GF Godwin	148
1957	*No competition*		1980	GM Dunsire ⎱ tie B Nicholson ⎰	149
1958	KR Mackenzie ⎱ tie BAF Pelmore ⎰	158	1981	JM Baldwin	146
1959	D Johnstone	149	1982	SG Homewood	145
1960	CG Moore	162	1983	M Davis	141
1961	RH Bazell	151	1984	DH Niven ⎱ tie F Wood ⎰	146
1962	Dr J Pittar	154			
1963	Sq Ldr WE McCrea	155	1985	RJ Tickner	141
1964	NA Paul	153	1986	JM Baldwin	149
1965	NA Paul ⎱ tie VE Barton ⎰	150	1987 1988	S Finch MP Palmer	148 144
1966	P Townsend	150	1989	T Lloyd ⎱ tie NA Farrell ⎰	143
1967	MF Bonallack	141			
1968	GC Marks ⎱ tie NA Paul ⎰	144	1990	BS Ingleby ⎱ tie SG Homewood ⎰	145
1969	MF Attenborough	152			

Purbeck Swords

INAUGURATED 1977

at Isle of Purbeck, Dorset

YEAR	WINNER	YEAR	WINNER
1977	D Barnes	1984	K Weeks
1978	D Barnes	1985	N Howie
1979	ND Owers	1986	K Weeks
1980	K Weeks	1987	K Weeks
1981	K Weeks	1988	S Amor
1982	T Wenham	1989	M Pooley
1983	K Weeks	1990	S Amor

Purley Trophy

INAUGURATED 1977

at Bognor Regis, West Sussex

YEAR	WINNER	YEAR	WINNER
1970	B Morrison	1981	B Caiger ⎱ tie
1971	R Revell		K Elvin ⎰
1972	C Strang	1982	MJ Christmas
1973	RL Glading	1983	SD Keppler ⎱ tie
1974	R Revell ⎱ tie		S Bowen ⎰
	B Winteridge ⎰	1984	K Bowen
1975	B Winteridge	1985	A Broadway
1976	R Mummery	1986	P Hurring
1977	P Wynn	1987	K Weeks
1978	P Hammond	1988	G Evans
1979	J Pinsent	1989	G Evans
1980	K Weeks	1990	S Graham

Queen Elizabeth Coronation Schools' Trophy

INAUGURATED 1953

at Barnton, Edinburgh

YEAR	WINNERS	YEAR	WINNERS
1953	Watsonians	1972	Merchistonians
1954	Daniel Stewart's College FP	1973	Merchistonians
1955	Watsonians	1974	Old Carthusians
1956	Watsonians	1975	Old Lorettonians
1957	Hillhead High School FP	1976	Watsonians
1958	Watsonians	1977	Glasgow High School FP
1959	Glasgow High School FP	1978	Old Lorettonians
1960	Glasgow High School FP	1979	Gordonians
1961	Watsonians	1980	George Heriots FP
1962	Glasgow High School FP	1981	Ayr Academicals
1963	Glasgow High School FP	1982	George Heriots FP
1964	Dollar Academicals	1983	Perth Academy FP
1965	Old Lorettonians	1984	Glasgow High School FP
1966	Merchistonians	1985	Glasgow High School FP
1967	Merchistonians	1986	Watsonians
1968	Glasgow Hillhead High School FP	1987	Stewarts Melville FP
1969	Kelvinside Academicals	1988	Watsonians
1970	Dollar Academicals	1989	Kelvinside Academicals
1971	Merchistonians	1990	Hutchesons FP

Rosebery Challenge Cup

INAUGURATED 1933

at Ashridge, Hertfordshire

YEAR	WINNER	YEAR	WINNER
1933	GA Hill	1966	A Holmes
1934	JS Rowell	1967	A Holmes
1935	PB Lucas	1968	A Holmes
1936	LG Crawley	1969	A Holmes
1937	JO Levinson	1970	PW Bent
1938	AS Anderson	1971	AW Holmes
1939	AS Anderson	1972	AW Holmes
1940–48	*No competition*	1973	AJ Mason
1949	AA McNair	1974	G Stradling
1950	RAR Black	1975	JA Watts
1951	JW Taylor	1976	G Stradling
1952	R Pattinson	1977	J Ambridge
1953	R Pattinson	1978	RJ Bevan
1954	C Ostler	1979	JB Berney
1955	D Gray	1980	JA Watts
1956	WCdr CH Beamish	1981	RY Mitchell
1957	GH Foster	1982	DG Lane
1958	JT Anderson	1983	N Briggs
1959	RW Acton	1984	DG Lane
1960	EJ Wiggs	1985	P Wharton
1961	KT Warren	1986	JE Ambridge
1962	PR Johnston	1987	HA Wilkerson
1963	CA Murray	1988	N Leconte
1964	A Millar	1989	C Slattery
1965	EJ Wiggs	1990	C Tingey

St David's Gold Cross

INAUGURATED 1930

at Royal St David's, Harlech

YEAR	WINNER	YEAR	WINNER
1930	GC Stokoe	1946	SB Roberts
1931	EW Fiddian	1947	G Mills
1932	Dr W Tweddell	1948	CH Eaves
1933	IS Thomas	1949	SB Roberts
1934	SB Roberts	1950	DMG Sutherland
1935	IS Thomas	1951	JL Morgan
1936	RMW Pritchard	1952	SB Roberts
1937	IS Thomas	1953	S Lunt
1938	SB Roberts	1954	GB Turner
1939	IS Thomas	1955	JL Morgan
1940–45	*Not played due to Second World War*	1956	W Cdr CH Beamish
		1957	CD Lawrie

YEAR	WINNER	YEAR	WINNER
1958	GB Turner	1975	CP Hodgkinson
1959	MSR Lunt	1976	JR Jones
1960	LJ Ranells	1977	JA Fagan
1961	MSR Lunt	1978	S Wild
1962	PD Kelley	1979	MA Smith
1963	JKD Povall	1980	CP Hodgkinson
1964	MSR Lunt	1981	G Broadbent
1965	MSR Lunt	1982	MW Calvert
1966	MSR Lunt	1983	RD James
1967	MSR Lunt	1984	RJ Green
1968	AW Holmes	1985	KH Williams
1969	AJ Thomson	1986	RN Roderick
1970	AJ Thomson	1987	SR Andrew
1971	A Smith	1988	MW Calvert
1972	EN Davies	1989	AJ Barnett
1973	RD James	1990	MA Macara
1974	GC Marks		

St George's Challenge Cup

INAUGURATED 1888

at Royal St George's, Sandwich

This was the earliest open club trophy in England to attract the best amateur golfers. It was first contested in 1888, the year after the club's foundation. The winner then and for the following three years was John Ball, the best amateur in the land, from the Royal Liverpool Club at Hoylake. His 1888 winning score of 180 for 36 holes reflected the near-gale conditions and the immature nature of the course.

The list of winners reads like a roll-call of past and future amateur champions. In 1926 and 1930 the US Walker Cup team competed, but in neither year was an American the winner. Francis Ouimet had won in 1923 and the youthful Jack Nicklaus, still an amateur, took the cup in 1959. John C. Davies had a fine flow of six successive victories 1972–77.

YEAR	WINNER	SCORE	YEAR	WINNER	SCORE
1888	J Ball	180	1903	CK Hutchison	158
1889	J Ball	169	1904	J Graham Jr	154
1890	J Ball	175	1905	R Harris	154
1891	J Ball	174	1906	S Mure Fergusson	155
1892	FA Fairlie	167	1907	CE Dick	161
1893	HH Hilton	165	1908	AC Lincoln	157
1894	HH Hilton	167	1909	SH Fry	153
1895	E Blackwell	176	1910	Capt CK Hutchison	157
1896	FG Tait	165	1911	E Martin Smith	148
1897	CE Hambro	162	1912	Hon Michael Scott	146
1898	FG Tait	163	1913	HD Gillies	153
1899	FG Tait	155	1914	J Graham Jr	146
1900	R Maxwell	155	1915–19	*Not played due to Great War*	
1901	SH Fry	165	1920	R Harris	162
1902	H Castle	162	1921	WB Torrance	154

YEAR	WINNER	SCORE	YEAR	WINNER	SCORE
1922	WI Hunter	156	1959	J Nicklaus (USA)	149
1923	F Ouimet (USA)	153	1960	JG Blackwell	152
1924	RH Wethered	149	1961	Sq Ldr WE McCrea	143
1925	D Grant	149	1962	Sq Ldr WE McCrea	145
1926	Maj CO Hezlet	158	1963	Sq Ldr WE McCrea	150
1927	WL Hartley	153	1964	Maj DA Blair	153
1928	D Grant	146	1965	MF Bonallack	144
1929	TA Torrance	148	1966	P Townsend	148
1930	RW Hartley	148	1967	Maj DA Blair	154
1931	WL Hartley	149	1968	MF Bonallack	142
1932	HG Bentley	151	1969	PJ Benka	150
1933	JB Beck	151	1970	PJ Hedges	150
1934	AGS Penman	153	1971	EJS Garrett	143
1935	Maj WHH Aitken	158	1972	JC Davies	149
1936	DHR Martin	150	1973	JC Davies	141
1937	DHR Martin	144	1974	JC Davies	140
1938	JJF Pennink	142	1975	JC Davies	147
1939	AA McNair	153	1976	JC Davies	158
1940–46	*Not played due to Second World War*		1977	JC Davies	154
			1978	C Phillips	145
1947	PB Lucas	147	1979	GF Godwin	146
1948	M Gonzalez	144	1980	J Simmance	150
1949	PF Scrutton	143	1981	MF Bonallack	151
1950	E Bromley-Davenport	148	1982	SJ Wood	145
1951	PF Strutton	142	1983	R Willison	155
1952	GH Micklem	148	1984	SJ Wood	142
1953	Major DA Blair	148	1985	SJ Wood	144
1954	H Berwick (Aus)	141	1986	RC Claydon	143
1955	PF Scrutton	150	1987	MR Goodwin	147
1956	DAC Marr	148	1988	T Ryan	143
1957	PF Scrutton	148	1989	S Green	149
1958	PF Scrutton	144	1990	P Sullivan	144

Seaton Salver

INAUGURATED 1969

at Seaton Carew, Cleveland

YEAR	WINNER	YEAR	WINNER
1969	MJ Kelley	1980	NBJ Fick
1970	R Webster	1981	D Oughton
1971	S Rolley	1982	JR Ellwood
1972	MJ Kelley	1983	R Duxfield
1973	D Oughton	1984	RH Teschner
1974	DP Davidson	1985	A Robertson Jr
1975	D Oughton	1986	A Robertson Jr
1976	*No competition*	1987	RA Pritchard
1977	MJ Kelley	1988	DH Curry
1978	JR Crawshaw	1989	J Metcalfe
1979	J Craggs	1990	C Chalk

Selborne Salver

INAUGURATED 1976

at Blackmoor, Hampshire

YEAR	WINNER	YEAR	WINNER
1976	A Miller	1984	D Curry
1977	CS Mitchell	1985	SM Bottomley
1978	GM Brand	1986	TE Clarke
1979	P McEvoy	1987	A Clapp
1980	P McEvoy	1988	NE Holman
1981	A Sherborne	1989	M Stamford
1982	IA Gray	1990	J Metcalfe
1983	DG Lane		

Stoneham Trophy

INAUGURATED 1982

at Stoneham, Southampton

YEAR	WINNER	YEAR	WINNER
1982	AE Long	1987	S Richardson
1983	R Park	1988	ADA Mew
1984	K Weeks	1989	S Richardson
1985	K Weeks	1990	I Donnelly
1986	M Wiggett		

Sudbury Salver

INAUGURATED 1968

at Sudbury, Middlesex

YEAR	WINNER	YEAR	WINNER
1968	J McBeath	1980	ML Weir
1969	P Bent	1981	R Boxall
1970	BA Price	1982	R Willison
1971	PS Middup	1983	RDA Smith
1972	IM Stungo	1984	R Willison
1973	PA Dew	1985	ACE Peake
1974	IF Kinlay	1986	MR Johnson
1975	MJ Toole	1987	JC Dulieu
1976	AJ Mason	1988	PR Thomas
1977	PR Morris	1989	GS Pooley
1978	IM Stungo	1990	L White
1979	ML Weir		

Sunningdale Open Foursomes

INAUGURATED 1934

at Sunningdale

This tournament is the only foursomes event in which men and women, professionals, amateurs and assistant professionals can play in competition together in any combination. Each category is allotted a set handicap and eleven of the possible twenty-one pairings have won over the sixty years it has been played, with a male amateur paired with a male professional the winners more often than others. This combination is less likely to win now with the arrival of the woman professional in the last fifteen years.

The tournament occurs very early in the season, but it is not one in which touring professionals are likely to be among the entries. Fancied partners often fail and unexpected pairs surface as winners. The meeting is a cheerful and popular event, supported by the club professionals and assistants, women professionals, and amateurs of both sexes, and is an ideal early season fixture for all.

YEAR	FINALS
1934	Miss D Fishwick and EN Layton beat Miss M Gourlay and Capt GE Hawkins, 2 and 1
1935	Miss J Wethered and JSF Morrison beat Miss P Barton and LG Garrett, 3 and 2
1936	Miss J Wethered and JSF Morrison beat DH Kyle and Maj WHH Aitken, 5 and 4
1937	AS Anderson and Dai Rees beat GD Hanney and RG French, 5 and 4
1938	Miss P Barton and Alf Padgham beat LG Crawley and F Francis, 19th hole
1939	C Rissik and EWH Kenyon beat CM Bell and C Denny, 19th hole
1940–47	*Not played due to Second World War*
1948	Miss Wanda Morgan and Sam King beat Peter Risdom and Dick Burton, 2 and 1
1949	RG French and SS Field beat Miss Jacqueline Gordon and J Knipe, 1 hole
1950	M Faulkner and J Knipe beat F Francis and A Lees, 1 hole
1951	Miss J Donald and TB Haliburton beat RG French and AE Poulton, 3 and 2
1952	PF Scrutton and Alan Waters beat AE Poulton and RG French, 2 and 1
1953	Miss J Donald and TB Haliburton beat G Knipe and DG Smalldon 3 and 2
1954	PF Scrutton and Alan Waters beat P Mills and T Harman, 4 and 3
1955	W Sharp and SS Scott beat RG French and E Ward, 2 and 1
1956	G Knipe and DG Smalldon beat LG Crawley and GH Foster, 3 and 2
1957	BGC Huggett and R Whitehead beat R Galloway and S Robertson, 2 holes
1958	Miss J Donald and Peter Alliss beat DMP Beard and B Bamford, 1 hole
1959	MF Bonallack and D Sewell beat WA Slark and PE Gill, 5 and 3
1960	Miss B McCorkindale and MJ Moir beat HC Squirrell and SD Mouland, 19th hole
1961	Mrs J Anderson and Peter Alliss beat W Dubabney and A Grubb, 2 and 1
1962	ER Whitehead and NC Coles beat MJ Christmas and MJ Burgess, 3 and 2
1963	L Platts and D Snell beat KA MacDonald and ID MacDonald, 1 hole
1964	B Critchley and R Hunter beat MJ Burgess and PO Green, 2 and 1
1965	Mrs AD Spearman and T Fisher beat MJ Burgess and PO Green, 1 hole
1966	RRW Davenport and A Walker beat G Burroughs and F Sunderland, 4 and 3
1967	NC Coles and K Warren beat Mlle B Varangot and CA Clark, 19th hole
1968	JC Davies and W Humphreys beat M Faulkner and BW Barnes, 6 and 4
1969	P Oosterhuis and PJ Benka beat JM Larretche and Mlle C Lacoste, 3 and 2
1970	R Barrell and Miss A Willard beat R Hunter and Miss M Everard, 2 and 1
1971	A Bird and H Flatman beat J Putt and Miss K Phillips, 3 and 2
1972	JC Davies and MG King beat JK Tullis and AJ Howard, 6 and 5
1973	J Putt and Miss M Everard beat HK Clark and SC Mason, 6 and 5
1974	PJ Butler and CA Clark beat HK Clark and DN Brunyard, 1 hole
1975	*Cancelled due to snow*

YEAR	FINALS
1976	CA Clark and M Hughesdon beat BJ Hunt and IM Stungo, 2 and 1
1977	GN Hunt and D Matthew beat D Huish and G Logan, 3 and 2
1978	GA Caygill and Miss J Greenhalgh beat A Stickley and Mrs C Caldwell, 5 and 4
1979	G Will and R Chapman beat NC Coles and D McClelland, 3 and 2
1980	NC Coles and D McClelland beat SC Mason and J O'Leary, 2 and 1
1981	A Lyddon and G Brand Jr beat MG King and MH Dixon, 1 hole
1982	Miss MA McKenna and Miss M Madill beat Miss C Langford and Miss M Walker, 1 hole
1983	J Davies and M Devetta beat M Hughesdon and Mrs L Bayman, 4 and 3
1984	Miss M McKenna and Miss M Madill beat Miss M Walker and Miss C Langford, 3 and 2
1985	J O'Leary and S Torrance beat B Gallacher and P Garner, 25th hole
1986	R Rafferty and R Chapman beat Mrs M Garner and Miss M McKenna, 1 hole
1987	I Mosey and W Humphreys beat Miss G Stewart and D Huish, 3 and 2
1988	SC Mason and A Chandler beat Miss M McKenna and Mrs M Garner, 5 and 3
1989	AD Hare and R Claydon beat Mrs V Thomas and Miss J Wade, 4 and 3
1990	Miss D Reid and Miss C Dibnah beat Miss T Craik and P Hughes, 7 and 6

Tenby Golden Eagle Trophy

INAUGURATED 1985

at Tenby

YEAR	WINNER	YEAR	WINNER
1985	W Farrell	1988	RN Roderick
1986	J Peters	1989	J Peters
1987	JP Price	1990	MA Macara

The Tennant Cup

INAUGURATED 1880

The Tennant Cup, one of the oldest open amateur stroke play competitions in the world, was inaugurated in 1880, and was played for the hundredth time in 1990, allowing for eleven years not played during the two world wars.

In its first decade it was played over two rounds of the 10-hole Alexandra Park course in Glasgow. It continued there over 18 holes from 1885 to 1892 when it moved to Blackhill (now no more) until 1905. Since then it has always been played at Glasgow Killermont. It became a 36-hole competition in 1927 and was extended again in 1976 to 72 holes, with the additional 36 being played at Glasgow Gailes. The 1990 winner, C. Everett of Cambuslang, had a record score of 270, 139 at Gailes and 131 at Killermont.

As evidence of the remarkably high standard of the field in the Tennant Cup, since 1922 it has been won by a Walker Cup player on 27 occasions. In addition in 1967 the winner was Bernard Gallacher, the current Ryder Cup captain, then a young amateur.

YEAR	WINNER	YEAR	WINNER
1880	AW Smith	1936	JNW Dall
1881	AW Smith	1937	WS McLeod
1882	AM Ross	1938	A Jamieson Jr
1883	J Kirk	1939	GB Peters
1884	W Doleman	1940–45	*Not played due to Second*
1885	TR Lamb		*World War*
1886	D Bone	1946	JB Stevenson
1887	JR Motion	1947	JC Wilson
1888	D Bone	1948	J Wallace
1889	W Milne	1949	W Irvine
1890	W Marshall	1950	JW Mill
1891	D Bone	1951	WS McLeod
1892	D Bone	1952	GT Black
1893	W Doleman	1953	AD Gray
1894	W Doleman	1954	H McInally
1895	JA Shaw	1955	LG Taylor
1896	J Thomson	1956	JM Dykes
1897	D Bone	1957	LG Taylor
1898	R Bone	1958	Dr FWG Deighton
1899	W Hunter	1959	JF Milligan
1900	JG Macfarlane	1960	Dr FWG Deighton
1901	R Bone	1961	R Reid Jack
1902	CB Macfarlane	1962	WS Jack
1903	CB Macfarlane	1963	SWT Murray
1904	WS Colville	1964	DR FWG Deighton
1905	TW Robb	1965	J Scott Cochran
1906	JG Macfarlane	1966	AH Hall
1907	R Andrew	1967	BJ Gallacher
1908	R Carson	1968	CW Green
1909	WS Colville	1969	J Scott Cochran
1910	R Andrew	1970	CW Green
1911	WS Colville	1971	Andrew Brodie
1912	R Scott Jr	1972	Allan Brodie
1913	SO Shepherd	1973	PJ Smith
1914	John Caven	1974	D McCart
1915–19	*Not played due to Great War*	1975	CW Green
1920	G Lockhart	1976	IC Hutcheon
1921	R Scott Jr	1977	S Martin
1922	WD Macleod	1978	IA Carslaw
1923	FW Baldie	1979	G Hay
1924	J Barrie Cooper	1980	A Brodie
1925	R Scott Jr	1981	G MacDonald
1926	W Tulloch	1982	LS Mann
1927	W Tulloch	1983	CR Dalgleish
1928	A Jamieson Jr	1984	E Wilson
1929	R Scott Jr	1985	CJ Brooks
1930	JE Dawson	1986	P Girvan
1931	GNS Tweedale	1987	J Rasmussen
1932	SL McInlay	1988	CR Dalgleish
1933	H Thomson	1989	DG Carrick
1934	K Lindsay Jr	1990	C Everett
1935	JM Dykes Jr		

Trubshaw Castle

INAUGURATED 1989

Awarded for the best combined score of the Tenby Golden Eagle Trophy and the Ashburnham Trophy

YEAR	WINNER
1989	MA Macara
1990	SM Wilkinson ⎫ tie D McLean ⎭

WC Roe Trophy

INAUGURATED 1973

at West Middlesex

YEAR	WINNER	YEAR	WINNER
1973	GE Ward	1982	N Pimm
1974	WJ Reid	1983	T Greenwood
1975	NC McLean	1984	N Pimm
1976	GE Ward	1985	W Grant
1977	AB Simmonds	1986	J O'Shea
1978	RF Bevan	1987	R Goldie
1979	W MacIntyre	1988	JG Walsh
1980	D Chatterton	1989	N Pimm
1981	R Willison	1990	N Pimm

Wem Bowl

INAUGURATED 1972

at Hawkstone Park, Shropshire

YEAR	WINNER	YEAR	WINNER
1972	I Pearce	1982	M Hassall
1973	AWB Lyle	1983	CA Banks
1974	AF Warde	1984	P Flockhart
1975	AWB Lyle	1985	MA Smith
1976	AWB Lyle	1986	D Eddiford
1977	S Wild	1987	D Harvey
1978	P Dennett	1988	D Harvey
1979	J Wilson	1989	M Hassall
1980	GC Moore	1990	D Probert
1981	T Allen		

West of England Open Amateur Championship

INAUGURATED 1912

at Burnham and Berrow

YEAR	WINNER	YEAR	WINNER
1912	RA Riddell	1957	D Gardner
1913	Hon Michael Scott	1958	AJN Young
1914–18	*Not played due to Great War*	1959	DM Woolmer
1919	Hon Michael Scott	1960	AW Holmes
1920	Hon D Scott	1961	JM Leach
1921	CVL Hooman	1962	Sq Ldr WE McCrea
1922	Hon Michael Scott	1963	KT Warren
1923	D Grant	1964	DC Allen
1924	D Grant	1965	DE Jones
1925	D Grant	1966	A Forrester
1926	K Whetstone	1967	A Forrester
1927	GC Brooks	1968	SR Warrin
1928	JA Pierson	1969	SR Warrin
1929	DE Landale	1970	C Ball
1930	RH de Montmorency	1971	G Irlam
1931	DR Howard	1972	JA Bloxham
1932	R Straker	1973	SC Mason
1933	DM Anderson	1974	CS Mitchell
1934	Hon Michael Scott	1975	MR Lovett
1935	JJF Pennink	1976	*Cancelled because of damage to*
1936	PH White		*course by drought*
1937	O Austreng	1977	AR Dunlop
1938	HJ Roberts	1978	R Broad
1939–45	*Not played due to Second World*	1979	N Burch
	War	1980	JM Durbin
1946	JH Neal	1981	M Mouland
1947	WF Wise	1982	M Higgins
1948	WF Wise	1983	C Peacock
1949	J Payne	1984	GB Hickman
1950	EB Millward	1985	AC Nash
1951	J Payne	1986	J Bennett
1952	EB Millward	1987	D Rosier
1953	F Griffin	1988	N Holman
1954	EB Millward	1989	N Holman
1955	SJ Fox	1990	I West
1956	SJ Fox		

West of England Open Amateur Stroke Play Championship

INAUGURATED 1968

at Saunton and Westward Ho!

YEAR	WINNER	SCORE	YEAR	WINNER	SCORE
1968	PJ Yeo	297	1980	P McEvoy	288
1969	A Forrester	304	1981	N Taee (3 rounds)	245
1970	PJ Yeo	312	1982	MP Higgins	286
1971	P Berry	303	1983	P McEvoy	298
1972	P Berry	310	1984	A Sherborne	288
1973	SC Mason	287	1985	P McEvoy	307
1974	R Abbott	301	1986	P Baker	282
1975	BG Steer	290	1987	G Wolstenholme	
1976	R Abbott	304	1988	M Evans	
1977	P McEvoy	298	1989	AD Hare	
1978	JG Bennett	291	1990	J Payne	
1979	R Kane	296			

Whitelaw Trophy

INAUGURATED 1964

at Penrith, Cumbria

YEAR	WINNER	YEAR	WINNER
1964	WD Longcake	1978	J Oliver
1965	SG Birtwell	1979	S Sinclair
1966	WR Sharp	1980	S Sinclair
1967	GJ Clark	1981	RM Roper
1968	JM Nutter	1982	RM Roper
1969	GJ Clark	1983	AR Morrison
1970	DP Davidson	1984	M Ruddick
1971	MP Walls	1985	G Shuttleworth
1972	MP Walls	1986	AR Morrison
1973	MP Walls	1987	M Ruddick
1974	MP Walls	1988	G Shuttleworth
1975	DJ Steele	1989	AR Morrison
1976	MP Walls	1990	M Ruddick
1977	MP Walls		

Whittington Trophy

INAUGURATED 1962

at Whittington Barracks, Staffordshire

YEAR	WINNER	YEAR	WINNER
1962	M Edwards	1977	R Hiatt
1963	M Edwards	1978	D Evans
1964	D Kelley	1979	A Carman
1965	I Fernyhough	1980	M Payne
1966	MSR Lunt	1981	A Stubbs
1967	A Smith	1982	C Banks
1968	M Payne	1983	A Allen
1969	I Fernyhough	1984	A Allen
1970	L Shelley	1985	D Gilford
1971	R Fitton	1986	C Poxon
1972	J Fisher	1987	C Poxon
1973	T Homer	1988	IR Lyner
1974	A Smith	1989	M Maguire
1975	G Gibberson	1990	M Maguire
1976	M Payne		

WI Tucker Trophy

INAUGURATED 1987

at Newport, Gwent

YEAR	WINNER
1987	RN Roderick
1988	K Jones
1989	P Price
1990	CJ Dinsdale ⎱ tie R Baird ⎰

Wimborne Cup

INAUGURATED 1911

at Parkstone, Dorset

YEAR	WINNER	YEAR	WINNER
1911	EP Sugden	1956	C McInerney
1912	JJ Lane	1957	K Longmore
1913	FW Beckford	1958	KV Robshaw
1914–18	*Not played due to Great War*	1959	C McInerney
1919	WE Johnson	1960	CW Cole
1920	T Homer	1961	Dr DM Holmes
1921	CH Armstrong	1962	CW Cole
1922	CH Armstrong	1963	K Longmore
1923	EF Rees-Mogg	1964	K Longmore
1924	V Weldon	1965	JB Airth
1925	DA Turpin	1966	R Lawford
1926	Maj CEM Morrison	1967	R Lawford
1927	EJ Dobson	1968	RE Searle
1928	NG Holt	1969	JC Davies
1929	NG Holt	1970	JC Davies
1930	NG Holt	1971	NLR Cook
1931	SH Vine	1972	J Nash
1932	SH Vine	1973	NLR Cook
1933	SH Vine	1974	Dr DM Holmes
1934	SH Vine	1975	P Edgington
1935	SH Vine	1976	B Crutcher
1936	SH Vine	1977	B Winteridge
1937	R Williams-Freeman	1978	RE Searle
1938	K Longmore	1979	RE Searle
1939–45	*Not played due to Second World War*	1980	B Townsend
		1981	RE Searle
1946	K Longmore	1982	K Weeks
1947	EB Millward	1983	R Hearn
1948	EB Millward	1984	RA Latham
1949	HC Neilson	1985	I Jones
1950	K Longmore	1986	R Guy
1951	EB Millward	1987	A Raitt
1952	EB Millward	1988	T Spence
1953	K Longmore	1989	J Nash
1954	JH Wyllie	1990	A Mew
1955	SJ Fox		

Worman Sword

INAUGURATED 1980

at Wyke Green, Middlesex

YEAR	WINNER	YEAR	WINNER
1980	JV Quilter	1986	S Walker
1981	DC Black	1987	J Jones
1982	M Rapley	1988	G Stacey
1983	R Willison	1989	J Smith
1984	G Griffiths	1990	P Lowrance
1985	M Rapley		

Worplesdon Mixed Foursomes

INAUGURATED 1921

at Worplesdon

This event, always played in October and first contested in 1921, was dominated by the Wethereds, Roger and Joyce, until the Second World War. During the 18 tournaments until 1938 either brother or sister were in the final on eleven occasions. Joyce won eight of them with seven different partners, one of whom was Roger; she appeared once again in the final as Lady Heathcoat-Amory, playing with her husband Sir John, in 1948.

While the tournament has lost none of its charm, it no longer enjoys quite the standing it once had when there were usually Walker and Curtis Cup players in the final. Even so, it still attracts leading amateurs of both sexes.

Only two married couples have won, the Bonallacks and the Thornhills in 1958 and 1975 respectively, and the Uziellis reached the final in 1973 as did the Becks in 1947 and the Beharrels in 1960. In 1963–65 Mrs Jessie Valentine and John Behrend won three years in succession.

YEAR	FINALS
1921	Miss Helme and TA Torrance beat Miss Joyce Wethered and R Wethered, 3 and 2
1922	Miss Joyce Wethered and R Wethered beat Mrs Patey and EN Layton, 2 and 1
1923	Miss Joyce Wethered and CJ Tolley beat Mrs Macbeth and B Darwin, 6 and 5
1924	Miss SR Fowler and EN Layton beat Miss J Winn and F Mead, 8 and 7
1925	Miss Cecil Leitch and E Esmond beat Miss Joan Gow and GD Hannay, 2 and 1
1926	Mlle de la Chaume and R Wethered beat Miss M Gourlay and Maj CO Hezlet, 2 holes
1927	Miss Joyce Wethered and CJH Tolley beat Mlle Thion de la Chaume and R Wethered 3 and 2
1928	Miss Joyce Wethered and JSF Morrison beat Mrs A Gold and EN Layton, 1 hole
1929	Miss M Gourlay and Maj CO Hezlet beat Miss J Winn and VC Longstaffe, 39th hole
1930	Miss M Gourlay and Maj CO Hezlet beat Miss Diana Esmond and RH Wethered, 5 and 4
1931	Miss J Wethered and Hon M Scott beat Miss Doris Park and S Forsyth, 4 and 3
1932	Miss J Wethered and RH Oppenheimer beat Miss A Regnart and Cdr Johnstone, 8 and 7
1933	Miss J Wethered and B Darwin beat Mrs MR Garon and A McNair, 8 and 7
1934	Miss M Gourlay and TA Torrance beat Miss K Garnham and EN Layton, 6 and 5
1935	Miss G Craddock-Hartopp and J Craddock-Hartopp beat Miss J Hamilton and S Forsyth, 2 and 1

YEAR	FINALS
1936	Miss J Wethered and Hon T Coke beat Miss D Wilkins and CJ Anderson, 3 and 2
1937	Mrs Heppel and LG Crawley beat Miss K Garnham and ASG Thompson, 5 and 4
1938	Mrs MR Garon and EF Storey beat Miss W Morgan and KAS Morrice, 6 and 5
1939–45	*Not played due to Second World War*
1946	Miss J Gordon and AA Duncan beat Miss J Pemberton and HC Longhurst, 4 and 3
1947	Miss J Gordon and AA Duncan beat Mrs Beck and JB Beck, 8 and 7
1948	Miss W Morgan and EF Storey beat Lady Heathcoat-Amory and Sir John Heathcoat-Amory, 5 and 4
1949	Miss F Stephens and LG Crawley beat Mrs AC Critchley and CJH Tolley, 4 and 3
1950	Miss F Stephens and LG Crawley beat Miss E Johnston and Peter MacDonald, 6 and 5
1951	Mrs AC Barclay and G Evans beat Mrs RT Peel and GW Mackie, 1 hole
1952	Mrs RT Peel and GW Mackie beat Miss F Stephens and WA Slark, 3 and 2
1953	Miss J Gordon and G Knipe beat Mrs M Spearman and JCE Atkins, 1 hole
1954	Miss F Stephens and WA Slark beat Miss J McIntyre and PF Scrutton, 2 holes
1955	Miss P Garvey and PF Scrutton beat Mrs A van Oss and GT Duncan, 2 and 1
1956	Mrs L Abrahams and Maj WD Henderson beat Mlle O Semelaigne and GH Micklem, 3 and 1
1957	Mrs B Singleton and WD Smith beat Miss J Gordon and HB Ridgley, 5 and 4
1958	Mr and Mrs M Bonallack beat Mrs B Singleton and WD Smith, 4 and 3
1959	Miss J Robertson and I Wright beat Signora I Goldschmid and Tudor Davies, 4 and 3
1960	Miss B Jackson and MJ Burgess beat Mr and Mrs JC Beharrel, 2 and 1
1961	Mrs R Smith and B Critchley beat Miss J Woodside and J Thornhill, 3 and 2
1962	Viscomtesse de Saint Sauveur and DW Frame beat Miss W Clark and KT Warren, 5 and 3
1963	Mrs G Valentine and JE Behrend beat Signora I Goldschmid and MJ Burgess, 4 and 3
1964	Mrs G Valentine and JE Behrend beat Mrs AD Spearman and A Thirlwell, 3 and 2
1965	Mrs G Valentine and JE Behrend beat Miss J Anderson and CA Clark, 1 hole
1966	Mrs C Barclay and DJ Miller beat Miss E Mountain and PJ Benka, 19th hole
1967	JF Gancedo and Mlle C Lacoste beat DJ Miller and Mrs C Barclay, 1 hole
1968	JD van Heel and Miss Dinah Oxley beat RPF Brown and Mrs G Valentine, 2 and 1
1969	Mrs R Ferguson and Alistair Wilson beat Miss P Tredinnick and B Critchley, 4 and 3
1970	Miss R Roberts and RL Glading beat Mrs J Roberts and Sir George Cole, 2 and 1
1971	Mrs D Frearson and A Smith beat Miss J de Witt Puyt and J Ward, 3 and 2
1972	Miss B Le Garreres and CA Strang beat Mrs CA Barclay and P Garner, 1 hole
1973	Miss T Perkins and RJ Evans beat Mr and Mrs WJ Uzielli, 3 and 2
1974	Mrs S Birley and RL Glading beat Mr and Mrs JR Thornhill, 4 and 3
1975	Mr and Mrs JR Thornhill beat Mrs S Birley and R Glading, 20th hole
1976	Mrs B Lewis and J Caplan beat Miss T Perkins and R Jones, 1 hole
1977	Mrs D Henson and J Caplan beat Miss P Light and M Chugg, 4 and 3
1978	Miss T Perkins and R Thomas beat Mrs C Caldwell and JC Davies, 2 and 1
1979	Miss J Melville and A Melville beat Miss G Gunby and D Robson, 2 and 1
1980	Mrs L Bayman and I Boyd beat Mrs L Davies and R Hurst, 1 hole
1981	Mrs J Nicholsen and MN Stern beat Mrs S Birley and RL Glading, 2 and 1
1982	Miss B New and K Dobson beat Miss S Cohen and J Tarbuck, 2 and 1
1983	Miss B New and K Dobson beat Miss N McCormack and N Briggs, 19th hole
1984	Mrs L Bayman and MC Hughesdon beat Miss N McCormack and N Briggs, 5 and 4
1985	Mrs H Kaye and D Longmuir beat Mrs J Collingham and GS Melville, 5 and 3
1986	Miss P Johnson and RN Roderick beat Miss C Duffy and L Hawkins, 2 and 1
1987	Miss J Nicholson and B White beat Miss T Craik and P Hughes, 4 and 3
1988	Mme A Larrezac and JJ Caplan beat Miss S Bennett and BK Turner, 4 and 3
1989	Miss J Kershaw and M Kershaw beat Mrs H Kaye and D Longmuir, 2 and 1
1990	Miss S Keogh and A Rodgers beat Miss J Rhodes and C Banks, 3 and 1

York Rose Bowl

INAUGURATED 1977

at York

YEAR	WINNER	YEAR	WINNER
1977	MI Mackenzie	1984–85	*Not played*
1978	AR Morrison	1986	S East
1979	L Walker	1987	J Mee
1980	MJ Kelley	1988	P Wardle
1981	JL Plaxton	1989	S East
1982	L Walker	1990	R Jones
1983	JJ Gaunt		

Young Masters Tournament

INAUGURATED 1978

Sand Moor, Leeds

YEAR	WINNER	YEAR	WINNER
1978	R Roper	1985	W Frost
1979	D Currey	1986	W Frost
1980	DG Muscroft	1987	S Raybould
1981	DG Muscroft	1988	SA Pullan
1982	G Harland	1989	RJ Bennett
1983	C Nolan	1990	AE Robinson
1984	D Bray		

Part Three
Women's Professional Events

Women's Professional Golf European Tour

The Women's Professional Golf Association was formed in late 1978 and it launched its first tournaments the next year. Its few very humble beginnings seemed doubtful but in the face of many difficulties and disappointments it has survived. After three years of partial success it was decided by the Committee of Players to seek assistance from the PGA, its male counterpart, which came to the rescue. It had been reduced to ten tournaments and was heading for final failure. Under the direction of Colin Snape, the PGA Executive Director, the Tour recovered. In the next five years more sponsors were found, 72-hole Tournaments became normal and continental Europe came forward with many more events. Prize money rose to £930,000 in 1987.

Later that year, the players decided to break away and form their own organisation. Ambitious and chancy as the decision appeared at the time, it has survived well. Contributing to its success has been the wide spread of countries in Europe where half the tournaments are now played, the resulting increase in the number of overseas players, including several from the Antipodes who have joined the Tour which now has over 200 members. No less important has been the leadership of the Director since 1988, Joe Flanagan, who has brought his wide experience to bear on the fledgling organisation, now named the Women's Professional Golf European Tour (WPGET).

Its development can be gauged by the increase in prize money which more and more sponsors have provided. In 1979 it amounted to £80,000; in 1991 it will be nearly £2 million. In the 1980s the leading players have been Beverly Huke, Dale Reid, Muriel Thomson, Cathy Panton and Alison Nicholas. Outshining them with their achievements are Laura Davies and Liselotte Neumann who won the US Ladies' Open in 1988 and 1989 respectively and Marie-Laure de Lorenzi (formerly Taya) (France) who has won many tournaments in Europe and led the Order of Merit in the last three years.

Given its present cohesion and drive, the WPGET is likely to grow in strength and possibly later to rival the LPGA Tour in the USA.

Ladies' British Open Stroke Play Championship

INAUGURATED 1976

This championship has had a chequered history with several changes of sponsorship. In 1983 it had to miss a year through lack of one, but is now firmly established under the Weetabix umbrella.

Since it began in 1976 there have been more winners from abroad than patriots would have liked, but there is no doubt about the quality of those who have won in the 1980s. In 1984 Ayako Okamoto, a diminutive Japanese, beat her nearest rival, Betsy King (USA), by 11 strokes at Woburn. Next year King herself won at Moor Park. Two of the best British professionals, Laura Davies and Alison Nicholas, won in 1986 and 1987, breaking the run of overseas successes, but since then the title has been taken abroad to Australia, USA and Sweden.

In its earlier years it was three times won by amateurs, Jenny Lee-Smith, Janet Melville and Marta Figueras-Dotti of France.

1976 *at Fulford, York*

WINNER	SCORE
Jenny Lee-Smith (Am)	299

1977 *at Lindrick, Sheffield*

WINNER	SCORE
Vivien Saunders	306

1978 *at Foxhills, Surrey*

WINNER	SCORE
Janet Melville (Am)	310

1979 *at Southport and Ainsdale*

WINNER	SCORE
Alison Sheard (USA)	301

1980 *at Wentworth (East)*

WINNER	SCORE
Debbie Massey (USA)	294

1981 *at Ganton, N. Yorks*

NAME					SCORE
Debbie Massey (USA)	71	71	81	72	295
Belle Robertson (Am)	72	75	78	74	299
Jenny Lee-Smith	73	74	74	72	295

1982 *at Birkdale*

NAME					SCORE
Marta Figueras-Dotti (Am) (Fra)	72	73	75	76	296
Rose Jones	78	73	73	73	297
Jenny Lee-Smith	73	72	81	72	297
Jane Cole	72	73	77	76	298
Catherine Panton	69	80	75	75	299
Debbie Massey (USA)	75	75	75	74	299

1983 *Not played*

1984 *at Woburn, Beds*

NAME					SCORE
Ayako Okamoto (Jpn)	71	71	70		289
Betsy King (USA)	75	76	76	73	300
Dale Reid	72	71	81	76	300
Jan Stephenson (Aus)	74	74	78	75	301
Pat Bradley (USA)	75	75	73	78	301

1985 *at Moor Park*

NAME					SCORE
Betsy King (USA)	75	76	76	73	300
Marta Figueras-Dotti (Am) (Fra)	77	73	78	74	302
Muffin Spencer-Devlin (USA)	81	80	70	73	303
Marie Wennersten (Swe)	75	76	77	76	304
Sandra Young (Can)	78	74	74	78	304

1986 *at Royal Birkdale*

NAME					SCORE
Laura Davies	71	73	69	70	283
Marta Figueras-Dotti (Fra)	68	72	74	73	287
Peggy Conley (USA)	70	69	71	77	287
Beverley New	69	77	76	66	288
Vicki Thomas (Am)	75	73	71	70	289

1987 *at St Mellion, Cornwall*

NAME					SCORE
Alison Nicholas	74	76	73	73	296
Laura Davies	73	73	79	73	297
Muffin Spencer-Devlin (USA)	79	68	75	75	297
N Little (USA)	69	80	74	75	298
Corinne Dibnah (Aus)	77	74	78	71	300
Jane Connachan	77	74	75	74	300

1988 *Lindrick, S. Yorks*

NAME					SCORE
Corinne Dibnah (Aus)	73	73	74	75	295
(After play-off)					
Sally Little (USA)	73	77	69	76	295
Alison Nicholas	76	73	75	72	296
Karen Lunn (Aus)	72	79	75	73	299
Janet Soulsby	75	77	75	73	300

1989 *at Ferndown, Dorset*

NAME					SCORE
Janet Geddes (USA)	67	67	72	68	274
Florence Descampe (Bel)	73	66	70	67	276
Marie-Laure de Lorenzi (Fra)	68	71	67	72	278
Patti Rizzo *(USA)*	71	69	68	71	279
Muffin Spencer-Devlin (USA)	72	69	67	71	279

1990 *at Woburn, Beds*

NAME					SCORE
Helen Alfredsson (Swe)	70	71	74	73	288
(After play-off)					
Jane Hill (Zim)	77	74	69	68	288
Laura Davies	75	73	73	70	291
Dana Lofland (USA)	73	70	75	73	291
Kitrina Douglas	69	71	75	76	291

WPGET Tour Events

1979

TOURNAMENT	NAME	SCORE	VENUE
Carlsberg European Championship	M Anderson	145	Tyrrells Wood
	Catherine Panton	151	Willingdon
	Christine Langford	73	Long Ashton
	Jo Smurthwaite	147	Baberton
	Christine Langford	142	Whitecraigs
	Jane Panter	146	Coventry
	Vanessa Marvin	143	South Staffs
	Beverly Huke	146	Ballater
	Christine Langford	148	St Annes Old Links
	Michelle Walker	140	York
	Alison Sheard	147	Sand Moor
	Jenny Lee-Smith	140	Arcot Hall
McEwans Welsh Classic	Alison Sheard	144	Dinas Powis
Hitachi	Christine Trew	145	Downshire
State Express	Catherine Panton	166	Portrush
WPGA European Championship	Susan Moon	292	Valbonne, Cannes
Lambert and Butler Match Play	Jane Panter		Moor Park

1980

TOURNAMENT	NAME	SCORE	VENUE
Carlsberg European Championship	Muriel Thomson	141	Tyrrells Wood
	Christine Trew	150	Queen's Park, Bournemouth
	Beverly Huke	144	Blairgowrie
	Wilma Aitken (Am)	147	Gleddoch House
	Christine Langford	142	Knowle
	Dale Reid	139	Coventry
	Maxine Burton	144	Arcot Hall
	Jenny Lee-Smith	142	Shifnal
	Christine Trew	148	Sand Moor
	R Barry	140	Tyrrells Wood
Billingham Championship	Christine Sharp	150	South Staffs
Elizabeth Ann Classic	Catherine Panton	289	Pannal
Robert Winsor Productions Championship	Jenny Lee-Smith	146	Finchley
McEwan's Lager Welsh Classic	Karstin Ehrnlund	142	Whitchurch
Hitachi Championship	Susan Moon	222	Walsall
Viscount Double Glazing Championship	Muriel Thomson	236	Portrush
Barnham Broom Championship	Muriel Thomson	230	Barnham Broom
Lambert and Butler Match Play	Michelle Walker	3 and 2	Moor Park
Volvo Invitational Tournament	Jenny Lee-Smith	149	Gothenburg
Manchester Evening News Pro-Am Classic	Jenny Lee-Smith	220	Mere

1981

TOURNAMENT	NAME	SCORE	VENUE
Carlsberg European Championship	Michelle Walker	222	St Pierre
	Catherine Panton	223	Queen's Park, Bournemouth
	Catherine Panton	213	Moortown
	Dale Reid	219	Gleneagles
Sports Space Championship	Jenny Lee-Smith	72	Dyrham Park
Smirnoff Ulster Open	S LeVeque	228	Royal Portrush
United Friendly Insurance Championship	S LeVeque	220	Moretonhampstead
Volvo Invitational Tournament	Beverly Lewis	147	Gothenburg
McEwan's Lager Welsh Classic	Jenny Lee-Smith	216	Whitchurch
Elizabeth Ann Classic	Muriel Thomson	293	Pannal, Harrogate
Moben Kitchen's Classic	Dale Reid	213	Mere
Lambert and Butler Match Play	Jenny Lee-Smith	3 and 1	Moor Park

1982

TOURNAMENT	NAME	SCORE	VENUE
Ford Ladies' Golf Classic	Jenny Lee-Smith	305	Woburn
United Friendly Worthing Open	Rose Jones	217	Hill Barn, Brighton
Smirnoff Ulster Open	Linda Bowman	225	Portstewart
United Friendly Insurance Championship	Beverley New (Am)	212	Walmley
Guernsey Open	Dale Reid	219	Royal Guernsey
Spanish Open	Rose Jones	224	Sotogrande
Dunhill Classic	Bridget Cooper	147	Woburn
Moben Kitchen's Classic	Catherine Panton	216	Mere
Nat West East Anglia Open	Linda Bowman	215	Lark Valley

1983

TOURNAMENT	NAME	SCORE	VENUE
Ford Ladies' Golf Classic	Barbara Helbig	298	Woburn
Smirnoff Irish Open	Catherine Panton	224	Portstewart
United Friendly Tournament	Marta Figueras-Dotti	217	Hill Barn, Brighton
UBM Northern Classic	Catherine Panton	210	Arcot Hall
Dunham Forest Pro-Am	Catherine Panton	142	Dunham Forest
Caldy Classic	Dale Reid	225	Caldy
Woodhall Hills	Debbie Dowling	142	Woodhall Hills
Clandeboye Pro-Am	Christine Sharp	154	Clandeboye
White Horse Whisky Challenge	Beverly Huke	207	Selsdon Park
Lilley Brooke International Ladies' Classic	Dale Reid	139	Lilley Brook
British Olivetti	Sandra Mackenzie	223	Old Thorns
United Friendly	Dale Reid	216	Moortown
Middlesbrough Municipal Ladies' Classic	Beverly Lewis	144	Middlesbrough
Playford Lark Valley Classic	Beverly Huke ⎱ tie Judy Statham ⎰	138	Lark Valley
Guernsey Open	Marta Figueras-Dotti	209	Royal Guernsey
Colt Cars Jersey Open	Debbie Dowling	215	Royal Jersey
Sands International	Michelle Walker	233	Saunton

1984

TOURNAMENT	NAME	SCORE	VENUE
Ford Ladies' Golf Classic	Kitrin Douglas	292	Woburn
Ulster Volkswagen Classic	Peggy Conley	216	Belvoir Park, Belfast
McEwan's Lager Manchester Classic	Rica C0mstock	286	Heaton Park
British Olivetti	Jenny Lee-Smith	294	Old Thorns
United Friendly	Rae Hast	283	Hill Barn, Brighton
UBM Classic	Dale Reid	291	Arcot Hill
Guernsey Open	Muriel Thomson	280	Royal Guernsey
Baume & Mercier Ladies' International Golf Classic	Michelle Walker	138	Lilley Brook
Wirral Caldy Classic	Lori Castillo	215	Caldy
JS Bloor Eastleigh Classic	Dale Reid	254	Fleming Park
United Friendly	Karstin Ehrnlund	288	Southport and Ainsdale
White Horse Whisky Challenge	Federica Dassu	283	Burnham Beeches
Cold Cars Jersey Open	Jane Connachan	279	Royal Jersey
Hoganas Sweden Open	Kitrina Douglas	288	Molle
IBM European Open	Gillian Stewart (Am)	299	The Belfry
LBS Ladies' German Open	Bevery Huke	219	Schloss Braunfels
Lorne Stewart Match Play Championship	Michelle Walker	2 and 1	Sudbury
Sands International	Muriel Thomson	307	Saunton
Smirnoff Ladies' Irish Open	Kathy Whitworth	285	Clandeboye
La Manga Club Spanish Open	Maxine Burton	286	La Manga
Elizabeth Ann Day	Susan Moon	134	Pannal

1985

TOURNAMENT	NAME	SCORE	VENUE
Ford Ladies' Classic	Gillian Stewart	296	Woburn
Hennessy Cognac Ladies' Cup	Jan Stephenson	283	St Cloud
Ulster Volkswagen Classic	Dale Reid	213	Belvoir Park, Belfast
British Olivetti	Jane Connachan	284	Moor Hall
Vale do Lobo Portuguese Ladies' Open	Debbie Dowling	285	Vale do Lobo
McEwan's Lager Wirral Caldy Classic	Catherine Panton	291	Caldy
Bowring Birmingham Ladies' Classic	Federica Dassu	280	Pype Hayes, Sutton Coldfield
Belgian Ladies' Open	Laura Davies	286	Royal Waterloo
LBS Ladies' German Open	Julie Brown	288	Braunfels
Bloor Homes Eastleigh Classic	Christine Sharp	261	Fleming Park, Southampton
Trusthouse Forte Ladies' Classic	Beverly Huke	289	Campo Villa de Madrid
Mitsubishi Colt Cars Jersey Open	Marie Wennersten	211	Royal Jersey
Delsjo Open	Catherine Panton	210	Gothenburg
Hoganas Open	Liselotte Neumann	283	Molle
IBM Ladies' European Open	Liselotte Neumann	290	Kingswood
Brend Hotels International	Dale Reid	288	Saunton
415/Vantage Ladies' European Match Play	Jane Connachan	1 hole	Bramhall
Laing Ladies' Classic	Muriel Thomson	282	Stokes Poges
La Manga Club Spanish Open	Alison Sheard	285	La Manga

1986

TOURNAMENT	NAME	SCORE	VENUE
Ford Ladies' Classic	Muriel Thomson	290	Woburn
Hennessy Cognac Cup	Kelly Leadbetter	293	Chantilly
Portuguese Ladies' Open	Catherine Panton	286	Vilamoura
British Olivetti	Dale Reid	285	Moor Hall
Ulster Volkswagen Classic	Beverley Huke	213	Belvoir Park, Belfast
British Midland Ladies' Irish Open	Muriel Thomson	290	City of Derry
McEwan's Wirral Classic	Laura Davies	285	Caldy
Belgian Ladies' Open	Penny Grice-Whittaker	275	Royal Waterloo
Volmac Dutch Ladies' Open	Jane Forrest	282	Hilversum
Trusthouse Forte Ladies' Classic	Corinne Dibnah	280	Cologne
Bloor Homes Eastleigh Classic	Debbie Dowling	254	Fleming Park, Southampton
BMW Ladies' German Open	Liselotte Neumann	282	Olching, Munich
Kristianstad Ladies' Open	Corinne Dibnah	288	Kristianstad, Sweden
Borlange Ladies' Open	Karen Lunn	212	Falun-Borlange, Sweden
Bowring Scottish Ladies' Open	Meredith Marshall	283	Dalmahoy
Greater Manchester Tournament	Laura Davies	268	Haigh Hall, Wigan
Mitsubishi Colt Cars Jersey Open	Kitrina Douglas	278	Royal Jersey
Laing Ladies' Classic	Debbie Dowling	274	Stoke Poges
La Manga Club Spanish Open	Laura Davies	268	La Manga

1987

TOURNAMENT	NAME	SCORE	VENUE
Ford Ladies' Classic	Gillian Stewart	289	Woburn
Letting France First Open de France Feminin	Liselotte Neumann	293	Fourqueux
British Olivetti	Jane Connachan	286	Moor Hall
Ulster Volkswagen Open	Dale Reid	283	Belvoir Park, Belfast
McEwan's Wirral Classic	Trish Johnson	292	Caldy
Belgian Ladies' Open	Marie Laure de Taya	285	Waterloo
Volmac Ladies' Open	Dale Reid	283	The Hague
Portuguese Ladies' Open	Catherine Panton	210	Vale do Lobo
Hennessy Cognac Ladies' Cup	Kitrina Douglas	283	St Germain
La Manga Club Ladies' European Open	Dale Reid	272	Ferndown
Bloor Homes Eastleigh Classic	Trish Johnson	242	Fleming Park, Southampton
BMW Ladies' German Open	Marie Laure de Taya	275	Wendlohe, Hamburg
Bowring Ladies' Scottish Open	Dale Reid	285	Cawder
First Italian Ladies' Open	Laura Davies	285	Croara
Laing NSPCC Charity Ladies' Classic	Alison Nicholas	281	Stoke Poges
James Capel (CI) Guernsey Open	Corinne Dibnah	275	Royal Guernsey
Qualitair Ladies' Spanish Open	Corinne Dibnah	210	La Manga
Woolmark Ladies' Match Play Championship	Trish Johnson	1 hole	Moor Park

1988

TOURNAMENT	NAME	SCORE	VENUE
Marbella Ladies' Open	Laurette Maritz	283	Los Naranjos
Ford Ladies' Classic	Laura Davies	292	Woburn
Ems Masters	Laurette Maritz	213	Quinta da Marinha
Portuguese Ladies' Open	Peggy Conley	291	Vilamoura
British Olivetti	Alison Nicholas	283	Moor Hall
BMW Ladies' German Open	Liselotte Neumann	290	Hubbelrath
Broadway Group Wirral Classic	Beverley New	283	Caldy
Letting France Ladies' French Open	Marie-Lauvre de Taya	290	Fourqueux
Volmac Ladies' Open	Marie-Lauvre de Taya	295	Rosendaelsche, Arnhem
St Moritz Classic	Janice Arnold	285	St Moritz
Birchgrey Ladies' European Open	Dale Reid	283	Kingswood
Hennessy Ladies' Cup	Marie-Laure de Taya	284	St Germain
Bloor Homes Eastleigh Classic	Corinne Dibnah	256	Fleming Park, Southampton
Danish Ladies' Open	Marie-Laure de Taya	275	Delsjo, Gothenburg
Gothenberg Ladies' Open	Florence Descampe	285	Ringstead
Bowring Ladies' Scottish Open	Catherine Panton	293	Cawder
Variety Club Celebrity Classic	Alison Nicholas	204	Calcot Park
Godiva European Masters	Karen Lunn	276	Royal Antwerp
Italian Open	Laura Davies	269	Ca'Della Nave
Toshiba Players' Championship	Dale Reid	294	Old Thorns
James Capel Guernsey Open	Alison Nicholas	274	Royal Guernsey
Laing Charity Ladies' Classic	Marie-Laure de Taya	203	Stoke Poges
Biarritz Ladies'Open	Laura Davies	267	Biarritz
Woolmark Match Play Championship	Marie-Laure de Taya	4 and 2	Vallromanas
Qualitair Ladies' Spanish Open	Marie-Laure de Taya	207	La Manga

1989

TOURNAMENT	NAME	SCORE	VENUE
Rome Ladies' Classic	Sofia Gronberg	210	Olgiata
Ford Ladies' Classic	Marie-Laure de Lorenzi (formerly Taya)	210	Woburn
Hennessy Ladies' Cup	Marie-Laure de Lorenzi	279	St Germain
BMW Ladies' Classic	Marie-Laure de Lorenzi	277	Hubbelrath
Third Ladies' French Open	Suzanne Strudwick	285	Fourqueux
St Moritz Ladies' Classic	Kitrina Douglas	286	St Moritz
TEC Players' Championship	Anna Oxenstierna-Rhodin	286	The Tytherington Club
Bloor Homes Eastleigh Classic	Debbie Dowling	261	Fleming Park
Lufthansa Ladies' German Open	Alison Nicholas	269	Worthsee
Ladies' Danish Open	Tania Abitbol	285	Rungsted
Gislaved Ladies' Open	Alison Nicholas	288	Isaberg, Sweden
Variety Club Celebrity Classic	Corinne Dibnah	279	Calcot Park
Godiva European Masters	Kitrina Douglas	287	Bercuit, Brussels
Expedier Ladies' European Open	Jane Connachan	279	Kingswood
Third Ladies' Italian Open	Xonia Wunsch-Ruiz	278	Carimate, Milan
Laing Charity Ladies' Classic	Laura Davies	276	Stoke Poges
Woolmark Ladies' Match Play	Dennise Hutton	2 holes	Vallromanas
AGF Biarritz Ladies' Open	Dennise Hutton	274	Biarritz
Qualitair Ladies' Classic	Alison Nicholas	213	La Manga

1990

TOURNAMENT	NAME	SCORE	VENUE
WPG European Tour Classic	Tania Abitbol	213	The Tytherington Club
Hennessy Ladies' Cup	Trish Johnson	285	St Germain
Ford Ladies' Classic	Maria-Laure de Lorenzi	284	Woburn
Valextra Classic	Florence Descampe	279	Olgiata, Rome
Bonment Ladies' Classic	Evelyn Orley	289	Bonment
BMW European Masters	Karen Lunn	285	Bercuit, Brussels
BMW Ladies' Classic	Diane Barnard	278	Hubbelrath
Laing Ladies' Charity Classic	Laurette Maritz	275	Stoke Poges
Bloor Homes Eastleigh Classic	Trish Johnson	249	Fleming Park, Southampton
Lufthansa Ladies' German Open	Ayako Okamoto	274	Worthsee
Haninge Ladies' Open	Dale Reid	291	Haninge, Stockholm
Variety Club Celebrity Classic	Alison Nicholas	275	Calcot Park
TEC Players' Championship	Anne Jones	281	Patshull Park
Expedier Ladies' European Open	Trish Johnson	276	Kingswood
Trophée International Coconut Skol	Corinne Dibnah	284	Fourqueux
Italian Ladies' Open	Florence Descampe	282	Gardagolf
Woolmark Match Play Championship	Florence Descampe		Club de Campo
AGF Biarnitz Ladies' Open	Laura Davies	136	Biarritz
Longines Classic	Trish Johnson	286	Nice

Solheim Cup

at Lake Nona, Florida

Foursomes

UNITED STATES	Matches	EUROPE	Matches
Pat Bradley and Nancy Lopez	0	Laura Davies and Alison Nicholas (2 and 1)	1
Cathy Gerring and Dottie Mochrie (6 and 5)	1	Pam Wright and Liselotte Neumann	0
Patti Shehan and Rosie Jones (6 and 5)	1	Dale Reid and Helen Alfredsson	0
Beth Daniel and Betsy King (5 and 4)	1	Trish Johnson and Marie-Laure de Lorenzi	0
	3		1

Four-balls

	Matches		Matches
Patti Shehan and Rosie Jones (2 and 1)	1	Trish Johnson and Marie-Laure de Lorenzi	0
Pat Bradley and Nancy Lopez (2 and 1)	1	Dale Reid and Helen Alfredsson	0
Betsy King and Beth Daniel (4 and 3)	1	Laura Davies and Alison Nicholas	0
Cathy Derring and Dotti Mochrie		Liselotte Neumann and Pam Wright (4 and 2)	1
	3		1

Singles

	Matches		Matches
Cathy Derring (4 and 3)	1	Helen Alfredsson	0
Rosie Jones	0	Laura Davies (3 and 2)	1
Nancy Lopez (6 and 4)	1	Alison Nicholas	0
Betsy King	½	Pam Wright	½
Beth Daniel (7 and 6)	1	Liselotte Neumann	0
Patti Sheehan	0	Dale Reid (2 and 1)	1
Dotti Mochrie (4 and 2)	1	Marie-Laure de Lorenzi	0
Pat Bradley (8 and 7)	1	Trish Johnson	0
	—		—
	5½		2½

Aggregate: USA 11½, Europe 4½.
Captains: USA, Kelly Whitworth; Europe, Mickey Walker.

Part Four
Ladies' Amateur Events

Ladies' British Championships

Ladies' British Open Amateur Championship

INAUGURATED 1893

The first Championship was played soon after the formation of the Ladies' Golf Union in 1893 by representatives of 14 clubs from all over the United Kingdom including Lytham, a club which had already come forward with the idea of a championship for ladies. Lytham gave a Silver Challenge Cup and the first Championship was played there. Thirty-eight ladies took part and over three days the winner proved to be Lady Margaret Scott who had learned her golf playing with her three brothers, Michael, Osmond and Denys, all scratch golfers at Westward Ho!.

Play was over the Lytham Ladies course of 9 holes. Clothed in the garb of the day with ankle-length dresses, tight waists, long flowing sleeves and straw boaters pinned to the head, given the circumstances the scoring was excellent. Lady Margaret's rounds of 9 holes averaged 41. Few champions of today wearing such clothes could match her play even on the short course it was then.

The Champion won again the next year at Littlestone playing the men's course from shortened tees and defeating Isette Pearson, the LGU secretary, for the second time. After her third consecutive win, at Portrush in Ireland, Lady Margaret did not appear again and the next year the Championship was played in Scotland at Gullane where the two Orr sisters met in the final. The Championship returned to Ireland every four years until 1914 and continues to be played there regularly. The three Hezlet sisters and Rhona Adair, all Irish girls, were often winners or runners-up during this period. May Hezlet won it on three occasions, beating her sister, Florence, in the 1907 final, and Rhona Adair won twice.

The Irish LGU had been formed as early as 1893 and the Championship has gone to Portrush or Newcastle, Co Down on seven occasions each and Portmarnock once. Both courses have staged the Championship more than any other. Apart from these it has also been played at Harlech and Hunstanton on five occasions each and St Andrews and Troon four times. In recent years it has not been confined to links courses – Ganton, Sunningdale, Walton Heath and Woodhall Spa being among those visited. The final was played over 36 holes from 1913 to the early 1960s.

In the 1920s two outstanding players Cecil Leitch and Joyce Wethered were often in combat. They were both Champions four times and each beat the other in the final once. While Cecil Leitch was first on the scene – she won at Hunstanton in 1914 when Joyce Wethered was much too young to have entered – and was recognised as the first woman to hit the ball like a man, Joyce Wethered is acknowledged as the outstanding woman player of her time and by many of all time. Her unmatched swing and supremely calm temperament were unique in her day. Like Bobby Jones, who was a great admirer of her play, she retired at 28 with no further fields to conquer. The 1920s also saw the first successful overseas competitors, among them the French ladies Nanette Le Blan and Thion de la Chaume, later Mme René Lacoste. In 1969 the winner was Catherine Lacoste, her daughter, the only mother and daughter to have both won the Championship. Glenna Collett (USA) was twice in the final but lost on both occasions, and it was not until 1947 that Mrs G. Zaharias ('Babe' Didrikson, the Olympic athlete) became the first American winner. Since then there have been several.

The 1930s saw Enid Wilson, Helen Holm and Pam Barton win seven titles between them. Enid Wilson took the title three years in succession, the first to do so since Lady Margaret Scott. Pam Barton, just 19 when she won in 1936, was the only British woman to hold both the British and US Ladies Championships at the same time after the First War in 1938. But for her tragic death in a war-time flying accident, she could well have won again.

Since 1946 only six ladies have won more than once; Frances Stephens, who also died young, Jessie Valentine who had won in 1937 as Jessie Anderson, Marley Spearman (now Mrs Harris), Brigitte Varangot of France, Elizabeth Chadwick and Mickey Walker. The latter turned professional and last year captained the Solheim Cup team in the USA.

Far greater numbers both in the UK and overseas now play the game which means that there is less domination by a few players than in the first half of the century. With the honourable exceptions of Belle Robertson and Lynda Bayman, winners in the last ten years have tended to be younger than before. This is no doubt due to many more competitive opportunities which young golfers now have and opportunities for better instruction which gives talent the chance to blossom earlier.

YEAR	WINNER	RUNNER-UP	MARGIN	VENUE
1893	Lady Margaret Scott	Miss Isette Pearson	7 and 5	Lytham St Annes
1894	Lady Margaret Scott	Miss Isette Pearson	3 and 2	Littlestone
1895	Lady Margaret Scott	Miss E Lythgoe	5 and 4	Portrush
1896	Miss Pascoe	Miss L Thomson	3 and 2	Hoylake
1897	Miss EC Orr	Miss Orr	4 and 2	Gullane
1898	Miss L Thomson	Miss EC Neville	7 and 5	Yarmouth
1899	Miss M Hezlet	Miss Magill	2 and 1	Newcastle, Co. Down
1900	Miss R Adair	Miss EC Neville	6 and 5	Westward Ho!
1901	Miss Graham	Miss R Adair	3 and 1	Aberdovey
1902	Miss M Hezlet	Miss EC Neville	19th hole	Deal
1903	Miss R Adair	Miss F Walker-Leigh	4 and 3	Portrush
1904	Miss L Dod	Miss M Hezlet	1 hole	Troon

YEAR	WINNER	RUNNER-UP	MARGIN	VENUE
1905	Miss B Thompson	Miss M E Stuart	3 and 2	Cromer
1906	Mrs Kennion	Miss B Thompson	4 and 3	Burnham and Berrow
1907	Miss M Hezlet	Miss F Hezlet	2 and 1	Newcastle, Co. Down
1908	Miss M Titterton	Miss D Campbell	19th hole	St Andrews
1909	Miss D Campbell	Miss F Hezlet	4 and 3	Birkdale
1910	Miss Grant Suttie	Miss L Moore	6 and 4	Westward Ho!
1911	Miss D Campbell	Miss V Hezlet	3 and 2	Portrush
1912	Miss G Ravenscroft	Miss S Temple	3 and 2	Turnberry
Final played over 36 holes after 1912				
1913	Miss M Dodd	Miss Chubb	8 and 6	Lytham St Annes
1914	Miss C Leitch	Miss G Ravenscroft	2 and 1	Hunstanton
1915-18	*No Championship owing to the Great War*			
1919	*Should have been played at Burnham in October, but abandoned owing to railway strike*			
1920	Miss C Leitch	Miss Molly Griffiths	7 and 6	Newcastle, Co. Down
1921	Miss C Leitch	Miss J Wethered	4 and 3	Turnberry
1922	Miss J Wethered	Miss C Leitch	9 and 7	Princes, Sandwich
1923	Miss D Chambers	Miss A Macbeth	2 holes	Burnham and Berrow
1924	Miss J Wethered	Mrs Cautley	7 and 6	Portrush
1925	Miss J Wethered	Miss C Leitch	37th hole	Troon
1926	Miss C Leitch	Mrs Garon	8 and 7	Harlech
1927	Miss Thion de la Chaume (Fra)	Miss Pearson	5 and 4	Newcastle, Co. Down
1928	Miss Nanette Le Blan (Fra)	Miss S Marshall	3 and 2	Hunstanton
1929	Miss J Wethered	Miss G Collett (USA)	3 and 1	St. Andrews
1930	Miss D Fishwick	Miss G Collett (USA)	4 and 3	Formby
1931	Miss E Wilson	Miss W Morgan	7 and 6	Portmarnock
1932	Miss E Wilson	Miss CPR Montgomery	7 and 6	Saunton
1933	Miss E Wilson	Miss D Plumpton	5 and 4	Gleneagles
1934	Mrs AM Holm	Miss P Barton	6 and 5	Porthcawl
1935	Miss W Morgan	Miss P Barton	3 and 2	Newcastle, Co. Down
1936	Miss P Barton	Miss B Newell	5 and 3	Southport and Ainsdale
1937	Miss J Anderson	Miss D Park	6 and 4	Turnberry
1938	Mrs AM Holm	Miss E Corlett	4 and 3	Burnham and Berrow
1939	Miss P Barton	Mrs T Marks	2 and 1	Portrush
1940-45	*No Championship owing to the Second World War*			
1946	Mrs G W Hetherington	Philomena Garvey	1 hole	Hunstanton
1947	Babe Zaharias (USA)	Jacqueline Gordon	5 and 4	Gullane
1948	Louise Suggs (USA)	Jean Donald	1 hole	Lytham St Annes
1949	Frances Stephens	Val Reddan	5 and 4	Harlech
1950	Vicomtesse de Saint Sauveur (Fra)	Jessie Valentine (*née* Anderson)	3 and 2	Newcastle, Co. Down
1951	Catherine MacCann	Frances Stephens	4 and 3	Broadstone
1952	Moira Paterson	Frances Stephens	39th hole	Troon
1953	Marlene Stewart (Can)	Philomena Garvey	7 and 6	Porthcawl
1954	Frances Stephens	Elizabeth Price	4 and 3	Ganton
1955	Jessie Valentine	Barbara Romack (USA)	7 and 6	Portrush
1956	Margaret Smith (USA)	Mary P Janssen	8 and 7	Sunningdale
1957	Philomena Garvey	Jessie Valentine	4 and 3	Gleneagles
1958	Jessie Valentine	Elizabeth Price	1 hole	Hunstanton
1959	Elizabeth Price	Belle McCorkindale	37th hole	The Berkshire
1960	Barbara McIntire (USA)	Philomena Garvey	4 and 2	Harlech
1961	Marley Spearman	Diane Robb	7 and 6	Carnoustie
1962	Marley Spearman	Angela Bonallack	3 and 1	Birkdale
1963	Brigitte Varangot (Fra)	Philomena Garvey	4 and 3	Newcastle, Co Down
1964	Carol Sorenson (USA)	Bridget Jackson	19th hole	Princes, Sandwich
1965	Brigitte Varangot (Fra)	Belle Robertson (*née* McCorkindale)	4 and 3	St Andrews
1966	Elizabeth Chadwick	Vivien Saunders	3 and 2	Ganton
1967	Elizabeth Chadwick	Mary Everard	1 hole	Harlech
1968	Brigitte Varangot (Fra)	Catherine Rubin (Fra)	20th hole	Walton Heath

YEAR	WINNER	RUNNER-UP	MARGIN	VENUE
1969	Catherine Lacoste (Fra)	Ann Irvin	1 hole	Portrush
1970	Dinah Oxley	Belle Robertson	1 hole	Gullane
1971	Mickey Walker	Beverly Huke	3 and 1	Alwoodley
1972	Mickey Walker	Catherine Rubin (Fra)	2 holes	Hunstanton
1973	Anne Irvin	Mickey Walker	3 and 2	Carnoustie
1974	Carol Semple (USA)	Angela Bonallack	2 and 1	Porthcawl
1975	Nancy Syms (USA)	Suzanne Cadden	3 and 2	St Andrews
1976	Catherine Panton	Alison Sheard	1 hole	Silloth
1977	Angela Uzielli	Vanessa Marvin	6 and 5	Hillside
1978	Edwina Kennedy (Aus)	Julia Greenhalgh	1 hole	Hollinwell
1979	Maureen Madill	J Lock (Aus)	2 and 1	Nairn
1980	Anne Sander (USA)	L Wollin (Swe)	3 and 1	Woodhall Spa
1981	Belle Robertson	Wilma Aitken	20th hole	Conwy
1982	Kitrina Douglas	Gillian Stewart	4 and 2	Walton Heath
1983	Jill Thornhill	Regine Lautens (Switz)	4 and 2	Silloth
1984	Jody Rosenthal (USA)	Julie Brown	4 and 3	Troon
1985	Lilian Behan	Claire Waite	1 hole	Ganton
1986	M McGuire (NZ)	L Briers (Aus)	2 and 1	Pulborough
1987	Janet Collingham	Susan Shapcott	19th hole	Harlech
1988	Joanne Furby	Julie Wade	4 and 3	Deal
1989	Helen Dobson	Elaine Farquharson	6 and 5	Hoylake
1990	Julie Hall (neé Wade)	Helen Wadsworth	3 and 2	Dunbar

Ladies' British Open Amateur Stroke Play

INAUGURATED 1969

Inaugurated in 1969 as the first 72-hole amateur stroke play event for ladies this side of the Atlantic, the British Open Amateur has been won each year by a British Isles player, except in 1973 when Ann Stant (USA), won at Ipswich. In that decade Belle Robertson, Mary Everard and Julia Greenhalgh each won twice. Belle won again in 1985, making her the only player to have won three times.

In the years 1976–78, it was played concurrently with the Ladies' British Open Championship. Since it set out on its own again, it has been won by a British or Irish Curtis Cup International every year except 1988. After numerous attempts Vicki Thomas of Wales was the victor in 1990 at Strathaven, Lanarkshire.

YEAR	WINNER	SCORE	VENUE
1969	Ann Irvin	295	Gosforth Park, Northumberland
1970	Mary Everard	313	Birkdale
1971	Belle Robertson	302	Ayr Belleisle
1972	Belle Robertson	296	Silloth, Cumbria
1973	Ann Stant (USA)	296	Purdis Heath, Ipswich
1974	Julia Greenhalgh	302	Seaton Carew, Cleveland
1975	Julia Greenhalgh	298	Gosforth Park, Northumberland
1976	Jenny Lee-Smith	299	Fulford, York
1977	Mary Everard	306	Lindrick, South Yorks
1978	Janet Melville	310	Foxhills, Surrey
1979	Mary McKenna	305	Moseley, West Midlands
1980	Maureen Madill	304	Brancepeth Castle, Co Durham

1981 at Royal Norwich

NAME	SCORE
Janet Soulsby	83 69 73 75 300
Jane Connachan	79 76 77 70 302
Maureen Madill	76 75 75 77 303
Mary McKenna	75 78 75 76 304
Wilma Aitken	76 75 79 75 305
Alison Gemmill	75 75 79 76 305
Claire Waite	76 77 78 74 305

1982 at Downfield, Dundee

NAME	SCORE
Jane Connachan	79 73 70 72 294
Barbara Bunkowsky	78 78 70 73 299
Pamela Wright	84 72 75 71 302
Kimberley Gardner	79 75 70 79 303
Claire Waite	75 78 78 73 304

1983 *at Moortown, Leeds*

NAME	SCORE
Alison Nicholas	71 75 70 76 292
Jane Connachan	71 76 74 73 294
Kitrina Douglas	72 75 75 73 295
Claire Hourihane	76 75 73 71 295
Wilma Aitken	76 71 74 75 296

1984 *at Caernarvonshire, Conwy*

NAME	SCORE
Claire Waite	75 74 75 71 295
Mary McKenna	73 74 77 73 297
Claire Hourihane	75 74 72 77 298
Laura Davies	78 73 75 74 300
Nicola McCormack	73 77 74 77 301

1985 *at Formby, Lancs*

NAME	SCORE
Belle Robertson	75 76 80 74 305
Cindy Scholefield	78 79 76 76 309
Claire Hourihane	75 78 81 77 311
Patricia Johnson	73 81 76 81 311
Susan Shapcott	81 80 73 78 312

1986 *at Blairgowrie (Lansdowne), Perthshire*

NAME	SCORE
Claire Hourihane	73 72 72 74 291
Patricia Johnson	72 74 73 72 291
(Claire Hourihane won play-off)	
Shirley Lawson	76 72 72 72 292
Kathryn Imrie	79 70 71 74 294
Vicki Thomas	76 79 72 72 299

1987 *at Ipswich, Suffolk*

NAME	SCORE
Linda Bayman	75 74 76 72 297
Jill Thornhill	75 77 75 79 299
Nicola Way	78 74 71 76 299
Joanne Morley	75 77 75 74 301
Janet Collingham	74 74 78 75 301

1988 *at Porthcawl, Glamorgan*

NAME	SCORE
Karen Mitchell	79 84 78 76 317
Julie Wade	78 83 80 78 319
Mary McKenna	78 81 81 79 319
Terril Samuel (Can)	80 84 81 77 322
Catriona Lambert	83 79 83 78 323
Helen Wadsworth	81 88 76 78 323

1989 *at Southerness, Dumfries*

NAME	SCORE
Helen Dobson	78 77 72 71 298
N Hall	79 79 73 69 300
Julie Hall (*née* Wade)	82 81 69 71 303
A van der Haegen (Neth)	82 77 71 73 303
Julie Forbes	80 81 72 71 304

1990 *at Strathaven, Lanarkshire*

NAME	SCORE
Vicki Thomas	72 72 70 73 287
Claire Hourihane	72 73 70 73 288
E Valera	76 72 71 71 290
P Carlson	72 73 73 72 290
Helen Wadsworth	74 73 68 77 292

Senior Ladies' British Open Championship

INAUGURATED 1981

The LGU launched the Senior Ladies' British Open Championship in 1981 at Formby. Since then it has been played four times in England and twice each in Scotland and Wales.

The first winner was Mrs B M King of the Pleasington Club. Although an open championship it has only been won twice, in 1984 and 1987, by an overseas player, Mme Odile Semelaigne, who has won many titles in her native France.

Only twice has a former Curtis Cup International won the Seniors, Ann Howard (*née* Phillips) in 1989 and Angela Uzielli (*née* Carrick) in 1990 at her first attempt; she has the unique double of taking the English and Senior titles in the same year. Also her mother, Peggy Carrick, gained third place in 1985.

The most consistently successful competitor has been Pru Riddiford of Royal Ashdown Forest, who won twice and has been second four times between 1982 and 1988. Catherine Bailey came second in 1986, third in 1987 and won in 1988 and in 1989.

YEAR	WINNER	SCORE	VENUE
1981	B King	159	Formby
1982	Pru Riddiford	161	Ilkley
1983	Margaret Birtwistle	167	Troon, Portland
1984	Odile Semelaigne (Fra)	152	Woodbridge
1985	Geraldine Costello	158	Prestatyn
1986	Pru Riddiford	154	Longniddry
1987	Odile Semelaigne (Fra)	152	Copt Heath
1988	Catherine Bailey	156	Littlestone
1989	Catherine Bailey	154	Wrexham
1990	Angela Uzielli	155	Harrogate

The Curtis Cup

INAUGURATED 1932

When Harriet and Margaret Curtis, sisters who were among the best players in the USA, came to Cromer for the British Ladies' Championship in 1905, they were so pleased with their reception and the impromptu match which they and five other US competitors played against seven of the best British players, that they dreamed of a challenge trophy for such a match. However it was not until after it had been mooted several times and another unofficial match was played in 1930 that the Curtis sisters presented a trophy 'to stimulate friendly rivalry among the women golfers of many lands'.

The first official match was played at Wentworth in 1932, one of four biennial games before the war. The Americans won three and halved the one at Gleneagles in 1936, when Jessie Anderson (later Mrs Valentine) holed a fine putt on the 18th green to finish one up and thus saved the match. In the Wentworth encounter two great players, Joyce Wethered (Lady Heathcoat-Amory) and Glenna Collett Vare, had another battle in the top singles match, but on this occasion Miss Wethered won comfortably; both had retired from tournament play when the next match was played.

Since the war the USA has certainly had the best results, but many of them were better for the British than those of the Walker and Ryder Cup teams during the same period. Britain won twice in the 1950s at Muirfield and Prince's, Sandwich. At Brae Burn in 1970 they halved the match, their best effort in the USA up to that point.

The 1960s and 1970s brought the Americans a steady flow of successes, sometimes by close margins. It was not until Diane Bailey inspired her team to a resounding 13–5 victory at Prairie Dunes, Kansas, in 1986, that the Curtis Cup side became the first British golf team to beat the Americans on their own soil. Diane Bailey followed her success there with a second win at St George's, Sandwich, two years later, but, hard as the new Captain Jill Thornhill tried, the winning spell was broken at Somerset Hills, New Jersey in 1990.

The Curtis Cup is always keenly contested and greatly enjoyed by all competitors, officials and spectators.

1932 *at Wentworth, Surrey*

Foursomes

GREAT BRITAIN & IRELAND	Matches	USA	Matches
Joyce Wethered and Wanda Morgan	0	Glenna Collett Vare and Mrs O S Hill (1 hole)	1
Enid Wilson and JB Watson	0	Virginia Van Wie and Helen Hicks (2 and 1)	1
Molly Gourlay and Doris Park	0	Maureen Orcutt and Mrs LD Cheney (1 hole)	1
	0		3

Singles

Joyce Wethered (6 and 4)	1	Glenna Collett Vare	0
Enid Wilson (2 and 1)	1	Helen Hicks	0
Wanda Morgan	0	Virginia Van Wie (2 and 1)	1
Diana Fishwick (4 and 3)	1	Maureen Orcutt	0
Molly Gourlay	½	Mrs OS Hill	½
Elsie Corlett	0	Mrs LD Cheney (4 and 3)	1
	3½		2½

Match aggregate: Great Britain & Ireland 3½, USA 5½
Captains: Joyce Wethered, Great Britain & Ireland; Marion Hollins, USA

1934 *at Chevy Chase, Maryland*

Foursomes

USA	Matches	GREAT BRITAIN & IRELAND	Matches
Virginia Van Wie and Charlotte Glutting	½	Molly Gourlay and Pamela Barton	½
Maureen Orcutt and Mrs LD Cheney (2 holes)	1	Diana Fishwick and Wanda Morgan	0
Mrs OS Hill and Lucile Robinson	0	Diana Plumpton and Charlotte Walker (2 and 1)	1
	1½		1½

Singles

Virginia Van Wie (2 and 1)	1	Diana Fishwick	0
Maureen Orcutt (4 and 2)	1	Molly Gourlay	0
Mrs LD Cheney (7 and 5)	1	Pamela Barton	0
Charlotte Glutting (3 and 2)	1	Wanda Morgan	0
Mrs OS Hill (3 and 2)	1	Diana Plumpton	0
Aniela Goldthwaite	0	Charlotte Walker (3 and 2)	1
	5		1

Match aggregate: USA 6½, Great Britain & Ireland 2½
Captains: Glenna Collett Vare, USA; Doris Chambers, Great Britain & Ireland

1936 *at Gleneagles, Perthshire*

Foursomes

GREAT BRITAIN & IRELAND	Matches	USA	Matches
Wanda Morgan and Marjorie Garon	½	Glenna Collett Vare and Patty Berg	½
Pamela Barton and Charlotte Walker	0	Maureen Orcutt and Mrs LD Cheney (2 and 1)	1
Jessie Anderson and Helen Holm (3 and 2)	1	Mrs OS Hill and Charlotte Glutting	0
	1½		1½

Singles

	Matches		Matches
Wanda Morgan	0	Glenna Collet Vare (3 and 2)	1
Helen Holm (4 and 3)	1	Patty Berg	0
Pamela Barton	0	Charlotte Glutting (1 hole)	1
Charlotte Walker	0	Maureen Orcutt (1 hole)	1
Jessie Anderson (1 hole)	1	Mrs LD Cheney	0
Marjorie Garon (7 and 5)	1	Mrs OS Hill	0
	3		3

Match aggregate: Great Britain & Ireland 4½, USA 4½
Captains: Doris Chambers, Great Britain & Ireland, Glenna Collett Vare, USA

1938 *at Essex, Massachusetts*

Foursomes

USA	Matches	GREAT BRITAIN & IRELAND	Matches
Mrs JA Page Jr and Maureen Orcutt	0	Helen Holm and Clarrie Tiernan (2 holes)	1
Glenna Collett Vare and Patty Berg	0	Jessie Anderson and Elsie Corlett (1 hole)	1
Marion Miley and Kathryn Hemphill	½	Charlotte Walker and Phyllis Wade	½
	½		2½

Singles

	Matches		Matches
Mrs JA Page Jr (6 and 5)	1	Helen Holm	0
Patty Berg (1 hole)	1	Jessie Anderson	0
Marion Miley (2 and 1)	1	Elsie Corlett	0
Glenna Collett Vare (2 and 1)	1	Charlotte Walker	0
Maureen Orcutt	0	Clarrie Tiernan (2 and 1)	1
Charlotte Glutting (1 hole)	1	Nan Baird	0
	5		1

Match aggregate: USA 5½, Great Britain & Ireland 3½
Captains: Frances E Stebbins, USA; Mrs R H Wallace-Williamson, Great Britain & Ireland

1948 *at Birkdale*

Foursomes

BRITISH ISLES	Matches	**USA**	Matches
Jean Donald and Jacqueline Gordon (3 and 2)	1	Louise Suggs and Grace Lenczyk	0
Philomena Garvey and Zara Bolton	0	Dorothy Kirby and Glenna Vare (4 and 3)	1
Maureen Ruttle and Val Reddan	0	Estelle Page and Dorothy Kielty (5 and 4)	1
	1		2

Singles

	Matches		Matches
Philomena Garvey	½	Louise Suggs	½
Jean Donald (2 holes)	1	Dorothy Kirby	0
Jacqueline Gordon	0	Grace Lenczyk (5 and 3)	1
Helen Holm	0	Estelle Page (3 and 2)	1
Maureen Ruttle	0	Polly Riley (3 and 2)	1
Zara Bolton	0	Dorothy Kielty (2 and 1)	1
	1½		4½

Match aggregate: British Isles 2½, USA 6½
Captains: Doris Chambers, British Isles; Glenna Vare, USA

1950 *at Buffalo, New York*

Foursomes

USA	Matches	**BRITISH ISLES**	Matches
Beverley Hanson and Dorothy Porter (3 and 2)	1	Jessie Valentine and Jean Donald	0
Helen Sigel and Peggy Kirk	0	Frances Stephens and Elizabeth Price (1 hole)	1
Dorothy Kirby and Dorothy Kielty (6 and 5)	1	Philomena Garvey and Jeanne Bisgood	0
	2		1

Singles

	Matches		Matches
Dorothy Porter	½	Frances Stephens	½
Polly Riley (7 and 6)	1	Jessie Valentine	0
Beverley Hanson (6 and 5)	1	Jean Donald	0
Dorothy Kielty (2 and 1)	1	Philomena Garvey	0
Peggy Kirk (1 hole)	1	Jeanne Bisgood	0
Grace Lenzcyk (5 and 4)	1	Elizabeth Price	0
	5½		½

Match aggregate: USA 7½, British Isles 1½
Captains: Glenna Vare, USA; Diana Critchley, British Isles

1952 *at Muirfield, East Lothian*

Foursomes

BRITISH ISLES		**USA**	
	Matches		Matches
Jean Donald and Elizabeth Price (3 and 2)	1	Dorothy Kirby and Grace De Moss	0
Frances Stephens and Jessie Valentine	0	Claire Doran and Majorie Lindsay (6 and 4)	1
Moira Paterson and Philomena Garvey (2 and 1)	1	Polly Riley and Patricia O'Sullivan	0
	2		1

Singles

Jean Donald	0	Dorothy Kirby (1 hole)	1
Frances Stephens (2 and 1)	1	Marjorie Lindsay	0
Moira Paterson	0	Polly Riley (6 and 4)	1
Jeanne Bisgood (6 and 5)	1	Mae Murray	0
Philomena Garvey	0	Claire Doran (3 and 2)	1
Elizabeth Price (3 and 2)	1	Grace De Moss	0
	3		3

Match aggregate: British Isles 5, USA 4
Captains: Lady Katherine Cairns, British Isles; Aniela Goldthwaite, USA

1954 *at Merion, Ardmore, Pennsylvania*

Foursomes

USA		**BRITISH ISLES**	
	Matches		Matches
Mary Lena Faulk and Polly Riley (6 and 4)	1	Frances Stephens and Elizabeth Price	0
Claire Doran and Patricia Lesser (6 and 5)	1	Philomena Garvey and Jessie Valentine	0
Dorothy Kirby and Barbara Romack (6 and 5)	1	Marjorie Peel and Janette Robertson	0
	3		0

Singles

Mary Lena Faulk	0	Frances Stephens (1 hole)	1
Claire Doran (4 and 3)	1	Jeanne Bisgood	0
Polly Riley (9 and 8)	1	Elizabeth Price	0
Dorothy Kirby	0	Philomena Garvey (3 and 1)	1
Grace Smith (*née* De Moss) (4 and 3)	1	Jessie Valentine	0
Joyce Ziske	0	Janette Robertson (3 and 1)	1
	3		3

Match aggregate: USA 6, British Isles 3
Captains: Edith Flippin, USA; Baba Beck, British Isles

1956 *at Prince's, Sandwich*

Foursomes

BRITISH ISLES	Matches	USA	Matches
Jessie Valentine and Philomena Garvey	0	Patricia Lesser and Margaret Smith (2 and 1)	1
Frances Smith (neé Stephens) and Elizabeth Price (5 and 3)	1	Polly Riley and Barbara Romack	0
Janette Robertson and Veronica Anstey	0	Mary Ann Downey and Carolyn Cudone (6 and 4)	1
	1		2

Singles

BRITISH ISLES	Matches	USA	Matches
Jessie Valentine (6 and 4)	1	Patricia Lesser	0
Philomena Garvey	0	Margaret Smith (9 and 8)	1
Frances Smith (1 hole)	1	Polly Riley	0
Janette Robertson	0	Barbara Romack (6 and 4)	1
Angela Ward (6 and 4)	1	Mary Ann Downey	0
Elizabeth Price (7 and 6)	1	Jane Nelson	0
	4		2

Match aggregate: British Isles 5, USA 4
Captains: Zara Bolton, British Isles; Edith Flippin, USA

1958 *at Brae Burn, Massachusetts*

Foursomes

USA	Matches	BRITISH ISLES	Matches
Polly Riley and Barbara Romack	0	Angela Bonallack (née Ward) and Elizabeth Price (2 and 1)	1
JoAnne Gunderson and Anne Quast	0	Janette Robertson and Frances Smith (3 and 2)	1
Les Johnstone and Barbara McIntire (6 and 5)	1	Bridget Jackson and Jessie Valentine	0
	1		2

Singles

USA	Matches	BRITISH ISLES	Matches
JoAnne Gunderson (2 holes)	1	Jessie Valentine	0
Barbara McIntire	½	Angela Bonallack	½
Anne Quast (4 and 2)	1	Elizabeth Price	0
Anna Johnstone	0	Janette Robertson (3 and 2)	1
Barbara Romack (3 and 2)	1	Bridget Jackson	0
Polly Riley	0	Frances Smith (2 holes)	1
	3½		2½

Match aggregate: USA 4½, British Isles 4½
Captains: Virginia Dennehy, USA; Daisy Ferguson, British Isles

1960 *at Lindrick, Yorkshire*

Foursomes

BRITISH ISLES	Matches	USA	Matches
Elizabeth Price and Angela Bonallack (1 hole)	1	JoAnne Gunderson and Barbara McIntire	0
Janette Robertson and Belle McCorkindale	0	Judy Eller and Anne Quast (4 and 2)	1
Frances Smith and Ruth Porter	0	Joanne Goodwin and Anna Johnstone (3 and 2)	1
	1		2

Singles

	Matches		Matches
Elizabeth Price	½	Barbara McIntire	½
Angela Bonallack	0	JoAnne Gunderson (2 and 1)	1
Janette Robertson	0	Anne Quast (2 holes)	1
Philomena Garvey	0	Judy Eller (4 and 3)	1
Belle McCorkindale	0	Judy Bell (8 and 7)	1
Ruth Porter (1 hole)	1	Joanne Goodwin	0
	1½		4½

Match aggregate: British Isles 3½, USA 8½
Captains: Maureen Garrett, British Isles; Mildred Prunaret, USA

1962 *at Broadmoor, Colorado Springs*

Foursomes

USA	Matches	BRITISH ISLES	Matches
Anne Decker (*née* Quast) and Barbara McIntire (7 and 5)	1	Marley Spearman and Angela Bonallack	0
Jean Ashley and Anna Johnstone (8 and 7)	1	Ruth Porter and Diane Frearson	0
Clifford Ann Creed and JoAnne Gunderson (4 and 3)	1	Sheila Vaughan and Ann Irvin	0
	3		0

Singles

Judy Bell	0	Diane Frearson (8 and 7)	1
JoAnne Gunderson (2 and 1)	1	Angela Bonallack	0
Clifford Ann Creed (6 and 5)	1	Sally Bonallack	0
Anne Decker (5 and 4)	1	Marley Spearman	0
Phyllis Preuss (1 hole)	1	Jean Roberts	0
Barbara McIntire (5 and 4)	1	Sheila Vaughan	0
	5		1

Match aggregate: United States 8, British Isles 1
Captains: Polly Riley, USA; Frances Smith, British Isles

1964 *at Porthcawl, Glamorgan*

First Day – Foursomes

BRITISH ISLES	Matches	USA	Matches
Marley Spearman and Angela Bonallack (2 and 1)	1	Barbara McIntire and Phyllis Preuss	0
Sheila Vaughan and Ruth Porter (3 and 2)	1	JoAnne Gunderson and Nancy Roth	0
Bridget Jackson and Susan Armitage	0	Carol Sorenson and Barbara White (8 and 6)	1
	2		1

Singles

Angela Bonallack	0	JoAnne Gunderson (6 and 5)	1
Marley Spearman	½	Barbara McIntire	½
Julia Greenhalgh	0	Barbara White (3 and 2)	1
Bridget Jackson (4 and 3)	1	Carol Sorenson	0
Joan Lawrence	0	Peggy Conley (1 hole)	1
Ruth Porter (1 hole)	1	Nancy Roth	0
	2½		3½

First day total: British Isles 4½, USA 4½

Second Day – Foursomes

Marley Spearman and Angela Bonallack (6 and 5)	1	Barbara McIntire and Phyllis Preuss	0
Susan Armitage and Bridget Jackson	0	JoAnne Gunderson and Nancy Roth (2 holes)	1
Ruth Porter and Sheila Vaughan	½	Carol Sorenson and Barbara White	½
	1½		1½

Singles

Marley Spearman	½	JoAnne Gunderson	½
Joan Lawrence	0	Barbara McIntire (4 and 2)	1
Julia Greenhalgh (5 and 3)	1	Phyllis Preuss	0
Angela Bonallack	0	Barbara White (3 and 2)	1
Ruth Porter	0	Carol Sorenson (3 and 2)	1
Bridget Jackson	0	Peggy Conley (1 hole)	1
	1½		4½

Second day total: British Isles 3, USA 6
Grand aggregate: British Isles 7½, USA 10½
Captains: Elsie Corlett, British Isles; Helen Hawes, USA

1966 *at Hot Springs, Virginia*

First Day – Foursomes

USA	Matches	GREAT BRITAIN & IRELAND	Matches
Jean Ashley and Phyllis Preuss (1 hole)	1	Angela Bonallack and Susan Armitage	0
Anne Welts (*née* Quast) and Barbara McIntire	1/2	Belle Robertson (*née* McCorkindale) and	
Barbara Boddie (*née* White) and Carol Flenniken		Joan Hastings	1/2
(*née* Sorenson) (1 hole)	1	Elizabeth Chadwick and Pam Tredinnick	0
	2 1/2		1/2

Singles

USA	Matches	GREAT BRITAIN & IRELAND	Matches
Jean Ashley (1 hole)	1	Belle Robertson	0
Anne Welts	1/2	Susan Armitage	1/2
Barbara Boddie (3 and 2)	1	Angela Bonallack	0
Nancy Syms (*née* Roth) (2 holes)	1	Elizabeth Chadwick	0
Helen Wilson	0	Ita Burke (3 and 1)	1
Carol Flenniken (3 and 1)	1	Marjory Fowler	0
	4 1/2		1 1/2

First day total: USA 7, Great Britain & Ireland 2

Second Day – Foursomes

USA	Matches	GREAT BRITAIN & IRELAND	Matches
Jean Ashley and Phyllis Preuss (2 and 1)	1	Angela Bonallack and Susan Armitage	0
Barbara McIntire and Anne Welts	0	Elizabeth Chadwick and Ita Burke (1 hole)	1
Barbara Boddie and Carol Flenniken (2 and 1)	1	Belle Robertson and Joan Hastings	0
	2		1

Singles

USA	Matches	GREAT BRITAIN & IRELAND	Matches
Jean Ashley	0	Angela Bonallack (2 and 1)	1
Anne Welts	1/2	Belle Robertson	1/2
Barbara Boddie (3 and 2)	1	Susan Armitage	0
Nancy Syms	1/2	Pam Tredinnick	1/2
Phyllis Preuss (3 and 2)	1	Elizabeth Chadwick	0
Carol Flenniken (2 and 1)	1	Ita Burke	0
	4		2

Second day total: USA 6, Great Britain & Ireland 3
Grand aggregate: USA 13, Great Britain & Ireland 5
Captains: Marie Porter, USA; Zara Bolton, Great Britain & Ireland

1968 *at Newcastle, Co Down*

First Day – Foursomes

GREAT BRITAIN & IRELAND	Matches	USA	Matches
Belle Robertson and Ann Irvin (6 and 5)	1	Shelley Hamlin and Anne Welts	0
Margaret Pickard and Vivien Saunders (3 and 2)	1	Mary Lou Dill and Peggy Conley	0
Ann Howard and Pam Tredinnick	0	Phyllis Preuss and Joan Ashley (1 hole)	1
	2		1

Singles

Ann Irvin (3 and 2)	1	Anne Welts	0
Vivien Saunders	0	Shelley Hamlin (1 hole)	1
Belle Robertson	0	Roberta Albers (1 hole)	1
Bridget Jackson	$^1/_2$	Peggy Conley	$^1/_2$
Dinah Oxley	$^1/_2$	Phyllis Preuss	$^1/_2$
Margaret Pickard (2 holes)	1	Joan Ashley	0
	—		—
	3		3

First day total: Great Britain & Ireland 5, USA 4

Second Day – Foursomes

Pam Tredinnick and Dinah Oxley	0	Phyllis Preuss and Joan Ashley (5 and 4)	1
Belle Robertson and Anne Irvin	$^1/_2$	Mary Lou Dill and Peggy Conley	$^1/_2$
Margaret Pickard and Vivien Saunders	0	Shelley Hamlin and Anne Welts (2 and 1)	1
	—		—
	$^1/_2$		$2^1/_2$

Singles

Ann Irvin (3 and 2)	1	Shelley Hamlin	0
Belle Robertson	$^1/_2$	Anne Welts	$^1/_2$
Vivien Saunders	$^1/_2$	Roberta Albers	$^1/_2$
Ann Howard (née Phillips)	0	Mary Lou Dill (4 and 2)	1
Margaret Pickard	0	Peggy Conley (1 hole)	1
Bridget Jackson	0	Phyllis Preuss (2 and 1)	1
	—		—
	2		4

Second day total: Great Britain & Ireland $2^1/_2$, USA $6^1/_2$
Grand aggregate: USA $10^1/_2$; Great Britain & Ireland $7^1/_2$
Captains: Zara Bolton, Great Britain & Ireland; Evelyn Monsted, USA

1970 at Brae Burn, Massachusetts

First Day – Foursomes

USA		GREAT BRITAIN & IRELAND	
	Matches		Matches
Shelley Hamlin and Jane Bastanchury	0	Dinah Oxley and Mary McKenna (4 and 3)	1
Phyllis Preuss and Martha Wilkinson (4 and 3)	1	Belle Robertson and Ann Irvin	0
Cindy Hill and Jane Fassinger	0	Mary Everard and Julia Greenhalgh (5 and 3)	1
	—		—
	1		2

Singles

Jane Bastanchury (5 and 3)	1	Dinah Oxley	0
Martha Wilkinson (1 hole)	1	Ann Irvin	0
Shelley Hamlin	$^1/_2$	Belle Robertson	$^1/_2$
Phyllis Preuss	0	Mary McKenna (4 and 2)	1
Nancy Hager (5 and 4)	1	Margaret Pickard	0
Alice Dye (1 hole)	1	Julia Greenhalgh	0
	—		—
	$4^1/_2$		$1^1/_2$

First day total: USA $5^1/_2$, Great Britain & Ireland $3^1/_2$

Second Day – Foursomes

Phyllis Preuss and Martha Wilkinson (6 and 4)	1	Dinah Oxley and Mary McKenna	0
Cindy Hill and Alice Dye	½	Mary Everard and Julia Greenhalgh	½
Shelley Hamlin and Jane Bastanchury (1 hole)	1	Belle Robertson and Ann Irvin	0
	2½		½

Singles

Jane Bastanchury (4 and 3)	1	Ann Irvin	0
Shelley Hamlin	½	Dinah Oxley	½
Phyllis Preuss (1 hole)	1	Belle Robertson	0
Martha Wilkinson	0	Julia Greenhalgh (6 and 4)	1
Nancy Hager	0	Mary Everard (4 and 3)	1
Cindy Hill (2 and 1)	1	Mary McKenna	0
	3½		2½

Second day total: USA 6, Great Britain & Ireland 3
Grand aggregate: USA 11½, Great Britain & Ireland 6½
Captains: Carolyn Cudone, USA; Jeanne Bisgood, Great Britain & Ireland

1972 at Western Gailes

First Day – Foursomes

GREAT BRITAIN & IRELAND		USA	
	Matches		Matches
Mary Everard and Beverly Huke	0	Laura Baugh and Martha Kirouac (née Wilkinson) (2 and 1)	1
Belle Robertson and Diane Frearson (2 and 1)	1	Jane Booth (née Bastanchury) and Barbara McIntire	0
Mickey Walker and Mary McKenna (1 hole)	1	Beth Barry and Hollis Stacy	0
	2		1

Singles

Mickey Walker	½	Laura Baugh	½
Belle Robertson	0	Jane Booth (3 and 1)	1
Mary Everard	0	Martha Kirouac (4 and 3)	1
Dinah Oxley	0	Barbara McIntire (4 and 3)	1
Kathryn Phillips (2 holes)	1	Lancy Smith	0
Mary McKenna	0	Beth Barry (2 and 1)	1
	1½		4½

First day total: Great Britain & Ireland 3½, USA 5½

Second Day – Foursomes

Mickey Walker and Mary McKenna (3 and 2)	1	Laura Baugh and Martha Kirouac	0
Mary Everard and Beverly Huke	0	Jane Booth and Barbara McIntire (5 and 4)	1
Belle Robertson and Diane Frearson	½	Beth Barry and Hollis Stacy	½
	1½		1½

Singles

Belle Robertson	0	Laura Baugh (6 and 5)	1
Mary Everard (6 and 5)	1	Barbara McIntire	0
Mickey Walker (1 hole)	1	Jane Booth	0
Mary McKenna (3 and 1)	1	Martha Kirouac	0
Diane Frearson	0	Lancy Smith (3 and 1)	1
Kathryn Phillips	0	Beth Barry (3 and 1)	1
	—		—
	3		3

Second day total: Great Britain & Ireland 4½, USA 4½
Grand aggregate: USA 10, Great Britain & Ireland 8
Captains: Frances Smith, Great Britain & Ireland; Jean Crawford, USA

1974 at San Francisco, California

First Day – Foursomes

USA	Matches	GREAT BRITAIN & IRELAND	Matches
Carol Semple and Cindy Hill	½	Mary McKenna and Julia Greenhalgh	½
Anne Sander (née Quast) and Jane Booth (6 and 5)	1	Jenny Lee-Smith and Carol Le Feuvre	0
Mary Budke and Bonnie Lauer	0	Mickey Walker and Mary Everard (5 and 4)	1
	—		—
	1½		1½

Singles

Carol Semple	0	Mickey Walker (2 and 1)	1
Jane Booth (5 and 3)	1	Mary McKenna	0
Debbie Massey (1 hole)	1	Mary Everard	0
Bonnie Lauer (6 and 5)	1	Jenny Lee-Smith	0
Beth Barry (1 hole)	1	Julia Greenhalgh	0
Cindy Hill	½	Tegwen Perkins	½
	—		—
	4½		1½

First day total: USA 6, Great Britain & Ireland 3

Second Day – Foursomes

Anne Sander and Jane Booth (5 and 4)	1	Mary McKenna and Mickey Walker	0
Mary Budke and Bonnie Lauer (5 and 3)	1	Mary Everard and Carol Le Feuvre	0
Carol Semple and Cindy Hill	0	Julia Greenhalgh and Tegwen Perkins (3 and 2)	1
	—		—
	2		1

Singles

Anne Sander (4 and 3)	1	Mary Everard	0
Jane Booth (7 and 5)	1	Julia Greenhalgh	0
Debbie Massey (6 and 5)	1	Carol Le Feuvre	0
Carol Semple (2 and 1)	1	Mickey Walker	0
Mary Budke (5 and 4)	1	Tegwen Perkins	0
Bonnie Lauer	0	Mary McKenna (2 and 1)	1
	—		—
	5		1

Second day total: USA 7, Great Britain & Ireland 2
Grand aggregate: USA 13, Great Britain & Ireland 5
Captains: Alison Choate, USA; Belle Robertson, Great Britain & Ireland

1976 *at Lytham St Annes*

First Day – Foursomes

GREAT BRITAIN & IRELAND	Matches	USA	Matches
Mary McKenna and Julia Greenhalgh	0	Beth Daniel and Cindy Hill (3 and 2)	1
Dinah Henson (*née* Oxley) and Suzanne Cadden	0	Debbie Massey and Donna Horton (6 and 5)	1
Ann Irvin and Tegwen Perkins (3 and 2)	1	Nancy Syms and Carol Semple	0
	1		2

Singles

	Matches		Matches
Ann Irvin	0	Beth Daniel (4 and 3)	1
Dinah Henson (1 hole)	1	Cindy Hill	0
Suzanne Cadden	0	Nancy Lopez (3 and 1)	1
Mary McKenna	0	Nancy Syms (1 hole)	1
Tegwen Perkins	0	Debbie Massey (1 hole)	1
Julia Greenhalgh	¹/₂	Barbara Barrow	¹/₂
	1¹/₂		4¹/₂

First day total: Great Britain & Ireland 2¹/₂, USA 6¹/₂

Second Day – Foursomes

Ann Irvin and Suzanne Cadden	0	Beth Daniel and Cindy Hill (4 and 3)	1
Dinah Henson and Tegwen Perkins (2 and 1)	1	Carol Semple and Nancy Syms	0
Mary McKenna and Anne Stant	0	Nancy Lopez and Barbara Barrow (4 and 2)	1
	1		2

Singles

Dinah Henson	0	Beth Daniel (3 and 2)	1
Julia Greenhalgh (2 and 1)	1	Nancy Syms	0
Suzanne Cadden	0	Donna Horton (6 and 5)	1
Jenny Lee-Smith	0	Debbie Massey (3 and 2)	1
Tegwen Perkins (1 hole)	1	Cindy Hill	0
Mary McKenna (1 hole)	1	Carol Semple	0
	3		3

Second day total: Great Britain and Ireland 4, USA 5
Grand aggregate: USA 11¹/₂, Great Britain & Ireland 6¹/₂
Captains: Belle Robertson, Great Britain & Ireland; Barbara McIntire, USA

1978 *at Apawamis, New York*

First Day – Foursomes

USA	MATCHES	GREAT BRITAIN & IRELAND	MATCHES
Beth Daniel and Brenda Goldsmith	0	Julia Greenhalgh and Vanessa Marvin (3 and 2)	1
Cynthia Hill and Lancy Smith	0	Mary Everard and Muriel Thomson (2 and 1)	1
Patricia Cornett and Carolyn Hill	¹/₂	Tegwen Perkins and Mary McKenna	¹/₂
	¹/₂		2¹/₂

Singles

Beth Daniel (5 and 4)	1	Vanessa Marvin	0
Noreen Uihlein	0	Mary Everard (7 and 6)	1
Lancy Smith (4 and 3)	1	Angela Uzielli	0
Cynthia Hill (2 and 1)	1	Julia Greenhalgh	0
Carolyn Hill	½	Carole Caldwell	½
Judith Oliver (2 and 1)	1	Tegwen Perkins	0
	—		—
	4½		1½

First day total: USA 5, Great Britain & Ireland 4

Second Day – Foursomes

Cynthia Hill and Lancy Smith (1 hole)	1	Mary Everard and Muriel Thomson	0
Brenda Goldsmith and Beth Daniel (1 hole)	1	Tegwen Perkins and Mary McKenna	0
Noreen Uihlein and Judith Oliver (4 and 3)	1	Julia Greenhalgh and Vanessa Marvin	0
	—		—
	3		0

Singles

Beth Daniel (2 and 1)	1	Mary McKenna	0
Patricia Cornett (3 and 2)	1	Carole Caldwell	0
Cynthia Hill	0	Muriel Thomson (2 and 1)	1
Lancy Smith (2 holes)	1	Tegwen Perkins	0
Judith Oliver	½	Julia Greenhalgh	½
Noreen Uihlein	½	Mary Everard	½
	—		—
	4		2

Second day total: USA 7, Great Britain & Ireland 2
Grand aggregate: USA 12, Great Britain & Ireland 6
Captains: Helen Wilson, USA; Carol Comboy, Great Britain & Ireland

1980 *at St Pierre, Chepstow*

First Day – Foursomes

GREAT BRITAIN & IRELAND		USA	
	Matches		Matches
Mary McKenna and Claire Nesbitt	½	Lancy Smith and Terri Moody	½
Tegwen Thomas (née Perkins) and Gillian Stewart	0	Patty Sheehan and Lori Castillo (5 and 3)	1
Maureen Madill and Carole Caldwell	½	Judith Oliver and Carol Semple	½
	—		—
	1		2

Singles

Mary McKenna	0	Patty Sheehan (3 and 2)	1
Claire Nesbitt	½	Lancy Smith	½
Jane Connachan	0	Brenda Goldsmith (2 holes)	1
Maureen Madill	0	Carol Semple (4 and 3)	1
Linda Moore	½	Mary Hafeman	½
Carole Caldwell	0	Judith Oliver (1 hole)	1
	—		—
	1		5

First day total: Great Britain & Ireland 2, USA 7

Second Day – Foursomes

Carole Caldwell and Maureen Madill	0	Patty Sheehan and Lori Castillo (3 and 2)	1
Claire Nesbitt and Mary McKenna	0	Lancy Smith and Terri Moody (6 and 5)	1
Tegwen Thomas and Linda Moore	0	Judith Oliver and Carol Semple (1 hole)	1
	—		—
	0		3

Singles

Maureen Madill	0	Patty Sheehan (5 and 4)	1
Mary McKenna (5 and 4)	1	Lori Castillo	0
Jane Connachan	0	Mary Hafeman (6 and 5)	1
Gillian Stewart (5 and 4)	1	Lancy Smith	0
Linda Moore (1 hole)	1	Brenda Goldsmith	0
Tegwen Thomas	0	Carol Semple (4 and 3)	1
	—		—
	3		3

Second day total: Great Britain & Ireland 3, USA 6
Grand aggregate: USA 13, Great Britain & Ireland 5
Captains: Carol Comboy, Great Britain & Ireland; Nancy Syms, USA

1982 at Denver, Colorado

First Day – Foursomes

USA	Matches	GREAT BRITAIN & IRELAND	Matches
Juli Inkster and Carol Semple (5 and 4)	1	Belle Robertson and Mary McKenna	0
Kathy Baker and Lancy Smith	½	Kitrina Douglas and Janet Soulsby	½
Amy Benz and Cathy Hanlon (2 and 1)	1	Gillian Stewart and Jane Connachan	0
	—		—
	2½		½

Singles

Amy Benz (2 and 1)	1	Mary McKenna	0
Cathy Hanlon (5 and 4)	1	Jane Connachan	0
Mari McDougall (2 holes)	1	Wilma Aitken	0
Kathy Baker (7 and 6)	1	Belle Robertson	0
Judith Oliver	0	Janet Soulsby (2 holes)	1
Juli Inkster (7 and 6)	1	Kitrina Douglas	0
	—		—
	5		1

First day total: USA 7½, Great Britain & Ireland 1½

Second Day – Foursomes

Juli Inkster and Carol Semple (3 and 2)	1	Jane Connachan and Wilma Aitken	0
Kathy Baker and Lancy Smith (1 hole)	1	Kitrina Douglas and Janet Soulsby	0
Amy Benz and Cathy Hanlon	0	Mary McKenna and Belle Robertson (1 hole)	1
	—		—
	2		1

Singles

Juli Inkster (7 and 6)	1	Kitrina Douglas	0
Kathy Baker (4 and 3)	1	Gillian Stewart	0
Judith Oliver (5 and 4)	1	Vicki Thomas	0
Mari McDougall (2 and 1)	1	Janet Soulsby	0
Carol Semple (1 hole)	1	Mary McKenna	0
Lancy Smith	0	Belle Robertson (5 and 4)	1
	5		1

Second day total: USA 7, Great Britain & Ireland 2
Grand aggregate: USA 14½, Great Britain & Ireland 3½
Captains: Betty Probasco, USA; Maire O'Donnell, Great Britain & Ireland

1984 *at Muirfield, East Lothian*

First Day – Foursomes

GREAT BRITAIN & IRELAND		USA	
	Matches		Matches
Claire Waite and Beverley New (2 holes)	1	Joanne Pacillo and Anne Sander	0
Jill Thornhill and Penny Grice	½	Lancy Smith and Jody Rosenthal	½
Mary McKenna and Laura Davies	0	Mary Anne Widman and Heather Farr (1 hole)	1
	1½		1½

Singles

Jill Thornhill	½	Joanne Pacillo	½
Claire Waite	0	Penny Hammel (4 and 2)	1
Claire Hourihane	0	Jody Rosenthal (3 and 1)	1
Vicki Thomas (2 and 1)	1	Dana Howe	0
Penny Grice (2 holes)	1	Anne Sander	0
Beverley New	0	Mary Anne Widman (4 and 3)	1
	2½		3½

First day total: Great Britain & Ireland 4, USA 5

Second Day – Foursomes

Claire Waite and Beverley New	0	Lancy Smith and Jody Rosenthal (3 and 1)	1
Jill Thornhill and Penny Grice (2 and 1)	1	Mary Anne Widman and Heather Farr	0
Vicki Thomas and Claire Hourihane	½	Dana Howe and Penny Hammel	½
	1½		1½

Singles

Jill Thornhill	0	Joanne Pacillo (3 and 2)	1
Laura Davies (1 hole)	1	Anne Sander	0
Claire Waite (5 and 4)	1	Lancy Smith	0
Penny Grice	0	Dana Howe (2 holes)	1
Beverley New	0	Heather Farr (6 and 5)	1
Claire Hourihane (2 and 1)	1	Penny Hammel	0
	3		3

Second day total: Great Britain and Ireland 4½, USA 4½
Grand aggregate: USA 9½, Great Britain & Ireland 8½
Captains: Diane Bailey, Great Britain & Ireland; Phyllis Preuss, USA

1986 *at Prairie Dunes, Kansas*

First Day – Foursomes

USA	Matches	GREAT BRITAIN & IRELAND	Matches
Kandi Kessler and Cindy Schreyer	0	Lilian Behan and Jill Thornhill (7 and 6)	1
Danielle Ammaccapane and Dottie Mochrie	0	Patricia Johnson and Karen Davies (2 and 1)	1
Kim Gardner and Kathleen McCarthy	0	Belle Robertson and Mary McKenna (1 hole)	1
	0		3

Singles

	Matches		Matches
Leslie Shannon	0	Patricia Johnson (1 hole)	1
Kimberley Williams	0	Jill Thornhill (4 and 3)	1
Danielle Ammaccapane	0	Lilian Behan (4 and 3)	1
Kandi Kessler (3 and 2)	1	Vicki Thomas	0
Dottie Mochrie	½	Karen Davies	½
Cindy Schreyer (2 and 1)	1	Claire Hourihane	0
	2½		3½

First day total: USA 2½, Great Britain & Ireland 6½

Second Day – Foursomes

	Matches		Matches
Danielle Ammaccapane and Dottie Mochrie	0	Patricia Johnson and Karen Davies (1 hole)	1
Leslie Shannon and Kimberley Williams	0	Lilian Behan and Jill Thornhill (5 and 3)	1
Kim Gardner and Kathleen McCarthy	½	Belle Robertson and Mary McKenna	½
	½		2½

Singles

	Matches		Matches
Leslie Shannon	½	Jill Thornhill	½
Kathleen McCarthy	0	Patricia Johnson (5 and 3)	1
Kim Gardner (1 hole)	1	Lilian Behan	0
Kimberley Williams	0	Vicki Thomas (4 and 3)	1
Kandi Kessler	½	Karen Davies	½
Cindy Schreyer	0	Claire Hourihane (5 and 4)	1
	2		4

Second day total: USA 2½, Great Britain & Ireland 6½
Grand aggregate: Great Britain & Ireland 13, USA 5
Captains: Judy Bell, USA; Diane Bailey, Great Britain & Ireland

1988 *at St George's, Sandwich*

First Day – Foursomes

GREAT BRITAIN & IRELAND	Matches	USA	Matches
Linda Bayman and Julie Wade (2 and 1)	1	Tracy Kerdyk and Kathleen Scrivner (*née* McCarthy)	0
Susan Shapcott and Karen Davies (5 and 4)	1	Cindy Scholefield and Carol Thompson (*née* Semple)	0
Jill Thornhill and Vicki Thomas	½	Leslie Shannon and Caroline Keggi	½
	2½		½

Singles

Linda Bayman	½	Tracy Kerdyk	½
Julie Wade (2 holes)	1	Cindy Scholefield	0
Susan Shapcott	0	Carol Thompson (1 hole)	1
Karen Davies	0	Pearl Sinn (4 and 3)	1
Shirley Lawson (1 hole)	1	Patricia Cornett	0
Jill Thornhill (3 and 2)	1	Leslie Shannon	0
	—		—
	3½		2½

First day total: Great Britain & Ireland 6, USA 3

Second Day – Foursomes

Linda Bayman and Julie Wade	0	Tracy Kerdyk and Kathleen Scrivner (1 hole)	1
Susan Shapcott and Karen Davies (2 holes)	1	Leslie Shannon and Caroline Keggi	0
Jill Thornhill and Vicki Thomas (6 and 5)	1	Cindy Scholefield and Carol Thompson	0
	—		—
	2		1

Singles

Julie Wade	0	Tracy Kerdyk (2 and 1)	1
Susan Shapcott (3 and 2)	1	Caroline Keggi	0
Shirley Lawson	0	Kathleen Scrivner (4 and 3)	1
Vicki Thomas (5 and 3)	1	Patricia Cornett	0
Linda Bayman (1 hole)	1	Pearl Sinn	0
Jill Thornhill	0	Carol Thompson (3 and 2)	1
	—		—
	3		3

Second day total: Great Britain & Ireland 5, USA 4
Grand aggregate: Great Britain & Ireland 11, USA 7
Captains: Diane Bailey, Great Britain & Ireland; July Bell, USA

1990 *at Somerset Hills, New Jersey*

First Day – Foursomes

USA	Matches	GREAT BRITAIN & IRELAND	Matches
Vicki Goetze and Anne Sander (4 and 3)	1	Helen Dobson and Catriona Lambert	0
Karen Noble and Margaret Platt	0	Julie Hall and Kathryn Imrie (2 and 1)	1
Carol Thompson and Robin Weiss (3 and 1)	1	Elaine Farquharson and Helen Wadsworth	0
	—		—
	2		1

Singles

Vicki Goetze	0	Julie Hall (2 and 1)	1
Katie Peterson (3 and 2)	1	Kathryn Imrie	0
Brandie Burton (3 and 1)	1	Linzi Fletcher	0
Robin Weiss (4 and 3)	1	Elaine Farquharson	0
Karen Noble (1 hole)	1	Catriona Lambert	0
Carol Thompson	0	Vicki Thomas (1 hole)	1
	—		—
	4		2

First day total: USA 6, Great Britain & Ireland 3

Second Day – Foursomes

Vicki Goetze and Anne Sander (3 and 1)	1	Julie Hall and Kathryn Imrie	0
Karen Noble and Margaret Platt	0	Catriona Lambert and Helen Dobson (1 hole)	1
Katie Peterson and Brandie Burton (5 and 4)	1	Elaine Farquharson and Helen Wadsworth	0
	—		—
	2		1

Singles

Vicki Goetze (4 and 3)	1	Helen Dobson	0
Brandie Burton (4 and 3)	1	Catriona Lambert	0
Katie Peterson (1 hole)	1	Kathryn Imrie	0
Karen Noble (2 holes)	1	Julie Hall	0
Robin Weiss (2 and 1)	1	Elaine Farquharson	0
Carol Thompson (3 and 1)	1	Vicki Thomas	0
	—		—
	6		0

Second day total: USA 8, Great Britain & Ireland 1
Grand aggregate: United States 14, Great Britain & Ireland 4
Captains: Lesley Shannon USA; Jill Thornhill, Great Britain & Ireland

Individual Records

Great Britain and Ireland

Name		Year	Played	Won	Lost	Halved
Jean Anderson (Donald)	Scot	1948	6	3	3	0
Diane Bailey [Frearson] (Robb)	Eng	1962-72-(84)-(86)-(88)	5	2	2	1
Sally Barber (Bonallack)	Eng	1962	1	0	1	0
Pam Barton	Eng	1934-36	4	0	3	1
Linda Bayman	Eng	1988	4	2	1	1
Baba Beck (Pym)	Ire	(1954)	0	0	0	0
Charlotte Beddows [Watson] (Stevenson)	Scot	1932	1	0	1	0
Lilian Behan	Ire	1986	4	3	1	0
Veronica Beharrell (Anstey)	Eng	1956	1	0	1	0
Pam Benka (Tredinnick)	Eng	1966-68	4	0	3	1
Jeanne Bisgood	Eng	1950-52-54-(70)	4	1	3	0
Zara Bolton (Davis)	Eng	1948-(56)-(66)-(68)	2	0	2	0
Angela Bonallack (Ward)	Eng	1956-58-60-62-64-66	15	6	8	1
Ita Butler (Burke)	Ire	1966	3	2	1	0
Lady Katherine Cairns	Eng	(1952)	0	0	0	0
Carole Caldwell (Redford)	Eng	1978-80	5	0	3	2
Doris Chambers	Eng	(1934)-(36)-(48)	0	0	0	0
Carol Comboy (Grott)	Eng	(1978)-(80)	0	0	0	0
Jane Connachan	Scot	1980-82	5	0	5	0
Elsie Corlett	Eng	1932-38-(64)	3	1	2	0
Diana Critchley (Fishwick)	Eng	1932-34-(50)	3	1	2	0
Karen Davies	Wales	1986-88	7	4	1	2
Laura Davies	Eng	1984	2	1	1	0
Helen Dobson	Eng	1990	.3	1	2	0
Kitrina Douglas	Eng	1982	4	0	3	1
Marjorie Draper [Peel] (Thomas)	Scot	1954	1	0	1	0
Mary Everard	Eng	1970-72-74-78	15	6	7	2
Elaine Farquharson	Scot	1990	.4	0	4	0
Daisy Ferguson	Ire	(1958)	0	0	0	0
Marjory Ferguson (Fowler)	Scot	1966	1	0	1	0
Elizabeth Price Fisher (Price)	Eng	1950-52-54-56-58-60	12	7	4	1
Linzi Fletcher	Eng	1990	1	0	1	0
Maureen Garner (Madill)	Ire	1980	4	0	3	1
Marjorie Ross Garon	Eng	1936	2	1	0	1
Maureen Garrett (Ruttle)	Eng	1948-(60)	2	0	2	0
Philomena Garvey	Ire	1948-50-52-54-56-60	11	2	8	1
Carol Gibbs (Le Feuvre)	Eng	1974	3	0	3	0
Jacqueline Gordon	Eng	1948	2	1	1	0
Molly Gourlay	Eng	1932-34	4	0	2	2
Julia Greenhalgh	Eng	1964-70-74-76-78	17	6	7	4
Penny Grice-Whittaker (Grice)	Eng	1984	4	2	1	1

Name		Year	Played	Won	Lost	Halved
Julie Hall (Wade)	Eng	1988-90	8	4	4	0
Marley Harris						
[Spearman] (Baker)	Eng	1960-62-64	6	2	2	2
Dorothea Hastings						
(Sommerville)	Scot	1958	0	0	0	0
Lady Heathcoat-Amory						
(Joyce Wethered)	Eng	1932	2	1	1	0
Dinah Henson (Oxley)	Eng	1968-70-72-76	11	3	6	2
Helen Holm (Gray)	Scot	1936-38-48	5	3	2	0
Claire Hourihane	Ire	1984-86-88-90	5	2	2	1
Ann Howard (Phillips)	Eng	1956-68	2	0	2	0
Beverley Huke	Eng	1972	2	0	2	0
Kathryn Imrie	Scot	1990	4	1	3	0
Ann Irvin	Eng	1962-68-70-76	12	4	7	1
Bridget Jackson	Eng	1958-64-68	8	1	6	1
Patricia Johnson	Eng	1986	4	4	0	0
Catriona Lambert	Scot	1990	4	1	3	0
Susan Langridge						
(Armitage)	Eng	1964-66	6	0	5	1
Joan Lawrence	Scot	1964	2	0	2	0
Shirley Lawson	Scot	1988	2	1	1	0
Wilma Leburn (Aitken)	Scot	1982	2	0	2	0
Jenny Lee Smith	Eng	1974-76	3	0	3	0
Kathryn Lumb (Phillips)	Eng	1970-72	2	1	1	0
Mary McKenna	Ire	1970-72-74-76-78-80-82-				
		84-86	30	10	16	4
Suzanne McMahon						
(Cadden)	Scot	1976	4	0	4	0
Sheila Maher (Vaughan)	Eng	1962-64	4	1	2	1
Vanessa Marvin	Eng	1978	3	1	2	0
Moira Milton (Paterson)	Scot	1952	2	1	1	0
Wanda Morgan	Eng	1932-34-36	6	0	5	1
Beverley New	Eng	1984	4	1	3	0
Maire O'Donnell	Ire	(1982)	0	0	0	0
Margaret Pickard						
(Nichol)	Eng	1968-70	5	2	3	0
Diana Plumpton	Eng	1934	2	1	1	0
Elizabeth Pook						
(Chadwick)	Eng	1966	4	1	3	0
Doris Porter (Park)	Scot	1932	1	0	1	0
Clarrie Reddan (Tiernan)	Ire	1938-48	3	2	1	0
Joan Rennie (Hastings)	Scot	1966	2	0	1	1
Maureen Richmond						
(Walker)	Scot	1974	4	2	2	0
Jean Roberts	Eng	1962	1	0	1	0
Belle Robertson						
(McCorkindale)	Scot	1960-66-68-70-72-(74)-				
		(76)-82-86	24	5	12	7
Claire Robinson						
(Nesbitt)	Ire	1980	3	0	1	2
Vivien Saunders	Eng	1968	4	1	2	1
Susan Shapcott	Eng	1988	4	3	1	0
Linda Simpson (Moore)	Eng	1980	3	1	1	1
Ruth Slark (Porter)	Eng	1960-62-64	7	3	3	1
Anne Smith [Stant]						
(Willard)	Eng	1976	1	0	1	0
Frances Smith (Stephens)	Eng	1950-52-54-56-58-60-				
		(62)-(72)	11	7	3	1

Name		Year	Played	Won	Lost	Halved
Janet Soulsby	Eng	1982	4	1	2	1
Gillian Stewart	Scot	1980-82	4	1	3	0
Tegwen Thomas						
(Perkins)	Wales	1974-76-78-80	14	4	8	2
Vicki Thomas (Rawlings)	Wales	1982-84-86-88-90	10	5	3	2
Muriel Thomson	Scot	1978	3	2	1	0
Jill Thornhill	Eng	1984-86-88	12	6	2	4
Angela Uzielli (Carrick)	Eng	1978	1	0	1	0
Jessie Valentine						
(Anderson)	Scot	1936-38-50-52-54-56-58	13	4	9	0
Helen Wadsworth	Wales	1990	2	0	2	0
Claire Waite	Eng	1984	4	2	2	0
Mickey Walker	Eng	1972	4	3	0	1
Pat Walker	Ire	1934-36-38	6	2	3	1
Verona Wallace-						
Williamson	Scot	(1938)	0	0	0	0
Nan Wardlaw (Baird)	Scot	1938	1	0	1	0
Enid Wilson	Eng	1932	2	1	1	0
Janette Wright						
(Robertson)	Scot	1954-56-58-60	8	3	5	0
Phyllis Wylie (Wade)	Eng	1938	1	0	0	1

Bold print: captain; bold print in brackets: non-playing captain
Maiden name in parentheses, former surname in square brackets

United States of America

Player	Year	Played	Won	Lost	Halved
Roberta Albers	1968	2	1	0	1
Danielle Ammaccapane	1986	3	0	3	0
Kathy Baker	1982	4	3	0	1
Barbara Barrow	1976	2	1	0	1
Beth Barry	1972-74	5	3	1	1
Larua Baugh	1972	4	2	1	1
Judy Bell	1960-62-(86)-(88)	2	1	1	0
Peggy Kirk Bell (Kirk)	1950	2	1	1	0
Amy Benz	1982	3	2	1	0
Patty Berg	1936-38	4	1	2	1
Barbara Fay Boddie					
(White)	1964-66	8	7	0	1
Jane Booth (Bastanchury)	1970-72-74	12	9	3	0
Mary Budke	1974	3	2	1	0
Brandie Burton	1990	3	3	0	0
JoAnne Carner					
(Gunderson)	1958-60-62-64	10	6	3	1
Lori Castillo	1980	3	2	1	0
Leona Cheney (Pressler)	1932-34-36	6	5	1	0
Sis Choate	(1974)	0	0	0	0
Peggy Conley	1964-68	6	3	1	2
Mary Ann Cook					
(Downey)	1956	2	1	1	0
Patricia Cornett	1978-88	4	1	2	1
Jean Crawford (Ashley)	1962-66-68-(72)	8	6	2	0
Clifford Ann Creed	1962	2	2	0	0
Grace Cronin (Lenczyk)	1948-50	3	2	1	0
Carolyn Cudone	1956-(70)	1	1	0	0
Beth Daniel	1976-78	8	7	1	0

Player	Year	Played	Won	Lost	Halved
Virginia Dennehy	(1958)	0	0	0	0
Mary Lou Dill	1968	3	1	1	1
Alice Dye	1970	2	1	0	1
Heather Farr	1984	3	2	1	0
Jane Fassinger	1970	1	0	1	0
Mary Lena Faulk	1954	2	1	1	0
Carol Sorensen					
Flenniken (Sorensen)	1964-66	8	6	1	1
Edith Flippin (Quier)	(1954)-(56)	0	0	0	0
Kim Gardner	1986	3	1	1	1
Charlotte Glutting	1934-36-38	5	3	1	1
Vicki Goetze	1990	4	3	1	0
Brenda Goldsmith	1978-80	4	2	2	0
Aniela Goldthwaite	1934-(52)	1	0	1	0
Joanne Goodwin	1960	2	1	1	0
Mary Hafeman	1980	2	1	0	1
Shelley Hamkin	1968-70	8	3	3	2
Penny Hammel	1984	3	1	1	1
Nancy Hammer (Hager)	1970	2	1	1	0
Cathy Hanlon	1982	3	2	1	0
Beverley Hanson	1950	2	2	0	0
Patricia Harbottle					
(Lesser)	1954-56	3	2	1	0
Helen Hawes	(1964)	0	0	0	0
Kathryn Hemphill	1938	1	0	0	1
Helen Hicks	1932	2	1	1	0
Carolyn Hill	1978	2	0	0	2
Cindy Hill	1970-74-76-78	14	5	6	3
Opel Hill	1932-34-36	6	2	3	1
Marion Hollins	(1932)	0	0	0	0
Dana Howe	1984	3	1	1	1
Juli Inkster	1982	4	4	0	0
Ann Casey Johnstone	1958-60-62	4	3	1	0
Mae Murray Jones					
(Murray)	1952	1	0	1	0
Caroline Keggi	1988	3	0	2	1
Tracy Kerdyk	1988	4	2	1	1
Kandi Kessler	1986	3	1	1	1
Dorothy Kielty	1948-50	4	4	0	0
Dorothy Kirby	1948-50-52-54	7	4	3	0
Martha Kirouac					
(Wilkinson)	1970-72	8	5	3	0
Nancy Knight (Lopez)	1976	2	2	0	0
Bonnie Lauer	1974	4	2	2	0
Marjorie Lindsay	1952	2	1	1	0
Patricia Lucey					
(O'Sullivan)	1952	1	0	1	0
Mari McDougall	1982	2	2	0	0
Barbara McIntire	1958-60-62-64-66-72-(76)	16	6	6	4
Lucile Mann (Robinson)	1934	1	0	1	0
Debbie Massey	1974-76	5	5	0	0
Marion Miley	1938	2	1	0	1
Dottie Mochrie (Pepper)	1986	3	0	2	1
Evelyn Monsted	(1968)	0	0	0	0
Terri Moody	1980	2	1	0	1
Karen Noble	1990	4	2	2	0
Judith Oliver	1978-80-82	8	5	1	2
Maureen Orcutt	1932-34-36-38	8	5	3	0

Player	Year	Played	Won	Lost	Halved
Joanne Pacillo	1984	3	1	1	1
Estelle Page (Lawson)	1938-48	4	3	1	0
Katie Peterson	1990	3	3	0	0
Margaret Platt	1990	2	0	2	0
Frances Pond (Stebbins)	(1938)	0	0	0	0
Dorothy Germain Porter	1950-(66)	2	1	0	1
Phyllis Preuss	1962-64-66-68-70-(84)	15	10	4	1
Betty Probasco	(1982)	0	0	0	0
Mildred Prunaret	(1960)	0	0	0	0
Polly Riley	1948-50-52-54-56-58-(62)	10	5	5	0
Barbara Romack	1954-56-58	5	3	2	0
Jody Rosenthal	1984	3	2	0	1
Anne Sander [Welts]					
[Decker] (Quast)	1958-60-62-66-68-74-84-90	22	11	7	4
Cindy Scholefield	1988	3	0	3	0
Cindy Schreyer	1986	3	1	2	0
Kathleen McCarthy					
Scrivner (McCarthy)	1986-88	6	2	3	1
Leslie Shannon	1986-88-90	6	0	4	2
Patty Sheehan	1980	4	4	0	0
Pearl Sinn	1988	2	1	1	0
Grace De Moss Smith					
(De Moss)	1952-54	3	1	2	0
Lancy Smith	1972-78-80-82-84	16	7	5	4
Margaret Smith	1956	2	2	0	0
Hollis Stacy	1972	2	0	1	1
Claire Stancik (Doran)	1952-54	4	4	0	0
Judy Street (Eller)	1960	2	2	0	0
Louise Suggs	1948	2	0	1	1
Nancy Roth Syms (Roth)	1964-66-76-(80)	9	3	5	1
Carol Thompson					
(Semple)	1974-76-80-82-90	17	9	6	2
Noreen Uihlein	1978	3	1	1	1
Virginia Van Wie	1932-34	4	3	0	1
Glenna Collett Vare					
(Collett)	1932-(34)-36-38-48-(50)	7	4	2	1
Jane Weiss (Nelson)	1956	1	0	1	0
Robin Weiss	1990	3	3	0	0
Donna White (Horton)	1976	2	2	0	0
Mary Anne Widman	1984	3	2	1	0
Kimberley Williams	1986	3	0	3	0
Helen Sigel Wilson					
(Sigel)	1950-66-(78)	2	0	2	0
Joyce Ziske	1954	1	0	1	0

Bold print: captain; bold print in brackets: non-playing captain.
Maiden name in parenthesis; former surname in square brackets.

Ladies' International Amateur Events

Commonwealth Tournament

INAUGURATED 1959

The trophy was presented by Lady Astor in 1959 and the tournament is played every four years in Australia, Canada, New Zealand or Great Britain. Each country plays the other in matches of 18 holes of two foursomes and four singles. Great Britain won on the first five occasions, but has not since 1975.

1959 *at St Andrews, Scotland*

MATCHES

Australia beat New Zealand	4–2
Canada beat South Africa	4–2
Great Britain beat Australia	4–2
Canada beat New Zealand	4½–1½
Great Britain beat New Zealand	6–0
South Africa beat Australia	4½–1½
Great Britain beat Canada	5–1
South Africa beat New Zealand	4–2
Australia drew with Canada	3 each
Great Britain beat South Africa	4–2

Great Britain 4 pts; Canada 2½ pts; South Africa 2 pts; Australia 1½ pts; New Zealand 0 pts.

1963 *at Melbourne, Australia*

MATCHES

Great Britain beat Canada	5–0 (1 halved)
Great Britain beat Australia	4–2
Great Britain beat New Zealand	6–0
Australia beat Canada	3–2 (1 halved)
Australia beat New Zealand	4–2
Canada beat New Zealand	5–0 (1 halved)

Great Britain 3 pts; Australia 2 pts; Canada 1 pt; New Zealand 0 pts.

1967 *at Ancaster, Ontario, Canada*

MATCHES

Great Britain beat New Zealand	4–2
Great Britain beat Australia	3–2 (1 halved)
Great Britain beat Canada	3–2 (1 halved)
Canada beat Australia	6–0
Canada halved with New Zealand	3–3
Australia beat New Zealand	5–1

Great Britain 3 pts; Canada 1½ pts; Australia 1 pt; New Zealand ½ pt.

1971 *at Hamilton, New Zealand*

MATCHES

Great Britain beat Canada	4–1 (1 halved)
Great Britain beat New Zealand	4–1 (1 halved)
Great Britain beat Australia	5–0 (1 halved)
Canada halved with New Zealand	3 each
Canada beat Australia	3–2 (1 halved)
New Zealand halved with Australia	3 each

Great Britain 3 pts; Canada 1½ pts; New Zealand 1 pt; Australia ½ pt.

1975 *at Ganton, Yorkshire, England*

MATCHES

Great Britain beat Australia	4–2
Great Britain beat New Zealand	4¹/₂–1¹/₂
Great Britain beat Canada	4–2
Australia beat New Zealand	3¹/₂–1¹/₂
Australia beat Canada	6–0
New Zealand beat Canada	4–2

Great Britain 3 pts; Australia 2 pts; New Zealand 1 pt; Canada 0 pts.

1983 *at Glendale, Canada*

MATCHES

Australia beat New Zealand	3¹/₂–2¹/₂
Great Britain beat Canada	4–2
New Zealand halved with Canada	3–3
Australia halved with Great Britain	3–3
Australia beat Canada	4¹/₂–1¹/₂
New Zealand beat Great Britain	3¹/₂–2¹/₂

Australia 2¹/₂ pts; Canada 1¹/₂ pts; Great Britain 1¹/₂ pts; New Zealand 1¹/₂ pts.

1979 *at Lake Karrinyup, Australia*

MATCHES

Canada beat Australia	4–2
Canada beat Great Britain	4¹/₂–1¹/₂
Canada beat New Zealand	4–2
Australia beat Great Britain	5¹/₂–1¹/₂
Australia beat New Zealand	5–1
Great Britain beat New Zealand	3¹/₂–2¹/₂

Canada 3 pts; Australia 2 pts; Great Britain 1 pt; New Zealand 0 pts.

1987 *at Christchurch, New Zealand*

MATCHES

Canada beat Great Britain	4–2
Australia beat New Zealand	5–1
New Zealand beat Great Britain	4–2
Canada beat Australia	3¹/₂–2¹/₂
Great Britain halved with Australia	3–3
Canada halved with New Zealand	3–3

Canada 2¹/₂ pts; Australia1¹/₂ pts; New Zealand 1¹/₂ pts; Great Britain ¹/₂ pt.

The Continent of Europe v Great Britain & Ireland

Vagliano Trophy

INAUGURATED 1959

In 1959 Monsieur André Vagliano, the father of Lally Segard (formerly Vicomtesse de Saint Sauveur) donated this trophy for competition between the teams. It replaced two annual matches: Great Britain & Ireland v France (1947–57) and Great Britain & Ireland v Belgium (1949–57) where the results had all been one-sided in favour of Britain. Played biennally Europe has won four times and halved one, but usually Britain and Ireland has fielded stronger teams.

YEAR	WINNER	VENUE	RESULT
1959	GB & Ireland	Wentworth, England	12–3
1961	GB & Ireland	Villa d'Este, Italy	8–7
1963	GB & Ireland	Muirfield, Scotland	20–10

YEAR	WINNER	VENUE	RESULT
1965	Continent of Europe	Cologne, Germany	17–13
1967	Continent of Europe	Lytham St Annes, England	15½–14½
1969	Continent of Europe	Chantilly, France	16–14
1971	GB & Ireland	Worplesdon, England	17½–12½
1973	GB & Ireland	Eindhoven, Netherlands	20–10
1975	GB & Ireland	Muirfield, Scotland	13½–10½
1977	GB & Ireland	Malmo, Sweden	15½–8½
1979	Halved	Porthcawl, Wales	12–12
1981	Continent of Europe	Puerta de Hierro, Spain	14–10
1983	GB & Ireland	Woodhall Spa, England	14–10
1985	GB & Ireland	Hamburg, Germany	14–10
1987	GB & Ireland	The Berkshire, England	15–9
1989	GB & Ireland	Venice, Italy	14½–9½

Great Britain v France

INAUGURATED 1931

YEAR	WINNER	VENUE	RESULTS
1931	Great Britain	Oxhey, England	8½–½
1932	Great Britain	St Germain, France	7–1
1933	Great Britain	St George's Hill, England	7–2
1934	Halved	Chantilly, France	4–4
1935	Great Britain	Worplesdon, England	5–4
1936	Great Britain	St Cloud, France	6–3
1937	Great Britain	West Sussex, England	6½–2½
1938	Great Britain	Morfontaine, France	7–2

Great Britain & Ireland v France

YEAR	WINNER	VENUE	RESULT
1947	Great Britain & Ireland	St Cloud, France	6½–2½
1948	Great Britain & Ireland	Royal Mid-Surrey, England	6½–2½
1949	Great Britain & Ireland	Morfontaine, France	8½–½
1951	Great Britain & Ireland	St George's Hill, England	8–1
1953	Great Britain & Ireland	Chantilly, France	5½–3½
1955	Great Britain & Ireland	Gullane, Scotland	7–2
1957	Great Britain & Ireland	Morfontaine, France	5½–3½

Women's World Amateur Team Championship (Espirito Santo Trophy)

Mme Ricardo Espirito Santo of Portugal presented the trophy for teams of two or three from a country, playing four rounds of stroke play, the winners to be the team with the two lowest scores over 72 holes. The match is played biennally alternately in the Americas, Australasia and Africa or Europe. The USA has dominated the competition, winning ten out of the fourteen occasions it has been played. The British and Irish team has never won, but has the excellent record of finishing in the top five ten times. As many as 28 countries have taken part in one meeting.

YEAR	WINNER	RUNNER-UP	SCORE	VENUE
1964	France	USA	588	St Germain, France
1966	USA	Canada	580	Mexico City, Mexico
1968	USA	Australia	616	Melbourne, Australia
1970	USA	France	598	Madrid, Spain
1972	USA	France	583	Buenos Aires, Argentina
1974	USA	Great Britain } South Africa	620	Dominican Republic
1976	USA	France	605	Vilamoura, Portugal
1978	Australia	Canada	596	Fiji
1980	USA	Australia	588	Pinehurst, USA
1982	USA	New Zealand	579	Geneva, Switzerland
1984	USA	France	585	Hong Kong
1986	Spain	France	580	Caracas, Venezuela
1988	USA	Sweden	587	Drottningholm, Sweden
1990	USA	New Zealand	585	Russley, New Zealand

European Ladies' Amateur Team Championship

Played biennally, England and France completely dominated the championship from 1965 to 1977. Subsequently, however, Ireland and Sweden have each won twice. In its thirteen meetings ten different countries have played host.

Play starts with two qualifying rounds of 18 holes stroke play, with the best five scores taken out of six. The leading eight teams then play two foursomes and five singles over three days.

YEAR	WINNER	RUNNER-UP	VENUE
1965	England	France	Haagsche, Netherlands
1967	England	France	Penina, Portugal
1969	France	England	Tylosand, Sweden
1971	England	France	Ganton, England

YEAR	WINNER	RUNNER-UP	VENUE
1973	England	France	Brussels, Belgium
1975	France	Spain	St Cloud, France
1977	England	Spain	Sotogrande, Spain
1979	Ireland	Germany	Hermitage, Ireland
1981	Sweden	France	Troia, Portugal
1983	Ireland	England	Waterloo, Belgium
1985	England	Italy	Stavanger, Norway
1987	Sweden	Wales	Turnberry, Scotland
1989	France	England	Pals, Spain

Ladies' Home International Matches

The four Home Countries Unions have played each other since 1909, with England the strongest overall and Scotland coming next in the total number of wins. Although many gifted golfers have emanated from both Ireland and Wales, neither country has had sufficient strength in depth to win outright except on two occasions when Ireland won at Cruden Bay in 1980 and at Whittington Barracks in 1986. In some years the championship has been shared by two countries and in 1974 there was a three-way tie between England, Scotland and Ireland.

Although each side has always played the three other countries over three days in matches of three foursomes and six singles, the method of scoring has changed. It was not until 1971 at Longniddry that halved matches counted half a point for each side and were included in the total. Many courses, picked at random, in each country have hosted the event.

1948 *at Lytham St Annes*

Winners: England

RESULT	SCORE
England beat Scotland	5–4
England beat Ireland	7–2
England beat Wales	8–1
Scotland beat Ireland	7–2
Scotland beat Wales	7–2
Ireland beat Wales	6–3

1949 *at Harlech*

Winners: England

RESULT	SCORE
England beat Scotland	5–4
England beat Ireland	7–2
England beat Wales	8–1
Scotland beat Ireland	8–1
Scotland beat Wales	8–1
Ireland beat Wales	8–1

1950 *at Newcastle, Co Down*

Winners: Scotland

RESULT	SCORE
Scotland beat England	6–3
Scotland beat Ireland	6–3
Scotland beat Wales	8–1
England beat Ireland	6–3
England beat Wales	8–1
Ireland beat Wales	6–3

1951 *at Broadstone, Dorset*

Winners: Scotland

RESULT	SCORE
Scotland beat England	9–0
Scotland beat Ireland	5–4
Scotland beat Wales	6–3
England beat Ireland	6–3
England beat Wales	9–0
Ireland beat Wales	6–3

1952 *at Troon*

Winners: Scotland

RESULT	SCORE
Scotland beat England	6–3
Scotland beat Ireland	5–4
Scotland beat Wales	6–3
England beat Wales	9–0
Ireland beat England	6–3
Ireland beat Wales	7–2

1953 *at Porthcawl*

Winners: England

RESULT	SCORE
England beat Ireland	6–3
England beat Scotland	5–4
England beat Wales	7–2
Scotland beat Ireland	6–3
Scotland beat Wales	8–1
Ireland beat Wales	7–2

1954 *at Ganton*

Winners: England

RESULT	SCORE
England beat Ireland	5–4
England beat Scotland	7½–1½
England beat Wales	9–0
Scotland beat Ireland	5–4
Scotland beat Wales	9–0
Ireland beat Wales	7–2

1955 *at Portrush*

Winners: England, Scotland (tie)

RESULT	SCORE
Scotland halved with England	4½ each
Scotland beat Wales	9–0
Scotland beat Ireland	6–3
England beat Wales	6½–2½
England beat Ireland	6½–2½
Ireland beat Wales	6½–2½

1956 *at Sunningdale*

Winners: Scotland

RESULT	SCORE
Scotland beat England	5–4
Scotland beat Ireland	8–1
Scotland beat Wales	7½–1½
England beat Wales	8½–½
England halved with Ireland	4½ each
Ireland beat Wales	7–2

1957 *at Troon*

Winners: Scotland

RESULT	SCORE
Scotland beat England	4–3
Scotland beat Ireland	5–2
Scotland beat Wales	7–0
England beat Ireland	5–2
England beat Wales	5–2
Ireland beat Wales	5–2

1958 *at Hunstanton*

Winners: England

RESULT	SCORE
England beat Wales	6–1
Ireland beat Scotland	4–3
Ireland beat Wales	5–2
England beat Scotland	6–1
England beat Ireland	4–3
Scotland beat Wales	6–1

1959 *at Hoylake*

Winners: England

RESULT	SCORE
Scotland beat Wales	9–0
England beat Ireland	6–3
England beat Scotland	6–3
Ireland beat Wales	8–1
England beat Wales	9–0
Scotland beat Ireland	5½–3½

1960 at Gullane

Winners: England

RESULT	SCORE
England beat Scotland	7–2
England beat Ireland	8½–½
England beat Wales	7–2
Scotland beat Wales	7–2
Scotland beat Ireland	7–2
Ireland beat Wales	4–3

1961 at Portmarnock

Winners: Scotland

RESULT	SCORE
Scotland beat Wales	8–0
Scotland beat Ireland	8–1
Scotland beat England	4–2
England beat Ireland	5–4
England beat Wales	9–0
Ireland beat Wales	7–1

1962 at Porthcawl

Winners: Scotland

RESULT	SCORE
Scotland beat England	4–3
Scotland beat Ireland	6–3
Scotland beat Wales	6–1
England beat Ireland	8–0
England beat Wales	9–0
Ireland beat Wales	7–1

1963 at Formby

Winners: England

RESULT	SCORE
England beat Scotland	5–3
England beat Ireland	6–2
England beat Wales	8–1
Scotland beat Ireland	5–2
Scotland beat Wales	9–0
Ireland beat Wales	6–2

1964 at Troon

Winners: England

RESULT	SCORE
England beat Scotland	7–1
England beat Wales	7–1
England beat Ireland	7–2
Scotland beat Ireland	6–1
Scotland beat Wales	6–3
Ireland halved with Wales	4 each

1965 at Portrush

Winners: England

RESULT	SCORE
England beat Ireland	7–0
England beat Scotland	5–3
England beat Wales	7–2
Scotland beat Ireland	5–4
Scotland beat Wales	9–0
Ireland beat Wales	7–2

1966 at Woodhall Spa

Winners: England

RESULT	SCORE
England beat Ireland	6–2
England beat Scotland	5–3
England beat Wales	9–0
Scotland beat Wales	7–1
Scotland beat Ireland	7–1
Ireland halved with Wales	4 each

1967 at Sunningdale

Winners: England

RESULT	SCORE
England halved with Scotland	4 each
England beat Wales	8–1
England beat Ireland	6–2
Scotland beat Ireland	6–2
Scotland beat Wales	7–0
Ireland halved with Wales	4 each

1968 at Porthcawl

Winners: England

RESULT	SCORE
England halved with Scotland	4 each
England beat Ireland	4–3
England beat Wales	7–2
Scotland beat Ireland	5–4
Scotland beat Wales	6–3
Ireland beat Wales	6–3

1969 at Western Gailes

Winners: England, Scotland (tie)

RESULT	SCORE
Scotland beat Ireland	8–0
Scotland beat Ireland	7–2
England beat Scotland	4–2
England beat Wales	8–0
Ireland beat England	5–4
Ireland halved with Wales	4 each

1970 at Killarney

Winners: England

RESULT	SCORE
England beat Ireland	7–1
England beat Scotland	8–0
England beat Wales	6–2
Ireland beat Scotland	5–3
Ireland beat Wales	8–1
Scotland beat Wales	7–1

1971 at Longniddry

Winners: England

RESULT	SCORE
England beat Scotland	6–3
England beat Ireland	6½–2½
England beat Wales	8–1
Scotland beat Ireland	8–1
Scotland beat Wales	7–2
Ireland beat Wales	5½–3½

1972 at Lytham St Annes

Winners: England

RESULT	SCORE
England beat Scotland	5½–3½
England beat Ireland	9–0
England beat Wales	8–1
Scotland halved with Ireland	4½ each
Scotland beat Wales	8–1
Ireland beat Wales	5–4

1973 at Harlech

Winners: England

RESULT	SCORE
England beat Scotland	5½–3½
England beat Wales	7–2
England beat Ireland	8–1
Scotland halved with Wales	4½ each
Scotland beat Ireland	5–4
Wales beat Ireland	5–4

1974 at Prince's, Sandwich

Winners: England, Scotland, Ireland (tie)

RESULT	SCORE
Scotland beat Ireland	7–2
Scotland beat Wales	7½–1½
England beat Scotland	5½–3½
England beat Wales	5½–3½
Ireland beat England	5–4
Ireland beat Wales	5–4

1975 at Newport, Gwent

Winners: England

RESULT	SCORE
England beat Wales	5½–3½
England beat Ireland	6–3
England beat Scotland	6–3
Wales beat Ireland	7–2
Ireland beat Scotland	6–3
Scotland beat Wales	5–4

1976 *at Troon*

Winners: England

RESULT	SCORE
England halved with Wales	4½ each
England beat Ireland	7½–1½
England beat Scotland	5–4
Wales halved with Ireland	4½ each
Wales halved with Scotland	4½ each
Ireland beat Scotland	5–4

1977 *at Cork*

Winners: England

RESULT	SCORE
England beat Ireland	5½–3½
England beat Scotland	6–3
England beat Wales	7½–1½
Ireland beat Scotland	7½–1½
Ireland beat Wales	7–2
Scotland beat Wales	8–1

1978 *at Moortown*

Winners: England

RESULT	SCORE
England beat Ireland	5½–3½
England beat Scotland	5–4
England beat Wales	5½–3½
Ireland beat Scotland	5½–3½
Ireland beat Wales	6½–2½
Scotland beat Wales	6½–2½

1979 *at Harlech*

Winners: Scotland, Ireland (tie)

RESULT	SCORE
Scotland beat Wales	5–4
Scotland beat England	7–2
Ireland beat Scotland	5½–3½
Ireland beat England	5–4
Wales beat Ireland	5½–3½
England beat Wales	6–3

1980 *at Cruden Bay*

Winners: Ireland

RESULT	SCORE
Ireland beat Scotland	6½–2½
Ireland beat England	5–4
Ireland beat Wales	7½–1½
Scotland beat England	5½–3½
Scotland beat Wales	5–4
England halved with Wales	4½ each

1981 *at Portmarnock*

Winners: Scotland

RESULT	SCORE
Scotland beat England	5½–3½
Scotland beat Ireland	6–3
Scotland beat Wales	8½–½
England beat Ireland	5½–3½
England halved with Wales	4½ each
Ireland beat Wales	7–2

1982 *at Burnham and Berrow*

Winners: England

RESULT	SCORE
England beat Scotland	5–4
England halved with Ireland	4½ each
England beat Wales	7–2
Scotland beat Ireland	5½–3½
Scotland beat Wales	6½–2½
Ireland beat Wales	7–2

1983 *Abandoned*

1984 *at Gullane*

Winners: England

RESULT	SCORE
England beat Wales	6½–2½
Scotland beat Ireland	7½–1½
Ireland beat Wales	9–0
England beat Scotland	5½–3½
Scotland beat Wales	5½–3½
England beat Ireland	7–2

1985 *at Waterville, Co Kerry*

Winners: England

RESULT	SCORE
England beat Scotland	7–2
England beat Wales	6½–2½
Ireland beat England	5½–3½
Ireland beat Wales	6–3
Scotland beat Ireland	5–4
Scotland beat Wales	6–3

1986 *at Whittington Barracks, Staffs*

Winners: Ireland

RESULT	SCORE
England halved with Scotland	4½ each
England beat Wales	7½–1½
Wales beat Ireland	5–4
Ireland beat Scotland	6½–2½
Ireland beat England	5–4
Scotland beat Wales	6–3

1987 *at Ashburnham, Dyfed*

Winners: England

RESULT	SCORE
England beat Scotland	5½–3½
England beat Ireland	5½–3½
England beat Wales	6–3
Scotland beat Ireland	6–3
Scotland beat Wales	7–2
Ireland beat Wales	8–1

1988 *at Barassie, Ayrshire*

Winners: Scotland

RESULT	SCORE
Scotland beat England	5½–3½
Scotland beat Ireland	5–4
Scotland beat Wales	7½–1½
England beat Ireland	6½–2½
England beat Wales	7–2
Ireland halved with Wales	4½ each

1989 *at Westport, Co Mayo*

Winners: England

RESULT	SCORE
Scotland beat Ireland	7–2
England beat Wales	6½–2½
Scotland beat Wales	5–4
England beat Ireland	5½–3½
England beat Scotland	8–1
Ireland beat Wales	6–3

1990 *at Hunstanton, Norfolk*

Winners: Scotland

RESULT	SCORE
England halved with Ireland	4½ each
Scotland beat Wales	5–4
Scotland beat Ireland	5–4
England beat Wales	6–3
Ireland halved with Wales	4½ each
Scotland beat England	6–3

British Isles International Players, Amateur Ladies

Abbreviations:

Eur L T Ch   played in European Ladies Amateur Team Championship
Home Int   played in Home International matches
CW   played in Commonwealth International
Previous surnames are shown in brackets.

Aitken, E (Young)
(Scotland): Home Int 1954

Alexander, M
(Ireland): Home Int 1920-21-22-30

Allen, F
(England): Home Int 1952

Allington Hughes, Miss
(Wales): Home Int 1908-09-10-12-14-22-25

Anderson, E
(Scotland): Home Int 1910-11-12-21-25

Anderson, F
(Scotland): Home Int 1977-79-80-81-83-84-86-87-88-89-90;
Eur L T Ch 1987. (GBI): in Vagliano Trophy 1987

Anderson, H
(Scotland): Home Int 1964-65-68-69-70-71; Eur L T Ch 1969.
(GBI): in Vagliano Trophy 1969

Anderson, J (Donald)
(Scotland): Home Int 1947-48-49-50-51-52-53. (GBI): in
Curtis Cup in 1948-50-52

Anderson, L.
(Scotland): Home Int 1986-87-88-89; Eur L T Ch 1987-89

Anderson, VH
(Scotland): Home Int 1907

Arbuthnot, M
(Ireland): Home Int 1921

Archer, A (Rampton)
(England): Home Int 1968 (Captain)

Armstrong, M
(Ireland): Home Int 1906

Ashcombe, Lady
(Wales): Home Int 1950-51-52-53-54

Aubertin, Mrs
(Wales): Home Int 1908-09-10

Bailey, D [Frearson] (Robb)
(England): Home Int 1961-62-71; Eur L T Ch 1968. (GBI): in
Curtis Cup 1962-72-84 (Captain)-86(Captain)-88(Captain); in
Vagliano Trophy 1961-83(Captain)-85(Captain); in
CW 1983

Baker, J
(Wales): Home Int 1990

Bald, J
(Scotland): Home Int 1968-69-71; Eur L T Ch 1969

Barber, S (Bonallack)
(England): Home Int 1960-61-62-68-70-72-77-78 (Captain);
Eur L T Ch 1969-71. (GBI): in Curtis Cup 1962; in Vagliano
Trophy 1961-63-69

Barclay, C (Brisbane)
(Scotland): Home Int 1953-61-68

Bargh Etherington, B (Whitehead)
(England): Home Int 1974

Barlow, Mrs
(Ireland): Home Int 1921

Barron, M
(Wales): Home Int 1929-30-31-34-35-36-37-38-39-47-48-49-
50-51-52-53-54-55-56-57-58-60-61-62-63

Barry, L
(England): Home Int 1911-12-13-14

Barry, P
(England): Home Int 1982

Barton, P
(England): Home Int 1935-36-37-38-39. (GBI): in Curtis Cup
1934-36

Bastin, G
(England): Home Int 1920-21-22-23-24-25

Bayliss, Mrs
(Wales): Home Int 1921

Bayman, L (Denison Pender)
(England): Home Int 1971-72-73-83-84-85-87-88; Eur L T Ch
1985-87-89. (GBI) in Curtis Cup 1988; in Vagliano Trophy
1971-85-87; in Espirito Santo 1988

Baynes, Mrs CE
(Scotland): Home Int 1921-22

Beck, B (Pim)
(Ireland): Home Int 1930-31-32-33-34-36-37-47-48-49-50-51-
52-53-54-55-56-58-59-61

Beckett, J
(Ireland): Home Int 1962-66-67-68; Eur L T Ch 1967

Beddows, C [Watson] (Stevenson)
(Scotland): Home Int 1913-14-21-22-23-27-29-30-31-32-33-
34-35-36-37-39-47-48-49-50-51. (GBI): in Curtis Cup 1932

Behan, L
(Ireland): Home Int 1984-85-86. (GBI): in Curtis Cup 1986; in
Vagliano Trophy 1985

Beharrell, V (Anstey)
(England): Home Int 1955-56-57-61(Captain). (GBI): in Curtis
Cup 1956

Benka, P (Tredinnick)
(England): Home Int 1967. (GBI): in Curtis Cup 1966-68; in
Vagliano Trophy 1967

Bennett, L
(Scotland): Home Int 1977-80-81

Benton, MH
(Scotland): Home Int 1914

Birmingham, M
(Ireland): Home Int 1967(Captain)

Bisgood, J
(England) Home Int 1949-50-51-52-53-54-56-58. (GBI): in
Curtis Cup 1950-52-54-70(Captain)

Blair, N (Menzies)
(Scotland): Home Int 1955

Blake, Miss
(Ireland): Home Int 1931-32-34-35-36

Blaymire, J
(England): Home Int 1971-88-89(Captain)

Bloodworth, D (Lewis)
(Wales): Home Int 1954-55-56-57-60

Boatman, EA (Collis)
(England): Home Int 1974-80-84 (Captain)-85 (Captain)-90
(Captain); Eur L T Ch 1985 (Captain)-87 (Captain). (GBI): CW
1987 (Captain)

Bolton, L
(Ireland): Home Int 1981-82-88-89

Bolton, Z (Bonner Davis)
(England): Home Int 1939-48-49-50-51-55-(Captain)-56.
(GBI): in Curtis Cup 1948-56(Captain)-66(Captain)-
68(Captain);CW 1967

Bonallack, A (Ward)
(England): Home Int 1956-57-58-59-60-61-62-63-64-65
(Captain)-66-72. (GBI): in Curtis Cup 1956-58-60-62-64-66; in
Vagliano Trophy 1959-61-63

Bostock, M
(England): Home Int 1954(Captain)

Bourn, Mrs
(England): Home Int 1909-12

Bowhill, M (Robertson-Durham)
(Scotland): Home Int 1936-37-38

Boyd, J
(Ireland): Home Int 1912-13-14

Bradley, K (Rawlings)
(Wales): Home Int 1975-76-77-78-79-82-83

Bradshaw, E
(Ireland): Home Int 1964-66-67-68-69-70-71-74-75-80
(Captain)-81(Captain); Eur L T Ch 1969-71-75. (GBI): in
Vagliano Trophy 1969-71

Brandom, G
(Ireland): Home Int 1965-66-67-68; Eur L T Ch 1967. (GBI) in
Vagliano Trophy 1967

Brearley, M
(Wales): Home Int 1937-38

Brennan, R (Hegarty)
(Ireland): Home Int 1974-75-76-77-78-79-81

Brice, Mrs
(Ireland): Home Int 1948

Bridges, Mrs
(Wales): Home Int 1933-38-39

Briggs, A (Brown)
(Wales): Home Int 1969-70-71-72-73-74-75-76-77-78-79-80-
81(Captain)-82(Captain)-83(Captain)-84; Eur L T Ch 1971-75.
(GBI): in Vagliano Trophy 1971-75

Brinton, Mrs
(Ireland): Home Int 1922

Bromley-Davenport, I (Rieben)
(Wales): Home Int 1932-33-34-35-36-48-50-51-52-53-54-55-56

Brook, D
(Wales): Home Int 1913

Brooks, E
(Ireland): Home Int 1953-54-56

Broun, JG
(Scotland): Home Int 1905-06-07-21

Brown, B
(Ireland): Home Int 1960

Brown, E (Jones)
(Wales): Home Int 1947-48-49-50-52-53-57-58-59-60-61-62-
63-64-65-66-68-69-70

Brown, Mrs FW (Gilroy)
(Scotland): Home Int 1905-06-07-08-09-10-11-13-21

Brown, J
(Wales): Home Int 1960-61-62-64-65; Eur L T Ch
1965-69

Brown, J
(England): Home Int 1984

Brown, TWL
(Scotland): Home Int 1924-25

Brown, Mrs
(Wales): Home Int 1924-25-27

Brownlow, Miss
(Ireland): Home Int 1923

Bryan-Smith, S
(Wales): Home Int 1947-48-49-50-51-52-56

Burrell, Mrs
(Wales): Home Int 1939

Burton, H (Mitchell)
(Scotland): Home Int 1931-55-56-59(Captain). (GBI): in
Vagliano Trophy 1961

Burton, M
(England): Home Int 1975-76

Butler, I (Burke)
(Ireland): Home Int 1962-63-64-65-66-68-70-71-72-73-76-77-
78-79-86(Captain)-87(Captain): Eur L T Ch 1967. (GBI): in
Curtis Cup 1966; in Vagliano Trophy 1965; in Espirito Santo
1964-66

Byrne, A (Sweeney)
(Ireland): Home Int 1959-60-61-62-63-90 (Captain)

Cadden, G
(Scotland): Home Int 1974-75

Cairns, Lady Katherine
(England): Home Int 1947-48-50-51-52-53-54. (GBI): in
Curtis Cup 1952(Captain)

Caldwell, C (Redford)
(England): Home Int 1973-78-79-80. (GBI): in Curtis Cup
1978-80; in Vagliano Trophy 1973

Callen, L
(Ireland): Home Int 1990

Campbell, J (Burnett)
(Scotland): Home Int 1960

Cann, M (Nuttall)
(England): Home Int 1966

Carrick, P (Bullard)
(England): Home Int 1939-47

Caryl, M
(Wales): Home Int 1929

Casement, M (Harrison)
(Ireland): Home Int 1909-10-11-12-13-14

Cautley, B (Hawtrey)
(England): Home Int 1912-13-14-22-23-24-25-27

Chambers, D
(England): Home Int 1906-07-09-10-11-12-20-24-25.
(GBI): in Curtis Cup 1934(Captain)-36(Captain)-38(Captain)

Christison, D
(England): Home Int 1981

Chugg, P (Light)
(Wales): Home Int 1973-74-75-76-77-78-86-87-78; Eur L T Ch
1975-87

Clark, G (Atkinson)
(England): Home Int 1955

Clarke, Mrs ML
(England): Home Int 1933-35

Clarke, P
(England): Home Int 1981

Clarke, Mrs
(Ireland): Home Int 1922

Clarkson, H (Reynolds)
(Wales): Home Int 1935-38-39

Clay, E
(Wales): Home Int 1912

Clement, V
(England): Home Int 1932-34-35

Close, M (Wenyon)
(England): Home Int 1968-69; Eur L T Ch 1969. (GBI) in
Vagliano Trophy 1969

Coats, Mrs G
(Scotland): Home Int 1931-32-33-34

Cochrane, K
(Scotland): Home Int 1924-25-28-29-30

Collett, P
(England): Home Int 1910

Collingham, J (Melville)
(England): Home Int 1978-79-81-84-86-87; Eur L T Ch 1989.
(GBI): in Vagliano Trophy 1979-87; CW 1987

Colquhoun, H
(Ireland): Home Int 1959-60-61-63

Comboy, C (Grott)
(England): Home Int 1975(Captain)-76(Captain). (GBI): in
Curtis Cup 1978(Captain)-80(Captain); in Vagliano Trophy
1977(Captain)-1979(Captain); in Espirito Santo
1978(Captain); CW 1979

Connachan, J
(Scotland): Home Int 1979-80-81-82-83. (GBI): in Curtis Cup
1980-82; in Vagliano Trophy 1981-83; in Espirito Santo 1980-
82; CW 1983

Coote, Miss
(Ireland): Home Int 1925-28-29

Copley, K (Lackie)
(Scotland): Home Int 1974-75

Corlett, E
(England): Home Int 1927-29-30-31-32-33-35-36-37-38-39.
(GBI): in Curtis Cup 1932-38-64(Captain)

Costello, G
(Ireland): Home Int 1973-84(Captain)-85(Captain)

Cotton, S (German)
(England): Home Int 1967-68; Eur L T Ch 1967. (GBI): in
Vagliano Trophy 1967

Couper, M
(Scotland): Home Int 1929-34-35-36-37-39-56

Cowley, Lady
(Wales): Home Int 1907-09

Cox, Margaret
(Wales): Home Int 1924-25

Cox, Nell
(Wales): Home Int 1954

Craik, T
(Scotland): Home Int 1988

Cramsie, F (Hezlet)
(Ireland): Home Int 1905-06-07-08-09-10-13-20-24

Crawford, I (Wylie)
(Scotland): Home Int 1970-71-72

Cresswell, K (Stuart)
(Scotland): Home Int 1909-10-11-12-14

Critchley, D (Fishwick)
(England): Home Int 1930-31-32-33-35-36-47. (GBI): in
Curtis Cup 1932-34-50(Captain)

Croft, A
(England): Home Int 1927

Cross, M
(Wales): Home Int 1922

Cruickshank, DM (Jenkins)
(Scotland): Home Int 1910-11-12

Crummack, Miss
(England): Home Int 1909

Cuming, Mrs
(Ireland): Home Int 1910

Cunninghame, S
(Wales): Home Int 1922-25-29-31

Cuthell, R (Adair)
(Ireland): Home Int 1908

Dampney, S
(Wales): Home Int 1924-25-27-28-29-30

David, Mrs
(Wales): Home Int 1908

Davidson, B (Inglis)
(Scotland): Home Int 1928

Davies, K
(Wales): Home Int 1981-82-83; Eur L T Ch 1987. (GBI): in
Curtis Cup 1986-88; in Vagliano Trophy 1987; CW 1987

Davies, L
(England): Home Int 1983-84. (GBI): in Curtis Cup 1984; CW
1987

Davies, P (Griffiths)
(Wales): Home Int 1965-66-67-68-70-71-73; Eur L T Ch 1971

Deacon, Mrs
(Wales): Home Int 1912-14

Denny, A (Barrett)
(England): Home Int 1951

Dering, Mrs
(Ireland): Home Int 1923

Dermott, Lisa
(Wales): Home Int 1987-88-89

Dickson, M
(Ireland): Home Int 1909

Dobson, H
(England): Home Int 1987-88-89; Eur L T Ch 1989. (GBI): in
Vagliano Trophy 1989; in Curtis Cup 1990

Dod, L
(England): Home Int 1905

Douglas, K
(England): Home Int 1981-82-83. (GBI): in Curtis Cup 1982;
in Vagliano Trophy 1983

Dowling, D
(England): Home Int 1979

Draper, M [Peel] (Thomas)
(Scotland): Home Int 1929-34-38-49-50-51-52-53-
54(Captain)-55(Captain)-56-57-58-61(Captain)-62.
(GBI): in Curtis Cup 1954; in Vagliano Trophy 1963(Captain)

Duncan, B
(Wales): Home Int 1907-08-09-10-12

Duncan, M
(Wales): Home Int 1922-23-28-34

Duncan, MJ (Wood)
(Scotland): Home Int 1925-27-28-39

Durlacher, Mrs
(Ireland): Home Int 1905-06-07-08-09-10-14

Durrant, B [Green] (Lowe)
(England): Home Int 1954

Dwyer, Mrs
(Ireland): 1928

Eakin, P (James)
(Ireland): Home Int 1967

Eakin, T
(Ireland): Home Int 1990

Earner, M
(Ireland): Home Int 1960-61-62-63-70

Edwards, E
(Wales): Home Int 1949-50

Edwards, J
(Wales): Home Int 1932-33-34-36-37

Edwards, J (Morris)
(Wales): Home Int 1962-63-66-67-68-69-70-77(Captain)
-78 (Captain)-79(Captain); Eur L T Ch 1967-69

Ellis, E
(Ireland): Home Int 1932-35-37-38

Ellis Griffiths (Mrs)
(Wales): Home Int 1907-08-09-12-13

Emery, MJ
(Wales): Home Int 1928-29-30-31-32-33-34-35-36-37-38-47

Evans, H
(England): Home Int 1908

Evans, N
(Wales): Home Int 1908-09-10-13

Everard, M
(England): Home Int 1964-67-69-70-72-73-77-78; Eur L T Ch
1967-71-77. (GBI): in Curtis Cup 1970-72-74-78; in Vagliano
Trophy 1967-69-71-73; in Espirito Santo 1968-72-78; CW
1971

Fairclough, L
(England): Home Int 1988-89-90; Eur L T Ch 1989. (GBI):
Vagliano Trophy 1989

Falconer, V (Lamb)
(Scotland): Home Int 1932-36-37-47-48-49-50-51-52-53-54-
55-56

Fallon, Gaynor, Z
(Ireland): Home Int 1952-53-54-55-56-57-58-59-60-61-62-63-
64-65-68-69-70-72 (Captain). (GBI): in Espirito Santo 1964

Farie-Anderson, J
(Scotland): Home Int 1924

Farquharson, E
(Scotland): Home Int 1987-88-89-90; Eur L T Ch 1989. (GBI):
in Vagliano Trophy 1989; in Curtis Cup 1990

Ferguson, A
(Ireland): Home Int 1989

Ferguson, D
(Ireland): Home Int 1927-28-29-30-31-32-34-35-36-37-38-61
(Captain). (GBI): in Curtis Cup 1958(Captain)

Ferguson, M (Fowler)
(Scotland): Home Int 1959-62-63-64-65-66-67-69-70-85; Eur
L T Ch 1965-67-71. (GBI): in Curtis Cup 1966; in Vagliano
Trophy 1965

Ferguson R (Ogden)
(England): Home Int 1957

Fitzgibbon, M
(Ireland): Home Int 1920-21-29-30-31-32-33

FitzPatrick, O (Heskin)
(Ireland): Home Int 1967

Fletcher, L
(England): Home Int 1989-90. (GBI) in Curtis Cup 1990

Fletcher, P (Sherlock)
(Ireland): Home Int 1932-34-35-36-38-39-54-55-66(Captain)

Forbes, J
(Scotland): Home Int 1985-86-87-88-89; Eur L T Ch 1987-89

Foster, C
(England): Home Int 1905-06-09

Foster, J
(Wales): Home Int 1984-85-86-87; Eur L T Ch 1987

Fowler, J
(England): Home Int 1928

Franklin Thomas, E
(Wales): Home Int 1909

Freeguard, C
(Wales): Home Int 1927

Furby, J
(England): Home Int 1987-88; Eur L T Ch 1987

Fyshe, M
(England): Home Int 1938

Gallagher, S
(Scotland): Home Int 1983-84

Gardiner, A
(Ireland): Home Int 1927-29

Garfield Evans, PR (Whittaker)
(Wales): Home Int 1948-49-50-51-52-53-54-55(Captain)-56
(Captain)-57 (Captain)-58(Captain)

Garner, M (Madill)
(Ireland): Home Int 1978-79-80-81-82-83-84-85. (GBI): in
Curtis Cup 1980; in Vagliano Trophy 1979-81-85; in Espirito
Santo 1980; CW 1979

Garon, MR
(England): Home Int 1927-28-32-33-34-36-37-38. (GBI); in
Curtis Cup 1936

Garrett, M (Ruttle)
(England): Home Int 1947-48-50-53-59(Captain)-60(Captain)-
63(Captain). (GBI): in Curtis Cup 1948-60(Captain); in
Vagliano Trophy 1959

Garvey, P
(Ireland): Home Int 1947-48-49-50-51-52-53-54(Captain)-56-
57(Captain)
-58(Captain)-59(Captain)-60(Captain)-61-62-63-68-69. (GBI):
in Curtis Cup 1948-50-52-54-56-60; in Vagliano Trophy 1959-
63

Gear Evans, A
(Wales): Home Int 1932-33-34

Gee, Hon. J (Hives)
(England): Home Int 1950-51-52

Gemmill, A
(Scotland): Home Int 1981-82-84-85-86-87-88-89

Gethin Griffith, S
(Wales): Home Int 1914-22-23-24-28-29-30-31-35

Gibb, M (Titterton)
(England): Home Int 1906-07-08-10-12

Gibbs, C (Le Feuvre)
(England): Home Int 1971-72-73-74. (GBI): in Curtis Cup
1974; in Vagliano Trophy 1973

Gibbs, S
(Wales): Home Int 1933-34-39

Gildea, Miss
(Ireland): Home Int 1936-37-38-39

Glendinning, D
(Ireland): Home Int 1937-54

Glennie, H
(Scotland): Home Int 1959

Glover, A
(Scotland): Home Int 1905-06-08-09-12

Gold, N
(England): Home Int 1929-31-32

Gordon, J
508(England): Home Int 1947-48-49-52-53. (GBI): in Curtis
Cup 1948

Gorman, S
(Ireland): Home Int 1976-79-80-81-82

Gorry, Mary
(Ireland): Home Int 1971-72-73-74-75-76-77-78-79-80-88-89
(Captain); Eur L T Ch 1971-75. (GBI): in Vagliano Trophy
1977

Gotto, Mrs C
(Ireland): Home Int 1923

Gotto, Mrs L
(Ireland): Home Int 1920

Gourlay, M
(England): Home Int 1923-24-27-28-29-30-32-33-34-38-57
(Captain). (GBI): in Curtis Cup 1932-34

Gow, J
(Scotland): Home Int 1923-24-27-28

Graham, MA
(Scotland): Home Int 1905-06

Graham, N
(Ireland): Home Int 1908-09-10-12

Granger Harrison, Mrs
(Scotland): Home Int 1922

Grant-Suttie, E
(Scotland): Home Int 1908-10-11-14-22-23

Grant-Suttie, R
(Scotland): Home Int 1914

Green, B (Pockett)
(England): Home Int 1939

Grice-Whittaker, P (Grice)
(England): Home Int 1983-84. (GBI): in Curtis Cup 1984; in
Espirito Santo 1984

Griffith, W
(Wales): Home Int 1981

Griffiths, M
(England): Home Int 1920-21

Greenlees, E
(Scotland): Home Int 1924

Greenlees, Y
(Scotland): Home Int 1928-30-31-33-34-35-38

Guadella, E (Leitch)
(England): Home Int 1908-10-20-21-22-27-28-29-30-33

Gubbins, Miss
(Ireland): Home Int 1905

Hackney, L
(England): Home Int 1990

Haig, J (Mathias Thomas)
(Wales): Home Int 1938-39

Hall, CM
(England): Home Int 1985

Hall, J (Wade)
(England): Home Int 1987-88-89-90; Eur L T Ch 1987-89.
(GBI): in Curtis Cup 1988-90; in Espirito Santo 1988-90; in
Vagliano Trophy 1989

Hall, Mrs
(Ireland): Home Int 1927-30

Hamilton, S (McKinven)
(Scotland): Home Int 1965

Hambro, W (Martin Smith)
(England): Home Int 1914

Hamilton, J
(England): Home Int 1937-38-39

Hammond, T
(England): Home Int 1985

Hampson, M
(England): Home Int 1954

Hanna, D
(Ireland): Home Int 1987-88

Harrington, D
(Ireland): Home Int 1923

Harris, M [Spearman] (Baker)
(England): Home Int 1955-56-57-58-59-60-61-62-63-64-65;
Eur L T Ch 1965-71. (GBI): in Curtis Cup 1960-62-64; in
Vagliano Trophy 1959-61-65; in Espirito Santo 1964

Harrold, L
(England): Home Int 1974-75-76

Hartill, D
(England): Home Int 1923

Hartley, E
(England): Home Int 1964(Captain)

Hartley, R
(Wales): Home Int 1958-59-62

Hastings, D (Sommerville)
(Scotland): Home Int 1955-56-57-58-59-60-61-62-63.
(GBI): in Curtis Cup 1958; in Vagliano Trophy 1963

Hay, J (Pelham Burn)
(Scotland): Home Int 1959

Hayter, J (Yuille)
(England): Home Int 1956

Hazlett, VP
(Ireland): Home Int 1956(Captain)

Healy, B (Gleeson)
(Ireland): Home Int 1980-82

Heathcoat-Amory, Lady (Joyce Wethered)
(England): Home Int 1921-22-23-24-25-29. (GBI): in Curtis
Cup 1932(Captain)

Hedges, S (Whitlock)
(England): Home Int 1979. (GBI): in Vagliano Trophy 1979;
CW 1979

Hedley Hill, Miss
(Wales): Home Int 1922

Hegarty, G
(Ireland): Home Int 1955-56-64(Captain)

Helme, E
(England): Home Int 1911-12-13-20

Heming Johnson, G
(England): Home Int 1909-11-13

Henson, D (Oxley)
(England): Home Int 1967-68-69-70-75-76-77-78; Eur L T Ch
1971-77. (GBI): in Curtis Cup 1968-70-72-76; in Vagliano
Trophy 1967-69-71; in Espirito Santo 1970; CW 1967-71

Heskin, A
(Ireland): Home Int 1968-69-70-72-75-77-82(Captain)-83
(Captain)

Hetherington, Mrs (Gittens)
(England): Home Int 1909

Hewett, G
(Ireland): Home Int 1923-24

Hezlet, Mrs
(Ireland): Home Int 1910

Hickey, C
(Ireland): Home Int 1969-75(Captain)-76(Captain)

Higgins, E
(Ireland): Home Int 1981-82-83-84-85-86-87-88; Eur L T Ch
1987

Hill, J
(England): Home Int 1986

Hill, Mrs
(Wales): Home Int 1924

Hodgson, M
(England): Home Int 1939

Holland, I (Hurst)
(Ireland): Home Int 1958

Holm, H (Gray)
(Scotland): Home Int 1932-33-34-35-36-37-38-47-48-50-51-
55-57. (GBI): in Curtis Cup 1936-38-48

Holmes, A
(England): Home Int 1931

Holmes, J [Hetherington] (McClure)
(England): Home Int 1957-66-67(Captain)

Hooman, EM [Gavin]
(England): Home Int 1910-11

Hope, LA
(Scotland): Home Int 1975-76-80-84-85-86-87-88(Captain)
-89 (Captain)-90 (Captain)

Hort, K
(Wales): Home Int 1929

Hourihane, C
(Ireland): Home Int 1979 to 1990; Eur L T Ch 1987. (GBI): in
Curtis Cup 1984-86-88-90; in Vagliano Trophy 1981-83-85-87-
89; in Espirito Santo 1986-90

Howard, A (Phillips)
(England): Home Int 1953-54-55-56-57-58-79(Captain)-80
(Captain). (GBI): in Curtis Cup 1956-58

Huggan, S (Lawson)
(Scotland): Home Int 1985-86-87-88-89; Eur L T Ch 1985-87-
89. (GBI): in Curtis Cup 1988, in Vagliano Trophy 1989

Hughes, J
(Wales): Home Int 1967-71-88-89(Captain); Eur L T Ch 1971

Hughes, Miss
(Wales): Home Int 1907

Huke, B
(England): Home Int 1971-72-75-76-77. (GBI): in Curtis Cup
1972; in Vagliano Trophy 1975

Hulton, V (Hezlet)
(Ireland): Home Int 1905-07-09-10-11-12-20-21

Humphreys, A (Coulman)
(Wales): Home Int 1969-70-71

Humphreys, D (Forster)
(Ireland): Home Int 1951-52-53-55-57

Hunter, D (Tucker)
(England): Home Int 1905

Hurd, D [Howe] (Campbell)
(Scotland): Home Int 1905-06-08-09-11-28-30

Hurst, Mrs
(Wales): Home Int 1921-22-23-25-27-28

Hyland, B
(Ireland): Home Int 1964-65-66

Imrie, K
(Scotland): Home Int 1984-85-89. Eur L T Ch 1987-89 (GBI):
in Vagliano Trophy 1989; in Curtis Cup 1990

Inghram, E (Lever)
(Wales): Home Int 1947-48-49-50-51-52-53-54-55-56-57-58-
64-65

Irvin, A
(England): Home Int 1962-63-65-67-68-69-70-71-72-73-75;
Eur L T Ch 1965-67-69-71. (GBI): in Curtis Cup 1962-68-70-
76; in Vagliano Trophy 1961-63-65-67-69-71-73-75; in
Espirito Santo 1982(Captain); CW 1967-75

Irvine, Miss
(Wales): Home Int 1930

Isaac, Mrs
(Wales): Home Int 1924

Isherwood, L
(Wales): Home Int 1972-76-77-78-80-86-88-89-90

Jack, E (Philip)
(Scotland): Home Int 1962-63-64-81(Captain)-82(Captain)

Jackson, B
(Ireland): Home Int 1937-38-39-50

Jackson, B
(England): Home Int 1955-56-57-58-59-63-64-65-66-73
(Captain)-74(Captain). (GBI): in Curtis Cup 1958-64-68; in
Vagliano Trophy 1959-63-65-67-73(Captain)-75(Captain);
Espirito Santo 1964; CW in 1959-67

Jackson, D
(Scotland): Home Int 1990

Jackson, Mrs H
(Ireland): Home Int 1921

Jackson, J
(Ireland): Home Int 1912-13-14-20-21-22-23-24-25-27-28-29-
30

Jackson, Mrs L
(Ireland): Home Int 1910-12-14-20-22-25

Jameson, S (Tobin)
(Ireland): Home Int 1913-14-20-24-25-27

Jenkin, B
(Wales): Home Int 1959

Jenkins, J (Owen)
(Wales): Home Int 1953-56

John, J
(Wales): Home Int 1974

Johns, A
(England): Home Int 1987-88-89

Johnson, A (Hughes)
(Wales): Home Int 1964-66-67-68-69-70-71-72-73-74-75-76-
78-79-85; Eur L T Ch 1965-67-69-71

Johnson, J (Roberts)
(Wales): Home Int 1955

Johnson, M
(England): Home Int 1934-35

Johnson, R
(Wales): Home Int 1955

Johnson, T
(England): Home Int 1984-85-86; Eur L T Ch 1985. (GBI): in
Curtis Cup 1986; in Vagliano Trophy 1985; in Espirito Santo
1986

Jones, A (Gwyther)
(Wales): Home Int 1959

Jones, K
(Wales): Home Int 1959(Captain)-1960(Captain)-61(Captain)

Jones, M (De Lloyd)
(Wales): Home Int 1951

Jones, Mrs
(Wales): Home Int 1932-35

Justice, M
(Wales): Home Int 1931-32

Kaye, H (Williamson)
(England): Home Int 1986(Captain)-87(Captain)

Keenan, D
(Ireland): Home Int 1989

Keiller, G [Style]
(England): Home Int 1948-49-52

Kelway Bamber, Mrs
(Scotland): Home Int 1923-27-33

Kennedy, D (Fowler)
(England): Home Int 1923-24-25-27-28-29

Kennion, Mrs (Kenyon Stow)
(England) Home Int 1910

Kerr, J
(Scotland): Home Int 1947-48-49-54

Kidd, Mrs
(Ireland): Home Int 1934-37

King Mrs
(Ireland): Home Int 1923-25-27-29

Kinloch, Miss
(Scotland): Home Int 1913-14

Kirkwood, Mrs
(Ireland): Home Int 1955

Knight, Mrs
(Scotland): Home Int 1922

Kyle, B [Rhodes] (Norris)
(England): Home Int 1937-38-39-48-49

Kyle, E
(Scotland): Home Int 1909-10

Laing, A
(Scotland): Home Int 1966-67-70-71-73(Captain)-74(Captain);
Eur L T Ch 1967. (GBI): in Vagliano Trophy 1967

Lambert, C
(Scotland): Home Int 1989-90; Eur L T Ch 1989. (GBI): in
Curtis Cup 1990

Lambert, S (Cohen)
(England): Home Int 1979-80. (GBI): in Vagliano Trophy 1979

Lambie, S
(Scotland): Home Int 1976

Laming Evans, Mrs
(Wales): Home Int 1922-23

Langford, Mrs
(Wales): Home Int 1937

Langridge, S (Armitage)
(England): Home Int 1963-64-65-66; Eur L T Ch 1965. (GBI):
in Curtis Cup 1964-66; in Vagliano Trophy 1963-65

Large, P (Davies)
(England): Home Int 1951-52-81(Captain)-82(Captain)

Larkin, C (McAuley)
(Ireland): Home Int 1966-67-68-69-70-71-72; Eur L T Ch
1971

Latchford, B
(Ireland): Home Int 1931-33

Latham Hall, E (Chubb)
(England): Home Int 1928

Lauder, G
(Ireland): Home Int 1911

Lauder, R
(Ireland): Home Int 1911

Lawrence, JB
(Scotland): Home Int 1959-60-61-62-63-64-65-66-67-68-69-70-77(Captain); Eur L T Ch 1965-67-69-71. (GBI): in Curtis Cup 1964; in Vagliano Trophy 1963-65; in Espirito Santo 1964; CW 1971

Lawson, H
(Wales): Home Int 1989-90

Lebrun, W (Aitken)
(Scotland): Home Int 1978-79-80-81-82-83-85. (GBI): in Curtis Cup 1982; in Vagliano Trophy 1981-83

Leaver, B
(Wales): Home Int 1912-14-21

Lee Smith, J
(England): Home Int 1973-74-75-76. (GBI): in Curtis Cup 1974-76; in Espirito Santo 1976; CW 1975

Leete, Mrs IG
(Scotland): Home Int 1933

Leitch, C
(England): Home Int 1910-11-12-13-14-20-21-22-24-25-27-28

Leitch, M
(England): Home Int 1912-14

Llewellyn, Miss
(Wales): Home Int 1912-13-14-21-22-23

Lloyd, J
(Wales): Home Int 1988

Lloyd, P
(Wales): Home Int 1935-36

Lloyd Davies, VH
(Wales): Home Int 1913

Lloyd Roberts, V
(Wales): Home Int 1907-08-10

Lloyd Williams, Miss
(Wales): Home Int 1909-10-12-14

Lobbett, P
(England): Home Int 1922-24-27-29-30

Lowry, Mrs
(Ireland): Home Int 1947

Luckin, B (Cooper)
(England): Home Int 1980

Lugton, C
(Scotland): Home Int 1968-72-73-75(Captain)-76(Captain)-77-78-80

Lumb, K (Phillips)
(England): Home Int 1968-69-70-71; Eur L T Ch 1969. (GBI): Curtis Cup 1972; in Vagliano Trophy 1969-71

Lyons, T (Ross Steen)
(England): Home Int 1959. (GBI): in Vagliano Trophy 1959

MacAndrew, F
(Scotland): Home Int 1913-14

Macbeth, M (Dodd)
(England): Home Int 1913-14-20-21-22-23-24-25

MacCann, K
(Ireland): Home Int 1984-85-86

MacCann, K (Smye)
(Ireland): Home Int 1947-48-49-50-51-52-53-54-56-57-58-60-61-62-64-65(Captain)

McCarthy, A
(Ireland): Home Int 1951-52

McCarthy, D
(Ireland): Home Int 1988-90

McCulloch, J
(Scotland): Home Int 1921-22-23-24-27-29-30-31-32-33-35-60(Captain)

McDaid, E (O'Grady)
(Ireland): Home Int 1959

McDaid, ER
(Ireland): Home Int 1987-88-89-90; Eur L T Ch 1987

Macdonald, F
(England): Home Int 1990

Macdonald, K
(Scotland): Home Int 1928-29

MacGeach, C
(Ireland): Home Int 1938-39-48-49-50

McGreevy, V
(Ireland): Home Int 1987-90

McIntosh, B (Dixon)
(England): Home Int 1969-70; Eur L T Ch 1969. (GBI): in Vagliano Trophy 1969

McIntyre, J
(England): Home Int 1949-54

MacKean, Mrs
(Wales): Home Int 1938-39-47

McKenna, M
(Ireland): Home Int 1968 to 1990; Eur L T Ch 1969-71-75-87. (GBI): in Curtis Cup 1970-72-74-76-78-80-82-84-86; in Vagliano Trophy 1969-71-73-75-77-79-81-85-87; in Espirito Santo 1970-74-76-86(Captain)-90(Captain)

Mackenzie, A
(Scotland): Home Int 1921

McKinlay, M
(Scotland): Home Int 1990

McLarty, E
(Scotland): Home Int 1966(Captain)-67(Captain)-68(Captain)

McMahon, S (Cadden)
(Scotland): Home Int 1974-75-76-77-79. (GBI): in Curtis Cup 1976; in Vagliano Trophy 1975

McNair, W
(England): Home Int 1921

McNeil, K
(Scotland): Home Int 1969(Captain)-70(Captain)

McNeile, CL
(Ireland): Home Int 1906

McQuillan, Y
(Ireland): Home Int 1985-86

MacTier, Mrs
(Wales): Home Int 1927

Madeley, M (Coburn)
(Ireland): Home Int 1964-69; Eur L T Ch 1969

Madill, Mrs
(Ireland): Home Int 1920-24-25-27-28-29-33

Magill, J
(Ireland): Home Int 1907-11-13

Maher, S (Vaughan)
(England): Home Int 1960-61-62-63-64. (GBI): in Curtis Cup 1962-64; in Vagliano Trophy 1961; CW 1963

Mahon, D
(Ireland): Home Int 1989-90

Main, M (Farquhar)
(Scotland): Home Int 1950-51

Maitland, M
(Scotland): Home Int 1905-06-08-12-13

Mallam, Mrs S
(Ireland): Home Int 1922-23

Marks, Mrs T
(Ireland): Home Int 1950

Marks, Mrs
(Ireland): Home Int 1930-31-33-35

Marley, MV (Marley)
(Wales): Home Int 1921-22-23-30-37

Marr, H (Cameron)
(Scotland): Home Int 1927-28-29-30-31

Martin, P [Whitworth Jones] (Low)
(Wales): Home Int 1948-50-56-59-60-61

Marvin, V
(England): Home Int 1977-78; Eur L T Ch 1977. (GBI): in Curtis Cup 1978; in Vagliano Trophy 1977

Mason, Mrs
(Wales): Home Int 1923

Mather, H
(Scotland): Home Int 1905-09-12-13-14

Mellis, Mrs
(Scotland): Home Int 1924-27

Menton, D
(Ireland): Home Int 1949

Menzies, M
(Scotland): Home Int 1962(Captain)

Merrill, J (Greenhalgh)
(England): Home Int 1960-61-63-66-69-70-71-75-76-77-78; Eur L T Ch 1971-77. (GBI): in Curtis Cup 1964-70-74-76-78; in Vagliano Trophy 1961-65-75-77; in Espirito Santo 1970-74(Captain)-78; CW 1963

Millar, D
(Ireland): Home Int 1928

Milligan, J (Mark)
(Ireland): Home Int 1971-72-73

Mills, I
(Wales): Home Int 1935-36-37-39-47-48

Milton, M (Paterson)
(Scotland): Home Int 1948-49-50-51-52. (GBI): in Curtis Cup 1952

Mitchell, J
(Ireland): Home Int 1930

Moodie, J
(Scotland): Home Int 1990

Mooney, M
(Ireland): Home Int 1972-73; Eur L T Ch 1971. (GBI): in Vagliano Trophy 1973

Moorcroft, S
(England): Home Int 1985-86; Eur L T Ch 1985-87

Moore, S
(Ireland): Home Int 1937-38-39-47-48-49-68(Captain)

Moran, V (Singleton)
(Ireland): Home Int 1970-71-73-74-75; Eur L T Ch 1971-75

Morant, E
(England): Home Int 1906-10

Morgan, S
(England): Home Int 1989; Eur L T Ch 1989

Morgan, W
(England): Home Int 1931-32-33-34-35-36-37. (GBI): in Curtis Cup 32-34-36

Morgan, Miss
(Wales): Home Int 1912-13-14

Moriarty, M (Irvine)
(Ireland): Home Int 1979

Morley, J
(England): Home Int 1990

Morris, L (Moore)
(England): Home Int 1912-13

Morris, Mrs de B
(Ireland): Home Int 1933

Morrison, G (Cheetham)
(England): Home Int 1965-69(Captain). (GBI): in Vagliano Trophy 1965

Morrison, G (Cradock-Hartopp)
(England): Home Int 1936

Mountford, S
(Wales): Home Int 1989-90

Murray, Rachel
(Ireland): Home Int 1952

Murray, S (Jolly)
(England): Home Int 1976

Musgrove, Mrs
(Wales): Home Int 1923-24

Myles, M
(Scotland): Home Int 1955-57-59-60-67

Neill-Fraser, M
(Scotland): Home Int 1905-06-07-08-09-10-11-12-13-14

Nes, K (Garnham)
(England): Home Int 1931-32-33-36-37-38-39

Nevile, E
(England): Home Int 1905-06-08-10

New, B
(England): Home Int 1980-81-82-83. (GBI): in Curtis Cup 1984; in Vagliano Trophy 1983

Newell, B
(England): Home Int 1936

Newman, L
(Wales): Home Int 1927-31

Newton, B (Brown)
(England): Home Int 1930-33-34-35-36-37

Nicholls, M
(Wales): Home Int 1962(Captain)

Nicholson, J (Hutton)
(Scotland): Home Int 1969-70; Eur L T Ch 1971; CW 1971

Nicholson, Mrs WH
(Scotland): Home Int 1910-13

Nimmo, H
(Scotland): Home Int 1936-38-39

Norris, J (Smith)
(Scotland): Home Int 1966-67-68-69-70-71-72-75-76-77-78-79-83(Captain)-84(Captain)-84(Captain); Eur L T Ch 1971. (GBI): in Vagliano Trophy 1977

Norwell, I (Watt)
(Scotland): Home Int 1954

Nutting, P (Jameson)
(Ireland): Home Int 1927-28

O'Brien, A
(Ireland): Home Int 1969

O'Brien Kenney, S
(Ireland): Home Int 1977-78-83-84-85-86

O'Donnell, M
(Ireland): Home Int 1974-77(Captain)-78(Captain)-79
(Captain); Eur L T Ch 1980(Captain). (GBI): in Curtis Cup
1982; in Vagliano Trophy 1981(Captain)

O'Donohoe, A
(Ireland): Home Int 1948-49-50-51-53-73(Captain)-74
(Captain)

O'Hare, S
(Ireland): Home Int 1921-22

O'Reilly, T (Moran)
(Ireland): Home Int 1977-78-86-88; Eur L T Ch 1987

O'Sullivan, A
(Ireland): Home Int 1982-83-84

O'Sullivan, P
(Ireland): Home Int 1950-51-52-53-54-55-56-57-58-59-60-63-
64-65-66-67-69 (Captain)-70(Captain)-71(Captain); Eur L T
Ch 1971(Captain)

Oliver, M (Jones)
(Wales): Home Int 1955-60-61-62-63-64-65-66.
(GBI): in Espirito Santo 1964

Ormsby, Miss
(Ireland): Home Int 1909-10-11

Orr, P (Boyd)
(Ireland): Home Int 1971

Orr, Mrs
(Wales): Home Int 1924

Owen, E
(Wales): Home Int 1947

Panton, C
(Scotland): Home Int 1972-73-76-77-78. (GBI): in Vagliano
Trophy 1977; in Espirito Santo 1976

Park, Mrs
(Scotland): Home Int 1952

Parker, S
(England): Home Int 1973

Patey, Mrs
(Scotland): Home Int 1922-23

Pearson, D
(England): Home Int 1928-29-30-31-32-34

Percy, G (Mitchell)
(Scotland): Home Int 1927-28-30-31

Perriam, A
(Wales): Home Int 1988-90

Phelips, M
(Wales): Home Int 1913-14-21

Phillips, ME
(England): Home Int 1905

Phillips, Mrs
(Wales): Home Int 1921

Pickard, M (Nichol)
(England): Home Int 1958-59-60-61-67-69-83(Captain).
(GBI): in Curtis Cup 1968-70; in Vagliano
Trophy 1959-61-67

Pim, Mrs
(Ireland): Home Int 1908

Pook, E (Chadwick)
(England): Home Int 1963-65-66-67; Eur L T Ch 1967.
(GBI): in Curtis Cup 1966; in Vagliano Trophy 1963-67;
CW 1967

Porter, D (Park)
(Scotland): Home Int 1922-25-27-29-30-31-32-33-34-35-37-
38-47-48. (GBI): in Curtis Cup 1932

Porter, M (Lazenby)
(England): Home Int 1931-32

Powell, M
(Wales): Home Int 1908-09-10-12

Price, M (Greaves)
(England): Home Int 1956(Captain)

Price Fisher, E (Price)
(England): Home Int 1948-51-52-53-54-55-56-57-58-59-60.
(GBI): in Curtis Cup 1950-52-54-56-58-60; in Vagliano Trophy
1959; CW 1959

Proctor, Mrs
(Wales): Home Int 1907

Provis, I (Kyle)
(Scotland): Home Int 1910-11

Purcell, E
(Ireland): Home Int 1965-66-67-72-73

Purvis-Russell-Montgomery, C
(Scotland): Home Int 1921-22-23-25-28-29-23-31-32-33-34-
35-36-37-38-39-47-48-49-50-52

Pyman, B
(Wales): Home Int 1925-28-29-30-32-33-34-35-36-37-38

Rabbidge, R
(England): Home Int 1931

Rawlings, M
(Wales): Home Int 1979-80-81-83-84-85-86-87.
(GBI): in Vagliano Trophy 1981

Rawlinson, T (Walker)
(Scotland): Home Int 1970-71-73-76. (GBI): in Vagliano
Trophy 1973

Read, P
(England): Home Int 1922

Reddan, C (Tiernan)
(Ireland): Home Int 1935-36-38-39-47-48-49. (GBI): in Curtis
Cup 1938-48

Reddan, MV
(Ireland): Home Int 1955

Reece, P (Millington)
(England): Home Int 1966(Captain)

Rees, G
(Wales): Home Int 1981

Rees, MB
(Wales): Home Int 1927-31

Reid, A (Lurie)
(Scotland) Home Int 1960-61-62-63-64-66. (GBI): in Vagliano
Trophy 1961

Reid, A (Kyle)
(Scotland): Home Int 1923-24-25

Reid, D
(Scotland): Home Int 1978-79

Remer, H
(England): Home Int 1909

Rennie, J (Hastings)
(Scotland): Home Int 1961-65-66-67-71-72; Eur L T Ch 1967.
(GBI): in Curtis Cup 1966; in Vagliano Trophy 1961-67

Rhys, J
(Wales): Home Int 1979

Rice, J
(Ireland): Home Int 1924-27-29

Richards, J
(Wales): Home Int 1980-82-83-85

Richards, S
(Wales): Home Int 1967

Richardson, Mrs
(England): Home Int 1907-09

Richmond, M (Walker)
(Scotland): Home Int 1972-73-74-75-77-78. (GBI): in Curtis Cup 1974; in Vagliano Trophy 1975

Rieben, Mrs
(Wales): Home Int 1927-28-29-30-31-32-33

Rigby, F (Macbeth)
(Scotland): Home Int 1912-13

Ritchie, C (Park)
(Scotland): Home Int 1939-47-48-51-52-53-64(Captain)

Roberts, B
(Wales): Home Int 1984(Captain)-85(Captain)-86(Captain)

Roberts, E (Pentony)
(Ireland): Home Int 1932-33-34-35-36-39

Roberts, E (Barnett)
(Ireland): Home Int 1961-62-63-64-65; Eur L T Ch 1964

Roberts, G
(Wales): Home Int 1949-52-53-54

Roberts, M (Brown)
(Scotland): Home Int 1965(Captain). (GBI): in Espirito Santo 1964

Roberts, P
(Wales): Home Int 1950-51-53-55-56-57-58-59-60-61-62-63-64(Captain)-65 (Captain)-66(Captain)-67(Captain)-68-69-70; Eur L T Ch 1965-67-69. (GBI) in Espirito Santo 1964

Roberts, S
(Wales): Home Int 1983-84-85-86-87-88-89-90; Eur L T Ch 1983-87

Robertson, B (McCorkindale)
(Scotland): Home Int 1958-59-60-61-62-63-64-65-66-69-72-73-78-80-81-82-84 -85-86; Eur L T Ch 1965-67(Captain)-69-71(Captain). (GBI): in Curtis Cup 1960-66-68-70-72-74 (Captain)-76(Captain)-82-86; in Vagliano Trophy 1959-63-69-71-81-85; in Espirito Santo 1959-63-69-71-81-85; CW 1971-75(Captain)

Robertson, D
(Scotland): Home Int 1907

Robertson, E
(Scotland): Home Int 1924

Robertson, G
(Scotland): Home Int 1907-08-09

Robinson, C (Nesbitt)
(Ireland): Home Int 1974-75-76-77-78-79-80-81. (GBI): in Curtis Cup 1980; in Vagliano Trophy 1979

Robinson, R (Bayly)
(Ireland): Home Int 1947-56-57

Robinson, S
(England): Home Int 1989

Roche, Mrs
(Ireland): Home Int 1922

Rogers, J
(Wales): Home Int 1972

Rose, A
(Scotland): Home Int 1990

Roskrow, M
(England): Home Int 1948-50

Ross, M (Hezlet)
(Ireland): Home Int 1905-06-07-08-11-12

Roy, S (Needham)
(Scotland): Home Int 1969-71-72-73-74-75-76-83. (GBI): in Vagliano Trophy 1973-75

Rudgard, G
(England): Home Int 1931-32-50-51-52

Rusack, J
(Scotland): Home Int 1908

Sabine, D (Plumpton)
(England): Home Int 1934-35. (GBI): in Curtis Cup 1934

Saunders, V
(England): Home Int 1967-68; Eur L T Ch 1967. (GBI): in Curtis Cup 1968; in Vagliano Trophy 1967; CW 1967

Scott Chard, Mrs
(Wales) Home Int 1928-30

Seddon, N
(Wales): Home Int 1962-63-74(Captain)-75(Captain)-76 (Captain)

Selkirk, H
(Wales): Home Int 1925-28

Shapcott, A
(England): Home Int 1989

Shapcott, S
(England): Home Int 1986-88; Eur L T Ch 1987. (GBI): in Curtis Cup 1988; in Vagliano Trophy 1987; CW 1987; in Espirito Santo 1988

Shaw, P
(Wales): Home Int 1913

Sheldon, A
(Wales): Home Int 1981

Sheppard, E (Pears)
(England): Home Int 1947

Simpson, L (Moore)
(England): Home Int 1979-80

Singleton, B (Henderson)
(Scotland): Home Int 1939-52-53-54-55-56-57-58-60-61-62-63-64-65

Slade, Lady
(Ireland): Home Int 1906

Slark, R (Porter)
(England): Home Int 1959-60-61-62-64-65-66-68-78; Eur L T Ch 1965. (GBI): in Curtis Cup 1960-62-64; in Vagliano Trophy 1959-61-65; in Espirito Santo 1964-66(Captain); CW 1963

Slocombe, E (Davies)
(Wales): Home Int 1974-75

Smalley, Mrs A
(Wales): Home Int 1924-25-31-32-33-34

Smillie, P
(England): Home Int 1985-86

Smith, A [Stant] (Willard)
(England): Home Int 1974-75-76. (GBI): in Curtis Cup 1976; in Vagliano Trophy 1975; CW 1959-63

Smith, F (Stephens)
(England): Home Int 1947-48-49-50-51-52-53-54-55-59-62 (Captain)-71(Captain) -72(Captain). (GBI): in Curtis Cup 1950-52-54-56-58-60-62(non-playing Captain)-72 (non-playing Captain); in Vagliano Trophy 1959-71; CW 1959-63

Smith, Mrs L
(Ireland): Home Int 1913-14-21-22-23-25

Smythe, M
(Ireland): Home Int 1947-48-49-50-51-52-53-54-55-56-58-59-62(Captain)

Sowter, Mrs
(Wales): Home Int 1923

Speir, M
(Scotland): Home Int 1957-64-68-71(Captain)-72(Captain)

Starrett, L (Malone)
(Ireland): Home Int 1975-76-77-78-80

Stavert, M
(Scotland): Home Int 1979

Steel, Mrs DC
(Scotland): Home Int 1925

Steel, E
(England): Home Int 1905-06-07-08-11

Stewart, G
(Scotland): Home Int 1979-80-81-82-83-84; Eur L T Ch 1982-84. (GBI): in Curtis Cup 1980-82; in Vagliano Trophy 1979-81-83; CW 1979-83

Stewart, L (Scraggie)
(Scotland): Home Int 1921-22-23

Stocker, J
(England): Home Int 1922-23

Stockton, Mrs
(Wales): Home Int 1949

Storry, Mrs
(Wales): Home Int 1910-14

Stroud, N
(Wales): Home Int 1989

Stuart, M
(Ireland): Home Int 1905-07-08

Stuart-French, Miss
(Ireland): Home Int 1922

Sugden, J (Machin)
(England): Home Int 1953-54-55

Summers, M (Mackie)
(Scotland): Home Int 1986

Sumpter, Mrs
(England): Home Int 1907-08-12-14-24

Sutherland Pilch, R (Barton)
(England): Home Int 1947-49-50-58(Captain)

Swallow, C
(England): Home Int 1985; Eur L T Ch 1985

Tamworth, Mrs
(England): Home Int 1908

Taylor, I
(Ireland): Home Int 1930

Teacher, F
(Scotland): Home Int 1908-09-11-12-13

Tebbet, K
(England): Home Int 1990

Temple, S
(England): Home Int 1913-14

Temple Dobell, G (Ravenscroft)
(England): Home Int 1911-12-13-14-20-21-25-30

Thomas, C (Phipps)
(Wales): Home Int 1959-63-64-65-66-67-68-69-70-71-72-73-76-77-80

Thomas, I
(Wales): Home Int 1910

Thomas, O
(Wales): Home Int 1921

Thomas, S (Rowlands)
(Wales): Home Int 1977-82-84-85

Thomas, T (Perkins)
(Wales): Home Int 1972-73-74-75-76-77-78-79-80-81-82-83-84; Eur L T Ch 1975. (GBI): in Curtis Cup 1974-76-78-80; in Vagliano Trophy 1973-75-77-79; in Espirito Santo 1979; CW 1975-79

Thomas, V (Rawlings)
(Wales): Home Int 1971 to 1990; Eur L T Ch 1975-87. (GBI): in Curtis Cup 1982-84-86-88-90; in Vagliano Trophy 1979-83 -85-87-89; CW 1979-83-87. Espirito Santo 1990

Thompson, M
(Wales): Home Int 1937-38-39

Thompson, M (Wallis)
(England): Home Int 1948-49

Thompson, M
(Scotland): Home Int 1949

Thomson, D
(Scotland): Home Int 1982-83-85-87

Thomson, M
(Scotland): Home Int 1907

Thomson, M
(Scotland): Home Int 1974-75-76-77-78; Eur L T Ch 1978. (GBI): in Curtis Cup 1978; in Vagliano Trophy 1977

Thornhill, J (Woodside)
(England): Home Int 1965-74-82-83-84-85-86-87-88; Eur L T Ch 1965-85-87. (GBI): in Curtis Cup 1984-86-88; in Vagliano Trophy 1965-83-85-87-89(Captain); CW 1983-87

Thornhill, Miss
(Ireland): Home Int 1924-25

Thornton, Mrs
(Ireland): Home Int 1924

Todd, Mrs
(Ireland): Home Int 1931-32-34-35-36

Thomlinson, J [Evans] (Roberts)
(England): Home Int 1962-64. (GBI): in Curtis Cup 1962; in Vagliano Trophy 1963

Treharne, A [Mills]
(Wales): Home Int 1952-61

Turner, B
(England): Home Int 1908

Turner, S (Jump)
(Wales): Home Int 1982-84-85-86

Tynte, V
(Ireland): Home Int 1905-06-08-09-11-12-13-14

Uzielli, A (Carrick)
(England): Home Int 1976-77-78-90; Eur L T Ch 1977. (GBI): in Curtis Cup 1978; in Vagliano Trophy 1977

Valentine, J (Anderson)
(Scotland): Home Int 1934-35-36-37-38-39-47-49-50-51-52-53-54-55-56 (Captain)-57-58. (GBI): in Curtis Cup 1938-48-50-52-54-56-58; CW 1959

Valentine, P (Whitley)
(Wales): Home Int 1973-74-75-77-78-79-80-90 (Captain)

Veitch, F
(Scotland): Home Int 1912

Wadsworth, H
(Wales): Home Int 1987-88-89-90; Eur L T Ch 1987-90. (GBI): in Curtis Cup 1990

Waite, C
(England): Home Int 1981-82-83-84, Eur L T Ch 1985. (GBI): in Curtis Cup 1984; in Vagliano Trophy 1983; in Espirito Santo 1984; CW 1983

Wakelin, H
(Wales): Home Int 1955

Walker, B (Thompson)
(England): Home Int 1905-06-07-08-09-11

Walker, M
(England): Home Int 1970-72; Eur L T Ch 1971. (GBI): in Curtis Cup 1972; in Vagliano Trophy 1971; CW 1971

Walker, P
(Ireland): Home Int 1928-29-30-31-32-33-34-35-36-37-38-39-48. (GBI): in Curtis Cup 1934-36-38

Walker-Leigh, F
(Ireland): Home Int 1907-08-09-11-12-13-14

Wallace-Williamson, V
(Scotland): Home Int 1932. (GBI): in Curtis Cup 1938 (Captain)

Walsh, R
(Ireland): Home Int 1987

Walter, J
(England): Home Int 1974-79-80-82-86

Wardlaw, N (Baird)
(Scotland): Home Int 1932-35-36-37-38-39-47-48. (GBI): in Curtis Cup 1938

Watson, C (Nelson)
(England): Home Int 1982

Webster, S (Hales)
(Wales): Home Int 1968-69-72

Wesley, N
(Wales): Home Int 1986

Westall, S (Maudsley)
(England): Home Int 1973

Weston, R
(Wales): Home Int 1927

Whieldon, Miss
(Wales): Home Int 1908

Wickham, C
(Ireland): Home Int 1983-89

Wickham, P
(Ireland): Home Int 1976-83-87; Eur L T Ch 1987

Williams, M
(Wales): Home Int 1936

Williamson, C (Barker)
(England): Home Int 1979-80-81

Willock-Pollen, G
(England): Home Int 1907

Wilson, A
(Scotland): Home Int 1973-74-85 (Captain)

Wilson, E
(England): Home Int 1928-29-30. (GBI): in Curtis Cup 1932

Wilson, Mrs
(Ireland): Home Int 1931

Wilson Jones, D
(Wales): Home Int 1952

Winn, J
(England): Home Int 1920-21-23-25

Wooldridge, W (Shaw)
(Scotland): Home Int 1982

Wragg, M
(England): Home Int 1929

Wright, J (Robertson)
(Scotland): Home Int 1952-53-54-55-56-57-58-59-60-61-63-65-67-73-78 (Captain)-79(Captain)-80(Captain)-86(Captain); Eur L T Ch 1965. (GBI): in Curtis Cup 1954-56-58-60; in Vagliano Trophy 1959-61-63; CW 1959

Wright, M
(Scotland): Home Int 1990

Wright, N (Cook)
(Wales): Home Int 1938-47-48-49-51-52-53-54-57-58-59-60-62-63-64-66-67-68-71 (Captain)-72(Captain)-73(Captain); Eur L T Ch 1965-71 (Captain). (GBI): in Espirito Santo 1964

Wright, P
(Scotland): Home Int 1981-82-83-84; Eur L T Ch 1987. (GBI): in Vagliano Trophy 1981

Wylie, P (Wade)
(England): Home Int 1934-35-36-37-38-47. (GBI): in Curtis Cup 1938

Ladies' National Championships

English Ladies' Close Amateur Championship

INAUGURATED 1912

The English Ladies' Golf Association, founded in 1952, now has nine championships for which it is responsible. The Association took over the English Ladies' Close Amateur, which was first played in 1912, in 1953. The great Cecil Leitch won in 1914 and again in 1919 when it was resumed after the Great War. The next year at Sheringham she lost to Joyce Wethered who went on to win for the next four years, but did not compete again. Nearly all subsequent winners have been Curtis Cup internationals.

YEAR	WINNER	RUNNER-UP	MARGIN	VENUE
1912	Miss M Gardner	Mrs Cautley	20th hole	Prince's, Sandwich
1913	Mrs F W Brown	Mrs McNair	1 hole	Hollinwell
(The 1912 and 1913 Championships were run by the National Golf Alliance)				
1914	Miss Cecil Leitch	Miss Bastin	2 and 1	Walton Heath
1915–18	*No Championship owing to the Great War*			
1919	Miss Cecil Leitch	Mrs Temple Dobell	10 and 8	St Annes, Old Links
1920	Miss J Wethered	Miss Cecil Leitch	2 and 1	Sheringham
1921	Miss J Wethered	Mrs Mudford	12 and 11	Lytham St Annes
1922	Miss J Wethered	Miss J Stocker	7 and 6	Hunstanton
1923	Miss J Wethered	Mrs TA Lodge	8 and 7	Ganton
1924	Miss J Wethered	Miss DR Fowler	8 and 7	Cooden Beach
1925	Miss DR Fowler	Miss J Winn	9 and 7	Westward Ho!
1926	Miss M Gourlay	Miss E Corlett	6 and 4	Woodhall Spa
1927	Mrs H Guedalla	Miss E Wilson	1 hole	Pannal
1928	Miss E Wilson	Miss D Pearson	9 and 8	Walton Heath
1929	Miss M Gourlay	Miss D Fishwick	6 and 5	Broadstone
1930	Miss E Wilson	Mrs RO Porter	12 and 11	Aldeburgh
1931	Miss W Morgan	Miss M Gourlay	3 and 1	Ganton
1932	Miss D Fishwick	Miss B Brown	5 and 4	Royal Ashdown Forest
1933	Miss D Pearson	Miss M Johnson	5 and 3	Westward Ho!
1934	Miss P Wade	Miss M Johnson	4 and 3	Seacroft
1935	Mrs M Garon	Miss E Corlett	38th hole	Birkdale
1936	Miss W Morgan	Miss P Wade	2 and 1	Hayling Island
1937	Miss W Morgan	Miss M Fyshe	4 and 2	St Enodoc
1938	Miss E Corlett	Miss J Winn	2 and 1	Aldeburgh
1939–46	*No Championship owing to the Second World War*			

YEAR	WINNER	RUNNER-UP	MARGIN	VENUE
1947	M Wallis	Elizabeth Price	3 and 1	Ganton
1948	Frances Stephens	Zara Bolton	1 hole	Hayling Island
1949	Diana Critchley	Lady Katherine Cairns	3 and 2	Burnham and Berrow
1950	Hon Mrs A Gee	Pamela Davies	8 and 6	Sheringham
1951	Jeanne Bisgood	A Keiller	2 and 1	St Annes Old Links
1952	Pamela Davies	Jacqueline Gordon	6 and 5	Westward Ho!
1953	Jeanne Bisgood	J McIntyre	6 and 5	Prince's, Sandwich
1954	Frances Stephens	Elizabeth Price	37th hole	Woodhall Spa
1955	Frances Smith (née Stephens)	Elizabeth Price	4 and 3	Moortown
1956	Bridget Jackson	Ruth Ferguson	2 and 1	Hunstanton
1957	Jeanne Bisgood	Margaret Nichol	10 and 8	Bournemouth
1958	Angela Bonallack	Bridget Jackson	3 and 2	Formby
1959	Ruth Porter	Frances Smith	5 and 4	Aldeburgh
1960	Margaret Nichol	Angela Bonallack	3 and 1	Burnham and Berrow
1961	Ruth Porter	Peggy Reece	2 holes	Littlestone
1962	Jean Roberts	Angela Bonallack	3 and 1	Woodhall Spa
1963	Angela Bonallack	Elizabeth Chadwick	7 and 6	Liphook
1964	Marley Spearman	Mary Everard	6 and 5	Lytham St Annes
1965	Ruth Porter	G Cheetham	6 and 5	Whittington Barracks
1966	Julia Greenhalgh	Jean Holmes	3 and 1	Hayling Island
1967	Ann Irvin	Margaret Pickard (née Nichol)	3 and 2	Alwoodley
1968	Sally Barber	Dinah Oxley	5 and 4	Hunstanton
1969	Barbara Dixon	M Wenyon	6 and 4	Burnham and Berrow
1970	Dinah Oxley	Sally Barber	3 and 2	Rye
1971	Dinah Oxley	Sally Barber	5 and 4	Hoylake
1972	Mary Everard	Angela Bonallack	2 and 1	Woodhall Spa
1973	Mickey Walker	Carol Le Feuvre	6 and 5	Broadstone
1974	Ann Irvin	Jill Thornhill	1 hole	Sunningdale
1975	Beverly Huke	Lynne Harrold	2 and 1	Birkdale
1976	Lynne Harrold	Angela Uzielli	3 and 2	Hollinwell
1977	Vanessa Marvin	Mary Everard	1 hole	Burnham and Berrow
1978	Vanessa Marvin	Ruth Porter	2 and 1	West Sussex
1979	Julia Greenhalgh	Susan Hedges	2 and 1	Hoylake
1980	Beverley New	Julie Walker	3 and 2	Aldeburgh
1981	Diane Christison	S Cohen	2 holes	Cotswold Hills
1982	Julie Walker	C Nelson	4 and 3	Brancepeth Castle
1983	Linda Bayman	C Mackintosh	4 and 3	Hayling Island
1984	Claire Waite	Linda Bayman	3 and 2	Hunstanton
1985	Patricia Johnson	Linda Bayman	1 hole	Ferndown
1986	Jill Thornhill	Susan Shapcott	3 and 1	Prince's, Sandwich
1987	Joanne Furby	Maria King	4 and 3	Alwoodley
1988	Julie Wade	Susan Shapcott	19th hole	Little Aston
1989	Helen Dobson	Simone Morgan	4 and 3	Burnham and Berrow
1990	Angela Uzielli	Linzi Fletcher	2 and 1	Rye

English Ladies' Close Amateur Stroke Play Championship

INAUGURATED 1984

The Under-23 Stroke Play began in 1978 and was contested over three rounds. When the English Ladies' Stroke Play was inaugurated in 1984, the Under-23 was merged with it and both are now played over four rounds, with the Under-21 and Under-18 also played concurrently.

ELGA is also responsible for the Intermediate Match Play Championship, begun in 1982, for players aged between 18 and 25, the English Girls' Match Play (1964) and the recently started English Ladies' Seniors over 36 holes stroke play.

YEAR	WINNER	SCORE	VENUE
1984	Penny Grice	300	Moor Park
1985	Patricia Johnson	301	Church Brampton
1986	Susan Shapcott	301	Broadstone
1987	Julie Wade	296	Gosforth Park
1988	Sally Prosser	297	Wentworth
1989	Sara Robinson	302	Hollinwell
1990	Katie Tebbet	299	Saunton

English Ladies' Intermediate Championship

INAUGURATED 1982

YEAR	WINNER	MARGIN	VENUE
1982	Lesley Rhodes	19th hole	Headingley
1983	Laura Davies	2 and 1	Worksop
1984	Penny Grice	3 and 2	Whittington Barracks
1985	Sarah Lowe	2 and 1	Caldy
1986	Susan Moorcroft	6 and 5	Hexham
1987	Julie Wade	2 and 1	Sheringham
1988	Simone Morgan	20th hole	Enville, Staffs
1989	Lorna Fairclough	4 and 3	Warrington
1990	Linzi Fletcher	7 and 6	Whitley Bay

English Ladies' Under-23 Stroke Play Championship

INAUGURATED 1978

YEAR	WINNER	SCORE	VENUE
1978	S Bamford	228	Caldy
1979	B Cooper	223	Coxmoor
1980	B Cooper	226	Porters Park
1981	Janet Soulsby	220	Willesley Park
1982	M Gallagher	221	High Post
1983	Penny Grice	219	Hallamshire
1984	Patricia Johnson	300	Moor Park
1985	Patricia Johnson	301	Church Brampton
1986	Susan Shapcott	301	Broadstone
1987	Julie Wade	296	Gosforth Park
1988	Julie Wade	299	Wentworth
1989	Alison Shapcott	302	Hollinwell
1990	Katie Tebbet	299	Saunton

English Senior Ladies' Championship

INAUGURATED 1986

YEAR	WINNER	SCORE	VENUE
1986	Catherine Bailey	170	Broadstone
1987	Catherine Bailey	164	Gosforth Park
1988	A Thompson	158	Wentworth
1989	Catherine Bailey	163	Hollinwell
1990	A Thompson	162	Fairhaven

Irish Ladies' Championship

INAUGURATED 1894

The Irish Ladies were the first to hold a close championship, as early as 1894. Between 1899 and 1908 the winner was either Rhona Adair or May Hezlet, with one or the other two Hezlet sisters the runner-up. May beat her sister Florence twice in the final.

Between the wars no one player stood out, but afterwards, Philomena Garvey was a frequent winner – 14 victories in 18 years from 1946; she was never in the final without winning it! Since her day the two most frequent winners have been Mary McKenna, eight wins and four times runner-up, and Claire Hourihane, four wins and once the losing finalist. Mary McKenna has played more matches, 30, in the Curtis Cup than any other player except Anne Quast (USA). Most of the best Irish courses have been among the venues from the start.

The Irish Girls' Championship started in 1951, but was suspended from 1954 to 1960. Since then several of the winners have been successful in senior golf. The five District Tournaments are well supported.

YEAR	WINNER	RUNNER-UP	MARGIN	VENUE
1894	Miss Mullingan	Miss N Graham	3 and 2	Carnalea
1895	Miss Cox	Miss MacLaine	3 and 2	Portrush
1896	Miss N Graham	Miss E Brownrigg	4 and 3	Newcastle, Co Down
1897	Miss N Graham	Miss Magill	4 and 3	Dollymount
1898	Miss Magill	Miss M Hezlet	1 hole	Malone
1899	Miss M Hezlet	Miss R Adair	5 and 4	Newcastle, Co Down
1900	Miss R Adair	Miss V Hezlet	9 and 7	Portrush
1901	Miss R Adair	Miss F Walker-Leigh	4 and 2	Portmarnock
1902	Miss R Adair	Miss ME Stuart	9 and 7	Newcastle, Co Down
1903	Miss R Adair	Miss V Hezlet	7 and 5	Portrush
1904	Miss M Hezlet	Miss F Walker-Leigh	3 and 2	Lahinch
1905	Miss M Hezlet	Miss F Hezlet	2 and 1	Portsalon
1906	Miss M Hezlet	Miss F Hezlet	2 and 1	Newcastle, Co Down
1907	Miss F Walker-Leigh	Mrs Fitzgibbon	4 and 3	Dollymount
1908	Miss M Hezlet	Miss F Hezlet	5 and 4	Portrush
1909	Miss Ormsby	Miss V Hezlet	4 and 2	Lahinch
1910	Miss M Harrison	Miss Magill	5 and 4	Newcastle, Co Down
1911	Miss M Harrison	Miss F Walker-Leigh	6 and 4	Malahide
1912	Miss M Harrison	Mrs Cramsie	5 and 3	Portsalon
1913	Miss J Jackson	Miss M Harrison	4 and 3	Lahinch
1914	Miss J Jackson	Miss Meldon	3 and 2	Castlerock
1915–18	No championship owing to the Great War			
1919	Miss J Jackson	Mrs M Alexander	5 and 4	Portmarnock
1920	Miss J Jackson	Mrs Cramsie	5 and 4	Portrush
1921	Miss Stuart French	Miss M Fitzgibbon	4 and 3	Hermitage
1922	Mrs C Gotto	Mrs MR Hirsch	2 holes	Newcastle, Co Down
1923	Miss J Jackson	Mrs Babington	5 and 4	Portmarnock
1924	Miss CG Thornton	Miss Hewitt	4 and 3	Castlerock
1925	Miss J Jameson	Mrs JF Jameson	2 and 1	Lahinch
1926	Miss P Jameson	Mrs CH Murland	5 and 3	Newcastle, Co Down
1927	Miss McLoughlin	Miss F Blake	2 holes	Dollymount
1928	Mrs Dwyer	Mrs H Clark	3 and 2	Cork
1929	Mrs MA Hall	Miss I Taylor	1 hole	Rosapenna

YEAR	WINNER	RUNNER-UP	MARGIN	VENUE
1930	Mrs JB Walker	Mrs JF Jameson	2 and 1	Portmarnock
1931	Miss E Pentony	Mrs JH Todd	2 and 1	Rosses Point
1932	Miss B Latchford	Miss D Ferguson	7 and 5	Ballybunion
1933	Miss E Pentony	Miss F Blacke	3 and 2	Newcastle, Co Down
1934	Mrs P Sherlock Fletcher	Mrs JB Walker	3 and 2	Portmarnock
1935	Miss D Ferguson	Miss Ellis	2 and 1	Rospenna
1936	Miss C Tiernan	Miss S Moore	7 and 6	Ballybunion
1937	Mrs HV Glendinning	Mrs EL Kidd	37th hole	Portrush
1938	Mrs J Beck	Miss B Jackson	5 and 4	Portmarnock
1939	Miss C MacGeagh	Miss E Gildea	1 hole	Bundoran
1940–45	*No championship owing to the Second World War*			
1946	Philomena Garvey	Val Reddan (*née* Tiernan)	39th hole	Lahinch
1947	Philomena Garvey	Kitty Smye	5 and 4	Portrush
1948	Philomena Garvey	Val Reddan	9 and 7	Rosslare
1949	Kitty Smye	Barbara Beck	9 and 7	Baltray
1950	Philomena Garvey	Josephine Marks	6 and 4	Rosses Point
1951	Philomena Garvey	Dorothy Forster	12 and 10	Ballybunion
1952	Dorothy Forster	Kitty McCann (*née* Smye)	3 and 2	Newcastle, Co Down
1953	Philomena Garvey	Monica Hegarty	8 and 7	Rosslare
1954	Philomena Garvey	Dorothy Glendinning	13 and 12	Portmarnock
1955	Philomena Garvey	Audrey O'Donohoe	10 and 9	Rosses Point
1956	Pat O'Sullivan	Monica Hegarty	14 and 12	Killarney
1957	Philomena Garvey	Kitty McCann	3 and 2	Portrush
1958	Philomena Garvey	Zelie Fallon	7 and 6	Carlow
1959	Philomena Garvey	Helen Colhoun	12 and 10	Lahinch
1960	Philomena Garvey	Kitty McCann	5 and 3	Cork
1961	Kitty McCann	Ann Sweeney	5 and 3	Newcastle, Co Down
1962	Philomena Garvey	Moira Earner	7 and 6	Baltray
1963	Philomena Garvey	Elizabeth Barnett	9 and 7	Killarney
1964	Zelie Fallon	Pat O'Sullivan	37th hole	Portrush
1965	Elizabeth Purcell	Pat O'Sullivan	3 and 2	Mullingar
1966	Elaine Bradshaw	Pat O'Sullivan	3 and 2	Rosslare
1967	Gwen Brandom	Pat O'Sullivan	3 and 2	Castlerock
1968	Elaine Bradshaw	Mary McKenna	4 and 3	Lahinch
1969	Mary McKenna	Catherine Hickey	3 and 2	Ballybunion
1970	Philomena Garvey	Moira Earner	2 and 1	Portrush
1971	Elaine Bradshaw	Maisie Mooney	3 and 1	Baltray
1972	Mary McKenna	Ita Butler	5 and 4	Killarney
1973	Maisie Mooney	Mary McKenna	2 and 1	Bundoran
1974	Mary McKenna	Vivienne Singleton	3 and 2	Lahinch
1975	Mary Gorry	Elaine Bradshaw	1 hole	Tramore
1976	Claire Nesbitt	Mary McKenna	20th hole	Rosses Point
1977	Mary McKenna	Rhona Hegarty	2 holes	Ballybunion
1978	Mary Gorry	Ita Butler	4 and 3	Grange
1979	Mary McKenna	Claire Nesbitt	6 and 5	Donegal
1980	Claire Nesbitt	Claire Hourihane	1 hole	Lahinch
1981	Mary McKenna	Mary Kenny	1 hole	Laytown and Bettystown
1982	Mary McKenna	Maureen Madill	19th hole	Rosses Point
1983	Claire Hourihane	Valerie Hassett	6 and 4	Cork
1984	Claire Hourihane	Maureen Madill	19th hole	Rosses Point
1985	Claire Hourihane	Mary McKenna	4 and 3	Waterville
1986	Therese O'Reilly	Eavan Higgins	4 and 3	Castlerock
1987	Claire Hourihane	Catherine Hickey	5 and 4	Lahinch
1988	Laura Bolton	Eavan Higgins	2 and 1	Tramore
1989	Mary McKenna	Carol Wickham	19th hole	Westport
1990	Eileen Rose McDaid	Lesley Callen	2 and 1	The Island

Irish Ladies' Seniors

at Athlone, Co Roscommon

INAUGURATED 1988

YEAR	WINNER
1988	Margot Magan
1989	Dr Geraldine Costello
1990	Ann Heskin

Irish Ladies' Inter-Provincial Tournament

INAUGURATED 1964

YEAR	WINNER	VENUE
1964	Leinster	Carlow, Co Carlow
1965	Leinster	Carlow, Co Carlow
1966	Leinster	Louth, Co Louth
1967	Leinster	Lahinch, Co Clare
1968	Leinster	Rosses Point, Co Sligo
1969	*no matches*	
1970	Leinster	Tullamor, Co Offaly
1971	Ulster	Cork, Co Cork
1972	*no matches*	
1973	Leinster	Birr, Co Offaly
1974	Leinster	Athlone, Co Roscommon
1975	Leinster	Hermitage, Co Dublin
1976	Leinster	Kilkenny, Co Kilkenny
1977	Ulster	Connemara, Co Galway
(after a tie with Munster and Leinster)		
1978	Leinster	Mallow, Co Cork
1979	Leinster	Mullingar, Co Westmeath
1980	Munster	Waterford, Co Waterford
1981	Ulster	Rosses Point, Co Sligo
1982	Leinster	Athlone, Co Roscommon
1983	Leinster	Carlow, Co Carlow
1984	Leinster	Tullamore, Co Offaly
(after a tie with Munster and Ulster)		
1985	Munster	Clandyboye, Co Down
(after a tie with Leinster)		
1986	Munster	Cork, Co Cork
1987	Leinster	Dundalk, Co Louth
(after a tie with Munster and Ulster)		
1988	Leinster	Donegal, Co Donegal
1989	Ulster	Carlow, Co Carlow
1990	Leinster	Mullingar, Co Westmeath

Scottish Ladies' Close Amateur Championship

INAUGURATED 1903

Inaugurated in 1903, nearly twenty years before the Mens' Close Championship, some winners of the Scottish Ladies have been successful over long periods. Helen Holm, five times between 1930 and 1950, Jessie Valentine (*née* Anderson) six from 1938 to 1956 and Belle Robertson seven between 1965 to 1986 are the most prominent. Until well after the Second World War, the Championship was contested by match play throughout, but now, as with many others, 36 holes stroke play for all competitors produces the 32 who proceed to the match play stages.

The venues selected through the years have included nearly all the leading Scottish links courses with no ventures inland.

The Scottish LGU is also responsible for the Scottish Girls' Close Match Play Championship and the Scottish Girls' Open Stoke Play Championship, consisting of three rounds of 18 holes. While the latter is open, no winner has yet come from outside Scotland.

YEAR	WINNER	RUNNER-UP	MARGIN	VENUE
1903	Miss AM Glover	Miss MA Graham	1 hole	St Andrews
1904	Miss MA Graham	Miss M Bishop	6 and 5	Prestwick, St Nicholas
1905	Miss D Campbell	Miss MA Graham	19th hole	North Berwick
1906	Miss D Campbell	Miss AM Glover	3 and 1	Cruden Bay
1907	Miss FS Teacher	Miss D Campbell	21st hole	Troon
1908	Miss D Campbell	Miss MA Cairns	7 and 6	Gullane
1909	Miss EL Kyle	Miss D Campbell	3 and 1	Machrihanish
1910	Miss EL Kyle	Miss AM Glover	4 and 3	Nairn
1911	Miss E Grant-Suttie	Miss EL Kyle	1 hole	St Andrews
1912	Miss DM Jenkins	Miss M Neil Fraser	4 and 2	Lossiemouth
1913	Miss JW McCulloch	Miss R MacKintosh	4 and 3	Machrihanish
1914	Miss ER Anderson	Miss FS Teacher	20th hole	Muirfield
1915–19	*No Championship owing to the Great War*			
1920	Mrs JB Watson	Miss L Scroggie	5 and 3	Cruden Bay
1921	Mrs JB Watson	Mrs M Martin	1 hole	Machrihanish
1922	Mrs JB Watson	Miss A Kyle	2 and 1	St Andrews
1923	Mrs WH Nicholson	Mrs JB Watson	2 and 1	Lossiemouth
1924	Miss CPR Montgomery	Miss H Cameron	5 and 4	Turnberry
1925	Miss J Percy	Miss E Grant-Suttie	2 holes	Gullane
1926	Miss MJ Wood	Mrs J Cochrane	2 and 1	Cruden Bay
1927	Miss B Inglis	Miss H Cameron	1 hole	Machrihanish
1928	Miss JW McCulloch	Miss P Ramsay	3 and 1	St Andrews
1929	Mrs JB Watson	Miss D Park	3 and 1	Nairn
1930	Mrs AM Holm	Miss D Park	1 hole	Turnberry
1931	Miss J McCulloch	Miss D Park	19th hole	Gullane
1932	Mrs AM Holm	Mrs G Coates	23rd hole	Cruden Bay
1933	Miss MJ Couper	Mrs AM Holm	22nd hole	Turnberry
1934	Miss N Baird	Miss J Andrews	1 hole	North Berwick
1935	Miss M Robertson-Durham	Miss N Baird	20th hole	Lossiemouth
1936	Miss D Park	Miss CPR Montgomery	19th hole	Turnberry
1937	Mrs AM Holm	Mrs I Bowhill	3 and 2	Gleneagles
1938	Miss J Anderson	Mrs AM Holm	2 holes	Nairn
1939	Miss J Anderson	Miss CM Park	19th hole	Turnberry

YEAR	WINNER	RUNNER-UP	MARGIN	VENUE
1940–46	*No Championship owing to the Second World War*			
1947	Jean Donald	J Kerr	5 and 3	Elie
1948	Helen Holm	Vivien Falconer	5 and 4	Gleneagles
1949	Jean Donald	Helen Holm	6 and 4	Troon
1950	Helen Holm	Charlotte Beddows		
		(formerly Mrs JB Watson)	6 and 5	St Andrews
1951	Jessie Valentine (*née* Anderson)	Moira Paterson	3 and 2	Nairn
1952	Jean Donald	Marjory Peel	13 and 11	Gullane
1953	Jessie Valentine	Jean Donald	8 and 7	Carnoustie
1954	Marjory Peel	Jessie Valentine	7 and 6	Turnberry
1955	Jessie Valentine	Millicent Couper	8 and 6	North Berwick
1956	Jessie Valentine	Helen Holm	8 and 7	Dornoch
1957	Marigold Speir	Helen Holm	7 and 5	Troon
1958	Dorothea Sommerville	Janette Robertson	1 hole	Elie
1959	Janette Robertson	Belle McCorkindale	6 and 5	Nairn
1960	Janette Robertson	Dorothea Sommerville	2 and 1	Turnberry
1961	Janette Wright (*née* Robertson)	A Lurie	1 hole	St Andrews
1962	Joan Lawrence	Marjorie Draper	5 and 4	Dornoch
1963	Joan Lawrence	Belle Robertson		
		(*née* McCorkindale)	2 and 1	Troon
1964	Joan Lawrence	Ansley Reid	5 and 3	Gullane
1965	Belle Robertson	Joan Lawrence	5 and 4	Nairn
1966	Belle Robertson	Marjorie Fowler (*née* Draper)	2 and 1	Machrihanish
1967	Joan Hastings	Annette Laing	5 and 3	North Berwick
1968	Joan Smith	Joan Rennie (*née* Hastings)	10 and 9	Carnoustie
1969	Jean Anderson	Kathleen Lackie	5 and 4	West Kilbride
1970	Annette Laing	Belle Robertson	1 hole	Dunbar
1971	Belle Robertson	Marjory Ferguson	3 and 2	Dornoch
1972	Belle Robertson	Constance Lugton	5 and 3	Machrihanish
1973	Janette Wright	Dr Aileen Wilson	2 holes	St Andrews
1974	Dr Aileen Wilson	Kathleen Lackie	22nd hole	Nairn
1975	Lesley Hope	Joan Smith	1 hole	Elie
1976	Sandra Needham	Tina Walker	3 and 2	Machrihanish
1977	Constance Lugton	Muriel Thomson	1 hole	Dornoch
1978	Belle Robertson	Joan Smith	2 holes	Prestwick
1979	Gillian Stewart	Lesley Hope	2 and 1	Gullane
1980	Belle Robertson	Fiona Anderson	1 hole	Carnoustie
1981	Alison Gemmill	Wilma Aitken	2 and 1	Stranraer
1982	Jane Connachan	Pamela Wright	19th hole	Troon
1983	Gillian Stewart	Fiona Anderson	3 and 1	North Berwick
1984	Gillian Stewart	Alison Gemmill	3 and 2	Dornoch
1985	Alison Gemmill	Donna Thomson	2 and 1	Barassie
1986	Belle Robertson	Lesley Hope	3 and 2	St Andrews
1987	Fiona Anderson	Christine Middleton	4 and 3	Nairn
1988	Shirley Lawson	Fiona Anderson	3 and 1	Southerness
1989	Shirley Huggan	Lesley Anderson	5 and 4	Lossiemouth
1990	Elaine Farquharson	Shirley Huggan	3 and 2	Machrihanish

Ladies' Amateur Championship of Wales

INAUGURATED 1905

Founded in 1904, the Welsh Ladies' Close event was first played in 1905 at Penarth. The next year Blanche Duncan won the first of her five titles in seven years, the last one before her sister-in-law, Mrs John Duncan, won three times in the 1920s. In 32 years since 1950, the Championship has been largely the preserve of three competitors – Nancy Wright (*née* Cook), Pat Roberts and Audrey Briggs. In all but four of those years one of them has been in the final. Between them they have won fourteen and been beaten finalist also on fourteen occasions. Pat Roberts has been secretary of the Welsh LGU since 1971.

From 1979, the Rawlings sisters have taken over, Vicki (now Mrs Thomas) has won six times and Mandy, twice. In 1982 Vicki beat her sister in the final.

The Welsh Ladies' Open Amateur Stroke Play was first played in 1976 with the number of Welsh and English winners nearly level. The Welsh Girls' Match Play started in 1960. The Team Championship also originated in 1905. Teams of five from each club play singles matches on a knock-out basis.

YEAR	WINNER	RUNNER-UP	MARGIN	VENUE
1905	Miss E Young	Miss B Duncan	2 and 1	Penarth
1906	Miss B Duncan	Mrs Storry	5 and 4	Radyr
1907	Miss B Duncan	Mrs Wenham	5 and 4	Porthcawl
1908	Miss B Duncan	Miss Lloyd Williams	4 and 2	Conwy
1909	Miss B Duncan	Mrs Ellis Griffiths	4 and 3	Southerndown
1910	Miss Lloyd Roberts	Miss Leaver	4 and 3	Rhyl
1911	Miss Clay	Miss Allington-Hughes	2 and 1	Porthcawl
1912	Miss B Duncan	Miss P Williams	4 and 2	Llandrindod Wells
1913	Miss Brooke	Miss Shaw	19th hole	Rhos-on-Sea
1914	Mrs Vivian Phelips	Miss Morgan	4 and 3	Tenby
1915–9	*No Championship owing to the Great War*			
1920	Mrs Rupert Phillips	Miss M Marley	8 and 6	Porthcawl
1921	Miss M Marley	Mrs Rieben	7 and 5	Aberdovey
1922	Mrs J Duncan	Mrs H Franklyn Thomas	9 and 8	Llandrindod Wells
1923	Miss MR Cox	Miss M Marley	39th hole	Southerndown
1924	Miss MR Cox	Miss B Pyman	11 and 10	Rhyl
1925	Miss MR Cox	Mrs J Rhys	9 and 7	Tenby
1926	Miss MC Justice	Mrs A Smalley	4 and 3	Aberdovey
1927	Mrs J Duncan	Mrs Blake	1 hole	Porthcawl
1928	Mrs J Duncan	Mrs I Rieben	2 and 1	Harlech
1929	Mrs I Rieben	Miss B Pyman	2 and 1	Tenby
1930	Miss MJ Jeffreys	Mrs I Rieben	2 holes	Llandudno
1931	Miss MJ Jeffreys	Miss B Pyman	4 and 3	Southerndown
1932	Mrs I Rieben	Miss MJ Jeffreys	2 and 1	Aberdovey
1933	Miss MJ Jeffreys	Mrs Bridge	2 and 1	Porthcawl
1934	Mrs I Rieben	Miss MJ Jeffreys	3 and 2	Harlech
1935	*Abandoned in third round due to snowstorm*			Tenby
1936	Mrs I Rieben	Miss M Thompson	2 and 1	Prestatyn
1937	Mrs GS Emery	Dr P Whitaker	10 and 9	Porthcawl
1938	Miss B Pyman	Mrs GS Emery	1 hole	Llandudno
1939	Mrs B Burrell	Miss H Reynolds	2 and 1	Swansea

YEAR	WINNER	RUNNER-UP	MARGIN	VENUE
1940–46	*No Championship owing to the Second World War*			
1947	M Barron	E Jones	1 hole	Prestatyn
1948	N Seely	M Barron	12 and 11	Prestatyn
1949	S Bryan Smith	E Brown	3 and 2	Newport
1950	Dr Garfield Evans	Nancy Cook	2 and 1	Porthcawl
1951	E Bromley-Davenport	Nancy Cook	1 hole	Harlech
1952	Elsie Lever	Pat Roberts	6 and 5	Southerndown
1953	Nancy Cook	Elsie Lever	3 and 2	Llandudno
1954	Nancy Cook	E Brown	1 hole	Tenby
1955	Nancy Cook	Pat Roberts	2 holes	Holyhead
1956	Pat Roberts	M Barron	2 and 1	Porthcawl
1957	M Barron	Pat Roberts	6 and 4	Harlech
1958	Nancy Wright (*née* Cook)	Pat Roberts	1 hole	Newport
1959	Pat Roberts	A Gwyther	6 and 4	Conwy
1960	M Barron	E Brown	8 and 6	Tenby
1961	M Oliver	N Seddon	5 and 4	Aberdovey
1962	M Oliver	Pat Roberts	4 and 2	Radyr
1963	Pat Roberts	N Seddon	7 and 5	Harlech
1964	M Oliver	Nancy Wright	1 hole	Southerndown
1965	Nancy Wright	E Brown	3 and 2	Prestatyn
1966	Ann Hughes	Pat Roberts	5 and 4	Ashburnham
1967	Nancy Wright	C Phipps	21st hole	Harlech
1968	S Hales	Nancy Wright	3 and 2	Porthcawl
1969	Pat Roberts	Ann Hughes	3 and 2	Caernarvonshire
1970	Audrey Briggs	J Morris	19th hole	Newport
1971	Audrey Briggs	E Davies	2 and 1	Harlech
1972	Ann Hughes	J Rogers	3 and 2	Tenby
1973	Audrey Briggs	J John	3 and 2	Holyhead
1974	Audrey Briggs	Dr H Lyall	3 and 2	Ashburnham
1975	Ann Johnson (*née* Hughes)	K Rawlings	1 hole	Prestatyn
1976	Tegwen Perkins	Ann Johnson	4 and 2	Porthcawl
1977	Tegwen Perkins	P Whitley	5 and 4	Aberdovey
1978	Pamela Light	Audrey Briggs	2 and 1	Newport
1979	Vicki Rawlings	Audrey Briggs	2 holes	Caernarvonshire
1980	Mandy Rawlings	Audrey Briggs	2 and 1	Tenby
1981	Mandy Rawlings	Audrey Briggs	5 and 3	Harlech
1982	Vicki Thomas (*née* Rawlings)	Mandy Rawlings	7 and 6	Ashburnham
1983	Vicki Thomas	Tegwen Thomas (*née* Perkins)	1 hole	Llandudno
1984	Sharon Roberts	Karen Davies	5 and 4	Newport
1985	Vicki Thomas	S Jump	1 hole	Prestatyn
1986	Vicki Thomas	L Isherwood	7 and 6	Porthcawl
1987	Vicki Thomas	Sharon Roberts	3 and 1	Aberdovey
1988	Sharon Roberts	F Connor	4 and 2	Tenby
1989	Helen Lawson	Vicki Thomas	2 and 1	Conwy
1990	Sharon Roberts	Helen Wadsworth	3 and 2	Ashburnham

Welsh Ladies' Open Amateur Stroke Play Championship

INAUGURATED 1976

YEAR	WINNER	SCORE	VENUE
1976	Pamela Light	227	Aberdovey
1977	Julia Greenhalgh	239	Aberdovey
1978	Susan Hedges	208 (47 holes)	Aberdovey
1979	S Crowcroft	228	Aberdovey
1980	Tegwen Thomas	223	Aberdovey
1981	Vicki Thomas	224	Aberdovey
1982	Vicki Thomas	224	Aberdovey
1983	Jill Thornhill	239	Aberdovey
1984	Laura Davies	230	Aberdovey
1985	Carole Swallow	219	Aberdovey
1986	Helen Wadsworth	223	Aberdovey
1987	Susan Shapcott	225	Newport
1988	Susan Shapcott	218	Newport
1989	Vicki Thomas	220	Newport
1990	L Hackney	218	Newport

Ladies' County and District Championships

The LGU County organisations operate happily alongside their male counterparts and like them the LGU has not adjusted its county boundaries to include those formed in 1971, such as Avon, Merseyside and Cleveland. In addition there are certain anomalies in the areas where counties are paired. For instance, in the LGU Herefordshire clubs are in the Worcestershire Association and in the EGU they join Shropshire as one County Union. To emphasise the inconsistency the Shropshire PGA has an affiliation with Staffordshire.

The same thing occurs also in Scotland. Dumbarton and Argyll are one in the SLGU, whereas the SGU merges Argyll and Bute and has a separate championship for Dumbartonshire. In Wales the LGU county areas differ from those of the WGU, while the Irish Ladies go one better and have introduced a new Midlands 'province' to compete with the other four – Connacht, Leinster, Munster and Ulster.

As with so many British institutions, the LGU, the Home Unions and County Professional Associations recognise boundaries, but use them variously to suit themselves. Nevertheless together they form a strong basis of the game, their clubs being the nurseries of most successful amateurs and, in these days, also many of those who join the professional ranks.

English Ladies' County Championships

Most of the Ladies' County Championships were started between 1920 and 1926, following the first English Ladies' Championships in 1920, but four counties, Cornwall and Yorkshire in 1896, Isle of Wight 1897 and Midland Counties 1898 were the pioneers. Only six more, Lancashire 1907, Chester and Norfolk 1912, Gloucester and Somerset 1913 and Middlesex 1914 joined them before the first war. The reasons for so tentative a beginning are obscure. It may be that Cornwall and the Isle of Wight were early popular holiday centres; yet many of the twenty counties inaugurating championships in that decade also contained holiday areas. By 1937 each English county branch of the LGU had its championship, including a South-Western Counties group started in 1931. Since 1945, only the Channel Islands and South-Eastern areas have been added.

Women's county golf with its keen competitive element is the basis from which most top class women players are nurtured. The formation of the ELGA (English Ladies' Golf Association) in 1951, with Mrs Joan de Rothschild in the lead, has provided the organisation for competition at several levels of ability, including Senior and Girls, to the improvement and advantage of the ladies' game.

Bedfordshire Ladies' Championship

INAUGURATED 1923

YEAR	WINNER	VENUE	YEAR	WINNER	VENUE
1923	Mrs Antliff		1940–46	*Not played due to Second World War*	
1924	Mrs JP White		1947	Mrs Oakins	South Beds
1925	Miss M Dalton		1948	Miss Walsh	Dunstable
1926	Mrs Payne	South Beds	1949	Miss Walsh	Bedfordshire
1927	Mrs Antliff	Bedford & County	1950	Mrs Seale	Dunstable Downs
1928	Miss M Dalton	Dunstable	1951	Mrs Crew	John O'Gaunt
1929	Miss M Dalton	Bedfordshire	1952	Mrs Crew	South Beds
1930	Mrs Antliff	South Beds	1953	Mrs Crew	Bedfordshire
1931	Miss M Dalton	Bedford & County	1954	Mrs B Allen	Dunstable Downs
1932	Miss M Dalton	South Beds	1955	Mrs Arnold	Bedford & County
1933	Miss R Payne	Bedfordshire	1956	Mrs Greer	John O'Gaunt
1934	Miss M Dalton	Dunstable	1957	Mrs Greer	South Beds
1935	Mrs Hedges	Bedford & County	1958	Mrs FW Wood	Bedfordshire
1936	Miss B Gorrell	South Beds	1959	Mrs L Cook	Dunstable
1937	Miss N Sanderson	Bedford & County	1960	Mrs Turner	Bedford & County
1938	Mrs Crew	Dunstable	1961	Mrs Turner	John O'Gaunt
1939	Mrs Crew	Bedfordshire	1962	Mrs Bevan	South Beds

YEAR	WINNER	VENUE	YEAR	WINNER	VENUE
1963	Mrs Murray	Bedfordshire	1979	Mrs J Latch	Apsley Guise and
1964	Mrs Greer	Dunstable			Woburn Sands
1965	Mrs G Brandom	Bedford & County	1980	Miss S Kiddle	Dunstable Downs
1966	Mrs G Brandom	John O'Gaunt	1981	Miss S Kiddle	John O'Gaunt
1967	Mrs G Brandom	South Beds	1982	Miss S Kiddle	Bedfordshire
1968	Mrs S Kempster	Bedfordshire	1983	Mrs S White	
1969	Mrs S Kempster	Dunstable Downs		(née Kiddle)	Bedfordshire
1970	Mrs B Hawkins	Bedford & County	1984	Mrs S White	Aspley Guise and
1971	Mrs S Kempster	John O'Gaunt			Woburn Sands
1972	Mrs P Deman	South Beds	1985	Mrs S White	John O'Gaunt
1973	Mrs J Hawkins	Bedfordshire	1986	Mrs C Westgate	South Beds
1974	Mrs S Kempster	Bedford & County	1987	Mrs S White	Bedfordshire
1975	Mrs P Deman	Dunstable Downs	1988	Miss S Cormack	Bedford & County
1976	Mrs S Kempster	John O'Gaunt	1989	Miss T Gale	Dunstable Downs
1977	Mrs P Deman	Bedfordshire	1990	Mrs C Cummings	Aspley Guise and
1978	Mrs P Deman	Bedford & County			Woburn Sands

Berkshire Ladies' Championship

INAUGURATED 1925

YEAR	WINNER	VENUE	YEAR	WINNER	VENUE
1925	Mrs Oldman	Sonning	1964	Mrs AC Marks	Temple
1926	Mrs Morris	Sonning	1965	Mrs M Garnett	East Berks
1927	Mrs Morris	Sonning	1966	Mrs D O'Brien	Sunningdale
1928	Miss J Cave	Maidenhead	1967	Mrs W Henney	Calcot
1929	Mrs Morris	Maidenhead	1968	Mrs M Garnett	The Berkshire
1930	Miss J Cave	Sonning	1969	Mrs D Hanbury	The Berkshire
1931	Miss J Cave	Sonning	1970	Mrs M Garnett	The Berkshire
1932	Miss J Cave	Maidenhead	1971	Mrs D Hanbury	The Berkshire
1933	Miss Timberg	The Berkshire	1972	Mrs D Hanbury	The Berkshire
1934	Miss Slade	Calcot	1973	Mrs P Cardy	The Berkshire
1935	Miss Timberg	Sonning	1974	Mrs Leatham	The Berkshire
1936	Miss Timberg	Temple	1975	Miss S Jolly	The Berkshire
1937	Miss N Gibbons	Calcot	1976	Mrs A Uzielli	The Berkshire
1938	Miss N Gibbons	East Berks	1977	Mrs A Uzielli	The Berkshire
1939	Miss Stokes	Temple	1978	Mrs A Uzielli	East Berks
1940–49	Not played due to the Second World War		1979	Mrs A Uzielli	The Berkshire
1950	Mrs Tegner	Ascot	1980	Mrs A Uzielli	The Berkshire
1951	Miss Bryant	Temple	1981	Mrs A Uzielli	The Berkshire
1952	Mrs Simmons	East Berks	1982	Mrs C Caldwell	The Berkshire
1954	Miss Bryant	East Berks	1983	Mrs A Uzielli	The Berkshire
1955	Mrs Van Oss	The Berkshire	1984	Mrs A Uzielli	East Berks
1956	Miss Bryant	Calcot	1985	Mrs A Uzielli	Reading
1958	Miss I Clifton	East Berks	1986	Mrs A Uzielli	Temple
1959	Mrs E Simmons	Ascot	1987	Mrs A Uzielli	Calcot Park
1960	Mrs M Garnett	Sonning	1988	Miss T Smith	The Berkshire
1961	Mrs D Buchanan	Sunningdale	1989	Miss L Watson	Sunningdale
1962	Miss E Clifton	The Berkshire	1990	Mrs A Uzielli	Sonning
1963	Mrs AC Marks	East Berks			

Bucks Ladies' Championship

INAUGURATED 1924

YEAR	WINNER	VENUE	YEAR	WINNER	VENUE
1924	Mrs Kelway Bamber	Denham	1961	Mrs E Braithwaite	Denham
1925	Miss P Cotgrave	Beaconsfield	1962	Mrs AWH Baucher	Beaconsfield
1926	Mrs Kelway Bamber	Gerrards Cross	1963	Mrs AWH Baucher	Stoke Poges
1927	Mrs Kelway Bamber	Stoke Poges	1964	Miss A Mobbs	Burnham Beeches
1928	Mrs Gold	Denham	1965	Mrs B Dutton	Denham
1929	Not played		1966	Miss A Mobbs	Beaconsfield
1930	Mrs Adams	Beaconsfield	1967	Miss A Mobbs	Stoke Poges
1931	Mrs Gold	Stoke Poges	1968	Mrs RB Parton	
1932	Mrs Gold	Denham		(née Mobbs)	Burnham Beeches
1933	Mrs Greenly	Burnham Beeches	1969	Mrs P Newman	Denham
1934	Mrs Gold	Harewood Downs	1970	Mrs AWH Baucher	Beaconsfield
1935	Mrs O Jones	Stoke Poges	1971	Mrs M Baxter	Stoke Poges
1936	Mrs Gold	Burnham Beeches	1972	Mrs J Marshall	Burnham Beeches
1937	Mrs Gold	Beaconsfield	1973	Mrs G Gordon	Denham
1938	Mrs A Scott	Denham	1974	Miss L Harrold	Beaconsfield
1939	Mrs Barnes	Burnham	1975	Miss L Harrold	Stoke Poges
1940–46	*Not played due to Second World War*		1976	Miss L Harrold	Burnham Beeches
1947	Mrs Gold	Denham	1977	Miss L Harrold	Denham
1948	Mrs Whitworth Jones		1978	Mrs M Purdy	Ellesborough
1949	Mrs Whitworth		1979	Miss J Lee	Flackwell Heath
	Jones	Stoke Poges	1980	Mrs K Copley	Gerrards Cross
1950	Mrs Gold	Denham	1981	Miss J Warren	Harewood Downs
1951	Mrs Gold	Beaconsfield	1982	Miss J Warren	Stoke Poges
1952	Mrs Braddon	Burnham Beeches	1983	Miss G Bonallack	Woburn
1953	Miss DM Speir	Burnham Beeches	1984	Miss J Warren	Beaconsfield
1954	Mrs WM Paul	Denham	1985	Miss E Franklin	Buckingham
1955	Mrs CW Stothert	Beaconsfield	1986	Miss A Tyreman	Burnham Beeches
1956	Mrs AWH Baucher	Burnham Beeches	1987	Mrs C Watson	Denham
1957	Mrs AWH Baucher	Denham	1988	Miss C Hourihane	Ellesborough
1958	Mrs M Baxter	Beaconsfield	1989	Miss C Hourihane	Flackwell Heath
1959	Miss A Mobbs	Stoke Poges	1990	Mrs C Watson	Gerrards Cross
1960	Miss A Mobbs	Burnham Beeches			

Cambridgeshire and Hunts Ladies' Championship

INAUGURATED 1932

YEAR	WINNER	VENUE	YEAR	WINNER	VENUE
1932	Mrs AB Coote	Gog Magog	1937	Miss Goodliff	Gog Magog
1933	Mrs WB Carter	Gog Magog	1938	Miss D Drew	Gog Magog
1934	Mrs Hamblyn Smith	Gog Magog	1939	Miss D Drew	Gog Magog
1935	Mrs Hamblyn Smith	Gog Magog	1940–46	*Not played due to Second World War*	
1936	Mrs WB Carter	Gog Magog	1947	Mrs Holland	Gog Magog

YEAR	WINNER	VENUE	YEAR	WINNER	VENUE
1948	Mrs Baker	Gog Magog	1970	Mrs M Gray	Links (Newmarket)
1949	Mrs A Newport	Gog Magog	1971	Mrs S Stephenson	
1950	Mrs Holland	Links (Newmarket)	1972	Mrs M Gray	Links (Newmarket)
1951	Mrs Baker	Gog Magog	1973	Mrs D Baker	Gog Magog
1952	Mrs Holland	Newmarket	1974	Miss Julie Walter	Royston
1953	Mrs Holland	Gog Magog	1975	Miss M Maddocks	Links (Newmarket)
1954	Mrs Hill	Links (Newmarket)	1976	Miss Julie Walter	Ely
1955	Mrs Croxton	Gog Magog	1977	Miss Julie Walter	Links (Newmarket)
1956	Mrs Baker	Links (Newmarket)	1978	Miss Julie Walter	Gog Magog
1957	Mrs Baker	Gog Magog	1979	Miss Julie Walter	Royston
1958	Mrs Baker	Links (Newmarket)	1980	Miss J Richards	Ely
1959	Mrs Baker	Gog Magog	1981	Miss Julie Walter	Saffron Walden
1960	Mrs Thomas	Links (Newmarket)	1982	Miss Julie Walter	Links (Newmarket)
1961	Mrs Croxton	Gog Magog	1983	Miss Julie Walter	Royston
1962	Mrs Baker	Links (Newmarket)	1984	Miss Julie Walter	Gog Magog
1963	Mrs Nan Richmond	Gog Magog	1985	Miss Julie Walter	Links (Newmarket)
1964	Miss Janet Peck	Links (Newmarket)	1986	Miss Julie Walter	Ely City
1965	Mrs J Sedgwick	Gog Magog	1987	Mrs R Farrow	Saffron Walden
1966	Mrs VJ Mackenzie	Gog Magog	1988	Miss S Meadows	Gog Magog
1967	Mrs VJ Mackenzie	Links (Newmarket)	1989	Miss J Hatcher	Ely City
1968	Mrs VJ Mackenzie	Links (Newmarket)	1990	Miss Julie Walter	St Neots
1969	Mrs J Honey	Gog Magog			

Channel Islands Ladies' Championship

INAUGURATED 1937

YEAR	WINNER	VENUE	YEAR	WINNER	VENUE
1937	Mrs JP Ross	La Moye	1968	Mrs A Lindsay	Royal Guernsey
1938	Mrs HM de la Rue	Royal Guernsey	1969	Mrs A Lindsay	La Moye
1939	Mrs HP Ross	Royal Jersey	1970	Mrs A Lindsay	Royal Guernsey
1940–48	*Not played due to Second World War*		1971	Mrs A Lindsay	Royal Jersey
1949	Mrs NB Grant	La Moye	1972	Mrs A Lindsay	Royal Guernsey
1950	Mrs JA McDade	Royal Guernsey	1973	Mrs A Lindsay	Royal Jersey
1951	Mrs WF Mauger	Royal Jersey	1974	Mrs P Haley	Royal Jersey
1952	Mrs DWM Randell	Royal Guernsey	1975	Miss M Darbyshire	Royal Jersey
1953	Mrs JA McDade	La Moye	1976	Miss M Darbyshire	Royal Guernsey
1954	Mrs DWM Randell	Royal Guernsey	1977	Miss M Darbyshire	La Moye
1955	Mrs D Porter	Royal Jersey	1978	Mrs E Roberts	Royal Guernsey
1956	Mrs JA McDade	Royal Guernsey	1979	Mrs J Bunbury	Royal Jersey
1957	Mrs JA McDade	La Moye	1980	Mrs E Roberts	Royal Guernsey
1958	Mrs JA McDade	Royal Guernsey	1981	Miss L Cummins	La Moye
1959	Hon Mrs Siddeley	Grouville	1982	Miss V Bougourd	
1960	Miss P Stacey	Royal Guernsey	1983	Mrs D Heaton	
1961	Mrs D Porter	La Moye	1984	Mrs E Roberts	Royal Guernsey
1962	Miss P Stacey	Royal Guernsey	1985	Miss L Cummins	La Moye
1963	Mrs JA McDade	Royal Jersey	1986	Miss V Bougourd	Royal Guernsey
1964	Mrs A Lindsay	Royal Guernsey	1987	Miss L Cummins	Royal Jersey
1965	Mrs A Lindsay	La Moye	1988	Miss L Cummins	Royal Guernsey
1966	Mrs A Lindsay	Royal Guernsey	1989	Miss L Cummins	La Moye
1967	Mrs A Lindsay	Grouville	1990	Miss L Cummins	Royal Guernsey

Cheshire County Ladies' Championship

INAUGURATED 1912

YEAR	WINNER	VENUE	YEAR	WINNER	VENUE
1912	Miss G Ravenscroft	Wallasey	1956	Miss M Wolff	Delamere Forest
1913	Miss G Ravenscroft	Wallasey	1957	Miss Lewis	Wilmslow
1914	Miss G Ravenscroft	Wallasey	1958	Miss S McNicoll	Hoylake
1915–19	*Not played due to Great War*		1959	Miss C Grott	Prestbury
1920	Mrs Temple-Dobell	Wallasey	1960	Mrs T Briggs	Wallasey
1921	Mrs Temple-Dobell	Wallasey	1961	Mrs C Comboy	Sandiway
1922	Mrs A Macbeth	Wallasey	1962	Mrs C Comboy	Hoylake
1923	Mrs A Macbeth	Wallasey	1963	Miss E Chadwick	Mere
1924	Miss D Chambers	Wilmslow	1964	Miss E Chadwick	Hoylake
1925	Miss Bridgford	Wallasey	1965	Miss E Chadwick	Wilmslow
1926	Mrs Temple-Dobell	Stockport	1966	Miss E Chadwick	Hoylake
1927	Mrs A Macbeth	Hoylake	1967	Miss E Chadwick	Sandiway
1928	Mrs Temple-Dobell	Sandiway	1968	Mrs C Comboy	Hoylake
1929	Mrs Clement	Hoylake	1969	Mrs C Comboy	Wilmslow
1930	Mrs Cooper	Prestbury & Upton	1970	Mrs C Comboy	Eaton
1931	Mrs Clement	Wallasey	1971	Mrs A Briggs	Bramall Park
1932	Mrs A Macbeth	Sandiway	1972	Dr H Lyall	Hoylake
1933	Miss E Wilson	Hoylake	1973	Mrs A Briggs	Mere
1934	Mrs Clement	Prestbury & Upton	1974	Mrs S Graveley	Delamere Forest
1935	Mrs A Macbeth	Hoylake	1975	Mrs E Wilson	Wilmslow
1936	Mrs Hartley	Wilmslow	1976	Mrs A Briggs	Caldy
1937	Mrs A Macbeth	Wallasey	1977	Miss H Latham	Stockport
1938	Mrs Whitfield	Mere	1978	Mrs J Hughes	Wallasey
1939	Mrs JB Hartley	Wallasey	1979	Miss H Latham	Wilmslow
1940–46	*Not played due to Second World War*		1980	Mrs A Briggs	Hoylake
1947	Miss J Pemberton	Prestbury & Upton	1981	Mrs A Briggs	Sandiway
1948	Miss J Pemberton	Hoylake	1982	Miss H Latham	Wallasey
1949	Mrs Cowper	Mere	1983	Miss H Latham	Prestbury
1950	Mrs Horabin	Hoylake	1984	Miss J Hill	Caldy
1951	Miss B Lloyd	Prestbury & Upton	1985	Miss L Percival	Prestbury
1952	Mrs Horabin	Hoylake	1986	Miss J Hill	Warrington
1953	Mrs M Appleby	Mere	1987	Miss S Robinson	Wilmslow
1954	Miss A Christian-Jones	Hoylake	1988	Miss J Morley	Hoylake
1955	Miss B Lloyd	Sandiway	1989	Miss J Morley	Mere
			1990	Miss J Morley	Wallasey

Cornwall Ladies' Championship

INAUGURATED 1896

YEAR	WINNER	VENUE	YEAR	WINNER	VENUE
1896	Miss Every	Royal Cornwall	1949	Mrs Wills	Lelant
1897	Miss Parker Smith	Bude	1950	Miss M Roskrow	Looe Bin Down
1898	Miss Parker Smith	Falmouth	1951	Miss H Trant	Trevose
1899	Miss NM Carter	Lelant	1952	Miss M Roskrow	Tehidy Park
1900	Miss Parker Smith	Royal Cornwall	1953	Miss M Roskrow	Carlyon Bay
1901	Miss O Miles	Bude	1954	Miss B Soper	St Enodoc
1902	Miss O Miles	Falmouth	1955	Miss M Roskrow	Newquay
1903	Mrs Michael	Lelant	1956	Miss M Roskrow	Lelant
1904	Miss O Miles	Newquay	1957	Miss M Roskrow	Trevose
1905	Miss KS Horn	Royal Cornwall	1958	Miss M Roskrow	Tehidy Park
1906	Miss O Miles	Bude	1959	Miss M Roskrow	St Enodoc
1907	Miss G Cary	Mullion	1960	Mrs J Rodgers	Newquay
1908	Miss KS Horn	Lelant	1961	Miss M Roskrow	Lelant
1909	Miss HS Rogers	Newquay	1962	Miss M Roskrow	St Enodoc
1910	Miss HS Rogers	Royal Cornwall	1963	Miss M Roskrow	Tehidy Park
1911	Miss Hardwick	Bude	1964	Mrs WA Tomlinson	Trevose
1912	Miss HS Rogers	Falmouth	1965	Miss M Roskrow	Newquay
1913	Miss O M Rogers	Lelant	1966	Miss M Roskrow	Lelant
1914–19	*Not played due to Great War*		1967	Miss E Luxon	Trevose
1920	Mrs Wise	St Enodoc	1968	Mrs MC Rowe	Tehidy Park
1921	Mrs Le Messurier	Bude	1969	Miss S Mitchell	St Enodoc
1922	Mrs Wise	Lelant	1970	Mrs D Luxon	Newquay
1923	Mrs Le Messurier	Newquay	1971	Mrs D Luxon	Lelant
1924	Mrs Wallace	St Austell	1972	Miss S Mitchell	Trevose
1925	Mrs Prideaux	Mullion	1973	Mrs J Clowes	Tehidy Park
1926	Mrs VB Hilton	St Enodoc	1974	Miss J Dodd	St Enodoc
1927	Miss Notman	Bude	1975	Miss E Luxon	Newquay
1928	Mrs HS Prideaux	Lelant	1976	Miss J Ryder	Lelant
1929	Miss E Ratcliffe	Newquay	1977	Miss J Ryder	Carlyon Bay
1930	Miss Cornwell	Camborne	1978	Miss S Cann	Tehidy Park
1931	Miss E Ratcliffe	Mullion	1979	Miss L Moore	Trevose
1932	Mrs Cornelius	St Enodoc	1980	Miss L Moore	St Enodoc
1933	Miss Cornwell	Bude	1981	Miss L Moore	Newquay
1934	Mrs Cornelius	St Austell	1982	Miss S Cann	Lelant
1935	Miss E Ratcliffe	Lelant	1983	Miss J Ryder	Launceston
1936	Miss E Ratcliffe	Newquay	1984	Miss J Fernley	Tehidy Park
1937	Miss K Roskrow	Camborne	1985	Miss J Fernley	Bude
1938	Miss K Roskrow	Trevose	1986	Miss J Ryder	Newquay
1939	Miss M Roskrow	Mullion	1987	Miss J Ryder	Lelant
1940–46	*Not played due to Second World War*		1988	Mrs S Currie	St Enodoc
1947	Miss M Roskrow	St Enodoc	1989	Mrs S Currie	Tehidy Park
1948	Miss M Roskrow	Newquay	1990	Mrs S Currie	Launceston

Cumbria Ladies' Championship

INAUGURATED 1928

YEAR	WINNER	VENUE	YEAR	WINNER	VENUE
1928	Miss M Howe	Carlisle	1963	Mrs J Stafford	Seascale
1929	Miss E Hartlet	Cockermouth	1964	Miss MA Peile	Penrith
1930	Miss M Howe	Silloth	1965	Mrs WJ Ward	Silloth
1931	Miss M Howe	Penrith	1966	Miss P Brough	Carlisle
1932	Mrs RD Burgess	Carlisle	1967	Miss P Brough	Seascale
1933	Mrs D Jordan	Cockermouth	1968	Miss P Brough	Penrith
1934	Miss M Howe	Penrith	1969	Miss MA Peile	Silloth
1935	Miss H Howe	Silloth	1970	Miss P Brough	Carlisle
1936	Miss LB Clark		1971	Miss P Brough	Seascale
1937	Miss LB Clark	Carlisle	1972	Miss M Stavert	Penrith
1938	Miss LB Clark	Silloth	1973	Miss M Stavert	Silloth
1939	Miss LB Clark	Penrith	1974	Miss H Long	Carlisle
1940–46	*Not played due to Second World War*		1975	Miss J Allison	Seascale
1947	Miss H Scott	Silloth	1976	Miss J Allison	Penrith
1948	Miss H Scott	Penrith	1977	Miss H Long	Silloth
1949	Miss JI Johnstone	Carlisle	1978	Miss N Pieri	Carlisle
1950	Miss LB Clark	Workington	1979	Miss D Thomson	Seascale
1951	Miss LB Clark	Silloth	1980	Miss D Thomson	Penrith
1952	Miss LBClark	Penrith	1981	Miss D Thomson	Silloth
1953	Miss LB Clark	Carlisle	1982	Miss D Thomson	Carlisle
1954	Mrs PE Gillman	Penrith	1983	Miss P Brumwell	Seascale
1955	Miss LB Clark	Silloth	1984	Miss D Thomson	Workington
1956	Miss LB Clark	Carlisle	1985	Miss J Currie	Carlisle
1957	Mrs JH French	Penrith	1986	Mrs H Porter	Brampton
1958	Miss LB Clark	Silloth	1987	Miss J McColl	Silloth
1959	Miss LB Clark	Carlisle	1988	Miss D Thomson	Penrith
1960	Mrs J Stafford	Penrith	1989	Miss S Tuck	Seascale
1961	Miss LB Clark	Silloth	1990	Miss S Tuck	Workington
1962	Miss LB Clark	Carlisle			

Derbyshire Ladies' Championship

INAUGURATED 1921

YEAR	WINNER	VENUE	YEAR	WINNER	VENUE
1921	Mrs W Abell	Chevin	1931	Miss G Craddock-Hartopp	Derbyshire
1922	Mrs Fryer	Derbyshire	1932	Miss G Craddock-Hartopp	Chevin
1923	Mrs Farrington	Chesterfield			
1924	Miss Bennett	Chevin	1933	Miss Spalding	Buxton and High Peak
1925	Miss E Wilson	Burton-on-Trent			
1926	Miss E Wilson	Matlock	1934	Miss G Craddock-Hartopp	Burton-on-Trent
1927	Miss Reah	Erewash Valley			
1928	Mrs Ellis	Markeaton	1935	Miss B Newell	Derby Municipal
1929	Miss G Craddock-Hartopp	Burton-on-Trent	1936	Miss P Shand	Mickleover
1930	Mrs Ellis	Markeaton	1937	Miss J Hives	Matlock

YEAR	WINNER	VENUE	YEAR	WINNER	VENUE
1938	Miss J Hives	Erewash Valley	1968	Hon Mrs J Gee	Chesterfield
1939–46	Not played due to Second World War		1969	Miss M Wenyon	Buxton and High
1947	Mrs A Gee				Peak
	(née Hives)	Cavendish	1970	Miss D Rose	Burton-on-Trent
1948	Mrs A Gee	Chevin	1971	Mrs EMJ Wenyon	Erewash Valley
1949	Mrs A Gee	Chesterfield	1972	Miss M Mason	Matlock
1950	Mrs A Gee	Buxton and High	1973	Miss E Clark	Kedleston Park
		Peak	1974	Miss E Colledge	Derby
1951	Mrs A Gee	Burton-on-Trent	1975	Mrs A Bemrose	Chevin
1952	Mrs A Gee	Matlock	1976	Mrs M Close	Chesterfield
1953	Hon Mrs J Gee	Erewash Valley	1977	Mrs M Close	Mickleover
1954	Mrs EM Jones	Derby Municipal	1978	Mrs M Close	Cavendish
1955	Mrs J Dickie	Erewash Valley	1979	Mrs M Close	Burton-on-Trent
1956	Hon Mrs J Gee	Burton-on-Trent	1980	Miss A Howe	Matlock
1957	Mrs ECS Pedley	Kedleston Park	1981	Miss A Howe	Erewash Valley
1958	Hon Mrs J Gee	Cavendish	1982	Miss V McWilliams	Kedleston Park
1959	Mrs R Gascoyne	Chevin	1983	Miss J Williams	Buxton and High
1960	Mrs JH Gibbs	Chesterfield			Peak
1961	Hon Mrs J Gee	Buxton and High	1984	Miss J Williams	Chesterfield
		Peak	1985	Miss L Holmes	Mickleover
1962	Mrs J Burns	Erewash Valley	1986	Miss E Robinson	Chevin
1963	Hon Mrs J Gee	Burton-on-Trent	1987	Miss E Clark	Burton-on-Trent
1964	Hon Mrs J Gee	Derby	1988	Miss A Howe	Cavendish
1965	Miss M Grey	Kedleston Park	1989	Miss D Andrews	Matlock
1966	Hon Mrs J Gee	Chevin	1990	Miss D Andrews	Kedleston Park
1967	Miss M Wenyon	Cavendish			

Devon Ladies' Championship

INAUGURATED 1900

YEAR	WINNER	VENUE	YEAR	WINNER	VENUE
1922	Mrs Dering	Budleigh Salterton	1951	Miss M Taylor	Westward Ho!
1923	Mrs Dering	Yelverton	1952	Mrs Anstey	The Warren
1924	Miss Hewitt	Saunton	1953	Mrs Anstey	Budleigh Salterton
1925	Miss Hewitt	Churston	1954	Mrs Anstey	Thurleston
1926	Miss M Hingston	Budleigh Salterton	1955	Miss P Morris	Saunton
1927	Mrs S H Murphy	Tavistock	1956	Miss P Morris	
1928	Miss P Williams	Westward Ho!	1957	Miss A Nicholson	Exeter
1929	Mrs Dering	Torquay	1958	Mrs B Ord	Tavistock
1930	Miss B Radford	Exeter	1959	Mrs K Sharp	Westward Ho!
1931	Miss L Foster	Thurlestone	1960	Mrs Anstey	Churston
1932	Miss B Radford	Westward Ho!	1961	Mrs Greenwood	Budleigh Salterton
1933	Miss P Williams	Churston	1962	Mrs R Emerson	Yelverton
1934	Miss B Radford	Budleigh Salterton	1963	Mrs TW Slater	Saunton
1935	Miss P Williams	Yelverton	1964	Miss J Buswell	Churston
1936	Miss P Williams	Saunton	1965	Mrs Anstey	Teignmouth
1937	Miss Dent	Dawlish	1966	Mrs Anstey	Yelverton
1938	Miss Dent	Budleigh Salterton	1967	Mrs Fox	Westward Ho!
1939	Miss M Foster	Thurleston	1968	Mrs J Mason	Torquay
1940–46	Not played due to Second World War		1969	Mrs J Mason	Exeter
1947	Mrs Ord	Westward Ho!	1970	Mrs J Mason	Yelverton
1948	Miss Pyman	Churston	1971	Mrs J Dymond	Tiverton
1949	Miss M Taylor	Exeter	1972	Mrs B Saltz	Teignmouth
1950	Mrs Anstey	Yelverton	1973	Mrs R Coleman	Budleigh Salterton

YEAR	WINNER	VENUE	YEAR	WINNER	VENUE
1974	Mrs J Lawson	Thurleston	1983	Miss J Hurley	Westward Ho!
1975	Mrs J Mason	Westward Ho!	1984	Miss J Hurley	Churston
1976	Miss M Wardrop	Churston	1985	Miss L Lines	Tiverton
1977	Mrs J Mason	Exeter	1986	Miss J Hurley	Bigbury
1978	Mrs D Baxter	Yelverton	1987	Miss G Jenkinson	Saunton
1979	Miss S Tyler	Saunton	1988	Miss J Hurley	Teignmouth
1980	Mrs J Mason	Teignmouth	1989	Miss S Germain	Budleigh Salterton
1981	Miss C Stephens	Budleigh Salterton	1990	Miss V Holloway	Thurleston
1982	Miss J Hurley	Thurleston			

Dorset Ladies' Championship

INAUGURATED 1923

YEAR	WINNER	VENUE	YEAR	WINNER	VENUE
1923	Miss Arkell	Broadstone	1960	Mrs J Cooper	Yeovil
1924	Miss Arkell	Came Down	1962	Mrs PM Crow	Ferndown
1925	Mrs Peppercorn	Parkstone	1963	Mrs PM Crow	Broadstone
1926	Mrs Morant	Ferndown	1964	Mrs J Sugen	Came Down
1927	Mrs Morant	Broadstone	1965	Mrs S Smith	
1928	Miss M Beard	Came Down	1966	Miss B Dixon	Parkstone
1929	Miss K Beard	Parkstone	1967	Mrs PM Crow	Broadstone
1930	Miss K Beard	Ferndown	1968	Miss B Dixon	Ferndown
1931	Mrs Latham Hall	Broadstone	1969	Mrs A Humphreys	Came Down
1932	Mrs Morant	Came Down	1970	Miss B Dixon	Sherborne
1933	Mrs Latham Hall	Parkstone	1971	Mrs PM Crow	Parkstone
1934	Miss Arkell	Ferndown	1972	Miss D Chalkley	Broadstone
1935	Mrs Jones	Came Down	1973	Mrs P Crow	Came Down
1936	Mrs Morant	Broadstone	1974	Mrs W Russell	Yeovil
1937	Mrs Jones	Parkstone	1975	Mrs J Sugden	Ferndown
1938	Mrs C Beard	Came Down	1976	Mrs J Sugden	Sherborne
1939	Mrs C Beard	Ferndown	1977	Mrs W Russell	Lyme Regis
1940–46	Not played due to Second World War		1978	Mrs W Russell	Parkstone
1947	Miss Bannister	Broadstone	1979	Miss S Reeks	Isle of Purbeck
1948	Mrs Stuart Smith	Parkstone	1980	Mrs C Stirling	Came Down
1949	Mrs McPherson	Ferndown	1981	Mrs R Page	Weymouth
1950	Mrs McPherson	Broadstone	1982	Mrs B Langley	Yeovil
1951	Mrs Stuart Smith	Parkstone	1983	Mrs J Sugden	Broadstone
1952	Mrs PM Crow	Came Down	1984	Miss S Lowe	Ferndown
1953	Dr E Kyle	Ferndown	1985	Miss S Lowe	Came Down
1954	Mrs PM Crow	Broadstone	1986	Miss H Delew	Yeovil
1955	Mrs M Crow	Came Down	1987	Miss J Sugden	Parkstone
1956	Mrs PM Crow	Parkstone	1988	Miss H Delew	Broadstone
1957	Miss J Alexander	Broadstone	1989	Miss T Loveys	Ferndown
1958	Mrs S Smith	Ferndown	1990	Miss T Loveys	Lyme Regis
1959	Mrs J Cooper	Came Down			

Durham Ladies' Championship

INAUGURATED 1923

YEAR	WINNER	VENUE	YEAR	WINNER	VENUE
1923	Miss Walker	Seaton Crew	1961	Mrs Riddell	South Moor
1924	Miss S Newlands	Dinsdale Spa	1962	Miss E Reed	Seaton Carew
1925	Mrs CWM Potts	Wearside	1963	Mrs Riddell	South Shields
1926	Miss Walker	Ryton	1964	Mrs Riddell	Brancepeth Castle
1927	Miss Westall	Dinsdale Spa	1965	Mrs Bennett	Seaton Carew
1928	Mrs Morton	Brancepeth Castle	1966	Miss P Dinning	Wearside
1929	Miss Rowland	West Hartlepool	1967	Mrs M Whitehead	Brancepeth Castle
1930	Miss Walker	Seaham Harbour	1968	Mrs P Twinn	Brancepeth Castle
1931	Miss Walker	Seaton Carew	1969	Mrs D Harrison	Seaton Carew
1932	Miss Sardler	Cox Green	1970	Miss L Hope	Bishop Auckland
1933	Mrs Waugh	Brancepeth Castle	1971	Mrs M Thompson	Tyneside
1934	Mrs Waugh	Hartlepool	1972	Miss R Kelly	Brancepeth Castle
1935	Mrs Waugh	Seaham Harbour	1973	Miss C Barker	South Moor
1936	Mrs Waugh	Seaton Carew	1974	Mrs C Bowerbank	Seaton Carew
1937	Mrs Richardson	Wearside	1975	Mrs A Biggs	Tyneside
1938	Miss Curry	Brancepeth Castle	1976	Miss R Kelly	Eaglescliffe
1939	Miss Bell	Dinsdale Spa	1977	Miss C Barker	Brancepeth Castle
1940–47	*Not played due to Second World War*		1978	Miss C Barker	Seaton Carew
1948	Miss Curry	Seaton Carew	1979	Miss P Hunt	Tyneside
1949	Mrs JH Carter	Brancepeth Castle	1980	Miss L Still	Wearside
1950	Mrs Birbeck	Seaton Carew	1981	Miss C Barker	Brancepeth Castle
1951	Mrs JH Carter	Brancepeth Castle	1982	Miss P Hunt	Eaglescliffe
1952	Mrs Butler	Seaton Carew	1983	Miss P Hunt	Castle Eden
1953	Mrs JH Carter	Brancepeth Castle	1984	Miss B Mansfield	Bishop Auckland
1954	Mrs C Wright	Seaton Carew	1985	Miss M Scullan	Beamish Park
1955	Mrs Birbeck	Brancepeth Castle	1986	Miss L Chesterton	Tyneside
1956	Miss Paton	Seaton Carew	1987	Miss B Mansfield	Darlington
1957	Mrs Riddell	Seaton Carew	1988	Miss L Chesterton	Bishop Auckland
1958	Mrs Riddell	Wearside	1989	Mrs L Still	Seaton Carew
1959	Mrs Riddell	Seaton Carew	1990	Miss B Mansfield	Brancepeth Castle
1960	Mrs J Kinsella	Brancepeth Castle			

Essex Ladies' Championship

INAUGURATED 1923

YEAR	WINNER	VENUE	YEAR	WINNER	VENUE
1923	Miss M Parkinson	Romford	1931	Miss D Wilkins	Wanstead
1924	Mrs P Garon	Thorpe Hall	1932	Miss K Garnham	Chigwell
1925	Mrs P Garon	Thorndon Park	1933	Miss K Garnham	Frinton
1926	Mrs Simpson	Chelmsford	1934	Mrs P Garon	Thorndon Park
1927	Mrs P Garon	Thorndon Park	1935	Miss D Wilkins	Romford
1928	Mrs P Garon	Romford	1936	Miss D Wilkins	Orsett
1929	Mrs P Garon	Thorndon Park	1937	Miss K Garnham	Thorndon Park
1930	Mrs P Garon	Rochford Hundred	1938	Miss K Garnham	Chigwell

YEAR	WINNER	VENUE	YEAR	WINNER	VENUE
1939	Miss K Garnham	Rochford Hundred	1968	Mrs A Bonallack	Thorndon Park
1940–46	*Not played due to Second World War*		1969	Mrs A Bonallack	Colchester
1947	Mrs Kenneth Hawes	Thorndon Park	1970	Mrs S Barber	Rochford Hundred
1948	Mrs S Munro	Romford	1971	Mrs S Barber	Romford
1949	Miss MA McKenny	Thorndon Park	1972	Mrs B Lewis	Chigwell
1950	Mrs S Munro	Thorndon Park	1973	Mrs A Bonallack	Thorpe Hall
1951	Miss A Barrett	Thorndon Park	1974	Mrs A Bonallack	Colchester
1952	Mrs P Garon	Thorndon Park	1975	*Not played*	
1953	*Not played*		1976	Mrs A Bonallack	Rochford Hundred
1954	Mrs Hanson-Abbott	Thorndon Park	1977	Mrs A Bonallack	Maylands
1955	Mrs J Willis	Thorndon Park	1978	Mrs A Bonallack	Romford
1956	Mrs J Hetherington	Thorndon Park	1979	Miss B Cooper	Colchester
1957	Mrs J Hetherington	Wanstead	1980	Mrs E Boatman	Chelmsford
1958	Miss S Bonallack	Orsett	1981	Mrs P Jackson	Orsett
1959	Miss S Bonallack	Romford	1982	Mrs A Bonallack	Romford
1960	Miss S Bonallack	Orsett	1983	Mrs E Boatman	Thorndon Park
1961	Miss S Bonallack	Romford	1984	Mrs S Barber	Thorpe Hall
1962	Miss S Bonallack	Thorndon Park	1985	Mrs S Barber	Rochford Hundred
1963	Mrs S Barber		1986	Miss S Moorcroft	Chigwell
	(*née* Bonallack)	Thorpe Hall	1987	Miss M King	Colchester
1964	Miss E Collis	Romford	1988	Miss W Dicks	Romford
1965	Miss E Collis	Chelmsford	1989	Miss A MacDonald	Frinton
1966	Mrs S Barber	Romford	1990	Miss S Bennett	Chelmsford
1967	Mrs S Barber	Orsett			

Gloucestershire Ladies' Championship

INAUGURATED 1913

YEAR	WINNER	VENUE	YEAR	WINNER	VENUE
1913	Miss Barry	Cotswold Hills	1937	Miss C Bramwell	Long Ashton
1914	Miss Bryan	Henbury	1938	Mrs Whitley	Cotswold Hills
1915–19	*Not played due to Great War*		1939	Mrs Collier	Henbury
1920	Miss Bryan	Minchinhampton	1940–46	*Not played due to Second World War*	
1921	Mrs Whitley	Long Ashton	1947	Mrs SL Dickinson	Stinchcombe Hill
1922	Miss Prince	Cotswold Hills	1948	Mrs Whitley	Long Ashton
1923	Mrs Whitley	Minchinhampton	1949	Miss LE Chamberlain	Cotswold Hills
1924	Miss V Bramwell	Long Ashton	1950	Mrs Whitley	Bristol & Clifton
1925	Miss V Bramwell	Cotswold Hills	1951	Mrs SL Dickinson	Minchinhampton
1926	Miss V Bramwell	Bristol & Clifton	1952	Mrs P Reece	Henbury
1927	Mrs Whitley	Stinchcombe Hill	1953	Mrs P Reece	Stinchcombe Hill
1928	Miss V Bramwell	Gloucester	1954	Mrs P Reece	Cotswold Hills
1929	Mrs Whitley	Long Ashton	1955	Mrs P Reece	Cotswold Hills
1930	Miss V Bramwell	Cotswold Hills	1956	Mrs P Reece	Bristol & Clifton
1931	Miss V Bramwell	Bristol & Clifton	1957	Miss R Porter	Minchinhampton
1932	Miss W Williams	Stinchcombe Hill	1958	Mrs B Popplestone	Knowle
1933	Miss V Bramwell	Henbury	1959	Miss R Porter	Cotswold Hills
1934	Miss V Bramwell	Minchinhampton	1960	Mrs P Reece	Henbury
1935	Mrs Whitley	Stinchcombe Hill	1961	Miss R Porter	Stinchcombe Hill
1936	Miss C Bramwell	Stinchcombe Hill	1962	Miss R Porter	Bristol & Clifton

YEAR	WINNER	VENUE	YEAR	WINNER	VENUE
1963	Miss R Porter	Minchinhampton	1977	Miss R Porter	Cirencester
1964	Miss R Porter	Long Ashton	1978	Miss D Park	Henbury
1965	Mrs P Reece	Cotswold Hills	1979	Mrs P Reece	Lilleybrook
1966	Miss R Porter	Knowle	1980	Miss K Douglas	Bristol & Clifton
1967	Miss R Porter	Cirencester	1981	Miss K Douglas	Stinchcombe Hill
1968	Mrs P Reece	Shirehampton Park	1982	Miss K Douglas	Long Ashton
1969	Miss R Porter	Stinchcombe Hill	1983	Miss K Douglas	Minchinhampton
1970	Mrs P Reece	Henbury	1984	Miss K Douglas	Knowle
1971	Mrs P Reece	Minchinhampton	1985	Miss C Griffiths	Cotswold Hills
1972	Miss B Huke	Bristol & Clifton	1986	Miss S Shapcott	Long Ashton
1973	Miss R Porter	Cotswold Hills	1987	Mrs R Page	Ross-on-Wye
1974	Miss R Porter	Long Ashton	1988	Miss S Elliott	Bristol & Clifton
1975	Miss R Porter	Broadway	1989	Miss S Elliott	Cirencester
1976	Miss R Porter	Knowle	1990	Miss M Mayes	Henbury

Hampshire Ladies' Championship

INAUGURATED 1924

YEAR	WINNER	VENUE	YEAR	WINNER	VENUE
1924	Miss Pearce	Hayling Island	1961	Mrs B Green	Blackmoor
1925	Mrs Lamplough	Fleet	1962	Mrs JSF Morrison	Sandown & Shanklin
1926	Miss A Kyle	Sandown	1963	Mrs B Green	Queen's Park
1927	Miss S Lamplough	Meyrick Park	1964	Mrs B Bavin	Brokenhurst Manor
1928	Miss Aitchinson	Lee-on-the-Solent	1965	Mrs B Bavin	Liphook
1929	Mrs WH Hunt	Stoneham	1966	Mrs B Bavin	North Hants, Fleet
1930	Miss Uthoff	Liphook	1967	Miss H Clifford	Meyrick Park
1931	Mrs Clark	Hayling Island	1968	Miss P Shepherd	Hayling Island
1932	Mrs WH Hunt	Blackmoor	1969	Miss H Clifford	Stoneham
1933	Miss P Wade	Brokenhurst Manor	1970	Miss C Le Feuvre	Sandown & Shanklin
1934	Mrs Clark	Hayling Island	1971	Miss C Le Feuvre	Blackmoor
1935	Miss P Wade	Liphook	1972	Miss C Le Feuvre	Brokenhurst Manor
1936	Miss N Diamond	Stoneham	1973	Miss C Le Feuvre	Basingstoke
1937	Miss P Wade	Lee-on-the-Solent	1974	Miss C Le Feuvre	Royal Winchester
1938	Miss P Wade	Liphook	1975	Miss S Thurston	Liphook
1939	Miss RS Morgan	Meyrick Park	1976	Mrs C Gibbs	
1940–46	*Not played due to Second World War*			(*née* Le Feuvre)	Hayling Island
1947	Miss M Wallis	Hayling Island	1977	Miss CM Mackintosh	Queen's Park
1948	Mrs Bavin	Liphook	1978	Miss CM Mackintosh	North Hants, Fleet
1949	Mrs Bavin	Meyrick Park	1979	Miss C Mackintosh	Stoneham
1950	Mrs JSF Morrison	North Hants, Fleet	1980	Miss C Mackintosh	Sandown & Shanklin
1951	Mrs JSF Morrison	Stoneham	1981	Miss S Pickles	Brokenhurst Manor
1952	Mrs F Allen	Blackmoor	1982	Miss A Wells	Blackmoor
1953	Miss B Lowe	Brokenhurst Manor	1983	Miss C Hayllar	Hockley
1954	Mrs Bavin	Hayling Island	1984	Miss C Mackintosh	Hayling Island
1955	Mrs Bavin	Meyrick Park	1985	Mrs C Stirling	Liphook
1956	Miss B Lowe	Liphook	1986	Miss C Hayllar	Basingstoke
1957	Mrs B Green	North Hants, Fleet	1987	Mrs C Stirling	Meon Valley
1958	Mrs Bavin	Meyrick Park	1988	Mrs C Stirling	Meon Valley
1959	Mrs B Green	Hayling Island	1989	Mrs S Pickles	Rowlands Castle
1960	Mrs B Green	Stoneham	1990	Miss A MacDonald	Shanklin & Sandown

Hertfordshire Ladies' Championship

INAUGURATED 1924

YEAR	WINNER	VENUE	YEAR	WINNER	VENUE
1924	Mrs R Fleming	Sandy Lodge	1961	Mrs R Oliver	Brookmans Park
1925	Mrs K Farquharson	Berkhamsted	1962	Mrs R Oliver	Sandy Lodge
1926	Mrs E Martin-Smith	Moor Park	1963	Mrs R Oliver	Berkhamsted
1927	Mrs Brindle	West Herts	1964	Mrs R Oliver	Porters Park
1928	Mrs Brindle	Oxhey	1965	Mrs M Cunneen	South Herts
1929	Mrs V Miles	Berkhamsted	1966	Miss M Paton	Ashridge
1930	Miss K Harley	Porter's Park	1967	Mrs P Rumble	Moor Park
1931	Miss P Horpfield	West Herts	1968	Mrs R Oliver	Hartsbourne
1932	Miss G Flint	Oxhey	1969	Mrs R Oliver	West Herts
1933	Miss G Flint	Berkhamsted	1970	Mrs B Smith	Brookmans Park
1934	Mrs P Gilbertson	Porters Park	1971	Mrs J Kaye	Berkhamsted
1935	Miss Z Bonner Davies	Sandy Lodge	1972	Mrs R Turnbull	Sandy Lodge
1936	Mrs V Miles	Oxhey	1973	Miss S Parker	Porters Park
1937	Mrs P Gilbertson	Ashridge	1974	Mrs R Turnbull	South Herts
1938	Miss B Goddard	West Herts	1975	Mrs P Rumble	Ashridge
1939	Mrs P Gilbertson	Porters Park	1976	Mrs R Turnbull	Moor Park
1940–46	*Not played due to Second World War*		1977	Miss J Smith	Knebworth
1947	Mrs A Mawson	Sandy Lodge	1978	Miss J Smith	Hartsbourne
1948	Mrs Clerke	Porters Park	1979	Miss S Latham	West Herts
1949	Miss E Dixon	West Herts	1980	Mrs H Kaye	Verulam
1950	Mrs HJ Davies	Sandy Lodge	1981	Mrs U Pearson	Berkhamsted
1951	Mrs R Oliver	Berkhamsted	1982	Miss N McCormack	Ashridge
1952	Mrs HJ Davies	Ashridge	1983	Mrs E Provan	Harpenden
1953	Mrs B Bostock	Porters Park	1984	Miss K Hurley	Brookmans Park
1954	Mrs HJ Davies	Sandy Lodge	1985	Mrs H Kaye	Dyrham Park
1955	Mrs R Oliver	West Herts	1986	Miss T Jeary	Sandy Lodge
1956	Mrs E Beck	Moor Park	1987	Mrs H Kaye	Porters Park
1957	Miss A Gardner	Berkhamsted	1988	Miss T Jeary	South Herts
1958	Mrs R Oliver	Ashridge	1989	Mrs H Kaye	Hadley Wood
1959	Miss P Lane	Old Ford Manor	1990	Mrs S Allison	
1960	Miss P Lane	West Herts		(*née* Latham)	Moor Park

Isle of Wight Ladies' Championship

INAUGURATED 1897

at Shanklin and Sandown (from 1901)

YEAR	WINNER	VENUE	YEAR	WINNER	VENUE
1897	Miss C Henry	Bembridge Ladies	1900	Mrs C Wingfield	
1898	Mrs C Wingfield			Stratford	Needles
	Stratford	Freshwater	1901	Miss J Gordon	
1899	Mrs C Wingfield	Royal Isle of Wight,	1902	Miss E Hull	
	Stratford	St Helens	1903	Mrs M Wilkinson	

YEAR	WINNER	YEAR	WINNER
1904	Miss L Alexander	1957	Mrs D Boyd
1905	Mrs J Lee White	1958	Miss H Day
1906	Miss Dauntesey	1959	Mrs V Webb
1907	Miss C Bloxsome	1960	Miss H Day
1908	Mrs Laidlay	1961	Mrs V Webb
1909	Mrs J Lee White	1962	Miss H Day
1910	Mrs Laidlay	1963	Mrs K Webb
1911	*Not played*	1964	Miss H Day
1912	Miss M Tankard	1965	Miss H Day
1913	Mrs J Lee White	1966	Mrs M Dinham
1914	Mrs Laidlay	1967	Mrs AB Oliveira
1915–22	*Not played due to Great War*	1968	Miss H Day
1923	Miss E Buck	1969	Miss L Baker
1924	Mrs Trinder	1970	Mrs AB Oliveira
1925	Mrs Newnham	1971	Mrs AB Oliveira
1926	Mrs Trinder	1972	Mrs R Matthews
1927	Mrs M White	1973	Mrs R Matthews
1928	Mrs Fishwick	1974	Miss G Wright
1929	Mrs P Snelling	1975	Mrs R Matthews
1930	Mrs P Snelling	1976	Miss G Wright
1931	Mrs THT Buchanan	1977	Mrs P Oliveira
1932	Miss L Storr	1978	Mrs R Matthews
1933	Miss L Storr	1979	Mrs M Butler
1934	Miss L Storr	1980	Miss G Wright
1935	Miss L Storr	1981	Miss G Wright
1936	Miss L Storr	1982	Miss G Wright
1937	Miss L Storr	1983	Miss G Wright
1938	Mrs M White	1984	Mrs M Butler
1939	Miss L Storr	1985	Miss G Wright
1940–52	*Not played due to Second World War*	1986	Miss M Ankers
1953	Mrs WM Driver	1987	Miss M Ankers
1954	Mrs WJ Bennett	1988	Mrs M Butler
1955	Mrs WJ Bennett	1989	Miss M Ankers
1956	Miss H Day	1990	Miss M Ankers

Kent Ladies' Championship

INAUGURATED 1906

YEAR	WINNER	VENUE	YEAR	WINNER	VENUE
1906	Mrs Arkwright	Barnehurst	1922	Miss N Wickenden	Littlestone
1907	Miss D Evans	Sundridge Park	1923	Mrs K Morrice	Chislehurst
1908	Miss Absolom	Eltham	1924	Mrs Cautley	Sidcup
1909	Miss Ryder		1925	Mrs JR Mason	Hythe
	Richardson	Littlestone	1926	Mrs JR Mason	Langley Park
1910	Miss L Jackson	Chislehurst	1927	Miss L Doxford	Knole Park
1911	Miss B Hawtrey	Eltham	1928	Miss Oswald	Littlestone
1912	Miss L Jackson	Sundridge Park	1929	Miss D Pearson	Sundridge Park
1913	Mrs Cautley	Hythe	1930	Miss W Morgan	Rochester and
1914–19	Not played due to Great War				Cobham
1920	Mrs Cautley	Sidcup	1931	Miss W Morgan	Prince's, Sandwich
1921	Miss H Prest	Sundridge Park	1932	Miss I Doxford	Sundridge Park

YEAR	WINNER	VENUE	YEAR	WINNER	VENUE
1933	Miss W Morgan	Wildernesse	1967	Miss Shirley Ward	Littlestone
1934	Miss D Fishwick	Hythe	1968	Miss L Denison-Pender	Langley Park
1935	Miss W Morgan	Knole Park	1969	Miss S German	Canterbury
1936	Miss W Morgan	Sidcup	1970	Miss C Redford	Deal
1937	Miss W Morgan	Canterbury	1971	Miss M Walker	West Kent
1938	Miss B Mackenzie	Rochester and Cobham	1972	Miss L Denison-Pender	Rochester and Cobham
1939	Miss Jackson	Prince's, Sandwich			
1940–47	*Not played due to Second World War*		1973	Miss L Denison-Pender	Prince's, Sandwich
1948	Mrs Z Bolton	Langley Park	1974	Miss A Langford	Sundridge Park
1949	Mrs M Richards	Rochester and Cobham	1975	Miss C Redford	Faversham
1950	Miss B Jackson	Royal Blackheath	1976	Mrs S Hedges	Littlestone
1951	Miss B Jackson	Knole Park	1977	Mrs C Caldwell	
1952	Miss B Jackson	Sundridge Park		(*née* Redford)	Cherry Lodge
1953	Miss W Morgan	Prince's, Sandwich	1978	Mrs L Bayman	
1954	Mrs C Falconer	Wildernesse		(*née* Denison-Pender)	Deal
1955	Miss A Ward	Chislehurst	1979	Mrs S Hedges	Canterbury
1956	Miss A Ward	Prince's, Sandwich	1980	Mrs A Robinson	West Kent
1957	Miss SB Smith	Langley Park	1981	Mrs J Guntrip	Prince's, Sandwich
1958	Mrs A Bonallack		1982	Mrs S Hedges	Rochester and Cobham
	(*née* Ward)	Littlestone			
1959	Mrs C Falconer	Rochester and Cobham	1983	Mrs J Guntrip	Wildernesse
1960	Miss E Hearn	West Kent	1984	Mrs S Kitchin	Littlestone
1961	Mrs R Brown	Deal	1985	Mrs L Bayman	Faversham
1962	Mrs R Brown	Sundridge Park	1986	Mrs C Caldwell	Langley Park
1963	Mrs M Richards	Knole Park	1987	Mrs L Bayman	Deal
1964	Miss Shirley Ward	Prince's, Sandwich	1988	Mrs C Caldwell	Littlestone
1965	Mrs D Neech	Blackheath	1989	Miss S Sutton	Canterbury
1966	Mrs D Neech	Wildernesse	1990	Miss H Wadsworth	West Kent

Lancashire Ladies' Championship

INAUGURATED 1912

YEAR	WINNER	VENUE	YEAR	WINNER	VENUE
1912	Miss Maudsley	Hesketh	1935	Miss WM Berry	Formby
1913	Miss Marsden	Manchester	1936	Miss WM Berry	Worsley
1914	Mrs Catlow	Lytham St Annes	1937	Miss JD Firth	Lytham St Annes
1915–19	*Not played due to Great War*		1938	Miss Robinson	Pleasington
1920	Mrs ACP Medrington	Formby	1939	Miss P Edwards	Blundellsands
1921	Miss B Brown	Ormskirk	1940–46	*Not played due to Second World War*	
1922	Mrs ACP Medrington	Birkdale	1947	Miss P Edwards	Formby
1923	Mrs ES Catlow	St Annes	1948	Miss F Stephens	Hillside, Southport
1924	Miss B Brown	Formby			
1925	Miss B Brown	Lytham St Annes	1949	Miss F Stephens	Lytham St Annes
1926	Miss B Brown	Hesketh	1950	Miss F Stephens	Southport and Ainsdale
1927	Miss E Corlett	Withington			
1928	Miss B Brown	Blundellsands	1951	Miss F Stephens	St Annes Old Links
1929	Miss E Corlett	Lytham St Annes			
1930	Mrs DEB Soulby	Pleasington	1952	Miss F Stephens	Ormskirk
1931	Miss B Brown	Ormskirk	1953	Miss F Stephens	Lytham St Annes
1932	Miss JD Firth	Manchester	1954	Miss F Stephens	Formby
1933	Miss JD Firth	Lytham St Annes	1955	Mrs F Smith	
1934	Miss WM Berry	Bolton		(*née* Stephens)	Fairhaven

YEAR	WINNER	VENUE	YEAR	WINNER	VENUE
1956	Miss S Stewart	Worsley	1975	Miss J Greenhalgh	Preston
1957	Mrs D Howard	Birkdale	1976	Miss J Greenhalgh	Pleasington
1958	Miss S Vaughan	St Annes Old Links	1977	Miss J Greenhalgh	Formby
1959	Mrs F Smith	Hillside	1978	Miss J Greenhalgh	Fairhaven
1960	Mrs F Smith	Pleasington	1979	Miss A Norman	Birkdale
1961	Miss J Greenhalgh	Lytham St Annes	1980	Miss A Brown	Bolton Old Links
1962	Miss J Greenhalgh	Formby	1981	Miss A Brown	Blackpool North
1963	Miss S Vaughan	Fairhaven			Shore
1964	Miss S Vaughan	Bolton	1982	Dr G Costello	Pleasington
1965	Miss A Irvin	Birkdale	1983	Miss J Melville	Southport and
1966	Miss J Greenhalgh	Lancaster			Ainsdale
1967	Miss A Irvin	Ormskirk	1984	Mrs A Goucher	Worsley
1968	Miss J Greenhalgh	Pleasington	1985	Mrs A Bromilow	Fairhaven
1969	Miss A Irvin	Manchester	1986	Mrs J Collingham	
1970	Miss P Burrows	Lytham St Annes		(née Melville)	Wilpshire
1971	Miss A Irvin	Formby	1987	Mrs J Collingham	Hillside
1972	Miss A Irvin	St Annes Old Links	1988	Miss L Fairclough	Manchester
1973	Miss J Greenhalgh	Bolton	1989	Miss C Blackshaw	St Annes Old Links
1974	Miss A Irvin	Hesketh	1990	Miss L Fairclough	Clitheroe

Leicestershire and Rutland Ladies' Championship

INAUGURATED 1922

YEAR	WINNER	VENUE	YEAR	WINNER	VENUE
1922	P Harrison		1953	Mrs A Kerslake	Wallasey
1923	P Harrison		1954	Mrs A Kerslake	Luffenham Heath
1924	P Harrison		1955	Miss F Brunton	Kirby Muxloe
1925	Mrs Morton		1956	Miss F Brunton	Birstall
1926	Mrs Lytton Baker	Rothley Park	1957	Miss F Brunton	Leicestershire
1927	Mrs Lytton Baker	Willesley Park	1958	Miss F Brunton	Longcliffe
1928	Mrs Sturgess Wells	Birstall	1959	Mrs W Howard	Luffenham Heath
1929	Mrs Sturgess Wells	Leicestershire	1960	Mrs A Kerslake	Rothley Park
1930	Mrs Sturgess Wells	Longcliffe	1961	Mrs JF Walton	Willesley Park
1931	Mrs Sturgess Wells	Luffenham Heath	1962	Mrs JF Walton	Birstall
1932	Mrs Lytton Baker	Rothley Park	1963	Mrs A Marion	Kirby Muxloe
1933	Mrs Lashmor	Willesley Park	1964	Mrs GA Wheatley	Leicestershire
1934	Mrs Lytton Baker	Birstall	1965	Mrs GA Wheatley	Luffenham Heath
1935	Miss V King	Kirby Muxloe	1966	Miss M Howard	Rothley Park
1936	Mrs Duncan	Leicestershire	1967	Mrs R Reed	Willesley Park
1937	Miss E Martin	Luffenham Heath	1968	Mrs R Reed	Birstall
1938	Mrs A Kerslake	Longcliffe	1969	Mrs H McKay	Kirby Muxloe
1939–46	*Not played due to Second World War*		1970	Mrs P Martin	Glen Gorse
1947	Mrs A Kerslake	Rothley Park	1971	Miss J Stevens	Leicestershire
1948	Mrs L Baxter	Leicestershire	1972	Miss J Stevens	Longcliffe
1949	Mrs L Baxter	Willesley Park	1973	Miss J Stevens	Luffenham Heath
1950	Mrs A Kerslake	Birstall	1974	Mrs O Sturton	Rothley Park
1951	Miss F Brunton	Longcliffe	1975	Mrs J Chapman	Willesley Park
1952	Mrs A Kerslake	Rothley Park	1976	Mrs J Chapman	Birstall

YEAR	WINNER	VENUE	YEAR	WINNER	VENUE
1977	Mrs J Chapman	Glen Gorse	1984	Mrs P Martin	Glen Gorse
1978	Mrs R Reed	Kirby Muxloe	1985	Miss A Walters	Birstall
1979	Mrs A Mansfield	Leicestershire	1986	Mrs V Davis	Kirby Muxloe
1980	Mrs J Roberts	Longcliffe	1987	Miss M Page	Leicestershire
1981	Mrs R Reed	Luffenham Heath	1988	Miss A Walters	Longcliffe
1982	Miss P Gray	Rothley Park	1989	Miss M Page	Luffenham Heath
1983	Mrs R Reed	Willesley Park	1990	Mrs R Reed	Rothley Park

Lincolnshire Ladies' Championship

INAUGURATED 1910

YEAR	WINNER	VENUE	YEAR	WINNER	VENUE
1910	Hon Mrs Jervis		1957	Mrs C Jones	Woodhall Spa
1911	Phyllis Ashton		1958	Mrs L Jones	Lincoln
1912	Mrs Stuart-MacRae		1959	Miss R Gale	North Shore,
1913	Mrs VE Royston-Mills				Skegness
1914	Hon Mrs Jervis		1960	Miss R Gale	Grimsby
1915–21	*Not played due to Great War*		1961	Miss R Gale	Seacroft, Skegness
1922	Mrs VE Royston-Mills		1962	Mrs B Watson	Holme Hall
1923	Kathleen EC Fearn		1963	Mrs B Watson	Lincoln
1924	Edna Dickinson		1964	Mrs B Watson	Woodhall Spa
1925	Mrs HE Sparrow		1965	Mrs R Winn	North Shore,
1926	EC Neville				Skegness
1927	GE Wood		1966	Mrs D Frearson	Seacroft, Skegness
1928	Mrs S Scott		1967	Mrs D Frearson	Lincoln
1929	Mrs WH Worthington		1968	Mrs B Watson	Woodhall Spa
1930	Mrs D Marshall		1969	Mrs B Dawson	Seacroft, Skegness
1931	Mrs D Marshall		1970	Mrs B Watson	Lincoln
1932	Mrs D Marshall		1971	Mrs E Annison	Woodhall Spa
1933	Mrs T Edwards	Woodhall Spa	1972	Mrs P Chatterton	Seacroft, Skegness
1934	Mrs HE Sparrow	North Shore,	1973	Mrs P Harvey	Seacroft, Skegness
		Skegness	1974	Mrs B Watson	Lincoln
1935	Mrs HE Sparrow	Seacroft, Skegness	1975	Mrs P Harvey	Spalding
1936	Mrs HE Sparrow	Cleethorpes	1976	Mrs P West	Holme Hall
1937	Mrs D Taylor	Lincoln	1977	Mrs B Hix	Seacroft, Skegness
1938	Miss C King	Grimsby	1978	Mrs P West	Lincoln
1939	Mrs HE Sparrow	Seacroft, Skegness	1979	Mrs B Hix	Woodhall Spa
1939–46	*Not played due to Second World War*		1980	Mrs E Annison	Holme Hall
1947	Miss D Taylor	Woodhall Spa	1981	Miss R Broughton	Seacroft, Skegness
1948	Miss J Johnson	North Shore,	1982	Mrs B Hix	Lincoln
		Skegness	1983	Mrs B Hix	Grimsby
1949	Miss FE Kearney	Seacroft, Skegness	1984	Mrs A Burtt	Woodhall Spa
1950	Mrs C Jones	Woodhall Spa	1985	Miss H Dobson	North Shore,
1951	Mrs C Jones	Grimsby			Skegness
1952	Mrs P Powell	Lincoln	1986	Miss A Johns	Holme Hall
1953	Miss J Johnson	Seacroft, Skegness	1987	Miss H Dobson	Seacroft, Skegness
1954	Mrs C Jones	North Shore,	1988	Miss H Dobson	Lincoln
		Skegness	1989	Miss H Dobson	Grimsby
1955	Miss J Johnson	Woodhall Spa	1990	Miss A Johns	Holme Hall
1956	Mrs P Powell	Grimsby			

Middlesex Ladies' Championship

INAUGURATED 1923

YEAR	WINNER	VENUE
1923	Miss E Leitch	Fulwell
1924	Miss C Leitch	Stanmore
1925	Mrs WA Gavin	Ashford Manor
1926	Miss A Croft	Fulwell
1927	Miss A Croft	Hadley Wood
1928	Miss Ramsden	Ashford Manor
1929	Miss Clayton	Fulwell
1930	Mrs H Guedalla	Hendon
1931	Miss R Rabbidge	Ashford Manor
1932	Mrs J Fleming	Sudbury
1933	Miss Daniell	Hadley Wood
1934	Miss AC Regnart	Stanmore
1935	Miss R Harris	Pinner Hill
1936	Miss B Taylor	Hendon
1937	Mrs JB Beck	Hadley Wood
1938	Mrs C Eberstein	Pinner Hill
1939	Miss M Ruttle	Hendon
1940–46	*Not played due to Second World War*	
1947	Miss J Gordon	Fulwell
1948	Miss J Gordon	West Middlesex
1949	Mrs CR Eberstein	Hadley Wood
1950	Miss J Gordon	Stanmore
1951	Mrs Bromley-Davenport	Fulwell
1952	Miss J Gordon	Hadley Wood
1953	Mrs RE Garrett (*née* Ruttle)	Ashford Manor
1954	Miss J Gordon	Crews Hill
1955	Mrs M Spearman	Pinner Hill
1956	Mrs M Spearman	Hendon
1957	Mrs M Spearman	Mill Hill
1958	Mrs M Spearman	Crews Hill
1959	Mrs M Spearman	Ashford Manor
1960	Mrs M Barton	Hadley Wood
1961	Mrs M Spearman	
1962	Mrs M Barton	Stanmore
1963	Miss P Moore	Crews Hill
1964	Mrs M Spearman	Potters Bar
1965	Mrs M Spearman	Northwood
1966	Mrs A Denny	Hadley Wood
1967	Mrs B Hayhurst	Hendon
1968	Mrs B Jones	Crews Hill
1969	Miss S Hills	Potters Bar
1970	Mrs M Barton	Hendon
1971	Miss S Hills	Ashford Manor
1972	Miss C Macintosh	Northwood
1973	Mrs RE Garrett	Finchley
1974	Miss A Daniel	Ashford Manor
1975	Miss A Daniel	Sudbury
1976	Miss J Boulter	Northwood
1977	Miss A Daniel	Crews Hill
1978	Mrs A Gems	Grim's Dyke
1979	Mrs C Turnbull	Hendon
1980	Mrs C Turnbull	Mill Hill
1981	Mrs A Gems	Highgate
1982	Mrs A Gems	Finchley
1983	Miss C McGillivray	Sudbury
1984	Miss C Nelson	Crew's Hill
1985	Miss C Nelson	Grim's Dyke
1986	Mrs A Gems	Northwood
1987	Mrs A Gems	Finchley
1988	Miss S Keogh	Fulwell
1989	Miss S Keogh	Enfield
1990	Miss S Keogh	Pinner Hill

Norfolk Ladies' Championship

INAUGURATED 1912

YEAR	WINNER	VENUE
1912	Mrs Steinmetz	Sheringham
1913	Miss Cooper	Hunstanton
1914	Miss Stocker	Royal Norwich
1915–19	*Not played due to Great War*	
1920	Miss S Marshall	Hunstanton
1921	Miss S Marshall	Brancaster
1922	Miss Watts	Sheringham
1923	Miss J Kerr	Cromer
1924	Miss J Kerr	Hunstanton
1925	Miss V Kerr	West Runton
1926	Miss EG Gower	Royal Norwich
1927	Mrs Barnard	Brancaster
1928	Miss VS Reeve	Sheringham
1929	Mrs Cross	Cromer
1930	Miss M Kerr	Hunstanton

YEAR	WINNER	VENUE	YEAR	WINNER	VENUE
1931	Miss M Kerr	Great Yarmouth and Caister	1964	Miss AM Rust	Sheringham
			1965	Mrs P Carrick	Royal Norwich
1932	Miss M Kerr	Royal Norwich	1966	Mrs M Leeder	Great Yarmouth and Caister
1933	Miss G Watts	Brancaster			
1934	Miss G Watts	Sheringham	1967	Mrs M Leeder	Hunstanton
1935	Mrs VM Cross	Hunstanton	1968	Mrs M Leeder	Eaton
1936	Miss G Watts	Cromer	1969	Mrs N Rains	Sheringham
1937	Mrs Jackson	Great Yarmouth and Caister	1970	Mrs N Rains	King's Lynn
			1971	Miss VE Cooper	Royal Norwich
1938	Miss P Bullard	Royal Norwich	1972	Mrs N Rains	Great Yarmouth and Caister
1939	Mrs P Carrick	Brancaster			
1940–46	*Not played due to Second World War*		1973	Mrs N Rains	Eaton
1947	Mrs P Carrick	Sheringham	1974	Mrs M Davies	Hunstanton
1948	Mrs Richardson	Royal Norwich	1975	Mrs M Davies	Sheringham
1949	Mrs P Carrick	Hunstanton	1976	Mrs N Rains	Thetford
1950	Mrs JH Martin	Sheringham	1977	Mrs P Carrick	Royal Norwich
1951	Miss J Cowell	Royal Norwich	1978	Mrs M Davies	King's Lynn
1952	Mrs P Carrick	Hunstanton	1979	Mrs D Sutton	Great Yarmouth and Caister
1953	Miss JM Harrison	Eaton			
1954	Mrs P Carrick	Sheringham	1980	Miss VE Cooper	Eaton
1955	Miss M Harrison	Royal Norwich	1981	Mrs AM Davies	Hunstanton
1956	Mrs P Carrick	Great Yarmouth and Caister	1982	Miss VE Cooper	Sheringham
			1983	Mrs M Davies	Thetford
1957	Mrs P Carrick	Eaton	1984	Mrs L Elliott	Royal Norwich
1958	Mrs P Carrick	Hunstanton	1985	Mrs M Whybrow	King's Lynn
1959	Miss H Smith	Sheringham	1986	Mrs N Clarke	Eaton
1960	Miss H Smith	Royal Norwich	1987	Mrs M Davies	Great Yarmouth and Caister
1961	Mrs P Carrick	Hunstanton			
1962	Miss AM Rust	Great Yarmouth and Caister	1988	Mrs L Elliott	Cromer
			1989	Miss T Keeley	Sheringham
1963	Miss VE Cooper	Eaton	1990	Miss T Ireland	King's Lynn

Northamptonshire Ladies' Championship

INAUGURATED 1932

YEAR	WINNER	VENUE
1932	Mrs RT Phipps	Church Brampton
1933	Miss DR Wooding	Church Brampton
1934	Mrs C Everard	Church Brampton
1935	Mrs RT Phipps	Church Brampton
1936	Mrs GE Dazeley	Church Brampton
1937	Mrs WT Swannell	Church Brampton
1938	Mrs RT Phipps	Church Brampton
1939	Mrs WT Swannell	Church Brampton
1940–45	*Not played due to Second World War*	
1946	Mrs WT Swannell	Church Brampton
1947	Mrs AM Troup	Church Brampton
1948	Mrs WT Swannell	Church Brampton
1949	Mrs AM Troup	Church Brampton
1950	Mrs W Taylor	Church Brampton

YEAR	WINNER	VENUE
1951	Mrs R Larratt	Church Brampton
1952	Mrs K Lock	Church Brampton
1953	Marchioness Northampton	Church Brampton
1954	Marchioness Northampton	Church Brampton
1955	Miss Spencer	Kettering
1956	Marchioness Northampton	Kingsthorpe
1957	Mrs L Everard	Church Brampton
1958	Mrs WT Swannell	Northampton
1959	Mrs L Everard	Peterborough Milton
1960	Mrs L Everard	Kettering
1962	Mrs G Hollingsworth	Church Brampton
1963	Mrs L Everard	Kettering
1964	Mrs L Everard	Kettering
1965	Mrs N Paton	Peterborough
1966	Mrs S Stephenson	Kingsthorpe
1967	Mrs S Stephenson	Church Brampton
1968	Mrs J Sugden	Northampton
1969	Mrs S Stephenson	Peterborough Milton
1970	Mrs K Lock	Kettering
1971	Mrs J Blezard	Kingsthorpe
1972	Mrs A Duck	Church Brampton
1973	Mrs J Sugden	Northampton
1974	Miss J Dicks	Peterborough Milton
1975	Miss J Lee	Kettering
1976	Miss J Lee	Kingsthorpe
1977	Miss J Lee	Church Brampton
1978	Miss J Dicks	Northampton
1979	Miss J Dicks	Peterborough Milton
1980	Mrs M Hutheson	Wellingborough
1981	Miss J Dicks	Kettering
1982	Mrs P Coles	Kingsthorpe
1983	Miss J Dicks	Church Brampton
1984	Mrs A Duck	Northampton
1985	Mrs A Duck	Peterborough Milton
1986	Mrs P Le Var	Staverton Park
1987	Mrs J Kendrick	Kettering
1988	Mrs A Duck	Wellingborough
1989	Mrs C Gibbs	Kingsthorpe
1990	Mrs C Gibbs	Church Brampton

Northumberland Ladies' Championship

INAUGURATED 1921

YEAR	WINNER	VENUE	YEAR	WINNER	VENUE
1921	Mrs BH Fraser	Hexham	1927	Miss M Moorhouse	Hexham
1922	Miss Middlemass	Gosforth	1928	Mrs H Percy	City of Newcastle
1923	Miss M Coning	Alnmouth	1929	Mrs H Percy	Alnmouth
1924	Miss Middlemass	Benton Park	1930	Miss M Tate	Gosforth
1925	Mrs H Percy	Whitley Bay	1931	Mrs Bird	Northumberland
1926	Mrs H Percy	Gosforth	1932	Mrs H Percy	Alnmouth

YEAR	WINNER	VENUE	YEAR	WINNER	VENUE
1933	Mrs H Percy	City of Newcastle	1966	Miss M Nichol	Hexham
1934	Mrs H Percy	Hexham	1967	Mrs M Pickard	
1935	Mrs H Percy	Northumberland		(*née* Nichol)•	City of Newcastle
1936	Miss M Hodgson	Morpeth	1968	Miss A Mortimer	Morpeth
1937	Mrs H Percy	Gosforth	1969	Mrs M Pickard	Alnmouth
1938	Mrs H Percy	Alnmouth	1970	Mrs M Pickard	Gosforth
1939	Miss M Hodgson	City of Newcastle	1971	Mrs M Pickard	Whitley Bay
1940–46	*Not played due to Second World War*		1972	Miss J Lee-Smith	Ponteland
1947	Mrs A Dodds	Hexham	1973	Miss J Lee-Smith	Tynemouth
1948	Mrs G Moore	Northumberland	1974	Miss J Lee-Smith	Hexham
1949	Mrs AMH Wardlaw	City of Newcastle	1975	Mrs E Elliott	Northumberland
1950	Mrs Storey	Morpeth	1976	Mrs M Pickard	City of Newcastle
1951	Mrs Storey	Gosforth	1977	Mrs M Pickard	Alnmouth
1952	Mrs AMH Wardlaw	Alnmouth	1978	Mrs E Elliott	Gosforth
1953	Mrs AMH Wardlaw	Northumberland	1979	Miss H Wilson	Morpeth
1955	Mrs Thatcher	City of Newcastle	1980	Mrs D Glenn	Ponteland
1956	Miss M Nichol	Hexham	1981	Mrs E Elliott	Arcot Hall
1957	Miss M Nichol	Gosforth	1982	Mrs M Pickard	Northumberland
1958	Miss M Nichol	Whitley Bay	1983	Miss J Soulsby	Alnmouth
1959	Mrs G Kennedy	Morpeth	1984	Miss CM Hall	Tynemouth
1960	Mrs G Kennedy	Alnmouth	1985	Miss CM Hall	Westerhope
1961	Miss M Nichol	Ponteland	1986	Miss CM Hall	Hexham
1962	Miss M Nichol	Northumberland	1987	Mrs C Breckon	City of Newcastle
1963	Mrs G Kennedy	Tynemouth	1988	Miss D Glenn	Alnmouth
1964	Miss M Nichol	Arcot Hall	1989	Miss D Glenn	Ponteland
1965	Miss M Nichol	Northumberland	1990	Miss L Fletcher	Gosforth

Nottinghamshire Ladies' Championship

INAUGURATED 1925

YEAR	WINNER	VENUE	YEAR	WINNER	VENUE
1925	Mrs Bristowe	Chilwell	1949	Mrs GW Hetherington	Sherwood Forest
1926	Miss K Watson	Hollinwell	1950	Mrs GW Hetherington	Hollinwell
1927	Miss Tate	Sherwood Forest	1951	Mrs GW Hetherington	Wollaton Park
1928	Mrs Bloomer	Hollinwell	1952	Mrs CHV Elliott	Sherwood Forest
1929	Miss D Snook	Sherwood Forest	1953	Miss J Redgate	Hollinwell
1930	Mrs Bingley	Hollinwell	1954	Miss J McIntyre	Wollaton Park
1931	Miss D Snook	Sherwood Forest	1955	Mrs B Baker	Sherwood Forest
1932	Mrs Bristowe	Hollinwell	1956	Miss J McIntyre	Hollinwell
1933	Mrs Bristowe	Sherwood Forest	1957	Mrs GR Needham	Wollaton Park
1934	Miss N Watson	Hollinwell	1958	Mrs B Baker	Wollaton Park
1935	Mrs AS Bright	Hollinwell	1959	Mrs B Baker	Hollinwell
1936	Mrs Elliott	Sherwood Forest	1960	Miss J Redgate	Wollaton Park
1937	Mrs Elliott	Hollinwell	1961	Miss J Redgate	Sherwood Forest
1938	Mrs AH Bloomer	Wollaton Park	1962	Mrs B Brewer	
1939	Mrs AS Bright	Sherwood Forest		(*née* Redgate)	Hollinwell
1940–46	*Not played due to Second World War*		1963	Mrs B Brewer	Wollaton Park
1947	Mrs RH Taylor	Hollinwell	1964	Mrs B Brewer	Sherwood Forest
1948	Miss Lowe	Wollaton Park	1965	Miss A Payne	Hollinwell

YEAR	WINNER	VENUE	YEAR	WINNER	VENUE
1966	Mrs B Brewer	Coxmoor	1979	Miss M Elswood	Wollaton Park
1967	Mrs B Brewer	Wollaton Park	1980	Miss M Elswood	Sherwood Forest
1968	Mrs G Marshall	Sherwood Forest	1981	Miss K Horberry	Hollinwell
1969	Miss K Horberry	Hollinwell	1982	Miss K Horberry	Coxmoor
1970	Mrs B Brewer	Coxmoor	1983	Miss M Elswood	Wollaton Park
1971	Miss V O'Sullivan	Wollaton Park	1984	Miss M Elswood	Sherwood Forest
1972	Miss RM Clay	Sherwood Forest	1985	Miss K Horberry	Hollinwell
1973	Mrs B Brewer	Hollinwell	1986	CG Palmer	Coxmoor
1974	Miss K Horberry	Coxmoor	1987	Miss M Elswood	Kettering
1975	Miss K Horberry	Wollaton Park	1988	Miss A Ferguson	Sherwood Forest
1976	Miss K Horberry	Sherwood Forest	1989	Miss A Peters	Hollinwell
1977	Miss K Horberry	Hollinwell	1990	Miss L Broughton	Coxmoor
1978	Mrs J Brewer	Coxmoor			

Oxfordshire Ladies' Championship

INAUGURATED 1927

YEAR	WINNER	VENUE	YEAR	WINNER	VENUE
1929	Mrs Barrington-Ward	Huntercombe	1963	Mrs J Grandison	Southfield
1930	Mrs Woodward	Huntercombe	1964	Mrs L Abrahams	Tadmarton Heath
1931	Mrs Evers	Huntercombe	1965	Mrs G Hanks	Huntercombe
1932	Mrs Woodward	Huntercombe	1966	Miss TR Ross Stein	Southfield
1933	Mrs Woodward	Huntercombe	1967	Mrs J Glennie	Frilford Heath
1934	Mrs Evers	Southfield	1968	Mrs A Delany	Henley
1935	Mrs Evers	Huntercombe	1969	Mrs L Davies	Huntercombe
1936	Mrs Coggins	Southfield	1970	Mrs A Delany	Tadmarton Heath
1937	Mrs Evers	Southfield	1971	Mrs L Davies	Burford
1938	Mrs Woodward	Huntercombe	1972	Mrs L Davies	Frilford Heath
1939	Mrs Coggins	Southfield	1973	Miss N Sparks	Southfield
1940–47	*Not played due to Second World War*		1974	Mrs L Davies	Henley
1948	Mrs Trepte	Southfield	1975	Mrs L Davies	Huntercombe
1949	Mrs Halban	Huntercombe	1976	Mrs L Davies	Tadmarton Heath
1950	Mrs W Bamberger	Southfield	1977	Mrs L Davies	Burford
1951	Mrs Richards	Huntercombe	1978	Mrs L Davies	Frilford Heath
1952	Mrs L Abrahams	Huntercombe	1979	Mrs L Davies	Southfield
1953	Mrs L Abrahams	Huntercombe	1980	Mrs L Davies	Henley
1954	Mrs L Abrahams	Frilford Heath	1981	Miss N Sparks	Tadmarton Heath
1955	Mrs L Abrahams	Huntercombe	1982	Mrs M Glennie	Humtercombe
1956	Mrs Nightingale	Huntercombe	1983	Mrs M Glennie	Frilford Heath
1957	Mrs L Abrahams	Frilford Heath	1984	Miss T Craik	Burford
1958	Mrs L Abrahams	Henley	1985	Miss N Sparks	Henley
1959	Mrs L Abrahams	Southfield	1986	Miss T Craik	Huntercombe
1960	Miss V Morris	Tadmarton Heath	1987	Miss T Craik	Southfield
1961	Mrs L Abrahams	Frilford Heath	1988	Miss T Craik	Frilford Heath
1962	Mrs L Abrahams	Huntercombe	1989	Miss L King	Tadmarton Heath
			1990	Miss N Sparks	Burford

Shropshire Ladies' Championship

INAUGURATED 1923

YEAR	WINNER	VENUE	YEAR	WINNER	VENUE
1923	Mrs Beard	Wrekin	1961	Mrs J Shrimpton	Shrewsbury
1924	Miss H Corser	Wrekin	1962	Mrs M Scott	Hawkstone Park
1925	Mrs Beard	Wrekin	1963	Mrs M Wynne-Thomas	Oswestry
1926	Miss M Deedes	Wrekin	1964	Mrs M Wynne-Thomas	Wrekin
1927	Miss M Deedes	Wrekin	1965	Mrs M Wynne-Thomas	Ludlow
1928	Miss M Barnes	Wrekin	1966	Mrs M Wynne-Thomas	Shrewsbury
1929	Miss M Barnes	Hawkstone Park	1967	Mrs G Geddes	Oswestry
1930	Miss M Barnes	Wrekin	1968	Mrs G Geddes	Wrekin
1931	Miss M Barnes	Wrekin	1969	Mrs G Geddes	Hawkstone Park
1932	Mrs AR Blockley	Church Stretton	1970	Mrs J Shrimpton	Ludlow
1933	Miss M Barnes	Shrewsbury	1971	Mrs G Geddes	Shrewsbury
1934	Miss M Black	Hawkstone Park	1972	Miss J Foster	Lilleshall Hall
1935	Miss M Black	Oswestry	1973	Mrs D Watkin	Shifnal
1936	Mrs Wycherley	Wrekin	1974	Mrs G Geddes	Bridgnorth
1937	Miss M Black	Church Stretton	1975	Mrs G Geddes	Wrekin
1938	Miss M Black	Shrewsbury	1976	Miss S McLachlin	Oswestry
1939	Mrs AR Blockley	Hawkstone Park	1977	Mrs J Shrimpton	Ludlow
1940–47	*Not played due to Second World War*		1978	Miss J Dingley	Shrewsbury
1948	Mrs V Jones	Oswestry	1979	Mrs S Pidgeon	Lilleshall Hall
1949	Mrs Argles	Wrekin	1980	Mrs S Pidgeon	Shifnal
1950	Miss M Loy	Ludlow	1981	Mrs S Pidgeon	Bridgnorth
1951	Mrs Argles	Shrewsbury	1982	Mrs S Pidgeon	Wrekin
1952	Mrs Argles	Hawkstone Park	1983	Miss C Gauge	Oswestry
1953	Mrs Beetham	Oswestry	1984	Mrs A Johnson	Ludlow
1954	Mrs Beetham	Wrekin	1985	Mrs A Johnson	Llanymynech
1955	Mrs Argles	Ludlow	1986	Mrs S Pidgeon	Shrewsbury
1956	Miss M Loy	Shrewsbury	1987	Mrs S Pidgeon	Lilleshall Hall
1957	Mrs AM Argles	Hawkstone Park	1988	Miss A Jackson	Shifnal
1958	Miss M Loy	Oswestry	1989	Miss C Gauge	Bridgnorth
1959	Mrs AM Argles	Hawkstone Park	1990	Miss J Marvell	Wrekin
1960	Mrs M Wynne-Thomas	Ludlow			

Somerset Ladies' Championship

INAUGURATED 1913

YEAR	WINNER	VENUE	YEAR	WINNER	VENUE
1913	Mrs Hart	Burnham and Berrow	1922	Miss DR Fowler	Burnham and Berrow
1914	Miss B May	Weston-super-Mare	1923	Miss DR Fowler	Weston-super-Mare
1915–19	*Not played due to Great War*		1924	Miss DR Fowler	Burnham and Berrow
1920	Mrs RE Tomkinson	Burnham and Berrow			
1921	Miss DR Fowler	Weston-super-Mare	1925	Miss DR Fowler	Weston-super-Mare
			1926	*Not played*	

YEAR	WINNER	VENUE	YEAR	WINNER	VENUE
1927	Miss Penruddock	Weston-super-Mare	1960	Mrs FR Brown	Burnham and Berrow
1928	Miss Brownlow	Burnham and Berrow	1961	Mrs R Watford	Burnham and Berrow
1929	Miss Penruddock	Weston-super-Mare	1962	Mrs FR Brown	Burnham and Berrow
1930	Miss P Reed	Burnham and Berrow	1963	Mrs R Watford	Weston-super-Mare
1931	Miss P Reed	Weston-super-Mare	1964	Miss J Jurgens	Knowle
1932	Mrs Skrimshire	Burnham and Berrow	1965	Mrs C Walpole	Burnham and Berrow
1933	Mrs Skrimshire	Knowle	1966	Miss A Alford	Bath
1934	Mrs Skrimshire	Weston-super-Mare	1967	Mrs R Watford	Weston-super-Mare
1935	Miss DR Fowler	Burnham and Berrow	1968	Miss K Counsell	Burnham and Berrow
1936	Miss DR Fowler	Bath	1969	Mrs C Walpole	Knowle
1937	Miss M Wall	Weston-super-Mare	1970	Mrs M Perriam	Weston-super-Mare
1938	Lady Katherine		1971	Mrs S Chambers	Bath
	Cairns	Knowle	1972	Mrs S Chambers	Minehead and West
1939	Lady Katherine				Somerset
	Cairns	Burnham and Berrow	1973	Mrs S Chambers	Knowle
1940–46	Not played due to Second World War		1974	Mrs S Chambers	Burnham and Berrow
1947	Mrs B Popplestone	Knowle	1975	Miss C Hammond	Bath
1948	Mrs B Popplestone	Burnham and Berrow	1976	Mrs M Perriam	Weston-super-Mare
1949	Mrs B Popplestone	Sham Castle	1977	Miss C Trew	Knowle
1950	Lady Katherine		1978	Miss C Trew	Enmore Park
	Cairns	Weston-super-Mare	1979	Miss B New	Burnham and Berrow
1951	Mrs G Lovell	Burnham and Berrow	1980	Miss B New	Bath
1952	Mrs G Lovell	Knowle	1981	Miss B New	Weston-super-Mare
1953	Lady Katherine		1982	Miss B New	Minehead
	Cairns	Bath	1983	Miss B New	Lansdown
1954	Lady Katherine		1984	Mrs M Perriam	Burnham and Berrow
	Cairns	Weston-super-Mare	1985	Miss K Nicholls	Enmore Park
1955	Mrs S Jones	Burnham and Berrow	1986	Miss K Nicholls	Bath
1956	Mrs G Lovell	Weston-super-Mare	1987	Miss K Nicholls	Clevedon
1957	Mrs G Lovell	Bath	1988	Mrs C Whiting	Burnham and Berrow
1958	Mrs P Watford	Burnham and Berrow	1989	Miss K Nicholls	Minehead
1959	Mrs FR Brown	Knowle	1990	Miss K Nicholls	Weston-super-Mare

Staffordshire Ladies' Championship

INAUGURATED 1926

YEAR	WINNER	VENUE	YEAR	WINNER	VENUE
1926	Mrs EB Bayliss	Brocton Hall	1939	Mrs AE Parkes	Trentham
1927	Miss Dobson	Sandwell Park	1940–46	Not played due to Second World War	
1928	Mrs EB Bayliss	Trentham	1947	Miss M Evershed	Little Aston
1929	Miss Dobson	Oxley Park	1948	Miss M Evershed	South Staffs
1930	Miss Dobson	Handsworth	1949	Mrs G Parrott	Brocton Hall
1931	Miss Dobson	Leek	1950	Mrs H Pritchards	Sandwell Park
1932	Mrs AE Parkes	South Staffs	1951	Mrs F King	Drayton Park
1933	Miss Dobson	Beau Desert	1952	Mrs A Denham	Whittington Barracks
1934	Miss Birkett	Walsall	1953	Miss M Evershed	Handsworth
1935	Miss Dobson	Brocton Hall	1954	Miss B Jackson	Leek
1936	Miss Dobson	Sandwell Park	1955	Mrs A Denham	Beau Desert
1937	Miss M Evershed	Bloxwich	1956	Miss B Jackson	Enville
1938	Miss Dobson	Whittington	1957	Miss B Jackson	Brocton Hall
		Barracks	1958	Miss B Jackson	Sandwell Park

YEAR	WINNER	VENUE	YEAR	WINNER	VENUE
1959	Miss B Jackson	South Staffs	1976	Miss B Jackson	Trentham
1960	Miss A Higgott	Trentham	1977	Mrs A Booth	Beau Desert
1961	Miss D Robb	Little Aston	1978	Mrs A Stant	Brocton Hall
1962	Miss A Higgott	Handsworth	1979	Mrs A Smith	
1963	Miss B Jackson	Beau Desert		(formerly Stant)	Leek
1964	Miss B Jackson	Whittington Barracks	1980	Mrs A Booth	Walsall
1965	Miss A Coxhill	Sandwell Park	1981	Miss J Brown	Oxley Park
1966	Miss B Jackson	South Staffs	1982	Miss J Brown	Little Aston
1967	Miss B Jackson	Trentham	1983	Miss D Christison	Trentham
1968	Miss B Jackson	Brocton Hall	1984	Miss D Boyd	Enville
1969	Miss B Jackson	Handsworth	1985	Miss L Hackney	Handsworth
1970	Mrs A Booth	Beau Desert	1986	Mrs A Booth	Whittington
1971	Mrs A Booth	Enville			Barracks
1972	Mrs A Booth	Little Aston	1987	Miss D Christison	Brocton Hall
1973	Miss M Hood	Whittington Barracks	1988	Miss D Boyd	Sandwell Park
1974	Mrs B Bargh	Sandwell Park	1989	Miss R Bolas	Leek
1975	Mrs A Stant	South Staffs	1990	Miss R Bolas	Beau Desert

Suffolk Ladies' Championship

INAUGURATED 1926

YEAR	WINNER	VENUE	YEAR	WINNER	VENUE
1926	Mrs Long	Woodbridge	1962	Miss S Dawson	Woodbridge
1927	Miss J Winn	Rushmere	1963	Mrs M Openshaw	Ipswich
1928	Miss J Winn	Aldeburgh	1964	Mrs A Eddis	Woodbridge
1929	Mrs Garrett	Woodbridge	1965	Miss S Dawson	Aldeburgh
1930	Miss Griffiths	Ipswich	1966	Mrs A Eddis	Thorpeness
1931	Miss J Winn	Aldeburgh	1967	Miss A Willard	Ipswich
1932	Miss Griffiths	Woodbridge	1968	Mrs RDR Biggar	Woodbridge
1933	Lady Eddis	Ipswich	1969	Miss A Willard	Aldeburgh
1934	Lady Eddis	Aldeburgh	1970	Miss A Willard	Thorpeness
1935	Miss J Winn	Woodbridge	1971	Miss A Willard	Ipswich
1936	Miss J Winn	Ipswich	1972	Mrs A Eddis	Woodbridge
1937	Lady Eddis	Felixstowe	1973	Mrs J Biggar	Aldeburgh
1938	Mrs A Eddis	Aldeburgh	1974	Miss S Dawson	Thorpeness
1939	Lady Eddis	Thorpeness	1975	Miss S Dawson	Ipswich
1940–46	*Not played due to Second World War*		1976	Mrs V Cullen	Bury St Edmunds
1947	Lady Eddis	Ipswich	1977	Miss S Dawson	Aldeburgh
1948	Miss P Marsh	Woodbridge	1978	Miss S Field	Woodbridge
1949	Mrs Evans	Aldeburgh	1979	Miss S Dawson	Thorpeness
1950	Mrs Gaskell	Thorpeness	1980	Miss S Field	Ipswich
1951	Mrs Gaskell	Ipswich	1981	Miss D Marriott	Bury St Edmunds
1952	Mrs Wilkins	Woodbridge	1982	Miss D Marriott	Stowmarket
1953	Lady Eddis	Aldeburgh	1983	Miss D Marriott	Woodbridge
1954	Mrs A Smith	Thorpeness	1984	Dr J Gibson	Thorpeness
1955	Miss J Winn	Ipswich	1985	Dr J Gibson	Ipswich
1956	Miss J Winn	Woodbridge	1986	Miss J Wade	Bury St Edmunds
1957	Mrs A Eddis	Aldeburgh	1987	Miss W Day	Stowmarket
1958	Mrs Wilkins	Thorpeness	1988	Miss S Dawson	Felixstowe Ferry
1959	Mrs M Openshaw	Ipswich	1989	Miss J Hall	Woodbridge
1960	Mrs Gaskell	Woodbridge	1990	Miss J Hall	Aldeburgh
1961	Mrs M Openshaw	Aldeburgh			

Surrey Ladies' Championship

INAUGURATED 1921

YEAR	WINNER	VENUE	YEAR	WINNER	VENUE
1921	Miss J Wethered	Burhill	1961	Mrs CA Barclay	Camberley Heath
1922	Miss J Wethered	Worplesdon	1962	Mrs J Thornhill	St George's Hill
1923	Miss M Gourlay	Woking	1963	Miss A Rampton	Worplesdon
1924	Miss J Wethered	Walton Heath	1964	Mrs J Thornhill	Sunningdale
1925	Mrs Latham Hall	St George's Hill	1965	Mrs J Thornhill	Hindhead
1926	Miss M Gourlay	Wentworth	1966	Miss C Denneny	Walton Heath
1927	Miss M Gourlay	West Hill	1967	Miss D Oxley	Woking
1928	Mrs Potter	Burhill	1968	Mrs R Sutherland-	
1929	Miss J Wethered	Worplesdon		Pilch	West Hill
1930	Mrs Atherton	West Surrey	1969	Miss J Bisgood	St George's Hill
1931	Miss M Gourlay	Camberley Heath	1970	Miss D Oxley	Worplesdon
1932	Miss J Wethered	Wentworth	1971	Miss D Oxley	West Byfleet
1933	Miss M Gourlay	West Hill	1972	Mrs S Birley	Royal Wimbledon
1934	Miss M Gourlay	Worplesdon	1973	Mrs J Thornhill	Walton Heath
1935	Miss P Barton	Kingswood	1974	Mrs J Thornhill	Hindhead
1936	Miss I, Fishwick	Byfleet	1975	Miss D Strickland	Burhill
1937	Miss J Hamilton	St George's Hill	1976	Mrs D Henson	
1938	Miss M Gourlay	Burhill		(née Oxley)	Tandridge
1939	Miss J Kerr	Walton Heath	1977	Mrs J Thornhill	West Hill
1940–45	*Not played due to Second World War*		1978	Mrs J Thornhill	Croham Hurst
1946	Mrs D Critchley		1979	Miss S Peters	Walton Heath
	(née Fishwick)	West Hill	1980	Miss D Dowling	St George's Hill
1950	Mrs Style	Walton Heath	1981	Mrs J Thornhill	Wentworth
1951	Miss J Bisgood	Camberley Heath	1982	Mrs J Thornhill	Coombe Hill
1952	Mrs CA Barclay	Royal Wimbledon	1983	Mrs J Thornhill	Worplesdon
1953	Miss J Bisgood	Worplesdon	1984	Mrs J Thornhill	Hankley Common
1954	Miss E Price	West Hill	1985	J Nicholson	Walton Heath
1955	Miss E Price	Addington	1986	Miss S Prosser	Wentworth
1956	Miss E Price	Wentworth	1987	Mrs W Wooldridge	Hankley Common
1957	Miss E Price	St George's Hill	1988	Mrs C Bailey	Tandridge
1958	Miss E Price	West Hill	1989	Mrs J Thornhill	Burhill
1959	Miss E Price	Walton Heath	1990	Mrs W Wooldridge	Sunningdale
1960	Miss E Price	Hankley Common			

Sussex Ladies' Championship

INAUGURATED 1923

YEAR	WINNER	VENUE	YEAR	WINNER	VENUE
1923	Miss CM Archer	Seaford	1930	Miss CM Archer	Royal Ashdown Forest
1924	Miss W Sarson	Brighton and Hove	1931	Mrs F de Winton	Worthing
1925	Mrs VG Davies	Seaford	1932	Mrs VG Davies	Cooden Beach
1926	Mrs F de Winton	Royal Ashdown	1933	Mrs L Rowand Harker	West Hove
		Forest	1934	Mrs Gallatley	Rye
1927	Mrs VG Davies	Littlehampton	1935	Mrs VG Davies	Pulborough
1928	Miss S Marshall	Seaford	1936	Mrs J Grant-White	Royal Ashdown Forest
1929	Mrs O Hambro	Cooden Beach	1937	Miss B Norris	Cooden Beach

YEAR	WINNER	VENUE	YEAR	WINNER	VENUE
1938	Miss B Norris	Worthing	1969	Audrey Brown	Piltdown
1939	Miss R Powell	Seaford	1970	Pam Tredinnick	Worthing
1940–46	*Not played due to Second World War*		1971	Elizabeth Mountain	Rye
1947	Rosemary Dennler	Worthing	1972	Pru Riddiford	Pulborough
1948	Sylvia Cleary	Cooden Beach	1973	Pru Riddiford	Piltdown
1949	Linda Jerdein	West Sussex	1974	Pru Riddiford	Dyke
1950	Linda Jerdein	Crowborough	1975	Sue Tredinnick	Royal Ashdown
1951	Rosemary Dennler	Seaford			Forest
1952	Rosemary Dennler	Pulborough	1976	Carol Larkin	Seaford
1953	Pru Riddiford	Crowborough	1977	Sue Bamford	Pulborough
1954	Morag Groom	Royal Ashdown	1978	Jenny Tate	Dyke
		Forest		*Dyke became snowbound so final rounds played*	
1955	Joan Grant-White	Pulborough		*West Sussex*	
1956	Jane Yuille	Crowborough	1979	Shirley Sutton	Cooden Beach
1957	Beryl Strange	Seaford	1980	Caroline Pierce	Worthing
1958	Beryl Strange	Worthing	1981	Carol Larkin	Willingdon
1959	Jane Hayter (*née* Yuille)	Piltdown	1982	Carol Larkin	Royal Ashdown
1960	Beryl Strange	Seaford			Forest
1961	Pru Riddiford	Littlehampton	1983	Mary Gallagher	East Brighton
1962	Pru Riddiford	Cooden Beach	1984	Christine Rolph	Littlehampton
1963	Pam Tredinnick	Pulborough	1985	Nicola Way	Nevill
1964	Pru Riddiford	Royal Ashdown	1986	Mary-Jane Cornelius	Seaford
		Forest	1987	Karen Mitchell	Royal Ashdown
1965	Mary Tredinnick	Littlehampton			Forest
1966	Pru Riddiford	Crowborough	1988	Mary-Jane Cornelius	Dyke
1967	Pru Riddiford	Cooden Beach	1989	Mary-Jane Cornelius	Worthing
1968	Pru Riddiford	Pulborough	1990	Mary-Jane Cornelius	Cooden Beach

Warwickshire Ladies' Championship

INAUGURATED 1901

YEAR	WINNER	VENUE	YEAR	WINNER	VENUE
1901	Miss A Steedman	Coventry	1933	Mrs M Peppercorn	Sutton Coldfield
1902	Miss F Smith		1934	Miss E Pears	Stratford-on-Avon
1903	Miss A Wilks		1935	Miss E Pears	Walmley
1908	Miss A Wilks		1936	Miss E Pears	Moor Hall
1913	Miss A Swanston		1937	Miss E Pears	Olton
1914–20	*Not played due to Great War*		1938	Mrs M Peppercorn	Harborne
1921	Miss E Haddelsey		1939	Miss M Fyshe	Copt Heath
1923	Miss D Hartill	Leamington	1940–46	*Not played due to Second World War*	
1924	Miss D Hartill	Edgbaston	1947	Mrs E Sheppard	
1925	Miss D Hartill	Castle Bromwich		(*née* Pears)	Sutton Coldfield
1926	Miss D Hartill	Harborne	1948	Mrs E Sheppard	Edgbaston
1927	Mrs D Hartill	Olton	1949	Mrs E Sheppard	Ladbrook Park
1928	Mrs M Peppercorn	Copt Heath	1950	Mrs E Sheppard	Moor Hall
1929	Miss D Hartill	Robin Hood	1951	Mrs E Sheppard	Stratford-on-Avon
1930	Mrs M Peppercorn	Finham Park	1952	Miss P Davies	Olton
1931	Mrs M Peppercorn	Olton	1953	Mrs M Peppercorn	Harborne
1932	Miss M Fyshe	Castle Bromwich	1954	Mrs E Sheppard	Finham Park

YEAR	WINNER	VENUE	YEAR	WINNER	VENUE
1955	Miss V Anstey	Edgbaston	1974	Mrs S Westall	Leamington and
1956	Miss V Anstey	Copt Heath			County
1957	Miss V Anstey	Moor Hall	1975	Mrs V Beharrell	Moor Hall
1958	Miss V Anstey	Edgbaston	1976	Mrs MF Roles	Robin Hood
1959	Miss S Armstrong	Ladbrook Park	1977	Miss A Middleton	Harborne
1960	Miss V Anstey	Olton	1978	Mrs S Westall	Edgbaston
1961	Mrs J Roles	Hall Green	1979	Mrs S Nicholson	Ladbrook Park
1962	Miss J Roberts	Finham Park	1980	Miss T Hammond	Olton
1963	Miss J Roberts	Hearsall	1981	Mrs J Evans	Shirley
1964	Miss J Roberts	Harborne	1982	Miss T Hammond	Kenilworth
1965	Miss J Roberts	Moor Hall	1983	Miss T Hammond	Leamington and
1966	Mrs J Roles	Olton			County
1967	Mrs J Tomlinson	Stratford-on-Avon	1984	Miss M Stevens	Robin Hood
1968	Mrs J Tomlinson	Edgbaston	1985	Mrs S Seville	Copt Heath
1969	Miss J Roberts	Harborne	1986	Miss T Hammond	Sutton Coldfield
1970	Mrs J Roles	Olton	1987	Mrs M Button	Ladbrook Park
1971	Mrs V Beharrell		1988	Miss S Morgan	Finham Park
	(*née* Anstey)	Sutton Coldfield	1989	Miss S Morgan	Moor Hall
1972	Mrs V Beharrell	Stratford-on-Avon	1990	Miss S Morgan	Stratford-on-Avon
1973	Mrs S Westall	Copt Heath			

Wiltshire Ladies' Championship

INAUGURATED 1936

YEAR	WINNER	VENUE	YEAR	WINNER	VENUE
1936	Mrs Hart	Salisbury and South	1966	Mrs RJA Morris	High Post
		Wilts	1967	Miss A Mackenzie	Warminster
1937	Mrs Potts	High Post	1968	Mrs A Bucher	Swindon
1938	Miss Pywell	Swindon	1969	Miss P Lord	Salisbury and South
1939	Miss Pywell	Warminster			Wilts
1940–46	*Not played due to Second World War*		1970	Miss P Lord	Tidworth Garrison
1947	Mrs Evans	High Post	1971	Mrs V Morgan	High Post
1948	Mrs Potts	Salisbury and South	1972	Mrs P Board	Warminster
		Wilts	1973	Mrs A Bucher	Swindon
1949	Mrs Kennard	Warminster	1974	Mrs V Morgan	Kingsdown
1950	Mrs Greenland	Ogbourne	1975	Mrs J Lawrence	Salisbury and South
1951	Mrs Greenland	High Post			Wilts
1952	Mrs Glendinning	Salisbury and South	1976	Mrs V Morgan	High Post
		Wilts	1977	Mrs J Lawrence	Tidworth Garrison
1953	Mrs Glendinning	Warminster	1978	Mrs P Millar	Warminster
1954	Mrs Greenland	Swindon	1979	Mrs P Board	North Wilts
1955	Mrs Curnick	Tidworth	1980	Miss C Waite	Swindon
1956	Mrs Curnick	High Post	1981	Miss C Waite	High Post
1957	Mrs J Taunton	Salisbury and South	1982	Miss F Dawson	Marlborough
		Wilts	1983	Miss C Waite	Kingsdown
1958	Mrs J Taunton	Warminster	1984	Mrs V Morgan	Salisbury and South
1959	Mrs J Taunton	Swindon			Wilts
1960	Mrs J Taunton	Tidworth Garrison	1985	Miss C Waite	Tidworth Garrison
1961	Mrs J Taunton	High Post	1986	Miss S Marks	North Wilts
1962	Mrs M Strong	Warminster	1987	Mrs J Lawrence	Swindon
1963	Mrs M Morris	Swindon	1988	Mrs S Sutton	Warminster
1964	Mrs C Jones	Warminster	1989	Mrs J Lawrence	High Post
1965	Mrs J Taunton	Tidworth	1990	Mrs M Johnson	Kingsdown

Worcestershire Ladies' Championship

INAUGURATED 1903

YEAR	WINNER	VENUE	YEAR	WINNER	VENUE
1924	Miss Robinson	Blackwell	1961	Miss M Hampson	Blackwell
1925	Miss K Nicholls	Moseley	1962	Mrs G Strang	Worcester
1926	Miss K Nicholls	Stourbridge	1963	Mrs J Odell	Stourbridge
1927	Miss K Nicholls	Northfield	1964	Mrs RL Brinton	King's Norton
1928	Miss K Nicholls	Kidderminster	1965	Mrs C Banner	North Worcestershire
1929	Mrs Fieldhouse	Malvern	1966	Mrs C Banner	Moseley
1930	Miss B Law	Moseley	1967	Miss J Blaymire	Stourbridge
1931	Mrs Challen	Blackwell	1968	Mrs M Hayes	Gay Hill
1932	Mrs Challen	Stourbridge	1969	Miss J Blaymire	Worcester
1933	Miss M Fieldhouse	Worcester	1970	Miss J Blaymire	King's Norton
1934	Miss B Law	Brand Hall	1971	Miss J Blaymire	North Worcestershire
1935	Mrs E Fiddian	King's Norton	1972	Miss J Blaymire	Kidderminster
1936	Mrs Brinton	North Worcestershire	1973	Miss J Blaymire	Moseley
1937	Mrs E Fiddian	Malvern	1974	Mrs V Cotterill	Blackwell
1938	Mrs Challen	Moseley	1975	Miss J Blaymire	Stourbridge
1939	Miss M Hampson	Blackwell	1976	Miss J Blaymire	Fulford Heath
1940–46	*Not played due to Second World War*		1977	Miss J Blaymire	Worcester
1947	Miss M Hampson	Stourbridge	1978	Miss S Crowcroft	Gay Hill
1948	Miss M Hampson	Kidderminster	1979	Miss J Blaymire	Malvern
1949	Miss M Hampson	Blackwell	1980	Mrs R West	King's Norton
1950	Miss M Hampson	Worcester	1981	Miss J Blaymire	North Worcestershire
1951	Mrs Challen	North Worcestershire	1982	Miss J Blaymire	Moseley
1952	Miss M Fyshe	Moseley	1983	Miss S Nicklin	Redditch
1953	Miss M Hampson	Kidderminster	1984	Miss S Nicklin	Kidderminster
1954	Miss M Fyshe	Blackwell	1985	Miss L Waring	Stourbridge
1955	Miss M Hampson	Worcester	1986	Miss K Cheetham	Blackwell
1956	Miss M Hampson	Stourbridge	1987	Miss L Waring	Fulford Heath
1957	Miss M Hampson	King's Norton	1988	Miss J Blaymire	Worcester
1958	Mrs M Downing	North Worcestershire	1989	Miss L Waring	Gay Hill
1959	Miss A Cawsey	Moseley	1990	Miss J Deceley	Worcester
1960	Miss M Hampson	Kidderminster			

Yorkshire Ladies' Championship

INAUGURATED 1896

YEAR	WINNER	VENUE	YEAR	WINNER	VENUE
1896	Miss N Haigh	Redcar	1949	Mrs Kyle	Pannal
1897	Miss KG Moeller	Lindrick	1950	Mrs E Hartley	Ganton
1898	Miss KG Moeller	Huddersfield	1951	Miss G Rudgard	Lindrick
1899	Miss HM Firth	Ganton	1952	Miss A Scargill	Alwoodley
1900	Miss KG Moeller	Ilkley	1953	Mrs E Hartley	Brough
1901	Mrs HJ Lister	Lindrick	1954	Miss J Mitton	Abbeydale
1902	Miss B Thompson	Huddersfield	1955	Mrs E Hartley	Sand Moor
1903	Miss E Steel	Ganton	1956	Mrs E Hartley	Ganton
1904	Miss E Steel	Lindrick	1957	Miss P Bagley	Hallamshire
1905	Miss E Steel	Cleveland	1958	Mrs E Hartley	Huddersfield
1906	Mrs Swayne	Huddersfield	1959	Mrs E Hartley	Fulford
1907	Miss KG Moeller	Bradford	1960	Mrs E Hartley	Pannal
1908	Miss E Steel	Hallamshire	1961	Mrs P Foster	Ganton
1909	Miss B Thompson	Ganton	1962	Miss G Coldwell	Lindrick
1910	Miss E Steel	Lindrick	1963	Miss G Hickson	Moortown
1911	Mrs Melrose	Cleveland	1964	Miss M Everard	Hull
1912	Miss Branson	Huddersfield	1965	Mrs TJ Briggs	Hallamshire
1913	Mrs Gwynne	Ganton	1966	Miss C Bell	Huddersfield
1914	Miss Heaton	Cleveland	1967	Miss M Everard	Ganton
1915–18	*Not played due to Great War*		1968	Miss K Phillips	Doncaster
1919	Mrs Harrop	Harrogate	1969	Miss K Phillips	Pannal
1920	Miss Heaton	Lindrick	1970	Mrs J Hunter	Fulford
1921	Miss M Wragg	Pannal	1971	Miss G Ringstead	Lindrick
1922	Mrs White	Alwoodley	1972	Miss M Everard	Moortown
1923	Mrs White	Ganton	1973	Miss M Everard	Ganton
1924	Miss M Wragg	Huddersfield	1974	Mrs B Allison	Hallamshire
1925	Miss E Griffiths	Bradford	1975	Miss V Marvin	Alwoodley
1926	Mrs Shalders	Pannal	1976	Miss P Wrightson	Brough
1927	Miss M Wragg	Abbeydale	1977	Miss M Everard	Sand Moor
1928	Miss M Wragg	Wakefield	1978	Miss V Marvin	Lindrick
1929	Miss M Wragg	Huddersfield	1979	Miss J Rhodes	Ganton
1930	Miss M Wragg	Lindrick	1980	Miss L Batty	Moor Allerton
1931	Miss M Wragg	Ganton	1981	Miss P Grice	Abbeydale
1932	Miss M Johnson	Moortown	1982	Miss P Grice	Hull
1933	Miss Swincoe	Hallamshire	1983	Miss P Grice	Moortown
1934	Miss M Johnson	Hull	1984	Miss A Nicholas	Doncaster
1935	Miss Platts	Bradford	1985	Miss A Farmery	Hornsea
1936	Mrs Rhodes	Lindrick	1986	Miss P Smillie	Alwoodley
1937	Mrs Rhodes	Cleveland	1987	Miss J Copley	Lindrick
1938	Miss K Merry	Sand Moor	1988	Miss J Furby	Ganton
1939–46	*Not played due to Second World War*		1989	Miss K Firth	Pannal
1947	Miss J McIntyre	Huddersfield	1990	Miss N Buxton	Hallamshire
1948	Mrs Kyle	Hallamshire			

East Anglian Ladies' Championship

INAUGURATED 1986

YEAR	WINNER
1986	Miss J Walter
1987	Miss J Walter
1988	Mrs R Farrow
1989	Mrs W Fryer
1990	Miss J Sheldrick

Midland Divisional Championship

INAUGURATED 1897

YEAR	WINNER	VENUE	YEAR	WINNER	VENUE
1897	Miss E Nevile	King's Norton	1934	Miss G Craddock-Hartopp	Seacroft, Skegness
1898	Miss E Nevile	Malvern	1935	Miss Bentley	Hawkstone Park
1899	Miss L Smith	Minchinhampton	1936	Miss B Newall	Aldeburgh
1900	Miss N Wobley	Handsworth	1937	Miss E Pears	Hollinwell
1901	Miss E Nevile	Cheltenham	1938	Miss E Pears	Sutton Coldfield
1902	Mrs Phillips	Sandwell Park	1939	Mrs Jackson	Church Brampton
1903	Miss E Nevile	Buxton	1940–46	*Not played due to Second World War*	
1904	Miss E Nevile	King's Norton	1947	Mrs Sheppard	Little Aston
1905	Miss Bryant	Hollinwell	1948	Miss M Hampson	Cavendish
1906	Miss Foster	Malvern	1949	Mrs Sheppard	Sheringham
1907	Miss L Moore	Sutton Coldfield	1950	Mrs Gaskell	Stourbridge
1908	Miss L Moore	Cheltenham	1951	Mrs Denham	Seacroft, Skegness
1909	Miss Foster	Sandwell Park	1952	Miss P Davies	Aldeburgh
1910	Miss Hemingway	Hollinwell	1953	Hon Mrs A Gee	Edgbaston
1911	Miss L Moore	Olton	1954	Miss B Jackson	Hollinwell
1912	Miss L Moore	Harborne	1955	Mrs Beeson	Hunstanton
1913	Mrs Barry	Cheltenham	1956	Miss B Jackson	Whittington Barracks
1914	Mrs Bell Scott	King's Norton	1957	Miss B Jackson	Woodhall Spa
1915–19	*Not played due to Great War*		1958	Miss B Jackson	Thorpeness
1920	Mrs EB Bayliss	Moseley	1959	Miss B Jackson	Hawkstone Park
1921	Mrs EB Bayliss	Finham Park	1960	Miss B Jackson	Seacroft, Skegness
1922	Mrs EB Bayliss	Sandwell Park	1961	Miss S Armitage	Church Brampton
1923	Miss Harthill	Stourbridge	1962	Miss A Higgott	Moseley
1924	Miss Robinson	King's Norton	1963	Miss A Higgott	Luffenham Heath
1925	Miss Harthill	Leamington	1964	Miss A Coxill	Gog Magog
1926	Miss E Wilson	Handsworth	1965	Miss S Armitage	Stratford-on-Avon
1927	Miss B Law	Beau Desert	1966	Mrs D Frearson	Woodhall Spa
1928	Miss E Wilson	Blackwell	1967	Mrs R Tomlinson	Royal Norwich
1929	Miss E Wilson	Hollinwell	1968	Mrs J Roles	South Staffordshire
1930	Miss E Wilson	Olton	1969	Miss B Jackson	Sherwood Forest
1931	Mrs M Peppercorn	Trentham	1970	Miss J Blaymire	Dunstable Downs
1932	Miss M Fieldhouse	Moseley	1971	Miss J Stant	Shifnal
1933	Miss G Craddock-Hartopp	Hunstanton	1972	Miss J Blaymire	Chesterfield

YEAR	WINNER	VENUE	YEAR	WINNER	VENUE
1973	Mrs A Stant	Woodbridge	1982	Miss S Kiddle	Seacroft, Skegness
1974	Mrs B Baugh	Stourbridge	1983	Miss T Hammond	Dunstable Downs
1975	Mrs A Stant	Church Brampton	1984	Miss L Waring	Bridgnorth
1976	Mrs J Chapman	Gog Magog	1985	Miss L Waring	Cavendish
1977	Mrs S Westall	Stratford-on-Avon	1986	Mrs J Collingham	Sherwood Forest
1978	Mrs S Westall	Longcliffe	1987	Miss S Roberts	Aldeburgh
1979	Mrs M Carr	Hunstanton	1988	Miss S Roberts	Moseley
1980	Miss J Walters	Prestatyn	1989	Miss R Bolas	Church Brampton
1981	Miss J Walters	Handsworth	1990	Miss J Hockley	Gog Magog

Northern Women's Championship

INAUGURATED 1957

YEAR	WINNER	VENUE	YEAR	WINNER	VENUE
1957	Miss M Nichol	Mere	1975	Miss V Marvin	Carlisle
1959	Mrs S Wood	Birkdale	1976	Mrs A Briggs	Warrington
1960	Mrs F Ferguson	Alwoodley	1977	Miss C Barker	Gosforth Park
1961	Miss J Greenhalgh	Llandudno	1978	Miss L Ghent	Eaglescliffe
1962	Miss J Greenhalgh	Carlisle and Silloth	1979	Miss H Wilson	Pannal
1963	Miss Ann Irvin	Wilmslow	1980	Miss C Barker	Bolton
1964	Miss Ann Irvin	Hexham	1981	Miss A Brown	Carlisle
1965	Miss E Chadwick	Formby	1982	Miss C Swallow	
1966	Miss E Chadwick	Brancepeth Castle	1983	Miss C Hall	Whitley Bay
1967	Miss E Chadwick	Moortown	1984	Miss C Hall	Tyneside
1968	Mrs E Brown	Caernarvonshire	1985	Miss C Hall	Huddersfield
1969	Miss P Burrows	Seascale	1986	Miss L Fairclough	Bolton Old Links
1970	Mrs F Smith	Hoylake	1987	Miss S Robinson	Brampton
1971	Mrs V Stone	Alnmouth	1988	Miss K Tebbet	Prestbury
1972	Miss M Everard	Hesketh	1989	Miss L Fletcher	Arcot Hall
1973	Mrs V Stone	Bishop Auckland	1990	Miss L Fairclough	Brancepeth Castle
1974	Mrs C Comboy	Birkdale			

South-Eastern Ladies' Championship

INAUGURATED 1950

YEAR	WINNER	VENUE	YEAR	WINNER	VENUE
1950	Miss J Bisgood	Sunningdale	1971	Miss H Clifford	Stoneham
1951	Lady K Cairns	Pulborough	1972	Miss H Clifford	Northwood
1952	Miss J Bisgood	West Hill	1973	Miss C Redford	Wildernesse
1953	Miss B Lowe	Woking	1974	Miss C Le Feuvre	Hankley Common
1954	Miss B Jackson	Royal Wimbledon	1975	Miss W Pithers	Stoke Poges
1955	Miss E Price	Worplesdon	1976	Miss L Harrold	Calcot Park
1956	Mrs A Spearman	Royal Mid-Surrey	1977	Miss S Bamford	Ashridge
1957	Miss A Ward	Moor Park	1978	Mrs C Caldwell	
1958	Mrs M Spearman	Wildernesse		(née Redford)	Liphook
1959	Miss E Price	Sunningdale	1979	Miss B Cooper	Royal Ashdown Forest
1960	Miss E Price	West Hill	1980	Miss J Rumsey	Huntercombe
1961	Mrs M Spearman	Liphook	1981	Mrs C Caldwell	Chigwell
1962	Mrs B Green	Ashridge	1982	Mrs J Nicholson	Hendon
1963	Mrs J Thornhill	Hankley Common	1983	Miss L Davies	Tandridge
1964	Mrs J Thornhill	Chigwell	1984	Miss L Davies	Burnham Beeches
1965	Mrs A Bonallack		1985	Mrs J Thornhill	Temple
	(née Ward)	Wildernesse	1986	Miss S Moorcroft	Ashridge
1966	Miss H Clifford	East Berks	1987	Mrs N Way	Seaford
1967	Mrs J Baucher	Beaconsfield	1988	Mrs C Stirling	Blackford
1968	Miss E Collis	Walton Heath	1989	Miss A MacDonald	North Foreland
1969	Mrs E Price-Fisher	Rye	1990	Miss A MacDonald	Thorpe Hall
1970	Mrs A Warren	Porters Park			

South-Western Ladies' Championship

INAUGURATED 1931

YEAR	WINNER	VENUE	YEAR	WINNER	VENUE
1931	Miss M Beard	Ferndown	1949	Miss M Roskrow	High Post
1932	Mrs G Jones	Long Ashton	1950	Miss P Roberts	Newport
1933	Mrs V Bramwell	Newquay	1951	Miss P Roberts	Budleigh Salterton
1934	Miss B Pyman	High Post	1952	Mrs P Reece	Porthcawl
1935	Mrs M J Jeffreys	Newport	1953	Lady Katherine	
1936	Mrs G Emery	Westward Ho!		Cairns	Long Ashton
1937	Mrs G Emery	Porthcawl	1954	Mrs P Crow	Burnham and Berrow
1938	Mrs C Beard	Long Ashton	1955	Mrs P Crow	Broadstone
1939	Mrs V Bramwell	Burnham and Berrow	1956	Miss R Porter	Newport
1940–46	*Not played due to Second World War*		1957	Miss R Porter	St Enodoc
1947	Miss M Roskrow	Ferndown	1958	Miss T Ross Steen	High Post
1948	Mrs B Wills	St Enodoc	1959	Mrs P Reece	Burnham and Berrow

YEAR	WINNER	VENUE	YEAR	WINNER	VENUE
1960	Miss R Porter	Porthcawl	1976	Miss T Perkins	Porthcawl
1961	Miss R Porter	Budleigh Salterton	1977	Miss R Porter	Saunton
1962	Miss R Porter	Long Ashton	1978	Miss P Light	Bristol and Clifton
1963	Mrs P Reece	Parkstone	1979	Mrs R Slark	
1964	Miss R Porter	Newport		(née Porter)	Parkstone
1965	Miss R Porter	St Enodoc	1980	Miss L Isherwood	Newport
1966	Miss R Porter	High Post	1981	Miss L Moore	Tehidy Park
1967	Miss R Porter	Burnham and Berrow	1982	Miss L Moore	North Wilts
1968	Mrs P Reece	Pyle and Kenfig	1983	Miss P Johnson	Bath
1969	Miss R Porter	Budleigh Salterton	1984	Miss P Johnson	Porthcawl
1970	Mrs S Chambers	Cirencester	1985	Miss S Shapcott	Saunton
1971	Mrs P Reece	Ferndown	1986	Miss K Nicholls	Henbury
1972	Miss R Porter	Newport	1987	Miss J Fernley	Broadstone
1973	Miss T Perkins	Tehidy Park	1988	Mrs V Thomas	St Mellion
1974	Miss T Perkins	High Post	1989	Miss C Hall	Newquay
1975	Miss P Light	Minehead	1990	Mrs V Thomas	High Post

England and Wales (Ladies')
County Championship

INAUGURATED 1908

ELGA also runs the England and Wales Ladies' County Championship when the winning counties in each of the four divisions – North, Midlands, South-East and South-West – meet in round-robin finals. Both Midlands and South-West absorb Welsh counties to their areas. Over the years the South-East with 34 wins, and the North with 27, have dominated the tournament, although since 1978 Glamorgan of the South-West has won four times. Surrey lead the winners' table with 23 victories.

YEAR	WINNERS	VENUE	YEAR	WINNERS	VENUE
1908	Lancashire	Wallasey	1930	Surrey	Aldeburgh
1909	Surrey	Littlestone	1931	Middlesex	Burnham and
1910	Cheshire	Hollinwell			Berrow
1911	Cheshire	Burnham and	1932	Cheshire	Royal Ashdown
		Berrow			Forest
1912	Cheshire	Ganton	1933	Yorkshire	Westward Ho!
1913	Surrey	Sandwich	1934	Surrey	Seacroft, Skegness
1914–19	*Not played due to Great War*		1935	Essex	Birkdale
1920	Middlesex	Sandwell Park	1936	Surrey	Hayling
1921	Surrey	Lytham St Annes	1937	Surrey	St Enodoc
1922	Surrey	Hunstanton	1938	Lancashire	Aldeburgh
1923	Surrey	Ganton	1939–46	*Not played due to Second World War*	
1924	Surrey	Cooden Beach	1947	Surrey	Ganton
1925	Surrey	Westward Ho!	1948	Yorkshire	Hayling
1926	Surrey	Woodhall Spa	1949	Surrey	Burnham and
1927	Yorkshire	Pannal			Berrow
1928	Cheshire	Walton Heath	1950	Yorkshire	Sheringham
1929	Yorkshire	Broadstone	1951	Lancashire	St Annes Old Links

YEAR	WINNERS	VENUE	YEAR	WINNERS	VENUE
1952	Lancashire	Westward Ho!	1972	Kent	Moortown
1953	Surrey	Prince's, Sandwich	1973	Northumberland	Frilford Heath
1954	Warwickshire	Woodhall Spa	1974	Surrey	Burnham and
1955	Surrey	Hillside			Berrow
1956	Kent	Pulborough	1975	Glamorgan	Church Brampton
1957	Middlesex	Hawkstone Park	1976	Staffordshire	Prestbury
1958	Lancashire	Ferndown	1977	Essex	Deal
1959	Middlesex	Lindrick	1978	Glamorgan	Saunton
1960	Lancashire	Worplesdon	1979	Essex	Gog Magog
1961	Middlesex	Worcester	1980	Lancashire	Formby
1962	Staffordshire	Parkstone	1981	Glamorgan	Thorpe Hall
1963	Warwickshire	Mere	1982	Surrey	Parkstone
1964	Lancashire	Royal Ashdown	1983	Surrey	Hunstanton
		Forest	1984	Surrey }tie	Lindrick
1965	Staffordshire	Lindrick		Yorkshire	
1966	Lancashire	Saunton	1985	Surrey	Walton Heath
1967	Lancashire	Prestbury	1986	Glamorgan	Cotswold Hills
1968	Surrey	Hillside	1987	Lancashire	Copt Heath
1969	Lancashire	Seaford	1988	Surrey	Stockport
1970	Yorkshire	St Enodoc	1989	Cheshire	Frilford Heath
1971	Kent	Kedleston Park	1990	Cheshire	Budleigh Salterton

Ireland

Leinster Scratch Cup

YEAR	WINNER	VENUE	YEAR	WINNER	VENUE
1931	Mrs NL Todd		1961	Moira Earner	Grange
1932	Mrs NL Todd		1962	Ita Burke	Hermitage
1933	Miss Blake		1963	Ita Burke	Castle
1934	Mrs NL Todd		1964	Ita Burke	Portmarnock
1935	Miss Blake		1965	Barbara Hyland	Grange
1936	Mrs NL Todd		1966	Barbara Hyland	Milltown
1937	Miss Gildea		1967	Ita Butler (née Burke)	Royal Dublin
1938	Miss Gildea		1968	Elaine Bradshaw	Co Louth
1939	no winner		1969	Elaine Bradshaw	Woodbrook
1940	Miss C Carroll		1970	Vivienne Singleton	Edmondstown
1941	Sybil Moore		1971	Josephine Mark	Woodbrook
1942	Sybil Moore		1972	Josephine Mark	Newlands
1943	Miss M O'Neil Donnellon		1973	Moira Earner	Dun Laoghaire
1944	Clarrie Reddan		1974	Susan Gorman	Greystones
1945	Philomena Garvey		1975	Geraldine Costello	Co Louth
1946	Philomena Garvey		1976	Susan Gorman	The Island
1947	Philomena Garvey		1977	Mary Gorry	Grange
1948	Kitty Smye		1978	Sheena O'Brien Kenney	Milltown
1949	Philomena Garvey		1979	Mary Gorry	Castle
1950	Philomena Garvey		1980	Claire Hourihane	Hermitage
1951	Dorothy Forster		1981	Mary McKenna	Royal Dublin
1952	Pat O'Sullivan		1982	Mary McKenna	Elm Park
1953	Philomena Garvey		1983	Phil Wickham	Grange
1954	Ena Brooks		1984	Lillian Behan	Portmarnock
1955	Pat O'Sullivan		1985	Claire Hourihane	Hermitage
1956	Pat Fletcher		1986	Yvonne McQuillan	Royal Dublin
1957	Clarrie Reddan		1987	Susan Gorman	Portmarnock
1958	Kitty MacCann		1988	Mary McKenna	Royal Dublin
	(née Smye)		1989	Mary McKenna	Castle
1959	Ena Brooks	Royal Dublin	1990	Mary McKenna	Hermitage
1960	Moira Earner	Dun Laoghaire			

Midland District Ladies' Championship

INAUGURATED 1949

YEAR	WINNER	VENUE	YEAR	WINNER	VENUE
1949	Audrey Donohoe		1970	Mrs M Fogan	Mullingar
1950	Mrs A McCarthy		1971	Miss G Smyth	Kilkenny
1951	Philomena Garvey		1972	Mrs V Hassett	Birr
1952	Kitty McCann		1973	Miss M Moran	Courtown
1953	Pat O'Sullivan		1974	Miss M Gorry	Carlow
1954	Pat O'Sullivan		1975	Miss LM Malone	Waterford
1955	Miss R Bayly		1976	Miss J Hodder	Mullingar
1956	Moira Earner		1977	Mrs M Lambie	Kilkenny
1957	Kitty McCann		1978	Mrs K Reilly	Birr
1958	Kitty McCann		1979	Miss M Gorry	Courtown
1959	Miss A O'Brien	Rosslare	1980	Mrs J Gillespie	Curragh
1960	Kitty McCann	Tullamore	1981	Miss A Reynolds	Tullamore
1961	Pat O'Sullivan	Carlow	1982	Miss C Daly	Carlow
1962	Miss A Heskin	Waterford	1983	Miss B Gleeson	Waterford
1963	Miss M Fogan	Mullingar	1984	Miss D O'Brien-Kenney	Mullingar
1964	Miss J Bourke	Tramore	1985	Miss B Gleeson	Tramore
1965	Miss J Lambert	Kilkenny	1986	Miss D O'Brien-Kenney	Kilkenny
1966	Miss P Quinlan	Birr	1987	Miss R Walsh	Birr
1967	Miss P Quinlan	Courtown	1988	Miss K Maguire	The Heath
1968	Miss C Hickey	Carlow	1989	Miss J Murphy	Rosslare
1969	Mrs P Flanagan	Waterford	1990	Miss S Kenny	Curragh

Munster Ladies' Championship

YEAR	WINNER	VENUE	YEAR	WINNER	VENUE
1949	Miss S McCloughry	Cork	1970	Miss A Heskin	Thurles
1950	Mrs JK Brice	Killarney	1971	Miss A Heskin	Douglas
1951	Philomena Garvey	Cork	1972	Mrs AJ Elmes	Castletroy
1952	Miss M O'Riordan	Cork	1973	Valerie Hassett	Muskerry
1953	Pat O'Sullivan	Cork	1974	Miss A Heskin	Mallow
1954	Pat O'Sullivan	Cork	1975	Miss A Heskin	Limerick
1955	Zelie Fallon	Cork	1976	Rhona Hegarty	Killarney
1956	Zelie Fallon	Cork	1977	Valerie Hassett	Thurles
1957	Zelie Fallon	Cork	1978	Miss A Heskin	Douglas
1958	Kitty McCann	Castletroy	1979	Rhona Hegarty	Lahinch
1959	Zelie Fallon	Killarney	1980	Miss B Gleeson	Muskerry
1960	Pat Quinlan	Thurles	1981	Miss R Brennan	Limerick
1961	Zelie Fallon	Douglas	1982	Eavan Higgins	Killarney
1962	Helen Colhon	Lahinch	1983	Miss B Gleeson	Mallow
1963	Miss A O'Brien	Cork	1984	Miss A O'Sullivan	Ballybunion
1964	Mrs AJ Elmes	Limerick	1985	Eileen Rose McDaid	Cork
1965	Ita Burke	Cork	1986	Mrs C Keating	Thurles
1966	Pat Quinlan	Castletroy	1987	Mrs B Gleeson Healey	Killarney
1967	Miss A O'Brien	Douglas	1988	Eavan Higgins	Castletroy
1968	Mrs AJ Elmes	Limerick	1989	Miss A O'Sullivan	Monkstown
1969	Mrs O Heskin	Cork	1990	Eavan Higgins	Mallow

Ulster Championship

INAUGURATED 1923

YEAR	WINNER	VENUE	YEAR	WINNER	VENUE
1923	Mrs D B Corbett	Malone	1961	*Not Played*	
1924	Jean Rice	Bangor	1962	Ann Sweeney	Royal Belfast
1925	Jean Rice	Balmoral	1963	Ann Sweeney	Shandon Park
1926	AH Cuthell	Holywood	1964	Miss H Colhoun	Knock
1927	Jean Rice	Knock	1965	Sandra Owen	Belvoir Park
1928	Betty Gardiner	Royal Belfast	1966	Joan Beckett	Malone
1929	Jean Rice	Malone	1967	Miss EC Barnett	Newcastle, Co Down
1930	Jean Marks (*née* Rice)	Bangor	1968	Carol McAuley	Kirkistown Castle
1931	Miss D Ferguson	Belvoir Park	1969	Mrs D Madeley	Newcastle, Co Down
1932	Jean Marks	Knock	1970	Carol McAuley	Kirkistown Castle
1933	Miss D Ferguson	Royal Belfast	1971	Maeve McConnell	Castlerock
1934	Joan Mitchell	Malone	1972	Deirdrie Morton	Kirkistown Castle
1935	Mrs J Lee	Belvoir Park	1973	Paula Rooney	Newcastle, Co Down
1936	Jean Marks	Knock	1974	Ann McLean	Massereene
1937	Miss E Ellis	Shandon Park	1975	Lilian Malone	Portrush
1938	Jean Marks	Royal Belfast	1976	Claire Nesbitt	Newcastle, Co Down
1939	Jean Marks	Malone	1977	Deirdre Morton	Belvoir Park
1940–46	*Not played due to Second World War*		1978	Claire Nesbitt	Kirkistown Castle
1947	Zara Bolton	Knock	1979	Mary Gorry	Castlerock
1948	Zara Bolton	Malone	1980	Maureen Madill	Newcastle, Co Down
1949	Zara Bolton	Belvoir Park	1981	Lilian Starrett	
1950	Zara Bolton	Shandon Park		(*née* Malone)	Portrush
1951	Moira Smyth	Royal Belfast	1982	Claire Robinson	
1952	Dorothy Forster	Knock		(*née* Nesbitt)	Kirkistown Castle
1953	Dorothy Forster	Malone	1983	Maureen Madill	Newcastle, Co Down
1954	Jean Marks	Belvoir Park	1984	Claire Robinson	Portrush
1955	Jean Marks	Royal Belfast	1985	Maureen Garner	
1956	Zara Bolton	Shandon Park		(*née* Madill)	Clandeboye
1957	Dorothy Humphreys		1986	Jane Allen	Portstewart
	(*née* Forster)	Malone	1987	Yari McGreevy	Kirkistown Castle
1958	Moira Smyth	Clandeboye	1988	Debbie Hanna	Newcastle, Co Down
1959	Moira Smyth	Knock	1989	Laura Bolton	Castlerock
1960	Zara Bolton	Belvoir Park	1990	Paula Gorman	Belvoir Park

Scotland

As with England the inauguration dates of Scottish county championships vary widely from East Lothian's in 1909 to Galloway's 64 years later. Those of the Area and District Championships began in 1928 with the South of Scotland and Western Divisions, but the Southern Division was not started until 1976.

A glance at the county results will reveal many winners with familiar names, some of them for a wide span of years, including those who were successful several times in succession. Joan Lawrence was Fife Champion every year from 1957 to 1965 and on four other occasions, while Belle Robertson first won the Western Division in 1957 and for the fifth time 28 years later. Her record also included the Dumbarton and Argyll event eleven times over 21 years from 1958.

Aberdeen Ladies' Championship

INAUGURATED 1927

YEAR	WINNER	VENUE	YEAR	WINNER	VENUE
1927	Miss MA Cruickshank	Balnagask	1954	Mrs DT Bruce	Hazlehead
1928	Miss KM Cochrane	Balgownie	1955	Mrs JL Moffat	Balgownie
1929	Miss KM Cochrane	Murcar	1956	Miss EP Davidson	Cruden Bay
1930	Miss KM Cochrane	Cruden Bay	1957	Miss EP Davidson	Deeside
1931	Mrs M Mellis	Balnagask	1958	Mrs JL Moffat	Murcar
1932	Mrs C Tocher	Deeside	1959	Miss L Patterson	Peterhead
1933	Miss KM Cochrane	Balgownie	1960	Miss JL Brown	Hazlehead
1934	Miss KM Cochrane	Murcar	1961	Mrs DT Bruce	Balgownie
1935	Mrs KM Christie		1962	Mrs DT Bruce	Cruden Bay
	(née Cochrane)	Cruden Bay	1963	Mrs JP Kennaway	Deeside
1936	Mrs M Mellis	Balnagask	1964	Miss JL Brown	Peterhead
1937	Mrs M Mellis	Peterhead	1965	Miss AV Laing	Peterhead
1938	Mrs McPherson	Deeside	1966	Miss AV Laing	Hazlehead
1939	Mrs Watt Duffus	Balgownie	1967	Miss AV Laing	Balgownie
1940–45	Not played due to Second World War		1968	Miss AV Laing	Cruden Bay
1946	Mrs Watt Duffus	Murcar	1969	Miss AV Laing	Deeside
1947	Miss M Brown	Peterhead	1970	Miss AV Laing	Murcar
1948	Mrs DT Bruce	Hazlehead	1971	Mrs N Henderson	Hazlehead
1949	Mrs JL Williams	Balgownie	1972	Miss AV Laing	Peterhead
1950	Mrs J Kennaway	Cruden Bay	1973	Mrs N Henderson	Balgownie
1951	Mrs DT Bruce	Deeside	1974	Mrs D Robertson	Cruden Bay
1952	Miss M Brown	Murcar	1975	Mrs RJ Milne	Deeside
1953	Miss GJ Taylor	Peterhead	1976	Miss CA Stewart	Murcar

YEAR	WINNER	VENUE	YEAR	WINNER	VENUE
1977	Miss M Thomson	Peterhead	1984	Mrs J Self	Cruden Bay
1978	Miss AV Laing	Balgownie	1985	Miss P Wright	Balgownie
1979	Mrs J Self	Cruden Bay	1986	Miss E Farquharson	Cruden Bay
1980	Mrs JB Rennie	Deeside	1987	Miss E Farquharson	Deeside
1981	Miss CA Stewart	Murcar	1988	Miss L Urquhart	Murcar
1982	Miss P Wright	Hazlehead	1989	Miss J Forbes	Fraserburgh
1983	Miss E Farquharson	Aboyne	1990	Miss E Farquharson	Cruden Bay

Angus Ladies' Championship

INAUGURATED 1934

YEAR	WINNER	VENUE	YEAR	WINNER	VENUE
1934	Miss L Harris	Carnoustie	1966	Miss K Lackie	Carnoustie
1935	Miss D Millikin	Carnoustie	1967	Miss J Smith	Carnoustie
1936	Mrs C Tocher	Carnoustie	1968	Miss S Chalmers	Montrose
1937	Mrs C Tocher	Carnoustie	1969	Miss I Taylor	Carnoustie
1938	Miss D Millikin	Carnoustie	1970	Miss J Smith	Monifieth
1939	Miss D Millikin	Carnoustie	1971	Miss K Lackie	Downfield
1940–47	*Not played due to Second World War*		1972	Miss K Lackie	Montrose
1948	Mrs BM Henderson	Carnoustie	1973	Miss K Lackie	Forfar
1949	Mrs O Wright	Carnoustie	1974	Miss N Duncan	Arbroath
1950	Mrs EF Duncan	Carnoustie	1975	Miss JW Smith	Camperdown
1951	Mrs C Johnston	Carnoustie	1976	Miss B Huke	Carnoustie
1952	Miss L Harris	Carnoustie	1977	Miss JW Smith	Monifieth
1953	Mrs EF Duncan	Carnoustie	1978	Miss JW Smith	Downfield
1954	Mrs EF Duncan	Carnoustie	1979	Miss JW Smith	Montrose
1955	Mrs EF Duncan	Carnoustie	1980	Miss N Duncan	Forfar
1956	Mrs EF Duncan	Carnoustie	1981	Miss K Sutherland	Arbroath
1957	Mrs EF Duncan	Carnoustie	1982	Miss K Imrie	Monifieth
1958	Mrs M Walker	Carnoustie	1983	Miss K Imrie	Montrose
1959	Mrs EF Duncan	Carnoustie	1984	Miss K Imrie	Carnoustie
1960	Miss S Cushnie	Downfield	1985	Miss M Mackie	Kirriemuir
1961	Miss E Allan	Arbroath	1986	Mrs F Farquharson	Panmure Barry
1962	Mrs A Beattie	Montrose	1987	Mrs F Farquharson	Downfield
1963	Miss E Allen	Carnoustie	1988	Miss C Hay	Monifieth
1964	Miss J Smith	Montrose	1989	Miss K Hope	Carnoustie
1965	Miss N Duncan	Carnoustie	1990	Miss K Sutherland	Panmure Barry

Ayrshire Ladies' Championship

INAUGURATED 1923

YEAR	WINNER	VENUE	YEAR	WINNER	VENUE
1923	Miss J McCulloch	Prestwick, St Nicholas	1928	Miss J McCulloch	Troon
1924	Miss J McCulloch	Troon, Portland	1929	Mrs G Coats	Barassie
1925	Miss C Martin	Barassie	1930	Mrs W Greenlees	Western Gailes
1926	Miss J Gow	Western Gailes	1931	Mrs W Greenlees	Troon, Portland
1927	Miss J McCulloch	Prestwick, St Nicholas	1932	Miss J McCulloch	Prestwick, St Nicholas

YEAR	WINNER	VENUE	YEAR	WINNER	VENUE
1933	Miss J McCulloch	Bogside	1965	Mrs ID Hamilton	West Kilbride
1934	Mrs JB Walker	Troon	1966	Miss J Hastings	Troon
1935	Mrs AM Holm	Barassie	1967	Miss J Hastings	Barassie
1936	Mrs AM Holm	Prestwick, St Nicholas	1968	Mrs ID Hamilton	Prestwick, St Nicholas
1937	Mrs JB Walker	Prestwick, St Nicholas	1969	Miss I Wylie	Troon, Portland
1938	Mrs JB Walker	Troon, Portland	1970	Miss I Wylie	Bogside
1939	Mrs B Henderson	Barassie	1971	Miss I Wylie	West Kilbride
1940–46	*Not played due to Second World War*		1972	Miss I Wylie	Troon, Portland
1947	Mrs AM Holm	Troon	1973	Miss I Wylie	Prestwick, St Nicholas
1948	Mrs AM Holm	Troon	1974	Mrs JM Sharp	Barassie
1949	Mrs A McCall	Bogside	1975	Miss S Lambie	Ayr Belleisle
1950	Mrs AM Holm	Western Gailes	1976	Miss S Lambie	Troon, Darley
1951	Mrs AM Holm	Troon	1977	Miss T Walker	West Kilbride
1952	Mrs M Park	Barassie	1978	Miss S Lambie	Barassie
1953	Mrs B Singleton	West Kilbride	1979	Miss S Lambie	Ballachmyle
1954	Mrs PH Wylie	Prestwick, St Nicholas	1980	Miss A Gemmill	Troon, Portland
1955	Mrs A McCall	Troon	1981	Miss A Gemmill	West Kilbride
1956	Mrs B Singleton	Bogside	1982	Miss A Gemmill	Ardeer
1957	Mrs B Singleton	Prestwick, St Nicholas	1983	Miss A Gemmill	Prestwick, St Nicholas
1958	Mrs B Singleton	West Kilbride	1984	Miss A Gemmill	Ayr Belleisle
1959	Mrs B Singleton	Troon, Portland	1985	Miss J Leishman	Troon, Darley
1960	Miss J Hastings	Troon, Portland	1986	Miss A Gemmill	Bogside
1961	Miss J Hastings	Bogside	1987	Miss A Gemmill	Troon, Portland
1962	Mrs B Singleton	Prestwick, St Nicholas	1988	Miss M Wilson	Prestwick, St Cuthbert
1963	Miss J Hastings	Ayr Belleisle	1989	Miss A Gemmill	Prestwick, St Nicholas
1964	Miss J Hastings	West Kilbride	1990	Miss C Gibson	Barassie

Dumfriesshire Ladies' Championship

INAUGURATED 1973

YEAR	WINNER	VENUE	YEAR	WINNER	VENUE
1973	Mrs A Barclay	Dumfries and County	1981	Mrs E Hill	Dumfries and County
1974	Miss McCalley	Dumfries and Galloway	1982	Mrs E Hill	Dumfries and Galloway
1975	Mrs A Barclay	Powfoot	1983	Miss DM Hill	Powfoot
1976	Mrs A Barclay	Dumfries and County	1984	Miss DM Hill	Dumfries and County
1977	Mrs A Barclay	Dumfries and Galloway	1985	Mrs R Morrison	Dumfries and Galloway
			1986	Mrs M McKerrow	Powfoot
1978	Mrs E Hill	Powfoot	1987	Mrs M McKerrow	Dumfries and County
1979	Miss DM Hill	Dumfries and County	1988	Miss D Douglas	Dumfries and County
1980	Mrs A Barclay	Dumfries and Galloway	1989	Miss D Douglas	Powfoot
			1990	Mrs L Armstrong	Dumfries and County

Dumbartonshire & Argyll Ladies' Championship

INAUGURATED 1909

YEAR	WINNER	VENUE	YEAR	WINNER	VENUE
1913	Miss T Ward	Milngavie	1958	Miss B McCorkindale	Milngavie
1914–19	Not played due to Great War		1959	Miss B McCorkindale	Hilton Park
1920	Mrs Elderson }tie	Glasgow, Killermont	1960	Miss B McCorkindale	Douglas Park
	Mrs Dykes		1961	Mrs IC Robertson	
1921				(née McCorkindale)	Cardross
1922			1962	Mrs IC Robertson	Milngavie
1923	Miss Johnstone	Bearsden	1963	Mrs IC Robertson	Hilton Park
1924	Miss Johnstone	Hillfoot	1964	Miss I Keywood	Cardross
1925	Miss Hay	Cardross	1965	Mrs IC Robertson	Milngavie
1926	Miss Adam	Milngavie	1966	Mrs IC Robertson	Hayston
1927	Mrs Philips	Cardross	1967	Miss E Low	Helensburgh
1928	Miss Johnstone	Milngavie	1968	Mrs IC Robertson	Hayston
1929	Miss Johnstone	Cardross	1969	Mrs IC Robertson	Hilton Park
1930	Miss Johnstone	Hilton Park	1970	Miss V McAlister	Douglas Park
1931	Mrs White	Milngavie	1971	Miss F Jamieson	Hayston
1932	Miss Hendry	Cardross	1972	Miss V McAlister	Milngavie
1933	Miss Hendry	Douglas Park	1973	Miss V McAlister	Clydebank and
1934	Miss Goldie	Helensburgh			District
1935	Miss Herbert	Milngavie	1974	Miss V McAlister	Helensburgh
1936	Miss Adam	Cardross	1975	Miss V McAlister	Hayston
1937	Mrs Turnbull	Milngavie	1976	Miss S Cadden	Cardross
1938	Miss Adam	Hilton Park	1977	Miss S Cadden	Milngavie
1939	Mrs Turnbull	Cardoss	1978	Mrs IC Robertson	Helensburgh
1940–46	Not played due to Second World War		1979	Mrs S McMahon	Hilton Park
1947	Mrs S Cochran	Hilton Park	1980	Mrs MP Grant	Douglas Park
1948	Mrs S Cochran	Glasgow, Killermont	1981	Miss V McAlister	Hayston
1949	Miss M Paterson	Douglas Park	1982	Miss V McAlister	Cardross
1950	Mrs TS Currie	Cardross	1983	Miss V McAlister	Milngavie
1951	Mrs S Cochran	Milngavie	1984	Miss V McAlister	Windyhill
1952	Miss M Bell	Cardross	1985	Miss V McAlister	Hilton Park
1953	Miss I Keywood	Milngavie	1986	Miss J Kinloch	Windyhill
1954	Miss I Keywood	Cardross	1987	Miss S McDonald	Douglas Park
1955	Mrs TS Currie	Douglas Park	1988	Miss V McAlister	Cardross
1956	Miss B Geekie	Cardross	1989	Miss V McAlister	Cardross
1957	Miss I Keywood	Hardgate	1990	Miss M McKinlay	Hilton Park

East Lothian Ladies' Championship

INAUGURATED 1934

YEAR	WINNER	VENUE	YEAR	WINNER	VENUE
1934	Miss MJ Couper	Gullane	1966	Miss M Fowler	Gullane
1935	Miss MJ Couper	Longniddry	1967	Miss M Fowler	Gullane
1936	Miss MM Robertson	Gullane	1968	Miss CJ Lugton	North Berwick
1937	Mrs IH Bowhill	Gullane	1969	Mrs AJR Ferguson	Longniddry
1938	Miss MJ Couper	Longniddry	1970	Miss CJ Lugton	Gullane
1939	Mrs EC Mackean	Gullane	1971	Miss CJ Lugton	Dunbar
1940–47	*Not played due to Second World War*		1972	Miss C Lugton	Royal Musselburgh
1948	Miss J Donald	Gullane	1973	Miss CJ Lugton	North Berwick
1949	Miss J Donald	Gullane	1974	Mrs AJR Ferguson	Dunbar
1950	Mrs RT Peel	Gullane	1975	Mrs D McIntosh	Gullane
1951	Miss J Donald	Gullane	1976	Miss CJ Lugton	North Berwick
1952	Miss J Donald	Gullane	1977	Miss CJ Lugton	Dunbar
1953	Miss J Donald	Gullane	1978	Miss J Connachan	North Berwick
1954	Mrs E Woodcock	North Berwick	1979	Miss J Connachan	Gullane
1955	Mrs E Woodcock	Longniddry	1980	Miss CJ Lugton	Dunbar
1956	Mrs Paton	Gullane	1981	Mrs AJR Ferguson	North Berwick
1957	Miss M Fowler	Gullane	1982	*Null and void*	
1958	Miss M Fowler	Longniddry	1983	Mrs M Thomson	Dunbar
1959	Miss M Fowler	Dunbar	1984	Miss M Ferguson	Gullane
1960	Miss M Fowler	Gullane	1985	Miss M Ferguson	Dunbar
1961	Miss M Fowler	Longniddry	1986	Miss P Lees	Longniddry
1962	Miss M Fowler	North Berwick	1987	Miss J Ford	Dunbar
1963	Miss M Fowler	Gullane	1988	Miss CJ Lugton	Gullane
1964	Miss M Fowler	Longniddry	1989	Miss CJ Lugton	Gullane
1965	Miss CJ Lugton	Dunbar	1990	Miss C Lambert	Dunbar

Fife County Championship

INAUGURATED 1930

YEAR	WINNER	VENUE	YEAR	WINNER	VENUE
1930	Marion Alexander	Dunfermline	1950	Meryll C Cowan	Elie
1931	Meryll Cook	Elie	1951	Helen Burton	Dunfermline
1932	Mary G Fortune	Lundin Links	1952	Helen Burton	Lundin Links
1933	Madeline Everard	Scotscraig	1953	Joan B Lawrence	Kirkcaldy
1934	Alison Hopwood	Dumfermline	1954	Helen Burton	Elie
1935	Alison Hopwood	St Andrews	1955	Frances L Dornan	Dunfermline
1936	Madeline Everard	Elie	1956	Ethel Thomson	Lundin Links
1937	Ellen RK Orr	Lundin Links	1957	Joan B Lawrence	Kirkcaldy
1938	Ellen RK Orr	Scotscraig	1958	Joan B Lawrence	Elie
1939	Ellen RK Orr	Torrie	1959	Joan B Lawrence	Scotscraig
1940–46	*Not played due to Second World War*		1960	Joan B Lawrence	Kirkcaldy
1947	Frances L Dornan	Scotscraig	1961	Joan B Lawrence	St Andrews
1948	Ethel Thomson	St Andrews	1962	Joan B Lawrence	Dunfermline
1949	Meryll C Cowan	Lundin Links	1963	Joan B Lawrence	St Andrews

YEAR	WINNER	VENUE	YEAR	WINNER	VENUE
1964	Joan B Lawrence	Dunfermline	1978	Diane Mitchell	Scotscraig
1965	Joan B Lawrence	Leven	1979	Jean Bald	Glenrothes
1966	Jean Bald	St Andrews	1980	Jennifer Louden	St Andrews
1967	Joan B Lawrence	Dunfermline	1981	Jean Bald	Scotscraig
1968	Joan B Lawrence	Scotscraig	1982	Jean Bald	Dunfermline
1969	Joan B Lawrence	St Andrews	1983	Rosemary Scott	Glenrothes
1970	Jean Bald	Dunfermline	1984	Elaine Hunter	Dunfermline
1971	Jean Bald	Lundin Links	1985	Lorna Bennett	Scotscraig
1972	Jennifer Neil	Dunfermline	1986	Lorna Bennett	Dunnikier Park
1973	Jean Bald	St Andrews	1987	Lorna Bennett	Ladybank
1974	Jennifer Neil	Scotscraig	1988	Joan B Lawrence	Dunfermline
1975	Marigold Speir	Leven	1989	Dorothy Ford	Scotscraig
1976	Jennifer Louden	Glenrothes	1990	Joan B Lawrence	Glenrothes
1977	Jennifer Louden	St Andrews			

Galloway Ladies' Championship

INAUGURATED 1973

YEAR	WINNER	VENUE	YEAR	WINNER	VENUE
1974	Mrs MP Rennie	Southerness and Stranraer	1982	Miss M Clement	Portpatrick
			1983	Miss S McDonald	Kirkcudbright
1975	Miss M Clement	Stranraer	1984	Miss S McDonald	Stranraer
1976	Miss M Clement	Stranraer	1985	Miss M Wright	Southerness
1977	Miss M Clement	Southerness	1986	Miss M Wright	Portpatrick
1978	Miss FM Rennie	Dunskey	1987	Miss M Wright	Kirkcudbright
1979	Miss FM Rennie	Stranraer	1988	Miss M Wright	Stranraer
1980	Miss FM Rennie	Kirkcudbright	1989	Miss FM Rennie	Kirkcudbright
1981	Miss M Clement	Southerness	1990	Miss FM Rennie	Wigtownshire

Lanarkshire Ladies' Championship

INAUGURATED 1928

YEAR	WINNER	VENUE	YEAR	WINNER	VENUE
1928	Miss H Gray	Douglas Park	1938	Miss W Morrison	Hamilton
1929	Mrs AM Holm (née Gray)	Douglas Park	1939	Mrs A Ballantine	Hamilton
			1940–46	*Not played due to Second World War*	
1930	Miss M Fogo	Douglas Park	1947	Miss J Hill	Sandyhills
1931	Mrs TM Burton	Douglas Park	1948	Miss J Hill	Drumpellier
1932	Mrs AM Holm	Drumpellier	1949	Miss S Conacher	Hamilton
1933	Mrs W Reid	Drumpellier	1950	Miss G Galbraith	Hamilton
1934	Miss W Morrison	Hamilton	1951	Miss H Murdoch	Cathkin Braes
1935	Miss N Forrest	Hamilton	1952	Miss H Murdoch	Cathkin Braes
1936	Miss W Morrison	Hamilton	1953	Miss J Cadzow	Cathkin Braes
1937	Mrs Ballantine	Hamilton	1954	Miss J Robertson	Cathkin Braes

YEAR	WINNER	VENUE	YEAR	WINNER	VENUE
1955	Miss J Robertson	Sandyhills	1974	Mrs W Norris	Cathkin Braes
1956	Miss J Robertson	Drumpellier	1975	Mrs W Norris	Drumpellier
1957	Miss J Robertson	Sandyhills	1976	Mrs A Burden	Strathaven
1958	Miss J Robertson	Cathkin Braes	1977	Miss S Needham	Sandyhills
1959	Miss J Robertson	Drumpellier	1978	Miss B McCormack	Drumpellier
1960	Miss H Murdoch	Cathkin Braes	1979	Mrs W Norris	Kirkhill
1961	Miss H Murdoch	Cawder	1980	Mrs JC Scott	Lanark
1962	Miss H Murdoch	Cathkin Braes	1981	Miss E Dunn	East Kilbride
1963	Miss B McCormack	Drumpellier	1982	Mrs W Norris	
1964	Miss J Smith	Cawder	1983	Mrs S Roy	
1965	Miss M Park	Cathkin Braes		(née Needham)	Strathaven
1966	Mrs W Norris	Hamilton	1984	Mrs S Roy	Cawder
1967	Miss B McCormack	Bothwell	1985	Miss P Hutton	Crow Wood
1968	Mrs W Norris	Drumpellier	1986	Mrs JC Scott	Kirkhill
1969	Miss S Needham	Sandyhills	1987	Mrs A Hendry	Sandyhills
1970	Mrs W Norris	Cathkin Braes	1988	Miss F McKay	Cathkin Braes
1971	Mrs W Norris	Lenzie	1989	Mrs K Dallas	Lanark
1972	Miss S Needham	Bothwell Castle	1990	Mrs A Hendry	Hamilton
1973	Miss S Needham	Hamilton			

Midlothian Ladies' Championship

INAUGURATED 1909

YEAR	WINNER	VENUE	YEAR	WINNER	VENUE
1924	Miss MJ Wood	Murrayfield	1960	Miss P Dunn	Prestonfield
1925	Miss MJ Wood	Prestonfield	1961	Miss E Philip	Baberton
1926	Miss MJ Wood	Turnhouse	1962	Mrs J Milton	Murrayfield
1927	Miss Q Smith	Cramond Brig,	1963	Mrs M Duthie	Baberton
		Edinburgh	1964	Mrs D Antonio	Dalmahoy
1928	Miss D Park	Murrayfield	1965	Miss F Miller	Turnhouse
1929	Miss D Park	Turnhouse	1966	Miss E Philip	Murrayfield
1930	Miss D Park	Craigmillar Park	1967	Miss M Norval	Baberton
1931	Miss D Park	Dalmahoy	1968	Mrs E Jack	Dalmahoy
1932	Mrs JN Duncan	Murrayfield	1969	Miss M Norval	Turnhouse
1933	Miss CM Park	Prestonfield	1970	Miss S MacDonald	Kingsknowe
1934	Miss CM Park	Bruntsfield	1971	Mrs J Marshall	Ratho Park
1935	Miss CM Park	Murrayfield	1972	Miss C Hardwick	Newbattle
1936	Miss CM Park	Kingsknowe	1973	Miss C Hardwick	Musselburgh
1937	Miss M Nicoll	Prestonfield	1974	Dr M Norval	Musselburgh
1938	Miss CM Park	Dalmahoy	1975	Miss J More	Dalmahoy
1939	Mrs SH Morton	Murrayfield	1976	Miss M Stavert	Kingsknowe
1940–46	*Not played due to Second World War*		1977	Miss M Stavert	Ratho Park
1947	Miss CM Park	Baberton	1978	Miss M Stavert	Newbattle
1948	Miss CM Park	Murrayfield	1979	Miss M Stavert	Turnhouse
1949	Mrs J Scott	Turnhouse	1980	Mrs BM Marshall	Dalmahoy
1950	Miss E McLarty	Craigmillar Park	1981	Miss MF Allen	Prestonfield
1951	Mrs WC Ritchie	Dalmahoy	1982	Miss S Little	Musselburgh
1952	Miss JL Dunbar	Prestonfield	1983	Mrs J Marshall	Broomieknowe
1953	Mrs WC Ritchie	Murrayfield	1984	Mrs F de Vries	Kingsknowe
1954	Mrs JJG Thomson	Ratho Park	1985	Mrs F de Vries	Murrayfield
1955	Mrs JB Cormack	Turnhouse	1986	Mrs J Marshall	Craigmillar Park
1956	Mrs WC Ritchie	Baberton	1987	Miss M Stavert	Newbattle
1957	Mrs JB Cormack	Murrayfield	1988	Miss M Stavert	Broomieknowe
1958	Mrs WC Ritchie	Craigmillar	1989	Mrs E Bruce	Prestonfield
1959	Miss E Philip	Kingsknowe	1990	Mrs E Jack	Dalmahoy

Perth & Kinross Ladies' Championship

INAUGURATED 1921

YEAR	WINNER	VENUE	YEAR	WINNER	VENUE
1921	Mysie L Brown		1961	Mrs J Norwell	Blairgowrie
1922	BS Graham		1962	Mrs J Aitken	Blairgowrie
1923	M Vallings		1963	Mrs J Hay	Blairgowrie
1924	Mysie L Brown		1964	Mrs J Norwell	Gleneagles
1925	Mysie L Brown		1965	Mrs J Hay	Blairgowrie
1926	SG Scott		1966	Mrs N Gibb	Blairgowrie
1927	SG Scott		1967	Mrs J Norwell	Blairgowrie
1928	M Mickle		1968	Mrs J Norwell	Blairgowrie
1929	Mysie L Brown		1969	Mrs J Norwell	Alyth
1930	CPR Montgomery		1970	Mrs J Norwell	Dunblane
1931	Mysie L Brown		1971	Mrs J Aitken	Crieff
1932	Jessie Anderson		1972	Mrs J Aitken	Blairgowrie
1933	Jessie Anderson		1973	Mrs J Hay	Taymouth Castle
1934	Jessie Anderson		1974	Mrs J Hay	Blairgowrie
1935	CPR Montgomery		1975	Miss FC Anderson	Blairgowrie
1936	Jessie Anderson		1976	Mrs J Hay	Gleneagles
1937	CPR Montgomery		1977	Miss FC Anderson	Blairgowrie
1938	Sheila B Scott		1978	Miss FC Anderson	Gleneagles
1939–49	*Not played due to Second World War*		1979	Miss FC Anderson	Crieff
1950	Elsie Crawford	Gleneagles	1980	Mrs J Aitken	King James VI, Perth
1951	Evelyn Young	Gleneagles	1981	Mrs J Aitken	Blairgowrie
1952	Evelyn Young	Gleneagles	1982	Mrs J Aitken	Craigie Hill
1953	Evelyn Young	Gleneagles	1983	Miss FC Anderson	Blairgowrie
1954	Elsie Crawford	Blairgowrie	1984	Mrs J Aitken	Murrayshall
1955	Mrs N Gibb	Gleneagles	1985	Miss A Guthrie	Crieff
1956	Mrs N Gibb	Blairgowrie	1986	Mrs I Shannon	Blairgowrie
1957	Mrs J Aitken	Gleneagles	1987	Miss FC Anderson	Crieff
1958	Mrs J Hay	Blairgowrie	1988	Mrs V Pringle	Murrayshall
1959	Mrs J Aitken	Blairgowrie	1989	Miss A Sharp	King James VI, Perth
1960	Mrs N Gibb	Gleneagles	1990	Miss S Mailer	Crieff

Renfrewshire Ladies' Championship

INAUGURATED 1927

YEAR	WINNER	VENUE	YEAR	WINNER	VENUE
1927	Miss D Herbert	Kilmacolm	1964	Miss JH Anderson	Ranfurly Castle
1928	Mrs Houston Rowan	Pollok	1965	Miss E Gibb	Paisley
1929	Mrs Fleming	Old Ranfurly	1966	Mrs JH Anderson	East Renfrewshire
1930	Miss V Lamb	Erskine	1967	Mrs JH Anderson	Ranfurly Castle
1931	Mrs Fleming	Kilmacolm	1968	Mrs JH Anderson	Kilmacolm
1932	Mrs Fleming	Old Ranfurly	1969	Miss E Gibb	Erskine
1933	Miss V Lamb	East Renfrewshire	1970	Mrs JH Anderson	Old Ranfurly
1934	Mrs Fleming	Ranfurly Castle	1971	Mrs JH Anderson	East Renfrewshire
1935	Miss J McLintock	Erskine	1972	Mrs JH Anderson	Ranfurly Castle
1936	Miss M Pearcy	Kilmacolm	1973	Mrs JH Anderson	Kilmacolm
1937	Mrs CM Falconer	Old Ranfurly	1974	Dr AJ Wilson	Whitecraigs
1938	Miss J McLintock	East Renfrewshire	1975	Miss L Bennett	Ranfurly Castle
1939	Mrs Fleming	Kilmacolm	1976	Dr AJ Wilson	Erskine
1940–48	*Not played due to Second World War*		1977	Miss L Bennett	Paisley
1949	Mrs J Drummond	East Renfrewshire	1978	Miss W Aitken	Haggs Castle
1950	Mrs J Drummond	Old Ranfurly	1979	Miss W Aitken	Kilmacolm
1951	Mrs J Drummond	Fereneze	1980	Miss W Aitken	Ralston
1952	Mrs AR Gray	Erskine	1981	Miss W Aitken	Whitecraigs
1953	Miss M Pearcy	Kilmacolm	1982	Miss W Aitken	Old Ranfurly
1954	Mrs J Drummond	Ranfurly Castle	1983	Mrs JL Hastings	
1955	Miss N Menzies	Erskine		(*née* Sommerville)	Kilmacolm
1956	Miss D Sommerville	East Renfrewshire	1984	Dr AJ Wilson	Ranfurly Castle
1957	Miss D Sommerville	Old Ranfurly	1985	Miss S Lawson	Erskine
1958	Miss D Sommerville	Kilmacolm	1986	Miss S Lawson	Paisley
1959	Miss D Sommerville	Ranfurly Castle	1987	Miss S Lawson	Whitecraigs
1960	Miss J Anderson	Erskine	1988	Miss S Lawson	Cochrane Castle
1961	Miss D Sommerville	East Renfrewshire	1989	Miss D Jackson	Renfrew
1962	Miss L Lethem	Old Ranfurly	1990	Miss D Jackson	Renfrew
1963	Miss D Sommerville	Kilmacolm			

Stirling & Clackmannan Ladies' Championship

INAUGURATED 1969

YEAR	WINNER	VENUE	YEAR	WINNER	VENUE
1969	Mrs D Smith	Falkirk Tryst	1980	Miss E Miskimmin	Falkirk Tryst
1970	Mrs GE Mitchell	Stirling	1981	Miss E Miskimmin	Stirling
1971	Mrs D Smith	Tulliallan	1982	*Not played*	
1972	Mrs GE Mitchell	Falkirk	1983	Miss J Harrison	Tulliallan
1973	Mrs D Smith	Glenbervie	1984	Mrs W McCallum	Falkirk
1974	Mrs GE Mitchell	Falkirk Tryst	1985	Miss S Michie	Glenbervie
1975	Miss E Miskimmin	Stirling	1986	Miss S Michie	Falkirk Tryst
1976	Mrs R Frame	Alloa	1987	Miss J Harrison	Stirling
1977	Mrs D Smith	Tulliallan	1988	Miss J Harrison	Alloa
1978	Mrs J MacCallum	Falkirk	1989	Mrs J Abernethy	Grangemouth
1979	Mrs J MacCallum	Glenbervie	1990	Miss A Rose	Braehead

South of Scotland Ladies' Championship

INAUGURATED 1928

YEAR	WINNER	VENUE
1928	Miss Cleland	Dumfries and County
1929	Mrs Wilson	New Galloway
1930	Mrs Wilson	Stranraer
1931	Mrs JJ Dykes	Moffat
1932	Miss R Lamb	Powfoot
1933	Mrs Williamson	Stranraer
1934	Mrs MC Allan	Dumfries and County
1935	Mrs Wilson	Moffat
1936	Miss Coltart	Stranraer
1937	Miss G Douglas	Dumfries and Galloway
1938	Miss Coltart	Powfoot
1939	Mrs Gavigan	Portpatrick Dunskey
1940–41	*Not played due to Second World War*	
1947	Dr R Donaldson	Dumfries and County
1948	Dr R Donaldson	Dumfries and Galloway
1949	Dr R Donaldson	Portpatrick Dunskey
1950	Dr R Donaldson	Powfoot
1951	Dr R Donaldson	Dumfries and County
1952	Miss H Bissett	Dumfries and Galloway
1953	Mrs DC Coubrough	Moffat
1954	Mrs P Vivers	Powfoot
1955	Mrs J Kerr	Dumfries and County
1956	Mrs M Drummond	Portpatrick Dunskey
1957	Mrs P Vivers	Dumfries and Galloway
1958	Mrs DC Coubrough	Stranraer
1959	Mrs DC Coubrough	Moffat
1960	Miss C McCelland	Powfoot
1961	Miss M McCallay	Dumfries and County
1962	Mrs DC Coubrough	Portpatrick Dunskey
1963	Mrs DC Coubrough	Dumfries and Galloway
1964	Mrs DC Coubrough	Southerness
1965	Mrs DC Coubrough	Moffat
1966	Mrs DC Coubrough	Stranraer
1967	Mrs DC Coubrough	Powfoot
1968	Miss VML McAlister	Dumfries and County
1969	Miss VML McAlister	Portpatrick Dunskey
1970	Mrs A Barclay	Dumfries and Galloway
1971	Miss DM Hill	Southerness
1972	Mrs I Anderson	Moffat
1973	Miss VML McAlister	Stranraer
1974	Miss VML McAlister	Powfoot
1975	Mrs A Barclay	Dumfries and County
1976	Mrs A Barclay	Portpatrick Dunskey
1977	Mrs A Barclay	Dumfries and Galloway
1978	Mrs A Barclay	Southerness
1979	Mrs E Hill	Moffat
1980	Mrs E Hill	Stanraer
1981	Mrs A Barclay	Powfoot
1982	Miss DM Hill	Dumfries and County
1983	Miss S McDonald	Portpatrick Dunskey
1984	Miss M Wright	Dumfries and Galloway
1985	Miss FM Rennie	Kirkcudbright
1986	Miss FM Rennie	Thornhill
1987	Mrs S McMurtrie	Southerness
1988	Miss M Wright	Moffat
1989	Miss M Wright	Stranraer
1990	Miss M Wright	Powfoot

Border Counties Ladies' Championship

INAUGURATED 1974

YEAR	WINNER	VENUE
1974	Mrs MAT Sanderson	Hawick
1975	Mrs S Simpson	Selkirk
1976	Mrs S Simpson	Hawick
1977	Miss S Gallacher	Selkirk
1978	Miss S Gallacher	Torwoodlee
1979	Miss S Gallacher	Duns
1980	Miss S Gallacher	Hawick
1981	Miss A Hunter	Hirsel
1982	Miss S Simpson	Innerleithen
1983	Mrs E White	Jedburgh
1984	Miss S Gallacher	Kelso
1985	Miss S Gallacher	Peebles
1986	Miss S Gallacher	Minto
1987	Mrs S Simpson	Minto
1988	Miss A Hunter	Kelso
1989	Mrs A Fleming	Peebles
1990	Miss J Anderson	Minto

Northern Counties (Scotland) Ladies' Championship

INAUGURATED 1967

YEAR	WINNER	VENUE	YEAR	WINNER	VENUE
1967	Mrs B Drakard		1979	Mrs I McIntosh	Inverness
1968	Miss J Cumming		1980	Mrs I McIntosh	Nairn Dunbar
1969	Mrs I McIntosh		1981	Miss S Ross	Forres
1970	Mrs I McIntosh		1982	Miss G Stewart	Lossiemouth
1971	Miss M Kirk		1983	Miss L Anderson	Inverness
1972	Miss J Cumming		1984	Miss J Buist	Nairn
1973	Mrs I McIntosh		1985	Miss A Shannon	Elgin
1974	Mrs I McIntosh	Lossiemouth	1986	Miss F McKay	Forres
1975	Mrs I McIntosh	Nairn Dunbar	1987	Mrs I McIntosh	Nairn
1976	Miss G Stewart	Nairn	1988	Mrs I McIntosh	Lossiemouth
1977	Miss S Ross	Forres	1989	Mrs E Fiskin	Inverness
1978	Miss G Stewart	Elgin	1990	Miss F McKay	Elgin

Eastern Division Ladies' Championship

INAUGURATED 1931

YEAR	WINNER	VENUE	YEAR	WINNER	VENUE
1931	Mrs JB Watson	Longniddry	1959	Miss M Fowler	Glenbervie
1932	Mrs JB Watson	Bruntsfield Links	1960	Miss M Fowler	Gullane
1933	Miss D Park	Gullane	1961	Mrs M Draper	Gullane
1934	Miss H Nimmo	Dalmahoy	1962	Miss M Fowler	Dalmahoy
1935	Mrs RH Wallace		1964	Miss B Crichton	Prestonfield
	Williamson	Gullane	1965	Miss J Bald	Dunfermline
1936	Miss J Anderson	Bruntsfield Links	1966	Miss A Laing	Glenbervie
1937	Miss CPR Montgomery	Murrayfield	1967	Mrs A McIntosh	
1938	Miss J Anderson	Longniddry	1968	Miss N Duncan	Ratho Park
1939	Miss J Anderson	Murrayfield	1969	Miss J Hutton	Dumfermline
1940–46	*Not played due to Second World War*		1970	Miss J Hutton	Tulliallan
1947	Miss J Donald	Gullane	1971	Miss J Lawrence	Gullane
1948	Miss J Donald	Murrayfield	1972	Miss J Lawrence	Kirkcaldy
1949	Miss J Donald	Longniddry	1973	Miss J Bald	Craigmillar Park
1950	Mrs G Valentine		1974	Miss C Lugton	Falkirk Carmuirs
	(*née* Anderson)	Bruntsfield Links	1975	Mrs AJR Ferguson	Dunbar
1951	Mrs RT Peel	Gullane	1976	Miss C Panton	Dunfermline
1952	Mrs RT Peel	Longniddry	1977	Miss L Hope	Turnhouse
1953	Miss J Donald	Gullane	1978	Miss L Hope	Falkirk Tryst
1954	Mrs RT Peel	Gullane	1979	Miss M Stavert	
1955	Mrs RT Peel	Dalmahoy	1980	Mrs J Marshall	
1956	Mrs RT Peel	Gullane	1981	Miss E Kimmen	
1957	Mrs R T Peel	St Andrews	1982	Miss J Bald	
1958	Mrs J Aitken		1983	Mrs J Marshall	

YEAR	WINNER	VENUE	YEAR	WINNER	VENUE
1984	Miss L Hope		1988	Miss J Ford	
1985	Miss L Bennett		1989	Miss A Rose	
1986	Miss J Harrison		1990	Mrs A Hendry	
1987	Miss A Rose				

Northern Division Ladies' Championship (Scotland)

YEAR	WINNER	VENUE	YEAR	WINNER	VENUE
1970	Mrs I Wright	Edzell	1981	Miss F McNab	
1971	Mrs I McIntosh	Nairn	1982	Miss G Stewart	
1972	Miss AV Laing	Blairgowrie	1983	Miss G Stewart	
1973	Miss M Thomson	Murcar	1984	Miss P Wright	
1974	Miss M Thomson	Montrose	1985	Miss A Shannon	
1975	Miss G Stewart	Elgin	1986	Miss C Middleton	
1976	Miss AV Laing	Blairgowrie	1987	Mrs A Murray (née Shannon)	
1977	Miss F Anderson	Cruden Bay	1988	Miss K Imrie	
1978	Miss G Stewart	Forfar	1989	Miss S Wood	
1979	Mrs J Self		1990	Miss K Imrie	
1980	Miss G Stewart				

South Division Ladies' Championship (Scotland)

INAUGURATED 1976

YEAR	WINNER	VENUE	YEAR	WINNER	VENUE
1976	Mrs S Simpson	Hawick	1983	Miss S McDonald	Dumfries and County
1977	Mrs A Barclay	Dumfries and Galloway	1984	Miss F Rennie	Southerness
			1985	Mrs S Simpson	Peebles
1978	Miss S Gallagher	Southerness	1986	Miss M Wright	Thornhill
1979	Miss S Gallagher	Peebles	1987	Miss M Wright	Stranraer
1980	Miss DM Hill	Powfoot	1988	Mrs S Simpson	Kelso
1981	Miss S Gallagher	Stranraer	1989	Miss F Rennie	Dumfries and County
1982	Miss A Hunter	Hawick	1990	Miss F Rennie	Kirkcudbright

West Divisional Ladies' Championship (Scotland)

YEAR	WINNER	VENUE	YEAR	WINNER	VENUE
1928	Mrs G Coats	Western Gailes	1964	Mrs IC Robertson	
1929	Miss J McCulloch	Troon		(née McCorkindale)	East Renfrewshire
1930	Miss J McCulloch	Cardross	1965	Mrs ID Hamilton	Prestwick St Nicholas
1931	Miss N Baird	Glasgow Gailes	1966	Mrs IC Robertson	Milngavie
1932	Mrs W Greenless	Ranfurly Castle	1967	Miss S Needham	Drumpellier
1933	Mrs AM Holm	Troon	1968	Mrs W Norris	Whitecraigs
1934	Mrs AM Holm	Cardross	1969	Mrs IC Robertson	Barassie
1935	Mrs AM Holm	Glasgow Killermont	1970	Miss F Jamieson	Cardross
1936	Mrs AM Holm	Ranfurly Castle	1971	Miss S Needham	Hamilton
1937	Mrs AM Holm	Troon Portland	1972	Miss S Needham	Paisley
1938	Miss B Henderson	Helensburgh	1973	Miss S Needham	West Kilbride
1939–46	*Not played due to Second World War*		1974	Miss G Cadden	Douglas Park
1947	Miss J McCulloch	Hayston	1975	Miss S Needham	East Kilbride
1948	Mrs AM Holm	Erskine	1976	Miss S Lambie	Cochrane Castle
1949	Mrs AM Holm	Troon Portland	1977	Miss S Lambie	Barassie
1950	Mrs AM Holm	Helensburgh	1978	Miss W Aitken	Cardross
1951	Mrs B Singleton	Cathkin Braes	1979	Miss S Lambie	Strathaven
1952	Miss K McNeil	East Renfrewshire	1980	Miss W Aitken	East Renfrewshire
1953	Mrs B Singleton	Troon	1981	Miss W Aitken	Troon Portland
1954	Mrs J Drummond	Milngavie	1982	Miss S Lawson	Helensburgh
1955	Miss B Geakie	Cathkin Braes	1983	Miss S Lawson	Hamilton
1956	Miss J Robertson	Ranfurly Castle	1984	Dr A Wilson	East Renfrewshire
1957	Miss B McCorkindale	Barassie	1985	Mrs IC Robertson	Old Prestwick
1958	Miss J Robertson	Cardross	1986	Miss S Lawson	Cardross
1959	Miss J Robertson	Cawder	1987	Mrs A Hendry	Lanark
1960	Mrs B Singleton	Kilmacolm	1988	Miss S Lawson	Cathkin Braes
1961	Miss DT Sommerville	Troon	1989	Mrs K Dallas	West Kilbride
1962	Miss S McKinven	Hilton Park	1990	Miss S Spiewak	Dullatur
1963	Mrs B Singleton	Cathkin Braes			

Scottish Ladies' Foursomes

YEAR	WINNER	VENUE	YEAR	WINNER	VENUE
1958	Falkirk	Troon Portland	1972	West of Scotland	
1959	Gullane	Gullane		Girls' Assoc	Hilton Park
1960	Caldwell	Douglas Park	1973	Troon	Turnhouse
1961	Elie and Earlsferry	Dunblane		*After 1974 became 36 hole stroke play under*	
1962	Milngavie	Glenbervie		*auspices of SLGA*	
1963	Caldwell	Barassie	1974	Edinburgh University	West Kilbride
1964	Gullane	Dalmahoy	1975	Aberdour	Ratho Park
1965	Troon	Erskine	1976	Panmure, Barry	Tulliallan
1966	Gullane	Longniddry	1977	Gullane	Downfield
1967	Haggs Castle	Old Ranfurly	1978	Dumfries and	
1968	Gullane	Hamilton		County	Dumfries and County
1969	Dumfries and		1979	Craigie Hill	Crow Wood
	County	Baberton	1980	Dumfries and	
1970	Hamilton	Prestwick St		County	Dalmahoy
		Nicholas	1981	Baberton	Dunfermline
1971	Gullane	Prestonfield	1982	Aberdour	Livingstone

YEAR	WINNER	VENUE	YEAR	WINNER	VENUE
1983	Hamilton	Ratho Park	1987	Baberton	Dunfermline
1984	Gullane	Buchanan Castle	1988	Gullane	Bonnyton
1985	*Not played*		1989	Gullane	Eastwood
1986	Blairgowrie	Crieff	1990	Gullane	Carnoustie

Scottish Ladies' County Championship

INAUGURATED 1909

YEAR	WINNERS	VENUE	YEAR	WINNERS	VENUE
1909	Lanarkshire	Western Gailes	1958	Fife	Troon
1910	Fife	St Andrews	1959	Renfrewshire	Gullane
1911	Ayrshire	Troon	1960	Renfrewshire	Carnoustie
1912	Ayrshire	St Andrews	1961	Renfrewshire	Troon
1913	Fife		1962	Ayrshire	Gullane
1914–19	*Not played due to Great War*		1963	Dunbartonshire	
1920	Ayrshire	Cruden Bay		and Argyll	Cruden Bay
1921	Midlothian	Troon	1964	Ayrshire	Western Gailes
1922	Midlothian	Gleneagles	1965	Fife	Elie
1923	Midlothian	Western Gailes	1966	Fife	Carnoustie
1924	Midlothian	Longniddry	1967	Fife	Kilmacolm
1925	Midlothian	Balgownie	1968	Ayrshire	Longniddry
1926	Lanarkshire	Gleneagles	1969	Dunbartonshire and	
1927	Midlothian	Turnberry		Argyll	Blairgowrie
1928	Midlothian	Gleneagles	1970	Ayrshire	Troon
1929	Midlothian	Gleneagles	1971	Aberdeenshire	Elie
1930	Ayrshire	Gleneagles	1972	Aberdeenshire	Cruden Bay
1931	Ayrshire	Gleneagles	1973	Dunbartonshire and	
1932	Midlothian	Gleneagles		Argyll	Troon
1933	Midlothian	Gleneagles	1974	Fife	Dumfries and County
1934	Ayrshire	Gleneagles	1975	Lanarkshire	Ladybank
1935	Midlothian	Gleneagles	1976	Lanarkshire	Cruden Bay
1936	East Lothian	Gleneagles	1977	Lanarkshire	Lanark
1937	Ayrshire	Gleneagles	1978	East Lothian	Stranraer
1938	Ayrshire	Gleneagles	1979	Dunbartonshire and	
1940–46	*Not played due to Second World War*			Argyll	Prestonfield
1947	East Lothian	St Andrews	1980	Northern Counties	Nairn
1948	Ayrshire	Gleneagles	1981	Northern Counties	Douglas Park
1949	East Lothian	Gleneagles	1982	Renfrewshire	Peebles
1950	East Lothian	Gleneagles	1983	Lanarkshire	Longniddry
1951	Perth and Kinross	Gleneagles	1984	Lanarkshire	Murrayshall
1952	Perth and Kinross	Gleneagles	1985	East Lothian	Erskine
1953	Perth and Kinross	Gleneagles	1986	Aberdeenshire	Powfoot
1954	Renfrewshire	Gleneagles	1987	Renfrewshire	St Andrews
1955	Ayrshire	Gleneagles	1988	Lanarkshire	Carnoustie
1956	Renfrewshire	Elie	1989	Lanarkshire	Prestwick
1957	Renfrewshire	Balgownie	1990	East Lothian	Portpatrick, Dunskey

Wales

Brecon and Radnor Ladies' Championship

YEAR	WINNER	VENUE	YEAR	WINNERS	VENUE
1986	Mrs G Gibb	Brecon	1989	Mrs B Brain	Llandrindod Wells
1987	Miss S Beetham	Cradoc	1990	Mrs H Phillips	Brecon
1988	Mrs S Coe	Builth Wells			

Caernarvonshire and Anglesey Ladies' Championship

INAUGURATED 1934

YEAR	WINNER	VENUE	YEAR	WINNER	VENUE
1934			1956	Miss EHA Lever	Bull Bay
1935			1957	Miss N Seddon	St Deiniol
1936			1958	Miss N Seddon	Pwllheli
1937			1959	Mrs DV Ingham	Rhos-on-Sea
1938			1960	Mrs BJ Jenkin	Anglesey
1939			1961	Mrs M Wright	North Wales
1940–46	*Not played due to Second World War*		1962	Mrs DV Ingham	Holyhead
1947	Miss A Stockton	Maesdu	1963	Miss N Seddon	Nefyn
1948	Miss N Cook	Caernarvonshire	1964	Mrs A Hughes	Maesdu
1949	Miss EHA Lever	St Deiniol	1965	Mrs M Wright	Caernarvonshire
1950	Miss EHA Lever	Rhos-on-Sea	1966	Mrs JH Brown	Pwllheli
1951	Miss EHA Lever	North Wales	1967	Mrs JH Brown	Bull Bay
1952	Miss EHA Lever	Holyhead	1968	Miss A Hughes	Nefyn
1953	Miss N Cook	Maesdu	1969	Miss A Hughes	Holyhead
1954	Mrs JH Brown	Nefyn	1970	Mrs M Wright	Maesdu
1955	Miss EHA Lever	Caernarvonshire	1971	Mrs JH Brown	Bull Bay

YEAR	WINNER	VENUE	YEAR	WINNER	VENUE
1972	Miss A Hughes	North Wales	1982	Miss F Connor	Pwllheli
1973	Mrs JH Brown	Nefyn	1983	Miss S Roberts	North Wales
1974	Miss VJ Brammer	Holyhead	1984	Miss S Jump	Harlech
1975	Mrs R Ferguson	Conwy	1985	Miss A Lewis	Conwy
1976	Mrs M Wright	Harlech	1986	Mrs S Turner	Maesdu
1977	Miss A Thomas	Bull Bay	1987	Miss S Roberts	Holyhead
1978	Mrs A Johnson	Maesdu	1988	Mrs S Turner	Pwllheli
1979	Miss A Thomas	Nefyn	1989	Miss S Roberts	North Wales
1980	Miss A Thomas	North Wales	1990	Miss S Roberts	Bull Bay
1981	Miss S Jumo	Holyhead			

Denbighshire Ladies' Championship

INAUGURATED 1924

YEAR	WINNER		YEAR	WINNER	VENUE
1924	Mrs O Brown		1961	Mrs M Hartley	
1925	Mrs Byford		1962	Mrs HM Bellis	
1926	Miss Baldwin		1963	Mrs M Hartley	
1927	Miss Baldwin		1964	Mrs OW Jones	
1928	Mrs Ashe		1965	Mrs OW Jones	
1929	Miss Baldwin		1966	Mrs OW Jones	
1930	Mrs MacAlpine		1967	Mrs HM Bellis	
1931	Mrs CR Taylor		1968	Miss M Lea	
1932	Mrs CR Taylor		1969	Miss M Lea	
1933	Mrs CR Taylor		1970	Mrs OW Jones	
1934	Mrs D Evans		1971	Mrs OW Jones	
1935	Miss M Brearley		1972	Miss P Whitley	
1936	Miss Turner		1973	Miss P Whitley	
1937	Miss Appleby		1974	Miss P Whitley	
1938	Mrs CR Taylor		1975	Miss M Hayes	
1939	Mrs CR Taylor		1976	Mrs E Davies	
1940–46	*Not played due to Second World War*		1977	Miss P Whitley	Wrexham
1947	Mrs M Hartley		1978	Miss P Whitley	Abergele
1948	*Not played*		1979	Miss P Whitley	Vale of Llangollen
1949	Mrs B Haberreiter		1980	Mrs K Davies	Wrexham
1950	Mrs M Hartley		1981	Mrs E Higgs	Abergele
1951	Mrs M Hartley		1982	Mrs K Davies	Vale of Llangollen
1952	Mrs M Hartley		1983	Mrs E Davies	Wrexham
1953	Mrs M Hartley		1984	Mrs C Ellis	Abergele
1954	Mrs J Johnson		1985	Mrs E Davies	Vale of Llangollen
1955	Mrs M Hartley		1986	Mrs H Higgs	Wrexham
1956	Mrs M Hartley		1987	Mrs S Thomas	Abergele
1957	Mrs J Johnson		1988	Mrs S Thomas	Prestatyn
1958	Mrs J Johnson		1989	Mrs S Thomas	Wrexham
1959	Mrs J Johnson		1990	Miss Lisa Dermott	Vale of Llangollen
1960	Mrs M Hartley				

Flintshire Ladies' Championship

YEAR	WINNER	VENUE	YEAR	WINNER	VENUE
1977	Mrs P Davies	Rhuddlan	1982	Mrs P Davies	Prestatyn
1978	Mrs P Davies	Prestatyn	1983	Miss S Rowlands	Rhuddlan
1979	Miss P Strange	Rhuddlan	1984	Mrs S Thomas	Prestatyn
1980	Mrs P Davies	Prestatyn	1985	Mrs S Thomas	Rhuddlan
1981	Mrs P Davies	Rhuddlan	1986	Mrs S Thomas	Prestatyn

Glamorgan County Ladies' Championship

INAUGURATED 1927

YEAR	WINNER	VENUE	YEAR	WINNER	VENUE
1927	Mrs M Duncan	Porthcawl	1964	Mrs J Treharne	Southerndown
1928	Mrs M Barron	Radyr	1965	Mrs J Treharne	Porthcawl
1929	Miss B Pyman	Southerndown	1966	Miss Jill Morris	Pyle and Kenfig
1930	Miss B Pyman	Porthcawl	1967	Miss C Phipps	Southerndown
1931	Miss G Ricardo	Southerndown	1968	Miss Jill Morris	Pyle and Kenfig
1932	Miss B Pyman	Porthcawl	1969	Miss C Phipps	Porthcawl
1933	Miss J Jeffreys	Southerndown	1970	Miss V Rawlings	Radyr
1934	Miss J Jeffreys	Southerndown	1971	Miss V Rawlings	Southerndown
1935	Miss J Jeffreys	Porthcawl	1972	Miss T Perkins	Pyle and Kenfig
1936	Mrs GS Emery	Southerndown	1973	Miss C Phipps	Porthcawl
1937	Mrs GS Emery	Southerndown	1974	Miss T Perkins	Southerndown
1938	Mrs GS Emery	Porthcawl	1975	Miss T Perkins	Pyle and Kenfig
1939	Miss M Thompson	Southerndown	1976	Miss L Isherwood	Southerndown
1940–47	*Not played due to Second World War*		1977	Miss T Perkins	Porthcawl
1948	Mrs RB Roberts	Glamorganshire	1978	Miss T Perkins	Southerndown
1949	Mrs RB Roberts	Southerndown	1979	Miss V Rawlings	Pyle and Kenfig
1950	Miss E Owen	Radyr	1980	Mrs T Thomas	
1951	Mrs RB Roberts	Southerndown		(*née* Perkins)	Porthcawl
1952	Mrs H Jenkins	Porthcawl	1981	Mrs T Thomas	Southerndown
1953	Mrs H Jenkins	Southerndown	1982	Miss V Rawlings	Pyle and Kenfig
1954	Mrs RB Roberts	Porthcawl	1983	Mrs T Thomas	Porthcawl
1955	Mrs RB Roberts	Southerndown	1984	Miss J Foster	Southerndown
1956	Miss H Wakelin	Southerndown	1985	Miss P Johnson	Pyle and Kenfig
1957	Miss C Phipps	Porthcawl	1986	Miss P Johnson	Porthcawl
1958	Mrs CR Robinson	Southerndown	1987	Mrs V Thomas	
1959	Miss E Owen	Porthcawl		(*née* Rawlings)	Southerndown
1960	Mrs J Treharne	Pyle and Kenfig	1988	Mrs V Thomas	Pyle and Kenfig
1961	Mrs M Fisher	Southerndown	1989	Mrs V Thomas	Porthcawl
1962	Miss E Owen	Porthcawl	1990	Miss A Perriam	Southerndown
1963	Mrs J Treharne	Pyle and Kenfig			

Monmouthshire Ladies' Championship

INAUGURATED 1920

YEAR	WINNER	VENUE	YEAR	WINNER	VENUE
1920	Miss EL Clay	Newport	1958	Mrs P Inglis	Tredegar Park
1921	Miss D Thomas	Newport	1959	Miss P Roberts	Abergavenny
1922	Miss EL Clay	West Monmouthshire	1960	Mrs R Hartley	Newport
			1961	Mrs R Hartley	Tredegar Park
1923	Mrs F Phillips	Abergavenny	1962	Miss P Roberts	Abergavenny
1924	Mrs F Phillips	Tredegar Park	1963	Miss P Roberts	Newport
1925	Miss L Newman	Newport	1964	Miss P Roberts	Monmouthshire
1926	Miss C Freeguard	Pontypool	1965	Miss P Roberts	St Mellons
1927	Mrs RW Meacock	Tredegar Park	1966	Miss P Roberts	St Pierre
1928	Mrs W Phillips	Newport	1967	Mrs G Galliers	Newport
1929	Miss L Newman	Pontypool	1968	Miss P Roberts	Monmouthshire
1930	Miss G Evan	Tredegar Park	1969	Mrs B Chambers	St Mellons
1931	Mrs ET Rees	Blackwood	1970	Miss P Roberts	Monmouthshire
1932	Miss L Newman	Newport	1971	Dr M Smith	Newport
1933	Mrs RW Meacock	Llanwern	1972	Miss P Roberts	Tredegar Park
1934	Mrs RW Meacock	Newport	1973	Miss E Davies	Pontypool
1935	Dr P Whitaker	Newport	1974	Miss E Davies	St Mellons
1936	Miss M Williams	Pontypool	1975	Mrs B Chambers	Pontypool
1937	Mrs JG Meredith	Tredegar Park	1976	Miss E Davies	Monmouthshire
1938	Mrs G Evans	St Mellons	1977	Miss C Parry	Newport
1939	Miss H Reynolds	Newport	1978	Miss E Davies	St Mellons
1940–46	*Not played due to Second World War*		1979	Miss E Davies	Pontypool
1947	Miss MP Roberts	Newport	1980	Miss M Davis	St Mellons
1948	Mrs Garfield Evans	Tredegar Park	1981	Miss K Beckett	St Pierre
1949	Miss P Roberts	Newport	1982	Miss M Davis	Tredegar Park
1950	Miss P Roberts	Tredegar Park	1983	Miss K Beckett	Newport
1951	Mrs Garfield Evans	Abergavenny	1984	Miss J Lapthorne	Monmouthshire
1952	Miss P Roberts	Newport	1985	Miss P Lord	Pontypool
1953	Miss P Roberts	Abergavenny	1986	Miss H Buckley	Pontypool
1954	Miss P Roberts	Tredegar Park	1987	Miss H Buckley	St Pierre
1955	Miss P Roberts	Newport	1988	Miss H Armstrong	Tredegar Park
1956	Miss P Roberts	Abergavenny	1989	Miss B Chambers	Monmouthshire
1957	Miss P Roberts	Newport	1990	Miss W Wood	Newport

Mid-Wales Ladies' Championship

INAUGURATED 1987

YEAR	WINNER	VENUE
1987	Miss A Hubbard	
1988	Miss S James	Cradoc
1989	Miss S Wilson	Borth
1990	Miss P Morgan	Aberystwyth

Welsh Ladies' Team Championship

INAUGURATED 1905

YEAR	WINNER	VENUE	YEAR	WINNER	VENUE
1922	Tenby	Llandrindod Wells	1963	Royal St David's	Harlech
1923	Glamorganshire	Southerndown	1964	Newport	Southerndown
1924	Rhos-on-Sea	Rhyl	1965	Royal St David's	Prestatyn
1925	Tenby	Tenby	1966	Royal St David's	Ashburnham
1926	Glamorganshire	Aberdovey	1967	North Wales	Glamorganshire
1927	Glamorganshire	Porthcawl	1968	Prestatyn	Llandudno (Maesdu)
1928	Aberdovey	Harlech	1969	Prestatyn	Pyle and Kenfig
1929	Glamorganshire	Tenby	1970	Newport	Newport
1930	Southerndown	Llandudno (Maesdu)	1971	Prestatyn	Harlech
1931	Southerndown	Southerndown	1972	Tenby	Tenby
1932	Aberdovey	Aberdovey	1973	Royal Porthcawl	Holyhead
1933	Royal Porthcawl	Porthcawl	1974	Royal St David's	Ashburnham
1934	Aberdovey	Harlech	1975	Royal Porthcawl	Prestatyn
1935	Tenby	Tenby	1976	Whitchurch	Porthcawl
1936	Aberdovey	Prestatyn	1977	Whitchurch	Aberdovey
1937	Southerndown	Porthcawl	1978	Whitchurch	Newport
1938	Newport	Llandudno (Maesdu)	1979	Bargoed	Caernarvonshire
1939	Newport	Swansea Bay	1980	Monmouthshire	Tenby
1940–46	*Not played due to Second World War*		1981	Royal Porthcawl	Harlech
1947	Radyr	Prestatyn	1982	Royal St David's	Ashburnham
1948	North Wales	Prestatyn	1983	Llandudno	
1949	Newport	Newport		(Maesdu)	Maesdu
1950	North Wales	Porthcawl	1984	Monmouthshire	Newport
1951	North Wales	Harlech	1985	Llandudno	
1952	Royal Porthcawl	Southerndown		(Maesdu)	Prestatyn
1953	North Wales	North Wales	1986	Royal Porthcawl	Porthcawl
1956	Radyr	Porthcawl	1987	Whitchurch	Aberdovey
1958	Monmouthshire		1988	Pennard	Tenby
1959	Radyr	Conwy	1989	Llandudno	
1960	Tenby	Tenby		(Maesdu)	Conwy
1961	Royal St David's	Aberdovey	1990	Llandudno	
1962	Radyr	Radyr		(Maesdu)	Harlech

Ladies' Open Amateur Tournaments

With so many commitments to county and club fixtures, which are carefully organised throughout the LGU, there is little space in the calendar for Amateur Open Scratch events which draw competitors from far and wide. It is hoped that the more important are included here. There are probably some which have not yet reached the status of those listed, which are all of considerable maturity and well established. One reason for the apparent lack of such tournaments may be the efficient LGU handicap system, under which so many ladies' events are played.

Astor Salver

INAUGURATED 1951

at The Berkshire

YEAR	WINNER	YEAR	WINNER
1951	Jeanne Bisgood	1972	Jill Thornhill
1952	Jeanne Bisgood	1973	Linda Denison-Pender } tie
1953	Jeanne Bisgood		Angela Uzielli
1954	Jean Donald	1974	Cathy Barclay
1955	Elizabeth Price	1975	Jill Thornhill
1956	J Barton } tie	1976	Heather Clifford
	Elizabeth Price	1977	Angela Uzielli
1957	Angela Ward	1978	Mary Everard
1958	Angela Bonallack (*née* Ward)	1979	Julia Greenhalgh
1959	Elizabeth Price	1980	Jane Lock
1960	Angela Bonallack	1981	Angela Uzielli
1961	Angela Bonallack	1982	*Abandoned*
1962	Ruth Porter	1983	Linda Bayman
1963	Ruth Porter	1984	Linda Bayman
1964	Marley Spearman	1985	Helen Wadsworth
1965	Marley Spearman	1986	Caroline Pierce
1966	Angela Bonallack	1987	Vicki Thomas
1967	Mary Everard	1988	Jill Thornhill
1968	Mary Everard	1989	Sarah Sutton
1969	Julia Greenhalgh	1990	Julie Hall } tie
1970	B Whitehead		J Morley
1971	Angela Uzielli		

Avia Foursomes Championship

INAUGURATED 1966

at The Berkshire

This early season foursomes tournament was a feature in the Ladies Amateur programme for 24 years from 1966. It will be seen that in several years poor weather caused curtailment of play, but this in no way inhibited the quality field returning year after year. Unfortunately for various reasons it was not possible to continue the event after 1989.

YEAR	WINNERS	SCORE
1966	Vicomtesse Lally St Sauveur and Brigitte Varangot	307
1967	Bridget Jackson and Vivien Saunders	314
1968	Ruth Porter and Ann Irvin	317
1969	Corinne Reybroeck and Linda Denison-Pender	319
1970	Gillian Cheetham and Jill Thornhill	305
1971	Corinne Reybroeck and Linda Denison-Pender	150 (36 holes)
1972	Belle Robertson and Diane Frearson	303
1973	Michelle Walker and Linda Denison-Pender	307
1974	Carole Redford and Carol Le Feuvre	268 (63 holes)
1975	*Abandoned due to snow*	
1976	Angela Bonallack and Sally Barber	307
1977	Tegwen Perkins and Mary McKenna	312
1978	Vivien Saunders and Mary Everard	310
1979	Linda Bayman (*née* Denison-Pender) and Anne Sander	302
1980	Linda Bayman and Maureen Madill	266 (63 holes)
1981	Belle Robertson and Winnie Wooldridge	309
1982	Angela Uzielli and Wilma Aitken	298
1983	Jill Thornhill and Jillian Nicolson	305
1984	Mary McKenna and Belle Robertson	298
1985	Linda Bayman and Maureen Garner (*née* Madill)	149 (36 holes)
1986	Belle Robertson and Mary McKenna	298
1987	Susan Moorcroft and Tracey Hammond	301
1988	Karen Mitchell and Nicola Way	305
1989	Joanne Morley and Lora Fairclough	224 (54 holes)
1990	*Not played*	

Hampshire Rose

INAUGURATED 1973

at North Hants, Fleet

YEAR	WINNER	YEAR	WINNER
1973	Carole Redford	1977	Julia Greenhalgh
1974	Pru Riddiford	1978	Vanessa Marvin }tie
1975	Vanessa Marvin		Heather Glyn-Jones (*née* Clifford)
1976	Heather Clifford } tie	1979	Carol Larkin
	Wendy Pithers	1980	Beverley New

YEAR	WINNER		YEAR	WINNER
1981	Jillian Nicolson		1986	Claire Hourihane
1982	Jill Thornhill		1987	Jill Thornhill
1983	J Pool		1988	Jill Thornhill
1984	Carole Caldwell (*née* Redford)		1989	Alison MacDonald
1985	Angela Uzielli		1990	S Keogh

Helen Holm Trophy

INAUGURATED 1973

at Portland and Royal Troon

The Helen Holm Trophy was given in memory of one of Scotland's great lady golfers, who twice won the British Open Amateur Championship in the 1930s. It is a 54-hole stroke play tournament and is always played at Troon, the club from which she always entered any championship. It consists of two rounds on Royal Troon's Portland course and one on the Championship course.

YEAR	WINNER		YEAR	WINNER
1973	Belle Robertson		1982	Wilma Aitken
1974	Sandra Needham		1983	Jane Connachan
1975	Muriel Thomson		1984	Gillian Stewart
1976	Muriel Thomson		1985	Pamela Wright
1977	Beverly Huke		1986	Belle Robertson
1978	Wilma Aitken		1987	Elaine Farquharson
1979	Belle Robertson		1988	Elaine Farquharson
1980	Wilma Aitken		1989	Sara Robinson
1981	Gillian Stewart		1990	Catriona Lambert

Roehampton Gold Cup

INAUGURATED 1926

at Roehampton

YEAR	WINNER		YEAR	WINNER
1926	Mrs WM McNair		1940–47	*Not played due to Second World War*
1927	Miss M Gourlay		1948	Maureen Ruttle
1928	Miss C Leitch		1949	Frances Stephens
1929	Miss I Doxford		1950	Maureen Garrett (*née* Ruttle)
1930	Miss E Wilson		1951	Jeanne Bisgood
1931	Miss V Lamb		1952	Jeanne Bisgood
1932	Mrs A Gold		1953	Jeanne Bisgood
1933	Miss A Ramsden		1954	Isabella Bromley Davenport
1934	Miss J Hamilton		1955	Louisa Abrahams
1935	Miss P Barton		1956	Shirley Allom
1936	Miss B Newell		1957	Mary Roberts
1937	Miss P Barton		1958	Patricia Moore
1938	Miss P Barton		1959	Mavis Glidewell
1939	Miss P Barton		1960	Elizabeth Price

YEAR	WINNER	YEAR	WINNER
1961	Louisa Abrahams	1977	Angela Uzielli
1962	Louisa Abrahams	1978	Carole Caldwell (*née* Redford) } tie
1963	Ruth Porter		Belle Robertson
1964	Miss RC Archer	1979	Belle Robertson
1965	Marley Spearman	1980	Angela Bonallack
1966	Gwen Brandon	1981	Belle Robertson
1967	Ann Irvin	1982	Belle Robertson
1968	Ann Irvin	1983	Beverley New } tie
1969	Ann Irvin		Vicki Thomas
1970	Mary Everard	1984	Beverley New
1971	Beverly Huke	1985	Vicki Thomas
1972	Ann Irvin	1986	Katherine Harridge } tie
1973	Carole Redford } tie		Patricia Johnson
	Ann Irvin	1987	Diane Barnard
1974	Lyn Harrold	1988	Alison Johns
1975	Wendy Pithers } tie	1989	Catherine Panton } tie
	Carole Redford		Catriona Lambert
1976	Ann Irvin } tie	1990	Kathryn Imrie
	Vanessa Marvin		

Part Five
Juniors and Youths

Boys' Events

The Boys' Championship

INAUGURATED 1921

The Boys' Championship was the result of an idea of Major T South in 1920, strongly supported by Mr DM Mathieson, the Editor of *Golf Monthly*. At first it was open to boys under sixteen, then seventeen and by 1923 under eighteen, as it remains today.

For the first two years it was played at Royal Ascot on the course surrounded by the track and the grandstands. It then moved north to Dunbar, East Lothian, and has been played alternately in England and Scotland ever since, except for 1984 when it moved to Porthcawl in South Wales.

Many boys, who subsequently became top class amateurs and, in more recent times, professionals, have shown early promise in winning the Boys'. Names such as John Lindsay, Hector Thomson, PB (Laddie) Lucas, John Langley, Jimmy Bruen before the War, and Michael Bonallack, Peter Townsend, Howard Clark, Ronan Rafferty and Jose Maria Olazabal since, are a good guide to the standard of player to be found among the winners.

The handicap limit for entry, which was not introduced until 1964, has been steadily reduced in keeping with the much higher general standard of play among boys.

YEAR	WINNER	RUNNER-UP	MARGIN	VENUE
1921	ADD Mathieson	GH Lintott	37th hole	Royal Ascot
1922	HS Mitchell	W Greenfield	4 and 2	Royal Ascot
1923	ADD Mathieson	HS Mitchell	3 and 2	Dunbar
1924	RW Peattie	P Manuevrier	2 holes	Coombe Hill
1925	RW Peattie	A McNair	4 and 3	Barnton
1926	EA McRuvie	C W Timmis	1 hole	Coombe Hill
1927	EW Fiddian	K Forbes	4 and 2	Barnton
1928	S Scheftel	A Dobbie	6 and 5	Formby
1929	J Lindsay	J Scot-Riddell	6 and 4	Barnton
1930	J Lindsay	J Todd	9 and 8	Fulwell
1931	H Thomson	F McGloin	5 and 4	Killermont

YEAR	WINNER	RUNNER-UP	MARGIN	VENUE
1932	IS MacDonald	LA Hardie	2 and 1	Lytham St Annes
1933	PB Lucas	W McLachlan	3 and 2	Carnoustie
1934	RS Burles	FB Allpass	12 and 10	Moortown
1935	JD A Langley	R Norris	6 and 5	Balgownie
1936	J Bruen	W Innes	11 and 9	Birkdale
1937	IM Roberts	J Stewart	8 and 7	Bruntsfield
1938	W Smeaton	T Snowball	3 and 2	Moor Park
1939	SB Williamson	KG Thom	4 and 2	Carnoustie
1940–45	*No Championship due to Second World War*			
1946	AFD MacGregor	DF Dunstan	7 and 5	Bruntsfield
1947	J Armour	I Caldwell	5 and 4	Hoylake
1948	JD Pritchett	DH Reid	37th hole	Barassie
1949	H MacAnespie	NV Drew	3 and 2	St Andrews
1950	J Glover	I Young	2 and 1	Lytham St Annes
1951	N Dunn	MSR Lunt	6 and 5	Prestwick
1952	MF Bonallack	AE Shepperson	37th hole	Formby
1953	AE Shepperson	AT Booth	6 and 4	Dunbar
1954	AF Bussell	K Warren	38th hole	Hoylake
1955	SC Wilson	BJK Aitken	39th hole	Barassie
1956	JF Ferguson	CW Cole	2 and 1	Sunningdale
1957	D Ball	J Wilson	2 and 1	Carnoustie
1958	RV Braddon	IM Stungo	4 and 3	Moortown
1959	AR Murphy	EM Shamash	3 and 1	Pollok
1960	P Cros	PO Green	5 and 3	Olton
1961	FS Morris	C Clark	3 and 2	Dalmahoy
1962	PM Townsend	DC Penman	1 hole	Mid-Surrey
1963	AH C Soutar	DI Rigby	2 and 1	Prestwick
1964	PM Townsend	RD Gray	9 and 8	Formby
1965	GR Milne	DK Midgley	4 and 2	Gullane
1966	A Phillips	A Muller	12 and 11	Moortown
1967	LP Tupling	SC Evans	4 and 2	Western Gailes
1968	SC Evans	K Dabson	3 and 2	St Annes Old Links
1969	M Foster	M Gray	37th hole	Dunbar
1970	ID Gradwell	JE Murray	1 hole	Hillside
1971	HK Clark	G Harvey	6 and 5	Barassie
1972	G Harvey	R Newsome	7 and 5	Moortown
1973	DM Robertson	S Betti	5 and 3	Blairgowrie
1974	TR Shannon	AWB Lyle	10 and 9	Hoylake
1975	B Marchbank	AWB Lyle	1 hole	Bruntsfield
1976	M Mouland	G Hargreaves	6 and 5	Sunningdale
1977	I Ford	CR Dalgleish	1 hole	Downfield
1978	S Keppler	M Stokes	3 and 2	Seaton Carew
1979	R Rafferty	D Ray	6 and 5	Barassie
1980	D Muscroft	A Llyr	7 and 6	Formby
1981	J Lopez	R Weedon	4 and 3	Gullane
1982	M Grieve	G Hickman	37th hole	Burnham and Berrow
1983	JM Olazabal	M Pendaries	6 and 5	Glenbervie
1984	L Vannett	A Mednick	2 and 1	Porthcawl
1985	J Cook	W Henry	5 and 4	Barnton
1986	L Walker	G King	5 and 4	Seaton Carew
1987	C O'Carrol	P Olsson	3 and 1	Barassie
1988	S Pardoe	D Haines	3 and 2	Formby
1989	C Watts	C Fraser	5 and 3	Nairn
1990	M Welch	M Ellis	3 and 1	Hunstanton

English Boys' Amateur Open Stroke Play Championship

(formerly Carris Trophy)

INAUGURATED 1935

at Moor Park
(Brancepeth Castle, 1988; Luffenham Heath, 1990)

YEAR	WINNER	YEAR	WINNER
1935	R Upex	1965	G McKay
1936	JDA Langley	1966	A Black
1937	RJ White	1967	RP Brown
1938	IP Garrow	1968	P Dawson
1939	CW Warren	1969	ID Gradwell
1940–45	*No Championship due to Second*	1970	MF Foster
	World War	1971	RJ Evans
1946	AH Perowne	1972	L Donovan
1947	I Caldwell	1973	S Hadfield
1948	I Caldwell	1974	KJ Brown
1949	PB Hine	1975	AWB Lyle
1950	J Glover	1976	H Stott
1951	I Young	1977	R Mugglestone
1952	N Thygesen	1978	J Plaxton
1953	N Johnson	1979	P Hammond
1954	K Warren	1980	MP McLean
1955	ID Wheater	1981	D Gilford
1956	G Maisey	1982	M Jarvis
1957	G Maisey	1983	P Baker
1958	J Hamilton	1984	J Coe
1959	RT Walker	1985	P Baker
1960	PM Baxter	1986	G Evans
1961	DJ Miller	1987	D Bathgate
1962	FS Morris	1988	P Page
1963	EJ Threlfall	1989	I Garbutt
1964	PM Townsend	1990	M Welch

Irish Boys' Close Amateur

INAUGURATED 1983

YEAR	WINNER	SCORE	VENUE	YEAR	WINNER	SCORE	VENUE
1983	J Carvill	144	Curragh	1987	G McNeill	143	Warrenpoint
1984	E O'Connell	142	Mullingar	1988	D McGrane	219	Birr
1985	K Kearney	145	Athlone	1989	D Higgins	221	Mullingar
1986	D Errity	147	Royal Tara	1990	R Burns	213	Kilkenny

Scottish Boys' Championship

INAUGURATED 1935

YEAR	WINNER	RUNNER-UP	MARGIN	VENUE
1935	DA Blair	AG Lowe	5 and 3	North Berwick
1936	R Stewart	AH Nesbit	8 and 6	North Berwick
1937	RG Inglis	J Sibbald	1 hole	North Berwick
1938	RG Inglis	W Smeaton	1 hole	North Berwick
1939	KW Walker	JM Steel	9 and 8	North Berwick
1940–46	*No Championship due to Second World War*			
1947	J Brydone	DH Reid	38th hole	North Berwick
1948	R Nicol	DH Reid	3 and 1	North Berwick
1949	DH Reid	R Nicol	5 and 4	North Berwick
1950	A Miller	R Brotherston	3 and 1	North Berwick
1951	I Young	DS Blair	12 and 10	North Berwick
1952	CB Thomson	IP A Rodger	38th hole	North Berwick
1953	R Aitken	J Carter	5 and 4	North Berwick
1954	MJ Moir	H McCrae	8 and 6	North Berwick
1955	G Will	JB Neish	8 and 6	North Berwick
1956	RDBM Shade	AJ Hanley	7 and 6	North Berwick
1957	JR Young	I Leitch	8 and 7	North Berwick
1958	J Grant	HC Brownlee	4 and 2	North Berwick
1959	HB Stuart	RT Walker	3 and 2	North Berwick
1960	L Carver	S Wilson	6 and 5	North Berwick
1961	K Thomson	G Wilson	10 and 8	North Berwick
1962	HF Urquhart	S MacDonald	3 and 2	North Berwick
1963	FS Morris	I Clark	9 and 8	North Berwick
1964	WR Lockie	MD Cleghorn	1 hole	North Berwick
1965	RL Penman	J Wood	9 and 8	North Berwick
1966	J McTear	DG Greig	4 and 3	North Berwick
1967	DG Greig	I Cannon	2 and 1	North Berwick
1968	RD Weir	M Grubb	6 and 4	North Berwick
1969	RP Fyfe	IF Doig	4 and 2	North Berwick
1970	S Stephen	M Henry	38th hole	North Berwick
1971	JE Murray	AA Mackay	4 and 3	North Berwick
1972	DM Robertson	G Cairns	9 and 8	North Berwick
1973	R Watson	H Alexander	8 and 7	North Berwick
1974	DM Robertson	J Cuddihy	6 and 5	North Berwick
1975	A Brown	J Cuddihy	6 and 4	North Berwick
1976	B Marchbank	J Cuddihy	2 and 1	Dunbar
1977	JS Taylor	GJ Webster	3 and 2	Dunbar
1978	J Huggan	KW Stables	2 and 1	Dunbar
1979	DR Weir	S Morrison	5 and 3	West Kilbride
1980	R Gregan	AJ Currie	2 and 1	Dunbar
1981	C Stewart	G Mellon	3 and 2	Dunbar
1982	A Smith	J White	39th hole	Dunbar
1983	C Gillies	C Innes	38th hole	Dunbar
1984	K Buchan	L Vannet	2 and 1	Dunbar
1985	AD McQueen	FJ McCulloch	1 hole	Dunbar
1986	AG Tait	EA McIntosh	6 and 5	Dunbar
1987	AJ Coltart	SJ Bannerman	37th hole	Dunbar
1988	CA Fraser	F Clark	9 and 8	Dunbar
1989	M King	D Brolls	8 and 7	Dunbar
1990	B Collier	D Keeney	281 (*stroke play*)	West Kilbride

Scottish Boys' Open Amateur Stroke Play Championship

INAUGURATED 1970

YEAR	WINNER	SCORE	VENUE	YEAR	WINNER	SCORE	VENUE
1970	D Chillas	298	Carnoustie	1981	J Gullen	296	Bellshill
1971	JE Murray	274	Lanark	1982	D Purdie	296	Monifieth
1972	S Martin	280	Montrose	1983	L Vannet	286	Barassie
1973	S Martin	284	Barnton	1984	K Walker	280	Carnoustie
1974	PW Gallacher	290	Lundin	1985	G Matthew	297	Baberton
			Links	1986	G Cassells	294	Edzell
1975	A Webster	286	Barassie	1987	C Ronald	287	Lanark
1976	A Webster	292	Forfar	1988	M Urquhart	280	Dumfries
1977	J Huggan	303	Renfrew				and County
1978	R Fraser	283	Arbroath	1989	F Burntside	283	Stirling
1979	L Mann	289	Stirling	1990	N Archibald	292	Monifieth
1980	ASK Glen	288	Forfar				

Welsh Boys' Championship

INAUGURATED 1954

YEAR	WINNER	RUNNER-UP	MARGIN	VENUE
1954	JWH Mitchell	DA Rees	8 and 6	Llandrindod Wells
1955	EW Griffith	DA Rees	3 and 2	Llandrindod Wells
1956	DA Rees	JP Hales	2 and 1	Llandrindod Wells
1957	P Waddilove	JG Jones	2 and 1	Llandrindod Wells
1958	P Waddilove	J Williams	1 hole	Llandrindod Wells
1959	C Gilford	JG Jones	6 and 4	Llandrindod Wells
1960	C Gilford	JL Toye	5 and 4	Llandrindod Wells
1961	AR Porter	JL Toye	3 and 2	Llandrindod Wells
1962	RC Waddilove	W Wadrup	20th hole	Harlech
1963	G Matthews	R Witchell	6 and 5	Penarth
1964	D Lloyd	M Walters	2 and 1	Conwy
1965	G Matthews	DG Lloyd	7 and 6	Wenvoe Castle
1966	J Buckley	DP Owen	4 and 2	Holyhead
1967	J Buckley	DL Stevens	2 and 1	Glamorganshire
1968	J Buckley	C Brown	1 hole	Maesdu
1969	K Dabson	P Light	5 and 3	Glamorganshire
1970	P Tadman	A Morgan	2 and 1	Conwy
1971	R Jenkins	T Melia	3 and 2	Ashburnham
1972	MG Chugg	RM Jones	3 and 2	Wrexham
1973	R Tate	N Duncan	2 and 1	Penarth
1974	D Williams	S Lewis	5 and 4	Maesdu
1975	G Davies	PG Garrett	20th hole	Glamorganshire
1976	JM Morrow	MG Mouland	1 hole	Conwy
1977	JM Morrow	MG Mouland	2 and 1	Glamorganshire
1978	JM Morrow	A Laking	2 and 1	Harlech

YEAR	WINNER	RUNNER-UP	MARGIN	VENUE
1979	P Mayo	M Hayward	24th hole	Penarth
1980	A Llyr	DK Wood	2 and 1	Maesdu
1981	M Evans	P Webborn	5 and 4	Pontypool
1982	CM Rees	KH Williams	2 holes	Prestatyn
1983	MA Macara	RN Roderick	1 hole	Radyr
1984	GA Macara	D Bagg	1 hole	North Wales
1985	B Macfarlane	R Herbert	1 hole	Cardiff
1986	C O'Carroll	GA Macara	1 hole	Rhuddlan
1987	SJ Edwards	A Herbert	19th hole	Abergavenny
1988	C Platt	P Murphy	2 and 1	Holyhead
1989	R Johnson	RL Evans	2 holes	Southerndown
1990	M Ellis	C Sheppard	3 and 2	Maesdu

Boys' Internationals

INAUGURATED 1923

The first Boys' International was played by England and Scotland at Dunbar in 1923. It has always been played at the same time and on the same course as the Boys' Championship, which has alternated between England and Scotland, except for a foray to Porthcawl in 1964. Until that year it was a match of 12 games, four foursomes and eight singles, but since then it has been contested between sides each of ten players, making five foursomes and ten singles.

England has won 34 of the 62 matches which have been staged, Scotland has won 25 and three halved. Before the war Scotland was the stronger side, winning 12 against England's four, with one halved. Subsequently England has drawn ahead with 20 wins against 12.

Ireland and Wales did not begin their encounters until 1972. They have been evenly matched and each side has won nine times, but Ireland is just ahead with ten victories. It is always played concurrently with the England v Scotland match.

Since 1958 a British side has been selected to play a Continent of Europe representative Boys' side. Until 1966 it was a very one-sided encounter with the Continentals losing every year. The match was dropped for ten years, but when resurrected in 1977, Europe won for two years and were again successful in 1986 at Seaton Carew.

The British team was renamed Great Britain and Ireland in 1983. The match is a popular preliminary to the Boys' Championship and those selected for both sides consider it an honour to play for their team.

England v Scotland

INAUGURATED 1923

YEAR	WINNER	VENUE	RESULT	YEAR	WINNER	VENUE	RESULT
1923	Scotland	Dunbar	7½–4½	1960	England	Olton	10–2
1924	Scotland	Coombe Hill	7–5	1961	Scotland	Dalmahoy	7–5
1925	England	Barnton	7–5	1962	England	Mid-Surrey	6½–5½
1926	England	Coombe Hil	6½–5½	1963	Scotland	Prestwick	9–3
1927	Scotland	Barnton	7–5	1964	England	Formby	9–3
1928	England	Formby	6½–5½	1965	England	Gullane	10–5
1929	Scotland	Barnton	9½–2½	1966	England	Moortown	12–3
1930	Scotland	Fulwell	8–4	1967	Scotland	Western Gailes	8–7
1931	Scotland	Killermont	7½–4½	1968	England	St Annes	
1932	Scotland	Lytham St Annes	8–4			Old Links	10–5
1933	Scotland	Carnoustie	7–5	1969	England	Dunbar	12–3
1934	England	Moortown	9–3	1970	England	Hillside	12–3
1935	halved	Balgownie	6–6	1971	halved	Barassie	7½–7½
1936	Scotland	Birkdale	8½–3½	1972	England	Moortown	13½–½
1937	Scotland	Bruntsfield	9½–2½	1973	England	Blairgowrie	9–6
1938	Scotland	Moor Park	7½–4½	1974	England	Hoylake	11–4
1939	Scotland	Carnoustie	7–5	1975	England	Bruntsfield	9½–5½
1940–45	No championship due to Second			1976	Scotland	Sunningdale	8–7
	World War			1977	England	Downfield	8–7
1946	England	Bruntsfield	8½–3½	1978	Scotland	Seaton Carew	8½–6½
1947	England	Hoylake	7–5	1979	England	Barassie	11–4
1948	England	Barassie	9–3	1980	England	Formby	9–6
1949	Scotland	St Andrews	8–4	1981	halved	Gullane	7½–7½
1950	Scotland	Lytham St Annes	8½–3½	1982	England	Burnham and	
1951	England	Prestwick	7–5			Berrow	8–7
1952	England	Formby	6½–5½	1983	England	Glenbervie	8–7
1953	Scotland	Dunbar	7–5	1984	England	Porthcawl	9½–5½
1954	England	Hoylake	6½–5½	1985	England	Barnton	10–5
1955	Scotland	Barassie	9–3	1986	Scotland	Seaton Carew	8½–6½
1956	England	Sunningdale	7½–4½	1987	Scotland	Barassie	8–7
1957	Scotland	Carnoustie	7½–4½	1988	England	Formby	11–4
1958	England	Moortown	7–5	1989	England	Nairn	8–7
1959	England	Pollok	8½–3½	1990	Scotland	Hunstanton	10½–4½

Ireland v Wales

INAUGURATED 1972

YEAR	WINNER	VENUE	RESULT	YEAR	WINNER	VENUE	RESULT
1972	Ireland	Moortown	5–4	1982	Wales	Burnham	
1973	Ireland	Blairgowrie	5½–3½			and Berrow	9–3
1974	Wales	Hoylake	5–4	1983	Ireland	Glenbervie	7–5
1975	Wales	Bruntsfield	6½–2½	1984	Wales	Porthcawl	6½–5½
1976	Wales	Sunningdale	7½–1½	1985	Ireland	Barnton	11½–3½
1977	Ireland	Downfield	6½–5½	1986	Ireland	Seaton Carew	8½–6½
1978	Wales	Seaton Carew	8–4	1987	Wales	Barassie	10½–4½
1979	Ireland	Barassie	9½–2½	1988	Wales	Formby	8–7
1980	Wales	Formby	6½–5½	1989	Wales	Nairn	10½–4½
1981	Ireland	Gullane	8–4	1990	Ireland	Hunstanton	8½–6½

R & A Trophy

INAUGURATED 1985

YEAR	WINNER	VENUE	RESULT	YEAR	WINNER	VENUE	RESULT
1985	England } tie Ireland	Barnton	7½–7½	1988	England	Formby	14–1
				1989	England	Nairn	11½–3½
1986	Ireland	Seaton Carew	8½–6½	1990	Scotland	Hunstanton	12½–2½
1987	Scotland	Barassie	10½–4½				

Great Britain & Ireland v Continent of Europe, Boys'

INAUGURATED 1958

YEAR	WINNER	VENUE	RESULT	YEAR	WINNER	VENUE	RESULT
1958	Great Britain & Ireland	Moortown	11½–½	1980	Great Britain & Ireland	Formby	7–5
1959	Great Britain & Ireland	Pollok	7–2	1981	Great Britain & Ireland	Gullane	8–4
1960	Great Britain & Ireland	Olton	8–7	1982	Great Britain & Ireland	Burnham and Berrow	11–1
1961	Great Britain & Ireland	Dalmahoy	11–4	1983	Great Britain & Ireland	Glenbervie	6½–5½
1962	Great Britain & Ireland	Mid-Surrey	11–4	1984	Great Britain & Ireland	Porthcawl	6½–5½
1963	Great Britain Ireland	Prestwick	12–3	1985	Great Britain & Ireland	Barnton	7½–4½
1964	Great Britain & Ireland	Formby	12–1	1986	Continent of Europe	Seaton Carew	8½–3½
1965	Great Britain & Ireland	Gullane	12–1	1987	Great Britain & Ireland	Barassie	7½–4½
1966	Great Britain & Ireland	Moortown	10–2	1988	Great Britain & Ireland	Formby	5½–2½
1967–76	*Not played*			1989	Great Britain & Ireland	Nairn	7½–4½
1977	Continent of Europe	Downfield	7–6	1990	Great Britain & Ireland	Hunstanton	10–2
1978	Continent of Europe	Seaton Carew	7–6				
1979	Great Britain & Ireland	Barassie	9½–2½				

European Boys' Team Championship

INAUGURATED 1989

YEAR	WINNER	RUNNER-UP	VENUE	YEAR	WINNER	RUNNER-UP	VENUE
1989	England	Spain	Lyckoma, Sweden	1990	Spain	Scotland	Reykjavik, Iceland

Peter McEvoy Trophy

INAUGURATED 1984

at Copt Heath

YEAR	WINNER	YEAR	WINNER
1984	W Henry	1988	P Sefton
1985	A Morley	1989	D Bathgate
1986	C Mitchell	1990	P Sherman
1987	W Henry		

Connacht Boys' Open Amateur

INAUGURATED 1950

YEAR	WINNER	VENUE	YEAR	WINNER	VENUE
1950	M Hegarty	Galway	1971	J Lynch	Athlone
1951	B Donnellon	Galway	1972	R McCormack	Co Sligo
1952	H McIlree	Co Sligo	1973	P O'Hagen	Galway
1953	J Kinsella	Galway	1974	P O'Hara	Ballina
1954	J Kinsella	Co Sligo	1975	J O'Mahony	Athlone
1955	*Not played*		1976	V Buggy	Co Sligo
1956	D Brennan	Co Sligo	1977	J Jones	Galway
1957	N Baker	Athlone	1978	B Hobson	Enniscrone
1958	P Morgan	Co Sligo	1979	P Walton	Athlone
1959	C McDonagh	Athlone	1980	R Culligan	Co Sligo
1960	C Devins	Co Sligo	1981	N Coey	Galway
1961	B O'Brien	Athlone	1982	J O'Neill	Westport
1962	B O'Brien	Galway	1983	M Sheridan	Athlone
1963	B O'Brien	Co Sligo	1984	K Kearney	Co Sligo
1964	I Elliott	Galway	1985	B Gilligan	Galway
1965	I Elliott	Athlone	1986	L Walker	Enniscrone
1966	M Hanway	Co Sligo	1987	G Sproule	Ballinasloe
1967	W O'Brien	Galway	1988	R Conway	Tuam
1968	M Frost	Galway	1989	R Burns	Galway
1969	MA Gannon	Galway	1990	R Couglan	Athlone
1970	P Egan	Galway			

Leinster Boys' Open Amateur

INAUGURATED 1949

YEAR	WINNER	VENUE	YEAR	WINNER	VENUE
1949	R Hayden	Grange	1971	H Duggan	Tullamore
1950	R Hayden	Grange	1972	R McCormack	Edmondstown
1951	D Donnellon	Grange	1973	P Osborne	Birr
1952	M Craddock	Hermitage	1974	C Moylan	Clontarf
1953	NC Hayes	Hermitage	1975	J Mahony	Laytown and
1954	W Kinsella	Hermitage			Bettystown
1955	F Fagan	Dun Laoghaire	1976	T Corridan	Donabate
1956	F Fagan	Dun Laoghaire	1977	A Hogan	Kilkenny
1957	W Kinsella	Sutton	1978	P Walton	Birr
1958	M McGuirk	Sutton	1979	P Walton	The Island
1959	S Cooney	Edmondstown	1981	P Murphy	Donabate
1960	S Cooney	Edmondstown	1982	N Goulding	Tullamore
1961	R Kane	Milltown	1983	J McKinstry	Elm Park
1962	J Mahon	Elm Park	1984	J Farrell	Mullingar
1963	R Hutton	Donabate	1985	L Walker	Clontarf
1964	A Black	Howth	1986	JP Fitzgerald	Laytown and
1965	I Elliott	Newlands			Bettystown
1966–68	*No Championship to enable the Boys'*		1987	G McNeill	Grange
	(Amateur) Open Championship of Ireland to be		1988	P Harrington	Royal Tara
	played		1989	R Burns	Headfort
1969	D Smyth	Donabate	1990	D Higgins	Laytown and
1970	H Duggan	Clontarf			Bettystown

Munster Boys' Open Amateur

INAUGURATED 1950

YEAR	WINNER	VENUE	YEAR	WINNER	VENUE
1950	T Skerritt	Castletroy	1966	J Lower	Douglas
1951	D Kelliher	Muskerry	1967	K Allen	Limerick
1952	J Harrington	Limerick	1968	RJ O'Brien	Muskerry
1953	J Harrington	Douglas	1969	D Smyth	Castletroy
1954	G McGlennon	Castletroy	1970	J Lynch	Cork
1955	M Walsh	Ennis	1971	RJ Leonard	Limerick
1956	N Baker	Thurles	1972	J Lynch	Douglas
1957	WM Kinsella	Ennis	1973	P M O'Boyle	Castletroy
1958	JD McDermott	Ennis	1974	T Corridan	Tramore
1959	M Wall	Ennis	1975	M Kavanagh	Muskerry
1960	SM Coghlan	Thurles	1976	A Hogan	Ballybunion
1961	C O'Loughlin	Ennis	1977	G O'Connor	Thurles
1962	B O'Brien	Ennis	1978	B McDaid	Killarney
1963	B O'Brien	Ennis	1979	R Rafferty	Tramore
1964	D Coen	Ennis	1980	K McDaid	Thurles
1965	P Soden	Castletroy	1981	C Fitzsimons	Ballybunion

YEAR	WINNER	VENUE	YEAR	WINNER	VENUE
1982	P McDonald	Bandon	1987	D Cunningham	Castletroy
1983	K Sheehan	Limerick	1988	M Riseley	Mallow
1984	D Kelleher	Monkstown	1989	R Burns	Youghal
1985	S Keane	Tramore	1990	S Quinlivan	Cork
1986	L Walker	Shannon			

Ulster Boys' Open Amateur

INAUGURATED 1949

YEAR	WINNER	VENUE	YEAR	WINNER	VENUE
1949	NV Drew	Royal Belfast	1970	DC Long	Fortwilliam
1950	J Glover	Shandon Park	1971	B Brennan	Warrenpoint
1951	B Donnellon	Donaghadee	1972	R McCormack	Balmoral
1952	AHG Love	Malone	1973	WAY Pope	Royal Belfast
1953	WH Rainey	Bangor	1974	K Campbell	Shandon Park
1954	T McAllister	Knock	1975	E Crawford	Donaghadee
1955	JFD Madeley	Ballycastle	1976	T Corridan	Malone
1956	M McAuley	Belvoir Park	1977	N Anderson	Knock
1957	JA McDade	Holywood	1978	C Glasgow	Ballycastle
1958	RC McAnoy	Fortwilliam	1979	P Brunton	Holywood
1959	NM Timms	Warrenpoint	1980	PG Barry	Belvoir Park
1960	NS Kelly	Balmoral	1981	P Mitchell	Royal Belfast
1961	B O'Brien	Royal Belfast	1982	P Stevenson	Co Armagh
1962	C McCormack	Shandon Park	1983	J McKinstry	Fortwilliam
1963	R Hutton	Donaghadee	1984	P Gribben	Warrenpoint
1964	A Black	Malone	1985	A Maney	Shandon Park
1965	A Rea	Bangor	1986	R Hutton	Knock
1966	M Bloom	Knock	1987	D Errity	Ardglass
1967	JC Brewer	Ballycastle	1988	M Davis	Donaghadee
1968	J McDonald	Belvoir Park	1989	R Burns	Balmoral
1969	D Campbell	Holywood	1990	G Sproule	Cairndhu

West of Scotland Boys' Championship

INAUGURATED 1964

YEAR	WINNER	YEAR	WINNER
1964	G McKay	1970	S Torrance
1965	WR Lockie	1971	D Stratton
1966	RA Bennett	1972	I Gillan
1967	IA Carslaw	1973	P McNiven
1968	PY Reed	1974	D Carrick
1969	M Gray	1975	A Taylor

YEAR	WINNER	YEAR	WINNER
1976	A Taylor	1984	G Orr
1977	G Haugh	1985	D O'Callaghan
1978	J Queen	1986	G King
1979	T Reid	1987	C Ronald
1980	J Milligan	1988	M King
1981	S Thompson	1989	S Dundas
1982	P Gorvan	1990	D Keeney
1983	G Collinson		

Girls' Events

Girls' British Open Amateur Championship

INAUGURATED 1919

This event was due to be played in August 1914 but the outbreak of the Great War intervened. It was started at the first opportunity afterwards in 1919 at Stoke Poges, the venue used without a break up to 1938. Ever since it has been played in England or Scotland until 1970 when Wales joined the rota.

Many of the winners, including six from France, have gone on to gain international honours; over twenty of them later played for Great Britain and Ireland in the Curtis Cup. Others disappeared from the golf scene after their success. One of the remarkable wins was that of Nancy Jupp in 1934 when she was only 13 years old. Pauline Doran won three times in succession 1931–33.

The French girls included three who went on to win the British Ladies Amateur: Thion de la Chaume (Mme Rene Lacoste), Lally Vagliano (Vicomtesse de Saint Sauveur, now Mme Segard) and Brigitte Varangot, co-incidentally each in a year when the venue was Newcastle Co. Down.

YEAR	WINNER	RUNNER-UP	MARGIN	VENUE
1919	Audrey Croft	C Clark	1 hole	Stoke Poges
1920	C Clark	A Croft	21st hole	Stoke Poges
1921	W Sarson	M Parkinson	5 and 3	Stoke Poges
1922	M Wickenden	B Griffiths	4 and 3	Stoke Poges
1923	M Mackay	Miss Strohmenger	3 and 2	Stoke Poges
1924	Miss Thion de la Chaume	D Pearson	4 and 2	Stoke Poges
1925	Enid Wilson	KM Nicholls	5 and 3	Stoke Poges
1926	Diana Esmond	M Ramsden	6 and 5	Stoke Poges
1927	Diana Fishwick	Irene Taylor	7 and 6	Stoke Poges
1928	Diana Fishwick	M Jolly	3 and 2	Stoke Poges
1929	Nan Baird	S Bailey	4 and 3	Stoke Poges
1930	Pauline Doran	D Wilkins	19th hole	Stoke Poges
1931	Pauline Doran	D Wilkins	2 and 1	Stoke Poges
1932	Pauline Doran	A de Gunzbourg	19th hole	Stoke Poges
1933	Jessie Anderson	EM Pears	5 and 3	Stoke Poges
1934	Nancy Jupp	J Mountford	3 and 1	Stoke Poges
1935	P Falkner	J Pemberton	1 hole	Stoke Poges
1936	P Edwards	Jacqueline Gordon	3 and 2	Stoke Poges

YEAR	WINNER	RUNNER-UP	MARGIN	VENUE
1937	Lally Vagliano	P Edwards	5 and 4	Stoke Poges
1938	S Stroyan	J Pemberton	4 and 3	Stoke Poges
1939–48	*No championship due to Second World War*			
1949	Pamela Davies	Arlette Jacquet	1 hole	Beaconsfield
1950	Janette Robertson	Ann Phillips	5 and 4	Formby Ladies
1951	Jane Redgate	Janette Robertson	19th hole	Gullane
1952	Ann Phillips	S Marbrook	7 and 6	Stoke Poges
1953	Susan Hill	Angela Ward	3 and 2	Woodhall Spa
1954	Bridget Jackson	D Winsor	20th hole	West Kilbride
1955	Angela Ward	Alison Gardner	5 and 4	Beaconsfield
1956	Ruth Porter	Annette Nicholson	5 and 4	Seaton Carew
1957	Brigitte Varangot	Ruth Porter	3 and 2	North Berwick
1958	T Ross-Stein	Brigitte Varangot	2 and 1	Cotswold Hills
1959	Sheila Vaughan	Julia Greenhalgh	1 hole	Nottingham
1960	S Clarke	Ann Irvin	2 and 1	Barassie
1961	Diane Robb	Jean Roberts	3 and 2	Beaconsfield
1962	S McLaren-Smith	A Murphy	2 and 1	Foxton Hall
1963	Dinah Oxley	B Whitehead	2 and 1	Gullane
1964	Pam Tredinnick	K Cumming	2 and 1	Camberley Heath
1965	Anne Willard	Shirley Ward	3 and 2	Formby Ladies
1966	Jillian Hutton	Dinah Oxley	20th hole	Troon Portland
1967	P Burrows	Jillian Hutton	2 and 1	Liphook
1968	C Wallace	C Reybroeck	4 and 3	Leven
1969	J de Witt Puyt	C Reybroeck	2 and 1	Ilkley
1970	Carol Le Feuvre	Michelle Walker	2 and 1	North Wales
1971	Jean Mark	Maureen Walker	4 and 3	North Berwick
1972	Maureen Walker	Suzanne Cadden	2 and 1	Royal Norwich
1973	A Palli	N Jeanson	2 and 1	Church Brampton
1974	R Barry	Tegwen Perkins	1 hole	Dunbar
1975	Suzanne Cadden	L Isherwood	4 and 3	Henbury
1976	Gillian Stewart	S Rowlands	5 and 4	Pyle and Kenfig
1977	Wilma Aitken	S Bamford	2 and 1	Formby Ladies
1978	Marie Laure de Lorenzi	D Glenn	2 and 1	Largs
1979	S Lapaire	P Smillie	19th hole	Edgbaston
1980	Jane Connachan	L Bolton	2 holes	Wrexham
1981	Jane Connachan	Penny Grice	20th hole	Woodbridge
1982	Claire Waite	M Mackie	6 and 5	Edzell
1983	E Orley	A Walters	7 and 6	Leeds
1984	Carole Swallow	Elaine Farquharson	1 hole	Llandudno (Maesdu)
1985	Susan Shapcott	Elaine Farquharson	3 and 1	Hesketh
1986	Stefania Croce	S Bennett	5 and 4	West Kilbride
1987	Helen Dobson	Stefania Croce	19th hole	Barnham Broom
1988	Alison Macdonald	J Posener	3 and 2	Pyle and Kenfig
1989	M McKinlay	S Eriksson	19th hole	Carlisle
1990	S Cavalleri	E Valera	5 and 4	Penrith

English Girls' Championship

INAUGURATED 1964

YEAR	WINNER	RUNNER-UP	MARGIN	VENUE
1964	Shirley Ward	Pam Tredinnick	2 and 1	Wollaton Park
1965	Dinah Oxley	A Payne	2 holes	Edgbaston
1966	B Whitehead	Dinah Oxley	1 hole	Woodbridge
1967	A Willard	G Holloway	1 hole	Burhill
1968	Kathryn Phillips	Carol Le Feuvre	6 and 5	Harrogate
1969	Carol Le Feuvre	Kathryn Phillips	2 and 1	Hawkstone Park
1970	Carol Le Feuvre	Michelle Walker	2 and 1	High Post
1971	C Eckersley	J Stevens	4 and 3	Liphook
1972	C Barker	R Kelly	4 and 3	Trentham
1973	S Parker	S Thurston	19th hole	Lincoln
1974	C Langford	Lynne Harrold	2 and 1	Knowle
1975	Maxine Burton	R Barry	6 and 5	Formby
1976	H Latham	D Park	3 and 2	Moseley
1977	S Bamford	S Jolly	21st hole	Chelmsford
1978	P Smillie	J Smith	3 and 2	Willesley Park
1979	Linda Moore	P Barry	1 hole	Cirencester
1980	P Smillie	Janet Soulsby	3 and 2	Kedleston Park
1981	Janet Soulsby	Claire Waite	7 and 5	Worksop
1982	Claire Waite	Penny Grice	3 and 2	Wilmslow
1983	Penny Grice	K Mitchell	2 and 1	West Surrey
1984	Carole Swallow	S Duhig	3 and 1	Bath
1985	Lorna Fairclough	K Mitchell	6 and 5	Coventry
1986	Susan Shapcott	N Way	7 and 6	Huddersfield
1987	Susan Shapcott	S Morgan	1 hole	Sandy Lodge
1988	Helen Dobson	Susan Shapcott	1 hole	Long Ashton
1989	Helen Dobson	Alison MacDonald	3 and 1	Edgbaston
1990	C Hall	J Hockley	20th hole	Bolton Old Links

Irish Girls' Championship

INAUGURATED 1951

YEAR	WINNER	RUNNER-UP	MARGIN	VENUE
1951	Jocelyn Davies	Irene Hurst	3 and 2	Milltown
1952	Jane Redgate	Ann Phillips	22nd hole	Grange
1953	Jane Redgate	Irene Hurst	4 and 3	Grange
1954–60	*Suspended*			
1961	M Coburn	C McAuley	6 and 5	Portrush
1962	Pearl Boyd	Patricia Atkinson	4 and 3	Elm Park
1963	Patricia Atkinson	C Scarlett	8 and 7	Donaghadee
1964	C Scarlett	A Maher	6 and 5	Milltown

YEAR	WINNER	RUNNER-UP	MARGIN	VENUE
1965	V Singleton	P McKenzie	7 and 6	Ballycastle
1966	M McConnell	D Hulme	3 and 2	Dun Laoghaire
1967	M McConnell	C Wallace	6 and 5	Portrush
1968	C Wallace	A McCoy	3 and 1	Louth
1969	E McGregor	M Sheenan	6 and 5	Knock
1970	E McGregor	J Mark	3 and 2	Greystones
1971	J Mark	C Nesbitt	3 and 2	Royal Belfast
1972	P Smyth	M Governey	1 hole	Elm Park
1973	M Governey	R Hegarty	3 and 1	Mullingar
1974	R Hegarty	M Irvine	2 holes	Castletroy
1975	M Irvine	P Wickham	2 and 1	Carlow
1976	P Wickham	R Hegarty	5 and 3	Castle
1977	A Ferguson	R Walsh	3 and 2	Birr
1978	C Wickham	B Gleeson	1 hole	Killarney
1979	L Bolton	B Gleeson	3 and 2	Milltown
1980	B Gleeson	L Bolton	5 and 3	Kilkenny
1981	B Gleeson	E Lynn	1 hole	Donegal
1982	D Langan	S Lynn	5 and 4	Headfort
1983	E McDaid	S Lynn	20th hole	Ennis
1984	S Sheehan	L Tormey	6 and 4	Thurles
1985	S Sheehan	D Hanna	5 and 4	Laytown and Bettystown
1986	D Mahon	T Eakin	4 and 3	Mallow
1987	V Greevy	B Ryan	8 and 7	Galway
1988	L McCool	P Gorman	3 and 2	Courtown
1989	A Rogers	R MacGuigan	2 and 1	Athlone
1990	G Doran	L McCool	3 and 1	Royal Portrush

Scottish Girls' Open Stroke Play Championship

In the early years of the Scottish Girls' Open Stroke Play, which started in 1955, the home players often failed to fend off the English and others; until 1971 the invaders won more often than the Scots. Since then, however, they have been much more successful in keeping the title at home.

The Close Girls' Championship (match play) contains the names of many winners who have gone on to succeed in senior competitions. The venues for both Championships have been at nearly as many inland courses as links.

INAUGURATED 1955

YEAR	WINNER	VENUE	YEAR	WINNER	VENUE
1955	Marjory Fowler	Erskine	1962	Susan Armitage	Dalmahoy
1956	Belle McCorkindale	Erskine	1963	Ann Irvin	Dumfries and County
1957	Marjory Fowler	Kilmacolm			
1958	Ruth Porter	Ranfurly Castle	1964	M Nuttall	Dalmahoy
1959	Diane Robb	Helensburgh	1965	I Wylie	Carnoustie
1960	Julia Greenhalgh	Ranfurly Castle	1966	J Smith	Douglas Park
1961	Diane Robb	Whitecraigs	1967	J Bourassa	Dunbar

YEAR	WINNER	VENUE	YEAR	WINNER	VENUE
1968	Kathryn Phillips	Dumfries and County	1980	Jane Connachan	Kirkcaldy
			1981	Kitrina Douglas	Downfield
1969	Kathryn Phillips	Prestonfield	1982	J Rhodes	Dumfries and Galloway
1970	Beverly Huke	Leven			
1971	Beverly Huke	Dalmahoy	1983	Shirley Lawson	Largs
1972	Lesley Hope	Troon Portland	1984	Shirley Lawson	Dunbar
1973	G Cadden	Edzell	1985	Kathryn Imrie	Ballater
1974	S Lambie	Stranraer	1986	Kathryn Imrie	Dumfries and County
1975	G Cadden	Lanark			
1976	Suzanne Cadden	Prestonfield	1987	Kathryn Imrie	Douglas Park
1977	Suzanne Cadden	Edzell	1988	Catriona Lambert	Baberton
1978	Jane Connachan	Peebles	1989	Catriona Lambert	Dunblane
1979	Alison Gemmill	Troon Portland	1990	J Moodie	Royal Troon

Scottish Girls' Close Amateur Championship

INAUGURATED 1960

YEAR	WINNER	RUNNER-UP	MARGIN	VENUE
1960	Joan Hastings	A Lurie	6 and 4	Kilmacolm
1961	I Wylie	W Clark	3 and 1	Murrayfield
1962	I Wylie	U Burnet	3 and 1	West Kilbride
1963	M Norval	S MacDonald	6 and 4	Carnoustie
1964	J Smith	C Workman	2 and 1	West Kilbride
1965	J Smith	I Walker	7 and 5	Leven
1966	Jillian Hutton	F Jamieson	2 holes	Arbroath
1967	Jillian Hutton	K Lackie	4 and 2	West Kilbride
1968	M Dewar	J Crawford	2 holes	Dalmahoy
1969	Catherine Panton	A Coutts	23rd hole	Edzell
1970	Michelle Walker	L Bennett	3 and 2	Largs
1971	Michelle Walker	S Kennedy	1 hole	Edzell
1972	G Cadden	Catherine Panton	3 and 2	Stirling
1973	Michelle Walker	M Thomson	1 hole	Cowal, Dunoon
1974	Suzanne Cadden	Dale Reid	3 and 1	Arbroath
1975	Wilma Aitken	Suzanne Cadden	1 hole	Leven
1976	Suzanne Cadden	D Mitchell	4 and 2	Dumfries and County
1977	Wilma Aitken	G Wilson	2 holes	West Kilbride
1978	Jane Connachan	D Mitchell	7 and 5	Stirling
1979	Jane Connachan	G Wilson	3 and 1	Dunbar
1980	Jane Connachan	P Wright	21st hole	Dumfries and County
1981	D Thomson	P Wright	2 and 1	Barassie
1982	Shirley Lawson	D Thomson	1 hole	Montrose
1983	Kathryn Imrie	D Martin	2 and 1	Leven
1984	T Craik	D Jackson	3 and 2	Peebles
1985	Elaine Farquharson	E Moffat	2 holes	West Kilbride
1986	Catriona Lambert	F McKay	4 and 3	Nairn
1987	S Little	L Moretti	3 and 2	Stirling
1988	J Jenkins	F McKay	4 and 3	Dumfries and County
1989	J Moodie	V Melvin	19th hole	Kilmacolm
1990	M McKay	J Moodie	3 and 2	Duff House Royal

Welsh Girls' Amateur Championship

INAUGURATED 1957

YEAR	WINNER	RUNNER-UP	MARGIN	VENUE
1957	A Coulman	S Wynne-Jones	1 hole	Newport
1958	S Wynne-Jones	A Coulman	3 and 1	Conwy
1959	C Mason	T Williams	3 and 2	Glamorgan
1960	Ann Hughes	D Wilson	6 and 4	Llandrindod Wells
1961	Jill Morris	Ann Hughes	3 and 2	North Wales
1962	Jill Morris	Peta Morgan	4 and 3	Southerndown
1963	Ann Hughes	Audrey Brown	8 and 7	Conwy
1964	Ann Hughes	M Leigh	5 and 3	Holyhead
1965	Ann Hughes	A Reardon-Hughes	19th hole	Swansea Bay
1966	S Hales	J Rogers	1 hole	Prestatyn
1967	E Wilkie	L Humphreys	1 hole	Pyle and Kenfig
1968	L Morris	J Rogers	1 hole	Portmadoc
1969	L Morris	L Humphreys	5 and 3	Wenvoe Castle
1970	Tegwen Perkins	Pamela Light	2 and 1	Rhuddlan
1971	Pamela Light	P Whitley	4 and 3	Glamorganshire
1972	P Whitley	Pamela Light	2 and 1	Maesdu
1973	Vicki Rawlings	Tegwen Perkins	19th hole	Whitchurch
1974	L Isherwood	S Rowlands	4 and 3	Wrexham
1975	L Isherwood	S Rowlands	1 hole	Swansea Bay
1976	K Rawlings	C Parry	5 and 4	Rhuddlan
1977	S Rowlands	D Taylor	7 and 5	Clyne
1978	S Rowlands	G Rees	3 and 2	Abergele
1979	Mandy Rawlings	J Richards	19th hole	St Mellons
1980	Karen Davies	Mandy Rawlings	19th hole	Vale of Llangollen
1981	Mandy Rawlings	F Connor	4 and 3	Radyr
1982	Karen Davies	K Beckett	6 and 5	Wrexham
1983	N Wesley	J Foster	4 and 2	Whitchurch
1984	J Foster	J Evans	6 and 5	Pwllheli
1985	J Foster	S Caley	6 and 5	Langland Bay
1986	J Foster	L Dermot	3 and 2	Holyhead
1987	J Lloyd	S Bibbs	2 and 1	Cardiff
1988	Lisa Dermot	A Perriam	2 holes	Builth Wells
1989	Lisa Dermot	N Stroud	4 and 2	Carmarthen
1990	Lisa Dermot	N Stroud	6 and 4	Padeswood and Buckley

Ireland v Wales

YEAR	WINNER	VENUE	RESULT
1967	Ireland	Liphook	7–2
1968	Ireland	Leven	$6^1/_2$–$2^1/_2$

From 1969 became included in Girls' Home Internationals

Home International Matches

1969 at Ilkley

Winners: England

RESULT	SCORE
England beat Scotland	$5^1/_2$–$1^1/_2$
England beat Ireland	5–2
England beat Wales	7–0
Scotland beat Ireland	5–2
Scotland beat Wales	5–2
Ireland beat Wales	6–1

1970 at North Wales

Winners: England

RESULT	SCORE
England beat Scotland	4–3
England beat Ireland	5–2
England beat Wales	6–1
Scotland beat Ireland	$4^1/_2$–$2^1/_2$
Scotland beat Wales	6–1
Ireland beat Wales	$6^1/_2$–$^1/_2$

1971 at North Berwick

Winners: England

RESULT	SCORE
England beat Scotland	$4^1/_2$–$2^1/_2$
England beat Ireland	5–2
England beat Wales	5–2
Scotland beat Ireland	$4^1/_2$–$2^1/_2$
Scotland beat Wales	$5^1/_2$–$1^1/_2$
Ireland beat Wales	4–3

1972 at Royal Norwich

Winners: Scotland

RESULT	SCORE
Scotland beat England	5–2
Scotland beat Wales	$5^1/_2$–$1^1/_2$
Scotland beat Ireland	$6^1/_2$–$^1/_2$
England beat Wales	5–2
England beat Ireland	$6^1/_2$–$^1/_2$
Wales beat Ireland	4–3

1973 at Church Brampton

Winners: Scotland

RESULT	SCORE
Scotland beat England	5–2
Scotland beat Ireland	6–1
Scotland beat Wales	5–2
England beat Ireland	$4^1/_2$–$2^1/_2$
England beat Wales	4–3
Ireland beat Wales	$6^1/_2$–$^1/_2$

1974 at Dunbar

Winners: England

RESULT	SCORE
England beat Scotland	5–2
England beat Ireland	$5^1/_2$–$1^1/_2$
England beat Wales	4–3
Scotland beat Ireland	$6^1/_2$–$^1/_2$
Scotland beat Wales	5–2
Ireland beat Wales	5–2

1975 at Henbury

Winners: England

RESULT	SCORE
England halved with Scotland	$3^1/_2$–$3^1/_2$
England beat Ireland	$6^1/_2$–$^1/_2$
England beat Wales	6–1
Scotland beat Ireland	5–2
Scotland beat Wales	5–2
Ireland beat Wales	5–2

1976 at Pyle and Kenfig

Winners: Scotland

RESULT	SCORE
Scotland beat England	$4^1/_2$–$2^1/_2$
Scotland beat Wales	5–2
Scotland beat Ireland	4–3
England beat Wales	6–1
England beat Ireland	$6^1/_2$–$^1/_2$
Wales beat Ireland	4–3

1977 *at Formby*

Winners: England

RESULT	SCORE
England halved with Scotland	$3^1/_2$–$3^1/_2$
England beat Wales	7–0
England beat Ireland	6–1
Scotland beat Wales	5–2
Scotland beat Ireland	7–0
Wales beat Ireland	5–2

1981 *at Woodbridge*

Winners: England

RESULT	SCORE
England beat Scotland	$4^1/_2$–$2^1/_2$
England beat Ireland	$5^1/_2$–$1^1/_2$
England beat Wales	$6^1/_2$–$^1/_2$
Scotland halved with Ireland	$3^1/_2$–$3^1/_2$
Scotland beat Wales	5–2
Ireland beat Wales	5–2

1978 *at Largs*

Winners: England

RESULT	SCORE
England beat Scotland	5–2
England beat Wales	6–1
England beat Ireland	7–0
Scotland beat Wales	6–1
Scotland beat Ireland	$4^1/_2$–$2^1/_2$
Wales beat Ireland	5–2

1982 *at Edzell*

Winners: England

RESULT	SCORE
England beat Ireland	7–0
England beat Scotland	5–2
England beat Wales	6–1
Ireland beat Scotland	4–3
Ireland beat Wales	$4^1/_2$–$2^1/_2$
Scotland beat Wales	6–1

1979 *at Edgbaston*

Winners: England

RESULT	SCORE
England halved with Wales	$3^1/_2$–$3^1/_2$
England beat Ireland	7–0
England beat Scotland	$5^1/_2$–$1^1/_2$
Wales beat Ireland	$4^1/_2$–$2^1/_2$
Wales beat Scotland	$4^1/_2$–$2^1/_2$
Ireland beat Scotland	4–3

1983 *at Alwoodley*

Winners: England

RESULT	SCORE
England beat Ireland	$4^1/_2$–$2^1/_2$
England beat Scotland	4–3
England beat Wales	7–0
Ireland beat Scotland	4–3
Ireland beat Wales	6–1
Scotland beat Wales	$5^1/_2$–$1^1/_2$

1980 *at Wrexham*

Winners: England

RESULT	SCORE
England beat Scotland	$5^1/_2$–$1^1/_2$
England halved with Ireland	$3^1/_2$–$3^1/_2$
England beat Wales	$5^1/_2$–$1^1/_2$
Scotland beat Ireland	4–3
Scotland beat Wales	6–1
Ireland beat Wales	$4^1/_2$–$2^1/_2$

1984 *at Maesdu*

Winners: Scotland

RESULT	SCORE
Scotland beat England	
Scotland beat Ireland	
Scotland beat Wales	
England beat Ireland	
England beat Wales	
Wales beat Ireland	

1985 *at Hesketh*

Winners: England

RESULT	SCORE
England beat Scotland	5–2
England beat Ireland	5^1/$_2$–1^1/$_2$
England beat Wales	6–1
Ireland beat Scotland	4–3
Ireland beat Wales	4–3
Scotland beat Wales	6^1/$_2$–^{1}/$_2$

1986 *at West Kilbride*

Winners: England

RESULT	SCORE
England beat Scotland	4–3
England beat Wales	4^1/$_2$–2^1/$_2$
England beat Ireland	5–2
Scotland beat Wales	5–2
Scotland beat Ireland	5–2
Wales beat Ireland	5–2

1987 *at Barnham Broom*

Winners: England

RESULT	SCORE
England beat Scotland	6^1/$_2$–^{1}/$_2$
England beat Ireland	7–0
England beat Wales	6–1
Scotland beat Ireland	4–3
Ireland beat Wales	4^1/$_2$–2^1/$_2$
Wales beat Scotland	4–3

1988 *at Pyle and Kenfig*

Winners: England

RESULT	SCORE
England beat Ireland	4–3
England beat Wales	4–3
England halved with Scotland	3^1/$_2$–3^1/$_2$
Ireland beat Wales	4–3
Ireland beat Scotland	5–2
Wales beat Scotland	4–3

1989 *at Carlisle*

Winners: England

RESULT	SCORE
Ireland beat Scotland	4^1/$_2$–2^1/$_2$
England beat Wales	4–3
Ireland beat Wales	4^1/$_2$–2^1/$_2$
England beat Scotland	5–2
Scotland beat Wales	4–3
England beat Ireland	4^1/$_2$–2^1/$_2$

1990 *at Penrith*

Winners: England

RESULT	SCORE
England beat Wales	7–2
Ireland beat Scotland	6–3
England beat Scotland	8–1
Ireland beat Wales	9–0
England beat Ireland	7^1/$_2$–1^1/$_2$
Scotland beat Wales	7–2

Youths' Events

To play in the Youths' Championship and international matches competitors must be under 21 years of age. The Championship provides an excellent test for those no longer eligible to compete in Boys' events, but who may not feel they have the experience, skill or confidence yet to play in the Home Union Championships. The Youths' is a 72 hole stroke play competition for 150 players of 3 handicap or less, playing a round each on Thursday and Friday and then the 40 lowest scores qualifying for 36 holes on the Saturday.

The Championship is preceded by the Youths' England versus Scotland match of which England has won 17 times and Scotland 15. Following the Championship a side is selected to represent Great Britain & Ireland Youths' against the Continent of Europe in a match which takes place at a different venue a few weeks later.

It will be seen that some past Youths' Champions have graduated to be top class professionals; they include Brian Barnes, Peter Townsend, Peter Oosterhuis, Nick Faldo, Sandy Lyle, Gordon Brand Jr and Jose Maria Olazabal. Equally others such as Alan Bussell, Peter Benka, who won two years in succession, John Cook and David Gilford have been successful in the amateur world.

British Youths' Open Amateur Championship

INAUGURATED 1954

YEAR	WINNER	SCORE	VENUE
1954	JS More	287	Dumfries and County
1955	B Stockdale	297	Pannal
1956	AF Bussell	287	Barnton
1957	G Will	290	Pannal
1958	RH Kemp	281	Dumfries and County
1959	RA Jowle	286	Pannal
1960	GA Caygill	279	Pannal
1961	JS Martin	284	Bruntsfield

YEAR	WINNER	SCORE	VENUE
1962	GA Caygill	287	Pannal
1963	AJ Low	283	Pollok
1964	BW Barnes	290	Pannal
1965	PM Townsend	281	Northumberland
1966	PA Oosterhuis	219 (54 holes)	Dalmahoy
1967	PJ Benka	278	Copt Heath
1968	PJ Benka	281	Ayr Belleisle
1969	JH Cook	289	Lindrick
1970	B Dassu	276	Barnton
1971	P Elson	277	Church Brampton
1972	AH Chandler	281	Glasgow Gailes
1973	SC Mason	284	Southport and Ainsdale
1974	DM Robertson	284	Downfield
1975	NA Faldo	278	Pannal
1976	ME Lewis	277	Gullane
1977	AWB Lyle	285	Moor Park
1978	B Marchbank	278	East Renfrewshire
1979	G Brand Jr	291	Woodhall Spa
1980	G Hay	303	Troon
1981	T Antevik (Swe)	290	Gullane
1982	AP Parkin	280	St Andrews New
1983	P Mayo	290	Sunningdale
1984	R Morris	281	Blairgowrie
1985	JM Olazabal (Spa)	281	Ganton
1986	D Gilford	283	Carnoustie
1987	J Cook	283	Hollinwell
1988	C Cevaer (Fra)	275	Royal Aberdeen
1989	M Smith	285	Ashburnham
1990	M Gronberg	275	Southerness

Youths' Internationals England V Scotland

INAUGURATED 1955

YEAR	WINNER	RESULT	VENUE
1955	England	13–5	Pannal
1956	Scotland	17 holes	Barnton
1957	*Not played*		
1958	England	4 holes	Dumfries and County
1959	Scotland	12–6	Pannal
1960	Scotland	11½–6½	Pannal
1961	England	11½–6½	Bruntsfield
1962	England	9½–8½	Pannal
1963	Scotland	9–6	Pollok
1964	Scotland	9–6	Pannal
1965	Scotland	10½–4½	Gosforth Park
1966	England	9½–5½	Dalmahoy
1967	Halved	7½–7½	Copt Heath
1968	Scotland	8½–6½	Ayr Belleisle

YEAR	WINNER	RESULT	VENUE
1969	England	8½–6½	Lindrick
1970	Scotland	8½–6½	Barnton
1971	England	11–4	Church Brampton
1972	England	11–4	Glasgow Gailes
1973	England	10–5	Southport and Ainsdale
1974	England	9–6	Downfield
1975	Scotland	11–4	Pannal
1976	England	8½–6½	Gullane
1977	Scotland	9½–5½	Moor Park
1978	Scotland	8½–6½	East Renfrewshire
1979	Halved	7½–7½	Woodhall Spa
1980	Scotland	9–6	Troon
1981	Scotland	8–7	West Lancs
1982	Halved	7½–7½	St Andrews New
1983	Scotland	8½–6½	Sunningdale
1984	Scotland	9–6	Blairgowrie
1985	Halved	7½–7½	Ganton
1986	Scotland	8–7	Carnoustie
1987	England	9½–5½	Hollinwell
1988	England	10–5	Balgownie
1989	England	9–6	Ashburnham
1990	Scotland	9–6	Southerness

Great Britain & Ireland v Continent of Europe, Youths'

INAUGURATED 1967

YEAR	WINNER	RESULT	VENUE
1967	Great Britain & Ireland	8–7	Copt Heath
1968	Great Britain & Ireland	11–4	Ayr Belleisle
1969	Great Britain & Ireland	13½–1½	Lindrick
1970	Great Britain & Ireland	10½–4½	Barnton
1971	Great Britain & Ireland	10–5	Church Brampton
1972	Great Britain & Ireland	11½–3½	Glasgow Gailes
1973	Great Britain & Ireland	10–5	Southport and Ainsdale
1974	Great Britain & Ireland	10–5	Downfield
1975	Great Britain & Ireland	9–6	Pannal
1976	Great Britain & Ireland	17–13	Chantilly, France
1977	Great Britain & Ireland	11½–3½	Moor Park
1978	Great Britain & Ireland	12½–2½	East Renfrewshire
1979	Great Britain & Ireland	12–3	Woodhall Spa
1980	Europe	13–11	Lunds Akademiska Sweden
1981	Great Britain & Ireland	7½–4½	West Lancs
	Singles curtailed owing to weather		
1982	Great Britain & Ireland	7½–4½	St Andrews New
1983	Great Britain & Ireland	13–11	Punta Ala, Italy
1984	Halved	6–6	Blairgowrie

YEAR	WINNER	RESULT	VENUE
1985	Great Britain & Ireland	8–4	Ganton
1986	Great Britain & Ireland	13^1/$_2$–10^1/$_2$	Bilbao, Spain
1987	Continent of Europe	7–5	Hollinwell
1988	Great Britain & Ireland	13^1/$_2$–10^1/$_2$	Copenhagen, Denmark
1989	Great Britain & Ireland	8^1/$_2$–3^1/$_2$	Ashburnham
1990	Great Britain & Ireland	14^1/$_2$–9^1/$_2$	Oporto, Portugal

Scottish Youths' Open Amateur Stroke Play Championship

INAUGURATED 1979

YEAR	WINNER	SCORE	VENUE
1979	A Oldcorn	217	Dalmahoy
1980	G Brand Jr	281	Monifieth and Ashludie
1981	S Campbell	279	Cawder and Keir
1982	LS Mann	270	Leven and Scoonie
1983	A Moir	284	Mortonhall
1984	B Shields	280	Eastwood, Renfrew
1985	H Kemp	282	East Kilbride
1986	A Mednick	282	Cawder
1987	K Walker	291	Bogside
1988	P McGinley	281	Ladybank and Glenrothes
1989	J Mackenzie	281	Longniddry
1990	S Bannerman	213 (54 holes)	Portpatrick and Stranraer

Irish Youths' Open Amateur

INAUGURATED 1969

YEAR	WINNER	SCORE	VENUE	YEAR	WINNER	SCORE	VENUE
1969	D Branigan	142	Delgany	1979	R Rafferty	293	Tullamore
Following the inaugural event the Championship				1980	J McHenry	296	Clandeboye
was extended to 72 holes				1981	J McHenry	303	Westport
1970	LA Owens	286	Tullamore	1982	K O'Donnell	286	Mullingar
1971	MA Gannon	277	Athlone	1983	P Murphy	287	Cork
1972	MA Gannon	291	Mullingar	1984	JC Morris	292	Bangor
1973	J Purcell	289	Tullamore	1985	J McHenry	287	Co Sligo
1974	S Dunlop	293	Athlone	1986	JC Morris	280	Carlow
1975	P McNally	287	Mullingar	1987	C Everett	300	Killarney
1976	R McCormack	294	Tullamore	1988	P McGinley	283	Malone
1977	B McDaid	290	Athlone	1989	A Mathers	279	Athlone
1978	T Corridan	279	Thurles	1990	D Errity	293	Dundalk

Connacht Youths' Open Amateur

INAUGURATED 1979

YEAR	WINNER	SCORE	VENUE	YEAR	WINNER	SCORE	VENUE
1979	D Parr	304	Co Sligo	1985	G Moore		Co Sligo
1980	J McHenry	140	Athlone	1986	G McNeill	245	Westport
1981	MF Sludds	150	Athlone	1987	G McNeill	297	Enniscrone
1982	C Fitzsimons	141	Galway	1988	K Kearney	296	Galway
1983	J McHenry	282	Athlone	1989	R Slone	295	Athlone
1984	C Fitzsimons	305	Co Sligo	1990	R Coughlan	248	Athlone

Leinster Youths' Open Amateur

INAUGURATED 1979

YEAR	WINNER	SCORE	VENUE	YEAR	WINNER	SCORE	VENUE
1979	P Walton	138	Delgany	1985	P McGinley	279	Delgany
1980	C Carew	283	Delgany	1986	T Kelliher	293	Delgany
1981	S King	285	Delgany	1987	P McGinley	283	Delgany
1982	P Errity	283	Delgany	1988	S Hogan	287	Delgany
1983	J Hutchinson	291	Delgany	1989	G McNeil	277	Delgany
1984	M Curran	286	Delgany	1990	G Murphy	281	Greystones

Munster Youths' Open Amateur

INAUGURATED 1980

YEAR	WINNER	SCORE	VENUE	YEAR	WINNER	SCORE	VENUE
1980	B McDaid	296	Muskerry	1986	J Morris	283	Nenagh
1981	B McDaid	292	Ballybunion	1987	J Morris	293	Mallow
1982	P Congdon	299	Lahinch	1988	P Gribben	293	Killarney
1983	K Mulcahy	263	Thurles	1989	D Errity	307	Tramore
1984	P Murphy	304	Killarney	1990	L Walker	280	Nenagh
1985	E O'Connell	307	Lahinch				

Ulster Youths' Open Amateur

INAUGURATED 1969

YEAR	WINNER	RUNNER-UP	MARGIN	VENUE
1969	JE O'Leary	WI Ritchie	6 and 5	Portrush
1970	PB Malone	AR Hope	4 and 3	Belvoir Park
1971	PB Malone	S Dijon	1 hole	Newcastle
1972	M Patterson	RJ Heggarty	1 hole	Portrush
1973	RJ Heggarty	B Warwick	5 and 4	Belvoir Park
1974	RJ Heggarty	NR Martin	2 and 1	Newcastle
1975	RJ Heggarty	G McGimpsey	19th hole	Portrush
1976	P O'Hagen	C Buller	3 and 1	Belvoir Park
1977	P O'Hara	P O'Hagen	3 and 2	Newcastle
1978	P Leckey	J Gray	3 and 1	Portrush
1979	R Rafferty	R Hanna	21st hole	Belvoir Park
1980	J Jones	J Breen	5 and 6	Newcastle
1981	M Windebank	C Murphy	8 and 7	Portrush
1982	G Hamill	P Grant	2 and 1	Belvoir Park
1983	M Froggatt	C Murphy	2 holes	Newcastle
1984	GJ Clarke	M Curran	3 and 2	Portrush
1985	J Carvill	CT Farr	4 and 3	Belvoir Park
1986	DA Mulholland	GJ Clarke	20th hole	Portrush
1987	J Carvill	S Paul	3 and 2	Malone
1988	G McAllister	A McFeeley	2 and 1	Belvoir Park
1989	G Moore	R Dorman	1 hole	Clandeboye
1990	N Crawford	C Feenan	3 and 2	Newcastle

Part Six
Overseas Championships

Overseas Championships

While mainly a book of British golf records, the results of the Open, Amateur and Ladies' Amateur Championships of Australia, Canada, New Zealand, South Africa, the United States and the Open of Japan have been included. Space prevents more detailed coverage of overseas events, but those listed are open to all nationalities and have sometimes been won by competitors from Britain and other countries.

Open Championship of Australia

INAUGURATED 1904

YEAR	WINNER	VENUE	SCORE
1904	Hon Michael Scott (Am)	Australian, Sydney	324
1905	D Soutar	Royal Melbourne	337
1906	C Clark	Royal Sydney	322
1907	Hon Michael Scott (Am)	Royal Melbourne	318
1908	C Pearce (Am)	Australian, Sydney	311
1909	C Felstead (Am)	Royal Melbourne	316
1910	C Clark	Royal Adelaide	306
1911	C Clark	Royal Sydney	321
1912	I Whitton (Am)	Royal Melbourne	321
1913	I Whitton (Am)	Royal Melbourne	302
1914–19	*No Championship due to Great War*		
1920	JH Kirkwood	Australian, Sydney	290
1921	A Le Fevre	Royal Melbourne	295
1922	C Campbell	Royal Sydney	307
1923	TE Howard	Royal Adelaide	301
1924	A Russell (Am)	Royal Melbourne	303
1925	F Popplewell	Australian, Sydney	299
1926	I Whitton (Am)	Royal Adelaide	297
1927	R Stewart	Royal Melbourne	297
1928	F Popplewell	Royal Sydney	295
1929	I Whitton (Am)	Royal Adelaide	309
1930	FP Eyre	Metropolitan, Melbourne	306
1931	I Whitton (Am)	Australian, Sydney	301
1932	MJ Ryan (Am)	Royal Adelaide	296
1933	ML Kelly	Royal Melbourne	302

YEAR	WINNER	VENUE	SCORE
1934	WJ Bolger	Royal Sydney	283
1935	FW McMahon	Royal Adelaide	293
1936	G Sarazen (USA)	Metropolitan, Melbourne	282
1937	G Naismith	Australian, Sydney	299
1938	JB Ferrier (Am)	Royal Adelaide	283
1939	JB Ferrier (Am)	Royal Melbourne	285
1940–45	*No Championship due to Second World War*		
1946	HO Pickworth	Royal Sydney	289
1947	HO Pickworth	Royal Queensland, Brisbane	285
1948	HO Pickworth	Kingston Heath, Victoria	289
1949	E Cremin	Australian, Sydney	287
1950	NG Von Nida	Kooyonga, Adelaide	286
1951	PW Thomson	Metropolitan, Melbourne	283
1952	NG Von Nida	Lake Karrinyup, Perth	278
1953	NG Von Nida	Royal Melbourne	278
1954	HO Pickworth	Kooyonga, Adelaide	280
1955	AD Locke (SA)	Gailes, Brisbane	290
1956	BS Crampton	Royal Sydney	289
1957	F Phillips	Kingston Heath, Victoria	287
1958	G Player (SA)	Kooyonga, Adelaide	270
1959	KDG Nagle	Australian, Sydney	284
1960	BW Devlin (Am)	Lake Karrinyup, Perth	282
1961	F Phillips	Victoria, Melbourne	275
1962	G Player (SA)	Royal Adelaide	281
1963	G Player (SA)	Royal Melbourne	278
1964	J Nicklaus (USA)	The Lakes, Sydney	287
1965	G Player (SA)	Kooyonga, Adelaide	264
1966	A Palmer (USA)	Royal Queensland, Brisbane	276
1967	PW Thomson	Commonwealth, Melbourne	281
1968	J Nicklaus (USA)	Lake Karrinyup, Perth	270
1969	G Player (SA)	Royal Sydney	288
1970	G Player (SA)	Kingston Heath, Victoria	280
1971	J Nicklaus (USA)	Royal Hobart	269
1972	PW Thomson	Kooyonga, Adelaide	281
1973	JC Snead	Royal Queensland, Brisbane	280
1974	G Player (SA)	Lake Karrinyup, Perth	277
1975	J Nicklaus (USA)	Australian, Sydney	279
1976	J Nicklaus (USA)	Australian, Sydney	286
1977	D Graham	Australian, Sydney	284
1978	J Nicklaus (USA)	Australian, Sydney	284
1979	J Newton	Metropolitan, Melbourne	288
1980	G Norman	The Lakes, Sydney	284
1981	W Rogers	Victoria, Melbourne	282
1982	R Shearer	Australian, Sydney	287
1983	P Fowler	Kingston Heath, Victoria	285
1984	T Watson (USA)	Royal Melbourne	281
1985	G Norman	Royal Melbourne	212

1986 *at Metropolitan, Melbourne*

NAME	SCORE
R Davis	278
G Marsh	279
I Baker-Finch	279
B Shearer	279
M Persson (Swe)	280

1987 *at Royal Melbourne*

NAME	SCORE
G Norman	273
AWB Lyle (GB)	283
R Wood	286
G Brand Jr (GB)	286
R Davis	287

1988 *at Royal Sydney*

NAME	SCORE
M Calcavecchia (USA)	269
M McCumber (USA)	275
W Grady	276
D Graham	278
R Rafferty (GB)	278

1989 *at Kingston Heath, Victoria*

NAME	SCORE
P Senior	271
P Fowler	278
B Ogle (NZ)	279
M Calcavecchia (USA)	280
N Faldo (GB)	281

1990 *at Australian, Sydney*

NAME	SCORE
J Morse	283
(After play-off)	
C Parry	283
G Norman	286
W Riley	286
I Baker-Finch	287
J Maggert	287
R Davis	287

Amateur Championship of Australia

INAUGURATED 1894

YEAR	WINNER	VENUE	MARGIN
1894	LA Whyte	Royal Melbourne	6 down
1895	RAA Balfour-Melville		
1896	HA Howden	Royal Melbourne	1 hole
1897	HA Howden	Royal Melbourne	348
1898	HA Howden	Royal Melbourne	360
1899	CES Gillies	Royal Sydney	314
1900	LA Whyte	Royal Adelaide	382
1901	HA Howden	Australian, Sydney	352
1902	H MacNeil		
1903	D Soutar	Royal Adelaide	3 and 1
	After 1903 decided by Match Play		
1904	JD Howden	Australian, Sydney	3 and 2
1905	Hon Michael Scott	Royal Melbourne	347
1906	EA Gill	Royal Sydney	5 and 4
1907	Hon Michael Scott	Royal Melbourne	318
1908	C Pearce	Australian, Sydney	10 and 8
1909	Hon Michael Scott	Royal Melbourne	37th hole
1910	Hon Michael Scott	Royal Adelaide	10 and 8
1911	JD Howden	Royal Sydney	4 and 3
1912	H Morrison		
1913	AR Lempriere	Royal Melbourne	2 and 1
1914–1919	*No Championship due to Great War*		
1920	EL Apperly	Australian, Sydney	4 and 3
1921	CL Winser	Royal Melbourne	6 and 5
1922	I Whitton	Royal Sydney	3 and 2
1923	I Whitton	Royal Adelaide	3 and 2
1924	HR Sinclair	Royal Melbourne	2 and 1
1925	HR Sinclair	Australian, Sydney	12 and 10
1926	L Nettlefold	Royal Adelaide	2 holes
1927	WS Nankivell	Royal Melbourne	38th hole
1928	L Nettlefold	Royal Sydney	4 and 2
1929	MJ Ryan	Royal Adelaide	2 and 1
1930	HW Hattersley	Metropolitan, Melbourne	3 and 1
1931	HL Williams	Australian, Sydney	3 and 2
1932	Dr RA Bettington	Royal Adelaide	2 and 1
1933	L Hope	Royal Melbourne	6 and 5
1934	TS McKay	Royal Sydney	5 and 4
1935	J Ferrier	Royal Adelaide	2 and 1
1936	J Ferrier	Metropolitan, Melbourne	9 and 8
1937	HL Williams	Australian, Sydney	1 hole
1938	J Ferrier	Royal Adelaide	8 and 6
1939	J Ferrier	Royal Melbourne	6 and 5
1940–45	*No Championship due to Second World War*		
1946	AN Waterson	Royal Sydney	2 and 1
1947	HW Hattersley	Royal Adelaide	1 hole
1948	DW Bachli	Metropolitan, Melbourne	7 and 6
1949	WD Ackland-Horman	Royal Sydney	38th hole
1950	HW Berwick	Royal Adelaide	4 and 3

YEAR	WINNER	VENUE	MARGIN
1951	PF Heard	Royal Melbourne	4 and 3
1952	RF Stevens	Lake Karrinyup, Perth	7 and 6
1953	PF Heard	New South Wales	8 and 7
1954	PA Toogood	Royal Adelaide	5 and 4
1955	J Rayner	Royal Queensland	4 and 2
1956	HW Berwick	Australian, Sydney	1 hole
1957	BW Warren	Commonwealth, Melbourne	3 and 1
1958	KW Hartley	Royal Adelaide	39th hole
1959	BW Devlin	Royal Sydney	2 holes
1960	EA Ball	Lake Karrinyup, Perth	5 and 4
1961	TL Crow	Royal Melbourne	3 and 2
1962	DW Bachli	Kooyonga, Adelaide	7 and 6
1963	JO Hayes	Kingston Heath, Victoria	8 and 7
1964	BJ Baker	Australian, Sydney	2 and 1
1965	KL Donohoe	Royal Melbourne	4 and 2
1966	WJ Britten	Royal Queensland	2 and 1
1967	JA Muller	Royal Perth	1 hole
1968	R Stott	Royal Hobart	3 and 1
1969	RA Shearer	Royal Adelaide	6 and 5
1970	HA Bennett	Australian, Sydney	2 holes
1971	R Hicks	Metropolitan, Melbourne	5 and 4
1972	CR Kaye	Gailes, Brisbane	37th hole
1973	RA Jenner	Lake Karrinyup, Perth	4 and 2
1974	TR Gale	Royal Hobart	8 and 7
1975	C Bonython	Royal Adelaide	1 hole
1976	P Sweeney	New South Wales	5 and 4
1977	AY Gresham	Victoria	40th hole
1978	M Clayton	Royal Queensland	1 hole
1979	J Kelly	Royal Perth	37th hole
1980	RJ Mackay	Royal Hobart	3 and 1
1981	OD Moore	Royal Adelaide	8 and 7
1982	E Couper	Australian	8 and 6
1983	W Smith	Commonwealth	37th hole
1984	B King	Royal Queensland	1 hole
1985	B Ruangkit	Royal Perth	2 and 1
1986	D Ecob	Glenelg, Adelaide	37th hole
1987	B Johns	Royal Hobart	3 and 2
1988	S Bouvier	Royal Canberra	2 and 1
1989	S Conran	Victoria	1 hole
1990	C Gray	Royal Queensland	

Australian Ladies' Amateur Championship

INAUGURATED 1894

YEAR	WINNER	VENUE	MARGIN
1894	Miss EB Mackenzie	Geelong	9 down
1895	Miss EB Mackenzie	Royal Melbourne	1 hole
1896	Miss EB Mackenzie	Geelong	6 down

YEAR	WINNER	VENUE	MARGIN
1897	Miss Jean Davie	Royal Melbourne	square
1898	Miss EB Mackenzie	Geelong	2 and 1
1899	Miss L Shaw		
1900	Miss E Calder		
1901	Miss E Guthrie	Bondi	
1902	Miss E Calder	Royal Melbourne	
1903	Mrs HF DeLittle	Glenelg, Adelaide	282
1904	Miss M Trevor Jones	Bondi	272
1905	Miss M Blackhouse	Royal Melbourne	299
1906	Miss E Whitesides	Royal Sydney	282
1907	Miss L Wray	Royal Melbourne	268
1908	Miss L Wray	Australian, Sydney	268
1909	Mrs A Gatehouse	Royal Melbourne	172
1910	Miss N Parbury	Royal Adelaide	5 and 3
1911	Miss N Parbury	Royal Sydney	
1912	Miss V Binnie	Royal Melbourne	280
1913	Mrs P A Harrison	Royal Melbourne	269
1914–19	*No Championship due to Great War*		
1920	Mrs Guy Williams	Australian, Sydney	261
1921	Miss Mona MacLeod	Royal Melbourne	259
1922	Miss G Hay	Royal Sydney	268
1923	Miss L Gordon	Royal Adelaide	273
1924	Mrs Newton Lees	Royal Melbourne	251
1925	Mrs A Gatehouse	Australian, Sydney	253
1926	Miss Mona MacLeod	Royal Adelaide	241
1927	Miss Mona MacLeod	Royal Melbourne	249
1928	Mrs A Gatehouse	Royal Sydney	9 and 8
1929	Miss L Wray	Royal Adelaide	1 hole
1930	Miss Susie Tolhurst	Commonwealth	1 hole
1931	Miss Susie Tolhurst	Australian, Sydney	7 and 6
1932	Miss Mona MacLeod	Kooyonga, Adelaide	4 and 2
1933	Miss Oliver Kay	Victoria	9 and 8
1934	Mrs Clive Robinson	Royal Sydney	4 and 3
1935	Miss JB Walker	Royal Melbourne	4 and 3
1936	Miss Oliver Kay	Royal Adelaide	5 and 4
1937	Miss B Kernot	Metropolitan, Melbourne	6 and 5
1938	Miss B Kernot	Australian, Sydney	7 and 6
1939	Miss Joan Lewis	Kooyonga, Adelaide	2 and 1
1940–46	*No Championship due to Second World War*		
1947	Joan Fisher (*née* Lewis)	Royal Adelaide	3 and 1
1948	Pat Borthwick	Commonwealth	5 and 4
1949	Pat Borthwick	Royal Sydney	2 and 1
1950	Janette Wellard	Royal Queensland	6 and 4
1951	Maxine Bishop	Kooyonga, Adelaide	2 holes
1952	Joan Fisher	Kingston Heath	7 and 5
1953	Pat Borthwick	Royal Perth	6 and 4
1954	Judith Percy	Brisbane	5 and 4
1955	Veronica Anstey	Australian, Sydney	10 and 9
1956	Pat Borthwick	Kingston Beach	2 and 1
1957	Burtta Cheney	Royal Adelaide	1 hole
1958	Margaret Masters	Royal Melbourne	6 and 5
1959	Eileen Dawson	Royal Perth	9 and 8
1960	Judith Percy	Royal Sydney	1 hole
1961	Beatrice Haley	Royal Queensland	13 and 11
1962	Judith Percy	Glenelg, Adelaide	6 and 4
1963	Marlene Streit	Royal Sydney	8 and 7
1964	Marea Hickey	Kingston Beach	5 and 4
1965	Gail Corry	Royal Perth	4 and 3

YEAR	WINNER	VENUE	MARGIN
1966	Gail Corry	Commonwealth	37th hole
1967	Judy Perkins	Royal Adelaide	7 and 6
1968	Betty Dalgleish	Royal Queensland	3 and 2
1969	Marea Hickey	Royal Hobart	5 and 4
1970	Judy Perkins	Royal Sydney	7 and 6
1971	Lindy Goggin	Mount Lawley	2 and 1
1972	Sandra McCaw	Barwon Heads	7 and 5
1973	Maisie Mooney	Metropolitan, Melbourne	37th hole
1974	Sandra McCaw	Grange	1 hole
1975	Jane Lock	Indooroopilly	6 and 5
1976	Jane Lock	Australian, Sydney	6 and 5
1977	Lindy Goggin	Lake Karrinyup, Perth	4 and 2
1978	Karen Permezel	Royal Hobart	37th hole
1979	Jane Lock	Royal Adelaide	4 and 3
1980	Lindy Goggin	Victoria	3 and 2
1981	Corinne Dibnah	Royal Queensland	5 and 4
1982	Regine Lautens (Switz)	Royal Canberra	6 and 5
1983	Sandra McCaw	Royal Perth	1 hole
1984	Sandra McCaw	Tasmania	8 and 6
1985	Helen Greenwood	Peninsula Country	2 holes
1986	Edwina Kennedy	Grange	5 and 4
1987	Elizabeth Cavill	Royal Queensland	2 and 1
1988	Caroline Bourtayre	Australian, Sydney	3 and 2
1989	Jan Higgins	Mount Lawley	11 and 9
1990	MJ Shearwood		

Canadian Open Championship

INAUGURATED 1904

YEAR	WINNER	VENUE	SCORE
1904	JH Oke	Royal Montreal	156
1905	G Cumming	Toronto	148
1906	C Murray	Royal Ottawa	170
1907	P Barrett	Lambton, Toronto	306
1908	A Murray	Royal Montreal	300
1909	K Keffer	Toronto	309
1910	D Kenny	Lambton, Toronto	303
1911	C Murray	Royal Ottawa	314
1912	G Sargent	Rosedale, Toronto	299
1913	A Murray	Royal Montreal	295
1914	K Keffer	Toronto	300
1915–18	*No Championship due to Great War*		
1919	JD Edgar	Hamilton	278
1920	JD Edgar	Rivermead, Ottawa	298
1921	WH Trovinger	Toronto	293
1922	A Watrous	Mt Bruno, Montreal	303
1923	C W Hackney	Lakeview, Toronto	295
1924	L Diegel	Mt Bruno, Montreal	285
1925	L Diegel	Lambton, Toronto	295
1926	M Smith	Royal Montreal	283

YEAR	WINNER	VENUE	SCORE
1927	T Armour	Toronto	288
1928	L Diegel	Rosedale, Toronto	282
1929	L Diegel	Kanawaki, Montreal	274
1930	T Armour	Hamilton	277
1931	W Hagen	Mississaugua, Toronto	292
1932	H Cooper	Ottawa Hunt Club	290
1933	J Kirkwood	Royal York, Toronto	282
1934	T Armour	Lakeview, Toronto	287
1935	G Kunes	Summerlea, Montreal	280
1936	L Little	St Andrews, Toronto	271
1937	H Cooper	St Andrews, Toronto	285
1938	S Snead	Mississaugua, Toronto	277
1939	H McSpaden	Riverside, Saint John	282
1940	S Snead	Scarboro, Toronto	281
1941	S Snead	Lambton, Toronto	274
1942	C Wood	Mississaugua, Toronto	275
1943–44	*No Championship due to Second World War*		
1945	B Nelson	Thornhill, Toronto	280
1946	G Fazio	Beaconsfield, Montreal	278
1947	AD Locke	Scarboro, Toronto	268
1948	CW Congdon	Shaughnessy Heights	280
1949	EJ Harrison	St George's, Toronto	271
1950	J Ferrier	Royal Montreal	271
1951	J Ferrier	Mississaugua, Toronto	273
1952	J Palmer	St Charles	263
1953	D Douglas	Scarboro, Toronto	273
1954	P Fletcher	Point Grey, Vancouver	280
1955	A Palmer	Weston, Toronto	265
1956	D Sanders (Am)	Beaconsfield, Montreal	273
1957	G Bayer	Westmount, Kitchener	271
1958	W Ellis Jr	Mayfair, Edmonton	267
1959	D Ford	Islesmere	276
1960	A Wall Jr	St George's, Toronto	269
1961	J Cupit	Niakwa, Winnipeg	270
1962	T Kroll	LeClub Laval-sur-le-Lac, Montreal	278
1963	D Ford	Scarboro, Toronto	280
1964	KDG Nagle	Pinegrove, St Luc	277
1965	G Littler	Mississaugua, Toronto	273
1966	D Massengale	Shaughnessy, Vancouver	280
1967	W Casper	Montreal Municipal	279
1968	RJ Charles	St George's, Toronto	274
1969	T Aaron	Pinegrove, St Luc	275
1970	D Zarley	London	279
1971	L Trevino	Richelieu Valley	275
1972	G Brewer, Jr	Cherry Hill	275
1973	T Weiskopf	Richelieu Valley	278
1974	B Nichols	Mississaugua, Toronto	270
1975	T Weiskopf	Royal Montreal	274
1976	J Pate	Essex, Windsor	267
1977	L Trevino	Glen Abbey, Oakville	280
1978	B Lietzke	Glen Abbey, Oakville	283
1979	L Trevino	Glen Abbey, Oakville	281
1980	B Gilder	Royal Montreal	274
1981	P Oosterhuis	Glen Abbey, Oakville	280
1982	B Lietzke	Glen Abbey, Oakville	277

1983 *at Glen Abbey, Oakville*

NAME	SCORE
J Cook	277
J Miller	277
J Nicklaus	278
A Bean	279
D Graham	279
R Landrum	279

1984 *at Glen Abbey, Oakville*

NAME	SCORE
G Norman	278
J Nicklaus	280
M Pfeil	283
N Price	283
R Zokol	284
C Rose	284
C Pavin	284
J Cook	284

1985 *at Glen Abbey, Oakville*

NAME	SCORE
C Strange	279
J Nicklaus	281
G Norman	281
F Zoeller	282
T Valentine	282
J Miller	282
W Sander	282
P Jacobsen	282

1986 *at Glen Abbey, Oakville*

NAME	SCORE
B Murphy	280
G Norman	283
A Bean	284
D Love III	284
M Donald	284

1987 *at Glen Abbey, Oakville*

NAME	SCORE
C Strange	276
J Mudd	279
D Frost	279
N Price	279
M McCullough	281
M McCumber	281

1988 *at Glen Abbey, Oakville*

NAME	SCORE
K Green	275
S Verplank	276
B Glasson	276
M Sullivan	277
D Barr	277

1989 *at Glen Abbey, Oakville*

NAME	SCORE
S Jones	271
M Hulbert	273
C Burroughs	273
M Calcavecchia	273
J Sindelar	274
M McCumber	274
M Brooks	274

1990 *at Glen Abbey, Oakville*

NAME	SCORE
W Levi	278
I Baker-Finch	279
J Woodward	279
A North	281
P Azinger	282
B Faxon	282
B Gardner	282
B Tennyson	282
B Wadkins	282
M Wiebe	282

Canadian Amateur Championship

INAUGURATED 1895

YEAR	WINNER	MARGIN	VENUE
1895	TM Harley	7 and 5	Royal Ottawa
1896	S Gillespie	4 and 3	Quebec
1897	WAH Kerr	5 and 4	Royal Montreal
1898	GS Lyon	12 and 11	Toronto
1899	VC Brown	5 and 3	Royal Ottawa
1900	GS Lyon	38th hole	Royal Montreal
1901	WAH Kerr	38th hole	Toronto
1902	FR Martin	38th hole	Royal Montreal
1903	GS Lyon	10 and 8	Toronto
1904	P Taylor	3 and 1	Royal Montreal
1905	GS Lyon	12 and 11	Toronto
1906	GS Lyon	5 and 4	Royal Ottawa
1907	GS Lyon	3 and 2	Lambton, Toronto
1908	A Wilson, Jr	1 hole	Royal Montreal
1909	E Legge	1 hole	Toronto
1910	F Martin	37th hole	Lambton, Toronto
1911	GH Hutton	39th hole	Royal Ottawa
1912	GS Lyon	6 and 5	Royal Montreal
1913	GH Turpin	1 hole	Toronto
1914	GS Lyon	8 and 7	Royal Ottawa
1913–18	*No Championship due to Great War*		
1919	W McLuckie	6 and 4	Lambton, Toronto
1920	CB Grier	5 and 4	Beaconsfield, Montreal
1921	F Thompson	38th hole	Winnipeg
1922	CC Fraser	37th hole	Hamilton
1923	WJ Thompson	3 and 2	Kanawaki, Montreal
1924	F Thompson	3 and 1	Rosedale, Toronto
1925	DD Carrick	5 and 4	Royal Ottawa
1926	CR Somerville	4 and 3	Toronto
1927	DD Carrick	9 and 8	Hamilton
1928	CR Somerville	3 and 2	Summerlea, Montreal
1929	E Held	3 and 2	Jasper Park, Jasper
1930	CR Somerville	11 and 10	London
1931	CR Somerville	3 and 2	Royal Montreal
1932	GB Taylor	5 and 3	Lambton, Toronto
1933	A Campbell	3 and 2	Shaughnessy Heights, Vancouver
1934	A Campbell	1 hole	Laval-sur-le-Lac, Montreal
1935	CR Sommerville	7 and 6	Hamilton
1936	F Haas Jr	8 and 7	St Charles, Winnipeg
1937	CR Somerville	2 and 1	Ottawa
1938	T Adams	39th hole	London
1939	K Black	8 and 6	Mount Bruno, Montreal
1940–45	*No Championship due to Second World War*		
1946	H Martell	6 and 5	Mayfair, Edmonton
1947	F Stranahan	6 and 5	Royal Quebec
1948	F Stranahan	9 and 7	Hamilton
1949	RD Chapman	38th hole	Riverside, Saint John
1950	B Mawhinney	6 and 4	Saskatoon
1951	W McElroy	2 and 1	Royal Ottawa
1952	L Bouchey	37th hole	Capilano, Vancouver
1953	D Cherry	1 hole	Kanawaki, Montreal
1954	H Ward Jr	5 and 4	London

YEAR	WINNER	MARGIN	VENUE
1955	M Norman	39th hole	Calgary
1956	M Norman	5 and 4	Edmundston
1957	N Weslock	9 and 8	St Charles, Winnipeg
1958	B Castator	1 hole	Scarboro, Toronto
1959	J Johnston	1 hole	Marine Drive, Vancouver
1960	RK Alexander	4 and 3	Ottawa Hunt
1961	G Cowan	1 hole	Edmonton
1962	R Taylor	4 and 2	Sunningdale, London
1963	N Weslock	7 and 6	Riverside, Saint John
1964	N Weslock	1 hole	Riverside, Saint John
1965	G Henry	1 hole	Pine Ridge, Winnipeg
1966	N Weslock	1 hole	Summerlea, Dorion
1967	SG Jones	3 and 2	Royal Colwood, Victoria
1968	J Doyle	4 and 3	Mayfair, Edmonton
After 1968 decided by stroke play			
1969	W McDonald	284	Westmount, Kitchener
1970	A Miller	274	Ottawa Hunt
1971	R Siderowf	293	Oakfield, Grand Lake
1972	D Roxburgh	276	Earl Grey, Calgary
1973	G Burns III	284	Summit, Old Ridges
1974	D Roxburgh	280	Naikwa, Winnipeg
1975	J Nelford	280	Riverside, Saint John
1976	J Nelford	287	Royal Colwood, Victoria
1977	R Spittle	279	The Hamilton, Ancaster
1978	R Spittel	276	Laval-sur-le-Lac, Montreal
1979	R Alarcon	282	Brantford
1980	G Olson	290	Ashburn, Halifax
1981	R Zokol	271	Calgary
1982	D Roxburgh	287	Kanawaki, Caughnawaga
1983	D Mijovic	277	Capilano, West Vancouver
1984	B Swartz	285	Sunningdale, London
1985	B Franklin	283	Riverside, Saskatoon
1986	B Franklin	286	Mactaquac, Fredericton
1987	B Franklin	283	Derrick, Edmonton
1988	D Roxburgh	285	Gallaghers Canyon, Kelowna
1989	P Major	279	Oakfield, Halifax
1990	W Sye	281	Western Ontario

Canadian Ladies' Amateur Championship

INAUGURATED 1901

YEAR	WINNER	MARGIN	VENUE
1901	Miss L Young	2 and 1	Royal Montreal
1902	Miss M Thomson	8 and 7	Toronto
1903	Miss F Harvey	2 and 1	Royal Montreal
1904	Miss F Harvey	3 and 1	Toronto
1905	Miss M Thomson	3 and 2	Royal Montreal
1906	Miss M Thomson	21st hole	Toronto

YEAR	WINNER	MARGIN	VENUE
1907	Miss M Thomson	2 holes	Royal Montreal
1908	Miss M Thomson	4 and 2	Lambton, Toronto
1909	Miss VH Anderson	5 and 4	Royal Montreal
1910	Miss Dorothy Campbell	2 and 1	Toronto
1911	Miss Dorothy Campbell	7 and 5	Royal Ottawa
1912	Miss Dorothy Campbell	5 and 4	Rosedale, Toronto
1913	Miss M Dodd	7 and 6	Royal Montreal
1914–18	*No Championship due to Great War*		
1919	Miss Ada Mackenzie	19th hole	Beaconsfield, Montreal
1920	Miss Alexa Stirling	5 and 3	Hamilton
1921	Miss Cecil Leitch	17 and 15	Rivermead, Ottawa
1922	Mrs WA Gavin	2 holes	Toronto
1923	Miss Glenna Collett	2 and 1	Mount Bruno, Montreal
1924	Miss Glenna Collett	9 and 8	Hamilton
1925	Miss Ada Mackenzie	5 and 4	Royal Ottawa
1926	Miss Ada Mackenzie	8 and 6	Elmhurst, Winnipeg
1927	Miss Helen Payson	3 and 2	Lambton, Toronto
1928	Miss Virginia Wilson	5 and 4	Beaconsfield, Montreal
1929	Miss Helen Hicks	7 and 6	Hamilton
1930	Miss Maureen Orcutt	7 and 6	Laval-sur-le-Lac, Montreal
1931	Miss Maureen Orcutt	6 and 4	Rosedale, Toronto
1932	Miss Margery Kirkham	3 and 2	Kanawaki, Montreal
1933	Miss Ada Mackenzie	8 and 6	Pine Ridge, Winnipeg
1934	Alexa Fraser (*née* Stirling)	38th hole	Toronto
1935	Miss Ada Mackenzie	8 and 7	Jericho, Vancouver
1936	Mrs AB Darling	4 and 2	Royal Montreal
1937	Mrs J Rogers	8 and 7	St Charles, Winnipeg
1938	Mrs FJ Mulqueen	1 hole	Royal Ottawa
1939–46	*No Championship due to Second World War*		
1947	Grace Lenczyk	12 and 11	Toronto
1948	Grace Lenczyk	3 and 2	Riverside, Saint John
1949	Grace de Moss	2 and 1	Capilano, Vancouver
1950	Dorothy Kielty	5 and 4	St Charles, Winnipeg
1951	Marlene Stewart	1 hole	Laval-sur-le-Lac, Montreal
1952	Edean Anderson	9 and 8	Mayfair, Edmonton
1953	Barbara Romack	2 and 1	London
1954	Marlene Stewart	9 and 8	Brightwood, Dartmouth
1955	Marlene Stewart	11 and 9	Royal Colwood, Victoria
1956	Marlene Stewart	38th hole	Niakwa, Winnipeg
1957	Betty Stanhope	5 and 4	Royal Montreal, Dorval
1958	Marlene Streit (*née* Stewart)	8 and 6	Saskatoon
1959	Marlene Streit	7 and 6	St George's, Islington
1960	Judy Darling	1 hole	Riverside, East Riverside
1961	Judy Darling	2 holes	Point Grey, Vancouver
1962	Gayle Hitchens	5 and 3	Glendale, St Charles
1963	Marlene Streit	6 and 5	Royal Ottawa
1964	Margaret Masters	1 hole	Calgary
1965	Jocelyn Bourassa	5 and 3	Westmount, Kitchener
1966	Helene Gagnon	37th hole	Ashburn, Halifax
1967	Bridget Jackson	37th hole	Riverside, Saskatoon
1968	Marlene Streit	4 and 3	Kanawaki, Caughnawaga
1969	Marlene Streit	6 and 5	Moncton
	After 1969 decided by stroke play		
1970	Gail Moore	296	Oakdale Downsview
1971	Jocelyn Bourassa	295	Capilano, Vancouver
1972	Marlene Streit	295	Niakwa, Winnipeg
1973	Marlene Streit	317	Belvedere, Charlottetown
1974	Debbie Massey	291	Edmonton

YEAR	WINNER	SCORE	VENUE
1975	Debbie Massey	293	Oakfield, Grand Lake
1976	Debbie Massey	276	Cooke Municipal, Prince Albert
1977	Cathy Sherk	302	Hillsdale, Boisbriand
1978	Cathy Sherk	292	Mactaquac Provincial Park, Fredericton
1979	Stacey West	294	Bally Haly, St John's
1980	Edwina Kennedy	287	London
1981	Jane Lock	291	St Charles, Winnipeg
1982	Cindy Pleger	288	Brudenell Golf Resort, Cardigan
1983	Dawn Coe	290	Victoria
1984	Kimberly Williams	295	Willow Park, Calgary
1985	Kimberly Williams	302	Ashburn, Armdale
1986	Marilyn O'Connor	291	Riverside, Saskatoon
1987	Tracy Kerdyk	286	Kanawaki, Caughnawaga
1988	Michiko Hattori	293	Shaughnessy, Vancouver
1989	Cheryll Damphouse	304	Bally Haly, St John's
1990	S Lebrun		

Japanese Open Championship

INAUGURATED 1927

YEAR	WINNER	SCORE	VENUE
1927	R Akahoshi (Am)	309	Hodogaya
1928	R Asami	301	Tokyo
1929	T Miyamoto	298	Ibaraki
1930	T Miyamoto	287	Ibaraki
1931	R Asami	281	Hodogaya
1932	T Miyamoto	298	Ibaraki
1933	N Nakamura	294	Kasumigaseki
1934	*Not Played*		
1935	T Miyamoto	296	Asaka
1936	T Miyamoto	293	Inagawa
1937	Chin Sai Sui	284	Sagami
1938	RM Fuku	294	Fujisawa
1939	T Toda	287	Hirono
1940	T Miyamoto	285	Asaka
1941	ET Shun	290	Hodogaya
1942–49	*No Championship due to Second World War*		
1950	Y Hayashi	288	Abiko
1951	SS Kin	288	Inagawa
1952	T Nakamura	279	Kawana
1953	SS Kin	291	Takarazuka
1954	Y Hayashi	293	Tokyo
1955	K Ono	291	Hirono
1956	T Nakamura	285	Kasumigaseki
1957	H Kobari	288	Aichi
1958	T Nakamura	288	Takanodai
1959	C Ching-Po	296	Sagamihara
1960	H Kobari	294	Hirono
1961	K Hosoishi	289	Takanodai
1962	T Sugihara	287	Chiba

YEAR	WINNER	SCORE	VENUE
1963	T Toda	283	Yokkaichi
1964	H Sugimoto	288	Tokyo
1965	T Kitta	284	Miyoshi
1966	S Sato	285	Sodegaura
1967	T Kitta	282	Hirono
1968	T Kono	284	Sobu
1969	H Sugimoto	284	Ono
1970	M Kitta	282	Musashi
1971	Y Fujii	282	Aichi
1972	H Chang-Sang	278	Iwai City
1973	B Arda	278	Osaka
1974	M Ozaki	279	Central
1975	T Murakami	278	Kasugai
1976	K Shimada	288	Central
1977	S Ballesteros	284	Narashino
1978	S Ballesteros	281	Yokohama
1979	K Chie–Hsiung	285	Hino GC, Kyoto
1980	K Kikuchi	296	Sagamihara
1981	Y Hagawa	280	Nihon Rhine
1982	A Yabe	277	Musashi
1983	I Aoki	281	Rokkokokusai
1984	K Uehara	283	Ranzan
1985	T Nakajima	285	Higashinagoya
1986	T Nakajima	284	Tozuka
1987	I Aoki	279	Arima
1988	M Ozaki	288	Tokyo
1989	M Ozaki	274	Nagoya
1990	T Nakajima	281	Otaru

New Zealand Open Championship

INAUGURATED 1907

YEAR	WINNER	SCORE	VENUE
1907	ADS Duncan (Am)	159	Napier
1908	JA Clements	333	Otago
1909	JA Clements	324	Auckland
1910	ADS Duncan (Am)	295	Christchurch
1911	ADS Duncan (Am)	319	Wanganui
1912	JA Clements	321	Wellington
1913	ES Douglas	303	Otago
1914	ES Douglas	313	Auckland
1915–18	*No Championship due to Great War*		
1919	ES Douglas	327	Napier
1920	JH Kirkwood	304	Hamilton
1921	ES Douglas	302	Christchurch
1922	A Brooks	308	Manawatu
1923	A Brooks	312	Wanganui
1924	EJ Moss	301	Auckland
1925	EM Macfarlane (Am)	308	Christchurch
1926	AJ Shaw	307	Miramar

YEAR	WINNER	SCORE	VENUE
1927	EJ Moss	300	Hamilton
1928	S Morpeth (Am)	303	Otago
1929	AJ Shaw	299	Wanganui
1930	AJ Shaw	284	Manawatu
1931	AJ Shaw	287	Christchurch
1932	AJ Shaw	289	Wellington
1933	EJ Moss	300	Titirangi
1934	AJ Shaw	288	Wanganui
1935	A Murray	286	Christchurch
1936	AJ Shaw	292	New Plymouth
1937	JP Hornabrook (Am)	299	Hamilton
1938	AD Locke	288	Otago
1939	JP Hornabrook (Am)	291	Miramar
1940–45	*No Championship due to Second World War*		
1946	RH Glading (Am)	306	Manawatu
1947	RH Glading (Am)	291	New Plymouth
1948	A Murray	294	Otago
1949	J Galloway	283	Hastings
1950	P Thomson	280	Christchurch
1951	P Thomson	288	Titirangi
1952	A Murray	293	Wanganui
1953	P Thomson	295	Otago
1954	RJ Charles (Am)	280	Wellington
1955	P Thomson	280	Auckland
1956	HW Berwick (Am)	292	Christchurch
1957	KDG Nagle	294	Manawatu
1958	KDG Nagle	278	Hamilton
1959	P Thomson	287	Paraparaumu
1960	P Thomson	281	Invercargill
1961	P Thomson	267	New Plymouth
1962	KDG Nagle	281	Titirangi
1963	B Devlin	273	Wanganui
1964	KDG Nagle	266	Christchurch
1965	P Thomson	278	Auckland
1966	RJ Charles	273	Paraparaumu
1967	KDG Nagle	275	Hamilton
1968	KDG Nagle	272	Christchurch
1969	KDG Nagle	273	Wanganui
1970	RJ Charles	271	Auckland
1971	P Thomson	276	Dunedin
1972	W Dunk	279	Paraparaumu
1973	RJ Charles	288	Palmerston North
1974	R Gilder	283	Christchurch
1975	W Dunk	272	Hamilton
1976	S Owen	284	Wellington
1977	B Byman	290	Auckland
1978	R Shearer	277	Wanganui
1979	S Ginn	278	Dunedin
1980	B Allin	274	New Plymouth
1981	R Shearer	285	Wellington
1982	T Gale	284	Christchurch
1983	I Baker-Finch	280	Auckland
1984	C Pavin	269	Paraparaumu Beach
1985	C Pavin	277	Russley
1986	R Davis	262	Auckland
1987	R Rafferty	279	Dunedin

YEAR	WINNER	SCORE	VENUE
1988	I Stanley	273	Wanganui
1989	G Turner	277	Wellington
1990	*Not Played*		

New Zealand Amateur Championship

INAUGURATED 1893

YEAR	WINNER	VENUE
1893	JA Somerville	Otago
1894	H Macneil	Christchurch
1895	G Gossett	Hutt
1896	MS Todd	Otago
1897	D Pryde	Auckland
1898	W Pryde	Christchurch
1899	ADS Duncan	Wellington
1900	ADS Duncan	Otago
1901	ADS Duncan	Auckland
1902	SH Gollan	Christchurch
1903	K Tareha	Napier
1904	AH Fisher	Otago
1905	AD S Duncan	Auckland
1906	SH Gollan	Christchurch
1907	ADS Duncan	Napier
1908	HC Smith	Otago
1909	ADS Duncan	Auckland
1910	HB Lusk	Christchurch
1911	ADS Duncan	Wanganui
1912	BB Wood	Wellington
1913	BB Wood	Otago
1914	ADS Duncan	Auckland
1915–18	*No Championship due to Great War*	
1919	H Cross	Napier
1920	S Morpeth	Hamilton
1921	AG Sime	Christchurch
1922	ADS Duncan	Manawatu
1923	J Goss Jr	Wanganui
1924	L Quin	Auckland
1925	TH Horton	Christchurch
1926	ADS Duncan	Miramar
1927	S Morpeth	Hamilton
1928	TH Horton	Otago
1929	S Morpeth	Wanganui
1930	HA Black	Manawatu
1931	R Wagg	Christchurch
1932	R Wagg	Wellington
1933	BV Wright	Titirangi
1934	BM Silk	Wanganui
1935	JP Hornabrook	Christchurch

YEAR	WINNER	VENUE
1936	JP Hornabrook	New Plymouth
1937	BM Silk	Hamilton
1938	PGF Smith	Otago
1939	JP Hornabrook	Miramar
1940–45	*No Championship due to Second World War*	
1946	WG Horne	Manawatu
1947	BM Silk	New Plymouth
1948	A Gibbs	Otago
1949	J Holden	Hastings
1950	DL Woon	Christchurch
1951	DL Woon	Titirangi
1952	H Berwick	Wanganui
1953	DL Woon	Otago
1954	DL Woon	Wellington
1955	SG Jones	Auckland
1956	PA Toogood	Christchurch
1957	EJ McDougall	Manawatu
1958	WJ Godfrey	Hamilton
1959	SG Jones	Paraparaumu
1960	R Newdick	Invercargill
1961	SG Jones	New Plymouth
1962	SG Jones	Titirangi
1963	J Durry	Wanganui
1964	SG Jones	Hamilton
1965	J Durry	Miramar
1966	SG Jones	Russley
1967	J Durry	Hastings
1968	BA Stevens	Titirangi
1969	G Stevenson	Nelson
1970	EJ McDougall	Manawatu
1971	SG Jones	Hutt, Wellington
1972	RC Murray	Waitikiri
1973	MN Nicholson	Springfield, Rotorua
1974	RM Barltrop	Manukau
1975	SF Reese	Nelson
1976	TR Pulman	New Plymouth
1977	TR Pulman	Russley
1978	F Nobilo	Hastings
1979	J Durry	Paraparaumu Beach
1980	PE Hartstone	Lochiel
1981	T Cochran	Timaru
1982	I Peters	Manawatu
1983	C Taylor	Titirangi
1984	J Wagner	St Clair
1985	G Power	Mt Maunganui
1986	P O'Malley	Hutt, Wellington
1987	O Kendall	Waitikiri
1988	B Hughes	North Shore
1989	L Peterson	Taupo
1990	M Long	Nelson

New Zealand Ladies' Championship

INAUGURATED 1893

YEAR	WINNER	VENUE	YEAR	WINNER	VENUE
1893	Mrs Lomax Smith	Dunedin	1949	Miss Z Hudson	Invercargill
1894	Mrs C Wilder	Christchurch	1950	Miss Z Hudson	Hastings
1895	Mrs Malland	Dunedin	1951	Miss M Bishop	Auckland
1896	Miss L Wilford	Wellington	1952	Miss M Hughes	Dunedin
1897	Miss L Wilford	Christchurch	1953	Miss M Bishop	Wanganui
1898	Miss K Rattray	Dunedin	1954	Miss A Nash	Miramar
1899	Miss K Rattray	Hutt	1955	Miss V Anstey	Christchurch
1900	Miss K Rattray	Christchurch	1956	Miss M Masters	New Plymouth
1901	Miss ES Gillies	Auckland	1957	Miss S Grigg	Hamilton
1902	Mrs Bidwill	Dunedin	1958	Miss N Campbell	Invercargill
1903	Mrs AE Pearce	Wellington	1959	Miss U Wickham	Poverty Bay
1904	Miss E Lewis	Christchurch	1960	Miss N Campbell	Paraparaumu
1905	Miss A Stephenson	Napier			Beach
1906	Miss Bidwill	Christchurch	1961	Miss N Campbell	Nelson
1907	Mrs G Williams	Auckland	1962	Miss P Harrison	Napier
1908	Miss Christie	Dunedin	1963	Miss JA Greenhalgh	Titirangi
1909	Mrs Bevan	Manawatu	1964	Miss M Hickey	Dunedin
1910	Miss Collins	Christchurch	1965	Miss G Taylor	Wanganui
1911	Miss Brandon	Wellington	1966	Miss NB White	Whangarei
1912	Miss Collins	Nelson	1967	Mrs DA Whitehead	Christchurch
1913	Mrs G Williams	Napier	1968	Mrs J Perkins	Hastings
1914	Mrs G Williams	Dunedin	1969	Miss U Wickham	New Plymouth
1915–18	*No Championship due to Great*		1970	Mrs ND Cullen	Invercargill
	War		1971	Mrs IC Robertson	Auckland
1919	Miss NE Wright	Auckland	1972	Mrs H Gosse	Manawatu
1920	Miss NE Wright	Christchurch	1973	Mrs DA Whitehead	Nelson
1921	Mrs G Williams	Wellington	1974	Miss C Sullivan	Paraparaumu
1922	Mrs G Williams	Wanganui			Beach
1923	Miss E Vigor-Brown	Nelson	1975	Miss R Low	Napier
1924	Mrs JW Peake	Hamilton	1976	Mrs WR Douglas	Russley
1925	Mrs H Dodgshun	Miramar	1977	Miss K Maxwell	New Plymouth
1926	Mrs EG Kerr	Dunedin	1978	Miss J Crafter	Springfield
1927	Mrs H Collinson	Manawatu	1979	Miss S Tonkin	St Clair
1928	Miss D Chrystall	Auckland	1980	Mrs B Rhodes	Wanganui
1929	Mrs H Dodgshun	Christchurch	1981	Mrs B Rhodes	Whakatane
1930	Miss O Kay	Wellington	1982	Miss J Arnold	Auckland
1931	Miss B Gaisford	Rotorua	1983	Miss C Dibnah	Harewood
1932	Mrs JC Templer	Timaru	1984	Mrs D Smith	Paraparaumu
1933	Miss O Kay	Wanganui			Beach
1934	Miss B Gaisford	Titirangi	1985	Miss E Kennedy	Hamilton
1935	Miss J Anderson	Wellington	1986	Miss A Kita	Nelson
1936	Miss E White-Parsons	Dunedin	1987	Miss J Wyatt	Manawatu
1937	Mrs GW Hollis	Napier	1988	Mrs E Cavill	Titirangi
1938	Miss S Collins	New Plymouth	1989	Mrs W Sook	
1939–45	*No Championship due to Second*		1990	L Brooky	
	World War				
1946	Miss J Horwell	Christchurch			
1947	Miss E Wilkinson	Hamilton			
1948	Mrs Jackson Ball	Manawatu			

South African Open Championship

INAUGURATED 1903

YEAR	WINNER	SCORE	VENUE
1903	LB Waters	163	Port Elizabeth
1904	LB Waters	143	Johannesburg
1905	AG Gray		Bloemfontein
1906	AG Gray	151	East London
1907	LB Waters	146	Kimberley
1908	G Fotheringham	163	Johannesburg
1909	J Fotheringham	306	Potchefstroom
1910	G Fotheringham	315	Wynberg
1911	G Fotheringham	301	Durban
1912	G Fotheringham	305	Potchefstroom
1913	JAW Prentice (Am)	304	Kimberley
1914	G Fotheringham	299	Wynberg
1915–18	*No Championship due to Great War*		
1919	WH Horne	320	Durban
1920	LB Waters	302	Johannesburg
1921	J Brews	316	Port Elizabeth
1922	F Jangle	310	Port Alfred
1923	J Brews	305	Royal Cape
1924	BH Elkin	316	Durban
1925	SF Brews	295	Johannesburg
1926	J Brews	301	Port Elizabeth
1927	SF Brews	301	Maccauvlei
1928	J Brews	297	Durban
1929	A Tosh	315	Royal Cape
1930	SF Brews	297	East London
1931	SF Brews	302	Port Elizabeth
1932	C McIlvenny	304	Mowbray
1933	SF Brews	297	Maccauvlei
1934	SF Brews	319	Port Elizabeth
1935	AD Locke (Am)	296	Johannesburg
1936	CE Olander	297	Royal Cape
1937	AD Locke (Am)	288	East London
1938	AD Locke	279	Maccauvlei
1939	AD Locke	279	Royal Durban
1940	AD Locke	293	Port Elizabeth
1941–45	*No Championship due to Second World War*		
1946	AD Locke	285	Royal Johannesburg
1947	RW Glennie (Am)	293	Mowbray, Cape Town
1948	M Janks (Am)	298	East London
1949	SF Brews	291	Maccauvlei
1950	AD Locke	287	Durban
1951	AD Locke	275	Houghton
1952	SF Brews	300	Humewood
1953	JR Boyd (Am)	302	Cape Town
1954	RC Taylor (Am)	289	East London
1955	AD Locke	283	Zwartkop
1956	G Player	286	Durban
1957	H Henning	289	Humewood
1958	AA Stewart (Am)	281	Bloemfontein
1959	D Hutchinson	282	Johannesburg
1960	G Player	288	Mowbray
1961	R Waltman	289	East London

YEAR	WINNER	SCORE	VENUE
1962	H Henning	285	Royal Johannesburg
1963	R Waltman	281	Royal Durban
1964	A Henning	278	Bloemfontein
1965	G Player	273	Mowbray, Cape Town
1966	G Player	274	Royal Johannesburg
1967	G Player	279	East London
1968	G Player	278	Houghton
1969	G Player	273	Royal Durban
1970	T Horton	285	Royal Durban
1971	S Hobday	276	Mowbray, Cape Town
1972	G Player	274	Royal Johannesburg
1973	RJ Charles	282	Royal Durban
1974	R Cole	272	Royal Johannesburg
1975	G Player	278	Mowbray, Cape Town
1976	D Hayes	287	Houghton
(with alteration in timing played twice in 1976)			
1976	G Player	280	Royal Durban
1977	G Player	273	Royal Johannesburg
1978	H Baiocchi	285	Mowbray, Cape Town
1979	G Player	279	Houghton
1980	R Cole	279	Durban
1981	G Player	272	Royal Johannesburg
1982	*With alteration in date, not played*		
1983	C Bolling	278	Mowbray, Cape Town
1984	A Johnstone	274	Houghton
1985	G Levenson	280	Royal Durban
1986	D Frost	275	Royal Johannesburg
1987	M McNulty	278	Mowbray, Cape Town
1988	W Westner	275	Durban
1989	F Wadsworth	278	Glendower
1990	T Dodds	285	Royal Cape

South African Amateur Championship

INAUGURATED 1892

YEAR	WINNER	SCORE	VENUE
1892	D Walker		Kimberley
1893	DG Proudfoot		Port Elizabeth
1894	DG Proudfoot		Port Elizabeth
1895	DG Proudfoot		Port Elizabeth
1896	DG Proudfoot		King William's Town
1897	DG Proudfort		Port Elizabeth
1898	DG Proudfoot		East London
1899	DG Proudfoot	320	Kimberley
1900–01	*No Championship due to War*		
1902	DG Proudfoot	361	King William's Town
1903	R Law	336	Port Elizabeth
1904	JR Southey	301	Johannesburg

YEAR	WINNER	SCORE	VENUE
1905	HCV Nicholson	322	Bloemfontein
1906	HM Ballinghall		East London
1907	HM Ballinghall	307	Kimberley
1908	JAW Prentice	310	Port Elizabeth
1909	JAW Prentice	321	Potchefstroom
1910	Dr EL Steyn	330	Cape Golf Club
1911	JAW Prentice	318	Durban
1912	HG Stewart	326	Potchefstroom
1913	JAW Prentice	304	Kimberley
1914	SM MacPherson	324	Royal Cape
1915–18	*No Championship due to Great War*		
1919	HG Stewart	329	Durban
1920	HG Stewart	315	Johannesburg
1921	AL Forster	322	Port Elizabeth
1922	WCE Stent	324	Royal Port Alfred
1923	WCE Stent	322	Royal Cape
1924	AL Forster	329	Durban
After 1924 decided by match play			
1925	TG McLelland	2 and 1	Johannesburg
1926	WS Bryant	2 and 1	Port Elizabeth
1927	GJ Chantler	4 and 3	Maccauvlei
1928	B Wynne	9 and 7	Durban
1929	C Hunter	8 and 6	Royal Cape
1930	B Wynne	4 and 3	East London
1931	C Coetzer	4 and 3	East Rand
1932	CE Olander	37th hole	Royal Port Alfred
1933	B Wynne	38th hole	Durban
1934	CE Olander	3 and 2	Humewood
1935	AD Locke	38th hole	Parkview
1936	CE Olander	4 and 3	Royal Cape
1937	AD Locke	4 and 3	East London
1938	B Wynne	8 and 7	Maccauvlei
1939	O Hayes	3 and 1	Durban
1940	HEP Watermeyer	5 and 4	Humewood
1941–45	*No Championship due to Second World War*		
1946	JR Boyd	4 and 3	Royal Johannesburg
1947	C de G Watermeyer	9 and 8	Mowbray
1948	BR Ryan	3 and 2	East London
1949	RW Glennie	3 and 2	Maccauvlei
1950	EL Dalton	5 and 4	Durban
1951	ES Irwin	4 and 3	Houghton
1952	M Janks	2 and 1	Humewood
1953	R Brews	4 and 3	Royal Cape
1954	AD Jackson	37th hole	East London
1955	BM Keyter	10 and 9	Zwartkop
1956	RC Taylor	37th hole	Durban
1957	AA Stewart	41st hole	Humewood
1958	JR Boyd	5 and 4	Bloemfontein
1959	A Walker	11 and 10	Royal Johannesburg
1960	WM Grindrod	3 and 2	Mowbray
1961	JG le Roux	3 and 2	East London
1962	J Hayes	2 and 1	Houghton
1963	D Symons	5 and 4	Durban
1964	JR Langridge	1 hole	Bloemfontein
1965	P Vorster	7 and 6	Humewood
1966	C du Toit	1 hole	Mowbray
1967	D Kemp	7 and 6	Royal Johannesburg
1968	R Williams	5 and 3	Bloemfontein
1969	DS Thornton	2 and 1	Humewood

YEAR	WINNER	SCORE	VENUE
1970	H Baiocchi	37th hole	Mowbray
1971	C Dreyer	6 and 5	Durban
1972	N Sundelson	3 and 2	East London
1973	A Oosthuizen	1 hole	Houghton
1974	T Lagerwey	1 hole	Port Elizabeth
1975	P Vorster	3 and 2	Bloemfontein
1976	R Kotzen	8 and 7	Mowbray
1977	T Webber	37th hole	Bryanston
1978	T Webber	3 and 2	Durban
1979	L Norval	5 and 4	Humewood
1980	E Groenewald	9 and 8	Royal Johannesburg
1981	D Suddards	2 and 1	Oppenheimer Park
1982	N James	37th hole	East London
1983	C-C Yuan	6 and 5	Royal Durban
1984	M Wiltshire	3 and 1	Humewood
1985	N Clarke	3 and 1	Royal Cape
1986	E Els	5 and 3	East London
1987	B Fouchee	1 hole	Glendower
1988	N Clarke	40th hole	Oppenheimer Park
1989	C Rivett	38th hole	Maritzburg
1990	R Goosen	2 and 1	Port Elizabeth

South African Amateur Stroke Play Championship

INAUGURATED 1969

YEAR	WINNER	SCORE	VENUE
1969	D Hayes	314	Humewood
1970	D Hayes	291	Mowbray
1971	K Suddards	291	Durban
1972	P Dunne	292	East London
1973	G Harvey	281	Houghton
1974	N Sundelson	288	Port Elizabeth
1975	G Levenson	217 (54 holes)	Bloemfontein
1976	G Harvey	292	Mowbray
1977	M McNulty	280	Bryanston
1978	D Suddards	290	Durban
1979	D Suddards	285	Humewood
1980	E Groenewald	293	Royal Johannesburg
1981	C-C Yuan	291	Oppenheimer Park
1982	W-S Li	290	East London
1983	P van der Riet	288	Royal Durban
1984	D James	287	Humewood
1985	D van Staden	285	Royal Cape
1986	C-S Hsieh	289	East London
1987	B Fouchee	211 (54 holes)	Glendower
1988	N Clarke	283	Oppenheimer Park
1989	E Els	279	Maritzburg
1990	P Pascoe	288	Port Elizabeth

South African Ladies' Championship

INAUGURATED 1909

YEAR	WINNER	VENUE	YEAR	WINNER	VENUE
1909	Miss Crozier	Grahamston	1954	R Green	Bethlehem
1910	Miss R Armstrong	Kimberley	1955	P Easton	Royal Cape
1911	Miss R Armstrong	Royal Cape	1956	I Kay	Durban
1912	Miss AG Brinton	Johannesburg	1957	M Masters	Royal
1913	Mrs JAP Gibb	Durban			Johannesburg
1914	Mrs JAP Gibb	Port Elizabeth	1958	Rita Levetan	Humewood
1915–19	*No Championship due to Great*		1959	Mrs Blumberg	Durban
	War		1960	Rita Easton	Bloemfontein
1920	Mrs Willey	Parkview	1961	Jean Tindal	Houghton
1921	Mrs Brinton	Royal Cape	1962	M Clemence	Mowbray
1922	Mrs Vernon	Durban	1963	J Mercer	Royal Durban
1923	Miss R Armstrong	Port Elizabeth	1964	Jeanette Burd	East London
1924	Mrs LK Harvey	Johannesburg	1965	M Palliser	Royal
1925	Mrs Vernon	Mowbray			Johannesburg
1926	Mrs Vernon	Durban	1966	Judy Angel	Durban
1927	Mrs Williams	Royal Port	1967	Jeanette Burd	Durban
		Alfred	1968	Rita Easton	Royal Cape
1928	Mrs Warner	Portview	1969	Marea Hickey	Bryanston
1929	Mrs Williams	Wynberg	1970	Jeanette Burd	Humewood
1930	Mrs RB Crosbie	Natal	1971	Sally Little	Royal Durban
1931	Miss M Juta	Royal Port	1972	J Nellmapius	Royal
		Alfred			Johannesburg
1932	Mrs Leete	Houghton	1973	J Bruce	Oppenheimer
1933	Miss Burwell	Raspenburg			Park
1934	Mrs AF Vernon	Maccauvlei	1974	J Mercer	Mowbray
1935	Mrs LA Witherow	Durban	1975	J Bruce	Durban
1936	Miss B Bentel	East London	1976	Alison Sheard	East London
1937	Mrs JA Douglas	Royal	1977	Alison Sheard	Houghton
		Johannesburg	1978	Alison Sheard	Schoeman Park
1938	Mrs A Hockey	Royal Cape	1979	J Mercer	Port Elizabeth
1939	Mrs R Wrighton	Beachwood,	1980	V Farrell	
		Durban	1981	Marie Laure de Lorenzi	
1940–46	*No Championship due to Second*		1982	Rae Hast	
	World War		1983	L Copeman	
1947	R Green	Royal	1984	G Whitfield	
		Johannesburg	1985	W Warrington	
1948	Jacqueline Smith	Port Elizabeth	1986	W Warrington	
1949	B Peltz	Maccauvlei	1987	C Louw	
1950	Rita Levetan	Mowbray	1988	G Tebbutt (*née* Whitfield)	
1951	Rita Levetan	Royal Durban	1989	L Rose	
1952	R Green	Houghton	1990	G Tebbutt	Mowbray
1953	Rita Levetan	East London			

South African Ladies' Stroke Play Championship

INAUGURATED 1969

YEAR	WINNER	VENUE
1969	Jeanette Burd	Humewood
1970	L Whitfield	Durban
1971	Sally Little	Royal Durban
1972	Judy Angel	Royal Johannesburg
1973	C Gerber	Oppenheimer Park
1974	Alison Sheard	Mowbray
1975	Alison Sheard	Durban
1976	Alison Sheard	East London
1977	J Bruce	Houghton
1978	Alison Sheard	Schoeman Park
1979	Alison Sheard	Port Elizabeth
1980	Rae Hast } tie S Muirhead	Hwletts
1981	Marie Laure de Lorenzi } tie N LeRoux	Royal Johannesburg
1982	Rae Hast	Royal Cape
1983	L Copeman	East London
1984	E Orley	Durban
1985	A vd Haegen	Randpark
1986	G Whitfield	Kimberley
1987	V Holland	Royal Johannesburg
1988	I Norval } tie W Warrington	
1989	G Tebbutt	Humewood
1990	J Keyter } tie G Tebbutt	Mowbray

United States Amateur Championship

INAUGURATED 1893

YEAR	WINNER	RUNNER-UP	MARGIN	VENUE
1893	WG Lawrence	CB Macdonald	4 and 3	Newport, RI
1894	LB Stoddart	CB Macdonald	5 and 4	St Andrews, NY
1895	CB Macdonald	C Sands	12 and 11	Newport, RI
1896	HJ Whigham	JG Thorp	8 and 7	Shinnecock Hills
1897	HJ Whigham	WR Betts	8 and 6	Wheaton, IL
1898	FS Douglas	WB Smith	5 and 3	Morris County, NJ
1899	HM Harriman	FS Douglas	3 and 2	Onwentsia, IL

YEAR	WINNER	RUNNER-UP	MARGIN	VENUE
1900	WJ Travis	FS Douglas	2 holes	Garden City, NY
1901	WJ Travis	WE Egan	5 and 4	Atlantic City
1902	LN James	EM Byers	4 and 3	Glen View, IL
1903	WJ Travis	EM Byers	4 and 3	Nassau, NY
1904	H Chandler Egan	F Herreschoff	8 and 6	Baltusrol, NJ
1905	H Chandler Egan	DE Sawyer	6 and 5	Wheaton, IL
1906	EM Byers	GS Lyon	2 holes	Englewood, NJ
1907	JD Travers	A Graham	6 and 5	Cleveland
1908	JD Travers	Max H Behr	8 and 7	Garden City, NY
1909	R Gardner	H Chandler Egan	4 and 3	Wheaton, IL
1910	WC Fownes, Jr	WK Wood	4 and 3	The Country Club, Brookline
1911	HH Hilton (GB)	F Herreshoff	37th hole	Apawamis, NY
1912	JD Travers	C Evans	7 and 6	Wheaton, IL
1913	JD Travers	JG Anderson	5 and 4	Garden City, NY
1914	F Ouimet	JD Travers	6 and 5	Ekwanok, VT
1915	RA Gardner	JG Anderson	5 and 4	Detroit
1916	C Evans	RA Gardner	4 and 3	Merion, PA
1917–18	*No Championship due to Great War*			
1919	SD Herson	RT Jones Jr	5 and 4	Oakmont PA
1920	C Evans	F Ouimet	5 and 4	Engineers Club, NY
1921	J Guildford	R Gardner	7 and 6	Clayton, MO
1922	J Sweetser	C Evans	3 and 2	The Country Club, Brookline
1923	MR Marston	J Sweetser	38th hole	Flossmoor, IL
1924	RT Jones Jr	G von Elm	9 and 8	Merion, PA
1925	RT Jones Jr	W Gunn	8 and 7	Oakmont, PA
1926	G von Elm	RT Jones Jr	2 and 1	Baltusrol, NJ
1927	RT Jones Jr	C Evans	8 and 7	Minikahda, MN
1928	RT Jones Jr	TP Perkins	10 and 9	Brae Burn, MA
1929	HR Johnson	Dr OF Willing	4 and 3	del Monte, CA
1930	RT Jones Jr	EV Homans	8 and 7	Merion
On and after 1931 Sectional Qualifying Competitions over 36 holes medal play were inaugurated				
1931	F Ouimet	J Westland	6 and 5	Beverley, IL
1932	CR Somerville	J Goodman	2 and 1	Baltimore, NJ
1933	GT Dunlap	MR Marston	6 and 5	Kenwood, OH
1934	W Lawson Little	D Goldman	8 and 7	The Country Club Brookline
1935	W Lawson Little	W Emery	4 and 2	Cleveland
1936	JW Fischer	J McLean (GB)	37th hole	Garden City, NY
1937	JW Goodman	RE Billows	2 holes	Portland, OR
1938	WP Turnesa	BP Abbott	8 and 7	Oakmont, PA
1939	MH Ward	RE Billows	7 and 5	Glenview, IL
1940	RD Chapman	WB McCullough	11 and 9	Winged Foot, NY
1941	MH Ward	BP Abbott	4 and 3	Omaha, NE
1942–45	*No Championship due to Second World War*			
1946	SE Bishop	SL Quick	37th hole	Baltusrol, NJ
1947	RH Riegel	J Dawson	2 and 1	Pebble Beach, CA
1948	WP Turnesa	RE Billows	2 and 1	Memphis, TN
1949	CR Coe	R King	11 and 10	Rochester
1950	S Urzetta	FR Stranahan	39th hole	Minneapolis
1951	WJ Maxwell	J Cagliardi	4 and 3	Saucon Valley, PA
1952	J Westland	A Mengert	3 and 2	Seattle, WA
1953	GA Littler	D Morey	1 hole	Oklahoma City
1954	A Palmer	RJ Sweeney Jr	1 hole	Detroit
1955	E Harvie Ward	W Hyndman III	9 and 8	Richmond, VA
1956	E Harvie Ward	C Kocsis	5 and 4	Lake Forest, IL
1957	H Robbins	Dr F Taylor	5 and 4	The Country Club Brookline

YEAR	WINNER	RUNNER-UP	MARGIN	VENUE
1958	CR Coe	T Aaron	5 and 4	San Francisco
1959	J Nicklaus	CR Coe	1 hole	Broadmoor, CO
1960	DR Beman	RW Gardner	6 and 4	St Louis, MO
1961	J Nicklaus	HD Wysong	8 and 5	Pebble Beach, CA
1962	LE Harris, Jr	D Gray	1 hole	Pinehurst, NC
1963	DR Beman	RH Sikes	2 and 1	Des Moines, IA
1964	WC Campbell	E Tutweiler	1 hole	Canterbury, OH
After 1965 decided by stroke play				
1965	RJ Murphy Jr		291	Tulsa, OK
1966	G Cowan		285	Merion, PA
1967	RB Dickson		285	Broadmoor, CO
1968	B Fleisher		284	Columbus, OH
1969	SN Melnyk		286	Oakmont, PA
1970	L Wadkins		280	Portland, OR
1971	G Cowan		280	Wilmington, DE
1972	M Giles		285	Charlotte, NC
After 1973 decided by match play				
1973	C Stadler	D Strawn	6 and 5	Inverness, OH
1974	J Pate	JP Grace	2 and 1	Ridgewood, NJ
1975	F Ridley	K Fergus	2 holes	Richmond, VA
1976	B Sander	CP Moore Jr	8 and 6	Bel-Air, CA
1977	J Fought	D Fischesser	9 and 8	Aronimink, PA
1978	J Cook	S Hoch	5 and 4	Plainfield, NJ
1979	M O'Meara	J Cook	8 and 7	Canterbury, OH
1980	H Sutton	B Lewis	9 and 8	Pinehurst, NC
1981	N Crosby	B Lyndley	37th hole	Olympic, CA
1982	J Sigel	D Tolley	8 and 7	The Country Club, Brookline
1983	J Sigel	C Perry	8 and 7	North Shore, Chicago
1984	S Verplank	S Randolph	4 and 3	Oak Tree, OK
1985	S Randolph	P Persons	1 hole	Montclair, NJ
1986	S Alexander	C Kite	5 and 3	Shoal Creek, AL
1987	W Mayfair	E Rebmann	4 and 3	Jupiter Hills, FL
1988	E Meeks	D Yates	7 and 6	Hot Springs, VA
1989	C Patton	D Green	3 and 1	Merion, PA
1990	P Mickelson	M Zerman	5 and 4	Cherry Hills, Denver

United States Ladies' Open Championship

INAUGURATED 1946

YEAR	WINNER	VENUE
1946	Patty Berg	Spokane, WA
1947	Betty Jameson	Greensboro, NC
1948	Babe Zaharias	Atlantic City, NJ
1949	Louise Suggs	Landover, MD
1950	Babe Zaharias	Wichita, KS
1951	Betsy Rawls	Atlanta, GA
1952	Louise Suggs	Bala, PA
1953	Betsy Rawls	Rochester, NY
1954	Babe Zaharias	Peabody, MA
1955	Fay Crocker (Uruguay)	Wichita, KS
1956	Kathy Cornelius	Duluth, MN
1957	Betsy Rawls	Winged Foot, NY
1958	Mickey Wright	Bloomfield Hills, MI
1959	Mickey Wright	Pittsburgh, PA
1960	Betsy Rawls	Worchester, MA
1961	Mickey Wright	Springfield, NJ
1962	Murle Lindstrom	Myrtle Beach, SC
1963	Mary Mills	Kenwood, OH
1964	Mickey Wright	San Diego, CA
1965	Carol Mann	Northfield, NJ
1966	Sandra Spuzich	Hazeltine National, MN
1967	Catherine Lacoste (France)	Hot Springs, VA
1968	Susie Berning	Moselem Springs, PA
1969	Donna Caponi	Scenic Hills, FL
1970	Donna Caponi	Muskogee, OK
1971	JoAnne Carner	Erie, PA
1972	Susie Berning	Winged Foot, NY
1973	Susie Berning	Rochester, NY
1974	Sandra Haynie	La Grange, IL
1975	Sandra Palmer	Northfield, NJ
1976	JoAnne Carner	Springfield, PA
1977	Hollis Stacy	Hazeltine, MN
1978	Hollis Stacy	Indianapolis, IN
1979	Jerilyn Britz	Brooklawn, CT
1980	Amy Alcott	Richland, TN
1981	Pat Bradley	La Grange, IL
1982	Janet Alex	Del Paso, CA

1983 at Cedar Ridge, Tulsa, Oklahoma

NAME	SCORE
Jan Stephenson (Aus)	290
JoAnne Carner	291
Patty Sheehan	291
Patti Rizzo	292
Cathy Morse	293

1984 at Salem, Peabody Massachusetts

NAME	SCORE
Hollis Stacy	290
Rosie Jones	291
Lori Garbacz	292
Amy Alcott	292
Patty Sheehan	294
Penny Pulz	294
Betsy King	294

1985 at Baltusrol, Springfield, New Jersey

NAME	SCORE
Kathy Baker	280
Judy Clark	283
Vicki Alvarez	287
Janet Coles	288
Nancy Lopez	288

1986 *at NCR, Kettering Ohio*

NAME	SCORE
Jane Geddes *(after play-off)*	287
Sally Little	287
Ayako Okamoto (Jpn)	288
Betsy King	288
Pat Bradley	290
Jodi Rosenthal	290
Amy Alcott	290
Judy Dickinson	290

1987 *at Plainfield, New Jersey*

NAME	SCORE
Laura Davies (Eng) *(after play-off)*	285
Ayako Okamoto (Jpn)	285
JoAnne Carner	285
Betsy King	289
Jodi Rosenthal	289

1988 *at Baltimore, Maryland*

NAME	SCORE
Liselotte Neuman (Swe)	277
Patty Sheehan	280
Dottie Mochrie	283
Colleen Walker	283
Jan Stephenson	284

1989 *at Indianwood, Lake Orion, Michigan*

NAME	SCORE
Betsy King	278
Nancy Lopez	282
Penny Hammel	283
Pat Bradley	283
Dottie Mochrie	284
Lori Garbacz	284

1990 *at Atlantic Athletic Club, Duluth, Georgia*

NAME	SCORE
Betsy King	284
Patty Sheehan	285
Dottie Mochrie	286
Danielle Ammaccapane	286
Mary Murphy	287

United States Ladies' Amateur Championship

INAUGURATED 1895

YEAR	WINNER	RUNNER-UP	MARGIN	VENUE
1895	Miss CG Brown	Miss NC Sargeant	132	Meadowbrook, NY
In 1895 the Championship was decided by stroke play				
1896	Miss B Hoyt	Mrs A Tunure	2 and 1	Morristown, NJ
1897	Miss B Hoyt	Miss NC Sargent	5 and 4	Essex Co, NH
1898	Miss B Hoyt	Miss MK Wetmore	5 and 3	Ardsley-on-Hudson, NY

YEAR	WINNER	RUNNER-UP	MARGIN	VENUE
1899	Miss R Underhill	Mrs C Fox	2 and 1	Philadelphia, PA
1900	Miss Griscom	Miss M Curtis	6 and 5	Shinnecock Hills, NY
1901	Miss G Hecker	Miss L Herron	5 and 3	Baltusrol, NJ
1902	Miss G Hecker	Miss LA Wells	4 and 3	The Country Club Brookline
1903	Mrs B Anthony	Miss JA Carpenter	7 and 6	Wheaton, IL
1904	Miss G Bishop	Mrs EF Sanford	5 and 3	Merion, PA
1905	Miss P Mackay	Miss M Curtis	1 hole	Morristown, NJ
1906	Miss H Curtis	Miss MB Adams	2 and 1	West Newton, MA
1907	Miss M Curtis	Miss H Curtis	7 and 6	Blue Island, IL
1908	Miss K Harley	Mrs TH Polhemus	6 and 5	Chevy Chase, MD
1909	Miss D Campbell	Mrs RH Barlow	3 and 2	Merion, PA
1910	Miss D Campbell	Mrs GN Martin	2 and 1	Flossmoor, IL
1911	Miss M Curtis	Miss LB Hyde	5 and 4	Baltusrol, NJ
1912	Miss M Curtis	Mrs RH Barlow	3 and 2	Manchester, MA
1913	Miss G Ravenscroft	Miss M Hollins	2 holes	Wilmington,DE
1914	Mrs HK Jackson	Miss EV Rosenthal	1 hole	Nassau, NY
1915	Mrs CH Vanderbeck	Mrs WA Gavin (Eng)	3 and 2	Onwentsia, IL
1916	Miss A Stirling	Miss M Caverley	2 and 1	Belmont, MA
1917–18	*No Championship due to Great War*			
1919	Miss A Stirling	Mrs WA Gavin (Eng)	6 and 4	Shawnee, PA
1920	Miss A Stirling	Mrs DC Hurd (*née* Campbell)	4 and 3	Mayfield,Cleveland
1921	Miss M Hollins	Miss A Stirling	5 and 4	Deal, NJ
1922	Miss G Collett	Mrs WA Gavin (Eng)	5 and 4	Greenbrier, WN
1923	Miss E Cummings	Miss A Stirling	2 and 1	Westchester, NY
1924	Mrs DC Hurd	Miss Browne	7 and 6	Nyatt, RI
1925	Miss G Collett	Mrs A Fraser (*née* Stirling)	9 and 8	Clayton, MO
1926	Mrs GH Stetson	Mrs AH Goss	2 and 1	Merion, PA
1927	Mrs MB Horn	Miss G Collett	5 and 4	Garden City, NY
1928	Miss G Collett	Miss V Van Wie	13 and 12	Hot Springs, VA
1929	Miss G Collett	Mrs L Pressler	4 and 3	Oakland Hills, MI
1930	Miss G Collett	Miss V Van Wie	2 and 1	Beverley Hills, CA
1931	Miss H Hicks	Mrs GC Vare (*née* Collett)	2 and 1	Buffalo, NY
1932	Miss V Van Wie	Mrs GC Vare	10 and·8	Peabody, MA
1933	Miss V Van Wie	Miss H Hicks	4 and 3	Exmoor, IL
1934	Miss V Van Wie	Miss D Traung	2 and 1	Whitemarsh Valley, PA
1935	Mrs GC Vare	Miss P Berg	3 and 2	Interlachen, MN
1936	Miss P Barton (Eng)	Mrs M Orcutt	4 and 3	Canoe Brook, NJ
1937	Mrs JA Page	Miss P Berg	7 and 6	Memphis City, TN
1938	Miss P Berg	Mrs JA Page	6 and 5	Westmoreland, IL
1939	Miss B Jameson	Miss D Kirby	3 and 2	Wee Burn, Darien, CT
1940	Miss B Jameson	Miss J Cochran	6 and 5	Pebble Beach, CA
1941	Mrs H Newell (*née* Hicks)	Miss H Sigel	5 and 3	The Country Club, Brookline
1942–1945	*No Championship due to Second World War*			
1946	Babe Zaharias	C Sherman	11 and 9	Southern Hills, Tulsa, OK
1947	Louise Suggs	Dorothy Kielty	2 holes	Detroit, MI
1948	Grace Lenczyk	Helen Sigel	4 and 3	Pebble Beach, CA
1949	Dorothy Porter	Dorothy Kielty	3 and 2	Merion, PA
1950	Beverley Hanson	Mae Murray	6 and 4	Atlanta, GA
1951	Dorothy Kirby	Claire Doran	2 and 1	St Paul, MN
1952	Jacqueline Pung	Shirley McFedters	2 and 1	Portland, OR
1953	Mary Faulk	Polly Riley	3 and 2	West Barrington, RI
1954	Barbara Romack	Mickey Wright	4 and 2	Allegheny, PA

YEAR	WINNER	RUNNER-UP	MARGIN	VENUE
1955	Pat Lesser	Jane Nelson	7 and 6	Charlotte, NC
1956	Marlene Stewart	JoAnne Gunderson	2 and 1	Indianapolis, IN
1957	JoAnne Gunderson	Ann Johnstone	8 and 6	Del Paso, CA
1958	Anne Quast	Barbara Romack	3 and 2	Wee Burn, Darien, CT
1959	Barbara McIntire	Joanne Goodwin	4 and 3	Washington DC
1960	JoAnne Gunderson	Jean Ashley	6 and 5	Southern Hills Tulsa, OK
1961	Anne Decker (*née* Quast)	Phyllis Preuss	14 and 13	Tacoma, WA
1962	JoAnne Gunderson	Anne Baker	9 and 8	Rochester, NY
1963	Mrs Anne Welts (*née* Quast)	Peggy Conley	2 and 1	Williamstown, MA
1964	Barbara McIntire	JoAnne Gunderson	3 and 2	Prairie Dunes, KA
1965	Jean Ashley	Anne Welts	5 and 4	Lakewood,Denver, CO
1966	JoAnne Carner (*née* Gunderson)	Marlene Streit (*née* Stewart)	41st hole	Sewickley, PA
1967	Mary Lou Dill	Jean Ashley	5 and 4	Pasadena, CA
1968	JoAnne Carner	Anne Welts	5 and 4	Birmingham, MI
1969	Catherine Lacoste (Fra)	Shelley Hamlin	3 and 2	Las Colinas, TX
1970	Martha Wilkinson	Cinthia Hill	3 and 2	Wee Burn, Darien, CT
1971	Laura Baugh	Beth Barry	1 hole	Atlanta, GA
1972	Mary Budke	Cinthia Hill	5 and 4	St Louis, MO
1973	Carol Semple	Anne Sander (*née* Quast)	1 hole	Montclair, NJ
1974	Cinthia Hill	Carol Semple	5 and 4	Broadmoor, Seattle
1975	Beth Daniel	Donna Horton	3 and 2	Brae Burn, MS
1976	Donna Horton	Marianne Bretton	2 and 1	Del Paso, CA
1977	Beth Daniel	Cathy Shark	3 and 1	Cincinnati
1978	Cathy Shark	Judith Oliver	4 and 3	Sunnybrook, PA
1979	Cinthia Hill	Patty Sheehan	7 and 6	Memphis, TN
1980	Juli Inkster	Patti Rizzo	2 holes	Prairie Dunes, KN
1981	Juli Inkster	Lindy Goggan (Aus)	1 hole	Portland, OR
1982	Juli Inkster	Cathy Hanlon	4 and 3	Colorado Springs
1983	Joanne Pacillo	Sally Quinlan	2 and 1	Canoe Brook, NJ
1984	Debbie Richard	Kimberley Williams	37th hole	Broadmoor, Seattle
1985	Michikol Hattori	Cheryl Stacy	5 and 4	Chapel, Pittsburgh, PA
1986	Kay Cockerill	Katherine McCarthy	9 and 7	Pastiempo, CA
1987	Kay Cockerill	Tracy Kerdyk	3 and 2	Barrington, RI
1988	Pearl Sinn	Karen Noble	6 and 5	Minikahde, MN
1989	Vicki Goetze	Brandie Burton	4 and 3	Pinehurst, NC
1990	Pat Hurst	Stephanie Davis	37th hole	Canoe Brook, NJ

Index

Listed in the Index are the championships and tournaments as well as the names of all individuals mentioned in the various introductions to events.